AN ENGLISH-PERSIAN DICTIONARY

AN ENGLISH-PERSIAN DICTIONARY

COMPILED FROM ORIGINAL SOURCES

BY

ARTHUR N. WOLLASTON, C.I.E.

H.M.'S INDIAN (HOME) SERVICE

TRANSLATOR OF THE "ANVAR-I-SUHAILI," EDITOR OF THE MIRACLE PLAY OF "HASAN AND HUSAIN," ETC.

GYAN

Published by

GYAN

Gyan Publishing House
5, Ansari Road
Daryaganj, New Delhi-110002
Phone: 011-47034999, 9811692060
E-mail: books@gyanbooks.com

Distribution Network
gyanbooks.com
India, USA, Canada, UK, Australia, France

ISBN : 978-81-212-4337-7 (PB)
First Published, 1922

2nd Impression 2020

Printed at: Gyan Press, Delhi.

An English-Persian Dictionary
Author: Arthur N. Wollaston

TO THE

MEMORY OF A MOTHER

IS DEDICATED ALL THAT IS WORTHY OF ACCEPTANCE
IN A VOLUME IN WHICH SHE TOOK A LIVELY
INTEREST, AND WHICH, WITH ALL ITS
DEFECTS AND IMPERFECTIONS, SHE
WOULD HAVE WELCOMED AS
THE WORK OF

HER SON.

PREFACE.

THE need of a modern English-Persian Dictionary can scarcely be questioned, the massive volumes edited many years ago by Richardson and Wilkins respectively being out of print and well-nigh unprocurable; in any case, also, for various reasons, they are by no means suited to the requirements of the present day, while the few other works which have appeared are, for the most part, compilations by natives of India, unacquainted with the spirit of the English language, and at best they rise but little beyond the level of vocabularies. In these circumstances, as I know from personal experience, a student is beset with difficulties, and from this point of view no apology is needed for an attempt to fill a void so serious and perplexing. There is, however, another aspect of the case, respecting which an explanation is due to the public. Reference has been made to the attempts of foreigners to cope with the difficulties of a strange tongue; the failure of an Englishman to grasp the endless shades of meaning of so ornate and mellifluous a language as Persian would scarcely be less conspicuous. Indeed, for my part, I am quite prepared to admit that a Dictionary should be the joint work of two individuals, responsible each in his own sphere for the accuracy of the work. Why, then, it may be asked, have I attempted single-handed a task for which I avow that a coadjutor is incumbent? The question is reasonable, and, considering that, by the inherent nature of things, a Dictionary must of necessity, for good or ill, leave "footprints on the sands of time," the answer is important. It seems right, therefore, that I should state precisely the grounds upon which I am tempted to hope for the accompanying work that approbation with which the public have been kind enough to receive my former efforts in the path of Oriental lore. It must be confessed that, from the very first, I was conscious that the fact that I have never had an opportunity of studying the language in the country where it is spoken placed me under an immense disadvantage, as compared with others more fortunate, who, from long residence in Persia, had the means of gaining a critical knowledge, which can scarcely be otherwise acquired. So fully alive was I to the difficulties of my position in this respect, that, had a more competent person been disposed to take the matter in hand, I should not have ventured to commence a task which, under the most favourable circumstances, could not be otherwise than tedious and, in some measure, unsatisfactory. As, however, time passed without an indication that anyone was willing to undertake the duty of compiling an English-Persian Dictionary, I determined, though with diffidence, to make the attempt myself, and I resolved to reverse a Persian-English Dictionary. But, on reflection, it at once became evident that such a mode of procedure would not ensure a practical result, for the obvious reason that, when translating from Persian into English, the student needs the use of every word, however pedantic and scarce, which is to be found in any author of note; on the other hand, as regards rendering from English into Persian, the introduction of obsolete or neglected phraseology into a Dictionary would retard rather than assist the learner, who would not be likely to possess that knowledge and experience which alone could enable him to select fitting and suitable equivalents.

These considerations, while they induced me to abandon the idea of reversing a Persian-English Dictionary, impelled me to adopt, if possible, some course which should at once ensure the omission of what was superfluous, and the introduction of such words as experience might dictate to be requisite and advantageous. The dilemma was perplexing, and ultimately, as my only resource, I determined to enter upon an extensive course of reading, with the view of culling from newspapers and modern works as many terms as within a reasonable time might be possible. The labour was enormous, extending over a period of years; and in the end, so considerable a mass of material was collected as to justify the commencement of the undertaking upon which I had resolved. In this portion of the work I received much assistance from Lieut.-Colonel Ross, H.B.M.'s Political Resident in the Persian Gulf, who obtained for me collections of words and idioms the value of which it would be difficult to overrate. Matters were in a fragmentary and unsettled state, when, about two years ago, the native translator to the Bushire Residency, by name Mirza Baker, came to this country, and, on his arrival, placed himself in communication with me, in order to assist in a work rumours of which had reached him. A very short conversation served to indicate that my new acquaintance was a ripe scholar. Not only was he familiar with the Arabic and Turkish languages, which supply so many of the words in modern use in Persia, but, possessing a truly remarkable critical knowledge of his own tongue, he was enabled to afford the explanations so necessary to me. I gladly availed myself of his services, and, trusting to his revision, I also added to my collection some thousands of words, respecting which, as I had not absolutely met with them in the course of my reading, I had some doubts whether they should be introduced or omitted. I may mention—not in any spirit of arrogance or presumption, but simply as a fact which may tend to enable the public to form an estimate of the value of the work now presented to them—that six months were consumed in the mere revision of the fragmentary matter which I had collected, a task which Mirza Baker conducted throughout in personal communication with myself. At this stage I deemed myself justified in allowing an announcement to appear in a literary journal, intimating that the Dictionary was approaching completion. But, alas! for the vanity of human plans and schemes. A few months after the statement to this effect was published in the *Athenæum*, I found that the task of working up the rough notes would involve a labour, not of days or of months, but of years. In despair, I almost contemplated abandoning such a Herculean task, when one morning, to my surprise, I received an offer from an unknown correspondent in this country to place at my disposal papers which were deemed of possible use in connection with the work which I was understood to have in hand.

In due course the documents arrived, and, to my amazement,

they turned out to be nothing less than a miniature Dictionary, compiled some years ago by a gentleman during a residence in Persia. I examined the production most critically, and could find scarce a fault therein. Somewhat perplexed as to what course to pursue, I ultimately determined to defer the publication of my own larger work, and to revise this "Pocket Dictionary," intending to resume my own labours on the appearance of its less pretentious companion, an event which I had hoped would not be long delayed. My correspondent was Mr R. Monro Binning, and I can only regret that it did not fall to his lot to undertake a task for which he is so eminently qualified, whether as regards practical experience gained during a residence in Persia, or critical knowledge of the minutiæ of the language. Commencing the revision of his Dictionary, I soon perceived that, accurate as it was in all respects, it was too concise for my purpose; indeed, with the modesty which has characterised all his proceedings in the matter, Mr Binning would never allow that his book was more than a mere vocabulary. In these circumstances, I was again compelled to change my plans, and instead of placing before the world a Dictionary which I felt was very far from complete, I determined to add thereto to a degree sufficient for ordinary requirements; the result is the work now before the public. As, however, I increased the bulk of Mr Binning's text to at least twice its original size, I did not deem it fair to that gentleman to burden him with the responsibility of authorship, seeing that many of the sins—at any rate, of commission—must be laid to my charge.

I should wish to guard myself against the presumption that the present volume is in any degree complete; as previously stated, the preparation of a Dictionary of such magnitude as would be requisite to ensure the introduction of all the words in common use must of necessity be a labour of years. In my own case, the comparatively limited amount of time at my disposal will still further tend to defer the appearance of the larger work which I have undertaken; meanwhile, the accompanying compilation is presented in the hope that it may serve for ordinary purposes of reference. Small and insignificant as it is, a considerable degree of care and labour has been expended in its preparation. That numerous omissions will be found I freely acknowledge; but I should wish to state, with reference to the faults of "commission," that I have inserted nothing on my own individual authority, so far, that is, as "coining" words is concerned. I do not attempt to disguise that, not improbably, in some instances, I may have placed erroneous interpretations upon terms with which I have met in the course of my reading, in which case errors would, as an inevitable consequence, have crept into the Dictionary; however, when any doubt existed in my mind, I have preferred to omit rather than to mislead. With regard to the large array of words in colloquial use, which now for the first time have received "a local habitation," I am privileged to quote, as the authority for their introduction, the names of Mirza Baker, Mr Binning, and Lieut.-Colonel Ross, each of whom has supplied me with information derived from a residence in the districts where the words in question are used in ordinary conversation. As to the mode of spelling and the accuracy of transliteration in such cases, I cannot avoid assuming a large degree of responsibility; indeed, it was impossible to do otherwise than choose a path for myself, in a direction where none had preceded to mark the way. As, however, Mirza Baker was constantly at hand to guide and counsel, I have some confidence as to the soundness of the results.

It will be observed that there are comparatively few renderings given for verbs, the object being to save space; but the omission will not, it is thought, occasion much inconvenience to the student, who can refer to the substantive, and add thereto an auxiliary verb, a process of "coining" which is strictly legitimate, and not more open to objection than the construction of such English phrases as, to "do repairs," to "make way," to "have confidence," etc.

For a similar reason, also, it has not been deemed necessary to give numerous equivalents for words which can be found under their various synonyms. A compendious Dictionary must be deficient in some points, and omissions of this nature commended themselves, with the view of providing for the introduction of more uncommon words, the absence of which would not unlikely occasion the student difficulty and embarrassment.

It may be urged as an objection that, in the transliteration, no attempt has been made to discriminate between the various letters which, though entirely distinct in Persian, are rendered by the same equivalent in the Roman character. It was thought, however, that, as the original words are always at hand in case of doubt, no difficulty would be likely to arise, and the adoption of a strict system of transliteration, owing to the numerous diacritical marks which it involves, would have materially added to the size and cost of the work, a consideration which also rendered necessary the omission of any marks to indicate the language to which the various words owe their origin.

The adoption of a "v" in place of a "w" as the equivalent of the Persian letter و is open to criticism. Mirza Ibrahim, in his Persian Grammar, uses the former equivalent, while Mr Binning, who, having resided in the country for a considerable period, is of necessity a high authority upon such a point, also adopts the "v." It is true that words of Arabic origin not unfrequently retain the original pronunciation of "w" assigned to them in that language, while in some districts the use of the "v" is comparatively rare; but I have been unable to gather that there is any fixed and invariable rule on the subject. On the whole, it seemed to me preferable to use a "v" as the equivalent of و, as being, in most cases, nearer to accuracy. Should the student have occasion to visit Persia, he will probably find no difficulty in adapting his pronunciation in this respect to the usages of the people by whom he may be surrounded. It is a matter of regret that the inquiries which resulted in this determination on my part were not completed till several pages of the Dictionary had been printed, an explanation which will, it is hoped, account for numerous inconsistencies in the earlier sheets of the Dictionary, and screen the author from the charge of want of care in the revision of the work. It would be hopeless to attempt an apology for the many errors which are to be found scattered throughout the pages of this volume, especially as regards the transliteration into Roman characters, a task, in some measure, hurriedly undertaken at the last moment, in deference to the views of those whose authority it would have been presumption on my part to have questioned. I can

PREFACE TO THE SECOND EDITION.

NEARLY a quarter of a century ago I published a concise English-Persian Dictionary. At the time I explained at considerable length both the need for such a work and also the reasons which had induced me to undertake the task. My efforts were so far successful that, as I am informed on the highest authority, the not inconsiderable number of words which of necessity were coined have been gradually accepted and are now incorporated into the current language of the country.

If, in these circumstances, I am tempted to indulge in feelings of pride, it is but fair to associate with myself Mirza Baker, who, as I announced at the time, materially helped me in the difficult task of adapting a language of untold antiquity to the requirements of modern life in all its varied and ever varying phases. I have already avowed, and I am proud to repeat, my obligations to a scholar—now alas! no more—whom I make bold to say has seldom, if ever, been approached as regards a close and intimate knowledge of Persian, and a familiarity with English which would put to shame many of our fellow-countrymen.

The first edition has now been exhausted, and as, so far as I know, the mistakes are neither numerous nor important, I have ventured to issue a reprint by a process which does not admit of corrections. I hope the public will continue to the new volume the patronage which for so long a term of years has been extended to its predecessor.

A. N. W.

GLEN HILL, WALMER,
6th March 1904.

AN

ENGLISH-PERSIAN DICTIONARY.

A.

Aback, پشت pusht, عقب 'akab.

Abaft, پشت pusht, عقب 'akab.

To Abandon, گذاشتن guzáshtan, ترک کردن tark kardan (*vide* To Leave).

Abandoned, متروك matrúk, مخذول makhzúl, گذاشته guzáshtah.—(*shameless*) بی شرم bí-sharm, بی آبرو bí-áb-rú, بی حیا bí-hayá.

Abandoner, تارك tárik.

Abandonment, ترك tark, هجر hajr, هجران hijrán.

To Abase, فرود آوردن furúd áwardan, خوار گردانیدن khwár gardánídan, پست کردن past kardan.

Abasement, پستی pastí, خواری khwárí.

To Abate, *vide* To Diminish (*lessen*).

Abatement, کمی kamí, تخفیف takhfíf.—(*in price*) تنزیل tanzíl, رعایت ri'áyat.

Abbey, خانقاه khánakáh.

Abbot, اسقف uskuf.

To Abbreviate, اختصار کردن ikhtisár kardan, مختصر کردن mukhtasar kardan.

Abbreviation, اختصار ikhtisár, مختصر mukhtasar.

To Abdicate, *vide* To Leave, To Withdraw, To Resign.

Abdomen, شکم shikm, معده mi'dah.

Aberration, خرامت kharámat, ضلالت zalálat.

To Abet, مساعد نمودن musá'id nimúdan, مدد کردن madad kardan.

To Abhor, کراهیت داشتن karáhíyat dáshtan, نفرت بردن nifrat burdan, منفور داشتن manfúr dáshtan, مکره شدن mukrih, shudan, متنفر بودن mutanaffir búdan, نفرت ورزیدن nifrat warzídan.

Abhorrence, نفرت nifrat, کره karih, کراهیت karáhíyat, استکراه istikráh, بغض bughz, رغم raghm, کینه kínah.

To Abide (*dwell*), وطن گرفتن watan giriftan, توطن کردن tawattun kardan.—(*stay*) ماندن mándan, توقف شدن tawakkuf shudan.

Abiding, (*permanent*), مستمر mustamirr.

Ability, توانائی tawáná,í, دست dast, تاب táb, قدرت kudrat, اقتدار iktidár, مقدور makdúr, قابلیت kábilíyat, لیاقت liyákat, مجال mijál, قوت kúwat, سر رشته sar-rishtah.—(*faculties*) عقل 'akl, فراست firásat, ادراك idrák, ذهن zihn, زکاوت zakáwat.

Abject, دون dún, پست past, خوار khwár, ذلیل zalíl.

Abjectness, پستی pastí, دونی dúní, رذالت razálat, خواری khwárí.

Abjuration, برگشتگی bar-gashtagí.

To ABJURE, بر گشتن bar-gashtan.
ABLATIVE (*case*), مفعول به maf'úlu bihi, مفعول عنه maf'úlu 'anhu.
ABLAZE, سوزان súzán.
ABLE, زرنگ zaring, زیرك zírak, چابك chábuk, چست chust.—(*capable*) قادر kádir, توانا tawáná.
To be ABLE, توانستن tawánistan, بقوت خود دیدن bi-kúwat-i-khúd dídan, قابل بودن kábil búdan.
ABLUTION (*previous to prayer*), وضو wuzú, آبدست áb-dast, دست نماز dast namáz. — (*after defilement*) طهارت tahárat, تطهیر tathír, استنجا istinjá.—(*of the whole body*) غسل ghusl.—(*with sand, in default of water*) تیمم tayammum.
ABNEGATION, امتناع imtiná'.
ABNORMAL, استثنائی istisná,í.
ABODE, مکان makán, منزل manzil, مسکن maskan, مقام makám, خانه khánah, ماء بد má,bid, مقر makarr, مستقر mustakarr, ماوا máwá, بود باش búd-básh.
To ABOLISH, منسوخ کردن mansúkh kardan, نسخ نمودن naskh nimúdan, معدوم ساختن ma'dúm sákhtan, نا بود کردن ná-búd kardan, موقوف کردن maukúf kardan, مبطل گردانیدن mubtal gardánídan.
ABOLITION, منسوخ mansúkh, معدوم ma'dúm, نسخ naskh.
ABOMINABLE, مکروه makrúh, کریه karíh, منفور manfúr.
To ABOMINATE, منفور داشتن manfúr dáshtan, مکروه داشتن makrúh dáshtan.
ABOMINATION, نفرت nifrat, کره karih, استکراه istikráh.
ABORTION (*miscarriage*), اسقاط حمل iskát-i-haml, سقوط حمل sakút-i-haml, اسقاط جنین iskát-i-janín.—(*fruit of a miscarriage*) جنین janín, جنین غیر کامل janín-i-ghair kámil, جنین نارسیده janín-i-ná-rasídah.
ABORTIVE, ضائع zá,i', بی فائده bí-fá,idah.
To ABOUND, موفور شدن maufúr shudan, کثیر شدن kasír shudan, وافر شدن wáfir shudan.

ABOUT (*around*), گرداگرد gird-á-gird, برگرد bar-gird, حوالی hawálá, دور daur, پیرامن pairámun.—(*nearly*) قریب karíb, مشرف mushrif, نزدیك nazdík. — (*concerning*) در خصوص dar khusús, در حق dar hakk, در باره dar bárah, بابت bábat, بر سر bar sar.
ABOVE (*upon*), بر bar, بر سر bar sar, بالا bálá, رو rú, در روی dar rúí.—(*over*) بالا bálá, زبر zabar, علی 'alá, فوق fauk, فراز faráz.
ABOVE-MENTIONED, مذکور mazkúr, مزبور mazbúr, مسفور masfúr, مقول makúl, مشار الیه mushár ilaihi, مومی الیه múmá ilaihi, سابق الذکر sábiku-'z-zikr.
ABRASION, خراش khirásh.
To ABRIDGE, اختصار نمودن ikhtisár nimúdan, مختصر کردن, mukhtasar kardan.
ABRIDGED, مختصر mukhtasar, مجمل mujmal, موجز míjaz, ملخص mulakhkhas, وجیز wajíz.
ABRIDGMENT, اختصار ikhtisár, ایجاز íjáz, اجمال ijmál, قصارت kasárat.
ABROAD, بیرون bírún, بسفر bi-safar.
To go ABROAD, سفر کردن safar kardan, سیاحت کردن siyáhat kardan.
To ABROGATE, *vide* To ABOLISH.
ABRUPT, *vide* STEEP, SUDDEN.
ABRUPTLY, ناگاه ná-gáh, ناگهان nágahán, بغتةً baghtatan.
ABRUPTNESS (*in answer*), جواب حاضری jawáb-háziri.
ABSCESS, دمل dummal, دنبل dumbal.
To ABSCOND, پنهان شدن panhán shudan, مخفی شدن makhfí shudan, فرار کردن firár kardan, رو پوش شدن rú-púsh shudan.
ABSENCE, غیبت ghaibat, غیاب ghiyáb, غیر حاضری ghair házirí.
ABSENT, غائب ghá,ib, جدا judá, غیر حاضر ghair házir, لا موجود lá maujúd.
To ABSENT (*oneself*), غائب شدن ghá,ib shudan.
ABSOLUTE (*having free power*), مختار mukhtár, مستقل mustakill, مطلق mutlak.

ABSOLUTELY, قطعاً kat'an, کاملا ká-milan.
ABSOLUTION, مغفرت maghfirat, عفو 'afw, آمرزش ámurzish.
To ABSOLVE, عفو کردن 'afw kardan, معذور داشتن ma'zúr dáshtan, معاف کردن mu'áf kardan, بخشیدن bakh-shidan.
To ABSORB, خیسانیدن khísánídan نوشیدن núshídan.
ABSORBENT, جاذب jázib.
ABSORPTION, نشف nashf, جذب jazb.
To ABSTAIN, پرهیز نمودن parhíz ni-múdan, احتراز نمودن ihtiráz nimú-dan, اجتناب کردن ijtináb kardan.
ABSTEMIOUS, پرهیز گار parhíz-gár, حصور hasúr, محتاط muhtát, مرتاض murtáz.
ABSTINENCE, پرهیز parhíz, پرهیز گاری parhíz-gárí, اجتناب ijtináb, ریاضت riyázat.
ABSTRACT, مختصر mukhtasar, ایجاز íjáz, مجمل mujmal.
In the ABSTRACT, علی وجه التجرد 'alá wajhu-'t-tajarrud.
To ABSTRACT (*abridge*), مختصر کردن mukhtasar kardan, مجمل ساختن mujmal sákhtan. —(*carry off*) ربودن rubúdan, بر داشتن bar-dásh-tan.
ABSTRACTION, تجرد tajarrud, تجرید tajríd. — (*abduction*) ربودگی ru-búdagí, ربایندگی rubáyandagí.
ABSTRUSE, دقیق dakík, مغلق mugh-lak, گنگ gung (*vulg.*).
ABSTRUSELY, بدقت bi-dikkat.
ABSTRUSENESS, دقت dikkat.
ABSURD, بیهوده bíhúdah, هرزه harzah, نا معقول ná-ma'kúl, پوچ púch, عبث 'abas, ول wil, بیمعنی bí-ma'ní, چرند charand, لیچار líchár, جفنگ jafang, نا موجه ná-muwajjah. — (*an absurd explanation*) توجیه نا موجه taujíh-i-ná-muwajjah, تفصیل نا معقول tafsíl-i-ná-ma'kúl.
ABSURDITY, بطلان butlán, بیهودگی bí-húdagí, نا ساز کاری ná-sáz-kárí.
ABSURDLY, بیهودانه bíhúdánah.
ABUNDANCE, *vide* PLENTY, EXCESS.
ABUNDANT, *vide* NUMEROUS, MUCH, MANY, PLENTEOUS, LIBERAL.

ABUSE (*bad language*), دشنام dush-nám, فحش fuhsh, سب sabb.— (*ill-usage*) بد رفتاری bad-raftárí, بد استعمالی bad-isti'málí, بد سلوکی bad-sulúkí.
To ABUSE, دشنام دادن dushnám dá-dan, دشنامیدن dushnámídan, فحش دادن fuhsh dádan.
ABUSER, مفتری muftarí, دشنام دهنده dushnám dihandah.
ABUSIVE, بد زبان bad-zabán, زبان دراز zabán-diráz.
To ABUT, نزدیك شدن nazdík-shudan.
ABYSS, قعر ka'r, حضیض hazíz, لجه lujjah, ورطه wartah.
ACACIA (*gum-tree*), طلح talh, سنط sant.—(*silk-tasselled acacia*) گل ابریشمی gul-i-abríshumí.—(*sweet-scented*) گل فتنه gul-i-fitnah.
ACADEMICIAN, اهل مدرسه ahl-i-ma-drasah.
ACADEMY, دار العلوم dáru-'l-'ulúm, مدرسه madrasah, مکتب maktab.
To ACCEDE, *vide* To AGREE, To ALLOW.
ACCENT, *vide* ARTICULATION, PRO-NUNCIATION.
To ACCENT, تلفظ کردن talaffuz kar-dan.
To ACCEPT, قبول کردن kabúl kardan, اجابت نمودن ijábat nimúdan, پذیرفتن pazíruftan. —(*monetary term*) قبولیت کردن kabúlíyat kar-dan.
ACCEPTABLE, مقبول makbúl, مطبوع matbú', منظور manzúr, پسندیده pa-sandídah.
ACCEPTATION, اجابت ijábat.—(*sense of a word*) معنی ma'ní, فحوائی کلام fahwá,í-i-kalám.
ACCEPTER, قائل ká,il.
ACCESS, بار bár, راه ráh, تقرب takar-rub, قدوم kudúm, دخول dukhúl, مدخلیت madkhalíyat.
ACCESSIBLE, ممکن الدخول mumkinu-'d-dukhúl.
ACCESSION (*increase*), اضافت izáfat, فزونی fuzúní.—(*to throne*), جلوس julús, تخت نشینی takht-nishíní.
ACCESSORY, ضمیم zamím; زیاده ziyá-dah. (*Vide* ACCOMPLICE.)

ACCIDENT, حادثه hádisah, سانحه sánihah, عارضه 'árizah, سهو sahw, سر گذشت sar-guzasht, اتفاق ittifák, خطا khatá.

ACCIDENTALLY, سهواً sahwan, اتفاقاً ittifákan, عارضاً 'árizan, نا گاهانه ná-gáhánah, خطاً khatan, بنا دانستگی bi-ná-dánistagí.

ACCLAMATION, آفرین áfirín, تحسین tahsín.

To ACCOMMODATE (*settle a dispute amicably*), مصالحه کردن musálahah kardan. (*Vide* To AGREE, To ADAPT.)

ACCOMMODATION (*fitness*), مناسبت munásabat, موافقت muwáfakat, لیاقت liyákat.

To ACCOMPANY, همراه رفتن hamráh raftan, مصاحب بودن musáhib búdan, بصحابت رفتن bi-sahábat raftan, صحبت داشتن suhbat dáshtan, رفاقت کردن rafákat kardan, باهم رفتن bá-ham raftan, مرافقت کردن muráfakat kardan.

ACCOMPLICE, شریک sharík, رفیق rafík, هم عهد ham-'ahd, هم شرط ham-shart.

To ACCOMPLISH, پرداختن pardákhtan, برآوردن bar-áwardan, بر رسانیدن bar-rasánídan, تتمیم نمودن tatmím nimúdan, تمام کردن tamám kardan.

ACCOMPLISHED, *vide* ABLE.

ACCOMPLISHMENT, اتمام itmám, اختتام ikhtitám, اکمال ikmál. (*Vide* GRACE, SKILL, LEARNING.)

To ACCORD, فراخور آمدن farákhúr ámadan.

ACCORDING TO, موافق muwáfik, بر وفق bar wafk, از قرار az karár, بحسب bi-hasb, حسب hasb, فراخور farákhúr, بقدر bi-kadr, مناسب munásib, بر طبق bar tibk.

ACCORDINGLY, لهذا lihází, علی هذا 'alá házá, بنا بر این banábar ín.

To ACCOST, خطاب کردن khitáb kardan, مخاطب نمودن mukhátib nimúdan.

ACCOUCHEMENT, تولید taulíd.

ACCOUCHEUSE, مولده muwallidah, قابله kábilah, ماماچه mámáchah.

ACCOUNTANT, مستوفی mustaufí, محرر muharrir, محاسب muhásib, مشرف mushrif.

ACCOUNT-BOOK, دفتر daftar, دستک حساب dastak-i-hisáb.

ACCOUNTS, حساب hisáb, شمار shimár.—(*to settle accounts*), محاسبه کردن muhásabah kardan.—(*narrative*) خبر khabar, قصه kissah, حکایت hikáyat, نقل nakl.

To ACCOUTRE, سلاح پوشانیدن siláh púshánídan.

ACCOUTRED (*equipped*), قبراغ kibrágh, آماده ámádah, مستعد musta'idd.

ACCOUTREMENTS, یراق yarák, سلاح siláh (pl. اسلحه aslihah).

ACCREDITED (*diplomatic term*), مقیم mukím.

To ACCRUE, وارد آمدن wárid ámadan.

To ACCUMULATE (*trans.*) جمع کردن jam' kardan, چیدن chídan, فراهم آوردن faráham áwardan.—(*intr.*) جمع شدن jam' shudan.

ACCUMULATION, ادخار iddikhár, جمع jam', مجمع majma'.

ACCUMULATOR, جامع jámi'.

ACCURACY, دقت dikkat, درستی durustí, متانت matánat, صحت sihhat, صحاح saháh.

ACCURATE, درست durust, راست rást, صحیح sahíh, کامل kámil, دقیق dakík.

ACCURATELY, صحیحاً sahíhan, بدرستی bi-durustí, براستی bi-rástí, بدقت bi-dikkat.

ACCURSED, ملعون mal'ún, لعین la'ín, مطعون mat'ún.

ACCUSATION, شکایت shikáyat, شکوی shakwá, تهمت tuhmat, ذم zamm, اسناد isnád.

ACCUSATIVE (*case*), مفعول maf'úl.

To ACCUSE, شکایت کردن (بر) shikáyat kardan (bar), نالش نمودن (بر) nálish nimúdan (bar), تهمت زدن tuhmat zadan. — (*to accuse falsely*) افترا بستن iftirá bastan, تهمت زدن tuhmat zadan, بهتان بستن buhtán bastan.

ACCUSER, مدعی mudda'í, ملامت زن malámat-zan.

ADORER (*worshipper*), عابد 'ábid, ساجد sájid.—(*lover*) عاشق 'áshik, محب muhibb, معشوق ma'shúk, معشوقه ma'shúkah.

To ADORN, آراستن árástan, پیراستن pírástan, زینت دادن zínat dádan, آرایش کردن áráyish kardan.

ADORNED, آراسته árástah, پیراسته pírástah, مزین muzayyan, محلی muhallá.

ADORNMENT, آرایش áráyish, زینت zínat, زیب zíb, پیرایش píráyish.

ADROIT, چشمبند chashm-band, چالاک دست chálák-dast, چیره دست chírah-dast.

ADROITNESS, چشمبندی chashm-bandí, چالاک دستی chálák-dastí, چیره دستی chírah-dastí.

ADULT (*adj.*), کبیر kabír, بالغ báligh. (*sub.*) صاحب ریش sáhib-rísh.

To ADULTERATE, مخلوط ساختن makhlút sákhtan.

ADULTERATED, مخلوط makhlút, مغشوش maghshúsh, فاسد fásid, مزور muzawwar.

ADULTERATION, فساد fasád, تغلب taghallub.

ADULTERER, زانی zání, زناکار ziná-kár.

ADULTERESS, زانیه záníyah.

ADULTERY, زنا ziná, زنا کاری ziná-kárí, زنائی محصنه ziná,í-i-muhsinah, سفاح sifáh.

To commit ADULTERY, زنا کردن ziná kardan, زنا کاری کردن ziná-kárí kardan.

ADVANCE (*of money*), پیشگی píshgí, سلف salaf.—(*to peasants to enable them to cultivate*) مساعده musá'adah, واسازی wá-sází.

To ADVANCE, پیش رفتن písh raftan, پیش آمدن písh ámadan, تقدیم نمودن takdím nimúdan.

ADVANCED-GUARD, پیشرو písh-rav, طلایه taláyah.

ADVANCEMENT (*promotion*), ترقی tarakkí, ارتقا irtiká, سرفرازی sar-farází, برتری bartarí.

ADVANTAGE, فائده fá,idah, نفع naf', منفعت manfa'at, سود súd, صرفه sarfah.

ADVANTAGEOUS, مفید mufíd, نافع náfi', نفع رسان naf'-rasán.

ADVENTURE, وقعه wak'ah, حادثه há-disah, ما جرا má-jará.

ADVENTURER, اوباش aubásh, نابکار ná-bi-kár.

ADVERB, ظرف zarf.

ADVERSARY, *vide* ENEMY, RIVAL.

ADVERSE, مخالف mukhálif, مغایر mugháyir, ناموافق ná-muwáfik, مناقض munákiz.

ADVERSITY, بدبختی bad-bakhtí, سختی sakhtí, شقاوت shakáwat, مخالفت mukhálafat, مشقت ma-shakkat, بلا balá, نکبت nakbat, مصیبت musíbat.

To ADVERTISE, اشتهار نمودن ishtihár nimúdan, اعلام نمودن i'lám nimúdan, اعلان نمودن i'lán nimúdan.

ADVERTISEMENT, اشتهار ishtihár, اعلام i'lám, اعلان i'lán.

ADVICE, پند pand, نصیحت nasíhat, رای rá,í تدبیر tadbír, مصلحت mas-lahat, وعظ wa'z, اندرز anduraz, صلاح saláh, موعظه mau'izah.

ADVISABLE, مناسب munásib, لایق láík.

ADVISABLENESS, مناسبت munása-bat, صلاح saláh.

To ADVISE, پند دادن pand dádan, نصیحت نمودن nasíhat nimúdan.

ADVOCATE, وکیل wakíl.

To ADVOCATE, طرف گرفتن taraf gi-riftan.

ADZE, تیشه tíshah.

AERONAUT, مرد بالون mard-i-bálún.

ÆSTHETICS, علم محسنات 'ilm-i-mah-sinát.

AFFABLE, *vide* KIND.

AFFAIR, کار kár, امر amr, عمل 'amal, معامله mu'ámalah, سر و کار sar wa kár, خصوص khusús, باب báb, بابت bábat, حال hál, ماده máddah.

To AFFECT (*feign*), بهانه کردن bahá-nah kardan, تقلید کردن taklíd kar-dan. — (*produce effect*) اثر کردن asar kardan, تاثیر کردن tá,sír kardan.

AFFECTION, *vide* LOVE, FRIEND-SHIP, CHARITY.

AFFECTIONATE, مهربان mihrbán,

شفیق shafík, مشفق mushfik, رؤف rú,úf.

To Affiance, نامزد فرمودن nám-zad firmúdan.

Affinity, نسبت nisbat, وابستگی wá-bastagí, جهت jihat, مناسبت munásabat.

Affirmation, تصدیق tasdík, ایجاب íjáb, اثبات isbát.

Affirmative, مثبت musbit, موئید mu,ayyid.—(*particle*) حرف اثبات harf-i-isbát, حرف تاکید harf-i-tákíd, حرف ایجاب harf-i-íjáb.

To Afflict, پریشان ساختن paríshán sákhtan, مبتلا ساختن mubtalá sákhtan, آزردن ázurdan, الم رسانیدن alam rasánídan.

Afflicted, غمناك gham-nák. غمگین gham-gín, غمزده gham-zadah, دلگیر dil-gír, رنجیده ranjídah, ملول malúl, اندوهناك andúh-nák, مضطرب muztarib, مخبط mukhabbat مکدر mukaddar, متالم mutá,llim.

Affliction, *vide* Grief.

Affront, هتك آبرو hatk-i-áb-rú, شتم shatm, خفت khiffat, سر شکستگی sar-shikastagí, بی ساختگی bí-sákhtagí.

To Affront, هتك آبرو کردن hatk-i-áb-rú kardan, دشنام دادن dushnám dádan.

Afire, سوزان súzán.

Afraid, ترسان tarsán, ترسناك tars-nák, خائف khá,if, هراسان hirásán.

Afresh, مجدداً mujaddadan, از سر نو az sar-i-nau.

After, پس pas, بعد ba'd, پی pai, عقب 'akab, اثر asar, دنبال dumbál.—(*one after the other*) پی در پی pai dar pai, متواتر mutawátir.

Afternoon, بعد ظهر ba'd-i-zuhr, عصر 'asr.

Afterwards, بعد از آن ba'd az án, من بعد min ba'd, از آن پس az án pas, بعده ba'dahu.

Again, باز báz, دیگر dígar, دگر digar, وا wá, واپس wá-pas, مکرراً mukarraran, بار دگر bár-i-digar, دیگر بار dígar-bár.

Against, خلاف khiláf, علی 'alá, مقابل mukábil, بضد bi-zidd, بر ضد bar zidd.

Agate, یشم yashm.

Age, عمر 'umr, ساله sálah, سن sinn, زاد zád.—(*era, time*) عهد 'ahad, زمان zamán.—(*old age*) پیری pírí, کبر السن kibaru-'s-sinn, هرم haram, مشیب mashíb.

To Age, پیر شدن pír shudan, مسن شدن musinn shudan.

Aged, مسن musinn, پیر pír, معمر mu'ammar, سالدیده sál-dídah.

Agency, وکالت wakálat, کار گذاری kár-guzárí.

Agent, وکیل wakíl, گماشته gumáshtah, نائب ná,ib, کارکن kár-kun, سر کار sar-kár, مباشر mubáshir.

To Aggravate, بدتر کردن badtar kardan.

Aggregate, جمله jumlah, مجموع majmú'.

Aggression, زبر دستی zabar-dastí, ظلم zulm, حمله hamlah.

Aghast, سر آسیمه sar-ásímah, متحیر mutahayyir, مضطرب muztarib.

Agile, چابك chábuk, چالاك chálák, چست chust.

Agility, چابکی chábukí, چالاکی chálákí, چستی chustí.

Agio (*difference in value of money*), صرف sarf.

To Agitate (*put in motion*), جنبانیدن jumbánídan, تحریك نمودن tahrík nimúdan. — (*distress*) آشوفتن áshúftan, پریشان ساختن paríshán sákhtan.

Agitation, تشویش tashwísh, اضطراب iztiráb, آشفتگی áshuftagí.—(*motion*), جنبش jumbish, تحریك tahrík.

Ago (*lately*), *vide* Newly.—(*past time*) گذشته guzashtah, ماضی mází, قبل kabl, سابق sábik.—(*a little while ago*) یکچندی پیش از این yak chandí písh az ín, اندکی قبل این andakí kabl-i-ín.—(*a few days ago*) چند روز پیش از این chand rúz písh az ín, چند روز قبل از این chand rúz kabl az ín, چند روز است chand rúz ast, چند روز شد chand rúz shud.—(*long ago*) *vide* Long.

Agony, *vide* Pain.—(*of death*) نزع naz', سکرات sakrát, جان کندنی ján-kandaní.

To Agree, قبول کردن kabúl kardan, راضی شدن rází shudan, موافقت نمودن muwáfakat nimúdan, قائل بودن ká,il búdan, پذیرفتن pazíruftan, قرار دادن karár dádan, کنار آمدن kanár ámadan.

Agreeable, پسندیده pasandídah, دلپذیر dil-pazír, دلپسند dil-pasand, مناسب munásib, موافق muwáfik, ساز گار sáz-gár, لایق láík, مقبول makbúl, مطبوع matbú', مرضی marzí.

Agreement, اتفاق ittifák, موافقت muwáfakat, وفاق wifák, اتحاد ittihád, عهد 'ahd, معاهدت mu'áhadat, شرط shart, پیمان paimán, وثیقه wasíkah, قول kaul, قرار karár, قرارداد karár-dád, بنا biná.

Agriculture, زراعت zirá'at, کشتکاری kisht-kárí, فلاحت faláhat.

Agriculturist, دهقان dihkán, کشتکار kisht-kár.

Ague, تب و لرز tab wa larz.

Aid, *vide* Assistance.

Aigrette (*ornament worn by women*), تیطه tiyatah.—(*royal, worn by princes*), جیغه jíká.

To Ail, نا خوش شدن ná-khúsh shudan, بیمار شدن bímár shudan.

Ailment, *vide* Complaint.

Aim, نشان nishán, شست shist.—(*to take aim*) دید کردن díd kardan, رو گرفتن rú giriftan.—(*to take aim from a rest or support to a gun*) دیاق کردن dayák kardan, دایاق گرفتن dáyák giriftan.

Air, هوا hawá, باد bád.—(*melody*) آوازه áwázah, نوا nawá.—(*deportment*) وجه wajh, وضع waz'.—(*to give oneself airs*) لاف زدن láf zadan, تکبر ورزیدن takabbur warzídan.

To Air, ترویح نمودن tarwíh nimúdan, تشمس نمودن tashammus nimúdan.

Air-bed, دوشك بادی dúshak-i-bádí.

Air-gun, تفنگ بادی tufang-i-bádí.

Air-hole, منفس manfas.

Airy, با روح bá-rúh.

Akin, برابر bar-á-bar, شبیه shabíh.

Alabaster, مرمر marmar.

Alacrity, *vide* Speed.

Alarm, آشفتگی áshuftagí, تحیر tahayyur.—(*call to arms, signal*) آوازه جنگ áwázah-i-jang, آهنگ áhang.

To Alarm, ترسانیدن tarsánídan, هراس ساختن hirás sákhtan.

Alarming, مهیب mahíb, هولناك haul-nák.

Alas! آه áh, واه wáh, دریغ dirígh, دریغا dirígh á, وای wáí, افسوس afsús, ویله wailah, فغان fighán, واویلا wá-wailá, ای وای ai-wáí, آوخ áwakh, هیهات haihát.

Albumen, سفیده تخم safídah-i-tukhm.

Alchemist, کیمیا گر kímiyá-gar.

Alchemy, الکیمیا al-kímiyá, کیمیا و سیمیا kímiyá wa símiyá.

Alcohol, عرق 'arak.

Alcove, شاهنشین sháh-nishín, طاق ták, محراب mihráb.

Alder-tree, درخت گز dirakht-i-gaz.

Alembic, *vide* Still.

Alert, زنده دل zindah-dil, چاق chák, هوشیار húsh-yár, گرم garm.

Alertness, هوشیاری húsh-yárí, هوشمندی húsh-mandí.

Algebra, الجبر al-jabr, الجبر و المقابلة al-jabr wa-'l-mukábalah.

Alien, بیگانه bígánah, غریب gharíb.

To Alight, پائین آمدن pá,ín ámadan, نزول نمودن nuzúl nimúdan, نشستن nishistan, فرود آمدن furúd ámadan.

Alike, برابر bar-á-bar, یکسان yaksán, نظیر nazír, مثال misál, مماثل mumásil.

Alimony, کابین kábín, نفقه nafakah.

Alive, زنده zindah, حی hayy.

Alkali, قلیا kalyá.

All, همه hamah, کل kull, جمیع jamí', جمله jumlah, تمام tamám, کلا و طرا kullan wa turran, اجمعین ajma'ína, جمهور jumhúr, همکنان hamkunán.

To Allay, تسکین دادن taskín dádan, نشاندن nishándan.

ALLEGATION, اسناد isnád, اقرار ikrár, تقریر takrír.

To ALLEGE, اسناد نمودن isnád nimúdan, اقرار کردن ikrár kardan, تقریر نمودن takrír nimúdan.

ALLEGIANCE, فرمان برداری firmán-bardárí.

ALLEGORIC, متشابه mutashábih.

ALLEGORY, تمثیل tamsíl, مثال misál, کنایه kináyah, مجاز majáz.

To ALLEVIATE, تخفیف دادن takhfíf dádan, تسکین نمودن taskín nimúdan, آرام دادن árám dádan.

ALLEVIATION, تخفیف takhfíf, تسکین taskín, آرام árám.

ALLEY, کوچه kúchah, خیابان khiyábán.

ALLIANCE (*connexion*), علاقه 'alákah, تعلق ta'alluk, دخل dakhl, نسبت nisbat. (*Vide* TREATY.)

ALLIGATOR, نهنگ nahang.

ALLITERATION, تجنیس tajnís.

To ALLOT, حصه کردن hissah kardan, دادن dádan, تقسیم کردن taksím kardan.

ALLOTMENT, حصه hissah, تقسیم taksím.

To ALLOW, گذاشتن guzáshtan, دادن dádan, دستور دادن dastúr dádan, اجازت دادن ijázat dádan, قائل بودن ká,il búdan, اذن دادن izn dádan, وا گذاشتن wá-guzáshtan, فرصت دادن fursat dádan, هشتن hishtan.

ALLOWABLE, مجاز mujáz, روا rawá, حلال halál.

ALLOWANCE, مبلغ مقرری mablagh-i-mukarrarí, بهره bahrah.

ALLOY, مخلوط makhlút, آمیزش ámízish.

To ALLUDE TO, کنایه کردن kináyah kardan, اشاره نمودن ishárah nimúdan.

To ALLURE, اغوا کردن ighwá kardan, ترغیب کردن targhíb kardan, فریفتن firíftan, کشیدن kashídan, جذب نمودن jazb nimúdan.

ALLUREMENT, اغوا ighwá, ترغیب targhíb, کشش kashish.

ALLURER, دل فریب dil-firíb.

ALLUSION, ایما ímá, رمز ramz, اشاره ishárah, ایهام íhám, عبارت 'ibárat, کنایه kináyah.

ALLY, دوست dúst, متفق muttafik, شریك sharík, رفیق rafík, همدم hamdam.

ALMANAC, تقویم takwím.

ALMIGHTY, قادر مطلق kádir-i-mutlak, حق تعالی hakk ta'álá.

ALMOND, بادام bádám, لوز lauz.—(*wild almond*) ارجن arjun, ارجین arjín.

ALMOND-CAKE (*made of almonds pounded, and a paste of sugar, cream, &c.*), باقلوا bákliwá.—(*of split almonds and brown sugar*) ساهون sáhún.

ALMOST, قریب karíb, نزدیك nazdík, تقریباً takríban, عنقریب 'an-karíb.

ALMS, صدقه sadakah, خیرات khairát, دهش dihish, زکات zikát.—(*alms prescribed by law*) زکات zikát.—(*voluntary alms*), صدقه sadakah.

ALMS-HOUSE, لنگر خانه langar-khánah.

ALOE (*plant*), درخت صبر dirakht-i-sabir.— (*drug*) صبر sabir.—(*lignum aloes*), عود 'úd.

ALOFT, فراز faráz, بالا bálá.

ALONE, تنها tanhá, تن تنها tan-i-tanhá, منفرد munfarid, مجرد mujarrad, منحرد munharid, وحد wahd, واحد wáhid, یگانه yagánah, بانفراده bi-infirádah.

ALONG WITH, *vide* TOGETHER.

ALOOF, دور dúr, کناره kanárah.

ALOUD, بلند buland.

ALPHABET, حروف تهجی hurúf-i-tahajjí, هجاء hijá,. (*Vide* LETTER.)

ALPHABETICAL, بقاعده تهجی bi-ká'idah-i-tahajjí.

ALREADY, هنوز hanúz, همینوقت hamín-wakht. (*Vide* YET.)

ALSO, هم ham, نیز níz, ایضاً aizan.

ALTAR, مذبح mazbah (*pl.* مذابح mazábih), قربانگاه kurbán-gáh.

To ALTER, تغییر نمودن taghyír nimúdan, تبدیل کردن tabdíl kardan, عوض کردن 'awaz kardan.

ALTERATION, تغیر taghayyur, تبدیل tabdíl.

ALTERCATION, مباحثه mubáhasah,

مناقشه munákashah, منازعه muná-za'ah, نزاع nizá', مذاکره muzákarah. مجادله mujádalah, تکرار takrár, قیل و قال kíl-u-kál, دعوی da'wá, ستیزه sitízah.

ALTERNATE, یك در میان yak dar miyán. — (*alternate days*) غباً ghibban, یکروز در میان yak rúz dar miyán.

ALTERNATELY, بنوبه bi-naubah, نوبتاً naubatan.

ALTHOUGH, اگرچه agarchih, گرچه garchih, هر چند که har-chand kih, علی آن 'alá án, با وجود که bá-wujúd-kih.

ALTITUDE, ارتفاع irtifá', بلندی bu-landí. — (*to take the altitude*) اندازهٔ ارتفاع کردن andázah-i-irtifá' kardan.

ALTOGETHER, بالکل bi-'l-kull, بالمره bi-'l-marrah, جمیعاً jamí'an, سراسر sar-á-sar, بالتمام bi-'t-tamám, همه رویهم رفته hamah rúí-ham raftah, کلاً kullan, کلاً و قاطبةً kul-lan wa kátibatan.—(*taking all into consideration*), بهمه جهت bi-hamah jihat.

ALUM, زاج سفید záj-i-safíd, شب shibb.

ALWAYS, همیشه hamíshah, همواره hamwárah, هر وقت har wakht, هر زمان har zamán, مدام mudám, دائم dá,im, هر دم har dam, علی الدوام 'alá-'d-dawám, پیوسته paiwastah, دمبدم dam bi-dam, متصلاً muttasilan, همیشه اوقات hamíshah aukát.

AMALGAM, ملغمه malghamah (*eur.*), مخلوط makhlút.

To AMALGAMATE, آمیختن ámíkhtan.

AMANUENSIS, کاتب kátib.

To AMASS, جمع کردن jam' kardan, فراهم آوردن faráham áwardan.

AMATEUR, مفت muft.

AMATIVE, عاشق 'áshik.

AMATIVENESS, عاشقی 'áshikí, عشق 'ishk.

To AMAZE, تعجب نمودن ta'ajjub nimúdan, حیرت کردن hairat kar-dan, متعجب نمودن muta'ajjib nimúdan.

AMAZED, حیران hairán, متحیر muta-hayyir, متعجب muta'ajjib, سراسیمه sar-ásímah, سرگردان sar-gardán, مات mát, آشفته áshuftah, مدهوش madhúsh, دنگ dang.

AMAZEMENT, آشفتگی áshuftagí, حیرت hairat, تحیر tahayyur, عجب 'ajab, تعجب ta'ajjub, هکر hakar, دهشت dihshat, ششدر shish-dar, تلواسه talwásah.

AMAZING, *vide* WONDERFUL.

AMAZON, زنکه zanakah.

AMBASSADOR, ایلچی ílchí, رسول rasúl, سفیر safír, پیك paik.—(*extraordi-nary*) سفیر کبیر safír-i-kabír.

AMBER, کهربا kah-rubá, عنبر 'ambar.

AMBERGRIS, عنبر 'ambar, عبیر 'abír.

AMBIGUITY, اشتباه ishtibáh, ایهام íhám.

AMBIGUOUS, مبهم mubham, مشتبه mushtabih, مشکوك mashkúk مغلق mughlak.

AMBITION, علو همت 'uluw-i-himmat, حوصله hausalah, بلند همتی buland-himmatí.

AMBITIOUS, استکبار istikbár, بلند همت buland-himmat.

To AMBLE, یرغه رفتن yurghah, raftan.

AMBUSCADE, کمین kamín, مکمن makman, کمینگاه kamín-gáh.

To AMELIORATE, بهتر کردن bihtar kardan, خوبتر کردن khúbtar kar-dan.

AMELIORATION, بهتری bihtarí.

To AMEND (*trans.*), درست کردن du-rust kardan, تصحیح کردن tashíh kardan.—(*intrans.*) بر سر ایستاده نمودن bar sar ístádah nimúdan.

AMENDMENT, اصلاح isláh, تصحیح tas-híh, بهتری bihtarí.

AMETHYST, یاقوت خمری yákút-i-khamrí, یاقوت رمانی yákút-i-rum-máni, یاقوت کبود yákút-i-kabúd, جبلقوم jaballakúm.

AMICABLE, لطیف latíf, شیرین shírín, مرغوب marghúb, مهربان mihrbán.

AMICABLENESS, شیرینی shíríní, مهر mihr, مهربانی mihrbání.

AMMONIAC (*plant*), اشق ushak.—(*salt*), نوشادر naushádur.

AMMUNITION, اسباب جنگ asbáb-i-jang.—(*pouch*) کیب kíf, گله دان gullah-dán.
AMNESTY, عفو نامه 'afw-námah, عفو 'afw.
AMONG, میان miyán, در میان dar miyán, بین bain, مابین má-bain, اندر andar, لا lá (*vulg.*)
AMOROUS, عاشق 'áshik, دلبسته dil-bastah, شیفته shíftah.
AMOUNT (*sum*), جمله jumlah, جمع jam', حاصل hásil, مبلغ mablagh.
AMOUR, عشقبازی 'ishk-bází, تعشق ta'ashshuk, معاشقه mu'áshakah.
AMPHIBOLOGY, ایهام íhám.
AMPHITHEATRE, مظهر mazhar.
AMPLE (*space*), پهن pahn, واسع wási', عریض 'aríz, بسیط basít.—(*quantity*), فراخ farákh, وافر wáfir, وفور wufúr.
AMPLENESS (*space*), پهنه pahnah, عرض 'arz.—(*quantity*) فراخی farákhí, وفرت wafrat.
To AMPUTATE, *vide* To CUT.
AMPUTATION, قطع kat', انقطاع inkitá'.
AMULET, تعوید ta'wíz, حرز hirz, حمایل hamáíl.
To AMUSE, صفا دادن safá dádan, خوش کردن khúsh kardan, لذت دادن lazzat dádan.
AMUSEMENT, بازی bází, تفرج tafarruj, صفا safá, لعب la'b.
AMUSING, تفرج نما tafarruj-nimá, دلکش dil-kash.
ANACHRONISM, غلط در زمان ghalat dar zamán, اشتباه ishtibáh.
ANAGRAM, تحریف tahríf.
ANAGRAMMATIST, محرف muharrif,
ANALOGOUS, متشبه mutashabbih, مناسب munásib.
ANALOGY, تمثیل tamsíl, نسبت nisbat.
To ANALYSE, تجزیه نمودن tajziyah nimúdan.
ANALYSIS, تفصیل tafsíl, تقسیم taksím, تفریق tafrík.—(*chemical*) تحلیل tahlíl, تجزیه tajziyah.
ANALYST, تجزیه کننده tajziyah kunandah.
ANARCHY, غدر ghadr, بی سیاست bí-siyásat, شورش shúrish.
ANATOMIST, تشریحدان tashríh-dán.
ANATOMY (*the science*), علم تشریح 'ilm-i-tashríh.
ANCESTOR, اب ab (*pl.* آبا ábá), جد jadd (*pl.* اجداد ajdád), سلف salaf (*pl.* اسلاف asláf), متقدم mutakaddim (*pl.* متقدمین mutakaddimín).
ANCESTRY, نسب nasab, نسبت nisbat.
To ANCHOR, لنگر انداختن langar andákhtan.
ANCHOR, لنگر langar. — (*to weigh anchor*) لنگر بر داشتن langar bar dáshtan.
ANCHORAGE, لنگرگاه langar-gáh.
ANCHORITE, زاهد záhid, عابد 'ábid.
ANCIENT, قدیم kadím, پیشین píshín, عتیق 'atík, دیرینه dírínah, سلف salaf.
The ANCIENTS, اولیان avvaliyán, پیشینان píshínán, اسلاف asláf, متقدمین mutakaddimín.
AND, و wa, و u.—(*and so forth, &c.*) وغیره waghairah, الخ alakh.
ANECDOTE, داستان dástán, نکته nuktah, افسانه áfsánah.
ANEMONE, شقائق shaká,ik, شقائق النعمان shaká,iku-'n-nu'mán.
ANGEL, فرشته firishtah, ملك malak.—(*angel of death*) ملك الموت malaku-'l-maut, عزرائل 'izrá,il, قابض الارواح kábizu-'l-arwáh. — (*guardian angel, attendant on man*), قعید ka'íd, تابع tábi'.—(*two angels who interrogate the dead*) منکر و نکیر munkar wa nakír.—(*invisible angel whose voice is heard*) سروش surúsh, هاتف hátif.
ANGELIC, ملکی malakí, فرشته وش firishtah-wash.
ANGER, غضب ghazab, کین kín, کینه kínah, خشم khishm, غیظ ghaiz, قهر kahr, رنجش ranjish, سورت saurat, تغیر taghayyur, سخط sukht, حدت hiddat.
ANGLE, گوشه gúshah, کنج kunj, زاویه záwiyah.—(*acute angle*) زاویه حاده záwiyah-i-háddah. — (*obtuse angle*) زاویه منفرجه záwiyah-i-munfarijah. —(*right angle*) زاویه قائمه záwiyah-i-ká,imah.

ANGRY, غضبناک ghazab-nák, خشمناک khishm-nák, بر آشفته bar-áshuftah, کجخلق kaj-khulk, متنفر mutan-affir, گرم garm, آزرده ázurdah, مکدر mukaddar, رنجیده ranjídah, در هم dar-ham, خفا khafá (*obs.*).

ANGUISH, *vide* GRIEF, PAIN.

ANGULAR, زاویه دار záwiyah-dár, گوشه دار gúshah-dár.

ANIMAL (*living being*), جاندار ján-dár, ذو حیات zú-hayát, ذی نفس zí nafas.—(*domestic animal, cattle or fish*) حیوان haiwán.—(*wild animal, reptile or insect*) جانور jánwar.

To ANIMATE, زنده کردن zindah kardan, جان دادن ján dádan, حیات دادن hayát dádan. — (*incite*) تحریک نمودن tahrík nimúdan, انگیختن angíkhtan.

ANIMOSITY, *vide* ENMITY.

ANISE, شبت shabt, سبت sabt, انیسون anísún, رازیانهٔ رومی rázi-yánah-i-rúmí.

ANKLE, اشتالنگ ishtálang, مچ پا much-i-pá, قوزک پا kúzak-i-pá, کعب ka'b, گوزک gúzak.

ANKLET, پای برنجن pái-baranjan, پا زیب pá-zíb, خلخال khalkhál. —(*of small bells*) سوسک súsk.

ANNALIST, اخباری akhbárí, راوی ráwí.

ANNALS, اخبار akhbár, تواریخ tawá-rikh.

To ANNEAL, گرم کوفتن garm kúftan.

To ANNEX, الحاق کردن ilhák kardan.

ANNEXATION, الحاق ilhák, اضافه izá-fah.

To ANNIHILATE, معدوم کردن ma'dúm kardan, نا بود کردن ná-búd kardan, سلب نمودن salb nimúdan, منقلع گردانیدن munkali' gardánídan.

To be ANNIHILATED, سلب شدن salb shudan, مسلوب شدن maslúb shu-dan, معدوم شدن ma'dúm shudan, منقلع بودن munkali' búdan.

ANNIHILATION, نیستی nístí, اعدام i'dám.

ANNIVERSARY, سالگانی sáligání.

To ANNOTATE, حاشیه نوشتن háshiyah niwishtan.

ANNOTATION, حاشیه háshiyah, شرح sharh, بیان bayán.

ANNOTATOR, شارح shárih.

To ANNOUNCE, آگاه ساختن ágáh sákhtan.

To ANNOY, *vide* To VEX.

ANNOYANCE, ضرر zarar, رنج ranj, زحمت zahmat, ایذا ízá, آزار ázár. (*Vide* TROUBLE.)

ANNUAL, سالیانه sáliyánah, سنوی sanawí.

ANNUITANT, وظیفه خور wazífah-khúr, سالیانه دار sáliyánah-dár.

To ANNUL, باطل کردن bátil kardan, نسخ نمودن naskh nimúdan, منسوخ کردن mansúkh kardan.

ANNULAR, حلقه وار halkah-wár.

ANNULLED, معطل mu'attal, منسوخ mansúkh.

ANNULMENT, ابطال ibtál, محو mahw, نسخ naskh.

To ANOINT, روغن مالیدن raughan málídan, مسح نمودن mash nimú-dan.

ANOMALOUS, خلاف طبیعت khiláf-i-tabí'at.

ANOMALY, خرق عادت khark-i-'ádat.

ANONYMOUS, اسمی نا معلوم ísmí-ná-ma'lúm.

ANOTHER, دیگر dígar, دگر digar, غیر ghair.

ANSWER, جواب jawáb, پاسخ pásukh.

To ANSWER, جواب دادن jawáb dádan. — (*succeed*) راست افتادن rást uftádan.

ANSWERABLE (*responsible*), جوابدار jawáb-dár, ضامن zámin, ملتزم mul-tazim.

ANT, مور múr, مورچه múrchah. — (*large black ant*) مور سواری múr-i-suwárí.—(*white ants*) موریانه múr-yánah, مورجنه múrjanah.—(*ant-hill or nest*) چال مورچه chál-i-múrchah.

ANTAGONIST, *vide* ENEMY.

ANTARCTIC, قطب جنوبی kutb-i-janúbí.

To ANTECEDE, پیش رفتن písh raf-tan, مقدم شدن mukaddam shudan.

ANTECEDENT (*grammatical term*), اسم فاعل ism-i-fá'il.

ANTECHAMBER, کفش کن kafsh-kun,
ANTEDILUVIAN, قبل از طوفان kabl az túfán.
ANTELOPE, آهو áhú, غزال ghazál.
ANTERIOR (*antecedent*) مقدم mukaddam, پیشین píshín, سابق sábik, اول avval.
ANTHEM, نعت na't, تسبیح tasbíh.
ANTICHRIST, دجال dajjál.
To ANTICIPATE, پنداشتن pindáshtan, پیش گمان کرده شدن písh gumán kardah shudan.
ANTICIPATION, پیش وقتی písh-waktí.—(*by anticipation*) پیش از وقت písh az wakt.
ANTIDOTE, تریاق tiryák, طریاق tiryák, دافع زهر dáfi'-i-zahr.
ANTIMONY, راسخت rásukht.—(*powder for the eyes*) سرمه surmah, کحل kuhl.
ANTIPATHY, نفرت nifrat, تنفر tanaffur, کره karih, رغم raghm.
ANTIQUARY, جامع العجایبات jámi'u-'l-'ajáíbát.
ANTIQUATED, *vide* OLD.
ANTIQUITIES (*ruins of ancient buildings, &c.*), آثار قدیم ásár-i-kadím.
ANTIQUITY, ما تقدم má-takaddum, ایام سابق ayyám-i-sábik, زمان قدیم zamán-i-kadím.
ANTITHESIS, ضد zidd, تضاد tazádd.
ANTLER, شاخ shákh.
ANTLERED, شاخ دار shákh-dár.
ANUS, کون kún, ماتحت má-taht, موضع معتاد mauza'-i-mu'tád, محل قعود mahall-i-ku'úd.
ANVIL, سندان sindán.
ANXIETY, دلتنگی dil-tangí, اضطراب iztiráb, غم gham, فکر fikr, تشویش tashwísh.
ANXIOUS, دلتنگ dil-tang, مضطرب muztarib, مکدر mukaddar, مشوش mushawwash, متفکر mutafakkir.
ANY, هیچ hích.—(*anyone*) کسی kasí, هیچ کس hích kas, شخصی shakhsí.—(*anything*) چیزی chízí.—(*anywhere*) بجای bi-jáí.—(*negative*) بهیچ جا bi-hích já. — (*anyhow*) بوجهی bi-wajhí, بهر نوع bi-har nau'.
—(*negative*) بهیچ وجه bi-hích wajh. بهیچ طور bi-hích taur.
AORIST (*of a verb*), مضارع muzári'.
APACE, زود zúd.
APART, جدا jidá, علیحده 'aláhiddah, مفصل mufassal, مباین mubáín, جداگانه jidáganah.—(*aside*) درکنار dar kanár, برطرف bartaraf.
APARTMENTS, منزل manzil.
APATHETIC, سرد sard, بی میل bí-mail.—(*to be apathetic*) ذهول نمودن zuhúl nimúdan.
APATHY, سردی sardí, مساهله musáhalah.
APE, *vide* MONKEY.
To APE, تقلید کردن taklíd kardan.
APERIENT, مسهل mus-hil, سهول sahúl.
APERTURE, سوراخ súrákh, شکاف shikáf.
APEX, اوج auj.
APHORISM, مثل masal, مثال misál, تمثیل tamsíl.
APOCHRYPHAL, مزور muzawwar, جعلی ja'lí.
APOCOPE (*cutting off the final syllable*), حذف hazf.—(*cutting off a short vowel*) جزم jazm.
APOGEE, اوج auj.
APOLOGETIC, پوزش پذیر púzish-pazír.
To APOLOGIZE, اعتذار کردن i'tizár kardan, معذرت خواستن ma'zirat khwástan, عذر کردن 'uzr kardan, پوزش نمودن púzish nimúdan.
APOLOGUE, مثل masal, مثال misál, تمثیل tamsíl.
APOLOGY, عذر 'uzr, اعتذار i'tizár, معذرت ma'zirat, پوزش púzish.
APOPLECTIC, سکته زده saktah-zadah.
APOPLEXY, سکته saktah.
APOSTACY, انکار دین inkár-i-dín, ترک ملت tark-i-millat, ارتداد irtidád.
APOSTATE, منکر دین munkir-i-dín, مرتد murtadd.
To APOSTATIZE, ارتداد نمودن irtidád nimúdan, مرتد شدن murtadd shudan.
APOSTLE, رسول rasúl.—(*of Christ*) حواری hawárí.
APOSTLESHIP, رسالت rasálat.

Apostolic, پیغمبری paigham-barí, پیغامبری paighám-barí.
Apothecary, عطار 'attár, دوا فروش dawá-furúsh. — (*apothecary's shop*) دوا خانه dawá-khánah.
Appanage, ملك milk.
Apparatus, یراق yarák, اسباب asbáb, رخت rakht, آلات álát, ساز sáz.
Apparel, *vide* Clothes.
Apparent, هویدا huwaidá, پدید padíd, آشکار áshkár, آشکاره áshkárah, ظاهر záhir, عیان 'iyán, فاش fásh, روشن raushan, واضح wázih, علانی 'aláni, مبین mubín, بدیهی badíhí, پیدا paidá.
Apparently, ظاهراً záhiran, عیاناً 'iyánan.
Apparition, خیال khiyál, تجلی tajallí.
Appeal, طلب talab, مراجعت murája'at, رجوع rujú', حوالت hawálat.
To Appeal, در خواستن dar khwástan. — (*legal term*) رجوع فرمودن rujú' firmúdan, مراجعت نمودن murája'at nimúdan.
To Appear, نمودن nimúdan, ظاهر شدن záhir shudan, پدید آمدن padíd ámadan, معلوم شدن ma'lúm shudan, مرئی شدن mara,í shudan.
Appearance, ظهور zuhúr, صورت súrat, اشکال ashkál, پیدائش paidá,ish.
To Appease, آرامیدن árámídan, تسلی دادن tasallí dádan.
Appellation, لقب lakab, نام nám.
To Append, آویز کردن áwíz kardan, الحاق نمودن ilhák nimúdan.
Appendage, ضمیمه zamímah, الحاق ilhák, وصل wasl.
Appendix, ذیل zail, ضمیمه zamímah.
To Appertain, راجع نمودن ráji' nimúdan, مربوط شدن marbút shudan.
Appetite, اشتها ishtihá, هوس hawas, میل mail.
To Applaud, تحسین کردن tahsín kardan, بلند آواز گردیدن buland-áwáz gardídan, توصیف کردن tausíf kardan, مرحبا گفتن marhabá guftan.
Applause, تحسین tahsín, آفرین áfirín.

Apple, سیب síb, سیو sív (*vulg.*).—(*crab-apple*) سیب جنگلی síb-i-jangalí.—(*of the eye*) مردمك چشم mardumak-i-chashm, بوبو búbú.
Appliances, اسباب asbáb, آلات álát, ساز sáz, یراق yarák.
Applicable to, مخصوص makhsús, منحصر munhasir.
Application (*assiduity*), توجه tawajjuh, اقدام ikdám, تقید takayyud, اشتغال ishtighál.
To Apply, در خواستن dar khwástan.
To Appoint, تعیین نمودن ta'yín nimúdan, نصب کردن nasb kardan; مقرر کردن mukarrar kardan, ممتاز کردن mumtáz kardan.
Appointment (*office*), منصب mansib, تعیین ta'yín, عهده 'uhdah.
To Apportion, *vide* To Allot.
Apposite, مناسب munásib, موافق muwáfik.
To Appreciate, غنیمت دانستن ghanímat dánistan.
To Apprehend, *vide* To Seize, To Fear, To Suppose.
Apprentice (*to a trade, &c.*), شاگرد shágird.
To Apprentice, شاگرد ساختن shágird sákhtan.
Apprenticeship, شاگردی shágirdí.
Approach, تقرب takarrub, قربت kurbat, دخول dukhúl.
To Approach, نزدیك آمدن nazdík ámadan, تقریب نمودن takríb nimúdan, تقدیم نمودن takdím nimúdan.
Approbation, استصواب istiswáb; پسند pasand, قبول kabúl.
Appropriate, مناسب munásib, قابل kábil, سزاوار sazáwar, موافق muwáfik.
To Appropriate, تخصیص کردن takhsís kardan, اختصاص نمودن ikhtisás nimúdan, مخصوص کردن makhsús kardan.
Approval, *vide* Approbation.
To Approve of, پسندیدن pasandídan, تحسین کردن tahsín kardan, میل داشتن mail dáshtan, دوست داشتن dúst dáshtan, نیکو داشتن níkú dáshtan.

APPROXIMATE, نزدیك nazdík, نزد nazd, قریب karíb.

APPROXIMATION, تقریب takríb, تقارب takárub, نزدیکی nazdíkí.

APPURTENANCES, متعلقات muta'allikát, ملتزمین multazimín.

APRICOT, زردآلو zard-álú.—(*preserved and dried*) قیسی kaisí, خوبانی khúbání.

APRIL, اوریل avríl, نیسان naisán.

APRON, فوته fútah, پیش دامنی písh-dámaní, دامن بند dáman-band.

A PROPOS, با محل bá-mahall, بجا bijá, بر وقت bar wakt.

APT, زرنگ zaring, زیرك zírak, واقف wákif, ماهر máhir.—(*suitable*) مناسب munásib, موافق muwáfik, لایق láík, قابل kábil.

APTITUDE, زرنگی zaringí, هنر hunar, فراست firásat. — (*suitability*) مناسبت munásabat, موافقت muwáfakat.

AQUAFORTIS, *vide* VITRIOL.

AQUARIUM, ماهی خانه máhí-khánah.

AQUATIC, آبی ábí.

AQUEDUCT, نهر nahr, آبگذر áb-guzar, جوی júí, جدول jadwal, جوب júb (*vulg.*).—(*channel leading over a hollow*) پلخنگ pulkhung, سواره suwárah.—(*subterraneous aqueduct*) قنات kanát, کاریز káríz.—(*a channel of stonework built in an inclined plane, through which water flows into tanks or cisterns at intervals*), شرشرك shurshurak.

AQUILINE, نسری nasrí.

ARABESQUE (*ornamental pattern*), نقش naksh.

ARABIA, عرب 'arab, عربستان 'arabistán.

ARABIAN, عربی 'arabí, تازی tází.—(*an Arab*) عرب 'arab.—(*a Bedouin or desert Arab*) اعراب a'ráb, بدوی badawí.

ARBITRARY (*despotic*), مختار mukhtár, مطلق mutlak, مستقل mustakill.

ARBITRATION, محاکمه muhákamah, فیصل faisal, حکم hukm.

ARBITRATOR, ثالث sális, میانچی miyán-chí, حکم hakam, منصف munsif, مصلح muslih.

ARBOUR, چفته chiftah, چار طاق chár-ták, سایابان sáyábán.

ARC, قوس kaus.

ARCADE, طاق ták, گنبد gumbad.

ARCH, کمان kamán, طاق ták, محراب mihráb, عرش 'arsh, قطاع kitá'.—(*of a bridge*) چشمه chashmah.—(*false arches, indented pattern on a wall*) طاقنما ták-nimá.

To ARCH, طاق زدن ták zadan.

ARCHAIC, عتیق 'atík.

ARCHANGEL, مقرب mukarrab.

ARCHBISHOP, اسقف بزرگ uskuf-i-buzurg, مطران matrán.

ARCHDEACON, پیش نماز písh-namáz.

ARCHDUKE, ارشیدوك arshídúk.

ARCHED, مقوس mukawwas.

ARCHER, تیر انداز tír-andáz, کماندار kamán-dár.

ARCHERY, تیر اندازی tír-andází, کمان کشی kamán-kashí.

ARCHETYPE, اصل asl, نسخه nuskhah.

ARCH-FIEND, شیطان shaitán.

ARCHITECT, استاد بنا ustád-i-banná, معمار باشی mi'már-báshí.

ARCHIVES, دیوان díwán, دفتر خانه daftar-khánah.—(*Keeper of the Archives*) دفتر دار daftar-dár.

ARCHWAY (*narrow passage or close in a street leading under an arch*), سائبات sá,'ibát, سهبات sahbát.

ARCTIC, طرف شمال taraf-i-shimál.

ARDENT, غیرت کش ghairat-kash, غیرت مند ghairat-mand.

ARDOUR, غیرت ghairat, رغبت raghbat.

ARDUOUS, *vide* DIFFICULT.

AREA (*expanse*), عرصه 'arsah, فضا fazá, ساحت sáhat, حیز hayyiz.—(*of a house, &c.*) صحن sahn, حیاطه hiyátah.

ARENA, میدان maidán, عرصه 'arsah.

To ARGUE, بحث کردن bahs kardan, منازره کردن munázarah kardan.—(*argument according to reason*) دلیل عقلی dalíl-i-'aklí.—(*according to hearsay or tradition*) دلیل نقلی dalíl-i-naklí.—(*to argue ac-*

cording to reason) بطور عقلی بحث کردن bi-taur-i-'aklí bahs kardan.

Argument, بحث bahs, مباحثه mubáhasah, حجت hujjat, دلیل dalíl (*pl.* ادله adillah).—(*disputation*) *vide* Altercation, Dispute.

Arid, خشک khushk, سوخته súkhtah.

Aridness, خشکی khushkí.

Aright, راست rást, درست durust.

To Arise, بر آمدن bar ámadan, بر خاستن bar khástan, صادر شدن sádir shudan, بر پا شدن bar pá shudan.

Aristocracy, امرا umará.

Arithmetic, علم حساب 'ilm-i-hisáb, علم اعداد 'ilm-i-a'dád.

Arithmetical, حسابی hisábí.

Arithmetician, حسابگر hisáb-gar.

Ark (*coffer*) صندوق sandúk, تابوت tábút.—(*of Noah*) کشتیء نوح kashtí-i-núh, سفینهء نوح safínah-i-núh.

Arm, بازو bázú, بال bál.—(*from elbow to wrist*) ساعد sá'id, عضد 'azud.—(*armpit*) بغل baghal, ابط ibt.—(*to cross the arms*) دست بر سینه نهادن dast bar sínah nihádan.

To Arm, مسلح کردن musallah kardan, سلاح پوشیدن siláh púshídan.

Armadillo, نهنگ دشتی nahang-i-dashtí.

Armful, آغوش ághúsh.

Armistice, متارکه mutárakah.

Armorial-bearings, نشان nishán, علامت 'alámat.

Armory, جبه خانه jabbah-khánah, سلاح خانه siláh-khánah, خانه اسلحه khánah-i-aslihah.

Armour, زره zirah, جوشن jaushan, سلاح siláh, جبه jabbah, درع dir'.—(*chain armour*) زره zirah.—(*plate armour*) چهار آئنه chahár á,inah.

Armour-bearer, سلاحدار siláh-dár.

Armourer, جیشگر jaish-gar, صیقل saikal.

Arms, سلاح siláh, یراق yarák, برگ barg, آلات álát, ساز sáz.—(*fire-arms*), اسلحهء ناریه aslihah-i-náríyah.

Army, سپاه sipáh, سپه sipah, لشکر Lishkar, عسکر 'askar, فوج fauj, جیش jaish, جند jund, قشون kushún. (*Vide* Regiment.)

Aroma, بو bú, رائحه rá,ihah.

Aromatic, خوش بو khúsh-bú, معطر mu'attar, مشموم mashmúm.

Aromatics, ابزار abzár.

Around, گرد gird, گرداگرد gird-á-gird, اطراف atráf, دور daur, حوالی hawálá, پیرامن pairámun, بهر جانب bi-har jánib, در دورة dar daurah, دوران dauran.

To Arouse, *vide* To Rouse.

To Arraign, متهم ساختن muttahim sákhtan, تهمت دادن tuhmat dádan.

Arraignment, تهمت tuhmat.

To Arrange, آراستن árástan, ترتیب نمودن tartíb nimúdan, نصب کردن nasb kardan, تدارک نمودن tadáruk nimúdan, انتظام نمودن intizám nimúdan, پیراستن pírástan.

Arrangement, انتظام intizám, ترتیب tartíb, آراستگی árástagí, تنظیم tanzím.

Arrant, بدترین badtarín.—(*an arrant knave*) نابکار ná-bi-kár, اوباش aubásh, دستکج dast-kaj, شریر sharír.

Array, صف saff.—(*attire*) رخت rakht, لباس libás, پوشاک púshák.

To Array, صف آراستن saff árástan.—(*attire*) پیراستن pírástan, آراستن árástan, پوشیدن púshídan, پوشانیدن púshánídan.

Arrears, باقی bákí, بقایا bakáyá, تتمه tatimmah, ما بقی má-baká.

Arrest, حبس habs, گرفتگی giriftagí, قبض kabz.

To Arrest, گرفتار کردن giriftár kardan, گیر نمودن gír nimúdan, کسیل کردن kisíl kardan, سر راه گرفتن sar-i-ráh giriftan.

Arrival, ورود wurúd, اتیان ityán, دخول dukhúl.

To Arrive, رسیدن rasidan, داخل شدن dákhil shudan, وارد گشتن wárid gashtan, ورود نمودن wurúd nimúdan.

ARROGANCE, کبر kibr, تکبر takabbur, غرور ghurúr, استکبار istikbár, گستاخی gustákhí.

ARROGANT, متکبر mutakabbir, مغرور maghrúr, گستاخ gustákh.

ARROGANTLY, متکبرانه mutakabbi-ránah, گستاخانه gustákhánah, مغروراً maghrúran.

To ARROGATE, فخر نمودن fakhr ni-múdan, سر کشی کردن sar-kashí kardan.

ARROW, تیر tír, سهم sahm, ناوك náwak, خدنگ khadang.—(*head of an arrow*) پیکان paikán.—(*shaft*) قلم kalam.—(*feathers*) پر par, تالش talish.—(*notch*) سوفار súfár, جای زه já,í-i-zih.—(*storm of arrows*), تیر باران tír-bárán.

ARSENAL, جبه خانه jabbah-khánah, توپخانه túp-khánah, قور خانه kúr-khánah.

ARSENIC, مرگ موش marg-i-músh, تراب الهالك turábu-'l-hálik.

ARSON, سوزندگی súzindagí.

ART, فن fann, حرفت hirfat, هنر hunar, کسب kasb, صنعت san'at (*pl.* صنائع saná,i'). (*Vide* ARTIFICE, DECEIT, TRICK.)

ARTERY, شریان shiryán (*pl.* شرایین shiráyín).—(*main-artery*) شاهرگ sháh-rag. — (*pulmonary-artery*) رگ شش rag-i-shush.

ARTFUL, حیله ساز hílah-sáz, دغا پیشه daghá-píshah.

ARTFULLY, حیلتاً hílatan, بمکر bi-makr.

ARTFULNESS, مکاری makkárí.

ARTICHOKE, کنگر kangar, انگنار anginár.—(*Jerusalem artichoke*) سیب زمین ایرانی síb-i-zamín-i-íráni.

ARTICLE (*rule*), قانون kánún, قاعده ká'idah, ماده máddah.—(*in grammar*), معرفت ma'rifat. (*Vide* THING).—(*literary*) مقاله makálah, فصل fasl.—(*leading article*) عرض مخصوص 'arz-i-makhsús, مقاله مخصوص makálah-i-makhsús. (*ware*) متاع matá' (*pl.* امتعه amti'ah.—(*articles de luxe*) اسباب تجمل asbáb-i-tajammul.

To ARTICLE, اجیر ساختن ajír sákhtan.

To ARTICULATE, تلفظ کردن talaffuz kardan.

ARTICULATION (*pronunciation, utterance*), تلفظ talaffuz.—(*proper accent when reading*) قراءت kira,at; تجوید tajwíd.

ARTIFICE, حیله hílah, فریب fíríb, بهانه bahánah, کید kaid, گول gúl, ساخته sákhtah, مکر makr, دمدمه damdamah, نیرنگ nairang.

ARTIFICER, کاریگر kárí-gar, پیشه ور píshah-war, صنعتگر san'at-gar.

ARTIFICIAL, صناعی saná'í, عملی 'amalí, ساختگی sákhtagí, جعلی ja'lí.

ARTILLERY, توپخانه túp-khánah.—(*commandant of artillery*) توپچی باشی túp-chí-báshí.

ARTILLERYMAN, توپچی túp-chí.

ARTIST, صنعتگر san'at-gar, استاد ustád. (*Vide* PAINTER.)

ARTLESS, ساده دل sádah-dil, ساده لوح sádah-lúh, پاك دل pák-dil.

ARTLESSNESS, ساده دلی sádah-dilí, پاك دلی pák-dilí.

AS, چو chú, چون chún, همچو ham-chú, چنانکه chunán-kih, چنانچه chunán-chih, چونکه chún-kih.—(*as soon as*) همان hamán, همانکه hamán-kih, همین hamín, همینکه hamín-kih, بمحض bi-mahz, بمجرد bi-mujarrad.—(*as if it were*) کما کان kamá kána, گویا gúyá, اگر چنانچه agar chunán-chih.—(*as before*) ایضاً aizan, کالاول ka-'l-av-val.—(*as long as*) مادام mádám, مادامیکه mádámí-kih.—(*as much as*) آنقدر án-kadar, آنچندان án-chandán, مساوی musáwí, مقابله mukábalah.—(*twice as much as*) دو مقابله dú mukábalah, دو مساوی dú musáwí. — (*ten times as much*) ده مقابله dih mukábalah, ده چندان dih chandán, ده مساوی dih musáwí.—(*as follows, videlicet*) یعنی ya'ní, اعنی a'ní.—(*as much or far as possible*) حتی الوسع hattá-'l-wus', بقدر مقدور bi-kadar-i-makdúr.

Asbestos, سنگ پنبه sang-i-pambah.

To Ascend, بالا رفتن bálá raftan, صعود نمودن sa'úd nimúdan, عروج کردن 'urúj kardan, بر آمدن bar ámadan, متصاعد شدن mutasá'id shudan.

Ascendancy, غلبت ghalabat.

Ascendant, طالع táli', معرج ma'raj

Ascension, معراج mi'ráj.

Ascent, معرج ma'raj, صعود sa'úd.—(*slope*) فراز faráz.

To Ascertain, تحقیق کردن tahkík kardan, تنقیح نمودن tankíh nimúdan, تجویز کردن tajwíz kardan.

Ascetic, زاهد záhid, اهل ریاضت ahl-i-riyázat.

Asceticism, ریاضت riyázat, زاهدی záhidí, زهد zuhd.

Asclepias (*swallow wort*), خرک khark, خرگ kharg, عشر 'ushar, اشخر ishkhir.

To Ascribe to, توصیف کردن tausíf kardan, نسبت دادن nisbat dádan, اسناد نمودن isnád nimúdan.

Ash (*tree*), اهر ahar, زبان گنجشک zabán-i-gunjashk.

Ashamed, شرمنده sharmandah, شرمسار sharm-sár, خجل khijil, منفعل munfa'il, متخفر mutakhaffir.

Ashes, خاکستر khákistar, رماد ramád.

Ash-pit (*place where ashes, sweepings, and rubbish are thrown out*), جای رشت ریزی já,í-i-rasht-rízí, مزبله mazbalah.

Aside, در کنار dar kanár, بر طرف bar taraf.—(*in speaking*) بگوش bigúsh, مخصوص makhsús.

Asinine, حماری himárí, خری kharí.

To Ask, پرسیدن pursídan, سوال کردن su,ál kardan, استفهام نمودن istifhám nimúdan, استفسار نمودن istifsár nimúdan.—(*beg, demand*) خواستن khwástan, طلبیدن talbídan. (*Vide also*, To Beg.)

Askew, کج kaj, نا راست ná-rást.

Aslant, کج kaj, مائل má,il.

Asleep, در خواب dar khwáb, خوابیده khwábídah, خفته khuftah.

Asp, مار mar, افعی af'á.

Asparagus, مار چوبه már-chúbah, هوا جیوه hawa-i-jíwah, اسفرج isfaraj.

Aspect, وجه wajh, چهره chihrah, روی rúí, منظر manzar, صورت súrat, ظهور zuhúr.

Aspen, سپیدار sapídár.

Asperity, درشتی durushtí, خشونت khushúnat, تندی tundí, تیزی tízí.

To Asperse, تهمت دادن tuhmat dádan, بد گفتن bad guftan, دشنام دادن dush-nám dádan.

Aspersion, بد زبان bad-zabán, دشنام dush-nám, افترا iftirá, فحش fuhsh.

Asphyxia, خناق khunák.

To Aspirate, تلفظ ها کردن talaffuz-i-há kardan.

To Aspire, آرزو داشتن árzú dáshtan, تمنا کردن tamanná kardan.

Ass, خر khar, حمار himár, دراز گوش diráz-gúsh, الاغ ulágh.—(*riding ass*) الاغ سواری ulágh-i-suwárí.—(*wild ass*) گور خر gúr-khar, گور gúr.

Assafœtida, انگوزه angúzah, انگسا ingisá, چرخمالی charkhmálí (*vulg.*).

Assassin, خونی khúní, سفاك saffák, قتال kattál.

To Assassinate, کشتن kushtan, قتل کردن katl kardan.

Assassination, کتل katl, کشش kushish, خونریزی khún-rízí.

Assault, یورش yúrish, حمله hamlah, هجوم hujúm.—(*robbery*) راهزنی ráh-zaní, سرقه sarikah.—(*night attack*) شبخونی shab-khúní, بوق bauk.

To Assault (*attack*), حمله کردن hamlah kardan, حمله ور شدن hamlah-war shudan, هجوم آور شدن hujúm-áwar shudan, هجوم آوردن hujúm áwardan, یورش کردن yúrish kardan, بر سر ریختن bar sar ríkhtan.

Assay, عیار 'iyár, چاشنی cháshní, آزمایش ázmáyish.

To Assay, چاشنی کردن cháshní kardan, عیار کردن 'iyár kardan.

Assayer, صاحب عیار sáhib-i-'iyár.

To Assemble, (*trans.*) فراهم آوردن

faráham áwardan, جمع کردن jam' kardan, (*intrans.*) فراهم آمدن faráham ámadan, جمع شدن jam' shudan.—(*court*), اجلاس کردن ijlás kardan.

ASSEMBLY, گروه gurúh, جماعت jamá'at, جمعیت jam'íyat, مجمع majma', دیوان díwán, بزم bazm, شورا shúrá, مجلس majlis, محفل mahfil, معشر ma'shar, انجمن anjuman, ملا mala,.

ASSEMBLY-ROOM, مجلس majlis.

ASSENT, *vide* CONSENT.

To ASSERT, اقرار کردن ikrár kardan, تقریر نمودن takrír nimúdan, یقین گفتن yakín guftan, تحقیق نمودن tahkík nimúdan.

ASSERTION, تقریر takrír, اقرار ikrár, گفتار guftár, مدعا mudda'á, توجیه taujíh.—(*mere assertion without proof*) تحکم tahakkum.

To ASSESS, خراج کردن khiráj kardan.

ASSESSMENT (*land-tax*), خراج khiráj.

ASSESSOR, شاهد عادل sháhid-i-'ádil.

ASSETS, اموال amwál, املاک amlák.

To ASSEVER, تعریف نمودن ta'ríf nimúdan, اعتراف نمودن i'tiráf nimúdan.

ASSEVERATION, اعتراف i'tiráf, تعریف ta'ríf, تقریر takrír.

ASSIDUITY, *vide* PERSEVERANCE.

ASSIDUOUS, *vide* INDUSTRIOUS.

To ASSIGN, محول کردن muhawwal kardan, دادن dádan, عطا کردن 'atá kardan.

ASSIGNATION, مهلت muhlat, تعیین ta'yín.

ASSIGNEE, وکیل wakíl.

ASSIGNMENT (*of goods, &c.*), تنخواه tankhwáh.

To ASSIMILATE, برابر ساختن bar-ábar sákhtan, تشبیه آوردن tashbíh áwardan.

ASSIMILATION, موافقت muwáfakat, تمثیل tamsíl, مماثلت mumásalat.

To ASSIST, مدد کردن madad kardan, امداد نمودن imdád nimúdan, پشتی کردن pushtí kardan, کمك دادن kumak dádan, اعانت نمودن i'ánat nimúdan, معاونت نمودن mu'áwanat nimúdan, مساعدت نمودن musá'adat nimúdan.

ASSISTANCE, مدد madad, امداد imdád, پشتی pushtí, کمك kumak, عون 'aun, اعانت i'ánat, معاونت mu'áwanat, یاری yárí, تایید ta,ayyud, نصرت nusrat, دستگیری dastgírí.—(*pecuniary assistance*) واسازی wá-sází, مساعده musá'adah, بیعانه bai'ánah.

ASSISTANT, مددگار madad-gár, معین mu'ín, معاون mu'áwin, عوان 'iwán, یار yár, دستگیر dast-gír, یاور yáwar, نصیر nasír, نائب ná'ib, ناصر násir (*pl.* انصار ansár).

ASSIZE, محکمه mahkamah.

ASSOCIATE, رفیق rafík, شریك sharík, همدم ham-dam, مصاحب musáhib, همراه ham-ráh انیس anís, یار yár, همسر ham-sar, انباز ambáz.

To ASSOCIATE with, مرافقت کردن muráfakat kardan, معاشرت کردن mu'áasharat kardan, اختلاط کردن ikhtilát kardan, صحبت کردن suhbat kardan, الفت نمودن ulfat nimúdan, انس داشتن uns dáshtan, دمساز بودن dam-sáz búdan.

ASSOCIATION, صحبت suhbat, رفقت rafkat. — (*public company*) دار التجاره dáru-'t-tijárah.

ASSONANCE, جناس jinás.

To ASSORT, چیدن chídan, ترتیب دادن tartíb dádan, آماده نمودن ámádah nimúdan, آراستن árástan.

ASSORTMENT, تبعیض tab'íz, ترتیب tartíb, تدارك tadáruk.

To ASSUAGE, آرامیدن árámídan, آرام دادن árám dádan, تسلی دادن tasallí dádan, تخفیف کردن takhfíf kardan.

ASSUAGEMENT, تخفیف takhfíf, قرار karár, آرام árám, تسلی tasallí.

ASSUASIVE, تسکین بخش taskín-bakhsh, آرام بخش árám-bakhsh.

To ASSUME, پنداشتن pindáshtan, تصور کردن tasawwur kardan.

ASSUMPTION, اخذ akhz.

ASSURANCE (*certainty of fulfilment*), استکمال istikmál.—(*commercial term*) بیمه bímah.

To Assure, حقیقت گفتن hakíkat guftan.

Assuredly, یقینا yakínan, یقینی yakíní, قطعا kat'an, بالقطع bi-'l-kat', لا محاله lá-mahálah.

Asterisk, نشان nishán.

Asthma, دما damá, ضیق النفس zíku-'n-nafas, زحیر zahír.

Asthmatic, دما بر damá-bar.

Astonished, Astonishment, *vide* Amazed and Amazement.

Astragalus (*tragacanth plant*), گون gawan.—(*the gum*) کتیرا katírá.

Astral, نجومی nujúmí, نجوم پیوند nujúm-paiwand.

Astray, گمراه gum-ráh, بیراه bí-ráh.—(*to lead astray*) فریفتن firíftan, فریب دادن firíb dádan, اضلال کردن izlál kardan.

Astride, سوار suwár.

Astringency, تندی tundí, تیزی tízí, قبضیت kabzíyat.

Astringent, قابض kábiz, کشنده kashandah.

Astrolabe, اصطرلاب usturláb, استرلاب usturláb.

Astrologer, منجم munajjim, فالچی fál-chí, اخترگو akhtar-gú.

Astrology, علم نجوم 'ilm-i-nujúm, تنجیم tanjím, علم استخراج 'ilm-i-istikhráj.

Astronomer, اهل هئت 'ahl-i-hai,at, رصاد rassád, ستاره شناس sitárah-shinás, رصد بند rasad-band.

Astronomical-tables, زیج zíj, جدول jadwal.

Astronomy, علم هئت 'ilm-i-hai,at.

Astute, *vide* Able.

Asunder, جدا jidá, مفصل mufassal.

Asylum, پناه panáh, بست bast, ملجا maljá, ملاذ maláz, مفر mafirr, مامن ma,man.

At, ب bi, در dar, نزد nazd, فی fí.—(*at least*) اقلا akallan, باری bárí, لا اقل lá-akall.—(*at most*) نهایت niháyat, زاید záíd, اکثر aksar.—(*at all*) هیچ hích.—(*at present, just now*) حال hal, اکنون aknún, در این وقت dar ín wakt, هنوز hanúz.—(*at all events*) بهر صورت bi-har súrat, بهر قسم bi-har kism, بهر نوع bi-har nau'.—(*at length*) آخر akhar, بالاخره bi-'l-ákhirah, عاقبة الامر 'ákibatu-'l-amr, نهایت niháyat, باری bárí.—(*at once*) دفعتا daf'atan, یك باره yák bárah, یك بارگی yak báragí, یکسره yak sarah.

Atheism, دهر dahr, الحاد ilhád.

Atheist, زندیق zindík, دهری dahrí. Neither of these words properly expresses an atheist, for which there is no Persian term. It must be expressed by a periphrase, such as منکر وجود خدای munkir-i-wujúd-khudáí, *a denier of the existence of a God*, &c.

Athlete, پهلو pahlav, پهلوان pahlaván, کشتی گر kushtí-gar.

Atmosphere, هوا hawá, جو jaww.

Atom, ذره zarrah, شمه shammah.

To Atone, کفاره کردن kaffárah kardan.

Atonement, کفاره kaffárah, تکفیر takfír.

Atrocious, شریر sharir, بد bad, سخت sakht, ظالم zálim.

Atrocity, ظلم zulm, تعدی ta'addí, فساد fasád, ستم sitam.

Atrophy, *vide* Consumption.

To Attach, *vide* To Join, To Arrest.

Attaché, وا بسته wá-bastah.

Attachment, *vide* Friendship, Love, Union, Favour, Inclination.

Attack, *vide* Assault.—(*medical term*) نزول nuzúl.

To Attain, *vide* To Acquire.

Attainable, ممکن mumkin, یافتنی yáftaní.

Attainment, تحصیل tahsíl, اکتساب iktisáb, حصول husúl, اقتنا iktiná.

To Attemper, موافق کردن muwáfik kardan, معتدل کردن mu'tadil kardan.

Attempt, سعی sa'í, قصد kasd, عزم 'azm, کوشش kúshish, تلاش talásh, سر sar.

To Attempt, کوشیدن kúshídan, قصد کردن kasd kardan, آزمودن ázmúdan, سعی نمودن sa'í nimúdan.

To ATTEND, گوش دادن gúsh dádan, ملتفت شدن multafit shudan, متوجه بودن mutawajjih búdan, اعتنا نمودن i'tiná nimúdan, التفات نمودن iltifát nimúdan.—(*to be present*) حاضر شدن házir shudan.—(*wait upon*) خدمت کردن khidmat kardan.

ATTENDANCE (*waiting upon*), پرستاری parastárí, خدمت khidmat, تیمار tímár.

ATTENDANT (*consequent*), منوط manút, منسوب mansúb, قرین karín, متعلق muta'allik.—(*a servant*) پیشخدمت písh-khidmat, خادم khádim, تابع tábi', تابین tábín (*vulg.*).

ATTENDANTS (*dependants, retinue*), خدام khuddám, خدم و حشم khadam wa hasham, لواحق lawáhik, اتباع atbá', توابع tawábi', نوکر باب naukar-báb, متعلقین muta'allikín, تابینها tábínhá (*vulg.*).

ATTENTION, توجه tawajjuh, اشتغال ishtighál, دل بستگی dil-bastagí, التفات iltifát, مبالات mubálát.

ATTENTIVE, متوجه mutawajjih, مشغول mashghúl, آگاه ágáh, ملتفت multafit.

ATTENTIVELY, بدقت bi-dikkat, روبکار rú-bi-kár.

ATTENUATE, رقیق rakík.

To ATTENUATE, رقیق کردن rakík kardan.

To ATTEST, اقرار نمودن ikrár nimúdan.

ATTESTATION, تقریر takrír, تصدیق tasdík, شاهدی sháhidí, شهادت shahádat.

To ATTIRE, پیراستن pírástan.

ATTITUDE, وضع waz'.

ATTORNEY, وکیل wakíl.—(*power of attorney*) وکالت نامه wakálat-námah, مختار نامه mukhtár-námah.

To ATTRACT, کشیدن kashídan, جذب نمودن jazb nimúdan, جلب نمودن jalb nimúdan.

ATTRACTION, جذب jazb, جلب jalb, کشش kashish.

ATTRACTIVE, جاذب jázib, جالب jálib.

ATTRIBUTE, صفت sifat, وصف wasf.

To ATTRIBUTE to, اسناد نمودن isnád nimúdan, نسبت دادن nisbat dádan, منسوب کردن mansúb kardan.

AUCTION, هراج harráj, مزاد mazád, لیلام lailám (*eur.*).

AUCTIONEER, هراجی harrájí.

AUDACIOUS, *vide* BOLD.

AUDIBLE, مسموع masmú'.

AUDIENCE, سامعین sámi'ín, حاضرین házirín.—(*interview*) حضور huzúr, بار bár.

To AUDIT, محاسبه کردن muhásabah kardan.

AUDITOR, مستمع mustami', سمیع samí'. (*Vide* ACCOUNTANT.)

AUGER, برمه barmah, مته matah.

To AUGMENT, زیاد کردن ziyád kardan, افزودن afzúdan.

AUGMENTATION, افزونی afzúní, زیاد ziyád.

AUGUR (*soothsayer*), فالچی fál-chí, اختر گو akhtar-gú.

To AUGUR, فال گرفتن fál giriftan.

AUGURY, فال fál, شگون shugún.

AUGUST, اعظم a'zam, مبارك mubárak, همایون humayún.—(*month*) آب áb, اغست aghust, اگوست agúst.

AUNT (*paternal*), عمه 'ammah.—(*maternal*) خاله khálah.

AU REVOIR, تا بباز دید tá bi-báz-díd.

AURICULAR, سماع samá'.

AURORA, صبح دم subh-dam, شفق shafak.

AURORA BOREALIS, شفق شمالی shafak-i-shimálí, نور شمالی núr-i-shimálí.

AUSPICES, سایه sáyah, حمایت himáyat.

AUSPICIOUS, فرخنده farkhundah, همایون humáyún, نیك اختر ník-akhtar, خجسته khujistah, میمون maimún, مبارك mubárak, سعید sa'íd, بختیار bakht-yár, فرخ farrukh.

AUSTERE, متعبس muta'abbis, درشت durusht, موقر muwakkar.

AUSTERITY, درشتی durushtí, تندی tundí, سختی sakhtí.

AUTHENTIC, صحیح sahíh, محقق muhakkak, یقین yakín, مسلم musallam.

BAGATELLE (*trifle*), شی قلیل shai-i-kalíl.—(*game*) نرد nard.

BAGGAGE, رخت rakht, سامان sámán.—اثاث asás, اسباب asbáb, احمال و اثقال ahmál wa askál.—(*travelling, tents, &c.*) بارخانه bár-khánah. — (*of an army*) بنه bunah, آغروق ághrúk.—(*small quantity of baggage carried by a traveller*) خردی مردی khurdí-murdí, خورده ریز khúrdah-ríz.

BAGPIPE, نی انبانه nai-i-ambánah, نی مشك nai-i-mashk.

BAIL (*security*), ضمانت zamánat, کفالت kafálat.—(*sponsor*) ضامن zámin, کفیل kafíl, متکفل muta-kaffil.

To BAIL, ضامن شدن zámin shudan.

BAILIFF (*dun*), محصل muhassil.—(*agent*) وکیل wakíl.

BAIT, طعمه tu'mah, دانه dánah, چینه chínah.

To BAIT, دانه نهادن dánah nihádan, چینه نهادن chínah nihádan.

BAIZE, پشمینه pashmínah.

To BAKE, پختن pukhtan, طبخ کردن tabkh kardan.

BAKEHOUSE, تنور خانه tannúr-khánah.

BAKER, نانپز nán-paz, نانوای nán-wáí, خباز khabbáz.

BALANCE (*scales*), ترازو tarázú, میزان mízán.—(*large balance for weighing heavy goods*) قبان kabbán. (*Vide* REMAINDER.)

To BALANCE, (*trans.*) وزن کردن wazn kardan, (*intrans.*) موازن شدن muwázin shudan.—(*to balance oneself*) سنجیدن sanjídan.

BALCONY, بالا خانه bálá-khánah, کاخ kákh.—(*flat terraced roof*) بام bám, بان bán. (*Vide* VERANDAH.)

BALD, کل kal, اصلع asla', اقرع akra', سر طاس sar-i-tás.

BALDNESS, صلعت sala'at, طاسی سر tásí-i-sar.

BALE (*of cloth, goods, &c.*), بسته bastah.

To BALK, نقاضت کردن nakázat kardan, دست کوتاه کردن dast kútáh kardan, محروم گردانیدن mahrúm gardánídan.

BALL, گوی gúí, گو gú, کره kurrah.—(*for fire-arms*) غلوله ghulúlah, گلوله gulúlah, گله gullah.—(*of thread*) گروك gurúk.—(*for playing with*) طوپه túpah, طوپه کاشی túpah-káshí.—(*dance*) رقص raks.

BALLAD, *vide* SONG.—(*ballad-singer*) *vide* SINGER, MINSTREL.

BALLAST (*of a ship*), نیلام nílám, طعان ta'án.

To BALLAST, وزن نهادن wazn nihádan.

BALLOON, بالون bálún.

BALLOT, قرعه kur'ah.

BALM, بلسان balasán.

BALMY, معطر mu'attar, مشموم mashmúm.

BALSAM, بلسان balasán.

BALUSTER, دست انداز dast-andáz.

BAMBOO, نی هندی nai-i-hindi, خیزران khaizurán.

BAN, اعلان i'lán, اعلام i'lám.

BANANA, میوه موز míwah-i-múz.

BAND (*tie*), بند band, پیوند paiwand, رفاده rifádah.—(*company*) طائفه tá,ifah, گروه gurúh, خیل khail, دسته dastah.—(*of music*) موسقیان músikiyán.

To BAND, بستن bastan.—(*together*) اتحاد دادن ittihád dádan, متحد ساختن muttahid sákhtan.

BANDAGE, رفاده rifádah, بند band, عصابه 'isábah.

BAND-BOX, صندوقچه sandúk-chah.

BANDIT, راه زن ráh-zan.

To BANDY words, رد بدل کردن radd-badal kardan.

BANDY-LEGGED, کجپا kaj-pá.

BANE, زهر zahr, سم samm.

BANEFUL, زهر دار zahr-dár, مضر muzirr.

BANG (*blow*), ضرب zarb, لطمه latmah, مشت musht, طپانچه tapánchah, لس lus.

To BANG (*trans.*), ضرب کردن zarb kardan, لت نمودن latt nimúdan.—(*intrans.*) آواز کردن áwáz kardan.

To BANISH, نفی کردن nafí kardan, اخراج بلد کردن ikhráj-i-balad kardan, بدر کردن bi-dar kardan, جلای وطن نمودن jalái-i-watan nimúdan, راندن rándan.

BANISHMENT, نفی nafí, جلای jalái, اخراج بلد ikhráj-i-balad.

BANJO, طنبور tambúr.

BANK (*mound*), تل tall, پشته pushtah.—(*dam*) بند band.—(*of a river, &c.*) کنار kanár, کناره kanárah, شط shatt, لب lab, ساحل sáhil, کران karán.—(*place where money is stored*) صرافخانه sarráf-khánah, خزانه khizánah.

BANK-BILL, خط صراف khatt-i-sarráf.

BANKER (*or money changer*), صراف sarráf.

BANK-NOTE, قایمه káímah.—(*hundred pound note*) قایمه صد فروشی káímah-i-sad-furúshí.

BANKRUPT, مفلس muflis, نا دار nádár, ور شکسته war-shikastah, ادبار گرفته idbár-giriftah.

BANKRUPTCY, افلاس iflás, ور شکستگی war-shikastagí, ادبار idbár.

BANNER, نشان nishán, علامه 'alámah, علم 'alam, لوا liwá.

BANQUET, ضیافت ziyáfat, مهمانی mihmání, سور súr, ولیمه walímah. (*Vide* FEAST.)

To BANQUET, سور بر پا کردن súr bar pá kardan, ولیمه دادن walímah dádan.

BANQUET-CHAMBER, بزمگاه bazmgáh, ضیافت خانه ziyáfat-khánah.

BANTER, طنز tanz, ظرافت zaráfat, استهزا istihzá.

To BANTER, طنز کردن tanz kardan, ظرافت کردن zaráfat kardan, استهزا نمودن istihzá nimúdan.

BANTERER, مسخره maskharah, ساخر sákhir.

BANYAN-TREE, درخت بنن dirakht-i-banan.

BAPTISM, تعمید ta'míd, معمودیه ma'múdíyah, صبغت sabghat, اصطباغ istibágh.

BAPTIST, معمد mu'ammid. تعمید دهنده ta'míd-dihandah.

To BAPTIZE, صبغ کردن sabgh kardan, اصطباغ نمودن istibágh nimúdan, آب کشیدن áb kashídan, تعمید نمودن ta'míd nimúdan.—(*to be baptized*) اصطباغ یافتن istibágh yáftan, تعمید یافتن ta'míd yáftan.

BAR, تیر tír, مفتول maftúl.—(*of wood*), چوب بست chúb-bast.—(*of a door*) *vide* BOLT.—(*bar fastened on a gate, &c., to strengthen it*) پشت بند pusht-band.

To BAR, بستن bastan, چفت کردن chift kardan.—(*prevent*) منع کردن mana' kardan.

BARB (*of an arrow, hook, &c.*), خار khár.

BARBARIAN (*sub.*), اعجمی a'jamí, (*adj.*) دشتی dashtí, بیمروت bí-murúwat.

BARBARITY, ظلم zulm, ستم sitam.

BARBAROUS, وحشی wahshí. (*Vide* IGNORANT, CRUEL, WILD, SAVAGE.)

BARBER, دلاك dallák, حجام hajjám, مزین muzayyin, سلمانی salmání (*vulg.*)

BARBERRY, زرشك zirishk.

BARD, شاعر shá'ir.

BARE, برهنه barahnah, عریان 'uryán, عاری 'árí, مجرد mujarrad, لخت lukht, لوخت lúkht (*vulg.*)

To BARE, برهنه کردن barahnah kardan, مجرد نمودن mujarrad nimúdan.

BAREFACED, گستاخ gustákh, بی شرم bí-sharm, شوخ shúkh.

BAREFACEDNESS, گستاخی gustákhí, بی شرمی bí-sharmí, شوخی shúkhí.

BAREFOOT, برهنه پا barahnah-pá.

BAREHEADED, برهنه سر barahnah-sar.

BARENESS, برهنگی barahnagí.

BARGAIN, شرط shart, قرار karár, عهد 'ahd.—(*money transaction*) معامله mu'ámalah, معاهده mu'áhadah.

To BARGAIN, بازار نمودن bázár nimúdan.

BARGE, قلس kals, نو nú.

BARGEMAN, ملاح malláh, نوتی nútí.

BARK, پوست púst, قشر kishr.—(*dog*) عفعف 'af'af, عوعو 'au'au.—(*ship*) سفینه safínah, کشتی kashtí.

To BARK (*a dog*), عفعف کردن 'af'af kardan, غوغو کردن ghaughau kardan, عوعو نمودن 'au'au nimúdan, لائیدن lá,ídan.

BARLEY, جو jau, شعیر sha'ír.—(*barley-bread*) نان جوین nán-i-javín, کشکینه kashkínah.—(*barley-corn*) جوی javí, شعیره sha'írah.—(*barley-meal*) آرد جو árd-i-jau.—(*young shoots of barley, on which horses are fed*) خصیل khasíl, قصیر kasír.—(*chopped straw and green barley shoots mixed, for horses*) تلیت tilít, تلید tilíd.—(*chopped straw and dried barley grain mixed*) کاه جو káh-jau.—(*barley-sugar*) آب دندان áb-i-dandán.—(*barley-water, decoction of barley*) ما شعیر má-sha'ír, آب جو áb-i-jau.

BARN, انبار ambár.

BARRACKS, سرباز خانه sarbáz-khánah.

BARREL, خمرهٔ چوبین khumrah-i-chúbín, تاپوی چوبین tápúí-i-chúbín, برمیل barmíl, پیپ píp (*eur.*).—(*of a gun*) لوله lúlah.

BARREN, بی بر bí-bar, شوره shúrah, غیر مثمر ghair-musmir, عقیم 'akím, ویرانه wairánah.—(*woman*) یائسه yá,isah, عقیمه 'akímah, عاقره 'ákirah.

BARRENNESS, بی حاصلی bi-hásilí.—(*woman*) خشک پستانی khushk-pistání.

BARRICADE, بند band, سد sadd, ضیق سد zík-i-sadd.

To BARRICADE (*fortify*), محارست نمودن muhárasat nimúdan, محافظت نمودن muháfazat nimúdan.

BARRISTER, وکیل wakíl.

BARROW, گاری کوچک gárí-i-kúchik.

BARTER, تجارت tijárat.

To BARTER, تجارت کردن tijárat kardan, فروختن furúkhtan.

BARTERER, بازارگان bázárgán.

BASE (*vile*), کمین kamín, کمینه kamínah, فرومایه furú-máyah, رذیل rizíl, مذم muzimm, خسیس khasís, خوار khwár, دنی daní, دون dún, ذلیل zalíl, سفله siflah, حقیر hakír, پدر سگ pidar-sag (*vulg.*).

To BASE, موسس داشتن mu'assas dáshtan.

BASENESS, خساست khasásat, خست khissat, دونی dúní, ذلت zillat, شنعت shan'at, خواری khwárí, خباثت khabásat, ذل zull, سگیت sagíyat (*vulg.*).

BASHFUL, شرمسار sharm-sár, خجل khijil, متخفر mutakhaffir, حیی hayí.

BASHFULNESS, خجلت khijlat, خجالت khijálat, شرمساری sharm-sárí.

BASIL (*ocymum basilicum*) ریحان raihán.

BASIN, لگن lagan, طشت tasht, طاس tás.—(*of a river*) مبدا mabdá, مجرا majrá.

BASIS, پایه páyah, اساس asás, بنیاد bunyád, بنیان bunyán.

To BASK, آفتاب خوردن áftáb khwurdan.

BASKET, سبد sabad, زنبیل zambíl, سله sallah, گیره gírah.

BASKET-MAKER, سله باف sallah-báf, سبدگر sabad-gar.

BAS-RELIEF (*figures, &c. carved in slight relief*), منبت munabbat, منبتکاری munabbat-kárí.

BASTARD, حرامزاده harám-zadah, ولد زنا walad-i-ziná.

BASTARDY, حرامزادگی harám-zádagí.

To BASTE (*sew in wide stitches*), بخیه کردن bakhyah kardan.—(*meat*) تبلیل نمودن tablíl nimúdan.

BASTINADO, فلاکه falákah.

To BASTINADO (*beat on the soles of the feet*), کف پا زدن kaf-i-pá zadan, چوب زدن chúb zadan, بچوب بستن bi-chúb bastan.—(*to be bastinadoed*) چوب خوردن chúb khúrdan.

BASTION, برج burj.

BAT (*animal*), شبپره shab-parah, سپره sapparah, شبکور shab-kúr, خفاش khuffásh, موشک کور múshk-kúr.—(*club*) چوگان chaugán, کتک kutk, چماق chumák.

BATCH, دسته dastah.

BATH, حمام hammám, غسلخانه ghusl-khánah.—(*foot-bath*) پا شویه pá-shúyah.—(*outer apartment, or undressing room of bath*) بینه bínah.—(*inner or bathing room*) گرمخانه garm-khánah.—(*tank of hot water*) خزانه khizánah, قلتین kullatain.—(*bathing dress*) رخت حمام rakht-i-hammám.—(*wrapper worn while bathing*) لنگ lung, لنگ رشتی lung-i-rashtí.—(*wrapper put on after bathing*) قطیفه katífah.—(*person who scrubs, shampoos, &c. bathers*). دلاک dallák.—(*Order of the Bath*) نشان حمام nishán-i-hammám. — (*the First Class of the Order of the Bath*) کوردن بزرگ ملکیه نشان حمام kúrdun-i-buzurg - i - malakíyah - i-nishán-i-hammám.

To Bathe, غسل کردن ghusl kardan, شستشو کردن shust-shú kardan, آب تنی کردن áb-taní kardan.

Bather, مغتسل mughtasil, حمامچی hammám-chí.

Bathing, غسل ghusl, شست و شو shust u shú.

Baton, عصا 'asá, چوب chúb.

Battalion, باطالیان bátáliyán (*eur.*).

Batter, خمیر khamír.

To Batter, *vide* To Beat.

Battery (*raised works on which cannons are placed*), مورچه múrchah, دمدمه damdamah.—(*electrical*), باطری bátarí.

Battle, جنگ jang, نبرد nabard, رزم razm, حرب harb, محاربه muhárabah, پرخاش purkhásh, هیجا haija, کار زار kár-zár, جهاد jihád, پیکار paikár, قتال kitál, مقاتلت mukátalat, وغا waghá, غزا ghazá.

Battle-array, صف آرای saff-árái, تیپ آرای típ-árái.

Battle-axe, تبر tabar, تبر زین tabar-i-zín.

Battle-field, *vide* Field, List.

Battlement, کنگره kungurah.

Bauble, ناچیز ná-chíz, بازیچه bází-chah.

Bawd, دلاله dallálah.

Bawdiness, فحش fuhsh, فسق fisk.

Bawdy (*obscene*), فاحش fáhish, پوچ púch, هرزه harzah, هزل hazil.

Bawdy-house, زنا خانه ziná-khánah, خیل خانه khail-khánah, کاولی خانه káwalá-khánah.

To Bawl, آواز دادن áwáz dádan, بانگ کردن báng kardan.

Bay (*gulf*), خور khaur, مرسی marsá, کنج دریا kunj-i-daryá, خلیج khalíj. —(*tree*), غار ghár, دهمست dah-mast.—(*colour*) احوی ahwá.—(*horse*) کهر kahar.—(*light bay horse*) کمیت kumait.—(*to keep at bay*) باز داشتن báz dáshtan.

Bayonet, نیزه naizah, سر نیزه sar-naizah, سر نیزه تفنگ sar-naizah-i-tufang.—(*present bayonets*) نیزه پیش naizah-písh.

Bay-window, شاهنشین sháh-nishín.

Bazaar, بازار bázár.

To Be, بودن búdan, شدن shudan.—(*be it so*) باشد báshad.

Beach, ساحل sáhil, لب دریا lab-i-daryá, کنار kanár.

Beacon, نشان nishán, علامت 'alámat, منارت manárat.

Bead, دانه dánah, مهره muhrah, شبه shabah.

Beadle, شاطر shátir, پاکار pá-kár, فراش farrásh.

Beak, منقار minkár, نوک nauk, تک tak.

Beaked, منقار دار minkár-dár, چنگ دار ching-dár.

Beam (*of wood, &c.*), شه تیر shah-tír, تیر tír, ورگه wargah.—(*of a balance*) شاهین ترازو sháhín-i-tarázú.—(*of the sun*) پرتو partav, قرن karn, شعاع shu'á'.

To Beam, درخشیدن dirakhshídan, شعله زدن shu'lah zadan.

Beaming, روشن raushan, درخشان dirakhshán, لامع lámi'.

Bean, باقلا bákilá, باقله bákilah, لوبیه lúbiyah.

Bear, خرس khirs, دب dubb.—(*Great Bear, star*) دب اکبر dubb-i-akbar.—(*Little Bear, star*) دب اصغر dubb-i-asghar.

To Bear, بر داشتن bar dáshtan, بردن burdan.—(*suffer*) بر داشتن bar dáshtan, تحمل نمودن tahammul nimúdan, کشیدن kashídan, خوردن khúrdan. — (*bring forth*), زادن zádan, وضع حمل کردن waz'-i-haml kardan.

Beard, ریش rísh, لحیه lahyah, محاسن mahásin, خط khatt. — (*young beard, or first appearance of the beard*) دم خط dam-i-khatt.

Bearded, ریشدار rísh-dár.

Beardless, بی ریش bí-rísh.

Bearer (*porter*), حمال hammál, بار کش bár-kash, بار بردار bár-bardár.

Bearing (*mien*), وضع waz', وجه wajh.

Beast, چرنده charandah, بهیمه bahímah, جانور jánwar, حیوان haiwán, چهارپای chahár-pái, دد dad.

Beastliness, فحش fuhsh, فسق fisk.

Beastly, ناپاك ná-pák, غلیظ ghalíz, نجس najs, مردار murdár.

To **Beat**, زدن zadan, کوفتن kúftan, کوبیدن kúbídan.—(*conquer*) فتح کردن fath kardan, غالب آمدن ghálib ámadan, ظفر یافتن zafar yáftan.—(*to beat down*) پایمال کردن pái-mál kardan, پست کردن past kardan.—(*to beat for game*) بر خیزانیدن bar khízánídan. — (*to excel or surpass*) سبقت بردن (بر) sibkat burdan (bar), بهتر بودن bihtar búdan (*vide also* To Excel).—(*throb*) نبضان کردن nabazán kardan.

To **Beatify**, مسعود کردن mas'úd kardan, مبارك ساختن mubárak sákhtan.

Beating (*waves*), تلاطم talátum.—(*pulse*) نبضان nabazán.

Beatitude, سعادت sa'ádat, مبارکی mubárakí.

Beau, طاؤس tá,us; مرد نازنین mard-i-náznín, قشنگ kashang. (*Vide also* Fop.)

Beautiful, خوشمنظر khúsh-manzar, خوبصورت khúb-súrat, خوبروی khúb-rúí, منقه munakkah, قشنگ kashang, خوشگل khúsh-gil, نیکمنظرník-manzar, زیب zíb, زیبا zíbá, حسین hasín, جمیل jamíl, لطیف latíf, رعنا ra'ná, نغز naghz, انیق aník, قسیم kasím, بهلول buhlúl, وجیه wajíh, مقبول makbúl, خجیر khujír, جون jún (*vulg.*).

Beauty, حسن husn, جمال jamál, لطافت latáfat, نزاکت nazákat, زیب zíb, زیبائی zíbá,í, رونق raunak, نضارت nazárat, وجاهت wajáhat, زینت zínat, جونی júní (*vulg.*)—(*regularity of features*), صباحت sabáhat.—(*sprightly look, fascination*) ملاحت maláhat.

Beaver, سگ آبی sag-i-ábí.

Because, چراکه chirá kih, زیراکه zírá kih, زیرا zírá, بنابر banábar, از بسکه az bas kih, از این جهت که az ín jihat kih.

To **Beckon**, اشارت کردن ishárat kardan.

To **Become**, شدن shudan, گشتن gashtan, گردیدن gardídan.—(*befit*), زیبیدن zíbídan, شایستن sháyistan, لایق بودن láík búdan.

Becoming, درخور darkhwur, سزاور sazáwar, مناسب munásib.

Bed, بستر bistar, فرش farsh, رخت خواب rakht-i-khwáb.—(*bedstead*) پلنگ palang (*hind.*), سریر sarír. —(*of a garden*) لته lattah, آبخوران áb-khúrán.—(*border of a garden-bed*) مرز marz.—(*of a river*) رودخانه rúd-khánah.—(*for a horse*) تخت پئین takht-i-pi,ín.—(*to go to bed*) خوابانیدن khwábánídan, برخت خواب رفتن bi-rakht-i-khwáb raftan.

Bed-chamber, خوابگاه khwáb-gáh.

Bedding, اسباب خواب asbáb-i-khwáb, پوشش púshish.

To **Bedew**, تر کردن tar kardan, مرطوب کردن martúb kardan.

Bedouin, بدوی badawí, اعراب a'ráb.

Bed-ridden, بستری bistarí.

Bee, زنبور عسل zambúr-i-'asal.—(*a swarm of bees*) خیل زنبور khail-i-zambúr.—(*Queen-bee*) جحل jahl.

Beef, گوشت گاو gúsht-i-gáv.

Beef-tea, جوهر گوشت jauhar-i-gúsht, آب گوشت áb-i-gusht.

Bee-hive, کند kund. کند عسل kund-i-'asal, مش mash.

Beer, بوزه búzah.

BEER-SHOP, میخانه mai-khánah.
BEES-WAX, موم múm, شمع sham'.
BEETLE, جعل ju'al, گوه لوله کنک gúh-lúlah-kunak, گوزد gauzad. — (*small beetle, very destructive to plants*) سین sín.
BEET-ROOT, چقندر chukundur, چوندر chúndar (*vulg.*).
To BEFAL, *vide* To HAPPEN.
BEFORE, پیش písh, قبل kabl, اول avval, پیشاپیش písh-á-písh.—(*in front*) جلو jilav, در پیش dar písh, مقابل mukábil.—(*sooner*) زودتر zúdtar, پیش از písh az písh, قبل kabl.—(*in presence of, opposite to*) محاذی muházá, روبرو rú-bi-rú, مقابل mukábil, مواجه muwájih. — (*mentioned, vide* ABOVE-MENTIONED).
To BEFRIEND, دوستی کردن dúští kardan, شفقت کردن shafakat kardan, مهربانی کردن mihrbání kardan.
To BEG, خواستن khwástan, درخواست نمودن dar-khwást nimúdan, التماس کردن iltimás kardan, تمنا نمودن tamanná nimúdan, نیاز کردن niyáz kardan, نیازیدن niyázídan, التجا نمودن iljá, nimúdan, مستدعی بودن mustadi' búdan, دعا کردن du'á kardan, استدعا نمودن istid'á nimúdan.—(*alms*) خواستن khwástan, گدائی کردن gadá,í kardan, دریوزه کردن daryúzah kardan.
To BEGET, تولید نمودن taulíd nimúdan. (*Vide* To PRODUCE.)
BEGGAR, گدا gadá, سائل sá,il, دربدر dar-bi-dar. فقیر fakír.
BEGGARY, *vide* POVERTY, DESTITUTION.
To BEGIN, گرفتن giriftan, شروع کردن shurú' kardan, آغاز نمودن ágház nimúdan, ابتدا کردن ibtidá kardan, بنا کردن biná kardan, مبادرت ورزیدن mubádarat warzídan.
BEGINNER, مبتدی mubtadí, نو آموز nau-ámúz.
BEGINNING, آغاز ágház, بنا biná, شروع shurú', اول avval, اوایل aváíl, سر sar, بدو badw, ابتدا ibtidá, مبدا mabda, مبادی mabádí, بدا badá, بداءت badá,at, مبادرت mubádarat, مباشرت mubásharat.
BEHALF, حق hakk, واسطه wásitah, پاس خاطر pás-i-khátir, بهر bahr, برای baráí.
To BEHAVE towards, حرکت کردن (به) harakat kardan (bi), رفتار کردن (به) raftár kardan (bi).
BEHAVIOUR, وضع waz', اطوار atwár, رفتار raftár, حرکت harakat, عمل 'amal, سلوک sulúk.—(*bad behaviour*) ترک ادب tark-i-adab.—(*good behaviour*) ادب adab.
To BEHEAD, سر بریدن sar burídan, گردن زدن gardan zadan.
BEHEST, امر amr, حکم hukm, فرمان firmán.
BEHIND, پس pas, در پس dar pas, خلف khalf, در عقب dar 'akab, وراء wará, دنبال dumbál.
BEHOLD! اینک ínak, هان hán, هین hín.
To BEHOLD, *vide* To SEE, To LOOK, To OBSERVE.
BEHOLDEN, ممنون mamnún, منتدار minnat-dár.
BEHOLDER, ناظر názir.
To BEHOVE, شایستن sháyistan, بایستن báyistan.
BEING (*creature*), کائنت ká,inat. مخلوق makhlúk. — (*existence*) بودنی búdaní, وجود wujúd, هستی hastí.
BELCH, آروغ árúgh.
To BELCH, آروغ کردن árúgh kardan.
BELFRY, جرس خانه jaras-khánah.
BELIEF, *vide* RELIGION, FAITH, TRUST, CONFIDENCE.
To BELIEVE, باور کردن báwar kardan, اعتقاد نمودن i'tikád nimúdan, اقرار کردن ikrár kardan, عقیدت داشتن 'akídat dáshtan, گرویدن girawídan, ایمان آوردن ímán áwardan, مسلم داشتن musallam dáshtan. (*Vide* To THINK.)
BELIEVER, معتقد mú'takid, مومن m,umin.
BELL, جرس jaras, زنگ zang, درای daráí.—(*small bells*) زنگوله zan-

gúlah, سوسک súsk.—(*hung round the neck of cattle*) ناقوس nákús.—(*diving-bell*) شیشه غواصی shíshah-i-ghawwásí. —(*bell-metal*) طوج túj, چدن chudan, مفرق mafrak.
Belle, خوبرو khúb-rú, خرام khirám, زن نازنین zan-i-náznín.
Belles-lettres, علم ادب 'ilm-i-adab.
Bellicose, and Belligerent, جنگ جو jang-jú, جنگ آور jang-áwar.
Bellow, نعره na'rah, بانگ báng.
To Bellow, نعره زدن na'rah zadan, بانگ زدن báng zadan.
Bellows, منفاخ minfákh, دمزن dam-zan.
Belly, شکم shikm, معده mi'dah, بطن batn.
To Belong to, مال بودن mál búdan, از آن بودن az án búdan, متعلق بودن muta'allik búdan, عاید شدن 'áid shudan, نسبت داشتن nisbat dáshtan, مخصوص بودن makhsús búdan, باب بودن báb búdan.
Belonging, متعلق muta'allik, منسوب mansúb.
Beloved (*mistress*), محبوبه mah-búbah, جانان jánán, معشوقه ma'-shúkah.
Below, زیر zír, در زیر dar zír, پائین pá,ín, در پائین dar pá,ín, فرو furú, تحت taht, دامن dáman, دومن dúman (*vulg.*).
Below-mentioned, در ذیل dar zail.
Belt, کمر بند kamar-band, کمر kamar, منطق mintak, حزام hizám.—(*leathern strap*) دوال duwál, تسمه tasmah.
To Bemoan, ناله کردن nálah kar-dan, نالش کردن nálish kardan, زاری کردن zárí kardan.
Bench, سکو sakú, نشیمن nishíman. —(*legal term*) دیوان díwán, محکمه mahkamah.
Bend, پیچ pích, پیچش píchish.
To Bend (*trans.*), خم کردن kham kardan, پیچانیدن pícháнídan, منحنی کردن munhaní kardan.—(*intrans.*), خمیدن khamídan, خم شدن kham shudan, پیچیدن píchí-dan, مائل بودن má,il búdan.
Beneath, *vide* Below, Under.
Benediction, برکت barakat, تبریک tabrík, مبارکی mubárakí, درود durúd.
Benefaction, نعمت ni'mat, احسان ihsán, تبرک tabarruk.
Benefactor, ولی نعمت walí-i-ni'mat, منعم mun'im.
Beneficent, *vide* Kind.
Beneficial, مفید mufíd, سودمند súd-mand, نافع náfi'.
Benefit, احسان ihsán, نعمت ni'-mat, انعام in'ám, کرم karam, الا alá.—(*advantage*) فائده fá,idah, سود súd, نفع naf', منفعت man-fa'at.
Benevolent, *vide* Kind.
Bent, کج kaj, اعوج a'waj.—(*bias*) میل mail, رغبت raghbat.
To Benumb, افسرده کردن afsurdah kardan.
Benzoin, جاوی jáwí, انگیان angu-yán, انگو angú, لبان lubán.
To Bequeath, توصیه نمودن tausiyah nimúdan.
Bequest, وقف wakf, وصایت wasáyat, موقوفه maukúfah.
To Bereave, محروم ساختن mahrúm sákhtan, برهنه کردن barahnah kardan.
Bereavement, محرومیت mahrúmí-yat.
Bereft, داغ دیده dágh-dídah, محروم mahrúm, فقید fakíd.
Berry, دانه dánah, حب habb.
Beryl, سنگ ترشیش sang-i-tarshísh.
To Beseech, *vide* To Beg, To Intreat.
To Beset, احاطه کردن ihátah kardan, شامل نمودن shámil nimúdan.
Beside, در جنب dar jamb, نزد nazd, در پهلو dar pahlú.
Besides (*moreover*), علاوه 'aláwah, سوائی آن siwá,í-i-án, بجز آن bi-juz-i-án, قطع نظر kat'-i-nazar.—(*except*) مگر magar, سوا siwá, بدون bidún, بغیر bi-ghair, جز juz, الا illá.
To Besiege, گرد کردن gird kardan, دور آمدن daur ámadan, محاصره کردن

muhásarab kardan, حصر نمودن hasr nimúdan, محصور ساختن mahsúr sákhtan.
To **Bespeak**, حکم کردن hukm kardan, امر کردن amr kardan.
Best, بهترین bihtarín, خوبترین khúbtarín, نیکوترین níkútarín, احسن ahsan, افضل afzal, اعلی a'lá.
Bestial, حیوانی haiwání, وحشی wahshí.
Bestiality, حیوانیت haiwáníyat.
To **Bestow**, بخشیدن bakhshídan, دادن dádan, ارزانی داشتن arzání dáshtan, عطا نمودن 'atá nimúdan.
Bet, شرط shart, بحث bahs.
To **Bet**, شرط بستن shart bastan, بحث کردن bahs kardan, نذر بستن nazr bastán.
Betel-nut, فوفل faufal.—(*leaf*) تنبول tambúl (*hind.*).
To **Bethink**, یاد آوردن yád áwardan.
Betimes, زود zúd, بر وقت bar wakt.
To **Betoken**, اشارت نمودن ishárat nimúdan.
To **Betray**, خیانت کردن khiyánat kardan, غدر کردن ghadr kardan.
Betrayal, خیانت khiyánat.
Betrayed, مطروک matrúk.
Betrayer, خائن khá,in.
To **Betroth**, منسوب کردن mansúb kardan, نامزد کردن nám-zad kardan, مخطوب نمودن makhtúb nimúdan.
Better, به bih, بهتر bihtar, خوبتر khúbtar, نیکتر níktar, اخیر akhyar, احسن ahsan.—(*so much the better*) آن بهتر án bihtar.—(*better and better*) به اندر به bih andar bih, بهتر از بهتر bihtar az bihtar.
To **Better**, بهتر کردن bihtar kardan, خوبتر نمودن khúbtar nimúdan.
Between, میان miyán, در میان dar miyán, بین bain, مابین má-bain, در خلال dar khilál, در اثنا dar asná.
Bevel, هنجار hanjár.
Beverage, شراب sharáb, شرب shurb.
Bevy, گروه gurúh, طائفه tá,ifah.—(*of birds*) سیله sílah.

To **Beware**, حذر کردن hazar kardan, پر حذر بودن pur-hazar búdan, خبردار بودن khabar-dár búdan, پرهیز کردن parhíz kardan, احتیاط نمودن ihtiyát nimúdan.
To **Bewitch**, نیرنگ کردن nairang kardan, افسون کردن afsún kardan.
Beyond, آنطرف án-taraf, آنسو án-sú, وراء wará,.—(*exceeding*) زیاده ziyádah, علاوه 'aláwah.
Bezoar, باد زهر bád-zahr, پا زهر pázahr, زهر مهره zahr-muhrah.
Bias, میل mail, رغبت raghbat.
To **Bias**, میل کردن mail kardan.
Bib, دوشوان dúshwán.
Bibber, می پرست mai-parast.
Bible, کتاب مقدس kitáb-i-mukaddas.—(*Old Testament*) عهد العتیق 'ahdu-'l-'atík, توریت taurát, پیمان قدیم paimán-i-kadím.—(*New Testament*) عهد الجدید 'ahdu-'l-jadíd, وثیقه جدید wasíkah-i-jadíd, انجیل anjíl, پیمان تازه paimán-i-tázah.
Bibulous, جاذب jázib, خیسنده khísandah.
To **Bicker**, ستیز کردن sitíz kardan, منازعت کردن munáza'at kardan.
Bickering, ستیز sitíz, منازعت munáza'at.
Bicoloured, دو رنگ dú-rang.
To **Bid**, *vide* To **Command**.—(*at a sale*) سوام کردن suwám kardan.
Bidder, سوام کننده suwám-kunandah.
Bier, تابوت tábút, نعش na'sh.
Bifold, دو تا dú-tá.
Bifurcate, دو شاخه dú-shákhah.
Big, بزرگ buzurg, کبیر kabír, عظیم 'azím, کلان kalán, جسیم jasím, خطیر khatír, کلفت kuluft.—(*vide* **Bulky**).—(*pregnant*) آبستن ábistan, حامله hámilah.—(*big-bellied, fat*) قمطره kumatrah, قطور katúr, بجباج bajbáj.
Bigness, بزرگی buzurgí, جسامت jasámat.
Bigot, وسواسی waswásí, متعصب muta'assib, خشک khushk, خر صالح khar-sálih.
Bigoted, وسواسی waswásí.

BIGOTRY, تعصب ta'assub.
BILE, صفرا safrá, زهره zahrah.
BILGE-WATER, آب خن áb-i-khan.
BILIOUS, صفرائی safráí.
BILL, *vide* BEAK, ACCOUNTS.—(*of exchange*), برات barát, هندوی hundaví (*hind.*), کاغذ زر kághaz-i-zar. — (*of sale*) قباله kabálah, بیعنامه bai'-námah. — (*note of hand*) دستاویز dast-áviz.—(*bond*) تمسك tamassuk, حجت hujjat.—(*Parliamentary*) لایحه láíhah.
To BILL, بوسه دادن búsah dádan.
BILLET (*note*), مراسله murásalah, رقعه ruk'ah. — (*of wood*) دسته dastah.
To BILLET (*military term*), در خانه اقامت کردن dar khánah ikámat kardan.
BILL-HOOK, داس dás.
BILLOW, موج mauj.
BILLOWY, مواج mavváj, متلاطم mutalátim.
To BIND, بستن bastan, بند کردن band kardan, ربط کردن rabt kardan. —(*a book*) جلد کردن jild kardan.—(*one's self by a vow, promise, &c.*) خودرا مقید ساختن khwudrá mukayyad sákhtan.—(*over, legal term*) کفیل کردن kafíl kardan.—(*an apprentice*), شاگرد کردن shágird kardan.
BINDER (*of books*) مجلد mujallid, جلد گر jild-gar, صحاف sahháf.
BINDING (*of a garment, &c.*), لبك labak.—(*stitching of the leaves of a book*), ته بندی tah-bandí.—(*silk cord at top and bottom of the leaves*), شیرازه shírázah.
BINOCULAR (*glass*), دور بین dúr-bín.
BIOGRAPHER, مورخ muvarrikh, اهل سیر ahl-i-siyar.
BIOGRAPHY, سیر siyár, تاریخ táríkh.
BIPARTITE, مناصفه munásafah.
BIRCH, *vide* ROD.
BIRCH-TREE, غوشه ghúshah.
BIRD, مرغ murgh, پرنده parandah, طیر tair. — (*bird-lime*) کشمشك کاولی kishmishk-i-kávalí.
BIRD'S-EYE VIEW, چشم انداز chashm andáz.

BIRTH, پیدایش paidáyish, ولادت viládat, میلاد míládd, تولد tavallud. (*Vide* DESCENT.)—(*to give birth to*) تولید نمودن taulíd nimúdan, زادن zádan, زائیدن záídan.
BIRTHDAY, روز ولادت rúz-i-viládat, سالگره sál-girih, روز تولد rúz-i-tavallud.
BIRTH-PLACE, مولد maulid, زاد بوم zád-búm.
BIRTHRIGHT, حق بکوریت hakk-i-bukúriyat, حق اول زادگی hakk-i-avval-zádagí.
BIRTH-WORT (*aristolochia*), زراوند zarávand.
BISCUIT, کماج خشك kumáj-i-khushk, بقسومات baksúmát (*only used in the plural*).—(*small sweet biscuit*) کلوچه kulúchah.
To BISECT, بریدن burídan, مناصفه کردن munásafah kardan.
BISECTION, قطعه kit'ah, مناصفه munásafah.
BISHOP, اسقوف uskúf.
BISHOPRICK, اسقوفیت uskúfíyat.
BISON, گاو دشتی gáv-i-dashtí, بیزون bízún (*eur.*).
BISSEXTILE YEAR, سال کبیسه sál-i-kabísah.
BIT, پاره párah, پارچه párchah, تکه tikkah, لفچه lafchah, ریزه rízah, قراضه kurázah, لقمه lukmah, ذره zarrah, شرحه sharhah, قطعه kat'ah, جزوی juzví. — (*in bits*) پاره پاره párah párah.—(*of a bridle*) دهنه dahanah, آبخور áb-khwur.
BITCH, سگ ماده sag-i-mádah, لاس lás.
BITE, گزیدگی gazídagí, گزندگی gazandagí.
To BITE, گزیدن gazídan, جاویدن jávídan, خائیدن khá,ídan, جائیدن já,ídan, دندان گرفتن dandán giriftan.—(*be pungent*) تیز شدن tíz shudan.
BITTER, تلخ talkh, مر murr.
BITTERN, بوتیمار bútímár.
BITTERNESS, تلخی talkhí, مراره marárah.
BITUMEN, نفط naft, نفطه naftah, قفر kafr.

BLACK, سیاه siyáh, سیه siyah, تیره tírah, اسود asvad, هندوی hindaví.—(*black and blue*) کبود kabúd.—(*black and white*) ابلق ablak, سیاه و سفید siyáh va safíd.—(*lamp-black*) دوده dúdah.

To BLACK, سیاه کردن siyáh kardan.—(*boots*) رنگ زدن rang zadan.

BLACKBERRY (*bramble*), توت کوهی tút-i-kúhí.

BLACKBIRD, سار sár.

BLACKGUARD, اوباش aubásh, بد نهاد bad-nihád, لوطی lútí.

BLACKING, سیاهی siyáhí, رنگ کفش rang-i-kafsh.

BLACKNESS, سیاهی siyáhí, سودا saudá, سواد savád, تیرگی tíragí.

BLACKSMITH, آهنگر áhan-gar, حداد haddád.

BLADDER, مثانه masánah. (*Vide* BLISTER.)

BLADE (*of grass, &c.*), برگ barg, ورق varak, پر گیاه par-i-giyáh, خس گیاه khas-i-giyah.—(*of a sword, &c.*), تیغه tíghah. — (*of the shoulder*), شانه shánah.

BLAIN, آبله ábilah, تول tuvul, اوله aulah (*vulg.*).

BLAMABLE, مقصر mukassar, لایق ملام láík-i-malám, سزاوار ملامت sazá-var-i-malámat.

BLAME (*fault*), تقصیر taksír, گناه gunáh, خطا khatá, عیب 'aib, قصور kusúr.—(*censure*), زجر zajr, ملامت malámat, سر زنش sar-zanish, مواخذه mu,ákhazah, پیغاره pai-ghárah, عتاب 'itáb.

To BLAME, ملامت کردن malámat kardan, عیب گفتن 'aib guftan, ذم کردن zamm kardan.

BLAMELESS, بی گناه bí-gunáh, بی عیب bí-'aib, بی تقصیر bí-taksír, پاك pák.

BLAMER, غماز ghammáz, عیبگو 'aib-gú.

To BLANDISH, عشوه کردن 'ishvah kardan, تملق نمودن tamalluk ni-múdan.

BLANDISHMENT, ناز náz, نوازش na-vázish, شیوه shívah, عشوه 'ish-vah.

BLANK, ساده sádah.—(*in lottery*) رقعهٔ ساده ruk'ah-i-sádah, بد بخت bad-bakht. — (*in writing*) خوا khavá.

BLANKET, گلیم gilím, مفرش mi-frash, لحاف liháf.—(*for a horse*) جل jul, جل نمد jul-i-namad.

To BLASPHEME, کفر گفتن kufr guf-tan.

BLASPHEMER, کفر گوی kufr-gúí.

BLASPHEMOUS, کافر káfir.

BLASPHEMY, کفر kufr, تجدیف taj-díf.

BLAST, باد سخت bád-i-sakht.

To BLAST, بر باد دادن bar bád dá-dan.

BLAZE, *vide* FLAME.

To BLAZE, *vide* To BURN.

To BLAZON, مشهور کردن mash-húr kardan, اشتهار کردن ishtihár kar-dan.

To BLEACH, گازری کردن gázurí kar-dan.

BLEAK, سرد sard, برد bard, بارد bárid.

BLEAKNESS, سردی sardí, سرما sar-má.

BLEAR-EYED, سرخ چشم surkh-chashm, چشم رمد دار chashm-i-ramad-dár.

To BLEAT (*as a sheep*), صدا زدن sadá zadan, باع کردن bá' kardan.

To BLEED (*open a vein*), فصد کردن fasd kardan, خون گرفتن khún giriftan, رگ زدن rag zadan.—(*in-trans.*) خون چکیدن khún chakí-dan, خون آمدن khún ámadan.

BLEEDING (*medical term*) حجامت hijámat, رگ زن rag-zan, فصد کن fasd-kun.

BLEMISH, عیب 'aib, جرم jurm, لکه lakkah.

BLEMISHED, معیوب ma'yúb.

To BLESS, برکت دادن barakat dá-dan, دعائی خیر گفتن du'á,í-i-khair guftan, درود گفتن durúd guftan, آفرین کردن áfirín kardan.—(*make prosper;*) مبارك ساختن mubárak sákhtan, بختیار کردن bakht-yár kardan.

BLESSED, مبارك mubárak, مسعود mas'úd, ميمون maimún.
BLESSEDNESS, سعادت sa'ádat, مبارکی mubárakí.
BLESSING, *vide* BENEDICTION.
BLIGHT (*mildew*), يرقان yarakán, زنگ zang, پورملك púrmík, پرملك purmik.
BLIGHTED, زنگ زده zang-zadah, پورملك زده púrmik-zadah.
BLIND, نابينا ná-bíná, کور kúr, اعمی a'má, ضرير zarír.—(*curtain*) پرده pardah.—(*Venetian blinds*) کرکری kirkirí (*hind.*).—(*blind of one eye*) يك چشمی yak-chashmí, اعور a'var, واحد العين váhidu-'l-'ain.—(*night-blind*), شبکور shab-kúr.
To BLIND, کور ساختن kúr sákhtan, چشم برآوردن chashm bar-ávardan. (*Vide* To DECEIVE.)
BLINDFOLD, چشم پوشيده chashm-púshídah.
To BLINDFOLD, چشم پوشيدن chashm púshídan, چشم بستن chashm bastan.
BLINDMAN'S BUFF, سر مامك sar-mámak.
BLINDNESS, نابينائی ná-bíná,í, کوری kúrí, عما 'amá.
BLISS, *vide* JOY.
BLISTER, تول tuvul, آبله ábilah, اوله aulah (*vulg.*).—(*plaster*) بلستر balastar (*eur.*).
BLOATED, ورم شده varam shudah, آماسيده ámásídah.
BLOCK (*of wood, &c.*), کنده kundah.
To BLOCK up, بستن bastan, مدروس کردن madrús kardan, مسدود ساختن masdúd sákhtan.
BLOCKADE, محاصره muhásarah, حصر hasr.
To BLOCKADE, *vide* To BESIEGE.
BLOCKHEAD, ابله ablah, کودن kaudan, نا دان ná-dán, نا فهم ná-fahm, بيوقوف bí-vukúf, خوپله khwaplah, احمق ahmak.
BLOOD, خون khún.—(*breed*) رگ rag, رگه ragah, نژاد nizhád.
BLOODLESS, بی خون bí khún.
BLOOD-MONEY, دية diyat, خونبها khún-bahá, معقلت ma'kulat.
BLOODSHED, قتل katl, خونريزی khún-rízí. (*Vide* SLAUGHTER, MURDER.)
BLOODSHOT, خون آلود khún-álúd, سرخ surkh.
BLOOD-STONE, حجر الدم hajaru-'d-dam.
BLOODTHIRSTY, قاتل kátil, ظالم zálim, خونفشان khún-fishán, خونخوار khún-khwár.
BLOODY, خونين khúnín, خون آلود khún-álúd.
BLOOM (*blossom*), شکوفه shikúfah, بهار bahár, غنچه ghunchah.—(*of youth*) عنفوان 'unfuván, ريعان شباب rai'án-i-shabáb.
To BLOSSOM, شکوفتن shikúftan, شکفتن shikuftan, غنچه زدن ghunchah zadan.
BLOT, لکه lakkah, داغ dágh.
To BLOT, داغدار کردن dágh-dár kardan.—(*to blot out*) محو ساختن mahv sákhtan, خط زدن khat zadan, پاك کردن pák kardan.
BLOTCH (*on the skin*), ککمل kakmal, ککمك kakmak.
BLOTTING-PAPER, کاغذ تر خشك کنك kághaz-i-tar-khushk-kunak.
BLOUSE, قميص kamís, پيراهن pírá-han.
BLOW, ضرب zarb, مشت musht, طپانچه tapánchah, لس lus, زد zad.
To BLOW, وزيدن vazídan, دميدن damídan.—(*with the breath*) پف کردن puf kardan, فوت کردن fút kardan.—(*as a flower*) شکوفتن shikúftan, دميدن damídan.—(*the nose*) استنشاق کردن istinshák kardan, دماغ گرفتن dimágh giriftan.—(*a trumpet, &c.*) نواختن navákhtan, دميدن damídan, کشيدن kashídan.—(*from the mouth of a cannon, a common mode of execution*), دم توپ گذاردن dam-i-túp guzárdan.—(*hot and cold*) تردد داشتن taraddud dáshtan.—(*out*) پوف کردن púf kardan.—(*the fire*) نفخ کردن nafkh kardan, فوت کردن fút kardan, پف کردن puf kardan. — (*to blow up, with gun-*

powder), بهوا افکندن bi-havá afkandan, بهوا بردن bi-havá burdan.

BLUBBER, چربی charbí, پیه píh.

BLUDGEON, چوب chúb.

BLUE, نیله nílah, نیل níl, نیلگون nílgún, کبود kabúd, سماوی samáví.—(*dark blue*) سرمه surmah, سورمئی súrma,í.—(*light blue*) آبی ábí, فیروزه fírúzah, آسمانی ásmání.—(*vivid or intense blue*) لاجوردی lájavardí.—(*Prussian blue*) نیل پروس níl-i-prús.

BLUE-BOOK, کتاب آبی kitáb-i-ábí.

BLUE-BOTTLE (*fly*), عنتر 'antar.

BLUENESS, نیلگونی níl-gúní, نیلفامی níl-fámí, کبودی kabúdí.

BLUNDER, ذلت zillat, غلط ghalat, سقت sakat, خطا khatá, سهو sahv.

To BLUNDER, خطا کردن khatá kardan, سهو کردن sahv kardan, تقصیر کردن taksír kardan, قصور ساختن kusúr sákhtan.

BLUNDERBUSS, قرابینه karábínah (*eur.*).

BLUNDERER, خطا کار khatá-kár, سهو کار sahv-kár.

BLUNT, کند kund.—(*stupid*) احمق ahmak, بی عقل bí-'akl.

To BLUNT, کند کردن kund kardan.

BLUNTNESS, کندی kundí.

BLUSH, خجلت khijlat, خجالت khijálat, شرم sharm.

To BLUSH, خجالت کشیدن khijálat kashídan, شرم داشتن sharm dáshtan, حیا داشتن hayá dáshtan.

BOAR, گراز guráz, خوک khúk, or خوگ khúg, خنزیر khinzír.—(*wild boar*) خوک وحشی khúk-i-vahshí.

BOARD, تخته takhtah, لوح lauh.—(*of a book*) مقوی mukavvá.—(*diet*) طعام ta'ám, سفره sufrah.

To BOARD, تخت بندی کردن takht-bandí kardan. [This term is not applied to a floor.] (*a person*) سفره دادن sufrah dádan.

BOARD-ROOM, اطاق نشیمنی uták-i-nishímaní, اوطاق مجلس úták-i-majlis, دیوانخانه díván-khánah.

BOARD-WAGES, خوراکی khwuráki.

BOARISH, روستا rústá, نا تراشیده ná-tiráshídah, بی ادب bí-adab.

BOAST, فخر fakhr, خود نمائی khúd-nimá,í, مفاخرت mufákharat, بلند پروازی buland-parvází.—(*of what one has done*) گذاف gizáf.—(*of what one can or will do*) لاف láf.

To BOAST, قل رفتن kul raftan, مفاخرت نمودن mufákharat nimúdan, گزاف زدن gizáf zadan, لاف زدن láf zadan.

BOASTER, فضول fuzúl, لافزن láf-zan.

BOASTFUL, لافزن láf-zan, فاخر fákhir, مفتخر muftakhir.

BOAT, کشتی kashtí, نو nau, مشوه mashuwwah (*hind.*). — (*ferry-boat*) معبر mi'bar.

BOATMAN, ملاح mallah, جاشو jáshú, نوتی nútí.

BOATSWAIN, سرهنگ sar-hang.

BOB, جنبش jumbish.

To BOB, جنبیدن jumbídan.

BOBBIN, چهره chihrah, ماسوره másúrah.

BODICE (*worn by women*), پستان بند pistán-band, بر بند bar-band.

BODILESS, بی تن bí-tan, بی بدن bí-badan, بی جسد bí-jasad, بی اندام bí-andám.

BODILY, متجسم mutajassim, جسمانی jismání, بدنی badaní. (*Vide* ENTIRELY.)

BODKIN, سوزن súzan.

BODY, تن tan, بدن badan, جسد jasad, جسم jism, اندام andám, وجود vujúd, شخص shakhs, قالب kálib.—(*corpse*) لاش lásh, لاشه láshah, میت mayyit, میته mayyitah, مردار murdár, جنازه janázah, جیفه jaifah. (*Vide* CROWD.)

BODY-GUARD, غلام رکابی ghulám-i-rikábí, غلام شاهی ghulám-i-sháhí.

BOG, گلابه gilábah, مشیله mashílah.

To BOGGLE, پس و پیش کردن pas va písh kardan.

BOHEMIAN (*bad character*) مرتکب بدزدی murtakib bi-duzdí.

BOIL (*tumour*), دمل dumal, دنبل dumbal, کورك kúrak.

To BOIL, (*trans.*) جوشانیدن júsháuídan, جوش کردن júsh kardan.

— (*intrans.*) جوشیدن júshídan, بجوش آمدن bi-júsh ámadan.
BOILED-MEAT, گوشت آب پز gúsht-i-áb-paz.
BOILER (*pot*), دیگ díg.
BOILING, جوش júsh, جوشش júshish.
BOISTEROUS, شدید shadíd, تند tund, سخت sakht.—(*sea*) متلاطم mutalátim.
BOISTEROUSNESS, تندی tundí, سختی sakhtí, شدت shiddat.
BOLD, دلیر dilír, دلاور dilávar, بیباك bí-bák, جانباز ján-báz, شجاع shujá', شجیع shají', جری jarí, بهادر bahádur, شیر مرد shír-mard, با جرات bá-jurát, رشید rashíd.
BOLDNESS, دلیری dilírí, دلاوری dilávarí, جرات jurát, جسارت jasárat, شجاعت shajá'at, غیرت ghairat, بیباکی bí-bákí, شراعت shará'at.
BOLSTER, بالش bálish, بالین bálín, ناز بالش náz-bálish.
BOLT (*of a door*), کلان kulán, کلند kuland.—(*of iron*) تملیك tamlík.
To BOLT, بستن bastan, بند کردن band kardan, چفت کردن chift kardan, کلند زدن kuland zadan.
BOMB, گلولهٔ قنبارہ gulúlah-i-kumbárah, گلولهٔ خمپاره gulúlah-i-khumpárah.
To BOMBARD, بتوپ بستن bi-túp bastan, توپ انداختن túp andákhtan.
BOMBARDIER, قنبارہ چی kumbárah-chí, خمپاره چی khumpárah-chí.
BOMBARDMENT, توپ انداختن túp andákhtan.
BOMBAST, مبالغه mubálaghah, اغراق ighrák.
BOMBASTIC, مطنطن mutantin.
BOMBAZINE, گرماسوف garmásúf, مشروع mashrú'.
BON-BON, شیرینی shíríní.
BOND (*contract*), تمسك tamassuk, حجت hujjat.—(*bond, tie*) ارتباط irtibát, رابطه rábitah, علاقه 'alákah.—(*obligation to pay*) حجت hujjat, تمسك نقدی tamassuk-i-nakdí, کاغذ التزام kághaz-i-iltizám.
BONDAGE, وا بستگی vá-bastagí, قید kaid, بند band, گرفتاری giriftárí, اسر usr, اسیری asírí, عبودیت 'ubúdíyat.
BONDMAID, کنیز kaníz.
BONDMAN, غلام ghulám.
BONE, استخوان ustukhwán, استخان ustukhán (*vulg.*), عظم 'azm.—(*bone-setter*) شکسته بند shikastah-band.
BONELESS, بی استخوان bí-ustukhwán.
BON-FIRE, آتش átish.
BONNET, کلاه kuláh, سر پوش sar-púsh.
BONY, پر استخوان pur ustukhwán.
BOOK, کتاب kitáb, نامه namáh, صحیفه sahífah.—(*section or chapter*) سفر safar.—(*account-book*) دفتر daftar, دستك حساب dastak-i-hisáb, سفینه safínah.—(*book-cover or envelope*) قوقلق kau,iluk, قولق kauluk. — (*memorandum - book*) مجمعه majma'ah, بیاض bayáz.
BOOK-BINDER, صحاف sahháf, مجلد mujallid, جلد گر jild-gar.
BOOK-BINDING, جلد گری jild-garí.
BOOKING-OFFICE, دفتر daftar, تیکت خانه tíkat-khánah.
BOOK-SELLER, کتاب فروش kitáb-furúsh, صحاف sahháf.
BOOK-WORM, کتابی kitábí.
BOOM, تیر tír, فروند farvand.
BOON, انعام in'ám, بخشش bakhshish.
BOOR, دهقان dihkán, ترك turk, روستائی rústá,í.
BOORISH, بی ادب bí-adab, جاهل jáhil.
BOORISHNESS, بی ادبی bí-adabí, دهقانیت dihkáníyat, نا تراشیدگی ná-tiráshídagí.
BOOT (*covering for leg and foot*), چکمه chakmah, موزه múzah (*obs.*). —(*top-boots*) چکمه chakmah.—(*Vide* GAIN).
BOOTH, کاشانه káshánah, کپر kappar, کمه kumah.
BOOTMAKER, چکمه دوز chakmah-dúz, چکمه ساز chakmah-sáz, کفش دوز kafsh-dúz.

Boots (*servant*), نوکر naukar, چاکر chákar.

Booty, *vide* Plunder.

Borax, تنکال tankál, بوراق búrák.

Border (*margin*), حاشیه háshiyah, کنار kanár, کناره kanárah, کران karán, کرانه karánah, زه zih, دامن dáman, لب lab, حد hadd, مرز marz. (*Vide* Bounds.)

To Border حاشیه نهادن háshiyah nihádan; (*adjoin*) نزدیک شدن nazdík shudan, نزد شدن nazd shudan.

Bordering, نزدیک nazdík, نزد nazd.

To Bore (*pierce*), سفتن suftan, سنبیدن sumbídan, سوراخ کردن súrákh kardan.

Boreas, باد شمال bád-i-shimál.

Borer, سوراخ کننده súrákh-kunandah.

Born, مولود maulúd, متولد mutavallid, پیدا paidá, زاد zád.

To be Born, زادن zádan, زائیدن zá,ídan, پیدا شدن paidá shudan, تولد یافتن tavallud yáftan, متولد شدن mutavallid shudan.

To Borrow (*an article which must itself be restored*), عاریت گرفتن 'árivat giriftan, استعارت کردن isti'árat kardan. — (*money or other things for which an equivalent is to be restored*) قرض گرفتن karz giriftan, وام گرفتن vám giriftan.

Borrower, قرضدار karz-dár.

Bosom, بر bar, سینه sínah, آغوش ághúsh. — (*of a female*) *vide* Breast.

Boss (*of a shield, &c., stud, ornament*) گلمیخ gul-míkh, قبه kubbah.

Botanist, علف چین 'alaf-chín, and

Botany, علف چینی 'alaf-chíní.— [These are contemptuous terms for a science which the Persians hold in no repute.]

Both, هر دو har dú, همدیگر hamdígar, اثنین isnain. (*Vide* Also.)

Bother, تشویش tashvísh.

To Bother, ایذا دادن ízá dádan, زحمت رسانیدن zahmat rasánídan, عذاب دادن 'azáb dádan.

Bottle (*of glass*), شیشه shíshah.— (*of earthenware*) بستو bastú.—(*of leather*) مطاره matárah, مطهره matharah, خیگ khíg. — (*long-necked bottle or phial*) صراحی surâhí.—(*large glass bottle or flask*) قرابه karábah.—(*smaller ditto*) بغلی baghalí.—(*English black glass bottle*) بطلی butlí (*eur.*), بطری butrí (*eur.*).—(*decanter*) تنگ tung.—(*square decanter or case bottle*) چارپر chárpar.

To Bottle, به شیشه ریختن bi-shíshah ríkhtan.

Bottom, ته tah, بن bun, پائین pá,ín, قعر ka'r, کف kaf.—(*of a coffee-cup, stand, or holder*) زیر فنجان zír-i-finján, ظرف zarf. — (*stand or foot of a vessel, &c.*) کعب ka'b.

Bottomless, بی ته bí-tah, بی بن bí-bun, بی قعر bí-ka'r, بی کف bí-kaf, بی پائین bí-pá,ín.

Bough, شاخ shákh, شاخه shákhah, فرع far' (*pl.* فروع furú').

Boulder, سنگ sang.

To Bounce, جستن jastan, جنبیدن jumbídan.

Bound (*leap*), جست jast, جنبش jumbish. — (*compelled*) مجبور majbúr, لابد lábudda, ناچار náchár.—(*book*) مجلد mujallad.

To be Bound to, بایستن báyístan, لابد شدن lábudda shudan.

To Bound, جستن jastan, جنبیدن jumbídan.

Boundless, بی حد bí-hadd, بی انتها bí-intihá, بی پایان bí-páyán, بی نهایت bí-niháyat.

Boundlessness, بی انتهائی bí-intihá,í, بی نهایتی bí-niháyatí.

Bounds, حد hadd, سرحد sar-hadd, ثغور sughúr, دهنه dahanah, کران karán, کنار kanár, مثال ma,ál, اقصی aksá, انتها intihá, مرزبوم marz-búm, مرز marz, سنور sunúr.

Bounteous, جاید jáid, کریم karím, جوانمرد javán-mard.

Bounty, کرم karam, کرامت karámat, عطا 'atá, سخا sakhá, سخاوت sakhávat, جود júd, بذل bazl, جوانمردی

javán - mardí, مروت murúvat, سماحت samáhat.
Bouquet, دسته dastah, گلدسته gul-dastah.
Bourse, صراف خانه sarráf-khánah, تجارتخانه tijárat-khánah, دار المعامله dáru-'l-mu'ámalah.
Bout, دفعه daf'ah, امتحان imtihán, کره karrah.
Bow, کمان kamán, قوس kaus.—(*violin*) کمان kamán. — (*pellet-bow*) گلوله کمان gulúlah - kamán, کمان گردها kamán - i - gardhá.—(*bow-string*) چله chillah, زه zih.—(*bow-case*) قربان kirbán, معوان mis-ván.—(*horns of a bow*), گوشه کمان gúshah-i-kamán.—(*bow or pom-mel of a saddle*) کوهه زین kúhah-i-zín, قربوس karabús.—(*rainbow*) قوس قزح kaus-i-kuzah, شمشیر علی shamshír-i-'alí, کمان فلک kamán-i-falak. — (*bow - maker*) کمان گر kamán-gar.
Bow (*reverence*), سر فرو sar-furú, کورنش kúrnish, رکوع rukú'.
To Bow, سلام کردن salám kardan, سر فرو کردن sar-furú kardan.
Bowels, روده rúdah (*pl.* رودها rúd-ahá), معی mi'á (*pl.* امعا am'á), حشا hashá (*pl.* احشا ahshá).
Bower, *vide* Arbour.
Bowl, کاسه kásah.
To Bowl, غلطانیدن ghaltánídan, گوی باز کردن gúí-báz kardan.
Bowler, گوی باز gúí-báz, طوپه باز túpah-báz.
Bowls (*game*) طوپه بازی túpah-bází.
Bowsprit, کمانه kamánah.
Box (*chest*), صندوق sandúk, یخدان yakhdán.—(*small chest or box*) صندوقچه sandúkchah, قاب káb.—(*tree*) شمشاد shimshád, بقس baks, کیشه دار kíshah-dár.—(*little box, such as snuff-box, pill-box, &c.*) قوطی kútí.—(*casket, or box bound with iron clamps*) مجری mijrí.—(*case or box of wood or leather*) جعبه ja'bah.—(*box or small press, like a medicine chest, full of drawers and compart-ments*) پیشتخته písh-takhtah.—(*earthenware box for saving money in*) کلک kulluk. — (*at theatre*) لژ lazh (*eur.*).—(*private box*) لژ مخصوص lazh-i-makhsús (*eur.*).
Box on the ear, سیلی sílí, گوشمال gúsh-mál.
To Box (*fight*), مشت زدن musht zadan.
Boxer, مشت زن musht-zan.
Boxing, مشت زدن musht-zadan.
Boy, پسر pisar, کودک kúdak. (*Vide* Servant.)
Boyhood, *vide* Babyhood.
Brace (*pair*), جفت juft, جور júr.
To Brace, بستن bastan.
Bracelet, دستبند dast-band, یاره yárah, النگو alangú.
Braces, شلوار بند shalvár-band.
Bracket, استاده istádah.
Brackish (*as water*), شور shúr.
Brad, میخ míkh.
To Brag, *vide* To Boast.
Brahman, برهمن barhaman.
Braid (*lace*), قیطان kaitán.
Brain, مغز maghz, دماغ dimágh, مخ mukhkh. — (*hare-brained*) بی مغز bí-maghz.
Bramble (*blackberry*), توت کوهی tút-i-kúhí.
Bran, سپوس sapús, نخاله nukhálah.
Branch, *vide* Bough.—(*of a river*) شعبت shu'bat, جوی júí, جوب júb (*vulg.*).
Brand (*mark of cautery*), داغ dágh.—(*burning stick*), نیمسوز ním-súz.
To Brand, داغ کردن dágh kardan.
To Brandish, افشاندن afshándan, کشیدن kashídan.
Brandy, عرق 'arak.
Brass, برنژ birinzh, برنج birinj, نحاس nahás.—(*brazen*) برنجین birinjín.
Brave, *vide* Bold.
Bravo, مرحبا marhaban, واه واه váh-váh, آفرین áfirín, شاباش shábásh, ماشالله máshállah. — (*a bravo*) آهن خور áhan-khwur.
Brawl, عربده 'arbadah, اغتشاش ightishásh.

To BRAY (*as an ass*), عرعر کردن ʻarʻar kardan, زاره دادن zárah dádan.

BRAZIER, مسگر mis-gar.

BRAZIL-WOOD (*a red dye*), بقم bakm.

BREACH, شکاف shikáf, رخنه rikhnah, شکستگی shikastagí, مغاره mughárah.

To BREACH (*a wall*), مغاره ساختن mughárah sákhtan.

BREAD, نان nán, چورك chúrak.—(*unleavened bread*), نان فطیری nán-i-fatírí.—(*leavened bread*) نان خمیری nán-i-khamírí.—(*thick bread cake*) کماج kumáj, کماچ kumách.—(*bread baked on an iron heater*) نان ساجی nán-i-sájí.—(*bread baked on heated gravel*) نان سنگك nán-i-sangak.—(*thin bread in sheets*) نان لواشی nán-i-lavāshí, نان یوخه nán-i-yúkhah.—(*barley bread*) نان جوین nán-i-javín, کشکینه kashkínah.—(*stale bread*) نان بیات nán-i-bayát, نان مانده nán-i-mándah.

BREADTH, پهن pahn, پهنائی pahná,í, عرض ʻarz, فراخی farákhí, قطر kutr.

BREAK OF DAY, سحر sahar, صبح subh.

To BREAK, (*trans.*) شکستن shikastan, پاره کردن párah kardan.—(*intrans.*) شکستن shikastan, پاره شدن párah shudan.—(*as a tough substance, to snap*), گسیختن gusíkhtan, گسستن gusustan.—(*trans.*) گسلانیدن gusilánídan.—(*a promise, &c.*) فسخ نمودن faskh nimúdan, شکستن shikastan, جر زدن jir zadan (*vulg.*).—(*tame*) تعلیم دادن taʻlím dádan, دست آموز کردن dast-ámúz kardan.—(*in pieces*), پاره پاره کردن párah párah kardan, خورد ساختن khwurd sákhtan, پخش کردن pakhsh kardan.—(*a seal*) بر داشتن bar-dáshtan.—(*to break with a person*) از کسی رو گردان شدن az kasí rú-gardán shudan.—(*to break up, as an assembly*) (*trans.*) سلام شکستن salám shikastan; (*intrans.*) برهم خوردن bar-ham khwurdan.—(*to break down*) (*intrans.*) شکسته بودن shikastah búdan.

BREAKFAST (*slight meal taken very early*), ناشتا náshtá.—(*meal taken near noon*) نهار nahár, چاشت chásht.

BREAST, سینه sínah, بر bar, صدر sadr.—(*breasts of a woman*) پستانها pistánhá, ثدیین sudyain.

BREASTWORKS, استحکامات istihkámát, سنگر sangur.

BREATH, دم dam, نفس nafas.—(*bad breath*) عفونت دهان ʻufúnát-i-dahán.—(*last breath*) رمق ramak.—(*short-breath*) ضیق النفس zíku-ʼn-nafas.

To BREATHE, دم زدن dam zadan, نفس کشیدن nafas kashídan.

BREECHES, شلوار shalvár.—(*knee-breeches*) شلوار نیم تنه shalvár-i-ním-tanah.

BREECH-LOADER, ته پر tah-pur.

BREED (*race*), اصل asl, نسل nasl, جنس jins, نژاد nizhád, ذریت zurríyat.—(*cross-breed*), دو رگ dú-rag. (*Vide* FAMILY, TRIBE.)

To BREED, *vide* To BRING FORTH.

BREEZE, نسیم nasím, باد bád.

BREVET, رتبی rutabí.

BREVITY, اختصار ikhtisár, اقتصار iktisár.

To BREW, ساختن sákhtan.

BRIBE, رشوت rishvat, ارش irsh, پاره párah.

BRICK (*unburnt*), خشت khisht.—(*burnt*) آجر ájur, آجور ájúr.—(*kiln*) کوره kúrah, کورهٔ آجر پزی kúrah-i-ajur-pazí.—(*dust*) سرخی surkhí.—(*brick-burner*) آجر پز ájur-paz.—(*bricklayer*) بنا banná.—(*brick-maker*) خشتزن khisht-zan.—(*brick-making*) خشتمالی khisht-málí.

BRIDAL TROUSSEAU, جهاز jaház, وردك vardak.

BRIDE, عروس ʻarús.

BRIDE-CHAMBER, حجله hijlah, جلوه jilvah, بیت السرور baitu-ʼs-surúr.

BRIDEGROOM, داماد dámád.
BRIDGE, پل pul, جسر jisr, کرپی kurpí, پرد purd.—(*suspension bridge*) پل زنجیری pul-i-zanjírí.—(*of the nose*) انفه anfah, بر آمدگی دماغ bar-ámadagí-i-dimágh.—(*of Paradise*) جنیور janívar, صراط sirát, پل صراط pul-i-sirát.
BRIDLE, عنان 'inán, زمام zimám.—(*bit of bridle*) دهنه dahanah, آبخور áb-khwur.—(*frontlet*) مگس پران magas-parán.—(*chain*) رشمه rashmah.—(*nose-bridle*), مهار mihár. — (*reins*) لجام lijám, لگام ligám, جلو jilau. — (*ornamented work on the head of a bridle*), کله گی killah-gí. — (*head-stall*), افسار afsár.
BRIEF, مختصر mukhtasar.
BRIEFLY, بطور اختصار bi-taur-i-ikhtisár.
BRIG (*two-masted vessel*) جهاز دو دقلی jaház-i-dú-dakalí.
BRIGADIER, میر لواء mír-i-livá,.
BRIGAND, رهزن rah-zan.
BRIGANDAGE, رهزنی rah-zaní, حرامی harámí.
BRIGHT, روشن raushan, منور munavvar, منیر munír, جوهردار jauhar-dár, لامع lámi', جلی jalí, درخشان dirakhshán, تابان tábán, تابدار táb-dár, ساطع sáti', رخشان rukhshán. (*Vide* MERRY, CLEVER.)
BRIGHTNESS, روشنی raushaní, تابانی tábání, تاب táb, تابش tábish, رخشندگی rukhshandagí.
BRILLIANT, *vide* BRIGHT.
BRIM, *vide* BRINK.
BRIMSTONE, گوگرد gúgird, کبریت kibrít.
BRINE, آب شور áb-i-shúr.
To BRING, آوردن ávardan, حاضر آوردن hazir ávardan.—(*forth, to bear*) زادن zádan, زائیدن zá,ídan, پیدا کردن paidá kardan, وضع حمل کردن vaz'-i-haml kardan.—(*up, to rear*) پروردن parvardan, تربیت نمودن tarbiyat nimúdan, حضانت نمودن hizánat nimúdan. — (*to bring back*) بر گردانیدن bar-gar-dánídan, نزدیك آوردن nazdík ávardan.—(*to bring before*) احضار کردن ihzár kardan.—(*to bring together*) نزدیك آوردن nazdík ávardan.
BRINJAL (*egg-plant*), بادنجان bádinján.
BRINK, لب lab, کنار kanár, کناره kanárah, کران karán.
BRINY, شور shúr.
BRIOCH, نان کوچك nán-i-kúchik, کماج kumáj.
BRISK, *vide* ACTIVE.—(*trade*) رواج raváj.
BRISTLE, مو mú.
To BRISTLE, بر پا شدن bar pá shudan, راست ایستادن rást ístádan.
BRISTLY, خشن khashin.
BRITISH AGENT, وکیل دولت بهیه انگلیسی vakíl-i-daulat-i-bahíyah-i-inglísí, بالیوس bályús.
BRITTLE, نازك nazuk, تنك tunuk, شکستنی shikastaní, ترد turd (*vulg.*).
BROAD, پهن pahn, پهنا pahná, عریض 'aríz, وسیع wasí', فراخ farákh.
BROADCLOTH, ماهوت máhút.
BROCADE (*cloth of gold, &c.*), زری zarí.
BROKEN-IN (*horse*), رام rám.
BROKER, دلال dallál, سمسار simsár.
BRONZE, چدن chudan.
BROOCH, گل سینه gul-i-sínah, سنجاق sanják.—(*to wear a brooch*), سنجاق زدن sanják zadan.
BROODING, غمگین gham-gín.
BROOK, جوی júí, جوب júb (*vulg.*).
BROOM, جاروب já-rúb. — (*plant*) بارشین barishín, رتم ratm.
BROTH, شوربا shurbá, آب گوشت áb-i-gúsht.—(*of rice*) شله shullah.
BROTHEL, خیل خانه khail-khánah, کاولی خانه kávalá-khánah, زنا خانه ziná-khánah.
BROTHER, برادر birádar, اخ ákh.—(*full*) برادر عین birádar-i-'ain.—(*half*) برادر صلبی birádar-sulbi, برادر بطنی birádar-i-batní. [The first is a brother by the father's, the second by the mother's, side.]—(*elder*) برادر مهتر birádar-i-mihtar, داداشی dádáshí, دادائش dádá,ish (*vulg.*). — (*younger*) برادر کهتر birádar-i-kihtar, کاکا káká (*vulg.*). — (*adopted*) برادر

خواندہ birádar-khwándah.—(*foster*), برادر همشیر birádar-i-hamshír, برادر رضاعی birádar-i-rizá'í.—(*-in-law, wife's brother*) برادر زن birádar-zan, همریش ham-rísh.—(*husband's brother*) برادر شوهر birádar-i-shauhar. — (*twin brother*) برادر توأم birádar-taua,m, برادر جمبولی birádar-jumbúlí. — (*sister's husband*) آیزنه áyaznah.—(*wife's sister's husband*) همداماں ham-dáman.

Brotherhood, برادری birádarí, اخوت ukhúvat, مواخات muvákhát. (*Vide* Society, Band.)

Brow, *vide* Forehead, Eyebrow.

Brown, بور búr, اسمر asmar, گندم گون gandum-gún, تیره رنگ tírah-rang.—(*dark brown*) میخکی míkhakí.—(*a horse*) قره کهر karah-kahar, بور búr.

To **Browse**, چریدن charídan.

Bruise, کوفتگی kúftagí.

To **Bruise**, کوفتن kúftan.

Brunette (*of dark complexion*), سبز sabz.

Brush, جاروب já-rúb, پاك كن pák-kun.—(*clothes-brush*) ماهوت صاف كن máhút-sáf-kun.—(*hair-brush*) موی صاف كن múí-sáf-kun.—(*painter's brush*) قلم مو kalam-i-mú.—(*nail brush*) ناخن صاف كن nákhun-sáf-kun.

To **Brush**, رفتن ruftan, با ماهوت صاف كن پاك كردن bá-mahút-sáf-kun pák kardan. — (*to brush off*) تكانیدن takánídan, پاك كردن pák kardan, افشاندن afshándan.

Brushwood, بوتها bútahá.

Brusque, بی ادب bí-adab.

Brusqueness, بی ادبی bí-adabí.

Brutal, حیوانی haiváni, درشت durusht.

Brutality, حیوانیت haiváníyat, درشتی durushtí.

Bryony, تاجریزی tájrízí.

Bubble, حباب hubáb.—(*to blow bubbles*) حباب ساختن hubáb sákhtan.

To **Bubble**, جوشیدن júshídan, بجوش آمدن bi-júsh ámadan, حباب بر آوردن hubáb bar-ávardan.

Bubo, خیارك khiyárak, باد bád.

Buck, گوزن gavazn.

Bucket, دلو dalv, دول dúl, بالدی báldí (*hind.*) — (*of metal*) سطل satl.—(*large leathern bucket for drawing water*) دول چاه گاو dúl-i-cháh-gáv.—(*bucket of flexible hide extended on a hoop*) دول سفره dúl-i-sufrah.

Buckle, سگك sagak.

Buckler, سپر sipar.

Bud, شكوفه shikúfah, غنچه ghunchah, تنزه tunzah, تكمه tukmah, گنپ gump.

To **Budge**, حركت كردن harakat kardan, جنبیدن jumbídan.

Budget, موازنه دخل و خرج muváza-nah-i-dakhl u kharj.

Buffalo, گامیش gámísh, جاموس jámús.

Buffet, دیوان díván, دفتر daftar.

Buffeting (*waves*), متلاطم mutalátim.

Buffoon, مسخره maskharah, لوطی lútí.

Bug, ساس sás, سرخك surkhak.—(*large poisonous bug*) مله millah.

Bugbear, غول ghúl, لولو lúlú.

Bugle (*horn*), شیفور shaifúr, شیپور shaipúr.—(*oblong bead*) لوله lúlah.

Bugler, شیفورچی shaifúr-chí.

Bugloss (*herb*), گاو زبان gáv-zabán, لسان الثور lisánu-'s saur.

To **Build**, ساختن sákhtan, عمارت كردن 'imárat kardan, تعمیر كردن ta'mír kardan, بنا كردن biná kardan.

Builder, بنا banná, بانی bání, معمار mi'már.

Building (*house*), بنا biná, عمارت 'imárat, بنیان bunyán.

Built, بنا شده biná-shudah, مبنی mabní, معمور ma'múr.

Bulb (*bulbous root*), پیاز piyáz, بصل basal.

Bulk, *vide* Bigness, Size.

Bulky, توفال túfál, جسیم jasím.

Bull, نر گاو nar-gáv, گاو نر gáv-i-nar, ثور saur.

Bullet, غلوله ghulúlah, گلوله gulúlah, گله gullah.

Bullock, گاو gáv.

BULLY, لاف زن láf-zan.
BULRUSH, هردی hirdí, خونگ khúnag, خنگ khunag.
BULWARK, سنگر sangur, بارو bárú, باره bárah, مترس matars.
BULWORKS (*of a ship*), دیواره dívárah.
BUMP, *vide* LUMP, SWELLING.
To BUMP, *vide* To DASH against.
BUMPTIOUS, طاغی tághí, مغرور maghrúr یاغی yághí, سر کش sar-kash.
BUN, قرص kurs.
BUNCH, خوشه khúshah, دسته dastah. —(*of grapes*) خوشه انگور khúshah-i-angúr.—(*of dates*) پنگ pang, عنقود 'ankúd.—(*a strand or portion of the bunch*) رساله risálah, تلنگه tilingah.
BUNDLE, بسته bastah, بقچه bukchah.
BURDEN, بار bár, حمل haml.—(*beast of burden*) بار بردار bár-bardár, بار گیر bár-gír.
BURDENSOME, سخت sakht.
BUREAU (*of administration, &c.*), دیوان díván, دفتر خانه daftar-khánah, کار خانه kar-khánah.
BURIAL, دفن dafn.
BURIED, دفین dafín, مدفون madfún.
BURLY, مجسم mujassam, ضخیم zakhím.
To BURN, (*trans.*) سوزانیدن súzání dan, (*intrans.*) سوختن súkhtan.
BURNING, سوزان súzán, محرق muhrik.
BURNING-GLASS, عینک آتشی 'ainak-i-átishí, عینک آتشگیر 'ainak-i-átish-gír.
To BURNISH, مجلا ساختن mujallá sákhtan, زدودن zidúdan, پرداختن pardákhtan, صیقل کردن saikal kardan.
BURROW, سوراخ súrákh, نقب nakb.
To BURROW, سوراخ کردن súrákh kardan, نقب زدن nakb zadan.
To BURST, ترقیدن tarkídan, چاک شدن chák shudan, پاره شدن párah shudan, تراکیدن tarákídan, پکیدن pakídan.—(*as a boil, or abscess*) منفجر شدن munfajir shudan, راه باز کردن ráh-báz kardan, پکیدن pakídan.—(*forth, as a spring of water, &c.*) بر جستن bar-jastan.

To BURY, دفن کردن dafn kardan, خاک کردن khák kardan.
BURYING-GROUND, گورستان gúristán, قبرستان kabristán, مقبره makbarah, مزارستان mazáristán, رمس rams, شهر خاموشان shahr-i-khámúshán. (*Literally, "city of the silent."*)
BUSH, بوته bútah, درخت dirakht.
BUSHY, پر شاخ pur-shákh, پر بوته púr-bútah.
BUSINESS, کار kár, کار و بار kár va bár, عمل 'amal, امر amr, شغل shughl, حال hál.—(*concern*) دخل dakhl, ربط rabt, کار kár, علاقه 'alákah.—(*important affair*) مهم muhimm (*pl.* مهام mahámm).—(*house of business*) کار خانه kár-khánah.—(*to do business*) معامله کردن mu'ámalah kardan.
BUST, مجسم mujassam, مجسم نصف تنه mujassam-i-nisf-tanah.
BUSTARD, حباری hubárá, هوبره húbarah, آهوبره áhúbarah. — (*large bustard, otis*) طوی túí, دوی داغ dúí-dágh. — (*small bustard or florican*) زنگبال zangibál, چرز charz.
BUSTLE (*hurry, tumult*), غوغا ghaughá, غلغله ghulghulah, شور shúr.—(*padding*) رفاعت rifá'at.
BUSY, مشغول mashghúl, سرگرم sar-garm.
BUSYBODY (*officious person*), فضول fuzúl, تفتاف taftáf.
BUT, لیکن líkin, لاکن lákin, اما ammá, ولی valí, بلکه balkih. (*Vide* EXCEPT, UNLESS.)
BUTCHER, قصاب kassáb.—(*butcher's stall*) دکان قصاب dukán-i-kassáb, قصاب خانه kassáb-khánah.—(*butcher's row of meat-hooks*), قناره kannárah.
BUTLER, نوکر naukar, سفره چی sufrah-chí.—(*royal butler, who accompanies the king when travelling*) آب دار áb-dár.
BUTT (*target*), هدف hadaf, نشانه nishánah. — (*wine*) بط bat (*eur.*), پیپا pípá (*eur.*).—(*of a musket*) ته قنداق tah-i-kundák.
To BUTT, کله زدن kalah zadan, سر زدن sar zadan.

BULLY, لاف زن láf-zan.
BULRUSH, هردی hirdí, خونک khúnag, خنک khunag.
BULWARK, سنگر sangur, بارو bárú, باره bárah, مترس matars.
BULWORKS (*of a ship*), دیواره dívárah.
BUMP, *vide* LUMP, SWELLING.
To BUMP, *vide* To DASH against.
BUMPTIOUS, طاغی tághí, مغرور maghrúr یاغی yághí, سرکش sar-kash.
BUN, قرص kurs.
BUNCH, خوشه khúshah, دسته dastah. —(*of grapes*) خوشهٔ انگور khúshah-i-angúr.—(*of dates*) پنگ pang, عنقود 'ankúd.—(*a strand or portion of the bunch*) رساله risálah, تلنگه tilingah.
BUNDLE, بسته bastah, بقچه bukchah.
BURDEN, بار bár, حمل haml.—(*beast of burden*) بار بردار bár-bardár, بار گیر bár-gír.
BURDENSOME, سخت sakht.
BUREAU (*of administration, &c.*), دیوان díván, دفتر خانه daftar-khánah, کار خانه kar-khánah.
BURIAL, دفن dafn.
BURIED, دفین dafín, مدفون madfún.
BURLY, مجسم mujassam, ضخیم zakhím.
To BURN, (*trans.*) سوزانیدن súzánídan, (*intrans.*) سوختن súkhtan.
BURNING, سوزان súzán, محرق muhrik.
BURNING-GLASS, عینک آتشی 'ainak-i-átishí, عینک آتشگیر 'ainak-i-átish-gír.
To BURNISH, مجلا ساختن mujallá sákhtan, زدودن zidúdan, پرداختن pardákhtan, صیقل کردن saikal kardan.
BURROW, سوراخ súrákh, نقب nakb.
To BURROW, سوراخ کردن súrákh kardan, نقب زدن nakb zadan.
To BURST, ترقیدن tarkídan, چاك شدن chák shudan, پاره شدن párah shudan, تراکیدن tarákídan, پکیدن pakídan.—(*as a boil, or abscess*) منفجر شدن munfajir shudan, راه باز کردن ráh-báz kardan, پکیدن pakídan.—(*forth, as a spring of water, &c.*) برجستن bar-jastan.

To BURY, دفن کردن dafn kardan, خاك کردن khák kardan.
BURYING-GROUND, گورستان gúristán, قبرستان kabristán, مقبره makbarah, مزارستان mazáristán, رمس rams, شهر خاموشان shahr-i-khámúshán. (*Literally,* "*city of the silent.*")
BUSH, بوته bútah, درخت dirakht.
BUSHY, پر شاخ pur-shákh, پر بوته púr-bútah.
BUSINESS, کار kár, کار و بار kár va bár, عمل 'amal, امر amr, شغل shughl, حال hál.—(*concern*) دخل dakhl, ربط rabt, کار kár, علاقه 'alákah.—(*important affair*) مهم muhimm (*pl.* مهام mahámm).—(*house of business*) کار خانه kár-khánah.—(*to do business*) معامله کردن mu'ámalah kardan.
BUST, مجسم mujassam, مجسم نصف تنه mujassam-i-nisf-tanah.
BUSTARD, حباری hubárá, هوبره húbarah, آهوبره áhúbarah. —(*large bustard, otis*) طوی túí, دوی داغ dúí-dágh. —(*small bustard or florican*) زنگبال zangibál, چرز charz.
BUSTLE (*hurry, tumult*), غوغا ghaughá, غلغله ghulghulah, شور shúr.—(*padding*) رفاعت rifá'at.
BUSY, مشغول mashghúl, سرگرم sar-garm.
BUSYBODY (*officious person*), فضول fuzúl, تفتاف taftáf.
BUT, لیکن líkin, لاکن lákin, اما ammá, ولی valí, بلکه balkih. (*Vide* EXCEPT, UNLESS.)
BUTCHER, قصاب kassáb.—(*butcher's stall*) دکان قصاب dukán-i-kassáb, قصاب خانه kassáb-khánah.—(*butcher's row of meat-hooks*), قناره kannárah.
BUTLER, نوکر naukar, سفره‌چی sufrah-chí.—(*royal butler, who accompanies the king when travelling*) آب دار áb-dár.
BUTT (*target*), هدف hadaf, نشانه nishánah. — (*wine*) بط bat (*eur.*), پیپا pípá (*eur.*).—(*of a musket*) ته قنداق tah-i-kundák.
To BUTT, کله زدن kalah zadan, سر زدن sar zadan.

bi-manzil raftan, دید و باز دید رفتن díd u báz-díd raftan. — (*to be called*) اسم داشتن ism dáshtan.

CALLED (*entitled*), مسمی musammá.

CALLIGRAPHY, رسم الخط rasmu-'l-khatt, خوشخط khwush-khatt.

CALLOSITY, دانه dánah. (*Vide* CORN.)

CALM (*placid*), آرمیده ármídah, آسوده ásúdah, ساکن sákin, آرام árám.—(*as weather*) ملایم mulá-yam.—(*to be calm*) خود داری نمودن khwud-dárí nimúdan.

To CALM, آرامیدن árámídan.—(*to calm oneself*) ارام گرفتن árám giriftan.

CALMNESS (*placidness*), آرمیدگی ármídagí, آسودگی ásúdagí, راحت ráhat, آرام árám.—(*sea*) ملایمت muláyamat.

CALOMEL, جیوه jívah, جیوه سفید jívah-i-safíd.

CALTHROPS (*a kind of thistle; also a ball of iron surrounded with spikes, to wound the feet of an invading army*), خسک khasak, خنجلک khanjak.

To CALUMNIATE, بد گفتن bad guftan, افترا کردن iftirá kardan, بهتان بستن buhtán bastan.

CALUMNIATOR, بهتان انداز buhtán-andáz, بد زبان bad-zabán, نمام nammám.

CALUMNIOUS, مفسد mufsid.

CALUMNY, تهمت tuhmat, افترا iftirá, بهتان buhtán, غیبت ghíbat, سعایت si'áyat.

CAMEL, شتر shutur, اشتر ushtur, جمل jamal, دوه divah.—(*riding*) بختی bukhtí, شتر سوار shutur-i-suvár. —(*she*) شتر ماده shutur-i-mádah, ناقه nákah.—(*camel-driver*) شتر بان shutur-bán, سار بان sárbán.

CAMELEON, حربا hirbá, بوقلمون bú-kalamún.

CAMELEOPARD, شتر گاو پلنگ shutur-gáv-palang, زراف zarráf.

CAMEL'S-THORN (*a prickly shrub*), خار شتر khár-i-shutur.

CAMEO, خاتم سازی khátim-sází.

CAMOMILE, بابونه bábúnah.

CAMP, لشکر گاه lashkar-gáh, معسکر mu'askar, اردو urdú, حشم hasham, اوتراق úturák. — (*camp-market*) اردو بازار urdú-bázár.—(*camp followers*) بنه گاه لشکر bunah-gáh-i-lashkar, رجاله rajjálah.

To CAMP, چادر زدن chádar zadan, اردو قرار دادن urdú karár dádan.

CAMPHOR, کافور káfúr.

CANAL, نهر nahr, جوی júí, جوب júb (*vulg.*). — (*subterraneous*) *vide* AQUEDUCT.

CANARY, هزار دستان hazár-dastán.

To CANCEL, محو کردن mahv kardan, بر داشتن bar-dáshtan, نسخ نمودن naskh nimúdan, فسخ کردن faskh kardan.

CANCER (*disease*), سرطان saratán, خوره khwurah.—(*sign of zodiac*) *vide* ZODIAC.

CANDELABRA, *vide* CHANDELIER.

CANDID, مخلص mukhlis, مخلصانه mukhlisánah, اخلاصمند ikhlás-mand, صادق sádik.

CANDIDATE, امیدوار umíd-vár.

CANDLE, شمع sham'. — (*stick*) شمعدان sham'-dán, پیسوز pí-súz. [The latter is a tall candelabrum, having a little cup on the top, in which a wick is placed in melted tallow.]

CANDOUR, راستبازی rást-bází, اخلاص ikhlás, صدق sidk.

CANE, نی nai.—(*stick*) چوب chúb, عصا 'asá.

CANNIBAL, مردم خوار mardum-khwár, آدم خوار ádam-khwár.

CANNON, توپ túp.

CANNON-BALL, گلوله توپی gulúlah-i-túpí.

CANOE, فلوقه falúkah.

CANON, قاعده ká'idah, قانون kánún.

CANONICAL, قانونی kánúní.

CANOPUS, سهیل suhail.

CANOPY, سایبان sáyabán, چتر chatr, شادروان shádurván.

CANT, *vide* HYPOCRISY.

CANTEEN, می خانه mai-khánah, شربخانه shurb-khánah.

To CANTER, یورطمه رفتن yúrtamah raftan, یورتمه رفتن yúrtamah raftan.

CANTHARIDES (*Spanish fly*), ذراح zurráh (*pl.* ذراریح zarárίh), آلا کلنک álá kulang.

CANTO, مقاله makálah.

CANTON, بلوك bulúk.

CANTONMENTS, اردو urdú, لشکر گاه lashkar-gáh.

CANVAS (*cloth*), پلاس palás.

CAP, کلاه kuláh, کله kulah, عرقچین 'arak-chín.—(*Persian cap of black lamb-skin*) کلاه پوستی kuláh-i-pústí.—(*cap of brown felt, worn by the poorer classes*) کلاه نمدی kuláh-i-namadí.—(*pinch or indentation in the Persian cap*) طرف کلاه taraf-i-kuláh, گوشه کلاه gúshah-i-kuláh.—(*cloth top of the Persian cap*), کلترك kallatark, کله کلاه kallah-i-kuláh. — (*skull-cap*) عرقگیر 'arak-gír, عرقچین 'arak-chín. — (*night-cap*) شبکلاه shab-kuláh.—(*Turkish cap*) قاوُق ká,uk, قلپق kalpak.—(*Darvish's cap*) تاج táj.—(*percussion cap*) کلاه تفنگ kuláh-i-tufang.

To CAP (*verses*), مشاعره کردن mushá-'arah kardan. [A favourite amusement with the Persians.]

CAPABILITY, قابلیت kábilíyat, قوت kúvat.

CAPABLE, قابل kábil, لایق láik, قادر kádir, توانا tavána.

CAPACIOUS, عریض 'aríz, وسیع vasí', واسع vási'.

CAPACITY, لیاقت liyákat, قابلیت kábilíyat, قدرت kudrat, اقتدار iktidár, مقدور makdúr, تاب táb, استعداد isti'dád, حیثیت haisíyat, سر رشته sar-rishtah.—(*size*) اندازه andázah, قدر kadr, گنجائش gunjá,ish.

CAPE (*point of land*), راس rás, سر sar, طرف taraf.

CAPER (*shrub*), کبر kabar.

CAPITAL (*chief city*), دار السلطنه dáru-'s-saltanah, دار الخلافه dáru-'l-khiláfat, دار الحکومه dáru-'l-hukúmah, پای تخت pái-takht.—(*of a pillar*) تاج táj.—(*stock*) *vide* STOCK.

To CAPITULATE, *vide* To SURRENDER.

CAPITULATION, تسلیم taslím.

CAPON, مرغ خصی murgh-i-khasí, خروس خصی khurús-i-khasí.

CAPRICE, وهم vahm, خیال khayál; خودسری khwud-sarí.

CAPRICIOUS, خود رای khwud-rái, متلون mutalavvin.

CAPRICIOUSNESS, خود رائی khwud-ra,í.

CAPRICORN, *vide* ZODIAC.

CAPSTAN, چرخ لنگر charkh-i-langar.

CAPTAIN, رئس ra,is, قپودان kapúdán (*eur.*).—(*naval*) رئس ra,is, ناخودا nákhúdá.

CAPTIVE, اسیر asír, گرفتار giriftár, برده bardah, محبوس mahbús, دیل díl (*vulg.*).

CAPTIVITY, گرفتاری giriftárí, بندگی bandagí, بند band, قید kaid, اسیری asírí, اسر usr, حبس habs, دستاق dusták.

CAPTOR, فاتح fátih.

CAPTURE, گرفتاری giriftárí.

To CAPTURE, *vide* To TAKE prisoner.

CAR, *vide* CARRIAGE.

CARAVAN, کاروان kárván, راحلهráhilah, قافله káfilah, عیر 'ír.

CARAVANSARY, کاروانسرای kárván-saráí, خان khán, رباط ribát, سرای saráí, وکاله vakálah. — (*small caravansary where manufacturers lodge*) تیمچه tímchah.

CARAWAY, کرویا karviyá.

CARBINE, تفنگ tufang, قرابینه karábínah (*eur.*).

CARBINEER, تفنگچی tufang-chí.

CARBONIC, زغالی zughálí, فحمی fahmí.

CARBUNCLE (*gem*) رواق ravák.

CARCASS, لاش lásh, لاشه láshah, مردار murdár, میت mayyit, میته mayyitah, جیفه jaifah, نعش na'sh.

CARD (*paste-board*), مقوا mukavvá. — (*English playing cards*) گنجیفه ganjífah, گنجفه ganjifah, ورق varak. — (*Persian playing cards*) آسناس ásnás.

To CARD (*cotton*), حلاجی کردن hallájí

kardan, پنبه زدن pambah zadan. (*Vide* Cotton.)

Cardamums, هیل híl, هل hil, قاقله kákulah.

Card-case, تیکت دان tikat-dán (*eur.*).

Carder, پنبه زن pambah-zan.

Care (*attention*), فکر fikr, آگهی ágahí, توجه tavajjuh, اندیشه andíshah, همت himmat, خبر khabar, شغل shughl, اشتغال ishtighál, مبالات mubálát, اعتنا i'tiná.—(*caution*) خبر khabar, خبرداری khabar-dárí, احتیاط ihtiyát, حذر hazar, انتباه intibáh, هوشیاری húsh-yárí, بصیرت basírat, دیده بانی dídah-báni.—(*anxiety or sorrow*) پروا parvá, غم gham, اندوه andúh, دلتنگی dil-tangí, تأنی ta.anní. اعتنا i'tiná, اضطراب iztiráb, الم alam, تشویش tashvísh.—(*attendance*) پرستاری parastárí, تیمار tímár, دیده بانی dídah-bání.—(*want of care, protection, or patronage*) بی صاحبی bí-sahibí.—(*to take care*) احتیاط کردن ihtiyát kardan, هوشیار بودن húsh-yár budan.—(*to take care of*) پرستاری کردن parastárí kardan.

To Care, پروا داشتن parvá dáshtan.

Career, طریقه taríkah, سلک silk.

Careful, خبردار khabar-dár, هوشیار húsh-yár, متوجه mutavajjih, آگاه ágáh, با حذر bá-hazar, محترز muhtariz, با هوش bá-húsh, معتنی mu'taní.

Careless, بیخبر bí-khabar, غافل gháfil, بیپروا bí-parvá, بی احتیاط bí-ihtiyát, بی اندیشه bí-andíshah, کاهل káhil, بیهوش bí-húsh, زاهل záhil, بی مبالات bí-mubálát, لاقید lá-kaid.

Carelessness, غفلت ghiflat, بی احتیاطی bí-ihtiyátí, بی پروائی bí-parvá,í.

Caress, دلنوازی dil-navází, تلطف talattuf, نواز naváz.

To Caress, نوازش کردن navázish kardan, نواختن navákhtan.

Cargo, بار جهاز bár-i-jaház, حمل کشتی haml-i-kashtí.

Caries, پوسیدگی استخوان púsídagí-i-ustukhwán.

Carnage, کشش kushish, کشتار kushtár.

Carnal, نفسی nafsí, نفسانی nafsání, جسمانی jismání.

Carnation, میخک صد پر míkhak-i-sad-par, قرنفل karanful.

Carnival, قرنوال karnavál (*eur.*).

Carnivorous, گوش خور gúsh-khwur.

Carp (*fish*), هاپور hapúr, کاپور kapúr, ماهی سیم mahí-i-sím.

Carpenter, نجار najjár, درودگر darúd-gar (*obs.*), درگر darú-gar (*obs.*)

Carpet (*large*), گلیم gilím.—(*fine carpet*) قالی kálí.—(*small carpet or rug*) قالیچه kalíchah, سوزنی súzaní.—(*large carpet in centre of a room*) قالی kálí, گلیم gilím.—(*side carpets of thick felt doubled*) نمد namad.—(*felt layer at upper end of the room*) سر انداز sar-andáz.—(*felt layers going down the sides of the room*) باریکه báríkah.—(*cotton cloth covering the felts*) حرمی haramí.—(*linen cloth covering the felts*) رو فرش rú-farsh.—(*praying carpet*) سجاده sujjádah, مصلا musallá.—(*carpet weaver*) قالیباف kálí-báf, گلیمباف gilím-báf.

To Carpet, فرش نمودن farsh nimúdan.

Carpeted, مفروش mafrúsh.

Carriage (*vehicle*), عرابه 'arábah, عراده 'arrádah, گاری gárí (*hind.*), کالسکه káliskah (*eur.*).—(*open*) کالسکه رو بازی káliskah-i-rú-bází. (*close*) کالسکه سر پوشیده káliskah-i-sar-púshídah.—(*line of carriages*) قطار kitár.—(*of loads, &c.*) بار برداری bár-bardárí.

Carrier (*porter*), حمال hammál, بار کش bár-kash.—(*pigeon*) کبوتر بار kabútar-i-bár, کفتر بار kaftar-i-bár.

Carrion, مردار murdár, میته maitah.

Carrot, گزر gazar, زردک zardak.

To Carry, بردن burdan, بر داشتن bar-dáshtan.—(*transport*) نقل کردن nakl kardan.—(*as a gun*)

اندختن andákhtan, زدن zadan, نشانه زدن nishánah zadan. — (*to carry out*) مجرا داشتن mujrá dáshtan, اجرا کردن ijrá kardan, وفا کردن vafá kardan.

CART, عرابه ʻarábah, عراده ʻarrádah, اراده arrádah.

CARTER, عراده چی ʻarrádah-chí.

CARTILAGE (*gristle*), غضروف ghuzrúf, کرکروک karkarúk, کتکتی kutkutí (*vulg.*). — (*of the nose*) خیشوم khaishúm.

CARTOGRAPHY, تصویر اراضی tasvír-i-arází.

CARTRIDGE, فیشنگ físhang, فیشک físhak.—(*box*) قاب فیشنگ káb-i-físhang, کیف kíf.

To CARVE (*meat, &c.*), بریدن burrídan, پارچه پارچه کردن párchah párchah kardan.—(*on stone, wood, &c.*) کندن kandan, تراشیدن tiráshídan, نقش کردن naksh kardan.

CARVED-WORK, منبت کاری munabbat-kárí.

CARVER, نقاش nakkásh.

CARVING (*sculpture*), نقش naksh.

CASCADE, آبشار áb-shár, آبشیب áb-shíb.

CASE (*box*), صندوق sandúk.—(*for sword*) غلاف ghiláf.—(*for instruments, &c.*) کنج ganj, جزدان juzdán, جزودان juzv-dán.—(*state of affairs*) حال hál, امر amr, مراتب marátib.—(*the truth of the case*) حقیقت حال hakíkat-i-hál, نفس الامر nafsu-l-'amr.—(*suppose the case!*) فرض بکن farz bi-kun, فرضاً farzan, اگر چنانچه ágar chunánchih.—(*in grammar*) حالت hálat, اعراب ʻiráb. —(*in case*) در صورت که dar súrat kih.—(*in any case*) در هر حال dar har hál, هر آینه har áyinah.

CASH, نقد nakd, پول púl, زر zar, نقدینه nakdínah. — (*book*) آورجه ávarjah.—(*keeper*) خزانچی khazánchí, خزانه دار khizánah-dár, تحویلدار tahvíl-dár.—(*to pay cash*) نقد دادن nakd dádan.

CASHIER, صندوقدار sandúk-dár.

To CASHIER, معزول کردن maʻzúl kardan.

CASHMERE (*cloth*), کشمیر شکن kashmír-shikan, کزمیر kazmír, ترمه tirmah.

CASK, *vide* BARREL.

CASKET, درج durj, حقه hukkah, جعبه jaʻbah.

CASSIA, خیار شنبر khiyár-shambar, فلوس fulús.

CAST, انداخت andákht, اندازی andází.

To CAST, افکندن afkandan, انداختن andákhtan.—(*in a mould*) ریختن ríkhtan. — (*anchor*) لنگر انداختن langar andákhtan. — (*lots*) قرعه افکندن kurʻah afkandan.

CASTANETS, زنگ zang.

CASTE, دودمان dúdmán, مذهب mazhab, فرقه firkah.

CASTELLAIN, قلعه دار kalʻah-dár, قلعه بیگی kalʻah-begí.

CASTLE, قلعه kalʻah, حصار hisár, حصن hisn, ارک ark.—(*garrison of a castle*) اهل قلعه ahl-i-kalʻah.—(*castle in the air, hope, or fanciful project*) پلو خیالی piláv-i-khayálí.

CASTOR (*plant*), بید انجیر bíd-anjír, کنتو kinnatú.—(*oil*) روغن بید انجیر raughan-i-bíd-anjír, روغن کنتو raughan-i-kinnatú.

To CASTRATE, خصی کردن khasí kardan.—(*men*) خواجه کردن khwájah kardan.—(*horses*) اخته کردن akhtah kardan.

CASTRATED, مخصی makhsí.

CASTRATION, اختصا ikhtisá.

CASUAL, حادث hádis, عارض ʻáriz.

CAT, گربه gurbah. — (*long-haired Ispahán cat*) گربه براق gurbah-i-burrák.—(*wild cat*), گربه دشتی gurbah-i-dashtí.

CATALOGUE, دفتر daftar, فهرست fihrist.

CATAMITE, ملوط mulút, مأبون maʼbún, مخنث mukhannas, مفعول mafʻúl.

CATAPULT, منجنیق manjaník.

CATARACT, آبشیب áb-shíb, آبشیبه áb-shíbah, آبشار áb-shár.—(*in the eye*) آب áb, آب مروارید áb-i-marvaríd.

CATARRH, *vide* COLD.

CATCH (*staple of a door*), رزه rizah, ریزه rízah.—(*chain or hasp fitting on the staple*) چفت chift.

To CATCH, گرفتن giriftan, گرفتار کردن giriftár kardan, قبض نمودن kabz nimúdan, اخذ کردن akhz kardan, ربودن rubúdan.

CATEGORICAL, قطعی kat'í, قطعیه kat'iyah.

CATEGORY, جنس jins, زمره zumrah, قبیل kabíl.

CATERPILLAR, کرم صد پا kirm-i-sad-pá, کرم درخت kirm-i-dirakht.

CATHARTIC, مسهل mus-hil.

CATHOLIC, کاتولیک kátúlík (*eur.*), پاپوئی pápú,í (*eur.*).

CAT-O'-NINE-TAILS, تازیانه táziyánah.

CATTLE, دواب davább, مواشی maváshí, حیوانات haivánát, عقار 'ikár, چهار پاها chahár-páhá.

CAUL (*of a child*), پرده pardah, مشیمه mashímah.

CAULDRON, دیگ díg, قزغان kazghán, تیان tiyán, پاتیل pátíl, مرجل mirjal. — (*smaller sized ditto*) پاتیلچه pátílchah, تیانچه tiyánchah.

CAULIFLOWER, کلم رومی kalam-i-rúmí, کلم گلدار kalam-i-gul-dár.

CAUSAL (*verb*), فعل مجبور fi'l-i-majbúr.

CAUSE, سبب sabab, موجب mújib, واسطه vásitah, وصیله vasílah, وسیله vásílah, جهت jihat, باعث bá'is, اجل ajl, اصل asl, مؤدی mú,addí, داعیه dá'iyah, علت 'illat, مورث múris, وجه vajh.—(*cause and effect*) اصل و فرع asl u far' (*pl.* اصول و فروع usúl u furú'.

To CAUSE, سبب شدن sabab shudan, مستلزم نمودن mustalzim nimúdan.

CAUSEWAY, سنگبست sang-bast, سنگفرش sang-farsh, تخته فرش takhtah-farsh, خیابان khiyábán.

CAUSTIC, تیز tíz, تند tund.

To CAUTERIZE, داغ کردن dágh kardan.

CAUTERY, داغ dágh, کی kayy.

CAUTION, CAUTIOUS, *vide* CARE, CAREFUL, WARNING, ATTENTIVE.

To CAUTION, *vide* To WARN.

CAVALCADE, حشم hasham, سواری suvárí, موکب maukib.

CAVALIER, سوار suvár.

CAVALRY, سواره suvárah.—(*body of cavalry*) دسته dastah, تیپ típ.

CAVERN, غار ghár, مغاره mughárah, کهف kahf.

CAVIARE, تخم ماهی tukhm-i-máhí, خاویار háviár, اشپل ashpil.

To CAVIL, اعتراض کردن i'tiráz kardan.

CAVILLER, خورده بین khwurdah-bín.

CAVITY, جوف jauf.

CAWING (*of a crow*), نعیق na'ík, قاقا káká.

To CEASE, موقوف بودن maukúf búdan, منقطع شدن munkati' shudan, وا ایستادن vá-ístádan, قطع شدن kat' shudan, فراغت کردن farághat kardan, باز ماندن báz-mándan, ساکت شدن sákit shudan, منقرض شدن munkariz shudan.—(*without ceasing*) بلا فاصله bilá fásilah, استمراراً istimráran.

CEDAR, سرو آزاد sarv-i-ázád.—(*red cedar*) کاج káj.

To CEDE, گذاشت نمودن guzásht nimúdan, وا گذاشتن vá-guzáshtan, تسلیم نمودن taslím nimúdan, حواله نمودن haválah nimúdan.

CEILING, سقف sakf, عرش 'arsh.—(*level ceiling*) سقف تخته sakf-i-takhtah.—(*ceiling with the beams rounded and carved*) سقف مرجوک sakf-i-marjavak.

To CELEBRATE, نگاه داشتن nigáh dáshtan.

CELEBRATED, مشهور mashhúr, معروف ma'rúf, موصوف mausúf, نامدار nám-dár, نامور nám-var, نیکنام ník-nám, ممدوح mamdúh.

CELEBRITY, شهرت shuhrat, اشتهار ishtihár.

CELERITY, *vide* SPEED.

CELERY, کرفس karafs.

CELESTIAL, *vide* HEAVENLY.

CELIBACY, عزبت 'uzbat, تجرد tajarrud, رهبانیت ruhbáníyat.

CELIBATE, عزب 'azab.

CELL (*of a recluse*), زاویه záviyah, گوشه gúshah, تکیه takyah, مقصوره maksúrah, صومعه sauma'ah.—

(*small room*) اوطاق útáк, اوتاغ útágh, اطاق uták.
CELLAR, ته خانه tah-khánah, زیر زمین zír-zamín, سردابه sardábah.
CEMENT (*for glass*), وصل vasl, پیوند paivand, سریش sarísh. (*Vide* GLUE, PLASTER.)
CEMETERY, *vide* BURYING-GROUND.
CENSER, بخوردان bakhúr-dán, مجمر mijmar (*pl.* مجامر majámir), منقل mankul.
CENSOR, نکته گیر nuktah-gír, عیب بین 'aib-bín.
CENSURE, *vide* BLAME, ACCUSATION, REBUKE.
CENSUS (*of population*), سر شماری sar-shimárí.
CENTIPEDE, صد پا sad-pá, هزار پای hazár-páí.
CENTRAL, مرکزی markazí.
CENTRE, وسط vasat, میانه miyánah, مرکز markaz, مدار madár, قلب kalb.
CENTURION, یوز باشی yúz-báshí.
CENTURY, صد سال sad sál, صده sadah, قرن karn.
CEREAL, غله ghallah.
CEREMONIAL (*adj.*), رسمی rasmí.
CEREMONY, رسم rasm, تکلف takalluf, ادب adab, تعارف ta'áruf.—(*without ceremony*) بی تکلف bí-takalluf, بی تکلیف bí-taklíf.—(*master of ceremonies*) تشریفاتچی tashrífát-chí, ایشك اقاسی باشی íshak-akásí-báshí.
CERTAIN, یقین yakín, مقرر mukarrar, محقق muhakkak, تحقیقی tahkíkí, معین mu'ayyan, صحیح sahíh, مسلم musallam, صریح saríh.—(*to make certain*) محقق نمودن muhakkak nimúdan.
CERTAINLY, البته albattah, بیشك bí-shak, بلاشك bilá-shak, بیگمان bí-gumán, یقینانه yakínánah, فی الحقیقت fí-'l-hakíkat, لامحالة lá-mahálata, حقاً hakkan.
CERTAINTY, یقین yakín, تحقق tahakkuk.
CERTIFICATE, تصدیق tasdík.—(*of forgiveness and safety*) خط الطمئنان khatt-i-itmi,nán.—(*recommendation*) اعتبار نامه i'tibár-námah, سفارش نامچه sifárish-námchah.
CERULEAN, کبود kabúd.
CESS, ابواب abváb.
CESSATION, توقف tavakkuf, مهلت muhlat, فراغت farághat.
CESSION, واگذار vá-guzár.
CHAFF, سپوس sapús, پوشال púshál.—(*fun*) مزاح mizáh, شوخی shúkhí.
To CHAFF, بنائی مزاح گذاشتن biná,í-i-mizáh guzáshtan, خنده نمودن khandah nimúdan.
CHAFING-DISH, منقل mankal.—(*of earthenware*) کلك kalak.
CHAGRIN, *vide* REMORSE, SORROW.
CHAIN, زنجیر zanjír, سلسله silsilah.—(*of hills*) سلسله کوه ها silsilah-i-kúh-há.—(*for door*) چفت chift.
To CHAIN, بستن bastan, زنجیر بستن zanjír bastan.
CHAIR, کرسی kursí, تخت takht, صندلی sandalí.
CHAISE, *vide* CARRIAGE.
CHALICE, *vide* CUP.
CHALK, گل سفید gil-i-safíd, تباشیر tabáshír.
CHALLENGE, دعوت da'vat, دعوی da'vá, ادعا iddi'á.
CHALLOP, *vide* CANOE.
CHALOT, گندنا gandaná, سیرمو sírmú.
CHAMBER, اوطاق útáк, اطاق uták, اوتاغ útágh, حجره hujrah.—(*Chamber of Deputies*) مبعوثان ملت مجلسی mab'úsán-i-millat-i-majlisí.
CHAMBERLAIN, ایشك اقاسی íshak-akásí.—(*Lord Chamberlain*) ایشك اقاسی باشی íshak-akásí-báshí.
CHAMPAGNE, شامپانیه shámpániyah (*eur.*).
CHAMPION, پهلوان pahlaván, غازی ghází.
CHANCE, *vide* ACCIDENT, FORTUNE, DESTINY, BY CHANCE.
CHANCELLERY, دیوان díván.
CHANCELLOR OF THE EXCHEQUER, وزیر مالیه vazír-i-máliyah.
CHANCRE (*venereal*), تاول távul.
CHANDELIER, چلچراغ chil-chirágh.
CHANDLER, بقال bakkál.

CHANGE, قلب kalb, انقلاب inkiláb, تبديل tabdíl.—(*small money*) خرده khurdah, پول خرده púl-i-khurdah.

To CHANGE, بدل كردن badal kardan, تبديل نمودن tabdíl nimúdan, عوض كردن 'ivaz kardan, تغيير نمودن taghyír nimúdan, آلش كردن álish kardan, مبدل گردانيدن mubaddal gardánídan.—(*one's mind*) تغيير به اراده دادن taghyír bi-irádah dádan.—(*money*) خرده كردن khurdah kardan. — (*hands*) استبعاد داشتن istib'ád dáshtan.—(*to be changed*) مبدل شدن mubaddal shudan, تبديل يافتن tabdíl yáftan, متغير شدن mutaghayyir shudan.

CHANGEABLE, *vide* INCONSTANT, VARIABLE.

CHANNEL, *vide* WATER, AQUEDUCT, PIPE, TUBE.

CHANT, نوا navá, ترانه tarána.

To CHANT, آوازه خواندن ávázah khwándan, سرائيدن saráyídan.

CHAOS, عدم 'adam, نيستى nístí.

CHAPEL, عبادتگاه 'ibádat-gáh, معبد ma'bad. — (*chapel-master*) مهتر باشى mihtar-báshí.

CHAPERONE, بدرقه badrakah.

To CHAPERONE, بدرقه كردن badrakah kardan.

CHAPLET, تاج گل táj-i-gul.

CHAPPED (*cracked, as the skin*), تفسيده tafsídah.

CHAPTER, فصل fasl, باب báb, سفر sifr, قسم kism.—(*of the Kur,án*) سوره súrah (*pl.* سور suvar).

CHARACTER (*written*), خط khatt, رقم rakm, نوشت nivisht, نوشته nivishtah. — (*reputation*) شهرت shuhrat, عرض 'irz, آبرو áb-rú, نام nám.—(*quality*) صفت sifat, وصف vasf, خصلت khaslat, خاصيت khássíyat, سيرت sírat, طبع tab', كيفيت kaifíyat.

CHARCOAL, زغال zughál.—(*burning*) آتش átish, زغال آتشين zughál-i-átishín, خرگ kharg, جمر jamr.

CHARGE (*custody*), حواله haválah, امانت amánat, نگهبانى nigah-bání. (*Vide* DEPOSIT, COMMAND, ACCUSATION, ASSAULT, EXPENSE.)

To CHARGE (*load*), زير بار كشيدن zír-i-bár kashídan.—(*a gun*) پر كردن pur kardan. — (*entrust*) گماشتن gumáshtan, سپردن sipurdan, حواله كردن haválah kardan.

CHARGÉ D'AFFAIRES, مصلحتگذار muslahat-guzár.

CHARIOT, *vide* CARRIAGE, CART.

CHARITABLE, عنايتكار 'ináyat-kár.

CHARITY (*affection*), محبت mahabbat. — (*alms-giving*) *vide* KINDNESS, ALMS, LIBERALITY. — (*charity commissioner*) وزير اوقاف vazír-i-aukáf.

CHARLATAN, عيار 'ayyár, آئينه چى á,inah-chí.

CHARLES'S WAIN (*the constellation*), بنات النعش banátu-'n-na'sh.

CHARM (*enchantment*), جادو jádú, سحر sihr, افسون afsún, طلسم tilism. — (*amulet*) تعويذ ta'víz, حمائل hamá,il.

To CHARM, *vide* To PLEASE.—(*enchant*) افسون كردن afsún kardan, سحر كردن sihr kardan.

CHARMING, *vide* PLEASANT.

CHART, نقشه nakshah.

CHARTER, سند sanad, برات barát, فرمان firmán. — (*royal*) توقيع taukí', منشور manshúr, فرمان عاليشان firmán-i-'álíshán.

CHASE, or CHACE, *vide* To HUNT.

CHASED ARTICLES, منقوش mankúsh.

CHASTE, پاك pák, پاكيزه pákízah, پاكدامن pák-dáman, پارسا pársá, عفيف 'afíf, عاصم 'ásim, طاهر táhir, پرهيزگار parhíz-gár, حصور hasúr, محتاط muhtát, معصوم ma'súm.

To CHASTISE, *vide* To BEAT, To FLOG.

CHASTISEMENT, *vide* PUNISHMENT.

CHASTITY, عصمت 'asmat, عفت 'iffat, پاكدامنى pák-dámaní, پارسائى pársá,í, زهد zuhd, تقاوت takávut, رهبانيت ruhbáníyat, پرهيزگارى parhíz-gárí.

CHAT, *vide* CONVERSATION.

CHATEAU, كوشك kúshk, قصر kasr.

CHATTEL, متاع matá' (*pl.* امتعه amti'ah), اسباب asbáb (*only used in the plural*).

To CHATTER (*prattle*), پر گفتن pur guftan, گپ زدن gap zadan (*hind.*). — (*as the teeth*) دندان فشردن dandán fishurdan.

CHATTY, حراف harráf.

CHEAP, ارزان arzán, کم بها kam-bahá.

CHEAPNESS, ارزانی arzání. کم بهائی kam-bahá,í.

CHEAT, *vide* FRAUD, ROGUE, TRICK, RASCAL, IMPOSTOR.

To CHEAT, *vide* To DEFRAUD, To WHEEDLE.

CHECK (*control*), ضبط zabt. (*Vide* CHESS.)

CHEEK, رخ rukh, رخساره rukhsárah, عارض 'áriz, عذار 'izár, خد khadd, گونه gúnah.

To CHEER, *vide* To APPLAUD.

CHEERFUL, خوش khwush, خوشوقت khwush-vakht, شاد shád, دلشاد dil-shád, شادمان shád-mán, فرحناک farah-nák, مسرور masrúr, خندان khandán.

CHEERFULNESS, مسرت masarrat, فرح farah, خوشی khwushí, بشاشت basháshat, شادی shádí, خوشوقتی khwush-vakhtí.

CHEESE, پنیر panír. — (*rennet of cheese*) پنیر مایه panír-máyah.— (*cream-cheese*) قروط kurút, کشک kushk.

CHEETAH, یوز yúz.

CHEMISE, قمیص kamís.

CHEMIST, عطار 'attár, اجزاچی ajzá-chí, کیمیا گر kímiyá-gar.

CHEMISTRY, کیمیا kímiyá.

CHEQUE (*draft*) برات barát, کاغذ زر kághaz-i-zar.

CHEQUERED, چهار خانه chahár-khá-nah.

To CHERISH, پروردن parvardan, نواختن navákhtan.

CHEROOT (*cigar*), سیغار síghár (*eur.*), چتہ chuttah (*hind.*).

CHERRY (*white*), گیلاس gílás.— (*sour*) وشنه vashnah. — (*black*) آلوبالو álúbálú. — (*eating*) گیلاس ماءکول gílás-i-ma,kúl.

CHERUB, کروب karrúb.

CHERVIL, علف معطر 'alaf-i-mu'attar.

CHESS, شطرنج shatranj.—(*board*) بساط شطرنج bisát-i-shatranj. — (*square on the board*) خانه khánah.— (*man, or piece*) مهره muhrah.— (*opening*) گشاد gushád. — (*king*) شاه sháh.—(*queen*) فرزین farzín, وزیر vazír. — (*bishop*) فیل fíl.— (*knight*) اسب asb. — (*castle*) رخ rukh.—(*pawn*) بیذق baizak, پیاده piyádah. — (*check*) کیش kísh.— (*check-mate*) مات mát.—(*to check-mate*) مات کردن mát kardan.—(*to be check-mated*) مات شدن mát shu-dan.—(*to move a piece*) حرکت دادن harakat dádan.—(*to take a piece*) بر داشتن bar-dáshtan. — (*stale-mate*) گیر آمده gír-ámadah.— (*chess-player*) شطرنج باز shatranj-báz.—(*to play at chess*) شطرنج بازی کردن shatranj-bází kardan.—(*to attack*) یورش بردن yúrish burdan, حمله آوردن hamlah ávardan.

CHEST (*box*), صندوق sandúk, یخدان yakhdán.—(*thorax*) سینه sínah, صدر sadr.

CHESTNUT, شاه بلوط sháh-balút.— (*colour of a horse*) کرن kuran.

CHEVALIER, بزرگ buzurg, خوب جوان khwub javán.

To CHEW, خائیدن khá,ídan, جائیدن já,ídan, جاویدن jávídan, خسیدن khasídan.—(*the cud*) نشخوار کردن nish-khwár kardan.

CHICANERY, فریب firíb, خیانت khi-yánat, نفاق nifák.

CHICKEN, جوجه júјah, چوزه chúzah (*obs.*).

CHICKEN-POX, زبرک zabrak.

CHICK-PEA, نخود nukhúd.

CHICKWEED, جل وزغ jul-i-vazagh.

CHICORY, هندبا hindabá, کاسنی kás-ní.

To CHIDE, *vide* To REBUKE, To WRANGLE.

CHIEF (*principal*), پیشین píshín, اول avval, مقدم mukaddam, مهتر mihtar.—(*chieftain*) سردار sar-dár, سالار sálár, کدخدا kad-khudá, امیر amír, رئیس ra,is, زعیم za'ím, مقدم mukaddam, پیشوا písh-vá, پیشرو písh-rau, شریف sharíf, قدوه kid-vah, کلانتر kalántar, سندید síndíd, هارون hárún, ضابط zábit, قائد ká,id, عین ʻain, قاعد káʻid, عقید ʻakíd, سرور sar-var.—(*chief of an army, commander-in-chief*) سپه سالار sipah-sálár, امیر نظام amír-nizám. —(*chief of nomadic or wandering tribes*) ایلخانی ílkhání, ایلبیگی ílbegí.—(*elder, or headman of a class of people*) استاد ustád, اوستاد ústád, شیخ shaikh, بزرگ buzurg, رئیس ra,is, مقدم mukaddam, کبیر kabír, مهتر mihtar, سرور sar-var.

CHIEFLY, اکثر aksar, اغلب aghlab, غالباً ghálíban, بیشتر bíshtar.

CHILD, بچه bachah, طفل tifl, کودک kúdak.

CHILD-BIRTH, وضع حمل vaz'-i-haml. —(*pains of child-birth*) درد زه dard-i-zih, طلق talk, مخاض makház.

CHILDHOOD, بچگی bachagí, طفولیت tufúlíyat, صغر sighr.

CHILD-LIKE, بچگانه bachagánah.

CHILLY, سرد sard, چاهیده cháhídah. — (*to be chilly, person*), چاهیدن cháhídan. — (*weather*) سرد شدن sard shudan.

To CHIME, صدائی زنگ کردن sadá,í-i-zang kardan.

CHIMERA, وهم vahm, خیال باطل khiyál-i-bátil.

CHIMNEY, دودکش dúd-kash, روزن rauzan. — (*fire-place*) بخاری bukhárí.

CHIN, زنخ zanakh, کچه kachah.— (*double-chin*) غبغب ghabghab.

CHINA (*porcelain ware*), ظروف چینی zurúf-i-chíní.—(*china-root*) چوب چینی chúb-i-chíní.—(*mender of broken china*) کلوا بند kalvá-band, کنگو گر gangú-gar.

CHINA-ASTER (*the flower*), گل مینا gul-i-míná.

CHINTZ, چیت chít, قلمکار kalamkár.

CHIP, چوب ریزه chúb-rízah, خراشه khiráshah, تراشه tiráshah.

To CHIP (*trans.*), تراشیدن tiráshídan, خراشیدن khiráshídan.—(*intrans.*) افتادن uftádan.

CHIROMANCY, علم کف ʻilm-i-kaf, طالع بینی táliʻ-bíní.

To CHIRP (*as a bird*), جقجق کردن jikjik kardan.

CHISEL, اشکنه ishkanah.

CHIT-CHAT, صحبت suhbat, قیل و قال kíl u kál, گپ gap.

CHIVALROUS, دلیر dilír, شهوار shahvár.

CHIVES, گندنا gandan

CHOCOLAT, شوکولا shúkúlá (*eur.*)

CHOICE, پسند pasand, اختیار ikhtiyár, گزین guzín. (*Vide* RARE, NICE, BEAUTIFUL.)

CHOIR, سرود خوانان surúd-khwánán.

To CHOKE (*be suffocated*), خفه شدن khafah shudan. — (*in eating, swallowing*) گلو گیر شدن gulú-gír shudan.—(*throttle*) خفه کردن khafah kardan, دم بستن dam bastan, نفسرا حبس کردن nafasrá habs kardan.

CHOLERA-MORBUS, وبا vabá.

CHOLERIC, محرور المزاج mahrúru-'l-mizáj, تیز مزاج tíz-mizáj, تند مزاج tund-mizáj.

To CHOOSE, پسند کردن pasand kardan, بر گزیدن bar-guzídan, اختیار نمودن ikhtiyár nimúdan, انتخاب نمودن intikháb nimúdan, اختصاص کردن ikhtisás kardan.

CHOPPER, تبر tabar.

CHORD (*of an arc or segment of a circle*), وتر vatar.

CHORUS (*of a song*), زمین zamín, زمینه zamínah. — (*at a theatre*) پیشخوانان písh - khwánán. — (*in chorus*) بهمان نوا bi-hamán navá.

CHRIST, عیسی ʻísá, مسیح masíh, مسیحا masíhá, عیسائی مسیح ʻísá,í-i-masíh.

CHRISTIAN, عیسوی ʻísaví, مسیحی masíhí, نصرانی nasrání (*pl.* نصاری nasárá), ترسا tarsá. — (*religion*) دین عیسوی dín - i - ʻísaví, ملت مسیحیه millat - i - masíhíyah.— (*priest*) قسیس kissís.

CHRISTIANITY, ملت عیسویه millat-i-ʻísavíyah, ملت مسیحیه millat-i-masíhíyah, نصرانیه nasráníyah.

CHRISTMAS, مولد عیسی maulud-i-

'ísá, عید میلاد عیسوی 'íd-i-mílád-i-'ísá.

CHRONIC, زمانه zamánah, مزمن muzmin.

CHRONICLE, تاریخ táríkh (*pl.* تواریخ tavárikh), اخبار akhbár, وقایع vakáí', روایت riváyat.

CHRONICLER, مورخ muvarrikh.

CHRONOLOGY, تاریخ táríkh.

CHRONOMETER, ساعت sá'at.

CHRYSALIS, بادامه bádámah.

CHRYSANTHEMUM (*flower*), گل داودی gul-i-dá,udí.

CHRYSOLITE, عقیق زرد 'akík-i-zard.

CHURCH, کلیسیا kalísiyá, کنیسه kanísah.

CHURL, تنگ چشم tang-chashm.

CHURN, خیگ khíg, مشك mashk. [These words both signify a vessel made of the entire skin of a sheep or goat. This, which, in Persia, supplies the place of a churn, is hung up and shaken to and fro till the milk it contains is churned.]

CHYLE, قیلوس kílús (*eur.*).

CHYME, قیموس kímús.

To CICATRIZE, داغ کردن dágh kardan.

CIDER, پالوده سیب pálúdah-i-síb, شراب سیب shiráb-i-síb.

CIGAR, سیگار sígár (*eur.*), سیغار síghár (*eur*).

CIGAR-CASE, قاب سیگار káb-i-sígár.

CINDER, خاکستر khákistar.

CINNABAR, زنجفره zinjifrah, شنجرف shanjiraf.

CINNAMON, دار چینی dár-chíní.

CIRCASSIA, چرکس charkas.

CIRCASSIAN, چرکسی charkasí, لگزی lagzí.

CIRCLE, دائره dá,irah, حلقه halkah, چنبر chambar, مدوره mudavvarah. — (*of people*) حلقه halkah. — (*centre of a circle*) مرکز markaz. —(*diameter*) قطر kutr.—(*radius*) نصف القطر nisfu-'l-kutr.—(*circumference*) دائره dá,irah.—(*segment*) قطاع kitá'.—(*semi-circle*) نصف دائره nisf-i-dá,irah, نیم دائره ním-dá,irah.—(*to form a circle*) دائره زدن dá,irah zadan.

CIRCUIT, گردش gardish, دور daur, دوره daurah, طواف taváf.—(*legal term*) دایر و سایر dáír va sáír.

CIRCULAR, دواری davvárí, مدور mudavvar, گرد gird.

To CIRCULATE, گشتن gashtan, گردیدن gardídan.—(*money*) ناشی شدن náshí shudan.—(*newspaper*) انتشار یافتن intishár yáftan, رائج شدن rá,ij shudan.

CIRCULATION, مداوره mudávarah, گردش gardish, میان miyán.—(*money*) رواج raváj.—(*newspaper*) انتشار intishár. — (*to put in circulation*) رواج دادن raváj dádan. —(*to take out of circulation*) از اعتبار انداختن az 'itibár andákhtan.

To CIRCUMCISE, ختنه نمودن khutnah nimúdan. — (*to be circumcised*) مختون شدن makhtún shudan, ختنه شدن khutnah shudan.

CIRCUMCISION, ختنه khutnah, *or* khatnah.

CIRCUMFERENCE, گرد gird, دائره dá,irah, اطراف atráf, حوالی haválí.

To CIRCUMSCRIBE, محدود ساختن mahdúd sákhtan.

CIRCUMSPECT, متنبه mutanabbih, مستبصر mustabsir, محترز muhtariz, کار شناس kár-shinás.

CIRCUMSPECTION, احتراز ihtiráz, احتیاط ihtiyát, بصیرت basírat, حزم hazm.

CIRCUMSTANCE, امر amr, حال hál, واقعه váki'ah, وقوع vukú', کیفیت kaifíyat, حقیقت hakíkat, باب báb, سر گذشت sar-guzasht.—(*in these circumstances*) در این صورت dar ín súrat.

To CIRCUMVENT, راه بستن ráh bastan, سر راه گرفتن sar-i-ráh giriftan.

CIRCUS, میدان maidán, جولانگاه jaulán-gáh.

CISTERN, حوض hauz, برکه birkah.—(*large reservoir*) آب انبار áb-ambár.

CITADEL, ارگ arg, ارك ark, قلعه kal'ah.

To CITE, ایراد نمودن írád nimúdan

—(*at law*) ادعا نمودن iddi'á nimúdan.
CITIZEN, شهری shahrí, بلدی baladí.
CITIZENSHIP, بلدیت baladiyat.
CITRON, ترنج turanj.
CITY, شهر shahr, بلده baldah, مدینه madínah.
CIVET, زباد zubád.
CIVIC, مدنی madaní.
CIVIL (*polite*), خلیق khalík, مؤدب mu'addab, لطیف latíf, خوش اخلاق khwush-akhlák.
CIVILIAN (*civil functionary, not military*), ارباب قلم arbáb-i-kalam, اهل قلم ahl-i-kalam.
CIVILITY, ادب adab, اخلاق akhlák, مدارا mudárá, لطافت latáfat.
CIVILIZATION, مدنیت madaníyat, تمدن tamaddun.
CIVILIZED, متمدن mutamaddin.
CIVILLY, ادبانه adabánah, با لطافت bá-latáfat.
CLAD, ملبس mulabbas.
CLAIM, دعوی da'vá, ادعا iddi'á, طلب talab, در خواست dar-khwást, اقتضا iktizá, مبتغا mubtaghá, مطالبه mutálabah.
CLAIMANT, مدعی mudda'í.
CLAMMINESS, لزوجت luzújat, چسبندگی chasbandagí.
CLAMMY, لزج lazij, چسبنده chasbandah.
CLAMOUR, فریاد faryád, غوغا ghaughá, های هوی hái-húí, شماته shamátah, شلوك shulúk (*vulg.*).
CLANDESTINE, *vide* SECRET.
CLAP, *vide* GONORRHŒA. — (*of thunder*) صاعقه sá'ikah.
To CLAP (*hands*), چپه زدن chapah zadan, دستك زدن dastak zadan.
CLARIFICATION, تصفیه tasfiyah.
To CLARIFY, تصفیه کردن tasfiyah kardan, مصفا ساختن musaffá sákhtan.
CLARIONET, سورنا súrná.
CLASHING (*of swords*), چاك چاك chák-chák.
CLASP (*fastening of a belt, &c.*), چپ و راست chap u rást, نر و لاس nar u lás.
To CLASP, *vide* To EMBRACE.
CLASS, جنس jins, قبیل kabíl, قسم kism.—(*school*) صنف sinf.—(*the middle classes*) اواسط ناس avásit-i-nás.
CLASSIFICATION, ترتیب tartíb, تقسیم taksím.
To CLASSIFY, ترتیب نمودن tartíb nimúdan, تقسیم کردن taksím kardan.
CLATTER, قال و مقال kál va makál. (*Vide* NOISE.)
CLAUSE (*sentence*), فقره fakarah, جمله jumlah.
CLAW, چنگ chang, چنگل changal, چنگال changál, ناخن nákhun, پنجه panjah, مخلب mikhlab, خنج khinj.
CLAY, گل gil, طین tín, وحل vahal.—(*pottery clay*) خاك چینی khák-i-chíní.
CLEAN, شسته shustah, پاك pák, پاکیزه pákízah, صاف sáf, نظیف nazíf, ساده sádah, نقی nakí.
CLEANNESS, پاکیزگی pákízagí, نظافت nazáfat.
To CLEANSE, پاك کردن pák kardan, تنقیه کردن tankiyah kardan, نجیدن najídan.
CLEAR (*transparent*), شفاف shaffáf. —(*limpid*) صاف sáf.—(*bright*) روشن raushan, منور munavvar, منیر munír, نورانی núrání, تابان tábán, تابدار táb-dár, جلی jalí, لامع lámi', ساطع sáti', درخشان dirakhshán.—(*evident*) آشکار áshkár, آشکاره áshkárah, ظاهر záhir, هویدا húvaidá, روشن raushan, مبین mubín, واضح vázih, لایح láíh, عیان 'iyán, باهر báhir, صریح saríh, بدیهی badíhí.
To CLEAR (*a drain, a well, &c.*), تنقیه کردن tankiyah kardan, روبیدن rúbídan.—(*to clear away, table*) بر چیدن bar-chídan.
CLEARLY, آشکارا áshkárá, واضحاً vázihan, جداً jiddan.
CLEARNESS, صفا safá, وضاحت vazá,at.
To CLEAVE, شکافتن shikáftan, شق کردن shakk kardan, چاك کردن chák kardan. (*Vide* To ADHERE, To CRACK.)
CLEAVING (*of the earth*), خسف khasf.

CLEFT, *vide* CRACK.

CLEMENCY, مرحمت marhamat, کرم karam.

CLEMENT, خطا بخش khatá-baksh, راحم ráhim, نرم‌دل narm-dil.

To CLENCH (*the fist*), دسترا مشت کردن dastrá musht kardan, پنجه بهم گذاشتن panjah bi-ham guzáshtan.

CLERGYMAN, پیش نماز písh-namáz, کشیش kashísh, قسیس kissís.

CLERK, اهل قلم ahl-i-kalam.

CLEVER, چابك chábuk, زیرك zírak, چست chust, زرنگ zaring, ذکی zakí, لوذعی lauza'í, چیره دست chírah-dast.

CLEVERNESS, زیرکی zírakí, زرنگی zaringí, فراست firásat, زکاوت zakávat, ذهن zihn.

CLEW (*of thread*), کلافه kaláfah.—(*guide*) دلالت dalálat, رهبری rahbarí, هدایت hidáyat, سراغ surágh.

CLIENT, موکل muvakkil, منیب muníb.

CLIMATE (*weather, &c.*), هوا havá.—(*clime of the world*) اقلیم iklím, کشور kishvar, خطه khuttah.—(*the seven climes*) هفت اقلیم haft iklím, هفت کشور haft kishvar.

To CLIMB, بالا رفتن bálá raftan, بر آمدن bar-ámadan.

CLIMBER (*plant*), عشقه 'ashikah.

CLIME, *vide* CLIMATE.

To CLINCH (*a nail*), پر چین کردن pur-chín kardan, پر چم کردن pur-cham kardan.

To CLING TO, چسبیدن chasbídan, پیوسته بودن paivastah búdan.

To CLIP, چیدن chídan, مقراض کردن mikráz kardan.—(*to clip one's words*) سخن خودرا خوردن sukhun-i-khwudra khwurdan.

CLITORIS, کین kain, زنبور zambúr.

CLOAK, بارانی báraní, جبه jubbah, چوغا chúghá, کاتبی kátibí, فرغل farghul, دراعت durrá'at, لباده libádah, عبا 'abá, برکان barrakán. (*Vide* RIDING-CLOAK.)

CLOCK, ساعت مجلسی sá'at-i-majlisí.—(*two o'clock, &c.*) ساعت دو sá'at-i-dú, &c. — (*clock-maker*) ساعت ساز sá'at-sáz. — (*to go by clock-work*) به قاعده ساعت کار کردن bi-ká'idah-i-sá'at kár kardan.

CLOD (*of earth*), کلوخ kulúkh.

CLOG, قبقاب kabkáb. (*Vide* OBSTACLE.)

CLOISTER, دیر dair.

CLOSE (*shut up*), بسته bastah, مسدود masdúd, بند band.—(*suffocating*) خفه khafah.—(*near to*) پیوسته paivastah, ملحق mulhak, قریب karíb, در جنب dar jamb, نزد nazd, متصل muttasil, نزدیك nazdík.—(*narrow*) تنگ tang, چست chust.—(*occult*) پنهان panhán, مخفی makhfí, پوشیده púshídah, نهان nihán. — (*stingy*) بخیل bakhíl, خسیس khasís, لئیم la'ím. — (*a passage in a street, leading under a building or archway*) ساباط sá,ibát, سهبات sahbát, بالا خانه خروجی bálá-khánah-i-khurújí.

To CLOSE, بستن bastan, بند کردن band kardan, مسدود ساختن masdúd sákhtan.—(*an account*), صاف کردن sáf kardan, مفروغ کردن mafrúgh kardan.

CLOSENESS (*narrowness*), تنگی tangí, چستی chustí.—(*nearness*) نزدیکی nazdíkí, اتصال ittisál.—(*stinginess*) بخل bukhl, خست khissat, لئامت la,ámat.

CLOSET, خلوتخانه khalvat-khánah, خلوتگاه khalvat-gáh.—(*for provisions, &c.*) حوائج خانه havá,ij-khánah, گنجه ganjah. — (*for clothes, valuables, and arms*) توشه خانه túshah-khánah, پستو pastú. — (*privy*) ادبخانه adab-khánah, خلا khalá, مبرز mabraz.

CLOTH, پارچه párchah.—(*piece or web of cloth*) طاقه tákah, پارچه párchah, توپ túp. — (*woollen cloth*) ماهوت máhút. — (*coarse woollen cloth*) پتو pattú. — (*of gold*), زری zarí.—(*of silk and cotton mixed*) گرمسوف garmasúf, مشروع mashrú'. — (*cotton stuff*) *vide* COTTON. — (*linen*) *vide* LINEN.—(*silk cloth*) *vide* SILK.

—(*sackcloth*) پلاس palás.—(*napkin*) فوته fútah, دستمال dast-mál, پیشگیر písh-gír.
CLOTH-MERCHANT, بزاز bazzáz.
To CLOTHE, پوشیدن púshídan, رخت پوشیدن rakht púshídan.
CLOTHES, جامه jámah, رخت rakht, پوشاک púshák, پوشش púshish, لباس libás, پوشن púshan, زی zí (*pl.* ازیاء azyá,).—(*old clothes*) کهنه kuhnah.—(*old clothes man*) کهنه فروش kuhnah-furúsh.—(*plain clothes*) لباس ساده libás-i-sádah.—(*under-clothes*) زیر پوش zír-púsh.
CLOUD, ابر abr, سحاب saháb, میغ mígh, غمامه ghamámah.—(*clouds in summer*) کوآر kúa,r.
CLOUDY, ابردار abr-dár, گرفته giriftah.
CLOUT, کهنه kahnah, پینه pínah, لته lattah.—(*nail*) میخ míkh.
CLOUTED (*patched*), پینه زده pínah zadah, مرقع murakka'.
CLOVE, میخک míkhak, قرنفل karanful.
CLOVEN (*divided*), شکافته شده shikáftah-shudah, چاکدار chák-dár, چاک شده chák-shudah, شق shakk.
CLOVER, طرفیل tarfíl, شفدر shafdar, شبدر shabdar, سه برگه sih-bargah.
CLOWN, روستائی rústá,í, دهقان dihkún.—(*buffoon*) مسخره maskharah.
CLUB, چوب chúb, کتک kutk, عصا 'asá, چماق chumák.—(*of metal*) *vide* MACE.
CLUE, *vide* TRACE.
CLUMSY, بی نزاکت bí-nazákat.
CLUSTER, خوشه khúshah, عقده 'ikdah.
To CLUSTER, گرد آمدن gird ámadan.
CLUTCH, *vide* CLAW.
CLYSTER, دستور dastúr, اماله imálah, حقنه huknah.
COACH, *vide* CARRIAGE.
COACH-HOUSE, خانه کالسکه khánah-i-káliskah, انبار ambár.
COACH-MAN, کالسکه چی káliskah-chí.
CO-ADJUTOR, یاور yávar.
To COAGULATE, بسته شدن bastah shudan, منجمد شدن munjamid shudan, غلیظ شدن ghalíz shudan, سفت شدن sift shudan, دلمه شدن dalamah shudan.
COAL, زغال zughál.—(*a live coal*) خرگ آتش kharg-i-átish, اخگر akhgar, جمر jamr, جذوه juzvah.
COAL-CELLAR, زغال دان zughál-dán.
COAL-MINE, معدن زغال ma'dan-i-zughál.
COARSE, کلفت kuluft, گنده gundah, درشت durusht, خشن khushn, *or* khashin.
COARSENESS, درشتی durushtí, خشونت khushúnat, گندگی gundagí.
COAST, کنار kanár, کران karán, ساحل sáhil, طرف taraf.
COAST-GUARD, ساحل بان sáhil-bán, مستحفظ ساحل mustahfiz-i-sáhil.
COAT, قبا kabá, قفتان kaftán, خفتان khuftán.—(*inner coat*) ارخالق arkhálik, الخالق alkhálik, الخلق alkhuluk (*vulg.*).—(*cut away coat*) نیمتنی nímtání.—(*frock-coat*) کلیجه kulíjah.—(*great-coat*) بالا پوشی bálá-púshí.—(*of paint, &c.*) پرده pardah.
To COAX, نواختن navákhtan, ریش خندی نمودن rísh-khandí nimúdan, چاپلوسی کردن cháplúsí kardan, دم بازی کردن dam-bází kardan, تملق نمودن tamalluk nimúdan, پیزر بپالان چپانیدن pízar bi-pálán chapánídan.
COBBLER (*mender of old shoes and leathern articles*), پینه دوز pínah-dúz.
COB-NUT, فندق funduk.
COBWEB, پرده عنکبوت pardah-i-'ankabút, کنتره kinatrah.
COCCULUS INDICUS (*poison-berry*), مرگ ماهی marg-i-máhí.
COCHINEAL, قرمز kirmiz.
COCK, خروس khurús.—(*of a match-lock gun*), ماشه máshah.—(*of a firelock*) چانه chánah, چونه chúnah, خروس khurús.—(*of a cistern, water-skin, &c.*) دهن شیر dahan-i-shír.—(*of a detonating gun*) دنگ ding, چکش chakush.
To COCK (*a gun*), چقماقرا سر پا آوردن chakmákrá sar-i-pá ávardan.—(*to half-cock a gun*) چقماقرا بر نیم

پا کشیدن chakmákrá bar ním-pá kashídan.

Cockroach, سوسك súsk.

Cocoa, قاقاوه kákávah (*eur.*).

Cocoa-nut, نارگیل nárgíl, نارجیل nárjíl, جوز هندی jauz-i-hindí.

Cocoon, پیله pílah, پیله کرم pílah-i-kirm.

Code, تنظیم tanzím, قانون kánún, قانون نامه kanún-námah, نظام nizám, آیین áyín.

Coffee, قهوه kahvah.—(*berries*) بن bunn. — (*shrub*) درخت قهوه dirakht-i-kahvah, درخت بن dirakht-i-bunn.—(*pot*) قهوه پز kahvah-paz, قهوه ریز kahvah-ríz.—(*cup*) فنجان finján.—(*stand for the cup*), ظرف zarf, زیر فنجان zír-finján.—(*house*) قهوه خانه kahvah-khánah.—(*coffee-house keeper*) قهوه چی kahvah-chí.

Coffers, انبار ambár.

Coffin, صندوق sanduk, تابوت tábút.

Cog, دندانه dandánah.

Cogitation, *vide* Thought.

Cognizance, خبر khabar, آگاهی ágáhí.

Cognomen (*family name*), کنیه kun-yah.

To Cohabit, مضاجعه نمودن muzája'ah nimúdán.

Cohabitation, مضاجعه muzája'ah, همخوابه ham-khwábah.

Coherence, ربط rabt, الحاق ilhák.

Coherent, مربوط marbút.

Cohesion (*uniting*), پیوستگی pai-vastagí, مواصلت muvásalat.

Coil (*of rope, &c.*), حلقه halkah.

Coin, پول púl, نقد nakd.—(*false coin*) پول قلابی púl-i-kullábí, پول مغشوش púl-i-maghshúsh.

To Coin, ضرب کردن zarb kardan.

Coincidence, موافقت muváfakat, اتفاق ittifák.

Coined (*word*), مخترع mukhtara'.

Coiner (*stamper of coin*), ضراب zarráb.—(*maker of false coin*) قلابی زن kullábí-zan.

Colander, پالونه pálúnah, پالاوان páláván.

Cold (*adj.*), سرد sard, بارد bárid.—(*subst.*) سرد sard, سردی sardí, برد bard. برودت burúdat, سرما sarmá.—(*catarrh*) سردی sardí, چاهش cháhish, زکام zukám.—(*to catch cold*) چاهیدن cháhídan, سرما خوردن sarmá khwurdan, زکام کردن zukám kardan. — (*cold region, high ground*), سرد سیر sard-sír, سر حد sar-hadd.

Coldness (*of manner, &c.*), برودت burúdat.

Coleric, صفروی safraví, آتش مزاج átish-mizáj.

Colic, دل دردی dil-dardí, قولنج kú-lunj, کولنج kúlinj, پیچ pích.

Collar (*of a coat, &c.*), گریبان girí-bán, یقه yakah, یقا yaká, یخه yakhah.—(*ring for the neck*) طوق tauk. — (*collar-bone*) ترقوه tur-kúvah (*pl.* تراقی tarákí)

To Collate, مقابل نمودن mukábil nímúdan.

Collation, مقابله mukábalah. (*Vide* Banquet.)

Colleague, شریك sharík, رفیق rafík, همراز ham-ráz.

To Collect, جمع کردن jam' kardan, فراهم آوردن faráham ávardan, چیدن chídan, کپیدن kapídan (*vulg.*).—(*to collect one's thoughts*) خیال کردن khiyál kardan.

Collection, جمع jam', اجتماع ijti-má', جمعیت jam'íyat, مجمع majma', جمله jumlah, جملگی jum-lagí. — (*of articles, &c.*) مجموعه majmú'ah.—(*of taxes*) تحصیل tah-síl.

Collectively, بالجمله bi-'l-jumlah, جمعا jam'an, جمیعا jamí'an.

Collector (*of revenue, taxes, &c.*), محصل muhassil, باجگیر báj-gír, عشار 'ashshár, داروغه dárúghah, مستوفی mustaufí.

College, مدرسه madrasah.

Collision, مصادمه musádamah, تصادم tasádum. — (*to come into collision*) بهم خوردن bi-ham-khwurdan.

Collusion, *vide* Intrigue, Con-spiracy, Plot.

Collyrium (*for the eyes*), سرمه surmah, کحل kuhl, توتیا tútiyá.
Colocynth, حنظل hanzal.
Colonel, میر آلای mír-áláí, سرتیپ sartíp, کولونل kúlúnal (*eur.*).
Colonnade, راهرو مسقف ráh-rau-i-musakkaf.
Colony, قبیله kabílah. — (*the colonies*) متصرفات mutasarrafát.
Colossal, ضخیم zakhím, بزرگ buzurg.
Colour, رنگ rang, لون laun.—(*in composition*) فام fám, گون gún.—(*to change colour*) رنگارنگ نمودن rang-á-rang nimúdan, ملون شدن mulavvan shudan.
To Colour, رنگ زدن rang zadan, رنگ کردن rang kardan.
Coloured, رنگین rangín, ملون mulavvan.
Colourless, بی رنگ bí-rang.
Colours, *vide* Flag.
Colt, کره kurrah.
Column, ستون sutún, رکن rukn, عمود 'amúd, عماد 'imád, میل míl. —(*base of a column*) پایه páyah. —(*capital*) تاج táj.—(*in a book*) جدول jadval.—(*to be drawn up in column*) بطور ستون ایستادن bi-taur-i-sutún ístádan.
Comb, شانه shánah. (*Vide* Curry-comb, Honeycomb.)—(*of a cock*) تاج táj. — (*comb-maker*) شانه ساز shánah-sáz.
To Comb, شانه زدن shánah zadan, شاندن shándan (*obs.*).—(*to comb one's hair*) زلف خودرا شانه کردن zulf-i-khwudrá shánah kardan.
Combat, *vide* War, Strife, Battle.
Combatant, مبارز mubáriz.
Combination, *vide* Union, Plot, Conspiracy, Agreement.
Combined with, ضمیمه zamímah.
Combustion, تحریق tahrík.
To Come, آمدن ámadan, رسیدن rasídan.—(*it came to pass*) چنین شد chunín shud, واقع شد váki' shud. —(*to come about*) بوقوع رسیدن bi-vukú' rasídan.—(*to come across*) افتادن uftádan.—(*to come down*) پائین آمدن pá,in ámadan. — (*to come up*) بالا آمدن bálá ámadan.
Comedian, *vide* Actor.
Comedy, بازی bází, لعبه بازی lu'bah-bází.
Comestibles, خوراکی khwurákí, اغذیه aghziyah.
Comet, ستاره دنباله دار sitárah-i-dumbálah-dár, ستاره دمدار sitárah-i-dum-dár.
Comfort, دلاسا dil-ásá, تسلی tasallí, خاطر جمعی khátir-jam'í, خوشی khwushí, آرام árám, آسایش ásáyish.
To Comfort, تسلی دادن tasallí dádan, فرح بخشیدن farah bakhshídan.
Comforter, تسلی دهنده tasallí dihandah.
Comic, مضحک muzhik. — (*comic journal*) روز نامه مزاح rúz-námah-i-mizáh.
Command, حکم hukm, فرمان firmán, فرمائش firmá,ish, فرموده firmúdah, امر amr, ارشاد irshád, وصیت vasiyat, قدغن kadghan, سفارش sifárish.
To Command (*order*), فرمودن firmúdan, حکم نمودن hukm nimúdan, امر نمودن amr nimúdan, ارشاد کردن irshád kardan, سفارش کردن sifárish kardan, قدغن کردن kadghan kardan.
Commander, فرمان فرمای firmán-firmáí, فرمان گذار firmán-guzár, حاکم hákim, رئیس ra,ís, امیر amír. —(*commander-in-chief*) امیر نظام amír-nizám, سپه سالار sipah-sálár. —(*of an Order of Chivalry*) صاحب نشان sáhib-i-nishán. —(*of an army*) لشکرکش lashkar-kash, سردار sardár.
To Commemorate, یاد آوری کردن yád-ávarí kardan, تذکیر نمودن tazkír nimúdan.
Commemoration, ذکر zikr, یاد گار yád-gár.
To Commence, *vide* To Begin.
Commendation, مدح madh. (*Vide also* Praise.)

COMMENSAL, همسفره ham-sufrah.

To COMMENT, شرح نمودن sharh nimúdan, تفسیر نمودن tafsír nimúdan.

COMMENTARY, تفسیر tafsír, تعبیر ta'bír, شرح sharh, تأویل ta,víl.

COMMENTATOR, مفسر mufassir, شارح shárih.

COMMERCE, سوداگری saudá-garí, تجارت tijárat, متجر matjar, معامله mu'ámalah, داد و ستد dád u sitad, بیع و شرا bai' va shirá, اشترا ishtirá. — (*Chamber of Commerce*) دار التجارت dárú-'t-tijárat.

COMMERCIAL, تجارتی tijáratí.

To COMMISERATE, رحمت نمودن rahmat nimúdan.

COMMISERATION, رحمت rahmat, رحم ruhm.

COMMISSARIAT, مباشره mubásharah.

COMMISSARY, گماشته gumáshtah, وکیل vakíl, داروغه dárúghah.—(*Commissary - General*) امین آذوقجات amín-i-ázúkaját.

COMMISSION, گماشتگی gumáshtagí.—(*on goods, sales, &c.*) حق السعی hakku-'s-sa'í. — (*body of men*), کومیسیون kumísiyún (*eur.*).—(*mixed commission*) کومیسیون مختلطی kumísiyún-i-mukhtalití.—(*to undertake a commission*) استحمال کردن istihmál kardan.

To COMMISSION, گماشتن gumáshtan.

COMMISSIONAIRE, گماشته gumáshtah.

COMMISSIONER, مباشر mubáshir.

To COMMIT (*intrust*), سپردن sipurdan, تفویض نمودن tafvíz nimúdan, حواله کردن haválah kardan, تسلیم کردن taslím kardan.—(*do*) ارتکاب نمودن irtíkáb nimúdan, کردن kardan, ساختن sákhtan, اقدام نمودن ikdám nimúdan.

COMMON, عام 'ámm, عموم 'umúm, مشترک mushtarak, معروف ma'rúf, متعارف muta'árif, متداول mutadával, مشهور mash-húr, معمول ma'múl.—(*people*) عام 'ámm, عوام الناس 'avvámu-'n-nás, اهالی ahálí, خلق khalk.—(*open space*) چمن chaman.—(*in common, indiscriminately*) مشترک mushtarak.

COMMONLY, عموماً 'umúman, اکثر aksar, بیشتر bishtar.

House of COMMONS, مجلس مبعوثان majlis-i-mab'úsán, اطاق عوام aták-i-'avámm.—(*an Address of the House of Commons*) بیاننامه از جانب اعضای اطاق عوام bayán-námah az jánib-i-a'zái-i-aták-i-'avámm.

COMMOTION, هنگامه hangámah, غوغا ghaughá.

To COMMUNICATE, سرایت نمودن siráyat nimúdan, راه داشتن ráh dáshtan. — (*message, &c.*) تبلیغ کردن tablígh kardan, ابلاغ کردن iblágh kardan.

COMMUNICATION, *vide* LETTER.

COMMUNICATIONS (*military term*), موارادات maváradát.

COMMUNION (*intercourse*), رفاقت rifákat, شراکت shirákat, مراودت murávadat, کار و بار kár va bár. (*Vide* INTERCOURSE.) — (*the Sacrament*), عشاء ربانی 'asha,-i-rabbání, قداس kuddás.

COMMUNIST, کومونیست kúmúníst (*eur.*).

COMMUNITY, مشارکت musharakat, ملت millat.

COMPACT, *vide* AGREEMENT, PROMISE, SOLID.

COMPANION, رفیق rafík, شریک sharík, همدم ham-dam, همال hamál, همدوش ham-dúsh, همراز ham-ráz, دمساز dam-sáz, همنشین ham-nishín, آشنا áshná, انباز ambáz, مصاحب musáhib, صاحب sáhib (*pl.* صحابه sahábah, *or* اصحاب asháb).

COMPANY, *Vide* SOCIETY, BAND.—(*of soldiers*) دسته dastah.

COMPARABLE, معادل mu'ádil, لائق تشبیه lá,ik-i-tashbíh, نظیر nazír.

COMPARATIVE (*degree*), حالت تفضیل hálat-i-tafzíl.

COMPARATIVELY, بالنسبه bi-'n-nisbah, بمقابله bi-mukábalah.

To COMPARE, مقابله نمودن mukábalah nimúdan, تشبیه کردن tashbíh kardan, بر آورد کردن bar-ávard kardan.

COMPARED with, نسبه به nisbah bi, بالنسبه به bi-'n-nisbah bi.

COMPARISON, تمثیل tamsíl, تشبیه tashbíh, مشابهه mushábahah, مقابله mukábalah, جور júr, برابری barábarí, تطبیق tatbík, بر آورد bar-ávard.—(*degrees of comparison*) مراتب تفصیل marátib-i-tafsíl.

COMPASS, پرگار pargár, پرکار parkár.—(*mariner's*), قطب نما kutb-nimá, قبله نما kiblah-nimá.—(*points of the compass*)—*N.* شمال shimál; *N.E.* ما بین شمال و مشرق má-bain-i-shimál va mashrik; *N.W.* ما بین شمال و مغرب má-bain-i-shimál va maghrib; *S.* جنوب junúb; *S.E.* ما بین جنوب و مشرق má-bain-i-junúb va mashrik; *S.W.* ما بین جنوب و مغرب má-bain-i-junúb va maghrib; *E.* مشرق mashrik, شرق shark, مطلع matla'; *W.* مغرب maghrib, غرب gharb.

COMPASSION, رقت rikkat, شفقت shafakat, مرحمت marahmat, رحم ruhm, مهربانی mihrbání, رأفت ra,fat, همدردی ham-dardí.

COMPASSIONATE, مشفق mushfik, شفیق shafík, رحیم rahím.

To COMPASSIONATE, شفقت نمودن shafakat nimúdan, رحم کردن ruhm kardan, (به) ترحم کردن tarahhum kardan (bi).

COMPEERS, امثال و اخران amsál va akhirán, اشباه ashbáh.

To COMPEL, جبرا کردن jabran kardan, بر آن داشتن bar án dáshtan, بزور کردن bi-zúr kardan, ابرام نمودن ibrám nimúdan, مجبور نمودن majbúr nimúdan.

COMPENDIUM, مجمل mujmal, موجز mújaz, مجموعه majmú'ah, وجیز vajíz.

To COMPENSATE, عوض دادن 'avaz dádan, معاوضت نمودن mu'ávazat nimúdan.

COMPENSATION, عوض 'avaz, جزا jazá, تلافی taláfí, پاداش pádásh, اجر ajr, اجرت ujrat, مکافات mukáfát.

To COMPETE, مسابقت کردن musábakat kardan, مجاهده نمودن mujáhadah nimúdan.

COMPETITION, مجاهده mujáhadah, مقابله mukábalah.

COMPILATION, تألیف ta,líf.

To COMPILE (*a book, &c., from other writings*), تألیف کردن ta,líf kardan.

To COMPLAIN, شکایت بردن shikáyat burdan, شکوی کردن shakvá kardan.

COMPLAINANT, *vide* PLAINTIFF.

COMPLAINT, گله gilah, نالش nálish, ناله nálah, شکوی shakvá, شکایت shikáyat, تظلم tazallum, فریاد faryád, زاری zárí.—(*malady*) مرض marz, بیماری bímárí, علت 'illat, رنج ranj, آزار ázár, درد dard, ناخوشی ná-khwushí, تکسر مزاج takassur-i-mizáj.

COMPLAISANCE, مهربانی mihrbání, تعطف ta'attuf.

COMPLAISANT, متواضع mutavází', مهربان mihrbán.

COMPLEMENT, تتمه tatammah.

COMPLETE, کامل kámil, تام támm, تمام tamám.—(*completely*) *vide* ENTIRELY.

To COMPLETE, تمام کردن tamám kardan, بانجام رسانیدن bi-anjám rasánídan.

COMPLETELY, تماما tamáman, بکلی bi-kullí.

COMPLETION, تتمه tatammah, انقراض inkiráz, اتمام itmám, اکمال ikmál, تکمیل takmíl, اختتام ikhtitám.

COMPLEXION, رنگ روی rang-i-rúí.

COMPLIANCE, رضا razá, رضامندی razámandí, قبول kabúl, ایجاب íjáb, اجابت ijábat, اتفاق ittifák, اتحاد ittihád, موافقت muváfakat.

COMPLICATED, متعسر muta'assir, مشکل mushkil, مختل mukhtall, مختلط mukhtalit, در هم dar-ham.

COMPLICATION, اشکال ishkál.

COMPLICITY, اتفاق ittifák.

COMPLIMENTS, سلام salám, دعا و سلام du'á u salám, خوش آمدی khwush-ámadí, ادب adab, تملق tamalluk, چم و خم cham va kham, تحیت tahíyat, مدارا mudárá.

To COMPOSE (*arrange*), ترتيب دادن tartíb dádan, مرتب ساختن murattab sákhtan, انتظام نمودن intizám nimúdan.—(*a book, &c.*) تصنيف كردن tasníf kardan, تاليف كردن ta,líf kardan. [This latter term signifies to compile from other books.] — (*to compose oneself*) آرام گرفتن árám giriftan.

COMPOSED of, مركب murakkab.

COMPOSER, ناظم názim.

COMPOSITION (*mixture, &c.*), اجزا ajzá, تركيب tarkíb. — (*of an author*) تصنيف tasníf, مصنف musannaf.

COMPOSITOR (*printer*), مرتب murattib.

COMPOSURE, امنيت amníyat, اطمئنان itmi,nán, آرامى árámí.

COMPOUNDED, مركب murakkab, سرشته sirishtah, مخلوط makhlút.

To COMPREHEND, *vide* To UNDERSTAND.

COMPREHENDING, *vide* CONTAINING.

COMPREHENSIBLE, معقول ma'kúl, مدرك mudrak, قابل ادراك kábil-i-idrák.

COMPREHENSION, فهم fahm, در يافت dar-yáft, عقل 'akl, هوش húsh, خرد khirad, فراست firásat, درك darak, ادراك idrák.

COMPREHENSIVE, شامل shámil.

To COMPRISE, احاطه كردن ihátah kardan, شامل بودن shámil búdan.

COMPROMISE, *vide* AGREEMENT, BARGAIN, CONCILIATION, PROMISE.

COMPULSION, زور zúr, جور jaur, تعدى ta'addí, ظلم zulm, ابرام ibrám, اضطرار iztirár, اقتضا iktizá, جبر jabr, قهر kahr.—(*by compulsion, forcibly, unwillingly*) زوركى zúrakí, جبراً jabran, قهراً kahran, عنفاً 'anfan, نخواسته na-khwástah, اضطراراً istirárán, كرهاً kirahan, بى اختيار bí-ikhtiyár.

COMPUTATION, حساب hísáb, شمار shimár.

To COMPUTE, حساب كردن hisáb kardan, شمردن shimurdan, شماريدن shimáridan.

COMRADE, *vide* COMPANION.

CONCATENATION, تسلسل tasalsul.

CONCAVE, مجوف mujavvaf, اجوف ajvaf, خالى khálí, مقعر muka''ar.

To CONCEAL, نهفتن nihuftan, پوشيدن púshídan, پنهان كردن panhán kardan, نهان كردن nihán kardan, اخفا نمودن ikhfá nimúdan, مخفى ساختن makhfí sákhtan, متوارى داشتن mutavárí dáshtan.

CONCEITED, *vide* PROUD, VAIN.

CONCEIVABLE, متصور mutasavvir.—قابل تصور kábil-i-tasavvur.

To CONCEIVE, يافتن yáftan, در يافت كردن dar-yáft kardan, فهميدن fahmídan.—(*in the womb*) نسل را بر گرفتن naslrá bar-giriftan, حامله شدن hámilah shudan.

To CONCENTRATE, فراهم آوردن faráham ávardan.

CONCENTRATION, فراهم faráham.

CONCEPTION, *vide* THOUGHT.—(*in the womb*) حمل haml.

CONCERN, *vide* BUSINESS, CARE, GRIEF.

To CONCERN, راجع نمودن ráji' nimúdan, تعلق داشتن ta'alluk dáshtan, دخل داشتن dakhl dáshtan, مختص بودن mukhtass búdan.

CONCERNING, در باب dar báb, در باره dar bárah, نسبت به nisbat bi, از az, در حق dar hakk, در خصوص dar khusús.

CONCERT, *vide* UNION.—(*music*) مهمانى ساز و آواز mihmání-i-sáz va áváz.

CONCESSION, ترخص tarakhkhus.—(*to make concessions*) گذشت كردن guzasht kardan.

CONCH (*shell*), بوق buk.

CONCILIATION, التيام iltiyám, مصالحه musálahah.

CONCISE, مختصر mukhtasar, مجمل mujmal, وجيز vajíz.

To CONCLUDE, *vide* To FINISH, To SUPPOSE.

CONCLUSION, *vide* END, RESULT.

CONCOCTION, *vide* DECOCTION.

CONCOMITANT, مقارن mukárin متفق muttafik, اتفاقى ittifákí.

CONCORD, موافقت muváfakat, وفاق

vífák, اتحاد ittihád, یگانگی yagánagí.
Concordance, مطابقت mutábakat.
Concourse, *vide* Crowd.
Concrete, جامد jámid.—(*grammatical term*) مقید mukayyad. (*Vide* Plaster.)
Concubine, متعه mut'ah, مدخوله madkhúlah, خاصه گی khássah-gí, پرستار parastár.
Concupiscence, *vide* Lust.
Concurrence, *vide* Consent.
Concussion, *vide* Shock.
To Condemn, تحکم نمودن tahakkum nimúdan, فتوی دادن fatvá dádan, مجرم نمودن mujram nimúdan.
Condensation, اختصار ikhtisár, مختصر mukhtasar.—(*water*) تکثیف taksíf.
To Condense, اختصار کردن ikhtisár kardan, مختصر کردن mukhtasar kardan. — (*water*) تکثیف نمودن taksíf nimúdan.
Condescension, توجه tavajjuh, تواضع tavázu'.
Condition (*state*), حال hál, حالت hálat, وضع váz'. — (*stipulation*), شرط shart, قرار karár, بنا biná, عهد 'ahd.
Conditional (*mood of a verb*), شرطی shartíy.
Conditionally, مشروط mashrút, علی ان 'alá án, بشرطیکه bi-shartíkih.
To Condole, عزاداری کردن 'azá-dárí kardan.
Condolence, عزا 'azá, تعزیت ta'ziyat, ماتم پرسی mátam-pursí, مواسات muvását.
To Condone, *vide* To Forgive.
Conduct (*guidance*), رهنمای rahnimái, رهبری rah-bari, دلالت dalálat, هدایت hidáyat.—(*behaviour*) وضع vaz', حرکت harakat, کردار kirdár, رفتار raftár, اطوار atvár, سلوك sulúk.
To Conduct, *vide* To Bear, To Lead.
Conductor, *vide* Guide.—(*of a band*) مهتر باشی mihtar-báshí.
Conduit, *vide* Aqueduct, Water-course, Drain.

Cone (*of fir, &c.*), جوز کلاغ jauz-i-kalágh, بر bar, گردوئی کلاغ girdú,í-i-kalágh.—(*conical body*) مخروطه makhrútah, قلمی kalamí.
Confectioner, قناد kannád, قنادی kannádí, حلوائی halvá,í.
Confectionery, شکری shakarí, شیرینی shíríní.
Confederacy, *vide* Conspiracy, Plot, Partnership, Society, Band.
To Confer, مزاکره نمودن muzákarah nimúdan, مکالمه نمودن mukálamah nimúdan, مشاوره نمودن mushávarah nimúdan. (*Vide* To Bestow.)
Conference, مذاکره muzákarah, مکالمه mukálamah, مشاوره mushávarah.
To Confess, *vide* To Acknowledge.
Confession, اقرار ikrár, اعتراف i'tiráf, تشهد tashahhud, اذعان iz'án.
Confidant (*subs.*), همراز ham-ráz, همدم ham-dam, محرم mahram.—(*adj.*) مطمئن mutma,inn.
To Confide in, اعتبار کردن i'tibár kardan, اعتماد نمودن i'timád nimúdan, اعتقاد بردن i'tikád burdan, واثق شدن vásik shudan, توکل نمودن tavakkul nimúdan, ایمان داشتن ímán dáshtan.
Confidence, باور bávar, اعتقاد i'tikád, اعتماد i'timád, اعتبار i'tibár, توکل tavakkul, استناد istinád, وثوق vusúk, ایمان ímán, امید umíd.
Confidential, مخفی makhfí.
Confined, محبوس mahbús. — (*limited*) محدود mahdúd.—(*air*) حبس habs. — (*to be confined, woman*) زادن zádan, زائدن zá,idan, در وضع حمل بودن dar vaz'-i-haml búdan.
Confinement, *vide* Imprisonment, Childbirth.
Confines (*limits*), حد hadd, حدود hudúd, سر حد sar-hadd, دهنه dahanah, کران karán, اقصی aksá, ثغور sughúr, انتها intihá, مرز marz, سنور sunúr.
To Confirm, تصدیق نمودن tasdík

nimúdan, ثابت کردن sábit kardan, محقق نمودن muhakkak nimúdan. —(*in an appointment*) بر قراری نمودن bar-karárí nimúdan.

CONFIRMATION, اثبات isbát, ثبوت subút, انضباط inzibát, تقویت takviyat, تصدیق tasdík.

CONFIRMED, *vide* ESTABLISHED, CERTAIN.

To CONFISCATE, مصادره نمودن musádarah nimúdan, ضبط کردن zabt kardan, قبض کردن kabz kardan.

CONFISCATION, ضبط zabt, قبض kabz, غصب ghasb.

CONFLAGRATION, حریق harík, سوزگی súzagí.

CONFLICT, *vide* BATTLE.

CONFLUENT, موصول mausúl.

To CONFORM, موافقت نمودن muváfakat nimúdan, متابعت شدن mutába'at shudan.

CONFORMABLY, موافق muváfik, بر وفق bar vafk, بر طبق bar tibk, مطابق mutábik, فراخور farákhwur, بحسب bi-hasab, مناسب munásib, از قرار az karár.

CONFORMITY, موافقت muváfakat, طبق tibk, وفق vafk.—(*in conformity with*) بر طبق bar tibk.

To CONFOUND, بر هم زدن bar-ham zadan, در هم کردن dar-ham kardan, مشوش ساختن mushavvash sákhtan, مختل گردانیدن mukhtall gardánídan.

To CONFRONT, رو برو کردن rú bi-rú kardan, مواجهه کردن muvájahah kardan.

To CONFUSE, *vide* To MIX.

CONFUSED, برهم زده bar-ham zadah, مختلط mukhtalit, مختل mukhtall, در هم dar-ham, پریشان paríshán, پیچاپیچ pích-á-pích, تار و مار tár u már.—(*in mind*) حیران hairán, مشوش mushavvash, آشفته áshuftah, دستپاچه dast-páchah.—(*to be confused*) خجل شدن khijil shudan, متحیر شدن mutahayyar shudan, حیران بودن hairán búdan, دستپاچه شدن dast-páchah shudan, بر آشفتن bar-áshuftan.

CONFUSION, پریشانی paríshání, اختلاط ikhtilát, خلل khalal, اختلال ikhtilál, بر همی bar-hamí, تشویش tashvísh, حیص بیص hais-bais, هرج مرج harj-marj, تار و مار tár u már, کژ و ویژ kazh u vízh (*vulg.*).

CONFUTATION, رد کلام radd-i-kalám.

To CONFUTE, ملزم کردن mulzam kardan, رد کلام نمودن radd-i-kalám nimúdan, جرح کردن jarh kardan.

To CONGEAL, *vide* To COAGULATE, To FREEZE.

To CONGRATULATE, تهنیت کردن tahniyat kardan, تبریك کردن tabrík kardan.—(*to congratulate oneself*) تهنیت دادن tahniyat dádan, استسعاد نمودن istis'ád nimúdan.

CONGRATULATION, تهنیت tahniyat, مژده muzhdah, مبارك بادی mubárak-bádí.

To CONGREGATE, جمع شدن jam' shudan.

CONGREGATION, جماعت jamá'at, مجمع majma', جمهور jamhúr, جمعیت jam'íyat, انجمن anjuman.

CONGRESS, مجلس مذاکره majlis-i-muzákarah, کونگره kúngarah (*eur.*).

CONGRUITY, مطابقت mutábakat.

CONIC sections, مخروطیات makhrútíyát.

CONJECTURAL, وهمی vahmí, خیالی khiyálí, قیاسی kiyásí.

To CONJECTURE, حدس نمودن hads nimúdan, تخمین کردن takhmín kardan. (*Vide* To IMAGINE.)

CONJECTURE, قیاس kiyás, گمان gumán, ظن zann, مظنه mazinnah, تخمین takhmín, حدس hads, اندازه andázah, وهم vahm, خیال khiyál.

CONJOINED, متوصل mutavassil, متواصل mutavásil, متصل muttasil.

CONJOINTLY with, بانضمام bi-inzimám.

To CONJUGATE, صرف کردن sarf kardan.

CONJUGATION (*of a verb*), تصریف tasríf.

CONJUNCTION (*part of speech*), عطف 'atf.

CONJUNCTIVE, وصلی vaslí.

CONJUNCTURE, *vide* OPPORTUNITY.

CONJURER, جادوگر jádú-gar, مشعبد musha'bid, شعبده باز shu'badah-báz, حقه باز hukkah-báz, ساحر sáhir, سحار sahhár, افسونگر afsún-gar.

CONJURING, *vide* MAGIC, CHARM, TRICK, FEAT.

To CONNECT, *vide* To JOIN.

CONNECTEDLY, متصلاً muttasilan, على الاتصال 'alá-'l-ittisál.

CONNECTION, وصل vasl, اتصال ittisál, دخل dakhl, نسبت nisbat, علاقه 'alákah, پیوند paivand, پیوست paivast, الحاق ilhák. — (*carnal*) مجامعه mujáma'ah, مقاربه mukárabah.

To CONNIVE at, اغماض نمودن ighmáz nimúdan, چشم پوشی کردن chashm-púshí kardan, تجاهل کردن tajáhul kardan, محابات کردن muhábát kardan.

CONNOISSEUR, واقف vákif, عارف 'árif.

To CONQUER, فتح کردن fath kardan, غلبه کردن ghalabah kardan, شکست دادن shikast dádan, ظفر یافتن zafar yáftan, گشادن gushádan, نصرت یافتن nusrat yáftan, فیروز شدن fírúz shudan, غالب آمدن ghálib ámadan.—(*to conquer a subject*) بر مطلب دست یافتن bar matlab dast yáftan.

CONQUEROR, فیروز fírúz, مظفر muzaffar, منصور mansúr.

CONSANGUINITY, همجنسی hamjinsí.

CONSCIENCE, دل dil, ضمیر zamír, قلب kalb.

CONSCIENTIOUS, منصف munsif.

CONSCRIPTION, نفر نامه nafar-námah.

To CONSECRATE, مقدس گردانیدن mukaddas gardánídan, تقدیس نمودن takhdís nimúdan, تخصیص نمودن takhsís nimúdan, منزه کردن munazzah kardan.

CONSECRATION, تقدیس takdís, تخصیص takhsís.

CONSECUTIVE, متوالی mutaválí, متواتر mutavátir, پی در پی paí dar paí.

CONSENSUS of opinion, ائتلاف افکاری i,tiláf-i-afkárí.

CONSENT, اجازت ijázat, رضا razá, رضامندی razá-mandí, استرضا istirzá, قبول kabúl, اجابت ijábat, اتفاق ittifák, موافقت muváfakat, خوشی khwushí, مطاوعه mutáva'ah. (*Vide* LEAVE.) — (*with one consent*) متفقاً muttafikan.

To CONSENT, *vide* To AGREE.

CONSEQUENCE (*result*), نتیجه natíjah, انجام anjám, اثر asar, مآل ma,ál. (*Vide* IMPORTANCE.)

CONSERVATOR, نگاهدار nigáh-dár.

CONSERVATORY, گرمخانه garm-khánah.

To CONSIDER, اندیشیدن andíshídan, اندیشه کردن andíshah kardan, فکر کردن fikr kardan, تأمل کردن ta,ammul kardan, غور کردن ghaur kardan. — (*deem*) محسوب کردن mahsúb kardan, دانستن dánistan, شمردن shimurdan.

CONSIDERABLE, *vide* MUCH.

CONSIDERATION, *vide* THOUGHT, DIGNITY.

To CONSIGN, *vide* To COMMIT.

To CONSIST, (به) بسته بودن bastah búdan (bi).

CONSISTENCY, توافق taváfuk, موافقت muváfakat, مناسبت munásabat.

CONSISTORY, مجلس majlis.

CONSOLATION, *vide* COMFORT.

To CONSOLIDATE, یکی کردن yakí kardan, استوار کردن ustuvár kardan, مستحکم نمودن mustahkim nimúdan, استحکام دادن istihkám dádan.

CONSOLIDATION, یکی شدن yakí shudan, استوار ustuvár, تمکین tamkín, تثبیت tasbít.

CONSONANT, *vide* LETTER.

CONSORT, *vide* WIFE, HUSBAND.

CONSPICUOUS, *vide* APPARENT, CLEAR.

CONSPIRACY, وفاق vifák, سازش sázish, معاهده mu'áhadah, همعهدی ham-'ahdí.

CONSPIRATOR, هم عهد ham-'ahd, هم شرط ham-shart.—(*to conspire against*) هم عهدی بستن ham-'ahdí bastan.

CONSTANCY, استواری ustuvárí, قرار karár, مداومت mudávamat.

CONSTANT, بر قرار bar-karár, راسخ rásikh, ثابت sábit, استوار ustuvár.

CONSTANTLY, *vide* ALWAYS.

CONSTELLATION, اختر akhtar, برج burj, الوا ulvá.

CONSTERNATION, *vide* ALARM.

To be CONSTIPATED, منقبض شدن munkabiz shudan.

CONSTIPATION, قبض kabs, شکم گرفتگی shikm-giriftagí, يبوست yubúsat.

CONSTITUENT, مفرد mufrad (*pl.* مفردات mufradát), منير munír.

CONSTITUTION (*government*), مملکت mamlakat, رياست riyásat, فرمانگذاری firmán-guzárí, حکمرانی hukm-rání.—(*of the body*) مزاج mizáj, نهاد nihád, طبيعت tabí'at, جبلت jibillat, طينت tínat, سرشت sirisht.

CONSTRAINT, *vide* COMPULSION, IMPRISONMENT.

To CONSTRUCT, *vide* To MAKE, To ERECT.

CONSUL, ايلچی ílchi, وکيل vakíl, باليوز bályúz (*eur.*), کونسل kúnsal (*eur.*).

CONSULATE, کونسلگری kúnsal-karí (*eur.*).

To CONSULT, استشاره نمودن istishárah nimúdan, مشورت کردن mashvarat kardan.

CONSULTATION, مشورت mashvarat, مشاوره mashávarah, شورا shúrá, مصلحت maslahat. — (*medical term*) مشورت اطبا mashvarat-i-atibbá.

To CONSUME, صرف کردن sarf kardan, تلف کردن talf kardan, خوردن khwurdan, خرج کردن kharj kardan. (*Vide* To BURN.) — (*to be consumed*) *vide* To be EXPENDED, To be ANNIHILATED, To WASTE.

To CONSUMMATE, منقضی ساختن munkazí sákhtan, تمام کردن tamám kardan, بانجام رسانيدن bi-anjám rasánídan. — (*marriage*) عروسی کردن 'arúsí kardan.

CONSUMMATION (*marriage*), عروسی 'arúsí. (*Vide* COMPLETION.)

CONSUMPTION, صرف sarf, تلف talf, (*disease*), سل sill, سحاف suháf.

CONSUMPTIVE, مسلول maslúl.

CONTAGION, تأثير ta,sír, اثر asar, اصابت isábat, سرايت siráyat.

CONTAGIOUS, ساری sárí, مسری musrí. — (*contagious diseases*) امراض ساريه amráz-i-sáriyah.

To CONTAIN, گنجانيدن gunjánídan, مشتمل بودن mushtamil búdan, داشتن dáshtan, متضمن بودن mutazammin búdan.—(*to be contained in*) گنجيدن gunjídan, مندرج بودن mundarij búdan, شامل بودن shámil búdan.—(*to contain oneself*) خودرا ضبط نمودن khwudrá zabt nimúdan.

CONTAINING, متضمن mutazammin, مشتمل mushtamil.

To CONTEMN, *vide* To DESPISE.

To CONTEMPLATE, *vide* To LOOK, To THINK.

CONTEMPLATION, انديشه andíshah, غور ghaur, تصور tasavvur, تأمل ta,ammul, ملاحظه muláhazah, فکر fikr, تفکر tafakkur, مراقبه murákabah, تلاوت tilávat.

CONTEMPLATIVE, *vide* THOUGHTFUL.

CONTEMPORARY, همزمان hamzamán, معاصر mu'ásir, قرين karín.

CONTEMPT, اهانت ihánat, استهزا istihzá, مذمت mazammat, تحقير tahkír, نکوهش nikúhish.

CONTEMPTIBLE, خوار khwár, ذليل zalíl, دون dún, حقير hakír, سفله siflah, فرومايه furú-máyah, مذموم mazmúm, مبتذل mubtazal, نکوهيده nikúhídah.

CONTENTED, راضی rází, خوش khwush, خوشنود khwush-núd, خرسند khursand, قانع káni', مستغنی mustaghní, سير sír, آسوده ásúdah, مطمئن mutma,inn.

CONTENTION, *vide* STRIFE.

CONTENTMENT, *vide* SATISFACTION TRANQUILLITY.

CONTENTS, ضمن zimn, مضمون maz-mún.
CONTEST, *vide* BATTLE.
CONTEXT, قرينه karínah.
CONTIGUOUS, متصل muttasil, نزد nazd, نزديك nazdík.
CONTINENCE, CONTINENT, *vide* CHASTITY, CHASTE.
CONTINGENCY (*what may happen*), درك dirk, عارضه 'árizah, واقعه váki'ah, موقع mauki'.
CONTINGENT, مشروط mashrút.—(*military*) قشون kushún.
CONTINUAL, *vide* PERPETUAL.
CONTINUALLY, *vide* CONTINUOUSLY.
CONTINUANCE, باقى bákí, دوام davám.
CONTINUATION, پيوستگى paivastagí.
To CONTINUE, *vide* To REMAIN, To LAST.
CONTINUITY, پيوستگى paivastagí. (*Vide also* CONTINUANCE.)
CONTINUOUSLY, على الاتصال 'alá-'l-ittisál, على التواتر 'alá-'t-tavátur, متواتر mutavátir, پيوسته paivastah.
CONTORTION, پيچ pích.
CONTRABAND goods, ممنوعات mamnú'át.
CONTRACT, *vide* AGREEMENT, BARGAIN.
CONTRACTION, *vide* ABBREVIATION. —(*grammatical*) ترخيم tarkhím.
To CONTRADICT, تكذيب كردن takzíb kardan, رد كلام كردن radd-i-kalám kardan, خلاف سخن كردن khiláf-i-sukhun kardan, بر ضد گفتن bar zidd guftan. — (*oneself*) تناقض گفتن tanákuz guftan.
CONTRADICTION, رد كلام radd-i-kalám, تخالف takháluf, تناقض tanákuz, تمرد قول tamarrud-i-kaul.
CONTRADICTORY, متناقض mutanákiz.
CONTRARIETY, ضديت ziddíyat, اختلاف ikhtiláf.
CONTRARY, خلاف khiláf, مخالف mukhálif, نقيض nakíz, مناقض munákiz, ضد zidd, بر عكس bar 'aks, مغاير mugháyir, مقابل mukábil.— (*on the contrary*) بر عكس bar 'aks, بلكه balkih, بر خلاف bar khiláf, بر ضد bar zidd.
CONTRAST, مخالفت mukhálafat, مضادت muzáddat.
CONTRAVENTION, مخالفت mukhálafat.
CONTRE-TEMPS, بى وقت bí-vakt, نا هنگام ná-hangám.
CONTRIBUTION, بذل bazl, تقسيم پول taksím-i-púl, حصه hissah, داد dád.
CONTRIBUTOR, اعانت دهنده i'ánat-dihandah. (*Vide* AUTHOR.)
CONTRIVANCE, ايجاد íjád, تجويز tajvíz, اختراع ikhtirá', ابداع ibdá', منصوبه mansúbah, تمهيد tamhíd.
To CONTRIVE, ايجاد نمودن íjád nimúdan, تجويز كردن tajvíz kardan, اختراع نمودن ikhtirá' nimúdan, انگيختن angíkhtan.
CONTROL, ضبط zabt, داورى dávarí, تدبير tadbír.
To CONTROL, ضبط كردن zabt kardan, داورى نمودن dávarí nimúdan, تدبير نمودن tadbír nimúdan, وا داشتن vá-dáshtan.
CONTROLLER, مستحفظ mustahfiz, سركار sar-kár.
CONTROVERSY, *vide* ARGUMENT, ALTERCATION.
CONTUMACIOUS, معاند mu'ánid
CONTUMACY, عناد 'inád.
To be CONTUSED, پرت خوردن part khwurdan.
CONTUSION, پرت part.
CONUNDRUM, لغز lughz, معمى mu'-ammá.
CONVALESCENCE, شفا shifá, صحت sihhat.
CONVALESCENT, بيمار خيز bímár-khíz, صحاح saháh.—(*to be convalescent*) شفا يافتن shifá yáftan, صحت يافتن sihhat yáftan.
CONVENIENT, مناسب munásib, انسب ansab, شايسته sháyistah, واجب vájib, روا ravá, سزا sazá, سزاوار sazávár, لائق lá,ik, موافق muváfik, لازم lázim.
CONVENT (*religious house, monastery*), دير dair, خانقاه khánkáh.

CONVENTION, *vide* TREATY.
CONVENTIONAL, مصطلح mustalah.
CONVERSATION, گفتگو guftugú, جواب سوال javáb su,ál, مکالمت mukálamat, معاشرت mu'ásharat, صحبت suhbat, قیل و قال kíl u kál.
CONVERSAZIONE, مجلس majlis, مجالست mujálasat.
To CONVERSE, صحبت کردن suhbat kardan, حرف زدن harf zadan, نطقی کردن nutkí kardan.
CONVERSION, قلب kalb, تغییر taghyír. — (*religious*) باز گشت báz-gasht, بدل badal.
CONVERT (*proselyte*), باز گشت کرده báz-gasht-kardah, بدل در یافته badal-dar-yáftah. — (*convert to Muhammadanism*) جدید jadíd.
To CONVERT, *vide* To CHANGE.— (*religious term*) باز گشت کردن báz-gasht kardan, بدل نمودن badal nimúdan.
CONVEX, مقبب mukabbab, ماهی پشت máhi-pusht, محدب muhaddab.
CONVEXITY, تحدب tahaddub.
To CONVEY, آوردن ávardan, رسانیدن rasánídan, نقل کردن nakl kardan.
To CONVICT, ملزم ساختن mulzam sákhtan, الزام کردن ilzám kardan, اثبات آوردن isbát ávardan, مجرم ساختن mujram sákhtan.
CONVICTED (*of a crime*), ملزم mulzam, ملتزم multazim, مجرم mujrim.
CONVICTION (*of a crime*), الزام ilzám. (*Vide* FAITH.)
To CONVINCE, مستدل گردانیدن mustadall gardánídan, ملزم ساختن mulzam sákhtan, مجاب گردانیدن mujáb gardánídan.
CONVINCED (*made sensible by proof*), مستدل mustadall, ملزم mulzam, مجاب mujáb.
CONVIVIAL, هم پیاله ham-piyálah.
CONVOCATION, اجماع ijmá'.
To CONVOKE, فراهم کردن faráham kardan, منعقد کردن mun'akid kardan.
CONVOY, بدرقه badrikah, مشایعت musháya'at.
To CONVOY (*nautical term*) بردیف آمدن bi-radíf ámadan.
CONVULSION (*spasm*), تشنج tashannuj.
COOK, آشپز ásh-paz, طباخ tabbákh.
To COOK, پختن pukhtan, طبخ کردن tabkh kardan.
COOKERY, طبخ tabkh.
COOKSHOP, آشخانه ásh-khánah.
COOL, خنک khunuk, سرد sard, چاهیده cháhídah.
To COOL, خنک کردن khunuk kardan, سرد کردن sard kardan.—(*oneself*) تازه ساختن tázah sákhtan.
COOP (*for fowls*), قفص kafas, قفس kafas.
COOT (*black diver, water-fowl*), غواص ghavváz.
COPARTNERSHIP, انبازی ambází, مشارکت musharakat, شراکت shirákat.—(*in profits of stock and labour*) مضاربه muzárabat.
COPING, لبه labah.
COPIOUS, *vide* PLENTEOUS.
COPPER, مس mis, نحاس nahás, صفر sifr. — (*boiler*) *vide* CAULDRON, KETTLE.—(*adj.*) مسین misín.
COPPERAS, زاج záj, توتیا tútiyá.
COPPERSMITH, مسگر mis-gar, صفار saffár.
To COPULATE, جماع کردن jimá' kardan, مباشرت نمودن mubásharat nimúdan, اجتماع کردن ijtimá' kardan, پیوستن paivastan, گادن gádan, گائیدن gá,ídan, جمع شدن jam' shudan, مضاجعت کردن muzája'at kardan, مجامعت کردن mujáma'at kardan.—(*as animals*) جفتی کردن juftí kardan.
COPULATION, مضاجعت muzája'at, مجامعت mujáma'at, جماع jimá'. — (*animals*) جفتی juftí.
COPULATIVE, وصلی vaslí.
COPY, نقل nakl, نسخه nuskhah.— (*rough copy*) سواد savád, مسوده musavvadah.—(*fair copy*) نسخه صاف nuskhah-i-sáf. — (*exercise to copy from*) مشق mashk.
To COPY (*imitate*), تقلید کردن taklíd kardan, نقل کردن nakl kardan.— (*a writing, &c.*) از رو نوشتن az rú

nivishtan, نقل بر داشتن nakl bar-dáshtan, نسخه کردن nuskhah kar-dan.
COPY-BOOK, مشق نامه mashk-námah.
COQUETRY, ناز náz, شیوه shívah, عشوه 'ishvah.
COQUETTE, عشقباز 'ishk-báz, شیوه باز shívah-báz, عشوهگر 'ishvah-gar.
To COQUETTE, عشوه کردن 'ishvah kardan, غمزه کردن ghamzah kar-dan.
CORAL, مرجان murján, بسد busadd, —(*child's coral*) لعبة lu'bah. بازیچه bázíchah.
CORD, ریسمان rísmán, رسن rasan. (*Vide* ROPE, STRING.) — (*silk cord*) قیطان kaitán.—(*maker of silk cord*) علاقه بند 'alákah-band, چرخ تاب charkh-táb.—(*umbilical cord*) خصم khasm, سره surrah.
CORDIAL, *vide* SINCERE, DRINK.
CORDIALLY, قلباً kalban.
CORDUROY, پتو pattú.
CORE, لب lubb.
CORIANDER, گشنیز gíshníz, کزبره kuz-burah.
CORK (*stopper*), سر شیشه sar-i-shíshah, بجلی bujlí.
CORKSCREW, پیچ pích, شیشه گوشا shíshah-gúshá.
CORMORANT, اکول ákúl. — (*bird*), اسفرود isfarúd, غواص ghavvás.
CORN (*grain*), غله ghallah, بذر bazr. —(*corn-chandler*) علاف 'alláf, غله فروش ghallah-furúsh.—(*bruised corn*) غله بلغور ghallah-i-bulghúr, پلکو palkú (*vulg.*). — (*parched corn*) غله برشته ghallah-i-burshtah. —(*ground corn*) *vide* MEAL, FLOUR.—(*on the foot*) پینه pínah, پنه pinah, سخت sakht (*obs.*).—(*corn-flower*) گل و دگمه gul-i-dug-mah.
CORNELIAN, عقیق 'akík.
CORNER, کنج kunj, گوشه gúshah, زاویه záviyah, پیغوله paighúlah, کش kash.
CORNICE, مقرنس mukarnas, شادروان shádurván.
CORONATION, جلوس julús.
CORONER, کشاف kashsháf.
CORPORATION, مجلس majlis, اصناف asnáf (*used only in plural*).
CORPOREAL, مجسم mujassam.
CORPS D'ARMÉE, قشون kushún, لشکر lashkar.
CORPS LEGISLATIF, مجلس شورای majlis-i-shúráí.
CORPSE, *vide* BODY, CARCASS.
CORPULENCE, جسوم jusúm, جسیم jasím, فربهی farbihí, قطور kutúr.
CORPULENT, فربه farbih, قطور katúr, قمطره kumatrah, بجباج bajbáj.
CORRECT, درست durust, راست rást, صحیح sahíh, کامل kámil, متین matín, بی غلط bí-ghalat.
To CORRECT, تصحیح کردن tas-hih kardan, تصلیح کردن taslíh kardan. —(*reprove*) عذاب نمودن 'azáb ni-múdan, تأدیب نمودن ta,dίb nimú-dan.
CORRECTION, اصلاح islah, تصحیح tas-hih. (*Vide* REBUKE.)
CORRESPONDENCE, مکاتبت muká-tabat, مراسلت murásalat.
CORRESPONDENT, محرر muharrir, اخبار نویس akhbár-nivís.
CORRESPONDING to, مطابق mutábik.
CORRIDOR, دالان dálán.
To CORROBORATE, تاکید نمودن tákíd nimúdan, تقویت دادن takviyat dádan.
CORROBORATING (*confirming or strengthening*), مؤید mu,ayyid, مقوی mukavví, معین mu'ayyan.
CORROBORATION, استحکام istihkám, تقویت takviyat, ثبوت subút, اثبات isbát.
CORRUPT, فاسد fásid, تباه tabáh, مختل mukhtall, خراب kharáb.— (*person*) رشوتخور rishvat-khwur.
To CORRUPT, افساد نمودن ifsád ni-múdan, خراب کردن kharáb kar-dan.
CORRUPTED (*language*), خرابه شده kharábah-shudah.
CORRUPTIBLE, فنا پذیر faná-pazír.
CORRUPTION, فساد fasád, افساد ifsád, تباهی tabáhí, عفونت 'ufú-nat.
CORTÉGE, موکب maukib.

COSMOGRAPHY, جهان نمای jahán-nimáí.

COST, مصرف masraf, خرج kharj, قیمت kaimat.

To COST, قیمت داشتن kaimat dáshtan, ارزیدن arzídan.

COSTIVE, منقبض munkabiz.

COSTIVENESS, انقباض inkibáz, قبض kabz.

COSTLY, vide DEAR, PRECIOUS.

COSTS (*law term*), مخارج makhárij.

COSTUME, vide CLOTHES.—(*in the costume of*) در زی dar zí.

COTTAGE, کلبه kulbah, سپنج sipanj. (*Vide* HUT.)

COTTON, پنبه pambah, قطن kutn.—(*plant*) درخت پنبه dirakht-i-pambah, درخت کتو dirakht-i-kitú (*vulg.*).—(*pod of cotton*) غوزه ghúzah, جوزق jauzak, کلوزه kulúzah. — (*cleaned cotton*) چله chillah, چله chullah.—(*dresser*) نداف naddáf, حلاج halláj, پنبه زن pambah-zan.—(*thread*) رشته پنبه rishtah-i-pambah.—(*calico*) چیت chít, قلمکار kalam-kár. — (*coarse stuff*) کرباس karbás, تفتی taftí.—(*cotton plantation*) پنبه زار pambah-zár, جوزق زار jauzak-zár, صحرائی کتو sahrá,í-i-kitú (*vulg.*). — (*cotton cloth*) پارچه پنبه párchah-i-pambah. — (*strong cotton stuff for coats, &c.*) قدك kadak. — (*white stuff for shirting*) چلواری chilvárí.

COUCH, مهاد mihád, سریر sarír, پلنگ palang (*hind.*).

COUGH, سعال su'ál, سرفه surfah.

To COUGH, خفیدن khafídan, سرفه کردن surfah kardan, سعال کردن su'ál kardan, تنحنح کردن tanahnuh kardan.

COUNCIL, مجلس majlis, دربار darbár, دیوان díván, محفل mahfil, شوری shúrá.—(*general council*) دربار عام darbár-i-'ámm, دیوان عام díván-i-'ámm.—(*privy council*) دیوان خاص díván-i-kháss. — (*member of council*) اهل دیوان ahl-i-díván.—(*room*) اطاق نشیمن uták-i-nishíman, دیوان خانه díván-khánah.

COUNCILLOR, *vide* MINISTER.—(*privy councillor*) اهل دیون ahl-i-díván.

COUNSEL, *vide* ADVICE. —(*to take counsel*) تدبیر نمودن tadbír nimúdan.

COUNSELLOR (*of State*), وزیر vazír, دبیر dabír, مدبر mudabbir, مشیر mushír, دستور dastur. (*Vide* MINISTER.)

COUNT, کنت kant (*eur.*).

To COUNT, شمردن shimurdan, حساب کردن hisáb kardan, تعداد نمودن ti'dád nimúdan.

COUNTENANCE, *vide* FACE.

COUNTER (*board*), تخته takhtah.

To COUNTERACT, مقابله کردن mukábalah kardan.

COUNTERACTION, مقابله mukábalah.

COUNTERFEIT (*fictitious*), جعلی ja'lí, ساختگی sákhtagí.—(*coin*) قلب kalb, قلابی kullábí, مغشوش maghshúsh.

COUNTERFEITER, قلاب kalláb.

COUNTER-JUMPER, اهل دکان ahl-i-dukán.

To COUNTERMAND, نسخ حکم کردن naskh-i-hukm kardan, خلاف امر کردن khiláf-i-amr kardan.

COUNTERPANE, لحاف liháf, رضائی razá,í.

COUNTERPART, نمونه nimúnah.

COUNTERPOISE (*equivalent weight*), مساوی musáví, موازنه muvázanah.

COUNTER-SCARP, دیوار dívár.

COUNTER-TENOR, بم bam.

COUNTESS, خانم khánam.

COUNTING-HOUSE, دفتر خانه daftar-khánah.

COUNTLESS, بیشمار bí-shimár.

COUNTRY (*region*), ملك mulk, ولایت valáyat, کشور kishvar, خطه khuttah, بلد balad, بلاد bilád, دیار diyár, اقلیم iklím, الکه ulkah, یورت yúrt, مرز و بوم marz u búm.—(*not town*) دهات dihát, اطراف atráf.

COUNTRYMAN, روستائی rústá,í.—(*fellow countryman*) هم وطنی ham-vataní, همشهری ham-shahrí.

COUNTRY-SEAT, یائلاق yá,ilák.

Coup d'œuil, منظر manzar.
Couple, دو تا dú-tá. (*Vide* Pair.)
Couples (*for hounds*), مروس miraus, مراس mirás, مرس maras.
Couplet (*verse*), بيت bait (*pl.* ابيات abyát).
Coupling, بند band.
Courage, مردانگی mardánagí, دليری dilírí, دلاوری dilávarí, همت himmat, جرات jur,at, شجاعت shujá'at, غيرت ghairat, جسارت jasárat, شهامت shahámat, حميت hamíyat, عصبيت 'asabíyat.
Courageous, *vide* Bold.
Courier (*footman*), قاصد kásid, شاطر shátir, پيك paik.—(*mounted*) چاپار chápár, چپر chapar.
Course (*progress, custom*), رفتار raftár, روش ravish, سيرت sírat, وجه vajh, رسم rasm.—(*of a river*) مجرا majrá. — (*of instruction*) صورت درس súrat-i-dars.—(*in the course of*) در بين dar bain, در ظرف dar zarf.
Courser, تازی tází.
Courses, *vide* Menses.
Court, درگاه dargáh, بارگاه bárgáh, دربار darbár, دولتخانه daulat-khánah, قصر kasr, عتبه 'atabah, آستان ásitán, سده suddah, ايوان aivan.—(*of justice*) محكمه mahkamah, خانه شرع khánah-i-shar'. —(*criminal court*) محكمه جرميه mahkamah-i-jarmiyah. — (*of audience*) ديوانخانه díván-khánah, دربار darbár, ديوان عام díván-i-'ámm.—(*yard*) صحن sahn, حياط hayát, ساحت sáhat, حظيره hazírah. —(*attendants of a prince*) حشم و خدم hashm va khadam, ملازمان mulázimán, توابع tavábi'. — (*to hold a court*) سلام نشستن salám nishastan.
Courteous (*polite*), خليق khalík, مؤدب mu,addab, خوش اطوار khwush-atvár, خوش اخلاق khwush-akhlák.
Courtesan, فاحشه fáhishah, قحبه kahbah, جافجاف jáfjáf, فاجره fájirah, لولی lúlí, كسبی kasbí, كاولی káwlí (*vulg.*), جنده jindah (*vulg.*).
Courtesy, مدارات mudárát.
Courtier, ملازم درگاه mulázim-i-dargáh, نديم nadím.
Cousin, عمو زاده 'ammú zádah, دختر عمو dukhtar-i-'ammú, ابن عمو ibn-i-'ammú, خالو زاده khálú-zádah, خالزاده khál-zádah, دختر عم dukhtar-i-'amm, ابن عم ibn-i-'amm, عم زاده 'amm-zádah.
Covenant, عهد 'ahd, عهده 'uhdah, پيمان paimán, قرار karár, قرار داد karár-dád, شرط shart.
Cover, پوشش púshish, پوش púsh, سر پوش sar-púsh, پوشه púshah.—(*envelope*) غلاف ghiláf, لفافه lifáfah.—(*of a book*) قوئلق kau,iluk, قولغ kaulugh.—(*boards*) مقوی mukavvá.
To Cover, پوشيدن púshídan, پوشانيدن púshánídan.
Coverlet, لحاف liháf, رضائی razá,í.
Covert (*subs.*), تكيه takyah.—(*adj.*) پوشيده púshídah.
To Covet, آرزو بردن árzú burdan, طمع ورزيدن tama' varzídan, طمعكار بودن tama'-kár búdan.
Covetous, طامع támi', طمعكار tama'-kár, آرزومند árzú-mand, حريص harís, لئيم la,ím, دانع dání', كنس kinis.
Covetousness, *vide* Avarice.
Covey (*of birds*), گله galah, خيل khail.
Cow, گاو gáv, گاو ماده gáv-i-má:lah, بقره bakarah.
Coward, نا مرد ná-mard, بز دل buz-díl, جبان jabbán, بيدل bí-dil, كمدل kam-dil, ترسو tarsú (*vulg.*).
Cowardice, نا مردی ná-mardí, بيدلی bí-dilí, جبن jubn.
Cowardly, بد دل bad-dil; كم زهره kam-zahrah.
Cowdung, سرگين sargín.—(*dried for fuel*), پاچلك páchak, تپاله tapálah, سازگار sáz-gár.
Cowherd, گاو چران gáv-charán.
Cow-house, جائی گاو já,í-i-gáv.
Cowl (*chimney*), باد گير bád-gír, دود كش dúd-kash.—(*head-piece*) كلاه كشيش kuláh-i-kashísh.
Coxcomb (*fop*), كشنگ kashang,

خودبين khwud-bín, اجلاف ijláf, خوشگل khwush-gil.

CRAB, خرچنگ khar-chang, کله چنگ kallah-chang, پنج پایک panj páyak, کرنجال karanjál, کلنجار kalanjár, سرطان saratán.

CRACK (*flaw*), شکاف shikáf, شق shakk, چاك chák, جرم jarm, ترك tarak, مو mú, درز darz.

To CRACK, شکافتن shikáftan, شق شدن shakk shudan, تراکیدن tarákídan, چاك شدن chák shudan, مو داشتن mú dáshtan.—(*the joints, by pulling the limbs*) اعضا شکستن a'zá shikastan.—(*as the ground from the heat of the sun, or to become chapped as the skin*), تفسیدن tafsídan. — (*a nut*) شکستن shikastan. — (*as a whip, &c.*) تراك کردن tarák kardan.

CRACKED, مودار mú-dár, شق شده shakk-shudah, ترکیده tarkídah.—(*to be cracked or light witted*) خبط دماغ داشتن khabt-i-dimágh dáshtan.

CRACKER (*firework*), طرقه tarakkah.

To CRACKLE, صدا کردن sadá kardan.

CRADLE, گهواره gahvárah, مهد mahd.

CRAFT, *vide* ART, ARTIFICE.

CRAFTY, مکار makkár, حیله ور hílah-var, حیله باز hílah-báz, نا پاك ná-pák.

CRAGGY (*uneven, as a hill-top, &c.*) دندانه dandánah.

To CRAM, انباشتن ampáshtan, آکندن ákandan, طپانیدن tapánídan, چپانیدن chapánídan.

CRAMP, پیچش píchish, تشنج tashannuj.—(*we were cramped*), جا تنگ بود já tang búd.

CRANE (*bird*), کلنگ kulang.—(*for raising weights*) منجنیق manjaník.

CRANNY, خلل khalal, منفذ manfaz, فرج farj, کنج kunj.

CRAPE, پارچه سیاه párchah-i-siyáh.

CRAVAT, گردنبند gardan-band.

To CRAVE, *vide* To BEG, To HANKER.

CRAVEN (*cowardly*), نا مرد ná-mard, بیدل bí-dil, ترسو tarsú, کمدل kam-dil.

CRAVING, اشتها ishtihá, آرزو árzú, خواهش khwáhish.

CRAWFISH, *vide* CRAB.

To CRAWL (*reptiles*), خزیدن khazídan.—(*men*) غژیدن ghazhídan.

CRAYON, قلم kalam.

CREAM, سر شیر sar-i-shír.—(*thickened or clouted*) قیماق kaimák, چربه charbah.—(*the best part of anything*) سلاله sulálah, خلاصه khulásah, زبده zubdah.

CREASE, تا tá, چین chín.

To CREASE, تا نمودن tá nimúdan, چین نمودن chín nimúdan.

To CREATE, آفریدن áfirídan, خلق کردن khalk kardan, پیدا کردن paidá kardan.

CREATION, تکوین takvín, آفرینش áfirínish, خلقت khilkat.—(*lord of creation*) اشرف مخلوقات ashraf-i-makhlúkát.

CREATOR, خالق khálik, خلاق khallák, آفریننده áfirínandah, آفریدگار áfirídagár, صانع sáni', مکون mukavvin.—(*Creator of the world*) جهان آفرین jahán-áfirín, خالق المخلوقات kháliku-'l-makhlúkát.

CREATURE, مخلوق makhlúk, مخلوقه makhlúkah, خلیقه khalíkah, کائنات ká,inat, آفریده áfirídah, موجود maujúd, بریه bariyah. — (*living creatures*), جنبندگان ذی حیات jumbandagán-i-zí-hayát.

CREDENTIALS, اختیار نامه ikhtiyár-námah, اعتماد نامه i'timád-námah.

CREDIBLE, واجب الاعتقاد vájibu-'l-i'tikád, قابل اعتبار kábil-i-i'tibár.

CREDIT, *vide* DIGNITY, TRUST, FAITH.—(*money*) نسئه nis,ah.

CREDITABLE, معتبر mu'tabar.

CREDITOR, طلبکار talab-kár, قرض خواه karz-khwáh, مداین mudáyin, بستان کار bisitán-kár (*vulg.*).

CREED, *vide* RELIGION.

CREEK (*small bay*), کنج دریا kunj-i-daryá. — (*back-water*) مرداب murd-áb.

To CREEP, *vide* To CRAWL.

CREEPER (*plant*), بنه bunah, بنلک bunak, بوته لمس bútah-i-lams.

CREPUSCLE (*red gleam before sunrise and after sunset*), شفق shafak (*pl.* اشفاق ashfák).

CRESCENT (*half-moon*), هلال hilál, ماه نو máh-i-nau.

CRESSES, تر تیزک tar-tízak.

CREST, زروه zirvah.—(*heraldic*) نشان nishán.

CRESTED (*bird*), تاج دار táj-dár.

CREVICE, *vide* CRANNY.

CREW, *vide* CROWD.—(*of ship*) عمله 'amalah.

CRICKET (*insect*), چرغد charghad, خزوک khazúk, سوسک súsk.

CRIER, جار چی jár-chí, منادی munádí.—(*to prayers*) موذن mu,azzin.

CRIME, گناه gunáh, گنه gunah, تقصیر taksír, قصور kusúr, جریمه jarímah, جرم jurm, جنایت janáyat, خطا khatá, اثم ism, ذنب zamb, عیب 'aib.

CRIMINAL, گناه کار gunáh-kár, خطا کار khatá-kár, مذنب muznib, اثیم asím, مفسد mufsid, فاسق fásik, روسیاه rú-siyah. (*Vide* CULPRIT.)

CRIMSON, لاکی lákí, قانی kání, قرمزی kirmizí.

CRIPPLE, شل shal. (*crippled by maiming*) چولاق chúlák, سقط sakat.

To CRIPPLE, ضعیف کردن za'íf kardan.

CRISIS, معرکه ma'rakah, هنگامه hangámah. — (*of a disease*), بحران buhrán.

CRITIC, نکته چین nuktah-chín, دقیقه شناس dakíkah-shinás.

CRITICISM, نکته چینی nuktah-chíní.

To CRITICIZE, نکته چینی کردن nuktah-chíní kardan.

CROCODILE, نهنگ nahang, تمساح timsáh.

CROCUS, زعفران za'farán.

CRONE, *vide* HAG.

CROOKED, خم kham, خمیده khamídah, کج kaj, کژ kazh, منحنی munhaní, معوج mu'avvaj, اعوج a'vaj, مائل má,il, گوژ gauzh (*vulg.*), چول chaul (*vulg.*), چوله chaulah (*vulg.*).

CROOKEDNESS, عوج 'avaj, خمیدگی khamídagí.

CROP (*of a field*), محصول mahsúl, حاصل hásil, پیدایش paidáyish, حصاد hasád.—(*of a bird*), حوصله hausalah, چینه دان chínah-dán.—(*reaped crop*) محصول درویده mahsúl-i-darvídah. —(*standing crop*) محصول نادرویده mahsúl-i-ná-darvídah.—(*crop sown and grown up*) کشت kisht.—(*estimate of growing crop*) بازدید حاصل bazdíd-i-hásil.

CROSS, چلیپا chalípá, صلیب salíb. (*Vide* ANGRY.)

To CROSS, عبور کردن 'ubúr kardan, از روی گذشتن az rúí guzashtan.

CROSSWAY (*place where four roads meet*), دهنه چهار راه dahanah-i-chahár-ráh, چار سو char-sú.

CROUP (*complaint in children*), خروسک khurúsak.

CROW, کلاغ kalágh.—(*grey-throated crow, like a jackdaw*) زاغ zágh.—(*iron lever*) دیلم dílum, اهرم ahrum.—(*of a cock*) بانگ خروس báng-i-khurús.

To CROW, بانگ زدن báng zadan.

CROWD, جماعت jamá'at, جمع jam', انبوه ambúh, هنگامه hangámah, گروه gurúh, غلبه ghalabah, ملاء mala,, بوش búsh, ازدحام izdihám, هجوم hujúm.—(*in crowds*) بازدحام bi-izdihám, گروه گروه gurúh gurúh.

CROWDED (*filled full*), پر pur, جنجال janjál (*vulg.*). — (*thick, close*) متصل muttasil. — (*suffocating*), خفه khafah.

CROWN, تاج táj, افسر afsar, اکلیل iklíl, اورند aurand.—(*of the head*) فرق fark, ناصیه násiyah.

To CROWN, تاج گذاری کردن táj-guzárí kardan.

CROWNED, بافسر bi-afsar, تاج دار táj-dár.

CRUCIBLE, بوته bútah.

CRUCIFIX, *vide* CROSS.

CRUCIFIXION, بصلیب زدن bi-salíb zadan.

To CRUCIFY, مصلوب ساختن maslúb sákhtan, تصلیب نمودن taslíb nimúdan, نمودن صلب salb nimúdan, صلیب کردن salíb kardan.

Crude, ناهنجار ná-hanjár, خام khám.

Cruel, جفا کار jafá-kár, بیرحم bí-ruhm, درشت durusht, سنگدل sang-dil, ظالم zálim, بیمروت bí-murúvat, جبار jabbár, ستمکار sitam-kár.

Cruelty, ظلم zulm, ستم sitam, سنگدلی sang-dilí, خشونت khushú-nat.

Cruet, کوزه kúzáh.

Crumb, ریزه rízah, خرده khurdah, قراضه kurázah. — (*soft part of bread*) خمیر khamír.

Crumpet, فطرا fatrá.

To Crumple, پیچ و چین پیدا کردن pích va chín paidá kardan.

Crupper (*of a saddle*), دنبالهٔ زین dumbálah-i-zín, قشقون kushkún.

Crusader, صلیبی salíbí, صلیب پرست salíb-parast.

Cruse, کوزه kúzah.

To Crush, خورد ساختن khwurd sákh-tan, نرم ساختن narm sákhtan, فشردن fishurdan, پخش کردن pakhsh kardan, سحق نمودن sahk nimú-dan. — (*to beat soft*) له کردن lih kardan. — (*to crush against a wall, &c.*) چسبانیدن chasbánídan.

Crushed, له lih, خورد khwurd, پخش pakhsh.

Crust, پوست púst.

Cry (*shout or exclamation*), بانگ báng, غریو gharív, نعره na'rah, فریاد faryád, آواز áváz.—(*of joy*) کل kill, هو hau, هبابک habábak, تهلیل tahlíl.

To Cry (*aloud*), بانگ زدن báng zadan, شماته کردن shamátah kar-dan, آواز دادن áváz dádan, صراخ زدن surákh zadan, غوغا کردن ghau-ghá kardan, صیحه زدن saihah zadan, نعره بر آوردن na'rah bar ávardan, فریاد بر آوردن faryád bar ávardan.—(*proclaim*) جار کشیدن jár kashídan, ندا کردن nidá kar-dan, اشتهار دادن ishtihár dádan. —(*weep*) گریستن girístan, گریه کردن giryah kardan.

Crypt, غار ghár, مغاره mughárah.

Crystal, بلور bulúr.—(*small crystallized body*) قلم kalam.

To Crystallize, قلم کردن kalam kardan.

Crystallized, منجمد munjamid.

Cub, بچه bachah.

Cube, کعب ka'b.

Cubebs, کبابه kabábah, کبابه چینی kabábah-i-chíní.

Cubic, مکعب muka''ab, کعبی ka'bí.

Cubit, ذرع zara', ذراع zirá', ارج araj, دست dast.

Cuckold, کلتبان kaltabán, دیوث dayyús, قرمساق kurmsák, زن بمزد zan-bi-muzd, کس ده زن kus-dih-i-zan.

Cuckoo, کوکو kúkú.

Cucumber, خیار khiyár, بالنگ bá-lang.

Cud (*of ruminating animals*), نشخوار nush-khwár, نوشخوار núsh-khwár.

Cuddy (*of a ship*), دبوس dabús, کده kadah.

Cudgel, *vide* Staff, Club.

Cue, اشاره ishárah.

Cuff, سر آستین sar-ástín.

Cuirasse, جوشن jaushan, زره zirah, چهار آینه chahár áyinah.

To Cull, چیدن chídan.

Culpability, تقصیر taksír.

Culpable, *vide* Blamable.

Culprit, گناه کار gunáh-kár, مجرم mujrim, اثم asim.

To Cultivate (*land, &c.*), زرع نمودن zar' nimúdan. — (*plants, &c.*) تربیت دادن tarbiyat dádan.

Cultivated (*as a country, district, &c.*), آباد ábád, دایر dáir, معمور ma'múr.

Cultivation, زراعت zirá'at, کشتکاری kisht-kárí, فلاحت faláhat.

Cultivator, زارع zári', فلاح falláh, بذرگر bazr-gar, کشتکار kisht-kár.

Cultivators (*peasantry*), حضرات زارع hazarát-i-zári', زارعین zári'ín, رعایا ri'áyá.

Culture, عمرانیت 'umráníyat, تربیت tarbiyat, ادب adab.

Cumin, زیره zírah.

Cunning, *vide* Crafty.

CUP, پیاله piyálah, جام jám, قدح kadah, ساغر sághir, کاسه kásah, پیمانه paimánah.—(*for tea, coffee, &c.*) فنجان finján.—(*large teacup*) کاسه kásah.

To CUP (*bleed*), حجامت کردن hajámat kardan.

CUP-BEARER, ساقی sákí.

CUPBOARD, تاکچه tákchah.

CUPIDITY, *vide* AVARICE.

CUPOLA, گنبد gumbad.

CUPPING-GLASS, محجم mihjam, شاخ حجام shákh-i-hajjám.

CURABLE, اصلاح پذیر isláh-pazír, قابل معالجه kábil-i-mu'álajah, ممکن الشفا mumkinu-'sh-shifá.

CURATOR, کافل káfil.

CURB, لگام ligám, لجام lijám, جلو jilau.

To CURDLE, منجمد شدن munjamid shudan, بستن bastan, افسردن afsurdan, سفت شدن sift shudan, دلمه شدن dalamah shudan.

CURDS, ماست mást, ماس más (*vulg.*).—(*dried and salted*) کشک kashk, قروت kurút.

CURE, شفا shifá, علاج 'iláj, معالجه mu'álajah, دارو dárú, چاره chárah, دوا davá.

To CURE, علاج نمودن 'iláj nimúdan, معالجه کردن mu'álajah kardan, شفا دادن shifá dádan, التئام نمودن ilti,ám nimúdan. — (*be cured*) التئام پذیرفتن ilti,ám pazíruftan, به شدن bih shudan, شفا یافتن shifá yáftan. — (*to salt*) نمک مالیدن namak málídan.

CURIOSITIES, تفاریق tafárik, نوادر navádir, نفیسات nafísát, امتعهٔ نفیسه amti'a-i-nafísah.

CURIOSITY, تفحص tafahhus, رازجوئی ráz-jú,í, استقصا istiksá.

CURIOUS (*inquisitive*), راز جو ráz-jú, مستفسر mustafsir, مستقصی mustaksí, سر جو sirr-jú, مفتش mufattish.—(*singular*) نادر nádir, غریب gharíb, عجب 'ajab, عجیب 'ajíb, بدیع badí'.

CURL (*of hair*), گیسو gísú, حلقه halkah, جعد ja'd. (*Vide* LOCK.)

To CURL, پیچیدن píchídan, پیچ دادن pích dádan, تاب دادن táb dádan.

CURLEW (*bird*), تلیله tallailah.

CURLING-PAPER, طره turrah.

CURRANTS, کشمش kishmish. [This word strictly means "*Sultana raisins.*"]

CURRENT, جاری jári, رائج rá,ij, مروج muravvaj, مستمری mustamarrí, روان raván, سره sarah.—(*stream*) سیل sail, جوی júí. — (*as money*) رائج rá,ij, جاری járí.

CURRIER, پوست پیرا púst-pírá, دباغ dabbágh.

CURRY (*the dish*), سالیانه sáliyánah (*hind.*), سالیان sáliyán (*hind.*).

To CURRY (*leather*), دبغ کردن dabgh kardan.—(*a horse*) تیمار کردن tímár kardan.

CURRY-COMB, قشو kashau, قشاوه kashávah.

CURSE, لعنت la'nat, نفرین nafrín, سب sabb.

To CURSE, لعنت نمودن la'nat nimúdan, لعن کردن la'n kardan, نفرین کردن nafrín kardan.

CURSED, ملعون mal'ún, لعین la'ín.

CURSORILY, عجالتاً 'ijálatan.

To CURTAIL, قصر نمودن kasr nimúdan.

CURTAIN, پرده pardah, حجاب hijáb, ستره sutrah, تجیر tijír, سردقه sardakah. — (*surrounding a tent*) سراپرده sarápardah, سرادق sarádak.

CURVATURE, عوج 'ivaj, اعوجاج i'vijáj.

CURVE, پیچش píchish, پیچ pích.

CURVED, کج kaj.

CUSHION, بالش bálish, تکیه takyah. متکا muttaká, بالین bálín.

CUSTODY, امانت amánat, حواله haválah, حراست hirásat, سپرد supurd. (*legal term*) حبس habs, قید kaid, دوساخ نظر dúsákh-nazar.

CUSTOM, رسم rasm, روش ravish, عادت 'ádat, شیوه shívah, طریق tarík, سلوک sulúk, وتیره vatírah, دستور dastúr, رواج raváj, قاعده ká'idah, آیین áyín, وضع vaz', خوی khúí, قانون kánún, ضابطه zábitah, پیشه píshah, داب dáb. — (*tax*) خراج khiráj, گمرک gumruk, باج báj,

محصول mahsúl. — (*custom-house*) گمرکخانه gumruk-khánah, باجگاه báj-gáh. — (*collector of customs*) گمرکچی gumruk-chí, باجگیر báj-gír. — (*fee to shop-boys, given by customers*) شاگردانگی shágirdá-nagí.

Customary, *vide* Usual.

Customer, مشتری mushtarí.

Cut, مجزوم majzúm.—(*as a jewel*) تراشیده tiráshídah.—(*in facets*) پخدار pakh-dár.—(*convex*), گل gul. —(*table-cut*) مسطح musattah, تخته takhtah.—(*sub.*) سوراخ súrákh.—(*of a coat*) برش burish.

To Cut, بریدن burídan, *or* burrí-dan, قطع کردن kat' kardan, تراشیدن tiráshídan. (*Vide* To Clip, To Pare).—(*to cut in two*) دو پاره کردن dú-párah kardan, قیچی کردن kaichí kardan, دو نیم کردن dú-ním kardan.—(*to cut short, abridge*) اختصار نمودن ikhtisár nimúdan.

Cute, *vide* Clever.

Cutlas, *vide* Sword.

Cutler, صیقلگر saikal-gar, سیاف sayyáf.

Cutter (*vessel*), جهاز یك دقلی jaház-i-yak-dakalí.

Cutting, *vide* Sharp, Chip.

Cycle (*period of time*), دور daur, دوره daurah.

Cylinder, اسطوانه ustuvánah, قلم kalam.

Cymbals, سنج sanj.

Cypher (*figure or number*), عدد 'adad, هندسه hindisah.—(*ought*) صفر sifr.

Cypress, سرو sarv, آزاد درخت ázád-dirakht.

D.

Daft, مجنون majnún.

Dagger (*straight, single-edged*), کارد kárd, سکین sikkín.—(*curved, double-edged*) خنجر khanjar, جنبیه jambiyah, دشنه dishnah.—(*large, or cutlass*), قمه kamah.—(*small, or poniard*), گزلك gazlak.

Dahlia (*flower*), گل کوکب gul-i-kaukab.

Daily, روزینه rúzínah, روزانه rúzánah, یومیه yaumíyah, هر روزه har rúzah, یوماً فیوماً yauman fi-yauman.—(*every day*) هر روز har rúz, روز بروز rúz bi-rúz, یوماً فیوماً yauman fi-yauman.

Dairy, شیرخانه shír-khánah.

Dais, شاه نشینی sháh-nishíní.

Daisy, بابونهٔ صحرائی bábúnah-i-sah-rá,í, گل داودی gul-i-dáúdí, هزار دانه hazár-dánah.

Dale, دره darrah.

Dalliance, ناز náz, نوازش navázish, عشقبازی 'ishk-bází.

Dam, *vide* Bank, Mother.

To Dam, وصله کردن vaslah kardan, بند کردن band kardan, مسدود کردن masdúd kardan.

Damage, زیان ziyán, آسیب ásíb, نقص naks, نقصان nuksán, گزند gazand, ضرر zarar, خلل khalal, خسارت khasárat.

To Damage, ضرر رسانیدن zarar rasání-dan.

Damaged, *vide* Spoilt.

Damasked (*silk*), مشجر mushajjar. —(*steel*) جوهر دار jauhar-dár, آبدار áb-dár.

Dame, خانم khánam, بی بی bíbí.

Damnation, عقوبت دوزخ 'ukúbat-i-dúzakh, عذاب جهنم 'azáb-i-jahan-nam.

Damned, دوزخ مآب dúzakh-ma,áb, اهل دوزخ ahl-i-dúzakh.

Damp, تر tar, نم nam, نمدار nam-dár, نمناك nam-nák. — (*subst.*) رطوبت rutúbat, نمی namí.

Damsel, دختر dukhtar, کنیز kaníz.

Damson, آلوچه álúchah.

Dance, رقص raks.—(*national dance*) رقص ملتی raks-i-millatí.—(*of der-*

vishes and religious fanatics) هروله harvalah.

To DANCE, رقص کردن raks kardan, رقصیدن raksídan, جست و خیز کردن jast u khíz kardan.

DANCER, رقاص rakkás, رقصنده rak-sandah, بازیگر bází-gar.

DANCING, رقص raks.—(*tight-rope dancing*) بند بازی band-bází.

DANDELION (*plant*), کله چماقی kal-lah chumákí, گل قاصدی gul-i-kásidí, هندبائی دشتی hindabá,i-i-dashtí.

To DANDLE, جنبانیدن jumbánídan, بچه نوازی کردن bachah-navází kar-dan.

DANDY, *vide* FOP.

DANGER, خطر khatar, خطره khatrah, مخاطره mukhátarah, بیم bím, خدشه khadashah, تشویش tashvísh, باك bák, تنگنائی tangná,í.—(*in danger of*) در بیم dar bím.

DANGEROUS, خطرناك khatar-nák, هولناك haulnák, مهلك muhlik.

DANGLING, معلق mu'allak.

DAPPLED, ابرش abrash, لکه دار lak-kah-dár, خالدار khál-dár.

To DARE, همت داشتن himmat dáshtan, جرأت داشتن jur,at dáshtan, دلیری نمودن dilírí nimú-dan.

DARING, *vide* BOLD.

DARK, تاریك tárík, تیره tírah, مظلم muzlim.—(*as a colour*), سیر sír, تیره tírah.—(*complexion*) سبز sabz.

To DARKEN, تیره کردن tírah kardan.

DARKNESS, تاریکی tárikí, تیرگی tíragí, تار tár, ظلمت zulmat, ظلام zalám, داج dáj.

DARLING, محبوب mahbúb, جانی jání, جانان jánán, عزیز 'azíz.

To DARN, *vide* To SEW.

DART, نیزه naizah, تیر tír.—(*blunt dart used in exercise*) جرید jaríd.

To DASH (*against*), بهم زدن bi-ham zadan, صدمه خوردن sadmah khwur-dan, تصادم نمودن tasádum nimú-dan. (*Vide* To FLING DOWN, To BREAK IN PIECES.)

DASHING, *vide* SMART.

DASTARD, *vide* COWARD.

DATE (*time*), تاریخ táríkh.—(*out of date*) متروك matrúk. — (*fruit*) خرما khurmá, تمر tamr.—(*green dates*) خلال khilál.—(*a little riper, but green*) بسر busr. — (*unripe dried dates*) خارك khárak.—(*ripe, but fresh*) رطب rutab.—(*date-stick, stem of leaf*) جرید jaríd, پوش púsh.—(*cluster of dates*) خوشه khúshah, پنگ pang. — (*each strand or portion of the cluster*) رساله risálah, تلنگه tilingah.—(*tree*) مخ mukh, درخت خرما dirakht-i-khurmá, نخل nakhl. — (*date-grove*) نخلستان nakhlistán.— (*fibre or coir of the date*) لیف líf, ریشه ríshah.—(*leaves of the date dried for thatch, &c.*) تاپول tápúl.

To DATE, تاریخ گذاشتن táríkh guzásh-tan.

DATED, مؤرخ mu,arrakh.

DATIVE (*case*), مفعول فیه maf'úl fíhi.

To DAUB, اندودن andúdan, مالیدن málídan, پالودن pálúdan, آلودن álúdan.

DAUGHTER, دختر dukhtar, بنت bint (*pl.* بنات banát).—(*in-law*) زن فرزند zan-i-farzand, عروس 'arús.

To DAWDLE, تأخیر کردن ta,khír kar-dan, مکث نمودن maks nimúdan, پا بپا کردن pá bi-pá kardan.

DAWN, *vide* MORNING.

DAY, روز rúz, یوم yaum (*pl.* ایام ayyám). — (*twenty-four hours*) شبانه روز shabánah-rúz.—(*opposed to night*) روز rúz, نهار nahár.—(*from day to day*) روز بروز rúz bi-rúz. —(*nowadays*), الان al,án, در ین وقت dar ín vakt.

DAY-BOOK, روز نامه rúz-námah, روز نامچه rúz-námchah.

DAY-BREAK, *vide* MORNING.

To DAZZLE, چشم خیره کردن chashm-khírah kardan.—(*to be dazzled*) چشم خیره شدن chashm-khírah shu-dan.

DEACON (*of a church*), شماس sham-más.

DEAD, مرده murdah, بی جان bí-ján,

متوفی mutavaffí, میت mayyit, فوت شده faut-shudah.—(*middle*) وسط vasat. — (*the dead*) آسودگان ásúdagán, مردگان murdagán, گذشتگان guzashtagán.

DEADLY (*fatal*), هلاهل haláhal, قاتل kátil, مهلك muhlik, مقاتل mukátil.

DEAF, کر kar, نا شنوا ná-shinavá, اصم asamm.—(*to be deaf*) گوش سنگین شدن gúsh-sangín shudan.

DEAL (*fir-wood*), چوب صنوبر chúb-i-sinaubar.

DEALER, تاجر tájir.—(*in composition*) فروش furúsh.

DEALING, *vide* AFFAIR, COMMERCE, BARGAIN, INTERCOURSE.

DEAR, گران girán, گرانمایه girán-máyah, گرانبها girán-bahá, ارجمند arjmand, غالی ghálí, قیمتی kaimatí.—(*beloved*) عزیز 'azíz, محبوب mahbúb, محبوبه mahbúbah, جانی jání.

DEARNESS, گرانی girání.

DEARTH, *vide* SCARCITY.

DEATH, مرگ marg, موت maut, ممات mamát, فوت faut, وفات vafát, قضا kazá, سام sám, اجل ajal, ارتحال irtihál.—(*natural death*) اجل ajal. —(*sudden death*) موت مفاجات maut-i-mufáját, ذاف záf, موت فجاءت maut-i-faj,at. — (*pains of death*) *vide* AGONY.

To DEBAR, محروم ساختن mahrúm sákhtan.

DEBATE, *vide* ALTERCATION, DISPUTE.

DEBAUCHED, بد زندگانی bad-zindagání.

DEBAUCHEE, رند rind, خوشگذران khwush-guzrán, قلاش kallásh, عیاش 'ayyásh, شید باز shaid-báz.

DEBAUCHERY, رندی rindí, خوش گذرانی khwush-guzrání, قلاشی kallàshí, عیاشی 'ayyáshí, هوسناکی havas-nákí.

DEBILITATED, ضعیف za'íf, نحیف nahíf, ناتوان ná-taván.

DEBILITY, *vide* WEAKNESS.

DEBT, قرض karz, بده bidih, وام vám, دین dain.—(*to be in debt*) مقروض شدن makrúz shudan, مدیون هستن madyún hastan. — (*to pay one's debts*) وام گذاریدن vám guzárídan, ادا نمودن adá nimúdan, مفروغ کردن mafrúgh kardan.

DEBTOR, بده کار bidih-kár, قرضدار karz-dár, مقروض makrúz, وام دار vám-dár, دیندار dain-dár, دائن dáín, متدین mutadayyin.

DECADENCE, زوال zavál.

DECAGON, معشر mu'ashshar.

DECANTER (*of glass*), تنگ tung.—(*square decanter*) چارپر chárpar.

To DECAPITATE, گردن زدن gardan zadan, سر بریدن sar burídan.

DECAPITATION, گردن زدن gardan-zadan, سر بریدن sar burídan.

DECAY, فنا fanà, زوال zavál.

To DECAY, کاستن kástan, کاهیدن káhídan, فرسودن farsúdan, زائل شدن zá,il shudan, ضایع شدن záí' shudan, سائیدن sá,ídan, کم شدن kam shudan, زوال کردن zavál kardan.

DECEASE, *vide* DEATH.

DECEIT, فریب firíb, ساخته sákhtah, گول gúl, مکر makr, حیله hílah, حیله بازی hílah-bází, بهانه bahánah, غدر ghadr, غبن ghaban, رنگ rang, کید kaid, روبه بازی rúbah - bází, خدعت khud'at, ریا riyá, دغا daghá, تلبیس talbís, غل ghill, دمدمه damdamah, غش ghishsh, دو رنگی dú-rangí, تقلب takallub.

DECEITFUL, *vide* TREACHEROUS.

To DECEIVE, فریفتن firiftan. (*Vide* To DEFRAUD, To WHEEDLE.)—(*to be deceived*) گول خوردن gúl khwurdan, فریب خوردن firíb khwurdan.

DECEIVER, فریبنده firíbandah.

DECENT, *vide* RESPECTABLE.

To DECIDE (*determine*), مصمم گردیدن musammam gardídan. — (*settle*) قرار دادن karár dádan, مقرر داشتن mukarrar dáshtan.

DECIDEDLY, آری árí. — (*firmly*) بسختی تمام bi-sakhtí-i-tamám.

DECIMAL, اعشار a'shár.

To DECIMATE, تعشیر نمودن ta'shír nimúdan.

DECISION, *vide* DECREE, DETERMINATION, RESOLUTION.
DECISIVE, قطعی kat'í, قاطع káti'.
DECK (*of a ship*), عرشه 'arshah.
To DECK, *vide* To ADORN.
To DECLAIM, انشاد نمودن inshád nimúdan.
DECLAMATION, انشاد inshád.
DECLARATION, اشتهار ishtihár, ایضاح ízáh, اعلان i'lán, اعلام i'lám.
To DECLARE, اعلان نمودن i'lán nimúdan, معلوم نمودن ma'lúm nimúdan, عرض کردن 'arz kardan.
DECLENSION, زوال zavál.—(*in grammar*), تصریف tasríf, تحویل tahvíl.
DECLINATION, انحراف inhiráf.
To DECLINE, *vide* To DECAY, To REFUSE.
DECLIVITY, نشیب nishíb, شیب shíb, پرت part.
DECOCTION, جوشانده júshándah.
DECOMPOSITION, انحلال inhilál, تعفن ta'affun, پوسیدگی púsídagí.
To DECORATE, آراستن árástan, پیراستن pírástan, زینت دادن zínat dádan, تزیین نمودن tazyín nimúdan, طرازیدن tirázídan, مزین ساختن muzayyan sákhtan.
DECORATION, *vide* ADORNMENT.—(*of honour*) نشان nishán.
DECORATOR, آراینده áráyindah, پیراینده piráyindah, مزین muzayyin.
DECOY, پرمشته parmushtáh. —(*decoy-bird*) مرغ دام murgh-i-dám.
To DECOY, *vide* To ALLURE.
DECREASE (*in quality*), نقص naks.—(*in quantity*) نقصان nuksán.
To DECREASE, *vide* To DIMINISH, To LESSEN.
DECREE, حکم hukm, فیصل faisal, انفصال infisál, قضا kazá, فتوی fatvá, امر amr, سجل sijil, حجت hujjat, سنور sunúr.
To DECREE, امر نمودن amr nimúdan, فتوی دادن fatvá dádan, حکم نمودن hukm nimúdan.
DECREPIT, فرتوت fartút, ضعیف za'íf.
DECREPITUDE, فرتوتی fartútí, ضعف za'f.

To DECYPHER, تاویل نمودن ta,víl nimúdan.
To DEDICATE (*consecrate*), تبرک نمودن tabarruk nimúdan, مقدس ساختن mukaddas sákhtan, تخصیص نمودن takhsís nimúdan, اختصاص کردن ikhtisás kardan, منزه کردن munazzah kardan.
To DEDUCE, تفریع نمودن tafrí' nimúdan.
To DEDUCT, منها کردن minhá kardan, کم کردن kam kardan.
DEDUCTION, استدلال istidlál. (*Vide* SUBTRACTION.)
DEED, کار kár, کردار kirdár, عمل 'amal, فعل fi'l, صنع san'.—(*written*) دستاویز dast-áviz, حجت hujjat.—(*of gift*) هبه نامه hibah-námah.—(*of sale*) قباله kabálah, بیعنامه bai'-námah, قباله نامچه kabálah-námchah.
To DEEM, دانستن dánistan, انگاشتن angáshtan.
DEEP, عمیق 'amík, ژرف zharf, قول kaul.—(*the deep, sea*) لجه lujjah.
DEER, گوزن gavazn.—(*antelope*) آهو áhú, غزال ghazál.
To DEFACE, محو کردن mahv kardan, سترون suturdan, پاك کردن pák kardan, ضایع کردن zái' kardan.
DEFAMATION, هتك عرض hatk-i-'irz, افترا iftirá.
To DEFAME, هتك عرض کردن hatk-i-'irz kardan.
DEFAULT (*failure*), نقص naks, قلت killat, عدم 'adam, قصور kusúr.
DEFEAT, شکست shikast, هزیمت hazímat.
To DEFEAT, هزیمت دادن hazímat dádan, شکست دادن shikast dádan. —(*to be defeated*) شکست خوردن shikast khwurdan.
DEFECT, *vide* FAULT, BLEMISH.
DEFECTIVE, نا تمام ná-tamám, ناقص nákis, مقصر mukassar.
DEFENCE, حفاظت hifázat, حفظ hifz, پناه panáh.
To DEFEND, حمایت دادن himáyat dádan, حفاظت نمودن hifázat nimúdan, صیانت کردن siyánat kardan, محارست نمودن muhárasat

nimúdan. — (*excuse*) معذور کردن ma'zúr kardan, اعتذار نمودن i'tizár nimúdan.

DEFENDANT (*at law*), مدعی الیه mudda'á ilaihi.

DEFENDER, حامی hámí, حافظ háfiz, دستگیر dast-gír.—(*of the faith*) غازی ghází.

DEFENSIVE, تدافع tadáfu', دفاع difá'.

To DEFER, *vide* To DELAY.

DEFERENCE, اعتبار i'tibár, تواضع tavázu', احترام ihtirám.

DEFERRED, موءجل mu,ajjal, معوق mu'avvak, در تعویق افتاده dar ta'vík uftádah, تاءخیر کرده شده ta,khír-kardah shudah.—(*to be deferred*) بتاءخیر افتادن bi-ta'khír uftádan.

DEFICIENCY, تقصیر taksír. (*Vide* DECREASE.)

DEFICIENT, کم kam, قاصر kásir.

DEFILE (*narrow pass*), تنگ راه tang-ráh, کتل kutal, گردن gardan, شعب sha'b, گدوک gadúk.

To DEFILE, یکی یکی آمدن yakí yakí ámadan.—(*stain*) آلودن álúdan, نا پاك کردن ná-pák kardan, ملوث ساختن mulavvas sákhtan, نجس کردن najs kardan.

To DEFINE, شرح کردن sharh kardan, بیان کردن bayán kardan.

DEFINITE, محدود mahdúd, معروف ma'rúf, معین mu'ayyan, مقرر mu-karrar.

DEFINITION, تعریف ta'ríf, وصف vasf, تفصیل tafsíl.

DEFINITIVE, *vide* DECISIVE.

DEFLEXION, انعطاف in'itáf.

To DEFLOWER, ازاله بکارت کردن izálah-i-bakárat kardan.

DEFORMED, چلاق chulák, چولاغ chú-lágh, معیوب ma'yúb.

To DEFRAUD, فریفتن firíftan, فریب دادن firíb dádan, گول خورانیدن gúl khwuránídan, گول زدن gúl zadan, غدر نمودن ghadar nimúdan, حیله کردن hílah kardan.

DEFUNCT, *vide* DEAD.

To DEFY, به مبارزت طلبیدن bi-mubá-razat talbídan, دعوت جنگ کردن da'vat-i-jang kardan.—(*brave, or slight*) *vide* To DESPISE, To OPPOSE.

DEGRADATION, *vide* DISGRACE BASENESS.

DEGRADED, *vide* ABANDONED.—(*military term*) از رتبه انداخته az rutbah andákhtah, پست گردانیده past gardánídah.

DEGREE, قدر kadr, مقدار mikdár, مرتبه martabah, مشابه masábah, اندازه andázah, حد hadd, مقابله mukábalah, درجه darajah.—(*proportion*) نسبت nisbat, مناسبت munásabat, مطابقت mutábakat, تساوی tasáví, وفق vafk, اندازه an-dázah.—(*rank*) درجه darajah, جاه jáh, شان shán, منزلت manzilat, طبقه tabakah, رتبه rutbah, مرتبه martabah, پایه páyah, قدر kadr. —(*mathematical*) درجه darajah.—(*by degrees*) قدم بقدم kadam bi-kadam, درجه بدرجه darajah bi-darajah, بتدریج bi-tadríj, تدریجا tadríjan, پایه پایه páyah páyah, آهسته آهسته áhistah áhistah, رفته رفته raftah raftah, سنگنك sang-nak. — (*to a degree*) بر مرتبه bar martabah. — (*to the last degree*) فوق الغایت fauku-'l-ghayat.

DEITY, *vide* GOD. — (*Godhead*) الوهیت ulúhíyat.

DEJECTED, *vide* SAD.

DELAY, دیری dírí, درنگی dirangí, توقف tavakkuf, تاءخیر ta,khír, مهل mahal, مهلت muhlat, امهال imhál, توانی taváni, تراخی tarákhí, اهمال ihmál, تعویق ta'vík, اناء ana,, تانی ta,anní, تهاون taháyun, خمول khu-múl, مکث maks, مکوث mukús, لیت و لعل lait u la'all, دفع الوقت daf'u-'l-vakt. — (*without delay*) بی درنگ bí-dirang, بلا تاءخیر bilá ta,khír.

To DELAY, در تعویق انداختن dar ta'vík andákhtan, تاءخیر نمودن ta'khír nimúdan, دیری کردن dírí kardan, توقف کردن tavakkuf kar-dan.—(*to be delayed*) در تعویق افتادن dar ta'vík uftádan, معوق شدن mu'avvak shudan, موءجل شدن

mu,ajjal shudan, گیر افتادن gír úftádan.

Delegate, مباشر mubáshir. (*Vide also* Ambassador, Agent.)

To Delegate, گماشتن gumáshtan.

Delegation, مباشره mubásharah.

To Deliberate, تدبیر نمودن tadbír nimúdan, استشاره نمودن istishárah nimúdan.

Deliberately, *vide* Intentionally.

Deliberation, *vide* Thought, Care.

Delicate, *vide* Fine, Soft, Gentle, Weak.

Delicious, لذیذ lazíz, مرغوب marghúb, خوشگوار khwush-guvár.

Delight, لذت lazzat, دلخوشی dil-khwushí, عیش 'aish, عشرت 'ishrat, حظ hazz, شادی shádí, ذوق zauk, لطافت latáfat, صفا safá.

To Delight, لذت دادن lazzat dádan, ممنون کردن mamnún kardan.—(*to be delighted*) محظوظ شدن mahzúz shudan, خوش آمدن khwush ámadan. [Generally used with the terminations م , ت , &c., affixed to the first word, thus خوشم آمد khwusham ámad, &c.]

Delightful, *vide* Pleasant.

Delimitation, حدود مفصله hudúd-i-mufassalah.

Delinquent, *vide* Culprit.

Delirious, مدهوش madhúsh, هذیان hazayán.

Delirium, سرسام sar-sám, هذی hazí.

To Deliver (*up*), تسلیم نمودن taslím nimúdan, تفویض کردن tafvíz kardan, حواله نمودن haválah nimúdan, سپردن sipurdan. — (*set free, save*) آزاد کردن ázád kardan, رهانیدن rihánídan, خلاص کردن khalás kardan, رها کردن rihá kardan, رسته گردانیدن rastah gardánídan, نجات دادن naját dádan.

Deliverance, رستگاری rastagárí, رها rihá, نجات naját.

Delivery (*goods*), تسلیم taslím.—(*speaking*) تقریر takrír. — (*child-birth*) تولد tavallud.

Delta, مصب masabb.

Deluge, طوفان túfán, سیلاب sailáb, سیل sail.—(*the Deluge*) طوفان نوح tufán-i-núh.

Delusion, *vide* Illusion, Sham.

Demand, در خواست dar-khwást, طلب talab, مطالبه mutálabah, دعوی d'avá, ادعا iddi'á استدعا istid'á, اقتضا iktizá. —(*to be in demand*) طالب داشتن tálib dáshtan.

To Demand, *vide* To Ask.

Demarcation, خط فاصل khatt-i-fásil.

Demeanour, *vide* Conduct.

Demented, *vide* Mad.

Demoiselle, دختر dukhtar.

To Demolish, *vide* To Destroy.

Demolition, هدم hadm, خرابت kharábat.

Demon, دیو dív, جن jinn, جان jánn, عفریت 'ifrít, غول ghúl.

Demoniac, مجنون majnún, دیوانه dívánah.

To Demonstrate, بیان نمودن bayán nimúdan, شرح کردن sharh kardan, واضح کردن vázih kardan.

Demonstration, اظهار izhár, دلیل dalíl, برهان burhán. — (*ocular demonstration*) مشاهده musháhadah, عیان 'iyán.

Den, غار ghár, مغاره mughárah, مصان masán, کمینگاه kamín-gáh.

Denial, انکار inkár, ابا ibá, حاشا hashá, نفی nafy.

Denominated, مسمی musammá.

Dense (*close, thick*), کثیف kasíf, متصل muttasil, جنجال janjál.

Density (*closeness*), کثافت kasáfat, سطبری sitabrí, قطر kutr.

Dentist, دندان ساز dandán-sáz.

Denuded, مجرد mujarrad.

To Deny, تکذیب کردن takzíb kardan, نفی کردن nafy kardan, انکار نمودن inkár nimúdan.—(*refuse*) دریغ نمودن dirígh nimúdan, وا داشتن vá-dáshtan, باز داشتن báz-dáshtan.

To Depart, روانه گشتن ravánah gashtan, رفتن raftan.

Departure, روانگی ravánagí, رحلت rihlat, جلا jalá, کوچ kúch, سفر safar.

To DEPEND on, موقوف بودن maukúf búdan, منوط بودن manút búdan, منسوب شدن mansúb shudan, بسته بودن bastah búdan. (*Vide* To CONFIDE.)

DEPENDENCE, وا بستگی vá-bastagí, تعلق ta'alluk, علاقه 'alákah. (*Vide* CONNECTION, RELIANCE, TRUST.)

DEPENDENCY (*part of a state or kingdom*), محال maháll.

DEPENDENT, موقوف maukúf.—(*to be dependent on another person*) متعلق بودن muta'allik búdan, متابع بودن mutábi' búdan.

DEPENDENTS (*retinue*), توابع tavábí', لواحق laváhik, متعلقان muta'allikán, تابینها tábínhá (*vulg.*).—(*family*) عیال 'iyál, خورنده khwurandah, اهل خانه ahl-i-khánah.

DEPICTER, چهره کشا chahrah-kashá, صورت آرا súrat-árá.

To DEPOPULATE, ویران ساختن vairán sákhtan, خراب کردن kharáb kardan.

To DEPOSE (*expel*), اخراج نمودن ikhráj nimúdan, معزول کردن ma'zúl kardan, دفع کردن daf' kardan, راندن rándan. —(*give testimony*) گواهی دادن gaváhí dádan, شهادت نمودن shahádat nimúdan.

DEPOSIT, ودیعت vadí'at, سپرد sipurd, امانت amánat, حواله haválah. —(*to keep in deposit*) محجر کردن muhajjar kardan, نگهداشتن nigahdáshtan.—(*to put in deposit*) حواله کردن haválah kardan, امانت گذاردن amánat guzárdan, ودیعت نهادن vadí'at nihádan, تفویض کردن tafvíz kardan.

DEPOSITION, تقریر takrír, زبان بندی zában-bandí.

DEPOSITOR, امانتدار amánat-dár.

DEPOSITORY, مخزن makhzan, انبار ambár, امانتگاه amánat-gáh.

DEPRAVED, تباه tabáh, خراب kharáb, مفسد mufsid, فاسد fásid.

DEPRAVITY, *vide* WICKEDNESS.

To DEPRECIATE (*trans.*), استخفاف کردن istikhfáf kardan.—(*intrans.*) کاستن kástan.

DEPRESSED, *vide* SAD.

DEPRESSION, فرود رفتگی furúd-raftagí. — (*of spirits*), *vide* MELANCHOLY.

To DEPRIVE, محروم گردانیدن mahrúm gardánídan, مفقود کردن mafkúd kardan, جدا کردن jidá kardan.

DEPTH, عمق 'umk *or* 'umuk, ژرفا zharfá, تك tak.

DEPUTATION, پیشواز píshváz, مراسله murásalah.

To DEPUTE, فرستادن firistádan, مامور کردن mámúr kardan, مبعوث کردن mab'ús kardan.

DEPUTY, نائب ná,ib, وکیل vakíl, گماشته gumáshtah, قائم مقام ká,im-makám, سر کار sar-kár.

DERANGEMENT, تشویش tashvísh.

DERISION, استهزا istihzá, مسخره maskharah, تمسخر tamaskhur, سخریه sukhríyah, ضحك zahak, توهین tauhín, خنده khandah, باردی báradí.

DERIVATION, صدور sudúr, اشتقاق ishtikák, اقتباس iktibás.

DERIVATIVE (*word*), مشتق mushtakk, مأخوذ ma,khúz.

To DERIVE, بر آوردن bar-ávardan, اخذ کردن akhz kardan.

DERVISH (*religious mendicant or ascetic*), درویش darvísh, قلندر kalandar. — (*dervish's gown*) دلق dalk.—(*high cap worn by dervishes*) تاج táj.—(*cup or calabash for alms, carried by dervishes*) کچکول kachkúl, کشکول kashkúl.

To DESCEND, فرود آمدن furúd ámadan, پائین آمدن pá,ín ámadan, بزیر آمدن bi-zír ámadan, نازل شدن názil shudan, نزول کردن nuzúl kardan, حاول بودن hávil búdan, زوال کردن zavál kardan.

DESCENDANTS (*offspring*), نسل nasl, خلف khalf, اخلاف akhláf, اولاد aulád, آل ál, بنی baní, نژاد nizhád, عقبه 'akabah, سلاله sulálah.

DESCENT, شیب shíb, نشیب nishíb, نزول nuzúl.—(*origin*) اصل asl, نسب nasab, تبار tabár, نسل nasl, نژاد nizhád.

To DESCRIBE, تعریف کردن ta'ríf kardan, وصف کردن vasf kardan, صفت

کردن sifat kardan, بیان کردن bayán kardan, توصیف کردن tausíf kardan.

DESCRIPTION, بیان bayán, تفصیل tafsíl, تقریر takrír, وصف vasf, تخطیط takhtít, تعریف ta'ríf, صفت sifat, تسطیر tastír.—(*beyond description*) که بوصف نمی آید kih bi-vasf namí-áyad, از حد توصیف بیرون az hadd-i-tausíf bírún, خارج از بیان khárij az bayán. (*Vide* KIND.)

DESERT, بیابان biyábán, ویرانه vairánah, دشت dasht, بادیه bádiyah, بیدا baidá, چول chaul, قاع ká', تیه tíh, بریه barriyah, مفازت mafázat, سهب sahab.—(*salt desert*) کویر kivír, کفه kaffah.

To DESERT, *vide* To ABANDON.—(*run away*) فرار کردن firár kardan, گریختن guríkhtan.

DESERTER, فراری firárí.

DESERTION, فرار firár.

To DESERVE, سزاوار بودن sazávár búdan, مستحق بودن mustahakk búdan, لائق شدن lá,ik shudan, سزیدن sazídan, واجب شدن vájib shudan, مستوجب شدن mustaujib shudan.

DESERVING, مستحق mustahakk, واجب vájib, قابل kábil, لائق lá,ik, سزاوار sazávár.

DESIGN, اراده irádah, مراد murád, قصد kasd, مقصد maksad, نیت níyat, عزم 'azm, آهنگ áhang, آرزو árzú, سعی sa'í, غرض gharaz, مدعا mudda'á, سر sar, بنا biná, صدد sadad, داعیه dá'iyah.—(*pattern*) نقش naksh.

To DESIGN, *vide* To INTEND.—(*pattern*) نقش کردن naksh kardan.

To DESIGNATE, تسمیه کردن tasmiyah kardan, نام گذاردن nám guzárdan.

DESIGNATION, *vide* NAME.

DESIGNEDLY, *vide* INTENTIONALLY.

DESIRABLE, دلخواه dil-khwáh, دلجو dil-jú, مرغوب marghúb, مقبول makbúl, مطبوع matbú'—(*to deem desirable*) صواب دانستن saváb dánistan.

DESIRE, خواهش khwáhish, آرزو árzú, کام kám, خاطر khátir, مراد murád, ارادت irádat, مقصود maksúd, هوس havas, نفس nafs, شوق shauk, اشتیاق ishtiyák, رغبت raghbat, مطلب matlab, امل amal, آرزومندی árzú-mandí, هویت havíyat, داعیه dá'iyah. — (*the desires*) اطماع atmá'. — (*sexual desire*), شهوت shahvat, نفس nafs, هوس havas.

To DESIRE, خواستن khwástan, آرزو کردن árzú kardan, خواهش داشتن khwáhish dáshtan.

DESIROUS, آرزومند árzú-mand, مشتاق mushták, هوسناك havasnák, جویا júyá, راغب rághib, طمعکار tama'-kár, شائق shá,ik, متشهی mutashahhí, مشتهی mushtahi.

To DESIST, باز ایستادن báz-ístádan, وا ماندن vá-mándan, توقف کردن tavakkuf kardan, دست بردار شدن dast-bardár shudan, آرامیدن árámídan.

DESK (*box containing correspondence, papers, &c.*), پیشتخته písh-takhtah.—(*stand for supporting books while reading*) رحل rahl.

DESOLATE, *vide* SAD. — (*place*) خرابه kharábah, ویرانه vairánah.

DESOLATION, *vide* MELANCHOLY.

DESPAIR, نا امیدی ná-umídí, نومیدی naumídí, یاس yás, قنوط kunút, انکسار inkisár.

To DESPAIR, نا امید شدن ná-umíd shudan, نومید شدن naumíd shudan.

DESPATCH, نوشته nivishtah, محرر muharrar. (*Vide* SPEED.)

To DESPATCH, *vide* To SEND.

DESPERADO, یارمز yáramaz, یارمباز yarmbáz, بردار و برو bardár u birau, شیر بی پیر shír-i-bí-pír, آذر بزین ázar bi-zín.

DESPERATE, نا امید ná-umíd, نومید naumíd.

DESPERATION, بی پروای bí-parvái, یدی yadí. (*Vide* DESPAIR.)

DESPICABLE, *vide* CONTEMPTIBLE.

To DESPISE, خوار دیدن khwár dídan, حقیر شمردن hakír shimurdan, تحقیر نمودن tahkír nimúdan, حقارت کردن

hikárat kardan, اهانت نمودن ihánat nimúdan, مذمت نمودن mazammat nimúdan, نکوهش نمودن nikúhish nimúdan.

DESPOT, *vide* TYRANT.

DESPOTIC, مستقل mustakill, خود رای khwud-ráí.

DESPOTISM, تسلط tasallut, استقلال istiklál, استبداد istibdád, تطاول tatávul, ظلم zulm.

DESSERT (*candied fruits, &c.*), نقل nukl.—(*dry fruit, nuts, &c.*) آجیل ájíl, خشکبار khushkibár.

To DESTINE, نامزد نمودن nám-zad nimúdan.

DESTINY, نصیب nasíb, قدر kadar, قدرت kudrat, تقدیر takdír, قسمت kismat, بخت bakht, قضا kazá, طالع táli', سر نوشت sar-nivisht.

DESTITUTE, بی نوا bí-navá, عاجز 'ájiz, بی کس bí-kas, مستأصل musta,sal.

DESTITUTION, بی نوائی bí-navá,í, بیچارگی bí-cháragí, عاجزی 'ájizí, فاقه fákah, استیصال istísál.

To DESTROY, نیست کردن níst kardan, معدوم کردن ma'dúm kardan, از هم ریختن az ham ríkhtan, تلف نمودن talaf nimúdan, نا بود گردانیدن ná-búd gardánídan, فنا کردن faná kardan, منهدم ساختن munhadim sákhtan, استیصال نمودن istísál nimúdan, پخش کردن pakhsh kardan.

DESTROYER, تباه کار tabáh-kár.

DESTRUCTION, خلل khalal, اخلال ikhlál, خسارت khasárat, قتل katl, اعدام i'dám.

To DETACH, جدا ساختن jidá sákhtan.

DETACHMENT (*of troops*), دسته dastah.

DETAIL, قرار داد karár-dád.—(*details*) جزئیات juz,iyát.—(*in detail*) علی التفصیل 'alá-'t-tafsíl.

DETAILED, مفصل mufassal.

To DETAIN, باز داشتن báz-dáshtan, وا داشتن vá-dáshtan, گیر کردن gír kardan, کسیل کردن kisíl kardan, نگاه داشتن nigáh dáshtan.

To DETECT, *vide* To DISCOVER, To CONVICT.

DETENTION, *vide* IMPRISONMENT.

To DETERIORATE, کاستن kástan, زائل شدن zá,il shudan, بزوال رفتن bi-zavál raftan.

DETERIORATION, زوال zavál.

DETERMINATION, عزم 'azm, عزیمت 'azímat, جزم jazm, خوض khauz, تصمیم tasmím. (*Vide* COURAGE.)

To DETERMINE (*resolve*), قراری دادن karárí dádan, مصمم گشتن musammim gashtan, تصمیم کردن tasmím kardan. (*Vide* To SETTLE.)

To DETEST, *vide* To ABHOR.

DETESTABLE, مکروه makrúh, کریه karíh, منفور manfúr, رجس rijs.

DETESTATION, *vide* ABHORRENCE.

DETHRONEMENT, خلع khal'.

DETOUR, عوج 'avaj.

DETRACTION, *vide* CALUMNY.

DETRACTOR, *vide* CALUMNIATOR.

DETRIMENT, ضرر zarar, زیان ziyán, خلل khalal, نقصان nuksán, آسیب ásíb.

To DEVASTATE, غارت کردن ghárat kardan, تاراج نمودن táráj nimúdan, خراب نمودن kharáb nimúdan.

DEVASTATION, غارت ghárat, خرابی kharábí.

To DEVELOP, پیدا نمودن paidá nimúdan, کشف کردن kashf kardan, آشکار کردن áshkár kardan.

To DEVIATE, انحراف نمودن inhiráf nimúdan.

DEVIATION, انحراف inhiráf, تجاوز tajávuz.

DEVIL, شیطان shaitán, ابلیس iblís, خناس khannás, خطاف khattáf, دیو dív.

DEVILISH, شیطانی shaitání.

DEVILRY, شیطنت shaitanat, شیطنلق shaitanlik.

To DEVISE, تدبیر کردن tadbír kardan, تمهید کردن tamhíd kardan.

To DEVOLVE, در عهده گذارده شدن dar 'uhdah guzárdah shudan.

To DEVOTE, *vide* To GIVE, To CONSUME.

DEVOTED (*appropriated*), مخصوص makhsús, مختص mukhtass, معین mu'ayyan.—(*attached*) محب muhibb.—(*thing devoted to God*) منذور

manzúr, مقدس mukaddas, قربانی kurbání. — (*bequeathed for religious purposes*) وقف vakf, موقوفه maukúfah.—(*servant*), فدوی fidví, بنده bandah.

DEVOTEE (*religious*), زاهد záhid, عابد 'ábid, پارسا pársá, گوشه نشین gúshah-nishín, مرتاض murtáz.—(*wandering devotee*) درویش darvísh, فقیر fakír, قلندر kalandar, آزاد ázád.

DEVOTION (*piety*), تقوی takvá, ریاضت riyázat, عبادت 'ibádat, زهد zuhd.

To DEVOUR, بلعیدن bal'ídan, خوردن khwurdan.

DEVOUT, معتکف mu'takif, متقی muttakí, خداترس khudá-tars.

DEW, شبنم shab-nam, ژاله zhálah.

DEW-LAP, غبغب ghabghab.

DEXTERITY, *vide* SKILL.

DEXTROUS, چابك chábuk, دستکار dast-kár, قابل kábil, زرنگ zaring, چست chust.

DIABETES, سلس البول salasu-'l-baul.

DIABOLIC, *vide* DEVILISH.

DIADEM, *vide* CROWN.

DIAGNOSIS, تشخیص tashkhís.

DIAGRAM, نمونه nimúnah.

DIAL, دائرهٔ هندی dá,irah-i-hindí, دائرهٔ ساعتی dá,irah-i-sá'ati, درجات darajját.

DIALECTICS, علم منطق 'ilm-i-mantik.

DIALOGUE, جواب سؤال javáb-su,ál, گفتگو guftugú, مکالمت mukálamat.

DIAMETER, قطر kutr.

DIAMOND, الماس almás.

DIARRHŒA, اسهال is-hál, جریان شکم jiryán-i-shikm, زحیر zahír.

DIARY, سفر نامه safar-námah, روز نامه rúz-námah.

DIBBLE, بیلچه bílchah.

DICE, ششدر shish-dar, جنگ jung, کعب ka'b.—(*one die*) کعبه ka'bah, طاس tás.

DICTATE, اغرا ighrá, تحریك tahrík.

To DICTATE (*letter*, *&c.*), املا کردن imlá kardan.

DICTATION, املا imlá.

DICTION, نطق nutk, تلفظ talaffuz.

DICTIONARY, لغت lughat, فرهنگ farhang.

DIE (*stamp*), سکه sikkah, مهر muhr.

To DIE, مردن murdan, فوت شدن faut shudan, وفات کردن vafát kardan, گشتن gashtan. [Also expressed by various phrases, such as: جان را تسلیم کردن ján-rá taslím kardan (*to resign life*); برحمت الهی پیوستن bi-rahmat-i-iláhí paivastan (*to be received into God's mercy*); لبیك اجابت گفتن labaik-i-ijábat guftan (*to pronounce the word of acceptance*); سر بتیرهٔ تراب کشیدن sar bi-tírah-i-turáb kashídan (*to withdraw one's head into the darkness of the grave*); دنیارا وداع کردن dunyárá vidá' kardan (*to bid adieu to the world*), &c.]

DIET, غذا ghizá, غدا ghadá, طعم ta'm, طعمت tu'mat.

DIFFERENCE, فرق fark, تفاوت tafávut, اختلاف ikhtiláf, توفیر taufír (*vulg.*). [This last word properly signifies increasing, multiplying.]. — (*misunderstanding*) نزاع nizá'.—(*of opinion*) کثرت آرا kasrat-i-árá, اختلاف آرا ikhtiláf-i-árá,.

DIFFERENT, متفرق mutafarrik, علیحده 'alá-hiddah, جدا jidá, مختلف mukhtalif, متباین mutabáyin, مغایر mugháyir, نا همتا ná-ham-tá, ور var (*vulg.*).—(*to be different from*) تفاوت داشتن (به) tafávut dáshtan (bi).

DIFFICULT, مشکل mushkil, دشوار dushvár, سخت sakht, شاق shákk, صعب sa'b, متعذر muta'azzir.

DIFFICULTY, مشکلی mushkilí, اشکال ishkál, دشواری dushvári, عسرت 'usrat, سختی sakhtí, صعوبت su'úbat.—(*with difficulty*) بوجهی صعب bi-vajhí-i-sa'b.

To DIFFUSE, افشاندن afshándan, ریختن ríkhtan, پاشیدن páshídan, پراکندن parákandan, نشر نمودن

nashr nimúdan, منتشر ساختن muntashir sákhtan.

DIFFUSELY, علی وجه التطویل ‘alá vajhu-’t-tatvíl.

DIFFUSION, انتشار intishár, نشر nashr.

To DIG, کند و کوب کردن kand u kúb kardan, کاویدن kávídan, کندن kandan, نطس کردن nuts kardan, کافتن káftan.—(*excavate*) حفر کردن hafr kardan, کاویدن kávídan. — (*up*) بر کندن bar-kandan, در آوردن dar-ávardan.

To DIGEST, هضم کردن hazm kardan, تحلیل کردن tahlíl kardan, گواریدن guvárídan, حل کردن hall kardan. —(*to be digested*) تحلیل رفتن tahlíl raftan, هضم شدن hazm shudan.

DIGESTION, هضم hazm, گوارش guvárish, تحلیل tahlíl.

DIGESTIVE, گوار guvár.

DIGNIFIED, معزز mu‘azzaz, با هیبت bá-haibat.

DIGNITY, جاه jáh, شان shán, سر افرازی sar-afrází, سر فرازی sar-farází, دولت daulat, حشمت hashmat, شکوه shukúh, مرتبه martabah, منصب mansab, شرف sharaf, رفعت rif‘at, جلال jalál, اقبال ikbál, اعلا a‘lá, قدر kadar, عزت ‘izzat, تشخص tashakhkhus.

DIGRESSION, انحراف inhiráf.

DIKE, *vide* DITCH.

DILAPIDATIONS, خراب kharáb.

To DILATE, مبسوط کردن mabsút kardan.

DILATION, تفصیل tafsíl, اطناب t náb.

DILATORY, *vide* LAZY.

DILEMMA, *vide* DIFFICULTY.

DILIGENCE, توجه tavajjuh, اهتمام ihtimám, تندهی tan-dihí, جهد jahd, جد jidd, اشتغال ishtighál.

DILIGENT, متوجه mutavajjih, ساعی sá‘í, مقید mukayyad, سر گرم sar-garm. — (*to be diligent*) اهتمام نمودن ihtimám nimúdan, متوجه بودن mutavajjih búdan, سر گرم بودن sar-garm búdan.

To DILLY-DALLY, دفع الوقت کردن daf‘u-’l-vakt kardan, دلدل کردن dildil kardan, لیت و لعل کردن lait u la‘all kardan.

DIM, *vide* OBSCURE, DARK.

To DIMINISH (*grow less*), کاستن kástan, کم شدن kam shudan.—(*make less*) *vide* To LESSEN.

DIMINUTION, *vide* DECREASE.

DIMINUTIVE, *vide* SMALL.—(*grammatical term*) تصغیر tasghír, مصغر musaghghar.

DIMPLE, چاه cháh.

DIN, *vide* NOISE (*clamour*). — (*din of battle*) دار و گیر dár u gír, هائی هوئی há,í hú,í.

To DINE, شام خوردن shám khwurdan.

DINING-ROOM, سفره خانه sufrah-khánah.

DINNER (*at noon*), چاشت chásht.—(*at night*) شام shám.

DINT (*bruise*), گود gaud, تو رفته tú-raftah.—(*by dint of*) از بس az bas, از کثرت az kasrat.

To DIP, فرو بردن furú burdan, خیسانیدن khísánídan.

DIPLOMA, نامه námah, برات barát.

DIPLOMACY, ایلچیگری ílchí-garí.

DIRECT, مستوی mustaví.

To DIRECT, ارشاد نمودن irshád nimúdan.

DIRECTION (*of a letter*), سر نامه sar-námah, نام و نشان nám u nishán, نام و مقام nám u makám.—(*place*) طرف taraf, سمت samt, جانب jánib, سو sú. — (*guiding*) رهنمائی rahnimá,í, رهبری rah-barí, هدایت hidáyat.

DIRECTLY, الان al,án.

DIRECTOR, مدبر mudabbir, مدیر mudír, رائیس rá,ís, سرکار sar-kar.

DIRGE, مرثیه marsiyah.

DIRHAM, درهم dirham.

DIRT, چرك chirk, لجن lajan, ادباری idbárí, کسافت kasáfat, دسومت dusúmat.

To DIRT, آلودن álúdan, چرکیدن chirkídan.—(*to get dirty*) از صفا افتادن az safá uftádan, نا پاك شدن ná-pák shudan, ملوث شدن mulavvas shudan, کسیف شدن kasíf shudan.

DIRTY, چرکین chirkín, کسیف kasíf, نا پاك ná-pák, غلیظ ghalíz. [This latter term is now applied only to fluids clotted or thickened.]

DISABLED, عاجز 'ájiz, نا توان ná-taván.

To DISAGREE, اختلاف کردن ikhtiláf kardan, مختلف شدن mukhtalif shudan.

DISAGREEABLE, نا پسند ná-pasand, نا مقبول ná-makbúl, نا موجه ná-muvajjah.

DISAGREEMENT, اختلاف ikhtiláf. (*Vide also* DIFFERENCE, DISPUTE.)

To DISAPPEAR, غائب شدن ghá,ib shudan, نا پدید شدن ná-padíd shudan.

DISAPPEARANCE, غیبت ghaibat.

DISAPPOINTED, نا مراد ná-murád, نا کام ná-kám, محروم mahrúm, مایوس máyús, بینصیب bí-nasíb, مخذول makhzúl.

DISAPPOINTMENT, محرومیت mahrúmíyat, نومیدی naumídí, دلشکستگی dil-shikastagí.

To DISAPPROVE, بد شمردن bad shimurdan, انکار داشتن inkár dáshtan.

To DISARRANGE, تخلیط نمودن takhlít nimúdan.

DISASTER, *vide* CALAMITY.

To DISAVOW, نفی کردن nafy kardan, حاشا کردن háshá kardan, انکار کردن inkár kardan.

DISAVOWAL, انکار inkár, نفی nafy, حاشا háshá.

To DISBURSE, *vide* To SPEND.

DISBURSEMENT, مصرف masraf, مخرج makhraj.

DISC, قرص kurs.

To DISCARD, *vide* To ABANDON.

To DISCERN, در یافت کردن dar-yáft kardan, از غیب دانستن az ghaib dánistan, فهمیدن fahmídan.

DISCERNMENT, تمییز tamyíz, امتیاز imtiyáz, فطانت fatánat, فراست firásat, ذهن zihn, بصیرت basírat, هوشمندی húsh-mandí.

DISCHARGE (*receipt*), ابرائی ذمت ibrá,í-i-zimmat.

To DISCHARGE (*dismiss*), اخراج کردن íkhráj kardan, جواب دادن javáb dádan, بیرون کردن bírún kardan, معزول کردن ma'zúl kardan, بر طرف کردن bar taraf kardan. (*Vide* To PERFORM.)—(*a debt*) مفروغ کردن mafrúgh kardan, ادا کردن adá kardan, کار سازی نمودن kár-sází nimúdan.—(*a gun*) خالی کردن khálí kardan. — (*a load*) تخفیف نمودن takhfíf nimúdan.

DISCIPLE, مرید muríd, تلمیذ talmíz, شاگرد shágird.—(*of Christ*) حواری havárí.

DISCIPLINE, نظام nizám, انتظام intizám, ضبط و ربط zabt u rabt.

DISCIPLINED, با نظم bá-nazm.

To DISCLOSE, بمیدان آوردن bi-maidán ávardan, کشف کردن kashf kardan, ظاهر ساختن záhir sákhtan.

DISCONTENT, نا رضامندی ná-rizámandí, بیزاری bízárí, بی حضوری bí-huzúrí.

DISCONTENTED, متنفر mutanaffir, بیزار bízár, رنجیده ranjídah, مکدر mukaddar, ملول malúl, دلتنگ dil-tang, نا خوشنود ná-khwushnúd, نا راضی ná-rází, بی حضور bí-huzúr.

DISCORD, اختلاف ikhtiláf, فتنه fitnah, ستیزه sitízah.

DISCORDANT, نا ساز ná-sáz.

DISCOUNT (*abatement*), تنزیل tanzíl, وضیعت vazí'at, رعایت ri'áyat, کمی kamí.—(*to allow a discount*) کم کردن kam kardan, رعایت کردن ri'áyat kardan, پا پائین گذاردن pá-pá,ín guzárdan (*vulg.*).

DISCOURSE, *vide* SPEECH (*harangue*).

To DISCOVER (*find out*), در یافت کردن dar-yáft kardan, پیدا کردن paidá kardan, استدراك نمودن istidrák nimúdan, یافتن yáftan, استنباط کردن istimbát kardan, ملتفت شدن multafit shudan.—(*display*) اظهار نمودن izhár nimúdan, کشف کردن kashf kardan, آشکاره کردن áshkárah kardan.

DISCOVERER, یابنده yábandah, کشف کننده kashf-kunandah. (*Vide* INVENTOR.)

DISCOVERY, کشف kashf. (*Vide* INVENTION.)

DISCREET, با تمییز bá-tamyíz, با بصیرت bá-basírat, با فراست bá-firásat.

DISCRETION, تمییز tamyíz, تدبیر tadbír, بصیرت basírat.
To DISCRIMINATE, تمییز کردن tamyíz kardan.
DISCRIMINATION, تباین tabáyun, امتیاز imtiyáz, تفریق tafrík.
To DISCUSS, رد و بدل شدن radd u badl shudan, مذاکره کردن muzákarah kardan.
DISCUSSION, مذاکره muzákarah, قیل و قال kíl u kál.
DISDAIN, *vide* CONTEMPT.
To DISDAIN, *vide* To DESPISE.
DISDAINFUL, مستغنی mustaghní, متکبر mutakabbir.
DISEASE, *vide* COMPLAINT.
DISEASED, مریض maríz.
To DISFIGURE, تبدیل صورت نمودن tabdíl-i-súrat nimúdan, دیگر گون کردن dígar gún kardan, خراب کردن kharáb kardan. (*Vide* To INJURE.)
DISGRACE, رسوائی rusvá,í, بی حرمتی bí-hurmatí, بی آبروئی bí-áb-rú,í, بی عزتی bí-'izzatí, ننگ nang, عار 'ár, بد نامی bad-námí, فضیحت fazíhat, تفضیح tafzíh.
To DISGRACE, فضیحت کردن fazíhat kardan.
DISGRACEFUL, رسوا rusvá.
DISGUISE, تبدیل tabdíl.
To DISGUISE, تبدیل نمودن tabdíl nimúdan.
DISGUST, نفرت nifrat, کراهیت karáhiyat, بیزاری bízárí.
To DISGUST, بیزار نمودن bízár nimúdan, تنفیر نمودن tanfír nimúdan.
DISGUSTING, مغص mughass, مکروه makrúh, نفرت انگیز nifrat-angíz.
DISH, ظرف zarf (*pl.* ظروف zurúf), دوری dúrí.—(*wooden dish*) طبق tabak.—(*tray*) مجموعه majmú'ah, سینی síní.—(*plate*) بشقاب bushkáb. — (*large plate*) قاب káb, نیمچه nímchah, لنگری langarí (*hind.*).—(*dish-clout*) صافی sáfí. —(*of food*) خورش khwurish, طعام ta'ám. — (*made dish*) طعام مهیا ta'ám-i-muhayyá. —(*hot dishes*) غذائی گرم پخته ghizá,í-i-garm-pakhtah.
To DISHEARTEN, ترسانیدن tarsánídan, دلتنگ کردن dil-tang kardan, انذار نمودن inzár nimúdan.
DISHONEST, بی ایمان bí-ímán, بی دیانت bí-diyánat, فریبنده firíbandah, حیله باز híláh-báz.
DISHONOUR, ذلت zillat, عیب 'aib, هتك آبرو hatk-i-áb-rú.
To DISHONOUR, تحقیر نمودن tahkír nimúdan.—(*a bill*) بر گشت کردن bar-gasht kardan, وا زدن vazadan.
To DISINHERIT, از میراث محروم ساختن az mírás mahrúm sákhtan.
DISINTERESTED, بی غرض bí-gharaz, خالص khális, صادق sádik.
To DISJOINT, قطع کردن kat' kardan.
DISJUNCTION, انقطاع inkitá'.
DISJUNCTIVE PARTICLE (*in grammar*), حرف تردید harf-i-tardíd, حرف استثنا harf-i-istisná.
DISK (*round surface*), قرص kurs, گرده girdah.
DISLIKE (*aversion*), ابا ibá, اعراض i'ráz, نفرت nifrat, تنفر tanaffur, کراهیت karáhiyat.
To DISLIKE, مکروه داشتن makrúh dáshtan.
To DISLOCATE, جابجا کردن já-bi-já kardan. — (*to be dislocated, a bone or limb*) در رفتن dar raftan, جابجا شدن já-bi-já shudan.
DISLOCATION, بیرون رفتن bírún raftan, جابجا شدن já-bi-já shudan.
DISLOYAL, عاصی 'ásí, طاغی tághí.
To DISMAY, *vide* To FRIGHTEN.
To DISMISS, *vide* To DISCHARGE.
DISMISSAL (*leave to go*), رخصت rukhsat.—(*discharge*) اخراج ikhráj, جواب javáb, نفی nafy.
DISMISSED, معزول ma'zúl.
To DISMOUNT, فرود آمدن furúd ámadan, پائین آمدن pá,ín ámadan, پیاده شدن piyádah shudan.
DISOBEDIENCE, نا فرمانی ná-firmání, عناد 'inád, سر کشی sar-kashí, معصیت ma'siyat.
DISOBEDIENT, نا فرمان ná-firmán, نا فرمان بردار ná-firmán-bardár, معاند mu'ánid, سر کش sar-kash, عاق 'ák.

To DISOBEY, سرکشی کردن sar-kashí kardan, سر از اطاعت کشیدن sar az itá'at kashídan, عاق شدن 'ákk shudan.

DISORDER, پریشانی paríshání, عدم نظام 'adam-i-nizám, تشویش tashvísh. (*Vide* COMPLAINT.)

To DISPARAGE, تعییب کردن ta'yíb kardan.

DISPARITY, تفاوت táfávut, فرق fark.

To DISPEL, رفع کردن raf' kardan, دور کردن dúr kardan.

DISPENSATION (*distribution, ordering*), تقسیم taksím, توزیع tauzí'.—(*method of Providence*) انتظام intizám, نظارت nazárat, توفیق taufík. —(*license*) *vide* LEAVE, EXCUSE.

To DISPENSE, *vide* To GIVE, To DISTRIBUTE.—(*to dispense with*) صرف نظر شدن sarf-i-nazar shudan, قطع نظر نمودن kat'-i-nazar nimúdan.

To DISPERSE, متفرق کردن mutafarrik kardan, تفریق نمودن tafrík nimúdan, پراکنده ساختن parákandah sákhtan, بر باد دادن bar bád dádan.

DISPERSED, پراکنده parákandah, منتشر muntashir, تار مار tár-már. (*Vide* SCATTERED.)

DISPERSION, پراکندگی parákandagí, تفرق tafarruk.

To DISPIRIT, بی دل ساختن bí-dil sákhtan.

To DISPLAY, *vide* To DISCOVER, To SHOW.

DISPLEASED, کجخلق kaj-khulk, متنفر mutanaffir, مکدر mukaddar, رنجیده ranjídah, آزرده ázurdah, بیزار bízár, تیره tírah, خشمناک khishm-nák.—(*to be displeased*) بد آمدن bad ámadan. [Generally used thus: *I am displeased, &c.*, بدم آمد badam ámad.]

DISPLEASURE, تکدر takaddur, آزردگی ázurdagí, بیزاری bízárí, تنفر tanaffur.

To DISPORT oneself, بازی کردن bází kardan.

DISPOSABLE, متصرف mutasarraf, منصرف munsarif.

DISPOSAL (*power, free will*), اختیار ikhtiyár, استقلال istiklál. — (*at one's disposal*) در دست dar dast.

To DISPOSE, *vide* To ARRANGE.

To DISPOSE of, *vide* To SELL.

DISPOSED, *vide* INCLINED.

DISPOSITION, *vide* INCLINATION, TENDENCY, TEMPER, ORDER.

DISPUTANT, مباحث mubáhis.

DISPUTE, دعوی da'vá, نزاع nizá', منازعت munáza'at, قضیه kazíyah, جدال jidál, مجادله mujádalah, لجاج lajáj, خرخشه kharkhishah, مباحثه mubáhasah, شلتاق shalták, ستیزه sitízah, ستیزگی sitízagí, شلوک shulúk (*vulg.*).

To DISPUTE, مباحثه در پیوستن mubáhasah dar paivastan, بحث نمودن bahs nimúdan.

DISQUIET, آشوفتگی áshúftagí, رنج ranj.

DISREGARD, تغافل tagháful, چشم پوشی chashm-púshí, اهمال ihmál.

DISRESPECT, بی عزتی bí-'izzatí, بی حرمتی bí-hurmatí, بی ساختگی bí-sákhtagí.—(*to treat with disrespect*) حقارت کردن hakárat kardan.

DISRUPTION, خرق khark, نقض nakz. (*Vide also* BREACH.)

To DISSECT, تشریح کردن tashríh kardan.

DISSECTION, تشریح tashríh, انفصال infisál.

To DISSEMBLE, ریا کردن riyá kardan, بهانه نمودن bahánah nimúdan.

To DISSEMINATE, *vide* To SCATTER.

DISSEMINATION, نشر nashr, انتشار intishár.

DISSENTION, غائله ghá,ilah.

DISSERTATION, *vide* SPEECH (*harangue*).—(*essay*), رساله risálah.

To DISSIMULATE, دروغی نمودن durúghí nimúdan, مدارات نمودن mudárát nimúdan, بهانه کردن bahánah kardan, تقلید کردن taklíd kardan.

DISSIMULATION, مدارات mudárát.

To DISSIPATE, دفع کردن daf' kardan. (*Vide* To SQUANDER, To SCATTER.)

DISSIPATION, *vide* DEBAUCHERY.
DISSOLUTE, *vide* ABANDONED (*shameless*).
DISSOLUTION, نقض nakz, انحلال inhilál. (*Vide* DEATH.)
DISSOLVANT, گدازنده gudázandah.
To DISSOLVE, *vide* To MELT, To DISPERSE.—(*a meeting*) (*trans.*) منحل ساختن munhall sákhtan, حل نمودن hall nimúdan.—(*intrans.*) انحلال یافتن inhilál yáftan.
DISSONANT, *vide* DISCORDANT.
To DISSUADE, انذار نمودن inzár nimúdan, منع کردن mana' kardan, باز داشتن báz-dáshtan, وا گردانیدن vá-gardánídan.
DISTAFF, دوك dúk, دوکچه dúkchah.
DISTANCE, دوری dúrí, مسافت masáfat, فاصله fásilah, بعد bu'd, تفاوت tafávut.—(*to keep at a distance*) رد نمودن radd nimúdan.
DISTANT, دور dúr, بعید ba'íd, متباین mutabáin.
DISTASTE, *vide* DISLIKE.
DISTEMPER, مرض maraz.
To DISTIL (*drop*), چکیدن chakídan, تراویدن tarávídan.—(*spirits*) عرق گرفتن 'arak giriftan, جوهر گرفتن jauhar giriftan.
DISTILLATION, تصعید tas'íd, استقطار istiktár.
DISTINCT, *vide* DIFFERENT, SEPARATE, CLEAR, APPARENT.
DISTINCTION, *vide* DIFFERENCE, HONOUR.
DISTINCTLY (*clearly*), تفصیلاً tafsílan, ظاهراً zahiran, مشروحاً mashrúhan, آشکاره áshkárah, عیاناً 'iyánan.
To DISTINGUISH, امتیاز کردن imtiyáz kardan, تشخیص نمودن tashkhís nimúdan, تفریق ساختن tafrík sákhtan, شناختن shinákhtan, تباین نمودن tabáyun nimúdan. — (*to distinguish oneself*) امتیاز یافتن imtiyáz yáftan, ممتاز شدن mumtáz shudan.
DISTINGUISHED, ممتاز mumtáz, ذی شان zí-shán.
To DISTORT, *vide* To PERVERT, To BEND, To ERR.

DISTRACTED, شوریده shúrídah, شیدا shaidá, حیران hairán, سرگردان sargardán, برآشفته bar-áshuftah.
DISTRESS, *vide* HARDSHIP, MISERY, PAIN, GRIEF, DIFFICULTY.
To DISTRESS, *vide* To AFFLICT.—(*to distress oneself*) خودرا پریشان ساختن khwudrá paríshán sákhtan. —(*to be distressed*) محنت کشیدن mihnat kashídan, رنجش یافتن ranjish yáftan.
To DISTRIBUTE, تقسیم کردن taksím kardan, حصه بخشیدن hissah bakhshídan.
DISTRIBUTION, تقسیم taksím, قسمت kismat.
DISTRICT (*large tract of country*), دیار diyár, کوره kúrah, ناحیه náhiyah.—(*smaller division*) بلوك bulúk.
To DISTURB, خلل رسانیدن khalal rasánídan, آشوب انداختن áshúb andákhtan, ازدحام نمودن izdihám nimúdan, آشوفتن áshúftan, مانع بودن máni' búdan, مغشوش گردانیدن maghshúsh gardánídan.
DISTURBANCE, *vide* RIOT, QUARREL.
DISTURBED (*as a country, town, &c., in a state of anarchy*), مغشوش maghshúsh, آشفته áshuftah.—(*turbid, as water, &c.*) تیره tírah, غلیظ ghalíz, مکدر mukaddar.
DISUNITED, بی اتفاق bí-ittifák.
DISUSED, معطل mu'attal, منسوخ mansúkh.
DITCH, خندق khandak, گود gaud, گودال gaudál, حفره hufrah, چاله chálah.
DITTO, ایضاً aizan.
To DIVE, غوطه خوردن ghútah khwurdan, غوص نمودن ghaus nimúdan.
DIVER, غواص ghavvás, غوطه خور ghútah-khwur.
DIVERGENCE, اختلاف ikhtiláf.
DIVERS, *vide* VARIOUS.
DIVERSION, انحراف inhiráf. — (*amusement*), بازیچه bází-chah, گشت gasht, تماشا tamáshá, تفرج tafarruj, سیر sair, لهو و لعب lahv va la'b, صفا safá, کیف kaif.

To DIVERT (*turn off*), گردانیدن gardánídan, وا راندن vá-rándan.

To DIVIDE, تقسیم کردن taksím kardan, دو قسمت کردن dú kismat kardan.

DIVIDEND (*arith.*), مقسوم maksúm.

DIVINATION, علم غیب 'ilm-i-ghaib, رمل ramal, فال fál, تفاؤل tafa,,ul.

DIVINE, الهی iláhí, سبحانی subhání, ربانی rabbání, قدسی kudsí, مقدس mukaddas.

To DIVINE, *vide* To DISCERN.

DIVINER, *vide* MAGICIAN.

DIVINITY, الوهیت ulúhíyat. (*Vide* GOD.)

DIVISION, قسم kism, تقسیم taksím, تفریق tafrík, تفرقه tafrikah, توزیع tauzí', توجیه taujih.—(*in arithmetic*) قسمت kismat, تقسیم taksím, قسم kasm.— (*of an army, river, &c.*) شعبه shu'bah. (*Vide* DISTRICT.)

DIVISOR, مقسوم به maksúm bihi.

DIVORCE, طلاق talák. — (*reversal of a divorce*) رجعت rij'at.—(*divorce by mutual agreement*) خلع khul', *or* khal', مبارات mubárát. —(*triple divorce, which cannot be revoked*) سه طلاق sih-talák.—(*the time of probation which a divorced woman must wait before she can engage in a second marriage*) عدت 'iddat.

DIVORCED (*woman*), مطلقه mutallakah.

To DIVULGE, *vide* To REVEAL.

DIZZINESS, *vide* GIDDINESS.

To DO, کردن kardan, ساختن sákhtan, عمل نمودن 'amal nimúdan, پرداختن pardákhtan, نمودن nimúdan.— (*how do you do?*) احوال شما چه طور است ahvál-i-shumá chih taur ast, احوال شریف ahvál-i-sharíf, دماغ شما چاق است dimágh-i-shumá chák ast, کیف شما کوک است kaif-i-shumá kúk ast.

DOCILE, *vide* TRACTABLE.

DOCILITY, مطاوعت mutáva'at.

DOCK (*plant*), سلمه تره sallamah-tarah, لیواس lívás, ریواس rívás.

DOCKYARD, کار خانهٔ کشتی سازی kár-khánah-i-kashtí-sází.

DOCTOR (*sage*), دانا dáná, دانشمند dánish-mand, عالم 'álim, حکیم hakím, فاضل fázil.—(*doctors, pl.*) علما 'ulamá, حکما hukamá, افاضل afázil, فضلا fuzalá, مشائخ mashá,-ikh, اکابر akábir. — (*physician*) طبیب tabíb (*pl.* اطبا atibbá), حکیم hakím (*pl.* حکما hukamá).—(*of laws*) فقیه fakíh, مفتی muftí, ملا mullá, اهل فقه ahl-i-fikah.

DOCTRINE, حکمت hikmat, تعلیم ta'lím.—(*religious*) مذهب mazhab.

DOCUMENT, دستاویز dast-áviz, کاغذ kághaz.

DODGE, تمهید tamhíd.

DODGER, با تمهید bá-tamhíd.

DOE, *vide* DEER.

DOG, سگ sag, کلب kalb. — (*hound*) تازی tází, طوله túlah.—(*pet dog*) بوجی búji.—(*shepherd's dog*) سگ گله sag - i - gallah. — (*watch-dog*) سگ خانه sag-i-khánah.— (*keeper*) مستحفظ تازی mustahfiz-i-tází, تازیبان tází-bán. — (*star, Sirius*) شعری sha'rá, الکلب al-kalb.

DOGMA, عقیده 'akídah, معالم الدین ma'álimu-'d-dín.

DOLEFUL, حزین hazín, اندوهناک andúh - nák, سهمگین sahm - gín, غمگین gham-gín, جگرسوز jigar-súz.

DOLL (*plaything, puppet*), عروسک 'arúsak, عروسچه 'arúschah, علوچک 'alúchik (*vulg.*).

DOLPHIN, دلفین dalfín.

DOLT (*stupid fellow*), خرف khirif, کودن kaudan, کند kund.

DOMAIN, ملک mulk.

DOME, گنبذ gumbaz, قبه kubbah.— (*raised on open arches*) چار طاق chár-ták.

DOMESTIC (*tame*), خانگی khánagí, انسی unsí. (*Vide* SERVANT.)

DOMICILE, *vide* ABODE.

DOMICILED, متوطن mutavattin.

To DOMINATE, مسلط کردن musallat kardan.

DOMINATION, تسلط tasallut.
DOMINION, *vide* AUTHORITY, POWER, GOVERNMENT, COUNTRY.
DONATION, *vide* GIFT.
DONKEY, *vide* ASS.
DONOR, دهنده dihandah, اعانه دهنده i'ánah dihandah, بخشنده bakhshandah.
DOOR, در dar, دروازه darvázah, باب báb, قاپو kápú, قاپی kápí.—(*to shut the door*) چفت کردن chift kardan.—(*door-post*) باهو báhú.—(*one leaf of a door*) لنگهٔ در lingah-i-dar. — (*folding doors*) در کتابی dar-i-kitábí. — (*hall-door*) درب darb.—(*door-keeper*) در بان darbán.
DOT, نقطه nuktah.
DOTAGE, خرافت khiráfat.
DOTARD, خرافت گوی khiráfat-gúí.
DOUBLE, دو تا dú-tá, دو چند dú-chand, مضاعف muzá'af, مثنی musanná, دو مقابله dú-mukábalah, ضعف zi'f.
To DOUBLE, مضاعف نمودن muzá'af nimúdan, تضعیف نمودن taz'íf nimúdan.—(*fold*), دو تا کردن dú-tá kardan.
DOUBLE-BARRELLED, دو لوله dú-lúlah.
DOUBLE-EDGED (*as a sword*), دو دمه dú-damah.
DOUBLE-ENTENDRE, ایهام íhám.
DOUBLET, جلیتکه jilítkah.
DOUBT, شبهه shubhah, گمان gumán, شك shak, *or* shakk, ریب raib, شائبه shá,ibah, اشتباه ishtibáh.
To DOUBT, شك کردن shak kardan, گمان نمودن gumán nimúdan.
DOUBTFUL, مشتبه mushtabih, مشکوك mashkúk, مبهم mubham.
DOUCEUR, *vide* GIFT.
DOUGH, خمیر khamír, آرد سرشته árd-i-sirishtah.
DOVE, کبوتر kabútar, کفتر kaftar, حمام hamám. — (*turtle*) فاخته fákhtah, قمری kumrí, تذرو tazarv. [This latter word has usually been taken to signify the pheasant.]—(*house, or cote*) کبوتر خانه kabútar-khánah, کفتر خانه kaftar-khánah, برج کفتر burj-i-kaftar.
DOWN, فرو furú, فرود furúd, پائین pá,ín, زیر zír, نشیب nishíb, دامن dáman, دومن dúman.—(*of birds, &c.*) پر ریزه par-i-rízah.—(*nap of velvet or cloth*) کلك kulk.
DOWNCAST, *vide* SAD.
DOWNWARDS, سرازیر sar-á-zír, نشیب nishíb, شیب shíb, پائین pá,ín.
DOWRY (*given by bridegroom to bride*), صداق sadák, مهر mahr, کابین kabín.—(*property which the bride brings with her*) جهیز jahíz, جهاز jaház.
DOZE, پینکی pínakí.
To DOZE, پینکی زدن pínakí zadan, چرت زدن churt zadan.
DRAGOMAN, ترجمان tarjumán, مترجم mutarjim.
DRAGON, اژدها azhdahá, اژدر azhdar, ثعبان su'bán, تنین tanín.
DRAGON-FLY, مشخره mashkhurah.
DRAGON'S BLOOD, دم الاخوین damu-'l-akhavain, خون سیاوشان khún-i-siyávushán.
DRAIN, آبراه áb-ráh, آبگذر áb-guzar, بدر رو bi-dar-raw, کاریز káríz.—(*sink of a house*) آبشی áb-shí, آبریز áb-ríz.
To DRAIN (*land, house, &c.*), خشك ساختن khushk sákhtan.
DRAMA and DRAMATIC, بازی bází, شبیه shabíh.
DRAPER, بزاز bazzáz.
DRAUGHT (*gulp*), شرب shurb, جرعه jur'ah, قرت kurt. — (*decoction*) جوشانده júshándah.—(*of a letter, &c.*) سواد savád, مسوده musavvadah. — (*for money*) برات barát, حواله haválah. — (*act of pulling*) کشش kashish.—(*of air*) رهگذر هوا rahguzar-i-havá.
DRAUGHTS (*the game*), نرد nard. [This game being played with dice, rather resembles backgammon than draughts.]—(*draughts-board*) تخته نرد takhtah-i-nard.—(*draughts-man*) مهره muhrah.
DRAUGHTSMAN (*drawer*), طراح tarráh.

To DRAW (*pull*), کشیدن kashídan. —(*attract*) کشیدن kashídan, جذب ساختن jazb sákhtan, جلب نمودن jalb nimúdan. — (*a sword*) بیرون کشیدن bírún kashídan, آختن ákhtan (*obs.*).—(*extract*) بر آوردن bar-ávardan, کندن kandan, قلع کردن kal' kardan, بر کشیدن bar-kashídan, استخراج کردن istikhráj kardan.—(*paint*) کشیدن kashídan, تصویر کردن tasvír kardan, انگاشتن angáshtan.—(*a fowl, &c.*) پاك کردن pák kardan. — (*to draw up an army*) صف بستن saff bastan, صف آرائی نمودن saff-árá,í nimúdan.—(*to draw back, show a white feather*) از میدان گریختن az maidan guríkhtan. (*Vide* To WITHDRAW, To RETREAT, To QUAIL, To AVOID.)—(*to draw, as tea or other decoction*) دم کشیدن dam kashídan.—(*to draw tight*) بزور کشیدن bi-zúr kashídan, سفت کشیدن sift kashídan, تنگ کشیدن tang kashídan.

DRAWER (*of a table, &c.*), خانه khánah. (*Vide* PAINTER.)

DRAWERS, زیر جامه zír-jámah, شلوار shalvár.

DRAWING, *vide* PICTURE.—(*figure-drawing*) تصویر اجسام tasvír-i-ajsám.

DREAD, *vide* FEAR.

DREADFUL, هولناك haul-nák, ترسناك tars-nák, مخوف mukhavvif, خطرناك khatar-nák, هائل há,il, مرهوب marhúb, مهیب muhíb.

DREAM, خواب khwáb, رؤیا ru,yá.

To DREAM, خواب دیدن khwáb dídan, در خواب دیدن dar khwáb dídan, رؤیا دیدن ru,yá dídan.

DREGS, درد durd, فضله fazlah, خلط khilt, لای láí, سفل sifl. — (*of the people*) اذناب الناس aznábu-'n-nás.

To DRENCH, تر کردن tar kardan.

DRESS, پوشاك púshák, پوشن púshan, لباس libás, جامه jámah. (*Vide* CLOTHES.) — (*change of dress*) واگردان vá-gardán.

To DRESS, پوشیدن púshídan, رخت پوشیدن rakht púshídan, پوشانیدن púshánídan, ملبس ساختن mulabbas sákhtan.—(*a wound*) مرهم گذاردن marham guzárdan.—(*victuals, &c.*) درست کردن durust kardan, آماده کردن ámádan kardan, طبخ کردن tabkh kardan, پختن pukhtan.

DRESSING, *vide* PLASTER (*for a wound*).

DRIED (*fruit, &c.*), خشك khushk.

DRIFT, مجموعه majmú'ah.—(*meaning*) معنی ma'ní, مطلب matlab.

To DRIFT, مجموع شدن majmú' shudan.

DRILL (*military exercise*), مشق سرباز mashk-i-sarbáz, مشق نظام mashk-i-nizám, تعلیم نظام ta'lím-i-nizám..—(*ground*) میدان مشق maidán-i-mashk. — (*instrument*) مثقب miskab.

To DRILL, مشق کردن mashk kardan. —(*a hole*) سوراخ کردن súrákh kardan.

DRINK (*anything drinkable*), شرب shurb, مشروب mashrúb, نوشیدنی núshídaní.—(*intoxicating drinks*) مسکرات muskirát.

To DRINK, نوشیدن núshídan, آشامیدن áshámídan, خوردن khwurdan.—(*speaking respectfully*) میل فرمودن mail firmúdan, نوش جان فرمودن núsh-i-ján firmúdan.

DRINKABLE, خوردنی khwurdaní.

DRINKER, نوشنده núshandah.—(*drunkard*) شرابخور sharáb-khwur, باده پیما bádah-paimá.

DRINKING-VESSEL, ظرف آبخوری zarf-i-áb-khwurí.

To DRIP, تقاطر شدن takátur shudan, چکیدن chakídan.

DRIPPING (*fat*), پیه píh, چربی charbí.—(*as water*) تراوش tarávish, تقاطر takátur.

To DRIVE, راندن rándan.—(*in a carriage*) سوار شدن suvár shudan.—(*away*) راندن rándan, دفع کردن daf' kardan, دور کردن dúr kardan, بر گردانیدن bar-gardánídan.

DRIVER, *vide* COACH-MAN.

DRIZZLE, باران نم نم bárán-i-namnam.

DROLL, مضحک muzhik, با مزه bá-mazah.

DROMEDARY, بختی bukhtí, جمازه jummázah, شتر تند رو shutur-i-tund-raw.

DROP, قطره katrah, چکه chakkah.—(*pendant*) آویزه ávízah.

To DROP, چکیدن chakídan, قطره قطره افتادن katrah katrah uftádan, چکه کردن chakkah kardan, ریختن ríkhtan.—(*to let go*) ول کردن vil kardan. (*Vide* To FALL.)

DROPSICAL, مستسقی mustaskí.

DROPSY, استسقا istiská.

DROSS (*of metal*), درد durd, فضله fazlah, فلز filizz, ریم rím.

DROUGHT, خشکی khushkí, عدم باران 'adam-i-bárán.

To DROWN, غرق کردن ghark kardan.—(*to be drowned*) غرق شدن ghark shudan, مستغرق شدن mustaghrak shudan.

DROWSINESS, پینکی pínakí, چرت churt, خواب آلودگی khwáb-álúdagí.

DROWSY, خواب آلوده khwáb-álúdah, پینکی زده pínakí-zadah.

DRUDGERY, محنت mihnat.

DRUG, دوا davá, دارو dárú.

DRUGGIST, عطار 'attár, دارو فروش dárú-furúsh.

DRUM, دهل duhl, طبل tabl. —(*drum-stick*) کجک kajak, چوگان chaugán.—(*kettle-drum*) نقاره nakkárah, کوس kús, روئین خم rú,ín-khum.—(*small drum played on with the fingers*) تمبک tumbak, دمبک dumbak.—(*big-drum*), طبل بزرگ سر بازی tabl-i-buzurg-i-sar-bází.

DRUMMER, نقارچی nakkár-chí, دهل زن duhl-zan, طبال tabbál, طبلچی tabl-chí, بالابانچی bálábán-chí.

DRUNK, مست mast, سر مست sar-mast, مخمور makhmúr, سر گران sar-girán, سر خوش sar-khwush.—(*dead drunk*) سیاه مست siyáh-mast, بد مست bad-mast.

DRUNKARD, شراب خور sharáb-khwur, می پرست mai-parast.

DRUNKENNESS, مستی mastí, سر گرانی sar-giráni, سر خوشی sar-khwushí.

DRY, خشک khushk, یابس yábis.—(*uninteresting*) بی مزه bí-mazah.—(*thirsty*) تشنه tishnah, عطشان 'atshán.—(*wine*) تلخ talkh, دبش dibsh.

To DRY, خشک کردن khushk kardan, خشکانیدن khushkánídan.

DUAL, تثنیه tasniyah.

DUBIOUS, *vide* DOUBTFUL.

DUCAT (*value generally about ten shillings sterling*), باجغلی bájughlí, باج اقلی báj-uklí, مجر majar.

DUCK, اوردک úrdak, بط bat, بطك batak, مرغابی murgh-ábí.

DUCT, *vide* CANAL.

DUCTILE, تلزج talazzuj.

DUE (*to be paid*), دادنی dádaní, واجب الادا vájibu-'l-adá. (*Vide* RIGHT, PROPER, TAX, TRIBUTE.)

DUEL, *vide* BATTLE.

DUGS (*breasts*), پستانها pistánhá, ثدیین sudyain.

DULCIMER, سنتور santúr, زنتور zan-túr.

DULCO-ACID (*as the juice of an orange, &c.*), میخوش mai-khwush.

DULL, *vide* BLUNT, STUPID.

DUMB, گنگ gung, لال lál, بیزبان bí-zabán, بکیم bakím (*pl.* بکمان bukmán).

DUMBNESS, بیزبانی bí-zabání, گنگی gungí, بکم bakam, بکامت baká-mat.

DUN (*coloured*), سمند samand.—(*importunate creditor*) متقاضی mu-takází.

To DUN (*importune*), تقاضا کردن ta-kázá kardan, پا پی شدن pá-pai shudan (*vulg.*).

DUNG, گوه gúh, گه guh, زبل zibl, براز biráz, فضله fazlah.—(*of cows*) سرگین sargín.—(*of horses*) پئین pa,ín, پین pain, پهین pahín.—(*of deer, sheep, camels, &c.*) پشکل pishkil.—(*of birds*) چلغوز chalghúz, پیخال píkhál, زلق zilk, فضله fazlah, زل zil (*vulg.*).—(*dried for fuel*) پاچك páchak, تپاله tapálah, تپله tapalah, جله jallah, ساز گار sáz-gár.

DUNGEON, سیاه چال siyáh-chál, زندان zindán, دستاقخانه dusták-khánah.

DUNG-HILL, مزبله mazbalah, دمن dumn.
DUPE, غبی ghabí, گول gúl, کودن kaudan.
DUPLICATE, مضاعف muzá'af.—(*of papers*) نقل nakl, دو نسخه dú nuskhah.
DUPLICITY, *vide* DECEIT.
DURABILITY, بقا baká, پایداری páy-dárí, استواری ustuvárí.
DURABLE, پایدار páy-dár, قائم ká,im, استوار ustuvár.
DURATION, استمرار istimrár, دوام davám, قرار karár.
DURING, مادام mádám, بین bain, تا tá, اثنا asná, درمیان dar miyán, در خلال dar khilál.
DUSK (*of evening*), تاریکی tárikí, ظلمت zulmat, تیرگی tíragí, شفق shafak, شبانگاه shabán-gáh, وقت گرگ و میش vakt-i-gurg u mísh (*literally* "*Time of wolf and sheep*"; *French*, "*Entre chien et loup.*")
DUST, خاک khák, تراب turáb, قتر katar, نقع nak', پلم palm.—(*flying dust*) گرد gard, غبار ghubár.—(*gold dust*) زرک zarak, ریزه طلا rizah-i-tilá. — (*to bite the dust*) زمین خوردن zamín khwurdan.—(*to dust*) گرد تکانیدن gard takání-dan, گرد افشاندن gard afshándan. —(*to kick up a dust*) آشوب کردن áshúb kardan.
DUST-HOLE, *vide* ASH-PIT.
DUSTY, غبار آلوده ghubár - álúdah, مغبر mughbarr.
DUTY, حق hakk, کار kár, پیشه píshah, ذمه zimmah, منصب man-sab, عهده 'uhdah, مبتغا mubtaghá, خدمت khidmat, منت minnat, وعده va'dah.—(*special duty*) کار معین kár - i - mu'ayyan. (*Vide* CUSTOM, TAX.)—(*to perform or fulfil a duty*) از عهدهٔ کار بر آمدن az 'uhdah - i - kár bar-ámadan, ایفای عهده نمودن ífá,í - i - 'uhdah nimúdan, کار بجا آوردن kár bi-já ávardan, وفا بوعده کردن vafá bi-va'dah kardan, اجرای امر نمودن ijrá,í-i-amr nimúdan, ادائی خدمت کردن adá,í-i-khidmat kardan.—(*to fail in a duty*) از عهده بر نیامدن az 'uhdah bar-nayámadán, از عهده عدول کردن az 'uhdah 'udúl kar-dan, کوتاهی کردن kútáhí kardan, قصور کردن kusúr kardan.
DWARF, کوتاه قد kútah-kad, مردک mardak, کتولی kutúlí, خپل khip-pil (*vulg.*).
To DWELL, *vide* To ABIDE.
DWELLER, متوطن mutavattin, ساکن sákin, باشنده báshandah, مقیم mukím.
DWELLING, *vide* ABODE.
DYE, رنگ rang, صبغت sibghat.
To DYE, رنگ زدن rang zadan, رنگین کردن rangín kardan, صبغت نمودن sibghat nimúdan.
DYER, رنگ زن rang-zan, رنگ ریز rang-ríz, صباغ sabbágh.
DYNASTY, طبقه tabakah, نسل nasl, سلسله silsilah.
DYSENTERY, اسهال is-hál, زحیر zahír.
DYSPEPSIA, *vide* INDIGESTION.

E.

EACH, هر har, هر یك har yak.
EAGER, آرزومند árzú-mand, شوقمند shauk-mand, مشتاق mushták, شائق shá,ik, سرگرم sar-garm.
EAGLE, عقاب 'ukáb, نسر nasr, دال dál, دالمن dálman, مود múd, قره قوش karah-kúsh. — (*two - headed eagle, Russian arms*) عقاب دو سر 'ukáb-i-dú-sar.
EAR, گوش gúsh.—(*of a pitcher or jug*) مشته mushtah, دسته dastah. —(*of corn*) خوشه khúshah, سنبله sumbulah.—(*by ear*) شفاهاً shifá-han.—(*to put one's fingers in one's*

ears) گوش گرفتن gúsh giriftan, پنبه در گوش کردن pambah dar gúsh kardan.—(to lend an ear) گوش دادن gúsh dádan.—(to set by the ears), بر هم زدن bar-ham zadan.

EARLY, زود zúd, زو zú (vulg.).—(in the morning) فجر صبح fajr-i-subh, علی الصباح 'alá-'s-sabáh, سحر گاهی sahar-gáhí, صبح زود subh-i-zúd.

To EARN, مداخل کردن mudákhil kardan, اندوختن andúkhtan, حاصل کردن hásil kardan.

EARNEST (true, really), حق hakk, فی الحقیقت fí-'l-hakíkat, جداً jiddan, راست rást, یقین yakín.—(advance of money) پیشگی písha-gí, بیعانه bai'ánah, عربون 'urbún, سلف salaf.

EARNESTLY, بطور جدی bi-taur-i-jiddí, جداً jiddan.

EARNING, تحصیل tahsíl, کسب kasb, اکتساب iktisáb.

EARRING, حلقه گوش halkah-i-gúsh, گوشواره gúshvárah.

EARTH, خاک khák, زمین zamín, ارض arz, پلم palm.

EARTHEN, خاکی khákí, سفالین sifálín.—(earthenware) از گل az gil, سفالی sifálí, گلین gilín.

EARTHLY, عالمی 'álamí, ارضی arzí.

EARTHQUAKE, زلزلهٔ زمین zalzalah-i-zamín, تزلزل tazalzul.

EARTHWORK, خاکریز khák-ríz.

EARWIG, گوش خزک gúsh-khazak.

EASE (facility), آسانی ásání, سهولت suhúlat, سلاست salásat.—(repose) آرام árám, آسایش ásáyish, راحت ráhat, فراغت farághat.—(at ease) مرفه البال muraffahu-'l-bál.—(to be at ease) آرامیدن árámídan.—(to take one's ease) مشغول عیش بودن mashghúl-i-'aish búdan.—(to ease oneself) ریدن rídan.

EASILY, آسان ásán, سهلاً sahlan, در عین صفا dar 'ain-i-safá.

EAST, مشرق mashrik, شرق shark, مطلع matla'.—(to the east of) در سمت شرقی dar samt-i-sharkí.—(the East, country) مشرق زمین mashrik-zamín.

EASTER, عید فطیر 'íd-i-fatír.

EASTERN, شرقی sharkí.—(countries) بلاد مشرقیه bilád-i-mashrikíyah.—(languages) السنهٔ شرقیه alsinah-i-sharkíyah.—(Question) مسلهٔ شرق masalah-i-shark.

EASY, آسان ásán, سهل sahl.

To EAT, خوردن khwurdan, تناول کردن tanávul kardan.—(speaking respectfully) میل فرمودن mail firmúdan, نوش جان فرمودن núsh-i-ján firmúdan.

EATABLE, خوردنی khwurdaní, قابل اکل kabil-i-akl.

EATABLES (provisions) خوراک khwurák, قوت kút, طعام ta'ám, خوراکی khwurákí (vulg.).—(prepared for a journey) زاد zád, توشه túshah.

EAU DE VIE, عرق 'arak, ماء الحیات má,u-'l-hayát.

EAVES (of a house), طره turrah, شادروان shádurván.

EBB, زوال zavál, جزر jazr.

EBONY, آبنوس ábnús.

EBULLITION, vide BOILING.

ECCENTRIC, خارج مرکز khárij-i-markaz, خارج دائره khárij-i-dá,irah, خارج العاده kháriju-'l-'ádah.

ECHO, صدائی کوه sadá,í-i-kúh, نوف núf, بنت الجبل bintu-'l-jabal.

ECLAT, vide SPLENDOUR.

ECLIPSE (of sun), کسوف kusúf, کسافت kasáfat, انکساف inkisáf.—(of moon) خسوف khusúf, انخساف inkhisáf.

ECLIPSED (sun), منکسف munkasif.—(moon) منخسف munkhasif.

ECLIPTIC (circle), طریق شمس taríki-shams, راه آفتاب ráh-i-áftáb.

ECONOMICAL, خانه دار khánah-dár, کم خرج kam-kharj.

To ECONOMISE, ادارت کردن idárat kardan.

ECONOMY, خانه داری khánah-dárí, باریک روی barík-rawí.

ECSTASY, وجد vajd, شعف sha'af, بی خودی bí-khwudí.

EDDY, موج ریزی mauj-rízí.

EDEN, باغ عدن bágh-i-'adan.

EDGE, دم dam, لب lab. (Vide BORDER, BOUNDS, TRIMMING.)—

(*to be set on edge, the teeth*) کند شدن kund shudan.
EDIBLE, *vide* EATABLE.
EDICT, تنظیم tanzím, امر amr. (*Vide* PROCLAMATION.)
EDIFICE, عمارت 'imárat, بنا biná.
To EDIFY (*to improve by teaching, to instruct*), معمور نمودن ma'múr nimúdan, تأدیب کردن ta,díb kardan.
EDITION (*of a book*), اجرا ijrá.
EDITOR (*of a book or periodical, &c.*), مؤلف mu,allif, مهتمم muhtamim, مدبر mudabbir, کارگذار kárguzár, محرر muharrir, مدیر mudír.
To EDUCATE, ترتیب کردن tartíb kardan, تربیت کردن tarbiyat kardan, پرورش کردن parvarish kardan.
EDUCATED, مؤدب mu,addab.
EDUCATION, تربیت tarbiyat, تعلیم ta'lím, تأدیب ta,díb, ترتیب tartíb.—(*of children*) حضانت hizánat.
EEL, مار ماهی már-máhí, یلان ماهی yalán-máhí.
To EFFACE, محو کردن mahv kardan, پاك کردن pák kardan.
EFFACED, منسوخ mansúkh, مندرس mundaris.
EFFACEMENT, ابطال ibtál, محو mahv.
EFFECT, اثر asar, تأثیر ta,sír, نتیجه natíjah, فرع far'.—(*to produce an effect*) تأثیر نمودن ta,sír nimúdan. —(*in effect*) واقعاً váki'an. — (*to this effect*) از این قرار az ín karár.
To EFFECT, *vide* To PERFORM.
EFFECTS, *vide* GOODS.
EFFECTUAL, کارگر kár-gar, مؤثر mu,assir, مفید mufíd.
EFFEMINACY, رخاوت rakhávat.
EFFEMINATE, رخو rakhv, زن طبیعت zan-tabí'at.
To EFFERVESCE, جوشیدن júshídan, بجوش آمدن bi-júsh ámadan.
EFFERVESCENCE, جوش júsh.
EFFICACIOUS, *vide* EFFECTUAL.
EFFICIENT, *vide* ABLE, CAPABLE.
EFFIGY, شکل shakl, صورت súrat, مجسمه mujassamah.
EFFORT, کوشش kúshish, سعی sa'í, قصد kasd, تلاش talásh, اهتمام ihtimám, عزم 'azm, همت himmat, جد jidd, جهد jahd.—(*a great effort*) سعی بلیغ sa'í-i-balígh.
EFFUSION, سفك safk, ریزش rízish. —(*of blood*) سفك دم safk-i-dam. —(*literary*) مقاله makálah, فصل fasl.
EGG, بیضه baizah, تخم tukhm, تخم مرغ tukhm-i-murgh. — (*rotten egg*) تخم لق tukhm-i-lak.—(*shell*) قشر kishr, پوست púst. — (*plant*) *vide* BRINJAL. (*Vide also* OMELET, POACHED EGG).
EGLANTINE (*sweetbriar*), نسرین nisrín.
EGOTISM, خود پرستی khwud-parastí, خود بینی khwud-bíní.
EGOTIST, *or* EGOTISTICAL, خود پرست khwud-parast, جود بین khwud-bín.—(*to be egotistical*) منم زدن manam zadan.
EITHER, خواه khwáh, یا yá.
EJACULATION, همهمه ذکر hamhamah-i-zikr, ندا nidá. — (*to mutter ejaculations*) همهمه ذکر کردن hamhamah-i-zikr kardan.
To EJECT, بیرون کردن bírún kardan, راندن rándan.
EJECTMENT, اخراج ikhráj, طرد tarad, اطراد itrád, نفی nafy.
To ELABORATE, ترتیب دادن tartíb dádan, تنظیم نمودن tanzím nimúdan.
To ELAPSE, طول کشیدن túl kashídan, گذشتن guzashtan.
ELASTIC, جهنده jihandah.
ELASTICITY, جهندگی jihandagí.
ELBOW, مرفق mirfak, آرنج áranj.
To ELBOW, غربیله کردن gharbílah kardan.
ELDER, مهتر mihtar, مهین mihín, اول avval. — (*head-man*) *vide* CHIEF.
ELDERS (*of the people*), مشائخ masha,ikh, بزرگان buzurgán, اکابر akábir.
ELDEST, بزرگترین buzurgtarín.
ELECT (*of God*), بر گزیده خدا barguzídah-i-khudá, خوانده شده خدا khwándah-shudah-i-khudá.

TO ELECT, بر گزیدن bar-guzídan, انتخاب نمودن intikháb nimúdan.

ELECTION, انتخاب intikháb.

ELECTRIC LIGHT, چراغ الکتریسیته chirágh-i-alaktrísítah.

ELECTRICITY, کهربایت kah-rubáyat, الکتریسیته alaktrísítah (*eur.*).

ELECTRO-PLATED, نقره نما nukrah-nimá.

ELECTUARY, معجون ma'jún.

ELEGANCE, نزاکت nazákat, لطافت latáfat, زینت zínat, نقاوت nakávat, حسن husn, قشنگی kashangí. (*vulg.*).

ELEGANT (*neat*), منقه munakkah, نازک názuk, خوشنما khwush-nimá, لطیف latíf, قشنگ kashang (*vulg.*).

ELEGY, مرثیه marsiyah.

ELEMENT, عنصر 'unsur (*pl.* عناصر 'anásir *or* عناصیر 'anásír).—(*the four elements*), چهار عناصیر chahár 'anásír, عناصیر اربع 'anásír - i - arba'.

ELEMENTARY, ابتدائی ibtidá,í, جهت مبتدیان jihat-i-mubtadiyán.

ELEPHANT, پیل píl, فیل fíl.—(*saddle of an elephant*) هوده haudah, هودج haudaj.—(*driver*) پیلبان píl-bán.

ELEPHANTIASIS (*kind of leprosy*), فیلپا fíl-pá, لری larrí, داءالفیل dá,u-'l-fíl.

TO ELEVATE, افراختن afrákhtan, افراشتن afráshtan, بلند ساختن buland sákhtan, بالا کشیدن bálá kashídan.

ELEVATED, *vide* EXALTED.

ELEVATION, رفعت rif'at, ارتفاع irtifá', بلندی bulandí, افرازی afrází, اعلا a'lá.—(*hill*) شامخ shámikh.

TO ELICIT, استنباط نمودن istimbát nimúdan, استدراک نمودن istidrák nimúdan, ملتفت شدن multafit shudan.

TO ELIMINATE, محذوف کردن mahzúf kardan, استخراج نمودن istikhráj nimúdan.

ELISION, حذف hazf.

ELITE, زبده zubdah.

ELIXIR, اکسیر iksír.

ELK, گوزن gauzan.

ELLIPTIC, بیضه baizah, بیضوی baizaví.

ELLIPSIS, مفهوم mafhúm, مقدر mukaddar.

ELM (*tree*), نارون náravan, ناروند nárvand.

ELOCUTION, معانی بیان ma'ání-bayán, طلاقت talákat.

ELOQUENCE, فصاحت fasáhat, بلاغت balághat, زبان آوری zabán-ávarí, خوش کلامی khwush-kalámí, طلاقت talákat, سخن پردازی sukhun-pardází.

ELOQUENT, فصیح fasíh, زبان آور zabán-ávar, شیرین ادا shírín-ádá, بلیغ balígh (*pl.* بلغا bulaghá).

ELSEWHERE, جائی دیگر já,í-i-dígar.

EMACIATED, لاغر lághir, زار و نزار zár va nizár, نحیف nahíf, مختل mukhtall.

TO EMANATE, صادر شدن sádir shudan, صدور کردن sudúr kardan.

EMANATION, ظهور zuhúr, صدور sudur.

TO EMBALM, تحنیط نمودن tahnít nimúdan, مومیا کردن múmiyá kardan.

EMBANKMENT, پشته pushtah, دمدمه damdamah, بند band.

TO EMBARK, بر جهاز رفتن bar jahaz raftan, در کشتی نشستن dar kashtí nishastan.

EMBARRASSED, پا در گل pá dar gil, معطل mu'attal.—(*to be embarrassed*) معطل ماندن mu'attal mándan, گیر افتادن gír uftádan.

EMBARRASSMENT, اشکال ishkál, دهشت dihshat, مضایقه muzáyakah, مضیق mazík.

EMBASSY, پیغام paighám, پیام payám, رساله risálah, سفارت sifárat, سفارت خانه sifárat - khánah.—(*Secretary of Embassy*) *vide* SECRETARY.

TO EMBELLISH, *vide* TO ADORN.

EMBELLISHMENT, زیب zíb, آرایش áráyish, زینت zínat, تزیین tazyín.

EMBERS, اخگر akhgar.

TO EMBEZZLE, دزدی کردن duzdí kardan, تصرف کردن tasarruf kardan.

EMBLEM, نشان nishán, اشاره ishárah, علامت 'alámat, کنایه kináyah.

EMBLEMATICAL, علامت 'alámat, نشانه nishánah.

EMBONPOINT, نار پستان nár-pistán, فربهی farbihí.

EMBOUCHURE, مخرج makhraj, بوغاز búgház.

EMBRACE, آغوش ághúsh.

To EMBRACE, آغوش کشیدن ághúsh kashídan, بغل گیری کردن baghal-gírí kardan, معانقه نمودن mu'ánakah nimúdan, کنار گرفتن kinár giriftan, در بر گرفتن dar bar giriftan. (*Vide* To INCLUDE, To ACCEPT.)

EMBRACING, *vide* CONTAINING.

EMBRASURE, بارو bárú.

To EMBROIDER, نقش دوختن naksh dúkhtan, طرازیدن tirázídan.

EMBROIDERER, مطرز mutarriz.

EMBROIDERY, نقش naksh, قلابدوزی kulláb-dúzí, قیطاندوزی kaitán-dúzí, بوته bútah, نقده دوزی nakdah-dúzí, طراز tiráz.—(*gold embroidery*) زر دوزی zar-dúzí.

To EMBROIL, گیر آوردن gír ávardan, دو چار کردن dú-chár kardan.—(*to become embroiled*) گیر آمدن gír ámadan, دو چار شدن dú-chár shudan.

EMBRYO, جنین janín.

EMERALD, زمرد zumurrud, مینو mínú.—(*colour*) زمرد رنگ zumurrud rang.

EMERGENCY, ضرورت zarúrat, حادثه hádisah (*pl.* حوادث havádis.)

EMERY, سنباده sumbádah.

EMETIC, دوائی قی davá,í-i-kai, دوائی مستفرغ davá,í-i-mustafrigh, دوائی مقیی davá,í-i-mukayyí.

EMEUTE, فتنه fitnah.

EMIGRANT, مهاجر muhájir.

To EMIGRATE, جلائی وطن نمودن jalá,í-i-vatan nimúdan, ترك وطن کردن tark-i-vatan kardan.

EMIGRATION, جلائی وطن jalá,í-i-vatan, ترك وطن tark-i-vatan.

EMINENCE (*high ground*), سر کوب sar-kúb, تپه tappah, پشته pushtah, گریوه girívah, قله kullah. (*Vide* DEGREE (*rank*), DIGNITY.)

EMINENCE (*term of respect*), جناب فضیلتماب janáb-i-fazílat-ma,áb.

EMINENT, *vide* FAMOUS, GREAT.

EMISSION (*sending forth*), اخراج ikhráj, ارسال irsál, انفاذ infáz. —(*seminal*) انزال inzál, مشع mash'.

EMOLUMENT, نفع naf'.

EMOTION, شغف خاطر shaghf-i-khátir.

EMPEROR, شاهنشاه sháhinsháh, سلطان sultán, خاقان khákán.—(*of Rome*) قیصر kaisar (*i.e.* *Cæsar*).—(*of China*) فغفور faghfúr, خاقان khákán.

EMPHASIS, تاکید ta,kíd.

EMPHATICALLY, بطور قطعی bi-taur-i-kat'í.

EMPIRE, *vide* GOVERNMENT, KINGDOM.

To EMPLOY, نگاه داشتن nigáh dáshtan, استخدام نمودن istikhdám nimúdan, مستخدم ساختن mustakhdam sákhtan.—(*to employ oneself*) مشتغل شدن mushtaghil shudan.—(*to be employed, idiom, &c.*) موضوع شدن mauzú' shudan.

EMPLOYÉ, کار گذار kár-guzár, وکیل vakíl.

EMPLOYMENT, کار kár, کار و بار kár u bár, شغل shughl, عمل 'amal.—(*office*) عهده 'uhdah, منصب mansab, خدمت khidmat.—(*out of employment*) معزول ma'zúl, بی کار bí-kár.

EMPRESS, قیصر kaisar.

EMPTY, تهی tuhí, خالی khálí, فارغ fárigh, پوك púk (*vulg.*).—(*empty-headed*) تهی مغز tuhí-maghz, تهی دماغ tuhí-dimágh.

To EMPTY, خالی کردن khálí kardan, تهی نمودن tuhí nimúdan.—(*into, like a river*) خالی کردن توی khálí kardan túí.

EMULATION, غیرت ghairat, رشك rashk.—(*competition*) مجاهده mujáhadah, مقابله mukábalah.

ENAMEL, مینا míná, کاشی káshí.

To ENAMEL, مینا نمودن míná nimúdan.

ENAMELLED, مینا míná, مینا کار míná-kár.

ENAMELLER, مینا کار míná-kár, دواتگر davát-gar.

ENAMOURED, شیفته shíftah, مشعوف mash'úf.

To ENCAMP, خیمه زدن khaimah zadan, اردو زدن urdú zadan, مقام کردن makám kardan.

ENCAMPMENT, اردو urdú, اوتراق úturák, لشکرگاه lashkar-gáh.

To ENCHANT, *vide* To DELIGHT, To PLEASE, To FASCINATE.

ENCHANTED, افسون کرده afsún kardah, جادو زده jádú-zadah.—(*pleased*) خوشوقت khwush-vakt, مبتهج mubtahij.

ENCHANTER, جادوگر jádú-gar, افسونگر afsún-gar, ساحر sáhir, سحار sahhár.

ENCHANTING, دلربا dil-rubá. دلاویز dil-áviz.

ENCHANTMENT, جادو jádú, جادوگری jádú-garí, سحر sihr, افسون afsún, عزیمت 'azímat.—(*fascination of the heart*) دلستانی dil-sitání, دلاویزی dil-ávízí, جانکشی ján-kashí, شیفتگی shíftagí.

ENCIENTE, *vide* PREGNANT.—(*military term*) خندق khandak.

To ENCLOSE, احاطه نمودن ihátah-nimúdan, حاوی بودن háví búdan, محاصره نمودن muhásarah nimúdan.

ENCLOSURE, حیاط hayát, احاطه ihátah.—(*for cattle*) آغل ághil, مربض marbaz, سول súl.—(*a letter, &c.*) ملفوف malfúf, مندرج mundarij.

ENCOMIAST, مدیحه سنج madíhah-sanj, مداح maddáh.

ENCOMIUM, مدیحه madíhah, مدح madh.

ENCORE, ایضاً aizan.

ENCOUNTER, تقابل takábul, مقابله mukábalah. (*Vide* BATTLE.)

To ENCOUNTER, دو چار شدن dú-chár shudan. (*Vide* To FIGHT.)

To ENCOURAGE, دلاسائی دادن dil-ásá,í dádan, تسلی نمودن tasallí nimúdan.

ENCOURAGEMENT, دلاسائی dil-ásá,í, تسلی tasallí.

To ENCROACH upon, تجاوز کردن tajávuz kardan, از حد گذشتن az hadd guzashtan, دخل کردن dakhl kardan.

ENCUMBRANCE, بار bár, حمل haml, مانع máni'.

ENCYCLOPÆDIA, دائرت العلوم dá,iratu-'l-'ulúm, دائرت المعارف dá,iratu-'l-ma'áríf.

END (*point or tip*), سر sar, نوک nauk.—(*conclusion*) آخر ákhir, آخرت ákhirat, عاقبت 'ákibat, اتمام itmám, تمام tamám, تتمه tatammah, سر sar, انصرام insirám, انتها intihá, نهایت niháyat, انجام anjám, سرانجام saranjám, ختم khatm, خاتمه khátimah, اختتام ikhtitám, فرجام farjám, مال ma,ál.—(*object*) غرض gharaz.—(*in the end*) عاقبت الامر 'ákibatu-'l-amr.—(*to the end*) الی آخره ilá ákhirah.

To END, *vide* To FINISH.—(*to end in*) (به) تمام شدن tamám shudan (bi).

ENDEAVOUR, *vide* EFFORT, ATTEMPT.—(*to use one's endeavours*) اهتمامرا بعمل آوردن ihtimámrá bi-'amal ávardan, بذل همت کردن bazl-i-himmat kardan.

To ENDEAVOUR, ساعی کردن sá'í kardan, کوشش نمودن kúshish nimúdan.

ENDEMIC, مرض متداول marz-i-mutadávil, مرض عمومی marz-i-'umúmí.

ENDIVE, کاسنی kásní.

ENDLESS, بی پایان bí-páyán, بی نهایت bí-niháyat, بلا نهایت bilá-niháyat.

To ENDORSE, مضبوط کردن mazbút kardan, امضا کردن imzá kardan.—(*a statement*) صحه گذاشتن zahah guzáshtan.

ENDOWMENT (*pious bequest*), وقف vakf, موقوفه maukúfah, خیرات khairát.

ENDURANCE, *vide* BOLDNESS.

To ENDURE, صبر کردن sabr kardan, بر داشت کردن bar-dásht kardan, طاقت داشتن tákat dáshtan, تحمل

نمودن tahammul nimúdan, تاب آوردن táb ávardan. (*Vide* To LAST.)

ENEMA, محقن mihkan, حقنه huknah, دستور dastúr, اماله imálah.

ENEMY, دشمن dushman, عدو 'adúv, *or* 'aduww, خصم khasm, معاند mu'ánid, غنيم ghaním, مخالف mukhálif, عوان 'aván, حريف haríf, مبغض mubghiz.

ENERGETIC, متجاهد mutajáhid.

ENERGY, قوت kúvat, *or* kuvvat, شدت shiddat, غيرت ghairat, اجتهاد ijtihád, شوق shauk.

ENFEEBLED, *vide* WEAK.

To ENFRANCHISE, مسلم نمودن musallam nimúdan, آزاد نمودن ázád nimúdan, رستگار كردن rastagár kardan.

To ENGAGE (*take into employ*), نگاه داشتن nigáh dáshtan, معين كردن mu'ayyan kardan. — (*settle*) عهد نمودن 'ahd nimúdan.

ENGAGED, *vide* BUSY.

ENGAGEMENT, عهده 'uhdah, عهد 'ahd, ميثاق mísák, كار kár, وعده va'dah.—(*to have an engagement*) وعده داشتن va'dah dáshtan.

ENGAGING, دلپسند dil-pasand.

To ENGENDER, توليد نمودن taulíd nimúdan.

ENGINE (*machine*), آلت álat, منجنيق manjaník.

ENGINEER, مهندس muhandis.

ENGLISH, انگليس inglís, انگليسی inglísí.

To ENGRAVE, كندن kandan, نقش كردن nakhsh kardan, حك كردن hakk kardan.

ENGRAVER, حكاك hakkák.

To ENGROSS, تحرير نمودن tahrír nimúdan.

To ENHANCE (*raise or increase*), زياد كردن ziyád kardan, افزودن afzúdan, اضافه نمودن izáfah nimúdan.

ENHANCEMENT, رفع raf', ترقی tarakkí, ترقيه tarkiyah.—(*enhancement of value of goods, by a fictitious tender of high price; a misdemeanour punishable by Muhammadan law*) نجش najsh.

ENIGMA, معما mu'ammá, رمز ramz, لغز lughz.

To ENJOIN, *vide* To COMMAND.

To ENJOY, لذت بردن *or* كشيدن lazzat burdan, *or* kashídan, متمتع شدن mutamatti' shudan, حظ كردن hazz kardan, برخوردن bar-khwurdan.—(*possess*) تصرف كردن tasarruf kardan.—(*to enjoy oneself*) عيش كردن 'aish kardan, دماغ كردن dimágh kardan.

ENJOYMENT, *vide* PLEASURE.

To ENLARGE, وسعت دادن vus'at dádan, بزرگتر كردن buzurgtar kardan.

ENLARGEMENT, توسيع tausí.

To ENLIGHTEN, روشنائی بخشودن rúshná,í bakhshúdan, روشن كردن raushan kardan, منور كردن munavvar kardan. (*Vide* To INFORM.)

To ENLIST (*raise soldiers*), جمع آوری نمودن jam'-ávarí nimúdan.—(*take service as a soldier*) سرباز شدن sarbáz shudan.

ENMITY, دشمنی dushmaní, عداوت 'adávat, عدوان 'udván, كينه kínah, كين kín, مخالفت mukhálafat, مخاصمت mukhásamat, خصومت khusúmat. — (*to bear enmity*) كين داشتن kín dáshtan.

ENNOBLED, مشرف musharraf.

ENNUI, دلتنگی dil-tangí, بيزاری bízári.

ENORMOUS, *vide* BIG.

ENOUGH, بس bas, كافی káfí.—(*exclamation!*) بس bas, بسا basá, باشد báshad.

To ENQUIRE, *vide* To ASK.

ENQUIRY, تفتيش taftísh, تجسس tajassus, تفحص tafahhus. (*Vide* QUESTION.)

ENRAGED, *vide* ANGRY.

To ENRICH, غنی ساختن ghaní sákhtan.

ENSIGN, *vide* FLAG.

To ENSLAVE, اسير كردن asír kardan.

To ENSNARE, *vide* To CATCH.

EN SUITE, تابع tábi', تبع taba'.

To ENTANGLE, پيچاپيچ كردن pích-á-pích kardan, بر هم زدن bar-ham zadan.—(*to be entangled*) محکم شدن muhkam shudan, بر هم زده شدن bar-ham-zadah shudan, گیر آمدن gír ámadan.

TO ENTER, اندر آمدن andar ámadan, داخل شدن dákhil shudan, تو رفتن tú raftan, دخل نمودن dakhl nimúdan, در شدن dar shudan.

ENTERPRIZE, عزیمت 'azímat, مبادرت mubádarat.

ENTERTAINMENT (*feast, &c.*), مهمانی mihmání, میهمانی mihmání, ضیافت ziyáfat, سور súr, ولیمه valímah.

ENTHRONEMENT, اجلاس ijlás.

ENTHUSIASM, *vide* ZEAL, INSPIRATION, GENIUS.

TO ENTICE, *vide* TO ALLURE, TO TEMPT.

ENTIRE, کامل kámil, تمام tamám, تام támm, مسلم musallam, صحیح sahíh, کل kull.

ENTIRELY, سراسر sar-á-sar, تماماً tamáman, بالکل bi-'l-kull, بالکلیت bi-'l-kulliyat, بالمره bi-'l-marrah, کلاً و قاطبةً kullan va kátibatan, همه رویهم رفته hamah rúí-ham raftah, کلیتاً kullíyatan, بعینه bi'ainihi.

ENTIRETY, درستی durustí, تمامیت tamámíyat.

TO ENTITLE, تسمیه کردن tasmiyah kardan.—(*entitled*) متلقب mutalakkib, مسمی musammá, موسوم mausúm.

TO ENTOMB, *vide* TO BURY.

ENTRAILS, امعا am'á.

ENTRANCE, *vide* ACCESS, DOOR, GATE.

TO ENTREAT, *vide* BEG.

ENTRÉE, دخول dukhúl.

ENTRENCHMENTS, استحکامات istihkámát.

ENTREPRENEUR, شبیه ساز shabíh-sáz.

TO ENTRUST, *vide* TO COMMIT.

ENTRY, دخول dukhúl.

ENUMERATION, تعداد ta'dád, احتساب ihtisáb.

ENUNCIATION, تعبیر ta'bír.

ENVELOPE (*cover*), لفافه lafáfah.

TO ENVELOPE, ملفوف نمودن malfúf nimúdan, اشتمال نمودن ishtimál nimúdan.

ENVIED, مغبوط maghbút, محسود mahsúd, رشکبرده rashk-burdah.

ENVIOUS, بد چشم bad-chashm, بد خواه bad-khwáh, حسود hasúd, رشکین rashkín.

ENVIRONS, نواحی naváhí, گرد و نواح gird ú naváh, حوالی haválí, حول و حوش haul u haush, اطراف atráf.

ENVOY, *vide* AMBASSADOR.

ENVY, حسد hasad, رشك rashk, حسرت hasrat, غل ghill.

TO ENVY, رشك بردن rashk burdan, حسد بردن hasad burdan.

EPAULETTE, علم 'alam, نشان دوش nishán-i-dúsh.

EPIDEMIC, مرض متداول marz-i-mutadávil, مرض عمومی marz-i-'umúmí.

EPIDERMIS, بشر bashar.

EPILEPSY, صرع sar'.

EPILEPTIC, مصروع masrú'.

EPILOGUE, خاتمه khátimah (*pl.* خواتم khavátim).

EPIPHANY, تجلی tajallí.

EPISTLE, *vide* LETTER.

EPITAPH, کتابه kitábah, کتابت قبر kitábat-i-kabr.

EPITHET, لقب lakab, وصف vasf, صفت sifat.

EPITOME, *vide* COMPENDIUM.

EPOCH, عصر 'asr, تاریخ táríkh, دور daur, زمانه zamánah.

EQUAL, برابر barábar, مساوی musáví, مثال misál, نظیر nazír, مطابق mutábik, زوج zauj, موازی mu,ází, یکسان yak-sán, مانند mánand, همتا ham-tá.—(*subs.*) نظیر nazír, مثل misl, هم تا ham-tá, عدیل 'adíl.

EQUAL to, معادل mu'ádil, موازی mu,ázi.

EQUALITY, مساوات musávát, معادلت mu'ádalat.

EQUALIZATION, مساوات musávát, تعدیل ta'díl.

EQUALLY, بسویت bi-savíyat, علی السویه 'alá-'s-savíyah, برابر barábar, علی السوا 'alá-'s-savá.

Equation (*in arithmetic*), مساوات musávát.
Equator, خط استوا khat-i-istivá.
Equerry, میراخور mír-ákhwur.
Equestrianism, اسب بازی asb-bází, اسب سواری asb-suvárí.
Equilibrium (*equipoise*), موازنه muvázanah, معادلت mu'ádalat.
Equinoctial, معدل mu'addil.
Equinox, اعتدال روز و شب i'tidál-i-rúz va shab, اعتدال اللیل و النهار i'tidálu-'l-lail-va-'n-nahár.
To Equip, تجهیز نمودن tajhíz nimúdan.
Equipage, *vide* Carriage.
Equipment, تجهیز tajhíz, کار سازی kár-sází, یراق yarák.
Equitable, *vide* Just.
Equivalent, *vide* Equal.
Equivocal, مشتبه mushtabih, متشابه mutashábih.
Equivocation, زبان بازی zabán-bází.
Era, *vide* Epoch.
To Eradicate, از بیخ بر کندن az bíkh bar-kandan, قلع نمودن kal' nimúdan, قمع کردن kam' kardan, استیصال نمودن istísál nimúdan, منزع نمودن munazzi' nimúdan.
To Erase, *vide* To Deface, Efface, Scratch out.
Ere, پیش písh, تا به tá-bi.
Erect, درست durust, راست rást, مستقیم mustakím.—(*penis*) راست rást.
To Erect, افراشتن afráshtan, بر داشتن bar-dáshtan, نصب کردن nasb kardan, بر پا کردن bar pá kardan, زدن zadan. — (*build*) عمارت کردن 'imárat kardan, تعمیر کردن ta'mír kardan, بنا کردن biná kardan.
Erection, *vide* Building.—(*penis*) راستی rástí.
Ermine, قاقم kákum.
To Err, غلط کردن ghalat kardan, خطا کردن khatá kardan, سهو کردن sahv kardan, زلت نمودن zallat nimúdan.—(*to cause to err, to mislead*) بر گردانیدن bar-gardánídan, اهباط نمودن ihbát nimúdan, اضلال کردن izlál kardan, گمراه کردن gum-ráh kardan.
Errant, آواره ávárah, گم راه gum-ráh.
Erroneously, سهواً sahvan.
Error, غلط ghalat, سهو sahv, خطا khatá, زلت zallat, ضلت zallat, مضلت mazallat, خبط khabt, قصور kusúr, تقصیر taksír.
Eructation, آروغ árúgh.
Erudite, *vide* Learned.
Eruption (*on the skin*), بثورات busúrát, آبله ábilah, دانها dánahá.—(*to break out in an eruption*) بثورات در آوردن busúrát dar-ávardan.
Erysipelas, بثور busúr.
Escape, رستگاری rastagárí, رها rihá, رهائی rihá,í, خلاص khalás, نجات naját.
To Escape, رستن rastan, رها یافتن rihá yáftan, نجات یافتن naját yáftan, خلاصی یافتن khalásí yáftan, رها گردیدن rihá gardídan.—(*flee*) گریختن guríkhtan, فرار کردن firár kardan, پهلو تهی کردن pahlú-tuhí kardan.—(*to let escape*) هشتن hishtan.
Escheat, باد آور bád-ávar.
Escort, *vide* Convoy.
Especially, خاصه khássah, خصوصاً khusúsan, علی الخصوص 'alá-'l-khusús, سیما síyamá, لاسیما lá-síyamá.
Espionage, جاسوسی jásúsí.
To Espouse, *vide* To Marry.—(*to espouse the cause of*) جانبداری کردن jánib-dárí kardan.
Esprit, قلب kalb.
Essay (*article*), مقاله makálah, فصل fasl. (*Vide* Attempt.)
Essence, عین 'ain, ذات zát, جوهر jauhar, روح rúh, عرق 'arak, خلاصه khulásah, پالوده pálúdah.—(*perfume*) عطر 'itr.
Essential, جوهری jauharí, ذاتی zátí.—(*obligatory*) مفروض mafrúz.
To Establish, اثبات نمودن isbát nimúdan, وضع کردن vaz' kardan, بر قرار نمودن bar-karár nimúdan.
Established, مقرر mukarrar, بر قرار bar-karár, منصوب mansúb, مترتب

mutarattib, متمکن mutamakkin, موکد mu,akkad, قائم ká,im, پایدار páyadár, ثابت sábit, استوار ustuvár, معین mu'ayyan.

ESTABLISHMENT, نصب nasb, تأسیس ta,sís.—(*household*) دستگاه dastgáh, عیال 'iyál, خدم و حشم khadam va hashm, تابینها tabínhá (*vulg.*).

ESTATE (*competence of means, cattle, &c., for which taxes must be paid*), نصاب nisáb. (*Vide* INHERITANCE, FIEF, LAND, PROPERTY, WEALTH.)

ESTEEM, حب hubb, مهر mihr, الفت ulfat, اخلاص ikhlás, التفات iltifát, اعزاز i'záz, احترام ihtirám.

To ESTEEM, محترم داشتن muhtaram dáshtan, مکرم داشتن mukarram dáshtan, معزز داشتن mu'azzaz dáshtan, احترام کردن ihtirám kardan.—(*deem*) محسوب کردن mahsúb kardan, دانستن dánistan, شمردن shimurdan.

ESTEEMED, معتبر mu'tabar, محترم muhtaram.

ESTIMABLE, مرغوب marghúb, عزتمند 'izzat-mand.

ESTIMATE, برآورد bar-ávard, تخمینه takhmínah, اندازه andázah. (*Vide* VALUE, OPINION.)

To ESTIMATE, برآورد کردن bar-ávard kardan, سنجیدن sanjídan.

ESTRANGEMENT, دوری dúrí, بعد ba'ad.

ESTUARY, خور khaur.

ET CÆTERA (*and so forth*), وغیره va ghairah, الخ alikh.

ETERNAL, ابدی abadí, ازلی azalí, دائم dá,im, دائمی dá,imí, مدام mudám, جاودان jávidán, صمدی samadí, صمد samad, سرمدی sarmadí, جاوید jávíd.

ETERNALLY, ابداً abadan, دهراً dahran.

ETERNITY (*without beginning*), ازل azal, ازلیت azalíyat.—(*without end*) ابد abad, ابدیت abadíyat, خلد khuld, بقا baká.

ETHER, اثیر asír.

ETHICS, اخلاق akhlák.

ETIQUETTE, تکلفات takallufát, اداب adáb, رسوم rusúm, مدارات mudárát, تعارف ta'áruf.

ETYMOLOGY (*of words*), اشتقاق ishtikák.—(*in grammar*) صرف sarf.

EUCHARIST, عشاء ربانی 'ashá,-i-rabbání, قداس kudás.

EUCLID, اقلیدس uklídas.—(*Euclid's Elements*) تحریر اقلیدس tahrír-i-uklídas.

To EULOGIZE, *vide* To PRAISE.

EUNUCH, خواجهٔ سرا khwájah-i-sará, خوجه khwajah, آغا ághá, آخته ákhtah, خصی khusí.—(*chief eunuch of a harem*) قزلر آغا kazlar-ághá, خواجه باشی khwájah-báshí.

EUROPE, فرنگ farang, فرنگستان farangistán.

EUROPEAN, فرنگی farangí.

To EVACUATE, تخلیه کردن takhliyah kardan.

To EVADE, کناره جستن kanárah jastan, دور کشی نمودن dúr-kashí nimúdan, حذر کردن hazar kardan.—(*one's business or duty*) طفره زدن tafrah zadan, تغافل نمودن tagháful nimúdan.

EVALUATION, تقویم takvím.

EVANGELIC and EVANGELIST, انجیلی anjílí.

To EVAPORATE (*trans.*), بخار ساختن bukhár sákhtan. — (*intrans.*) نشف نمودن nashf nimúdan.

EVAPORATION, نشف nashf.

EVASION, رها rihá, رهائی rihá,í, رستگاری rastagárí, خلاص khalás, نجات naját. — (*subterfuge*), بهانه bahánah, عذر 'uzr, حیله hílah, تجاهل tajáhul, چنان چنین chunán chunín, بهانه bahánah.

EVE, روز گذشته rúz-i-guzashtah, شام shám. — (*on the eve of*) شرف shuruf.

EVEN, *vide* LEVEL, SMOOTH, ALSO, ALIKE.—(*not odd*) جفت juft, زوج zauj, شفع shaf'.—(*even number*) عدد شفع 'adad-i-shaf', عدد زوج 'adad-i-zauj, عدد جفت 'adad-i-juft.—(*odd or even?*) طاق یا جفت ták yá juft, تك یا جفت tak yá juft.

EVENING, شام shám, عشا 'ishá, سر شب sar-i-shab.—(*evening star*) زهره zuhrah, ناهید náhíd.

EVENT, واقعه váki'ah, وقیعه vakí'ah, وقوع vukú', حادثه hádisah, عارضه 'árizah, ماجرا má-jará, قضیه kazíyah, سرگذشت sar-guzasht, اتفاق ittifák. — (*result*) *vide* CONSEQUENCE.—(*in the event of*) صورتیکه súratí kih.—(*at all events*) در بهر حال dar bi-har hál.

EVER (*at any time*), گاهی gáhí, هیچوقت hích vakt.—(*at no time*) هرگز hargiz, اصلاً aslan, ابداً abadan. —(*at all times*) همیشه hamíshah, همواره hamvárah, مدام mudám, دائماً dá,iman, هر وقت har vakt, هر دم har dam.—(*for ever*) ابد الاباد abadu-'l-ábád, تا بابد tá bi-abad, جاویدان jávidán.

EVERGREEN, همیشه سبز hamíshah sabz, خرم khurram.

EVERLASTING, مدام mudám.—(*in religious sense*) اخروی ukhraví.

EVERY, هر har, هر یك har yak, كل kull, همه hamah.

EVERYWHERE, همه جا hamah já, هر جا har já.

To EVICT, راندن rándan, دفع نمودن daf' nimúdan, منع کردن mana' kardan.—(*to be evicted*) محروم شدن mahrúm shudan, ممنوع شدن mamnú' shudan, رانده شدن rándah shudan.

EVICTION, منع mana', دفع daf'.

EVIDENCE, *vide* TESTIMONY.—(*to accept evidence*) تعدیل شاهد کردن ta'díl-i-sháhid kardan, شهادترا قبول کردن shahádatrá kabúl kardan.—(*to reject evidence*) جرح شاهد کردن jarh-i-sháhid kardan, شهادترا رد کردن shahádatrá radd kardan.

EVIDENT, *vide* APPARENT, CLEAR.

EVIDENTLY, ظاهراً záhiran.

EVIL, *vide* BAD, WICKED, WICKEDNESS, CALAMITY, INJURY.

EWE, میش mísh.

EWER, آفتابه áftábah, ابریق ibrík (*pl.* اباریق abárík).

EXACT, کامل kámil, درست durust, صحیح sahíh.

EXACTLY, بدرستی bi-durustí, با دقت bá-dikkat, نقیر و قطمیر nakír va katmír, بعینه bi-'ainihi, جخ jakh (*vulg.*).—(*in point of time*) *vide* IMMEDIATELY.

EXACTNESS, درستی durustí, دقت dikkat.

To EXAGGERATE, اغراق نمودن ighrák nimúdan, مبالغه نمودن mubálaghah nimúdan.

EXAGGERATION, اغراق ighrák, مبالغه mubálaghah.

To EXALT, افراشتن afráshtan, افراختن afrákhtan. (*Vide* To HONOUR.)

EXALTATION, سر افرازی sar-afrází.

EXALTED, عالی 'álí, معلی mu'allá, افراخته afrákhtah, مرتفع murtafi', مرفوع marfú', سر افراز sar-afráz, منیف muníf.

EXAMINATION, باز پرس báz purs, تجسس tajassus, تفتیش taftísh, تفحص tafahhus.—(*of candidates*) امتحان imtihán. — (*cross-examination*), حرف و اعتراض harf va i'tiráz, استنطاق istinták.—(*to pass an examination*), از امتحان بیرون آمدن az imtihán bírún ámadan.

To EXAMINE, تفحص کردن tafahhus kardan, آزمودن ázmúdan, تنقیح کردن tankíh kardan, تحقیق کردن tahkík kardan, تفتیش نمودن taftísh nimúdan, تجویز نمودن tajvíz nimúdan, امعان نظر کردن ím'án-i-nazar kardan, غور رسی کردن ghaur-rasí kardan.—(*candidates*) امتحان کردن imtihán kardan. — (*legal term*) استنطاق کردن istinták kardan.

EXAMINER, متفحص mutafahhis, تفتیشچی taftísh-chí.

EXAMPLE, مثال misál, تمثیل tamsíl, مثل masal. — (*for example*) بر فرض bar farz, فرضاً farzan, مثلاً masalan, اگر چنانچه agar chunánchih.—(*model or pattern*) نمونه nimúnah.—(*applicable to punishment*) عبرت 'ibrat.—(*to follow the example*) اقتدا نمودن iktidá nimúdan.

To EXASPERATE, مضطرب ساختن muz-

tarib sákhtan, متنفر گردانیدن mutanaffir gardánídan, برآشفتن bar-áshuftan.
EXASPERATION, اضطراب iztiráb, سر آسیمه‌گی sar-ásímah-gí.
To EXCAVATE, *vide* To DIG.
EXCAVATION, حفر hafr, حفرت hufrat.
To EXCEED, از حد گذشتن az hadd guzashtan, تجاوز نمودن tajávuz nimúdan, بیرون شدن bírún shudan.
EXCEEDING, (از) متجاوز mutajáviz (az).
EXCEEDINGLY, نهایت niháyat, بغایت bi-gháyat, کثیراً kasíran, فزون fuzún.
To EXCEL, رجحان داشتن rajahán dáshtan, (بر) سبقت بردن sibkat burdan (bar), فضیلت داشتن fazílat dáshtan, بهتر بودن bihtar búdan, قصب السبق ربودن kasabu-'s-sibk rubúdan, پیشی یافتن píshí yáftan, پیش دستی نمودن písh-dastí nimúdan, غالب شدن ghálib shudan, فائق بودن fá,ik búdan.
EXCELLENCE, خوبی khúbí, فضیلت fazílat, نیکی níkí, نیکوئی níkú,í.
EXCELLENCY, جناب janáb, عالی حضرت 'álí-hazrat, عالیشان 'álí-shán.
EXCELLENT, راجح rájih, فاضل fázil, بهتر bihtar, افضل afzal, اعلی a'lá, احسن ahsan.
EXCEPT, سوا savá, جز juz, بجز bi-juz, غیر ghair, بغیر bi-ghair, مگر magar, الا illá, ورائی vará,í.
EXCEPTION, استثنا istisná.
EXCEPTIONAL, استثنائی istisná,í.
EXCESS, افراط ifrát, افزونی afzúní, کثرت kasrat, نهایت niháyat, زیادتی ziyádatí.
EXCESSIVE, از حد بیرون az hadd bírún, مفرط mufrit.
EXCESSIVELY, بغایت bi-gháyat, از حد گذشته az hadd guzashtah.
EXCHANGE, تبدیل tabdíl, مبادله mubádalah, عوض 'ivaz, استبدال istibdál.—(*in exchange for*) بدلاً badalan, در عوض dar 'ivaz, عوضاً 'ivazan. — (*money*), صرف sarf, صرافیه saráfíyah. (*Vide* BOURSE.)
To EXCHANGE, عوض کردن 'ivaz kardan, معاوضه کردن mu'ávazah kardan, بدل کردن badal kardan, مبادله نمودن mubádalah nimúdan, تبدیل کردن tabdíl kardan.
EXCHEQUER, دیوان وزارت díván-i-vizárat.
EXCISE-OFFICER, مستوفی mustaufí, باجگیر báj-gír, گمرک چی gumruk-chí.
To EXCITE, برانگیختن bar-angíkhtan, خیزانیدن khízánídan, تحریک کردن tahrík kardan, تغیر ساختن taghayyur sákhtan.—(*to be excited*) به هیجان آمدن bi-hayaján ámadan, طغیان کردن tughyán kardan, برآشفتن bar-áshuftan, کوک شدن kúk shudan.
EXCITEMENT, شعف sha'af, هیجان hayaján, تغیر taghayyur.
EXCITING, روح افزا rúh-afzá.
To EXCLAIM, غریو نمودن ghariv nimúdan. (*Vide* To CRY ALOUD, To SAY.)
EXCLAMATION, فریاد faryád, بانگ báng, آواز áváz, غریو ghariv.
To EXCLUDE, محروم ساختن mahrúm sákhtan, خارج کردن khárij kardan, رد نمودن radd nimúdan, وا داشتن vá-dáshtan.
EXCLUDING, استثنا istisná, مانع máni'.
EXCLUSION, محرومیت mahrúmíyat, استثنا istisná.—(*to the exclusion of*) الا illá, بغیر از bi-ghair az, مستثنی mustasná.
EXCLUSIVE, منافی munáfí.
To EXCOMMUNICATE, لعنت نمودن la'nat nimúdan, مردود نمودن mardúd nimúdan.
EXCOMMUNICATION, لعنت la'nat, مردودیه mardúdiyah.
EXCORIATION, خراش khirásh, ریش rísh.
EXCREMENT, گوه gúh, گه guh, براز biráz, غائط ghá,it, فضله fazlah.
To EXCULPATE, ابرا نمودن ibrá nimúdan, رو سفید گردانیدن rú-safíd gardánídan, بیگناه بر آوردن bí-gunáh bar-ávardan. — (*oneself*) خودرا بری الذمه کردن khwudrá baríu-'z-zimmah kardan, عذر

عذر خواستن ‘uzr khwástan, اعتذار کردن i‘tizár kardan, عذر خواهی کردن ‘uzr-khwáhí kardan.

Exculpation, *vide* Excuse.

Excusable, متعذر muta‘azzir, لائق عذر lá,ik-i-‘uzr.

Excuse, عذر ‘uzr, اعتذار i‘tizár, معذرت ma‘zirat, پوزش púzish.

To Excuse, *vide* To Forgive.—(*to excuse oneself*) *vide* To Exculpate oneself.

Excused, معذور ma‘zúr.

Execrable, مکروه makrúh, مذموم mazmúm.

Execration, *vide* Curse.

To Execute, *vide* To Perform, To Kill, To Hang, To Do.

Executioner, نسقچی nasakchí, جلاد jallád, فراش غضب farrásh-i-ghazab.—(*chief executioner*) میر غضب mír-i-ghazab, نسقچی باشی nasakchí-báshí.

Executor, مجری mujrí, متولی mutavallí, وکیل vakíl, وصی vasí.

Exempt, بری barí, مبرا mubarrá, منزه munazzah, مستغنی mustaghní, مستثنی mustasná, معاف mu‘áf, آزاد ázád, مأمون ma,mún, معرا mu‘arrá.

To Exempt, مستثنی ساختن mustasná sákhtan, مسلم نمودن musallam nimúdan.

Exemption, آزادگی ázádagí, تبرئه tabri,ah.

Exequator, رقم rakam, فرمان firmán, مضبطه mazbatah.

Exercise, ورزش varzish. — (*task*) عبرت ‘ibrat. — (*habitual*) *vide* Practise. — (*military*) *vide* Drill. — (*a walk or ride for amusement; taking the air*) گردش gardish, تفرج tafarruj.—(*exercise in throwing the spear on horseback*) جرید بازی jaríd-bází, دوغله بازی dúghalah-bází.—(*exercise in shooting with bow or gun while riding at full speed*) قیقاج kaikáj.

Exhalation, بخار bukhár, نزم nizm. —(*breathing*) تنفس tanaffus.

To Exhale, *vide* To Breathe.

To Exhaust, *vide* To Expend.

Exhaustion, *vide* Fatigue, Weakness.

To Exhibit, اظهار نمودن izhár nimúdan, عرضه داشتن ‘arzah dáshtan. (*Vide* To Show).

Exhibition, اظهار izhár, نمایش namáyish.—(*place*) معرض ma‘raz. —(*Universal*), بازار عمومی bázár-i-‘umúmí.

Exhilarant, فرح ناک farah-nák.

To Exhort, تحریک کردن tahrík kardan, تشویق کردن tashvík kardan, ترغیب کردن targhíb kardan, موعظت نمودن mau‘izat nimúdan.

Exhortation, وعظ va‘z, موعظت mau‘izat, اندرز andurz.

Exhumation, نبش nabsh.

To Exhume, نبش نمودن nabsh nimúdan.

Exigence, اقتضا iktizá, داعیه dá,‘iyah. — (*exigencies of the case*) دواعی الدهر davá‘íu - ’d - dahr, مقتضیات وقت muktazíyát-i-vakt.

Exile, *vide* Banishment.

To Exile, *vide* To Banish.

To Exist, *vide* To Live, To Be.

Existence, هستی hastí, وجود vujúd, کون kaun, زندگانی zindagání.

Existent, موجود maujud.

Exit, مخرج makhraj.

Exodus, خروج khurúj, اخراج ikhráj.

To Exonerate, *vide* To Exculpate.

Exorbitance, تجاوز tajávuz.

Exorbitant, متجاوز mutajáviz.

Exorcism, مریرت marírat, عزیمت ‘azímat.

To Expand, گشادن gushádan, بسط نمودن bast nimúdan, گستردن gusturdan, وا شدن vá-shudan.

Expanse (*area*), فضا fizá, ساحت sáhat, عرصه ‘arsah.

Expatriation, جلا وطن jalá-i-vatan

To Expect, انتظار کشیدن intizár kashídan, منتظر بودن muntazir búdan, توقع داشتن tavakku‘ dáshtan, نگران شدن nigarán shudan, ترصد نمودن tarassud nimúdan, مترصد شدن mutarassid shudan, چشم داشتن chashm dáshtan.

Expectation, توقع tavakku‘ انتظار intizár.

To Expectorate, *vide* To Spit.

Expectoration, تف سازی tuf-sází.

Expedient, صواب saváb, مفید mufíd.—(*device*) تمهید tamhíd.

To Expedite, شتاب کردن shitáb kardan, روانه نمودن ravánah nimúdan.

Expedition, *vide* Journey, Haste.

To Expel, راندن rándan, اخراج کردن ikhráj kardan, دفع کردن daf' kardan, دور کردن dúr kardan, بدر کردن bi-dar kardan, نفی نمودن nafy nimúdan.—(*to be expelled*) خارج گشتن khárij gashtan.

To Expend, خرج کردن kharj kardan, صرف نمودن sarf nimúdan.—(*to be expended*) خرج شدن kharj shudan, منصرف بودن munsarif búdan, منقرض شدن munkariz shudan, مصروف شدن masrúf shudan, سپری شدن siparí shudan, منقلع بودن munkalí' búdan.

Expense, خرج kharj, اخراج ikhráj, صرف sarf, اسراف isráf, نفقه nafakah.—(*at the expense of*) بخرج bi-kharj.

Expensive, *vide* Dear.

Experience, تجربه tajribah, تدبیر tadbír, وقوف vukúf, خبرت khibrat.

Experienced, کار دیده kár-dídah, پخته pukhtah, آموخته ámúkhtah, کار آزموده kár-ázmúdah.

Experiment, آزمایش ázmáyish, تجربه tajribah.

To Experiment, *vide* To Try.

Expert, چابك chábuk, چست chust, چالاك chálák, چاق دست chák-dast, واقف vákif, کار گر kár-gar, ماهر máhir, زرنگ zaring.—(*subs.*) اهل وقوف ahl-i-vukúf, اهل خبرت ahl-i-khibrat.

Expiation, کفاره kaffárah, تکفیر takfír.

Expiration, انقضا inkizá. (*Vide* End, Death.)

To Explain, بیان نمودن bayán nimúdan, شرح نمودن sharh nimúdan, تعریف کردن (از) ta'ríf kardan (az).

Explanation, بیان bayán, تفسیر tafsír, تعبیر ta'bír, تأویل ta,víl, کشف kashf, تفصیل tafsíl, شرح sharh, مفاوضه mufávazah, توجیه taujíh.—(*an absurd explanation*) توجیه نا موجه taujíh-i-ná-muvajjah.—(*a lucid explanation*) شرح مبین sharh-i-mubín, بیان صریح bayán-i-saríh, توجیه موجه taujíh-i-muvajjah.—(*to demand an explanation*) باز خواست نمودن báz-khwást nimúdan.

Explicit, مبین mubín, مفصل mufassal.

Explicitly, تصریحاً tasríhan.

To Explode (*as gunpowder*), آتش گرفتن átish giriftan, بهوا رفتن bi-havá raftan.

Exploit, *vide* Deed.

Exploration, *vide* Examination.

To Export, بردن burdan, بیرون بردن bírún burdán.

Exportation, حمل بخارج haml bi-khárij.

To Expose, *vide* To Show.

Exposition, اظهار izhár, عرض 'arz.

Expostulation, *vide* Altercation.

To Expound, *vide* To Explain.—(*Scripture*), تفسیر نمودن tafsír nimúdan, شرح کردن sharh kardan.

Express, مخصوص makhsús.

To Express, ادا کردن adá kardan, نمودن nimúdan.

Expression (*by language, &c.*), تلفظ talaffuz, اصطلاح istiláh.

Expressly, مخصوصاً makhsúsan, عمداً 'amdan.

Expulsion, اخراج ikhráj, نفی nafy.

Exquisite, *vide* Beautiful, Rare.

Extant, وجود vujúd, موجود maujúd.

Extempore, بدیهی badíhí, بی اندیشه bí-andíshah, بلا فاصله bilá fásilah, بلا تأمل bilá tá,ammul, بدیها badíhan.

To Extemporize, شفاها سخن راندن shifáhan sukhun rándan.

To Extend, دراز کردن diráz kardan, کشیدن kashídan. (*Vide* To Reach, To Stretch, To Diffuse.)

Extension, مد madd, توسیع tausí', امتداد imtidád.

Extensive, گشاده gushádah, کشیده

kashídah, وسیع vasí', بسیط basít, پهن pahn.

EXTENT, وسعت vus'at, فراخی farákhí, بسطت bastat, پهنا pahná, مساحت misáhat. (*Vide* DEGREE). —(*to any extent*) بهر اندازه bi-har andázah.—(*to that extent*) بهمان قدر bi-hamán kadar.

EXTERIOR, خارج khárij, بیرون bírún, بیرونی bírúní, صورت súrat.

To EXTERMINATE, استئصال کردن isti,sál kardan, بر کندن bar-kandan.

EXTERMINATION, استئصال isti,sál, بر کندگی bar-kandagí.

EXTERNAL, خارج khárij, ظاهر záhir.

EXTERNALLY, ظاهراً záhiran, ظاهرانه zahiránah, صورتاً súratan, از بیرون az bírún.

EXTINCT (*annihilated*), معدوم ma'dúm, نا بود ná-búd, منطفی muntafí, منقطع munkati', محو mahv.

EXTINCTION (*of fire*), انطفا intifá. —(*of a family, &c.*), انقراض inkiráz.

To EXTINGUISH, نشاندن nishándan, کشتن kushtan, اطفا نمودن itfá nimúdan, منطفی ساختن muntafí sákhtan, خاموش کردن khámúsh kardan, ساکت کردن sákit kardan.

To EXTIRPATE, *vide* To EXTERMINATE.

To EXTORT, بزور گرفتن bi-zúr giriftan, ستم ورزیدن sitam varzídan, تعسف نمودن ta'assuf nimúdan, قلق گرفتن kulluk giriftan, سخت گیری نمودن sakht-gírí nimúdan, زیاد پا بستن ziyád pá bastan (*vulg.*), اواب کردن avváb kardan (*vulg.*).

EXTORTION, سختگیری sakht-gírí, اجحاف ijháf, جنیبه janíbah, ترجمان turjumán, اواب avváb (*vulg.*).

EXTORTIONER, اخاذ akhkház, سخت گیر sakht-gír.

EXTRA, زائد zá,id, فاضل fázil, افزون afzún, اضافه izáfah.

EXTRACT (*compendium*), تلخیص talkhís, اجمال ijmál, منتخب muntakhab, موجز mújaz. (*Vide* ESSENCE.) — (*from a book*) عبارت 'ibárat, فقره fakarah.

To EXTRACT, *vide* To DRAW.

EXTRACTION, کشیدن kashídan. (*Vide* DESCENT.)

EXTRAORDINARY, غیر معهود ghair-i-ma'húd, غیر معتاد ghair-i-mu'tád. (*rare*) نادر nádir, غریب gharíb.

EXTRAVAGANCE (*squandering*), خرج بی اندازه kharj-i-bí-andázah, تلف talaf, ول خرج vil-kharj.

EXTRAVAGANT, مسرف musrif, سرف saraf.

EXTREME, نهایت niháyat, غایت gháyat.

EXTREMELY, بغایت bi-gháyat, بنهایت bi-niháyat, از حد زیاده az hadd ziyádah, بی حد و حساب bí-hadd va hisáb.

EXTREMITY, *vide* END, DIFFICULTY.

To EXTRICATE, *vide* To PULL out.

EXUBERANCE, *vide* PLENTY, EXCESS.

To EXUDE, چکیدن chakídán, تراویدن tarávídan.

EYE, چشم chashm, عین 'ain, دیده dídah, چش chash (*vulg.*).—(*socket of eye*) چشمخانه chashm-khánah.—(*eye-ball or pupil*) مردمک چشم mardumak-i-chashm, چشمیلان chashmilán, حدقه hidkah, ببه bibih (*vulg.*). — (*eye-brow*) ابرو abrú, حاجب hájib.—(*eye-lid*) پلک palak, جفن jafn. — (*eye-lash*) مژه mizhah (*pl.* مژگان mizhagán).—(*eye-sight, vision*) دیدار dídár, دیده dídah, بینائی bíná,í, بصر basr, نظر nazar, رأی العین ra,íu-'l-'ain.—(*extent of vision*) مد البصر maddu-'l-basr, مد نظر madd-i-nazar.—(*glance of the eye*) رمز العین ramzu-'l-'ain, طرفة العین tarafatu-'l-'ain, چشمک chashmak.—(*the evil eye*) عین الکمال 'ainu-'l-kamál, چشم زخم chashm-i-zakhm, بد چشم bad-chashm.—(*of a needle*) سوراخ سوزن súrákh-i-súzan, چشم chashm, سم summ.—(*smitten with the evil eye*) چشم زده chashm-zadah.—(*as far as the eye will carry*) تا چشم کار میکند tá chashm kár mí-kunad, تا مد نظر tá madd-i-nazar.—(*with one's own eyes*) به رأى العين bi-ra,íu-'l-'ain.—(*to meet the eye*) ملحوظ افتادن malhuz uftádan.

EYE-GLASS, عینک 'ainak.

EYRIE, منسره mansarah.

F.

FABLE, قصه kissah, حکایت hikáyat, افسانه afsánah, مثل masal, داستان dástán, خرافه khiráfah, نقل nakl.

FABRIC (*material*), قماش kumásh. (*Vide* EDIFICE.)

FABULOUS, ساخته sákhtah, دروغ durúgh, مزور muzavvar, زور zúr, کاذب kázib.

FAÇADE, پیشگاه písh-gáh, عنوان 'unván.

FACE, رو rú, روی rúí, وجه vajh, چهره chihrah, جبین jabín, منظر manzar, رخ rukh, لقا liká, پیکر paikar, سیما símá, طلعت tal'at, صورت súrat. (*Vide* SURFACE).—(*face to face*) *vide* OPPOSITE. — (*open-faced*) پیشانی گشاده píshání-gushádah.—(*full face, portrait*) تصویر تمام tasvír-i-tamám.

To FACE, رو به ... شدن rú bi . . . shudan.

FACET (*cutting of a jewel*), پخ pakh.

FACETIOUS, خوشطبع khwush-tab', ظریف zaríf, لطیفه گو latífah-gú.

FACETIOUSNESS, *vide* FUN, JEST.

FACILE, ملائم mulá,im.

To FACILITATE, تسهیل نمودن tas-híl nimúdan.

FACILITY, *vide* EASE.

FACING (*fronting*), روبرو rú-bi-rú, محاذی muhází, مقابل mukábil, بالمشافهه bi-'l-musháfahah.

FACT (*deed*), کار kár, کردار kirdár, فعل fi'l, عمل 'amal, حرکت harakat. —(*reality*) حقیقت hakíkat, معنی ma'ní, حق hakk. — (*in fact*) فی الحقیقت fí-'l-hakíkat, الحق al-hakk, فی الواقع fí-'l-váki', معناً ma'nan, بعینه bi-'ainihi.

FACTOR, *vide* AGENT.

FACTORY, *vide* WORKSHOP, OFFICE.

FACULTY, *vide* ABILITY.

To FADE (*wither*), پژمردن pazhmurdan, افسردن afsurdan, خشکیدن khushkídan.

FAGGOT, بسته هیزم bastah-i-hízum.

FAIL or FAILURE, در ماندگی darmándagí, دریغ dirígh.—(*without fail*) بی تخلف bí-takhalluf.

To FAIL (*become deficient*), ناقص شدن nákis shudan, کم شدن kam shudan, زائل گشتن zá,il gashtan, قاصر شدن kásir shudan.—(*not succeed*) بر نیامدن bar-nayámadan, نا میسر شدن ná-muyassar shudan, ساقط شدن sákit shudan.—(*as crops or produce of the ground*) عمل نیامدن 'amal nayámadan, زمین خوردن zamín khwurdan.

FAINT (*feeble*), کم زور kam-zúr, سست sust, فاتر fátir, ضعیف za'íf.—(*as colour*) آبکی ábakí, واز váz.

To FAINT (*swoon*), غش کردن ghash kardan, بیهوش شدن bí-húsh shudan, غش شدن ghash shudan.

FAINTNESS, *vide* WEAKNESS.

FAIR (*in complexion*) سفید safíd.—(*handsome*) *vide* BEAUTIFUL.—(*prosperous, favourable*) موافق muváfik, مسعود mas'úd, فرخ farrukh, فرخنده farkhandah, بختیار bakht-yár. — (*as weather*) لطیف latíf, گشاده هوا gushádah-havá.—(*market*) بازار bázár. — (*the fair sex*) زن خوبرویان zan-i-khúb-rúíán.

FAIRLY (*honestly*), عادلانه 'ádilánah, بالصواب bis-'s-saváb, با راستی bá-rástí.

FAIRY, پری parí, جن jinn, جان jánn (*pl.* اجنه ajinnah).—(*fairyland*) جنستان jinnistán, شادهکام shádahkám, عنبراباد 'ambar-ábád, پریستان paristán.

FAITH (*religion*), مذهب mazhab,

ملت millat, دين dín, کيش kísh.—(*belief*) ايمان ímán, اعتقاد i'tikád, اعتماد i'timád, اعتبار i'tibár, باور bávar.—(*fidelity*) وفا vafá, وفاداری vafá-dárí, صدق sidk, صداقت sadákat.

FAITHFUL, وفادار vafá-dár, صادق sádik, با وفا bá-vafá, متدين mutadayyin, امين amín, مستقيم mustakím.–(*orthodox*) موءمن mu,min, ايماندار ímán-dár, ديندار dín-dár.

FAITHFULLY, مستقيماً mustakíman, صادقانه sádikánah.

FAITHLESS, بيوفا bí-vafá, نمك حرام namak-harám, بد عهد bad-'ahd.

FALCON, باز báz, بالابان bálábán, چرخ charkh, چرغ chargh, قوش kúsh.—(*royal falcon*) شاهين sháhín.—(*sea-falcon*) بحری bahrí.

FALCONER, بازدار báz-dár, قوشچی kúsh-chí.—(*glove*) بهله bahlah.

FALL, سقوط sukút, پرت part (*vulg.*).

To FALL, اوفتادن úftádan, افتادن uftádan, سقوط کردن sukút kardan, زمين خوردن zamín khwurdan, پرت شدن part shudan (*vulg.*).—(*be killed*) کشته شدن kushtah shudan, تلف شدن talaf shudan.—(*tumble in ruins*) خراب شدن kharáb shudan, رنبيدن rumbídan (*vulg.*).—(*back, to recede*) پس رفتن pas raftan, پس نشستن pas nishastan, قهقرا نمودن kahkará nimúdan.—(*in love*) عاشق شدن 'áshik shudan.—(*thermometer*) نازل شدن názil shudan.—(*into, as a river*) يکی شدن yakí shudan.—(*out*) برهم زدن bar-ham zadan.—(*upon*) *vide* To ASSAULT.

FALLACY (*deceitful argument*), فلسفت falsafat.

FALLOW (*ground*), بور baur, موات mavát.—(*colour*) اصفر asfar.

FALSE, دروغ durúgh, کاذب kázib, باطل bátil, مزور muzavvar, دغل daghal, قلب kalb, فريه firyah, زور zúr.—(*deceitful, knavish*) فريبنده firíbandah, مکار makkár, حيله باز hílah-báz, باسمه básmah, بی ايمان bí-ímán, غدار ghaddár, خائن khá,in.—(*base, as coin*) قلابی kul-lábí, قلب kalb, مغشوش maghshúsh, اشکيلی ishkílí.

FALSEHOOD, دروغ durúgh, کذب kizb, تزوير tazvír, غدر ghadr, ارجاف irjáf.

FALSIFIER, محرف muharrif.

FAME, نام nám, نيك نامی ník-námí, شهرت shuhrat, ناموس námús, ننگ nang, ذکر جميل zikr-i-jamíl.

FAMILIAR, متاءلف muta,allif, ماءلوف ma,lúf, همدم ham-dam, ماءنوس ma,nús. (*Vide* IMPUDENT.)

FAMILIARITY, الفت ulfat, انس uns, آشنائی áshná,í, موءانست mu,ánasat.

To FAMILIARIZE (*oneself*) ماءنوس ساختن ma,nús sákhtan.

FAMILY (*children*), اولاد aulád, اطفال atfál.—(*household, wives, dependants, &c.*) عيال 'iyál, خورنده khwurandah, اهل خانه ahl-i-khánah, خانوده khánvádah.—(*descendants of a common ancestor*) خاندان khándán, خانــواده khánvádah, اصل asl, نسل nasl, نسب nasab, قوم kaum, آل ál, ال ill, نژاد nizhád, دودمان dúdmán, تبار tabár, قبيله kabílah.—(*of good family*) اصيل asíl, اصلمند asl-mand, پاك نژاد pák-nizhád, نجيب najíb.—(*of low family*) بد تبار bad-tabár, بد جنس bad-jins, بد نژاد bad-nizhád.—(*head of the family*) کد خدا kad-khudá, بزرگ خانه buzurg-i-khánah.—(*without family*) بی کس bí-kas.

FAMINE, قحط kaht, گرانی girání, غلا ghalá.

FAMISHED, *vide* HUNGRY.

FAMOUS, نامدار nám-dár, نامور námvar, معروف ma'rúf, موصوف mausúf, مشهور mashhúr, ممدوح mamdúh, نيکنام ník-nám.

FAN, بادبزن bád-bizan, مروحه mirvahah (*pl.* مراوح marávih).—(*for winnowing grain*) طبق tabak.

FANATIC and FANATICAL, متعصب muta'assib, خشك دماغ khushk-dimágh.

FANATICISM, تعصب ta'assub, عصبيه 'asabíyah.

FANCY, خيال khayál, وهم vahm, توهم

tavahhum. — (*inclination*) میل mail, دماغ dimágh, صفا safá.

To FANCY, *vide* To IMAGINE.

FANTASTICAL, وسواسی vasvásí.

FANTASY, خود نمائی khwud-nimá,í.

FAR, دور dúr, بعید ba'íd, مبعد mub'ad, قاصی kásí, مستبعد mustab'ad, دور دست dúr-dast.—(*as far as*) تا tá, الی ilá.

FARCE, بیهودگی bíhúdagí.—(*play*) لعبه بازی la'bah-bází.

FARE, طعام ta'ám, خوراک khwurák, چاشته و ناشته cháshtah u náshtah. (*Vide* HIRE, PAY.)

FAREWELL, وداع vidá', پدرود pidrúd. —(*to bid farewell*) پدرود کردن pidrúd kardan, وداع کردن vidá' kardan.

FAR-FETCHED, دور و دراز dúr va diráz, دور از مطلب dúr az matlab.

FARINA, آرد árd.

FARINACEOUS, آردی árdí.

FARM, اجاره ijárah.

To FARM, باجاره دادن bi-ijárah dádan, ایجار نمودن íjár nimúdan.

FARMER (*of land*), مستاجر mustájir, اجاره دار ijárah-dár.

FARRIER, نعلبند na'l-band.—(*horse-doctor*) بیطار baitár.—(*farrier's knife*) سمتراش sum-tirásh.

FAR-SIGHTED, دور بین dúr-bín.

FAR-SIGHTEDNESS, دور بینی dúr-bíní.

FART, تیز tíz, گوز gúz.

To FART, گوزیدن gúzídan, تیزیدن tízídan, تیز دادن tíz dádan, گوز دادن gúz dádan.

FARTHER, دورتر dúrtar, پیشتر píshtar, اقصی aksá.

To FASCINATE, افسون کردن afsún kardan. (*Vide* To DELIGHT, To PLEASE.)

FASCINATED, مفتون maftún, افسون زده afsún-zadah, مسحور mas-húr. —(*enraptured*), شیفته shíftah, چشم بسته chashm-bastah, دلبسته dil-bastah, مغرم mughram.

FASCINATION, افسون afsún, نظرت nazrat. (*Vide* ENCHANTMENT.)

FASHION, *vide* CUSTOM, WAY.—(*cut of dress*) برش لباس burrish-i-libás.—(*man of fashion*) قشنگ kashang.—(*to be in fashion, like things in use*) رواج یافتن raváj yáftan.—(*clothes, &c.*) زی داشتن zí dáshtan.

To FASHION, تشکیل نمودن tashkíl nimúdan.

FASHIONABLE, متعارف muta'árif, به موجب قاعده bi-mújib-i-ká'idah. —(*old-fashioned*) بسبک قدیم bi-sabk-i-kadím.—(*new fashioned*) بسبک جدید bi-sabk-i-jadíd.

FAST (*firm*), مضبوط mazbút, مستحکم mustahkim, محکم muhkam, پایدار páyadár, استوار ustuvár, قائم ká,im, ثابت sábit, سفت sift (*vulg.*).—(*quick*) زود zúd, سریع sarí', چست chust, جلد jald, زرنگ zaring.—(*as watch*) تند tund.—(*swift of foot*) تیز رو tíz-rau, تند رو tund-rau, باد پا bád-pá.—(*abstinence from food*) روزه rúzah, صوم saum, پرهیز parhíz.

To FAST, روزه گرفتن rúzah giriftan, صیام کردن siyám kardan.

To FASTEN, *vide* To TIE.

FASTENING, *vide* KNOT.

FASTIDIOUS, ثاقل sákil, وسواسی vasvásí.

FASTING (*keeping a fast*), صائم sá,im, روزه دار rúzah-dár.—(*before eating anything*) ناشتا náshtá.

FAT (*subs.*), پیه píh, پی pí, چربی charbí, شحم shahm.—(*adj.*) فربه farbih, سمین samín, لنبه lumbah, چاق chák, جسیم jasím. — (*fattened, as an animal*), پرواری parvárí.—(*rich, greasy*) چرب charb, شحیم shahím.

FATAL, *vide* DEADLY, MORTAL.

FATE, *vide* DESTINY, FORTUNE, LUCK.

FATHER, پدر pidar, والد válid, اب ab, ابو abú, بابا bábá.—(*-in-law*) پدر زن pidar-i-zan, پدر شوهر pidar-i-shauhar, خسر khusur, بوسوره bausúrah (*vulg.*).—(*step-father*) عموئی شوهر مادر 'ammú,í-i-andar, شوهر مادر shauhar-i-mádar. — (*god-father*)

پدر خوانده pidar-khwándah. —(*from father to son*) پشت به پشت pusht-bi-pusht, نسلاً بعد نسل naslan ba'd naslin.

FATHOM (*measure of six feet*) بغل baghal.—(*the ordinary height of a man, about* 5½ *feet*) کله kallah.

To FATHOM, پیمودن paimúdan.

FATIGUE, ماندگی mándagí, خستگی khastagí, کوفتگی kúftagí, تعب ta'ab. — (*to undergo fatigue*) متحمل مشقت شدن mutahammil-i-mashakkat shudan.

FATIGUED, *vide* TIRED.

FATNESS, فربهی farbihí.—(*greasiness*) شحیمی shahímí, چربی charbí.

To FATTEN, فربه ساختن farbih sákhtan.

FAUBOURG, فبورگ fabúrg (*eur.*).

FAULT, عیب 'aib, خطا khatá, قصور kusúr, غلط ghalat, گناه gunáh, سهو sahv, ذنب zamb, ضل zall, تقصیر taksír, زلت zallat, نقص nuks.—(*commit a fault*) خبط کردن khabt kardan, غلط کردن ghalat kardan, گه خوردن guh khwurdan. — (*to find fault with*) مؤاخذه کردن mu,ákhazah kardan, الزام کردن ilzám kardan, زجر نمودن zajr nimúdan, پیغاره نمودن paigharah nimúdan, سر زنش کردن sar-zanish kardan.

FAULTLESS, بی تقصیر bí-taksír, بیگناه bí-gunáh, بیعیب bí-'aib.

FAULTY, زائل zá,il, با تقصیر ba-taksír, با گناه ba-gunáh.

FAVOUR, لطف lutf, ملاطفت mulátafat, الطاف iltáf, توجه tavajjuh, فضل fazl, کرم karam, مکرمت makrumat, شفقت shafakat, مهربانی mihr-bání, عنایت 'ináyat, نوازش navázish, نصرت nusrat, رأفت ra,fat, مرحمت marhamat, التفات iltifát, طرفگیری taraf-gírí, جانبداری jánib-dárí.—(*Divine favour*) توفیق الهی taufík-i-iláhí. — (*to find favour*) التفات یافتن iltifát yáftan, نوازش یافتن navázish yáftan.—(*to curry favour*) استعطاف نمودن isti'táf nimúdan, التفات طلبیدن iltifát talbídan, نوازش بودن طالب tálib-i-navázish búdan.—(*by favour of*) بدستیاری bi-dast-yárí, باستعانت bi-isti'ánat.

To FAVOUR, التفات نمودن iltifát nimúdan, لطف کردن lutf kardan.

FAVOURABLE, *vide* FAIR.

FAVOURED, محظوظ mahzúz, مقبول makbúl.—(*the most favoured nations*) دول کاملة الوداد duval-i-kámilahu-'l-vidád.

FAVOURITE, مرغوب marghúb, محبوب mahbúb, محبوبه mahbúbah, برگزیده bar-guzídah.—(*of a prince*) ندیم nadím, ملازم mulázim, خاص kháss, خاص الخواص khássu-'l-khaváss, مقرب mukarrab.

To FAWN, تملق کردن tamalluk kardan, چاپلوسی نمودن cháplúsí nimúdan.

FAYENCE, کاشی káshí.

FEALTY, وفاداری vafá-dárí, حق نمك hakk-i-namak.

FEAR, ترس tars, بیم bím, باك bák, دهشت dihshat, هول haul, هراس hirás, خوف khauf, ستوه sutúh, وحشت vahshat, نهیب nihíb, خشیت khashyat, هیبت haibat, مهابت mahábat.—(*fear and trembling*) ترس و لرز tars u larz.—(*fear of God*) تقوا takvá.

To FEAR, ترسیدن tarsídan, هراسان شدن hirásán shudan, ترس داشتن tars dáshtan.

FEARFUL, *vide* TERRIBLE, COWARD, CRAVEN.

FEARING, *vide* AFRAID.

FEARLESS, بی هراس bí-hirás, بی باك bí-bák.

FEASIBLE, شدنی shudaní, ممکن الحصول mumkinu-'l-husúl.

FEAST, ضیافت ziyáfat, مهمانی mihmání, میهمانی míhmání, سور súr, بزم bazm, جشن jashn, ولیمه valímah.—(*holiday*) عید 'íd, عید 'aid (*vulg.*). — (*feast days, holidays*) اعیاد a'yád.—(*marriage feast or merry-making*) سور súr, عیش 'aish. —(*feast given by great men to their dependants, &c.*) شیلان shílán.—(*feast given on certain occasions, such as the birth of a son, going into a new house, &c.*) ولیمه valímah.—(*to give a feast*) سور بر پا کردن súr bar pá kardan, شیلان کشیدن shílán kashídan, ولیمه دادن valímah dádan.

FEAT, بند band, کار kár, بازیچه bází-chah, نیرنگ nairang.

FEATHER, پر par.

FEATHERLESS, بی پر bí-par.

FEATHERY, پردار par-dár.

FEATURE, *vide* FACE.

FEBRUARY, شباط shabát.

FEDERATION, معاهده mu'áhadah.

FEE (*payment for duties performed*) حق السعی hakku-'s-sa'í, اجر ajr, مزد muzd. — (*douceur*) بخشش bakhshish, پول چای púl-i-chái.

FEEBLE, *vide* WEAK.

FEEBLY, ضعیفانه za'ífánah, عاجزانه 'ájizánah.

To FEED, خورانیدن khwuránídan, پروردن parvardan, تغذیه نمودن taghziyah nimúdan.—(*pasture*) چرانیدن charánídan, چرا کردن chará kardan.—(*a horse*) کاه و دانه دادن káh va dánah dádan.

To FEEL, احساس کردن ihsás kardan, جس کردن jass kardan. (*Vide* To PERCEIVE, To TOUCH.)

FEELING, حس hiss, قوهٔ لامسه kúvah-i-lámisah.

To FEIGN, بهانه نمودن bahánah nimúdan, تقلید کردن taklíd kardan.

FELICITATION, *vide* CONGRATULATION.

FELICITOUS, *vide* HAPPY.

FELLOW (*one of a pair*), جور júr, زوج zauj, لنگه lingah. — (*man*) مردکه mardakah.—(*fellow-traveller*) *vide* TRAVELLER.

FELLOWSHIP, شراکت shirákat, مشارکت mushárakat, رفاقت rafákat.

FELT (*unwoven woollen stuff*), نمد namad, لبد libd.

FEMALE, ماده mádah, مادینه mádínah, مؤنث mu,annas, اناث anás, انثی unsá. (*Vide* WOMAN.)

FEMININE, مؤنث mu,annas.

FENCE, *vide* HEDGE.

To FENCE, شمشیر بازی کردن shamshír-bází kardan. *Vid.* To ENCLOSE.

FENCING (*sword-play*), شمشیر بازی shamshír-bází.

FENNEL, شبت shibt, رازیانه ráz-yánah, بادیان bádyán.

FENUGREEK, شنبلید shambalíd, شنبلیله shambalílah, شملیز sham-liz (*vulg.*).

FERMENT (*agitation*), هیجان hayaján.

To FERMENT, بجوش آمدن bi-júsh ámadan.

FERMENTATION, جوشش júshish, تخمیر takhmír.

FERMENTED, مخمر mukhammar.

FERN, ثمامه sumámah.

FEROCIOUS, *vide* FIERCE.

FERRET, موش خرما músh-i-khurmá, راسو rású.

FERRULE, نصل nasl (pl. نصول nusúl).

FERRY, گذرگاه guzar-gáh, معبر ma'-bar, گذار guzár (*vulg.*).—(*ferry-boat*) کشتی گذاره kashtí-i-guzárah.

FERTILE, جید jayyid, خصیب khasíb, حاصل ده hásil-dih, برومند barú-mand, باروَر bár-var.

FERTILITY, برومندی barú-mandí, خصب khisb.

To FESTER, ریش شدن rísh shudan, خوره شدن khwarah shudan, فاسد شدن fásid shudan.

FESTIVAL, *vide* FEAST.

FESTIVITY, شادی shádí, خوشی khwushí, خوشوقتی khwush-vaktí, نشاط nashát.

FESTOON, هره hirah.

To FETCH, *vide* To BRING.

FÊTE, *vide* FEAST.

FETLOCK, پای páy.

FETTERS, پا بند pá-band, زنجیر zan-jír, غل ghull.

FEUDATORY, زیر دست zír-dast.

FEVER, تب tab.—(*ague*) تب و لرز tab u larz. — (*intermittent*) تب نوبتی tab-i-naubatí, تب غب tab-i-ghibb.—(*hectic*) تب دق tab-i-dikk.

FEW, کم kam, اندک andak, قلیل kalíl. —(*a few*) قدری kadrí, جزوی juzví.

FEZ (*cap*), فس fas (*eur.*).

FIANCÉE, مخطوبه makhtúbah, نام زد nám-zad.

FIB, *vide* FALSEHOOD.—(*to tell fibs*) چاپ زدن cháp zadan.

FIBRE, ريشه ríshah.
FICKLE, *vide* VARIABLE, INCONSTANT.
FICTION, افسانه afsánah.
FICTITIOUS, نقلی naklí, جعلی ja'lí.
FIDELITY, وفا vafá, وفاداری vafá-dárí, صداقت sadákat, حق نمك hakk-i-namak.
FIDGETTY, متزلزل mutazalzil.
FIE! وای váí, واه váh, اف uf, اخ ukh, تفو tafú.
FIEF (*estate, feudal tenure*), تیول tuyúl, تویل tuvíl (*vulg.*).
FIELD, صحرا sahrá, میدان maidán.—(*cultivated field*) مزرعه mazra'ah, کشت زار kisht-zár, زراعت zirá'at.—(*of battle*) میدان maidán, معرکه ma'rikah, نبرد گاه nabard-gáh, رزمگاه razm-gáh.
FIEND, شیطان shaitán.
FIERCE, تند tund, درشت durusht, شدید shadíd.—(*animal*) درنده darandah.—(*sun*) تند tund, زننده zanandah, تیز tíz.
FIERCENESS, تندی tundí, درشتی durushtí, شدت shiddat, صولت saulat.—(*animal*) درندگی darandagí.—(*sun*) تندی tundí, زنندگی zanandagí, تیزی tízí.
FIERY, آتشین átishín, آتشبار átish-bár, ناری nárí.
FIFE, نی nai.
FIFER, نیچی nai-chí.
FIG, انجیر anjír.
FIGHT, *vide* BATTLE, DISPUTE, WAR.
To FIGHT, جنگ کردن jang kardan, رزم ساختن razm sákhtan.
FIGURATIVE, رنگین rangín, تمثیل tamsíl.
FIGURE, شکل shakl, صورت súrat, کالبد kálbud, پیکر paikar, هیئت hai,at, هیکل haikal, قواره kuvárah, شخص shakhs, ریخت ríkht.—(*in arithmetic*) رقم rakam.
FILE, سوهان súhán.—(*of papers*) طبق tabak, طبقه tabakah, دسته dastah.
To FILE, سوهان زدن súhán zadan, سوهانکاری کردن súhán-kárí kardan.
FILINGS, براده burádah, ساوه sávah.
To FILL, پر کردن pur kardan, مملو نمودن mamlú nimúdan, ملا کردن malá kardan, مشحون کردن mashhún kardan.—(*cram*) آکندن ákandan, انپاشتن ampáshtan, طپانیدن tapánídan, چپانیدن chapánídan.
FILLET, سر بند sar-band, مباف mubáf.
To FILLIP, انگشتك دادن angushtak dádan, پلنگ زدن piling zadan.
FILLY, کره مادة kurrah-i-mádah, فلوه faluvah, طریح taríh.
FILM, فوف fúf, پرده pardah.
FILTER, مصفات misfát, صافی sáfí.
To FILTER, صاف کردن sáf kardan, پالودن pálúdan.
FILTERED, مروق muravvak.
FILTH, چرك chirk, نجاست najásat, لجن lajan, لوث laus, آلایش áláyish, جنابت janábat.
FILTHY, پلید palíd, چرکین chirkín, نا پاك ná-pák. (*Vide* INDECENT.)
FILTRATION, تصفیه tasfiyah.
FIN (*of a fish*), پر ماهی par-i-máhí, بال bál.—(*dorsal fin*) مازه mázah.
FINALLY, نهایت الامر niháyatu-'l-amr.
FINANCE, مالیات máliyát, ارتفاع مملکت irtifá'-i-mamlakat.—(*minister*) وزیر مالیه vazír-i-máli-yah.—(*financial arrangements*) خرج و مخارج kharj u makhárij, مداخل و مخارج madákhil u makhárij.
To FIND, یافتن yáftan, پیدا کردن paidá kardan, جستن justan, بهم رسانیدن bi-ham rasánídan.—(*to find out*) ملتفت شدن multafit shudan, منتقل شدن muntakil shudan, در یافتن dar-yaftan.
FINE (*not coarse*), نازك názuk, رقیق rakík, باریك bárík. (*Vide* DEAR, PRECIOUS, RARE, EXCELLENT.)—(*weather*) مساعد musá'id.—(*small*) باریك bárík, دقیق dakík, ریزه rízah.—(*pen*) نازك názuk.—(*mulct*) جریمه jarímah, جریمانه jarímánah, مصادره musádarah.—(*fine for manslaughter*) خونبها khún-bahá, دیت diyyat, معقله ma'-kulah.—(*for causing abortion*) غره ghurrah.—(*in fine*) غایتش ghá-yat-ash, الغرض al-gharaz, الحاصل al-hásil, الاخر al-ákhir.

To FINE, مصادرۀ نمودن musádarah nimúdan.—(*to be fined*) جريمانه كرده شدن jarímánah-kardah shudan.

To FINE-DRAW, رفو كردن rafú kardan.

FINENESS, دقت dikkat.

FINESSE, *vide* ARTIFICE.

FINGER, انگشت angusht.—(*fore-finger*) سبابه sabbábah, انگشت شهادت angusht-i-shahádat.—(*ring-finger*) بنصر binsir.—(*middle finger*) انگشت ميانه angusht-i-miyánah. — (*little finger*) خنصر khinsir, كلنج kilinj. — (*joint of the fingers*) بند انگشت band-i-angusht, مفصل mafsil (*pl.* مفاصل mafásil.—(*tip of finger*) بنانه banánah (*pl.* بنان bunán), انملت anmulat (*pl.* انامل anámil).

To FINGER, انگشت بردن angusht burdan, دست زدن dast zadan.

FINISH, *vide* END.

To FINISH, تمام كردن tamám kardan, باخر رسانيدن bi-ákhir rasánídan, پرداختن pardákhtan, منقرض ساختن munkariz sákhtan, انجاميدن anjámídan, انجام كردن anjám kardan, ختم نمودن khatm nimúdan, اختتام نمودن ikhtitám nimúdan.

FINISHED, *vide* POLITE.—(*to be finished, expended*) خلاص شدن khalás shudan, بسر آمدن bi-sar ámadan, خرج شدن kharj shudan, منقرض شدن munkariz shudan, باخر رسيدن bi-ákhir rasídan, تمام شدن tamám shudan.

FIR (*tree*), صنوبر sinaubar, كاج káj.

FIRE, آتش átish, نار nár, آذر ázar (*obs.*) (*Vide* CONFLAGRATION.) (*fire-place in a room*) بخاری bukhárí.—(*sunk in the floor*) تنور tannúr.—(*fire-place or oven*) اوجاق úják, چاله chálah.—(*fire-place formed of a pan of charcoal placed under a frame or low table, which is covered with a quilt*), كرسی kursí. — (*worshipper; priest; temple of worship*) *vide* MAGIAN. —(*fire-pan or brazier*) منقل mankal, آتشدان átish-dán.—(*of earthenware*) كلك kalak.—(*fire-brand*) آتشپاره átish-párah, نيمسوز nímsúz.—(*fire-fly*) مگس شبتاب magas-i-shab-táb.

To FIRE (*set on fire*), آتش زدن átish zadan, افروختن afrúkhtan, روشن كردن raushan kardan.—(*a gun*) خالی كردن khálí kardan. — (*to catch fire*) آتش در گرفتن átish dar giriftan.—(*to stir the fire*) آتش بهم زدن átish bi-ham zadan. —(*to blow the fire*) آتشرا پوف كردن átishrá púf kardan.—(*to make up the fire*) آتش كردن átish kardan.—(*to light the fire*) آتش روشن كردن átish raushan kardan. —(*to put out the fire*) آتشرا خاموش كردن átishrá khamúsh kardan, آتش نشاندن átish nishándan, آتشرا كشتن átishrá kushtan.

FIRE-DAMP, دمه damah.

FIRE-ENGINE, طولومبه túlúm bah.

FIREMAN (*extinguisher of fire*), آتش خاموش كن átish-khámúsh-kun.—(*company of firemen*) نظام آتش خاموش كن nizám-i-átish-khámúsh-kun, طولومبه چيان túlúmbah-chíán.

FIREWORKS, آتشبازی átish-bází.

FIRM (*company*), شركت shirkat. (*Vide* FAST, HARD.)—(*to make firm*) استوار كردن ustuvár kardán.

FIRMAMENT, رقيع rakí', سماوات samávát, جلد jalad, فضائی آسمان fazá,í-i-ásmán.

FIRMNESS, استواری ustuvárí, متانت matánat, قوت مندی kúvat-mandí.

FIRST, نخست nukhust, نخستين nukhustín, اول avval, يكم yakum, مقدم mukaddam.—(*firstly*) اولاً avvalan, مقدماً mukaddaman.—(*in the first place*) پيش از پيش písh az písh, اول بلا اول avval bilá avval.—(*first-fruits of the season*) نو بر nau-bar, نو باوه nau-bávah, پيش رس písh-ras.—(*at first*) در ابتدا dar ibtidá.—(*first day of month*) غره ghurrah, روز غرة rúz-i-ghurrah. — (*to come in first, racing*) پيش آمدن písh ámadan.

FIRSTBORN, اول زاده avval-zádah.
FISCAL, دیوانی díváni.
FISH, ماهی máhí. — (*dried and smoked fish*) کسیف kisíf, ماهی خشک máhí - i - khushk.— (*river fish*) ماهی شطی máhí-i-shatí.— (*sea fish*) ماهی بحری máhí-i-bahrí. —(*fish-hook*) قلابه kullábah, شص shass. — (*fishing-net*) دام dám, شبکه shabakah, طور túr, توره túrah. —(*fisherman*) ماهیگیر máhí-gír. —(*fish-pond*) تالاب táláb.—(*fish-monger*) ماهی فروش máhí-furúsh.
To FISH, صید نمودن said nimúdan, ماهی صید کردن máhí said kardan, شکار کردن shikár kardan.
FISSURE, *vide* CRACK.
FIST, مشت musht.—(*to clench the fist*) دسترا مشت کردن dastrá musht kardan, پنجه بهم گذاشتن panjah bi-ham guzáshtan.
FISTULA, ناسور násúr, ناسور násúr.— (*lacrymalis*) سیلان چشم sailán-i-chashm, دمعه dam'ah.
FIT, *vide* PAROXYSM, SWOON. — (*proper*), لائق lá,ik, واجب vájib, روا ravá, مناسب munásib, سزا sazá, سزاوار sazávár, شایسته sháyistah, لازم lázim. — (*to be fit*) شایستن sháyistan, لائق بودن lá,ik búdan, بکار خوردن bi-kár khwurdan, بایستن báyistan, سازکار شدن sáz-kár shudan.
To FIT, مناسب شدن munásib shudan, مناسبت داشتن munásabat dáshtan, موافقت داشتن muváfakat dáshtan, فراخور بودن farákhwur búdan. (*Vide* To BECOME (*befit*), To ADAPT.)
FITNESS, شایستگی sháyistagí, سازکاری sáz-kárí.
FITTINGS, اسباب asbáb.
FIX, کشمکش kash-ma-kash. — (*to be in a fix*) گیر آمدن gír ámadan, دو چار شدن dú-chár shudan.
To FIX, نشاندن nishándan, ثبت کردن sabt kardan, نصب کردن nasb kardan, اقامت کردن ikámat kardan.
FIXED, معین mu'ayyan, مقرر mukarrar.—(*usual*) موعود mau'úd.— (*to keep one's eyes fixed*) مراقب بودن murákib búdan.
FLABBINESS, نرمی narmí.
FLABBY, نرم narm.
FLAG, نشان nishán, علم 'alam, رایت ra,yat, لوا livá, بیرق bairak, بیراق bairák. — (*reed*) نی nai, هردی hurdí, پیزر pízur, لخ lukh, جگن jagan.--(*flag-staff*) دار علم dár-i-'alam.
To FLAG, *vide* To WITHER.
FLAGON, قرابه karábah.
FLAIL, گندم کوب gandum-kúb.
FLAMBEAU, *vide* TORCH.
FLAME, زبانه zabánah, شعله shu'lah, تف taf. — (*in flames*) مشتعل mushta'al.
FLANK, پهلو pahlú.—(*the flanks*) اضلاع azlá'.
FLANNEL, فنالن fanálan (*eur.*).
FLAP, دامن dáman, چین chín.
FLASH, آتش átish.
To FLASH, درخشیدن dirakhshídan, برق زدن bark zadan.—(*in the pan, a gun*), گل کردن gul kardan.
FLASHING, درخشان dirakhshán, بارق bárik.
FLASK, *vide* BOTTLE.
FLAT (*level*), برابر barábar, هموار hamvár, مساوی musáví, بسیط basít, مسطح musattah, پهن pahn. —(*trade*) کاسد kásid.
To FLATTEN, *vide* To ROLL OUT.
To FLATTER, *vide* To COAX, To WHEEDLE.
FLATTERER, چاپلوس cháplús.
FLATTERY, خوش آمد khwush-ámad, چاپلوسی cháplúsí, تملق tamallúk, چم و خم cham va kham, نوازش navázish, ریشخندی rísh-khandí.
FLATULENCY, نفخ شکم nafkh - i - shikm, باد شکم bád-i-shikm.
FLATULENT, نفاخ naffákh.
FLAUTIST, نی زن nai-zan.
FLAVOUR, مزه mazah, طعم ta'm, ذوق zauk, چاشنی cháshní.
FLAW, نقص naks, نقیصه nakísah, کاست kást, مو mú. (*Vide* CRACK.) —(*flawed*) مودار mú-dár, شق شده shakk-shudah, شکافته shikáftah.
FLAX, کتان kattán.

To FLAY, پوست کندن púst kandan, پوست بر کشیدن púst bar-kashídan, سلخ کردن salkh kardan.
FLEA, کیک kaik, کهک kahk.
To FLEE, گریختن guríkhtan, فرار کردن firár kardan, هزیمت نمودن hazímat nimúdan, پشت دادن pusht dádan.
FLEECE, پشم pashm.
To FLEECE, *vide* To SHEAR, To DEFRAUD.
FLEET (*of vessels*), دستهٔ کشتی dastah-i-kashtí. (*Vide* QUICK.)
FLEETING, فانی fání, نا پایدار ná-páyadár.
FLESH, گوشت gúsht, لحم lahm.
FLESHY, گوشتین gúshtín.
FLEXIBILITY, نرمی narmí.
FLEXIBLE, نرم narm, پیچخور píchkhwur.
FLEXION (*grammatical term*), صرف sarf.
FLIGHT (*escape*), فرار firár, گریز guríz, هرب harb.—(*act of flying*) پرواز parváz, طیران tayarán.—(*rout or defeat*) هزیمت hazímat, شکست shikast.—(*of arrows*) تیر باران tírbárán. — (*flock of birds*), گله galah, سیله sílah.—(*to put to flight*) منهزم گردانیدن munhazim gardánídan, هزیمت دادن hazímat dádan, گریزانیدن gurízánídán.
To FLINCH, *vide* To QUAIL.
To FLING, انداختن andákhtan, افکندن afkandan.—(*down*) انداختن andákhtan, بزیر افکندن bi-zír afkandan, پرت کردن part kardan (*vulg*).
FLINT, سنگ چخماق sang-i-chakhmák.—(*a skin flint*) نان کور nánkúr. (*Vide* MISER.)—(*to skin a flint*) مگسرا در هوا رگ زدن magasrá dar havá rag zadan.
FLIPPANT, گستاخ gustákh, شوخ shúkh.
FLIPPANTLY, غافلانه gháfilánah, غفلةً ghiflatan, گستاخانه gustákhánah, با شوخی bá-shúkhí.
FLIRT, شیوه باز shívah-báz, شیوه گر shívah-gar, عشوه باز 'ishvah-báz, عشوه گر 'ishvah-gar.
To FLOAT, بالائی آب رفتن bálá,í-i-áb raftan.
FLOCK (*of large cattle, horses, cows, mules, &c.*), رمه ramah. — (*of sheep, goats, birds, &c.*) گله galah.
To FLOG, تازیانه زدن táziyánah zadan. — (*tie up and chastise*) با سرمه زدن bá-surmah zadan.
FLOOD, سیلاب sailáb, طوفان túfán.—(*the Flood*) طوفان túfán.
FLOOR, زمین zamín, کف kaf, فرش farsh.—(*boarded*) تخته takhtah.—(*story of a house*) طبقه tabakah, طاقه tákah, بام bám.—(*ground-floor*) تحتانی tahtání, مرتبهٔ پائین martabah-i-pá,ín.
To FLOOR, از تخته مفروش کردن az takhtah mafrúsh kardan, با تخته فرش کردن ba-takhtah farsh kardan.
FLORICAN (*small species of bustard*), زنگبال zangibál, چرز charz.
FLOUR, آرد árd.—(*fine flour*) آرد رقیق árd-i-rakík. — (*place for storing flour*) کته kattah.
To FLOURISH, شکوفتن shikúftan. (*Vide* To BRANDISH.)—(*be prosperous*) بالیدن bálídan, خوشوقت بودن khwush-vakt búdan, بهره مند بودن bahrah-mand búdan.
FLOURISHING (*exchequer*), معمور ma'múr. (*Vide* HEALTHY, PROSPEROUS.)
FLOW (*of the sea*), مد madd.
To FLOW, جاری شدن járí shudan, جریان نمودن jiryán nimúdan, روان شدن raván shudan, سیلان شدن sayalán shudan, سیل نمودن sail nimúdan, ریزان شدن rízán shudan.
FLOWER, گل gul, نور naur, زهر zahr, شکوفه shikúfah.—(*of youth*) عنفوان 'unfuván, ریعان ray'án. — (*best part*) زبده zubdah, خلاصه khulásah, سلاله sulálah. — (*garden*) گلستان gulistán, بوستان bústán, گلزار gulzár, باغچه bághchah.—(*flower-pot*) گلدان gul-dán.—(*flower-box*) کوزه kúzah.— (*flower-work, embroidery*) بوته bútah, بوته کاری bútah-kárí.
FLOWING, جاری járí, روان raván.
FLUE, خالی khálí, دود کش dúd-kash.
FLUENCY (*of speech*), فصاحت fasáhat, زبان آوری zabán-ávarí.

FLUENT, فصیح fasíh, زبان آور zabán-ávar.
FLUID, سیال sayyál, جاری jári, آبی ábí. (*Vide* LIQUOR.)
FLURRY, های هوی háí-húí, آشوب áshúb, آشفتگی áshuftagí, همهمه hamhamah.—(*to be in a flurry*) طپیدن tapídan.
To FLURRY, ترسانیدن tarsánídan.
FLUTE, نی nai, نای náy.
To FLUTTER, طپیدن tapídan.
FLUVIAL, نهری nahrí.
FLUX (*water*) سیل sail.—(*blood*) رفتن خون raftan-i-khún, رفتگی خون raftagí-i-khún, اسهال is-hál.
FLY, مگس magas.—(*gad-fly*) خر مگس khar-magas.—(*dragon-fly*) مشخره mashkhurah. — (*fire-fly*) مگس شبتاب magas-i-shab-táb.—(*Spanish fly*) *vide* CANTHARIDES.—(*fly-flap*) باد بزن bád-bizan.
To FLY, پریدن parídan, *or* parrídan, پرواز نمودن parváz nimúdan, طیران نمودن tayarán nimúdan.—(*a kite*) هوا دادن havá dádan.
FOAL, کره kurrah. (*Vide* FILLY.)
FOAM, کف kaf, تفش tafish.
To FOAM, کف کردن kaf kardan.
FOB, جیب jíb.
FODDER, علف 'alaf, گیاه giyáh, علیق 'alík.
FOE, *vide* ENEMY.
FŒTUS, جنین janín.
FOG, دود dúd, غبار شبنم ghubár-i-shabnam, مه mih, بخار bukhár, طومان túmán, میغ mígh.
FOGGY, هوا مه havá-i-mih, میغناک mígh-nák.
FOIST, تیز تیز, گوز gúz.
FOLD (*for cattle*), آغل ághil, مربض marbaz, حظیره hazírah, آگل ágil, سول súl.—(*ply*) ته tah, تا tá, لای láí.—(*two-fold*) دو تا dú-tá, مضاعف muzá'af, دوگانه dú-gánah.—(*three-fold*) سه لای sih-láí, سه تا sih-tá.—(*ten-fold*) ده تا dih-tá, ده چندان dih-chandán, ده مقابله dih-mukábalah. —(*subterraneous fold for cattle*) کند kand.
To FOLD UP, پیچیدن píchídan, ته کردن tah kardan, تا کردن tá kardan, طی ساختن tai sákhtan, نوردیدن navardídan.
FOLIAGE, برگ barg, ورق varak.
To FOLLOW, عقب رفتن 'akab raftan, تعاقب کردن ta'ákub kardan, دنبال رفتن dumbál raftan, پیروی نمودن pay-raví nimúdan, در پی رفتن dar pay raftan, پس رفتن pas raftan, پی زدن pay zadan.—(*to the door on taking leave*) مشایعت نمودن musháya'at nimúdán, بدرقه رفتن badrikah raftan. — (*to follow after*) *vide* To PURSUE.—(*to follow as a mourner*) تشییع جنازه کردن tashyí'-i-janázah kardan.—(*as follows*) باین تفصیل bá-ín tafsíl, بتفصیل ذیل bi-tafsíl-i-zail.—(*following*) ذیل zail, آتیه átiyah, از این قرار az ín karár.
FOLLOWER, پس رو pas-rau, معاقب mu'ákib, تابع tábi', متابع mutábi', پی رونده pay-ravandah, پیزن pay-zan.—(*believer*) مقتدی muktadí, معتقد mu'takid, تلمیذ talmíz, مرید muríd, مقلد mukallid.
FOLLY, ابلهی ablahí, بلاهت baláhat, حماقت himákat, سفاهت safáhat, خبط khabt, قلت عقل killat-i-'akl, بیوقوفی bí-vukúfí, نادانی ná-dání, بیعقلی bí-'aklí, خریت kharíyat (*vulg.*).—(*height of folly*) کمال بی عقلی kamál-i-bí-'aklí.
FOND, مائل má,il, شائق shá,ik, مغرم mighram.
To FONDLE, جنبانیدن jumbánídan, بچه نوازی کردن bachah-navází kardan.
FOOD, قوت kút, خوراک khwurák, طعام ta'ám, غذا ghizá, خورد khwurd, آزوقه ázúkah, ماکول ma,kúl.—(*bodily*) غذائی جسمانی ghizá,í-i-jismání.—(*spiritual*) غذائی روحانی ghizá,í-i-rúhání.
FOOL, ابله ablah, کودن kaudan, احمق ahmak, نا دان ná-dán, نا فهم ná-fahm, سفیه safíh, خوپله khwaplah, بیوقوف bí-vukúf, پخت pakht (*vulg.*). (*Vide* JESTER.)
FOOLISH, *vide* STUPID, IGNORANT.
FOOLISHLY, احمقانه ahmakánah, بی عقلانه 'aklánah, بیهوده bíhúdah.

Foot, پا pá, پای páy.—(*as applied to things*) پاچه páchah. (*Vide* Basis, Pedestal, Verse.)—(*on foot*) پیاده piyádah.—(*at the foot of*) دم dam, پای páy.—(*to set on foot*) بر پای کردن bar páy kardan.—(*to go on foot*) پیاده رفتن piyádah raftan.

Foot-board, جا پا já-i-pá.

Footing, قاعده ká'idah, اساس asás, حالت hálat.

Footman, پیاده piyádah. (*Vide* Servant.)—(*runner*) شاطر shátir, پیک paik, قاصد kásid.

Footstep (*pace*), قدم kadam, گام gám.—(*mark*) نشان پای nishán-i-páy, اثر asar, خطوه khatvah, قدم kadam, سراغ surágh.

Footstool, قدمگاه kadam-gáh, کرسی زیر پا kursí-i-zír-pá.

Fop, قشنگ kashang, کج کلاه kaj-kuláh, خود بین khwud-bín, اجلاف ijláf, خوشگل khwush-gil.

Foppish, خویشتن بین khwíshtan-bín, قشنگ kashang.

For, برای baráí, از بهر az bahr, جهت jihat, بواسطه bi-vásitah, پاس خاطر pás-i-khátir, بخش bakhsh, تا tá, واسه vásah (*vulg.*).—(*for instance, for example*) مثلاً masalan, فرضاً farzan, بر فرض bar farz.—(*for long, for a long while*) از قدیم الایام az kadímu-'l-ayyám, دیر باز dír-báz.—(*for the sake of*) برای baráí, بنابر biná-bar, پاس خاطر pás-i-khátir, از بهر az bahr, بواسطه bi-vásitah.—(*for ever*) *vide* Ever.

Forage, علف 'alaf, گیاه giyáh, علیق 'alík.

Foray (*plundering expedition*), چپاو chapáw, غارت ghárat, تاراج táráj, یغما yaghmá, سلب salab, راهزنی ráh-zaní, انتهاب intiháb, چپاولی chapávali (*vulg.*).

To Forbear, وا ایستادن vá-ístádan, دست بر داشتن dast bar-dáshtan, پرهیز کردن parhíz kardan, تحمل نمودن tahammul nimúdan.

Forbearance, اجتناب ijtináb, احتراز ihtiráz, امتناع imtiná', تحمل tahammul, توقف tavakkuf, اهمال ihmál, پرهیزی parhízí.

To Forbid, منع کردن mana' kardan, حرمان نمودن harmán nimúdan, باز داشتن báz-dáshtan, نهی کردن nahy kardan, قدغن نمودن kadghan nimúdan.

Forbidden, ممنوع mamnú', منهی munhí, حرام harám, حریم harím, محظور mahzúr.—(*forbidden things*) محرمات muharramát, مناهی manáhí, ملاهی maláhí, نواهی naváhí, ممنوعات mamnú'át, محظورات mahzúrát.

Force (*strength*), *vide* Strength.—(*violence*) *vide* Compulsion, Violence.

To Force, *vide* To Compel.

Forced, مجبور majbúr.

Forces (*military*), فوج fauj, لشکر lashkar.—(*by force*) بزور bi-zúr, جبراً jabran.—(*to come into force*) مرعی الاجرا شدن mar'íu-'l-ijrá shudan.—(*to put in force*) مجرا کردن mujrá kardan.

Ford, گذار guzár, گذاره guzárah, گذرگاه guzar-gáh, معبر ma'bar, گدار gudár (*vulg.*).

Fordable, پایاب pá-yáb, ممکن گذار mumkin-i-guzár.

Fore, پیشین píshín.

Forefather, پیشین píshín, جد jadd (*pl.* اجداد ajdád).

To Forego, *vide* To Abandon.

Forehead, پیشانی písháni, جبین jabín, جبهه jabhah, ناصیه násiyah (*pl.* نواصی navásí).

Foreign, غریب gharíb, بیگانه bígánah, اجنب ajnab.—(*Foreign Minister*) وزیر خارجه vazír-i-khárijah.—(*Under Secretary of State for Foreign Affairs*) مستشار خارجیه mustashár-i-khárijíyah.—(*Foreign Office*) وزارتخانه خارجه دولتی vizárat-khánah-i-khárijah-i-daulatí.

Foreigner, اجنبی ajnabí.

Foreleg (*of an animal*), دست dast.

Foreman, سرکار sar-kár, استاد ustád.

Foremost, پیشترین píshtarín, اول

avval, مقدم mukaddam, پیشرو písh-rau.
FORENOON, پیش از ظهر písh az zuhr, ضحی zuhá.
FORERUNNER, پیشرو písh-rau.
To FORESEE, پیش دیدن písh dídan, از مآل اندیشی دانستن az ma,ál-andíshí dánistan.
FORESIGHT, بصیرت basírat.
FORESKIN, غلفت ghulfat, غلاف ghiláf.
FOREST, درختستان dirakhtistán, درختزار dirakht-zár, بیشه bíshah, جنگل jangal, اجم ujum.
FORETASTE, عربون 'urbún.
To FORETELL, از مآل اندیشی خبر دادن az ma,ál-andíshí khabar dádan, پیش گفتن písh guftan. — (*prophecy*) نبوت نمودن nubúvat nimúdan, اخبار نمودن ikhbár nimúdan, کهانت گفتن kahánat guftan.
FORFEIT, جریمه jarímah, جریمانه jarímánah.
To FORFEIT, گم کردن gum kardan.
FORGE (*of a blacksmith*), کوره kúrah.
To FORGE, ساختن sákhtan.
FORGED, *vide* COUNTERFEIT.
FORGER, قلاب kalláb, ساخته گر sákhtah-gar.
FORGERY, جعل ja'l, ساختگی sákhtagí, تزویر tazvír.
To FORGET, فراموش کردن farámúsh kardan, نسیان نمودن nisyán nimúdan.
FORGETFUL, ذاهل záhil, ناسی násí, فراموشکار farámúsh-kár.
FORGETFULNESS, فراموش farámúsh, نسیان nisyán, فراموشی farámúshí.
To FORGIVE, عفو کردن 'afv kardan, معاف کردن mu'áf kardan, بخشیدن bakhshídan, معذور داشتن ma'zúr dáshtan, در گذر کردن dar guzar kardan, آمرزیدن ámurzídan, مغفور گردانیدن maghfúr gardánídan.
FORK, چنگال changál.—(*for shifting corn, &c. while thrashing*) اوچوم auchúm, اوسی ausí ; سکو sikú. — (*of flame*) زبانه zabánah.
FORLORN, پریشان paríshán.—(*forlorn hope*) پیش افتاد písh-uftád, پیش آهنگ písh-áhang.

FORM, *vide* FIGURE, SHAPE.—(*ceremony*) رسم rasm, تکلف takalluf.—(*grammatical term*) بنا biná, مبنی mabní.—(*at school*) صنف sinf.
To FORM, تشکیل کردن tashkíl kardan, صورت دادن súrat dádan, ساختن sákhtan.—(*intrans.*) صورت بستن súrat bastan. — (*to be formed*) تشکیل یافتن tashkíl yáftan.
FORMALLY, صریحاً saríhan.
FORMER, پیشین píshín, سابق sábik, قدیم kadím, مقدم mukaddam.—(*as opposed to latter*) اولی aulá.
FORMERLY, سابق sábik, پیشتر píshtar, مقدماً mukaddaman, من قبل min kabl, پیش از این písh az ín, ایام گذشته ayyám-i-guzashtah, آنفاً ánifan.
FORMIDABLE, مهیب mahíb, هولناک haul-nák.
FORMIDABLENESS, هیبت haibat, هولناکی haul-nákí.
FORMIDABLY, بهیبت bi-haibat.
FORMULA, دستور العمل dastúru-'l-'amal.
To FORNICATE, زنا کردن ziná kardan.
FORNICATION, زنا ziná, زنا کاری ziná-kárí, حرام کاری harám-kárí, شید shaid, فاحشگی fáhishagí.
FORNICATOR, زنا کار ziná-kár, زانی zání, شید باز shaid-báz.
To FORSAKE, *vide* ABANDON.
FORSOOTH! به bih, بهی bihí.
FORT, قلعه kal'ah, حصار hisár, بارو bárú, حصن hisn.—(*on a hill*) دژ dizh, کلات kalát.
FORTE, رسم rasm, طریقه taríkah.
FORTHWITH, فی الفور fí-'l-faur.
FORTIFICATIONS (*of a town*) بارو bárú, باره bárah, حصن hisn, حصار hisár.
FORTIFIED (*a town, &c.*) محروسه mahrúsah, محصون mahsún, مشید mushayyad.
To FORTIFY, محصون کردن mahsún kardan, تحصین کردن tahsín kardan.
FORTITUDE, مروت murúvat. (*Vide* BOLDNESS.)
FORTNIGHT, دو هفته dú-haftah.

Fortunate, بختيار bakht-yár, نيك بختník-bakht, نيك اختر ník-akhtar, سعيد sa'íd, فرخ farrukh, برومند barú-mand, ميمون maimún, خجسته khujastah, كامران kámrán, طالعمند táli'-mand, خوشوقت khwush-vakt.

Fortunately, قضارا kazárá.

Fortune, روزگار rúzigár, روزی rúzí, نصيب nasíb, بخت bakht, طالع táli', قسمت kismat, بهره bahrah, فلك falak, دهر dahr, زمانه zamánah, دولت daulat.—(*bad fortune*) بد بختی bad-bakhti, بخت نامساعد bakht-i-ná-musá'id.—(*good fortune*) بخت سعيد bakht-i-sa'íd, بخت نيكو bakht-i-níkú.—(*to make one's fortune*) صاحب دولت شدن sáhib-i-daulat shudan.

Fortune-teller, فالگير fál-gír.

To Forward, *vide* to Send.

Forwards, در پيش dar písh, پيشتر píshtar, مقدم mukaddam.

Fosse, *vide* Ditch.

Foster (*mother*), دايه dáyah, شير ده shír-dih.—(*brother*) برادر همشير birádar-i-ham-shír, برادر رضاعی birádar-i-rizá'í. — (*child*) فرزند شير ده farzand-i-shír-dih, پسر رضاعی pisar-i-rizá'í.

To Foster, پرورش كردن parvarish kardan.

Foul, نا پاك ná-pák, آلوده álúdah, نجس najis, پليد pilíd, پلشت pilisht.—(*wicked*) فاسد fasid, قبيح kabíh, فضيح fazíh, شنيع shaní', ميشوم maishúm.

To Foul. ناپاك كردن ná-pák kardan, آلودن álúdan, چركين كردن chirkín kardan.—(*ships, &c.*) بهم خوردن bi-ham khwurdan.

Foul-mouthed, بد زبان bad-zabán.

Foulness, نا پاكی ná-pákí, نجاست najásat, آلودگی álúdagí.

To Found, تأسيس نمودن ta,sís nimudan.—(*metals*) ريختن ríkhtan.

Foundation, بنياد bunyád, بنيان bunyán, بن bun, پايه páyah, اساس asás, طرح tarh, اصل asl, قاعده ká'idah.—(*of a wall*) شالده sháldah.—(*foundation stone*) سنگ پايه دار sang-i-páyah-dár.

Founded, مبنی mabní.

Founder, بانی báni. — (*of metals*), ريخته گر ríkhtah-gar, قال كن kál-kun, قالگر kál-gar.

Foundling (*child*), لقيط lakít, بچهٔ منبوذ bachah-i-mambúz.

Fountain, چشمه chashmah, عين 'ain, منبع mamba', ينبوع yambú', خانی khání.—(*jet d'eau*) فواره favvárah, شادروان shádurván.

Fowl, مرغ murgh, پرنده parandah.

Fowler, صياد sayyád.

Fox, روباه rúbáh, روبه rúbah, رباه rubáh.

Fracas, *vide* Quarrel.

Fraction (*in arithmetic*), كسره kasrah, عدد مكسور 'adad-i-maksúr, كسور kusúr.—(*vulgar fractions*) كسور عادی kusúr-i-'ádí.

Fracture, شكستگی shikastagí, كسر kasr.

Fragile, *vide* Brittle, Inconstant.

Fragment, پاره párah, پارچه párchah, ريزه rízah, پرزه purzah, كسره kasrah, تكه tikkah.

Fragrance, خوشبوی khwush-búí, رائحه rá,ihah, نفحه nafhah, عطر 'itr.

Fragrant, مشموم mashmúm, معطر mu'attar.

Frail, *vide* Brittle, Inconstant.

Frame (*of wood, &c.*), كالبد kál-bud, قوام kavám.—(*frame for training vines, &c. on*) تالانه tálánah, داربست dár-bast, چفته chiftah.—(*frame on which lamps are arranged*) چلچراغ chil-chirágh.—(*frame of a window, picture, &c.*) چهار چوبه chahár-chúbah, چار چوبه chár-chúbah.—(*human*) جثه jussah, بنيه bunyah.

To Frame, چهار چوبه گذاردن chahár-chúbah guzárdan.

Franchise, آزادی ázádí, آزادگی ázádagí.

Frank, آزاده دل ázádah-dil; صديق sadík, صادق sádik, راستگو rást-gú.—(*European*) فرنگی farangí.

FRANKINCENSE, کندر kundur, لبان lubán.
FRANTIC, دیوانه díváhah, مجنون majnún.
FRATERNALLY, برادرانه birádaránah.
To FRATERNIZE, یکدل شدن yak-dil shudan, یکرائی شدن yak-ra,í shudan.
FRATRICIDE, قتل برادر katl-i-birádar.
FRAUD, فریب firíb, حیله hílah, تلبیس talbís, خدعه khud'ah, مکر makr, تزویر tazvír, زور zúr, دغا daghá, دغا بازی daghá-bází, غل ghill, غدر ghadr, کید kaid, رنگ rang, ریا riyá, غش ghishsh, مکاده makádah, زرق zirk, دخل dakhal, دغل daghal, گول gúl, تقلب takallub.
FRAUDULENT, دغاباز daghá-báz.
FRAUDULENTLY, حیلتاً hílatan.
FRECKLE, گندمه gandamah.
FREE, آزاد ázád, آزاده ázádah, رسته rastah, رستگار rastagár, رها rihá, مبرا mubarrá, بری barí, ایمن íman, منزه munazzah, معرا mu'arrá, مطلق mutlak, دست گشاده dast-gushádah, مخلا mukhallá, مسلم musallam, مجاز mujáz, مختار mukhtár, عتیق 'atík, مستقل mustakill.—(*void*), خالی khálí.—(*to become free*) رستن rastan, خلاص شدن khalás shudan.
To FREE, خلاص کردن khalás kardan, رستگار کردن rastagár kardan, رها کردن rihá kardan.
FREEDOM, آزادی ázádí, آزادگی ázádagí, خلاص khalás, خلاصی khalásí, امن aman, نجات naját, رهائی rihá,í, حریه hurríyah, اختیار ikhtiyár. (*Vide* MANUMISSION, LIBERTY.)—(*freedom of a company*) عادت مجلس 'ádat-i-majlis.
FREELY, بطور آزادی bi-taur-i-ázádí.
FREEMASON, فرماسون faramásún (*eur.*), فراموشی farámúshí.—(*Freemason's Hall*), فراموشخانه farámúsh-khánah.
FREE-THINKER (*a sect of sceptics who entertain peculiar views on religious matters, common in Persia*), صوفی súfí, اهل تصوف ahl-i-tasavvuf.—(*complete free-thinker who denies the Kur,án and divine mission of the Prophet*) صوفی مطلق súfí-i-mutlak.—(*free-thinker who admits the Kur,án and Prophet, but holds much of the doctrine to be metaphorical, and not requiring strict obedience*) صوفی متشرع súfí-i-mutasharri'. — (*doctrine of the Súfís or free-thinkers*) تصوف tasavvuf.
FREEWILL, اختیار ikhtiyár.
To FREEZE, یخ بستن yakh bastan, منجمد شدن munjamid shudan, فسردن fisurdan.—(*to be frozen*) یخ شدن yakh shudan.
FREIGHT, بار bár, حمل haml, نول naul.
FRENCH, فرانساوی faránsáví, فرنساوی faransáví.
FRENZY, دیوانگی dívánagí, جنون junún.
FREQUENT, *vide* NUMEROUS.
To FREQUENT, آمد و شد کردن ámad-va-shud kardan, متواتر شدن mutavátir shudan.
FREQUENTLY, بارها bárhá, اکثر aksar, بسیار بار bisyár bár, دفعةً daf'atan, اکثر اوقات aksar aukát.
FRESH, تازه tázah, سبز sabz.—(*air*) خنک khunuk, سرد sard, بارد bárid.—(*water*) شیرین shírín.
To FRESHEN (*trans.*), تازه ساختن tázah sákhtan.— (*intrans.*) تازه شدن tázah shudan.
FRESHNESS, تازگی tázagí, سبزی sabzí, شیرینی shíríní, سردی sardí.
To FRET, کج خلق شدن kaj-khulk shudan, خشم گرفتن khishm giriftan, بسر بردن bi-sar burdan.
FRETFUL, افسرده afsurdah, بد مزاج bad-mizáj, کجخلق kaj-khulk, مکدر mukaddar.
FRETFULNESS, افسردگی afsurdagí, تکدر takaddur.
FRIAR, *vide* MONK.
FRICTION, مالش málish, حک hakk.
FRIDAY, روز جمعه rúz-i-jum'ah, آدینه ádínah.
FRIEND, دوست dúst, یار yár, آشنا áshná, رفیق rafík, دلدار dil-dár,

مخلص mukhlis, خیر خواه khair-khwáh, حبیب habíb, محب muhibb, خلیل khalíl, همدم ham-dam, صدیق sadík, شفیق shafík, مشفق mushfik.—(*a true friend*) دوست حقیقی dúst-i-hakíkí, یار صادق yár-i-sádik, دوست معنوی dúst-i-ma'-naví, دوست باطنی dúst-i-bátiní.

FRIENDLESS, بی کس bí-kas, بیچاره bí-chárah, بی دوست bí-dúst.

FRIENDLY, دوستانه dústánah, خیر خواه khair-khwáh, مشفقانه mushfiká-nah.

FRIENDSHIP, دوستی dústí, یاری yárí, آشنائی áshná,í, محبت mahabbat, مهر mihr, خلت khullat, مودت mavaddat, تودد tavad-dud, وداد vidád, ولا vilá, موالات muválát, اتحاد ittihád.—(*with an inferior*) عنایت 'ináyat, لطف lutf, مرحمت marhamat, التفات iltifát, شفقت shafakat.—(*with a superior*) اخلاص ikhlás, ارادت irádat. —(*with an equal*) دوستی dústí, الفت ulfat, آشنائی áshná,í, محبت mahabbat. — (*mutual*) مصادقت musádakat, خلوص khulús, اتحاد ittihád, خیر خواهی khair-khwáhí.

FRIGATE, جهاز سه دقلی jaház-i-sih-dakalí.—(*man-o'-war*) منوار man-vár (*eur.*), جهاز جنگی jaház-i-jangí.

FRIGHT, *vide* FEAR.

To FRIGHTEN, ترسانیدن tarsánídan, تهدید کردن tahdíd kardan.—(*horse*) رم دادن ram dádan.—(*to be frightened—horses*), رم کردن *or* خوردن ram kardan, *or* khwurdan, بر جستن bar-jastan.

FRIGHTFUL, *vide* UGLY, TERRIBLE.

FRIGID, سرد sard.

FRIGIDITY, سردی sardí, سرما sarmá.

FRINGE, ریشه ríshah, سجاف sajáf.

FRISKY, جافی jáfí.

FRITH, *vide* BAY.

FRITTER, خاگینه khágínah.

FRIVOLITY, هرزگی harzagí, یاوه yá-vah.

FRIVOLOUS, سبك subuk, پوچ púch, خفیف khafíf, نا چیز ná-chíz.

To FRIZZLE (*hair*) تجعد نمودن taja''ud nimúdan.

FROCK, فستان fistán.

FROG, قرباقه kurbákah, قرباغه kur-bághah, غوك ghúk, وزغ vazagh.

FROM, از az, ز zi, من min, عن 'an.

FRONT, پیش písh, روی rúy, دهنه da-hanah, قدام kuddám.—(*in front, opposite, in presence of*) در پیش dar písh, مقابل mukábil, محاذی muhází, در حضور dar huzúr, روبرو rú-bi-rú.—(*in front, foremost*), اول avval, پیشین píshín, مقدم mukad-dam.—(*to go in front*) از جلو رفتن az jilau raftan.

FRONTIERS, دهنه dahanah, سر حد sar-hadd, اقصی aksá, ثغور sughúr, مرز marz, سنور sunúr, کران karán.

FRONTISPIECE (*ornamented first page*), سر لوح sar-i-lauh, عنوان 'un-ván, سر صفحه sar-i-safhah.

FROST, سرما sarmá. — (*hoar-frost*) پژه puzhah, گچك gachak (*vulg.*).

FROST-BITTEN, یخ بسته yakh-bas-tah.

FROTH, کف kaf, رغاوه raghávah, تفش tafish.

To FROTH, کف کردن kaf kardan.

FROWN, چین بجبین chín-bi-jabín, چین ابرو chín-abrú.

To FROWN, روی درهم کشیدن rúy dar-ham kashídan.

FRUGAL, خانه دار khánah-dár, کم خرج kam-kharj.

FRUGALITY, خانه داری khánah-dárí, میانه روی miyánah-raví, باریك روی, barík-raví.

FRUIT, میوه mívah, بر bar, بار bár, ثمره samrah, فاکهه fákihah (*pl.* فواکه favákih).—(*first-fruits*) نو بر nau-bar, نو باوه nau-bávah, پیش رس písh-ras. — (*dried or preserved fruit*) خشکبار khushk-bár, آجیل ájíl.—(*candied fruits, moist*) نقل nukl, مربا murabbá. — (*unripe fruit, which has not attained the proper size*) چاغاله chághálah, چغله chughulah.

FRUITERER, بقال bakkál, میوه فروشی mívah-furúshí.

FRUITFUL, بارور bár-var, مثمر mus-

mir, فراخ farákh, برومند barú-mand.
FRUITFULNESS, فراخی farákhí, برومندی barúmandí.
FRUITLESS, بی ثمر bí-samar. (*Vide* VAIN.)
To FRUSTRATE, محروم ساختن mah-rúm sákhtan.
FRUSTRATION, محرومیت mahrúmí-yat.
To FRY, بریان کردن biryán kardan. —(*frying-pan*) طابه tábah, تابه tábah, تاوه távah.
FUEL, هیمه hímah, هیزم hízum.
FUGITIVE, فراری firárí, گریخته guríkh-tah, هزیمتی hazímatí. — (*slave*) آبق ábik.
FULCRUM, مرکز markaz, گردان gar-dán.
To FULFIL, *vide* To PERFORM, To PAY.
FULL, پر pur, مملو mamlúw, ملان malán, آکنده ákandah, مشحون mash-hún.—(*to the brim*) لبریز lab-ríz, سر نثار sar-nisár.—(*sa-tiated*) سیر sír.—(*in full*) بالتمام bi-'t-tamám.
FULLER, قصار kassár, گازر gázur.
FULLER'S EARTH, گل سفید gil-i-safíd, رختشو rakht-shú.
FULLY, *vide* ENTIRELY.
FULNESS, امتلا imtilá, پری purí, آکندگی ákandagí.—(*satiety*) سیری sírí.
To FUMBLE, دست زدن dast zadan, دست مالیدن dast málídan.
FUME, دود dúd, دخان dukhán.
To FUMIGATE, تبخیر نمودن tabkhír nimúdan, دخنه کردن dukhnah kardan.
FUMIGATION, دخنه dukhnah, تبخیر tabkhír.
FUN, بازی bází, بازیچه bázíchah, تفرج tafarruj.
FUNCTIONARY, گماشته gumáshtah.
FUNCTION, کار kár, خدمت khid-mat.
FUNDAMENT, موضع معتاد mauza'-i-mu'tád, ماتحت má-taht, کون kún.
FUNDAMENTAL, اصلی aslí, اساسی asásí, از اصول az usúl.
FUNERAL, تدفین tadfín, جنازه janá-zah.
FUNGUS, قارچ kárch, چتر مار chatr-i-már, قارچ مار karch-i-már.
FUNNEL, قیف kíf.
FUNNY, شوخ shúkh, مضحك muzhik, بامزه bá-mazh. (*Vide* STRANGE).
FUR, پوست púst, خز khazz.—(*fine fur*) کرك kurk, کورك kúrk, کلك kulk.
To FURBISH, *vide* To POLISH.
FURIOUS, تند tund, متهور muta-havvir, دیوانه dívánah.—(*animal*) ژیان zhiyán. — (*to be furious*) خشمناك شدن khishm-nák shudan, غضبناك شدن ghazab-nák shudan, گرم شدن garm shudan, رنجیدن ran-jídan.
FURIOUSLY, دیوانه وار dívánah-vár, متهورانه mutahavvиránah, با تندی bá-tundí.
To FURL, پیچیدن píchídan.
FURLOUGH, رخصت rukhsat, اذن izn, تعطیل ta'tíl.—(*to be on furlough*) مرخص خانه شدن murakhkhas-i-khánah shudan, معطل بودن mu-'attal búdan.
FURNACE, کوره kúrah, تنور tannúr, تون tún.
To FURNISH, فرش نمودن farsh ni-múdan. (*Vide* To SUPPLY.)
FURNISHED, مفروش mafrúsh, باسباب bi-asbáb.
FURNITURE, رخت rakht, اثاث asás, اسباب asbáb, مخلفات خانه mukhal-lafát-i-khánah, اوضاع auzá'
FURRIER, پوستینه دوز pústínah-dúz, پوست پیرا púst-pirá.
FURROW, شیار shiyár, خط khatt.—(*ridge of a furrow*) کرزه kurzah, کردو kurdú.
FURTHERMORE, *vide* MOREOVER.
FURY, غیظ ghaiz, تهور tahavvur, قهر kahr, دیوانگی dívánagí.
FURZE, رتم ratm.
To FUSE, گداختن gudákhtan, ذوب نمودن zaub nimúdan.
FUSILIER, تفنگچی tufang-chí.
FUSION, ذوب zaub.
FUSS, های هوی hái-húí, همهمه ham-hamah, غوغا ghaughá, تشویش tashvísh.

FUTILE, *vide* VAIN.

FUTURE, مستقبل mustakbil, آینده áyandah, عاقبت 'ákibat. — (*in future*) آینده áyandah, از این باز az ín báz, بعد از این ba'd az ín, سپس sipas.—(*next*) آتیه átiyah.—(*grammatical term*) مستقبل mustakbil.

FUTURITY, استقبال istikbál, عاقبت 'ákibat.

G.

To GABBLE, *vide* To BABBLE.

GABBLING, چرند chirand, زیاده گوی ziyádah-gúí, پوچ púch, جفنگ jafang.

GABION (*basket or pannier filled with earth*), کفه kuffah.

GAIETY, *vide* JOY.

GAIN, فائده fá,idah, سود súd, حاصل hásil, صرفه sarfah, کسب kisb or kasb, مکسب maksab, نفع naf', منفعت manfa'at, انتفاع intifá'.

To GAIN, *vide* To GET, To WIN.—(*watch*) تند کار کردن tund-kár kardan.—(*to gain over*) متفق الرأی ساختن muttafiku-'r-ra,í sákhtan.

To GAINSAY, رد کلام کردن radd-i-kalám kardan, تخالف نمودن takhálluf nimúdan.

GAIT, *vide* PACE.

GAITERS, لبچین lab-chín, لفچین laf-chín, پا تابه pá-tábah.

GALE (*of wind*), باد bád, هوا havá.

GALL, زهره zahrah, زرداب zard-áb.

GALLANT, *vide* BOLD.—(*paramour*), مول múl, یار yár, دوستدار dúst-dár.

GALLANTRY, *vide* BOLDNESS, POLITENESS.

GALLERY, رواق ravák, غلام گردش ghulám-gardish.

GALLEY, *vide* BOAT.—(*galley-slave*) اسیر asír, گرفتار giriftár, دیل díl (*vulg.*).

GALLIPOT, حقه hukkah, قاب káb.

GALL-NUT, مازو mázú, مازی mází.

To GALLOP, دویدن davídan.—(*causal*) دوانیدن davánídan, تاختن tákhtan. (*Vide* HORSE.)

GALLOWS, دار dár, چوب دار chúb-i-dár.—(*pole erected in a public place, at the foot of which criminals are executed*) قاپوق kápúk.

To GAMBLE, قمار بازی کردن kimár-bází kardan, باختن bákhtán.

GAMBLER, *vide* GAMESTER.

GAMBLING, قمار بازی kimár-bází.

GAMBOL, بازی bází, بازیچه bazíchah.

To GAMBOL, بازی کردن bází kardan.

GAME (*sport*), لعب la'b, بازی bází.—(*gambling*) قمار بازی kimár-bází, بازی bází.—(*prey*) صید said, شکار shikár, نخچیر nakhchír.

GAME-COCK, خروس جنگی khurús-i-jangí.

GAMESTER, قمار باز kimár-báz, مقامر mukámir.

GAMUT, در مفصل durr-i-mufassal.

GANDER, قاز káz, قاز نر káz-i-nar.

GANG, طائفه tá,ifah.

GANGRENE, خوره khwarah, آکله ákilah.

GANGWAY, کوچه kúchah.

GAOL, زندان zindán, زندان خانه zindán-khánah, دستاق خانه dusták-khánah, حبس habs, محبس mahbas.

GAOLER, زندانبان zindán-bán, بزرگ زندانخانه buzurg-i-zindán-khánah, مستحفظ دستاقخانه mustahfiz-i-dusták-khánah.

GAP, چاک chák, شق shakk, شکاف shikáf. (*Vide* CRACK, INTERVAL.)

To GAPE (*trans.*), خمیازه کردن khamyázah kardan.—(*intrans.*) خمیازه شدن khamyázah shudan.

GARB, *vide* DRESS.

To GARBLE (*corrupt or alter a writing or statement, to suit a particular purpose*), تحریف کردن tahríf kardan.

GARBLED, محرف muharraf, تحریف

شده tahríf shudah, دست خورده dast khwurdah.

GARDEN, باغ bágh, باغچه bághchah, روضه rauzah, حديقه hadíkah, دوحت dauhat, جنت jannat. — (*flower-garden*) گلستان gulistán, بوستان bústán, بستان bustán, گلزار gulzár, گلشن gulshan. — (*kitchen garden*) باغچهٔ سبزها bághchah-i-sabzahá. — (*summer-house or lodge in a garden*) عمارت 'imárat, كوشك kúshk, ايوان aiván. — (*botanical gardens*) باغ نباتات bágh-i-nabátát. —(*public garden*) باغ عامه bágh-i-'ámah.

GARDENER, باغبان bágh-bán, ناطور nátúr (*pl.* نواطير navátír).

GARDENING, باغبانى bágh-báni.

To GARGLE, قلقله كردن kalkalah kardan, غرغره نمودن ghargharah nimúdan.

GARGLING (*rinsing the mouth and throat*), غرغره ghargharah.

GARLAND, تاج گل táj-i-gul, سهره sihrah.

GARLIC, سير sír.

GARMENT, پوشاك púshák, جامه jámah, لباس libás, كسوت kisvat, پوشن púshan. (*Vide* CLOTHES.)

GARNET, لعل la'l.

To GARNISH, *vide* To DECORATE.

GARRET, اوطاق بالا úták-i-bálá.

GARRISON (*of a castle*), اهل قلعه ahl-i-kal'ah, مستحفظان قلعه mustahfizán-i-kal'ah.

GARRULITY, زياده گوئى ziyádah-gú,í.

GARRULOUS, زياده گو ziyádah-gú.

GARTER, جورب بند jaurab-band, زانو بند zánú-band.

GAS, گاز gáz (*eur.*).

GASH, زخم zakhm, سوراخ súrákh.

To GASP, نفس زدن nafas zadan.

GATE, در dar, دروازه darvázah, قاپو kápú, قاپى kápí, باب báb, درب darb, درگاه dargáh, دهنه dahanah.

GATE-KEEPER, قاپچى kápchí, دربان dar-bán, بواب bavváb.

To GATHER, *vide* To COLLECT, To PLUCK. — (*to gather in harvest*) درويدن diravídan, درو كردن dirau kardan.

GAUGE, گرد gard.

GAUNTLET (*iron glove*), قلچاق kulchák.

GAUZE, برنجك birinjak.

GAY, *vide* MERRY.

GAZELLE, غزال ghazál, آهو áhú.

GAZETTE, روز نامه rúz-námah, گازت gázat (*eur.*).

GELATINE, سريشم ماهى siríshum-i-máhí, ماقوتى makútí.

To GELD, *vide* To CASTRATE.

GELDING (*horse*), اخته akhtah, آخته ákhtah, خصى khusí, اسب مخصى asb-i-makhsí.

GEM, *vide* JEWEL.

GENDARME, ژاندارم jándárm (*eur.*).

GENDER, جنس jins. (*Vide* MALE, FEMALE, NEUTER.)

GENEALOGIST, نساب nassáb.

GENEALOGY, *vide* PEDIGREE.

GENERAL (*of an army*), سردار sardár, سپه سالار sipah-sálár, لشكر كش lashkar-kash. (*Vide* UNIVERSAL, COMMON.)—(*to be general*) شيوعى داشتن shuyú'í dáshtan, مروج بودن muravvaj búdan, متداول بودن mutadávil búdan. — (*in general and in particular*) عموماً و خصوصاً 'umúman va khusúsan.

GENERALITY, عموم 'umúm, عموميت 'umúmíyat.

GENERALIZATION, تعميم ta'mím.

GENERALLY, *vide* COMMONLY, FREQUENTLY.

GENERATION (*begetting*), توليد taulíd.—(*race*) *vide* FAMILY. — (*a succession*) پشت pusht, طبقه tabakah, نسل nasl, دوره daurah, قرن karn. — (*from generation to generation*) دور الادوار dauru-'l-ádvár, نسلاً بعد نسل naslan ba'd-i-naslin, دور بدور daur-bi-daur.

GENERIC, جنسى jinsí.

GENEROSITY, *vide* LIBERALITY.

GENEROUS, *vide* LIBERAL.

GENIAL, روح افزا rúh afzá.

GENITIVE (*case*), اضافه izáfah.— (*noun in the genitive case*) مضاف اليه muzáf-ilaihi.—(*noun which governs another in the genitive*) مضاف muzáf.

GENIUS (*talent*), ادراک idrák, فراست firásat, ذهن zihn, زکاوت zakávat.—(*spirit*) جن jinn, جان jánn (*pl.* اجنه ajinnah).

GENTEEL, *vide* POLITE.

GENTIAN, کوشاد kúshád, جنطیانا jantiyáná.

GENTILES (*nations*), طوائف tavá,if, ملل milal, اقوام akvám, شعوب shu'úb.

GENTLE (*mild*), حلیم halím, ملایم muláyam, لطیف latíf.—(*horse*) رام rám, مطیع mutí'.

GENTLEMAN, بیگزاده beg-zádah, نجیب najíb.

GENTLENESS, حلم hilm, ملایمت muláyamat, لطف lutf.

GENTLY, آهسته áhistah, یواش yavásh, سنگنک sanganak.

GENUINE, خالص khális, اصیل asíl, عینی 'ainí, صحیح sahíh.

GENUINENESS, صحت sihhat, حق hakk, راستی rástí.

GENUS, جنس jins.

GEOGRAPHER, جغرافیا دان jughráfiyá-dán.

GEOGRAPHY, تخطیط بلاد takhtít-i-balád, علم جغرافیا 'ilm-i-jughráfiyá.

GEOMANCER, رمال rammál.

GEOMANCY, علم الرمل 'ilmu-'r-ramal.

GEOMETRICAL, هندسی handasí.

GEOMETRICIAN, مهندس muhandis.

GEOMETRY, علم مساحت 'ilm-i-masáhat, علم هندسه 'ilm-i-handasah.

GERM, نبت nabt.

GERUND (*in grammar*), اسم حالیه ism-i-háliyah.

GESTURE, وضع vaz'.

To GET, یافتن yáftan, حاصل کردن hásil kardan, بهم رسانیدن bi-ham rasánídan, پیدا کردن paidá kardan, اندوختن andúkhtan. — (*by heart*), یاد گرفتن yád giriftan, آموختن ámúkhtan, حفظ کردن hifz kardan, از بر کردن az bar kardan.—(*to be got*) دوچار شدن dú-chár shudan, گیر آمدن gír-ámadan, بدست آمدن bi-dast ámadan, یافته شدن yáftah shudan, همدست شدن ham-dast shudan, بهم رسیدن bi-ham rasídan, پیدا شدن paidá shudan.—(*to get down*) پائین آمدن pá,ín ámadan.—(*to get up*) *vide* To RISE. — (*from bed*) از خواب بر خاستن az khwáb bar-khástan, پا شدن pá shudan.

GHOST, روح rúh, عفریت 'ifrít.—(*the Holy Ghost*) روح القدس rúhu-'l-kuds.

GIANT, مرد بلند قد mard-i-buland-kadd, پتیاره patyárah (*obs.*).

To GIBBET, *vide* To HANG.

GIBE, *vide* TAUNT.

GIDDINESS, خیرگی khíragí, سرگردانی sar-gardání, دوران سر daurán-i-sar, دوار davár.

GIDDY, گیج gíj, گیچ gích, سرگردان sar-gardán.

GIFT, بخشش bakhshish, داد dád, دهش dihish, عطا 'atá, تحفه tuhfah, سوغات saughát, ارمغان armaghán, هدیه hadíyah, هبه hibah, موهبه mauhabah. —(*from superior to inferior*), انعام in'ám, عطا 'atá, بخشش bakhshish. — (*from inferior to superior*) پیشکش píshkash, نذر nazr, هدیه hadíyah, تعارف ta'áruf.—(*between equals*) داد dád, هدیه hadíyah, تعارف ta'áruf. — (*brought from a journey*) سوغات saughát, ارمغان armaghán.—(*given for good news*) مژده لک muzhdah - luk, مژدگانی muzhdagání.—(*bribe*) رشوت rishvat, ارش irsh.—(*power*) *vide* ABILITY.

To GILD, اندودن andúdan, تذهیب کردن tazhíb kardan, ملمع کردن mulamma' kardan, مطلا کردن mutallá kardan.

GILDER, ملمع کننده mulamma'-kunandah, مطلا کن mutallá-kun.

GILDING, طلا tilá, طلا کاری tilá-kárí.

GILL (*of fish*), گوش ماهی gúsh-máhí.

GILLIFLOWER, گل میخکی gul-i-míkhakí, قرنفل karanful.

GILT, مطلا mutallá, اندود andúd, غرق طلا gharak-i-tilá.

Gimlet, برمه barmah, مته mattah.
Gimp, غیطان ghaitán, قیطان kaitán.
Gin, سفید آب safíd-áb, عرق ‘arak. (*Vide* Snare.)
Ginger, زنجبیل zanjabíl.
Giraffe, زراف zarráf, شترگاو shutur-gáv.
To Gird, بستن bastan.
Girder, تیر tír.
Girdle, کمر بند kamar-band, کمر kamar, شال کمر shál-i-kamar, حزام hizám.—(*with shooting apparatus*) کیسه کمر kísah-i-kamar. [This contains two or three pouches for ball, &c., a powder-flask, and priming-flask.]
Girl, دختر dukhtar, صبیه sabíyah.—(*slave-girl*) کنیز kaníz, کنیزک kanízak, جاریه járiyah.
Girth, تنگ tang, کفه kaffah.
To Give, دادن dádan, بخشیدن bakh-shídan, ارزانی داشتن arzání dásh-tan, ارزانی کردن arzání kardan, عطا کردن ‘atá kardan, هبه نمودن hibah nimúdan.—(*to give up*) *vide* To Abandon, To Leave, To Deliver up, To Commit.—(*to give back*) پس دادن pas dádan, رد کردن radd kardan, وا گذار کردن vá-guzár kardan.
Giver, دهنده dihandah, بخشنده bakhshandah.
Glad, *vide* Happy, Merry.—(*to be glad*) اظهار مسرت کردن izhár-i-masarrat kardan.
Gladiator, پهلوان pahlaván.
Gladness, *vide* Joy, Rejoicing.
Glance, نگاه nigáh, لحظه lahzah, رمز ramz, طرفه tarfah, لمحه lam-hah.
To Glance, لحظه نمودن lahzah ni-múdan, لمحه نمودن lamhah nimú-dan.
Gland, غدت ghuddat (*pl.* غدود ghudúd).
Glanders (*disease in horses*), مکاو makkáw, سکاو sakkáw, مشمشه mishmishah, مخاط mukhát.
Glans (*of the penis*), حشفه hashfah, سر ذکر sar-i-zakar.
Glare, تاب táb, تابش tábish.
Glass, شیشه shíshah, آبگینه áb-gínah, زجاج zajáj.—(*wine-glass*) جنگ jung.—(*cup*) جام jám, پیاله piyálah.—(*tumbler*) استیکان istí-kán.—(*mirror*) آئنه á,inah, مرآت mir,át.—(*telescope*) دور بین dúr-bín.—(*hour-glass*) شیشه ساعت shíshah-i-sá‘at.—(*spectacles*) عینک ‘ainak.—(*burning or magnifying glass*) عینک آتشی ‘ainak-i-átishí, عینک آتشگیر ‘ainak-i-átish-gír.—(*cupping-glass*), شاخ حجام shákh-i-hajjám. [This implement is made of horn more commonly than of glass.]—(*urinal*) قاروره kárúrah.—(*glass beads*) شبه shabah.—(*glass-blower*) شیشه گر shíshah-gar.—(*glass-blowing*) شیشه گری shíshah-garí.—(*glass-house*) شیشه گر خانه shíshah-gar-khánah.—(*inlaying work of mirrors*) آئنه کاری á,inah-kárí.—(*room entirely inlaid with mirrors*) آئنه خانه á,inah-khánah.—(*cut glass, crystal*) بلور bulúr.—(*pane of glass*) جام jám.—(*glass shade*) لاله lálah, مردنگی mirdangí (*hind.*).—(*glass decanter*) تنگ tung.—(*plate glass*) بلور bulúr, آئنه سنگی á,inah-i-sangí.—(*sand-glass*) ریگدان ríg-dán, شیشه ساعتی shíshah-i-sá‘atí. (*glass-ware*) بلورات bulúrát, شیشه آلات shíshah-álát.
To Glaze (*smooth*), مهره کردن muh-rah kardan, جلا نمودن jilá nimú-dan, جلا دادن jilá dádan.
Glazier, شیشه بر shíshah-bar.
To Glean, خوشه چیدن khúshah chídan, خوشه چینی نمودن khúshah-chíní nimúdan.
Gleaner, خوشه چین khúshah chín.
Gleaning, خوشه چینی khúshah-chíní.
Glebe land, زمین وقف zamín-i-vakf, زمین موقوفه zamín-i-maukú-fah.
Glen, دره darrah, جلگه julgah, وادی vádí.
Glimmer, *vide* Ray.
Glitter, درخش dirakhsh, تاب táb.

17

To GLITTER, رخشیدن rakhshídan, تابیدن tábídan.
GLITTERING, شعله دار shu'lah-dár, بارق bárik, شعله زن shu'lah zan.
GLOBE, گوی gúy, کره kurrah, جرم jirm. (*Vide* EARTH.) — (*the terrestrial globe*) کرهٔ ارض kurrah-i-arz.—(*of a lamp*) حباب habáb.
GLOBULAR, مستدیر mustadír, مدور mudavvar.
GLOOMY, تیره tírah, مظلم muzlim. (*Vide* GRAVE, SULLEN.)
GLORIFICATION, افتخار iftikhár, تعریف ta'ríf, تمجید tamjíd.
To GLORIFY, تمجید نمودن tamjíd nimúdan, تکریم و تعظیم نمودن takrím va ta'zím nimúdan.
GLORIOUS, جلیل jalíl, عزیز 'azíz, مجید majíd, بزرگوار buzurgvár, فرخ farrukh, عالی 'álí, منیف muníf, ذو الجلال zú-'l-jalál, معظم mu'azzam.
GLORIOUSLY, مجیداً majídan.
GLORY (*praise*), تحمید tahmíd, تمجید tamjíd, تعظیم ta'zím, مدح madh, حمد hamd, ستایش sitáyish. —(*grandeur*) جلال jalál, عزت 'izzat, مجد majd, فر farr, ابهت ubhat, بزرگواری buzurgvárí, علا 'alá, فخر fakhr, افتخار iftikhár, کبریا kibriyá, مباهات mubáhát, عظمت 'azamat, حشمت hashmat.—(*halo round the head of a saint, &c., in a picture*) هاله hálah, حاله hálah.
GLOSSARY, لغت lughat, فرهنگ farhang.
GLOSSY, مهره دار muhrah-dár, مصقول maskúl, جلا داده jilá-dádah.
GLOVE, دستکش dast-kash, دستانه dastánah (*obs.*).—(*hair glove for scrubbing the body*) کیسه kísah.
To GLOW, *vide* To GLITTER.
GLOWING, سوزان súzán. (*Vide* GLITTERING.)
GLOWWORM, کرم شبتاب kirm-i-shab-táb.
GLUE, سیریشم sírishum, سریشم siríshum, سریش sirísh.
GLUTTON, شکم پرست shikm-parast, اکال akkál, بسیارخوار bisyár-khwár.
GLUTTONOUS, بسیار خوار bisyár-khwár, شکم پرست shikm-parast.
GLUTTONY, شکم پرستی shikm-parastí, بسیار خواری bisyár-khwárí.
To GNASH (*the teeth*), دندان فشردن dandán fishurdan, فشار دندان نمودن fishár-i-dandán nimúdan.
GNAT, پشه pashah, بعوضه ba'úzah.
To GNAW, خائیدن khá,ídan, جائیدن já,ídan, جاویدن jávídan.
To GO, رفتن raftan, روان شدن raván shudan. — (*to go, respectfully*) تشریف بردن tashríf-burdan, تشریف فرما شدن tashríf firmá shudan, قدم رنجه فرمودن kadam ranjah firmúdan.—(*as a watch*) کار کردن kár kardan.—(*to go away*) گم شدن gum shudan.—(*to let go*) ول کردن vil kardan, رها کردن rihá kardan, گذاشتن guzáshtan—(*to go down*) پائین رفتن pá,ín raftan.—(*to go forth*) بدر رفتن bi-dar raftan.—(*to go in*) میانش رفتن miyánash raftan, تو رفتن tú raftan, داخل شدن dákhil shudan.—(*to go out*) بیرون رفتن bírún raftan, خارج شدن khárij shudan.—(*to go round*) دور نمودن daur nimúdan. —(*to go up*) بالا رفتن balá raftan. —(*a go-between*) دلال dallál.
GOAD, آهن گاو ران áhan-i-gáv-rán, نیزهٔ گاو رانی naizah-i-gáv-rání.
To GOAD, مهمیز زدن mihmíz zadan.
GOAL (*destination*), منزل manzil, مآل ma,ál, مدار madár, متتا mi,tá, منتها muntahá.
GOAT, بز buz معز (*pl.* ma'z معیز ma'íz). —(*wild goat*) بز کوهی buz-i-kúhí, پازن pázan.—(*he-goat*) بز نر buz-i-nar, کبش kabsh, تیس tís, بز تگه buz-i-taggah.—(*she-goat*) بز ماده buz-i-mádah, جدی jadí. — (*chief he-goat of the flock*) شاه بز sháh-buz, شهاز shaház, بز تگه buz-i-taggah, دبر dubur.
GOAT-HERD, بزبان buz-bán.
To GOBBLE, بسیار خوردن bisyár khwurdan.
GOBLET, *vide* CUP, GLASS.
GOBLIN, غول ghúl, جن jinn.
GOD, خدا khudá, خدای khudáy, الله

alláh, حق hakk, باری bárí, رب rabb, مولی maulá, تنگری tangrí ایزد ízad, یزدان yazdán, داور dávar, خداوندگار khudávand-gár. — (*O God!*) خدایا khudáyá, یا الله yá alláh, الهی iláhí.—(*God knows*) خدا داند khudá dánad, الله اعلم alláhu a'lam.—(*please God*) انشاءالله insha,allah, ان شاء الله تعالی inshá, alláhu ta'álá.—(*for God's sake*) از برای خدا az baráy-i-khudá, فی سبیل الله fí sabíl alláh.—(*thank God!*) الحمد لله al-hamdu-'li'lláh, شکر خدا shukr-i-khudá.—(*God preserve you!*) خدا حافظ شما khudá háfiz-i-shumá.—(*God forbid!*) خدا نکند khudá na-kunad, خدا نخواسته khudá na-khwástah, حاشا háshá, استغفر الله astaghfiru-'lláh, نعوذ بالله na'úzu-bi-'lláh, عیاذا بالله 'iyázan bi-'lláh.

GOD-CHILD, پسر خوانده pisar-khwándah.

GOD-DAUGHTER, دختر خوانده dukhtar-khwándah.

GODDESS, خدا مادة khudá-i-mádah.

GODHEAD, الوهیت ulúhíyat.

GODLINESS, خدا پرستی khudá-parastí, زهد zuhd, دینداری dín-dárí, تقوی takvá.

GODLY, خدا پرست khudá-parast.

GOD-MOTHER, مادر خوانده mádar-khwándah.

GODSEND, خدا بخش khudá-bakhsh.

GOITRE (*tumour on the throat*), دشول dushvil, غده ghuddah.

GOLD, زر zar, طلا tilá.—(*pure gold*) زر خالص zar-i-khális. — (*gold thread*) قلابتون kulábatún, گلابتان gulábatán, دبیری dabírí.—(*small bit of gold*) تنکهٔ زر tunkah-i-zar.—(*gold-dust*) ریزهٔ طلا ríza-i-tilá, زرك zarak.—(*gold leaf*) ورق طلائی varak-i-tilá,í.—(*ingot of gold*) شمش زر shumsh-i-zar.—(*gold embroidery*) کار زر دوز kár-i-zar-dúz, زر تاری zar-tárí.—(*cloth of gold*) زری zarí.—(*inlaying of gold*), طلا کوب tilá-kúb, زر نشان zar-nishán.

GOLD-BEATER, زرکوب zar-kúb.

GOLDEN, زرین zarín, طلائی tilá,í.

GOLDSMITH, زر گر zar-gar, صائغ sá,igh (*pl.* صاغة sághah).

GOLOSHES, سر چکمه sar-chakmah چکمه پوش chakmah-púsh.

GONDOLA, زورق zaurak.

GONG, ناقوس nákús.

GONORRHŒA, سوزنك súzanak, آتشك átishak, گم سوزه gum-súzah (*vulg.*), سوزاك súzák (*obs.*).

GOOD (*adj.*), خوب khúb, نیك ník, نیکو níkú, نکو nikú, خیر khair, خوش khwush, حسن hasan, ملیح malíh, به bih, طیب tayyib.—(*subs.*) خوبی khúbí, نیکوی níkúí, نیکی níkí, فضیلة fazílah.—(*good-natured*) حلیم halím, مهربان mihr-bán. — (*good news*) خوش خبر khwush-khabar, بشارت bishárat, مژده muzhdah, تباشیر tabáshír, نوید navíd.

GOOD-BYE, خدا حافظ khudá háfiz.—(*to say Good-bye*) خدا حافظ گفتن khudá háfiz guftan.

GOOD MORNING, سلام علیکم salám 'alaikum, صباح الخیر sabáhu-'l-khair. — (*to say Good morning*) صباح الخیر گفتن sabáhu-'l-khair guftan.

GOODNESS, نیکی níkí, نیکوئی níkú,í, مهربانی mihr-bání.

GOOD-NIGHT, شب شما خوش باد shab-i-shumá khwush bád.

GOODS (*possessions*), مال mál, اموال amvál, اشیا ashyá, متاع matá', اجناس ajnás, ما یملك má-yamlik, ما ملك má-malak, ملك milk.—(*commodities, merchandise*), اجناس ajnás, تنخواه tankhváh, متاع matá', مال mál, اقمشه akmishah.

GOOD-WILL, نیت نیك níyat-i-ník, نیك نیتی ník-níyatí.

GOOSE, قاز káz, غاز gház.—(*wild-goose*) قاز وحشی káz-i-vahshí.

GORE, خون khún.

GORGE, *vide* PASS.

To GORGE, بسیار خوردن bisyár khwurdan.

GORGEOUS, جلیل jalíl.

GORGEOUSNESS, جلالت jalálat.

GOSHAWK, باز báz.

GOSLING, بچهٔ قاز bachah-i-káz.

Gospel, انجیل injíl.—(*the four Gospels*) اناجیل اربعه anájíl-i-arb'ah.

Gossamer (*substance like cobweb*), کنتره kinatrah, تار tár.

Gossip (*a tattler, tale-bearer*), تفتاف taftáf, حراف harráf. (*Vide* Tattle.)

Gouge, برمه barmah.

Gourd, کدو kadú.

Gourmand, *vide* Glutton.

Gout, نقرس nikris, شقاقلوس shakáklús.

Gouty, نقرسی nikrisí, شقاقلوسی shakáklúsí.

To Govern, حکومت کردن hukúmat kardan, حکمرانی کردن hukm-rání kardan, فرمانروائی کردن firmán-ravá,í kardan, اداره کردن idárah kardan. — (*grammatical term*) تعدی نمودن ta'addí nimúdan.

Government, حکومت hukúmat, حکمرانی hukm-rání, داوری dávarí, فرمانروائی firmán-ravá,í, فرمان گذاری firmán-guzárí, رئاست ri,ásat, تمشیت tamshíyat, عمل 'amal, ایالت iyálat, سلطنت saltanat, تسلط tasallut.

Governor (*of a province*), بیگلربیگ beglar-beg, بگلربگ baglar-bag, والی válí, حکمران hukm-rán, فرمانفرمای firmán-firmáí.— (*of a city*) حاکم hákim, متسلم mutasallim, ضابط zábit.—(*of a fort*) قلعدار kala'-dár, قلعه بیگی kal'ah-begí.—(*tutor*) استاد ustád, للا lálá, اتالیق atálík, لله lallah (*vulg.*), دده dadah (*vulg.*).—(*Governor-General*) فرمانفرمائی firmán-firmá,í. — (*Lieutenant-Governor*) متسلم mutasallim.

Gown, رخت زنانه rakht-i-zanánah. (*Vide* Garment.)

Grace (*elegance*), حسن husn, لطافت latáfat, نزاکت nazákat, ناز náz.—(*favour*) عنایت 'ináyat, لطف lutf, مهربانی mihrbání, فضل fazl, کرم karam. — (*excellence*) هنر hunar, فضیلت fazílat, کمال kamál.—(*of God*) توفیق taufík, فضل الهی fazl-i-illáhí.—(*with good grace*) قلباً kalban.

Graceful, لطیف latíf, جمیل jamíl, نازك názuk.

Gracefully (*elegantly*), نازکانه názukánah, خوش khwush, با لطافت bá-latáfat.

Gracelfss, بی جمیلت bí-jamílat, بی نزاکت bí-nazákat.

Gracious, کریم karím, لطیف latíf, رحیم rahím.—(*God*) رحمان rahmán.

Graciously, لطفاً lutfan.

Gradation, درجه darajah, مرتبه martabah.

Grade, پایه páyah, مرتبه martabah, طبقت tabakat, منزلت manzilat.

Gradual, تدریجی tadríjí.

Gradually, درجه بدرجه darajah-bi-darajah, آهسته آهسته áhistah-áhistah, تدریجاً tadríjan, رفته رفته raftah raftah.

Graft, قلمه kalamah.

To Graft, قلمه پیوند کردن kalamah paivand kardan.

Grain (*corn*), غله ghallah, بذر bazr.—(*single grain*) دانه dánah. —(*weight*) دانه گندم dánah-i-gandum.—(*of wood*) جوهر jauhar.

Grammar, صرف و نحو sarf va nahv.

Grammarian, نحوی nahví, صرفی sarfí.

Grammatical, نحوی nahví, صرفی sarfí. — (*grammatical terms*) اصطلاحات نحویه و صرفیه istiláhát-i-nahvíyah va sarfíyah.

Grammatically, با قاعدهٔ صرف و نحو bá ká'idah-i-sarf va nahv.

Granary, انبار ambár, مخزن makhzan.—(*place for storing flour*) کته kattah. — (*receptacle of wicker-work plastered with clay, resembling a large barrel, in which grain is stored*) تاپو tápú.

Grand, *vide* Great (*mighty*).

Grand-child, نبیره nabírah, پسرزاده pisar-zádah, دختر زاده dukhtar-zádah, نوه navah.

Grandee, اکبر akbar, امیر amír.

Grandeur, *vide* Glory (*grandeur*).

Grandfather, جد jadd.

Grandmother, جده jaddah, بیبی bíbí (*vulg.*).

Granite, سماق summák.

Grant, بخشش bakhshish, عطا 'atá.

—(*document*) سند sanad, فرمان firmán.
To GRANT, *vide* To BESTOW.
GRANTED (*in a problem*), معلوم ma'lúm. — (*granted that*) گیرم که gíram-kih.
GRANTEE, یابنده yábandah.
GRANTOR, دهنده dihandah, بخشنده bakhshandah.
GRANULOUS, دانه مانند danáh-mánand.
GRAPE, انگور angúr, عنب 'inab, ستة sattah.—(*white grapes*) ریش بابا rish-i-bábá.—(*unripe grape*) غوره ghúrah, باغچ bághich.—(*grape-stone*) دانهٔ انگور dánah-i-angúr, خستهٔ انگور khassah-i-angúr.—(*dried grapes, raisins*), مویز maviz.—(*bunch of grapes*) خوشهٔ انگور khúshah-i-angúr. — (*stalk of grapes*) چنبه chumbah, خوشهٔ خالی khúshah-i-khálí. — (*grape-skins, spit out while eating grapes*) تفاله tufálah. — (*grape-treacle*) شیره shírah, دوشاب dúsh-áb.—(*Sultana grape*), عسکری 'askrí.—(*Sultana grapes dried*) کشمش kishmish.
GRAPNELL, لنگر langar.
To GRAPPLE, گیر و دار کردن gír u dár kardan.
GRAPPLING-IRON, قلاب kulláb.
GRASP, قبض kabz, پنجه panjah, دستگیر dast-gír, قبضه kabzah, مشت musht.
To GRASP, بدست گرفتن bi-dast giriftan, پنجه گرفتن panjah giriftan.
GRASS, گیاه giyáh, علف 'alaf, کاه káh, سبزه sabzah.
GRASSHOPPER, ملخ malakh, جزو jazzú.
GRATE (*lattice*), شبکه shabakah, مشبك mushabbak.—(*fire-grate*) پنجره panjarah, بخاری bukhárí.
To GRATE, تراشیدن tiráshídan, تراش کردن tirásh kardan.
GRATEFUL, وفادار vafá-dár, حق شناس hakk-shinás, شکرگذار shukr-guzár, شکور shukúr, سپاسدار sipás-dár. (*Vide* AGREEABLE.)
GRATEFULLY, شکرانه shukránah.

GRATIFICATION, تفریح tafríh, تفرج tafarruj, سرور surúr, مسرت masarrat.
To GRATIFY, ممنون کردن mamnún kardan, دل شاد کردن dil-shád kardan, رضا دادن rizá dádan.—(*to be gratified*) محظوظ گشتن mahzúz gashtan, دل شاد شدن dil shád shudan.
GRATING, قفس kafas.
GRATIS, مفت muft, بلا عوض bilá-'ivaz, تطوع tatavvu', رایگان rá,igán.
GRATITUDE, شکرگذاری shukr-guzárí, حق شناسی hakk-shinásí, سپاسداری sipás-dárí.
GRATUITY, *vide* GIFT.
GRAVE, گور gúr, مزار mazár, قبر kabr, مرقد markad, سر sirr.—(*solemn*) موقر muvakkar, متعبس muta'abbis, عبوس 'abús.—(*sedate*) با وقار bá-vakár, با تمکین bá-tamkín.
GRAVE-DIGGER, گورکن gúr-kun.
GRAVEL, سنگریزه sang-rízah, ریگ ríg, حصی hassá, سنگك sangak.
GRAVER, قلم kalam, قلم حکاکی kalam-i-hakkákí.
GRAVE-STONE, سنگ قبر sang-i-kabr.
To GRAVITATE, ثقالت نمودن sakálat nimúdan.
GRAVITATION, ثقالت sakálat.
GRAVITY, *vide* WEIGHT.—(*centre of gravity*), مرکز ثقالت markaz-i-sakálat.—(*sedateness*), وقار vakár, تمکین tamkín.
GRAVY, آب گوشت ab-i-gúsht.
GRAY, خاکستری khákistarí, کبود kabúd, فلفل نمکی filfil-namakí.—(*a horse*) نیله nílah.—(*dark gray, horse*) سرخون sarkhún, سرخونك sarkhúnak.
To GRAZE, چریدن charídan.—(*scrape*) تراشیدن tiráshídan. — (*causal*) *vide* To FEED.
GRAZIER, شبان shabán.
GREASE, پیه píh, پی pí, چربی charbí.
To GREASE, چرب کردن charb kardan.
GREASY, چرب charb.
GREAT (*large*), *vide* BIG.—(*mighty*) عظیم 'azím, کبیر kabír, بزرگوار bu-

zurg-vár, بزرگ buzurg, جليل jalíl, شگرف shigarf, عالى 'álí, جزيل jazíl, الغ ulugh, معظم mu'azzam. —(*great deal*) *vide* MUCH.

GREATNESS, *vide* BIGNESS, DIGNITY.

GREED, *vide* AVARICE.

GREEDILY, با طمع bá-tama'.

GREEDY, حريص harís, طمعكار tama'-kár, آرزومند árzú-mand, شائق shá,ik.

GREEN, سبز sabz, اخضر akhzar.—(*dark green*) قره ماشى karah-máshí.—(*pea-green*) رنگ ماشى rang-i-máshí.—(*fresh*) تازه tázah.—(*not ripe*) نا رس ná-ras.

GREEN-GAGE (*plum*), آلوئى سبز álú,í-i-sabz, گوچه gauchah.

GREEN-GROCER, بقال bakkál.

GREEN-HOUSE, گرمخانه garm-khánah.

GREENS (*pot-herbs*), سبزى sabzí, تره tarah, بقل bakl.

To GREET, سلام كردن salám kardan, صلوت كردن salát kardan.

GREETING, صلوت salát, سلام salám.

GRENADE, رعد انداز ra'd andáz.—(*grenade-colour*) گلنارى gulnárí.

GREYHOUND, سگ تازى sag-i-tází, توله túlah.

GRIDIRON, سيخ síkh, مصبع musabba', مشوات mishvát.

GRIEF, غم gham, الم alam, اندوه andúh, ملال malál, ملالت malálat, تاسف ta,assuf, كدورت kudúrat, رنج ranj, رنجه ranjah, درد dard, آزار ázár, حزن huzn, احزان ihzán, حسرت hasrat, عزا 'azá, دلتنگى dil-tangí, هم hamm, وجع vaja', سوگ súg, تيمار tímár, هنجار hanjár, تنگنائى tangná,í.

GRIEVANCE, *vide* COMPLAINT.

To GRIEVE (*be sorrowful*), دل سوختن dil súkhtan, رنجيدن ranjídan, غم خوردن gham khwurdan, حسرت بردن hasrat burdan, تاسف خوردن ta,assuf khwurdan, دلتنگ شدن dil-tang shudan. (*Vide also* To VEX.)

GRIEVOUS, سخت sakht, شديد shadíd.

To GRILL, بريان كردن biryán kardan.

GRIM, زشت zisht, ترسناك tars-nák, مهيب mahíb.

GRIMACE, رو ترش rú-tursh. —(*to make a grimace*) رو ترش كردن rú-tursh kardan.

GRIME, *vide* DIRT.

To GRIME, *vide* To DIRT.

To GRIN, نيشك وا كردن níshak vá-kardan.

To GRIND, سائيدن sá,ídan, سابيدن sábídan. (*Vide* To POUND). —(*meal*) آس كردن ás kardan.—(*sharpen*) تيز كردن tíz kardan.

GRINDSTONE (*whetstone*), سنگ ساى sang-i-sáí, سنگ فسان sang-i-fisán.—(*of a mill*) سنگ آسيا sang-i-ásyá.

GRIPES, پيچش píchish, درد شكم dard-i-shikm.

GRISTLE, غضروف ghuzrúf, كركروك karkarúk, كتكتى kutkutí (*vulg.*).

GRIT, خاك khák, خاكستر khákistar.

GROAN, آه áh, انان anán, ناله nálah, زار zár.

To GROAN, آه كردن áh kardan, ناله نمودن nálah nimúdan.

GROCER, بقال bakkál.

GROIN, ورك varak, بيخ ران bíkh-i-rán.

GROOM, سائس sá,is, نفر nafar, مهتر mihtar.—(*head groom*), مير آخور mír-ákhwur, جلودار jilau-dár.

To GROOM, تيمار كردن tímár kardan.

GROOVE, خانه khánah, ناو náv, ناب náb.

GROSS, غليظ ghalíz, درشت durusht, كثيف kasíf.

GROSSNESS, غلظت ghalzat, درشتى durushtí, كثافت kasáfat.

GROTESQUE, *vide* STRANGE.

GROTTO, مغاره mughárah, غار ghár.

GROUND, زمين zamín, خاك khák, ارض arz, بر bar, تراب turáb.

GROUNDLESS (*false*), بيسبب bí-sabab, باطل bátil, دغل daghal, كاذب kázib.

GROUND-RENT, كرايه kiráyah.

GROUNDS, *vide* DREGS.—(*grounds of a house*) جلوخان jilau-khán.

GROUP, جماعت jamá'at, مجمع majma', انبوه ambúh, گروه gurúh.

GROUSE, کوکر kaukar, سیاه سینه siyáh-sínah, باغر قره baghir-i-karah.—(*pintailed grouse*) قل قوئرق kil-i-ku,iruk, کوکر kaukar, کاوکار káúkár.

GROVE, درختزار dirakht-zár, درختستان dirakhtistán, جای مشجر jáí-i-mushajjar.

To GROW, رستن rustan, روئیدن rú,ídan, نمو کردن nimú kardan, رشد نمودن rushd nimúdan, سر زدن sar zadan.—(*increase in size*) بالیدن bálídan, نشو و نما کردن nashv va nimá kardan, رشد نمودن rushd nimúdan.—(*increase in number or quantity*) زیاده شدن ziyádah shudan, افزودن afzúdan.—(*become*) گشتن gashtan, گردیدن gardídan, شدن shudan.—(*to grow up*) بزرگ شدن buzurg shudan.

To GROWL, غریدن ghurrídan.

GROWTH, نمو nimú, نشو و نما nashv va nimá.

To GRUB, *vide* To DIG.

GRUDGE, دشمنی dushmaní, عداوت 'adávat, کدورت kadúrat, حسد hasad.

To GRUDGE, رشك بردن rashk burdan, حسد بردن hasad burdan.

GRUDGINGLY, عداوتاً 'adávatan.

GRUEL, آش ásh, شوربا shúrbá.

GRUFF, درشت durusht, سخت sakht.

To GRUMBLE, لند لند کردن lund lund kardan, همهمه کردن hamhamah kardan, لنده زدن lundah zadan.

GRUMBLING IN THE STOMACH, نفخ nafkh.

To GRUNT, مخ مخ کردن mikh mikh kardan.

GUARANTEE, کفالت kafálat, ضمان zamán, قبالت kabálat.

To GUARANTEE, کفالت نمودن kafálat nimúdan, متکفل شدن mutakaffil shudan.

GUARD (*company of men*), کشیك kashík, پاس pás, قراول karávul, گزمه gazmah. — (*sentinel, watchman*) نگاهبان nigáh-bán, پاسبان pás-bán, کشیکچی kashík-chí, حارس háris, قراول karávul. — (*advanced guard*) مقدمه الجیش mukaddamahu-'l-jaish.— (*relieve guard*) بدل badal, عوض 'ivaz.—(*of railway*) مستحفظ mustahfiz.—(*keeper*) محافظ muháfiz, مستحفظ mustahfiz, نگاه بان nigáh-bán, نگهبان nigah-bán.—(*of roads*) راهدار ráh-dár, قراول karávul.—(*of a sword-hilt*) برچلك barchak, برچاك barchák. (*Vide* PROTECTION).

To GUARD, *vide* To DEFEND.—(*to be upon one's guard*), احتیاط کردن ihtiyát kardan.—(*to mount guard*) پاس داشتن pás dáshtan, به قراولی رفتن bi karávulí raftan.

GUARDHOUSE, کشیکخانه kashík-khánah, قراول خانه karávul-khánah, سر دم sar-i-dam.—(*place of confinement*) دستاقخانه dusták-khánah, حبس habs, زندان zindán.—(*on a public road*) راه دار خانه ráh-dár-khánah, قراول خانه karávul-khánah.

GUARDIAN (*who has care of an orphan*) وصی vasí, وکیل vakíl, قیم kayyim.—(*protector*) محافظ muháfiz, مربی murabbí, حامی hámí.

GUARDIANSHIP, محافظت muháfazat, نگاهبانی nigáh-báni. — (*legal*) وصیت vasíyat, وکالت vakálat.

GUESS, قیاس kiyás, مظنه mazinnah, تخمین takhmín, حدس hads.—(*at a guess*) تخمیناً takhmínan.

To GUESS, قیاس نمودن kiyás nimúdán, استنباط نمودن istimbát nimúdan, در یافت کردن dar-yáft kardan.

GUEST, مهمان mihmán, میهمان míhmán, ضیف zaif.

GUGLET (*earthenware water-jug*), کوزه kúzah.—(*small guglet*), پارچ párch, شربه sharbah.

GUIDANCE, هدایت hidáyat, راهنمائی ráh-nimá,í, راهبری ráh-barí.

GUIDE, راهبر ráh-bar, راهنما ráh-nimá, هادی hádí, بلد balad, بلدچی balad-chí, بدرقه badrikah.

To GUIDE, بدرقه نمودن badrikah nimúdan, بلدیت کردن baladíyat kardan, هدایت کردن hidáyat kardan, دلالت کردن dilálat kardan.

GUIDE-BOOK, كتاب دلالت kitáb-i-dilálat.
GUILE or GUILT, *vide* SIN.
GUILTLESS, بی گناه bí-gunáh, مبرا muharrá.
GUILTY, تقصیروار taksír-vár, مجرم mujrim, ملزم mulzam, گناه کار gunáh-kár.
GUINEA WORM, رشته ríshtah, پیوک payúk.
GUISE, طور taur, عادت 'ádat, لباس libás.
GUITAR, قیطار kítár, عود 'úd. —(*large guitar*) تار tár.—(*small guitar*) ستاره sitárah, ستار sitár.—(*body of the guitar*) کاسه kásah.—(*neck*) دسته dastah.—(*wires or cords*) سیم sím.—(*bridge*) خرک kharak.—(*pegs*) گوشه gúshah.—(*plectrum*) مضراب mizráb.
GULF, *vide* BAY, ABYSS.
GULL (*sea-bird*) یاغو yághú, مرغ نو روزی murgh-i-nau-rúzí, شالو shálú.
GULLET, *vide* THROAT.
GULLEY, دره darah or darrah, تنگ tang.
GULP (*swallow*), جرعه jur'ah, قرت kurt.
To GULP, فرو بردن furú burdan, جرعه نمودن jur'ah nimúdan, قرت نمودن kurt nimúdan.
GUM, صمغ samagh, زد zidd.—(*of the teeth*) گوشت دندان gúsht-i-dandán, لثه lisah.
GUMMINESS, لزوجت luzújat.
GUMMY, لزج lazij.
GUN (*cannon*) توپ túp. — (*swivel*) زنبورك zambúrak.—(*musket*) تفنگ tufang.—(*matchlock*) تفنگ فتیله tufang-i-fatílah. — (*fire-lock or flint-lock*) تفنگ چخماقی tufang-i-chakh-mákí. — (*double-barrelled gun*) تفنگ دو لوله tufang-i-dú-lúlah, چفته تفنگ chaftah tufang. —(*small guns*) تفنگچه tufangchah. (*breech-loader*) توپ ته پر túp-i-tah-pur. — (*muzzle-loader*) توپ دهن پر túp-i-dahan-pur.—(*needle-gun*) تفنگ سوزنی کار tufang-i-súzání-kár. — (*fowling-piece*) تفنگ ساچمه زن tufang-i-sáchmah-zan. —(*percussion gun*) تفنگ دنگی tufang-i-dingí, تفنگ چکشی tufang-i-chakkushí. — (*rifle*) تفنگ ششخانه tufang-i-shish-khánah.—(*smooth-bore*) تفنگ قوال tufang-i-kavvál.—(*long rifle, fired from a rest*) شمخال shamkhál, جزائر jazá,ir.—(*parts of a gun*) *vide* MUSKET.
GUN-METAL, چدن chudan.
GUNNER, توپچی túpchí.
GUNNERY, توپ اندازی túp-andází.
GUNPOWDER, باروت bárút.
GUN-SHOT (*range or distance*) پرتاب partáb, گلوله پرتاب gulúlah-partáb.
GUNSMITH, تفنگساز tufang-sáz.
To GURGLE, غرغره نمودن ghargharah nimúdan.
To GUSH, *vide* To FLOW.
GUSSET, باد گیر bád-gír.
GUST (*of wind*), نفحه nafhah, باد bád, ریح ríh, لطمت latmat.
GUT, روده rúdah, معی mi,á (*pl.* امعا am'á, حشا hashá, (*pl.* احشا ahshá).
GUTTA-PERCHA, صمغ samagh.
GUTTA-SERENA, سیاه دانه siyáh-dánah.
GUTTED, خالی khálí, خراب kharáb, ویران vairán.
GUTTER, آبریز áb-ríz, ناو دان náv-dán, میزاب mízáb.—(*gutter boy*) گلخنی gulkhaní.
GUTTURAL (*articulation*) حلقی halkí.
GYMNASIUM, زور خانه zúr-khánah.
GYMNASTICS (*exercise*) ورزش varzish, پهلوانی pahlavání.
GYPSUM, آهك áhak.
GYPSY, کاولی kávulí, قره چی karahchí, سسمانی susmání, زنگنه zanganah.

H.

HABERDASHER, پیله ور pílah-var.

HABIT, *vide* CUSTOM, DRESS.—(*to acquire a habit*) خو گرفتن khú giriftan, عادت کردن 'ádat kardan.

HABITABLE, قابل سکون kábil-i-sukún, لائق سکونت lá,ik-i-sukúnat.

HABITANT, ساکن sákin, متوطن mutavattin.

HABITATION, مسکن maskan, منزل manzil, مکان makán, بود باش búd-básh, ماوا máva, ماوی mává.

HABITUAL, مستعمل musta'mal, عادتی 'ádatí, معتاد mu'tád, مألوف ma,-lúf.

To HABITUATE oneself, عادت کردن 'ádat kardan.

HACKNEYED, مبتذل mubtazal.

HAG (*hideous old woman*), عجوز 'ajúz, پیر زن pír-zan.

HAGGARD, *vide* EMACIATED.

HAGGIS (*mincemeat, &c., cooked in the stomach of a sheep*) شیردان shírdán.

To HAGGLE (*in bargaining, &c.*), در معامله قیل و قال کردن dar mu'ámalah kíl va kál kardan, متردد بودن mutaraddid búdan.

HAIL, تگرگ tagarg, ژاله zhálah.—(*interjection*) سلام salám, مبارک mubárak.

To HAIL, تگرگ باریدن tagarg bárídan.

HAIR, مو mú, موی múí, شعر sha'r.—(*hair-breadth*) پهنائی مو pahná,í-i-mú.—(*lock of hair*) گیسو gísú, جعد ja'd, زلف zulf. (*Vide* RINGLET, TRESSES.)—(*of the pubes*) زهار zahár, رمگان ramagán, شعره shi'rah.—(*head of hair*) کله موی kallah-i-múí.

HAIR-DRESSER, مزین muzayyin, شانه زن shánah-zan, مشاط mashshát.

HAIRINESS, مویداری múí-dárí.

HAIRLESS, بی مو bí-mú.

HAIRY, مویدار múí-dár, مو دار mú-dár.

HALE, قوی بنیه kaví-bunyah.

HALF, نیم ním, نیمه nímah, نصف nisf.—(*half-and-half*) نیمچه ním-chah.

HALF-BLOOD, مادر زاد mádar-zád.

HALF-CASTE, دو رگ dú-rag.

HALF-WAY, نیم راه ním-ráh.

HALL, ایوان aiván, دالان dálán, تالار tálár, کفش کن kafsh-kun.—(*of audience*) دیوانخانه díván-khánah, دربار darbár.

To HALLOW, مقدس ساختن mukaddas sákhtan.

HALO, حاله hálah, هاله hálah.

HALT, لنگ lang.

To HALT (*stay*), ایستادن ístádan, توقف کردن tavakkuf kardan, ماندن mándan, وا ایستادن vá-ístádan, مکث نمودن maks nimúdan.—(*limp*) لنگیدن langídan.—(*for a day, during a journey*) لنگ کردن lang kardan.—(*to halt between two opinions*), متردد بودن mutaraddid búdan.

HALTER, خطام khutám, شکال shikál, پالهنگ pálahang.—(*for gallows*) ریسمان rísmán.

HALTING-PLACE, اوتراق úturák, مقام makám, منزل manzil.—(*house or station*) سرای saráí, رباط ribát, خان khán, منزلگاه manzil-gáh.

To HALVE, تنصیف نمودن tansíf nimúdan, دو نیم کردن dú ním kardan.

HALVING, تنصیف tansíf, دو نیم کردن dú ním kardan.

HAM, ران rán.—(*for eating*) پائی گراز pá,í-i-guráz.

HAMLET (*collection of huts*), حشم hasham, احشام ihshám, ده dih.

HAMMER (*large or sledge*), خائسک khá,isk, کله پا kallah-pá.—(*small*) چکش chakush, پتک putk.—(*of a gunlock*) قاشلق káshluk, قارشلوق kárshlúk.—(*steam-hammer*) چکش

بخار chakush-i-bukhár. — (*of a musical instrument*, چکش chakush.

HAMMOCK, ننو nanú, ننی naní.

HAMPER, سبد sabad, زنبیل zambíl. —(*wooden hampers for carrying fruit, &c.*) لوده laudah.

To HAMPER, باز داشتن báz-dáshtan, مانع بودن mání' búdan, گرفتن giriftan, مزاحم شدن muzahim shudan.

To HAMSTRING, پی کردن pay kardan.

HAND, دست dast, ید yadd (*pl.* ایدی aidí).—(*hollow of the hand*) کفت kiffat.—(*hands of a watch*) عقرب 'akrab.—(*to shake hands*) دست دادن dast dádan.—(*to stretch out the hand*) دست دادن dast dádan, دست درازکردن dast diráz kardan.—(*to lay hands on*), دست آویز نمودن dast áviz nimúdan. —(*measure*) وجب vajab.—(*at hand*) بدست bidast.—(*in hand*) در دست dar dast. —(*off hand*) بی تمهید مقدمه bítamhíd-i-mukaddamah.—(*handmade*) دستی dastí.—(*on the other hand*) از آن طرف az án taraf.—(*open-handed*) گشاده دست gusháhdah-dast.

To HAND, دادن dádan.

HANDCUFFS, *vide* MANACLES.

HANDFUL, مشت musht, مشتی mushtí, قبضه kabzah, پری دست purí-i-dast.

HANDICRAFT, صناعت siná'at.

HANDKERCHIEF, دستمال dast-mál, دستارچه dastár-chah. — (*worn by women on the head*) چار قد chárkadd.

HANDLE, دسته dastah, قبضه kabzah, عروه 'urvah, دستگیره dast-gírah. — (*of an organ, &c.*) پیچ کوك píchkúk.

To HANDLE, دست رسانیدن dast rasánídan, لمس کردن lams kardan.

HAND-MAID, *vide* GIRL.

HAND-MILL, دست آسیا dast-ásyá, دست آس dast-ás, رحی rahá, آسك ásak.

HANDSOME, *vide* BEAUTIFUL. — (*horse*) شکیل shakíl.

HAND-VICE, گیرهٔ دست gírah-i-dast.

HAND-WRITING, خط khatt, دستخط dast-khatt. — (*disguised handwriting*) خط جعلی khatt-i-ja'lí.

HANDY, *vide* CLEVER.— (*at hand*) حاضر házir, موجود maujúd.

To HANG (*suspend*), آویختن avíkhtan, آویزانیدن ávízánídan. — (*be suspended*) آویختن ávíkhtan, معلق بودن mu'allak búdan, آویخته شدن ávíkhtah shudan, هشتن hishtan. —(*execute*) بر دار کشیدن bar dár kashídan, بر دار آویختن bar dár ávíkhtan, آویزان کردن ávízán kardan.—(*a picture, &c.*) چسبانیدن chasbánídan.—(*to hang on as a dependant*) منوط شدن manút shudan.

HANGER-ON, متعلق muta'allik.

HANGINGS (*curtains, &c.*), پرده pardah, تجیر tijír.

HANGMAN, *vide* EXECUTIONER.

To HANKER, میل نمودن mail nimúdan, رغبت نمدن raghbat nimúdan.

HANKERING, رغبت raghbat, ارادت irádat.

HAPHAZARD, اتفاق ittífák, ناگهان nágahán.

HAPLESS, ناچار ná-chár, بیچاره bícharah.

HAPLY, شاید sháyad, اتفاقاً ittifákan.

To HAPPEN, واقع شدن váki' shudan, اتفاق افتادن ittifák uftádan, بظهور رسیدن bi-zuhúr rasídan, عارض شدن 'áriz shudan, بهم شدن bi-ham shudan, صادر شدن sádir shudan, سر زدن sar zadan, وارد شدن várid shudan, روی نمودن rúí nimúdan.

HAPPILY, تیمناً tayammunan.

HAPPINESS, *vide* JOY.

HAPPY, خوش khwush, خوشوقت khwush-vakt, خجسته khujastah, فرخنده farkhandah, نیك بخت níkbakht, بختیار bakht-yár, مسرور masrúr, برومند barú-mand, خرم khurram, شاد shád, دلشاد dil-shád, شادمان shádmán.—(*happy tidings*)

مژده. muzhdah, بشارت bishárat, خوش خبر khwush-khabar, نوید navíd, تباشیر tabáshír.

HARANGUE, مکالمه mukálamah, وعظ va'z, سخن sukhun, کلام kalám, خطاب khitáb, موعظه mau'izah.

To HARANGUE, کلام نمودن kalám nimúdan.

To HARASS, ایذا دادن ízá dádan, آزار رسانیدن ázár rasánídan, آزردن ázurdan, رنجانیدن ranjánídan.

HARBINGER, پیشرو písh-rau, طلایه taláyah.

HARBOUR, بندر bandar.

To HARBOUR, پناه دادن panáh dádan.

HARD, سخت sakht, صلب sulb, صلد suld.—(*Vide* NEAR, DIFFICULT.) —(*person*) زشت zisht.—(*with force*) به زور bi-zúr.—(*to be hard upon a person*) بر کسی سخت گرفتن bar kasí sakht giriftan.

To HARDEN, سخت کردن sakht kardan, سنگین ساختن sangín sákhtan.

HARD-HEARTED, دل سخت dil-sakht, سنگ دل sang-dil.

HARD-HEARTEDNESS, سنگدلی sang-dilí, سختدلی sakht-dilí.

HARDIHOOD, *vide* BOLDNESS.

HARDLY, با دشواری bá-dushvárí, مشکلانه mushkilánah, با دقت bá-dikkat.

HARDNESS, سختی sakhtí, صلابت salábat. (*Vide* DIFFICULTY).

HARDSHIP, سختی sakhtí, مصیبت musíbat, بلا balá, مشقت mushakkat.

HARDY, *vide* BOLD.

HARE, خرگوش khar-gúsh.

HARE-LIPPED, لب شکری lab-shakarí.

HAREM, حرم haram, زنانه zanánah.

HARK! الا ilá, اهای ahái, یواش yavásh, بشنو bi-shinú, هان hán, گوش ده gúsh-dih.

HARLEQUIN, بمبلی bambulí, بازی گر bází-gar.

HARLOT, *vide* COURTESAN.

HARM, ضرر zarar, عیب 'aib, اذیت azíyat, آسیب ásíb, زیان ziyán, نقصان nuksán, آزار ázár, گزند gazand, خسارت khasárat.

HARMFUL, مضر muzirr, موذی mu,zá.

HARMLESS, بی اذیت bí-azíyat, بی آسیب bí-ásíb.

HARMONIOUS, هم آهنگ ham-áhang.

To HARMONIZE, تطبیق داشتن tatbík dáshtan, مشابهت داشتن mushábahat dáshtan.

HARMONY, آهنگ áhang, توافق الالحان taváfuku-'l-alhán, موافقت اصوات muváfakat-i-asvát. — (*science of harmony*) علم نغمه پردازی 'ilm-i-naghmah-pardází.

HARNESS, ساز sáz, یراق yarák, برگ barg.

To HARNESS, ساختن sákhtan.

HARP, چنگ chang, بربط barbat.

HARPIST, چنگی changí, بربطی barbatí.

HARPOON, قلاب kulláb.

HARRIER, تازی tází.

HARROW, مازو mázú, واز váz, شاکول shákúl.

To HARROW, مازو نمودن mázú nimúdan.

HARSH, درشت durusht, ترش tursh, سخت sakht.

HARSHNESS, درشتی durushtí, ترشی turshí, سختی sakhtí.

HART, آهو áhú, غزال ghazál.

HARVEST, درو dirau, حاصل hásil, محصول mahsúl, حصاد hasád.— (*time*) وقت درو vakt-i-dirau, زمان حصاد zamán-i-hasád. (*Vide* CROP.)

HASH, خورش khwurish.

To HASH, پاره پاره کردن párah párah kardan, قیمه کردن kímah kardan.

HASP, چفت chift, ریزه rízah.

HASTE, زودی zúdí, شتاب shitáb, شتابی shitábí, تندی tundí, عجلت 'ajalat, تعجیل ta'jíl, سرعت sur'at, جلدی jaldí, چالاکی chálákí, مبادرت mubádarat.—(*in haste*) علی الفور 'alá-'l-faur, به تعجیل bi-ta'jíl, علی العجلة 'alá-'l-'ajalah. — (*to make haste*) شتافتن shitáftan, شتاب نمودن shitáb nimúdan, تعجیل نمودن ta'jíl nimúdan.

HASTY (*hurried*), دستپاچه dast-pá-

chah, پر شتاب pur-shitáb, عجول 'ajúl, تند tund.
HAT, کلاه فرنگی kuláh-i-farangí.—(*to raise one's hat*) کلاه بر داشتن kuláh bar-dáshtan.
HATCH (*of a ship*), خن khan.
To HATCH, تفریخ کردن tafríkh kardan, جوجه از تخم بر آوردن júјah az tukhm bar-ávardan, ایشانه بر آوردن íshánah bar-ávardan.
HATCHET, تبر tabar, تیشه tíshah.
To HATE, نفرت داشتن nifrat dáshtan, کین داشتن kín dáshtan, رغم داشتن raghm dáshtan, مکروه داشتن makrúh dáshtan.
HATEFUL, معیوب ma'yúb, بد bad, زبون zabún.
HATRED, بغض bughz, کین kín, کینه kínah, عداوت 'adávat, عدوان 'udván, دشمنی dushmaní, بد خواهی bad-khwáhí, خصومت khusúmut, نفرت nifrat, رغم raghm.
HAUGHTINESS, غرور gharúr, کبر kibr, تکبر takabbur.
HAUGHTY, مغرور maghrúr, متکبر mutakabbir, دماغدار dimágh-dár, خود بین khwud-bín.
To HAUL, کشیدن kashídan.
HAUNCH, گرده gurdah.
HAUTBOIS (*pipe or clarionet*), سرنا surná. — (*player*) سرنا زن surná-zan.
To HAVE, داشتن dáshtan.
HAVEN, کشتیگاه kashtí-gáh, بندر bandar.
HAVOC, *vide* INJURY (*hurt*).
HAWK, باز báz, قوش kúsh.—(*sea-hawk*) بحری bahrí. — (*sparrow-hawk*) موشگیر músh-gír. (*Vide* FALCON.)
HAWKER (*falconer*), باز دار báz-dár, قوشچی kúsh-chí. — (*pedlar*) پیلور pílavar, دستفروش dast-furúsh.
HAWTHORN (*small*), تنگز tangiz.—(*large, the hips of which are edible*) کیالك kiyálak, گویج gavíj.
HAY, علف خشك 'alaf-i-khushk, حشیش hashísh.
HAZARD, خطره khatrah, باك bák, بیم bím.—(*chance*) بخت bakht. — (*game of hazard*) قمار kimár.
To HAZARD, باختن bákhtan.
HAZARDOUS, *vide* DANGEROUS.
HAZY, *vide* FOGGY.
HE, او ú, وی vai, اوی úí.—(*he himself*) او خودش ú khwudash.
HEAD, سر sar, راس rás, کله kallah, فرق fark.—(*source*) مبدا mabdá. —(*to put heads together*) سازش کردن sázish kardan.
HEADACHE, درد سر dard-i-sar, صداع sudá'. — (*from drinking*) خمار khumár.
HEADING, عنوان 'unván.
HEADLONG, سر نگون sar-nigún.—(*rash*) سرکش sar-kash, متهور mutáhavvir, دستپاچه dast-páchah, خود سر khwud-sar, بی محابا bí-muhábá.
HEADMAN (*chief*), سردار sardár, سالار sálár, رئیس ra,ís, مقدم mukaddam.—(*of a village*) کد خدا kad-khudá, ده خدا dih-khudá, پیر ده pír-i-dih, رئیس ده rá,ís-i-dih.—(*of a trade or profession*) استاد ustád, اوستاد ústád, شیخ shaikh.
HEADSTALL (*of a bridle*), افسار afsár.
HEADSTRONG, سرکش sar-kash.
To HEAL, *vide* To CURE.
HEALTH, صحت sihhat, تندرستی tandurustí, سلامت salámat, عافیت 'áfiyat, اوغر úghur.—(*good health*) تناسانی tan-ásání, حسن صحت hasan-i-sihhat.—(*Board of Health*) حفظ الصحت hifzú-'s-sihhat.
HEALTHY, چاق chák, خوش khwush, تندرست tan-durust, صاغ ságh.
HEAP, توده túdah, جماعت jamá'at, کپه kuppah (*vulg.*).
To HEAP UP (*store*), جمع کردن jam' kardan, فراهم آوردن faráham ávardan.—(*gather in a heap*) کپه کردن kuppah kardan, انبوه کردن ambúh kardan, توده کردن túdah kardan.
To HEAR, شنیدن shinídan, شنودن shinúdan, شنفتن shinuftan, نیوشیدن niyúshídan, گوش دادن gúsh dádan, اصغا نمودن isghá nimúdan, استماع کردن istimá' kardan, مستمع بودن mustami' búdan

HEARER, شنونده shinavandah, سامع sámi'.
HEARING, سمع sam', سماعت samá'at.
To HEARKEN, گوش کردن gúsh kardan.
HEARSE, گاری مرده کشی gárí-i-murdah-kashí.
HEART, دل dil, خاطر khátir, قلب kalb, خواطر khwátir (*vulg.*).—(*to get by heart*) *vide* To GET.
HEART-BURN, دلسوزش dil-súzish.
HEARTH, بخاری bukhárí, آتشدان átish-dán.
HEARTLESS, بیدل bí-dil, ظالم zálim, ستمکار sitam-kár, سنگدل sang-dil.
HEARTLESSNESS, بیدلی bí-dilí, سنگدلی sang-dilí, ظلم zulm, ستم sitam.
HEARTY, قوی بنیه kaví-bunyah.
HEAT, گرمی garmí, گرما garmá, تاب táb, تابش tábish, حرارت harárat, حر harr, لهاب luháb, حراق hirák, حمیت hamíyat, آوار ávár.—(*to be on heat*) مست شدن mast shudan.
To HEAT, گرم ساختن garm sákhtan.
HEATHEN, کافر káfir, بیدین bí-dín, ملحد mulhid.—(*Pagan*) بت پرست but-parast. (*Vide* UNBELIEVER.)
To HEAVE, *vide* To RAISE, To CAST.
HEAVEN, بهشت bihisht, جنت jannat, فردوس firdaus.—(*sky*) آسمان ásmán, گردون gardún, سما samá, فلك falak, سپهر sipihr.—(*the highest heavens*) علیین 'illíyín, فلك الافلاك falaku-'l-aflák.
HEAVENLY, سماوی samávi, آسمانی ásmání, فلکی falakí, بهشتی bihishtí.
HEAVINESS, گرانی girání, سنگینی sangíní, ثقلت saklat.
HEAVY, گران girán, سنگین sangín, وزنی vazní, ثقیل sakíl.
HEBREW, عبری 'ibrí, عبرانی 'ibrání, عمرانی 'imrání, یهودی yahúdí.
HECTIC (*fever*), تب دق tab-i-dikk.
HEDGE, خار بست khár-bast, خار بند khár-band.
HEDGEHOG, خار پشت khár-pusht, قنفذ kunfuz.

HEED, *vide* ATTENTION.
To HEED, *vide* To ATTEND.
HEEDFUL, *vide* ATTENTIVE.
HEEDFULNESS, *vide* ATTENTION.
HEEDLESS, *vide* CARELESS.
HEEDLESSNESS, *vide* CARELESSNESS.
HEEL, پاشنه páshnah, عقب 'akb.—(*to heel over*) کج شدن kaj shudan, یك بری شدن yak barí shudan.
HEIFER, گوساله ماده gúsálah-i-mádah, کهره kahrah, گاو ماده gáv-i-mádah.
HEIGHT, بلندی bulandí, بالائی bálá,í, رفعت rif'at, ارتفاع irtifá', علو 'ulú, فرازی farází.
To HEIGHTEN, بلند ساختن buland sákhtan.
HEINOUS, بد bad, سنگین sangín, سخت sakht.
HEINOUSNESS, بدی badí, سنگینی sangíní, سختی sakhtí.
HEIR, وارث váris, ولی valí, خلف khalaf.—(*-apparent*) ولی عهد valí-i-'ahd, عصبه 'asabah, خلف الصدق khalafu-'s-sadk.—(*heirs and successors*) نسلاً بعد نسلاً naslan ba'd naslan.
HEIRESS, وارثه várisah.
HEIRLESS, بی وارث bí-váris.
HELIOTROPE, آفتاب پرست áftáb-parast.
HELL, جهنم jahannam, دوزخ dúzakh, سقر sakar, دار البوار dáru-'l-bavár, جحیم jahím.—(*lowest hell*) درك darak, اسفل السافلین asfalu-'s-sáfilín.
HELLEBORE, خربق kharbak.
HELLISH, دوزخی dúzakhí, جهنمی jahannamí.
HELM, خله khallah, سکان sukkán, دومن dúman.
HELMET, خود khúd, مغفر mighfar, ترگ targ.
HELMSMAN, دومنچی dúman-chí, سکانی sukkání.
HELP, مدد madad, امداد imdád, مدد گاری madad-gárí, یاری yárí, یاوری yávarí, پشتی pushtí, نصرت nusrat, کمك kumak, عون 'aun, اعانت i'ánat, استعانت isti'ánat.—

(*remedy*) چاره chárah.—(*interjection*) فریاد faryád.

To HELP, متعرض حال شدن muta-'arriz-i-hál shudan, مساعدت نمودن musá'adat nimúdan, کمک دادن kumak dádan, امداد کردن imdád kardan.

HELPER, مدد گار madad-gár.

HELPLESS (*without remedy*), لاچار láchár, مضطر muztarr, بیچاره bíchárah. (*Vide* WEAK.)

HELTER-SKELTER, بهم آمیخته biham-ámíkhtah, هرج مرج harj-marj.

HEM, قور بخیه kúr-bakhyah, کنار kanár, مغزی maghzí. — (*border*) حاشیه háshiyah, کناره kanárah, لبك labak, سجاف saját.

To HEM, دوختن dúkhtan, حاشیه بستن háshiyah bastan.

HEMISPHERE, نصف الارض nisfú-'l-arz.

HEMISTICH (*single verse*), مصراع misrá'.

HEMORRHAGE, رعاف ru'áf.

HEMORRHOIDS (*piles*), بواسیر bavásír, بواسیر bavásír.

HEMP, کنب kanab, کنف kanaf.—(*hemp-seed*) شهدانج shahdánaj.

HEN, ماکیان makíyán, مرغ murgh.—(*hen-house*) کله مرغ kullah-i-murgh, لانه lánah, کتونه katúnah.

HENCE (*from this place*), از اینجا az ín-já.—(*from this time*) از این پس az ín pas, بعد از این ba'd az ín, سپس sipas, از این باز az ín báz.—(*for this reason*) از این سبب az ín sabab, برای این baráy,i-ín, لهذا liházá.

HENNA (*the Lawsonia inermis, or Eastern privet, a plant from which a red dye is obtained*), حنا hinná.—(*seeds of the henna plant*) اسپند ispand.

HEN-PECKED (*ruled by one's wife*), زن مطیع zan-mutí', مطیع زن mutí'-i-zan.

HEPTAGON, مسبع musabba'.

HER, او ú.—(*possessive*) مال او mál-i-ú.

HERALD, جار چی jár-chí, چاؤش cha,úsh, منادی munádí, نسقچی nasak-chí.

HERB, رستنی rustaní, سبزی sabzí, علف 'alaf, نبات nabát.

HERBACEOUS, رستنی rustaní, نباتی nabátí.

HERBAGE, گیاه giyáh, علف 'alaf, سبزه sabzah, نباتات nabátát.

HERBALIST, بقال bakkál.

HERD, گله gallah, رمه ramah, جماعت jamá'at, فسیله fasílah.

HERDSMAN, گله بان gallah-bán, شبان shabán, راعی rá'í, گله دار gallah-dár, چوپان chaupán.

HERE, اینجا ín-já, اینسو ín-sú.

HEREABOUTS, از این طرف az ín taraf.

HEREAFTER, آینده áyandah, از این باز az ín báz, من الان min al,án, سپس sipas.

HEREBY, از ین az ín.

HEREDITARY, موروثی maurúsí, میراث mirás. — (*hereditary possessions*) میراث mírás.

HEREIN, بدین badín.

HERESY, بدعت bid'at, رفض rafaz, جدائی jidá,í, ضلال zalál.

HERETIC, رافضی rafizí, خارجی khárijí, اهل بدعت ahl-i-bid'at.

HERETOFORE, پیش از این písh az ín, قبل از این kabl az ín, مقدما mukaddaman.

HEREUNTO, بر این bar ín.

HEREWITH, با این bá-ín.

HERITAGE, ارث irs, میراث mírás, ارثیت irsíyat, وراثت virásat, عصوبت 'usúbat.

HERMAPHRODITE, خنثی khunsá, مخنث mukhannas.

HERMIT, گوشه نشین gúshah-nishín, زاهد záhid, ابدال abdál.

HERMITAGE, زاویه záviyah, صومعه sauma'ah, گوشه gúshah, تکیه takyah.

HERNIA, فتق fatk.

HERO, دلیر dilír, دلاور dilávar, پهلوان pahlaván, غازی ghází, یل yal, مبارز mubáriz, گرد gurd.

HEROIC, پهلوانی pahlavání, شجاع shujá', بهادر bahádur.—(*heroic verse, consisting of three dactyls and one iambic foot*) متقارب mutakárib.

HEROICALLY, دليرانه dilíránah, بهادرانه baháduránah.

HEROISM, شجاعت shujá'at, دلاوری dilávarí, غیرت ghairat, مردانگی mardánagí.

HERON, ماهی خوار máhí-khwár.

HERRING, شاه ماهی sháh-máhí.—(*herring-gutted*) پوك púk.

HERSELF, خود khwud.

To HESITATE, تردید داشتن tardíd dáshtan, وسواس نمودن vasvás nimúdan, تردد نمودن taraddud nimúdan, متردد بودن mutaraddid búdan, دو دل بودن dú-dil búdan.

HESITATING, متردد mutaraddid.

HESITATION, تردد taraddud.

HETEROGENEOUS, نا جنس ná-jins.

To HEW (*cut or hack*), بریدن burídan *or* burrídan, تراشیدن tiráshídan.

HEXAGON, مسدس musaddas.

HIBERNAL, زمستانی zamistání.

HICCUP, سکسکه saksakah, سکسك suksuk.

To HICCUP, سکسکه کردن saksakah kardan, سکسك کردن suksuk kardan.

HIDDEN, پنهان panhán, نهان nihán, نهفته nihuftah, مخفی makhfí, مختفی mukhtafí, مستور mastúr, مکتم mukattam, مختبی mukhtabí, متواری mutavárí.

HIDE (*skin*), چرم charm.

To HIDE, *vide* To CONCEAL.

HIDEOUS, زشت zisht, کریه المنظر taríhu-'l-manzar, قبیح kabíh, شنیع shaní', مکره mukrih, مغص mughass.

HIDEOUSLY, مکروهاً makrúhan.

HIDING-PLACE, مکمن makman, نهفتن گاه nihuftan-gáh.

HIERARCH, شیخ shaikh, پیر pír.

HIERARCHICAL, مذهبیه mazhabiyah.

HIERARCHY, طریقه taríkah.

HIGGLEDY-PIGGLEDY, تار و مار tár-u-már, درهم برهم darham barham.

HIGH, بلند buland, بالا bálá, فراز faráz, مرتفع murtafi', رفیع rafí', عالی 'álí, معلا mu'allá, سامی sámí, شامخ shámikh, برین barín.—(*the Most High*) علی الاعلی 'alá-'l-'álí, خدای متعال khudáí-i-muta'ál, المتعال al-muta'ál. — (*high and low*) خاص و عام kháss u 'ámm, اعلا و ادنا a'lá va adná.—(*on high*) بالا bálá, در فوق dar fauk.

HIGH-BORN, نجیب najíb.

HIGHNESS (*masc.*), اعلا حضرت a'lá hazrat.—(*fem.*) علیا حضرت 'ulyá hazrat.

HIGH TREASON, یاغی yághí.

HIGHWAY, شاهراه sháh-ráh, شارع shári', طریق عام tarík-i-'ámm.

HIGHWAYMAN, رهزن rah-zan, طرار tarrár.

HIJRA (*Muhammadan era*) هجرت hijrat.

HILARITY, بهجت bahjat, عیش 'aish, عشرت 'ishrat, بشاشت basháshat.

HILL, کوه kúh, تل tall, تپه tappah, گریوه girívah.—(*hill and dale*) دره و تپه darrah va tappah.—(*range of hills*) رشته کوه rishtah-i-kúh.

HILLOCK, تپه tappah, توده túdah, پشته pushtah.

HILLY, کوهی kúhí, پست و بلند past u buland, تپه مانند tappah-mánand.

HILT, *vide* HANDLE.

HIM, اورا úrá.

HIND, *vide* HINDER.—(*hind-leg*) پا pá.—(*animal*) مرل maral, مرال marál.

HINDER, پسین pasín, آخر ákhir, وا پسین vá-pasín, آخرین ákhirín.

To HINDER, منع کردن mana' kardan, مانع بودن máni' búdan, دفع کردن daf' kardan, باز داشتن báz-dáshtan, مزاحم شدن muzáhim shudan, تعرض نمودن ta'arruz nimúdan, وا داشتن vá-dáshtan.

HINDMOST, وا پسین vá-pasín.

HINDOO, هندو hindú.

HINDRANCE, منع mana', دفع daf'.

HINGE, لولا laulá, لولوه laulavah.

HINT, اشاره ishárah, ایما ímá.—(*to take a hint*) ملتفت مقصود شدن multafit-i-maksúd shudan.

To HINT, اشاره دادن ishárah dádan, ایما دادن ímá dádan.

HIPPODROME, میدان maidán, مضمار mizmár.

HIPPOPOTAMUS, اسب دریا asb-i-daryá.

HIPS, سرین surín, کفل kafal, دبر dubr, جائی نشستن já,í-i-nishastan, عجز 'ajuz, اعجاز a'jáz.

HIRE, کرایه kiráyah, کرا kirá, مزد muzd, اجر ajar, اجاره ijárah, اجرت ujrat, التزام iltizám, غله ghallah.

To HIRE (*take on hire*), بکرایه گرفتن bi-kiráyah giriftan, کرایه کردن kiráyah kardan, اجیر کردن ajír kardan, اجیر گرفتن ajír giriftan. —(*let on hire*) بکرایه دادن bi-kiráyah dádan, اجاره دادن ijárah dádan, مستغل دادن mustaghall dádan, غله کردن ghallah kardan.

HIRELING, اجیر ajír, مزدور muzdúr.

HIS, مال او mál-i-ú.

To HISS, صفیر زدن safír zadan, سوتك زدن sútak zadan.

HIST! خاموش khámúsh.

HISTORIAN, محدث muhaddis, مورخ muvarrikh, راوی ráví.

HISTORICAL, با تواریخ bá-taváríkh.

HISTORY, تاریخ ta,ríkh, تواریخ taváríkh, حدیث hadís, تذکره tazkarah, روایت riváyat, داستان dástán. (*Vide* ACCOUNT.)—(*natural history*) تاریخ طبیعی ta,ríkh-i-tabí'í.

HIT, ضرب zarb, زد zad.

To HIT, زدن zadan, ضرب کردن zarb kardan.—(*target, &c.*) خوردن khwurdan, به خوردن bi-khwurdan.—(*to hit it off*) سازش کردن sázish kardan.

HITHER, اینجا ín-já, اینسو ín-sú, اینطرف ín-taraf.

HITHERTO, تا حال tá-hál, تا هنوز tá-hanúz, تا این زمان tá-ín zamán, الی الان ilá-'l-án.

HIVE (*of bees*), کند kand, مش mash.

HOARD, گنج ganj, خزانه khizánah, ذخیره zakhírah, مایه máyah.

To HOARD, اندوختن andúkhtan, جمع کردن jam' kardan, فراهم آوردن faráham ávardan.

HOAR-FROST, پژه puzhah, جلید jalíd, گچك gachak (*vulg.*).

HOARSE, صدا گرفته sadá-giriftah, گلو گرفته gulú-giriftah.

HOARSENESS, گرفتگی گلو giriftagí-i-gulu.

HOARY, سفید safíd.

HOBGOBLIN, عفریت 'ifrít (*pl.* عفاریت 'afárít).

HOCK (*of horse*), پای páy, ساق sák.

HOCKEY, چوگان chaugán.

HOD, اجر کش ajur-kash.

HOE, بیل bíl, بیلچه bílchah.

To HOE, بیل کردن bíl kardan.

HOG, خوك khúk, خوگ khúg, گراز guráz, خنزیر khinzír.

To HOIST, *vide* To RAISE.

HOLD! یواش yavásh, باش básh, دست نگهدار dast-nigahdár.—(*of a ship*) خن khann, انبار ambár.

To HOLD, داشتن dáshtan.—(*to take hold*) گرفتن giriftan, دست بردن dast burdan, کپیدن kapídan (*vulg.*).—(*contain*) گنجانیدن gunjánídan.—(*to hold forth*) *vide* To EXTEND, To PREACH.—(*a pen, &c.*), نگاه داشتن nigáh-dáshtan. —(*to hold back*) وا پس استادن vá-pas istádan.—(*to hold up, rain*) کم کم آمدن kam kam ámadan.

HOLE, سوراخ súrákh, روزن rauzán, رخنه rikhnah, ثقب sakb.—(*hole in the ground*) گود gaud, سوراخ súrákh, نقب nakb.—(*hole in a garment, &c.*) سوراخ súrákh.—(*button-hole*) مادگی mádagí.

HOLIDAY, تعطیل ta'tíl, عید 'íd (*pl.* اعیاد a'yád), عید 'aid (*vulg.*).

HOLINESS, قدس kuds, پارسائی parsá,í, پاکی pákí, قدوسیت kuddúsíyat.

HOLLOW, خالی khálí, تهی tuhí, اجوف ajvaf, مجوف mujavvaf, پوك púk (*vulg.*).—(*cavity*) جوف jauf, روزنه rauzanah, گود gaud.

HOLLOWNESS, جوف javaf, پوکی púkí (*vulg.*).

HOLLYHOCK, گل خطمی gul-i-khatmí.

HOLM-OAK, سندیان sindiyán.

HOLTSTERS, قبل kubbul, قبل طپانچه kubbul-i-tapánchah, قبور kubur.

HOLY, قدس kuds, قدسی kudsí, قدوس kudús, مقدس mukaddas, منزه munazzah, پاک pák, مطهر mutah-har.—(*to keep holy*) جهت تقدیس نمودن نگاه داشتن jihat-i-takdís nimúdan nigáh dáshtan, تقدیس نمودن takdís nimúdan.

HOLY-DAY, عید 'íd, عید 'aid (*vulg.*).

HOLY GHOST, روح الله rúhu-'lláh, روح القدس rúhu-'l-kuds.

HOLY PLACE (*place where a saint or prophet has been; generally marked with a heap of stones*), نظر گاه nazar-gáh, قدم گاه kadam-gáh.—(*place of pilgrimage, &c.*) *vide* PILGRIMAGE.

HOMAGE, فرمانبرداری firmán-bar-dárí, اطاعت itá'at, بیعت bai'at.

HOME, خانه khánah, منزل manzil, مسکن maskan, ماوا mává, مقر makarr, ماءبد ma,bad.—(*native place*) وطن vatan, موله maulah. —(*to be at home*) منزل بودن manzil búdan, خانه بودن khánah búdan, تشریف شدن tashríf shudan.

HOME SECRETARY, وزیر داخله vazír-i-dákhilah.

HOMELINESS (*persons*) ساده دلی sádah-dilí.—(*things*) قشنگی ka-shangí.

HOMELY (*persons*) ساده دل sádah-dil.—(*things*) قشنگ kashang.

HOMEWARD, جانب وطن jánib-í-vatan, طرف خانه taraf-i-khánah.

HOMICIDE, خونی khúní, قتال kattál. —(*manslaughter*) خون khún, قتل katl. (*Vide* MURDER, SLAUGHTER.)

HOMOGENEOUS, مجانس mujánis, جنیس janís.

HOMOGENEOUSNESS, تجنس tajan-nus, جناس jinás.

HONE, مشحذ mish-haz.

HONEST, صادق sádik, صالح sálih, متدین mutadayyin, راست rást, راستباز rást-báz.

HONESTLY, بدیانت bi-diyánat, بصدق bi-sidk.

HONESTY, صدق sidk, صداقت sadákat, راستی rástí, دیانت diyánat, صلاح saláh.

HONEY, شهد shahd, عسل 'asal, انگبین angubín.—(*liquid honey*) عسل مصفا 'asal-i-musaffá, عسل ناب 'asal-i-náb.

HONEY-COMB, خانه عسل khánah-i-'asal, نانك عسل nának-i-'asal, شان shán.

HONORARIUM, مزد muzd.

HONOUR, *vide* REPUTATION, CHASTITY, DIGNITY.—(*reverence*) تعظیم ta'zím, تکریم takrím, اعزاز i'záz, اعتبار i'tibár, احترام ihtirám. —(*exaltation*) سر افرازی sar-afrází, ترقی tarakkí, ارتقا irtiká, تشریف tashríf.—(*dress of honour*) خلعت khil'at.—(*point of honour*) ننگ nang.—(*on my honour*) بمرگ اولادم bi-marg-i-auládam, بریش شما bi-rísh-i-shumá.

To HONOUR (*reverence*), محترم داشتن muhtaram dáshtan, اکرام نمودن ikrám nimúdan, تعظیم و تکریم کردن ta'zím va takrím kardan.—(*exalt, distinguish*) ممتاز کردن mumtáz kardan, مشرف ساختن musharraf sákhtan, سرفراز گردانیدن sar-faráz gardánídan.

HONOURABLE or HONOURED, معزز mu'azzaz, مشرف musharraf, محترم muhtaram, معتبر mu'tabar, معظم mu'azzam.—(*honourable mention*) ذکر جمیل zikr-i-jamíl.

HOOD, باشلق báshluk.

To HOODWINK, گول زدن gúl zadan.

HOOF, سم sum.—(*cloven*) سم چاکدار sum-i-chák-dár, ظلف zilf (*pl.* ظلوف zulúf).

HOOK, قلاب kulláb, قلابه kullábah.—(*reaping-hook*) داس dás, منجل minjal.—(*for fishing*) *vide* FISH-HOOK.—(*hook and eye*) نر و لاس nar u lás.

To HOOK, بقلاب کشیدن bi-kulláb kashídan.

HOOKED, کج kaj, خمیده khamí-dah.

HOOP, چنبر chambar, حلقه halkah.

HOOPING-COUGH, سرفه سیاه surfah-i-siyáh, سرفه سالی surfah-i-sálí.

HOOPOE (*bird*), هدهد hudhud, شانه

سر shánah-sar, مرغ سلیمانی murgh-i-sulaimání.

To Hoot, بانگ زدن báng zadan, آواز دادن áváz dádan.

To Hop, بر یك پا جستن bar yak pá jastan.

Hope, امید umíd, امیدواری umíd-várí, امل amal, رجا rajá, ارتجا irti-já, بوی búí, چشم chashm, توقع tavakku'.

To Hope, امید داشتن umíd dáshtan, امیدوار شدن umíd-vár shudan, توقع نمودن tavakku' nimúdan.

Hopeful, امیدوار umíd-vár, متوقع mutavakki'.

Hopeless, نومید naumíd, مأیوس ma,yús, محروم mahrúm.

Horde, *vide* Crowd.

Horizon, افق ufuk, خافق kháfik.

Horizontal, متسوی mutasavví, مسطح musattah, متساوی بالافق mutasáví bi-'l-ufuk.

Horn, شاخ shákh, سرو surú.—(*to butt with the horns*) شاخ زدن shákh zadan.—(*trumpet*) کرنا karná, بوق búk, سرنا surná.

Horned, شاخدار shákh-dár.

Hornet, زنبور zumbúr (*pl.* زنابیر zanábír).—(*hornet's nest*) چال زنبور chál-i-zumbúr.

Horoscope, زائچه zá,ichah, طالعنامه táli'-námah.

Horrible, *vide* Dreadful.

Horrified, *vide* Shocked.

Horror, هول haul, هیبت haibat, وحشت vahshat, واهمه váhimah.

Horse, اسب asb, اسپ asp, ستور sitúr, مرکب markab (*pl.* مراکب marákib), بارکی báraki, اس as (*vulg.*). — (*entire horse*) نریان naryán. — (*gelding*) آخته ákhtah, اخته akhtah, اسب مخصی asb-i-makhsí, اسب خصی asb-i-khusí. — (*blood horse*) اسب نجیب asb-i-najíb, اسب اصیل asb-i-asíl, توسن tausan. — (*draught-horse*) یابو yábú, اسب بارکش asb-i-bár-kash. — (*post-horse*) اسب چپری asb-i-chaparí, اسب چاپاری asb-i-chápárí. — (*carriage-horse*) اسب عرابه asb-i-'arábah. — (*saddle-horse*), اسب سواری asb-i-suvárí.—(*unsaddled horse*) اسب آلغ asb-i-álugh. — (*led horse*) اسب کوتل asb-i-kútal, یدك yadak, اسب مجنب asb-i-mujannab.—(*white horse*) سفید safíd. —(*gray*) نیله nílah, کبود kabúd.— (*dark gray*) سرخون surkhún, سرخونك surkhúnag.—(*black*) سیاه siyáh, مشکی mishkí. — (*bay*) کهر kahar. — (*light bay*) کمیت kumait.—(*chestnut*) کرن kuran.— (*brown*) قره کهر karah-kahar, بور búr. — (*dun*) سمند samand. — (*dappled*) ابرش abrash. — (*pie-bald*) ابلق ablak. — (*flea-bitten*) مگسی magasí.—(*roan*) قزل kizil, سرخثیره surkhitírah.—(*armour for a horse*) برگستوان bar-gustuván.— (*horse-breaker or jockey*) چابکسوار chábuk-suvár, سوارکار súvár-kár. —(*horse-dealer*) اسب فروش asb-furúsh, دلال dallál. — (*horse-keeper*) *vide* Groom. — (*horse-doctor*) بیطار baitár.—(*horse-dung*) پئین pa,ín, پین paín, پهین pahín. —(*horse-blanket*) جل jul, جل نمد jul-namad, شعار shi'ár, یال پوش yál-púsh. — (*horse-hair*) موی اسب múí,-i-asb.-(*horse-shoe*), نعل na'l. —(*paces of a horse:—to walk*) قدم رفتن kadam raftan.—(*to trot*) لکه رفتن lukkah raftan.-(*to amble*) یرغه رفتن yurghah raftan.—(*to canter*) یورطمه رفتن yúrtmah raftan.—(*to gallop*) دویدن davídan, سر شنو رفتن sar-i-shinau raftan.—(*horse exercise, in throwing a lance or stick while riding at full speed*) جرید بازی jaríd-bází, دوغله بازی dúghalah bází.—(*exercise in shooting with bow or gun while riding at full speed*) قیقاج kaikáj.—(*bed for a horse*) تخت پئین takht-i-pa,ín. [This is usually made of the animal's dung, dried and crumbled.]—(*on horseback*), روی اسب rúí-i-asb, سواره suvárah.—(*Master of the Horse*) میرآخور mír-ákhwur.

(*it is ... horse-power*) زور ... اسب بخار دارد zúr-i- . . . asb bukhár dárad.

Horseman, سوار suvár, فارس fáris. —(*good rider*) خوش سوار khwush-suvár, شهسوار shah-suvár.

Horsemanship, اسب بازی asb-bází.

Horse-radish, ترب turb.

Horticulture, زراعت zará'at, دهکانی dihkání.

Hosanna, سبحان الله sabhán-allah.

Hose, منفذ munfiz.—(*stocking*) جورب jaurab.

Hosier, پیله ور pílah-var.

Hospice, مهمانخانه mihmán-khánah.

Hospitable, مهمان پرور mihmán-parvar, مسافر نواز musáfir-naváz, مهمان دوست mihmán-dúst.

Hospitably, بنوازش bi-navázish.

Hospital, شفا خانه shifá-khánah.

Hospitality, مهمانداری mihmán-dárí, میز بانی míz-bání, مهمانی mihmání.

Host (*landlord*), میز بان míz-bán, مهماندار mihmán-dár.—(*who receives travellers*) خانه خواه khánah-khwáh.—(*company*) طائفه tá,ifah, گروه gurúh, جماعت jamá'at, انبوه ambúh, ازدحام izdihám.

Hostage, کفیل kafíl, گرو girav, ضامن zámin, ضمان zamán.

Hostess, زن مهماندار zan-i-mihmán-dár.

Hostile, مخالف mukhálif, مغایر mugháyir, مناقض munákiz.

Hostility, *vide* Enmity.

Hot, گرم garm, حار hárr.—(*pungent*) تیز tíz, تند tund.—(*glaring*) تند tund, تیز tíz, تابان tábán.—(*red hot*) سرخ surkh.—(*on heat*) مست mast.

Hotel, *vide* Inn.

Hot-house, تابخانه táb-khánah.

Houda, تخت takht.

Hound, سگ تازی sag-i-tází, طوله taulah.

Hour, ساعت sá'at.—(*twenty-four hours*) شب و روز shab u rúz.—(*from hour to hour*) دم بدم dam bi-dam, دمادم damádam.

Hour-glass, شیشه ساعت shíshah-i-sá'at.

Hourly, ساعت بساعت sá'at bi-sá'at.

House, خانه khánah, دار dár, سرا sará, منزل manzil, بیت bait, عمارت 'imárat.—The various parts of a Persian house are as follow:—(*suite of apartments appropriated to the men*) مردانه mardánah, بیرون bírún.—(*ladies' suite of apartments*) زنانه zanánah, حرم haram, اندرون andarún.—(*the court-yard*) صحن sahn, حیاط hayát.—(*passage entering the court*) دهلیز dihlíz, دالان dálán.—(*tank or cistern in the court*) حوض hauz.—(*chief room, fronting the court*) دیوانخانه díván-khánah.—(*steps leading up from court to chief room*) پله pillah, اورچین úrchín.—(*threshhold*) درگاه dargáh.—(*side rooms, on either side of the chief room*) کفش کن kafsh-kun, صف نعال saf-i-ni'ál.—(*large window, in sashes of coloured glass, looking on the court, and occupying the entire front of the room*) ارسی ursí.—(*alcove, at one end of room*), شاهنشین sháh-nishín.—(*small apartment above the alcove*) غرفه ghurfah, منظر manzar.—(*inner room, generally entered from the alcove*) تنبی tanabí, تنابی tanábí.—(*open room supported with pillars*) تالار tálár.—(*upper story*) بالا خانه bálá-khánah.—(*side rooms of upper story*) گوشواره gúshvárah.—(*flat roof of the house*) بام bám, پشت بام pusht-i-bám.—(*platform upon the roof*) سکوی بام sakkú,í-i-bám.—(*parapet of roof*) معجر ma'jar, محجر mahjar.—(*coping or border of roof*) رخبام rukh-bám.—(*gutter*) نابدان náb-dán, ناودان náú-dán.—(*eaves of roof*) طره turrah.—(*open hall or reception room*) ایوان aiván.—(*underground apartment, a retreat in hot weather*) سردابه sardábah, زیر زمین zír-zamín.—(*wind-tower or ventilator*) باد گیر bád-gír.—(*lumber room*), صندوقخانه sandúk-khánah, پستو pastú, میان پای miyán-i-páy.—(*closet where beds are stowed in daytime*) مفرشدان mafrash-dán.—(*outhouse where pipes and coffee are got ready*) قهوه خانه kahvah-khánah,—(*kitchen*) آشپز خانه ásh-paz khánah, مطبخ matbakh.—(*privy*) مبرز mabraz, مزبله mazbalah, متوضی mutavazzá, مستراح mustaráh, منجلابخانه manjaláb-khánah. (*Vide also* Wall, Ceiling, Cornice, Niche, Wainscot, Fireplace, Chimney, Roof, Carpet, Door, Bolt, Lock, Catch, Knocker, Stairs, Room).—(*House of Parliament*) مجلس مشورت majlis-i-mashvarat, دار الشورا dáru-'sh-shúrá.—(*country house*) ییلاق yílák.

To House, امانت گذاشتن amánat guzáshtan, ودیعت نهادن vadí'at nihádan.

Housebreaker, دزد duzd.

Household, خاندان khándán, اهل خانه ahl-i-khánah, خورنده khwurandah, خانواده khánavádah, خانه واده khánah-vádah.

Householder, اهل خانه ahl-i-khánah.

Housekeeper, وکیل خرج vakíl-i-kharj, مصرف musarrif.

Housekeeping, خانه داری khánah-dárí.

Housemaid, کنیز kaníz.

Housewife (*case for needles and thread*) جزدان juz-dán.

Hovel, خانهٔ پست رعیت khánah-i-past-i-ra'íyat.

To Hover, *vide* To Fly.

How? چگونه chigúnah, چون chún, چه طور chih taur, بچه وجه bi-chih vajh.—(*how much?*) چه قدر chih kadar, چه مقدار chih mikdár.—(*how many?*) چند chand.—(*how long?*) تا کی tá kai, تا بکی tá bi-kai, تا چند tá chand.—(*how often?*) چند بار chand bár, چند مرتبه chand martabah.—(*however*) مگر magar, و لیکن va líkin, مع هذا ma' házá, باری bárí.—(*how far?*) چقدر دور chi-kadar dúr, چقدر راه chi-kadar ráh, تا کجا tá kujá, تا بکو tá bi-kú.—(*how much the more, rather*) بچندین مرتبه افزون bi-chandín martabah-i-afzún, چه قدر بیشتر chih kadar bíshtar.—(*how much the less*) کجا مانده kujá mándah, تا چه رسد tá chih rasad.

Howl, ولوله valvalah, غریو gharív, عویل 'avíl, ویل vail.

To Howl, غریو کردن gharív kardan.

Hubbub, معرکه ma'rakah, غوغا ghaughá, همهمه hamhamah.

Huckle-bone (*of a sheep, used in playing*), کعب ka'b, قام kám (*vulg.*).

Huckster (*pedlar or dealer in small wares*), خرده فروش khurdah-furúsh, پیلور pílavar.

To Huddle, خزیدن khazídan.

Hue, غوغا ghaughá, همهمه hamhamah. (*Vide* Colour.)

To Hug, در آغوش نمودن dar ághúsh nimúdan, در سینه گرفتن dar sínah giriftan.

Huge, *vide* Big.

Hum, قال و مقال kál va makál.

To Hum (*as bees, &c.*), رنه کردن rinnah kardan.—(*a song*) ترانه کردن taránah kardan.

Human, انسانی insání, بشری basharí.—(*human being*) انسان insán (*pl.* ناس nás), آدمزاد ádam-zád, بشر bashar.—(*human nature*) انسانیت insáníyat, بشریت bashariyat, آدمیت ádmíyat.—(*human race*) نوع انسان nau'-i-insán, نوع بشر nau'-i-bashar.

Humane, صاحب مروت sáhib-i-murúvat, حلیم halím, کریم karím, نرم دل narm-dil.

Humanity, مروت murúvat, مردم دوستی mardum-dústí, آدمیت ádmíyat, انسانیت insáníyat.

Humanly, آدمیانه ádmíyánah.

Humble, مسکین miskín, فروتن furútan, غریب gharíb, متواضع mutavázi'.

To Humble, *vide* To Abase.

HUMBUG, *vide* DECEIT, NONSENSE.
To HUMBUG, گول زدن gúl zadan.
HUMID, *vide* MOIST.
HUMIDITY, *vide* MOISTURE.
To HUMILIATE, تحقیر نمودن tahkír nimúdan, پست کردن past kardan.
HUMILIATION, تحقیر tahkír, خشوع khushú'.
HUMILITY, فرو تنی furú-taní, مسکینی miskíní, خشوع khushú', خضوع khuzú', تواضع tavázu', انکسار inkisár, ضراعت zará'at, کوچکی kúchikí.
HUMMING-BIRD, مرغ مگس murgh-i-magas.
HUMOROUS, *vide* FACETIOUS.
HUMOUR (*of the body*), خلط khilt (*pl.* اخلاط aklát), — (*temper*) خو khú, مزاج mizáj, مشرب mashrab. —(*jocularity*) لطیفه latífah, بذله bazlah, ظرافت zaráfat.
To HUMOUR, *vide* To COAX.
HUMP, کوهه kúhah, کوهان kúhán, کوله kúlah.
HUMP-BACKED, کوز پشت kúz-pusht, گوژ پشت gúzh-pusht, قوزی kúzí (*vulg.*), قوزو kúzú (*vulg.*).
HUNGER, گرسنگی gurisnagí, گرس gurs, جوع jú', مجاعت majá'at, قحط kaht, اشتها ishtihá.
HUNGRY, گرسنه gurisnah, جوعان jú'án.
HUNT, شکار shikár.
To HUNT, شکار کردن shikár kardan, صید کردن said kardan. (*Vide* To PURSUE.)
HUNTER, شکارچی shikár-chí, صیاد sayyád, قناص kannás, نخچیروان nakhchír-ván, نخچیرگر nakhchír-gar.
HUNTING, صیادت siyádat, صید said, شکار shikár.
To HURL, افکندن afkandan, انداختن andákhtan.
HURLEY-BURLEY, همهمه hambamah, غوغا ghaughá, معرکه ma'rakah.
HURRAH, *vide* BRAVO.
HURRICANE, گرد باد gird-bád, باد گرد bád-i-gird, دیو باد dív-bád, طوفان túfán.
HURRY, *vide* HASTE.—(*to be in a hurry*) تعجیل داشتن ta'jíl dáshtan, زود بودن zúd búdan, شتافتن shitáftan.

HURT, *vide* INJURY.
To HURT, رنجانیدن ranjánídan, آزردن ázurdan, آزار رسانیدن ázár rasánídan, ایذا دادن ízá dádan, زیان کردن ziyán kardan, ضرر رسانیدن zarar rasánídan, آسیب دادن ásíb dádan.
HURTFUL (*injurious*), مضر muzirr, موذی mu,zí, زیان دار ziyán-dár.
HUSBAND, شوهر shauhar, شوی shúy, زوج zauj, شور shúr (*vulg.*).
HUSBANDMAN, زارع zári', مزارع muzári', فلاح falláh, برزگر bazr-gar.
HUSBANDRY, زراعت zará'at, دهکانی dihkání.
HUSH, خاموش khamúsh.
HUSH-MONEY, رشوت rishvat, ارش irsh, پاره párah.
HUSK, پوست púst, قشر kishr.
HUSKY, *vide* HOARSE.
HUSSAR, هوسار húsár (*eur.*).
HUT, کپر kappar, کمه kumah, عریش 'arísh, مظله mizallah.
HYACINTH, سنبل sumbul.
HYÆNA, کفتار kaftár.
HYDROCELE, باد خایه bád-kháyah, استسقا الخصیه istiská-'l-khusyah.
HYDROGEN, مولد الماء múlidu-'l-má, .
HYDROPHOBIA, خوف من الماء khauf minu-'l-má, , داء الکلب dá,u-'l-kalb, دیوانگی سگ dívánagí-i-sag.
HYMN, تسبیح tasbíh, ثنا saná.
HYPERBOLE, *vide* EXAGGERATION.
HYBERBOLICAL, بلیغ balígh.
HYPERCRITIC *and* HYPERCRITICAL, مو شکاف mú-shikáf.
HYPOCRISY, ریا riyá, ریاکاری riyá-kárí, رنگ rang, دو روی dú-rúí, نفاق nifák, سالوس sálús, مرائت mara,t, مداهنت mudáhanat.
HYPOCRITE, ریا کار riyá-kár, منافق munáfik, مرائی murá,í, مزور muzavvir, مکار makkár, دو رو dú-rú, اهل نفاق ahl-i-nifák, غاش ghásh, مداهن mudáhín.
HYPOCRITICAL, دو رنگ dú-rang, دو زبان dú-zabán, دو رو dú-rú.
HYPOTHESIS, فرض farz, تقدیر takdír.
HYPOTHETICAL, فرض farz, وهمی vahmí.
HYSSOP, زوفا zúfá.

I.

I, من man.—(*I myself*) من خود man-khwud, من خودم man-khúd-am.

Iambic (*measure in verse*), رجز rajaz.

Ibex (*mountain goat*), بزکوهی buz-i-kúhí.

Ice, یخ yakh.—(*ice-house*) یخچال yakh-chál. — (*ice-cream*) بستنی bastaní.—(*iced-water*) آب یخ áb-i-yakh.

Ichneumon (*species of pole-cat*), سمور گور کن samnúr-i-gúr-kun, موش خرما músh-i-khurmá.

Icicle, قلم یخ kalam-i-yakh.

Icy, سرد sard, بارد bárid.

Idea, خیال khayál, گمان gumán, حدس hads, تصور tasavvur, وهم vahm, ظن zann, فکر fikr, قیاس kiyás, ضمن zimn.—(*to have an idea*) پنداشتن pindáshtan.

Ideal, معناوی ma'náví, معناویه ma'náviyah, معنوی ma'naví, معنویه ma'naviyah.

Identical, همان hamán, همین hamín, عینی 'ainí, حقیقی hakíkí, صحیح sahíh.

Idiocy (*madness*), دیوانگی dívánagí, مجنونیت majnúníyat. — (*ignorance*) نادانی ná-dání, احمقی ahmakí, بیوقوفی bí-vukúfí.

Idiom, اصطلاح istiláh, محاورت muhávarat, ضرب المثل zarbu-'l-masal.

Idiomatic, موافق محاورت muváfik-i-muhávarat, بر وفق محاورت bar vafk-i-muhávarat, از قرار محاورت az karár-i-muhávarat.

Idiosyncrasy, مزاج مخصوص mizáj-i-makhsús.

Idiot, امی ummí, ابله ablah, بیوقوف bí-vukúf.

Idiotic (*mad*), دیوانه dívánah, مجنون majnún.—(*ignorant*) نا دان ná-dán, ابله ablah, احمق ahmak, بیوقوف bí-vukúf.

Idle (*unemployed*), بیکار bí-kár, معطل mu'attal. — (*lazy*) سست sust, کاهل káhil, تنبل tambal, زاهل záhil, بازی گوش bází-gúsh (*vulg.*).—(*to be idle*) تنبلی کردن tambalí kardan.

Idleness, سستی sustí, کاهلی káhilí, بطلان butlán, تنبلی tambalí, بازی گوشی bází-gúshí (*vulg.*).

Idler, مرد سست mard-i-sust. — (*scamp*) آواره ávárah, اوباش aubásh.

Idly, کاهلانه káhilánah.

Idol, بت but, صنم sanam (*pl.* اصنام asnám), نگار nigár.

Idolater *and* Idolatrous, بت پرست but-parast, عابد الاصنام 'ábidu-'l-asnám.

To Idolatrize, بت پرستی کردن but-parastí kardan.

Idolatry, بت پرستی but-parastí.

To Idolize, تکریم کردن takrím kardan, تعظیم نمودن ta'zím nimúdan.

If, اگر agar, گر gar, ار ar, ان in, اگر چنانچه agar chunán-chih.

Igneous, آتش نما átish-nimá.

To Ignite (*trans.*), سوزانیدن suzánídan.—(*intrans.*) سوختن súkhtan.

Ignition, سوز súz, سوزش súzish.

Ignoble, بد رگ bad-rag, بد سرشت bad-sirisht, بد تبار bad-tabár, دون dún, پست past, رذیل razíl.

Ignominious, رسوا rusvá, قبیح kabíh, بد bad, زبون zubún.

Ignominy, رسوائی rusvá,í, فضیحت fazíhat, عار 'ár.

Ignorance, نا دانی ná-dání, جهل jahl, جاهلی jáhilí.—(*presumptuous ignorance*) جهل مرکب jahl-i-murakkab.—(*to feign ignorance*) تجاهل کردن tajáhul kardan.

Ignorant, نا دان ná-dán, نا واقف ná-vákif, بیخبر bí-khabar, غافل gháfil, ناشی náshí, عاری 'árí.—(*unlearned*) نا خوانده ná-khwándah, امی ummí, نا دان ná-dán, بی سواد bí-savád, نبطی nabatí.

Ignorantly, نا دنستانه ná-danistánah.

Ill, عیب 'aib, ضرارت zarárat, بدی badí, زیان ziyán. (*Vide* Sick, Bad, Improper.)

Illegal, خلاف شرع khiláf-i-shar', حرام harám, نا حق ná-hakk.

ILLEGALITY, مخالفت شرع mukhálafat-i-shar', خلافت شرع khiláfat-i-shar'.

ILLEGIBLE, نا خوانا ná-khwáná.

ILLEGITIMACY, حرامزادگی harám-zádagí.

ILLEGITIMATE, حرامزاده harám-zádah, ولد الزنا valadu-'z-ziná.

ILL-FATED, بد بخت bad-bakht, بخت بر گشته bakht-bar-gashtah, بخت خفته bakht-khuftah.

ILL-FAVOURED, زشت zisht, مکروه makrúh.

ILLIBERAL, بخیل bakhíl.

ILLITERATE, امی ummí.

ILL-NATURE, بد خوئی bad-khú,í, بد مزاجی bad-mizájí, شرارت sharárat.

ILL-NATURED, کج خلق kaj-khulk, بد خو bad-khú, بد نهاد bad-nihád, تند خو tund-khú, شریر sharír.

ILLNESS, *vide* COMPLAINT.

ILLOGICAL, خلاف قیاس khiláf-i-kiyás.

To ILL-TREAT, ستم نمودن sitam nimúdan, بد رفتاری کردن bad-raftárí kardan, ظلم نمودن zulm nimúdan.

ILL-TREATMENT, ستم sitam, بد رفتاری bad-raftárí, ظلم zulm.

To ILLUMINATE, چراغان کردن chirághán kardan. (*Vide* To ENLIGHTEN.)

ILLUMINATED (*embellished with gilding and colours, &c., as fine manuscript books*), مذهب muzahhab, تذهیب شده tazhíb-shudah.—(*title-page of a book, &c.*) سر لوح sar-i-lauh, سر صفحه sar-i-safhah, عنوان 'unván.

ILLUMINATION (*of lamps*), چراغان chirághán.

ILLUSION, خیال khayál, بهانه bahánah, حیله hílah, نظر بند nazar-band, نظر بازی nazar-bází, نیرنگ nairang.

ILLUSIVE, خیالی khayálí, وهمی vahmí.

To ILLUSTRATE (*book, &c.*), منور کردن munavvar kardan.

ILLUSTRATION (*proof*), مثال misál, اثبات isbát, دلیل dalíl. (*Vide* EXAMPLE, PROOF.) — (*explanation*) تفسیر tafsír, تعبیر ta'bír, شرح sharh, توضیح tauzíh, بیان bayán. —(*ornament or picture*), تصویر tasvír, نقش naksh.

ILLUSTRIOUS, *vide* FAMOUS, GREAT.

IMAGE, صورت súrat, تمثال timsál, صنم sanam, بت but.

IMAGINABLE, متصور mutasavvir.

IMAGINARY, موهوم mauhúm, موهومه mauhúmah, خیالی khayálí.

IMAGINATION, *vide* IDEA, THOUGHT, ILLUSION. — (*in imagination*) در مرکز ایجاد dar markaz-i-íjád.

IMAGINATIVE, سریع التخیل sarí'u-'t-takhayyul.

To IMAGINE, تصور کردن tasavvur kardan, مظنه داشتن mazinnah dáshtan, قیاس کردن kiyás kardan, گمان بردن gumán burdan, پنداشتن pindáshtan, خیال کردن khayál kardan, خیال بستن khayál bastan.

IMBECILE (*mad*), دیوانه dívánah, مجنون majnún. — (*foolish*) ابله ablah, احمق ahmak, ضعیف العقل za'ífu-'l-'akl.

IMBECILITY (*madness*), دیوانگی dívánagí, مجنونیت majnúníyat. — (*folly*) ابلهی ablahí, بی حواسی bí-havássí.

To IMBIBE, *vide* To DRINK, To ABSORB.

IMITABLE, قابل تقلید kábil-i-taklíd.

To IMITATE, اقتدا نمودن iktidá nimúdan, تقلید کردن taklíd kardan, تقلید در آوردن taklíd-dar-ávardan.

IMITATION, تقلید taklíd, تتبع tatabbu', نقل nakl, اقتدا iktidá, تشبیه tashbíh, مماثله mumásalah.

IMITATOR, مقلد mukallid, تقلید چی taklíd-chí.

IMMACULATE, پاک pák, بی گناه bí-gunáh, بی عیب bí-'aib.

IMMATURE, خام khám, نا رس ná-ras.

IMMATURITY, خامی khámí, نارسی ná-rasí.

IMMEASURABLE, بی اندازه bí-andázah, بی حد bí-hadd.

IMMEDIATE, قریب karíb, حاضر házir.

IMMEDIATELY (*quickly*), بزودی bi-zúdí, در حال dar hál, بلا فاصله bilá fásilah, فی الفور fí-'l-faur, معاً

ma'án. — (*exactly upon time*) بمجرد bi-mujarrad, بمحض bi-mahz, همانکه hamán-kih, همینکه hamín-kih, جخ jakh (*vulg.*).
Immemorial, مستدام mustadám, قدیم kadím.
Immense, بی اندازه bí-andázah, شایگان shaígán, نا محصور ná-mahsúr, بزرگ buzurg.
Immensity, بزرگی buzurgí.
To Immerge, غوطه نمودن ghútah nimúdan, غرق کردن ghark kardan.
Immersed, غرق ghark, مستغرق mustaghrak.
Immersion, غوطه ghútah.
To Immigrate, *vide* To Emigrate.
Immigration, نقل nakl.
Imminent, مشرف mushrif, نزدیک nazdík.
Immobile, قائم ká,im.
Immobility, سکون sukún.
Immoderate, *vide* Immeasurable.
Immodest, بی ادب bí-adab, بی حیا bí-hayá.
Immodesty, بی ادبی bí-adabí, بی حیائی hayá,í.
To Immolate, قربان نمودن kurbán nimúdan.
Immoral, بد معاش bad-ma'ásh, فاسد fásid, فاحش fáhish, بد نهاد bad-nihád.
Immorality, بد معاشی bad-ma'áshí, فساد fasád.
Immortal, بی زوال bí-zavál, لا یموت lá-yamút, لا یزال lá-yazál.
Immortality, ابدی abadí, ابدیت abadíyat.
To Immortalize, مخلد نمودن mukhallad nimúdan.
Immovability, ثبات sabát, ثبوت subút.
Immovable, غیر متحرک ghair-i-mutaharrik.
Immunity, معافی mu'áfí, مخلصی mukhlisí, آزادی ázádí, امن aman, رهائی rihá,í.
Immutable, بی تغیر bí-taghayyur, لا یتبدل lá-yutabaddal.
Imp, عفریت 'ifrít.
Impact, صاف sáf.
To Impair, *vide* To Injure.
To Impale, خازوق زدن kházúk zadan, دار زدن dár zadan, بر دار کشیدن bar dár kashídan.—(*impaling stake*) خازوق khăzúk, دار dár.
To Impart, *vide* To Give.
Impartial, عادل 'ádil, راستباز rást-báz, داد رس dád-ras, بی غرض bí-gharaz, بی میل bí-mail, صادق sádik.
Impartiality, عدل 'adl, بی طرفی bí-tarafí, راست بازی rást-bází, داد رسی dád-rasí, صداقت sadákat.
Impassable, بی گذار bí-guzár, نا ممکن عبور ná-mumkin-i-'ubúr, غیر قابل مرور ghair-i-kábil-i-murúr.
Impatience, بیصبری bí-sabrí, اضطراب iztiráb.
Impatient, بیصبر bí-sabr, غیر تحمل ghair-i-tahammul, بی شکیب bí-shikíb.
To Impeach, تهمت دادن tuhmat dádan.
Impeachment, دعوی da'vá, اسناد isnad, تهمت tuhmat.
To Impede, *vide* To Hinder.
Impediment, منع mana', مانع máni', ممانعت mumána'at, مزاحمت muzáhamat, تعرض ta,arruz, بار bár.
To Impel, راندن rándan, ابرام نمودن ibrám nimúdan, تحریک ساختن tahrík sákhtan, بر آن داشتن bar án dáshtan.
Impenetrable, لا ممکن الدخول lá mumkinu-'d-dukhúl.
Impenitence *or* Impenitent, بغیر توبه bi-ghair-i-taubah.
Imperative (*mood*), امر amr.—(*needful*) *vide* Necessary.
Imperceptible, غیر محسوس ghair-i-mahsús.
Imperceptibly, رفته رفته raftah-raftah, بتدریج bi-tadríj, آهسته آهسته áhistah-áhistah.
Imperfect, نا تمام ná-tamám, ناقص nákis, قاصر kásir.—(*imperfect tense of a verb*) ماضی استمراری mází-i-istimrárí.
Imperfection, نقیصه nakísah, قصور kusúr.
Imperial, شاهی sháhí, قیصری kaisarí.

To IMPERIL, در خطر انداختن dar khatar andákhtan.—(*to be imperilled*) بخطر افتادن bi-khatar uftádan.

IMPERIOUS, امیرانه amíránah.

IMPERISHABLE, *vide* IMMORTAL.

To IMPERSONATE, تشبه کردن tashabbuh kardan.

IMPERSONATION, تشبه tashábbuh.

IMPERTINENCE, *vide* IMPUDENCE.

IMPETUOSITY, تندی tundí, تهور tahavvur.

IMPETUOUS, متهور mutahavvir, تند رو tund-rau, تند tund.

IMPETUS, زور zúr, شدت shiddat, قوت kúvat, هجوم hujúm, غلبه ghalabah, حمله hamlah.

IMPIETY, کفر kufr, نفاق nifák, بی دینی bí-díní.

IMPIOUS, بیدین bí-dín, کافر káfir, منافق munáfik, فاسق fásik.

IMPLACABLE, بی رحم bí-ruhm.

To IMPLANT, مرکوز کردن markúz kardan.

IMPLEMENT, آلت álat.

To IMPLICATE, تهمت زدن tuhmat zadan.—(*to be implicated*) مدخلیت داشتن madkhalíyat dáshtan.

To IMPLORE, *vide* To BEG.

To IMPLY, اشاره کردن isharah kardan.

IMPOLITE, بی ادب bí-adab, درشت durusht.

IMPOLITIC, نالائق ná-lá,ik, نا شایسته ná-sháyistah.

IMPORT, معنی ma'ní, مطلب matlab.—(*goods*) مدخل madkhal.

To IMPORT, پاین آوردن páyin ávardan.

IMPORTANCE (*matter, consequence*), قدر kadr, مضایقه muzáyakah, لازمت lázimat, مصرف masraf, گرانی giráni, مهمی muhammí (*Vide* DIGNITY, VALUE, SIZE.)

IMPORTANT, لازم lázim, مهم muhimm, گران girán, خطیر khatír, معتنی به mu'taná-bihi, عمده 'umdah.

IMPORTATION, حمل haml, مدخل madkhal.

IMPORTUNATE, متقاضی mutakází.

To IMPORTUNE, تقاضا نمودن takazá nimúdan.

IMPORTUNITY, تقاضا takázá, الحاح ilháh.

To IMPOSE, گذاشتن guzáshtan.—(*to impose upon*) فریفتن firíftan, فریب دادن firíb dádan, گول خورانیدن gúl khwuránídan, حیله کردن hílah kardan, غدر نمودن ghadar nimúdan.

IMPOSING (*structure, &c.*), مهیب mahíb.

IMPOSITION, *vide* FRAUD.

IMPOSSIBILITY, عدم امکان 'adam-i-imkán.

IMPOSSIBLE, نا ممکن ná-mumkin, محال muhál, ممتنع mumtani'.

IMPOST, *vide* TAX.

IMPOSTOR, مزور muzavvir, مکار makkár, عیار 'ayyár, فریبنده firíbandah, شیاد shayyád, قلابی kullábí, دولابی dúlábí.

IMPOSTURE, *vide* FRAUD.

IMPOTENCE (*physical*), عنت 'unnat, عنینت 'innínat.—(*practical*) نا توانائی ná-tavána,í.

IMPOTENT (*physically*), عنین 'anín.—(*practically*) نا توان ná-taván, عاجز 'ájiz.

To IMPOVERISH, محتاج ساختن muhtáj sákhtan

IMPRACTICABLE, *vide* IMPOSSIBLE.

To IMPRECATE, *vide* To CURSE.

IMPREGNABLE, منیع maní'.

To IMPREGNATE, آبستن ساختن ábistan sákhtan.—(*a flower*) بو دادن bú dádan.

IMPREGNATION, آبستنی ábistaní.—(*flower*) بو دادنی bú-dádaní.

IMPRESARIO, شبیه ساز shabíh-sáz.

To IMPRESS (*stamp*), مهر نمودن muhr nimúdan, نشان دادن nishán dádan.—(*force to serve*), سخره گرفتن sukhrah giriftan, بخدمت بی جیره گرفتن bi-khidmat-i-bí-jírah giriftan.

IMPRESSION (*stamp*), نقش naksh, نشان nishán, اثر asar, مهر muhr, چاپ cháp (*hind.*).—(*to make an impression*) تاثیر نمودن ta,sír nimúdan.

To IMPRISON, در زندان نهادن dar

zindán nihádan, حبس کردن habs kardan.

IMPRISONMENT, حبس habs, قید kaid.

IMPROBABILITY, دوری dúrí.

IMPROBABLE, غیر معقول ghair-i-ma'kúl, نا محتمل ná-muhtamal, دور dúr, بعید ba'íd.

IMPROMPTU, بدیهاً badíhan.—(*impromptu reply*) بدیهت badíhat.

IMPROPER, نا مناسب ná-munásib, نا شایسته ná-sháyistah, بیجا bí-já, نا موجه ná-muvajjah, مستهجن mustahjan.

IMPROPRIETY, نا مناسبت ná-munásabat, نا شایستگی ná-sháyistagí.

To IMPROVE (*trans.*), بهتر کردن bihtar kardan.—(*intrans.*), بهتر شدن bihtar shudan.

IMPROVEMENT, بهتری bihtarí, ترقی tarakkí, اصلاح isláh.

IMPROVIDENCE, غافلی ghátilí.

IMPROVIDENT, غافل ghátil, بی احتیاط bí-ihtiyát.

IMPRUDENCE, تهور tahavvur, غفلت ghiflat, بی تدبیری bí-tadbírí.

IMPRUDENT, بی تمییز bí-tamyíz, بی بصیرت bí-basírat, بی تدبیر bí-tadbír, بی احتیاط bí-ihtiyát.

IMPRUDENTLY, علی الغفلة 'alá-'l-ghiflah, غافلانه ghátilánah.

IMPUDENCE, شوخی shúkhí, گستاخی gustákhí, بی ادبی bí-adabí, وقاحت vakáhat, بی ساختگی bí-sákhtagí.

IMPUDENT, شوخ shúkh, گستاخ gustákh, بی ادب bí-adab, بی حیا bí-hayá, لا ابالی lá-ubálí, فضول fuzúl, بی شرم bí-sharm.

IMPULSE, تحریك tahrík, ترغیب targhíb.

IMPUNITY, بی سزائی bí-sazá,í, عدم عقوبت 'adam-i-'ukúbat. — (*with impunity*) بی سزا bí-sazá, ظلفاً zalafan, هدراً hadran.

IMPURE, نا پاك ná-pák, پلید palíd, نجس najis, ملوث mulavvas.

IMPURITY, نا پاکی ná-pákí, آلایش áláyish, غلاظت ghilázat, نجاست najásat, قذر kazar, قاذورات kázúrát, کدر kadar, لوث laus.

IMPUTATION, احتمال ihtimál, تهمت tuhmat, اتهام ittihám, اسناد isnád, نسبت nisbat.

To IMPUTE, منسوب کردن mansúb kardan, محتمل کردن muhtamal kardan, نسبت دادن nisbat dádan.

IN, در dar, اندر andar, درون darún, اندرون andarún, میان miyán, در میان dar miyán, داخل dákhil, تو tú, توی túí, فی fí, لا lá (*vulg.*).

INABILITY, در ماندگی dar-mándagí, نا توانائی ná taváná,í.

INACCESSIBLE, دور دست dúr-dast, منیع maní'.

INACCURACY, نا درستی ná-durustí, نا راستی ná-rástí.

INACCURATE, نا درست ná-durust, نا راست ná-rást.

INACTIVE, سست sust.

INACTIVITY, سستی sustí.

INADEQUATE, کم kam.

INADVERTENCE, غفلت ghiflat.—(*by inadvertence*) سهواً sahvan, غافلاً ghátilan.

INADVERTENT, غافل ghátil.

INANIMATE, بی جان bí-ján.

INAPPLICABLE, بی موقع bí-mauki'.

INASMUCH AS, بسکه bas-kih.

INATTENTION, غافلی ghátilí, غفلت ghiflat, تغافل tagháful.

INATTENTIVE, غافل ghátil.

INATTENTIVELY, غفلتاً ghiflatan.

To INAUGURATE, فتح نمودن fath nimudan.

INAUGURATION, فتح fath.

INCALCULABLE, بی حد bí-hadd.

INCANTATION, نیرنگ nairang, افسون afsún.

INCAPABLE, نا لائق ná-lá,ik, نا قابل ná-kábil, بیقدرت bí-kudrat, نا توان ná-taván.

INCAPACITY, عدم قابلیت 'adam-i-kábiliyat.

To INCARCERATE, *vide* To IMPRISON.

INCARNATE, مجسم mujassam.

INCARNATION, تجسم tajassum.

INCAUTIOUS, بی خبر bí-khabar, بی فکر bí-fikr.

INCENDIARISM, محترق سازی muhtarik-sází.

INCENDIARY, محترق ساز muhtarik-sáz.

INCENSE, بخور bakhúr. (*Vide also* PERFUME.)

INCENTIVE, تحریض tahríz, تحریک tahrík.

INCESSANT, مدام mudám, دائم dá,im, بلا فاصله bilá fásilah.

INCESSANTLY, دائماً dá,iman, لا تقطع lá-takattu‘, علی الدوام ‘alá-’d-davám, پیوسته paivastah.

INCEST, زنا ziná, فجور القرابه fujúru-’l-karábah.

INCH, وجب vajab.

INCIDENT, حادثه hádisah, ماجرا májará, واقعه váki‘ah, وقوع vukú‘, قضا kazá, سرگذشت sar-guzasht, اتفاق ittifák.

INCIDENTAL, اتفاقی ittifákí.

INCISION, شق shakk, قطع kat‘.

INCISIVE, قاطع káti‘.

To INCITE, ابرام نمودن ibrám nimúdan, اغوا کردن ighvá kardan, تحریک دادن tahrík dádan, خیزانیدن khízánídan, ترغیب نمودن targhíb nimúdan, انگیختن angíkhtan.

INCIVILITY (*rudeness, affront*), بی ساختگی bí-sákhtagí, بی تعارفی bí-ta‘árufí, بی ادبی bí-adabí.

INCLEMENT, درشت durusht, سخت sakht.

INCLEMENCY, درشتی durushtí, سختی sakhtí.

INCLINATION, میل mail, آرزو árzú, دماغ dimágh, هوا havá, اراده irádah, شوق shauk, صفا safá.—(*things*) میل mail, تمایل tamáyul.

To INCLINE, میل کردن mail kardan.—(*lean*) تکیه دادن takyah dádan.

INCLINED, مائل má,il, منعطف mun‘atif.—(*to be inclined*) مائل شدن má,il shudan, رغبت نمودن raghbat nimúdan.—(*it was inclined to be fine*) هوا رو بخوبی شد havá rú bi-khúbí shud.

To INCLUDE, داخل کردن dákhil kardan, درج نمودن darj nimúdan.—(*to be included*) داخل شدن dákhil shudan, شامل شدن shámil shudan, ملحق شدن mulhak shudan.

INCLUSIVE, مشتمل mushtamil, مندرج mundarij, متضمن mutazammin, شامل shámil.

INCOGNITO, در صورت نا شناسائی dar súrat-i-ná-shinásá,í, بطور نا شناس bi-taur-i-ná-shinás.—(*to go incognito*) تبدیل شدن tabdíl shudan.

INCOHERENCY, بی موافقت bí-muváfakat.

INCOHERENT, بی موافق bí-muváfik.

INCOME, آمدنی ámadaní, مداخل madákhil, حاصل hásil, جاچن jáchan.

INCOMPARABILITY, بیمثالی bí-misálí, یگانگی yagánagí.

INCOMPARABLE, لا ثانی lá-sání, بی نظیر bí-nazír, بی مثال bí-misál, یگانه yáganah, فرید faríd, بیمانند bí-mánand, بی اقران bí-akrán, بی همتا bí-ham-tá, بی شبیه bí-shabíh, بی بدل bí-badal.

INCOMPATIBLE, منافی munáfí.—(*to be incompatible with*) منافاتی داشتن munáfátí dáshtan.

INCOMPETENT, نا موافق ná-muváfik, غیر مطابق ghair-i-mutábik.

INCOMPLETE, ناقص nákis, نا تمام ná-tamám.

INCOMPREHENSIBLE, نا ممکن فهم ná-mumkin-i-fahm, بی قیاس bí-kiyás, از فهم دور az fahm dúr, بلا ادراک bilá idrák, لا یدرک lá-yudrik.

INCONGRUITY, نا سازی ná-sází.

INCONGRUOUS, نا سزا ná-sazá, نا ساز ná-sáz.

INCONSIDERABLE, قلیل kalíl.

INCONSIDERATE, بی بصیرت bí-basírat, متهور mutahavvir.

INCONSISTENCY, تناقض tanákuz.

INCONSISTENT (*things*), متناقض mutanákiz, منافی munáfí, نا مستقیم ná-mustakím.—(*persons*) مناقض munákiz.—(*to be inconsistent*) تناقض گفتن tanákuz guftan.

INCONSOLABLE, بیصبر bí-sabr.

INCONSTANCY, تلون talavvun.

INCONSTANT, بی قرار bí-karár, بی ثبات bí-sabát, نا پایدار ná-páyadár, متلون mutalavvin, متغیر mutaghayyir, دو رو dú-rú.

INCONTESTABLE, ثابت sábit.

INCONTINENCE, بد پرهیزی bad-parhízí, بد کاری bad-kárí.

INCONTINENT, بد پرهیز bad-parhíz, بد کار bad-kár.
INCONTROVERTIBLE, قطعی kat'í.
INCONVENIENCE, مشقت mashakkat, مضرت mazarrat, محنت mihnat.
INCONVENIENT, ثقیل sakíl, دشوار dushvár, متصدع mutasaddi'.
INCORPORATE, مجسم mujassam.
TO INCORPORATE, ضم نمودن zamm nimúdan.—(*to be incorporated*) ضمیمه گردیدن zamímah gardídan.
INCORPORATION, الحاق ilhák.
INCORRECT, نا صواب ná-saváb, نا راست ná-rást, نا درست ná-durust.
INCORRECTNESS, نا راستی ná-rástí, نا درستی ná-durustí, غلط ghalat.
INCORRUPTIBILITY (*things*), نا فنا ná-faná.— (*persons*) عفت 'iffat, پاك دامنی pák dámaní.
INCORRUPTIBLE (*things*), فنا ناپذیر faná-ná-pazír. — (*persons*) پاك دامن pák dáman.
INCREASE, افزایش afzáyish, افزونی afzúní, زیادتی ziyádatí, ازدیاد izdiyád, تزاید tazáyud, اضافه izáfah, ترقی tarakkí, انضمام inzimám.
TO INCREASE, افزودن afzúdan, مزید کردن mazíd kardan, زیاد کردن ziyád kardan, اضافه نمودن izáfah nimúdan.—(*to be increased*) زیاد شدن ziyád shudan.
INCREDIBILITY, عدم اعتبار 'adam-i-i'tibár.
INCREDIBLE, نا لائق اعتبار ná-lá,ik-i-i'tibár, نا واجب اعتقاد ná-vájib-i-i'tikád.
INCREMENT, ضمیمه zamímah.
TO INCRUST, اندودن andúdan.
INCRUSTATION, اندوده andúdah.
INCUMBENT (*duty*), لازم lázim, واجب vájib, مقتضی muktazí, متحتم mu-tahattam.
INCURABLE, لا علاج lá-'iláj, بی دوا bí-daváa, معالجه پذیر نه mu'álajah-pazír-nah.
INCURSION (*hostile*), هجوم hujúm, حمله hamlah. (*Vide* ASSAULT, INVASION.)—(*to make an incursion*) تاختن tákhtan.
INDEBTED, ممنون mamnún. — (*in debt*) مقروض makrúz.

INDECENCY (*in words*), هرزه harzah, پوچ púch, فحش fuhsh. — (*in deeds*) هرزگی harzagí, گستاخی gustákhí, وقاحت vakáhat, خباثت khabásat.
INDECENT, فاحش fáhish, نا شایسته ná-sháyistah, رکیك rakík, هرزه harzah, مستهجن mustahjan, خبیث khabís.
INDECLINABLE, غیر منصرف ghair-i-munsarif.
INDECOROUS, شوخ shúkh, بی ادب bí-adab.
INDEED, تحقیق tahkík, یقیناً yakínan, فی الواقع fí-'l-váki', آری árí, فی الحقیقة fí-'l-hakíkat, واقعاً váki'an, انصافاً insáfan.
INDEFATIGABLE, زحمت کش zahmat-kash.
INDEFENSIBLE, ممتنع العذر mam-tani'u-'l-'uzr.
INDEFINITE, نا محدود ná-mahdúd, نا محصور ná-mahsúr, غیر معین ghair-i-mu'ayyan. — (*grammatical term*) نکره nakirah.
INDEFINITELY, بلا مدت bilá muddat.
INDELIBLE, ثابت sábit.
INDELICATE, *vide* INDECENT.
INDEMNITY, مجازات mujázát.
INDEMONSTRABLE, غیر مدلول ghair-i-madlúl.
INDENTATION, *vide* DINT.
INDENTURE, عهد نامه 'ahd-námah, اقرار نامه ikrár-námah.
INDEPENDENCE, استبداد istibdád, آزادی ázádí, استقلال istiklál.
INDEPENDENT, خود مختار khwud-mukhtár, مستقل mustakill, مطلق mutlak, آزاد ázád.
INDESCRIBABLE, که بتعریف نمی آید kih bi-ta'ríf na-mí-áyad.
INDESTRUCTIBLE, لا یزال lá-yazál.
INDETERMINABLE (*grammatical term*), منکر munakkar.
INDEX, فهرست fihrist.—(*pointer*) شاخص shákhis.
INDIA, هند hind, هندوستان hindú-stán. — (*Secretary of State for India*) وزیر مستملکات هند vazír-i-mustamalkát-i-hind.
INDIAN, هندی hindí, هندوی hindúí.

INDIA-RUBBER, مداد پاك كن midád-pák-kun.
To INDICATE, اشارہ کردن ishárah kardan, نمودن nimúdan.
INDICATION, *vide* SIGN.
INDICATIVE, معرب mu'rib.—(*indicative mood*), فعل مطلق fi'l-mutlak.
INDICTMENT, حکم نامه hukm-námah.—(*Vide* ACCUSATION).
INDIFFERENCE, *vide* CARELESSNESS.
INDIFFERENT, *vide* CARELESS.
INDIGENCE, *vide* POVERTY.
INDIGENOUS (*as a plant*), خود رو khwud-rú.
INDIGENT, *vide* POOR.
INDIGESTIBLE, سنگین sangín, نا گوار ná-guvár.
INDIGESTION, بد هضمی bad-hazmí, وخامت vakhámat.
INDIGNANT, *vide* ANGRY.
INDIGNATION, خشم khishm, رنجش ranjish, تنفر tanaffur.
INDIGNITY, ذلت zillat, خفت khiffat.
INDIGO (*substance*), نیل níl. —(*leaves pounded, as a dye for the beard, &c.*) رنگ rang, وسمه vasmah.—(*plant*) درخت نیل dirakht-i-níl.
INDIRECT, نا راست ná-rást, پیچیده píchídah.
INDISCERNIBLE, غیر ظاهر ghair-i-záhir, بعید الفهم ba'ídu-'l-fahm.
INDISCREET, بی عقل bí-'akl, بی امتیاز bí-imtiyáz.
INDISCREETLY, بی تمیزانه bí-tamízánah.
INDISCRETION, *vide* FOLLY.
INDISCRIMINATING, بی امتیاز bí-imtiyáz, بیبصیرت bí-basírat, بیتدبیر bí-tadbír.
INDISPENSABLE, *vide* NECESSARY.
INDISPOSED, *vide* SICK.
INDISPUTABLE, لا شك lá-shak, بیشبهه bí-shabhah.
INDISPUTABLY, صریحاً saríhan.
INDISSOLUBLE, حل نا پذیر hall-ná-pazír.
INDISTINCT, نا صاف ná-sáf.
INDIVIDUAL, نفر nafar, کس kas, شخص shakhs.—(*adj.*) احد ahad.
INDIVIDUALITY, تعین ta'ayyun.
INDIVIDUALLY, یکیك yak-yak, منفرداً munfaridan.
INDIVISIBLE, لا یتجزی lá-yatajazá, غیر منقسم ghair-i-munkasim.
INDOLENCE, سستی sustí, کاهلی káhilí.
INDOLENT, سست sust, کاهل káhil, تنبل tambal.—(*to be indolent*) تنبلی کردن tambalí kardan, سستی کردن sustí kardan, کهالت ورزیدن kahálat varzídan.
INDOMITABLE, غیر مغلوب ghair-i-maghlúb.
INDUBITABLE, بیشبهه bí-shabhah, متواتر mutavátir.
To INDUCE, تحریك کردن tahrík kardan, ترغیب نمودن targhíb nimúdan, بر آن داشتن bar án dáshtan, چاره کردن chárah kardan.
INDUCEMENT, ترغیب targhíb, تحریك tahrík.
INDUCTION, استنباط istimbát, استدلال istidlál.
To INDUE, دادن dádan, بخشیدن bakhshídan.
INDULGENCE, مرحمت marhamat, شفقت shafakat, التفات iltifát.
INDULGENT, شفیق shafík, مهربان mihrbán. — (*to be indulgent*) عنایت داشتن 'ináyat dáshtan, ملاطفت نمودن mulátafat nimúdan.
INDUSTRIOUS, محنتی mihnatí, ساعی sá'í, جاهد jáhid.
INDUSTRY, محنت mihnat, سعی sa'í, جد و جهد jidd va jahd.
INEBRIATED, *vide* INTOXICATED.
INEFFABLE, بیچون bí-chún.
INEFFICACIOUS, بی ثمر bí-samar, بی تأثیر bí-ta,sír.
INEFFICACY, بی ثمری bí-samarí, بی تأثیری ta,sírí.
INELEGANCE, بد نمائی bad-nimá,í, نا زیبائی ná-zíbá,í, زشتی zishtí.
INELEGANT, بد نما bad-nimá, زشت zisht.
INELOQUENT, بی بلاغت bí-balághat.
INEPT, نا قابل ná-kábil, نا زرنگ ná-zaring, بی لیاقت bí-liyákat.

INEQUALITY, نا هموارۀ ná-hamvárah, فرق fark.
INERT, *vide* IDLE.
INESTIMABLE, بی بها bí-bahá, عزیز 'azíz.
INEVITABLY, لا محاله lá-muhálah, چار نا چار chár-ná-chár, بلا شك bilá shak.
INEXORABLE, ثابت sábit, سنگدل sang-dil.
INEXPEDIENT, بدشواری bi-dushvárí, نا مناسب ná-munásib, نا لائق ná-lá,ik, بیجا bí-já.
INEXPERIENCE, عدم تجربه 'adam-i-tajribah, عدم وقوف 'adam-i-vukúf.
INEXPERIENCED, کار ندیده kár-na-dídah, خام khám.
INEXPERT, نا آزموده کار ná-ázmúdah-kár, نا واقف ná-vákif, بی سر رشته bí-sar-i-rishtah.
INEXPLICABLE, نا قابل بیان ná-kábil-i-bayán, بلا تعبیر bilá-ta'bír, ممتنع الوصف mumtani'-'l-vasf.
INEXPRESSIBLE, ناگفتنی ná-guftaní, بی بیان bí-bayán, از حد بیان بیرون az hadd-i-bayán bírún.
IN EXTENSO, با التمام bi-'t-tamám.
INFALLIBILITY, بی خطائی bí-khatá,í, بلا خطائی bilá-khatá,í.
INFALLIBLE, بی خطا bí-khatá, محقق muhakkak, بلا خطا bilá-khatá, مسلم musallam.
INFAMOUS, رسوا rusvá, فضیح fazíh, رو سیاه rú-síyah, بی آبرو bí-áb-rú.
INFAMY, *vide* DISGRACE.
INFANCY, بچگی bachagí, طفولیت tufúlíyat.
INFANT, بچه bachah, طفل tifl.
INFANTICIDE, طفل کشی tifl-kashí.
INFANTILE, طفلی tiflí, کودکی kúdakí.
INFANTRY, سرباز sarbáz.
To INFATUATE, فریفتن firíftan, فریب دادن faríb dádan.
INFATUATED, دیوانه dívánah, شیفته shíftah, فریفته firíftah, مجنون majnún.
INFATUATION, عناد 'inád, شیفتگی shíftagí.
To INFECT, سرایت نمودن siráyat nimúdan.
INFECTION, سرایت siráyat, عفونت 'ufúnat, اصابت isábat, اثر asar, تأثیر ta,sír.
INFECTIOUS, ساری sárí, معدی mu'dí, موثر mu,assir.
To INFER, استنباط کردن istimbát kardan.
INFERENCE, *vide* INDUCTION.
INFERIOR, کهتر kihtar, کمتر kamtar, کوچکتر kúchiktar, اسفل asfal, ادنا adná, پست past.
INFERIORITY, دونی dúní, کهتری kihtarí, کمتری kamtarí, کوچکتری kúchiktarí, پستی pastí.
INFERNAL, دوزخی duzakhí.—(*infernal regions*) *vide* HELL.
INFIDEL, کافر káfir, بیدین bí-dín, گور gaur, زندیق zandík, مشرك mushrik. (*Vide* UNBELIEVER.)—(*infidel subjects under Muhammadan government*) ذمی zimmí.
INFIDELITY, *vide* IMPIETY.
INFINITE, بی انتها bí-intihá, بی نهایت bí-niháyat, نا متناهی ná-mutanáhí, بی پایان bí-páyán, بی اندازه bí-andázah, بلا قیاس bilá kiyás, بی حد bí-hadd.
INFINITELY, *vide* MUCH, VERY.
INFINITIVE (*of a verb*), مصدر masdar.
INFINITY, بسیاری bisyárí, بی نهایتی bí-niháyatí.
INFIRM, *vide* WEAK.
INFIRMARY, شفا خانه shifá-khánah.
INFIRMITY, *vide* WEAKNESS, SICKNESS.
To INFLAME, تاب دادن táb dádan.
INFLAMED, گرم garm, سرخ surkh.
INFLAMMABLE, تابناك táb-nák, سوزناك súz-nák.
INFLAMMATION, سوزش súzish, حرارت harárat.—(*medical*) التهاب iltíháb.
To INFLATE, نفخ کردن nafkh kardan.
INFLATION, نفخ nafkh.
To INFLECT, تصریف کردن tasríf kardan.
INFLECTED (*noun*), مفعول maf'úl, معمول ma'múl. — (*case*) حالت معمولیت hálat-i-ma'múlíyat.
INFLEXIBLE, سخت sakht.
INFLEXION (*of a noun or verb*),

صرف sarf, تصریف tasríf, تحویل tahvíl.

INFLUENCE, *vide* INTEREST, EFFECT, AUTHORITY.

To INFLUENCE, اثر کردن asar kardan, تاثیر کردن ta,sír kardan, تحریص نمودن tahrís nimúdan, قدرت داشتن kudrat dáshtan, تحریك کردن tahrík kardan, ترغیب نمودن targhíb nimúdan, چارہ کردن chárah kardan.

INFLUENZA, نزله nazlah, زکام zukám.

INFLUX, دخل dakhl, در آمد dar-ámad.

To INFORM, اطلاع دادن ittilá' dádan, خبر دادن khabar dádan, مطلع گردانیدن mutallí' gardánídan, آگاہ کردن ágáh kardan, آگاهی دادن ágáhí dádan, نیوشانیدن niyúshánídan, آگاهانیدن ágáhánídan, معروف گردانیدن ma'rúf gardánídan, منتقل گردانیدن muntakil gardánídan, مخبر ساختن mukhbar sákhtan.

INFORMAL, غیر رسم ghair-i-rasm.

INFORMATION, اطلاع ittilá', خبر khabar.

INFORMER (*spy*), جاسوس jasús, گوینده gúyandah.

To INFRINGE, فسخ کردن faskh kardan.

INFRINGEMENT, فسخ faskh.

To INFUSE, *vide* To MIX, To BOIL. —(*to be infused*) دم کشیدن dam kashídan.

INFUSION (*tincture*), جوشانده jushándah, خیسانده khísándah, خسانده khusándah.

INGENIOUS, ذکی zakí, حاذق házík, زهین zahín, ظریف zaríf, عاقل 'ákil, چابك chábuk.

INGENUOUS, صادق sádik, راست rást, راستباز rást-báz, بی غرض bí-gharaz.

INGOT (*of gold or silver*), شمس shums, سبیکه sabíkah, سبکه sabukah.

INGRATITUDE, بی وفائی bí-vafá,í, نا سپاسی ná-sipásí, نا حق شناسی ná-hakk-shinásí.

INGREDIENT, جزوی juzví, جز juz,.

INGRESS, مدخل madkhal, مداخله mudákhalah.

To INHABIT, ساکن بودن sákin búdan, سکونت داشتن sukúnat dáshtan, وطن ساختن vatan sákhtan, سکنی گرفتن sukná giriftan, قرار گرفتن karár giriftan, منزل گرفتن manzil giriftan, مستنزل بودن mustanzil búdan.

INHABITABLE, *vide* HABITABLE.

INHABITANT, ساکن sákin (*pl.* سکنه sakanah, *and* سکان sukkán), باشنده báshandah (*pl.* باشندگان báshandagán), مکین makín, متمکین mutamakkin, مقیم makím, متوطن mutavattin, قاطن kátin, اهل ahl.

INHABITED, مسکون maskún, معمور ma'múr, آباد ábád, آبادان ábádán.

To INHALE, دم زدن dam zadan.

INHARMONIOUS, نا آهنگ ná-áhang.

INHERENT, اصلی aslí, جبلی jiballí, ذاتی zátí, طبیعی tabí'í.

To INHERIT, میراث یافتن mírás yáftan.

INHERITANCE, میراث mírás, ارث irs, وراثت virásat, ورثه varsah, ترکه tarikah, عصوبت 'usúbat, ارثیت irsíyat.

INHERITOR, وارث váris.

To INHIBIT, غدغن کردن ghadghan kardan, تنبیه نمودن tambíh nimúdan, نهی کردن nahy kardan, مدافعه کردن mudáfa'ah kardan.

INHIBITION, تنبیه tambíh, غدغن ghadghan, منع mana', نهی nahy.

INHOSPITABLE, نا مهمان دوست ná-mihmán-dúst, لئیم la,ím.

INHOSPITABLENESS, نا مهمان دوستی ná-mihmán-dústí, لوم lu,m.

INHUMAN, *vide* CRUEL.

INIMICAL, مخالف mukhálif.

INIMITABLE, بی مثل bí-misl, بی نظیر bí-nazír.

INIQUITOUS, بد bad, شریر sharír.

INIQUITY, *vide* SIN.

INITIAL, ابتدائی ibtidáí.

To INITIATE, داخل مبادی نمودن dákhil-i-mabádí nimúdan, دخل دادن dakhl dádan. — (*Vide* To BEGIN.) — (*a person*) در مقدمات

تعلیم دادن dar mukaddamát ta'-lím dádan.
INITIATION, دخل dakhl, مداخله mu-dákhalah.—(*Vide* BEGINNING.) —(*a person*) تعلیم در مقدمات ta'-lím dar mukaddamát.
INJECTION, تنقیه tankiyah, *vide* CLYSTER.
INJUDICIOUS, بی بصیرت bí-basírat, بیتدبیر bí-tadbír, بی عقل bí-'akl.
INJUDICIOUSLY, احمقانه ahmakánah.
INJUNCTION, *vide* INHIBITION.
To INJURE, آزردن ázurdan, آزار رسانیدن ázár rasánídan, زیان کردن ziyán kardan, ضرر رسانیدن zarar rasánídan, ستم نمودن sitam nimú-dan, خستن khastan.
INJURIOUS, زیان ور ziyán-var, مضر muzirr, ضرر انگیز zarar-angíz.
INJURY (*hurt*), ضرر zarar, زیان ziyán, آزار ázár, آسیب ásíb, تطاول tatávul. (*Vide* LOSS.)—(*contumely*) مذمت muzammat, طعن ta'n, ملامت ma-lámat, زجر zajr.
INJUSTICE, بیداد bí-dád, حیف haif, مظلمه mazlimah, بی انصافی bí-insáfí.
INK, مرکب murakkab, مداد midád. —(*red ink*) شنجرف shanjarf, سرنج suranj.—(*Indian-ink*), مرکب چین marakkab-i-chín. — (*ink-bottle*) دوات davát.—(*inkstand, case for holding pens and ink, &c.*), قلمدان kalam-dán, آمه ámah.
INKLING, حدس hads.
INLAID (*with jewels*), مرصع murassa', جواهر آمود javáhir-ámúd. — (*with gold*) طلا کوفت tilá-kúft, طلا کوب tilá-kúb, زر نشان zar-nishán.— (*with mosaic work*) خاتمی khá-timí, خاتمبندی khátim-bandí.— (*with coloured tiles*), کاشیکاری káshí-kárí.
INLET, راه ráh.
IN LIEU OF, عوض 'ivaz.
INMATE, اهل ahl.
INN (*lodging for strangers*) مهمانخانه mihmán-khánah.—(*Vide* CARA-VANSARY.)
INNATE, طبیعی tabí'í, فطری fatrí, ذاتی zátí.
INNERMOST, درونی darúní, اندرونی andarúní, باطنی bátiní.
INNKEEPER, رباطی ribátí.
INNOCENCE, بی گناهی bí-gunáhí, سادگی sádagí, پاکی pákí.
INNOCENT, بیگناه bí-gunáh, بری الزمه baríu-'z-zimmah, معصوم ma'súm, مبرا mubarrá, مزکی muzakká, بیجرم bí-jurm.—(*pure*) پاک pák, ساده sádah, طاهر táhir, مزکی muzakká.
INNOVATION, بدعت bid'at.
INNOVATOR, متبدع mutábaddi'.
INNOXIOUS, بی مضر bí-muzirr, نا موذی ná-mu,zá.
INNUMERABLE, بی شمار bí-shimár, بی حساب bí-hisáb, بی حد bí-hadd, لا یعد lá-yu'add, لا یحصی lá-yuhsá.
To INOCULATE, آبله کوفتن ábilah kúftan.
INOCULATION, بر آوردن آبله bar-ávar-dan-i-ábilah, آبله کوبی ábilah-kúbí.
INODOROUS, بی بو bí-bú, بی شمیم bí-shamím.
INOFFENSIVE, نا مضر ná-muzirr, نا موذی ná-mu,zá.
INOPERATIVE, بی تاثیر bí-ta,sír, بی عمل bí-'amal.
INOPPORTUNE, بیمحل bí-mahall, بی وقت bí-vakt, بیموقع bí-maukí'.
INQUEST, تفتیش taftísh, تفحص ta-fahhus.
INQUIETUDE, اضطراب iztiráb, تنگی tangí, ضیق zík, رنج ranj.
To INQUIRE, *vide* To ASK.
INQUIRER, متلاشی mutaláshí, متفحص mutafahhis.
INQUIRY, پرسش pursish, پژوهش paz-vahish, استفسار istifsár, استفهام istifhám, استخبار istikhbár, تحقیق tahkík, تجویز tajvíz, تنقیح tankíh, تفحص tafahhus, استقصا istíksá, استدراک istidrák.
INQUISITIVE, *vide* CURIOUS.
INQUISITOR, متفحص mutafahhis, تفتیشچی taftísh-chí.
INROAD, *vide* INVASION.
INSALUBRIOUS, *vide* UNHEALTHY.
INSALUBRITY, وبالت vabálat.
INSANE, *vide* MAD.
INSATIABLE, طامع támi', حریص harís.
To INSCRIBE, مرقوم نمودن markúm

nimúdan, ثبت نمودن sabt nimúdan, نوشتن nivishtan.
Inscription, کتابت kitábat, نوشته nivishtah, کتیبه katíbah.
Insect, حشرت hashrat (*pl.* حشرات hashrát), هامه hámah (*pl.* هوام havám), جانورک jánvarak, جانور jánvar.
Insecure, نا محفوظ ná-mahfúz.
Insecurity, خطر khatar, مخاطره mukhátarah.
Insensibility, بیهوشی bí-húshí.
Insensible, بلا حس bilá-hiss, بیهوش bí-húsh.—(*dull*) کند kund, کور دل kúr-dil, کودن kaudan, خیره khírah.
Insensibly, رفته رفته raftah raftah, بتدریج bi-tadríj.
Inseparable, متصل muttasil.
To Insert, داخل کردن dákhil kardan, درج کردن darj kardan.
Insertion, درج darj, مندرج mundarij, داخل dákhil.
Inside, درون darún, اندرون andarún, توی túí, داخل dákhil, بطن batn.—(*inside out*) وارونه várúnah.
Insidious, بد اندیش bad-andísh, دغا باز daghá-báz.
Insidiousness, بد اندیشی bad-andíshí, دغا بازی daghá-bází.
Insignia, حمایل hamáíl.
Insignificance, حقر hakr, پستی pastí.
Insignificant, ول vil, محقر muhakkar, پست past.
Insincere, بیوفا bí-vafá, منافق munáfik.
Insincerity, بیوفائی bí-vafá,í, منافقت munáfakat.
To Insinuate, اشاره کردن isharah kardan.
Insinuation, اشاره isharah, کنایه kináyah, ایهام íhám.
Insipid, بیمزه bí-mazah.
Insipidity, بیمزگی bí-mazagí.
To Insist, اصرار نمودن israr nimúdan, مصر بودن musirr búdan, پا فشردن pá fishurdan (*vulg.*).
Insistance, اصرار isrár.
Insolent, *vide* Impudent.
Insoluble, لا حل lá-hall.
Insolvent, *vide* Bankrupt.
To Inspect, نگه کردن nigah kardan, مشاهده کردن musháhadah kardan, زیارت کردن ziyárat kardan, سیر کردن sair kardan, ملاحظه کردن muláhazah kardan, امعان نظر کردن im'án-i-nazar kardan, سیل کردن sail kardan (*vulg.*).
Inspection, ملاحظه muláhazah, نظر nazar, سیر sair, سیل sail (*vulg.*).
Inspector, ناظر názir, نگاهبان nigáhbán, سرکار sar-kár, پرستار parastár.
Inspiration (*revelation by an angel*), وحی vahí.—(*supernatural influence arising in the heart*) الهام ilhám.
To Inspire, الهام نمودن ilhám nimúdan.
Inspired, ملهم mulham.
To Inspirit, تحریص کردن tahrís kardan.
Instability, نا پایداری ná-páyadárí, بی قراری bí-karárí.
Instable, نا پایدار ná-páyadár, بی قرار bí-karár.
To Install, نصب کردن nasb kardan.
Installation, نصب nasb.
Instalment, قسط kist, پاره párah.
Instance (*example*), مثال misál, تمثال timsál, تمثیل tamsíl, نمونه nimúnah. — (*for instance*) مثلاً masalan, فرضاً farzan, بر فرض bar farz.—(*in the first instance*) در مبادی حل dar mabádí-i-hál.
Instant (*of time*), لحظه lahzah, لمحه lamhah, آن án, دم dam.
Instantaneous, یکدم yak dam.
Instantly, *vide* Immediately.
Instead, عوض 'ivaz, بدل badal, بجای bi-jáí, بجائزه bi-já,izah, بازاء bi,izá,, بمنزله bi-manzilah.
To Instigate, تحریك کردن tahrík kardan, تحریض نمودن tahríz nimúdan.
Instigation, تحریك tahrík, ترغیب targhíb, اغوا ighvá, تحریض tahríz.
Instigator, محرك muharrik.
To Instill, نهادن nihádan, نمودن nimúdan.
Instinct, عقل حیوانی 'akl-i-haiváni,

طبع میل mail-i-tab', فراست firásat.
INSTINCTIVE, ذاتی zátí.
INSTINCTIVELY, بطور فراست bi-taur-i-firásat.
To INSTITUTE, گماشتن gumáshtan, اختراع نمودن ikhtirá' nimúdan.
INSTITUTION, اختراع ikhtirá'.
INSTITUTIONS (*regulations, precepts*), آیین áyín, قانون kánún (*pl.* قوانین kavánín), دستور dastúr, قاعده ká'idah (*pl.* قواعد kavá'id), تزوکات tuzúkát.
INSTITUTOR, موجد mújid, مؤسس mu,assis.
To INSTRUCT, تعلیم کردن ta'lím kardan, تادیب نمودن ta,díb nimúdan, یاد دادن yád dádan, تربیت نمودن tarbiyat nimúdan.
INSTRUCTION, تربیت tarbiyat, تعلیم ta'lím, تادیب ta,díb, افاد ifád, افاده ifádah.—(*to give instructions*) دستور العمل دادن dastúru-'l-'amal dádan.
INSTRUCTIVE, دانش آموز dánish-ámúz, عبرت اندوز 'ibrat-andúz.
INSTRUCTOR, معلم mu'allim.
INSTRUMENT (*tool*), آلت álat, ابزار abzár, ادات adát (*pl.* ادوات adavát).—(*musical*) ساز sáz.—(*agent*) *vide* CAUSE, MEANS.
INSTRUMENTAL, آلت álat.
INSUBORDINATION, بغاوت baghávat, تمرد tamarrud.
INSUFFERABLE, بیتحمل bí-tahammul, لاتحمل lá-tahammul.
INSUFFICIENCY, قصور kusúr, کمی kamí.
INSUFFICIENT, قاصر kásir, کم kam.
INSULAR, جزیرائی jazírá,í.
To INSULATE (*telegraphic term*), خارج کردن khárij kardan.
INSULATOR, گرگری gargarí.
INSULT, هتک آبرو hatk-i-áb-rú, شتم shatm, خفت khiffat, سر شکستگی sar-shikastagí, بی ساختگی bí-sákhtagí.
To INSULT, آزردن ázurdan, شتم نمودن shatm nimúdan, دشنام دادن dushnám dádan.
INSULTING, شوخ shúkh, بی شرم bí-sharm.

INSUPPORTABLE, بیتحمل bí-tahammul, لا تحمل lá-tahammul.
INSURANCE (*on a ship, goods, &c.*), بیمه bímah.
To INSURE, بیمه کردن bímah kardan.
INSURED, بیمه bímah.—(*uninsured*) غیر بیمه ghair-i-bímah.
INSURRECTION, عصیان 'isyán, فتنه fitnah, شورش shúrish.
INTACT, سلیم salím.—(*to be intact*) بر جا ماندن bar já mándan
INTEGER, عدد صحیح 'adad-i-sahíh.
INTEGRAL, وافی váfí. — (*integral portion*) جز juz. — (*integral and differential calculus*) حساب تمامی و تفاوتی hisáb-i-tamámí va tafávutí.
INTEGRITY, درستی durustí, راستی rástí, صداقت sadákat, صلاح saláh. —(*entirety*) تمامیت tamámíyat, کمال kamál.
INTELLECT, عقل 'akl, هوش húsh, خرد khirad, ذهن zihn.
INTELLECTUAL, عقول 'akúl, عقلانی 'aklání, معقول ma'kúl.
INTELLECTUALLY, عقلاً 'aklan.
INTELLIGENCE, *vide* NEWS, ABILITY.
INTELLIGENT, عاقل 'ákil, دراك darrák, هوشیار húsh-yár, هوشمند húsh-mand, زیرك zírak, خردمند khirad-mand, عارف 'árif, دانا dáná, کار دان kár-dán, ذهین zahín, ذکی zakí, تیز فهم tíz-fahm, المعی alma'í.
INTELLIGIBILITY, اتضاح ittizáh.
INTELLIGIBLE, معقول ma'kúl, مدرك mudrak.
INTEMPERANCE, مستی mastí, بی پرهیزی bí-parhízí.
INTEMPERATE, بی پرهیز bí-parhíz, غیر اعتدال ghair-i-i'tidál.
To INTEND, بنا داشتن biná dáshtan, اراده داشتن irádah dáshtan, خواستن khwástan, قصد کردن kasd kardan.
INTENSE, سخت sakht, شدید shadíd.
INTENSELY, بشدت bi-shiddat.
INTENSITY, شدت shiddat, سورت saurat.
INTENTION, اراده irádah, مراد murád, عزم 'azm, عزیمت 'azímat, قصد

kasd, مقصود maksúd, کام kám, نیت níyat, غرض gharaz, خواست khwást, طویت taviyat, مرکوز markúz, آهنگ áhang, سر sar, آرزو árzú, مرام marám, همت himmat, طلب talab, مطلب matlab, بنا biná, داعیه dá'iyah.

INTENTIONAL, بالقصد bi-'l-kasd, دیده و دانسته dídah va dánistah.

INTENTIONALLY, قصداً kasdan, عمداً 'amdan, دیده و دانسته dídah va dánistah.

To INTER, دفن کردن dafn kardan.

INTERCALARY, کبیسه kabísah.

To INTERCEDE, شفاعت نمودن shifá'at nimúdan, تشفع نمودن tashaffu' nimúdan.

To INTERCEPT, گرفتن giriftan.

INTERCEPTION, گرفتگی giriftagí.

INTERCESSION, شفاعت shifá'at, وساطت vasátat, مباینت mubáyanat.

INTERCESSOR, شفیع shafí'. (*Vide* MEDIATOR.)

INTERCOURSE (*communication, associating*), کار و بار kár va bár, آمد و رفت ámad va raft, اختلاط ikhtilát, علاقه 'alákah, معاشرت mu'ásharat, مراودت murávadat, مناسبات munásabát. — (*carnal*) مضاجعت muzája'at.

INTERDICT, *vide* INHIBITION.

INTEREST, *vide* ADVANTAGE. — (*participation, business*) بهره bahrah, علاقه 'alákah, کار kár, رابطه rábitah. — (*concern, emotion*) دلبستگی dil-bastagí, اعتنا i'tiná.— (*on money*) سود súd, ربا ribá, ربح ribh, مرابحه murábahah.—(*influence*) وسیله vasílah, قدرت kudrat, چاره chárah. — (*regard to one's own wish or advantage*) غرض gharaz.

INTERESTING, دلچسب dil-chasb, مقبول makbúl.

To INTERFERE with (*hinder*), تعویق انداختن ta'vík andákhtan, معارض بودن mu'áriz búdan, مزاحم شدن muzáhim shudan.—(*intermeddle*) مداخله نمودن mudákhalah nimúdan, پا در میان گذاردن pá dar miyán guzárdan, دخل داشتن dakhl dáshtan.

INTERFERENCE, مداخله mudákhalah.

INTERIM, اثنا asná, اثنای وقت asná,í-i-vakt, در بین dar bain, در میان dar miyán.

INTERIOR, تحتانی tahtání, میان miyán, درونی darúní.

INTERJECTION, صوت saut, ندا nidá,.

To INTERLACE (*trans.*), مشبک نمودن mushabbak nimúdan.—(*intrans.*) تشابک شدن tashábuk shudan.

INTERLACED, مشبک mushabbak, تشابک tashábuk.

INTERLEAVED (*tree*), شاخ در شاخ shákh dar shákh.—(*book*) برگ در برگ barg dar barg.

INTERLOCUTION, مکالمه mukálamah.

INTERLOCUTOR, متکلم mutakallim.

INTERLOPER, مداخل mudákhil.

INTERMARRIAGE, وصلت vaslat.

To INTERMARRY, وصلت کردن vaslat kardan.

To INTERMEDDLE, مداخله کردن mudákhalah kardan.

INTERMEDIARY, متوسط mutavassit.

INTERMENT, دفن dafn.

INTERMINABLY, الی غیر النهایه ilá ghairu-'n-niháyah.

To INTERMINGLE, مخلوط کردن makhlút kardán, آمیختن ámíkhtan.

INTERMINGLED, ممزوج mamzúj, مخلوط بهم makhlút bi-ham.

INTERMISSION, وقف vakf, توقف tavakkuf, فراغت farághat, اهمال ihmál, تقطع takattu'.

INTERMITTING (*fever*), تب غب tab-i-ghibb, تب نوبت tab-i-naubat.

INTERNAL, اندرونی andarúní, داخلی dakhilí, باطنی bátiní.

INTERNALLY, داخلاً dákhilan, اندرون andarún, تو tú.

INTERNATIONAL, دولیه duvaliyah.— (*international obligations*) حقوق عمومی ملل hukúk-i-'umúmí-i-milal.

To INTERPOLATE, داخل ساختن dákhil sákhtan, درج نمودن darj nimúdan.

INTERPOLATION, الحاق ilhák, مخالطه mukhálatah.

To INTERPOSE, در میان آمدن dar miyán ámadan, مداخله نمودن mudákhalah nimúdan, دخل داشتن dakhl dáshtan.

INTERPOSITION, مداخله mudákhalah, دخل dakhl.

To INTERPRET, ترجمه نمودن tarjumah nimúdan, شرح نمودن sharh nimúdan.—(*dreams*) تعبیر نمودن ta'bír nimúdan.

INTERPRETATION, ترجمه tarjumah, تعبیر ta'bír, بیان bayán, شرح sharh, عبر 'abr.—(*of dreams*) تعبیر خواب ta'bír-i-khwáb, تعبیر رؤیا ta'bír-i-ru,yá.

INTERPRETER, مترجم mutarjim, ترجمان tarjumán, دلماج dilmáj.—(*of dreams, omens, &c.*) تعبیر کننده ta'bír-kunandah, فالچی fál-chí, اختر گو akhtar-gú.

INTERREGNUM, فترت fatrat.

To INTERROGATE, پرسش نمودن pursish nimúdan, استفسار نمودن istifsár nimúdan.

INTERROGATION, سؤال su,ál, استفسار istifsár, پرسش pursish, استفهام istifhám.—(*note of interrogation*) علامت استفهام 'alámat-i-istifhám.

INTERROGATIVE and INTERROGATIVELY, باستفهام bi-istifhám, باستفسار bi-istifsár.

To INTERRUPT, قطع نمودن kat' nimúdan.

INTERRUPTION, خلل khalal, ازدحام izdihám, مزاحمت muzáhamat, قطع kat', تقطع takattu'. — (*in speech*) قطع سخن kat'-i-sukhun.

To INTERSECT, قطع نمودن kat' nimúdan.

INTERSECTION, تقاطع takátu'.

To INTERSPERSE, موشح ساختن muvashshah sákhtan.

INTERSTICE, *vide* CRANNY.

INTERVAL, اثنا asná, بین bain, میانه miyánah, فاصله fásilah.—(*at intervals*) تك تك tak tak.

To INTERVENE, دخل نمودن dakhl nimúdan, مداخله کردن mudákhalah kardan.

INTERVENING, فاصله fásilah.

INTERVENTION, وساطت vasátat, توسط tavassut, دخل dakhl, مداخله mudákhalah.

INTERVIEW, ملاقات mulákát, مواصلت muvásalat, بار bar.

To INTERWEAVE, بهم مخلوط نمودن bi-ham makhlút nimúdan.

INTERWOVEN, مخلوط بهم makhlút bi-ham.

INTESTATE, بیوصیت bí-vasíyat.

INTESTINE, درونی darúní, باطنی bátiní, اندرونی andarúní.

INTESTINES, *vide* BOWELS.

INTIMACY, اختلاط ikhtilát, مخالطه mukhálatah, موانست muvánasat, آشنائی áshná,í.

INTIMATE, الیف alíf, محرم muhrim. —(*to become intimate*) تألف نمودن ta,alluf nimúdan, الفت نمودن ulfat nimúdan.

To INTIMATE, اشاره کردن ishárah kardan.

INTIMATION, شیوع shuyú', اشاره ishárah.

To INTIMIDATE, تخویف کردن takhvíf kardan, ترسانیدن tarsánídan.

INTIMIDATION, تخویف takhvíf.

INTO, در dar, اندر andar, در میان dar miyán, درون darún, تو tú, توی túí.

INTOLERABLE, لا یتحمل lá-yatahammul.

INTOLERABLY, لا یتحملا lá-yatahammulan.

To INTOMB, دفن کردن dafn kardan.

To INTOXICATE, مست کردن mast kardan, مخمور نمودن makhmúr nimúdan.

INTOXICATED, مست mast, سرمست sar-mast, مخمور makhmúr, سرگران sar-girán.—(*slightly intoxicated*) گیج gích, سر خوش sar-khwush.

INTOXICATING (*liquor, drug, &c.*), مسکر muskir.

INTOXICATION, مستی mastí, نشاء nashá, سکر sukr, مخموری makhmúrí.

INTRACTABLE, سر کش sar-kash, نا فرمان بردار ná-firmán-bardár.

INTRANSITIVE, لازم lázim.

INTRANSMUTABLE, لا ممکن التبدیل lá-mumkinu-'t-tabdíl.

To INTREAT, نیازیدن niyázídan, التجاء نمودن iljá, nimúdan, التماس کردن iltimás kardan, الحاح کردن ilháh kardan, مستدعی بودن mustadí' búdan, استدعا نمودن istid'á nimúdan.

INTREATY, التجاء iljá, التماس iltimás, الحاح ilháh, استدعا istid'a.

To INTRENCH, قلعه بندی کردن kal'ah-bandí kardan.

INTRENCHMENT, سنگر sangur.

INTREPID, *vide* BOLD, FEARLESS.

INTRICATE, *vide* DIFFICULT, RAVELLED.

INTRIGUE, سازش sázish, اتفاق ittifák, هم عهدی ham-'ahdí.—(*amour*) عشقبازی 'ishk-bází, تعشق ta'ashshuk, معاشقه mu'áshakah.

To INTRIGUE, هم عهدی بستن ham-'ahdi bastan.—(*have an amour*) عشقبازی نمودن 'ishk-bází nimúdan.

INTRIGUER, دغا باز daghá-báz.

INTRINSIC, ذاتی zatí, اصلی aslí.

To INTRODUCE, در آوردن dar-ávardan. — (*a person*) معرفی کردن mu'arrafí kardan.

INTRODUCER, معرف mu'arrif.

INTRODUCTION, وسیلت vasílat.— معرفی mu'arrafí. —(*appearance*) ظهور zuhúr.—(*preface*) دیباچه díbáchah, مقدمه mukaddamah.

INTRODUCTORY, مقدمه mukaddamah.

To INTRUDE, مداخل نمودن mudákhil nimúdan.

INTRUDER, مداخل mudákhil.

INTRUSION, مداخله mudákhalah, دخل dakhl.

To INTRUST, سپردن sipurdan, حواله کردن haválah kardan, تسلیم نمودن taslím nimúdan, تفویض نمودن tafvíz nimúdan.

INTUITION, خیال khayál.

INTUITIVE, خیالی khayálí.

To INTWINE (*trans.*) پیچانیدن píchánídan. — (*intrans.*) پیچیدن píchídan.

To INUNDATE, سیلاب نمودن sailáb nimúdan.

INUNDATION, سیلاب sailáb, سیل sail.

To INVADE, هجوم نمودن hujúm nimúdan, حمله کردن hamlah kardan, تاختن tákhtan, یورش کردن yúrish kardan.

INVADER, حمله آور hamlah-ávar, تاراج گر táráj-gar.

INVALID, نا خوش ná-khwush. —(*military term*) مانده mándah, عاجز 'ájiz.

To INVALIDATE, باطل کردن bátil kardan.

INVALIDITY, بطلان butlán.

INVALUABLE, بی بها bí-bahá, عزیز 'azíz, عالی قدر 'álí-kudr.

INVARIABILITY, دوام davám.

INVARIABLE, دائم dá,im.

INVARIABLY, *vide* ALWAYS.

INVASION, هجوم hujúm, حمله hamlah, تاخت tákht, یورش yúrish.

INVECTIVE, لعن la'n, لعنت la'nat.

To INVEIGH against, زباندرازی نمودن zabán-dirází nimúdan, ملامت کردن malámat kardan, طعنه زدن ta'nah zadan, شکایت کردن shikáyat kardan.

To INVEIGLE, اغوا نمودن igvá nimúdan, ور غلانیدن var-ghalánídan, فریفتن firíftan.

INVEIGLER, فریبنده firíbandah.

To INVENT, اختراع نمودن ikhtirá' nimúdan, ایجاد کردن íjád kardan.

INVENTION, ایجاد íjád, اختراع ikhtirá', صنعت san'at, ابداع ibdá', تدبیر tadbír.

INVENTIVE, ایجادی íjádí, اختراعی ikhtirá'í.

INVENTOR, موجد mújid, مخترع mukhtari', مبدع mubdi'.

INVENTORY, فهرست fihrist. — (*to draw up an inventory*) ثبت دفتر کردن sabt-i-daftar kardan.

INVERSE, مخالف mukhálif, منقلب munkalib.

INVERSION, عکس 'aks, انقلاب inkiláb, منقلب munkalab.

To INVERT, مقلوب کردن maklúb kardan, وارون کردن várún kardan.

INVERTED, واژگون vázhgún, مقلوب maklúb, وارون varún, وارونه várúnah, سر نگون sar-nigún, نگونسار nigún-sár, منعکس mun'akis, بر گشته bar-gashtah.

To INVEST, *vide* To BESIEGE.—(*with honours, &c.*) متقلد کردن mutakallid kardan.

To INVESTIGATE, تفحص نمودن tafahhus nimúdan, تحقیق نمودن tahkík nimúdan.

INVESTIGATION, تفحص tafahhus, تحقیق tahkík.

INVESTMENT, محاصرة muhásarah, حصر hisr.—(*with honours, &c.*) تقلید taklíd.

INVETERACY, کهنگی kuhnagi, سختی sakhtí.

INVETERATE, کهنه kuhnah, سخت sakht.

INVIDIOUS, حاسد hásid.

To INVIGORATE, قوت دادن kúvat dádan, تقویت کردن takviyat kardan.

INVIGORATION, قوت kúvat, تقویت takviyat.

INVINCIBLE, غیر مغلوب ghair-i-maghlúb.

INVIOLABLE, بی زوال bí-zavál, بی فتور bí-futúr.

INVIOLATE, بی قصور bí-kusúr, بی شکست bí-shikast.

INVISIBILITY, غیبت ghaibat, غیب ghaib.

INVISIBLE, نا پدید ná-padíd, غائب ghá,ib, نا پیدا ná-paidá, نا مرئی ná-mar,í.

INVITATION, دعوت da'vat, صلا silá.

To INVITE, دعوت کردن da'vat kardan, مهمان کردن mihmán kardan.

INVITER, داعی da,í, میزبان mízbán.

INVOCATION, دعا du'á, استدعا istid'á.

INVOICE, فهرست fihrist.

To INVOKE, دعا کردن du'á kardan, خواندن khwándan.

INVOLUNTARY, بی اختیار bí-ikhtiyár, بی ارادة bí-irádah, نا دانسته ná-dánistah.

To INVOLVE, مشتمل بودن mushtamil búdan, محتوی شدن muhtaví shudan.

INVOLVED (*complicated*), پیچ در پیچ pích dar pích, پیچاپیچ pích-a-pích.

INVULNERABILITY, معصومیت ma'súmíyat.

INVULNERABLE, معصوم ma'súm.

INWARD, درونی darúní, باطن bátin, تو tú, توی túí, داخل dákhil.

IRASCIBILITY, غضوبت ghazúbat, تسخط tasakhkhat, تغیظ taghayyuz.

IRASCIBLE, تند طبیعت tund-tabí'at, غضوب ghazúb.

IRE, غضب ghazab, کین kín, خشم khishm, حدت hiddat.

IRIS (*flower*), سوسن ازرق súsan-i-azrak, زنبق zambak.

IRKSOME, مشکل mushkil, سخت sakht.

IRON, آهن áhan, حدید hadíd.—(*for ironing clothes*) اتو uttú (*hind.*).—(*sheet iron*) آهن ورقه áhan-i-varakah.—(*for prisoners*) بخاو bakháv.—(*made of iron*) آهنی áhaní, آهنین áhanín.

To IRON, اتو کشیدن uttú kashídan.

IRONCLAD (*ship*), زره پوش zarah-púsh, زرهدار zarah-dár, آهن پوش áhan-púsh.

IRON-FOUNDRY, آهن ریزی áhan-rízí.

IRONICAL, هجو hajv, هجو آمیز hajv-ámíz.—(*to speak ironically*) گوشه زدن gúshah zadan.

IRONMONGER, آهن فروش áhan-furúsh.

IRONY, هجو hajv, استهزا istihzá.

IRRATIONAL, غیر ناطق ghair-i-nátik.

IRRATIONALITY, غیر نطق ghair-i-nutk.

IRRECLAIMABLE, غیر مسترد ghair-i-mustarrad.

IRRECONCILEABLE, لا یتصالح lá-yatasálah, صلح نا پذیر sulh-ná-pazír.

IRRECOVERABLE, لا یصلح lá-yaslah, اصلاح نا پذیر isláh-ná-pazír.—(*medical*) لا یعالج lá-yu'álaj, علاج نا پذیر 'iláj-ná-pazír.

IRREGULAR, بی قاعدة bí-ká'idah, بی ترتیب bí-tartíb, خلاف قیاس khiláf-i-kiyás, نا مانوس ná-ma,nús.—(*verb, phrase, &c., in grammar*), سماعی samá,í. — (*troops*) غیر نظامی ghair-i-nizámí.

IRREGULARITY, عدم نظام 'adam-i-

nizám, بی ترتیبی bí-tartíbí, پریشانی paríshání.—(*in a wall, side of a house, &c.*) قناس kanás, اعوجاج i'vijáj.
IRRELIGION, بی دینی bí-díní.
IRRELIGIOUS, بد دین bad-dín.
IRREMEDIABLE, بی درمان bí-darmán.
IRREMOVABLE, لا یتحول lá-yatahavval, تحویل نا پذیر tahvíl-ná-pazír.
IRREPROACHABLE, غیر معاتب ghair-i-mu'átab.
IRRESISTIBLE, لا یقاوم lá-yukávam, مقاومت نا پذیر mukávamat-ná-pazír.
IRRESOLUTE, مترددّ mutaraddid, مردد muraddad, دودل dú-dil, مذبذب muzabzib.
IRRESOLUTION, تذبذب tazabzúb, تردد taraddud.
IRREVERENCE, بی احترامی bí-ihtirámí.
IRREVERENT, بی احترام bí ihtirám.
IRREVERSIBLE, لا یفسخ lá-yufsakh, تبدیل نا پذیر tabdíl-ná-pazír.
IRREVOCABLE, بی درمان bí-darmán.
To IRRIGATE, آب دادن áb dádan.—(*to be irrigated*) مشروب شدن mashrúb shudan.
IRRIGATION, آبیاری áb-yárí, آبپاشی áb páshí, آبدهی áb-dihí.
IRRITABILITY, کج خلق kaj-khalk.
IRRITABLE, غضوب ghazúb.
To IRRITATE, بخشم آوردن bi-khishm ávardan, مضطرب ساختن muztarib sákhtan.
IRRITATION, آزار ázár, خراش khirásh, آشفتگی áshuftagí. (*Vide also* ANGER.)
IRRUPTION, *vide* INVASION.

ISH (*a termination—e.g reddish*), مائل به má,il bi.
ISINGLASS, سریش ماهی siríshi-máhí, سیرشم ماهی sírishum-i-máhí.
ISLAND, جزیره jazírah, اداك adák.
ISLANDER, اهل جزیره áhl-i-jazírah.
ISOLATED, مجرد mujarrad, تنها tanhá, فرید faríd, تك تك tak-tak.
ISOLATION, تفرد tafarrud, تجرد tajarrud.
ISSUE (*children*), اولاد aulád, ذریه zuríyah, نسل nasl.—(*Vide* SORE, WOUND, BOIL, ABSCESS, RESULT).—(*number issued*) شماره shimárah.—(*copy*) نسخه nuskhah.
To ISSUE, صادر شدن sádir shudan, جاری شدن járí shudan, صدور نمودن sudúr nimúdan, خروج کردن kharúj kardan, بارز بودن báriz búdan, بر آمدن bar-ámadan.
ISTHMUS, تنگه tangah.
IT, او ú, آن án.
ITCH, گر gar, جرب jarab, خارش khárish.—(*having the itch*) گرگین gargín.
To ITCH, خاریدن kháridan.
ITEM, چیز chíz, فرد fard, شی shay.
ITINERANT, خانه بدوش khánah-bidúsh.
ITINERARY, راه ráh.
ITSELF, خود khwud. — (*of itself*) بنفسه bi-nafsah.
IVORY, عاج 'áj, دندان فیل dandán-i-fíl. — (*of the walrus*) دندان شیر ماهی dandán - i - shír - máhí, شیر ماهی shír-máhí.
IVY, لبلاب labláb, پاپیتال pápítál, عشقه 'ashakah, پیچك píchak.

J.

To JABBER, قال و مقال نمودن kál u makál nimúdan.
JABBERER, *vide* BABBLER.
JACKALL, شغال shighál.
JACKDAW, زاغ zágh.
JACKET, کردی kurdí, کردك kurdak.—(*riding jacket*) کلیچه kulíchah.—(*long-skirted ditto*) ایمه uímah, تکمه tikmah.—(*of thick wool*) کپنك kapank, نمد دوش namud-i-dúsh.—(*of sheepskin*) پوستین púatín.—(*woman's*) چپکن

chapkun, بهاره buhárah, کردی kurdí.—(*strait-jacket*) بغلبند baghal-band.
JADE (*stone*), یشم yashm.—(*horse*) بار گیر bár-gír.
JADED, فروماندة furú-mándah.
JAGGED, نا هموار ná-hamvár.
JAIL, *vide* GAOL.
JAILOR, *vide* GAOLER.
JALAP (*flower, Marvel of Peru*), لاله عباسی lálah-i-'abbásí.—(*medicine*) جلاب jaláb.
JAM (*jelly*), مربا murabbá, شیره shírah.
JANUARY, کانون ثانی kánún-i-sání.
JAR, سبو sabú, بستو bastú, بلونی bulúní.—(*large jar*) خم khum, خمرة khumrah. — (*earthen pot*) کلوك kulúk, دیزی dízí.
JARGON (*broken speech, or patois*), کج زبان kaj-zabán.
JASPER, یسپ yasp, یشب yashb.
JAUNDICE, مرض زهره marz-i-zahrah, یرقان yarkán.
JAVELIN, نیزه naizah, حربه harbah.—(*blunt javelin used in sport*) جرید jaríd.
JAW, الوارة ilvárah, چانه chánah, کله kallah, کچه kachah (*vulg.*).
JAY (*bird*), سبزه قبا sabzah-kabá, رنگریز rang-r'·' بلوط خور balút-khwur.
JEALOUS (*envious*), حاسد hásid, حسود hasúd, رشکین rashkín.—(*suspicious*) غیور ghuyúr, غیرتمند ghairat-mand, بد گمان bad-gumán.
JEALOUSY (*envy*), رشك rashk, حسد hasad.—(*suspicion*) غیرت ghairat, بد گمان bad-gumán.
To JEER, ریشخند کردن rísh-khand kardan, استهزا نمودن istihzá nimúdan, مزاح کردن mizáh kardan, مسخره کردن maskharah kardan.
JEHOVAH, یاهو yáhuva, یهواه yihuváh.
JELLY, *vide* JAM.
JEOPARDY, *vide* DANGER.
JERBOA (*desert rat*), موش صحرائی músh-i-sahrá,í, موش دو پا músh-i-dú-pá, یربوع yarbú'.

JERK, تکان takán, جنبش jumbish.
To JERK, تکانیدن takánídan, تکان دادن takán dádan.
JERSEY (*dress*), بغلبند baghal-band.
JESSAMINE, یاسمن yásaman, سمن saman.
JEST, لطیفه latífah, بذله bazlah, مطائبه mutá,ibah, شوخی shúkhí, باردی bárdí, فسوس fisús, کنایه kináyah, هزل hazl, مسخره maskharah.
To JEST, شوخی کردن shúkhí kardan, مسخره کردن maskharah kardan, ظرافت کردن zaráfat kardan.
JESTER, مسخره maskharah, لطیفه گو latífah-gú, مستهزئی mustahz,í.
JESUS, عیسی 'ísá.
JET, شبه shabah, سنگ موسی sang-i-músá, سیاه کهربا siyáh-kah-rubá.
JET D'EAU, فوارة favvárah.
JETTY, اسکله askalah.
JEU DE MOTS, تجنیس tajnís.
JEW, یهودی yahúdí, جهودی jahúdí, اسرائلی isrá,ilí, عبرانی 'ibrání, نغوك nighúk.
JEWEL, جوهر jauhar, گوهر gauhar.—(*ornament*) زیور zívar.
JEWELLED, *vide* STUDDED.
JEWELLER, جوهری jauharí, جواهری javáhirí (*vulg.*).
JEWELLERY (*precious stones*), جواهر javáhir.—(*ornaments of gold, &c.*) زیورات zívarát.
JEWESS, زن جهودی zan-i-jahúdí.
JEWISH, موسوی músaví.
JIG BY JOWL, بردیف bi-radíf.
To JINGLE, زنگ زدن zang zadan, طنطنه کردن tantanah kardan.
JOB, شغل shaghl, کار kár.
JOB-MASTER, اسب فروش asb-furúsh.
JOCKEY, چابکسوار chábuk-suvár, مهتر mihtar, سوارکار suvár-kár.
JOCOSE, مسخره maskharah, طناز tannáz, شوخ shúkh.
JOCOSENESS, شوخی shukhí, بذله bazlah, لطیفه latífah, لطیفه گوی latífah-gúí.
To JOG, تکان دادن takán dádan.
To JOIN, پیوستن paivastan, پیوند کردن paivand kardan, وصل کردن vasl kardan, چسبانیدن chasbánídan,

ملحق کردن mulhak kardan, ملصق کردن mulsak kardan.—(*to join one's letters*) حروفرا متصل نوشتن hurúfrá muttasil nivishtan.

JOINED, *Vide* UNITED.

JOINER, *vide* CARPENTER.

JOINT, بند band, مفصل mufsal, عقد 'akd, شلو shilv (*pl.* اشلا ashlá).—(*limb*) عضو 'uzv.—(*of wrist or ancle*) مچ much.—(*of meat*) قطعة kit'ah, وصلة vaslah.

JOINTLY, باتفاق bi-ittifák.

JOINTURE (*income settled on a wife*) صداق sadák, مهر mahr.

JOIST (*beam*), شه تیر shah-tír, ورگه vargah.

JOKE, *vide* JEST.—(*to play a practical joke*), کوك کردن kúk kardan.

JOLLY, *vide* PLEASANT.

JOLT, تکان takán, جنبش jumbish.

To JOLT (*trans.*), تکان دادن takán dádan.—(*intrans.*) جنبیدن jumbídan.

To JOSTLE, غربیله کردن gharbílah kardan.

JOT (*tittle, particle*), شوشه shúshah, همزه hamzah, نکته nuktah, ذره zarrah, شمه shammah.

JOURNAL, روزنامه rúz-námah, روزنامچه rúz-námchah, دفتر daftar.—(*account-book*) دستك dastak.

JOURNALIST, اخبار نویس akhbár-nivís.

JOURNEY, سفر safar, سیر sair, مسیر masír, کوچ kúch, مسافرت musáfarat.

To JOURNEY, راه رفتن ráh raftan, طی مسافرت نمودن tai-i-musáfarat nimúdan.

JOURNEYMAN (*hired workman*), مزدور muzdúr, اجیر ajír.

JOVIAL, دلشاد dil-shád, عیاش 'ayyásh, خوشگذران khwush-guzrán.

JOVIALITY, *vide* JOY.

JOY, خوشی khwushí, خوشدلی khwush-dilí, دلخوشی dil-khwushí, شادی shádí, دلشادی dil-shádí, شادمانی shádmání, خرمی khurramí, بهجت bihjat, ابتهاج ibtiháj, سرور surúr, مسرت masarrat, فرح farah, نشاط nishát, ابتسام ibtishám, اهتزاز ihtizáz, انبساط imbisát, طرب tarab, حظ hazz, انشراح inshiráh.

JOYFUL, مسرور masrúr, مشعوف mash-'úf, شاد shád, فرحناك farah-nák.

JOYFULLY, مسرورا masrúran.

JUBILEE, عید 'íd.

JUDAISM, یهودیت yahúdíyat.

JUDAS-TREE (*arbor Judæ, or Cercis Siliquastrum*), ارغوان arghaván.

JUDGE, قاضی kazí, حاکم hákim, حکم hakam, منصف munsif, داور dávar.—(*chief judge*) قاضی القضات kazíu-'l-kuzzát, رئیس حکام ra,ís-i-hukkám.

To JUDGE, داوری کردن dávarí kardan, قضا کردن kazá kardan.

JUDGMENT, *vide* OPINION, THOUGHT, DISCRETION.—(*decision*) فتوی fatvá, حکم شرع hukm-i-shar', دینونت dainúnat, تحکم tahakkum.—(*Judgment hall*) محکمه mahkamah.—(*Judgment seat*) داد گاه dád-gáh.—(*Day of Judgment*) روز قیامت rúz-i-kiyámat.

JUDICATURE, شریعت sharí'at.

JUDICIAL, شرعی shar'í.—(*judicial system*) قوانین شرعیه kavánín-i-shar'iyah.

JUDICIOUS, *vide* SENSIBLE, PROPER.

JUDICIOUSLY, عقلا 'aklan.

JUG, کوزه kúzah.

To JUGGLE, حقه بازی کردن hukkah-bází kardan.

JUGGLER, *vide* CONJURER.

JUGULAR VEIN, حبل الورید hablu-'l-varíd, رگ جان rag-i-ján.

JUICE, شیره shírah, عصاره 'usárah, عصیر 'asír.

JUICELESS, خشك khashk, بی آب bí-áb.

JUICINESS, طراوت tarávat, رطوبت rutúbat.

JUICY, آبدار áb-dár, تر tar, مرطوب martúb.

JUJUBE (*tree*), کنار kunar, کونار kúnár, سدر sidr, نبق nabk.—(*species of red jujube*) سنجد sinjid, عناب 'unnáb.

JULY, تموز tamúz.

To JUMBLE, مخلوط کردن makhlút kardan.

Jump (*spring*), جست jast, خیز khíz.

To Jump, جستن jastan (*root* جه jih), خیز کردن khíz kardan.—(*to jump about, skip*) جست و خیز کردن jast u khíz kardan.—(*to jump up*) بر جستن bar-jastan.

Junction, یکی شدن yakí-shudan, اتصال ittisál.

Juncture, *vide* Contingency.

June, حزیران hazírán.

Jungle, جنگل jangal.

Junior, کهتر kihtar, کوچکتر kúchik-tar, اصغر asghar.

Juniper, اردج ardaj.

Jupiter (*the planet*), مشتری mushtarí, برجیس birjís.

Jurisconsult, فقیه fakiyah, مجتهد mujtahid.

Jurisdiction, داوری dávarí, حکمرانی hukm-rání, حکومت hukúmat, قلمرو kalam-rau, قضا kazá.

Jurisprudence, فقه fikah, شرع shar'.

Jurist, *vide* Jurisconsult.

Jury (*assembly for trying a case*), مجلس عدالت majlis-i-'adálat.

Juryman, نفر مجلس عدالت nafar-i-majlis-i-'adálat.

Just, عادل 'ádil, داور dávar, داد رس dád-ras, بر barr.—(*exactly*) بدرستی bi-durustí, با دقت bá-dikkat, عیناً 'ainan, مقرراً mukarraran, جخ jakh (*vulg.*).—(*equitable*) با داد bá-dád, با صواب bá-saváb, عادلانه 'ádilánah, از روی عدالت az rúí-i-'adálat, روا ravá, جائز já,iz, راست rást, درست durust, صحیح sahíh, با انصاف bá-insáf.—(*just as*) بوقتی که bi-vaktí-kih.—(*just as they are*) کما کان kamá-kána.—(*just then*) در این بین dar ín bain.

Justice, عدل 'adl, عدالت 'adálat, معدلت ma'dalat, داد dád, انصاف insáf, نصفت nasifat, حق hakk, شریعت sharí'at, رشادت rishádat.—(*to do justice*) داد دادن dád dádan.—(*Minister of Justice*) وزیر عدلیه vazír-i-'adlíyah.

Justifiable, درست durust, راست rást, حق hakk.

Justification, عذر 'uzr, اعتذار i'tizár, تبری tabarrí, تزکیت tazkíyat, تصدیق tasdík, تنزیه tanzíh.

To Justify (*clear from guilt*), تزکیت کردن tazkíyat kardan, ابرا نمودن ibrá nimúdan, تنزیه نمودن tanzíh nimúdan.—(*render just*) عادل شمردن 'ádil shimurdan, بعدالت منسوب گردانیدن bi-'adálat mansúb gardánídan, صادق شمردن sádik shimurdan.—(*excuse or defend*) اعتذار نمودن i'tizár nimúdan, معذور داشتن ma'zúr dáshtan.—(*absolve*) معاف کردن mu'áf kardan, عفو نمودن 'afv nimúdan, خلاص کردن khalás kardan, آمرزیدن ámurzídan.

Justly, بالصواب bi-'s-saváb, عادلانه 'ádilánah, حسب شرع hasb-i-shar', با حق bá-hakk.—(*justly or unjustly, right or wrong*) حق یا ناحق hakk yá ná-hakk.

Justness, راستی rastí, درستی durustí, حق hakk, انصاف insáf.

To Jut out, آمدن ámadan.

Juvenile, جوان javán, خورد سال khwurd-sál, جاهل jáhil (*vulg.*).

Juvenility, جوانی javání, شباب shabáb.

Juxta-position, مقابله mukábalah, محاذی muhází, موازات mu,ázát.

K.

Kalyan (*Persian pipe, for smoking through water, similar to the Indian hukah*), قلیان kalyán, غلیان ghalyán, قلیون kalyún, نارگیله nár-gílah. The component parts of this apparatus are as follow:—(*the bottle*) قلیان kalyán, غلیان ghalyán.—(*upright stem fitting into the bottle*) میانه miyánah.—(*tube dipping into the water*), میل

آب míl-áb, شکاری shakárí.—(*straight tube applied to the mouth*) نی nai.—(*long flexible snake, used sometimes instead of the straight tube aforesaid*) نیپیچ nai-pích, مار پیچ már-pích.—(*ornamented ends of the snake*) زلفک zulfak.—(*mouthpiece of the tube or snake*) سر نی sar-i-nai.—(*lower end of the tube or snake*) ته نی tah-i-nai.—(*bowl or cup*) سر قلیان sar-i-kalyán.—(*perforated bottom of the bowl*) پنجره panjarah.—(*foot of the bowl, fitting on the upright stem*) ته سر tah-i-sar.—(*cover of the bowl*) باد گیر bád-gír.—(*small kalyan, carried in the hand*) قلیان دستی kalyán-i-dastí.—(*larger ditto, placed on the floor, and used with a long snake tube*) قلیان نیپیچ kalyán-i-nai-pích.—(*servant who prepares the kalyan*) قلیانچی kalyán-chí.—(*kalyan, the vessel of which containing the water is made of the shell of a cocoa-nut*) نارگیله nárgílah.—(*cases or holsters for carrying the kalyan, and its apparatus, &c., on horse-back*) قبل kubbul.—(*small chafing-dish attached to the saddle, for lighting the kalyan when on a journey*) قبل منقل kubbul-mankal.—(*brush for cleaning the kalyan*) گلو شورک gulú-shúrak.

KEEL (*of a ship or boat*), کیل kíl (*eur.*).

KEEN (*sharp*), تیز tíz.—(*eager*) آرزو مند árzú-mand, شوقمند shauk-mand, سر گرم sar-garm, شائق shá,ik.

To KEEP, داشتن dáshtan.—(*preserve or maintain*) نگاه داشتن nigáh dáshtan, مرعی داشتن mar'í dáshtan, بجا آوردن bi-já ávardan.—(*a promise*) وفا نمودن vafá nimúdan, نگاه داشتن nigáh dáshtan, از عهده بر آمدن az 'uhdah bar-ámadan, ادا کردن adá kardan.—(*to keep away*) باز ماندن báz-mándan.—(*to keep back*) باز داشتن báz-dáshtan.

KEEPER, محافظ muháfiz, مستحفظ mustahfiz, دارنده dárandah, نگهبان nigah-bán, حارس háris, مربی murabbí.—(*in composition*) دار dár, بان bán, جی jí, چی chí.

KEEPSAKE, یاد گار yád-gár, تذکره tazkirah.

KENNEL, سگخانه sag-khánah, تازی خانه tází-khánah.

KERCHIEF (*cloth worn on the head by women*), چارقد chár-kadd.

KERNEL, مغز maghz, هسته hastah, خسه khassah, دانه dánah.

KETTLE, دیگ díg, دیگچه dígchah, قدر kidr, کتری katrí.—(*large kettle or cauldron*) قزغان kazghán, پاتیل pátíl.

KETTLE-DRUM, نقاره nakkárah, کوس kús.

KEY, کلید kilíd, مفتاح miftáh, اچار áchár.—(*keystone, of an arch, &c.*) سنگ سر طاق sang-i-sar-i-ták.—(*false key*) کلید عملی kilíd-i-'amalí.—(*for musical instrument*) پیچ کوك píeh-i-kúk.

KEY-HOLE, سوراخ کلید surákh-i-kilíd.

KICK, لگد lagad.

To KICK, لگد زدن lagad zadan, پا زدن pá zadan.—(*with both hind feet*) جفتك انداختن juftak andákhtan.—(*as a gun*) لگد زدن lagad zadan.

KID, بزغاله buz-ghálah, کهره kahrah.

To KIDNAP, دزدیدن duzdídan.

KIDNAPPER, دزد duzd.

KIDNEY, گرده gurdah, کلوه kulvah.—(*beans*) لوبیه lúbiyah.

To KILL, کشتن kushtan, قتل نمودن katl nimúdan, هلاك ساختن halák sákhtan, بقتل رسانیدن bi-katl rasánídan.—(*to kill animals for food in the manner prescribed by Muhammadan law*) ذبح کردن zibh kardan, بسمل کردن bismil kardan (*vulg.*).

KILLER, قاتل kátil.

KILN, کوره kúrah.—(*for lime*) کورۀ گچ پزی kúrah-i-gach-pazí.—(*of bricks*) کورۀ آجر kúrah-i-ájur.

KIN, خویش khwísh.

KIND (*sort, species*), نوع nau' (*pl.*

انواع anvá'), جنس jins, قسم kism (*pl.* اقسام aksám), گونه gúnah, صنف sinf, قبيل kabíl, طور taur, وجه vajh, نمط namat, جور júr.—(*benevolent*) مهربان mihr-bán, شفيق shafík, مشفق mushfik, كريم karím, لطيف latíf, منعم mun'im, خير خواه khair-khwáh, نيكو كار níkú-kár, محسن muhsin, احسان ihsán.—(*in kind*) جنسی jinsí.—(*to be kind enough to*) التفات كرده iltifát kardah, لطف كرده lutf kardah.

To KINDLE, افروختن afrúkhtan, روشن كردن raushan kardan, مشتعل كردن mushta'al kardan.

KINDLY, دوستانه dústánah, از روی آشتی az rúí-i-áshtí.

KINDNESS, مهربانی mihr-bání, شفقت shafakat, خير خواهی khair-khwáhí, نيكو كاری níku-kárí, لطف lutf, ملاطفت mulátafat, عطوفت 'utúfat, تفقد tafakkud, احسان ihsán, خاطر داری khátir-dárí.

KINDRED, خويش khwísh.

KING, پادشاه pádishah, شاه sháh, شه shah, ملك malik, سلطان sultán, خاقان khákan, كی kai.—(*title of kings of Persia*) شاهنشاه sháhinsháh, شهنشه shahinshah.

KINGDOM, پادشاهی padisháhí, پادشاهت padisháhat, ملك mulk, مملكت mamlakat, سلطنت sultanat, دولت daulat, ملكوت malakút, فرمانده‌ی firmán-dihí.—(*division of natural objects in natural history*) مولود maulúd (*pl.* مواليد maválíd).—(*the three kingdoms of Nature*) مواليد ثلاثه maválíd-i-salásah, مواليد سه گانه maválíd-i-sih-gánah.—(*vegetable*) مولود نبات maulúd-i-nabát.—(*mineral*) مولود جماد maulúd-i-jamád.—(*animal*) مولود حيوان maulúd-i-haiván.

KINGFISHER, ماهی خورك máhí-khwurak, چلك chillik.

KINGLY, پادشاهانه pádisháhánah, خسروانه khusravánah.

KING'S-EVIL (*disease*), مرض جلد maraz-i-jild.

KINGSHIP, پادشاهی padisháhí, سلطنت sultanat.

KINK, پيچ و تاب pich u táb.

KINSHIP, جنسيت jinsíyat.

KINSMAN, خويش khwísh.

KIOSK (*summer-house*), كوشك kúshk, قصر kasr, عمارت 'imárat.

KISS, بوسه búsah, بوس bús, كام kam, ماچ mách (*vulg.*).

To KISS, بوسيدن búsídan, بوسه دادن búsah dádan, ماچ دادن mách dádan (*vulg.*).

KITCHEN, آشپز خانه ásh-paz-khánah, مطبخ matbakh *or* mattabakh.

KITE (*bird*), لاشه خور láshah-khwur, لاش خوار lásh-khwár, غليواز ghalívázh.—(*of paper*) كاغذك kághazak.—(*to fly a kite*) كاغذك هوا كردن kághazak havá kardan.

KITTEN, گربه بچه gurbah-bachah.

KLICK, غوغا ghaughá, آواز áváz.

To KLICK, غوغا نمودن ghaughá nimúdan, آواز دادن áváz dádan.

KNACK, سليقه salíkah, بند band.

KNAPSACK, كوله بار kúlah-bár, توشه دان túshah-dán.

KNAVE, فريبنده firíbandah, دستكج dast-kaj, غدار ghaddár, سر همبند sar-ham-band, حيله باز hílah-báz, دولاب باز dúláb-báz, دولابی dúlábí.

KNAVERY, عياری 'ayyárí, حيله بازی hílah-bází, سر همبندی sar-ham-bandí, دولاب بازی dúláb-bází, خيانت khiyánat.

KNAVISH, شرير sharír, دغاباز daghá-báz.

To KNEAD, آشردن áshurdan, خمير كردن khamír kardan, آغشتن ághashtan.

KNEE, زانو zánú.—(*knee-pan*) سر زانو sar-i-zánú, كنده زانو kundah-i-zánú.

To KNEEL, زانو زدن zánú zadan.—(*to cause to kneel*) بزانو نشانيدن bi-zánú nishánídan.—(*small carpet for kneeling on at prayers*) سجاده sujjádah, مصلا musallá.

KNIFE, كارد kárd.—(*butcher's knife*) بغدا bughdá, ساطور sátúr.—(*carving-knife*) كارد kárd.—(*shoemaker's knife*) شفره shifrah, نشكرده nishkardah.—(*pen-knife*) چاقو

chákú, کزلک kizlik, قلم تراش kalam-tirásh.—(*small knife worn in the same sheath with a dagger*) چکچکی chikchikí.—(*knife with a curved blade*), خنجر khanjar, جنبیه jambíyah. — (*large double-edged knife*) قمه kamah. — (*farrier's knife for paring hoofs*) سمتراش sum-tirásh. — (*knife-grinder*) چرخگر charkh-gar.

KNIGHT (*of an Order*), حامل نشان بزرگ hámil-i-nishán-i-buzurg.

KNIGHTHOOD, حمل نشان بزرگ haml-i-nishán-i-buzurg.

To KNIT, بافتن báftan.—(*knit-work*) بافته báftah. — (*knitting wires or needles*) میل míl.

KNITTER, پارچه باف párchah-báf.

KNOB, قبه kubbah, گره girih, لك luk, برآمدگی bar-ámadagí.

KNOBBY, قبه دار kubbah-dár, گره دار girih-dár.

KNOCK (*blow*) ضرب zarb, زد zad, مصادمه musádamah.—(*at door*) دستك dastak. — (*with the fist*) مشت musht, طپانچه tapánchah.

To KNOCK, زدن zadan, کوبیدن kúbídan, کوفتن kúftan.—(*to knock to pieces*) خرد کردن khurd kardan.—(*to knock down*) زمین انداختن zamín andákhtan.—(*knocked up*) ضعیف zá'íf, علیل 'alíl, مانده mándah.

KNOCKER (*of a door*), کوبه kúbah, کوه kúvah.

KNOLCOLE (*vegetable*), کلم شهری kalam-i-shahrí, قمری kumrí.

KNOT, گره girih, عقد 'akd, عقده 'ukdah, بند band.—(*tight knot*) گره کور girih-i-kúr.

To KNOT, گره زدن girih zadan.

KNOTTED, گرهدار girih-dár.

KNOTTY, پر گره pur-girih.

To KNOW, دانستن dánistan, شناختن shinákhtan, فهمیدن fahmídan, آگاه بودن ágáh búdan, اطلاع داشتن ittilá' dáshtan, مطلع بودن muttalí' búdan, واقف شدن vákif shudan, معلوم کردن ma'lúm kardan.—(*to come to know*) ملتفت شدن multafit shudan, منتقل شدن muntakil shudan.—(*a language*) بلد شدن balad shudan.—(*to let know*) خبر کردن kardan.

KNOWING, *vide* CLEVER.

KNOWINGLY, دانسته dánistah.

KNOWLEDGE, علم 'ilm, دانش dánish, دانائی dáná,í, معرفت ma'rifat, فهم fahm, وقوف vukúf هنر hunar, شعور shu'úr, حکمت hikmat, فطانت fatánat, سر رشته sar-rishtah.—(*superficial knowledge*) دانش خام dánish-i-khám, علم نا تمام 'ilm-i-ná-tamám.

KNOWN, معلوم ma'lúm, معروف ma'rúf, دانسته dánistah, شناخته shinákhtah, مشهور mash-húr.

KNUCKLE, بند انگشت band-i-angusht.

KRAN, قران krán.

KRORE (*a number, which in India signifies ten millions, and in Persia only five hundred thousand*), کرور karúr (*hind.*).

KURAN, قرآن kur,án, القرآن al-ku,rán, فرقان furkán, مصحف mushaf. — (*verse of the Kuran*) آیة áyat (*pl.* آیات áyát).—(*chapter of Kuran*) سوره súrah (*pl.* سور suvar). [The hundred and fourteen chapters of the Kuran are all divided into thirty sections called جزء juz' (*pl.* اجزاء ajzá,); and each section is subdivided into two portions called حزب hizb (*pl.* احزاب ahzáb.]

L.

LABEL, سر نامه sar-námah.

LABIAL, شفی shafí, شفهی shafahí.—(*the labial letters*) حروف شفهیه hurúf-i-shafahiyah.

LABORATORY, کار خانه کیمیا گر kár khánah-i-kímiyá-gar.

LABORIOUS, کار کن kár-kun, ساعی sá'í, جاهد jáhid.

LABOUR (*work*), كار kár, شغل shughl, محنت mihnat, عمل 'amal.—(*endeavour, action*) جد jidd, جهد jahd, سعی sa'í, کوشش kúshish, مبادرت mubádarat.—(*child-birth*) درد زه dard-i-zih, وضع حمل vaz'-i-haml.

To LABOUR, عمل نمودن 'amal nimúdan, كار كردن kár kardan.

LABOURER, كار گر kár-gar, عامل 'ámil (*pl.* عمله 'amalah *or* عمال 'ummál), فاعل fá'il (*pl.* فعله fa'alah). — (*for hire*) مزدور muzdúr, اجير ajír.—(*fellow-labourer*) همكار ham-kár.

LABYRINTH, طريق tarík (*pl.* اطرق atruk.

LAC (*gum*), لك lak.

LACE (*fine netting*), توره túrah, طور túr, شبكه shabakah. — (*cord or braid*) قيطان kaitán, بافته báftah, غايتان gháítán.—(*gold lace*) قلابتون بافته kulábatún-i-báftah, قيطان زر kaitán-i-zar.

To LACE, مشبك نمودن mushabbak nimúdan. — (*tie*) بستن bastan.

LACED (*embroidered*), مطرز mutarraz, منقش munakkash.

LACEMAN, مطرز mutarriz.

To LACERATE, دريدن darídan.

LACERATION, دريدگی darídagí.

LACK, *vide* WANT.—(*number of one hundred thousand*) لك lak (*hind.*). [In India, one hundred lacks make a krore, equal to ten millions; but in Persia, the krore contains only five lacks.]

LACKEY, نوكر naukar.

LACONIC, مختصر mukhtasar.

LACONICALLY, مختصرا mukhtasaran.

LACQUER, روغن raughan, روغن كمان raughan-i-kamán.

LAD, كودك kúdak, طفل tifl, پسرك pisarak.

LADDER, نردبان nardubán, پله pillah, سد sidd, سلم sullam, اورچين úrchín.—(*rope-ladder*) كمند kamand. — (*scaling-ladder*), نردبان nardubán.—(*naval term*) پسله pillah.

To LADE, بار كردن bár kardan, حمل كردن haml kardan.

LADLE, معلقه ma'lakah, آبگردان áb-gar-dán.

LADY, بيبی bíbí, كريمه karímah.—(*of high rank*) خانم khánam, بيگم begum, بانو bánú. —(*of inferior rank*), خاتون khátún.

LADY-LIKE, لطيف latíf, مؤدب mu,-addab.

To LAG (*loiter behind*), عقب افتادن 'akab úftádan, در پس افتادن dar-pas uftádan.

LAIR, كنام kunám.

LAKE, درياچه daryáchah, غدر ghudar, بركه birkah.

LAMB, بره barrah. — (*newly born lamb*) بره املك barrah-i-amlik.

LAME, لنگ lang, شل shal, زمين گير zamín-gír.

To LAME, شل كردن shal kardan.

LAMENESS, لنگی langí, زمين گيری zamín-gírí.

To LAMENT, زاری نمودن zárí nimúdan, گريه كردن giryah kardan, نالش كردن nálish kardan.—افسوس خوردن afsús khwurdan.

LAMENTABLE, مستمند mustmand, دلسوز dil-súz, تاسف خيز ta,assuf-khíz.

LAMENTATION, نوحه nauhah, نوحه گری nauhah-garí, ناله nálah, عزا 'azá, عزا داری 'azá-dárí, گريه giryah, زاری zárí, شيون shívan, فغان fighán, جزع و فزع jaza' u faza', نياح niyáh, تعزيه داری ta'ziyah-dárí.

LAMENTER, ناله زن nálah-zan, نوحه گر nauhah-gar.

LAMP, چراغ chirágh, سراج siráj.—(*street lamp*) فانوس fánús.—(*small earthenware lamp*) چراغ مشكی chirágh-i-mushkí.

LAMP-BLACK, دوده dúdah.

LAMPOON, هجو hajv, بد نام bad-nám.

To LAMPOON, هجو نمودن hajv nimúdan.

LAMPOONER, هجو ساز hajv-sáz.

LAMPREY (*fish*), مرينه murínah (*eur.*).

LANCE, نيزه naizah, رمح rumh. (*Vide* JAVELIN.)

To LANCE, نيشتر زدن nishtar zadan.

LANCER (*soldier*), سرباز نیزه دار sar-báz-i-naizah-dár.

LANCET, نیشتر níshtar, نشطر nashtar (*obs.*).

LAND, *vide* EARTH, GROUND, COUNTRY. — (*opposed to sea*) خشکی khushkí, بر barr. — (*opposed to swamp*) جلگه julgah.—(*dry land, watered only by rains*) زمین دیمی zamín-i-daimí, زمین دیمانی zamín-i-daimání, زمین بخس zamín-i-bakhs.—(*wet land, watered by wells, rivers, &c.*) زمین فاریابی zamín-i-fáryábí, زمین آبی zamín-i-ábí.—(*land planted with trees*) زمین مشجر zamín-i-mushajjar, درختزار dirakht-zár. —(*hilly land*) زمین تلال zamín-i-talál.—(*barren land*) زمین غیر مثمر zamín-i-ghair-i-musmir, زمین بی بر zamín-i-bí-bar, شوره زمین shúrah-zamín.—(*unclaimed land, belonging to no one*) زمین مجهول المالك zamín-majhúlu-'l-málik.—(*by land*) از راه خشکی az ráh-i-khushkí, براً barran.

TO LAND (*trans.*) بر کنار نهادن bar kanár nihádan.— (*intrans.*) بکنار آمدن bi-kanár ámadan.

LANDING-STAGE, اسکله askalah.

LANDHOLDER, زمیندار zamín-dár, رب الارض rabbu-'l-arz, مالك زمین málik-i-zamín.

LANDLORD, *vide* HOST.

LANDMARK, نشان سر زمین nishán-i-sar-zamín, نشان حد nishán-i-hadd.

LANDSCAPE, چشم انداز chashm-andáz.

LAND-TAX, مال دیوان mál-i-díván.

LANE, کوچه kúchah, کو kú.

LANGUAGE, زبان zabán, لغت lughat, سخن sukhun, کلام kalám, لسان lisán.—(*vernacular*) لغت lughat, خاص زبان kháss-zabán.—(*teacher of languages*) مدرس mudarris, معلم mu'allim, منشی munshí. [This word properly signifies a secretary or scribe. It is used in the sense here given only in India.]

LANGUID, سست sust, فاتر fátir, مانده mándah.

LANGUOR, فتور futúr, فترت fatrat, نقاهت nakáhat, ماندگی mándagí, سستی sustí.

LANK, لاغر lághir, نزار nizár.

LANKNESS, لاغری lághirí, نزاری nizárí.

LANTERN, فانوس fánús.—(*portable folding lantern*) فانوس فنر fánús-i-fanar.—(*Chinese lantern*) قندیل kindíl. — (*magic lantern*) فانوس شعبده fánús-i-shu'badah.

LAP, دامن dáman, کنار kinár.

TO LAP, لیسیدن lísídan.

LAP-DOG, سگ کوچك sag-i-kúchik.

LAPIDARY, جواهری javáhirí, جوهری jauharí, سنگتراش sang-tirásh.

LAPIS-LAZULI, لاجورد lájavard.

LAPPET, چین chín, دامن dáman.

LAPSE, سهو sahv.—(*lapse of time*) مرور murúr.

TO LAPSE, افتادن uftádan, طول کشیدن túl kashídan. (*Vide* TO ELAPSE.)

LAPSUS LINGUÆ, زلت لسانی zallat-i-lisání.

LAPWING, هدهد hudhud, شانه سر shánah-sar, مرغ سلیمانی murgh-i-sulaimání.

LARBOARD, طرف چپ taraf-i-chap.

LARCENY, دزدی duzdí.

LARD, چربی خوك charbí-i-khúk.

LARDER, حوائج خانه hawá,ij-khánah, گنجه ganjah.

LARGE, *vide* BIG, NUMEROUS.

LARGENESS, *vide* BIGNESS.

LARGESSE, دهش dihish, انعام in'ám.

LARK, چکاوه chakávah, چکاوك chakávuk, قنبره kumbarah, قازلاق kázlák.—(*crested lark*) کلکلاتی kulkulátí.—(*large crested lark*) چغول chughúl.

LARKSPUR (*flower*), زبان در قفا zabán dar kafá.

LARYNX, نای گلو náí-i-gulú.

LASCIVIOUS, مست mast, شهوتی shahvatí, نفس پرست nafs-parast, بد نفس bad-nafs.

LASCIVIOUSNESS, مستی mastí, نفس

پرستی nafs-parastí, بد نفسی bad-nafsí.

LASH, زبان قمچی zabán-i-kamchí, زه قمچی zih-i-kamchí.

To LASH, قمچی زدن kamchí zadan.

LASS, دختر dukhtar, صبیه sabíyah.

LASSITUDE, خستگی khastagí, ماندگی mándagí, سستی sustí, تعب ta'b.

LASSO, کمند kamand.

LAST, پسترین pastarín, پسین pasín, آخر ákhir, آخرین ákhirín, موءخر mu,akhkhar, وا پسین vá-pasín.—(*at last*) نهایت niháyat, آخر ákhir, بالاخره bi-'l-ákhirah, عاقبة الامر ákibatu - 'l - amr, باری bárí. — (*last week*) هفته قبل haftah-i-kabl, هفته گذشته haftah-i-guzashtah.—(*last month*) ماه قبل máh-i-kabl, ماه گذشته máh - i - guzashtah.—(*last year*) سال قبل sál-i-kabl, سال گذشته sál - i - guzashtah.—(*last night*) دوش dúsh, دیشب díshab, دیشو díshav (*vulg.*).—(*last day of the month*) سلخ salkh.—(*shoemaker's last*) فرزوم furzúm.

To LAST (*continue*), ماندن mándan, پایدار بودن páyadár búdan, پاینده بودن páyandah búdan, دائم بودن da,im búdan, دوام داشتن davám dáshtan, قائم بودن ká,im búdan, بقا داشتن baká dáshtan, پائیدن pá,ídan, امتداد دادن imtidád dádan, طول کشیدن túl kashídan.—(*suffice*) کفایت کردن kifáyat kardan.

LASTING, مستمر mustamirr, مستدام mustadám, دائم dá,im.

LASTLY, آخر الامر ákhiru'-l-amr, حاصل الامر hásilu-'l-amr.

LATCH, قفل kufl (*pl.* اقفال akfál).

LATCHET, چکمه بند chakmah-band.

LATE, دیر dír, عصراً 'usran.—(*lately*) *vide* NEWLY, AGO. — (*deceased*) مرده murdah, فوت شده faut-shudah, متوفی mutavaffí, رفته raftah, سابق sábik.—(*deceased, alluding to a Musulman*) مغفور maghfúr (*the forgiven*), مرحوم marhúm (*one who has received mercy*), خلد مکان khuld-makán (*whose abode is in Paradise*), جنت آشیان jannat-áshyán (*whose resting-place is in the heavens*), بهشت معاد bihisht-mi'ád. — (*to be late*) تاخیر کردن ta,khír kardan, دیر شدن dír shudan, دیر آمدن dír ámadan.

LATENESS, دیری dírí.

LATENT, *vide* SECRET.

LATERAL, جانبی jánibí.

LATH, چوب chúb.

LATHE (*turner's*), خراد kharád, آلت خراطی álat-i-kharátí.

LATHER, کف kaf.—(*of soap*) کف صابون kaf-i-sábún.

LATIN, لاتن látin (*eur.*), لاتین látín (*eur.*).

LATITUDE, عرض 'arz, پهنائی pahná,í. —(*freedom*) آزادی ázádí.—(*degree of latitude*) درجه عرض darajah-i-'arz.

LATRINE, مخرج makhraj, ادبخانه adab-khánah.

LATTER, باز پس báz pas, آخرین ákhirín, ثانوی sánaví.

LATTERLY, چند وقت قبل از این chand vakt kabl az ín, چندی قبل از این chandí kabl az ín.

LATTICE, شبکه shabakah, شباکه shubbákah, مشبك mushabbak.—(*latticed window*) پنجره panjarah.

To LAUD, *vide* To PRAISE.

LAUDABLE, ستوده sitúdah, مستحسن mustahsan, حمید hamíd, واجب مدح vájib-i-madh.

LAUDANUM, لادن ládan, روح افیون rúh-i-ifyún, جوهر تریاك jauhar-i-tiryák.

To LAUGH, خندیدن khandídan, خنده کردن khandah kardan.—(*ridicule*) استهزا نمودن istihzá nimúdan, مزاح کردن mizáh kardan, مسخره کردن maskharah kardan, ریشخند کردن ríshkhand kardan.

LAUGHABLE, با خنده bá-khandah, مضحك muzhik.

LAUGHER, ضاحك záhik.

LAUGHING, متبسم mutabassim.—(*laughing-stock*) مضحکه muzhikah, مسخره maskharah.

LAUGHTER, خنده khandah, قهقهه kahkahah, ضحك zahak.

To LAUNCH, باب انداختن bi-áb andákhtan.
LAUNDRESS, رختشو rakht-shú, قصار kassár.
LAUNDRY, رخت شو خانه rakht-shú-khánah.
LAUREL, غار ghár, دهمست dahmast.
LAVA, مواد مذابه mavádd-i-muzábah.
LAVATION, غسل ghusl, شست و شو shust u shú.
LAVATORY, غسل خانه ghusl-khánah.
To LAVE, *vide* To WASH.
LAVER, لگن lagan, طشت tasht, طاس tás.
LAVISH, مسرف musrif, مسروف masrúf.
To LAVISH, اسراف کردن isráf kardan, بر باد دادن bar bád dádan.
LAVISHLY, مسروفاً masrúfan.
LAW (*Divine*) شرع shar', شریعت sharí'at. — (*common law*) عرف 'urf.—(*science of law*) فقه fikah, علم فقه 'ilm-i-fikah. (*Vide* CUSTOM, REGULATION.)
LAW-COURT, دیوانخانه عدلیه díván-khánah-i-'adlíyah.
LAWFUL, حلال halál, مسنون masnún مباح mubáh, روا ravá, جائز já,iz, شرعی shar'í, ندب nadb. [A man's actions are, by the Shi'ah doctors, pronounced to be: واجب vájib, *or* فرض farz, *a lawful and imperative act, which it is a sin to leave undone;* مستحب mustahabb, *or* سنت sunnat, *an act which it is lawful and right to do, but which to omit does not amount to a sin;* مباح mubáh, *or* حلال halál, *a lawful act, which it is neither meritorious to perform, nor sinful to omit;* حرام harám, *the reverse of* واجب vájib, *an unlawful act, which it is sinful to commit, and meritorious to avoid;* مکروه makrúh, *the reverse of* مستحب mustahabb, *an act which is not unlawful and sinful, but which had better be avoided.*]
LAWFULLY, شرعاً shar'an, موافق شرع muváfik-i-shar'.
LAWFULNESS, حل hill, حلالیت halálíyat.
LAW-GIVER, شارع shári', مدبر mudabbir.
LAWLESS, بیناموس bí-námús. — (*wicked*) شریر sharír, فاسد fásid.
LAW-SUIT, دعوی da'vá, مرافعه muráfa'ah, نزاع nizá', لجاج lajáj.
LAWN, چمن chaman.
LAWYER, اهل فقه ahl-i-fikah, فقیه fakíh, ملا mullá.
LAX, سست sust, رخو rakhv.
LAXATIVE, مسهل mus-hil, ملین mulayyin.
LAXITY, سستی sustí, رخاوت rakhávat.
LAY, *vide* SONG.
To LAY, گذاشتن guzáshtan, نهادن nihádan, وضع کردن vaz' kardan, گذاردن guzárdan, قرار دادن karár dádan.—(*eggs*) بیضه نهادن baizah nihádan, تخم کردن tukhm kardan. —(*a wager*) شرط بستن shart bastan, بحث کردن bahs kardan.—(*a meal*) غذا حاضر کردن ghizá házir kardan, سفرا پهن کردن sufarrá pahn kardan. — (*a telegraph*) کشیدن kashídan.—(*dust*) خاکرا فرو ماندن khákrá furú mándan.—(*to lay aside*) بر یك طرف نهادن bar yak taraf nihádan. — (*to lay before, submit*) پیش داشتن písh dáshtan, تقدیم نمودن takdím nimudan.—(*to lay out a garden*) ایجاد کردن íjád kardan.
LAYER, ته tah.—(*in layers*) به ته bi-tah.
LAZARET, بیمار خانه bímár-khánah.
LAZILY, بسستی bi-sustí, بکاهلی bi-káhilí, بتنبلی bi-tambalí.
LAZINESS, تنبلی tambalí, سستی sustí, کاهلی káhilí.
LAZY, تنبل tambal, سست sust, کاهل káhil.
LEAD, سرب surb, رصاص rasás.—(*white lead*) سفیدا safídá.—(*red lead*) شنگرف shangarf, سرنج suranj, زنجفره zinjifrah.—(*black lead*) سرمه surmah, کحل kuhl.—(*plummet for sounding at sea*) بلت bult.

To LEAD, بردن burdan, کشیدن kashídan, هدایت کردن hidáyat kardan, دلالت کردن dalálat kardan, راه نمودن ráh nimúdan.—(*to lead forth*) بدر بردن bi-dar burdan.

LEADEN, سربی surbí.

LEADER, *vide* CHIEF, GUIDE.—(*one who goes first*) پیشرو písh-rau, مقدم mukaddam, اول avval.

LEADING (*principal*), عمده 'umdah. — (*leading to, tending*) مؤدی mu,addí, مبلغ muballigh, مائل má,il. — (*leading-rein, long rein for a led horse*) یدك کشی yadak-kashí.

LEAF, برگ barg, ورق varak.—(*of paper, sheet*) ورق varak, تخته takhtah.—(*of a book*) صحیفه sahífah, ورق varak.—(*of a door*) لنگه در lingah-i-dar.

LEAFLESS, بی برگ bí-barg, برهنه barahnah.

LEAFY, برگ دار barg-dár, پر برگ pur-barg.

LEAGUE (*parasang, about three miles and three-quarters*), فرسخ farsakh, فرسنگ farsang. (*Vide also* PLOT, PARTNERSHIP.)

To LEAGUE, عهد نمودن 'ahd nimúdan, پیمان بستن paimán bastan.

LEAK, شکاف shikáf, رخنه rikhnah.

To LEAK (*exude*), تراویدن tarávídan, چکیدن chakídan, چکه کردن chakkah kardan.—(*ship*) آب تو دادن áb tú-dádan.

LEAKAGE, چکه chakkah.

LEAKY (*roof, &c.*) چکه دار chakkah-dár.—(*ship*) آب بالا دهنده áb-bálá-dihandah, که چکه میکند kih chakkah míkunad.

LEAN (*thin*), لاغر lághir, نزار nizár, ضعیف za'íf.

To LEAN (*trans.*), تکیه زدن takyah zadan, اتکا نمودن ittiká nimúdan. —(*intrans.*) مائل بودن má,il búdan.

LEANNESS, لاغری lághirí, نزاری nizárí, ضعیفی za'ífí.

To LEAP, جستن jastan, خیز کردن khíz kardan.

LEAP-YEAR, سال کبیسه sál-i-kabísah.

To LEARN, آموختن ámúkhtan, تحصیل کردن tahsíl kardan, یاد گرفتن yád giriftan.—(*study*) درس گرفتن dars giriftan, مطالعه کردن mutála'ah kardan, تعلیم کردن ta'lím kardan, اقتباس کردن iktibás kardan.

LEARNED, دانا dáná, عالم 'álim, عارف 'árif, دانشمند dánish-mand, فاضل fázil, حکیم hakím, علام 'allám, آموخته ámúkhtah, مسلط musallat, عاقل 'ákil.

LEARNER, متعلم muta'allim.

LEARNING, دانش dánish, علم 'ilm, تحصیل tahsíl, معرفت ma'rifat, حکمت hikmat.

LEASE, اجاره ijárah, کرایه kiráyah, سند sanad.

To LEASE (*trans.*) اجاره دادن ijárah dádan.—(*intrans.*) اجاره گرفتن ijárah giriftan.

LEAST, کمترین kamtarín, کوچکترین kúchiktarín, کهترین kihtarín, خردترین khurdtarín, اصغر asghar, اقل akall.—(*at least*) اقلاً akallan, باری bárí, لا اقل lá-akall, دست کم dast-i-kam.—(*not in the least*) هرگز نه hargiz nah, هیچ گاه نه híchgáh nah.

LEATHER, چرم chirm, پوست púst, جلد jild. — (*Russia leather*) بلغار bulghár, بلخال bulkhál (*vulg.*).—(*ox-hide leather*) جیر jír.—(*scented leather*) ادیم adím.—(*shagreen*) ساغری sághari, سغری saghari.—(*strong leather of horse or ass skin*) کیموخت kímúkht.—(*sheep-skin*) تیماج tímáj.—(*solid leather*) سختیان sákhtíán.—(*worker in leather—maker of belts, quivers, holsters, &c., in embroidered leather*) ترکش دوز tarkashdúz.

LEATHERN, چرمین chirmín.—(*leathern wallet*) انبان ambán. — (*leathern purse*) همیان himyán, همیانه himyánah.—(*leathern cover or bag, to protect a box or package from rain*) خام khám.

LEAVE, اجازت ijázat, اذن izn, پروانگی parvánagí, اباحت ibáhat, رضا razá, رخصت rukhsat, دستور dastúr, دستوری dastúri, جواز javáz.—(*on privilege leave*) ماذوناً و موقتاً ma,zúnan va muvakkatan.

To LEAVE, گذاشتن guzáshtan, ترك كردن tark kardan, هجر نمودن hajr nimúdan, دست بر داشتن dast bardáshtan.—(*bid adieu*) رخصت گرفتن rukhsat giriftan, مرخص شدن murakhkhas shudan, وداع كردن vidá' kardan, پدرود گفتن pidrúd guftan, هليدن hilídan.—(*to leave off, cease*) وا ايستادن vá-ístádan, باز ايستادن báz-ístádan, قطع شدن kat' shudan, منقطع شدن munkati' shudan, موقوف بودن maukúf búdan, فراغت كردن farághat kardan.—(*give up*) *vide* To ABANDON, To LEAVE.—(*to go on leave*) اذن گرفتن izn giriftan, مرخص شدن murakhkhas shudan.

LEAVEN, مايه máyah, خمير مايه khamír-máyah.—(*leavened bread*) نان خميرى nán-i-khamírí.

To LEAVEN, ور آوردن var-ávardan.—(*to be leavened*) ور آمدن var-ámadan.

LEAVINGS, بقيه bakíyah, باقيات bákiyát, بقايا bakáyá, پس مانده pasmándah, تتمه tatammah, فضله fazlah.—(*of a feast*) پس مانده pasmándah, ته سفره tah-i-sufrah, الوش ulúsh.

LECHEROUS, نفس پرست nafs-parast, شهوتى shahvatí, مست mast.

LECHERY, نفس پرستى nafs-parastí, شهوت shahvat, مستى mastí.

LECTURE, درس dars, سبق sabak, تقرير takrír.

To LECTURE, تدريس كردن tadrís kardan.

LECTURER, واعظ vá'iz, مدرس mudarris.

LEDGE, *vide* RIDGE.

LEDGER, دفتر daftar.

LEECH, زلو zalú, زالو zálú.—(*to apply a leech*) زالو انداختن zálú andákhtan.

LEEK, گندنا gandaná.

To LEER, چشمك زدن chashmak zadan.

LEES (*dregs*), درد durd, فضله fazlah, خلط khilt.

LEFT (*remaining*), باقى bákí, مانده mándah, تتمه tatammah, متروك matrúk.—(*not right*) چپ chap, يسار yasár, شمال shimál.—(*left-handed*) چپ دست chap-dast, شمالى shimálí, كار كن بدست چپ kár-kun bi-dast-i-chap.

LEG, ساق sák, پا pá.—(*bone of leg*) قلم پا kalam-i-pá.—(*to be on one's legs*) در سر پا بودن dar sar-i-pá búdan.

LEGACY, ميراث míras, ارث irs, تركة tarkah, متروكه matrúkah.

LEGAL, *vide* LAWFUL.

LEGALITY, مشروعيت mashrú'íyat.

To LEGALIZE, حلال ساختن halál sákhtan, شرعى ساختن shar'í sákhtan.

LEGATE, مرسل mursal, ايلچى ílchí, سفير safír.

LEGATEE, وارث váris, ارث گير irsgír.

LEGATION, سفارت sifárat, سفارت خانه sifárat-khánah.

LEGEND, افسانه áfsánah, روايت riváyat, حكايت hikáyat, تذكره tazkarah.—(*inscription*) رقم rakm, رسم rasm, كتابت kitábat.

LEGENDARY, افسانه آمیز áfsánah-ámíz.

LEGERDEMAIN, بازيگرى bází-garí, حقه بازى hukkah-bází.

LEGIBLE, خوانا khwáná, خونا khwaná.

LEGIBLY, صاف صاف sáf-sáf.

LEGION, گروه gurúh, تمن tuman.

To LEGISLATE, قانون ساختن kánún sákhtan, وضع احكام نمودن vaz'-i-ahkám nimúdan.

LEGISLATIVE, قوانينى kavánīní.

LEGISLATOR, واضع قانون ، vází'-i-kánún, واضع احكام vází'-i-ahkám, واضع الناموس vázi'u-'n-námús, واضع القانون vázi'u-'l-kánún.

LEGISLATURE, حكمرانى hukm-rání, حكومت hukúmat, فرمانروائى firmán-ravá,í, داورى dávarí.

LEGITIMACY, *vide* LAWFULNESS.—(*birth*) حلالزادگى halál-zádagí.

LEGITIMATE, *vide* LAWFUL.—(*born*) حلالزاده halál-zádah.

LEISURE, فراغت farághat, فرصت fursat.—(*at leisure*) هنگام بی کاری hangám-i-bí-kárí, به وقت فرصت bi-vakt-i-fursat.

LEISURELY, آهسته áhistah.

LEMON, ليمو límú, ليمون límún, شاه ليمو shah-límú. — (*sweet lemon*) بكرئى bakru,í.

LEMONADE, افشرده afshurdah, شربت آبليمو sharbat-i-áb-límú.

TO LEND (*money*), قرض دادن karz dádan. — (*things*) عاريت دادن 'áriyat dádan.

LENDER, قرض دهنده karz-dihandah.

LENGTH (*things*) طـول túl, درازى dirází.—(*time*) طول túl.—(*at full length*) على التفصيل 'alá.'t-tafsíl.

TO LENGTHEN, دراز كردن diráz kardan, طويل كردن tavíl kardan.

LENGTHENED, مديد madíd.

LENGTHWAYS, درازنه dirázanah.

LENIENT, ملايم muláyam, مورحم murahhim.

LENITIVE, ملين mulayyin.

LENITY, مدارات mudárát, ملايمت muláyamat.

LENS, عدسه 'adasah.

LENT (*fast*), روزه rúzah.

LENTILS, عدس 'adas.

LEOPARD, پلنگ palang, قپلان kaplán.—(*hunting leopard*) يوز yúz.

LEPER, مبروص mabrús, بريص barís, مجذوم majzúm, پيس pís.

LEPROSY (*white*), برص baras, مبروصى mabrúsí, پيسى písí.— (*black*) جذام juzám. [This is the eating leprosy, a fearful disease, in which the flesh rots from the bones.]

LEPROUS, پيس pís, ابرص abras.

LESS (*in quantity*), كم kam, كمتر kamtar, اقل akall.—(*less in size*) كوچكتر kúchiktar, خردتر khurdtar, اصغر asghar. — (*less in rank or degree*) كهتر kihtar.—(*rather less*) كسرى kasrí, خشكترك khushktarak, كمترك kamtarak. — (*much less*) تا چه رسد tá chih rasad, كجا ماند kujá mánad.

LESSEE, اجاره دار ijárah-dár, كرايه دار kiráyah-dár.

TO LESSEN, كم كردن kam kardan, كوچك كردن kúchik kardan, تخفيف نمودن takhfíf nimúdan. (*Vide* TO DIMINISH.)

LESSON, سبق sabak, درس dars.—(*to take lessons*) درسرا خواندن darsrá khwándan.

LESSOR, اجاره دهنده ijárah-dihandah, كرايه دهنده kiráyah-dihandah.

LEST, مبادا mabádá, تا كه tá kih, از ترسيكه az tarsí kih.

LET (*hired out*), مستغل mustaghall, اجير ajír, مكرى mukrá.

TO LET (*allow*), دادن dádan, گذاشتن guzáshtan, اجازت دادن ijázat dádan, اذن دادن izn dádan.—(*let on hire*) بكرايه دادن bi-kiráyah dádan, اجاره دادن ijárah dádan, غله كردن ghallah kardan, مستغل دادن mustaghall dádan.—(*let go*) ول كردن vil kardan, گذاشتن guzáshtan, رها كردن rihá kardan, خلاص كردن khalás kardan.—(*let loose*) رها كردن rihá kardan, گشاده كردن gushádah kardan, باز كردن báz-kardan, ول كردن vil kardan.—(*let down, from a height*) رها دادن rihá dádan, فرو هشتن furú hishtan, هليدن hilídan.—(*let alone*) گذاشتن guzáshtan, واگذاشتن vá-guzáshtan.—(*to be let loose*) رها شدن rihá shudan, ول شدن vil shudan, باز شدن báz shudan.—(*to let down, pull down*) انداختن andákhtan, پائين آوردن pá,ín ávardan, پرت كردن part kardan.

LETHARGIC, پينكى زده pínakí zadah, سست sust.

LETHARGY, پينكى pínakí, سستى sustí.

LETTER (*of the alphabet*), حرف harf (*pl.* حروف hurúf).—(*capital*) حرف بزرگ harf-i-buzurg.—(*consonant*) حرف صحيح harf-i-sahih, حرف معرب harf-i-mu'rab.—(*long vowel*) حرف علت harf-i-'illat.—(*short vowel*) اعراب i'ráb, حركت harakat (*pl.* حركات harakát). — (*epistle*) خط khatt, مكتوب maktúb, نامه námah, مراسله murásalah, رقعه

ruk'ah, صحیفه sahífah, کاغذ kághaz, مکاتبه mukátabah, نوشته nivishtah, تحریر tahrír. — (*of a king*) فرمان firmán, رقم همایون rakm-i-humáyún, منشور manshúr, شقه shukkah.—(*of a prince or noble*) فرمان firmán, تعلیقه ta'líkah, پروانه parvánah, رقم rakm.—(*of a superior*) شریفه sharífah, تعلیقه ta'líkah, مفاوضه mufávazah, رقم rakm, مشرفه musharrafah, عنایتنامه 'ináyat-námah, نوازشنامه navázish-námah.—(*of an inferior to a superior*) عرض 'arz, عریضه 'arízah, نیاز نامه niyáz-námah, عرضداشت 'arz-dásht, ذریعه zarí'ah. —(*of recommendation*) سفارش نامه sifárish-námah, اعتبار نامچه i'tibár-námchah.—(*of apology*) اعتذار نامه i'tizár-námah.—(*of reproof*) ملامت نامه malámat-námah, عتاب نامه 'itáb-námah, خط توبیخی khat-i-taubíkhí.—(*of victory*) فتح نامه fath-námah. — (*of permission, licence*) جواز نامه javáz-námah.—(*of consolation*) تسلیت نامه tasliyat-námah. — (*of attestation*) شهادت نامه shahádat-námah. — (*of forgiveness and safety*) نامه اطمینان námah-i-itmínán, کاغذ خاطر جمعی kághaz-i-khátir-jam'í. —(*of condolence*) تعزیت نامه ta'ziyat-námah. — (*of submission*) اطاعت نامه itá'at-námah, نوشته تسلیم nivishtah-i-taslím.— (*of credit*) برات barát, کاغذ زر kághaz-i-zár.—(*of congratulation*), تهنیت نامه tahniyat-námah.—(*of passport*) راهداری ráh-dárí, تذکره tazkirah.—(*tittle of a letter*) طره turrah, شوشه shúshah. — (*sweep or tail of a letter*) دامن dáman.—(*unpointed letter, as* ا, ح, و, *&c.*) مهمله muhmalah.—(*pointed or dotted letter, as* ب, ج, ش, *&c.*) معجمه mu'jamah. —(*letter with one dot, as* ب, ج, ن) حرف موحده harf-i-múhadat. —(*with two dots, as* ت, ق) مثناة musnát.—(*with three dots, as* ث, ش) مثلثه muslasat. —(*with two dots above, as* ت) مثناة من فوقها musnátu min faukihá. — (*with two dots below, as* ی) مثناة من تحتها musnátu min tahtihá.

LETTERED, دانا dáná, عالم 'álim.

LETTUCE, کاهو kábú.

LEVÉE, سلام عام salám-i-'ámm, سلام salám.

LEVEL, برابر barábar, هموار hamvár, مسطح musattah, متسوی mutasavví.—(*level of the sea*) سطح sath.

To LEVEL, برابر ساختن barábar sákhtan, هموار ساختن hamvár sákhtan, مسطح نمودن musattah nimúdan.—(*a gun*), دیاق کردن dayák kardan, رو گرفتن rú giriftan.

LEVELNESS, برابری barábarí, همواری hamvárí.

LEVER, اهرم ahrum, دیلم dílum.

LEVERET, خرگوش بچه khar-gúsh-i-bachah.

LEVIABLE, قابل تحصیل kábil-i-tahsíl.

LEVIATHAN, لیویاثان lívíásán (*eur.*).

LEVITY, بهجت bihjat, سبکی subukí.

LEVY, طائفه tá,ifah.

To LEVY (*troops*), جمع آوری سپاه نمودن jam'-ávarí-i-sipáh nimúdan. —(*taxes*) خراج گذاردن khiráj guzárdan, باج قرار دادن báj karár dádan.

LEWD, نفس پرست nafs-parast, شهوتی shahvatí, مست mast.

LEWDNESS, نفس پرستی nafs-parastí, شهوت shahvat, مستی mastí.

LEXICOGRAPHER, اهل لغت ahl-i-lughat.

LEXICOGRAPHY, علم لغت 'ilm-i-lughat.

LEXICON, کتاب لغات kitáb-i-lughát.

LIABLE to, معرض mu'arraz, مستوجب mustaujib, سزاوار sazávár, متحمل mutahammil.

LIAISON, علاقه 'alákah.

LIAR, دروغگو durúgh-gú, کاذب kázib, کذاب kazzáb.

LIBEL, بد نام bad-nám, دشنام dushnám, مذمت mazammat, هجو hajv.

LIBELLER, بد نام نویس bad-nám-nivís, دشنام نویس dush-nám-nivís, مفتری muftarí.

LIBELLOUS, بد نامی bad-námí, دشنامی dush-námí.

LIBERAL, سخی sakhí, کریم karím, جواد javvád, گشاده دست gushá-dah-dast, جوانمرد javán-mard, منعم mun'im, وهاب vahháb, فیاض fayyáz, سامح sámih.

LIBERALITY, سخاوت sakhávat, سخا sakhá, کرامت karámat, مکرمت makrumat, جود júd, بذل bazl, جوانمردی javán-mardí, سماحت samáhat.

LIBERALLY, جوانمردانه javán-mar-dánah.

To LIBERATE, خلاص کردن khalás kardan, رستگار کردن rastagár kar-dan, رها کردن rihá kardan.

LIBERTINE, خوش گذران khwush-guz-rán, قلاش kallásh, رند rind, شید باز shaid-báz.

LIBERTINISM, خوش گذرانی khwush-guzrání, رندی rindí, شید بازی shaid-bází, فسق fisk.

LIBERTY, آزادی ázádí, آزادگی ázá-dagí, رها rihá, رهائی rihá,í, خلاص khalás, مخلصی mukhlasí, رستگاری rastagárí. (*Vide* MANUMISSION.) —(*to be at liberty to do anything*) آزاد بودن ázád búdan, ماذون بودن ma,zún búdan, اختیار داشتن ikh-tiyár dáshtan.

LIBIDINOUS, نفس پرست nafs-parast, شهوتی shahvatí, مست mast.

LIBRA, میزان mízán.

LIBRARIAN, کتابچی kitáb-čhí.

LIBRARY, کتب خانه kutub-khánah.

LICE, *vide* LOUSE.

LICENSE, *vide* LEAVE.

To LICENSE, گماشتن gumáshtan.

LICHEN, گل سنگ gil-i-sang.

LICIT, *vide* LAWFUL.

To LICK, لیسیدن lísídan.

LICTOR, عساول 'asával.

LID, سرپوش sar-púsh, سر sar.

LIE, دروغ durúgh, کذب kizb, زور zúr, ارجاف irjáf (*pl.* اراجیف arájíf).

To LIE, دروغ گفتن durúgh guftan.—(*to lie on the back*) سر بالا خوابیدن sar-bálá khwábídan, بر پشت خوابیدن bar pusht khwábídan.—(*to lie on the face*) دم رو خوابیدن dam-i-rú khwábídan, بر رو خوابیدن bar rú khwábídan.—(*to lie on one side*) یکپهلو خوابیدن yak-pahlú khwábídan, یکجنبه خوابیدن yak-jambah khwábídan. — (*to lie down*) دراز شدن diráz shudan, خوابیدن khwábídan, خسبیدن khusbídan, آرام کردن árám kar-dan, استراحت نمودن istiráhat ni-múdan, کپه کردن kappah kardan (*vulg.*).—(*with a woman*) همخوابی شدن ham-khwábí shudan.

LIEGE (*sovereign*) پادشاه pádisháh, ملک malk.—(*subject*) رعیت ra'iyat, وفا کیش vafá-kísh.

LIEU, عوض 'ivaz, جا já, مقام makám.

LIEUTENANT, نائب ná,ib.

LIEUTENANT-COLONEL, سرهنگ sar-hang, سرکرده sar-kardah.

LIFE, زندگی zindagí, زندگانی zinda-gání, زی zí, زیست zíst, عمر 'umr, حیات hayát, جان ján, عیش 'aish, روح rúh, روان raván, هستی hastí.—(*written narrative*) تذکره tazkarah, تاریخ ta,ríkh.—(*to restore to life*) احیا کردن ihyá kardan.—(*life in-terest*) استمتاع istimtá'.

LIFE-GUARDSMAN, همرکاب ham-rikáb.

LIFELESS, بیجان bí-ján, مرده mur-dah.

LIFETIME, عمر 'umr, مدت حیات muddat-i-hayát.

To LIFT, بر داشتن bar-dáshtan, افراشتن afráshtan, بالا کردن bálá kardan, بلند ساختن buland sákh-tan.—(*a fallen person or animal*) بر خیزانیدن bar-khízánídan.

LIGAMENT, عصب 'asb.

LIGATURE, بند band, بست bast.

LIGHT (*subs.*), روشنی raushaní, روشنائی raushaná,í, نور núr, نورانی núrání, نیر nayyir, تجلی tajallí, جلوه jilvah, ضیا ziyá, فروغ furúgh, شعاع shu'á'.—(*adj.*) روشن raushan, پر نور pur-núr, منور munavvar, منیر munír.—(*candle, &c.*), شمع sham', چراغ chirágh. — (*not heavy*) سبک subuk, خفیف khafíf. — (*to bring to light*) بمیدان آوردن bi-maidán ávardan, کشف

کشف کردن kashf kardan, ظاهر ساختن záhir sákhtan.—(*as colour*) واز váz, آبکی ábakí.

To LIGHT, روشن کردن raushan kardan, افروختن afrúkhtan, سوزانیدن súzánídan, آتش کردن átish kardan.

To LIGHTEN (*flash*), درخشیدن dirakhshídan, جهیدن jihídan.—(*lessen the weight*) تخفیف نمودن takhfíf nimúdan.

LIGHT-FINGERED, دزد duzd.

LIGHT-FOOTED, سبکپا subuk-pá.

LIGHT-HEADED, سبکسار subuk-sár.

LIGHT-HEADEDNESS, سبکساری subuk-sárí.

LIGHT-HEARTED, آزاده دل ázádah-dil.

LIGHT-HOUSE, منارت manárat (*pl.* مناور manávir), فانوس fánús, فنار fanár.

LIGHTLY, آهسته áhistah, سبک سارانه subuk-sáránah.

LIGHTNESS, سبکی subukí, خفت khiffat.

LIGHTNING, برق bark, صاعقه sá'ikah, درخش dirakhsh, یلدرم yildiram.

LIGHTS (*of the body*), شش shush.

LIGNEOUS, چوبین chúbín.

LIKE, چون chún, چو chú, همچون ham-chún, چنان chunán (generally pronounced chinán), بکردار bi-kirdár, بسان bi-sán, مانند mánand, مثل misl, مثال misál, حکم hukm.—(*in composition*) سا sá, آسا ásá, سار sár, وار vár, وش vash, سان sán, آشام áshám.—(*adjective*) برابر barábar, یکسان yak-sán, موافق muváfik, مطابق mutábik, همتا ham-tá, مشابه mushábih, همانا hamáná, مانند mánand, مثل misl, مماثل mumásil, معادل mu'ádil.

To LIKE, پسندیدن pasandídan, دوست داشتن dúst dáshtan, میل داشتن mail dáshtan.

LIKELIHOOD, معقولت ma'kúlat, احتمال ihtimál.

LIKELY (*probable*), محتمل muhtamal, اغلب aghlab, معقول ma'kúl, گویا gúyá.

To LIKEN, برابر ساختن barábar sákhtan, موافق ساختن muváfik sákhtan, همتا ساختن ham-tá sákhtan.—(*compare*) مقابله نمودن mukábalah nimúdan, تشبیه کردن tashbíh kardan, بر آورد کردن bar-ávard kardan.

LIKENESS (*portrait*), شبیه shabíh, تصویر tasvír, شکل shakl (*pl.* اشکال ashkál).—(*resemblance*) برابری barábarí, تمثیل tamsíl, مثال misál, تشبیه tashbíh, مشابهه mushábahah, شبه shibh, موافقت muváfakat, شباهت shabáhat, نمایش nimáyish, حکم hukm.

LIKEWISE, هم ham, نیز níz, ایضا aizan.

LIKING, میل mail.

LILAC, یاس کبود yás-i-kabúd, گل یاس gul-i-yás.—(*colour*) ارغوان arghaván.

LILY, سوسن súsan, زنبق zambak.—(*large white lily*) گل مریم gul-i-maryam.—(*water lily*) نیلوفر nailúfar, آبو ábú.—(*small blue spring lily*) ایلچی سوسن ílchí-i-súsan.—(*Japan lily*) زنبق تخم ژاپونی zambak-i-tukhm-i-zhápúní.

LIMB, عضو 'uzv (*pl.* اعضا a'zá), شلو shilv (*pl.* اشلا ashlá), جزء تن juz-i-tan.

To LIMB, بریدن burídan *or* burrídan.

LIME, آهک áhak.—(*fine plaster*) گچ gach.—(*quick-lime*) آهک خام áhak-i-khám, نوره núrah.—(*bird-lime*) کشمشک کاولی kishmishk-i-kávalí, دق dakk.—(*fruit*) لیمو límú.—(*sweet lime*) بکرئی bakru,í.

LIME-KILN, کوره گچپزی kúrah-i-gach-pazí.

LIME-WATER, آب آهک áb-i-áhak.

LIMIT, *vide* BOUNDS.

To LIMIT, محدود داشتن mahdúd dáshtan.

LIMITATION, حصر hasr, حد hadd.

LIMITED, محدود mahdúd.—(*to be limited*) محدود ماندن mahdúd mándan.

LIMITROPHE, متلاقی mutalákí.

To LIMN, کشیدن kashídan, تصویر کردن tasvír kardan, انگاشتن angáshtan.

LIMNER, *vide* PAINTER.

LIMP, نرم narm, لسم lasm. — (*in walking*), لنگی langí.
To LIMP, لنگیدن langídan.
LIMPID, زلال zulál, پاك pák, ناب náb.
LIMPIDITY, پاکی pákí, صافی sáfí.
LINE, سطر satar, خط khatt.—(*measuring line*) شاول shávul, ریسمانکار rísmán-kár. (*Vide* PLUMB-LINE.) — (*cord*) ریسمان rísmán, رشته rishtah.—(*of battle*) صف saff (*pl.* صفوف sufúf).—(*of a composition*) فقره fakarah. — (*of ships*) دسته dastah.—(*of railway*) رشته rishtah.—(*lines on the face and hands*) اسرار asrár.—(*military lines*) حدود حربیه hudúd-i-harbiyah. — (*for writing*) سطربندی satar-bandí.—(*for clothes*) رخت rakht.
LINEAGE, *vide* FAMILY, TRIBE.
LINEAL, همجنس ham-jins.
LINEAMENT, رخ rukh, چهره chihrah.
LINEN, کتان kattán, بز bazz.—(*fine linen*) کتان نازك kattán-názuk.
LINEN-DRAPER, بزاز bazzáz, پیله ور pílah-var.
To LINGER, *vide* To LOITER.
LINGUAL, لسانی lisání.
LINGUIST, زبان دان zabán-dán, زبان شناس zabán-shinás.
LINIMENT, مرهم marham.
LINING (*of a garment*), آستر ástur, بطانه batánah, أستر a,star.
LINK (*of a chain*) حلقه halkah.—(*torch*) مشعل mash'al.
To LINK, پیوند داشتن paivand dáshtan.
LINKED with, منوط به manút bí.
LINSEED, تخم کتان tukhm-i-kattán, بزر کتان bazr-i-kattán, بزرك bazrak.
LINSTOCK (*match*), فتیله fatílah, فلیته falítah (*vulg.*).
LINT, کتان kattán, فتیله fatílah.
LINTEL, عتبه 'atabah, آستانه ásitánah.
LION, شیر shír, اسد asad, ارسلان arslán, حیدر haidar, هزبر hizabr, لیث lais, سبع sabu', غضنفر ghazanfar, غرین gharín.—(*lioness*) شیر مادة shír-i-mádah, لبوة labvah, اسدة asadah.—(*lion's cub*) شبل shibl, شیر بچه shír-bachah.—(*sea-lion*) شیر بحر shír-i-bahr.—(*Order of the Lion and Sun*) نشان شیر و خورشید nishán-i-shír u khúrshíd.
LIP, لب lab, شفه shifah.
LIQUID (*subs.*), آب áb, آبی ábí.—(*adj.*) مذاب muzáb, ذائب zá,ib, سیال sayyál.
To LIQUIFY, گداختن gudákhtan.
LIQUOR (*fluid*), آب áb, ما má.—(*spirits*) عرق 'arak, شراب sharáb.
LIQUORICE, سوس sús, مهك mahk.
LISP, لکنت luknat.
To LISP, بد تلفظ کردن bad-talaffuz kardan, لکنت کردن luknat kardan.
LIST (*catalogue*), فهرست fihrist, تفصیل tafsíl, فرد fard, سیاهه siyáhah.—(*arena*) میدان maidán, معرکه ma'rakah.
To LIST (*heel over*), کج شدن kaj shudan, یك بری شدن yak-barí shudan (*Vide* To LISTEN.)
To LISTEN, گوش دادن gúsh dádan, مستمع بودن mustami' búdan, استماع کردن istimá' kardan.—(*in a bad sense*) تسمع نمودن tasammu' nimúdan.
LISTENER, مستمع mustami', سامع sámi'.
LISTLESS, غافل gháfil, سست sust.
LISTLESSLY, غفلتاً ghiflatan.
LISTLESSNESS, غفلت ghiflat, سستی sustí.
LITANY, دعا du'á.
LITERAL, لفظی lafzí, اصلی aslí.
LITERALLY (*verbatim*), لفظاً بلفظ lafzan bi-lafz.
LITERARY, اهل علم ahl-i-'ilm.
LITERATE, ادیب adíb.
LITERATURE, علم 'ilm, ادب adab.
LITHARGE, مرده سنگ murdah-sang, مردار سنگ murdár-sang.
LITHOGRAPHY, چاپ سنگی cháp-i-sangí.
LITHOTOMY, اخراج سنگ مثانه ikhráj-i-sang-i-masánah.
LITIGANT, مدعی mudda'í.
To LITIGATE, منازعت نمودن munáza'at nimúdan, خصومت نمودن khusúmat nimúdan.
LITIGATION, دعوی da'vá, قضیه kazí-

yah, منازعت munáza'at, خصومت khusúmat, لجاج lajáj, نزاع nizá'.

LITIGIOUS, نزاع دوست nizá'-dúst, لجوج lajúj, گله جو gilah-jú.

LITIGIOUSNESS, گله جوی gilah-júí, لجاجت lajájat.

LITTER (*sedan*), محمل mahmil.—(*for an elephant*) هودج haudaj, حوده haudah.—(*carried by mules*) تخت روان takht-i-raván.—(*camel panniers*) کجاوه kajávah. — (*of cubs, &c.*) گروه gurúh, مجموعه majmú'ah.—(*sweepings, rubbish*) ادبار idbár, اشقال ashkál, رشت rasht, خاکروبه khák-rúbah. — (*straw*) پوشال púshál, علف النگ 'alaf-ulang, پوش púsh, کاه káh.

To LITTER, تولید نمودن taulíd nimúdan, زادن zádan, زایدن záídan.

LITTLE (*in quantity*), اندک andak, کم kam, قلیل kalíl, خورده khwurdah, ذره zarrah.—(*small*) خرد khurd, خورد kkwurd, کوچک kúchik, صغیر saghír, که kih, پاچه páchah.—(*a little, some*) قدری kadrí, اندکی andakí, خورده khwurdah, جزوی juzví, شطری shatrí.—(*a little, short time*) قدری kadrí, یکچندی yak-chandí, اندکی andakí, زمان قلیل zamán-i-kalíl.—(*little by little*) کم کم kam kam, رفته رفته raftah raftah, بتدریج bi-tadríj. — (*too little*) خیلی کم khailí kam, پر کم pur kam.—(*but little*) کمی kamí.—(*ever so little*) اندک andak, ذره zarrah, شمه shammah.

LITURGY, قداس kuddás.

LIVE, زنده zindah, حی hayy.

To LIVE (*be alive*), زیستن zístan, زنده بودن zindah búdan, زندگی نمودن zindagí nimúdan. — (*pass life*) اوقات گذرانیدن aukát guzránídan, بسر بردن bi-sar burdan, زندگانی کردن zindagání kardan.—(*gain a livelihood*), گذران کردن guzrán kardan, گذران پیدا کردن guzrán paidá kardan, معاش تحصیل کردن ma'ásh tahsíl kardan.—(*dwell*) ساکن بودن sákin búdan, سکونت داشتن sukúnat dáshtan, مقیم بودن búdan, منزل داشتن manzil dáshtan.

LIVELIHOOD, روزی rúzí, معیشت ma'íshat, مدد معاش madad-i-ma'ásh, مدار معاش madár-i-ma'ásh, گذران guzrán.

LIVELINESS, خوشطبعی khwush-tab'í.

LIVELONG, همه hamah, تمام tamám.

LIVELY (*gay*), جلف jilf, خوشطبع khwush-tab'.

LIVER, جگر jigar, کبد kabid.—(*liver complaint*) درد جگر dard-i-jigar, سده جگر sudah-i-jigar.—(*one who lives*) زنده zindah.—(*a free-liver*) اهل صفا ahl-i-safá.

LIVERY, لباس libás, رخت rahkt.

LIVERY-STABLE, اسطبل istabl.

LIVERY-STABLE KEEPER, چهار پا دار chahár-pá-dár.

LIVID, زرد zard, سفید safíd.

LIVIDNESS, زردی zardí, سفیدی safídí.

LIVING (*food, &c.*), خوراک khwurák. —(*alive*) زنده zindah, حی hayy. (*Vide* LIVELIHOOD.)

LIZARD, چلپاسه chalpásah.—(*guana lizard*) سوسمار súsmár, بزمجه buzmajah, بزدوش buz-dúsh.—(*speckled lizard*) سام ابرص sámm-abras, ابرص abras.

LO! اینک ínak, هان hán, هین hín.

LOAD, بار bár, حمل haml.—(*load of a camel*) شتر وار shutur-vár, بار شتر bár-i-shutur.—(*of an ass*) خروار khar-vár, خلوار khal-vár (*vulg.*).—(*of a man*) کوله بارچه kúlah-bárchah, کوله kúlah.

To LOAD, بار کردن bár kardan, حمل کردن haml kardan.—(*a gun*) پر کردن pur kardan.

LOADSTONE, سنگ آهنربا sang-i-áhan-rubá, سنگ مقناطیس sang-i-maknátís.

LOAF, نان nán, قرص نان kurs-i-nán.

LOAM, گل gil, خاک khák.

LOAMY, گلی gilí, خاکی khákí.

LOAN (*of money, &c.*), قرض karz, وام vám, بده bidih, دین dain.—(*of an article*) عاریت 'áriyat, استعاره isti'árah. — (*commercial term*) سندات استقراض sanadát-i-istikráz.

To LOATHE, مکروه داشتن makrúh dáshtan, نفرت کردن nifrat kardan.

LOATHING, *and* LOATHSOMENESS, ابا ibá, اعراض i'ráz, نفرت nifrat, تنفر tanaffur, کراهیت karáhíyat.

LOATHSOME, زشت zisht, مکروه makrúh.

LOBBY, ایوان aiván, دالان dálán, تالار tálár, کفش کن kafsh-kun.

LOBE (*of the ear*), نرمهٔ گوش narmah-i-gúsh.

LOBSTER, خر چنگ khar-chang, کله چنگ kallah-chang, پنج پایک panj-páyak, کرنجال karanjál, کلنجار kálanjár, سرطان saratán.

LOCAL, محلی mahallí, محلیه mahalliyah, موقعی mauki'í. — (*local government*) حکومت محلیه hukúmat-i-mahalliyah.

LOCALITY, *vide* PLACE.

LOCALLY, مکاناً makánan, از حیثیت محل az haisíyat-i-mahall.

To LOCATE, *vide* To PUT, To LAY. —(*to locate oneself*) جا گرفتن já giriftan.

LOCATION, اقامت ikámat, مقام makám.

LOCH, دریاچه daryáchah, غدر ghudar, برکه birkah.

LOCK, قفل kufl.—(*of hair*) حلقه halkah, طره turrah, جعد ja'd, تاب táb.—(*at the sides of the head*) زلف zulf.—(*on the crown of the head*) کاکل kákul, شوشه shúshah.—(*at the back of the head*) گیس gís, گیسو gísú.—(*on the forehead*) چلیپا chalípá. — (*of a gun*) چخماق chakhmák, چقماق chakmák.

To LOCK, قفلرا بند کردن kuflrá band kardan, چفت کردن chift kardan. —(*to put on a lock*) قفل چسبانیدن kufl chasbánídan.

LOCKER, صندوق sandúk.

LOCKET, موی دان múí-dán, زلف دان zulf-dán.

LOCK-JAW, لقوه lakvah.

LOCK-SMITH, قفل ساز kufl-sáz.

LOCOMOTION, انتقال intikál, ارتحال irtihál.

LOCOMOTIVE, لوکوموتیف lúkúmútíf (*eur.*).

LOCUST, ملخ malakh, میگ maig.—(*ravages of locusts*) ملخ خوری malakh-khwurí.

LODGE, خانه khánah, مکان makán.

To LODGE (*abide*), منزل داشتن manzil dáshtan.—(*to lodge a person*) اسکان نمودن iskán nimúdan, منزل دادن manzil dádan.

LODGER, کرایه چی kiráyah-chí.

LODGING, منزل manzil, خانه khánah, بود باش búd-básh, ماوا mává.

LOFT, بالا خانه bálá-khánah.

LOFTY, *vide* HIGH, EXALTED, PROUD.

LOG, کنده kundah, تنه tanah.

LOGARITHMS, انساب ansáb, نسبت nisbat, شمار اعداد متناسبه shimár-i-a'dád-i-mutanásabah.

LOGGERHEAD, احمق ahmak, بیوقوف bí-vukúf.

LOGIC, منطق mantik. — (*terms of logic*) اصطلاحات منطقیه istiláhát-i-mantikiyah.

LOGICAL, منطقی mantakí.

LOGICIAN, منطقی mantikí, اهل منطق ahl-i-mantik.

LOGWOOD, بقم bakm.

LOIN, کمر kamar, صلب sulb, میان miyán.

To LOITER, درنگ کردن dirang kardan, دیری نمودن dírí nimúdan, عقب افتادن 'akab uftádan.

LOITERER, عقب روان 'akab-raván. —(*bad character*) نابکار ná-bi-kár.

To LOLL, سستی کردن sustí kardan, آرام کردن árám kardan.

LONELINESS, *vide* SOLITUDE.

LONELY, تنها tanhá, منفرد munfarid, مجرد mujarrad, واحد váhid, وحد vahd.

LONG, دراز diráz, طول túl, طویل tavíl, مدید madíd, کشیده kashídah, بلند buland.—(*how long? till when?*) تا کی tá kai, تا چند tá chand, تا کجا tá kujá.—(*long ago*) مدتی muddatí, دیر باز dír-báz, از قدیم الایام az kadímu-'l-ayyám, مدتی مدید پیش از این muddatí-i-madíd písh az ín.—(*the long and short of it*), کلیات سخن kullíyát-i-sukhun.—(*to be long, time*), بطول انجامیدن bi-túl anjámídan.

To LONG, خواهش کردن khwáhish kardan, میل نمودن mail nimúdan.

LONGANIMITY, وقار vakár, صبر sabr, تحمل tahammul.

LONGING (*desire*), خواهش khwáhish, آرزومندی árzú-mandí, میل mail, اشتیاق ishtiyák.—(*of women in child-bed*) آرمه ármah.

LONGITUDE, درجه طول darajah-i-túl.

LONGITUDINAL, بطویل bi-tavíl.

LONGSUFFERING, صبر sabr, تحمل tahammul.

LOOK, نگاه nigáh, نظر nazár.—(*appearance*) ظهور zuhúr, صورت súrat, اشکال ashkál, پیدائش paidá,ish.—(*interj.*) اینک ínak, هان hán, هین hín, ده dah.

To LOOK, نگریستن nigrístan, دیدن dídan, نظر کردن nazar kardan, نگاه کردن nigáh kardan, مشاهده کردن musháhadah kardan. — (*seem*) نمودن nimúdan, پدید آمدن padíd ámadan, ظاهر شدن záhir shudan, معلوم شدن ma'lúm shudan. (*Vide* To INSPECT, To SEARCH, To EXPECT.)—(*to look after*) مواظبت نمودن muvázabat nimúdan.—(*to look into*, i.e. *overlook*) بسمت بودن bi-samt búdan.

LOOM, کار گه kár-gah, جولاه خانه júlah-khánah.

To LOOM, نمودن nimúdan, ظاهر شدن záhir shudan, پدید آمدن padíd ámadan.

LOOP, حلقه halkah, مادگی mádagí. —(*loop-holed*) مثقوب maskúb.

LOOSE (*unbound*), گشاده gushádah, محلول mahlúl, نا بسته ná-bastah, باز báz, واز váz, ول vil (*vulg.*).—(*slack, not tight*) سست sust, گشاده gúshádah, فراخ firákh, شل shul, لك lak.—(*not firm*) لك lak, نا محکم ná-muhkam. — (*hanging down*) فرو هشته furú-hishtah, آویخته ávíkhtah, ول شده vil-shudah (*vulg.*). — (*unconnected*) نا پیوسته ná-paivastah, نا مربوط ná-marbút, نا مقرون ná-makrún. — (*as leaves of a book, &c., unstitched*) ور آمده var-ámadah.—(*to hang loose*) هلیدن hilídan. — (*to be loose, unbound, free*) باز شدن báz shudan, ول شدن vil shudan, رها شدن rihá shudan.—(*infirm, shakey*) لکیدن lakídan, لك شدن lak shudan, نا محکم بودن ná-muhkam búdan.

To LOOSE, گشادن gushádan, گشودن gushúdan, باز کردن báz kardan, حل کردن hall kardan.—(*let go*) رها کردن rihá kardan, ول کردن vil kardan, خلاص کردن khalás kardan, گذاشتن guzáshtan.

LOOSELY, بطور گشاده bí-taur-i-gushádah.

LOOSENESS, گشادگی gushádagí, نا بستگی ná-bastagí, سستی sustí, فرو هشتگی furú-hishtagí, نا پیوستگی ná-paivastagí. — (*medical term*) اسهال ishál, جریان شکم jiryán-i-shikm, زحیر zahír.

To LOP, بریدن burídan, *or* burrídan.

LOQUACIOUS, مقوال mikvál, پر گو pur-gú.

LOQUACITY, پرگوئی pur-gú,í.

LORD, امیر amír, میر mír, خان khán, بیگ beg, والی válí, مولی maulá, آغا ághá, آقا áká, سید sayyid, خداوند khudávand, خاوند khávand, حضرت hazrat.—(*God*) خدا khudá, الله allah, رب rabb, حق hakk.—(*O Lord!*) یا رب yá-rabb.— (*House of Lords*) مجلس اعیان majlis-i-'a'yán.

LORDLINESS, کبر kibr, مغروری maghrúrí.

LORDLY, متکبر mutakabbir, مغرور maghrúr.

LORE, علم 'ilm, دانش dánish.

To LOSE, گم کردن gum kardan, ضایع کردن zái' kardan, فوت نمودن faut nimúdan, مفقود کردن mafkúd kardan. — (*squander or throw away*) باختن bákhtan, بر باد دادن bar bád dádan, تلف کردن talaf kardan.—(*sustain loss*) خسارت کشیدن khasárat kashídan, نقصان یافتن nuksán yáftan, زیان بردن ziyán burdan.—(*as a watch*) کند کار کردن kund kár kardan.—(*soldiers in battle*) تلفات دادن talafát dádan, تلف شدن talaf shudan.

Loser, زیان کار ziyán-kár, خاسر khásir, خسارت زده khasárat-zadah.

Loss, زیان ziyán, نقص naks, نقصان nuksán, خسارت khasárat, گزند gazand, تلف talaf, فوت faut.—(*military term*) تلفات talafát.—(*at a loss*) متحیر mutahayyir.

Lost, گم gum, مفقود mafkúd.—(*to be lost*) گم شدن gum shudan, غائب شدن ghá,ib shudan, ضایع شدن záí' shudan, فوت شدن faut shudan.

Lot (*chance or stake*), قرعه kur'ah, داو dáv. (*Vide* Part, Share.)—(*to cast lots*) قرعه انداختن kur'ah andákhtan.

Lote (*tree*), کنار kunár, نبق nabk, سدر sidr.

Lotion, اغتسال ightisál, دوا davá.

Lottery, قرعه بخت kur'ah-bakht.

Lotus (*water-lily*), نیلوفر nailúfar, لیلوپر lailúpar, ابو abú.

Loud, بلند buland.

Loudly, بابلندی bá-bulandí.

Loudness, بلندی bulandí.

Lounge (*place*), جای تعیش jái-i-ta'ayyush.

To Lounge, تنبل شدن tambal shudan, تنبلی نمودن tambalí nimúdan.

Louse, شپش shipish, قمل kaml. (*larvæ of lice*) رشك rishk.

Lousy, شپشو shipishú, شپش دار shipish-dár.

Lout, بی ادبی bí-adabí.

Loutish, بی ادب bí-adab.

Lovable, دل چسب dil-chasb.

Love, عشق 'ishk, محبت mahabbat, حب hubb, مودت ma-vaddat, وداد vidád, یاری yárí, دوستی dústí, مهر mihr, میلان mailán, الفت ulfat, صباب sibáb, هوا havá, شغف sha'f.

To Love, عاشق بودن 'áshik búdan, محبت داشتن mahabbat dáshtan, دوست داشتن dúst dáshtan, عزیز داشتن 'azíz dáshtan, میل داشتن mail dáshtan, مائل بودن má,il búdan, مغرم بودن mughram búdan.

Love-apple (*tomata*), پاتشگاه pátishgáh, بادنجان فرنگی bádinján-i-farangí.

Love-lies-bleeding (*flower*), زلف عروسان zulf-i-'arúsán.

Loveliness, دلفریبی dil-firíbí, لطف lutf, حسن husn, جمال jamál.

Lovely, مرغوب marghúb, مطبوع matbú', محبوب mahbúb.

Love-sick, مجنون majnún, شوریده shurídah, شیدا shaidá.

Lover, عاشق 'áshik, حبیب habíb, هوادار havá-dár, محب muhibb, یار yár.—(*lovers*) عاشق و معشوقه 'áshik va ma'shúkah, عشاق 'ushák, حبیب و محبوب habíb va mahbúb, یاران yárán.

Loving-cup, رطل گران ritl-i-girán.

Low, پست past, نشیب nishíb, زیر zír, فرو furú, پائین pá,ín, دومن dúman. (*Vide* Mean). —(*adv.*) آهسته áhistah. — (*low ground*) زمین منحدر zamín-i-munhadar, زمین پست zamín-i-past.—(*low in price*) کم kam, کم بها kam-bahá, نازل názil.

To Low, بانگ زدن báng zadan.

To Lower, پست کردن past kardan. —(*colours*) خوابانیدن khwábánídan.—(*one's head*) سر بزیر انداختن sar bi-zír andákhtan.

Lowliness, فروتنی furú-taní, مسکینی miskíní, خشوع khushú', خضوع khuzú', تواضع tavá'zu', انکسار inkisár, ضراعت zará'at, کوچکی kúchikí.

Lowly, مسکین miskín, فروتن furútan, غریب gharíb, متواضع mutavázi'.

Lowness, پستی pastí.

Low-spirited, مرده دل murdah-dil, دل تنگ dil-tang.

Loyal, مخلص mukhlis, مخلصانه mukhlisánah, صادق sádik.

Loyalty, مصافات musáfát, صادقی sádikí, وطن پرستی vatan-parastí.

Lozenge, كرص kurs.
Lubber, غافل gháfil, سست sust.
To Lubricate, چرب کردن charb kardan.
Lucerne (*grass*), يونجه yúnjah.
Lucid, صاف sáf.
Lucidness, صافی sáfí.
Lucifer (*match*), کبريت kibrít.
Luck, *vide* Fortune, Destiny.—(*good luck*) نيك بختی ník-bakhtí, نيك اختری ník-akhtarí, بختياری bakht-yárí, خوش نصيبی khwush-nasíbí, اقبال ikbál, طالع táli', نجاح nijáh.—(*bad luck*) بد بختی bad-bakhtí, کم بختی kam-bakhtí, نحوست nuhúsat.
Luckily, بيار بخت bi-yár-i-bakht.
Luckless, کم بخت kam-bakht, بيبخت bí-bakht.
Lucky, بختيار bakht-yár, خوشنصيب khwush-nasíb, نيك اختر ník-akhtar, نيکبخت ník-bakht, سعيد sa'íd, فرخ farrukh, کامران kámrán, اقبالمند ikbál-mand, خجسته khujastah, ميمون maimún.
Lucrative, سودمند súd-mand, نافع náfi', مفيد mufíd.
Lucre, فائده fá,idah, سود súd, حاصل hásil, صرفه sarfah, کسب kisb *or* kasb, مکسب muksab, نفع naf', منفعت manfa'at, انتفاع intifá'.
To Lucubrate, بشب محنت کردن bi-shab mihnat kardan.
Lucubration, محنت شب mihnat-i-shab.
Ludicrous, با خنده bá-khandah, مضحك muzhik.
Ludicrously, باخنده bá-khandah.
To Lug, کشيدن kashídan.
Luggage, اسباب asbáb, بارها bárhá, بنه bunah.
Lugubrious, *vide* Sad.
Lukewarm, شير گرم shír-garm, نيم گرم ním-garm, ملول malúl.
Lukewarmness, برودت burúdat, فتور futúr.
Lull, آرام árám.
To Lull, آرام گرفتن árám giriftan.—(*to lull to sleep*) خوابانيدن khwábánídan.

Lumber-room, پستو pastú, ميان پای miyán-i-páy.
Luminous, روشن raushan, درخشنده dirakhshandah, ضيادار ziyá-dár.
Lump, کنده kundah, تکه tikkah, لخته lakhtah, مضغه muzghah.—(*caused by the bite of an insect*) لك luk, برآمدگی bar-ámadagí.
Lumpy, کنده دار kundah-dár, لخته دار lakhtah-dár.
Lunacy, ديوانگی dívánagí, جنون junún, خبط khabt.
Lunar, قمری kamarí.
Lunatic, ديوانه dívánah, مجنون majnún.
Lunch, عصرانه 'asránah.—(*to take lunch*) صرف عصرانه نمودن sarf-i-'asránah nimúdan.
Lung, شش shush, رئيه ri,yah, رياه riyáh.
Lupine, ترمس tirmus, باقله مصری bákilah-i-misrí.
Lure, طعمه tu'mah, دانه dánah, چينه chínah.
To Lure, اغوا نمودن ighvá nimúdan, فريفتن firíftan, جذب نمودن jazb nimúdan.
Lurid, تيره tírah, مظلم muzlim.
To Lurk, پنهان شدن panhán shudan, کمين کردن kamín kardan, نهفته شدن nihuftah shudan, متواری بودن mutavárí búdan.
Lurker, کمين گر kamín-gar.
Lurking-place, کمين گاه kamín-gáh.
Luscious, لذيذ lazíz, مزه دار mazah-dár, نوشين núshín, شيرين shírín.
Lusciousness, لذت lazzat, شيرينی shíríní.
Lust, مستی mastí, شهوت shahvat, هوا havá, هوس havas, فسق fisk, نفس nafs, نفس اماره nafs-i-ammárah, طمع tama', آرزوئی نفسانی árzú,í-i-nafsání.
Lustful, مست mast, شهوت پرست shahvat-parast.—(*covetous*) طامع támi', طمعکار tama'-kár, آرزو مند árzú-mand, حريص harís, لئيم la,ím دانع dáni', کنس kinis.
Lustiness, قوت kúvat.
Lustre, روشنی raushaní, روشنائی

raushná,í, جلا jalá, جلوه jalvah, رونق raunak, ضیا ziyá, تاب táb, شعاع shu'á', نضارت nazárat.—(*of a sword, &c.*) آب áb.

LUSTY, با قوت bá-kúvat.

LUTE, عود 'úd, بربط barbat.

LUTHERAN, لوتران lútarán (*eur.*).

LUTIST, عواد 'avvád, بربط ساز barbat-sáz.

LUXURIANCE, افراط ifrát, کثرت kasrat, وفرت vafrat.

LUXURIANT (*abundant*), وافر váfir, موفور maufúr, فراوان faráván, کثیر kasír.

LUXURIES, آذوقه ázúkah.

LUXURIOUS, نفسانی nafsání, خوش گذران khwush-guzrán, عیاش 'ayyásh.

LUXURY, عیش 'aish, عشرت 'ishrat, عیاشی 'ayyáshí, خوش گذرانی khwush-guzrání.

LYING, دروغ گو durúgh-gú, کذب آمیز kizb-ámíz.

LYING-IN (*woman*), زاچه záchah, زچه zachah, زجه zajah.

LYMPH, ماده آبله mádah-i-ábilah.

LYNX, وشق vashk, سیاه گوش siyáh-gúsh.

LYRE, عود 'úd.

LYRICAL, بربطی barbatí.

LYRIST, عواد 'avvád, بربط ساز barbat-sáz.

M.

MACADAMISED, پخته pakhtah.

MACARONI, رشته rishtah.

MACE (*spice*), پوست جوز púst-i-jauz, بسباسه bisbásah, بزباز bizbáz.—(*metal club*) گرز gurz, طوپز túpuz, طپز tupuz, چماق chumák, گوپال gúpál.—(*staff of gold or silver*) عصا 'asá, چماق chumák.

MACE-BEARER, چماق دار chumák-dár, گرز دار gurz-dár.

To MACERATE (*sleep*), آغشتن ághushtan, آغاریدن ághárídan.—(*to make lean*) لاغر ساختن lághir sákhtan.

MACERATION, آغشتگی ághushtagí.

To MACHINATE, حیله نمودن hílah nimúdan.

MACHINATION, حیله hílah, مکیده makídah, مکر makr.

MACHINE, آلت álat, منجنیق manjaník.

MACHINERY, اسبابی asbábí.

MACHINIST, آلت کار álat-kár.

MAD, دیوانه dívánah, مجنون majnún, دلی dillí, جنونی junúní.—(*fascinated or distracted*) مجنون majnún, شوریده shúrídah, آلفته áluftah, مشغوف mashghúf, شیدا shaidá, شیفته shíftah, بیخود bí-khwud, جنونی junúní.

MADAM, خانم khánam, بانو bánú.

MADCAP, دیوانه dívánah.

To MADDEN, دیوانه ساختن dívánah sákhtan, مجنون ساختن majnún sákhtan.

MADDER (*a dye*), روناس rúnás.

MAD-HOUSE, تیمار خانه tímár-khánah.

MADLY, دیوانه وار dívánah-vár.

MADNESS, دیوانگی dívánagí, جنون junún, خبط khabt.

MADMAN, دیوانه dívánah.

MAGAZINE, مخزن makhzan, خزانه khizánah, خزینه khizínah, انبار ambár, گنجینه ganjínah, حاصل hásil. — (*of powder*) باروت خانه bárút-khánah, قور خانه kúr - khánah.—(*of arms*) سلاح خانه siláh-khánah, جبه خانه jabbah-khánah, قور خانه kúr-khánah.—(*pamphlet*) رساله risálah.

MAGGOT, کرم kirm.

MAGGOTY, کرم خورده kirm-khwurdah.

MAGIAN (*fire-worshipper*), مجوسی majúsí, آتش پرست átish-parast, مغ mugh, گبر gabr, گور gaur, در

کیش ázur-kísh, زردشتی zardushtí, زندیق zandík. — (*the Magi or Guebres, fire-worshippers*) مجوس majús, مغان mughán, گبران gabrán, اهل آتشپرست ahl-i-átish-parast, گوران gaurán. — (*Magian priest*) موبد múbid.—(*fire temple*) آتشکده átish-kadah, کنشت kunisht. — (*Magian cemetery*) دخمه dakhmah.—(*religion of the Magi*) مجوسیت majúsíyat, دین زردشت dín-i-zardusht. — (*sacred writings of the Magi*) زند zand. زنداوستا zandávastá, دساتیر dasátír. —(*Magian belt or girdle*) زنار zunnár.

MAGIC, جادو jádú, سحر sihr, جادوگری jádú-garí.

MAGICAL, افسونی afsúní.

MAGICIAN, جادو گر jádú-gar, ساحر sáhir, سحار sahhár, جادومان jádú-mán.

MAGISM, مجوسیه majúsíyah.

MAGISTRATE, حاکم hákim, ضابط zábit.

MAGNANIMITY, جوانمردی javán-mardí, همت himmat.

MAGNANIMOUS, جوانمرد javán-mard, بلند همت buland-himmat.

MAGNESIA, جوهر تباشیر jauhar-i-tabáshír, مغنیسیا maghnísíyá (*eur.*), مانگانز mángániz (*eur.*).

MAGNET, سنگ آهنربا sang-i-áhan-rubá, سنگ مقناطیسی sang-i-maknátís.

MAGNETIC, مقناطیسی maknátísí.

MAGNETISM, مغناطیسیه maghnátísíyah (*eur*).

MAGNIFIC and MAGNIFICENT, معظم mu'azzam, عظیم 'azím, جلیل jalíl, شگرف shigarf.

MAGNIFICENCE, لطافت latáfat, نزاکت nazákat, رونق raunak, جلالت jalálat.

To MAGNIFY, بزرگ کردن buzurg kardan. — (*honour*) ممتاز کردن mumtáz kardan, مشرف ساختن musharraf sákhtan.

MAGNIFYING GLASS, *vide* GLASS.

MAGNITUDE, بزرگی buzurgí, جسامت jasámat.—(*importance*) قدر kadr, مضایقه muzáyakah, لازمت lázimat, مصرف masraf, گرانی giráni, مهمی muhammí.

MAGPIE, کلاغ جرک kalágh-i-jarrak, کلاغ جیکو kalágh-i-jíkú, کلاغ زاغی kalágh-i-zághí, آلا قرغه álá-kurghah.

MAHOGANY, ماغون mághún (*eur.*).

MAHOMEDAN, اسلامی islámí, محمدی muhammadí, اهل اسلام ahl-i-islám. (*Vide* MUSULMAN.)

MAID, *vide* VIRGIN, SLAVE-GIRL.

MAIDENHOOD, *vide* VIRGINITY.

MAIL, زره zirah, جوشن jaushan, سلاح siláh; جبه jabbah, درع dir'. — (*post*) داک dák (*hind.*).

To MAIM, زخمی کردن zakhmí kardan, چولاق نمودن chúlák nimúdan.

MAIMED, چولاق chúlák, چلاق chulák, سقط sakat, زخمی zakhmí, افلیج iflíj.

MAIN, اول avval.—(*sea*) دریا daryá.

MAINLY, اکثر aksar.

To MAINTAIN, *vide* To ASSERT, To DEFEND, To KEEP.—(*support*) پروردن parvardan, پرورش کردن parvarish kardan.

MAINTENANCE, *vide* SUBSISTENCE.

MAIZE (*Indian corn*), ذرت zurrat, ذرت بلالی zurrat-i-ballálí, ذرت کلاک zurrat-i-kalák.—(*stalk of maize*) چوب ذرت chúb-i-zurrat. — (*head of corn*) سر ذرت sar-i-zurrat, خوشه ذرت khúshah-i-zurrat.

MAJESTIC, با وقار bá-vakár.

MAJESTY, سلطنت sultanat, جلالت jalálat, حضرت hazrat. — (*Your Majesty!*) قبله عالم kiblah-i-'álam, جهان پناه jahán-panáh.—(*Her Majesty*) علیا حضرت 'ulyá hazrat.— (*His Majesty*) اعلا حضرت á'lá hazrat.

MAJOR, یاور yávar.

MAJOR-DOMO, قهرمان kahramán.

MAJORITY, اکثر aksar, اغلب aghlab. —(*Parliamentary term*) طرف اغلب taraf-i-aghlab.

To MAKE, ساختن sákhtan, کردن kardan.—(*create*) آفریدن áfrídan, خلق کردن khalk kardan.—(*pud-

dings, &c.) درست کردن durust kardan. — (*cause to become*) گردانیدن gardánídan.—(*make it up*) صلح کردن sulh kardan.— (*make over*) محول کردن muhavval kardan.—(*make up an account*) جمع کردن jam' kardan.

MAKER, کننده kunandah, سازنده sázandah.—(*Creator*) خالق khálik, خلاق khallák, آفریننده áfirínandah, آفریدگار áfirídagár, صانع sáni', مکون mukavvin.

MALACHITE, ملخیت malakhít (*eur.*).

MALADY, مرض marz, بیماری bímárí, علت 'illat, درد dard.

MAL A PROPOS, بیمحل bí-mahall, بی جا bí-já, بی وقت bí-vakt.

MALARIA, بخار bukhár.

MALE, نر nar, مذکر muzakkar, ذکر zakr (*pl.* ذکور zukúr), نرینه narínah, مردانه mardánah.

MALEDICTION, لعنت la'nat, نفرین nafrín, سب sabb.

MALEFACTOR, گناه کار gunáh-kár, اثم asim, مجرم mujrim.

MALEVOLENCE, بد اندیشی bad-andíshí, بد خواهی bad-khwáhí, بد نهادی bad-nihádí.

MALEVOLENT, شریر sharír, بد نهاد bad-nihád, بد اندیش bad-andísh, بد خواه bad-khwáh, بد ذات bad-zát.

MALICE, بد خواهی bad-khwáhí, بد اندیش bad-andísh, کین kín, کینه kínah, حقد hikd, بغض bughz, عداوت 'adávat, شر sharr, شرر sharar, خبث khubs.

MALICIOUS *and* MALIGNANT, *vide* MALEVOLENT.

MALIGN, هلاهل haláhal, قاتل kátil, مهلک muhlik.

To MALIGN, هتک عرض کردن hatk-i-'irz kardan.

MALLEABLE, نرم narm.

MALLET, کلوخ کوب kulúkh-kúb.— (*of iron*) طوقماق túkmák, توقمق túkmak, توخماق túkhmák.

MALLOWS (*plant*), خبازی khabbází, نان کلاغ nán-i-kalágh, توله túlah, خطمی کوچک khatmí-i-kúchik.

MALVERSATION, غل ghill, غلول ghulúl.

MAMMA, مادر mádar, ماما mámá.

MAMMOTH, ماموت mámút (*eur.*).

MAN (*mankind*), بنی آدم baní-ádam, انسان insán, ناس nás, بشر bashar, جنس بشر jins-i-bashar, حیوان ناطق haiván-i-nátik. — (*human male*) آدم ádam, مرد mard, مردم mardum, نفر nafar, شخص shakhs.— (*piece, at chess, draughts, &c.*) مهره muhrah. — (*man-o'-war, ship*) جهاز جنگی jaház-i-jangí, کشتی جنگ kashtí-i-jang, جهاز حربی jaház-i-harbí, منوار manvár (*eur.*).

MANACLED, بسته زنجیر bastah-i-zanjír.

MANACLES (*fetters*), دست بند dast-band, غل ghull, زنجیر zanjír.

To MANAGE, کار گذاری نمودن kár-guzárí nimúdan, اجرائی کار کردن ijrá,í-i-kár kardan, سر براهی نمودن sar-bi-ráhí nimúdan.

MANAGEMENT, کارگذاری kár-guzárí, تدبیر tadbír, نظارت nazárat, سر براهی sar-bi-ráhí.

MANAGER, پیشکار písh-kár, ناظر názir, سرکار sar-kár, سر براه sar-bi-ráh.—(*body of managers*) اداره idárah.

MANDATE, حکم hukm, فرمان firmán, فرمائش firmá,ish, امر amr.

MANDRAKE, مردم گیاه mardum-giyáh, یبروج الصنم yabrúju-'s-sanam. [A fabulous plant, the root of which is said to resemble a man; and to which many wonderful properties are attributed.] —(*mandrake of Scripture, a small wild gourd, having a sweet smell, supposed to be the plant alluded to in Genesis* XXX. 14) دستنبو dastambú.

MANE (*of a horse*), یال yál, معرفه ma'rafah.

MANED, یال دار yál-dár.

MANES, غول ghúl, عفریت 'ifrít.

MANFUL, شجاع shujá', بهادر bahádur, دلیر dilír, رشید rashíd.

MANFULLY, دلیرانه dilíránah, بهادرانه baháduránah.

MANGE, گر gar, جرب jarab.
MANGEL-WURZEL, چقندر chukundur, چوندر chúndar (*vulg.*).
MANGER, آخر ákhur, آخور ákhwur, معلف ma'laf.
To MANGLE, دریدن darídan.
MANGO (*Indian fruit*), انبه ambah.
MANGY, گرگین gar-gín, جربان jar-bán.
MANHOOD, رجولیت rajúlíyat.—(*puberty*) بلوغت bulúghat, شباب shabáb. (*Vide* COURAGE, RESOLUTION.)
MANIA, عشق 'ishk, سودا saudá.
MANIAC, مجنون majnún, دیوانه dívánah.
MANIFEST, هویدار huvaidár, پدید padíd, آشکار áshkár, آشکاره ashkárah, ظاهر záhir, عیان 'iyán, پیدا paidá, مبین mubín.—(*nautical term*) قول kaul.
To MANIFEST, نمودن nimúdan, اظهار نمودن izhár nimúdan.
MANIFESTATION, اظهار izhár, توضیح tauzíh, پیدائش paidá,ish, بیان bayán.
MANIFESTLY, بالصراحة bi-'s-saráhat, صراحتاً saráhatan, واضحاً vázihan.
MANIFESTO, اظهارنامه izhár-námah.
MANIFOLD, عدید 'adíd, عدیده 'adídah, مستوفی mustaufí, متکاثر mutakásir.
MANIKIN, مردمک mardumak.
MANKIND, *vide* MAN.
MANLINESS, مردانگی mardánagí, مردی mardí, مردمی mardumí. (*Vide* BOLDNESS.)
MANLY, جوانمرد javán-mard, مردانه mardánah.
MANNA, من mann.—(*the drug*) شیر خشت shír-khisht, ترنجبین taranjubín.—(*of the tamarisk*) گز انگبین gaz-angubín.—(*a silicious substance found in the bamboo*), طباشیر tabáshír.
MANNER, طور taur, طرح tarah, وجه vajh, طریق tarík, منوال minvál, رسم rasm, وتیره vatírah, وضع vaz', روش ravish, طرز tarz, راه ráh, سبیل sabíl, سلوک sulúk, ضابطه zábitah, دستور dastúr, گونه gúnah, نهاد nihád, نمط namat, درایت dirâyat, اسلوب uslúb, قاعده ká'ídah, قسم kism.—(*in like manner*) اینچنین ín-chunín, هکذا hákazá.—(*after the manner*) بسان bi-sán.
MANNERLY, خوش اخلاق khwush-akhlák, تهذیب اخلاق tahzíb-akhlák.
MANNERS, آداب ádáb, رسوم rusúm, اخلاق akhlák, سیر siyar, قواعد kavá'id. — (*good manners*) تهذیب اخلاق tahzíb-akhlák, اخلاق پسندیده akhlák-i-pasandídah, خوش اخلاق khwush-akhlák.
MANŒUVRE, منوره manúrah (*eur.*).
MANSION, عمارت 'imárat.
MANSLAUGHTER, قتل katl.
MANTEL-PIECE, طاق ták.
MANTLE, ردا ridá, غاشیه gháshiyah.
MANUAL, دستی dastí.—(*pamphlet*) رساله risálah.
MANUFACTORY, کارخانه kár-khánah.
MANUFACTURE, عمل 'amal, صنعت san'at.—(*thing made*) مال mál.
To MANUFACTURE, معمول کردن ma'múl kardan, ساختن sákhtan.
MANUFACTURER, صانع sáni', کاریگر kárí-gar.
MANUMISSION (*of slaves*), عتاق 'iták, تحریر tahrír, اعتاق i'ták.
To MANUMIT, اعتاق کردن i'ták kardan.
MANURE, رشوه rishvah, کود kúd.—(*carrier of manure*) کود کش kúd-kash, گابره gábirah.
To MANURE, کود دادن kúd dádan, رشوه دادن rishvah dádan.
MANUSCRIPT, دستخط dast-khat, نوشته nivishtah, قلمی kalamí.
MANY, بسیار bisyár, فراوان farávân, بسی basí, خیلی khailí, کثیر kasír, موفور maufúr, جزیل jazíl, وفی vafí, عدید 'adíd, متعدد muta'addid, شگرف shigarf, انبوه ambúh.—(*how many?*) چند chand, چقدر chi-kadr.—(*so many*) چندین chandín, چندان chandán, آنقدر án-kadr, اینقدر ín-kadr.—(*as many as*) چندان chandán, چندانکه chandán-kih, بقدر bi-kadr.—(*twice as many*) دو چند dú-chand, مضعف

muza‘‘af, مضاعف muzá‘af, دو مقابله dú-mukábalah, دو گانه dú-gánah, دو مساوی dú-musáví.—(*one hundred times as many*) صد چندان sad-chandán. — (*many-coloured*) گوناگون gún-á-gún, رنگارنگ rang-á-rang. — (*many times*) بارها bárhá.

MAP, نقشه nakshah.— (*staff map*) نقشه ارکان حرب nakshah-i-arkán-i-harb.

MAPLE (*wood*), سارمه sármah, چیت chít.

To MAR, *vide* To SPOIL.

MARAUDER, غارت گر ghárat-gar, تاراج گر táráj-gar, حمله آور hamlah-ávar.

MARBLE, مرمر marmar, رخام rukhám.

MARCH (*of an army, &c.*), کوچ kúch, رحلت rihlat, رحیل rahíl, ارتحال irtihál, سفر safar, سیر sair, نهضت nuhzat. — (*forced march*) الغار ilghár, یلغار yalghár. — (*month*) آذار ázár, مارت márt.

To MARCH, کوچیدن kúchídan, کوچ کردن kúch kardan, رحلت کردن rihlat kardan.

MARCHES (*frontiers or boundary*), دهنه dahanah, مرز marz, سر حد sar-hadd, سنور sunúr.—(*Lord of the Marches*) مرزبان marzbán.

MARCHIONESS, بانو bánú.

MARE, مادیان mádiyán, اسب ماده asb-i-mádah.

MARGIN, *vide* BOUNDS, BORDER.— (*on the page of a book, &c.*) حاشیه háshiyah.—(*marginal lines*) جدول jadval.—(*having marginal lines or notes*) محشی muhashshá, جدول کرده شده jadval-kardah-shudah.

MARIGOLD, همیشه بهار hamíshah-bahár.—(*African marigold*) گل جعفری gul-i-ja‘farí.

MARINE, بحری bahrí, دریائی daryá,í. —(*naval force*), قشون بحری kushún-i-bahrí. — (*Minister of Marine*) وزیر بحریه vazír-i-bahriyah.

MARINER, جاشو jáshú, ملاح malláh.

MARINETTE, بازیچه bázíchah, لعبه la‘bah.

MARITAL, شوهری shauharí.

MARITIME, بحری bahrí, دریائی daryá,í.

MARJORAM, مرزنجوش marzanjúsh.

MARK, نشان nishán, علامت ‘alámat, اثر asar, سراغ surágh, نشانه nishánah.—(*on cattle, &c.*) داغ dágh. —(*target*) هدف hadaf, نشانه nishánah.—(*to leave a mark*) تاثیر نمودن ta,sír nimúdan. — (*to hit the mark*) نشانه خوردن nishánah khwurdan.—(*to miss the mark*) نشانه نخوردن nishánah na-khwurdan.

To MARK, نشان کردن nishán kardan, نشان دادن nishán dádan.

MARKET, بازار bázár, سوق súk, چهار سو chahár-sú, چار سوق chár-súk.— (*for slaves or cattle*) نخاس nakhás. —(*for cloth, &c.*) بزازستان bazzázistán.—(*vegetable market*) بازار سبزی فروش bázár-i-sabzí-furúsh.— (*market-price*) نرخ nirkh, قیمت متعارف kaimat-i-muta‘árif.

To MARKET, بازار نمودن bázár nimúdan.

MARKETABLE, رائج الوقت rá,iju-'l-vakt.

MARPLOT, برهم زن bar-ham-zan, مفتن muftin.

MARQUIS, امیر amír.

MARRIAGE, عروسی ‘arúsí, تاهل ta,ahhul, ازدواج izdiváj, زواج ziváj.—(*temporary*) متعه mut‘ah, صیغه síghah.—(*ceremony*) عقد ‘akd, نکاح nikáh, عروسی ‘arúsí. — (*written contract*) قباله kabálah, عقد نامه ‘akd-námah.—(*feast*) سور súr, عیش ‘aish. — (*portion*) کابین kábín, مهر mahr, صداق sidák. —(*property which the bride brings with her*) جهیز jahíz, جهاز jaház.

MARRIAGEABLE, بالغ báligh.

MARRIED (*man*), منکوح mankúh, زوج zauj, متاهل muta,ahhil, خانه دار khánah-dár.—(*woman*) منکوحه mankúhah, زوجه zaujah, زن مزوجه zan-i-muzavvajah.

MARROW, مغز maghz, مخ mukhkh.

To MARRY (*as a man*), زن گرفتن zan giriftan, تاهل ساختن ta,ahhul sákhtan, تأهل اختیار کردن ta,ahhul ikhtiyár kardan, عروسی کردن 'arúsí kardan, بزنی گرفتن bi-zani giriftan, نکاح نمودن nikáh nímúdan, زن کردن zan kardan, تزویج کردن tazvíj kardan.—(*as a woman*), تزویج کردن tazvíj kardan, شوهر کردن shauhar kardan, نکاح نمودن nikáh nimúdan.—(*to join a couple in matrimony*) عقد نکاح بستن 'akd-i-nikáh bastan.—(*to give in marriage*) بزنی دادن bizaní dádan, مقاربت نمودن mukárabat nimúdan.

MARS (*the planet*), مریخ mirríkh, بهرام bahrám, پهلوان سپهر pahlaván-i-sipihr.

MARSH, خلاب khaláb, وحل vahal, مشیله mashílah, مرز marz.

MARSHAL, صف آرا saff-árá.

To MARSHAL, صف آراستن saff árástan.

MARSHY, مشیله ور mashílah-var, مرزی marzí.

MART, صراف خانه sarráf-khánah, تجارتخانه tijárat-khánah, دار المعامله daru-'l-mu'ámalah.

MARTEN (*weasel*), سمور sammúr.

MARTIAL, جنگجو jang-jú, دلیر dilír, شجاع shujá'.

MARTIN, پرستك parastuk, پرستوك parastúk.

MARTINGALE, زیر بند zír-band, پیش بند písh-band.

MARTYR, شهید shahíd (*pl.* شهدا shuhadá).

MARTYRDOM, شهادت shahádat.—(*place of martyrdom*) مشهد mashhad.—(*to suffer martyrdom*) شهادت یافتن shahádat yáftan.

MARVEL, تعجب ta'ajjub, عجب 'ajab. (*Vide* MIRACLE).

MARVELLOUS, عجب 'ajab, عجیب 'ajíb.

MARVELLOUSLY, عجیباً 'ajíban.

MARVEL-OF-PERU (*jalap-flower*), لاله عباسی lálah-i-'abbásí.

MASCULINE, *vide* MALE.—(*gender*) مذکر muzakkar.

To MASH, کوبیدن kúbídan, پخش کردن pakhsh kardan, له کردن lih kardan.

MASK (*vizor*), برقع burka'.—(*play*) مسخره maskharah.

MASON (*stone-cutter*), سنگ تراش sang-tirásh.—(*builder*) بنا banná, معمار mi'már. — (*chief mason, architect*) معمارباشی mi'már-báshí, استاد بنا ustád-banná.—(*mason's rule*) گونیا gúnyá, سه گوش sih-gúsh.

MASONRY, معماری mi'márí.

MASS (*heap*), توده túdah, انبار ambár, کپه kuppah. — (*agglomeration*) جماعت jamá'at, اجتماع ijtimá', مجمع majma', جمله jumlah, جملگی jumlagí.—(*Church Service*), قداس kuddás.

To MASS, جمع آوری کردن jam'-ávarí kardan, جمع کردن jam' kardan.

MASSACRE, مقاتله múkátalah, قتل عام katl-i-'ámm, خونریزی khún-rízí, کشتار kushtár, اعدام i'dám.

To MASSACRE, قتل نمودن katl nimúdan, کشتن kushtan, مقاتله نمودن mukátalah nimúdan, اعدام نمودن i'dám nimúdan.

MASSIVE, ضخیم zakhím, بزرگ buzurg.

MASSIVENESS, ضخامت zakhámat, بزرگی buzurgí.

MAST, دگل dagal, دقل dakal, دول dúl (*hind.*).—(*to set up or ship a mast*) دگلرا سقب کردن dagalrá sukub kardan.—(*to strike or unship a mast*) دگلرا خزر کردن dagalrá khazar kardan.

MASTER, آغا ághá, آقا áká, صاحب sáhib, خداوند khudávand, مولی maulá, خاوند khávand.—(*owner*) مالك málik, صاحب sáhib.—(*chief workman or teacher*) استاد ustád, اوستاد ústád.—(*of a school*) معلم mu'allim, آخوند ákhwund, آخون ákhwun, ملا مکتبی mullá-i-maktabí.

To MASTER, غالب آمدن ghálib ámadan, گشادن gushádan.—(*to master a subject*) بر مطلب دست یافتن bar matlab dast yáftan.

MASTERLY, بی نظیر bí-nazír.

MASTER-PIECE, کار استاد kár-i-ustád.
MASTERY, فتح fath, غلبت ghalabat.
To MASTICATE, خائیدن khá,ídan, جائیدن já,ídan, جاویدن jávídan, خسیدن khasídan.
MASTICATION, خائیدگی khá,ídagí, خسیدگی khasídagí.
MASTICH (*gum*), مصطکا mastiká, ساقز sákiz, سقز sakkiz.—(*tree*), بن bann.
MASTIFF; سگ sag, کلب kalb.
MASTUPRATION, جلق jalk.
MAT, بوریا búryá, حصیر hasír, بساط bisát.
MATCH (*equal, rival*), حریف haríf, خصم khasm, طرف مقابل taraf-i-mukábil, مساوی musáví, زوج zauj, نظیر nazír, برابر barábar.—(*pair*) همتا ham-tá, جفت juft, زوج zauj. —(*marriage*) عروسی 'arúsí.—(*of a gun, &c.*) فتیله fatílah.—(*lucifer*) شمعچه sham'chah, کبریت kibrít. —(*matchlock*) *vide* GUN.—(*matchlockman*) *vide* MUSKETEER. —(*slow-match*) ماهتابی máhtábí.
To MATCH, برابر شدن barábar shudan.
MATCHLESS, بی نظیر bí-nazír.
MATE (*husband or wife*), زوج zauj.—(*of a ship*) معلم mu,allim.
MATERIAL, مجسم mujassam.—(*cloth, &c.*), قماش kumásh.
MATERIALITY, جسمانیت jismáníyat, جسمیت jismíyat.
MATERIALLY, در اصل dar asl.
MATERIALS, اسباب asbáb, لوازمه lavázimah, سامان sámán, سرنجام saranjám.
MATERNAL, مادران mádarán.
MATERNITY, امومت umúmat.
MATHEMATICIAN, مهندس muhandis, ریاضیت شناس riyázíyat-shinás.
MATHEMATICS, علم ریاضی 'ilm-i-riyází, ریاضیت riyázíyat.
MATRICIDE, مادرکشی mádar-kushí.
MATRIMONIAL, نکاحی nikáhí, زوجی zaují.
MATRIMONY, *vide* MARRIAGE.
MATRIX, رحم rihm, مشیمه mashímah, زهدان zihdán.

MATRON, خانم khánam, بانو bánú.
MATRONLY, خانم ور khánam-var, بانو ور bánú-var.
MATTER, *vide* AFFAIR, IMPORTANCE.—(*of a sore*) ریم rím. —(*what is the matter?*) چه شد chih shud.—(*no matter*) عیب ندارد 'aib-na-dárad, حرفی نیست harfí níst.
MATTOCK, تیشه tíshah, کلند kuland, کلنگ kulang.
MATTRESS, دوشك dúshak, توشك túshak.—(*spring-mattress*) دوشك فناری dúshak-i-fanárí.
MATURE, کامل kámil, رس ras.
To MATURE, کامل شدن kámil shudan, رسیدن rasídan.
MATURELY, کاملا kámilan.
MATURITY (*persons*), بلوغ bulúgh.—(*things*) بلوغیت bulúghíyat, کمال kamál, رسیدگی rasídagí.
MATUTINAL, بامدادی bámdádí.
MAUDLIN, نیم مست ním-mast.
To MAUL, زدن zadan, کوفتن kúftan.
MAUND (*weight of seven pounds and a half*), من man, من تبریزی man-i-tabrízí.—(*royal, fifteen pounds*) من شاهی man-i-sháhí.
MAUSOLEUM, مقبره makbarah, مزار mazár, ضریح zaríh.—(*of a saint*) روضه rausah, درگاه dargah, مزار mazár, امامزاده imám-zádah.
MAW, چینه دان chínah-dán.
MAWKISH, بد مزه bad-mazah.
MAXIM, مسئله mas,alah, مثل masal, مقوله makúlah.
MAY (*month*), آیار áyár, مایس máís.
MAY BE, شاید sháyad.
MAYOR, عین 'ain, کلانتر kalántar.
MAZE, حیرانی hairání, تفکر tafakkur, اندیشه andíshah.—(*place*) طریق tarík (*pl.* اطرق atruk).
ME, من man, مرا mará.
MEAD, چمن chaman, مرغزار marghzár.
MEADOW, چمن chaman, چمنزار chaman-zár, چراگاه chará-gáh, مرتع marta', مرغزار margh-zár, علفزار 'alaf-zár, صحرا sahrá, مغاز magház, جلگه julgah.
MEAGER, زبون zabún, لاغر lághir, حقیر hakír.

MEAGERNESS, زبونی zabúní, لاغری lághirí.

MEAL, آرد árd, دقیق dakík.—(*coarse meal or bruised grain*) بلغور bulghúr, پلکو palkú (*vulg.*)—(*a repast, food*) خوراکی khwurákí, طعام ta'ám, تغذیه taghziyah.—(*to take a meal*) تغذی نمودن taghazzí nimúdan.

MEALY, آرد سا árd-sá.

MEAN (*vile*), کمینه kamínah, فرومایه furú-máyah, پست past, خوار khwár, پوچ púch, دون dún, دنی daní, ذلیل zalíl, رذیل razíl, حقیر hakír.—(*middle*) واسطه vásitah, متوسط mutavassit.

To MEAN (*purpose*), قصد کردن kasd kardan.

MEANING, معنی ma'ní, فحوا fahvá, مطلب matlab.

MEANNESS, سفلگی siflagí, دونی dúní, کمینگی kamínagí.

MEANS, واسطه vásitah, وسیله vasílah, وصیله vasílah, موجب mújib, سبب sabab, رابطه rábitah, علت 'illat, وجه vajh, باعث bá'is, اصل asl, مورث mauris, وساطت vasátat, توسط tavassut.—(*by all means*) بهر وجه bi-har vajh, بهر صورت bi-har súrat.—(*by no means*) بهیچ وجه bi-hích vajh, اصلاً aslan, هرگز نه hargiz-nah, حاشا و کلا háshá va kallá.—(*by means of, through the agency of*) بوساطت bi-vasátat, از وسیله az vasílah.

MEANWHILE, *vide* WHILST.—(*in the meanwhile*) در این بین dar ín bain.

MEASLES, سرخک surkhak.

MEASURE, پیمایش paimáyish, میزان mízán, قیاس kiyás, اندازه andázah.—(*vessel for measuring*) پیمانه paimánah, مقیاس mikyás, معیار mi'yár, کیل kail, وزنه vaznah.—(*rod or stick*) نی پیمایش nai-i-paimáyish.—(*line*) شاول shávul, ریسمانکار rísmán-kár.—(*grammatical term*) میزان mízán, بحر bahr.—(*proceeding*) تدبیر tadbír, امر amr, کار kár.—(*beyond measure*) زیاده از حد ziyádah az hadd.—(*good measure*), وزن تمام vazn-i-tamám, وزن درست vazn-i-durust.—(*measure of length*) مقیاس طول mikyás-i-túl.—(*measure of quantity*) مقیاس کیل mikyás-i-kail.—(*superficial measure*) مقیاس سطح mikyás-i-sath.

To MEASURE, پیمودن paimúdan, پیمایش کردن paimáyish kardan, ذرع کردن zar' kardan.—(*land*) مساحت کردن misáhat kardan.—(*ascertain size or depth*) اندازه گرفتن andázah giriftan, قد گرفتن kadd giriftan.

MEASURELESS, بی انتها bí-intihá, بی حساب bí-hisáb.

MEASUREMENT, پیمایش paimáyish, مساحت misáhat.

MEASURER, پیما paimá.

MEAT, گوشت gúsht.

MECHANIC, پیشه ور píshah-var, کاریگر kárí-gar, صانع sání', کسبی kasbí.—(*mechanical powers*) قوائی منجنیق kuvá,í-i-manjaník.—(*lever*) اهرم ahrum.—(*wheel*) چرخ charkh, دولاب dúláb.—(*pulley*) غرغره ghargharah.—(*inclined plane*) تخته نشیبدار takhtah-i-nishíb-dár, بسیط مائل basít-i-má,il, صفحه مائل safhah-i-má,il.—(*wedge*) اخی akhí, گاوه gávah, گوه gavvah, گاز gáz.—(*screw*) پیچ pích.

MECHANICS, علم منجنیق 'ilm-i-manjaník.

MEDAL, مدال madál (*eur.*).

MEDALLION, سکه sikkah.—(*face*) روی rúí.—(*reverse*) پشت pusht.

MEDALLIST, مدال ساز madál-sáz.

To MEDDLE, دست زدن dast zadan, پس و پیش کردن pas va písh kardan.

MEDDLER, فضول fuzúl.

To MEDIATE, توسط کردن tavassut kardan, وساطت نمودن vasátat nimúdan.

MEDIATION, وساطت vasátat, شفاعت shifá'at, توسط tavassut, مباینت mubáyanat.

MEDIATOR, شفیع shafí', واسطه vásitah.—(*arbitrator*) حکم hakam,

منصف munsif, واسطه vásitah, مصلح muslih, میاندار miyán-dár.

Medical, طبی tabbí.

Medicinal, جهت دوا سازی jihat-i-davá-sází.

Medicine, علاج 'iláj, معالجه mu'álajah, دوا davá, درمان darmán.—(*the science*) طب tibb, طبابت tabábat. —(*drug*) دوا davá, دارو dárú.

Mediocrity, وساطه vasátah, اوسط úsat.

To Meditate, فکر کردن fikr kardan, تصور نمودن tasavvur nimúdan, اندیشه کردن andíshah kardan.

Meditation, فکر fikr, تفکر tafakkur, تلاوت tilávat, غور ghaur, تصور tasavvur, مراقبه murákabah, تأمل ta,-ammul, اندیشه andíshah.

Meditative, متفکر mutafakkir, متأمل muta,ammil.

Medium, واسطه vásitah, توسط tavassut.

Medjidie (*Order of*), نشان مجیدیه nishán-i-majídíyah.

Medlar, ازگیل azgíl, ازگل azgil, کونوس kúnús.

Medley, مخلوط makhlút, آمیزش ámízish.

Meed, بهره bahrah.

Meek, حلیم halím, سلیم salím, ملائم mulá,im, نرم narm.

Meekness, حلم hilm, ملایمت múláyamat, لطف lutf, نرمی narmí.

Meet, لائق lá,ik, واجب vájib, روا ravá, مناسب munásib, سزا sazá, سزاوار sazávár, شایسته sháyistah, لازم lázim.—(*to be meet*) شایستن sháyistan, لائق بودن lá,ik búdan, بکار خوردن bi-kár khwurdan, بایستن báyistan, ساز کار شدن sáz-kár shudan.

To Meet, ملاقات کردن mulákát kardan, دو چار شدن dú-chár shudan, بر خوردن bar-khwurdan.—(*go forth to meet*) استقبال کردن istikbál kardan, پیشواز کردن písh-váz kardan.

Meeting, مجلس majlis, جماعت jamá'at, مجمع majma', انجمن anjuman.—(*encounter*) ملاقات mulákát, وصال vasál.

Meetness, شایستگی sháyistagí, سازکاری sáz-kárí.

Megrim, درد سر dard-i-sar, صداع sudá'.

Melancholic, *vide* Sad.

Melancholy (*hypochondria*), ملنخولیه malankhúlíyah, سودا saudá.—(*as a sad tale, &c.*) سهمگین sahmgín, جگر سوز jigar-súz, دل خراش dil-khirásh.

Melange, مخلوط makhlút.

Melée, ناورد návard.

To Meliorate, بهتر کردن bihtar kardan, خوبتر کردن khúbtar kardan.

Melioration, بهتری bihtarí.

Melliferous, شهد آمیز shahd-ámíz.

Mellifluous, شیرین shírín.

Mellow (*ripe*), رس ras, رسیده rasídah.—(*soft*) نرم narm, ملائم mulá,im.

Mellowness (*ripeness*), رسیدگی rasídagí.—(*softness*) نرمی narmí, ملایمت muláyamat.

Melodious, خوشنوا khwush-navá, خوش الحان khwush-alhán.

Melodiousness, خوشنوائی khwush-navá,í, خوشآوازی khwush-ávází.

Melody, سجع saj', اسجاع asjá', نوا navá, نغمه naghmah.

Melon, خربوزه kharbúzah, خربز kharbuz.—(*small musk lemon*) گرمك garmak. —(*unripe melon*) کنبزه kumbizáh, کرکو karkú.—(*water-melon*) هندوانه hinduvánah, تربوزه tarbúzah, تربز tarbuz, قارپوز kárpúz. —(*melon-ground*) فالیز fálíz, پالیز pálíz, جالیز jálíz, خربزه زار kharbuzah-zár.

To Melt, گداختن gudákhtan, آب شدن áb shudan, حل شدن hall shudan. —(*causal*) گداختن gudákhtan, گدازانیدن gudázánídan, حل کردن hall kardan, آب کردن áb kardan.

Melter, گدازنده gudázandah.

Member, *vide* Limb. —(*fellow or partner*) شریك sharík, هم شرط ham-shart, رفیق rafík, صاحب sáhib, هم عهد ham-'ahd.—(*of a corporation,*

&c.) عضو 'uzv, نفر عضو nafar-i-'uzv, اجزا ajzá (*used in plural*).
MEMBERSHIP, عضویت 'uzvíyat.
MEMBRANE, پرده pardah.
MEMOIR, تذکره tazkirah, یاد داشت yád-dásht.
MEMORABLE, واجب الذکر vajibu-'z-zikr.
MEMORANDUM, یاد داشت yád-dásht, تذکره tazkirah.
MEMORIAL, *vide* PETITION, KEEPSAKE.
MEMORY, یاد yád, حفظ hifz, حافظ háfiz, خاطر khátir.—(*to escape the memory*) از خاطر رفتن az khátir raftan.—(*to retain in memory*) یاد داشتن yád dáshtan.
MENACE, *vide* THREAT.
MENAGERIE, شیر خانه shír-khánah.
To MEND (*repair, as buildings, &c.*), مرمت کردن marammat kardan, تعمیر کردن ta'mír kardan.—(*stitch*) رفو کردن rafv kardan, پیوند کردن paivand kardan.—(*improve*) اصلاح نمودن isláh nimúdan, به کردن bih kardan, افاقه نمودن ifákah nimúdán.—(*broken articles*) تصلیح کردن taslíh kardan, مرمت کردن marammat kardan, درست کردن durust kardan.
MENDACIOUS, *vide* LYING.
MENDACITY, فریب faríb, خیانت khiyánat, دروغ گری durúgh-garí.
MENDER, مرمت ساز marammat-sáz, رفو کن rafv-kun.
MENDICANT, گدا gadá, سائل sá,il, دربدر dar-bi-dar, فقیر fakír.
MENDICITY, گدائی gadá,í, گدایه gadáyah, فقیری fakírí.
MENIAL (*sub.*), نوکر naukar, پیشخدمت písh-khidmat.—(*adj.*) پست past.
MENSES (*a woman's monthly courses*), حیض haiz, طمث tums, عذر معین 'uzr-i-mu'ayyan.
MENSTRUOUS (*woman*), حائضه há,-izah.
MENSURATION, علم مساحت 'ilm-i-misáhat.
MENTAL, قلبی kalbí, دلی dilí.
MENTION, ذکر zikr, تذکره tazkirah, یاد yád, بازگوی báz-guí.—(*favourable mention*) ذکر جمیل zikr-i-jamíl, ذکر خیر zikr-i-khair.
To MENTION, ذکر کردن zikr kardan.
MENTIONED, مذکور mazkúr, ملفوظ malfúz, مزبور mazbúr.
MERCANTILE, تجارتی tijáratí.
MERCENARY, حریص harís, طمعکار tama'-kár, طامع támi', بخیل bakhíl, لئیم la,ím, ممسک mumsik, خسیس khasís.—(*soldier*) اجیر ajír, مزدور mazdúr.
MERCER, بزاز bazzáz, پیله ور pílah-var.
MERCHANDISE (*trade*), سوداگری saudá-garí, تجارت tijárat, متجر matjar, معامله mu'ámalah, داد و ستد dád u sitad, بیع و شرا bai' va shirá, اشترا ishtirá.—(*thing for sale*) فروختنی furúkhtaní, مال فروش mál-i-furúsh.—(*wares*) اجناس ajnás, تنخواه tankhwáh, متاع matá', مال mál, اقمشه akmishah.
MERCHANT, بازرگان bázargán, تاجر tájir, سوداگر saudá-gar, خواجه khwájah (*pl.* تجار tujjár, اصحاب تجارت asháb-i-tijárat).
MERCIFUL, رحیم rahím, رحمن rahmán, آمرزگار ámurzigár, شفیق shafík, کریم karím, رؤف ra,uf.
MERCIFULLY, کریمانه karímánah.
MERCILESS, بی رحم bí-rahm, بی شفقت bí-shafakat, سنگدل sang-dil, بی مروت bí-murúvat.
MERCURIAL, سیمابی símábí.
MERCURY (*quicksilver*), زیبق zíbak, جیوه jívah, سیماب símáb.—(*planet*) عطارد utárid, تیر tír, دبیر dabír.—(*alloy of mercury and tin-foil, used for looking-glasses, &c.*) کشته جیوه kushtah-i-jívah, زیبق کشته zíbak-i-kushtah.
MERCY, رحم rahm, رحمت rahmat, مرحمت marhamat, شفقت shafakat, ملایمت muláyamat, رقت rikkat, نرمدلی narm-dilí, رأفت ra,fat. (*Vide* PARDON).—(*to cry for mercy*) آمان آوردن ámán ávardan.
MERELY, فقط fakat, محض mahz, و بس va bas, تنها tanhá.
MERIDIAN, ظهر zuhr, نصف النهار nis-

fu-'n-nahár, نیمروز ním-rúz.—(*circle*) خط نصف النهار khatt-i-nisfu-'n-nahár.

MERIDIONAL, جنوبی janúbí.

MERIT, لیاقت liyákat, قدر kadr, فضیلت fazílat, سزاواری sazávarí.

To MERIT, سزاوار بودن sazávár búdan, مستحق بودن mustahakk búdan, لائق شدن lá,ik shudan, سزیدن sazídan, واجب شدن vájib shudan, مستوجب شدن mustaujib shudan.

MERITORIOUS, سزاوار sazávar, مستحق mustahakk, لائق lá,ik, واجب vájib, مستوجب mustaujib.

MERMAID, بنت البحر bintu-'l-bahr.

MERRILY, بشادی bi-shádí, بخوشی bi-khwushí.

MERRIMENT, *vide* MIRTH.

MERRY, شاد shád, شادمان shádmán, خوش khwush, دلخوش dil-khwush-خوشدل khwush dil, خرم khurram, بهیج bahíj, دلشاد dil-shád, فرحناک farah-nák, مشعوف mash'úf.

MERSION, غوطه ghútah.

MESH, شبکه shabakah.

MESS (*repast*), خوراکی khwurákí, طعام ta'ám, تغذیه taghziyah.—(*difficulty*) مشکلی mushkilí, سختی sakhtí, دشواری dushvárí.—(*stain*) آلودگی álúdagí, داغ dágh.

To MESS, طعام خوردن ta'ám khwurdan, تغذیه خوردن taghziyah khwurdan.—(*stain*) آلودن álúdan, نا پاک کردن ná-pák kardan, ملوث ساختن mulavvas sákhtan, نجس کردن najs kardan.

MESSAGE, پیام payám, پیغام paighám, رسالت rasálat.

MESSENGER, رسول rasúl, قاصد kásid, پیامبر payám-bar, پیغمبر paigham-bar, برید baríd.—(*mounted*) چاپار chápár, چپر chapar, پیك paik.

MESSIAH, مسیح masíh, المسیح al-masíh, مسیحا masíhá.

MESSMATE, ندیم nadím.

MESSUAGE, خانه khánah, منزل manzil, دار dar, سرا sará, بیت bait.

METAL, معدنی ma'daní, فلز filizz.—(*metalled road*) پخته pakhtah.

METALLIC, فلزی filizzí, معدنی ma'daní, کانی kání.

To METAMORPHOSE, تغیر دادن taghayyur dádan.

METAMORPHOSIS, تبدیل شکل tabdíl-i-shakl, مسخ maskh, نسخ naskh.

METAPHOR, استعاره isti'árah, کنایه kináyah, مجاز majáz, مجازت majázat.

METAPHORICAL, مجازی majází, کنایه آمیز kináyah-ámíz.

METAPHYSICS, الهیات iláhíyát, علم الاهی 'ilm-i-iláhí.

To METE, پیمودن paimúdan.

METEMPSYCHOSIS, تناسخ tanásukh.—(*in bad sense*) تماسخ tamásukh.

METEOR, شهاب shaháb (*pl.* شهبان shuhbán).

METEOROLOGICAL, شهابی shahábí.

METEOROLOGY, شهاب شناسی shaháb-shinásí.

METHINKS, گویا gúyá.

METHOD, *vide* MANNER.

METHODICAL, منتظم muntazim.

METRE (*measure of verse*), میزان mízán, بحر bahr.—(*rhyme*) قافیه káfiyah, سجع saj'.—(*measure of distance*) متر matar (*eur.*).

METRICAL, منظوم manzúm, موزون mauzún.

METROPOLIS, دار السلطنت dáru-'s-sultanat, دار الخلافت dáru-'l-khiláfat, دار الحکومت dáru-'l-hukúmat, پای تخت pá,í-i-takht, تختگاه takht-gáh, مدینه محروسه madínah-i-mahrúsah.

METROPOLITAN (*ecclesiastical term*), مطران matrán.

METTLE, جان ján, حدت hiddat.

MEW, مو مو mau mau.

To MEW, مو مو کردن mau mau kardan.

MIASMA, بخار bukhár.

MICROSCOPE, ذره بین zarrah-bín.

MID-DAY, *vide* MERIDIAN, NOON.

MIDDLE, میان miyán, میانه miyánah, وسط vasat, قلب kalb, اثنا asná, بطن batn.

MIDDLING, متوسط mutavassit.

MID-NIGHT, نیمه شب nímah-shab, نیم شب ním-shab, نصف الليل

nisfu-'l-lail, شبدار shab-dár, شبگیر shab-gír.

MID-SHIPS, مرکز جهاز markaz-i-jaház, تحت taht.

MIDST, میان miyán, میانه miyánah, وسط vasat, قلب kalb, اثنا asná, بطن batn.—(*in the midst of*) در بین dar bain, در صحن dar sahn.

MIDSUMMER, تابستان tábistán.

MIDWAY, متوسط mutavassit, تا نیمه راه tá-nímah-i-ráh.

MIDWIFE, ماماچه mámáchah, قابله kábilah.

MIEN, وجه vajh, چهره chihrah, روی rúí, منظر manzar, صورت súrat, ظهور zuhúr.

MIGHT, *vide* STRENGTH, SPLENDOUR, PRIDE.

MIGHTILY, نهایت niháyat.

MIGHTY, قوی kaví, قادر kádir, ذو القدر zú-'l-kadr, مقتدر muktadir, توانا taváná, عالی 'álí, کبیر kabír, اکبر akbar, عظیم 'azím, اعظم a'zam, بزرگوار buzurg-vár, معظم mu'azzam.—(*mighty deed*) فعل بزرگ fi'l-i-buzurg, عمل قوی 'amal-i-kaví.

To MIGRATE, نقل کردن nakl kardan.

MIGRATION, نقل کردن nakl kardan, انتقال intikál.—(*emigration*) جلاء وطن jalá,i-i-vatan, ترک وطن tark-i-vatan.

MILCH-COW, گاو شیرده gáv-i-shír-dih.

MILD, ملایم muláyam, *or* ملائم mulá,im, نرم narm, حلیم halím, سلیم salím.

MILDEW (*blight*), پرمک purmik, سم samm, یرقان yarakán.

MILDEWED, پرمک زده purmik-zadah, سم زده samm-zadah.

MILDLY, بانرمی bá-narmí, باملایمت bá-muláyamat.

MILDNESS, ملایمت muláyamat, نرمی narmí, حلم hilm.

MILE, میل míl (*eur.*).

MILITANT, جنگی jangí.

MILITARY, جنگی jangí, عسکری 'askarí, لشکری lashkarí.

MILITIA, عساکر ضبطیه 'asákir-i-zabtiyah.

MILK, شیر shír.—(*skimmed milk*) دوغ dúgh.

To MILK, دوشیدن dúshídan, دوختن dúkhtan (*obs.*).

MILK-CAN, شیر دان shír-dán.

MILKER, شیر کش shír-kash.

MILKINESS, شیر آسائی shír-ásáí.

MILK-MAID, زن شیر فروش zan-i-shír-furúsh.

MILK-MAN, شیر فروش shír-furúsh.

MILKY, شیر آسا shír-ásá, پر شیر pur-shír.

MILKY-WAY (*galaxy*), کهکشان kah-kashán, مجره majarrah, باب السماء bábu-'s-samá,.

MILL, آسیا ásyá, آس ás, مطحان mit-hán.—(*windmill*) آسیائی باد ásyá,í-i-bád.—(*cotton-mill*) کار خانه شعر بافی kár-khánah-i-sha'r-báfí.—(*paper-mill*) کاغذ خانه ká-ghaz-khánah.—(*water-mill*) آسیائی آب ásyá,í-i-áb.—(*ass-mill*) خر آس khar-ás.—(*hand-mill*) دست آس dast-ás, آسک ásak.—(*powder-mill*) دنگ خانه باروتی ding-khánah-i-bárútí.—(*oil-mill, or press*) معصر mi'sar, عصار خانه 'assár-khánah.

MILLENNIUM, رجعت raj'at.

MILLER, آسیا بان ásyá-bán, طحان tahhán.

MILLET (*large — holcus sorgum*), ذرت دانه ریزه zurrat-i-dánah-rízah, ذرت نان zurrat-i-nán.—(*small—panicum italicum*) الم allum, ارزن arzan, دخن dukhn.—(*Indian—holcus spicatus*) جاورس jávars, گاورس gávars, گارسک gársak.

MILLINER, خیاط زنانه khayyát-i-zanánah.

MILLION, میلیون míliyún (*eur.*).

MILL-STONE, سنگ آس sang-i-ás, آسیا سنگ ásyá-sang.

MIMIC, مقلد mukallid, تقلید چی tak-líd-chí.

To MIMIC, تقلید کردن taklíd kardan.

MIMICRY, تقلید taklíd.

MIMOSA (*gum-tree or acacia*), طلح talh, سنط sant.—(*scented flowering mimosa*) گل فتنه gul-i-fitnah.

MINARET (*spire*), مناره manárah (*pl.* مناور manávir), مأذنه ma,za-nah.

MINATORY, تهديد tahdíd.
MINCE (*stew*), قيمه kímah.
To MINCE, قيمه كردن kímah kardan.
MINCING STYLE, شيوه shívah.
MIND, ضمير zamír, خاطر khátir, دل dil, قلب kalb, رأى ra,í, عقل 'akl, هوش húsh, فكر fikr, بال bál.—(*interj.*) ده dah.
To MIND, ملتفت شدن multafit shudan.—(*never mind*) پيش مرو písh ma-rau, عيب ندارد 'aib na-dárad.—(*to have a mind to*) ميل داشتن mail dáshtan.
MINDFUL, هوشيار húsh-yár, خبردار khabar-dár.
MINDFULNESS, هوشيارى húsh-yárí, خبردارى khabar-dárí.
MINDLESS, غافل ghâfil, سست sust.
MINE, معدن ma'dan, كان kán.—(*gold mine*) معدن طلا ma'dan-i-tilá. — (*salt - mine*) معدن نمك ma'dan-i-namak. — (*silver-mine*) معدن نقره ma'dan-i-nukrah.—(*dug passage*) نقب nakb, لغم laghum.—(*belonging to me*) مال من mál-i-man.
To MINE, كندن kandan, نقب زدن nakb zadan.
MINER, معدنچى ma'dan - chí. — (*sapper*) لغمچى laghum-chí, نقاب nakkáb, نقبزن nakb-zan.
MINERAL, معدنى ma'daní, كانى káni, جماد jamád.—(*metal*) فلز filizz.
MINERALOGIST, معدن شناس ma'dan-shinás.
MINERALOGY, علم معادن 'ilm-i-ma'ádin.
To MINGLE, آميختن amíkhtan, سرشتن sirishtan, مخلوط ساختن makhlút sákhtan.
To MINISH, كم ساختن kam sákhtan.
MINISTER (*of State*), وزير vazír, مدبر mudabbir, وكيل vakíl, دستور dastúr, مشير mushír, دبير dabír.—(*an envoy or resident delegate*) ايلچى ílchí, وكيل vakíl, موكل muvakkal, باليوز bályúz (*eur.*). — (*Prime Minister*) وزير اعظم vazír-i-a'zam, اعتماد الدوله i'timádu-'d-daulah.—(*Second Minister*) امين الدوله amínu-'d-daulah. — (*Ministers of State*) وزرا vuzará, اركان دولت arkán-i-daulat, اعيان دوله a'yán-i-daulah, وكلائى دولت vukalá,í-i-daulat, امنائى دولت umaná,í-i-daulat, مدبران مملكت mudabbirán-i-mamlakat, اوليائى سلطنت auliyá,í-i-sultanat.—(*Minister of Foreign Affairs*) وزير امور خارجه vazír-i-umúr-i-khárijah, امير دول خارجه amír-i-duval-i-khárijah. — (*Minister of War*) وزير نظام vazír-i-nizám. — (*Minister or chief Envoy from another State*) وزير مختار vazír-i-mukhtár.
MINISTERIAL, وزيرى vazírí.
MINISTRATION, خدمت khidmat.
MINISTRY (*office of Ministry*), وزارت vazárat. — (*Parliamentary term*) وزارت خانه vazárat-khánah. (*Vide* PRIEST, PRIESTHOOD.)
MINOR (*petty*), صغير saghír, اصغر asghar, كه kih, كهتر kihtar, كم kam, كمتر kamtar.—(*under age*) كم سن kam - sinn, صغير السن saghíru-'s-sinn, خورد سال khwurd-sál, نا بالغ ná-báligh.—(*term of logic*) صغرى sughrá, تالى tálí.
MINORITY (*being under age*) خورد سالى khwurd-sálí, صغرالسن sighru-'s-sinn. — (*Parliamentary term*) طرف اقل taraf-i-akall.
MINSTREL, *vide* MUSICIAN.—(*singer of ballads*) خوانندہ khwánandah, قوال kavvál, عاشق 'áshik. [This latter term is applied to a class of wandering minstrels, who sing Turkish ballads.]
MINT (*plant*), پودينه púdínah, نعناع na'ná'. — (*for coinage*) دار الضرب dáru-'z-zarb, ضرابخانه zarráb-khánah.
MINUS (*in arithmetic*), تفريق tafrík (*as* پنج تفريق سه panj tafrík-i-sih, *five minus three*).
MINUTE (*of time*), دقيقه dakíkah.—(*memorandum*) تسويد tasvíd.—(*small*) دقيق dakík, رقيق rakík.—(*in a minute*) الآن al-án.
MINUTELY, با دقت bá-dikkat, نقير و قطمير nakír va katmír, على التفصيل 'alá-'t-tafsíl.

MINUTIÆ, نکات nikát.
MINX, نازنین názanín.
MIRACLE, کرامت karámat, اعجوبه u'júbah, آیت áyat.—(*wrought by a prophet*) معجزه mu'jizah.
MIRACULOUS, معجز نشان mu'jiz-nishán, عجیب 'ajíb.
MIRAGE (*fallacious appearance of water*) سراب saráb, کوراب kúráb, واله válah.
MIRE, گل gil.
MIRROR, آئنه á,inah, مرات mirát. —(*room inlaid with mirrors*) آئنه خانه á,inah- khánah.
MIRTH, خوشی khwushí, دلخوشی dil-khwushí, خرمی khurammí, سرور surúr, مسرت masarrat, نشاط nishát, انبساط imbisát, شادی shádí, شادمانی shádmání, عشرت 'ishrat, فراح faráh, بهجت bihjat, تنعم tana''um, فرح farah.
MIRTHFUL, شاد shád, شادمان shád-mán, خوش khwush, دلخوش dil-khwush, خوشدل khwush-dil, خرم khurram, بهیج bahíj, دلشاد dilshád, فرحناک farah-nák, مشعوف mash'úf.
MIRY, گلدار gil-dár.
MISADVENTURE, خطا khatá, سهو sahv, آفت áfat, بدبختی bad-bakhtí, بلا balá.
MISANTHROPE *and* MISANTHROPIC, ترش مزاج tursh-mizáj.
MISANTHROPY, ترش مزاجی tursh-mizájí, سختی sakhtí, درشتی du-rushtí.
MISAPPLIED, غیر محل ghair-i-ma-hall, بیجا bí-já, بی وجه bí-vajh, بی موقع bí-mauki'.
To MISAPPLY, بر باد کردن bar bád kardan, ضائع نمودن zá,i' nimúdan.
To MISAPPREHEND, بد فهمیدن bad fahmídan.
MISAPPREHENSION, خطا khatá, غلط ghalat.
To MISBEHAVE, بد رفتاری نمودن bad-raftárí nimúdan, بد سلوکی نمودن bad-sulúkí nimúdan.
MISBEHAVIOUR, بد رفتاری bad-raf-tárí, بد سلوکی bad-sulúkí, وضع نا سزا vaz'-i-ná-sazá, بی ساختگی bí-sákhtagí.

MISBELIEF, عدم اعتقاد 'adam-i-i'tikad, بی اعتقادی bí-i'tikádí, بی ایمانی bí-ímání.
MISBELIEVER, کافر káfir.
MISCARRIAGE (*abortion*), سقوط حمل sukút-i-haml, اسقاط حمل iskát-i-haml, سقط حمل sakt-i-haml.
To MISCARRY, سقط نمودن sakat ni-múdan.
MISCELLANEOUS, مختلف mukhtalif, مختلفه mukhtalifah, متفرق muta-farrik, متفرقه mutafarrikah, متنوع matanavvi', متنوعه mutanav-vi'ah.
MISCELLANY, اجتماع ijtimá'.
MISCHANCE, خطا khatá, سهو sahv, آفت áfat, بدبختی bad-bakhtí, بلا balá.
MISCHIEF, شرارت sharárat, قباحت kabáhat.—(*evil*) قبح kubh, ضرر zarar, گزند guzand, بدی badí.
MISCHIEVOUS, شریر sharír, مضر mu-zirr, مفسد mufsid.
MISCONCEPTION, بد فهمی bad-fahmí.
MISCONDUCT, بد رفتاری bad-raftárí, بد سلوکی bad-sulúkí, وضع نا سزا vaz'-i-ná-sazá, بی ساختگی bí-sákhtagí.
MISCREANT, اوباش aubásh.
MISDEED, بد کرداری bad-kirdárí.
MISDEMEANOUR, بد رفتاری bad-raf-tárí, بد سلوکی bad-sulúkí, وضع نا سزا vaz'-i-ná-sazá, بی ساختگی bí-sákhtagí. — (*crime*) گناه gunáh, تقصیر taksír, قصور kusúr, جریمه jarí-mah, جرم jurm.
MISER, بخیل bakhíl, ممسک mumsik, لئیم la,ím, جوکی júkí, طمعکار tama'-kár, خسیس khasís, حریص harís, طماع tammá', کنس kinis.
MISERABLE, شکسته حال shikastah-hál, پریشان حال paríshán-hál, مستمند mast-mand, مسکین mis-kín, بیچاره bí-chárah, خوار khwár, سیاه روز siyáh-rúz, شقی shakí.—(*to be miserable*) رنجیدن ranjídan, مبتلا شدن mubtalá shudan.
MISERY, بیچارگی bí-charagí, خواری khwárí, خرابی kharábí, مسکنت maskanat, شقاوت shakávat, در

ماندگی dar-mándagí, شکسته حالی shikastah-hálí, فلاکت falákat.

Misfortune, آفت áfat, کم بختی kam-bakhtí, بد بختی bad-bakhti, آسیب ásíb, بلا balá, مشقت mashakkat, حادثه hádisah, شقاوت shakávat, سختی sakhtí, نکبت nakbat, زمانت zamánat, شامت shámat, عنا 'aná, غائله ghá,ilah, مصیبت musíbat, فلاکت falákat.

Mishap, آفت áfat, بد بختی bad-bakhtí, بلا balá, آسیب ásíb.

To Misinform, دروغ گفتن durúgh guftan.

To Mislead, *vide* To Pervert.

Misrule, هرج مرج harj-marj, هنگامه hangámah, غوغا ghaughá.

Miss, خطا khatá, عیب 'aib.—(*girl*) دختر dukhtar.

To Miss, خطا کردن khatá kardan.—(*nearly get*) کم بودن kam búdan.

Missing, گم gum, مفقود mafkúd.—(*to be missing, lost, or wanting*) گم شدن gum shudan, غائب شدن ghá,ib shudan, مفقود بودن mafkúd búdan, نا بود گردانیدن ná-búd gardánídan.

Mission (*embassy*), سفارت sifárat, رسالت rasálat.—(*Special Mission*) مأموریت عمده ma,múríyat-i-'umdah.

Missionary, کشیش kashísh, قسیس kissís.

Missive, خط khatt, مکتوب maktúb, نامه námah, مراسله murásalah, رقعه ruk'ah, صحیفه sahífah, کاغذ kághaz, مکاتبه mukátabah, نوشته nivishtah, تحریر tahrír.

Mist, دود dúd, غبار شبنم ghubár-i-shabnam, مه mih, بخار bukhár, طومان túmán, میغ mígh.

Mistake, غلط ghalat, سهو sahv, خطا khatá, زلت zallat, ضلت zallat, مضلت mazallat, خبط khibt, قصور kusúr, تقصیر taksír.—(*by mistake*) سهوا sahvan, ندانسته na-dánistah.

To Mistake, خطا کردن khatá kardan, غلط کردن ghalat kardan.—(*to be mistaken*), غلط کردن ghalat kardan.

Mister, آقا áká, آغا ághá, میرزا mírzá.

Mistletoe, کاولی kávalí.

Mistress (*lady*), بیبی bíbí, بانو bánú, مالکه málikah, خاتون khátún, خانم khánam, بیگم begam.—(*chief lady of a harem*) بانوئی حرم bánú,í-i-haram.—(*sweetheart*) معشوقه ma'shúkah, محبوبه mahbúbah, نگار nigár, جانان jánán, شاهد sháhid, جانی jání.—(*tutoress*) آتون átún.—(*concubine*) خاصگی khássagí, مدخوله madkhúlah, متعه mut'ah.

Mistrust, بد گمانی bad-gumání.

To Mistrust, (از) متردد بودن mutaraddid búdan (az).

Mistrustful, بد گمان bad-gumán, بد ظن bad-zann.

Misty, پر مه pur-mih, میغ دار míghdár.

To Misunderstand, غلط دانستن ghalat dánistan, سهو کردن sahv kardan.

Misunderstanding, غلط ghalat, خطا khatá.—(*quarrel*) نزاع nizá', منازعت munáza'at, قضیه kazíyah, جدال jidál, مجادله mujádalah, لجاج lajáj, خرخشه kharkhishah, مباحثه mubáhasah, شلتاق shalták, ستیزه sitízah, شلوك shuluk (*vulg.*).

Mite (*insect*), کرم kirm.—(*mity, as cheese, &c.*) کرم زده kirm-zadah.—(*small quantity*) خورده khwurdah.

To Mitigate, تخفیف نمودن takhfíf nimúdan, آرامیدن árámídan, آرام دادن árám dádan, تسلی دادن tasallí dádan.

Mitigation, تخفیف takhfíf, آرام árám, تسلی tasallí.

Mitre, عمامه 'imámah, تاج táj.

Mittens, دستانه dastánah.

To Mix, آمیختن ámíkhtan, سرشتن sirishtan, مخلوط ساختن makhlút sákhtan.

Mixed, آمیخته ámikhtah, سرشته sirishtah, مخلوط makhlút, ممزوج mamzúj, مرکب murakkab.—(*to be mixed up with*) مدخلیت داشتن madkhalíyat dáshtan.

Mixture امتزاج imtizáj.—(*composition*) اجزا ajzá, اخلاط akhlát, ترکیب tarkíb.

MOAN, ناله nálah, آه áh, زار zár, انان anán.
To MOAN, آه کردن áh kardan, ناله نمودن nálah nimúdan.
MOAT, خندق khandak, گود gaud, گودال gaudál, حفره hufrah, چاله chálah.
MOB, جماعت jamá'at, جمع jam', انبوه ambúh, هنگامه hangámah, گروه gurúh, غلبه ghalabah, ملا mala, بوش búsh, ازدحام izdihám, هجوم hujúm.
MOBILE, متزلزل mutazalzil.
To MOCK, ریشخند کردن rísh-khand kardan, استهزا کردن istihzá kardan.—(*mimic*) تقلید کردن taklíd kardan.
MOCKER, سخره sukharah.
MOCKERY, خنده khandah, سخریه sukhríyah, مسخره maskharah, استهزا istihzá, تضحیك tazhík, مضحکه muzhikah, باردی bárdí, مزاح muzáh.
MODE, *vide* MANNER.—(*à la mode*) به وجه bi-vajh, موافق طرز muváfik-i-tárz.
MODEL, نمونه nimúnah, نقشه nakshah.
To MODEL, نقشه کردن nakshah kardan, نمونه کردن nimúnah kardan.
MODERATE, معتدل mu'tadil, مستوی mustaví.
To MODERATE, معتدل کردن mu'tadil kardan, بحد اعتدال آوردن bi-hadd-i-i'tidál ávardan, کم شدن kam shudan.
MODERATION, اعتدال i'tidál, سویت savíyat.
MODERN, نو nau, جدید jadíd, متأخر muta,akhkhir, تازه tázah.—(*people*) متأخرین muta,akhkhirín, ابنائی زمان abná,í-i-zamán.
MODEST, شرمسار sharm-sár, خجل khijil, مؤدب mu,addab, شرم رو sharm-rú.
MODESTLY, با حیا bá-hayá, با خجالت bá-khijálat.
MODESTY, شرم sharm, شرمساری sharm-sárí, حیا hayá, حجاب hijáb, خجالت khijálat, آزرم ázarm, زرانت zaránat, وقار vakár.

MODIFICATION, تعدیل ta'díl, تغییر taghyír.
To MODIFY, تعدیل دادن ta'díl dádan, تغییر دادن taghyír dádan.
To MODULATE, نغمه کردن naghmah kardan.
MODULATION, نوا navá.
MODULATOR, مطرب mutrib, نغمه پرداز naghmah-pardáz.
MOIETY, نیم ním, نیمه nímah, نصف nisf.
MOIRE ANTIQUE (*silk*), پرند parand.
MOIST, نم nam, نمگین nam-gín, تر tar.
To MOISTEN, تر کردن tar kardan, نم کردن nam kardan.
MOISTURE, رطوبت rutúbat, تری tarí, نمی namí.
MOLASSES, شیره shírah.
MOLE (*animal*), موش کور músh-i-kúr.—(*on the skin*) خال khál, کلف kalaf, شامت shámat.
MOLE-HILL, توده túdah.
To MOLEST, آزردن ázurdan, آزار رسانیدن ázár rasánídan, زیان کردن ziyán kardan, ضرر رسانیدن zarar rasánídan, ستم نمودن sitam nimúdan, خستن khastan.
MOLESTATION, آزار ázár, رنج ranj, ایذا ízá, اضطراب iztiráb, زحمت zahmat, جفا jafá.
To MOLLIFY, ملایم نمودن muláyam nimúdan, نرم ساختن narm sákhtan, آرامیدن árámídan, تسلی دادن tasallí dádan, آرام دادن árám dádan.
MOLTEN, ذائب zá,ib.
MOMENT (*of time*), دم dam, لمحه lamhah, لحظه lahzah.—(*importance*) قدر kadr, مضایقه muzáyakah, لازمت lázimat, مصرف masraf, گرانی giráni, مهمی muhammí.
MOMENTARY, آنی ání, یك دم yak-dam.
MOMENTOUS, لازم lázim, مهم muhimm, گران girán, خطیر khatír, عمده 'umdah.
MONARCH, پادشاه pádisháh, شاه sháh, شه shah, ملك malk, سلطان sultán, خاقان khákán, کی kai.

MONARCHICAL, سلطانی sultání, شاهی sháhí, خسروی khusraví.

MONARCHY, پادشاهی pádisháhí, پادشاهت padisháhat, ملك mulk, مملکت mamlakat, سلطنت sultanat, دولت daulat.

MONASTERY, خانقاه khánkáh, دیر dair, بقعه buk'ah, کشیشخانه kashísh-khánah.

MONASTIC (*life*), زهد zuhd, رهبانیت ruhbáníyat.

MONASTICISM, رهبانیت ruhbáníyat, زاهدی záhidí.

MONDAY, دو شنبه dú-shambah.

MONEY, زر zar, پول púl, نقد nakd, مایه máyah, تنخواه tankhwáh, وجه vajh.—(*ready cash*) نقد nakd, پول حاضر púl-i-házir, نقدینه nakdínah. —(*small money*) خرده khurdah, پول خرده púl-i-khurdah. —(*bad money*) زائف zá,if. — (*paper money*) قایمه káímah.

MONEY-CHANGER, صراف sarráf.

MONEYLESS, مفلس m uflis, تهی‌دست tuhí-dast.

MONEY-ORDER, برات barát.

MONGREL, دو رگه dú-ragah, دو نسله dú-naslah.

MONITION, پند pand, نصیحت nasíhat, تدبیر tadbír, مصلحت maslahat, وعظ va'z, اندرز anduraz, موعظه mau'izah.

MONITOR (*head-boy in a class at school*), خلیفه khalífah.

MONK (*recluse*), زاهد záhid, عابد 'ábid, گوشه نشین gúshah-nishín, ابدال abdál.—(*Christian monk*) راهب ráhib, کشیش kashísh, قسیس kissís, حبر hibr (*pl.* احبار ahbár).

MONKEY, بوزنه búzinah, بوزینه búzínah, میمون maimún.

MONODY, مرثیه marsiyah.

MONOLOGUE, تنها گوئی tanhá-gú,í.

MONOPOLIST, محتکر muhtakir.

MONOPOLY, انحصار inhisár.

MONOTHEIST, موحد muvahhid.

MONOTONE, عدیل المقام 'adílu-'l-makám.

MONOTONOUS, مکرر mukarrar.

MONOTONY, تکرار tatrár, وضع مکرر vaz'-i-mukarrar.

MONSIEUR, مسیو masíú (*eur.*), موسی músí (*eur.*).

MONSOON, موسم mausim (*pl.* مواسم mavásim).

MONSTER, خرق عادت khark-i-'ádat, عفریت 'ifrít.

MONSTROUS, غریب gharib, عجیب 'ajíb, بزرگ buzurg, عظیم a'zím, جسیم jasím, کلفت kuluft.

MONTH, ماه mah, شهر shahr.—(*every month*) هر ماهه har máhah. —(*first of the month*) غره ghurrah, اول ماه avval-i-mah, سر ماه sar-i-máh.—(*last of the month*) سلخ salkh, آخر ماه ákhir-i-máh. — (*this month*) این ماه ín máh, شهر حال shahr-i-hál. — (*last month*) ماه گذشته máh-i-guzashtah, ماه قبل máh-i-kabl. — (*next month*) ماه آینده máh-i-áyandah, ماه دگر mah-i-digar.

The Muhammadan months are lunar, and consist of twenty-nine and thirty days alternately. The whole year contains only three hundred and fifty-four days, and an intercalary day is added eleven times in the course of thirty years. The following are the names of the months, which do not correspond in any way with ours:—

1. محرم Muharram.
2. صفر Safar.
3. ربیع الاول Rabíu-'l-avval.
4. ربیع الثانی Rabíu-'s-sáni, ربیع الاخر Rabí'u-'l-ákhir.
5. جمادی الاولی Jumádáu-'l-úlá.
6. جمادی الثانی Jumádáu-'s-sání, جمادی الاخر Jumádáu-'l-ákhir.
7. رجب Rajab.
8. شعبان Sha'bán.
9. رمضان Ramazán.
10. شوال Shavvál.
11. ذو القعده Zú-'l-ka'dah, ذی قعد Zí-ka'd.
12. ذو الحجه Zú-'l-hijjah, ذی حج Zí-hajj.

Thirty-two of our years are very nearly equal to thirty-three

Muhammadan years. Their era dates from the morning after the هجره hijrah, or flight of the Prophet from Makkah to Madínah, that is, the 16th of July, A.D. 622. Every year begins earlier in the season than the preceding, so that a month occurring in summer in the present year, will, sixteen years afterwards, occur in winter.

The ancient Persian year is solar like ours, and consists of twelve months of thirty days each, five days being, moreover, added to complete the year, and a leap year occurring every four years, as with us. This year commences when the sun enters Aries, about the 21st of March, when the عيد نو روز 'íd-i-nau-rúz ("New Year's festival") is held. This feast is still kept up, although the solar year has fallen into desuetude, and has been superseded by the abovementioned lunar era, the Persians having changed their calendar with their religion.

1. فروردين Farvardín (March and April). [The first day of this month, the 21st of March, is the New Year's festival.]
2. اردیبهشت Urdí-bihisht (April and May).
3. خور داد Khwur-dád (May and June).
4. تير Tír (June and July).
5. مرداد Murdád (July and August).
6. شهريور Sharívar (August and September).
7. مهر Mihr (September and October).
8. آبان Abán (October and November). [The intercalation of five days, or six in leap-year, to complete the solar year, is inserted at the end of this month.]
9. آذر Ázur (November and December).
10. دی Dai (December and January).
11. بهمن Bahman (January and February).
12. اسفندارمذ Isfandármuz (February and March).

Days are reckoned in weeks as well as months. (*Vide* Monday, Tuesday, &c.) Friday is the Muhammadan Sabbath. Sunset is considered the close of one day, and the commencement of the next; so that what we call Monday evening, a Persian will maintain to be Tuesday, as, conformably with his theory, Monday had ended and Tuesday begun when the sun set. Their day and night, like ours, comprise twenty-four hours.

Monthly, ماهيانه máhiyánah, ماهانه máhánah, ماهی máhí, شهری shahrí, ماهواره máhvárah.—(*salary or pay*) مشاهره mushâharah, مواجب ماهانه mavájib-i-máhánah.

Monument, يادگار yád-gár, تذكره tazkirah, اثر asar, منار manár, مناره manárah.—(*tomb*) مرقد markad, تربت turbat, مقبره makbarah, مزار mazár.

Monumental, ياد گاری yád-gárí.

Mood (*tense*), حالت hálat, صيغه síghah.—(*disposition*) *vide* Temper.

Moon, ماه máh, مه mah, قمر kamar.—(*new moon or crescent*) ماه نو máh-i-nau, هلال hilál. — (*full moon*) ماه تام máh-i-támm, بدر badar, نخشب nakhshab.—(*change of the moon*) تحويل ماه tahvíl-i-máh.—(*wane of the moon*) محاق muhák.

Moonlight, مهتاب mah-táb, ماهتاب máh-táb, ضياء القمر ziyá,u-'l-kamar.

Moor, زنگی zangí.

To Moor, لنگر انداختن langar andákhtan, بستن bastan, بند کردن band kardan.

MORAL, فائدة fá,idah.—(*virtuous*) پاك دامن pák-dáman, پارسا pársá, صالح sálih.

MORALIST, پند گو pand-gú, واعظ vá'iz.

MORALITY, پاك دامنی pák-dámaní, پارسائی pársá,í, صلاح saláh.

MORALS, اخلاق akhlák, اطوار atvár.

MORASS, *vide* MARSH.

MORBID, مریض maríz.

MORBIDNESS, مرض marz.

MORE, بیش bísh, بیشتر bíshtar, زیادة ziyádah, ازید azyad, افزون afzún, اکثر aksar, بسیارتر bisyártar (*vulg.*).—(*more or less*) کم و بیش kam va bísh, کمابیش kamábísh.—(*neither more nor less*) بی کم و زیاد bí-kam va ziyád.—(*more and more*) بیشتر از بیشتر bíshtar az bíshtar.—(*a little more*) بیشترك bíshtarak, زیادترك ziyádatarak.—(*much more, rather*) بطریق اولیٰ bi-tarík-i-úlá, بمرتبهٔ افزون bi-martabah-i-afzún. — (*no more*) نه دیگر nah-dígar, دیگر نه dígar-nah.

MOREOVER, علاوة بر آن 'alávah bar án, جز آن juz-i-án, سوائی آن sava,í-i-án, مکررا mukarraran, قطع نظر kat'-i-nazar.

MORNING, صبح subh, صباح sabáh, بامداد bámdád. — (*early, before day-break*) سحر sahar, سحرگاه sahar-gáh.—(*day-break*) فجر صبح fajr-i-subh, فجر fajr, سپیده دم sapídah-dam, پگاه pagáh, مژگان سحر mizhagán - i - sahar.—(*the middle hour between sunrise and the meridian, or about 9 o'clock*) چاشت chásht, چاشتگاه chásht-gáh, ضحیٰ zuhá.—(*false dawn before sunrise*) صبح کاذب subh-i-kázib.—(*true dawn*) صبح صادق subh-i-sádik.—(*morning star*) زهرة zuhrah, شباهنگ shabáhang —(*early, before light*) هوائی گرگ و میش havá,í-i-gurg va mísh (*literally*, "*Time of the wolf and sheep.*")

MOROCCO (*leather*), انبان ambán, دیم dím.

MOROSE, ترش مزاج tursh-mizáj, سخت sakht.

MOROSENESS, سختی sakhtí, درشتی durushtí.

MORROW, فردا fardá, غد ghad, صباح sabáh.

MORSEL, لقمة lukmah, نوالة naválah, تکة tikkah.

MORTAL (*man*), آدم ádam, مرد mard.—(*subject to death*) فانی fání, معرض بمرگ mu'arraz-bi-marg, علوفة مرگ 'alúfah-i-marg. —(*deadly, fatal*) قاتل kátil, هلاهل haláhal, مهلك muhlik, مقاتل mu-kátil.—(*as a wound*) کاری kárí.

MORTALITY, هلکت halakat, اجل ajal, فنا faná, مرگ marg, موت maut, ممات mamát, فوت faut, وفات vafát, قضا kazá, سام sám, ارتحال irtihál. — (*human nature*) انسانیت insáníyat, بشریت ba-sharíyat, آدمیت ádmíyat.

MORTALLY, بشدت bi-shiddat, بنهایت bi-niháyat.

MORTAR (*for pounding*) هاون há-van, جوغن júghan, چوغن chú-ghan.—(*large mortar*) جوازة juvá-zah, جواز juváz. — (*gun*) قمبارة kumbárah, خمپارة khumpárah.—(*lime, plaster*) گچ gach, آهك áhak.—(*of lime and ashes*) ساروج sarúj. — (*of clay and chopped straw*) کاه گل káh-gil.

MORTGAGE, گرو girav, رهن rahn.

To **MORTGAGE**, رهن گذاشتن rahn guzáshtan.

MORTGAGED, رهین rahín.

MORTGAGEE, مرتهن murtahin.

MORTGAGOR, راهن ráhin.

MORTIFICATION (*abstinence*), ریاضت riyázat, پرهیز parhíz, پرهیز گاری parhíz-gárí, اجتناب ijtináb.—(*corruption*) فساد fasád, افساد ifsád, تباهی tabáhí, عفونت 'ufú-nat.—(*annoyance*) ضرر zarar, رنج ranj, زحمت zahmat, ایذا íza, آزار ázár.

To **MORTIFY** (*corrupt*), گندیدة شدن gandídah shudan, خورة شدن khwa-rah shudan, فاسد شدن fásid shu-dan.—(*suppress or restrain*) ضبط

کردن zabt kardan, باز داشتن báz-dáshtan, وا داشتن vá-dáshtan.—(*vex*) رنجانیدن ranjánídan, آزار دادن ázár dádan.

MORTMAIN, وقف vakf, وقفی vakfí, وقفیه vakfíyah.

MORTUARY, مرده خانه murdah khánah, غسال خانه ghassál-khánah.

MOSAIC (*inlaid work in tessellated pattern*) خاتمی khátimí, خاتمبندی khátim-bandí.

MOSQUE (*place of Musulman worship*), مسجد masjid, عبادتگاه 'ibádat-gáh, نماز گاه namáz-gáh, معبد ma'bad, مشکو mashkú.—(*great mosque*) مسجد جامع masjid-i-jámi', جامع jámi'.—(*small mosque*) تکیه takyah, زاویه záviyah.

MOSQUITO, پشه pashah, بعوضه ba'úzah.

MOSS, پوژه púzhah, پوده púdah, پرمك purmik, دکان dukán.

MOST, بیشتر bíshtar, بیشترین bíshtarín, اکثر aksar, اغلب aghlab.—(*at the most*) خیلی باشد khailí báshad, معادل mu'ádil.

MOTE, ذره zarrah.

MOTH (*butterfly*), پروانه parvánah, شبپره shab-parah.—(*small moth*) بید bíd.—(*moth-eaten*) بید خورده bíd-khwurdah, بید زده bíd-zadah.

MOTHER, مادر mádar, ام umm, والده válidah, مام mám, ننه nanah (*vulg.*).—(*mother-in-law*) مادر زن mádar-i-zan, مادر شوهر mádar-i-shauhar, خوشدامن khwush-dáman, خارسو khársú.

MOTHERLESS, بی مادر bí-mádar.

MOTHERLY, مادرانه mádaránah.

MOTHER-OF-PEARL, صدف sadaf, مادر در mádar-i-durr.

MOTION, جنبش jumbish, حرکت harakat. — (*of the sea*) انقلاب inkiláb.—(*perpetual motion*) دور دائم daur-i-dá,im, دور مدام daur-i-mudám.—(*in motion*) در حرکت dar harakat.—(*of bowels*) اطلاق itlák.

MOTIONLESS, بی حرکت bí-harakat, ساکن sákin.

MOTIVE, غرض gharaz, قصد kasd, آهنگ áhang, مطلب matlab, مقصود maksúd.

MOTLEY, غریب gharíb, عجیب 'ajíb.

MOTTO, نشان nishán, علامت 'alámat, ورد vird, ورد زبان vird-i-zabán.

MOULD, قالب kálab, رجه rijah.—(*for bullets*) قالب kálab, گلوله ریز gulúlah-ríz, رجه rijah.—(*soil*) خاك khák, تراب turáb, گل gil.

To MOULD, ریختن ríkhtan.

MOULDINESS, پرمك purmik, زنگ zang, موریانه múriyánah, مورجنه múrjanah.

MOULDING, حاشیه háshiyah (*pl.* حواشی havá shí).

MOULDY, پوسیده púsídah, پرمك بر آورده purmik-bar-ávardah, گندیده gandídah, زنگ زده zang-zadah.

To MOULT, پر ریختن par ríkhtan.

MOUND, پشته pushtah, گریوه garívah, سد sadd, دمدمه damdamah, تپه tappah.

To MOUNT (*horse*), سوار شدن suvár shudan.—(*ascend*) بالا رفتن bálá raftan, صعود نمودن sa'úd nimúdan, بر آمدن bar-ámadan.

MOUNTAIN, کوه kúh, که kuh, جبل jabal, شامخ shámikh.—(*summit of a mountain*) قله کوه kullah-i-kúh, سر کوه sar-i-kúh, راس الجبل rásu-'l-jabal, عرف 'urf, تیغ کوه tígh-i-kúh.—(*brow of a mountain*) کمر کوه kamar-i-kúh.—(*skirt of a mountain*) دامن کوه dáman-i-kúh, اتك atak, شیب کوه shíb-i-kúh.—(*mountain pass or road*) کتل kutal, گردن gardan.—(*defile between mountains*) دره darrah, تنگ tang, شعب sha'b, ثنیت saníyat.

MOUNTAINEER, کوهستانی kúhistání.

MOUNTAINOUS, کوهسار kúh-sár, کوهستان kúhistán, داغستان dághistán.

MOUNTEBANK, لوطی lútí.

MOUNTED, سوار suvár, سواره suvárah.

To MOURN (*lament*), زاری نمودن zárí nimúdan, گریه کردن giryah kardan, نالش کردن nálish kardan, افسوس خوردن afsús khwurdan.—

(*for the dead*) نوحه کردن nauhat kardan, ناله کردن nálah kardan.

Mourner, ماتمی mátamí, نوحه گر nauhah-gar, تعزیه دار ta'ziyah-dár. — (*mourner hired to bewail the dead*) نوحه گر nauhah-gar, نواح navváh.

Mournful, دلتنگ dil-tang, پریشان paríshán, ملول malúl, غمگین gham-gín, غمناک gham-nák.

Mourning, تاسف ta,assuf, غم gham, زاری zárí, ماتم mátam, نالش nálish.—(*for the dead*) عزا 'azá, گریه giryah, نوحت nauhat, ماتم mátam, ناله nálah, نوحه گری nauhah-garí, عزا داری 'azá-dárí, تعزیه داری ta'ziyah-dárí.—(*dress*) لباس ماتم libás-i-mátam. — (*in mourning*) ماتمی mátamí. — (*to be in mourning*) حالت عزائی داشتن hálat-i-'azá,í dáshtan.

Mouse, موش músh, مرزن marzan (*obs.*).

Mouse-trap, موش گیر músh-gír.

Mouth, دهان dahán, دهن dahan, کام kám, فم fam (*pl.* افواه afváh), پوز púz.—(*of a pit or well*) دهنه dahanah, لبه labah.—(*of a river*) دهنه رود خانه dahanah-i-rúd-khánah, خور khaur.

Mouthful, لقمه lukmah, نواله naválah, تکه tikkah.

Mouthless, بی دهن bí-dahan.

Movable, متحرک mutaharrik.

Movables, رخت rakht, اثاث asás, اسباب asbáb, اوضاع auzá'.

To Move (*trans.*), جنبانیدن jumbánídan, تکانیدن takánídan, حرکت دادن harakat dádan, اوضاع ساختن auzá' sákhtan, خلجان دادن khalján dádan, تکان دادن takán dádan.—(*intrans.*) جنبیدن jumbídan, حرکت کردن harakat kardan, متحرک شدن mutaharrik shudan, لاندن lándan (*obs.*). — (*from a house*) رخت کشیدن rakht kashídan.

Movement, جنبش jumbish, حرکت harakat.

To Mow, درویدن diravídan, درو کردن dirau kardan.

Mower, دروندہ diravandah,

Much, بسیار bisyár, خیلی khailí, بسا basá, کثیر kasír, وافر váfir, موفور maufúr, فراوان faráván, فره firah, وفی vafí, بسی basí, جزیل jazíl, پر pur.—(*much more, far rather*) بیشتر bíshtar, بمرتبه افزون bi-martabah-i-afzún, بطریق اولی bi-tarík-i-aulá.—(*much less*) کجا ماند kujá mánad, تا چه رسد tá-chih rasad.—(*that much*) آن قدر án kadr.—(*too much*) زیاد ziyád, پر pur, بافراط bi-afrát.

Mucilage, چربی charbí, لعاب lu'áb.

Mucous, لعابدار lu'áb-dár.

Mucus (*of the body*), خلط khilt.—(*of the nose*) خلط بینی khilt-i-khilt-i-bíní.

Mud, گل gil, گلاوه giláyah, لجن lajan, وحل vahl, شل shul. —(*to sink in the mud*) گلاب غرق شدن gil-áb ghark shudan.

Muddiness (*dirt*), شل آلودگی shul-álúdagí, گل آلودگی gil-álúdagí.—(*ground*) گل gil.—(*water*) تیرگی tíragí, کدرت kudrat, غلیظی ghalízí.

To Muddle, تیره ساختن tírah sákhtan, نیم مست کردن ním-mast kardan.

Muddled, در هم بر هم dar-ham bar-ham.

Muddy (*dirtied*), شل آلوده shul-álúdah, گل آلوده gil-álúdah.—(*as ground*) شل shul, شل و گل shul vá gil. — (*as water, turbid*), تیره tírah, مکدر mukaddar, غلیظ ghalíz.

To Muffle, پوشیدن púshídan, تسکیت نمودن taskít nimúdan.

Mug, کوزه kúzah.

Muggy, تیره tírah, تر tar, نم nam, نمگین nam-gín.

Mughul, مغل mughul.

Muhammad, *vide* Musulman.

Mulatto, دو رنگ dú-rang.

Mulberry, توت tút, شهتوت shah-tút.

Mulct, جریمه jarímah, جریمانه jarímánah, مصادره musádarah.

Mule, قاطر kátir, استر astar, بغل baghl.

MULETEER (*keeper of mules*), مکاری mukárí, چهار وا دار chahár-vá-dár, چار وا دار chár-vá-dár (*properly spelt* چهار پا دار chahár-pá-dár, چار پا دار chár-pá-dár). —(*mule-driver*) قاطرچی kátir-chí, استربان astar-bán.

MULLET (*fish*), سفید ماهی safíd-máhí, بیاح biyáh.

MULTIFOLD, *vide* NUMEROUS.

MULTIPLE, افزا afzá, تو بر تو tú bar tú.

MULTIPLICAND, مضروب mazrúb.

MULTIPLICATION (*in arithmetic*), ضرب zarb.—(*compound multiplication*) ضرب مرکب zarb-i-murakkab.—(*multiplication-table*) ضرب شبیکه zarb-i-shabíkah, ضرب زبانی zarb-i-zabání, ضرب اندر ضرب zarb andar zarb.

MULTIPLICATOR, مضروب فیه mazrúb-fíhi.

MULTIPLICITY, کثرت kasrat, بسیاری bisyárí.

To MULTIPLY (*increase*), افزودن afzúdan, افزائیدن afzá,idan, بسیار شدن bisyár shudan, زیاد شدن ziyád shudan.—(*arithmetic*) ضرب کردن zarb kardan.

MULTITUDE, *vide* CROWD, ASSEMBLY, PLENTY.

MUMMY, مومیا múmiyá, مومیائی múmiyá,í.

MUNDANE, دنیوی dunyaví, پست past, زمانی zamání.

MUNIFICENCE, سخاوت sakhávat, سخا sakhá, کرامت karámat, مکرمت makrumat, جود júd, بذل bazl, جوانمردی javán-mardí, سماحت samáhat.

MUNIFICENT, سخی sakhí, کریم karím, جواد javvád, گشاده دست gushádah-dast, جوانمرد javán-mard.

MUNITIONS, سامان جنگ sámán-i-jang.

MURAL, حجاری hijárí. — (*mural tablets*) حجر hajar.

MURDER, خون khún, خونریزی khún-rízí, قتل katl.—(*wilful murder*) قتل عمد katl-i-'amd.—(*accidental*) قتل خطا katl-i-khatá.

MURDERER, خونی khúní, قتال kattál.

MURDERESS, قاتله kátilah.

MURDEROUS, خونریز khún-ríz, خونخوار khún-khwár.

MURKY, تیره tírah.

MURMUR, همهمه hamhamah, فیچ فیچ fich fich, دمدمه damdamah.

To MURMUR, لندلند کردن lundalund kardan, همهمه کردن hamhamah kardan, لنده زدن lundah zadan, دمدمه کردن damdamah kardan. —(*complain*) شکایت بردن shikáyat burdan, شکوی کردن shakvá kardan.—(*like water*) صدا کردن sadá kardan.

MURMURER, شاکی shákí.

MURRAIN, مرگی margí.

MUSCLE (*of a body*), پی pay, عصب 'asab (*pl.* اعصاب a'sáb), عضلت 'azalat, حبل habl.—(*shell-fish*) صدف sadaf.

MUSCULAR, عضلت ناك 'azalat-nák.

To MUSE, *vide* To THINK.

MUSEUM, مجمع الصنائع majma'u-'s-saná,i', موزه múzah (*eur.*).

MUSHROOM, قارچ kárch, قارچ قلاتی kárch-i-kallátí.

MUSIC, غنا ghaná, طرب tarab, موسقی músikí. — (*instrumental music*) ساز sáz, رود rúd.—(*vocal music*) سماع samá', سرود surúd, الحان alhán.—(*science of music*) علم نغمه پردازی 'ilm-i-naghmah-pardází.

MUSICAL, موسقی músikí.

MUSICAL BOX, موزیك múzík (*eur.*).

MUSICAL INSTRUMENT, ساز sáz.

MUSICIAN, مطرب mutrib, مغنی mughanní, سازنده sázandah, موسقی músikí.

MUSK, مشك mishk, مسك misk.—(*musk-deer*) آهوئی مشکین áhú,í-i-mishkín, نافه náfah. — (*bag of musk*) نافه náfah.

MUSKET, تفنگ tufang, گلوله بار gulúlah-bár. The different parts of a musket are as follow:—(*the barrel*) لوله lúlah.—(*calibre*) دهنه dahanah, گلوله خور gulúlah-khwur.

—(*breeching*) دنباله dumbálah.—(*touch-hole*) برمه burmah, گداره gudárah.—(*chamber*) خزانه khizánah, خزینه khizínah.—(*nipple of percussion gun*) خروسك khurúsak. (*sight*) دید díd, دید پیش díd-i-písh.—(*hind sight*) دید پس díd-i-pas.—(*butt*) ته قنداق tah-i-kundák, ته تفنگ tah-i-tufang, زیر قنداق zír-i-kundák.—(*stock*) قنداق kundák, قنداغه kundághah.—(*grasp of stock*) قبضه kabzah.—(*ramrod*) سنبه sumbah, میل míl.—(*bands confining the stock and barrel*) بست bast.—(*lock*) چخماق chakhmák. — (*lock-plate*) صفحه چخماق safhah - i - chakhmák.—(*cock*) چونه chúnah, چانه chánah, خروس khurús.—(*cock of a percussion gun*) دنگ ding, چکش chakush. — (*cock of a match-lock*) ماشه máshah.—(*full cock*) چخماق سر پا chakhmák-sar-pá. — (*half cock*) چخماق نیم پا chakhmák ním-pá.—(*doghead*) سر چونه sar-i-chúnah. — (*hammer*) قاشلق káshluk, قارشلوق karshulúk. — (*pan*) گوشه gúshah, آتشخانه átish-khánah, چاله chálah, اوجاق úják.—(*spring*) کمان kamán.—(*tumbler*) چرخ charkh.—(*screw*) پیچ pích.—(*scear*) پایه páyah.—(*trigger*) پاشنه páshinah, ماشه máshah.—(*trigger - guard*) قرخلق kurkhuluk, قورخلوق kúrkhulúk.—(*plate opposite to the lock*) عقربه 'akrabah.—(*sling*) تسمهٔ تفنگ tasmah-i-tufang.

MUSKETEER, تفنگچی tufang-chí.

MUSKY, مشکین mishkín.

MUSLIN, برنجك birinjak, ململ malmal (*hind.*), آقابانو ákábánú.

MUSTACHIOS, سبیل sibíl, بروت burút, شارب sharib.

MUSTARD, خردل khardal.

MUSTER (*of forces, &c.*), سان sán, عرض لشکر 'araz - i - lashkar.—(*roll*) فهرست fihrist.

To MUSTER, سان دیدن sán dídan.—(*to be mustered*) سان دیده شدن sán-dídah shudan.

MUSTINESS, بوسیدگی búsídagí.

MUSTY, بوسیده búsídah.

MUSULMAN, مسلم muslim (*pl.* مسلمین muslimín), مسلمان musulmán, اهل اسلام ahl-i-islam, مومن múmin.—(*Musulman faith*) اسلام islám.—(*scriptures*) *vide* KURAN. — (*the founder of the faith—Muhammadanism*, مسلمانی musulmání—*whom we call Mahomet, Mahomed, or Mohammed*) محمد muhammad (*literally signifying "praiseworthy"*). He is also termed: حضرت محمد hazrat-i-muhammad (*the Lord Muhammad*); محمد مصطفی muhammad-i-mustafá (*Muhammad the Chosen*); رسول الله rasúlu-'llah (*the Prophet of God*); سید سادات sayyid-i-sádát (*Noble of Nobles*); سید المرسلین sayyidu-'l-mursalín (*Chief of prophets*), &c.

In addition to his own proper name, by which he is universally known, Muhammad allowed himself to be called: احمد ahmad (*most praised*); ابو القاسم abú-'l-Kásim (*father of Kasim, his eldest son, who like all of his children, except Fatimah, died young*); ماحی máhí (*the blotter out*, i.e. *of infidelity*); حاشر háshir (*the gatherer together*, i.e. *of the faithful*); عاقب 'ákib (*the last in succession*, i.e. *of the prophets*); نبی التوبة nabíyu-'t-taubah (*prophet of repentance*); and نبی الرحمة nabíyu-'r-rahmat (*prophet of mercy*).

MUTABILITY, تلون talavvun, تغییر taghyír, تغیر taghayyur.

MUTABLE, متغیر mutaghayyir, تبدیل پذیر tabdíl-pazír, تغیر پذیر taghayyur-pazír.

MUTATION, تبدیل tabdíl, تغییر taghyír.

MUTE, بی زبان bí-zabán, ساکت sákit, لال lál, گنگ gung, بکیم bakím, ابکم abkam.

To MUTILATE (*castrate*), خوجه کردن

khwajah kardan, خصی کردن khusí kardan, آخته کردن ákhtah kardan. —(*cut off nose, ears, hands; put out eyes, &c., according to the sentence of a chief*) نسق کردن nasak kardan.

MUTILATED, چولاق chúlák, زخمی zakhmí, سقط sakat, نسق کرده شده nasak-kardah-shudah.

MUTILATION, تجذیم tajzím, اجذام ijzám.

MUTINEER *and* MUTINOUS, یاغی yághí, باغی bághí, عاصی 'ásí, طاغی tághí, گردن کش gardan-kash, مفسد mufsid, منحرف munharif, سر کش sar-kash, متمرد mutamarrid.

MUTINY, یاغیگری yághí-gari, بغاوت baghávat, فتنه fitnah, طغیان tughyán, عصیان 'isyán, فساد fasád, گردنکشی gardan-kashí, دغدغه daghdaghah, سر کشی sar-kashí, قهقرا kahkará, هرزگی harzagí (*vulg.*).

To MUTINY, عصیان نمودن 'isyán nimúdan, عاصی شدن 'ásí shudan, طغی کردن taghí kardan, یاغی شدن yághí shudan.

To MUTTER, *vide* To GRUMBLE, To MURMUR.

MUTTON, گوشت گوسفند gúsht-i-gúsfand.

MUTUAL, جانبین jánibain, ما بین má-bain, طرفین tarafain.

MUZZLE (*for dogs, &c.*), دهن بند dahan-band.

To MUZZLE, دهن بستن dahan bastan.

MUZZLE-LOADER, دهن پر dahan-pur.

MY, مال من mál-i-man.

MYRIAD (*ten thousand*), تومان túmán, تمن tuman.

MYROBALAN (*tree*), هلیله halílah, آمله ámulah.

MYRRH, مر murr.

MYRTLE, مورد múrd, آس ás.

MYSELF, خود من khwud-i-man.

MYSTERIOUS, مخفی makhfí.

MYSTERIOUSLY, مرموزاً marmúzan, سراً sirran.

MYSTERY, راز ráz, رمز ramz, غیب ghaib, سر sirr.

MYSTICAL, باطن bátin, باطنی bátiní.

MYSTICISM, تصوف tasavvuf.

MYTHOLOGICAL, موهوم mauhúm.

MYTHOLOGIST, موهومات نویس mauhúmát-nivís, عالم موهومات 'álim-i-mauhúmát.

MYTHOLOGY, موهومات mauhúmát, علم موهومات 'ilm-i-mauhúmát.

N.

NADIR (*opposite to Zenith*), نظیر nazír, نظیر السمت nazíru-'s-samt.

NAG, اسب asb, اسپ asp, ستور sitúr, مرکب markab (*pl.* مراکب marákib), بارکی bárakí, اس as (*vulg.*).

NAIL (*of finger or toe*), ناخن nákhun.—(*hang-nail*) ریشه ríshah. —(*to cut one's nails*) ناخن تراشیدن nákhun tiráshídan. — (*of iron, &c.*) میخ míkh, مسمار mismár.

To NAIL, میخ کوبیدن míkh kúbídan.

NAIVE, سلیم salím.

NAKED, برهنه barahnah, عریان 'uryán, عاری 'árí, معرا mu'arrá, مجرد mujarrad, لوخت lúkht, لخت lukht.

NAKEDNESS, برهنگی barahnagí, عریت 'uryat, تجرد tajarrud.

NAME, نام nám, اسم ism (*pl.* اسامی asámí, *or* اسما asmá). — (*surname of relationship*) کنیه kunyah.—(*surname relating to family, trade, or country*) اسم منسوب ism-i-mansúb. — (*title or nickname*) لقب lakab (*pl.* القاب alkáb).—(*assumed name of a poet*) تخلص takhallus.—(*the names of God, of which there are ninety-nine*)

اسماء حسنی asmá-i-husná, اسماء عظمی asmá-i-'uzmá.—(*it bears out its name*) اسم با مسمی است ism bá-musammá ast.—(*to assume a name*) اسمرا گذاشتن ismrá guzáshtan, نام گرفتن nám giriftan.

To NAME, نامیدن námídan, نام گذاردن nám guzárdan, نام دادن nám dádan, اسم نهادن ism nihádan, مسمی نمودن musammá nimúdan.

NAMED (*called*), موسوم mausúm, مسمی musammá. — (*surnamed*) ملقب mulakkab, متلقب mutalakkib.

NAMELY, یعنی ya'ní, اعنی a'ní, ای ay.

NAMESAKE, سمی samíy, همنام hamnám.

NAP (*of cloth*), کلک kuluk, خواب khwáb, پرز purz.—(*sleep*) خواب khwáb, پینکی pínakí.—(*to take a nap*) پینکی زدن pínakí zadan, چرت زدن churt zadan.

NAPE (*of the neck*), قفا kafá, حیره hírah.

NAPHTHA, نفط naft.

NAPKIN, دستمال dast-mál, پیشگیر písh-gír.

NARCISSUS, نرگس nirgis.

NARCOTIC, مسکر muskir, خواب بخش khwáb-bakhsh.

To NARRATE, تقریر نمودن takrír nimúdan, گفتن guftan, وصف کردن vasf kardan.

NARRATION, وصف vasf.

NARRATIVE, تقریر takrír, نقل nakl.

NARRATOR, ناقل nákil, راوی ráví.

NARROW, تنگ tang, چست chust, ضیق zayyik.

NARROWLY, قریب karíb.

NARROWNESS, تنگی tangí, چستی chustí.

NASAL (*utterance*), غنه ghunnah.

NASTILY, کثیفا kasífan.

NASTINESS, نا پاکی ná-pákí, چرك chirk, کثافت kasáfat.

NASTY, نا پاك ná-pák, چرکین chirkín, کثیف kasíf, مغص mughass. کسیف kasíf.

NATATION, سباحت sibáhat, شنا shiná, شناوری shinávarí.

NATION, قوم kaum, ملت millat, شعبت shu'bat, امت ummat, تبار tabár, خلق khalk.—(*country*) ملك mulk, ولایت valáyat.

NATIONAL, ملتی millatí.

NATIVE (*of a country*), متوطن mutavattin, مولود maulúd.—(*native country or place*) وطن vatan, مولد maulad, زاد بوم zád-búm.

NATIVITY, ولادت viládat, میلاد mílád, تولد tavallud, پیدایش paidáyish.—(*horoscope*) بخت bakht, طالع táli'.

NATRON (*nitre*), نطرون natrún, شوره shúrah.

NATURAL, ذاتی zátí, اصلی aslí, طبیعی tabí'í, طبعی tab'í, جبلی jibillí, غریزی gharízí.—(*natural child*) حرامزاده harám-zádah, ولد الزنا valadu-'z-ziná.

NATURALIST, طبیعی tabí'í.

To NATURALIZE, محسوب ساختن mahsúb sákhtan, اهل بلد گردانیدن ahl-i-balad gardánídan.

NATURALIZED, محسوب mahsúb.

NATURE, ذات zát, طبع tab', طبیعت tabí'at, جوهر jauhar, جبلت jibillat, طینت tínat, سرشت sirisht, خلت khallat, وجود vujúd, شیمه shímah, نهاد nihád, خلقت khilkat, فطرت fitrat, سیرت sírat, مشرب mashrab, مزاج mizáj, سجیه sajíyah, جبلیت jibillíyat.—(*good-natured*) لطیف مشرب latíf-mashrab.—(*ill-natured*) بد خصال bad-khisál, بد خو bad-khú, کج خلق kaj-khulk.

NAUGHT, هیچ hích, چیزی chízí.

NAUGHTINESS, شرارت sharárat, بدی badí.

NAUGHTY (*as a child*), شریر sharír, بد bad.

NAUSEA, تهوع tahavvu'.

To NAUSEATE (*be sick*), استفراغ کردن istifrágh kardan, قی کردن kai kardan.—(*loathe*) مکروه داشتن makrúh dáshtan, نفرت داشتن nifrat dáshtan, متنفر بودن mutanaffir búdan.

NAUSEOUS, ثقیل sakíl.

NAUSEOUSNESS, ثقلت saklat.
NAUTICAL, بحرى bahrí, بحريه bahríyah.
NAVAL, بحرى bahrí, بحريه bahríyah. —(*naval college*) مدرسه بحرى madrasah-i-bahrí. — (*naval officer*) صاحب منصب بحرى sáhib-mansab-i-bahrí.
NAVE, قطب kutb.
NAVEL, ناف náf, سره surrah.—(*string*) خصم khasm.
NAVIGABLE, قابل عبور کشتی kabil-i-'ubúr-i-kashtí.
To NAVIGATE, کشتی راندن kashtí rándan.
NAVIGATION (*the art*), علم سير سفائن 'ilm-i-sair-i-safá,in, علم ملاحى 'ilm-i-mallahí, فن سفر دريا fann-i-safar-i-daryá.
NAVIGATOR, ملاح mallah, نوتى nútí, بحرى bahrí, جاشو jáshú.
NAVY, بحريه bahríyah.
NAY, نى nai, نه nah, خير khair. — (*nay more*) بلکه balkih.
NAZARENE, نصران nasarán.
NAZARITE (*one devoted by religious vows to a life of purity and austerity*), حصور hasúr.
NEAR, نزديك nazdík, نزد nazd, قريب karíb, مقارب mukárib, مشرف mushrif, در شرف dar sharaf, پهلوئى pahlú,í, مکاسر mukásir, موارق muvárik, در جنب dar jamb.
To NEAR, نزديك شدن nazdík shudan, نزديك آمدن nazdík ámadan.
NEARLY, قريب karíb, نزديك nazdík, تقريبا takríban, عنقريب 'an-karíb.
NEARNESS, نزديكي nazdíkí, قرب karb, مقاربت mukárabat, موارقت muvárakat.
NEAT, پاکيزه pákízah, منقه munakkah, آراسته árástah, قشنگ kashang, نظيف nazíf, خوشگل khwush-gil.
NEATLY, با نظافت bá - nazáfat, با قشنگی bá-kashangí.
NEATNESS (*elegance*), سليقت salíkat, نظافت nazáfat, تنقيه tankiyah, قشنگی kashangí.
NEBULOUS, ابر دار abr-dár, گرفته giriftah, پر ميغ pur-mígh.
NECESSARIES, لوازم lavázim.
NECESSARILY, بالضرورت bi-'z-zarúrat, لاجرم lájaram.
NECESSARY, ضرور zarúr, لازم lázim, ملتزم multazim, مقتضى muktazí, معتكد mu'takid, واجب vájib, درکار dar-kár, متحتم mutahattim. —(*privy*) جائی ضرور já,í-i-zarúr, بيت الخلا baitu-'l-khalá, مبرز mabraz, منجلاب خانه munjaláb-khánah.—(*to be necessary*) بايستن báyistan.
To NECESSITATE, واجب ساختن vájib sákhtan, ضرورت نمودن zarúrat nimúdan, لازم نمودن lázim nimúdan.
NECESSITOUS, نياز مند niyáz-mand, محتاج muhtáj, تهی دست tuhí-dast.
NECESSITY, ضرورت zarúrat, حاجت hájat, احتياج ihtiyáj, اقتضا iktizá, لازمت lázimat.—(*want*) بی نوائی bí-navá,í, بيچارگی bí-cháragí, عاجزی 'ájizí, فاقه fákah, استيصال istísál.
NECK, گردن gardan, عنق 'unuk.—(*throat*) گلو gulú, حلق halk, حلقوم hulkúm. — (*back of the neck*) قفاء گردن kafá - i - gardan, حيره hírah.
NECKLACE, گردن بند gardan-band, قلاده kiládah.
NECKTIE, گردنبند gardan-band.
NECROMANCER, جادو گر jádú-gar, ساحر sáhir.
NECROMANCY, نيرنج níranj, جادو jádú, نيرنگ nairang.
NECTAR, رحيق rahík.
NECTARINE, شليل shalíl.
NEED, *vide* NECESSITY.
To NEED, *vide* To REQUIRE.
NEEDLE, سوزن súzan, ميل míl.—(*packing needle*) جوالدوز javál-dúz.
NEEDLE-CASE, سوزندان súzan-dán.
NEEDLESS, بی جهت bí-jihat, بی ضرورت bí-zarúrat.
NEEDLESSLY, بی ضرورت bí-zarúrat.
NEEDLE-WORK (*embroidery*), بوته bútah, قلابدوزی kulláb-dúzí, نقش naksh, نقده دوزی nakdah-dúzí, لندره دوزی landarah-dúzí.

NEEDY, مفلس muflis, فقیر fakír, بی نوا bí-navá, عاجز ‘ájiz.

NEFARIOUS, شریر sharír, رسوا rusvá, فضیح fazíh, روسیاه rú-siyah, بی آبرو bi-áb-rú, بد bad.

NEGATION, انکار inkár, نفی nafy, ابا ibá.

NEGATIVE, منفی manfy, نفی nafy, منکر munkir.—(*of photograph*) شیشه shíshah.

NEGATIVELY, نفیاً nafyan.

NEGLECT, غفلت ghiflat, تغافل taghá-ful, بی پروائی bí-parvá,í, تهاون ta-hávun, اهمال ihmál, کاهلی káhilí, تساهل tasáhul, مساهلت musá-halat, مسامحت musámahat, مهلت muhlat.

To NEGLECT, غافل شدن gháfil shu-dan, اهمال نمودن ihmál nimúdan.

NEGLIGÉ, عاطل ‘átil.

NEGLIGENT, بیخبر bí-khabar, غافل gháfil, بیپروا bí-parvá, بی احتیاط bí-ihtiyát, بی اندیشه bí-andíshah, کاهل káhil, بیهوش bí-húsh, زاهل záhil.

To NEGOTIATE, معامله کردن mu‘áma-lah kardan, معاهده نمودن mu-‘áhadah nimúdan.

NEGOTIATION, معامله mu‘ámalah, کار بار kár-bár, مصلحت maslahat, معاهده mu‘áhadah.

NEGRO, زنگی zangí, حبشی habashí, سیاه siyáh, سیه siyah.—(*negro slave*), بنده حبشی bandah-i-habashí, کاکا سیه káká-i-siyah (*vulg.*).—(*slave girl*) کنیز حبشی kaníz-i-habashí, دده سیه dadah-i-siyah (*vulg.*).

NEIGH, شیهه shaihah, صهیل sahíl.

To NEIGH (*a horse*), شیهه کردن shaihah kardan, صهیل کردن sahíl kardan.

NEIGHBOUR, همسایه ham-sáyah, مجاور mujávir, جار jár (*pl.* جیران jírán), همخوار ham-khwár, مکاسر mukásir.

NEIGHBOURING, مجاور mujávir, متصل muttasil.

NEIGHBOURHOOD, همسایگی ham-sáyagí, جوار javár, مجاورت mujá-varat, قرب kurb, نواحی naváhí, نزدیکی nazdíkí, حوالی haválí, حول و حوش haul va haush.—(*in the neighbourhood of*) در اطراف dar atráf, در حوالی dar haválí.

NEIGHBOURLY, مهربان mihrbán, شفیق shafík.

NEITHER, نه nah.—(*neither one nor other*) نه آن نه این nah án nah ín, نه یك نه دگر nah yak nah digar.—(*neither more nor less*) نه کم نه زیاد nah kam nah ziyád.—(*nei-ther ... nor ...*) نه ... نه ... nah ... nah ...

NEOPHYTE, طالب العلم tálibu’-l-‘ilm.

NEPHEW (*brother's son*), برادر زاده birádar-zádah, پسر برادر pisar-i-birádar.—(*sister's son*) همشیره زاده hamshírah-zádah, خواهر زاده khwáhar-zádah, پسر خواهر pisar-i-khwáhar.

NEPOTISM, نفسانیت nafsáníyat.

NERVE, عصبه ‘asabah, پی pay, عضلت ‘azalat, ریشه ríshah, وتر vatar.

NERVELESS, بی قوت bí-kúvat, نا توان ná-taván, ضعیف za‘íf.

NERVOUS, پیناك pay-nák, ترسان tar-sán.

NEST, آشیانه áshyánah, لانه lánah.—(*of ants, wasps, &c.*) چال chál.

To NESTLE, آشیانه کردن áshyánah kardan.

NET, شبکه shabakah.—(*for fishing or fowling*) دام dám, توره túrah, طور túr, شص shass.—(*commercial term*) صافی sáfí.

NETHER, پست past, فرو furú, زیر zír.

NETTED, مشبك mushabbak.

NETTING, شبکه shabakah.—(*wire-netting*) شبکه با سیم کرده shaba-kah bá-sím kardah.

NETTLE, گزنه gaznah.

To NETTLE, بخشم آوردن bi-khishm ávardan, مضطرب ساختن muztarib sákhtan, آزردن ázurdan.

NET-WORK, شبکه shabakah.

NEUTER (*noun*), اسم بی جنس ism-i-bí-jins, اسم بلا تذکیر و تانیث ism-i-bilá tazkír va ta,nís.

NEUTRAL, بی طرف bí-taraf.

NEUTRALITY, بی طرفی bí-tarafí.
NEVER, هرگز hargiz, اصلاً aslan, ابداً abdan.
NEVERTHELESS, با وجود آن bá-vujúd-i-án, مع کل هذا ma' kull házá, هر چند که har chand kih.
NEW, نو nau, تازه tázah, جدید jadíd, ینگی yangí.—(*it is nothing new*) تازگی ندارد tázagí na-dárad.—(*New-Year's Day*) نو روز nau-rúz.—(*new comer*) خوشنشین khwush-nishín, تازه وارد tázah-várid, نو رسیده nau-rasídah.
NEW-FASHIONED, رسم جدید rasm-i-jadíd.
NEWLY, از نو az nau, مجدداً mujaddadan.—(*lately*) در این وقت dar ín vakt.
NEWS, خبر khabar, اخبار akhbár, افواه afváh, آوازه ávázah, حدیث hadís, آگهی ágahí.—(*newsmonger*) خبر گیر khabar-gír.—(*good news*) مژده muzhdah, خوش خبر khwush-khabar, بشارت bishárat, تباشیر tabáshír, نوید navíd.—(*a present for good news*) مژده لك muzhdah-luk, مژدگانی muzhdagání.—(*bad news*) خبر بد khabar-i-bad, خبر وحشت مدار khabar-i-vahshat-madár, حدیث شوم hadís-i-shúm.—(*newspaper*) روز نامچه اخبار rúz-námchah-i-akhbár, روز نامچه rúz-námchah, روز نامه rúz-námah, گازت gázit (*eur.*).
NEWS-WRITER, اخبار نویس akhbár-nivís.
NEXT (*adjoining*), متصل muttasil, پیوسته paivastah. — (*following*) دیگر dígar, دگر digar, عنقریب 'ankaríb, بعد ba'd, آینده áyandah, پس pas.—(*next day*) روز دگر rúz-i-digar, روز بعد rúz-i-ba'd.—(*next year*) سال آینده sál-i-áyandah, سال دگر sál-i-digar.
NIB (*point*), نوك nauk, سر sar.—(*piece of horn or ivory upon which pens are nibbed*) قطزن katzan, قطعزن kat'zan.
NIBBED, نوکدار nauk-dár.
TO NIBBLE, خائیدن khá,ídan, جائیدن já,ídan, گزیدن gazídan.

NICE, مرغوب marghúb, نیك ník, لذیذ lazíz, قشنگ kashang, مطبوع matbú'.
NICELY, به خوبی bi-khúbí.
NICENESS, لذت lazzat, نیکی níkí, قشنگی kashangí, لطافت latáfat.
NICETY, سلیقه salíkah, نکته nuktah.
NICHE, طاقچه tákchah, خلل khalal, — (*spaces between the niches in the wall of a room*) جرز jirz.
NICK (*of time*), عین وقت 'ain-i-vakt.
NICK-NACKS, چیزها ابله فریبانه chíza-há-i-ablah-firíbánah.
NIECE, دختر برادر dukhtar-i-birádar, دختر خواهر dukhtar-i-khwáhar, برادر زاده birádar-zádah, خواهر زاده khwáhar-zádah.
NIGGARD, بخیل bakhíl, ممسك mumsik, لئیم la,ím, جوکی júkí, خسیس khasís, حریص harís, طامع támi'.
NIGGARDLINESS, بخل bukhl, حرص hirs, طمع tama', خسیست khasísat, امساك imsák.
NIGGARDLY, طمعکار tama'-kár, لئیم la,ím, حریص harís, تنگ چشم tang-chashm, خسیس khasís.
NIGH, نزدیك nazdík, نزد nazd, قریب karíb, مقارب mukárib, مشرف mushrif, در شرف dar sharaf, پهلوئی pahlú,í, مکاثر mukásir, موارق muvárik, در جنب dar jamb.
NIGHT, شب shab, لیل lail (*pl.* لیالی liyálí), لیله lailah, شو shau (*vulg.*).—(*this night, to night*) امشب imshab, امشو imshav (*vulg.*).—(*last night*) دیشب dí-shab, دوش dúsh, دیشو díshav (*vulg.*).—(*night before last*) پریشب parí-shab.—(*at night*) وقت شب vakt-i-shab, هنگام شب hangám-i-shab.—(*to pass the night*) بیتوته کردن baitútah kardan, شب بسر بردن shab bi-sar burdan.
NIGHT-CAP, شبکلاه shab-kuláh.
NIGHT-DRESS, رخت خواب rakht-i-khwáb.
NIGHT-FALL, شبانگاه shabán-gáh.
NIGHTINGALE, بلبل bulbul, عندلیب 'andalíb, هزار داستان hazár-dástán, زند باف zand-báf.
NIGHT-LIGHT, قندیل kandíl (*eur.*).

NIGHTLY, در شب dar shab, لیلاً lailan.—(*every night*) هر شب har shab, شبینه shabínah, شبانه shabánah.

NIGHT-MAN (*cleanser of privies*), کناس kannás, خاصه چین khássah-chín (*vulg.*).

NIGHTMARE, کابوس kábús, بختک bakhtak.

NIGHTSHADE, طولیدون túlídún, سگ انگور sag-angúr, روا تربك ravá-turbak.

NIGHT-WALKER, شب گرد shab-gird.

NIGHT-WATCH (*guard*), عسس 'asas, پاسبان شب pásbán-i-shab, کشیکچی kashík-chí, گزمه gazmah.

NIHILIST, نهیلیست nihílíst (*eur.*).

NIMBLE, چابك chábuk, چالاك chálák, زرنگ zaring, شاطر shátir, قچاق ghuchák.

NIMBLY, بچابکی bi-chábukí, بچالاکی bi-chálákí.

NINNY, احمق ahmak, بیوقوف bí-vukúf.

To NIP (*things*), چیدن chídan.—(*persons*) پنجر گرفتن pinjar giriftan.

NIPPERS, *vide* PINCERS.

NIPPLE, سر پستان sar-i-pistán, ضرع zir' (*pl.* ضروع zurú').—(*of a percussion gun*) خروسك khurúsak.

NITRE, شوره shúrah, نطرون natrún.

NITROUS, با شوره bá-shúrah.

No, نه nah, نی nai, خیر khair, لا lá, ما má.

NOBLE, شریف sháríf, اشرف ashraf, عمده 'umdah, بزرگ buzurg, اصیل asíl, نجیب najíb, پاك نژاد pák-nizhád, کبیر kabír, کریم karím, عالی 'álí, عالیشان 'álí-shán, عالیجاه 'álí-jáh, امیر amír.—(*grand*) جلیل jalíl, شگرف shigarf, عالی 'álí, جزیل jazíl, اعلی a'lá, مکرم mukarram. (*nobles, nobility*) شرفا shurafá, اشراف ashráf, امرا umará, خواص khaváss, برایا baráyá, اعیان a'yán, ارکان دولت arkán-i-daulat, بزرگان buzurgán, موالی maválí, اکابر akábir.—(*nobles and commoners*) خواص و عام kháss va 'ámm, خواص و عوام khaváss va 'avámm, ادنی اعلی adná a'lá, وضیع و شریف vazí' va sharíf, خرد و بزرگ khurd va buzurg, اهالی و موالی ahálí u maválí.

NOBLENESS, نجابت najábat, شرافت sharáfat, بزرگی buzurgí.

NOBLY, امیرانه amíránah, شریفانه sháríífánah, مکرماً mukarraman.

NOBODY, هیچکس hích-kas.

NOCES, زفاف zifáf.

NOCTURNAL, شبی shabí, سمر samar.

NOCTURNALLY, شبانه shabánah.

NOD, جنبش jumbish.

To NOD, جنبانیدن jumbánídan.

NOISE (*sound*), آواز áváz, صدا sadá, صوت saut.—(*clamour*) شور shúr, شورش shúrish, بانگ báng, غوغا ghaughá, فریاد faryád, ولوله valvalah, هنگامه hangámah, هائی هوئی há,í hú,í, شماته shamátah.—(*to make a noise*) همهمه کردن hamhamah kardan.

NOISELESS, بی آواز bí-áváz, خاموش khámúsh.

NOISOME, متعفن muta'affin, زیان ور ziyán-var, مضر muzirr, ضرر انگیز zarar-angíz.

NOISY (*persons*), غوغائی ghaughá,í.—(*place*) پر غوغا pur-ghaughá.

NOLECOLE (*or knolcole, the vegetable turnip-rooted cabbage*), قمری kumrí, کلم شهری kalam-i-shahrí.

NOLENS VOLENS, طوعاً و کرهاً tau'an va kurhan, خواسته نخواسته khwástah na-khwástah.

NOMAD (*wandering tribe of Persia*), ال ill, ایل íl (*pl.* الیات ilyát).—(*a man of a nomadic tribe*) الیاتی ilyátí, صحرا نشین sahra-nishín.

NOM DE PLUME, اسم عملی ism-i-'amalí, تخلص takhallus.

NOMENCLATURE, فهرست اسامی fihrist-i-asámí.

NOMINAL, اسمی ismíy.

NOMINALLY, اسماً isman.

To NOMINATE, تسمیه کردن tasmiyah kardan.

NOMINATION, تسمیه tasmiyah.

NOMINATIVE, اسم فاعل ism-i-fá,il.—

(*case*) حالت فاعلیت hálat-i-fá'ilíyat.
NONAGE, خورد سالی khwurd-sálí, صغر السن sighru-'s-sinn.
NONCHALANCE, تکاهل takáhul, غافلی gháfilí, کسالت kasálat.
NONCHALANT, غافل gháfil, کسلان kaslán, کاهل káhil.
NONE, هیچ نه hích-nah, لا شی lá-shai, هیچ کدام hích-kudám.
NONENTITY, نیستی nístí, عدم 'adam.
NON-EXISTENT, نیست níst, منعدم mun'adim.
NONSENSE, پوچ púch, چرند charand, عبث 'abas, بیهودگی bíhúdagí, مهمل muhmal, یاوه yávah, هرزه harzah, لغو laghv, هذیان hazyán, جفنگ jafang, لیچار líchár, حرف مفت haraf-i-muft.—(*to talk nonsense*) چرند گفتن charand guftan, ابطال نمودن ibtál nimúdan, پوچ گفتن púch guftan, لیچار گفتن líchár guftan.
NONSENSICAL, احمق ahmak بیوقوف bí-vukúf.
NOOK, منفذ manfaz, خلل khalal, گوشه gúshah. — (*nooks and crannies*) خلل و فرج khilal va furaj.
NOON, ظهر zuhr, نیمروز ním-rúz, نصف النهار nisfu-'n-nahár.
NOOSE, کمند kamand, دام dám.
To NOOSE, کمند انداختن kamand andákhtan.
NOR, نه nah, و نه va nah.
NORMAL, معتاد mu'tád, طبعی tab'í. —(*medical term*) غریزی gharízí.
NORTH, شمال shimál.—(*pole*) قطب شمالی kutb-i-shimálí. — (*northeast*) ما بین شمال و مشرق má bain-i-shimál va mashrik. —(*northwest*) ما بین شمال و مغرب má bain-i-shimál va maghrib.
NORTHERLY, شمالاً shimálan.
NORTHERN, شمالی shimálí, شمالیه shamálíyah.
NORTHWARD, بسوی شمال bi-suví-i-shimál.
NOSE, بینی bíní, انف [illegible]f.—(*pug-nose*) اخنس akhnas.—(*..p of nose*) نوك بینی nauk-i-bíní.—(*bridge of nose*) بر آمدگی بینی bar-ámadagí-i-bíní.—(*upper part of nose*) دماغ dimágh. — (*he leads him by the nose*) بتصنیفش میرقصد bi-tasnífash mí-raksad.
NOSE-BAG (*of a horse*), توبره túbarah.
NOSEGAY, گلدسته gul-dastah.
NOSE-RING, حلقه بینی halkah-i-bíní, خزام khizám, برسن bursan (*obs.*).
NOSTRIL, پره بینی parrah-i-bíní, منخار mankhár. — (*septum, or division of the nostrils*) خیشیم khaishím.
NOT, نه nah, نا ná, لا lá, غیر ghair, ما má, نی nai.—(*not at all*) اصلاً aslan, مطلقاً mutlakan, هیچ hích, حاشا و کلا háshá va kallá.
NOTABLE, مشهور mash-húr, معروف ma'rúf.—(*notables*) *vide* NOBLES.
NOTABLENESS, شهرت shuhrat, عیان 'iyán.
NOTARY, تذکره چی tazkirah-chí, دفتر نویس daftar-nivís.
NOTATION, رقم rakam.
NOTCH, چوبخط chúb-khat, ناب náb, کنه kinah, چو خط chú-khat (*vulg.*). —(*of an arrow*) سوفار súfár, جائی زه já,í-i-zih.—(*in the blade of a sword or knife*) رخنه rikhnah, دمریزه damrízah, شلی shalí.
To NOTCH, کنه کردن kinah kardan.
NOTCHED, دندانه دار dandánah-dár, رخنه دار rikhnah-dár, کنه دار kinah-dár.
NOTE (*memorandum*), یاد داشت yád-dásht, تذکره tazkirah.—(*short letter*) رقعه ruk'ah.—(*enclosure in a letter*) ملفوفه malfúfah.—(*marginal gloss*) حاشیه háshiyah (*pl.* حواشی havášhí). — (*of hand*) تمسك tamassuk.—(*of music, of which, according to Persian musicians, there are twelve*) مقام makám, کوك kúk.—(*half-note, of which there are twenty-four*) پرده pardah.—(*diplomatic note*) لائحه lá,ihah, تقریر takrír, شرح دولتی sharh-i-daulatí.—(*circular note*) تحریرات عمومیه tahrírát-i-'umúmíyah. — (*joint note*) کاغذ متحد المالی kághaz-i-muttahidu-'l-

ma,álí. — (*money*) قايمه káímah. —(*of interrogation*) حرف استفهام haraf-i-istifhám. — (*to make a note of a thing*) نوشتن nivishtan.

NOTE-BOOK, كتابچه kitábchah.

NOTHING, هيچ hích, لا شى lá-shay.

NOTHINGNESS, عدم 'adam, نيستى nístí.

NOTICE (*observation*), نگاه nigáh, نظر nazar, ملاحظه muláhazah.—(*intelligence*) آگاهى ágáhí, آگهى ágahí, اطلاع ittilá', خبر khabar, اعلام i'lám, اعلان i'lán.

To NOTICE, امعان نظر نمودن im'án-i-nazar nimúdan, ملتفت شدن multafit shudan.

NOTIFICATION, اعلام i'lám, اعلان i'lán, اشتهار ishtihár, اشعار ish'ár.

To NOTIFY, اشتهار دادن ishtihár dádan, اعلان كردن i'lán kardan, اشعار كردن ish'ár kardan.

NOTION, خيال khayál, گمان gumán, حدس hads, تصور tasavvur, وهم vahm, ظن zann, فكر fikr, قياس kiyás.—(*to have a notion*) پنداشتن pindáshtan.

NOTORIETY, شهرت shuhrat, عيان 'iyán.

NOTORIOUS, معروف ma'rúf, مشهور mash-húr, منصوص mansús, نامزد nám-zad.

NOTORIOUSLY, مشهوراً mashúran, ظاهراً záhiran.

NOTWITHSTANDING, با وجود كه bá-vujúd kih, هر چند كه har chand kih, حال آنكه hál án kih, مع هذا ma' házá.

NOUGHT, هيچ hích, چيزى chízí.

NOUN, اسم ism (*pl.* اسما asmá).—(*substantive*) اسم ذات ism-i-zát. —(*definite noun*) اسم معروف ism-i-ma'rúf.—(*indefinite noun*) اسم منكر ism-i-munakkar. — (*generic noun*) اسم جنس ism-i-jins.—(*primitive noun*) اسم جامد ism-i-jámid, اسم اصلى ism-i-aslí.—(*derivative noun*) اسم مشتق ism-i-mushtakk, اسم ماخوذ ism-i-ma,khúz.—(*abstract noun*) حاصل مصدر hásil-i-masdar.—(*adjective*) صفت sifat.—(*variable or declinable noun*) اسم منصرف ism-i-munsarif.—(*indeclinable noun*) اسم غير منصرف ism-i-ghair-i-munsarif. —(*simple noun*) اسم مفرد ism-i-mufrad, اسم بسيط ism-i-basít.—(*verbal noun*) مصدر masdar.—(*noun of time*) اسم زمان ism-i-zamán.—(*noun of place*) اسم مكان ism-i-makán. — (*noun of instrument*) اسم آلت ism-i-álat.—(*noun of multitude*) اسم جمع ism-i-jam'.

To NOURISH, پروردن parvardan, پرورش كردن parvarish kardan.

NOURISHER, پرور parvar, پرورنده par-varandah.

NOURISHMENT, قوت kút, خوراك khwurák, طعام ta'ám, غذا ghizá, خورد khwurd, آذوقه ázúkah, ماكول ma,kúl.

NOVEL, نو nau, تازه tázah, جديد jadíd, ينگى yangí.—(*book*) قصه kissah, داستان dástán, كتاب نقل kitáb-i-nakl.

NOVELIST, نقال nakkál.

NOVELTY, تازگى tázagí.—(*it is a novelty*) تازگى دارد tázagí dárad.

NOVEMBER, تشرين ثانى tashrín-i-sání.

NOVICE, نو آموز nau-ámúz, جديد jadíd, مبتدى mubtadí.

NOVITIATE, نو آموزى nau-ámúzí. (*Vide* NOVICE).

NOW, اكنون aknún, كنون kanun, حال hál, حالا hálá, الحال al-hál, الان al,án, هنوز hanúz, در اين وقت dar ín vakt.—(*now-a-days*) در اين زمان dar ín zamán.—(*now and then*) *vide* SOMETIMES.

NOWHERE, هيچ جا hích-já.

NOWISE, بهيچ صورت bi-hích súrat, اصلاً aslan, هيچوجه hích-vajh.

NOXIOUS, مضر muzirr, موذى mu,zí, زيانكار ziyán-kár, ضاره zárrah.

NOXIOUSNESS, ضرر zarar, زيانكارى ziyán-kárí, زيان ziyán, آزار ázár.

NUANCES, جزئات juz,ivát.

NUBILE, بالغ bálígh, بحد تكليف رسيده bi-hadd-i-taklíf-rasídah, بسن شعور آمده bi-sinn-i-shu'úr-ámadah.

NUCLEUS, اصل asl, اساس asás, امهات ummahát.

NUDE, برهنه barahnah, عاری 'árí, عریان 'uryán, معری mu'arrá, مجرد mujarrad, لوخت lúkht, لخت lukht.

To NUDGE, تحریک نمودن tahrík nimúdan.

NUDITY, برهنگی barahnagí, تجرد tajarrud, عریت 'uryat.

NUGATORY, ابطال ibtál, باطل bátil.

NUISANCE, آفت áfat, آزار ázár, اذیت azíyat, ایذا ízá, وبال vabál.

NULL, نا چیز ná-chíz.—(*null and void*) ابطال ibtál.—(*to render null and void*) ابطال کردن ibtál kardan.

NULLITY, نا چیزی ná-chízí, بطلان butlán.

NUMB, بی حس bí-hiss, سست sust.

To NUMB, بی حس ساختن bí-hiss sákhtan, افسرده کردن afsurdah kardan.—(*to be numbed*) سست شدن sust shudan, بی حس شدن bí-hiss shudan.

NUMBER, عدد 'adad, شماره shimárah, حساب hisáb.—(*on a paper, &c.*) نمره numrah (*eur.*), نومره númrah (*eur.*).—(*even number*) عدد شفع 'adad-i-shaf', عدد زوج 'adad-i-zauj.—(*odd number*) عدد طاق 'adad-i-ták, عدد وتر 'adad-i-vitr.—(*mixed number*) عدد مرکب 'adad-i-marakkab.—(*round number*) عدد تام 'adad-i-támm.—(*ordinal number*) اسم عدد ism-i-'adad.—(*square number*) عدد مربع 'adad-i-murabba'.—(*whole number*) عدد تام 'adad-i-támm.—(*to the number of*) بقدر bi-kadr.—(*science of numbers*) علم اعداد و حساب 'ilm-i-a'dád va hisáb.

Numbers of different things are customarily denoted by certain technical classifications prefixed, corresponding with our terms Lot, Set, Head, Flock, Line, Suit, Stand, &c., as follow: دست dast (applicable to clothes, houses, chess or backgammon-men, and hawks), as یک دست رخوت yak dast rukhút (*one suit of clothes*), دو دست خانه dú dast khánah (*two houses*), &c.; راس rás (applied to horses, mules, sheep, cattle, and slaves), as پنج راس اسب panj rás asb (*five horses*), &c.; زنجیر zanjír (applied to elephants); مرس maras, or قلاده kiládah (hunting dogs, hounds); قطار kitár, or مهار mihár (camels), a term not much in use; بهله bahlah (hawks, falcons); باب báb (shops); فروند farvand (ships, boats, &c.); نفر nafar (persons, men; also teeth, and sometimes camels—more used in the latter sense than the term before mentioned); قبضه kabzah (swords, daggers, guns, and pistols); عراده 'arrádah (cannon); طاقه tákah (webs or pieces of cloth, shawls, handkerchiefs); تخته takhtah (carpets); دانه dánah (precious stones, and also used indiscriminately for anything); جلد jild (books); طغرا tughrá (papers, documents); رشته rishtah (railway); تا tá, عدد 'adad, دانه dánah (applicable indiscriminately to almost anything); جفت juft, or زوج zauj (a pair of anything).

To NUMBER, عدد نمودن 'adad nimúdan.

NUMBERER, حساب گر hisáb-gar, شمرنده shimurandah.

NUMBERING, عد 'add, تعداد ti'dád.

NUMBERLESS, بیعدد bí-'adad, بیشمار bí-shimár.—(*numerous*) بسیار bisyár, عدید 'adíd, متعدد muta'addid, متکثره mutakassarah, کثیر العدد kasíru-'l-'adad, خیلی khailí, خطیر khatír.

NUMERABLE, تعداد پذیر ti'dád-pazír.

NUMERAL (*figure*), هندسه hindasah, حساب رقومی hisáb-i-rukúmí.

NUMERATION, عد 'add, رقم rakam, تعداد ti'dád.

NUMERATOR, حساب گر hisáb-gar, عدد دان 'adad-dán.—(*in fractions*) شمار کننده shimár-kunandah.

NUMERICAL, عددی 'adadí.
NUMEROUS, بسیار bisyár, عدید 'adíd, متعدد muta'addid, متکثره mutakassarah, کثیر العدد kasíru-'l-'adad, خیلی khailí, خطیر khatír.
NUN, راهبه ráhibah.
NUNNERY, دیر dair, مسکن راهبات maskan-i-ráhibát.
NUPTIAL, عروسی 'arúsí, نکاحی nikáhí. (*Vide* MARRIAGE.)
NURSE, دایه dáyah, دده dadah.—(*monthly nurse*) ماماچه mámáchah, قابله kábilah.
To NURSE, بچه نوازی کردن bachah-navází kardan.
NURSERY, دایه خانه dáyah-khánah.—(*garden*) درختزار dirakht-zár, شجرستان shajaristán, باغچه bághchah.
NURSLING, بچه bachah, طفل tifl.
NURTURE, تربیت tarbiyat, پرورش parvarish.
To NURTURE, پرورش کردن parvarish kardan, پروریدن parvarídan, تربیت کردن tarbiyat kardan.
NUT, جوز jauz.—(*filbert*), فندق finduk.—(*pistachio*) پسته pistah, فستق fistuk.—(*walnut*) گردو girdú, گردگان girdgán.—(*cocoa-nut*) نارگیل nárgíl, نارجیل nárjíl.
NUT-CRACKER, فندق شکن finduk-shikan, جوز شکن jauz-shikan.
NUTMEG, جوز jauz, جوز الطیب jauzu-'t-tíb.
NUTRIMENT, قوت kút, خوراک khwurák, طعام ta'ám, غذا ghizá, خورد khwurd, آذوقه ázúkah, مأکول ma,kúl.
NUTRITIOUS, مغذی mughazzí.
NUTSHELL, پوست púst.
NUX VOMICA, فلوس ماهی fulús-i-máhí, جوز القی jauzu-'l-kay.
NYMPH (*of Paradise*), حور húr, حوری húrí.

O.

O! ای ai, یا yá, آوخ ávakh, اهای ahái.
OAF, خرف khirif, کودن kaudan, کند kund.
OAFISHNESS, ابلهی ablahí, حماقت himákat, بیوقوفی bí-vukúfí, نادانی ná-dání, خریت kharíyat (*vulg.*).
OAK, درخت بلوط dirakht-i-ballút.—(*evergreen oak*) سندیان sindiyán.
OAK-APPLE, مازو mázú, مازی mází.
OAKEN, بلوطی ballútí.
OAR, پارو parú, خاده khádah.
OASIS (*fertile spot in the desert*), وادی vádí, جزیره jazírah.
OATH, سوگند saugand, قسم kasam, یمین yamín, حلف half.—(*to take an oath*) قسم خوردن kasam khwurdan, سوگند یاد نمودن saugand yád nimúdan.
OATS, زن zann, زان zánn.—(*wild species of oats*) زنگوله zangúlah.—(*wild oats dried for fodder*) برمه burmah, بریده burídah.
OBDURATE, سنگدل sang-dil, سخت sakht, بیرحم bí-rahm, درشت durusht.
OBDURATENESS, سنگدلی sang-dilí, سختی sakhtí, بیرحمی bí-rahmí, درشتی durushtí.
OBEDIENCE, فرمانبرداری firmán-burdárí, حکمبرداری hukm-burdárí, طاعت tá'at, اطاعت itá'at, اتباع ittibá', انقیاد inkiyád, امتثال imtisál, اذعان iz'án.
OBEDIENT, فرمانبردار firmán-burdár, حکمبردار hukm-burdár, مطیع mutí', تابع tábi', متابع mutábi', رام rám, منقاد munkád.
OBEDIENTLY, تابعاً tábi'an.
OBEISANCE, کورنش kúrnish, سر فرو sar-furú, رکوع rukú', تکریم takrím.
OBELISK, میل míl, مناره manárah.
OBESE, فربه farbih, سمین samín, لنبه lumbah, چاق chák, جسیم jasím.
To OBEY, اطاعت کردن itá'at kardan,

فرمان بردار شدن firmán-burdár shudan.

OBITUARY, مرحومین marhúmín.

OBJECT (*thing seen*), منظر manzar, مظهر mazhar.—(*thing*) شی shay, باب báb, مادة mádah.—(*desire*) مقصد maksad, مقصود maksúd, مطمع matma', غرض gharaz, مدعا mudd'á, مراد murád, مطلب matlab, ارادة irádah, عزم 'azm, قصد kasd, نیت níyat, خواست khwást, آهنگ ahang. — (*grammatical term*) معمول ma'múl.

To **OBJECT** to, رد نمودن radd nimúdan, اعتراض کردن i'tiráz kardan, عیب دیدن 'aib dídan, نقص دیدن naks dídan, امتناع داشتن (از) imtiná' dáshtan (az), مخالف کردن mukhálif kardan.

OBJECTION, اعراض i'ráz, اعتراض i'tiráz. — (*fault*) عیب 'aib, نقص naks.

OBJECTIVE CASE, حالت معمولیت hálat-i-ma'múlíyat.

OBJECTOR, متعرض muta'arriz.

To **OBJURGATE**, تحدید نمودن tahdíd nimúdan, سرزنش نمودن sarzanish nimúdan.

OBJURGATION, تحدید tahdíd, سرزنش sarzanish.

OBLATION (*offering*), نذر nazr, عرس 'urs.

OBLIGATION, *vide* DUTY, FAVOUR, BOND.

OBLIGATORY, لازم lázim, واجب vájib, مقتضی muktazí, متحتم mutahattam.

To **OBLIGE**, جبراً کردن jabran kardan, بر آن داشتن bar án dáshtan, بزور کردن bi-zúr kardan, ابرام نمودن ibrám nimúdan, مجبور نمودن majbúr nimúdan.—(*confer favour*) ممنون ساختن mamnún sákhtan, مرهون منت گردانیدن marhún-i-minnat gardánídan, منت نهادن minnat nihádan, احسان کردن ihsán kardan, عنایت نمودن 'ináyat nimúdan.—(*I am much obliged*) منت دارم minnat dáram, مرهون منت میشوم marhún-i-minnat míshavam.

OBLIGING, کریم karím, مشفق mushfik, شفیق shafík, مهربان mihr-bán.

OBLIQUE, کج kaj, مائل má,il, غیر قائم ghair-i-ká,im, غیر مستقیم ghair-i-mustakím.—(*oblique case*) حالت معمولیت hálat-i-ma'múlíyat.

OBLIQUITY, اعوجاج i'vijáj.

To **OBLITERATE**, محو ساختن mahv sákhtan, خط زدن khat zadan, پاك کردن pák kardan.

OBLITERATION, محو mahv, نسخ naskh.

OBLIVION, نسیان nasyan, فراموشی farámúshí, ذهول zuhúl.

OBLIVIOUS, ذاهل záhil, ناسی násí, فراموشکار faramúsh-kár.

OBLONG, مطر mutirr, مستطیل mustatíl.

OBLOQUY, طعن ta'n, ملامت malámat, بهتان buhtán.

OBNOXIOUS, *vide* NOXIOUS.

OBSCENE, فاحش fáhish, پوچ púch, زشت zisht, هرزة harzah, هزل hazl, خبیث khabís.

OBSCENITY, فحش fuhsh, زشتی zishtí, هرزگی harzagí, خباثت khabásat.

OBSCURE (*dark*), تاریك tárík, تیرة tírah, مظلم muzlim, تار tár.—(*abstruse*) دقیق dakík, غامض ghámiz, مغلق mughlak.—(*unknown*) نا معروف ná-ma'rúf, مجهول majhúl.

To **OBSCURE**, تیرة داشتن tírah dashtan.

OBSCURELY, تاریکانة táríkánah.

OBSCURITY, تاریکی táríkí, تیرگی tíragí, ظلمت zulmat, تار tár, ظلام zalám, داج dáj.

OBSEQUIES, تدفین tadfín, جنازة janázah.

OBSEQUIOUS, مطیع mutí', متابع mutábi', متواضع mutavázi', فرو تن furú-tan, منقاد munkád.

OBSEQUIOUSNESS, کوچکی kúchikí, تواضع tavázu', فرو تنی furú-taní, انکسار inkisár.

OBSERVABLE, ظاهر záhir, هویدا huvaidá, پدید padíd, آشکار áshkár, آشکارة áshkárah, عیان 'iyán, فاش

fásh, روشن raushan, واضح vázih, علانی 'alání, مبین mubín, بدیهی badíhí, پیدا paidá.

OBSERVANCE (*respect*), رعایت ri'áyat, توجه tavajjuh, انقیاد inkiyád, اعتنا i'tiná.

OBSERVATION, مراقبه murákabah, مطالعه mutála'ah, نگاه nigáh.

OBSERVATORY, رصد خانه rasad-khánah.

To OBSERVE (*look on*), نگریستن nigrístan, مراقب بودن murákib búdan, ملاحظه کردن muláhazah kardan.—(*obey a rule*) رعایت نمودن ri'áyat nimúdan, نگاه داشتن nigáh dáshtan, صیانت نمودن siyánat nimúdan, فرا گرفتن fará giriftan, اطاعت کردن itá'at kardan, اجرا داشتن ijrá dáshtan.—(*to be observed, rule, &c.*) استنباط شدن istimbát shudan.

OBSERVER, مراقب murákib, دیده بان dídah-bán, راصد rásid.

OBSOLETE, منسوخ mansúkh, متروک matrúk, نا مانوس ná-ma,nús.

OBSTACLE, مانع máni', سد sadd, مزاحمت muzáhamat.

OBSTINACY, اصرار isrár, خود رائی khwud-rá,í, خود سری khwud-sarí, تمرد tamarrud, عناد 'inád.—(*perseverance*) استقرار istikrár, مداومت mudávamat, مواظبت muvázabat, اصرار isrár.

OBSTINATE, خود سر khwud-sar, مرید maríd, متمرد mutamarrid, حرون harún, منخرط munkharit, معاند mu'ánid, اخلال ikhlál, لجوج lajúj.—(*persevering*) مصر musirr, مواظب muvázib, ملازم mulázim, راسخ rásikh, مداوم mudávim.—(*horse*) سخت لگام sakht-ligám.

OBSTINATELY, عنادا 'inádan, بطور عناد bi-taur-i-'inád.

To OBSTRUCT, منع کردن mana' kardan, مسدود ساختن masdúd sákhtan.

OBSTRUCTION, بند band, سد sadd, ضیق سد zík-i-sadd.—(*medical term*) قبض kabz.

OBSTRUCTIVE, متعرض muta'arriz.

To OBTAIN, یافتن yáftan, حاصل کردن hásil kardan, تحصیل نمودن tahsíl nimúdan, نیل ساختن nail sákhtan, میسر نمودن muyassar nimúdan, اندوختن andúkhtan, بهم رسانیدن bi-ham rasánídan, پیدا کردن paidá kardan.

OBTAINABLE, یافتنی yáftaní.

To OBTRUDE (*trans.*), انداختن andákhtan, له دادن luh dádan (*vulg.*), هل دادن hul dádan (*vulg.*).—(*intrans.*) بی اذن داخل شدن bí-izn dákhil shudan, نا خواسته در آمدن ná-khwástah dar-ámadan.

OBTRUSION, دخل بیجا dakhl-i-bí-já.

OBTUSE, احمق ahmak, کند kund, کودن kaudan, بیوقوف bi-vukúf.

OBTUSELY, جاهلانه jáhilánah.

OBTUSENESS, ابلهی ablahí, حماقت himákat, بیوقوفی bí-vukúfí, نا دانی ná-dání, خریت kharíyat (*vulg.*).

To OBVIATE, تدارک نمودن tadáruk nimúdan, بر داشتن bar-dáshtan, علاج نمودن 'iláj nimúdan, چاره نمودن chárah nimúdan.

OBVIOUS, هویدا huvaidá, پدید padíd, آشکار ashkár, آشکاره ashkárah, ظاهر záhir, عیان 'iyán, فاش fásh, روشن raushan, واضح vázih, علانی 'alání, پیدا paidá.

OBVIOUSLY, ظاهرا záhiran.

OBVIOUSNESS, ظهور zuhúr.

OCCASION, *vide* LEISURE, CAUSE, NECESSITY, OPPORTUNITY.—(*there is no occasion for it*) وجهی ندارد vajhí na-dárad.—(*to seize the occasion*) فرصترا غنیمت شمردن fursatrá ghanímat shimurdan.—(*on the occasion of*) بموقع bi-mauki'.

To OCCASION, انگیختن angíkhtan.

OCCASIONALLY, گاه گاه gáh-gáh, احیانا ahyánan, گاه وقتی gáh-vaktí.

OCCIDENT, مغرب maghrib, غرب gharb.

OCCIDENTAL, مغربی maghribí, غربی gharbí.

OCCULT, *vide* SECRET.

OCCUPANCY, تصرف tasarruf, ضبط zabt.

OCCUPATION, کار kár, عمل 'amal,

شغل shughl, پیشه píshah.—(*possession*) ضبط zabt, تصرف tasarruf.

Occupier, متصرف mutasarrif.

To Occupy, ضبط نمودن zabt nimúdan, تصرف کردن tasarruf kardan.—(*to occupy oneself*) مشتغل شدن mushtaghil shudan.

To Occur, واقع شدن váki' shudan, اتفاق افتادن ittifák uftádan, بظهور رسیدن bi-zuhúr rasídan, عارض شدن 'áriz shudan, بهم شدن bi-ham shudan, صادر شدن sádir shudan, سر زدن sar zadan, وارد شدن várid shudan, روی نمودن rúy nimúdan.

Occurrence, سرگذشت sar-guzasht, اتفاق ittifák, واقعه váki'ah, ما جرا má-jará, رویدار rúy-dár, عارضه 'árizah, سانحه sánihah.

Ocean, بحر محیط bahr-i-muhít, دریای عظیم daryá,í-i-'azím, قاموس kámús.

Ochre, گل ماشی gil-i-máshí, گل زرد gil-i-zard.

O'clock, ساعت sá'at.

Octagon *and* Octagonal, مثمن musamman.

October, تشرین اول tashrín-i-avval.

Octopus, اختپوت akhtapút (*eur.*), هشتپای hasht-páy.

Octuple, مثمن musamman.

Ocular, با چشم bá-chashm, چشمی chasmí.

Oculist, کحال kahhál, حکیم چشم hakím-i-chashm.

Odd (*not even*), فرد fard, تك tak, طاق ták.—(*odd number*) عدد وتر 'adad-i-vitr, عدد طاق 'adad-i-ták, عدد تك 'adad-i-tak.—(*unusual*) غریب gharíb, نادر nádir, عجب 'ajab.

Oddity, غریبی gharíbí, عجیبه 'ajíbah.

Oddly, غریبانه gharíbánah, نادرانه nádiránah.

Ode, غزل ghazal. [This consists of from five to eighteen couplets.]—(*elegy or ode of unlimited length*) قصیده kasídah.

Odious, کریه karíh, مکروه makrúh, مغص mughass.

Odium, کراهیت karáhiyat, نفرت nifrat, تنفر tanaffur, عار 'ár.

Odoriferous, مشموم mashmúm, معطر mu'attar.

Odour, بو bú, بوی búí, رائحه rá,ihah.

Œsophagus, مری mari,.

Of, از az, ز zi, من min.

Off! (*interjection*), دور باش dúr-básh, برو bi-rau, گم بشو gum-bishau.—(*far*) دور dúr, بعید ba'íd.—(*from*) از az, ز zí, من min.

Offal, رشوه rishvah, مردار murdár, میته maitah, رشت rasht, فضله fazlah.

Offence, گناه gunáh, گنه gunah, تقصیر taksír, قصور kusúr, جریمه jarímah, جرم jurm, جنایت janáyat, خطا khatá, اثم ism, ذنب zamb, عیب 'aib.—(*insult*) هتك آبرو hatk-i-áb-rú, شتم shatm, خفت khiffat, بی ساختگی bí-sákhtagí.—(*to take offence*) خشم گرفتن khishm giriftan.

Offenceless, بیگناه bí - gunáh, بیقصور bí-kusúr, معصوم ma'súm.

To Offend, شتم نمودن shatm nimúdan, آزردن ázurdan, رنجانیدن ranjánídan.—(*to be offended*) متنفر بودن mutanaffir búdan, کجخلق بودن kaj-khulk búdan, بیزار شدن bízár shudan, آزرده شدن ázurdah shudan, لغزش گرفتن laghzish giriftan, سر شکسته بودن sar-shikastah búdan, منزجر شدن munzajir shudan, پا کوفتن pá kúftan (*vulg.*).

Offender, گناه کار gunáh-kár, خطا کار khatá-kár, مذنب muznib, اثیم asím, مفسد mufsid, فاسق fásik, رو سیه rú-siyah.

Offensive, کریه karíh, مکروه makrúh, مغص mughass.—(*to assume the offensive*) در خیال حرکات تعرض شدن dar khayál - i- harakát-i-ta'arruz shudan.

Offensively, مکروها makrúhan.

Offer, تقدیم takdím, پیش آوردگی písh-ávardagí.

To Offer, پیش آوردن písh ávardan, تقدیم کردن takdím kardan, تقریب نمودن takríb nimúdan.—(*to offer up as a sacrifice*) ذبح نمودن zibh nimúdan, قربان کردن kurbán, تصدق کردن tasadduk kardan.

OFFERING (*gift*), نذر nazr, پیشکش písh-kash.—(*sacrifice*) هدیه hadíyah, تصدق tasadduk, قربان kurbán, فدا fidá. — (*burnt-offering*) قربان سوختنی kurbán-i-súkhtaní.

OFFERTORY, نذر nazr, پیشکش písh-kash.

OFFICE (*public charge*), عهده ʻuhdah, منصب mansab, عمل ʻamal. —(*house of business*) دفتر خانه daftar-khánah, کار خانه kár-khánah.—(*good offices*) مساعی جمیله masáʻí-i-jamílah, مساعی خیریه masáʻí-i-khairíyah.—(*to use one's good offices*) مساعی جمیله مبذول داشتن masáʻí-i-jamílah mabzúl dáshtan.—(*to quit office*) عزل شدن ʻazl shudan.

OFFICER, عهده دار ʻuhdah - dár, منصبدار mansab-dár, صاحب منصب sáhib-mansab.—(*military*) صاحب منصب sáhib-mansab, سرهنگ sar-hang. — (*of police*) کشیکچی ka-shík-chí, پاسبان pás-bán.

OFFICIAL (*connected with duty, as business, documents, &c.*), رسامی rassámí, دولتی daulatí.—(*clerk, &c.*) مباشر mubáshir.

OFFICIALLY, رسماً rasman.

To OFFICIATE, وکالت کردن vakálat kardan, قائم مقام کردن ká,im-makám kardan.

OFFICIOUS, چابك chábuk, چالاك chálák, زرنگ zaring, شاطر shátir, گستاخ gustakh.

OFFICIOUSNESS, چابکی chábukí, چالاکی chálákí, زرنگی zaringí, جسارت jasárat, گستاخی gustákhí.

OFFSPRING, اولاد aulád, نسل nasl, صلب salab, ذریه zurríyah, اعقاب aʻkáb, سلاله sulálah.

OFTEN, بارها bárhá, بار بار bár-bár, اکثر aksar, اکثر اوقات aksar aukát, مکرر mukarrar, بکرات bi-kirrát, بسا basá, دفعاً dafʻan.

To OGLE, چشمك زدن chashmak zadan.

OGLING, کرشمه kirishmah, غمزه ghamzah, رمز العین ramzu-'l-ʻain.

OGRE, عفریت ʻifrít, غول ghúl, آدمخور ádam-khwur.

OH! دریغ dirígh, فغان fighán, ای ai, های háy, وای váy.

OIL, روغن raughan. — (*castor-oil*) روغن بید انجیر raughan-i-bíd-anjír, روغن کنتو raughan-i-kinnatú.—(*of olives*) روغن زیت raughan-i-zait, روغن زیتون raughan-i-zaitún. (*of linseed*) روغن کتان raughan-i-kattán. — (*lamp-oil*) روغن چراغ raughan-i-chirágh.

To OIL, چرب کردن charb kardan, روغن مالیدن raughan málídan.

OIL-FLASK, دبه روغن dabbah-i-raughan.

OILINESS, چربی charbí.

OILMAN, روغن فروش raughan-furúsh, بقال bakkál.

OIL-MILL, معصر miʻsar, معصار miʻsár.

OILY, چرب charb, روغنی raughaní.

OINTMENT, مرهم marham, روغن raughan.

OLD, سالدیده sál-dídah, سالخورده sál-khwurdah, کهنسال kuhan-sál, کهنه kuhnah, پیر pír, مسن musinn.— مزمن muzmin.—(*ancient*) قدیم kadím, دیرینه dírínah, پیشین píshín, سابق sábik, سلف salaf.— (*stale*) پوسیده púsídah, کهنه kuhnah, کهن kuhan, شبمانده shab-mándah. — (*worn - out*) مندرس mundaris, ساییده sábídah, فرسوده farsúdah.—(*to be . . . years old*) ... سال داشتن . . . sál dáshtan. —(*to grow old*) پیر شدن pír shudan, مسن شدن musinn shudan.— (*old age*) پیری pírí, کبر سن kibr-i-sinn, ضعیفی zaʻífí, هرم haram, مشیب mashíb.—(*old man*) پیر pír, زال zál, ریش سفید rísh-safíd, شیخ shaikh, سالخورده sál-khwurdah, فرتوت fartút, سالدیده sál-dídah. —(*old woman*) پیره pírah, پیر زن pír-zan, پیره زن pírah-zan, گیس سفید gís-safíd, پیره زال pírah-zál, عجوز ʻajúz, عجوزه ʻajúzah.—(*old clothes-man*) کهنه فروش kuhnah-furúsh, کهنه چین kuhnah-chín.

OLEAGINOUS, چرب charb.

OLEANDER, خر زهره khar-zahrah, دفله diflah.
OLIGARCHY, حکومت اشخاص hukúmat-i-ashkhás.
OLIVE, زیتون zaitún, زیت zait.
OMELET, کوکو kúkú.—(*sweet omelet*) خاگینه khágínah.
OMEN, فال fál, شگون shugún, اختر akhtar, طالع táli'.
OMINOUS, غیب نما ghaib-nimá, پر شگون pur-shugún.
OMISSION, فوت faut, سهو sahv.
To OMIT, در گذشتن dar-guzashtan, فرو گذاشت کردن furú-guzásht kardan, سهو کردن sahv kardan, ساقط داشتن sákit dáshtan, انداختن andákhtan.
OMNIPOTENCE, قدرت مطلق kudrat-i-mutlak.
OMNIPOTENT, قادر مطلق kádir-i-mutlak, قدیر kadír, جبار jabbár.
OMNIPRESENCE, هر جا حاضری har-já-házirí.
OMNIPRESENT, همه جا حاضر hamah-já-házir.
OMNISCIENCE, همه دانی hamah-dání, همه بینی hamah-bíní.
OMNISCIENT, همه دان hamah-dán, همه بین hamah-bín.
ON, بر bar, بالا bálá, علی 'alá, فرا fará, روی rúy.—(*on foot*) پیاده piyádah. — (*on horseback*) سواره suvárah, سوار suvár.
ONAGER, حمار وحشی himár-i-vahshí, گور gúr, گور خر gúr-khar.
ONCE, یکدفعه yak-daf'ah, یکبار yak-bár. — (*in former times*) سابق sábik, پیشتر píshtar, مقدما mukaddaman, باری bárí. — (*once upon a time*) باری bárí. — (*at once*) دفعتا daf'atan, یکباره yak-bárah, یکبارگی yak-báragí.—(*all at once*) یک بارگی yak-báragí.—(*Vide* SUDDENLY.)—(*once more*) بتکرار bi-takrár.
ON DIT, از قراری که مذکور میشود az karárí-kih mazkúr mí-shavad, میگویند mí-gúyand, نقل است nakl ast.
ONE, یک yak.—(*one by one*) یک یک yak yak, فردافرد fard-á-fard.—(*one another*), یکدیگر yak-dígar.—(*one with the other*) روی هم رفته rúy-ham-raftah.
To ONERATE, بار کردن bár kardan, حمل نمودن haml nimúdan.
ONEROUS, سخت sakht, ثقیل sakíl, گران girán.
ONION, پیاز piyáz, بصل basal.
ONLY (*singly*), یگانه yagánah, فرد fard, تنها tanhá, مجرد mujarrad, یکتا yak-tá.—(*merely*) فقط fakat, و بس va bas.
ONSET, یورش yúrish, حمله hamlah, خروش khurúsh, هجوم hujúm.
ONWARDS, پیش písh, پیشتر píshtar.
ONYX, عقیق 'akík, سلیمانی sulaimání.
OOZE, گل gil.
To OOZE, چکه کردن chakkah kardan.
OOZY, گلی gilí.
OPAL, عین الهره 'ainu-'l-hirrah, سراوی sarávi, عین الشمس 'ainu-'sh-shams.
OPAQUE, نا شفاف ná-shaffáf.
OPAQUENESS, نا شفافی ná-shaffáfí.
OPEN, باز báz, مفتوح maftúh, گشاده gushádah, واز váz. — (*candid*) مخلص mukhlis, مخلصانه mukhlisánah, اخلاصمند ikhlás-mand, صادق sádik.—(*open air*) بیرون bírún.
To OPEN (*trans.*), گشادن gushádan, گشودن gushúdan, باز کردن báz kardan, وا کردن vá kardan.—(*intrans.*) گشاده شدن gushádah shudan, باز شدن báz shudan, مفتوح شدن maftúh shudan, وا شدن vá shudan. — (*window*) بالا کردن bálá kardan.—(*window of train*) شیشه انداختن shíshah andákhtan. (*flower*) شکوفتن shikúftan, شکفتن shikuftan, غنچه زدن ghunchah zadan.—(*to open into*) راه داشتن ráh dáshtan. — (*to be opened—Parliament*) افتتاح شدن iftitáh shudan.
OPEN-HANDED *and* OPEN-HEARTED, سخی sakhí, کریم karím, جواد javvád, گشاده دست gushádah-dast, جوانمرد javán-mard, منعم mun'im, وهاب vahháb, فیاض fayyáz, سامح sámih.

OPENING, مفر mafarr.
OPENLY (*publicly*), ظاهرا záhiran, علانیه 'aláníyah, آشکاره áshkárah, عیانا 'ayánan.
OPEN-MOUTHED, طامع támi', حریص harís.
OPENNESS, گشادگی gushádagí. — (*candour*) راستبازی rást-bází, اخلاص ikhlás, صدق sidk.
OPERA, تماشا tamáshá. — (*opera-house*) تماشا خانه tamáshá-khánah.
To OPERATE, عمل کردن 'amal kardan, کار کردن kár kardan, ساختن sákhtan.—(*surgical term*), جراحی کردن jarráhí kardan.—(*be effectual*) کارگر آمدن kár-gar ámadan, اثر کردن asar kardan, موثر شدن mú,assir shudan.
OPERATION, عمل 'amal, کار kár.—(*surgical*), جراحی jarráhí.
OPERATIVE, موثر mú,assir, مفید mufíd, کارگر kár-gar.—(*artificer*) کاریگر kárí-gar, پیشه ور píshah-var, صنعتگر san'at-gar.
OPERATOR, عامل 'ámil.—(*surgical*) جراح jarráh.
OPHTHALMIA, آشوب چشم áshúb-i-chashm, رمد ramad, سبل sabal.
OPIATE, معجون ma'jún, دوائی خواب بخش davá,í-i-khwáb-bakhsh.
To OPINE, *vide* To SUPPOSE.
OPINION, رائی ra,í, رای ráy, گمان gumán, اندیشه andíshah, قیاس kiyás, خیال khayál, حدس hads, تصور tasavvur, ظن zann, مظنه mazannah, فکر fikr, وهم vahm, تدبیر tadbír, اعتقاد i'tikád, انگار angár, پندار pindár, تخمین takhmín, زعم za'm, استنباط istimbát.
OPINIONATED, متعصب muta'assib, خود سر khwud-sar, خود رائی khwud-ra,í.
OPIUM, افیون afyaun, تریاک tiryák, شیره خشخاش shírah-i-khashkhásh.
OPIUM-EATER, تریاکی tiryákí, افیونی afyauní.
OPPONENT, معارض mu'áriz, مخاصم mukhásim, مخالف mukhálif.
OPPORTUNE, با محل bá-mahall, با موقع bá-mauki', بجا bi-já.
OPPORTUNITY, فرصت fursat, قابو kábú, محل mahall, حباله habállah.
To OPPOSE, مخالفت نمودن mukhálafat nimúdan, مخالف بودن mukhálif búdan, مقاومت کردن mukávamat kardan, مزاحم شدن muzahim shudan, اعتراض نمودن i'tiráz nimúdan, بر ضد شدن bar zidd shudan. — (*as opposed to*) نقیض nakíz, در مقابل dar mukábil.
OPPOSITE, روبرو rú-bi-rú, محاذی muhází, مواجه muvájih, مقابل mukábil, عکس 'aks, نظیر nazír, موازی muvází, در برابر dar barábar. (*the opposite*) ضد zidd, خلاف khiláf.
OPPOSITION, مخالفت mukhálafat, مزاحمت muzáhamat, مقاومت mukávamat, مقابلت mukábalat, معارضه mu'árazah, ممانعت mumána'at, تناقض tanákuz, ضدیت ziddíyat, اعتراض i'tiráz, اختلاف ikhtiláf, تردد taraddud.—(*Parliamentary term*) مخالفان mukhálifán.— (*in opposition to*) بر خلاف bar khiláf, مخالف mukhálif.—(*to be in opposition*) بر ضد بودن bar zidd búdan.
To OPPRESS, دست درازی کردن dast-dirází kardan, ظلم نمودن zulm nimúdan, جفا کردن jafá kardan, اذیت دادن azíyat dádan.
OPPRESSION, ظلم zulm, تعدی ta-'addí, ستم sitam, اعتساف i'tisáf, جبر jabar, جور jaur, عنف 'unf, اذیت azíyat, بیز bíz, اجحاف ijháf, حیف و میل haif va mail, دراز دستی diráz-dastí.
OPPRESSIVE, ثقیل sakíl, سخت sakht. (*cruel*) جفا کار jafá-kár, بیرحم bí-rahm, درشت durusht, سنگدل sang-dil, ظالم zálim, بیمروت bí-murúvat, جبار jabbár, ستمکار sitam-kár.
OPPRESSOR, دست دراز dast-diráz, دراز دست diráz-dast, جفا کار jafá-kár, ظالم zálim.
OPPROBRIOUS, معیوب ma'yúb, شوخ shúkh, بد زبان bad-zabán, زبان دراز zabán-diráz.
OPPROBRIUM, فضیحت fazíhat, رسوائی rusvá,í, عار 'ár.

OPTATIVE, اختیاری ikhtiyárí.—(*optative mood*), فعل تمنی fi'l-i-tamanná, فعل دعائی fi'l-i-du'á,í.
OPTICAL, بصری basarí.
OPTICS (*the science*), علم بصر 'ilm-i-basar.
OPTION, خیار khiyár, اختیار ikhtiyár, پسند pasand, مرضی marzí.
OPTIONAL, اختیاری ikhtiyárí.
OPULENCE, *vide* WEALTH.
OR, یا yá, خواه khwáh, او au.—(*or else*) وگرنه va garnah, و الا va illá, ور نه var-nah.
ORACLE, خطاب الهی khitáb-i-iláhí, آیت áyat, وحی vahy.
ORACULAR, تنزیلی tanzílí.
ORAL, شفاهی shifáhí, شفاهیه shifáhíyah.
ORANGE, نارنگی nárangí.—(*sweet* مدنی madaní.—(*sour*) نارنج náranj.—(*blood*) توی سرخ túí surkh. —(*colour*) نارنگی nárangí.
ORANGERY, نارنگستان nárangistán.
ORANG-OUTANG, بوزینه búzinah, بوزینه búzínah, میمون maimún.
ORATION, خطاب khitáb, گفتار guftár, کلام kalam, سخن sukhun, نفس nafas (*pl.* انفاس anfás).—(*to make an oration*) خطابه خواندن khatábah khwándan.
ORATOR, سخن آور sukhun-ávar, سخن پرداز sukhun-pardáz.
ORATORICAL, خطبه khutbah.
ORATORY, سخن آوری sukhun-ávarí, سخن پردازی sukhun-pardází.—(*place of worship*) نماز گاه namáz-gáh.
ORB, جرم jirm, گوی gúí, کره kurrah.
ORBIT (*path of a planet*), دور daur, دوران daurán, گردش gardish.
ORCHARD, باغ bágh, بوستان búständ, بستان bustán.
ORCHESTRA, نوبت خانه naubat-khánah, نقاره خانه nakkárah-khánah.
To ORDAIN, امر نمودن amr nimúdan, حکم نمودن hukm nimúdan, فرمودن firmúdan.—(*clerical term*) نصب نمودن nasb nimúdan.
ORDEAL, *vide* TRIAL.
ORDER (*arrangement*), آرایش árá-yish, ترتیب tartíb, نظام nizám, انتظام intizám, تدارک tadáruk, تدبیر tadbír, تمشیت tamshíyat.—(*rule*) آیین áyín, قاعده ká'idah, قانون kánún, شرع shar'.—(*command*) حکم hukm, امر amr, فرمان firmán, قدغن kadghan, سنور sunúr, سفارش sifárish.—(*to put in order*) آراستن árástan, ترتیب نمودن tartíb nimúdan, نصب کردن nasb kardan, تدارک نمودن tadáruk nimúdan, انتظام نمودن intizám nimúdan, پیراستن pírástan.—(*religious*) طریقه taríkah.—(*of knighthood, &c.*) نشان nishán.—(*in order that*) تا tá, تا که tá kih.
To ORDER, فرمودن firmúdan, حکم نمودن hukm nimúdan, امر نمودن amr nimúdan, ارشاد کردن irshád kardan, سفارش کردن sifárish kardan, قدغن کردن kadghan kardan.
ORDERLESS, بی ترتیب bí-tartíb, بی انتظام bí-intizám.
ORDERLY, ترتیب tartíb.—(*servant*), غلام ghulám, اردل ardal (*eur.*).
ORDINAL, ترتیبی tartíbí, فرعی far'í.
ORDINANCE, آیین áyín, قاعده ká'idah, قانون kánún, شرع shar'.
ORDINARILY, عادتاً 'ádatan, از روی عادت az rúy-i-'ádat.
ORDINARY (*usual*), متداول mutadával, رائج rá,ij, مشترک mushtarak. —(*common, mean*) عام 'ámm, فرو مایه furú-máyah, پست past.
ORDINATION (*clerical term*), نصب nasb.
ORDNANCE (*artillery*), توپخانه túp-khánah.
ORDURE, گوه gúh, گه guh, زبل zibl, براز biráz, فضله fazlah. (*Vide also* DUNG).
ORE, فلز filizz, معدنی ma'daní.
ORGAN, آلت álat.—(*organ of sight*) چشم chashm.—(*of speech*) زبان zabán.—(*musical*) ارغنون arghanún (*eur.*).—(*barrel organ*) جعبه ساز ja'bah-sáz.—(*to play the organ*) ارغنونرا زدن arghanúnrá zadan.
ORGANIC, ترکیبی tarkíbí, تشکیلی tashkílí.
ORGANISATION, نظام nizám, ترتیب tartíb.

To Organise, نظام دادن nizám dádan, ترتب داشتن tarattub dáshtan.
Organism, ترکیب tarkíb, تشکیل tashkíl.
Organist, ارغنون زن arghanún-zan.
Orient, شرق shark, مشرق mashrik.
Oriental, شرقی sharkí, مشرقی mashrikí. — (*an Oriental*) اهل مشرق زمین ahl-i-mashrik-zamín, اهل شرق ahl-i-shark.
Orifice, دهنه dahanah, سوراخ súrákh.
Origin, اصل asl, بنیاد bunyád, بنیان bunyán, مصدر masdar, منشا manshá, سر sar, مبدا mabdá, اول avval, بیخ bíkh, آغاز ágház, حدر hadar, نصاب nisáb, منبع mamb'.
Original, اصلی aslí اول avval.
Originality, غرابت gharábat.
Originally, اولاً avvalan, ابتداً ibtidan, اصلاً aslan.
To Originate (*trans.*), ناشی کردن náshí kardan.—(*intrans.*) بر پا شدن bar pá shudan.
Originator, مبدع mubdi'.
Orion (*the constellation*), جبار jabbár, النسق an-nasak.
Orison, نماز namáz.
Ornament, آرایش áráyish, زیب zíb, زینت zínat, پیرایه píráyah, طراز tiráz, حلیه hulyah, فر farr, نقش naksh.
To Ornament, آراستن árástan, پیراستن pírástan, زینت دادن zínat dádan, تزیین نمودن tazyín nimúdan, طرازیدن tirázídan, مزین ساختن muzayyan sákhtan.
Ornamental, زینتی zínatí, زیوری zívarí.
Ornamented, آراسته árástah, پیراسته pírástah, مزین muzayyan, مطرز mutarraz, منقش munakkash.—(*with jewels*) مرصع murassa', جواهر آگین javáhir-ágín, جوهر آمود jauhar-ámúd.
Ornaments, اسباب تجمل asbáb-i-tajammul, زیور zívar, جواهر javáhir.
Orphan, یتیم yatím (*pl.* ایتام aitám, *or* یتامی yatámá).
Orthodox, مومن múmin, متشرع mutasharri', متدین mutadayyin.
Orthodoxy, راستی rástí, صدق sidk, دینداری dín-dárí, حق hakk, استحقاق istihkák.
Orthographer, املا دان imlá-dán.
Orthographical, املائی imlá,í.—(*orthographic mistake*) تصحیف tas-híf.
Orthography, املا imlá.
Ortolan, پرگیری pargírí.
To Oscillate, تکان نمودن takán nimúdan.
Oscillation, تکان takán, جنبش jumbish.
Osmani (*decoration*), عثمانیه 'usmáníyah.
Osprey (*sea-eagle*), نسر بحری nisr-i-bahrí.
Ossification, استخوان سازی ustukhwán-sází.
To Ossify (*trans.*), استخوان ساختن ustukhwán sákhtan.—(*intrans.*) استخوان شدن ustukhwán shudan.
Ostensible, پدید padíd, پیدا paidá, ظاهر záhir.
Ostentation, خود نمائی khwud-nimá,í, کبریا kibriyá, تکبر takabbur, خود پسندی khwud-pasandí.
Ostentatiously, با کبر bá-kibr.
Ostler, جلو دار jilau-dár.
Ostrich, شتر مرغ shutur-murgh, نعامه na'ámah.
Other, دیگر dígar, دگر digar, غیر ghair, علاحده 'alá-hiddah.
Otherwise (*if not*), وگر نه vagar nah, و الا va illá, ور نه var nah. — (*in another way*) دگر گونه digar-gúnah, طور دگر taur-i-digár, قسم دگر kism-i-digar, بطریق علاحده bi-taríḳ-i-'alá-hiddah.
Otter, سگ آبی sag-i-ábí.
Ottoman, عثمانی 'usmání.—(*Ottoman Empire*) دولت عثمانی daulat-i-'usmání.
Ought (*should*), باید báyad, لازم lázim, بایست báyist, شاید sháyad. —(*a cypher*) صفر sifr. — (*anything*) چیزی chízí, هیچ hích.
Ounce (*animal*) یوز yúz.
Our, مال ما mál-i-má, از ما az má, مان i-mán.
Ourselves, خود مان khwud-i-mán.

To Oust, راندن rándan, اخراج کردن ikhráj kardan, دور کردن dúr kardan, بدر کردن bi-dar kardan, نفی نمودن nafy nimúdan.—(*to be ousted*) خارج گشتن khárij gashtan.

Out, بیرون bírún, بدر bi-dar, خارج khárij. — (*out of doors*) بیرون bírún, خارج khárij.—(*to be out—flowers*) باز شدن báz shudan.

Outcast, مردود mardud, رانده rándah.

Outcry, غوغا ghaughá, غریو gharív, هنگامه hangámah.

To Outdo, مسابقت نمودن musábakat nimúdan, پیش گرفتن písh giriftan.

Outer, بیرون bírún, خارج khárij.

Outfall, ریزش rízish.

Outlandish, مستعجم musta'jim, بیگانه bígánah.

Outlaw, خارجی khárijí.

To Outlaw, محدود ساختن mahdúd sákhtan, ملعون ساختن mal'ún sakhtan.

Outlet, مفر mafarr.

Outline, دائره dá,irah, نقشه nakshah.

Outpost, قراول karávul.

Outrage, هتك عرض hatk-i-'irz, تعدی ta addí.

To Outrage, تعدی کردن ta'addí kardan, هتك عرض کردن hatk-i-'irz-kardan, دشنام دادن dushnám dádan, دشنامیدن dushnámídan. (*Vide* To Ravish).

Outrageous, طاغی tághí, باغی bághí.—(*violent*) تند مزاج tund mizáj, درشت خو durusht-khú.

Outright, سراسر sar-á-sar تماماً tamáman, بالكل bi-'l-kull, بالكليت bi-'l-kulliyat, بالمره bi-'l-marrah.

To Outroot, بر کندن bar-kandan, استئصال کردن isti,sál kardan.

Outside, بیرون bírún, خارج khárij.—(*just outside*) دم dam (*as* دم در dam-i-dar, *just outside the door*).

To Outstrip, پیش رو شدن písh-rau shudan, پیش بندی کردن písh-bandí kardan, گوئی سبقت بردن guí,i-i-sibkat burdan.

Outward, بیرون bírún, خارج khárij.

Outwardly, ظاهراً záhiran, در صورت dar súrat.

Outworks, حصار بند hisár-band.

Oval (*sub.*), شکل بیضوی shakl-i-baizaví.—(*adj.*) بیضوی baizaví, بادامی bádámí, بیضه baizah, بیضی baizí.

Ovarious, بیضه دار baizah-dár.

Oven, تنور tannúr, کوره kúrah.

Over, بالا bálá, علی 'alá, بر bar, زبر zabar, بر سر bar sar, فوق fauk, فراز faráz, روی rúy. — (*across*) عبور 'ubúr, آنطرف án-taraf, وراء vará, , آنسو án-sú. — (*exceeding*) بیش bísh, زیاده ziyádah, زائد zá,id. — (*to be over, remain*), ماندن mándan, باقی بودن bákí búdan.

To Overawe, ترسانیدن tarsánídan, تهدید کردن tahdíd kardan.

Overboard, از روی کشتی az rúy-i-kashtí.

Overcast, ابر دار abr-dár, گرفته giriftah.

To Overcharge (*overload*), زیاد بار کردن ziyád bár kardan.—(*in an account*) زیاد طلبیدن ziyád talbídan.

To Overcome, فتح کردن fath kardan, غلبه کردن ghalabah kardan, شکست دادن shikast dádan, ظفر یافتن zafar yáftan, گشادن gushádan, نصرت یافتن nusrat yáftan, فیروز شدن fírúz shudan, غالب آمدن ghálib ámadan.

To Overflow, لبریز بودن lab-ríz búdan, سیلان شدن sailán shudan.

Overflowing, لبریزی lab-rízí, سرشاری sar-shárí.

To Overgrow, روئیدن rú,ídan.—(*grow big*) پر بزرگ شدن pur buzurg shudan.

Over-hanging, مشرف mushrif, بر سر مائل sar má,il.

Overhead, بالا bálá, علی 'alá, بر سر bar sar, فوق fauk, فراز faráz.

To Over-hear, مستمع بودن mustami' búdan, استماع کردن istimá' kardan.—(*in a bad sense*) تسمع نمودن tasammuʻ nimúdan.

To OVERLOOK (*neglect*), غفلت نمودن ghiflat nimúdan, اهمال کردن ihmál kardan, صرف نظر نمودن sarf-i-nazar nimúdan. — (*connive at*) اغماض کردن ighmáz kardan, چشم پوشی نمودن chashm-púshí nimúdan. — (*forgive*) عفو کردن ʻafv kardan, در گذر کردن dar-guzar kardan, بخشیدن bakhshídan, معاف کردن muʻáf kardan.—(*as from a window, &c.*) مشرف بودن (به) mushrif búdan (bi).

OVER-MUCH, زیاده ziyádah, بسیار bisyár.

OVER-NIGHT, شبانه shabánah.

OVERPLUS, ما باقی má-bákí, فضله fazlah, ما بقی má-baká.

To OVER-REACH, فریفتن firíftan, فریب دادن firíb dádan, گول خورانیدن gúl khwuránídan, گول زدن gúl zadan, غدر نمودن ghadar nimúdan, حیله کردن hílah kardan.

To OVERRUN, ویران کردن vairán kardan, تاراج کردن táráj kardan.

OVERSEER, ناظر názir, داروغه dárúghah, کار گذار kár-guzár, مباشر mubáshir, سر کار sar-kár.

OVERSIGHT, غلط ghalat, سهو sahv, زلت zallat.

To OVERSLEEP, زیاد خوابیدن ziyád khwábídan.

To OVERSPREAD (*trans.*) پر کردن pur kardan, انتشار دادن intishár dádan. — (*intrans.*) انتشار یافتن intishár yáftan, پر شدن pur shudan, پهن شدن pahn shudan, سرایت کردن sirâyat kardan.

OVERT, آشکار áshkár, آشکاره áshkárah, ظاهر záhir, عیان ʻiyán, واضح vázih.

To OVERTAKE, پی اپی آمدن pay-á-pay ámadan, برابر آمدن barábar ámadan, ملحق شدن mulkik shudan, واصل شدن vásil shudan.

OVERTHROW, خلل khalal, اخلال ikhlál, خسارت khasárat, شکست shikast, هزیمت hazímat.

To OVERTHROW, *vide* To THROW DOWN, To CONQUER.

OVERTURE, پیش قدم písh-kadam, افتتاح iftitáh. — (*to make an overture*) افتتاح کردن iftitáh kardan.

To OVERTURN, سر نگون کردن sar-nigún kardan, سر زیر کردن sar-zír kardan, وارونه کردن várúnah kardan, واژگون ساختن vázhgún sákhtan, بر گشته ساختن bar-gashtah sákhtan, بر گردانیدن bar-gardánídán.—(*to be overturned*) افتادن uftádan, بر گشتن bar-gashtan, وارونه شدن várúnah shudan.

To OVERWHELM, غالب شدن ghálib shudan مستولی شدن mustaulí shudan, غلبه کردن ghalabah kardan.—(*drown*) غرق کردن gharak kardan.

To OWE, بده داشتن bidih dáshtan, بده کار بودن bidih-kár búdan, قرض داشتن karz dáshtan, قرضدار بودن karz-dár búdan, وام داشتن vám dáshtan, دین داشتن dain dáshtan, مقروض بودن makrúz búdan, متدین بودن mutadayyin búdan.

OWING to this, از این رهگذر az ín rah-guzar.

OWL, بوم búm, بوف búf, کوکومه kúkúmah (*vulg.*).—(*screech-owl*) جغد jughd, چغد chughd.

OWN, خود khwud, خویش khwísh, خویشتن khwíshtan, خاص kháss.—(*my own*) خود من khwud-i-man, خودم i-khwudam.—(*their own*) خود شان khwud-i-shán.

To OWN (*possess*), مالک بودن málik-búdan, داشتن dáshtan.—(*admit*) اقرار کردن ikrár kardan, مسلم داشتن musallam dáshtan, مقر بودن mukirr búdan, اعتراف کردن iʻtiráf kardan, معترف شدن muʻtarif shudan.

OWNER, مالک málik, صاحب sáhib, خاوند khávand.

OWNERSHIP, مالکیت málikíyat.

OX, گاو gáv, بقر bakar.—(*ploughing ox*) ورزاو varzáv, گاو فداد gáv-i-faddád.—(*wild ox*) گاو دشتی gáv-i-dashtí, بقر الوحش bakaru-'l-vahsh.—(*ox-goad*) نیزهٔ گاورانی naizah-i-gáv-rání.

OXIDE, زنگار zangár.

OXYGEN, مولد الحموضة muvallidu-'l-humúzah.

OXYMEL, سکنجبین sikanjabín.

OYSTER, صدف sadaf.

P.

PACE (*step*), قدم kadam, گام gám, خطوه khatvah.—(*gait*) رفتار raftár, روش ravish, ام gám, قدم kadam.—(*speed*) تندی tundí.

To PACE, قدم رفتن kadam raftan, قدم زدن kadam zadan.

PACIFIC, مصالح musálih, صلح آمیز sulh-ámíz.

PACIFICATION, مصالحت musálahat, مسالمت musálamat.

PACIFICATOR, مصلح muslih.

To PACIFY, آرامیدن árámídan, آرام دادن árám dádan, تسلی دادن tasallí dádan, تسکین کردن taskín kardan.

PACK, دسته dastah.

To PACK up, بستن bastan, ته نمودن tah nimúdan, بار درست کردن bár durust kardan.

PACKER, بسته بند bastah-band.

PACKET, بسته bastah, دسته dastah, بقچه bukchah.

PACK-HORSE, اسب بار کش asb-i-bár kash, یابو yábú.

PACKING-NEEDLE, جوالدوز javál-dúz.

PACK-SADDLE, پالان pálán.—(*cover of pack-saddle, made of ornamental worsted work*) آشرمه áshurmah.

PACK-THREAD, ریسمان rísmán.

PACT, *vide* TREATY.

PAD (*soft saddle*), تگل tagal, خوگیر khú-gír, تگلتی tagaltí.

To PAD, حشو کردن hashv kardan.

PADDLE (*oar*), پارو párú, خاده kháḍah.

PADDLE-WHEEL, چرخ بخار charkh-i-bukhár.

PADDOCK, چمن chaman, چمنزار chaman-zár, چراگاه chará-gáh, مرتع marta', مرغزار margh-zár, علفزار 'alaf-zár, صحرا sahrá, مغاز marghâz, جلگه julgah.

PADLOCK, قفل kufl.

PÆAN, فتح نامه fath-námah.

PAGAN, بت پرست but-parast, کافر káfir, مشرك mushrik.

PAGANISM, بت پرستی but-parastí, کفر kufr.

PAGE (*of a book*), صفحه safhah.—(*leaf or double page*) صحیفه sahífah, ورق varak.—(*boy*) پسر pisar, غلام ghulám, پیشخدمت písh-khidmat.

PAGEANT, تماشا tamáshá.

PAGEANTRY, شوکت shaukat, حشمت hashmat.

PAGODA, بتخانه but-khánah, بتکده but-kadah.

PAIL, دلو dalv, دول dúl, بالدی báldí (*hind.*).

PAIN, درد dard, رنج ranj, رنجش ranjish, عذاب 'azáb, آزار ázár, الم alam, زحمت zahmat, وجع vaja'.—(*anguish*) اذیت azíyat, محنت mihnat, تنگی tangí.

To PAIN, پریشان ساختن paríshán sákhtan, مبتلا ساختن mubtalá sákhtan, آزردن ázurdan, الم رسانیدن alam rasánídan.

PAINFUL, پر درد pur-dard, درد مند dard-mand, درد ناك dard-nák, الم زده alam-zadah, متألم muta,allim, وجیع vají'.—(*giving pain*) رنج آور ranj-ávar, آزار رسان ázár-rasán.

PAINLESS, بی درد bí-dard.

PAINS (*toil*), مشقت mashakkat, زحمت zahmat, محنت mihnat, رنج ranj.—(*to take pains*) مواظبت داشتن muvázabat dáshtan.

PAINS-TAKER, متجاهد mutajáhid, محنت کار mihnat-kár.

PAINS-TAKING, متقید mutakayyid, محنتی mihnatí, جاهد jáhid, مواظب muvázib, متجاهد mutajáhid.

PAINT, رنگ rang.—(*red paint*) سرخی surkhí.—(*white paint*) رنگ سفید rang-i-safíd.—(*rouge for the face*) غازه gházah.—(*for the eye-brows*) خطات khitát.

To PAINT (*draw*), کشیدن kashídan, نقش کردن naksh kardan.—(*colour*) رنگین کردن rangín kardan, رنگ دادن rang dádan.

PAINTER, مصور musavvir, نقاش nakkásh, رسام rassám, تمثالگر timsálgar.

PAINTING (*picture*), تصویر tasvír, نقش naksh, پرده اشکال pardah-i-ashkál, پرده نقاشی pardah-i-nakkáshí.—(*oil painting*) پرده اشکال روغن pardah-i-ashkál-i-raughan, پرده روغن pardah-i-raughan.

PAIR, جفت juft, جور júr, زوج zauj.—(*in pairs*) تک و جفت tak va juft.

To PAIR, جفت کردن juft kardan, زوج نمودن zauj nimúdan.

PALACE, بارگاه bárgáh, ایوان aiván, سرای saráí, قصر kasr, عمارت 'imárat.

PALACIOUS, قصر مانند kasr-mánand.

PALANQUIN, تخت روان takht-i-raván.

PALATABLE, گوار guvár, گوارا guvárá.

PALATABLENESS, گواری guvárí.

PALATE, کام kám, مذاق mazák, مشام mashámm.—(*roof of mouth*) سق sakk.

PALE, زرد zard, اصفر asfar, پریده parídah. — (*weak in colour*) آبکی ábakí, واز váz.—(*to turn pale*) زرد شدن zard shudan.

To PALE, زرد گشتن zard gashtan.

PALE-FACED, زرد رو zard-rú.

PALENESS, زردی zardí, پریدگی parídagí, اصفرار isfirár.

PALISADE, مترس matars, سد sadd, بند band, ضیق سد zík-i-sadd.

To PALL, بی مزه شدن bí-mazah shudan.

PALLETTE (*painter's*), تخته رنگدان takhtah-i-rang-dán.

To PALLIATE, عفو کردن 'afv kardan, معاف کردن mu'áf kardan, بخشیدن bakhshídan, معذور داشتن ma'zúr dáshtan, در گذر کردن dar guzar kardan, آمرزیدن ámurzídan, مغفور گردانیدن maghfúr gardánídan.

PALLIATION, عفو afv, معاف mu'áf. — (*mitigation*) تخفیف takhfíf, تسکین taskín.

PALLIATIVE, تسکین بخش taskín-bakhsh.

PALLID, زرد zard, پریده parídah.

PALM (*date tree*), درخت خرما dirakht-i-khurmá, نخل nakhl, مخ mukh. — (*palm leaves*) خوص khaus, تاپول tápúl, پوش púsh.—(*fibres of the palm, coir*) ریشه ríshah, لیف líf.—(*victory*) نصرت nusrat, ظفر zafar, فیروزی fírúzí, فتح fath, غلبه ghalabah.—(*of the hand*) کف kaf, راحت ráhat. — (*measure*) شبر shibr.

PALMA-CHRISTI, بید انجیر bíd-anjír, کنتو kinnatú.

PALMISTRY, علم کف 'ilm-i-kaf.

PALPABLE, متجسم mutajassim, ظاهر záhir, صریح saríh.

PALPABLY, ظاهراً záhiran, صریحاً saríhan.

To PALPITATE, طپیدن tapídan.

PALPITATION, طپش tapish.

PALSIED, افلیج iflíj, مفلوج maflúj.—(*to be palsied*) رعشه داشتن ra'shah dáshtan, فالج داشتن fálij dáshtan.

PALSY, فالج fálij, شل shall.—(*trembling*) رعشه ra'shah. — (*hemiphlegia*) فالج fálij.—(*of the mouth and face*) لقوه lakvah.

PALTRY, دون dún, پست past, زبون zabún.

To PAMPER, پروردن parvardan.

PAMPERED, پرورده parvardah.

PAMPHLET, رساله risálah.

PAMPHLETEER, رساله نویس risálah-nivís.

PAN (*earthen*), دیزی dízí.—(*large shallow pan*) حسین hasín, تغار taghár.—(*frying pan*) تاوه távah, تابه tábah. — (*of a gun*) کوشه

gúshah, آتشخانه átish-khánah, اوجاق úják, چاله chálah.
PANACÆA, کیمیائی اکبر kímiyá,í-i-akbar.
PANCAKE, خاگینه khágínah.
PANDER, *vide* PIMP, BAWD.
PANE (*of glass*), جام jám.—(*small coloured panes*) کتابی kitábí, داءود خانی da,úd-kháni.
PANEGYRIC, مدح madh, مدحنامه madh-námah.
PANEGYRICAL, مدح آمیز madh-ámíz.
PANEGYRIST, مداح maddáh.
PANEL, تخته takhtah.
PANG, درد dard.
PANIC, ترس tars, هول haul, فزع faza', هزیمت hazímat, بیم bím, باك bák, خوف khauf.
PANNIERS, زنبیل zambíl, سبد sabad. —(*large wooden panniers for carrying fruit*) لوده laudah.—(*travelling panniers, resembling cradles, and slung on both sides of a mule or camel; much used by women*) کجاوه kajávah.
PANORAMA, دور نما dúr-nimá.
To PANT, طپیدن tapídan.—(*draw breath quickly*) دم زدن dam zadan, نفس زدن nafas zadan, هنگه زدن hingah zadan.
PANTALOONS, شلوار shalvár.
PANTHER, پارس párs, قپلان kaplán, پلنگ palang.—(*hunting*) یوز yúz.
PANTRY, خوراك خانه khwurák-khánah.
PAP, پستان pistán.—(*food*) خوراك khwurák.
PAPA, پدر pidar, بابا bábá.
PAPER, کاغذ kághaz, قرطاس kartás. —(*glazed paper*) کاغذ مهره دار kághaz-i-muhrah-dár.—(*blotting-paper*) کاغذ تر خشك کنك kághaz-i-tar-khushk-kunak. — (*ship's-papers*) قول kaul.
PAPER-KNIFE, کاغذ بر kághaz-bur.
PAPER-MAKER, کاغذ ساز kághaz-sáz.
PAPER-MILL, کاغذ خانه kághaz-khánah.
PAPIST, پاپاوی pápáví (*eur.*).
PAPYRUS (*reed*), بردی bardí, حلفاء hafa,.
PAR, مساوات musávát.—(*on a par*) مساوی musáví. — (*at par*) قیمت درست kaimat-i-durust, قیمت واقعی kaimat-i-váki'í, قیمت حقیقی kaimat-i-hakíkí.
PARABLE, مثل masal (*pl.* امثال amsál), مثال misál, تشبیه tashbíh.
PARABOLA, قطع مکافی kat'-i-mukáfí.
PARABOLICAL, متشابه mutashábih.
PARACLETE, فارقلیط fáraklít (*eur.*).
PARADE (*of an army*), سان sán, عرض لشکر 'arz-i-lashkar.
PARADE-GROUND, جولانگاه jaulán-gáh, میدان maidán.
PARADISE, فردوس firdaus, جنت jannat, بهشت bihisht, روضه rauzah, خلد khuld.—(*boundary between paradise and hell*) عرف 'urf, اعراف a'ráf.
PARADOX, لغز lughz.
PARADOXICAL, معمی وش mu'ammá-vash, لغز مانند lughz-mánand.
PARAFFINE, پارافین páráfín (*eur.*).
PARAGON, نمونه nimúnah. — (*person*) بیمثال bí-misál.
PARAGRAPH, فصل fasl, فقره fakarah.
PARALLAX (*astronomical term*), اختلاف منظر ikhtiláf-i-manzar.
PARALLEL, برابر barábar, موازی muvází, متوازی mutavází, مساوی musáví. — (*parallel lines*) خطوط متوازی khutút-i-mutavází.
PARALLELISM, برابری barábarí, مساوات musávát.
PARALLELOGRAM, مربع مستطیل murabba'-i-mustatíl, مستطیل mustatíl.
PARALLELOPIPED, مجسم متساوی الاضلاع mujassam-i-mutasávi-'l-azlá'.
PARALYSIS, فالج fálij, فلج falj, رعشه ra'shah.
PARALYTIC, افلیج iflíj, مفلوج maflúj.
PARAMOUNT, قاهر káhir, علی الاطلاق 'ala-'l-itlák.
PARAMOUR, یار yár, عاشق 'áshik, مول múl.

PARAPET, كنگره kangurah, معجر ma'jar, محجر mahjar.
PARAPHERNALIA, سامان sámán, اسباب asbáb, يراق yarák.
PARAPHRASE, شرح sharh, تفسير tafsír, تفصيل tafsíl.
To PARAPHRASE, تفسير نمودن tafsír nimúdan, تفصيل نمودن tafsíl nimúdan.
PARASANG (*Persian league, about three miles and three-quarters*) فرسخ farsakh, فرسنگ farsang.
PARASITE, مفت خور muft-khwur, طفيلى tufailí, حاشيه نشين háshiyah-nishín.
PARASOL, چتر chatr, آفتابگير áftábgír.
PARCEL, بسته bastah, بوغچه búghchah.
To PARCEL, تقسيم كردن taksím kardan, دو قسمت كردن dú kismat kardan.
To PARCH, نيم سوختن ním-súkhtan, برشتن birishtan.
PARCHMENT, رق rakk *or* rikk, پوست púst.
PARDON, عفو 'afv, معافى mu'áfí, آمرزش ámurzish, بخشايش bakhsháyish, مسامحت musámahat, صفح safh, غفران ghafrán, مغفرت maghfirat, درگذر dar-guzar.—(*to beg pardon*) پوزش نمودن púzish nimúdan.
To PARDON, عفو كردن 'afv kardan, معاف كردن mu'áf kardan, بخشيدن bakhshídan, گذشتن guzashtan, در گذشتن dar-guzashtan.—(*pardon me! used in polite conversation*) چرا chirá, لبى laby.
PARDONABLE, قابل بخشش kábil-i-bakhshish, عفو پذير 'afv-pazír, سزاوار مغفرت sazávar-i-maghfirat.
To PARE (*strip off skin*), پوست كندن púst kandan, مقشر ساختن mukashshar sákhtan.—(*the nails*) ناخن گرفتن nákhun giriftan.—(*the hoofs of a horse*) قيار كردن kayár kardan, سم تراشيدن sum tiráshídan.
PARENTAGE, نسب nasab, انتساب intisáb, اصل asl.
PARENTAL, والدى válidí, والدينى válidainí.
PARENTHESIS, جمله معترضه jumlah-i-mu'tarizah.
PARENTHETICAL, معترض mu'tariz.
PARENTHETICALLY, بطور معترضه bi-taur-i-mu'tarizah.
PARENTICIDE, پدر كشى pidar-kushí, مادر كشى mádar-kushí.
PARENTS, والدين válidain, پدر و مادر pidar u mádar.
PARER, پوست كننده púst-kanandah, مقشر mukashshir.—(*nails*) ناخن گيرنده nákhun-gírandah.
PARING, تراشه tiráshah, خراشه khiráshah.
PARING-KNIFE (*for horse's hoofs*) سمتراش sum-tirásh.
PARISH, محله mahallah.
PARISHIONER, اهل محله ahl-i-mahallah.
PARITY, مساوات musávát, معادلت mu'ádalat.
PARK, چمن chaman, ميدان maidán. —(*public park*), باغ عامه bágh-i-'ámmah.
PARLANCE (*common talk*), عرف 'urf.
PARLEY, مكالمه mukálamah, قيل و قال kíl u kál, معاشرت mu'áshamat.
To PARLEY, مكالمه نمودن mukálamah nimúdan, معاشرت نمودن mu'ásharat nimúdan.
PARLIAMENT, دار الشورائى dáru-'sh-shúrá,í. — (*Member of Parliament*) عدم از اعضاء مجلس پارلمنت 'adam az a'zá,-i-majlis-i-párlamant.—(*Opening of Parliament*) باز شدن پارلمنت báz-shudan-i-párlamant.—(*to dissolve Parliament*) پارلمنترا متفرق ساختن párlamantrá mutafarrik sákhtán.
PARLOUR, اطاق uták, ديوانخانه díván-khánah, مشربه mashrabah.
PAROCHIAL, محلى mahallí.
PARODY, تقليد taklíd.
PAROLE, قول kaul.
PAROQUET, طوطى كوچك tú+í-i-kúchik.
PAROXYSM, نوبت naubat, حالت há-

lat, طغیان tughyán, شدت shiddat, غلبه ghalabah.

PARRICIDE, قطع ارحام kat'-i-arhám.

PARRICIDAL, قاطع ارحام káti'-i-arhám.

PARROT, طوطی túti.

To PARRY (*a stroke*), دفع کردن daf' kardan, رد کردن radd kardan, وا زدن vá-zadan.

To PARSE (*resolve grammatically*), ترکیب کردن tarkíb kardan.

PARSEE, گبر gabr, مجوسی majúsí.

PARSEEISM, مجوسیت majúsíyat.

PARSIMONIOUS, حریص harís, طمعکار tama'-kár, طامع támi', بخیل bakhíl, لئیم la'ím, ممسک mumsik, خسیس khasís.

PARSIMONIOUSLY, بخیل وار bakhíl-vár.

PARSIMONY, بخل bukhl, حرص hirs, آز áz, طمع tama', طمعکاری tama'-kárí, خسیست khasísat, خست khissat, امساک imsák, لوءم lu,m.

PARSLEY, کرفس kirafs, اجمود ajmúd, جعفری ja'farí.

PARSNIP, گزر gazar. [This is properly a carrot.]

PARSON, کشیش kashísh, قسیس kissís, پیش نماز písh-namáz.

PARSONAGE, کشیش خانه kashísh-khánah.

PART (*piece*), پاره párah, پارچه párchah, پرزه purzah, تکه tikkah, قطعه kat'ah, جز juz, حصه hissah, جزوی juzví, لخت lakht, بهره bahrah, قسم kism. — (*side, party*) طرف taraf, جانب jánib, قبل kibal.—(*business*) کار kár, عمل 'amal, امر amr, حال hál.—(*quarter or region*) ملک mulk, ولایت valáyat, اقلیم iklím, سمت samt.—(*share*) قسمت kismat, حصه hissah.—(*on the part of*) از جانب az jánib.—(*for the most part*) غالباً gháliban, اکثری aksarí.—(*I for my part*) من که man kih.—(*to take in good part*) پذیرفتن pazíruftan.

To PART, جدا ساختن jidá sákhtan. —(*to depart*) روانه گشتن ravánah gashtan, رفتن raftan.

To PARTAKE (*have a share in*), شریک بودن sharík búdan, شراکت داشتن shirákat dáshtan, حصه دار بودن hissah-dár búdan, بهره داشتن bahrah dáshtan. — (*eat*), میل نمودن mail nimúdan, تناول کردن tanávul kardan.

PARTAKER, شریک sharík, حصه دار hissah-dár.

PARTERRE, خیابان khiyábán.

PARTIAL, طرفدار taraf-dár, جانبدار jánib-dár.

PARTIALITY, جانبداری jánib-dárí, طرفداری taraf-dárí, تعصب ta'assub, میل mail, طرفگیری taraf-gírí, تمایل tamáyul.

PARTIALLY, قدری kadrí, فی الجمله fi-'l-jumlah.

PARTICIPANT, شریک sharík, حصه دار hissah-dár.

To PARTICIPATE, سهیم شدن sahím shudan, شریک شدن sharík shudan, بر خوردن bar-khwurdan.

PARTICIPATION, شراکت shirákat, مشارکت musharakat, مداخله mudákhalah.

PARTICIPLE (*active*), اسم فاعل ism-i-fá'il.—(*passive*) اسم مفعول ism-i-maf'úl.

PARTICLE, ذره zarrah, شوشه shúshah, همزه hamzah, شمه shammah, ریزه rízah.—(*in grammar*) حرف harf. —(*affirmative particle*) حرف تاکید harf-i-ta,kíd, حرف ایجاب harf-i-íjáb.

PARTICULAR, خاص kháss, مخصوص makhsús, مختص mukhtass. — (*fanciful*) مصر musirr, مبرم mubrim.—(*in general and in particular*) عموماً و خصوصاً 'umúman va khusúsan.

PARTICULARITY, مخصوصیت makhsúsíyat.

To PARTICULARIZE, تفصیل کردن tafsíl kardan.

PARTICULARLY, بخصوص bi-khusús, علی الخصوص 'ala-'l-khusús.

PARTICULARS, رموز rumúz, جزئیات juz,íát.

PARTING (*hair*), فرق fark.

PARTISAN, هوا دار havá-dár.—(*to be

a partisan of) جانبداری کردن jánib-dárí kardan.

PARTITION (*mutual division*), مقاسمت mukásamat. (*Vide* WALL, SCREEN.)

PARTLY, قسمی kismí, پاره párah, یکچندی yak-chandí.

PARTNER, شریک sharík, بهره دار bah-rah-dár, انباز ambáz.

PARTNERSHIP, شراکت shirákat, مشارکت mushárakat, انبازی am-bází.—(*unfair dealing in partnership*) ستم شریکی sitam-sharíkí.

PARTRIDGE (*red-legged or bartavelle*) کبك kabk.—(*of the valley, a very large species*) کبك دری kabk-i-darí.—(*black partridge or francolin*) دراج durráj.—(*desert partridge*) تیهو taihú, توهی túhí.—(*a covey of partridges*) گله کبك gallah-i-kabk.

PARTURITION, نتاج nitáj.

PARTY (*assembly*), گروه gurúh, جماعت jamá'at, جمیعت jam'íyat, مجمع majma', دیوان díván, بزم bazm, شورا shúrá, مجلس majlis, محفل mahfil, انجمن anjuman.—(*banquet*) ضیافت ziyáfat, مهمانی mihmání, سور súr, ولیمه valímah.—(*Parliamentary term*) دسته dastah, فرقه firkah. —(*party spirit*) عصبیه 'asabíyah.

PARVENU, نو کیسه nau-kísah.

PASHA, پاشا páshá.

PASHALIK, پاشالق páshálik.

PASS (*narrow road*), تنك راه tang-ráh, گدوك gadúk.—(*among mountains*) تنك tang, شعب sha'b, کتل kutal, کوتل kútal, گردن gardan.

To PASS, گذشتن guzashtan, گذر کردن guzar kardan, گذار آوردن guzár ávardan.—(*Parliamentary term*) پذیرفته شدن pazíruftah shudan.—(*across a river*) عبور کردن 'ubúr kardan, از رود خانه گذشتن az rúd-khánah guzashtan.—(*be current*) رائج بودن rá,ij búdan, مروج بودن muravvaj búdan.—(*the night*) بیتوته کردن baitútah kardan, شبرا بروز آوردن shabrá bi-rúz ávar-dan.—(*to pass over, neglect*) در گذشتن dar-guzashtan, ساقط داشتن sákit dáshtan, سهو کردن sahv kardan.—(*to pass off upon, to deceive*) حلق کردن halk kardan, گول زدن gúl zadan.

PASSABLE, قابل عبور kábil-i-'ubúr, قابل گذر kábil-i-guzar.—(*allowable*) مجاز mujáz, روا ravá, حلال halál.

PASSABLY, نزدیك nazdík, تقریباً tak-ríban.

PASSAGE (*in a book*), عبارت 'ibárat, مقالت makálat, فقره fakarah.—(*voyage*) سفر safar, سیر sair, سیل sail (*vulg.*).—(*passage in a street, leading under a building; a close*) ساباط sá,ibát, سهبات sahbát, بالا خانه خروجی bálá-khánah-i-khurújí.—(*in a house*) محل عبور mahall-i-'ubúr.

PASSAGE-MONEY (*fare*), کرایه kirá-yah, نول núl.

PASSENGER, مسافر musáfir, رونده ra-vandah, عابر 'ábir, سالك sálik, سیاح sayyáh.—(*in a ship*), عبری 'ibrí.

PASSION, *Vide* ANGER, LOVE, ZEAL.—(*the passions*) هوائی نفسانی havá,í-i-nafsání, اغراض aghráz.

PASSIONATE, تیز مزاج tíz-mizáj, غضبناك ghazab-nák, تند خو tund-khú, تند مزاج tund-mizáj.

PASSIONATELY, با خشم bá-khishm, غضبا ghazaban. — (*extremely*) بنهایت bi-niháyat, بغایت bi-ghá-yat.

PASSIVE (*unresisting*), متحمل mu-tahammil, ساکن sákin.—(*verb*) مجهول majhúl.

PASSIVENESS, تحمل táhammul, سکن sakan, صبر sabr.

PASSOVER (*feast*), عید فصح 'íd-i-fis-h.

PASSPORT, راهداری ráh-dárí, تذکره tazkirah, رقم rakm, تعلیقه ta'líkah.—(*for goods*) پته pattah (*hind.*), فته fattah, فراغنامه farágh-námah.

PAST (*beyond*), بلا bilá, فوق fauk, بیرون bírún.—(*gone by*) گذشته guzashtah, ماضی mází, سلف salaf, سابق sábik.—(*past all *hope*) بلا امید bilá-umíd.—(*past danger*) بلا خطر bilá-khatar.—(*the past*) سابق sábik, الماضی al-mází, سلف salaf, ایام گذشته ayyám-i-guzashtah.—(*past tense*) ماضی mází, ماضی مطلق mází-i-mutlak.

PASTE, خمیر khamír.—(*made of a root pounded*) سریش sirísh, سیرشم sírishum.

To PASTE up, چسبانیدن chasbánídan.

PASTEBOARD, *or* PAPIER-MACHÉ, مقوی mukavvá, مقوا mukavvá.

PASTERN (*of a horse*), خرده khurdah.

PASTIL, بخور bukhúr.

PASTIME, بازیچه bázíchah, تفرج tafarruj.

PASTOR, کشیش kashísh, قسیس kissís.

PASTORAL, بدوی badaví, بادیه نشین bádiyah-nishín.

PASTRY, خمیر khamír, آرد سرشته árd-i-sirishtah.

PASTURAGE, علوفه 'alúfah.—(*pasture*) مرغزار margh-zár, چراگاه chará-gáh.

PASTURE (*ground*), مرتع marta', مرعی mar'á, چراگاه chará-gáh, علفزار 'alaf-zár, مرغ margh, مرغزار margh-zár, قوروق kúrúk, چمن chaman.

To PASTURE, چریدن charídan.

PAT, کامل kámil, درست durust, صحیح sahíh.

To PAT, دست مالیدن dast málídan.

PATCH, پینه pínah, پیوند paivand, رقعه ruk'ah, وصله vaslah.—(*for a rifle-bullet*) کفن kafan.

To PATCH, وصله کردن vaslah kardan, پنبه انداختن pambah andákhtan.

PATCHED, مرقع murakka'.

PATCHER, لندره دوز landarah-dúz, قلابدوز kulláb-dúz, پینه دوز pinah-dúz.

PATCHWORK, لندره دوزی landarah-dúzí, قلابدوزی kulláb-dúzí.

PATE, سر sar, راس rás, کله kallah, فرق fark.

PATENT (*exclusive privilege*), سند sanad.—(*Royal patent*), یرلیغ yarlígh, توقیع taukí'.—(*evident*) آشکار áshkár, آشکاره áshkárah, ظاهر záhir, هویدا huvaidá, روشن raushan, مبین mubín, واضح vázih, لایح láih, عیان 'iyán, باهر báhir, صریح saríh, بدیهی badíhí.

PATENTEE, سند دار sanad-dár.

PATERNAL, پدری pidarí, پدرانه pidaránah.

PATERNITY, پدریه pidaríyah, ابوت abúvat.

PATH, *vide* ROAD.—(*of a garden*) معبر ma'bar, خیابان khiyábán.

PATHETIC, دلسوز dil-súz, دلاویز dil-áviz, سهمگین sahm-gín.

PATHETICALLY, با دلسوزی bá-dil-súzí.

PATHLESS, بیراه bí-ráh, بلا طریق bilá tarík.

PATIENCE, صبر sabr, صبوری sabúrí, شکیب shikíb, شکیبائی shikíbá,í, تحمل tahammul, طاقت tákat, برد باری burd-bárí.

PATIENT, صابر sábir, صبور sabúr, برد بار burd-bár, شکیبا shikíbá.—(*sick person*) مریض maríz, علیل 'alíl, نا خوش ná-khwush.—(*to be patient*) تحمل نمودن tahammul nimúdan, صبر نمودن sabr nimúdan.

PATIENTLY, با صبر bá-sabr, صبرا sabran.

PATRIARCH (*of a church*), بطرق batrak, پطریق patrík.

PATRIARCHAL, پطریقی patríkí.

PATRICIAN, امیر amír.

PATRIMONY, ارث irs, میراث mírás, ارثیت irsíyat, وراثت virásat, عصوبت 'usúbat.

PATRIOT, وطن دوست vatan-dúst, حبیب الوطن habíbu-'l-vatan.

PATRIOTISM, حب الوطن hubbu-'l-vatan.

PATROL (*night-watch*), پاسبان شب pásbán-i-shab, عسس 'asas, گزمه gazmah, کشیك kashík.

To PATROL, پاسبانی کردن pásbání kardan.

PATRON, مربی murabbí, حامی hámí, صاحب sáhib.

PATRONAGE, حمایت himáyat, توصیه tausíyah, صاحبی sáhibí.

To PATRONIZE, حمایت دادن himáyat dádan.

PATRONYMIC, نسبت nisbat, نام nám, اسم ism.

PATTENS (*clogs*), نعلین na'lain.

PATTERN, نمونه nimúnah, مثال misál, نقش naksh.

PAUCITY, کمی kamí, اندک andak.

PAUNCH, معده mi'dah, شکم shikm, بطن batn.

PAUPER, مسکین miskín, فقیر fakír.

PAUSE (*in reading*), وقف vakf. (*Vide* INTERMISSION, DELAY.)

To PAUSE, وقوف نمودن vukúf nimúdan, وقف کردن vakf kardan.

To PAVE, سنگفرش کردن sang-farsh kardan.

PAVED, سنگفرشی sang-farshí.

PAVEMENT, سنگفرش sang-farsh, سنگبست sang-bast. — (*tessellated pavement*) فرش منبت کار farsh-i-munabbat-kár.

PAVER, سنگ فرش کننده sang-farsh-kunandah.

PAVILION, *vide* AWNING, TENT, KIOSK.

PAW, پا pá, پای páy, پاچه páchah, پنجه panjah, چنگ chang.

To PAW, دست زدن dast-zadan, دست ماله کردن dast-málah kardan.—(*as a horse*) سم زدن sum zadan.

PAWN, رهن rahn, گرو girau.—(*thing pledged*) رهینه rahínah, تنخواه tankhwáh, گرو girau.—(*at chess*) بیذق baizak, پیاده piyádah.

To PAWN, رهن گذاردن rahn guzárdan, گرو گذاشتن girau guzáshtan.

PAWNBROKER, رهنگیر rahn-gír, گروگیر girau-gír, راهن ráhin.

PAWNER (*one who pawns*), مرتهن murtahin, رهن گذار rahn-guzár, گرو گذار girau-guzár.

PAY (*wages*), مواجب mavájib, اجرت ujrat, اجر ajr, وظیفه vazífah, علوفه 'alúfah, مزد muzd.—(*fare, hire*), کرایه kiráyah, کرا kirá, جیره jírah, اجرت ujrat, غله ghallah.—(*monthly*) مشاهره musháharah, ماهیانه máhiyánah. — (*yearly*) سالیانه sáliyánah.—(*daily*) یومیه yúmíyah, روزانه rúzánah.—(*half-pay*) مواجب نیمه mavájib-i-nímah. — (*advance of pay*) سلم silm, پیشگی píshagí, سلف salaf.

To PAY, کار سازی کردن kár-sází kardan, ادا کردن adá kardan, دادن dádan, مفروغ کردن mafrúgh kardan.

PAYABLE, ادا شدنی adá-shudaní.

PAYMASTER, خزانچی khizán - chí, بخشی bakhshí.

PAYMENT, ادا adá, تادیه ta,diyah.

PAY-OFFICE, دار الحساب dáru-'l-hisáb.

PEA, کرسنه karsanna, کسن kisan, گاو دانه gáv-dánah, باقله موشی bákilah-múshí. — (*English pea*), نخود فرنگی nukhúd-i-farangí.—(*chick-pea*) نخود nukhúd.—(*small field-pea*) گرگرو girgirú.—(*green pea*) ماش másh.

PEACE, آشتی áshtí, صلح sulh, امان amán, رفاه rafáh.—(*rest*) آرام árám, آسایش ásáyish, راحت ráhat, رفاه rafáh, رفاهیت rafáhiyat.—(*of God*) سلام الله salámu-'llah, امان الله amánu-'llah. — (*the conclusion of peace*) انعقاد صلح in'ikád-i-sulh.—(*peace-footing*) حال صلح hál-i-sulh.—(*to make peace*) عقد مصالحه نمودن 'akd-i-musálahah nimúdan.—(*to make overtures for peace*) در صدد مصالحه بر آمدن dar sadad-i-musálahah bar-ámadan.

PEACEABLE, سلیم salím, صلح جو sulh-jú.

PEACEABLY, بمصالحه bi-musálalah, صلحاً sulhan, از روی آشتی az rúy-i-áshtí.

PEACEFUL, ارمنده armandah.

PEACE-MAKER, مصلح muslih.

PEACH, شفتالو shaftálú.—(*woolly peach*) هلو hullú.

PEACH-COLOURED (*pale red*), شفتالو رنگ shaftálú-rang.

PEACOCK, طاؤس tá,us.

PEA-HEN, طاؤس ماده tá,us-i-mádah.

PEA-JACKET (*outer coat of felt or*

thick unwoven wool), كپنك kapanak, نمد دوش namad-i-dúsh.

PEAK (*of a mountain, &c.*), سر sar, قله kullah, راس rás, سر كوب sar-kúb, نوك nauk, بلندى bulandí, تيغ tígh.

PEAL, صدا مسلسل sadá-i-musalsal.

PEAR, گلابى gulábí, امرود amrúd.

PEARL, مرواريد marváríd, گوهر gauhar, لؤلؤ lu,lu, (*pl.* لآلى la,áli,) در durr (*pl.* درر durar).—(*small pearls*) بسد basad.—(*royal pearl*) لولوئى شاهوار lu,lu,í-i-sháh-vár, در مكنون durr-i-maknún, لؤلؤئى لاله lulu,í-i-lálah, در شهوار durr-i-shah-vár, شهدانه shah-dánah, گوشواره gúsh-várah.

PEARLY, مرواريد دار marvaríd-dár.

PEASANT, روستائى rústá,í, دهقان dih-kán, زارع zári', رعيت ra'íyat.

PEASANTRY, رعايا ra'áyá, حضرات زارع hazarát-i-zári', زارعين zári'ín.

PEA-SHOOTER, تفك tufak.

PEBBLE, ريگ ríg.

PECCABLE, گناهكار gunáh-kár.

PECCADILLO, عيب 'aib, خطا khatá, قصور kusúr, غلط ghalat, گناه gunáh, سهو sahv, ذنب zamb, ذل zall, تقصير taksír, زلت zallat, نقص nuks.

PECCANT, تقصير وار taksír-vár, مجرم mujrim, ملزم mulzam, گناه كار gunáh-kár.

To PECK, چنگ زدن chang zadan.

PECKER, منقار زننده minkár-zanan-dah.

PECTORAL, صدرى sadríy.

To PECULATE, دزدى كردن duzdí kardan.

PECULATION, دزدى duzdí, تصرف ta-sarruf.

PECULIAR, غريب gharíb, بديهى ba-díhí, عجيب 'ajíb.—(*peculiar to*) مخصوص makhsús, مختص mukh-tass, منحصر munhasir.

PECULIARITY, اختصاص ikhtisás, خاصيت khássíyat.

PECULIARLY, خصوصاً khusúsan.

PECUNIARY, پولى púlí, مالى málí.

PEDAGOGUE, ملا مكتبى mullá-i-maktabí, معلم mu'allim,

PEDANT, متفضل mutafazzil, مغرور از علم maghrúr az 'ilm, عالم خود پسند 'álim-i-khwud-pasand.

PEDANTIC, فضيلت فروش fazílat-furúsh.—(*to be pedantic*) اظهار فضيلت كردن izhár-i-fazílat kar-dan, فضيلت فروختن fazílat furúkh-tan.

PEDANTRY, فضيلت فروشى fazílat-furúshí.

PEDDLER, خورده فروش khwurdah-furúsh, پيلور pílavar, خراز kharráz.

PEDESTAL, بن ستون bunn-i-sutún, بنيان bunyán, پايه páyah.

PEDESTRIAN, راجل rájil, پياده piyá-dah.

PEDIGREE, نسبنامه nasab-námah, سلسله silsilah, تناسل tanásul, نسل nasl, حسب و نسب hasab va nasab. — (*to trace a pedigree*) استنساب كردن istinsáb kardan.

PEEL, قشر kishr, پوست púst.

To PEEL, پوست كندن púst kandan, مقشر ساختن mukashshar sákhtan.

PEELER, پوست كننده púst-kanandah, مقشر mukashshir.

PEEP, نظر nazar.

To PEEP, دزدانه نگريستن duzdánah nigrístan, از گوشه ديدن az gúshah dídan.

PEEP-HOLE, منظر manzar.

PEER, نظير nazír, مثل misl, هم تا عديل ham-tá-i-'adíl.

PEERLESS, بى نظير bí-nazír, لاثانى lá-sání.

PEEVISH, تند مزاج tund-mizáj, كجخلق kaj-khulk, افسرده afsur-dah.

PEEVISHNESS, افسردگى afsurdagí, تندى مزاج tundí-i-mizáj.

PEG, ميخ míkh, مسمار mismár.

PELF, زر zar, پول púl, نقد nakd, مايه máyah, تنخواه tankhváh, وجه vajh.

PELICAN, مرغ سقا murgh-i-sakká.

PELISSE (*kind of cloak*), بورمه búr-mah, كاتبى kátibí.

PELLET, گلوله gulúlah, گله gullah, غلوله ghulúlah.—(*pellet-bow*) كمان گردها kamán-i-gardahá, گلوله كمان gulúlah-kamán.

PELLICLE, پرده pardah.
PELL-MELL, بهم آمیخته bi-ham ámíkhtah, هرج مرج harj-marj.
PELLUCID, صاف sáf, روشن raushan. --(*transparent*) شفاف shifáf.
PELLUCIDNESS, صفا safá, روشنائی raushaná,í. — (*transparency*) شفافی shifáfí.
To PELT, زدن zadan, با سنگ زدن bá-sang zadan.
PELVIS (*lower part of the abdomen*), ته شکم tah-i-shikm, پائین شکم pá,ín-i-shikm. — (*pelvis bones*) قالیچه kálíchah, غالیچه ghálíchah.
PEN, قلم kalam, خامه khámah, کلك kilk, قصب kasab.—(*steel pen*), قلم پولاد kalam-i-púlád, قلم آهن kalam-i-áhan. — (*feather, quill*) پر par, شه پر shah-par.—(*pen-knife*) چاقو chákú, کزلك kizlak, قلمتراش kalam-tirásh.—(*nib of a pen*) نوك قلم nauk-i-kalam. — (*piece of bone on which pens are nibbed*), قطزن kat-zan, مقطع makta', قطعزن kat'-zan. — (*pen-case*) قلمدان kalam-dán, آمه ámah. — (*penholder*) دسته قلم dastah-i-kalam. (*to cut a pen*) قلم ساختن kalam sákhtan. — (*pen for cattle*), آغل ághil, آگل ágil, سول súl, حظیره hazírah.
To PEN, نوشتن nivishtan.
PENAL, عقوبتی 'ukúbatí.
PENALTY, جریمه jarímah, جریمانه jarímánah, مصادره musádarah. (*Vide* PUNISHMENT.)
PENANCE, حد کفاره hadd-i-kaffárah, جزائی شر jazá,í-i-sharr, تکفیر گناه takfír-i-gunáh.
PENCHANT (*inclination, liking*), میل mail, دماغ dimágh, شوق shauk.
PENCIL (*leaden*), قلم سرمه kalam-i-surmah, قلم سرب kalam-i-surb, قلم مدادی kalam-i-midádí, مداد midád.—(*of hair*) قلم مو kalam-i-mú.
PENDANT, *vide* TASSEL, EARRING, &c.
PENDENT, آویزان ávízán, آویخته ávíkhtah, معلق mu'allak, بردار bardár.
PENDING (*hanging*), معلق mu'allak. —(*during*) مادام mádám, بین bain, تا tá.
PENDULOUS, آویزان ávízán, معلق mu'allak.
PENDULUM, لنگر ساعت langar-i-sá'at, لنگر langar.
PENETRABLE, نفوذ پذیر nufúz-pazír, قابل سرایت kábil-i-siráyat.
To PENETRATE, اندرون رفتن andarún raftan, تو رفتن tú raftan, داخل شدن dákhil shudan, نفوذ نمودن nufúz nimúdan, گذر کردن guzar kardan, نافذ بودن náfiz búdan.
PENETRATING, نافذ náfiz, کارگر kár-gar.
PENETRATION, دخل dukhl, مداخله mudákhalah. — (*acuteness, sagacity*) فراست firásat, فطانت fatánat, ذهن zihn, ادراك idrák, زیرکی zírakí, ذکا zaká, جزالت jazálat, زکاوت zakávat, سرعت فهم sur'at-i-fahm.
PENINSULA, جزیره jazírah, نیم جزیره ním-jazírah.
PENIS, ذکر zakar (*pl.* ذکور zukúr), کیر kír, زردك zardak (*vulg.*).
PENITENCE, *vide* REPENTANCE.
PENMAN (*fine writer*), خوشنویس khwush-nivís, کاتب kátib.
PENNANT, نشان nishán, علم 'alam, رأیت ra,yat, لوا livá, بیرق bairak, بیراق bairák.
PENNILESS, مفلس muflis, محتاج muhtáj.
PENSION, وظیفه vazífah, علوفه 'alúfah, ادرار idrár.
PENSIONER, وظیفه خور vazífah-khwur, مواجب خور mavájib-khwur.
PENSIVE, *vide* THOUGHTFUL.
PENT, حبس habs.
PENTAGON, مخمس mukhammas, پنجگوشه panj-gúshah.
PENTATEUCH (*Books of Moses*), توراة taurát, توریت taurát.
PENTECOST, عید خمسین 'íd-i-khamsín.
PENURIOUS, طامع támi', طمعکار tama'-kár, آرزو مند árzú-mand, حریص harís, لئیم la,ím, دانع dáni', کنس kinis.
PENURIOUSNESS, حرص hirs, آز áz,

طمع tama', طمعکاری tama'-kárí, بخل bukhl, خسیست khasísat, خست khissat, امساك imsák, لوم lu,m.

PENURY, *vide* POVERTY.

PEOPLE, خلق khalk, خلقمان khalkamán, امت ummat, ملت millat, مردمان mardumán, حضرات hazarát.—(*common people*) عام 'ámm, عوام 'avámm, عوام الناس 'avámmu-'n-nás, اهالی aháli. — (*peopling and cultivating*) آبادی ábádí. — (*peopled place*) آبادانی ábádání, جائی معمور já,í-i-ma'múr.

To PEOPLE, آباد کردن ábád kardan.

PEPPER, فلفل filfil.—(*red pepper*) فلفل هندی filfil-i-hindí, فلفل سرخ filfil-i-surkh.—(*pepper and salt colour*) فلفل نمکی filfil-namakí.

To PEPPER, فلفل زدن filfil zadan.

PEPPERCORN, نقیر nakír, قطمیر kitmír, پشیز pishíz.

PEPPERMINT, نعنا na'ná, نعنع na'na'.

PERADVENTURE, شاید sháyad, مگر magar, بوکه bú-kih, باشد báshad, گویا gúyá, گاهست gáhast.

To PERAMBULATE, طواف نمودن taváf nimúdan, گرد گردیدن gird gardídan.

PERAMBULATION, طواف taváf.

To PERCEIVE, *vide* To SEE, To KNOW, To DISCOVER.—(*to feel*) احساس نمودن ihsás nimúdan, در یافتن dar-yáftan.

PER CENT., فی صد fí sad (*thus, five per cent.*, صد پنج sad-panj, صدرا پنج sadrá-panj, فی صد پنج fí-sad-panj).

PERCEPTIBLE, محسوس mahsús.

PERCEPTION, *vide* IDEA, SIGHT.

PERCEPTIVE, بصیر basír.

PERCH, چوب chúb.—(*fish*) ماهی خار دار máhí-i-khár-dár.

To PERCH, بر چوب نشستن bar chúb nishastan.

PERCHANCE, شاید sháyad, مگر magar, بوکه bú-kih, باشد báshad, گویا gúyá, گاهست gáhast.

To PERCOLATE, وقوب نمودن vukúb nimúdan.

PERCOLATION, وقوب vukúb.

PERCUSSION, صدمه sadmah. — (*percussion gun*), تفنگ طرقه دار tufang-i-tarakkah-dár, تفنگ چکشی tufang-i-chakkushí, تفنگ دنگی tufang-i-dingí.—(*cap*) کلاه طرقه kulah-i-tarakkah, چاشنی cháshní.

PERDITION, هلاکت halákat, اهلاك ihlák, خرابی kharábí, تباهی taDáhí, دمار damár, بوار bavár.

To PEREGRINATE, آواره گشتن ávárah gashtan.

PEREGRINATION, آوارگی áváragí.

PEREMPTORILY, باتاکید bá-ta,kíd.

PEREMPTORY, قاطع kátiʻ, شافی sháfí, موکد mu,akkad.

PERENNIAL, مدام mudám.

PERFECT, تمام tamám, تام támm, کامل kámil, سالم sálim, صحیح sahíh.—(*perfect tense*) ماضی قریب mází-i-karíb.

To PERFECT, پرداختن pardákhtan, اکمال نمودن ikmál nimúdan, تکمیل نمودن takmíl nimúdan, تتمیم نمودن tatmím nimúdan.

PERFECTION, فضیلت fazílat, اکمال ikmál, کمال kamál, کنه kunh.—(*completion*) اتمام itmám, اکمال ikmál, تکمیل takmíl, اختتام ikhtitám, انصرام insirám.

PERFECTLY, سراسر sar-á-sar, تماماً tamáman, بالکل bi-'l-kull, بالکلیت bi-'l-kulliyat, بالمره bi-'l-marrah, کلاً و قاطبةً kullan va kátibatan, همه رویهم رفته hamah ruy-ham raftah, کلیتاً kullíyatan, بعینه bi-'ainihi.

PERFIDIOUS, *vide* TREACHEROUS.

PERFIDY, *vide* TREACHERY.

To PERFORATE, سفتن suftan, سنبیدن sumbídan, سوراخ کردن súrákh kardan.

PERFORATION, سوراخ súrákh.

PERFORATOR, سوراخ کننده súrákh-kunandah.

To PERFORM, کردن kardan, ساختن sákhtan, بجا آوردن bi-já ávardan, بکار بردن bi-kár burdan, بسر بردن bi-sar burdan, پرداختن pardákhtan, اجرا نمودن ijrá nimúdan, ادا

کردن adá kardan, ایفا نمودن ífá nimúdan.

PERFORMANCE (*act*), کار kár, کردار kirdár, عمل 'amal, فعل fi'l.—(*completion*) اتمام itmám, اکمال ikmál, تکمیل takmíl, اختتام ikhtitám, انصرام insirám. — (*execution of a project or design*) سر براهی sar bi-ráhí, ادا adá, اتمام itmám, اجرا ijrá, ایفا ífá, کار kár. —(*of a promise, &c.*) وفا vafá, ایفا ífá, ادا adá, اجرا ijrá.—(*stage play*) تماشا tamáshá.

PERFORMER, فاعل fá'il, عامل 'ámil, کار کن kár-kun, سازنده sázandah. —(*stage performer*) بازی bází.

PERFUME, بخور bukhúr, خوشبوی khwush-búí, عطر 'itr, رائحه rá,ihah, نفحه nafhah, عبیر 'abír, غالیه ghá-liyah, نکهت nakhat.—(*censer for burning perfumes*) بخور دان bukhúr-dán.

To PERFUME, خوش بو کردن khwush-bú kardan, تبخیر نمودن tabkhír nimúdan.

PERFUMED, مشموم mashmúm, معطر mu'attar.

PERFUMER, عطار 'attár, عطر فروش 'itr-furúsh. — (*maker of perfumes*) عطر کش 'itr-kash.

PERFUNCTORILY, بغفلت bi-ghiflat.

PERFUNCTORY, غافل gháfil, بیخبر bí-khabar, بیپروا bí-parvá, بی احتیاط bí-ihtiyát, بی اندیشه bí-andíshah, کاهل káhil, بیهوش bí-húsh, زاهل záhil, بی مبالات bí-mubálát, لا قید lá-kaid.

PERHAPS, شاید sháyad, مگر magar, بوکه bú-kih, باشد báshad, گویا gúyá, گاهست gáhast.

PERICARDIUM, پرده دل pardah-i-dil.

PERIL, خطر khatar, خطره khatrah, مخاطره mukhátarah, بیم bím, خدشه khadashah, تشویش tashvísh, باك bák, تنگنائی tangná,í.—(*at the peril of one's life*) جان بهلاکت انداخته ján bi-halákat andákh-tah.

PERILOUS, خطر ناك khatar-nák, هولناك haulnák, مهلك muhlik.

PERIOD (*time*), وقت vakt, عرصه 'arsah, مدت muddat, حین hín, زمان zamán, هنگام hangám, *or* hungám, عهد 'ahad.—(*full sentence*) جمله jumlah. —(*circle of time*) دور daur, دوره daurah, گردش gardish, نوبت naubat.

PERIODICAL, دواری davvárí.

PERIODICALLY, بنوبت bi-naubat.

PERIPHERY, محیط muhít.

To PERISH, هلاك شدن halák shudan, تلف شدن talaf shudan, نا بود شدن ná-búd shudan, تباه شدن tabáh shudan, زائل گشتن zá,il gashtan, معدوم شدن ma'dúm shudan, فوت شدن faut shudan, ضایع شدن zái' shudan.

PERISHABLE, فانی fání, فانیه fání-yah, فنا پذیر faná-pazír, زائل zá,il.

To PERJURE oneself, سوگند دروغ خوردن saugand-i-durúgh khwur-dan, قسم زور خوردن kasam-i-zúr khwurdan.

PERJURER, سوگند دروغ گو saugand-i-durugh-gú.

PERJURY, سوگند دروغ saugand-i-durúgh, حلف کاذب half-i-kázib, قسم زور kasam-i-zúr.

PERMANENCE, بقا baká, برقراری bar-karárí, دوام davám, مداومت mudá-vamat.

PERMANENT, پایدار páyadár, پاینده páyandah, بقا دار baká-dár, استوار ustuvár, قایم káím, دائم dá,im, باقی bákí, ثابت sábit.

PERMANENTLY, بطور دائمی bi-taur-i-dá,imí.

PERMEABLE, نفوذ پذیر nufúz-pazír, قابل سرایت kábil-i-siráyat.

To PERMEATE, سرایت نمودن siráyat nimúdan.

PERMISSIBLE, مجاز mujáz, روا ravá, حلال halál.

PERMISSION, اجازت ijázat, اذن izn, پروانگی parvánagí, اباحت ibáhat, رضا razá, رخصت rukhsat, دستور dastúr, دستوری dastúrí, جواز javáz. —(*by permission*) مأذوناً ma,zú-nan.—(*to ask permission*) استجازه کردن istijázah kardan, اجازه خواستن

ijázah khwástan, اذن خواستن izn khwástan.

PERMISSIVE, اذنی izní.

PERMIT, *vide* PASSPORT.

To PERMIT, گذشتن guzashtan, دادن dádan, دستور دادن dastúr dádan, اجازت دادن ijázat dádan, قائل بودن ká,il búdan, اذن دادن izn dádan, واگذاشتن vá-guzáshtan, فرصت دادن fursat dádan, هشتن hishtan.

PERMUTATION, تبدیل tabdíl, تبدل tabaddul, عوض 'ivaz *or* 'avaz.

PERNICIOUS, ضرر انگیز zarar-angíz, مضر muzirr, موذی mu,zí.

PERNICIOUSLY, مفسدانه mufsidánah.

PERPENDICULAR, مستقیم mustakím, معمد mu'ammad.

To PERPETRATE, کردن kardan, ساختن sákhtan, بجا آوردن bi-já ávardan, بکار بردن bi-kár burdan, بسر بردن bi-sar burdan, پرداختن pardákhtan, اجرا نمودن ijrá nimúdan, ادا کردن adá kardan, ایفا نمودن ífá nimúdan.

PERPETRATION, ارتکاب irtikáb.

PERPETRATOR, مرتکب murtakib.

PERPETUAL, دائم dá,im, مدام mudám, جاودان jávidán, جاوید jávíd, سرمدی sarmadí, ابدی abadí, صمد samad.

PERPETUALLY, همیشه hamíshah, همواره hamvárah, هر وقت har vakt, هر زمان har zamán, مدام mudám, دائم dá,im, هر دم har dam, علی الدوام 'ala-'d-davám, پیوسته paivastah, دمبدم dam-bi-dam, متصلاً muttasilan, همیشه اوقات hamíshah-aukát.

To PERPETUATE, مستدام نمودن mustadám nimúdan, استمرار ساختن istimrár sákhtan.

PERPETUITY, دوام davám, مداومت mudávamat.—(*to all perpetuity*) بر سبیل استمرار bar sabíl-i-istimrár.

To PERPLEX, حیران کردن hairán kardan, پریشان ساختن paríshán sákhtan, متحیر گردانیدن mutahayyir gardánídan.

PERPLEXED, حیران hairán, متحیر mutahayyir, مضطرب muztarib, پریشان paríshán, مشوش mushavvash.

PERPLEXITY, حیرانی hairání, تحیر tahayyur, اضطراب iztiráb, پریشانی paríshání, تشویش tashvísh, سر گردانی sar-gardání, آشفتگی áshuftagí, توزع tavazzu', حیص بیص haiz-baiz.

PERQUISITE, مزد muzd, حق السعی hakku-'s-sa'í, تعارف ta'áruf.—(*king's perquisites, privy purse*) جیب شاهی jíb-i-sháhí.—(*fee to a police officer*) قلق kulluk, تکلف takalluf.—(*fee to a shop-boy, given by purchasers*) شاگردانگی shágirdánagí, شاگردگانی shágirdagání.

To PERSECUTE, ظلم نمودن zulm nimúdan, ستم کردن sitam kardan, تعاقب نمودن ta'ákub nimúdan, دست درازی کردن dast-dirází kardan, پاپی کردن pá-pay kardan (*vulg.*).

PERSECUTION, تعاقب ta'ákub, ظلم zulm, جفا jafá, ستم sitam, جبر jabr, اجحاف ijháf, پاپی pá-pay (*vulg.*).

PERSECUTOR, معاقب mu'ákib, ستمکار sitam-kár, ستمگار sitamgár, جفاکار jafá-kár, ظالم zálim.

PERSEVERANCE, مداومت mudávamat, مواظبت muvázabat, استقامت istikámat, استقرار istikrár, اصرار isrár.—(*obstinacy*) اصرار isrár, خود سری khwud-sarí, عناد 'inád.

To PERSEVERE, اقامت نمودن ikámat nimúdan, اصرار نمودن isrár nimúdan.

PERSEVERING, ثابت قدم sábit-kadam.

PERSIA, ایران írán, عجم 'ajam.—(*the whole kingdom of Persia*) مملکت ایران mamlikat-i-írán, ولایت عجم viláyat-i-'ajam.—(*a province*) ملک mulk; of these, the principal are: فارس fars, عراق عجمی 'irák-i-'ajamí, خراسان khurásán, آذربایجان ázarbá,iján, مازندران mázandarán, گیلان gílán, استراباد astarábád, خوزستان khúzistán, and کرمان kirmán.

PERSIAN, ایرانی írání, عجمی 'ajamí, تاجیك tájík.—(*language*) فارسی fársí, پارسی pársí.—(*court language*) دری darí.—(*ancient language*) پهلوی pahlaví.

To PERSIST, استبداد نمودن istibdád nimúdan, اصرار نمودن isrár nimúdan.

PERSISTENCE, اصرار isrár, مواظبت muvázabat, استبداد istibdád.

PERSISTING, مستمر mustamirr.

PERSON, شخص shakhs, نفر nafar, آدم ádam, کس kas. —(*external appearance*) شخص shakhs, صورت súrat, شکل shakl, سیما símá, قوارہ kavárah, پیکر paikar, اندام andám, بشرہ basharah, هیئت hai,at, هیکل haikal, ریخت ríkht.—(*of the Holy Trinity*), اقنوم aknúm (*pl.* اقانیم akáním).—(*of a verb or pronoun*) صیغه síghah, ضمیر zamír, اسم ضمیر ism-i-zamír.—(*first person*) متکلم mutakallim. — (*second person*) مخاطب mukhátab.—(*third person*) غائب ghá,ib.—(*in person*) فی ذاته fí zátihi, فی نفسه fí-nafsihi, شخصاً shakhsan, ذاتاً zátan.

PERSONAGE, امیر amír.—(*appearance*) صورت súrat, شخص shakhs, ریخت ríkht, شکل shakl.

PERSONAL, شخصی shakhsí, ذاتی zátí.

PERSONALITY, شخصیت shakhsíyat, ذات zát.

PERSONALLY, فی ذاته fí-zátihi, فی نفسه fí-nafsihi, شخصاً shakhsan, ذاتاً zátan.

To PERSONATE, نیابت کردن niyábat kardan.

PERSONIFICATION, تشبیه tashbíh.

To PERSONIFY, تشبیه نمودن tashbíh nimúdan.

PERSPECTIVE, منظرہ manzarah.

PERSPICACIOUS, تیز فهم tíz-fahm, زرنگ zaring, زیرك zírak, چست chust, چابك chábuk.

PERSPICACITY, کیاست kiyásat, فراست firásat, ذهن zihn, زکاوت zakávat.

PERSPICUITY, بینائی bíná,í, وضاحت vazáhat.

PERSPICUOUS, بینا bíná, واضح vázih, مبین mubín, پیدا paidá.

PERSPICUOUSLY, واضحاً vázihan, ظاهراً záhiran.

PERSPIRATION, عرق 'arak, خوی khwai.—(*in a perspiration*) عرق دار 'arak-dár.

To PERSPIRE, عرق کردن 'arak kardan.

To PERSUADE, تحریك کردن tahrík kardan, ترغیب نمودن targhíb nimúdan, اغوا کردن ighvá kardan, چارہ کردن chárah kardan, رائی زدن ra,í zadan.

PERSUASIBLE, ترغیب پذیر targhíb-pazír.

PERSUASION, تحریك tahrík, ترغیب targhíb, اغوا ighvá, تحریص tahrís.

PERSUASIVE, بلیغ balígh.

PERT, شوخ shúkh, گستاخ gustákh, تیز tíz.

To PERTAIN, راجع نمودن ráji' nimúdan, مربوط شدن marbút shudan.

PERTINACIOUS, مصر musirr, مواظب muvázib, ملازم mulázim, راسخ rásikh, مداوم mudávim.

PERTINACITY, استقرار istikrár, مداومت mudávamat, مواظبت muvázabat, اصرار isrár.

PERTINENCE, مناسبت munásabat, موافقت muváfakat.

PERTINENT, مناسب munásib, قابل kábil, سزاور sazávar, موافق muváfik.

PERTLY, بشوخی bi-shúkhí.

PERTNESS, شوخی shúkhí, گستاخی gustákhí, تیزی tízí.

To PERTURBATE, آشوفتن áshúftan, پریشان ساختن paríshán sákhtan.

PERTURBATION, حیرانی hairání, تحیر tahayyur, اضطراب iztiráb, پریشانی paríshání, تشویش tashvísh, سر گردانی sar-gardání, آشفتگی áshuftagí, توزع tavazzu', حیص بیص haiz-baiz.

PERUSAL, مطالعه mutála'ah, ملاحظه muláhazah.

To PERUSE, خواندن khwándan, ملاحظه کردن muláhazah kardan, مطالعه کردن mutála'ah kardan.

To PERVADE, ساری بودن sárí búdan, شمول بودن shumúl búdan.
PERVASION, سرایت sirâyat.
PERVERSE, خود سر khwud-sar, مرید marίd, متمرد mutamarid, حرون harún, منخرط munkharit, معاند mu'ánid, اخلال ikhlál, لجوج lajúj.
PERVERSELY, عناداً 'inádan, بطور عناد bi-taur-i-'inád.
PERVERSENESS, اصرار isrár, خود رأی khwud-ra,í, خود سری khwud-sarí, تمرد tamarrud, عناد 'inád.
PERVERSION, انحراف inhiráf.
To PERVERT (*defeat an object, distort, or mislead*), حبط کردن habt kardan, احباط نمودن ihbát nimúdan, حیف کردن haif kardan, اضلال کردن izlál kardan, بر گردانیدن bar-gardánídan, اعوج کردن a'vaj kardan, معوج گردانیدن mu'avvaj gardánídan.
PERVERTED, بر گشته bar-gashtah, معوج mu'vajj.
PERVIOUS, قابل سرایت kábil-i-sirá-yat, نفوذ پذیر nufúz-pazír.
PEST, آفت áfat, آزار ázár, اذیت azíyat, ایذا ízá, وبال vabál.
PESTIFEROUS, مضر muzirr.
PESTILENCE, طاعون tá'ún, وبا vabá.
PESTILENTIAL, طاعونی tá'úní.
PESTLE, دسته dastah, مدقه midakkah, مشته mushtah.
PET, عزیز 'azíz, معشوق ma'shúk.
To PET, نوازش کردن navázish kardan, دوست داشتن dúst dáshtan.
PETAL, برگ barg.
PETITION, عرض 'arz, در خواست dar-khwást, التماس iltimás, تمنا tamanná.—(*written*) عریضه 'arízah, عرضداشت 'arz-dásht.
To PETITION, در خواستن dar-khwástan, در خواست نمودن dar-khwást nimúdan.
PETITIONER, عارض 'áriz, ملتجی multaji,.
PETRIFACTION, تحجر tahajjur.
PETRIFIED, متحجر mutahajjir.
To PETRIFY, تحجیر نمودن tahjír nimúdan.
PETROLEUM, نفط naft, بترول batrúl (*eur.*).
PETTICOAT, فستان fistán.
PETTY, قلیل kalíl.
PETULANCE, کج خلق kaj-khulk, افسردگی afsurdagí, تندی مزاج tundí-i-mizáj.
PETULANT, تند مزاج tund-mizáj, کج خلق kaj-khulk, افسرده afsurdah. —(*to be petulant*) دوش بر زدن dúsh bar zadan.
PEWIT (*plover*), مرغ ملخ murgh-i-malakh, مرغ زیبا murgh-i-zíbá.
PEWTER, روح rúh, روی rúy.
PHAETON, عرابه 'arábah, عراده 'arrádah, گاری gárí (*hind.*), کالسکه káliskah (*eur.*).
PHALANX, صف saff.
PHANTOM, خیال khayál, تجلی tajallí, روح rúh.
PHARISAICAL, دو رنگ dú-rang, دو زبان dú-zabán, دو رو dú-rú.
PHARISEE, فریسی farísí (*eur.*).
PHARMACY, علم ادویه 'ilm-i-adviyah, علم اجزا 'ilm-i-ajzá.
PHASE, صورت súrat.
PHEASANT, تورنگ túrang, قرقاول karkával, تذرو tazarv. [This latter is an imaginary bird, mentioned by the poets. Some say it is meant for the dove, not the pheasant.]
PHENOMENON, علامت 'alámat.
PHIAL, شیشه shíshah. (*long-necked flask*) صراحی surâhí.
PHILANTHROPIC *and* PHILANTHROPIST, مردم دوست mardum-dúst.
PHILANTHROPY, مردم دوستی mardum-dústí.
PHILIPPIC, هجو hajv.
PHILOLOGIST, لسان آشنا lisán-áshná.
PHILOLOGY, علم ادبیه 'ilm-i-adabíyah, علم لغات 'ilm-i-lughát.
PHILOMEL, بلبل bulbul, عندلیب 'andalíb, هزار داستان hazár-dástán, زند باف zand-báf.
PHILOSOPHER, حکیم hakím, فیلسوف fa,lasúf, عالم 'álim, خردمند khird-mand, دانشمند dánish-mand, بزرگ buzurg, حکمت پیشه hikmat-píshah.
PHILOSOPHER'S STONE, اکسیر iksír, کیمیائی اکبر kímiyá,í-akbar. [This

stone is supposed to have the faculty of transmuting metals to gold.]

PHILOSOPHIC, دانشمند dánish-mand, عالم 'álim, دانا dáná, عاقل 'ákil, حکیم hakím.

PHILOSOPHY, حکمت hikmat, فلسفه falsafah, دانش dánish, علم 'ilm.

PHLEBOTOMY, فصد fasd.

PHLEGM, بلغم balgham.

PHLEGMATIC, بلغمی balghamí.

PHŒNIX, عنقا 'anká, سیمرغ símurgh, رخ rukh. [These three words signify a fabulous bird, of enormous size; the "Roc" of the "Arabian Nights."].—(*a fabulous bird, said never to alight on the ground. The head which it overshadows will wear a crown*) هما humá.

PHONOGRAPH, فونوگراف fúnúgráf (*eur.*)

PHOSPHORUS, کبریت kibrít, نفط naft. [Strictly speaking the first of these words is the equivalent for "brimstone," the second for "naphtha."]

PHOTOGRAPH, عکس 'aks, صورت عکس súrat-i-'aks.—(*to take a photograph*) شیشه عکس انداختن shísbah-i-'aks andákhtan.

PHOTOGRAPHER, عکاس 'akkás.

PHOTOGRAPHIC STUDIO, عکاسخانه 'akkás-khánah.

PHOTOGRAPHY, عکسی 'aksí.

PHRASE, اصطلاح istiláh, طرز قلام tarz-i-kalám, ضرب مثل zarb-i-masal.

PHRASEOLOGY, نطق nutk, تلفظ talaffuz.

PHYSIC, علاج iláj, معالجه mu'álajah, دوا davá, دارو dárú.—(*the science*) علم ادویه 'ilm-i-adviyah, علم اجزا 'ilm-i-ajzá.

PHYSICAL, طبیعی tabí'í.

PHYSICIAN, طبیب tabíb (*pl.* اطبا atibbá), حکیم hakím (*pl.* حکما hukamá).

PHYSIOGNOMIST, سیما شناس símá-shinás, قیافه شناس kiyáfah-shinás.

PHYSIOGNOMY, علم قیافه 'ilm-i-kiyáfah.

PHYSIOLOGY, علم موجودات 'ilm-i-maujúdát.

PHYSIQUE, مزاج mizáj, نهاد nihád, طبیعت tabí'at, جبلت jibillat, طینت tínat, سرشت sirisht.

PIANO, پیانو piyánú (*eur.*).

PIASTRE (*a silver coin*), قروش kurúsh, غروش ghurúsh.

TO PICK, تراشیدن tiráshídan, ستردن suturdan, پاك کردن pák kardan.—(*to pick up*), چیدن chídan, بر داشتن bar-dáshtan, بلند کردن buland kardan.—(*collect*) جمع کردن jam' kardan, فراهم آوردن faráham ávardan, چیدن chídan, کپیدن kapídan (*vulg.*)—(*choose*) گزیدن guzídan, بر چیدن bar-chídan, انتخاب کردن intikháb kardan, اختیار کردن ikhtiyár kardan.

PICKAXE, کلنگ kulung, کلند kulund, تیشه tíshah.

PICKER, چین chín.

PICKLE, ترشی turshí.

TO PICKLE, ترشی انداختن turshí andákhtan.

PICKPOCKET, کیسه بر kísah-burr.

PICQUET (*of an army*), طلایه taláyah, پیشرو písh-rau.

PICTURE, تصویر tasvír, نقش naksh, شبیه shabíh, نگار nigár, پرده نقاشی pardah-i-nakkáshí, پرده اشکال pardah-i-ashkál.—(*to picture to oneself*) انگاشتن ángáshtan.

PICTURE GALLERY, نگار خانه nigár-khánah, نگارستان nigáristán.

PIE, سنبوسه sambúsah.

PIEBALD, ابلق ablak.

PIECE, پاره párah, پارچه párchah, تکه tikkah, لفچه lafchah, ریزه rízah, قراضه kurázah, لقمه lukmah, ذره zarrah, شرحه sharhah, قطعه kat'ah, جزوی juzví.

PIECE-MEAL, پاره پاره párah-párah, یك یك yak-yak, فردافرد fard-á-fard.

PIE-MAN, سنبوسه چی sambúsah-chí.

PIER, اسکله askalah (*eur.*), سکو sakkú.

TO PIERCE, سفتن suftan, سنبیدن sumbídan, سوراخ کردن súrákh kardan, دوختن dúkhtan, فرو کردن furú kardan, گذر کردن guzar kardan.

PIERCED, مثقوب maskúb, سفته suftah, دوخته dúkhtah.

PIERCER, سوراخ کننده súrákh-kunandah.—(*instrument*) برمه barmah, مته mattah.

PIERCING, تیز tíz.

PIERCINGLY, بتیزی bi-tízí.

PIETY, تقوی takvá, تقاوت takávat, صلاح saláh, ریاضت riyázat, دیانت diyánat.

PIG, خنزیر khinzír, خوگ khúg, خوك khúk, گراز guráz.

PIGEON, کبوتر kabútar, کفتر kaftar (*vulg.*). — (*fantail pigeon*) کفتر چتری kaftar-i-chatrí. — (*carrier pigeon*) کبوتر بار kabútar-i-bár, کفتر بار kaftar-i-bár.—(*tumbler pigeon*) کفتر معلق kaftar-i-mu'allak.—(*pigeon-house*) کبوتر خانه kabútar-khánah, کفتر خانه kaftar-khánah, برج کفتر burj-i-kaftar. — (*wood-pigeon*) فاخته fákhtah, قمری kumrí.

PIGMENT, رنگ rang.

PIGMY (*subs.*), کوتاه قد kútáh-kad, مردك mardak, کتولی kutúlí, خپل khippil (*vulg.*). — (*adj.*) خرد khurd, خورد khwurd, کوچك kúchik, صغیر saghír, که kih, پاچه páchah.

PIKE, نیزه naizah, حربه harbah.

PIKEMAN, اهل نیزه ahl-i-naizah, نیزه ور naizah-var.

PIKESTAFF, چوب نیزه chúb-i-naizah, چوب chúb.

PILE (*heap*), توده túdah, کپه kuppah.—(*nap of cloth*) کلك kulk, خواب khwáb.—(*stake*) وتد vatad, چوب chúb, عمود 'amúd.—(*of an arrow*) پیکان paikán.

To PILE, کپه کردن kappah kardan, توده کردن túdah kardan.

PILES (*hæmorrhoids*), بواسیر bavásír, بواسیر bavásír.

To PILFER, دزدی کردن duzdí kardan, دزدیدن duzdídan.

PILFERER, دزدی duzdí.

PILGRIM (*to Makkah*), حاجی hájí, حاج hájj (*pl.* حجاج hujáj).—(*to minor places of sanctity*) زوار zavvár, زائر zá,ir (*pl.* زوار zuvár), سیاح sayyáh.—(*company or caravan of pilgrims*) حاج hájj, قافله زوار káfilah-i-zuvár.

PILGRIMAGE, زیارت ziyárat, سیاحت sayyáhat.—(*to Makkah*) حج hajj, عمرت 'umrat.—(*place of pilgrimage, tomb of holy personages, &c.*) زیارتگاه ziyárat-gáh, مزار mazár, روضه rauzah.

PILL, حب habb, حبه habbah.

PILLAGE, چپاو chapáw, غارت ghárat, تاراج táráj, نهب nahb, راهزنی ráhzaní, ترك تازی turk-i-tází.

PILLAR, ستون sutún, عمود 'amúd, رکن rukn, عضادت 'izádat.—(*pillars of the State, ministers*) ارکان دولت arkán-i-daulat, اعیان دولت a'yán-i-daulat.

PILL-BOX, قوطی kútí.

PILLORY, طوق tauk, پالاهنگ pálá-hang.

PILLOW, بالش bálish, بالین bálín, بالنج bálinj, زیر گوشی zír-i-gúshí.—(*large pillow for the back*) متکا muttaká, وساده vasádah, پشتی pushtí.—(*pillow-case*) غلاف بالش ghiláf-i-bálish.

PILOT, معلم mu'allim, کشتیبان kashtí-bán, حرکاتی harakátí.

PILOTAGE, کشتیبانی kashtí-bání, حرکات harakát.

PIMP, دلال dallál.—(*to one's own wife*) قرمساق kurmsák, قلتبان kaltabán, دیوث dayyús, کس ده زن kus-dih-i-zan, زن بمزد zan-bi-muzd.

PIMPLE, کورك kúrk, بثر basar, دانه dánah, جوش júsh.

PIN, سنجاق sanják, الفینه alfínah (*obs.*). — (*peg*) میخ míkh, مسمار mismár.—(*rolling-pin*) تیره tírah.

PINCERS, انبر ambur, گاز انبر gáz-ambur.—(*small tongs*) ماشه máshah.

PINCH, نشکنج nishkunj, پنجر pinjar. — (*small quantity*) خورده khwurdah, اندك andak, کم kam, قلیل kalíl.

To PINCH, نشکن گرفتن nishkun giriftan, نشکنج کردن nishkunj kardan, انبر گرفتن ambur giriftan, پنجر گرفتن pinjar giriftan.—(*live frugally*) باریك رو بودن bárík-rau búdan, کم خرج کردن kam-kharj kardan.—(*to pinch the top of the Persian cap*) طرف کلاه شکستن taráf-i-kulah shikastan.
PINCHBECK, رویین rúyín.
PIN-CUSHION, بالش سوزن bálish-i-súzan.
PINE (*tree*), صنوبر sinaubar.—(*red pine, a species of cedar*) کاج káj. —(*stone pine*) چلغوزه chalgúzah. —(*pitch-pine*) شجر القطران sha-jaru-'l-kitrán.
To PINE, خواهش کردن khwáhish kardan, میل نمودن mail nimúdan. —(*to pine away*) کاهیدن káhídan, کاهیده گردیدن káhídah gardídan, افسرده شدن afsurdah shudan, زائل شدن zá,il shudan.
PINE-APPLE, عین الناس 'ainu-'n-nás. [This fruit is scarcely known in Persia.]
PINION, بال bál, پر par, جناح janáh.
PINK, میخك míkhak, قرنفل karanful.—(*colour*) گلرنگ gul-rang, گلگون gul-gún.
To PINK (*a dress*), بخیه کردن bakhyah kardan.
PIN-MONEY, پول سوزن púl-i-súzan.
PINNACE, کشتی kashtí, نو nau.
PINNACLE (*of a tower*), کنگره kungurah, قله kullah, سر کوب sar-kúb.
PIONEER, بیلدار bíl-dár, پیش رو písh-rau.
To PIONEER, پیش رفتن písh-raftan.
PIOUS, متقی muttakí, صالح sálih, زکی zakí, معتکف mu'takif, خدا ترس khudá-tars, عابد 'ábid.
PIOUSLY, بتقاوت bi-takávat, بصلاح bi-saláh.
PIPE (*tube*), نی nay, لوله lúlah, ماشوره máshúrah.—(*musical*) نی nay, نای náy.—(*for conveying water*) لوله lúlah, تنبوشه tambúshah, آبریز áb-ríz.—(*Turkish, for smoking*) چبوق chibúk, شطب shatab, سبیل sabíl. [This latter is a very short pipe of clay, much used by the Arabs.]—(*Persian pipe*) قلیان kalyán, غلیان ghalyán, قلیون kalyún, نارگیله nár-gílah.
To PIPE, نی و سرنا زدن nay va surná zadan.
PIPE-CLAY, گل سفید gil-i-safíd.
PIPER, زمار zammár, نی زن nay-zan.
PIPKIN, دیزی dízí, کوأره ku,árah.
PIQUANT, تیز tíz, گوار guvár.
PIQUE, دشمنی dushmaní, عداوت 'adávat, کدورت kadúrat, حسد hasad.
To PIQUE, بخشم آوردن bi-khishm ávardan, مضطرب ساختن muztarib sákhtan.
PIRACY, دزدی دریا duzdí-i-daryá.
PIRATE, دزد دریا duzd-i-daryá, قرصان kursán.
PISCES, حوت hút.
To PISS, شاشه کردن sháshah kardan, بول کردن baul kardan, شاشیدن sháshídan.
PISTACHIO, پسته pistah, فستق fistuk.
PISTOL, طپانچه tapánchah.—(*pocket pistol*) طپانچه جیبی tapánchah-i-jíbí.—(*horse pistol*) طپانچه سر زین tapánchah-i-sar-i-zín, طپانچه قبل tapánchah-i-kubbal.—(*large pistol worn in the girdle*) پیشتاب píshtáb.—(*bell-mouthed or blunderbuss pistol*) قرابینه karábínah (*eur.*).
PIT, گود gaud, گودال gaudál, چاه cháh, چه chah, حفره hufrah, مغاك maghák, چال chál, چاله chálah, حفیره hafírah, ویل vail.—(*of theatre*) سطح زمین sath-i-zamín.
PITCH, زفت zift.—(*liquid*) قطران kitrán, قیر kír.—(*degree*) قدر kadr, مقدار mikdár, مرتبه martabah, مشابه masábah, اندازه andázah, حد hadd, مقابله mukábalah, درجه darajah.
To PITCH, بزفت مالیدن bi-zift málídan.—(*throw*) انداختن andákhtan, افکندن afkandan.—(*a tent*), زدن zadan, بر پا کردن bar pá kardan.—(*heave or toss, as a ship, &c.*) حرکت کردن harakat kardan,

تکان نمودن takán nimúdan, پیچ خوردن pích khwurdan, در تلاطم بودن dar talátum búdan.
PITCHER, سبو sabú, کوزه kúzah, بستو bastú.—(*of metal*) سطل satl.
PITCHFORK, چنگال changál.
PITCHY, زفتی ziftí.
PITEOUS, دلسوز dil-súz, حزین hazín, اندوهناک andúh-nák, سهمگین sahm-gín, جگرسوز jigar-súz.
PITFALL, دام dám.
PITH, مغز maghz, لب lubb.
PITHLESS, بی مغز bí-maghz, بی لب bí-lubb.
PITHY, مضبوط mazbút.
PITIABLE, لائق رحمت lá,ik-i-rahmat.
PITIFUL, رحم دل rahm-dil, رحمان rahmán.
PITIFULLY, برحمت bi-rahmat.
PITILESS, بیرحم bí-rahm.
PITTANCE, وظیفه قلیل vazífah-i-kalíl.
PITTED (*marked with small-pox*), مجدر mujaddar, آبله خورده ábilah-khwurdah, اوله زده aulah-zadah.
PITY, رحم rahm, رحمت rahmat, ترحم tarahhum, مرحمت marhamat, رقت rikkat, ملایمت muláyamat, شفقت shafakat, نرمدلی narm-dilí, رأفت ra,fat.—(*interj.*) حیف haif, دخیل dakhíl.—(*it is a pity*) حیف است haif ast.
To PITY, شفقت نمودن shafakat nimúdan, رحمت نمودن rahmat nimúdan, ترحم نمودن tarahhum nimúdan, بیچاره دانستن bí-chárah dánistan.
PIVOT, محور mihvar, مدار madár.
PLACABLE, رؤف ra,uf, با رأفت bá-ra,fat.
PLACARD, اعلام i'lám, اعلان i'lán.
To PLACARD, چسبانیدن chasbánídan.
PLACE, مکان makán, مقام makám, محل mahall, معرض ma'raz, موضع mauza', موقف maukif, حیز hayyiz مطرح matrah, جا já, جای jáy, جایگاه jáy-gáh, بقاع buká', موقع mauki'.—(*in composition*) گاه gáh, ستان stán, استان istán, جا já, گه gah, لاخ lákh.—(*market-place*) بازار bázár, چهارسو chahár-sú, سوق súk.—(*of meeting, rendezvous*) میعاد mí'ád, منزل manzil, مرجع marja'.—(*in place of*) عوض 'avaz, *or* 'ivaz, بجای bi-jáy, بدل badal, بازاء bi-izá,.—(*in the first place*) اولاً avvalan, نخستین nakhustín, مقدماً mukaddaman.—(*in place*) با محل bá-mahall, به موقع bi-mauki', بجا bi-já.—(*out of place*) بیمحل bí-mahall, بیموقع bí-mauki', بیجا bí-já.—(*in place and out of place*) گاه و ناگاه gáh va ná-gáh.
To PLACE, *vide* To PUT.—(*to get a place, servant*) نوکری کردن naukarí kardan.
PLACID, سلیم salím, ملایم muláyam, حلیم halím, خود دار khwud-dár.
PLACIDNESS, حلم hilm, ملایمت muláyamat, خود داری khwud-dárí.
PLAGIARISM, عبارت دزدی ibárat-duzdí, سخن دزدی sukhun-duzdí, سرقات sarikát.
PLAGIARIST, سخن دزد sukhun-duzd, عبارت دزد 'ibárat-duzd.
PLAGUE, طاعون tá'ún.—(*trouble*) ایذا ízá, تکلیف taklíf, آزار ázár, تصدیع tasdí', رنج ranj.
To PLAGUE, آزار کردن ázár kardan, آزردن ázurdan, اذیت کردن azíyat kardan.
PLAID, شطرنجی shatranjí, زیلو zailú. [The plaid is unknown in Persia, and there is no strict equivalent.]
PLAIN (*open ground*), میدان maidán, فضا fizá, جلگه julgah, صحرا sahrá.—(*smooth*) هموار hamvár, مساوی musáví.—(*unornamented*) ساده sádah.—(*artless*) ساده لوح sádah-lúh, ساده دل sádah-dil.—(*without relish*) خالی khálí.—(*person*) قبیح kabíh, زشت zisht.
PLAINLY, آشکارا ashkárá, واضحاً vázihan, ظاهراً záhiran.
PLAINNESS (*smoothness*), همواری hamvárí, مساوات musávát.—(*unornamentation*) سادگی sádagí.—(*artlessness*) ساده دلی sádah-dilí.
PLAINT, گله gilah, نالش nálish, ناله

nálah, شکوی shakvá, شکایت shikáyat, تظلم tazallum, فریاد faryád, زاری zárí.

PLAINTIFF, مدعی mudda'í, شاکی shákí, داد خواه dád-khwáh, متظلم mutazallim.

PLAINTIVE, مستمند must-mand.

PLAINTIVELY, زار زار zár zár.

PLAIT, ته tah, تا tá, چین chín, شکن shikan.

To PLAIT, بافتن báftan.

PLAITS (*in cloth*), اتو uttú (*hind.*), چین chín.

PLAN, *vide* MAP, PLOT, CONTRIVANCE.

PLANE (*carpenter's*), رنده randah. —(*superficies*) سطح sath, بسیط basít, تخته takhtah, صفحه safhah. —(*tree*) چنار chinár, چنال chinál (*vulg.*).

To PLANE (*wood, &c.*), رنده زدن randah zadan, رنده کاری کردن randah-kárí kardan.

PLANET, سیاره sayyárah, نجم سائر najm-i-sá,ir. (*Vide* JUPITER, MERCURY, MARS, VENUS, SATURN.) — (*conjunction of the planets*) قران kirán.

PLANK, تخته takhtah, خشب khashab.

To PLANK, از تخته مفروش کردن az takhtah mafrúsh kardan.

PLANKING (*woodwork*), چوب بست chúb-bast, تخته بندی takhtah-bandí.

PLANT, رستنی rustaní, نبات nabát, بنه bunah, سبزی sabzí.

To PLANT, غرس کردن ghars kardan, نشاندن nishándan, کاشتن káshtan. —(*a flag*) زدن zadan, افراختن afrákhtan.—(*to plant out, flowers*) در باغ گذاشتن dar bágh guzáshtan, تولک کردن túlak kardan.

PLANTAIN (*fruit*), موز múz.

PLANTATION (*of trees*), درختزار dirakht-zár, جائی مشجر já,í-i-mushajjar.

PLANTER, غارس ghária.

PLASTER (*lime*), آهك áhak.—(*fine plaster*) گچ gach.—(*for a wound*) مرهم marham, ضماد zamád. — (*of clay and chopped straw*) کاه گل káh-gil.—(*of lime and ashes*) ساروج sárúj.

To PLASTER (*a wall*), اندودن andúdan, کاه گل مالیدن káh-gil málídan, سفید کاری کردن safíd-kárí kardan.—(*plastering trowel*) ماله málah.—(*trough*) ناوه návah, نو nav.

PLASTERER, اندود کننده andúd-kunandah, گچ کار gach-kár.

PLAT (*of ground*), لته lattah, کرزه kurzah, آبخوران áb-khwurán, اوخرون aukhurún (*vulg.*).—(*division between plats or beds*) مرز marz.

PLATE, بشقاب bushkáb, سینی síní. — (*big plate*) قاب káb. — (*flat piece of metal*) صفحه safhah.— (*silver spoons, &c.*) نقره آلات nukrah-álát.

To PLATE, اندودن andúdan.

PLATFORM (*terrace*), سکو sakkú, سطح sath, ماهتابی máh-tábí, مسطبه mastabah.—(*wooden structure*) تلواره talvárah, تخته takhtah, دار بست dár-bast.

PLATINA, طلائی سفید tilá,í-i-safíd.

PLATTER, طبق tabak. — (*tray*) مجموعه majmú'ah, سینی síní.

PLAUDIT, شاباش shábásh, آفرین áfirín.

PLAUSIBILITY, صورت خوبی súrat-i-khúbí, استحسان istihsán.

PLAUSIBLE, مستحسن mustahsan, مقبول makbúl, مرغوب marghúb.

PLAUSIBLY, مقبولا makbúlan.

PLAY (*sport*), بازی bází, بازیچه bází-chah, لعب la'b, ملاعبه mulá'abah. (*gambling*) قمار kimár, بازی bází, برد و باخت burd va bákht.— (*stage - play*) تماشا tamáshá.— (*plaything*) *vide* TOY.—(*play of words*) تجنیس tajnís, تجنیس الفاظ tajnís-i-alfáz.

To PLAY, باختن bákhtan, بازی کردن bází kardan, لعب نمودن la'b nimúdan.—(*music*) نواختن navákhtan, زدن zadan. — (*fountain*) جستن jastan.

PLAYER, شخص بازی کن shakhs-i-bází-kun.

PLAYFELLOW, رفیق rafík, شریک sharík, همدم ham-dam, صاحب sáhib, مصاحب musáhib.

PLAYFUL, خوشدل khwush-dil, شاد shád, شادمان shád-mán, خوش khwush, دلخوش dil-khwush, خرم khurram, بهیج bahíj, دلشاد dil-shád, مشعوف mash'úf.

PLAYTHING, *vide* TOY.

PLEA, *vide* CLAIM, ARGUMENT, LAWSUIT.

To PLEAD (*a cause*), حجت بر آوردن hujjat bar-ávardan, دعوی کردن da'vá kardan, ادعا نمودن 'iddi'á nimúdan, محاکمه نمودن muhákamah nimúdan, مرافعه بر آوردن muráfa'ah bar-ávardan, داد خواستن dád khwástan.

PLEADER, وکیل vakíl.

PLEASANT, خوش khwush, لطیف latíf, دلاویز dil-ávíz, دلپسند dil-pasand, پسندیده pasandídah, دلپذیر dil-pazír, لذیذ lazíz, ملتذ multazz, مفرح mufarrih, نعیم na'ím, مقبول makbúl, مطبوع matbú'.

PLEASANTLY, بخوشی bi-khwushí.

PLEASANTRY, لطیفه latífah, بذله bazlah, مطائبه mutá,ibah, شوخی shúkhí, باردی bárdí, فسوس fisús, کنایه kináyah, هزل hazl, مسخره maskharah.

To PLEASE, خوش کردن khwush kardan, خوشنود کردن khwushnúd kardan, ملتذ گردانیدن multazz gardánídan.—(*if you please*) زحمت کشیده zahmat kashídah, التفات کرده iltifát kardah.—(*to choose, or take pleasure in*) خوش آمدن khwush ámadan, پسند اوفتادن pasand úftádan, پسندیدن pasandídan, صلاح دانستن saláh dánistan, دماغ داشتن dimágh dáshtan, صفا داشتن safá dáshtan, میل داشتن mail dáshtan.—(*hard to please*) مشکل پسند mushkil-pasand.

PLEASED, خوش khwush, خوشنود khwushnúd, راضی rází.

PLEASURE, خوشی khwushí, خرمی khurammí, شادی shádí, عیش 'aish, عشرت 'ishrat, نشاط nishát, صفا safá, سرور surúr, مسرت masarrat, بهجت bihjat, لذت lazzat, حظ hazz, تنعم tana'um. — (*with pleasure*) بچشم bi-chashm. — (*pleasure-party*) تفرج tafarruj.—(*pleasure seeker*) مردم عیاش mardum-i-'ayyásh, راحت طلب ráhat-talab, خوش گذران khwush-guzrán.

PLECTRUM (*of a musical instrument*), مضراب mizráb.

PLEDGE, رهن rahn, گرو girau.

To PLEDGE, رهن گذاردن rahn guzárdan, گرو گذاشتن girau guzáshtan.—(*to pledge one's word*) قول دادن kaul dádan.

PLEIADES, پروین parvín, پرو parv, پرنا parná, ثریا surayyá.

PLENARILY, بالکمال bi-'l-kamál, بالتمام bi-'t-tamám.

PLENARY, کامل kámil, تام támm, تمام tamám.

PLENIPOTENTIARY, وزیر مختار vazír-i-mukhtár, سفیر کبیر safír-i-kabír.

PLENITUDE, پری purí.

PLENTEOUS, فراخ farákh, وافر váfir, فیاض fayyaz, مثمر musmir.

PLENTEOUSLY, بکثرت bi-kasrat.

PLENTIFUL, وافر váfir, وافی váfí, فراوان faráván.

PLENTY (*abundance*), افراط ifrát, فراوانی farávání, کثرت kasrat, افزونی afzúní, بسیاری bisyárí, وفرت vafrat, غنیمت ghanímat, زیادتی ziyádatí.

PLEONASM, فضول fuzúl.

PLETHORIC, دموی damaví.

PLEURISY, جرسام jirsám.

PLIABLE, نرم narm, پیچخور píchkhwur.

PLIERS, انبر ambur, گاز انبر gáz-ambur.

PLIGHT, اشکال ishkál, دهشت dihshat, مضایقه muzáyakah, مضیق mazík.

To PLIGHT, عهد بستن 'ahd bastan.

To PLOD, ساعی نمودن sá'í nimúdan, کوشش نمودن kúshish nimúdan, اهتمام نمودن ihtimám nimúdan, متوجه بودن mutavajjih búdan, سر گرم بودن sar-garm búdan.

PLODDER, متجاهد mutajáhid, محنت کار mihnat-kár.

PLODDING, متوجه mutavajjih, ساعی sá'í, مقید mukayyad, سر گرم sar-garm.

PLOT, سازش sázish, معاهده mu'áhadah, وفاق vifák, اتفاق ittifák, توطئه tauti,ah, هم عهدی ham-'ahdí.

PLOUGH, خیش khísh, خویش khwísh, قلبه kulbah.—(*shaft of a plough*) دار خیش dár-i-khísh. — (*handle*) بوشه búshah, کلاکک kalákak.—(*yoke*) جوغ júgh, یوغ yúgh, گردن بند gardan-band.

To **PLOUGH**, شیاریدن shiyárídan, شخم کردن shukhm kardan, خیش کردن khísh kardan, نطس کردن nuts kardan.

PLOUGHING OX, ورزاو varzáv, فداد faddád.

PLOUGHMAN, زارع zári', خیش ران khísh-rán, قلبه ران kulbah-rán.

PLOUGHSHARE, گاو آهن gáv-áhan, سپار supár, بیخش bíkhash, لپک lapak.

PLOVER, مرغ زیبا murgh-i-zíbá, مرغ ملخ murgh-i-malakh.

PLUCK, مردانگی mardánagí, دلیری dilírí, دلاوری dilávarí, همت himmat, جرأت jur,at, شجاعت shujá'at, غیرت ghairat, جسارت jasárat, شهامت shahámat, حمیت hamíyat, عصبیت 'asabíyat.

To **PLUCK**, ربودن rubúdan, چیدن chídan, قپیدن kapídan. — (*a fowl*) پر کندن par kandan, پر کشیدن par kashídan.

PLUG, سداد sadád, سر sar.

PLUM, آلو álú.—(*green-gage*) آلوئی سبز álú,í-i-sabz, گوجه gaujah.—(*bullace*) آلوچه álúchah.—(*dried plum, prune*) آلوئی خشک álu,í-i-khushk, آلوئی بخارا álú,í-i-bukhárá.

PLUMAGE (*of a bird*), پر و بال par va bál.

PLUMBAGO (*black lead*), سرمه surmah.

PLUMBER, سرب ریز surb-ríz.

PLUMB-LINE, ریسمان کار rísmán-i-kár, بلد balad, هنجار hinjár, مقیاس mikyás.

PLUME, طره turrah.—(*royal plume*) جیکا jíká.

To **PLUME**, آراستن árástan, پیراستن pírástan, آرایش نمودن áráyish nimúdan. — (*to plume oneself*) افتخار نمودن iftikhár nimúdan.

PLUMP, فربه farbih, سمین samín, لنبه lumbah, چاق chák, جسیم jasím, تازه tázah.

PLUMPNESS, فربهی farbihí, تازگی tázagí.

PLUNDER (*rapine*), چپاو chapáw, غارت ghárat, تاراج táráj, نهب nahb, راهزنی ráh-zaní, ترک تازی turk-i-tází.—(*booty*) غنیمت ghanímat, یغما yaghmá, غارت ghárat, سلب salab, منهوبه manhúbah, سلیب salíb.

To **PLUNDER**, چپاو کردن chapáw kardan, غارت کردن ghárat kardan, یغما کردن yaghmá kardan, سلب گرفتن salab giriftan, تاراج نمودن táráj nimúdan, نهب کردن nahb kardan, چپاولی کردن chapávalí kardan (*vulg.*).

PLUNDERER, غارت کننده ghárat-kunandah, یغماچی yaghmá-chí.

PLUNGE, غوطه ghútah.

To **PLUNGE** (*dive*), غوطه خوردن ghútah khwurdan, غوص نمودن ghaus nimúdan, غرق شدن ghark shudan.

PLUPERFECT (*tense*), ماضی بعید mází-i-ba'íd.

PLURAL, جمع jam'.

PLURALITY, تعدد ta'addud.

PLUS (*in arithmetic*), جمع jam' (as سه جمع چهار sih-jam'-i-chahár, *three plus four*).

PLUSH, مخمل makhmal.

PLY, ته tah, تا tá, لای láy.

To **PLY**, تردد کردن taraddud kardan.

PNEUMATIC, بادی bádí, هوای haváí.

PNEUMATICS, علم طبیعت هوا 'ilm-i-tabí'at-i-havá.

To **POACH**, شکار دزدیدن shikár duzdídan, دزدانه شکار کردن duzdánah shikár kardan.—(*eggs*) نیم رو کردن ním-rú kardan, خاگینه کردن khágínah kardan.

Poached egg, تخم نیمرو tukhm-i-ním-rú, گوازه gavázah.

Poacher, دزد شکار duzd-i-shikár.

Pock, آبله ábilah, تورك túrk.—(*pock-marked*) آبله دار ábilah-dár.

Pocket, جیب jíb.

Pocket-book, جزدان juz-dán.

Pocket-handkerchief, دستمال dast-mál, دستارچه dastárchah.

Pod, تنزه tunzah, سر sar, پیله pílah. —(*of cotton*) جوزق jauzak, کلوزه kulúzah.

Poem, شعر shi'r, نظم nazm.

Poet, شاعر shá'ir.

Poetess, شاعره shá'irah.

Poetic, شعری shi'rí, شاعرانه shá'iránah.

Poetry, شعر shi'r, نظم nazm, عروض 'arúz.—(*the art*) علم عروض 'ilm-i-'arúz.

Poignancy, تیزی tízí, تندی tundí, سختی sakhtí.

Poignant, تیز tíz, تند tund, سخت sakht.

Poignard, گزلك gazlak.

Point, سر sar, نوك nauk.—(*dot*) نقطه nuktah.—(*nicety*) نکته nuktah, دقیقه dakíkah.—(*of land, cape*) رأس ra,s, سر sar, طرف taraf.—(*on the point of*) درصدد dar sadad. (*to be on the point of*) مشرف بودن به mushrif búdan bi.—(*point by point*) نقطه بنقطه nuktah-bi-nuktah.—(*chief points*) زبده zubdah.

To Point, دلالت کردن dalálat kardan, نمودن nimúdan, نشان دادن nishán dádan, اشارت کردن ishárat kardan.

Pointed, سر تیز sar-i-tíz.—(*pointed at*) انگشت نما angusht-nimá.

Pointer, اشارت کن ishárat-kun. —(*dog*) سگ شکاری sag-i-shikárí.

Pointless, بی نوك bí-nauk.—(*speech, &c.*) بینکته bí-nuktah.

To Poise, وزن کردن vazn kardan.

Poison, زهر zahr, سم samm.

To Poison, زهر دادن zahr dádan. —(*to take poison*) زهر خوردن zahr khwurdan.

Poisoned, مسموم masmúm.

Poisonous, زهر دار zahr-dár, زهر ناك zahr-nák, سام sámm.

Poitrel (*of a horse*), سینه بند sínah-band.

To Poke (*with a stick, &c., thrust*), سك دادن suk dádan, هل دادن hul dádan.

Poker, مهراك mihrák.

Polar, قطبی kutbí.—(*polar-star*) قطب kutb.

Pole (*of the heavens*), قطب kutb.—(*north pole*) قطب شمالی kutb-i-shimálí. — (*south pole*) قطب جنوبی kutb-i-janúbí. — (*a stick*) چوب دراز chúb-i-diráz. — (*tent-pole*) *vide* Tent. — (*boat-pole*) مردی mardí. — (*balancing pole*) لنگر langar.— (*telegraph pole*) تیر tír. — (*of a carriage*) تیر tír. — (*pole fixed in the centre of the market or other public place, and at the foot of which criminals are executed*) قاپوق kápúk, دار dár.

Polemic, حربی harbí.

Police (*of a town*), مستحفظان شهر mustahfizán-i-shahr, قراول karávul, عسس 'asas, کشیك kashík, گزمه gazmah. — (*policeman*) کشیکچی kashík-chí, قراول karávul, پاسبان pás-bán.—(*chief of police*) داروغه dárúghah, شحنه shahnah, میر عسس mír-i-'asas.— (*police-station*) قراول خانه karávul-khánah, گزمه gazmah.

Policy, حکمت hikmat, مصلحت maslahat, پولیتیك púlítík (*eur.*). —(*line of policy*) تعیین پولیتیك ta'yín-i-púlítík.

Polish (*gloss or brightness*), جلا jilá, جلوه jalvah.

To Polish, زدودن zadúdan, صیقل کردن saikal kardan, جلا دادن jilá dádan, پرداختن pardákhtan.

Polished, صیقلی saikalí, مصقول maskúl, براق barrák, پرداخته pardákhtah.

Polisher (*of arms, &c.*), صیقلگر saikal-gar, پرداختگر pardákht-gar. —(*of jewels*) حکاك hakkák.

Polite, ادیب adíb, مؤدب mu,addab, خلیق khalík, خوش اطوار

khwush-atvár, خوش اخلاق khwush-akhlák.
Politely, مؤدبانه mu,addabánah.
Politeness, ادب adab, مردمی mardumí, تربیت tarbiyat.
Politic (*discreet*), با تمیز bá-tamyíz, با بصیرت bá-basírat, با فراست bá-firásat.—(*expedient*) صواب saváb, مفید mufíd, مقرون بصواب makrún bi-saváb.
Politically, موجب علم سیاست mújib-i-'ilm-i-siyásat.
Politician, اهل سیاست ahl-i-siyásat.
Politics, معاملۀ مملکت mu'ámalah-i-mamlikat, تدبیر سلطنت tadbír-i-sultanat, علم سیاست مدن 'ilm-i-siyásat-i-mudun.
Polity, حکومت hukúmat, رئاست ri,ásat, سیاست siyásat.
Poll-tax, جزیه jizyah, سر شماری sar-shimárí.
To Pollute, آلودن álúdan, آلائیدن álá,ídan, پلید ساختن pilíd sákhtan, تفضیح نمودن tafzíh nimúdan, ملوث کردن mulavvas kardan, نا پاك کردن ná-pák kardan, نجس گردانیدن najis gardánídan, تنجیس کردن tanjís kardan, تدنیس نمودن tadnís nimúdan.
Polluted, نا پاك ná-pák, پلید pilíd, آلوده álúdah, ملوث mulavvas.
Polluter, ملوث mulavvis, تنجیس کار tanjís-kár.
Pollution, تنجیس tanjís, تفضیح tafzíh, لوث laus, جنابت janábat, آلایش áláyish, آلودگی álúdagí.
Poltroon, نا مرد ná-mard, بزدل buz-dil, جبان jabbán, بیدل bí-dil, کمدل kam-dil, ترسو tarsú (*vulg.*).
Polygamy, تعدد ازواج ta'addud-i-azváj.
Polygon, سطح کثیر الاضلاع sath-kasíru-'l-azlá'.
Polypus (*in the nose*), بواسیر انف bavásir-i-anf.
Polytechnic, مکتب علوم متنوعه maktab-i-'ulúm-mutanavvi'ah.
Polytheism, شرك shirk, ملت مشرك millat-i-mushrik.
Polytheist, مشرك mushrik.
Pomade, مرهم marham, روغن raughan.
Pomegranate, نار nár, انار anár, رمان rummán.—(*flower*) گل انار gul-i-anár, گلنار gul-nár.
Pomflet (*fish*), حلوا ماهی halvá-máhí.
Pommel (*of a saddle*), کوهۀ زین kúhah-i-zín, قربوس karabús.—(*of a sword*) قبضه kabzah.—(*knob or top of the handle*) کلاه kuláh.
To Pommel, زدن zadan.
Pomp, *vide* Pride, Splendour.
Pompous, مطنطن mutantin, مغرور maghrúr.
Pompously, متکبرانه mutakabbiránah, با دبدبه و طنطنه bá-dabdabah va tantanah.
Pond, دریاچه daryáchah, حوض hauz, آبگیر áb-gír.
To Ponder, *vide* To Think.
Ponderous, گران girán, سنگین sangín, وزنی vazní, ثقیل sakíl.
Ponderousness, گرانی girání, سنگینی sangíní, ثقلت saklat.
Pontiff, امام imám.
Pontifical, امامی imámí.
Pony, یابو yábú.
Pool, دریاچه daryáchah, حوض hauz, آبگیر áb-gír.
Poop (*of a ship*), دبوسه dabbúsah, تفر tafar.
Poor, مفلس muflis, مسکین miskín, بینوا bí-navá, غریب gharíb, فقیر fakír, تهی دست tuhí-dast, گدا gadá, مفلوك maflúk, نیازمند níyáz-mand, مستمند mustamand, مستأصل musta,sal, نا دار ná-dár.
Poorly, مفلسانه muflisánah.—(*ill*) نا خوش ná-khwush.
Pope, پاپ páp (*eur.*).
Popish, پاپی pápí (*eur.*).
Poplar (*white or Lombardy poplar*), سفیدار safídár.—(*Oriental poplar or plane*) چنار chinár, چنال chinál (*vulg.*).—(*grey poplar*) کبوده kabúdah.—(*poplar willow*) پادار بید pádár-bíd.
Poppy, کوکنار kúknár, خشخاش khashkhásh.

POPULACE, عام 'ámm, عوام 'avámm, خلق khalk, مردمان mardumán, اهالی ahálí.
POPULAR, عوام پسند 'avámm-pasand.
POPULARITY, اعتبار i'tibár, معروفیت ma'rúfiyat.
To POPULATE, آباد کردن ábád kardan.
POPULATION, جمعیت jam'íyat.
POPULOUS, آباد ábád, دائر dá,ir, معمور ma'múr.
PORCELAIN, ظروف چینی zurúf-i-chíní, چینی chíní.
PORCH, دهنهٔ خانه dahanah-i-khánah, رواق rivák, طاق ták.
PORCUPINE, خار پشت khár-pusht, قنفذ kunfuz, چوله chúlah (*vulg.*).
PORE (*of the skin*), مسام masámm (*pl.* مسامات masámmát).
To PORE, نظر کردن nazar kardan, نگاه کردن nigáh kardan.
PORK, گوشت خوک gúsht-i-khúg, لحم الخنزیر lahmu-'l-khinzír.
POROUS, پر مسام pur masámm.
PORPHYRY, سنگ سماق sang-i-sumák.
PORPOISE, گراز ماهی guráz-máhí, خوک دریائی khúg-i-daryá,í.
PORRIDGE, آش ásh.
PORRINGER, کاسه kásah, طاس tás.
PORT (*harbour*), بندر bandar, مینا míná.
PORTABLE, قابل حمل kábil-i-haml.
PORTAL, در dar, دروازه darvázah, قاپو kápú, قاپی kápí, باب báb, درب darb, درگاه dargáh, دهنه dahanah.
To PORTEND, دلالت کردن dalálat kardan, اشارت کردن ishárat kardan, وعده نمودن va'dah nimúdan.
PORTENT, فال fál, شگون shugún, اختر akhtar, طالع tálí'.
PORTENTOUS, غیب نما ghaib-nimá, پر شگون pur shugún.
PORTER (*of a gate*), دربان darbán, بواب bavváb, قاپیچی kápíjí, قاپوچی kápúchí.—(*of inner rooms*) حاجب hájib, پرده دار pardah-dár.—(*carrier*) حمال hammál, بارکش bár-kash.

PORTERAGE, حمالی himmálí.
PORTFIRE, مهتاب mahtáb.
PORTFOLIO, جزو کش juzv-kash, جزدان juz,-dán.
PORT-HOLE, پنجره panjarah.
PORTICO, دهنهٔ خانه dahanah-i-khánah, رواق rivák, طاق ták.
PORTION, *vide* PART, SHARE.
To PORTION, تقسیم کردن taksím kardan, حصه کردن hissah kardan, دادن dádan.
PORTIONLESS, بی نصیب bí-nasíb.
PORTLINESS, جلال jalál, سرافرازی sar-afrází, قدر kadr. — (*fatness*) فربهی farbihí.
PORTLY, معزز mu'azzaz, با هیبت bá-haibat.—(*fat*) فربه farbih, چاق chák, جسیم jasím.
PORTMANTEAU, خورجین khúrjín, بنه bunah.
PORTRAIT, شبیه shabíh, تصویر tasvír, پردهٔ صورت pardah-i-súrat.
To PORTRAY, نقش زدن naksh zadan.
PORTRAYER, چهره گشا chihrah-gushá, صورت آرا súrat-árá.
To POSE, نهادن nihádan.— (*confuse*) حیران ساختن hairán sákhtan.
POSITION, طرح tarah, وضع vaz'.—(*footing*) حالت hálat.
POSITIVE, ایجابی íjábí. (*Vide* SURE). — (*to be positive*) یقین داشتن yakín dáshtan, مسلم داشتن musallam dáshtan.
POSITIVELY, یقیناً yakínan, قطعاً kat'an, لا محاله lá-muhálah, بی همه چیز bí-hamah chíz.
To POSSESS, داشتن dáshtan.—(*get possession of*) ضبط نمودن zabt nimúdan, تصرف کردن tasarruf kardan, بهم رسانیدن bi-ham rasánídan.—(*to become possessed of*) اندوختن andúkhtan, بهم رسانیدن bi-ham rasánídan, حاصل کردن hásil kardan, تحصیل کردن tahsíl kardan, یافتن yáftan.
POSSESSING, متصرف mutasarrif, مالک málik.—(*in composition, prefixed*) صاحب sáhib, ذو zú, ذی zí, اهل ahl.—(*ditto, affixed*) دار dár, مند mand, آور ávar.

Possession, تصرف tasarruf, ضبط zabt, قبضه kabzah, عمل ʻamal, دست dast, معموریت maʻmúríyat.—(*property*) ملك milk, ما یملك má yamlik, ما ملك má malak, مال mál.

Possessive, مالکی málikí.—(*case*) اضافت izáfat.

Possessor, مالك málik, صاحب sáhib.

Possibility, امکان imkán, احتمال ihtimál, استطاعت istitáʻat.

Possible, ممکن mumkin, یمکن yumkin, یحتمل yahtamil, بودنی búdaní.—(*as ... as possible*) ... به هرچه تمامتر bi ... har chih tamám-tar.—(*to be possible*) امکان داشتن imkán dáshtan, ممکن شدن mumkin shudan, احتمال داشتن ihtimál dáshtan.

Possibly, شاید sháyad, باشد báshad.

Post (*carrier of letters*), قاصد kásid, نامه بر námah-bar, چاپار chápár, چپر chapar, برید baríd. — (*post-free*) بی اجرت پوست bí-ujrat-i-púst.—(*postmaster*) چپر چی cha-par-chí, چاپار چی chápár-chí. — (*post-office*) پوسته خانه púste-khá-nah.—(*Postmaster - General*) چپر چی باشی chapar-chí-báshí.—(*situ-ation*), مقام makám, موضع mauzaʻ, محل mahall.—(*office or service*) عهده ʻuhdah, منصب mansab, خدمت khidmat.—(*military sta-tion*) لشکر گاه lashkar-gáh, اوتراق úturák, معسکر maʻaskar.—(*stake*) چوب chúb, ستون sutún, عمود ʻamúd.—(*of a door*) باهو báhú.—(*station where horses are kept for travellers*) چپر خانه chapar-khá-nah, چاپار خانه chápár-khánah.—(*post-horse*) اسب چپری asb-i-chaparí, اسب چاپاری asb-i-chá-párí.—(*post-boy*) چپر شاگرد cha-par-shágird.—(*to travel by post*), چپر رفتن chapar raftan, چاپار رفتن chápár raftan.

To Post, در پوسته انداختن dar pústah andákhtan.

Postage, پوسته pústah (*eur.*).—(*to pay the postage*) محصول دادن mah-súl dádan.

Posterior, وا پسین vá-pasín.

Posteriority, تأخر ta,akhkhur.

Posteriors, دبر dubr, کفل kafal, سرین surín, اعجاز aʻjáz.

Posterity, اولاد aulád, عقب ʻakab, اعقاب aʻkáb, خلف khalaf, اخلاف akhláf, سلاله sulálah.

Postern, دار بچه dár-i-bachah.

Posthaste, علی الفور ʻala-'l-faur, به تعجیل bi-taʻjíl, علی العجله ʻala-'l-ʻajalah.

Posthumous, پس افتاده pas-uftá-dah.

Postillion, کالسکه چی káliskah-chí.

To Postpone, تعویق انداختن taʻvík andákhtan, تأخیر کردن ta,khír kar-dan, مهلت نمودن muhlat nimú-dan, توقف کردن tavakkuf kardan, دست بدست کردن dast bi-dast kardan.

Postscript, ذیل zail *or* zayl.

Posture, وضع vazʻ, طرح tarah, حالت hálat.

Posy, گلدسته gul-dastah.

Pot (*iron, &c., for cooking*), دیگ díg, دیگچه dígchah, پاتیلچه pátíl-chah, تیانچه tiyánchah.—(*earthen pot*) دیزی dízí, کوأره ku,árah, کوزه kúzah. — (*chamber - pot*) شاشدان shásh-dán, بولدان baul-dán. — (*flower - pot*) گلدان gul-dán. —(*jar*) کلوك kulúk, بلونی bu-lúní.—(*water pot*) ابریق ibrík, آفتابه áftábah.—(*large travelling pot*) دیگ برگ díg-barg, دیگبر díg-bar, قابلمه káblamah. [This consists of a nest of pots and other utensils, all fitting into one large one, and comprises the following articles: دیگ بزرگ díg-i-buzurg (the large outer pot); صماق پالان sumák-pálán *or* چلو صافی chaláw-sáfí (a vessel for boiling rice, consisting of two parts, one fitting into the other; the innermost being perforated with holes to strain off the water); دیگچه dígchah (a smaller pot or kettle); بادیه bádiyah (metal cup), of which there are two or three; and some other articles of cuisine.]

To POT (*flowers, &c.*) گل در گلدان کاشتن gul dar gul-dán káshtan.—(*meat, &c.*), گوشت نگاه داشتن gúsht nigáh dáshtan.

POTABLE, مشروب mashrúb, نوشیدنی núshídaní.

POTASH (*alkali*), شخار shakhár, قلی kilí, قلیا kilyá, حرض hurz.

POTATION, مشروب mashrúb, نوشت núsht.

POTATO, سیب زمینی síb-i-zamíní, سیب زیر زمین síb-i-zír-zamín, آلوئی مالکم álú,í-i-málkam (so called after Sir John Malcolm; but the name is now obsolete).

POTENCY, قوت kúvat.

POTENT, قادر kádir, کار گر kár-gar, موثر mu,assir.

POTENTATE, پادشاه pádisháh, شاه sháh, شه shah, ملك malk, سلطان sultán, خاقان khákán, کی kay.

POTENTIAL, ممکن mumkin.—(*mood*) فعل ممکن fi'l-i-mumkin.

POTENTLY, قویا kavíyan, قادرانه kádiránah.

POT-HERBS, سبزی sabzí, تره tarah, بقل bakl.

POTION, مشروب mashrúb, شربت sharbat.

POTSHERD, سفال safál, خزف khazaf, کندله kundilah (*vulg.*).

POTTAGE, آش ásh, شوربا shúrbá.—(*with chopped meat*) هلیم halím, هریسه harísah.

POTTER, کوزه پز kúzah-paz, کوزه گر kúzah-gar, فخار fakhkhár.—(*seller of earthenware*) کوزه گر kúzah-gar.

POTTERY (*manufactory*), کار خانهٔ چینی سازی kár-khánah-i-chíní-sází, کار خانهٔ کوزه گر kár-khánah-i-kúzah gar.—(*ware*) ظروف چینی zurúf-i-chíní, چینی chíní.

POUCH, کیسه kísah, جیب jíb.—(*for ammunition, bullets, &c.*) کیف kíf.

POULTERER, مرغ فروش murgh-furúsh.

POULTICE, پخته pukhtah, ضماد zamád.

POULTRY, مرغ و خروس murgh va khurús.

POUNCE, هجوم hujúm, حمله hamlah.

To POUNCE, هجوم آوردن hujúm ávardan, حمله آوردن hamlah ávardan.—(*persons*) بدست آوردن bi-dast ávardan.

POUND (*place of detention*), محبس mahbas. — (*sterling*) لیره lírah (*eur.*).

To POUND, کوبیدن kúbídan, کوفتن kúftan, سائیدن sá,ídan.

POUNDER, دسته dastah.—(*for rice or grain; a heavy iron pestle worked by the feet, and playing in a stone mortar*) دنگ ding.—(*person who pounds*) کوبنده kúbandah.

To POUR, ریختن ríkhtan.—(*rain*) تند باریدن tund báridan.

POURPARLERS, مذاکرات muzákarát.

To POUT (*sulk*), افسرده شدن afsurdah shudan, مکدر شدن mukaddar shudan, رنجیدن ranjídan.

POUTING (*of the lips*), عبوس لبها 'ubús-i-labhá.

POVERTY, بینوائی bí-navá,í, افلاس iflás, مفلسی muflisí, فقر fakr, فاقه fákah, تنگ دستی tang-dastí, نیازمندی niyáz-mandí, سختی sakhtí, مسکنت maskanat, مسکینی miskíní, استیصال istísál, نا داری ná-dárí. — (*poverty-stricken*) مفلوك maflúk, فقیر fakír, مفلس muflis, بی چاره bí-chárah.

POWDER, سفوف safúf, غبار ghubár, سوده súdah. — (*medicinal*) سفوف safúf. — (*gunpowder*) باروت bárút.

To POWDER, مالیدن málídan, کوفتن kúftan, کوبیدن kúbídan.—(*cover with powder*) گردك زدن gardak zadan.

POWDER-FLASK, دبه باروت dabbah-i-bárút, باروتدان bárút-dán. — (*small priming flask*) شاخدهنه shákh-dahanah, چاشنیدان cháshní-dán.

POWDER-MAGAZINE, باروتخانه bárút-khánah, قور خانه kúr-khánah.

Powder-mill, کار خانه باروت کوبی kár-khánah-i-bárút-kúbí.

Powdery, خاکه دار khákah-dár.

Power, زور zúr, قدرت kudrat, اقتدار iktidár, قوت kúvat, قوه kúvah, توانائی taváná,í, طاقت tákat, دست dast, مکنت miknat, نیرو nairú, مجال majál, زهره zahrah, یارا yárá, ایالت ayálat.—(*to the utmost of one's power*) حتی الوسع hatta-'l-vas', حتی المقدور hatta-'l-makdúr. — (*beyond one's power*) بیرون از حوصله bírún az hausalah. — (*within the power*) در داخل حوصله dar dákhil-i-hausalah. — (*deprived of power*) مسلوب الاختیار maslúbu-'l-ikhtiyár.

Powerful, زور آور zúr-ávar, توانا taváná, قوی kaví, قادر kádir, قدیر kadír, مقتدر muktadir, نیرو مند nairú-mand, متمکن mutamakkin, قهار kahhár, صاحب اقتدار sáhib-i-iktidár, ذو القدر zu-'l-kadr.

Powerfully, قویاً kavíyan, قادرانه kádiránah.

Powerless, نا توان ná-taván, بی تاب bí-táb, نا چار ná-chár, بی طاقت bí-tákat.

Powers (*functions*), حقوق hukúk, وظائف vazá,if.

Pox (*venereal*), مرض خبیثه marz-i-khabísah, کوفت kúft, قروحات شهدیه kurúhát-i-shahdíyah.—(*small-pox*) آبله ábilah, اوله aulah (*vulg.*).

Practicable, صورت پذیر súrat-pazír, شدنی shudaní, ممکن mumkin.

Practical, عملی 'amalí.

Practically, از روی بصیرت az rúy-i-basírat.

Practice, عادت 'ádat, مشق mashk, استعمال isti'mál, عمل 'amal.

To Practise (*exercise*), مشق کردن mashk kardan, استعمال کردن isti'mál kardan, پر کردن pur kardan.

Practitioner, طبیب tabíb (*pl.* اطبا atibbá), حکیم hakím (*pl.* حکما hukamá).

Prairie, مرغزار margh-zár, سبزه زار sabzah-zár, صحرا sahrá.

Praise, تعریف ta'ríf, توصیف tausíf, ستایش sitáyish, نیایش niyáyish, نعت na't, وصف vasf, حمد hamd, مدح madh, تحسین tahsín, آفرین áfirín, ثنا saná, محمدت mahmadat. — (*self-praise*) خود ستایش khwud-sitáyish.

To Praise, ستودن sitúdan, ستایش نمودن sitáyish nimúdan, توصیف کردن tausíf kardan, ثنا گفتن saná guftan.

Praiseworthy, لائق ستایش lá,ik-i-sitáyish, واجب المدح vájibu-'l-madah, مستحسن mustahsan, حمید hamíd, محمود mahmúd, محمد muhammad, ممدوح mamdúh.

To Prance, جست و خیز نمودن jast u khíz nimúdan.

Prank, لعب la'b, بازی bází.

To Prate, گپ زدن gap zadan (*hind.*), پر گفتن pur guftan.

Prattler, مقوال mikvál, پرگو pur-gú, حراف harráf, فضول fuzúl.

Prawn, روبیان rúbiyán, میگو maigú, ماهی میگو máhí-i-maigú.

Pray! (*I beg of you; I request or hope*), تمنا اینکه tamanná ín-kih, از شفقت خود az shafakat-i-khwud, از لطف خودت az lutf-i-khwudat, التماس اینکه iltimás ín-kih.

To Pray (*say prayers*), نماز گذاردن namáz guzárdan, صلوت خواندن salát-khwándan, دعا گفتن du'á guftan.—(*beseech*) خواستن khwástan, در خواست نمودن dar-khwást nimúdan, التماس کردن iltimás kardan, تمنا نمودن tamanná nimúdan, نیاز کردن niyáz kardan, نیازیدن niyázídan, الجاء نمودن ilja, nimúdan, دعا کردن du'á kardan.

Prayer (*intreaty*), نیاز niyáz, تمنا tamanná, التماس iltimás, دعا du'á, آرزو árzú, ابرام ibrám, الجا iljá.—(*to God*) نماز namáz, صلوت salát, دعا du'á.—(*leader in prayers, at a mosque*) پیش نماز písh-namáz, خطیب khatíb.—(*praying carpet*) سجاده sajjádah, مصلا musallá, تشلیج tashlíj.—(*small piece of clay, usually having the names of God, the Prophet, and twelve Imams stamped on it, used in praying)* مهر muhr.—*(rosary of ninety-nine beads, corresponding with the ninety-nine names of God, used in prayer)* سبحه sabhat, تسبيح tasbíh. — *(book of prayers)* صحيفهٔ دعوات sahífah-i-da'vát.—*(crier for prayers)* موٴذن mu'azzin.

The five appointed daily prayers of Musulmans are:—sunset prayer, نماز مغرب namáz - i - maghrib; evening prayer, نماز عشا namáz-i-'ishá; morning prayer, نماز صبح namáz-i-subh, نماز فجر namáz-i-fajr; noon prayer, نماز ظهر namáz-i-zuhr; afternoon prayer, نماز عصر namáz - i - 'asr. Besides these, there are certain other prayers, as follow:—prayer at midnight, نماز تهجد namáz - i - tahajjud; extra prayers not prescribed by law, نفل nafl, نافله náfilah (*pl.* نوافل navá fil). سنه sunnah; prayers performed to make up for omissions, as when sick, on a journey, at war, or other occasions, when it is lawful to postpone one's devotions, قضا kazá,; prayer on the ceremony of marriage, adoption of children, and some other events, سيغه síghah; separate prayers, generally said at night, not enjoined, وتر vitr; prayers commended but not enjoined, نماز مستحب namáz-i-mustahabb.

The positions of the body in prayer, are as follow:—1st., standing erect, with the hands down by the sides, قيام kiyám; 2nd., the hands raised on either side of the face, with the fingers extended, while declaring God's greatness, تكبير گفتن takbír-guftan; 3rd., inclination of the body, the hands placed on the knees, ركوع rukú'; 4th., standing with the head inclined forwards, and the hands on either side of the face, قنوت kunút; 5th., kneeling, with the hands downwards, دو زانو نشستن dú zánú-nishastan; 6th., prostration, with the forehead touching the ground, سجده sijdah.

To **Preach**, وعظ كردن va'z kardan, مواعظه نمودن muvá'azah nimúdan, موعظه كردن mau'izah kardan.

Preacher, واعظ vá'iz, خطيب khatíb. —*(a faithful preacher)* واعظ صادق vá'iz-i-sádik, واعظ امين vá'iz-i-amín.—*(a preacher who does not practise as he preaches)* واعظ غير متعظ vá'iz-i-ghair-i-mutta'iz.

Preaching, وعظ va'z.

Preamble (*exordium*), مقدمه mukaddamah, ديباچه díbáchah, منشا minshá,.

Precarious, نا پايدار ná-páyadár.

Precariously, نا پايدار ná-páyadár, غير دائم ghair-i-dá,im.

Precaution, دور انديشى dúr-andíshí, تدبير tadbír, انتباه intibáh, حذر hazar.—*(by way of precaution)* احتياطا ihtiyátan.

To **Precede**, پيش آمدن písh ámadan, پيش رفتن písh raftan, مقدم بودن mukaddam búdan, پيش واقع شدن písh-váki' shudan.

Precedence, پيشروى písh - raví, اقدام ikdám, تقدم takaddum, سبقت sibkat.

Precedent (*example*), نمونه nimúnah, مثل masal, پيشنهاد písh-nihád.

Preceding, سابق sábik, مقدم mukaddam.

Precept, پند pand, نصيحت nasíhat, اندرز anduraz, وصيت vasíyat.

Preceptor, استاد ustád, معلم mu'allim.—*(spiritual preceptor)* مرشد murshid.

Precinct, حد hadd, سر حد sar-hadd.

Precious, عزيز 'azíz, نفيس nafís, ارجمند arjmand, قيمتى kaimatí, ثمين samín, فاخر fákhir, گران girán, گرانبها girán-bahá, گرانمايه girán-máyah.

Preciousness, ارجمندى arjmandí, گرانبهائى girán-bahá,í.

Precious stone, جوهر jauhar, گوهر gauhar.

PRECIPICE, جائی سراشیب já,í-i-saráshíb, کوه سرازیر kúh-i-sarázír, کوه پرت kúh-i-part.

PRECIPITANCE, *vide* RASHNESS.

PRECIPITATE, *vide* STEEP, RASH, HEADLONG.

To PRECIPITATE (*hasten*), شتابانیدن shitábánídan. — (*to precipitate oneself*) خودرا سر نگون ساختن khwudrá sar-nigún sákhtan.

PRECIPITATION, شتاب shitáb, فور faur, تهور tahavvur.

PRECIPITOUS (*steep*), پرت part, سرازیر sarázír, سراشیب saráshíb.

PRÉCIS, محصل muhassal, مجمل mujmal, اجمال ijmál.

PRECISE (*exact*), مدقق mudakkak, صحیح sahíh, با دقت bá-dikkat.

PRECISELY, عیناً 'ainan, قطعاً kat'au, جخ jakh (*vulg.*).

PRECISENESS, دقت dikkat, درستی durustí.

To PRECLUDE, منع کردن mana' kardan, مانع بودن mání' búdan, دفع کردن daf' kardan, باز داشتن báz-dáshtan, وا داشتن vá-dáshtan.

PRECOCIOUS, بیوقت bí-vakt.

PRECOCITY, بیوقتی bí-vaktí.

To PRECONCEIVE, پیش اندیشیدن písh andíshídan, پیش بینی کردن písh-bíní kardan.

PRECONCEPTION, پیش اندیشی písh-andíshí, پیش بینی písh-bíní.

PRECURSOR, پیش آهنگ písh-áhang.

PREDATORY, یغمائی yaghmá,í, غارتی gháratí, تاراجی táráji.

PREDECESSOR, سلف salaf, متقدم mutakaddim.

PREDESTINATION, نصیب nasíb, قدر kadr, قدرت kudrat, تقدیر takdír, قسمت kismat, بخت bakht, قضا kazá, طالع táli', سر نوشت sar-nivisht.

To PREDESTINE, مقدر نمودن mukaddar nimúdan.

PREDICAMENT, کشمکش kash-makash.

PREDICATE (*in logic*), تالی tálí, خبر khabar, محمول mahmúl. — (*in grammar*), خبر khabar, محمول mahmúl, محکوم به mahkúm-bihi.

To PREDICT, استخراج کردن istikhráj kardan, از غیب خبر دادن az ghaib khabar dádan, از مال اندیشی خبر دادن az ma,ál andíshí khabar dádan, پیشی گفتن píshí guftan.

PREDICTION, کهانت kahánat, غیب گوی ghaib-gúí.

PREDICTOR, غیب گو ghaib-gú.

PREDILECTION, میل mail, رغبت raghbat.

To PREDISPOSE, آماده ساختن ámádah sákhtan.—(*to be predisposed*) آماده بودن ámádah búdan, میل داشتن mail dáshtan.

PREDISPOSITION, آمادگی ámádagí, میل mail.

PREDOMINANCE, استیلا istílá, سبقت sibkat.—(*prevalence*) غلبه ghalabah, استیلا istílá, عمومی 'umúmí.

PREDOMINANT, غالب ghálib.—(*prevalent*) مستولی mustaulí, مروج muravvaj, طاری tárí, متداول mutadával, عموم 'umúm.

To PREDOMINATE, غالب شدن ghálib shudan, غالب آمدن ghálib ámadan.

PRE-EMINENCE, سبقت síbkat, تفوق tafavvuk, استیلاً istílá, , پیش دستی písh-dastí, برتری bartarí.

PRE-EMINENT, سر فراز sar-faráz, ممتاز mumtáz.

PRE-EMINENTLY, بیش از همه bísh az hamah.

PRE-EMPTION (*right of purchase*), حق شفعه hakk-i-shuf'ah.

To PRE-ENGAGE, مواعدت نمودن muvá'adat nimúdan.

PRE - ENGAGEMENT, وعده va'dah, میثاق mísák.

PRE-EXISTENCE, قدامت kadámat.

PRE-EXISTENT, قدیم kadím.

PREFACE, مقدمه mukaddamah, دیباچه díbáchah.

To PREFACE, مقدمه ساختن mukaddamah sákhtan.

PREFECT, ناظم názim, حاکم hákim.

PREFECTURE, نظامت nizámat, حکومت hukúmat.

To PREFER, ترجیح دادن tarjíh dádan, تفضیل دادن tafzíl dádan, پیشتر دانستن píshtar dánistan, تقدم دادن takaddum dádan, پسندیدن pasandídan, اختیار کردن ikhtiyár kardan, مقدم دانستن mukaddam dánistan, رجحان دادن rujhán dádan, بیشتر دوست داشتن bíshtar dúst dáshtan, دوستتر داشتن dústtar dáshtan.

PREFERABLE, راجح rájih.—(*to be preferable*) ترجیح داشتن tarjíh dáshtan.

PREFERENCE, رجحان rujhán, ترجیح tarjíh.

PREFERMENT, ترقی tarakkí, سرفرازی sar-farází, اقبال ikbál.

PREFIGURATION, تشبیه tashbíh.

To PREFIGURE, تشبیه نمودن tashbíh nimúdan.

PREFIX, حرف وصل harf-i-vasl.

PREGNANCY, حمل haml, آبستنی ábistaní.

PREGNANT, آبستن ábistan, حامله hámilah, حبلی hublá.

To PREJUDGE, نا دانسته حکم کردن ná-dánistah hukm kardan.

PREJUDICE (*in favour of*), میل بی سبب mail-i-bí-sabab, ترجیح بلا مرجح tarjíh-i-bilá murajjah, تعصب ta'assub, رو داری rú - dárí.—(*against*) اکراه بی سبب ikráh-i-bí-sabab, تنفر بی سبب tanaffur-i-bí-sabab.

To PREJUDICE, بر انگیختن bar-angíkhtan, متعصب ساختن muta-'assib sákhtan.

PREJUDICIAL, وخیم vakhím, مضر muzirr, موذی mu,zí, زیانکار ziyán-kár.

PRELATE, اسقف uskúf.

PRELIMINARY (*sub.*), مقدمه mukad-damah.—(*adj.*) متقدم mutakad-dim, مقدم mukaddam.

PRELUDE, پیشرو písh-rau.

PREMATURE, بیوقت bí-vakt, قبل الوقت kablu-'l-vakt, پیش از وقت písh az vakt.

To PREMEDITATE, پیش اندیشیدن písh andíshídan, تدبیر نمودن tad-bír nimúdan.

PREMEDITATION, تدبیر tadbír, تدبر tadabbur, غور ghaur.

PREMIER, اول avval.

To PREMISE, پنداشتن pindáshtan, تصور کردن tasavvur kardan.

PREMISES, منزل manzil. — (*logic*) مقدمات mukaddamát.

PREMIUM, مزد muzd.

To PREMONISH, نصیحت کردن nasí-hat kardan, وعظ کردن va'z kardan, پند دادن pand dádan.

PREMONITION, پند pand, نصیحت nasíhat, تدبیر tadbír, وعظ va'z, موعظه mau'izah.

PREPARATION, آمادگی ámádagí, تهیه tahíyah, تدارك tadáruk, معموریت ma'múríyat, بسیج basíj, استعداد isti'dád.

PREPARATORY, ابتدائی ibtidá,í, موجب mújib, مقدمه mukadda-mah, تهیه tahíyah.

To PREPARE, ترتیب دادن tartíb dádan, حاضر کردن házir kardan, آماده کردن ámádah kardan, مهیا کردن muhayyá kardan.—(*to prepare for* ...) آهنگ ... کردن áhang-i- ... kardan.

PREPARED, آماده ámádah, مهیا mu-hayyá, تیار tayyár, مستعد musta'-idd, حاضر házir, درست durust, چاق chák, رو براه rú-bi-ráh.—(*to be prepared*) مستعد شدن musta'idd shudan.

PREPONDERANCE, استیلا istílá.

To PREPONDERATE, استیلا نمودن istílá nimúdan.

PREPOSITION (*in grammar*), حرف جر haraf-i-jarr, ادات adát.

To PREPOSSESS (*influence*), بر انگیختن bar-angíkhtan, بر آن داشتن bar án dáshtan.

PREPOSSESSION, میل mail, رغبت raghbat.

PREPOSTEROUS, معکوس ma'kús, بیهوده bíhúdah.

PREPOSTEROUSLY, به بیهودگی bi-bíhúdagí.

PREPUCE, غلفه ghulfah, غلاف ghiláf.

PREROGATIVE, مزیت mazíyat, امتیاز imtiyáz, حق hakk.

PRESAGE, فال fál, شگون shugún, اختر akhtar, طالع táli'.

To PRESAGE, تفول نمودن tafavvul nimúdan.

PRESBYTERY (*priesthood*), كشيشان kashíshán, كهنه kahanah.

PRESCIENCE, پیش بینی písh-bíní. — (*intelligence*) فراست firásat, بصیرت basírat.

PRESCIENT, پیش بین písh-bín.— (*intelligent*) صاحب بصیرت sáhib-i-basírat.

To PRESCRIBE, فرمودن firmúdan, حکم نمودن hukm nimúdan, امر نمودن amr nimúdan. — (*medical term*) نسخه دادن nuskhah dádan.

PRESCRIBED, مرسوم marsúm.

PRESCRIPTION (*of a physician*), نسخه nuskhah.

PRESENCE, حضور huzúr, وجود vujúd. —(*in the presence of*), رو برو rú-bi-rú, در حضور dar huzúr, مقابل mukábil.

PRESENT (*not absent*) حاضر házir, موجود maujúd, رو برو rú-bi-rú.— (*not past or future*) حال hál.—(*at present*) حالاً hálan, الحال al-hál, اکنون aknún, الان alán, در این وقت dar ín vakt.—(*gift*) بخشش bakhshish, داد dád, دهش dihish, عطا 'atá, تحفه tuhfah, سوغات saughát, هبه hibah.—(*not at present*) حالاً کمتر hálan kamtar.

To PRESENT, دادن dádan, بخشیدن bakhshídan, ارزانی داشتن arzání dáshtan, ارزانی کردن arzání kardan, عطا کردن 'atá kardan, هبه نمودن hibah nimúdan. — (*submit*) عرض نمودن 'arz nimúdan.— (*place before*) احضار کردن ihzár kardan. — (*to be present*) حضور داشتن huzúr dáshtan.

PRESENTABLE, قابل حضور kábil-i-huzúr.

PRESENTATION (*person*), احضار ihzár, تعارف ta'áruf.—(*offering*) تقدیم takdím.

PRESENTED, معروض ma'rúz.—(*to be presented at Court*) مشرف شدن musharraf shudan.

PRESENTER, دهنده dihandah, بخشنده bakhshandah.

PRESENTIMENT, خیال khayál, وهم vahm, توهم tavahhum.

PRESENTLY, عنقریب 'an-karíb.

PRESERVATION, محافظه muháfazah, حفاظت hifázat, حمایت himáyat.

PRESERVATIVE, حافظ háfiz, محافظ muháfiz, واقی vákí.

PRESERVE (*for game*), شکار گاه shikár-gáh.

To PRESERVE, نگاه داشتن nigáh dáshtan, نگاهبانی نمودن nigáh-báni nimúdan, حفظ کردن hifz kardan, حفاظت کردن hifázat kardan, محافظه نمودن muháfazah nimúdan, حراست کردن hirásat kardan. —(*fruit*) مربا ساختن murabbá sákhtan.

PRESERVED, محفوظ mahfúz.— (*fruit*) مربب murabbab, مربا murabbá.

PRESERVER, محافظ muháfiz, حامی hámí, حافظ háfiz, دستگیر dast-gír.

PRESERVES (*fruits dried*), خشکبار khushkibár, آجیل ájíl. — (*moist fruits*) نقل nukl.—(*confections*) مربا murabbá.

To PRESIDE, رئاست کردن ri,ásat kardan, نظارت کردن nazárat kardan.

PRESIDENCY, ولایت valáyat. — (*official term*) ولایت valáyat.

PRESIDENT, میر مجلس mír-i-majlis, رئیس ra,ís, والی válí. — (*Vice-President*) رئیس ثانی ra,ís-i-sání.

PRESS (*for wine*), شیره خانه shírah khánah, حوض hauz, آخوره انگور ákhwurah-i-angúr.—(*for olives, &c.*) معصر mi'sar, عصار خانه 'assár-khánah. — (*bookbinder's*) شکنجه shikanjah, قید kaid.—(*printer's*) چاپ خانه chháp-khánah, باسمه خانه básmah-khánah, مطبع matba'.— (*closet or store-room*) گنجه ganjah, حوائج خانه havá'ij-khánah.

To PRESS (*squeeze*), فشاردن fishárdan, افشردن afshurdan, چپانیدن chapánídan, چلاندن chilándan (*vulg.*). — (*impress*) مهر نمودن muhr nimúdan, نشان دادن nishán dádan.—(*throng*) افشاریدن afsharídan, افشار دادن afshár dádan, جمع شدن jam' shudan.

PRESSING (*earnest*), مبرم mubrim, مصر musir. — (*important*) مهم

muhimm, لازم lázim, عمده 'um-dah.

PRESSURE, فشار fishár.

PRESTIDIGITATOR, شعبده باز shu'ba-dah-báz.

PRESTO, با زودی bá-zúdí.

PRESUMABLE, محتمل muhtamal.

To PRESUME, پنداشتن pindáshtan, گمان بردن gumán burdan, مظنه داشتن mazannah dáshtan.—(*it may be presumed*) احتمال کل میرود که ihtimal-i-kull mí-ravad kih.

PRESUMPTION (*arrogance*), گستاخی gustákhí, غرور ghurúr, مغروری maghrúrí, جسارت jasárat, تکبر takabbur, هوا داری havá-dárí, رو rú.—(*idea*) مظنه mazannah, احتمال ihtimál.

PRESUMPTUOUS, مغرور maghrúr, متکبر mutakabbir, لاف زن láf-zan, گستاخ gustákh.

PRESUMPTUOUSLY, گستاخانه gustá-khánah, مغرورا maghrúran.

PRETENCE, بهانه bahánah.

To PRETEND, بهانه نمودن bahánah nimúdan, تقلید کردن taklíd kar-dan.

PRETENDER, لاف زن láf-zan.

PRETENTION, ادعا 'iddi'á, داعیه dá'iyah.

PRETENTIOUS, بلند نظر buland-nazar, بلند بین buland-bín.

PRETERITE (*tense*), ماضی قریب mází-i-karíb.

PRETERNATURAL, خلاف الطبیعت khi-láfu-'t-tabíyat.

PRETEXT, بهانه bahánah.—(*to make a pretext*) بهانه نمودن bahánah ni-múdan.—(*to find a pretext*) بهانه یافتن bahánah yáftan.

PRETTILY, لطیفا latífan, بلطافت bi-latáfat.

PRETTINESS, حسن husn, جمال jamál, لطافت latáfat, نزاکت nazá-kat, زیب zíb, رونق raunak, زینت zínat, جونی júní (*vulg.*).

PRETTY, زیب zíb, جمیل jamíl, لطیف latíf, خوبصورت khúb-súrat, قشنگ kashang, خوشگل khwush-gil, جون jún (*vulg.*).—(*pretty well, toler-able*) میانه miyánah, طوری taurí, همچنین ham-chunín, معتدل mu'-tadil.

To PREVAIL (*over*), غالب شدن ghá-lib shudan, استیلا یافتن istílá yáftan, مستولی شدن mustaulí shudan.—(*on, to induce*) تحریک کردن tahrík kardan, بر آن داشتن bar án dáshtan, ترغیب نمودن targhíb nimúdan, چاره کردن chárah kardan.—(*be prevalent*) متداول شدن mutadával shudan, شیوعی داشتن shuyú'í dáshtan, رواج داشتن raváj dáshtan.

PREVALENCE, غلبه ghalabah, استیلا istílá, عمومی 'umúmí.

PREVALENT, مستولی mustaulí, مروج muravvaj, طاری tárí, متداول muta-dával, عموم 'umúm.

To PREVARICATE, تناقض گفتن taná-kuz guftan, زبان بازی کردن zabán-bází kardan, لیت و لعل کردن lait u la'all kardan.

PREVARICATION, زبانبازی zabán-bází.

PREVARICATOR, زبان باز zabán-báz.

To PREVENT, باز داشتن báz-dásh-tan, مانع بودن máni' búdan, منع کردن mana' kardan, مزاحم شدن muzáhim shudan, سد کردن sadd kardan, معارضه نمودن mu'árazah nimúdan, وا داشتن vá-dáshtan.

PREVENTION, منع mana', دفع daf', مزاحمت muzáhamat.

PREVENTIVE, مانع máni', مزاحم mu-záhim.

PREVIOUS, سابق sábik, پیش písh.

PREVIOUSLY, قبل از این kabl az ín.

PREY, *vide* GAME, PLUNDER.

To PREY, شکار کردن shikár kardan, صید نمودن said nimúdan.

PRICE, قیمت kaimat, بها bahá, ارز arz, ارزش arzish, ارج arj, ثمن sa-man, مایه máyah.—(*current price of the market*) نرخ nirkh, قیمت متعارف kaimat-i-muta'árif.—(*price of blood*) دیت diyat, خونبها khún-bahá, معقلت ma'kulat.—(*fair price*) قیمت خوب kaimat-i-khúb.—(*a high price*) مبلغ خطیر mablagh-i-khatír, قیمت عالی kaimat-i-'álí, بهائی گران bahá,í-i-girán.—(*a low price*) قیمت پست kaimat-i-past, بهائی کم bahá,í-i-kam. — (*the very lowest price*) قیمت آخر آخر kaimat-i-ákhir-i-ákhir.—(*rate of prices*) فهرست نرخها fihrist-i-nirkhahá.

PRICELESS (*very valuable*), بی بها bí-bahá, بیش قیمت bísh-kaimat, گرانمایه girán-máyah.—(*having no fixed price, such as many works of art, &c.*) آب بردار áb-bardár.

To PRICK, خلیدن khalídan, زدن zadan, در رفتن dar-raftan.

PRICKLE, خار khár.

PRICKLY (*full of prickles*), خار دار khár-dár, پر خار pur-khár.

PRICKLY-PEAR, انجیر فرنگی anjír-i-farangí.

PRIDE, غرور ghurúr, مغروری maghrúrí, کبریا kibriyá,, تکبر takabbur, نفس nafs, خود پسندی khwud-pasandí, نخوت nakhvat, خود نمائی khwud-nimá,í, عجب 'ujb.

To PRIDE, قل رفتن kul raftan, مفاخرت نمودن mufákharat nimúdan, گزاف زدن gizáf zadan, لاف زدن láf zadan.—(*to pride oneself*) افتخار نمودن iftikhár nimúdan.

PRIEST, کاهن káhin, ملا mullá. [Properly speaking, there exists no priesthood among Muhammadans. Any person capable of reading the Kuran may act as a priest, but they have no crdination of clergy.] — (*chief priest of the faith*) امام imám (*pl.* ائمة a,immah), a title given to Ali, the cousin and son-in-law of Muhammad, and his descendants to the ninth generation—twelve Imâms altogether; the last of whom is supposed to be still living.—(*chief priest of recent times*) مجتهد mujtahid, مطران mitrán, رئیس کهنه ra,ís-i-kahanah. — (*Christian priest*) قسیس kissís, کشیش kashísh.

PRIESTHOOD (*office of priest*), کهانت kahánat. — (*presbytery*) کشیشان kashíshán, کهنه kahanah.

PRIG (*upstart*), خود پسند khwud-pasand.

PRIM, قشنگ kashang.

PRIMARILY, اولا avvalan.

PRIMARY, اول avval, اصلی aslí.

PRIME (*chief*), اول avval, اصل asl, مهتر mihtar. — (*beautiful*) خوب khúb, قشنگ kashang, فاضل fázil. —(*the prime*) بهار bahár.

To PRIME (*a gun*), چاشنی نمودن cháshní nimúdan. — (*a person*) تلقین نمودن talkín nimúdan.

PRIMER, کتاب مقدمه kitáb-i-mukaddamah.

PRIMEVAL, قدیم kadím.

PRIMING (*of a gun*), چاشنی cháshní. —(*small powder-horn for priming*) چاشنیدان cháshní-dán, شاخدهنه shákh-dahanah.

PRIMITIVE, پیشین píshín, قدیم kadím, سابق sábik, اول avval. — (*grammatical term*) جامد jámid, اصلی aslí.

PRIMITIVELY, قدیمانه kadímánah.

PRIMOGENITURE, حق اول زادگی hakk-i-avval-zádagí, حق بکوریت hakk-i-bukúríyat.

PRINCE, پادشاه pádisháh, شاه sháh, شه shah, ملک malk, سلطان sultán. —(*son of a king*) شاهزاده sháh-zádah, شهزاده shah-zádah, میرزا mírzá.

PRINCEDOM, سلطنت sultanat, پادشاهت pádisháhat.

PRINCELY, امیرانه amíránah.

PRINCESS, دختر شاه dukhtar-i-sháh, بیگم begum, بانو bánú, شاهزاده خانم sháhzádah-khánam. — (*Princess Royal*) شاه بیگم sháh-begum.

PRINCIPAL, اول avval, عینی 'ainí, مهتر mihtar, اصل asl, عمده 'umdah. —(*capital*) رأس المال ra,su-'l-mál, سر مایه sar-máyah.

PRINCIPALITY, امارت imárat.

PRINCIPALLY, غالبا gháliban, فی الغالب fi'l-ghálib.

PRINCIPLE, موجب mújib, سبب sabab, وجه vajh.—(*element*) عنصر 'unsur.—(*bad-principled*) بد اصل bad-asl.

PRINT (*of foot, &c.*), نشان nishán,

اثر asr. — (*paper*) چاپ cháp.— (*calico*) چیت chít. — (*out of print*) از چاپ افتاده az cháp uftádah.

To PRINT, باسمه کردن básmah kardan, چاپ کردن cháp kardan, طبع کردن tab' kardan.

PRINTED, مطبوع matbú'.—(*to be printed*) انطباع شدن intibá' shudan, چاپ کرده شدن cháp-kardah shudan, مطبوع شدن matbú' shudan.

PRINTER, طباع tabbá', چاپچی chápchí.

PRINTING, باسمه básmah, چاپ cháp, طبع tab'.

PRINTING - OFFICE, چاپخانه cháp-khánah.

PRINTING-PRESS, مطبعه matba'ah.

PRIOR, پیشینه píshínah.—(*preceding*) جلو jilau, در پیش dar písh, مقابل mukábil. — (*monk*) راهب ráhib, کشیش kashísh, قسیس kissís, حبر hibr.

PRIORITY, تقدم takaddum.

PRISM, موشور maushúr.

PRISMATIC, الماس تراش almás-tirásh, موشور آسا maushúr-ásá.

PRISON, زندان zindán, حبس خانه habs - khánah, محبس mahbas, دستاق خانه dusták - khánah, زندانخانه zindán-khánah.

PRISONER, محبوس mahbús, مقید mukayyad, زندانی zindání, دستاقی dustákí (*vulg.*).—(*of war*) اسیر asír, دیل díl (*vulg.*).—(*to take prisoner*) اسیر گرفتن asír giriftan, گرفتار کردن giriftár kardan, دیل کردن díl kardan (*vulg.*).

PRIVACY, خلوت khalvat.

PRIVATE, خاص kháss, مخصوص makhsús, مختص mukhtass.—(*private parts*) *vide* PUDENDUM. — (*not public or official*) دوستانه dústánah, نهان nihán. — (*common soldier*) سر باز sar-báz, سپاهی sipáhí.

PRIVATEER, کشتی دزد kashtí-i-duzd.

PRIVATELY, *vide* SECRETLY.

PRIVATION, محرومیت mahrúmíyat. (*Vide* POVERTY.)

PRIVILEGE, حق hakk, امتیاز imtiyáz.—(*written*) برات barát, منشور manshúr, تذکره tazkirah.

To PRIVILEGE, اذن دادن izn dádan, استحقاق بخشیدن istihkák bakhshídan, رتبه دادن rutbah dádan. —(*to be privileged*) استحقاق یافتن istihkák yáftan.

PRIVITY, آگاهی ágáhí.

PRIVY, جائی ضرور ja,í-i-zarúr, مبرز mabraz, مزبله mazbalah, بیت الخلا baitu-'l-khalá, مستراح mustaráh, متوضا mutavazzá, منجلاب خانه manjaláb - khánah. (*Vide* SECRET.)—(*to go to the privy*) متوضا رفتن mutavazzá raftan, بسر آب رفتن bi-sar-áb raftan, بقضای حاجت رفتن bi-kazá,í-i-hájat raftan.

PRIZE, *vide* REWARD, PLUNDER.

To PRIZE, قدر دانستن kadr dánistan.

PRIZE-MONEY, غنیمت ghanímat.

PROBABILITY, احتمال ihtimál, معقولات ma'kúlat.—(*in all probability*) علی حسب الاحتمال 'alá hasbu-'l-ihtimál.

PROBABLE, محتمل muhtamal, اغلب aghlab, معقول ma'kúl, گویا gúyá. — (*to be probable*) احتمال داشتن ihtimál dáshtan. — (*to appear probable*) محتمل بنظر آمدن muhtamal-bi-nazar ámadan.

PROBABLY, گویا gúyá, شاید sháyad, احتمال است ihtimál ast.

PROBATION, امتحان imtihán, ابتلا ibtilá. — (*on probation*) تحت امتحان taht-i-imtihán.

PROBATIONER, معروض امتحان ma'rúz-i-imtihán.

PROBE, میل míl, سبار sibár.

PROBITY, دیانت diyánat, راستی rástí, صدق sidk.

PROBLEM, مسئله mas,alah, مشکله mushkilah. — (*problems*) مسائل masá,il, مشکلات mushkilát.

PROBLEMATICAL, مشکوک mashkúk.

PROBOSCIS, خرطوم khurtúm, خلتوم khultúm (*vulg.*).

PROCEDURE, حرکت harakat, وضع vaz'.

To PROCEED, رفتار کردن raftár kardan, گذشتن guzashtan, پیشرفت نمودن písh-raft nimúdan.—(*issue forth*) صادر شدن sádir shudan, صدور کردن sudúr kardan.—(*arise*) ناشی شدن náshí shudan.

PROCEEDING, *vide* AFFAIR.—(*issuing forth*) صادر sádir, صدور sudúr.

PROCESS, وجه vajh, وضع vaz'.—(*legal*) محاکمه muhákamah.

PROCESSION, طواف taváf, طائفه tá,ifah.

To PROCLAIM, سخن رانی نمودن sukhun-rání nimúdan, شایع کردن sháí' kardan, تبلیغ نمودن tablígh nimúdan, اشاعت نمودن ishá'at nimúdan.—(*call*) جار کشیدن jár káshídan, منادا کردن manádá kardan, ندا کردن nidá kardan, اشتهار دادن ishtihár dádan.

PROCLAMATION, جار jár, اشتهار ishtihár, منادات munádát, ندا nidá.—(*written*) اشتهار نامه ishtihár-námah.

To PROCRASTINATE, تأنی نمودن ta,anní nimúdan, تأخیر انداختن ta,khír andákhtan.

PROCRASTINATION, لیت و لعل lait u la'all, تأخیر ta,khír, درنگی dirangí, تعویق ta'vík.

To PROCREATE, تولید نمودن taulíd nimúdan, زایدن záídan, زادن zádan.

PROCREATION, تولید taulíd, آفرینش áfirínish.

PROCREATOR, خالق khálik, آفریننده áfirínandah.

PROCTOR, وکیل vakíl.

PROCTORSHIP, وکالت vakálat.

PROCURABLE, یافتنی yáftaní.

PROCURATION, حکمرانی hukm-rání.

PROCURATOR, حکمران hukm-rán.

To PROCURE, بهم رسانیدن bi-ham rasánídan, همدست کردن ham-dast kardan, میسر کردن muyassar kardan, حاصل کردن hásil kardan, یافتن yáftan, پیدا کردن paidá kardan.

PROCURER, یابنده yábandah, تحصیل کننده tahsíl-kunandah.

PROCURESS, دلاله dallálah.

PRODIGAL, مسرف musrif, مبذر mubazzir, متلف mutlif, مصرف musrif.

PRODIGALITY, اسراف isráf, تبذیر tabzír.

PRODIGIOUS, بوالعجب bu-'l-'ajab, عجیب 'ajíb, غریب gharíb.—(*big*) عظیم 'azím, بزرگ buzurg.

PRODIGIOUSLY, بغایت bi-gháyat, بشدت bi-shiddat, زیاد از حد ziyád áz hadd.

PRODIGY, عجب العجائب 'ajabu-'l-'ajá'ib, استدراج istidráj.

PRODUCE, حاصل hásil, محصول mahsúl, پیدائش paidá,ish, مال mál.

To PRODUCE, بر آوردن bar-ávardan, پیدا کردن paidá kardan, موجود کردن maujúd kardan, بعمل آوردن bi-'amal-ávardan, بیرون آوردن bírún ávardan, زایدن záídan.

PRODUCT, محصول mahsúl, حاصل hásil.—(*in arithmetic*) حاصل ضرب hásil-i-zarb.

PRODUCTION, تولید taulíd.—(*literary*) انشا inshá,.

PRODUCTIVE, محصولدار mahsúl-dár.

PROFANATION, پلیدی pilídí, تنجیس tanjís, تدنیس tadnís.

PROFANE, فاسق fásik, کافر káfir, منافق munáfik, بی دین bí-dín.

To PROFANE, پلید ساختن pilíd sákhtan, تنجیس کردن tanjís kardan, تدنیس کردن tadnís kardan.

PROFANELY, پلیدانه pilídánah.

PROFANER, پلید ساز pilíd-sáz, تدنیس کن tadnís-kun.

PROFANITY, کفر kufr, نفاق nifák, بی دینی bí-díní.

To PROFESS, ادعا نمودن 'iddi'á nimúdan, اظهار کردن izhár kardan, اقرار کردن ikrár kardan.

PROFESSEDLY, ظاهراً záhiran.

PROFESSION (*calling*), پیشه píshah, حرفه hirfah, صنعت san'at, دکان dukán (*vulg.*).—(*of religion, belief, &c.*), شهادت shahádat, تشهد tashahhud.—(*declaration*)

اقرار ikrár, اظهار izhár, ادعا iddi'á, ایضاح ízáh.

PROFESSIONAL (*person*), صاحب پیشه sáhib-píshah, پیشه ور píshah-var.

PROFESSOR (*teacher*), مدرس mu-darris, معلم mu'allim, استاد ustád, اوستاد ústád.

PROFESSORSHIP, مدرسی mudarrisí, تدریس tadrís.

PROFFER, تقدیم takdím, پیش آوردگی písh-ávardagí.

To PROFFER, پیش آوردن písh ávar-dan, تقدیم کردن takdím kardan, تقریب نمودن takríb nimúdan.

PROFICIENCY, لیاقت liyákat, قابلیت kábilíyat, زکاوت zakávat, فراست firásat.

PROFICIENT, ماهر máhir, زرنگ zaring, چست chust, چابك chábuk.

PROFILE, نیم رو ním-rú, یك بری yak-barí.

PROFIT, سود súd, نفع naf', منفعت manfa'at, فائده fá,idah, صرفه sar-fah, مصرف masraf, حاصل hásil.—(*profit and loss*) سود و زیان súd u ziyán, جبر و نقصان jabar va nuksán. نفع و ضرر naf' u zarar.

To PROFIT (*benefit*), طرفی بستن tarafí bastan.—(*to make profit, to gain*), سود یافتن súd yáftan, حاصل گرفتن hásil giriftan, صرفه بهم رسانیدن sarfah bi-ham rasánídan, نفع یافتن naf' yáftan, جاچن زدن jáchan zadan (*vulg.*).

PROFITABLE, سودمند súd-mand, نافع náfi', مفید mufíd.

PROFITABLY, با منفعت bá-manfa'at.

PROFITLESS, بی فائده bí-fá,idah, بی نفع bí-naf'.

PROFLIGACY, فسق fisk, رندی rindí, بد کاری bad-kárí, فجور fujúr, خوش گذرانی khwush-guzrání.

PROFLIGATE, رند rind, فاسق fásik, بد کار bad-kár, فاجر fájir, شقی shakí, قلاش kallásh, زانی zání, خوش گذران khwush-guzrán, اوباش aubásh.

PROFOUND, کمال kamál.—(*learned*) علمدار 'ilm-dár.

PROFOUNDLY, بغایت bi-ghâyat, بنهایت bi-niháyat.

PROFUNDITY, کمالیت kamálíyat, بسیاری bisyárí.

PROFUSE (*extreme*), نهایت niháyat, غایت ghâyat.—(*prodigal*) مسرف musrif, مبذر mubazzir, متلف mutlif, مصرف musrif.

PROFUSION, بسیاری bisyárí, وفور vufúr.—(*prodigality*) اسراف isráf, تبذیر tabzír.

PROGENITOR, جد jadd (*pl.* اجداد ajdád), سلف salaf (*pl.* اسلاف asláf), اب ab (*pl.* آبا ábá).

PROGENY, اولاد aulád, نسل nasl, صلب salab, ذریه zurríyah, اعقاب a'káb, سلاله sulálah.

PROGNOSTIC, فال fál, شگون shugún.

To PROGNOSTICATE, *vide* To PRE-DICT.

PROGRESS, روش ravish, رفتار raftár, تدریج tadríj, تمشیت tamshiyat.—(*in acquirement*) ترقی tarakkí, ارتقا irtiká.

To PROGRESS, ترقی کردن tarakkí kardan.—(*move*) جنبیدن jumbí-dan, حرکت کردن harakat kardan, متحرك شدن mutaharrik shudan.

PROGRESSION, روش ravish, رفتار raftár. —(*arithmetical progression*) حساب سلسله جمع و تفریق hisáb-i-silsilah-i-jam' va tafrík. —(*geometrical progression*) حساب سلسله ضرب و تقسیم hisáb-i-silsilah-i-zarb va taksím.

PROGRESSIVE, مترقی mutarakkí.

PROGRESSIVELY, رفته رفته raftah raftah, بتدریج bi-tadríj.

To PROHIBIT, منع کردن mana' kar-dan, حرمان نمودن harmán nimú-dan, باز داشتن báz-dáshtan, نهی کردن nahy kardan, قدغن نمودن kadghan nimúdan.

PROHIBITION, قدغن kadghan, منع mana', نهی nahy.

PROHIBITORY, مانع máni'.

PROJECT, *vide* PLOT, CONTRIVANCE.

To PROJECT, ایجاد نمودن íjád nimú-dan, تجویز کردن tajvíz kardan, اختراع نمودن ikhtirá' nimúdan, انگیختن angíkhtan.

Projectile, تیر tír.

Projection; بر آمدگی bar-ámadagí.

Projector, موجد mújid.

Prolific, باروَر bár-var.

Prolix, طویل tavíl, مفصل mufassal, دراز diráz.

Prolixity, تفصیل tafsíl, اطناب itnáb, تطویل tatvíl.

Prolixly, تطویل tatvíl, علی التفصیل 'ala-'t-tafsíl, تفصیلاً tafsílan, علی الطویل 'ala-'t-tavíl.

Prologue, مقدمه mukaddamah.

To Prolong, امتداد کردن imtidád kardan, دراز نمودن diráz nimúdan.

Prolongation, امتداد imtidád, مد madd, تطویل tatvíl.

Prolonged, مدید madíd, طویل tavíl, ممتد mumtadd.—(*to be prolonged*) امتداد یافتن imtidád yáftan, طول کشیدن túl kashídan.

Promenade, گردش gardish, تماشا tamáshá, تفرج tafarruj, سیر sair.—(*place*) تفرجگاه tafarruj-gáh, تماشا گاه tamáshá-gáh, خیابان khiyábán.

To Promenade, سیر کردن sair kardan, گشت کردن gasht kardan.

Prominence, بر آمدگی bar-ámadagí.

Prominent (*men*), مشرف musharraf, عمده 'umdah.—(*things*) بر آمده bar-ámadah, پیش آمده písh-ámadah.

Promiscuous, آمیخته ámíkhtah.

Promiscuously, مخلوطاً makhlútan.

Promise, عهد 'ahd, پیمان paimán, وعده va'dah, قول kaul, میثاق mísák, اقرار ikrár, قرار karár.

To Promise, عهد نمودن 'ahd nimúdan, وعده کردن va'dah kardan.

Promised, موعود mau'úd, وعید va'íd, معهود ma'húd.

Promising (*propitious*), فرخنده farkhundah, همایون humáyún, نیک اختر ník-akhtar, خجسته khujistah, میمون maimún, مبارک mubárak, سعید sa,íd, بختیار bakht-yár, فرخ farrukh.

Promissory note, عهد نامه 'ahd-námah.

Promontory, راٴس الجبل ra,su-'l-jabal, راٴس ra,s, انف anf, طرف taraf.

To Promote, ترقی کردن tarakkí kardan, برتری مناسب دادن bartarí munásib dádan.

Promoter, موجد mújid.

Promotion, ترقی tarakkí, ارتقا irtiká, سر فرازی sar-faràzí, برتری bartarí.

Prompt, چیره دست chírah-dast, چالاک chálák, چابک chábuk, زرنگ zaring.

To Prompt, ترغیب نمودن targhíb nimúdan, تحریک نمودن tahrík nimúdan, اغوا نمودن ighvá nimúdan, بر انگیختن bar-angíkhtan.

Prompter, محرک muharrik.—(*theatrical*) مذکر muzakkir.

Promptitude, سرعت sur'at, تیز دستی tíz-dastí, تعجیل ta'jíl, شتاب shitáb, شتابی shitábí, زودی zúdí.

Promptly, سریعاً surí'an, فوراً fauran, زود zúd.

To Promulgate, شهرت دادن shuhrat dádan, اشتهار کردن ishtihár kardan, اظهار نمودن izhár nimúdan, شایع کردن sháí' kardan, آشکاره کردن áshkárah kardan, علانیت نمودن 'aláníyat nimúdan.

Promulgation, اشتهار ishtihár, اظهار izhár.

Prone, مائل má,il, راغب rághib.

Proneness, رغبت raghbat, میل mail.

Prong, چنگ chang.

Pronoun, ضمیر zamír. — (*separate pronoun*) ضمیر منفصل zamír-i-munfasil. — (*affixed*) ضمیر متصل zamír-i-muttasil. — (*demonstrative pronoun*) اسم اشاره ism-i-ishárah. — (*relative*) موصول mausúl.—(*interrogative*) اسم استفهام ism-i-istifhám.— (*reflective*) ضمیر مشترک zamír-i-mushtarak. — (*possessive*) ضمیر مضاف الیه zamír-i-muzáf-ilaihi.

To Pronounce, تلفظ کردن talaffuz kardan.

PRONOUNCER, متلفظ mutalaffiz, تلفظ کنندہ talaffuz-kunandah.

PRONUNCIATION, تلفظ talaffuz, مخرج makhraj, تکلم takallum, تجوید tajvíd.

PROOF, اثبات isbát, دلیل dalíl, برهان burhán, حجت hujjat.—(*positive proof*) برهان قاطع burhán-i-káti‘, حجت بینتی hujjat-i-bayyinatí, بینہ bayyinah.—(*proof according to reason*) دلیل عقلی dalíl-i-‘aklí.—(*proof according to report or tradition*) دلیل نقلی dalíl-i-naklí.

PROP, ازا izá, عمود ‘amúd, عمدت ‘umdat, پشتی pushtí.—(*for supporting the branch of a tree, a line, &c.*) دو شاخہ dú-shákhah.

To PROPAGATE (*trans.*), انتشار دادن intishár dádan.—(*intrans.*) منتشر شدن muntashir shudan.—(*procreate*) تولید نمودن taulíd nimúdan, زایدن záídan, زادن zádan.

PROPAGATION, سرایت siráyat.—(*procreation*) تولد tavallud.

PROPAGATOR, والد válid.

To PROPEL, راندن rándan.

PROPENSITY, میل mail, رغبت raghbat.

PROPER, لائق lá,ik, واجب vájib, روا ravá, سزا sazá, سزاوار sazá-vár, شایستہ sháyistah, مناسب munásib, انسب ansab, لازم lázim, موجہ muvajjah.—(*peculiar to*) مخصوص makhsús, منحصر munhasir.—(*to think proper*) صواب دانستن saváb dánistan, صلاح دانستن saláh dánistan.

PROPERLY, بطور مناسب bi-taur-i-munásib.

PROPERTY, ملک milk, ملکیت milkíyat, ما یملک má yamlik, مال mál, ما حصل má hasal.—(*quality*) خاصیت khassíyat, خصلت khaslat, جبلت jibillat. (*Vide* QUALITY.)—(*real property or fixtures*) عقار ‘akár.—(*moveable or personal property*) منقول mankúl.—(*property held in possession for a year, and consequently liable to be taxed*) حولان حول haulán-i-haul.—(*man of property*) صاحب املاک sáhib-amlák.

PROPHECY, اخبار ikhbár, انبا imbá, , نبوت nubúvat, غیب گوی ghaib-gúí, کهانت kahánat.—(*the gift or power*) نبوت nubúvat, کهانت kahánat, کرامت اخبار نمودن karámat-i-ikhbár nimúdan.

To PROPHESY, نبوت نمودن nubúvat nimúdan, از پیش خبر دادن az písh khabar dádan, غیب گفتن ghaib guftan.

PROPHET, پیغمبر paigham-bar, پیغامبر paighám-bar, پیمبر payambar, نبی nabíy, رسول rasúl.—(*the prophets*) پیغمبران paigham-barán, انبیا ambiyá,.

PROPHETIC, پیغامبری paighám-barí, پیغمبری paigham-barí.

PROPHETICALLY, پیغامبرانہ paighámbaránah, پیغمبرانہ paigham-baránah.

PROPINQUITY, نزدیکی nazdíkí, قرب karb, مقاربت mukárabat, موارقت muvárakat.

To PROPITIATE, تکفیر نمودن takfír nimúdan. — (*appease*) آرامیدن árámídan, تسلی دادن tasallí dádan.

PROPITIATION, کفارہ kaffárah, تکفیر takfír.

PROPITIOUS, فرخندہ farkhundah, همایون humáyún, نیک اختر ník-akhtar, خجستہ khujistah, میمون maimún, مبارک mubárak, سعید sa‘íd, بختیار bakht-yár, فرخ farrukh.

PROPITIOUSLY, بمساعدت bi-musá‘adat.

PROPITIOUSNESS, بختیاری bakht-yárí, مساعدت musá‘adat.

PROPORTION, قدر kadr, مقدار mikdár, وفق vafk, موافقت muváfakat, اندازہ andázah, تساوی tasáví, نسبت nisbat, مطابقت mutábakat, ازا izá, قرار karár.—(*in proportion*) بتناسب bi-tanásub.

To PROPORTION, موافق ساختن muváfik sákhtan.

PROPORTIONAL, مناسب munásib, موافق muváfik.

PROPORTIONALLY, بمناسبت bi-munásabat.

PROPORTIONATE, متناسب mutanásib, معادل mu'ádil.

PROPOSAL, مسئله mas,alah, عرض 'arz.

To PROPOSE, اقامت کردن ikámat kardan.

PROPOSITION, مسئله mas,alah.—(*propositions of Euclid*) تحریر اوقلیدس tahrír-i-úklídas.—(*proposition in logic*) موضوع mauzú', مسئله mas,alah. — (*affirmative proposition*) موجبه múijibah.—(*negative proposition*) سالبه sálibah.

PROPOSITIONAL, شرطی shartí.

To PROPOUND, پیش کردن písh kardan.

PROPRIETARY, ملاکی mulláki.

PROPRIETOR, مالک málik, موکل muvakkal, صاحب sáhib.

PROPRIETY, سازکاری sáz-kárí, شایستگی sháyistagí, مناسبت munásabat.

PROROGATION, امتداد imtidád, استمداد istimdád.

To PROROGUE, متفرق ساختن mutafarrik sákhtan. — (*to be prorogued*) تعطیل شدن ta'tíl shudan, معطل شدن mu'attal shudan.

PROSAIC, بی مزه bí-mazah.

PROSE, نثر nasr.—(*prose in poetic measure, blank verse*) مرجز murajjaz.—(*rhythmical prose without measure*) مسجع musajja'.

To PROSCRIBE, محدود ساختن mahdúd sákhtan, ملعون ساختن mal'ún sákhtan, تفضیح نمودن tafzíh nimúdan.

PROSCRIPTION, تفضیح tafzíh.

To PROSECUTE (*carry on*), اجرا نمودن ijrá nimúdan, بجا آوردن bi-já ávardan. — (*legal term*) محاکمه کردن muhákamah kardan, مرافعت نمودن muráfa'at nimúdan.

PROSECUTION, اتمام itmám, اکمال ikmál, تکمیل takmíl, اختتام iktitám, انصرام insirám.—(*legal term*) مرافعه muráfa'ah, محاکمه muhákamah.

PROSECUTOR مدعی mudda'í, شاکی shákí, داد خواه dád-khwáh, متظلم mutazallim. — (*Public Prosecutor*) مدعی عمومی mudda'í-i-'umúmí.

PROSELYTE, داخل طریق dákhil-i-tarík, مؤمن جدید mu,min-i-jadíd, جدید jadíd.

PROSODY, علم عروض 'ilm-i-'arúz.

PROSPECT, منظر manzar, مظهر mazhar, مطمح mutmah.

PROSPECTIVE, منتظر mantazar, مورد چشم داشت múrid-i-chashm-dásht.

PROSPECTUS, تفصیل tafsíl.

To PROSPER, نیک بخت شدن níkbakht shudan, اقبال نمودن ikbál nimúdan.

PROSPERITY, اقبال ikbál, سعادت sa'ádat, سعادتمندی sa'ádat-mandí, نیکبختی ník-bakhtí, بختیاری bakht-yárí, فرخندگی farkhundagí, دولت daulat, بهره مندی bahrahmandí, بهبودی bih-búdí, فیروزمندی fírúz-mandí, ترقی tarakkí, میمنت maimanat, فلاح faláh, برکت barakat, بر خور داری bar-khwur-dárí, خیریت khairíyat.

PROSPEROUS, کامران kámrán, سعادتمند sa'ádat-mand, کامگار kámgár, مسعود mas'úd, نیک بخت níkbakht, فرخنده farkhundah, همایون humáyún, نیک اختر ník-akhtar, خجسته khujistah, میمون maimún, مبارک mubárak, سعید sa'íd, بختیار bakht-yár, فرخ farrukh.

PROSTERNATION, افتادگی uftádagí.

PROSTITUTE, فاحشه fáhishah, زانیه zániyah, لولی lúlí, جافجاف jáfjáf, روسپی rúspí, قحبه kahbah, لوند lavand, کاولی kávalí (*vulg.*), جنده jindah (*vulg.*).

To PROSTITUTE, ضائع نمودن zá,i' nimúdan.—(*to prostitute oneself*) خودرا وقف کار بد نمودن khwudrá vakf-i-kár-i-bad nimúdan, جنده ساختن jindah sákhtan, مرتکب فحشا شدن murtakib-i-fahshá shudan.

PROSTITUTION, جندگی jindagí, جنده

بازی jindah-bází, فاحشگی fáhishagí.

PROSTRATE, افتاده uftádah.

To PROSTRATE, افکندن afkandan, انداختن andákhtan.—(*to prostrate oneself*) افتادن uftádan, خودرا افکندن khwudrá afkandan.

PROSTRATION, سجده sijdah, سجود sujúd, استلام istilám.—(*medical term*) صرع sar'.

To PROTECT, حمایت دادن himáyat dádan, حفاظت نمودن hifázat nimúdan, صیانت کردن siyánat kardan, محارست نمودن muhárasat nimúdan.

PROTECTION, حمایت himáyat, پناه panáh, نگاهبانی nigáh-báni, حفاظت hifázat, محافظت muháfazat, امان amán, صیانت siyánat, زنهار zinhár, حرس hirs, رعایت ri'áyat, مطا matá, دیده بانی dídah-báni.

PROTECTIVE, محافظ muháfiz.

PROTECTOR, پشتی pushtí, حامی hámí, محافظ muháfiz, مظاهر muzáhir, مربی murabbí.

PROTÉGÉ, سایه نشین sáyah-nishín, مربی murabbá, پرورده parvardah.

PROTEST, استشهاد istishhád. پرتست partast (*eur.*).

To PROTEST, شهادت دادن shahádat dádan, پرتست نمودن partast nimúdan.

PROTESTATION, اشتهار ishtihár, ایضاح ízáh.

PROTOCOL, صورت معاهده súrat-i-mu'áhadah, مضبطه mazbatah.

PROTOTYPE, نسخه nuskhah.

To PROTRACT, در تعویق انداختن dar ta'vík andákhtan, تاخیر نمودن ta,khír nimúdan, دیری کردن dírí kardan, توقف کردن tavakkuf kardan.

PROTRACTED, طول túl, دراز diráz.

PROTRACTION, تاخیر ta,khír, دیر dír.

To PROTRUDE, پیش آمدن písh ámadan.

PROTRUSION, بر آمدگی bar-ámadagí.

PROUD, مغرور maghrúr, متکبر mutakabbir, خود پسند khwud-pasand, خود بین khwud-bín, مدمغ mudammagh, دماغدار dimágh-dár.—(*to be proud*) دماغ داشتن dimágh dáshtan, تجبر نمودن tajabbur nimúdan.

PROUDLY, متکبرانه mutakabbiránah, با تکبر bá-takabbur.

To PROVE, ثابت کردن sábit kardan, اثبات نمودن isbát nimúdan, دلالت نمودن dalálat nimúdan, مدلل کردن mudallal kardan.—(*to be proved*) صحیح یافت شدن sahíh-yáft shudan, ثابت شدن sábit shudan.—(*to prove to be true*) تصدیق نمودن tasdík nimúdan.—(*to prove to be false*) تکذیب نمودن takzíb nimúdan.

PROVEABLE, قابل اثبات kábil-i-isbát, اثبات پذیر isbát-pazír.

PROVENDER (*for cattle*), علوفه 'alúfah, علف 'alaf, علیق 'alík, چرا chará.

PROVERB, مثل masal, ضرب المثل zarbu-'l-masal, مثله masalah (*pl.* امثال amsál).

PROVERBIAL, ضرب المثل zarbu-'l-masal.

To PROVIDE, تهیه نمودن tahiyah nimúdan, آماده کردن ámádah kardan.

PROVIDED that (*on condition*), بشرطیکه bi-shartí-kih, مشروط بانکه mashrút bi-án-kih, در صورت که dar súrat-kih.

PROVIDENCE (*Divine*), پیش بینی písh-bíní, تدبیر tadbír, قدرت kudrat.

PROVIDENT, عاقبت بین 'ákibat-bín, اندیشمند andísh-mand, احتیاط مند ihtiyát-mand.

PROVIDENTIAL, خدائی khudá,í, الهی iláhí.

PROVINCE, دیار diyár, ملک mulk.—(*subdivision of a province*) کوره kúrah.—(*smaller subdivision of the above*) بلوك bulúk.—(*the provinces*) ممالك محروسه mamálik-i-mahrúsah.

PROVINCIAL, ولایتی valáyatí.

PROVISION, تدبیر tadbír.

PROVISIONAL, موقت muvakkat, موقته muvakkatah.

PROVISIONALLY, موقتاً muvakkatan.

PROVISIONS, خوراک khwurák, غذا ghizá, اکل akl, طعام ta'ám, آذوقه ázúkah.—(*for a journey*), زاد zád, توشه túshah, ذخیره zakhírah.—(*salt provisions*) مملوحات mamlúhát, نمکسور namaksúr.

PROVISO, شرط shart.

PROVOCATION, تحریض tahríz, تحریک tahrík.

PROVOCATIVES (*aphrodisiacs*), مشتهیات mushtahíyát, مبهیات mubahíyát.

To PROVOKE, بر انگیختن bar-angíkhtan, خیزانیدن khízánídan, تحریک کردن tahrík kardan, تغیر ساختن taghayyur sákhtan.—(*enrage*) رنجانیدن ranjánídan, غضبناک کردن ghazab-nák kardan, خشمناک کردن khishm-nák kardan.

PROVOKINGLY, مسخطانه maskhitánah.

PROW (*of a vessel*), سر کشتی sar-i-kashtí, جلو jilau, راس ra,s.

PROWESS, مردانگی mardánagí, دلیری dilírí, دلاوری diláварí, همت himmat, جرأت jur,at, شجاعت shujá'at.

PROXIMATE, نزدیک nazdík.

PROXIMITY, نزدیکی nazdíkí, قربت kurbat, قرابت karábat, تقریب takríb.

PROXY (*person*), وکیل vakíl.—(*paper*) وکالت نامه vakálat-námah.

PRUDE or PRUDISH, عفت فروش 'iffat-furúsh, زهد فروش zuhd-furúsh.

PRUDENCE, تدبیر tadbír, تمییز tamyíz, امتیاز imtiyáz, هوشمندی húshmandí, خردمندی khird-mandí, فرهنگی farhangí, بصیرت basírat.

PRUDENT, هوشمند húsh-mand, هوشیار húsh-yár, عاقل 'ákil, صاحب تدبیر sáhib-tadbír, اهل تمییز ahl-tamyíz, زیرک zírak, خردمند khird-mand.—(*a prudent man*) اهل تدبیر ahl-tadbír.

PRUDENTLY, احتیاطاً ihtiyátan.

PRUDERY, عفت فروشی 'iffat-furúshí, عصمت فروشی 'ismat-furúshí.

PRUNE (*dried plum*), آلوی خشک álú,í-i-khushk, آلوی بخارا álú,í-i-bukhárá.

To PRUNE, حطاب کردن hitáb kardan, پائشت کردن pá,isht kardan, پاهشت کردن páhisht kardan.

PRURIENCE, شوق shauk, شهوت shahvat, هوس havas.

PRURIENT, هوس مند havas-mand, شهوت پرست shahvat-parast.

PRYING, سر جو sirr-jú, راز جو ráz-jú, مستفسر mustafsir, مستقصی mustaksí, مفتش mufattish.

To PRY, تفتیش کردن taftísh kardan.

PSALM, مزمور mazmúr, زمر zamr, زبور zabúr.—(*Psalms of David*) زبور داؤد zubúr-i-da,úd, مزامیر داؤد mazámír-i-da,úd.

PSALMIST, صاحب مزامیر sáhib-i-mizámír, زبوری zabúrí.

PSALTER, زبور zabúr, مزامیر mazámír.

PSHAW, واه váh.

PUBERTY, بلوغ bulúgh, بلوغت bulúghat, رسیدگی rasídagí, شباب shabáb.—(*age of puberty*), حد بلوغ hadd-i-bulúgh, حد تکلیف hadd-i-taklíf, سن شعور sinn-i-shu'úr.—(*to come to the age of puberty*), بالغ شدن báligh shudan, بسن شعور رسیدن bi-sinn-i-shu'úr rasídan, بحد تکلیف رسیدن bi-hadd-i-taklíf rasídan, بحد بلوغ آمدن bi-hadd-i-bulúgh ámadan.

PUBES, زهار zahár, عانت 'ánat.—(*hair on the pubes*) موئی زهار mú,í-i-zahár, رمگان ramgán, پشم pashm, شعره shi'rah.

PUBLIC (*common*), عام 'ámm, عموم 'umúm, مشترک mushtarak.—(*the public*) مردم mardum, قوم kaum.

PUBLICAN, میخانه چی mai-khánah-chí.

PUBLICATION, اظهار izhár, اعلام i'lám, اعلان i'lán.—(*literary*) جریده jarídah, کتاب kitáb, مطبوعه matbú'ah.

PUBLIC-HOUSE, میخانه mai-khánah.

PUBLICITY, عیان 'iyán, انتشا intishá, شیوع shuyú'.

PUBLICLY, ظاهراً záhiran, علانیه 'aláníyah, آشکاره áshkárah, عیاناً 'ayánan.

PUBLIC WORKS, انشاآت عمومیه insha,át-i-'umúmíyah. — (*Minister of Public Works*) وزیر فواید vazír-i-faváíd.

To PUBLISH, انتشار نمودن intishár nimúdan, آشکار نمودن áshkár nimúdan, نشر کردن nashr kardan, منتشر ساختن muntashir sákhtan. —(*a book*) انتشار دادن intishár dádan.—(*to be published*) شیوع داشتن shuyú' dáshtan.

PUBLISHER, انتشار دهنده intishár-dihandah.

PUBLISHING-HOUSE, دار الانشاءی dáru-'l-inshá,í, چاپخانه cháp-khánah, مطبعخانه matba'-khánah.

To PUCKER (*trans.*), پر چین کردن pur chín kardan.—(*intrans.*) پر چین شدن pur chín shudan.

PUDDING, پودنگ púding (*eur.*).

PUDDLE, آبگیر áb-gír, گوداب gaud-áb.

PUDENDUM (*virile*), آلت álat, ذکر zakar, کیر kír, عورت مرد 'aurat-i-mard, نره narah, نفس nafs, فلانه falánah, الفیه alfíyah, قضیب kazíb.—(*muliebre*) کس kus, عورت زن 'aurat-i-zan, فرج farj, شلفیه shalfíyah.

PUERILE, طفل وش tifl-vash, بچه مانند bachah-mánand.

PUERILELY, طفلانه tiflánah.

PUERILITY, طفلی tiflí.

PUFF, فوت fút, پف puff.

To PUFF (*blow*), پف کردن puff kardan, فوت کردن fút kardan. —(*praise extravagantly*) اغراق گفتن ighrák guftan, زیاد تعریف کردن ziyád ta'ríf kardan. — (*to puff oneself up*) آماسیدن ámásídan.—(*to be puffed up*) مغرور شدن maghrúr shudan, پر باد شدن pur bád shudan.

PUFFY, بادی bádí, آماسیده ámásídah.

PUGNACIOUS, *vide* QUARRELSOME.

PULL, کشش kashish.

To PULL, کشیدن kashídan.—(*off*) بر کشیدن bar-kashídan, کندن kandan, خلع کردن khal' kardan.— (*down*) تخریب کردن takhríb kardan, پرت کردن part kardan. — (*out*) بر کشیدن bar-kashídan, بر آوردن bar-ávardan, اخراج نمودن ikhráj nimúdan, قلع کردن kal' kardan.

PULLET, جوجه júјah, بچه خروس khurús-i-bachah.

PULLEY, غرغره ghargharah, بکره bakrah.

PULP (*of fruit, &c.*), گوشت gúsht, مغز maghz.—(*soft mass or mixture*) خمیر khamír.

PULPIT, منبر mimbar.

PULPY, مغز دار maghz-dár, نرم narm.

PULSATION, نبضه nabzah.

PULSE (*artery*), نبض nabz.—(*beating of the pulse*) حرکت نبض harakat-i-nabz. — (*to feel the pulse*) نبض گرفتن *or* دیدن nabz giriftan *or* dídan.—(*pea*) کرسنه karsannah, کسن kisan, گاو دانه gáv-dánah, باقله موشی bákilah-múshí. — (*leguminous plants in general, &c.*) حبوبات hubúbát.

To PULVERIZE, سحق نمودن sahk nimúdan, کوبیدن kúbídan.

PUMICE-STONE, سنگ پا مالہ sang-i-pá-málah.

PUMMEL, *vide* POMMEL.

PUMP, طلمبه tulumbah, بمبا bumbá (*eur.*), بمبو bambú (*eur.*).

To PUMP, ایجاد نمودن íjád nimúdan.—(*worm secrets from*) روبه بازی کردن rúbah-bází kardan.

PUMPKIN, کدو kaddú.

PUN, لطیفه latífah, بذله bazlah, کنایه kináyah.

To PUN, لطیفه نمودن latífah nimúdan, بذله نمودن bazlah nimúdan.

PUNCH, مثقب miskab.

To PUNCH, مثقب زدن miskab zadan.—(*strike*) زدن zadan.

PUNCH AND JUDY, پهلوان کچل pahlaván-i-kachal, قره گوز karah-gúz.

PUNCTUAL *or* PUNCTUALLY, بوقت bi-vakt, بالوقت bi-'l-vakt, با دقت bá-dikkat.

PUNCTUALITY, دقت dikkat.

To PUNCTUATE, نقط گذاشتن nukat guzáshtan.

PUNCTUATION, نقطه گذاری nuktah-guzárí.

PUNGENT, تیز tíz, تلخ talkh, حاد hádd, تند tund.

PUNGENCY, تیزی tízí, تلخی talkhí, تندی tundí.

To PUNISH, سیاست کردن siyásat kardan, بجزا رسانیدن bi-jazá rasánídan, سزا دادن sizá dádan, عقوبت نمودن 'ukúbat nimúdan.

PUNISHABLE, قابل سزا kábil-i-sizá.

PUNISHMENT, سزا sizá, سیاست siyásat, عقوبت 'ukúbat, تادیب ta,díb, عقاب 'ikáb, نکال nakál, سر زنش sar-zanish, تنبیه tambíh.—(*retaliatory*) قصاص kisás. — (*discretionary*) تعزیر ta'zír.—(*prescribed by law*) حد hadd.—(*capital*) قتل katl.—(*by blinding or mutilating*) نسق nasak.

PUNKAH, باد کش bád-kásh.

PUNNET, سبد sabad, زنبیل zambíl, سله sallah.

PUNSTER, مسخره maskharah, لطیفه گو latífah-gú, مستهزی mustahzí,.

PUNY, خرد khurd, خورد khwurd, کوچك kúchik, صغیر saghír, که kih, پاچه páchah.

PUP, بچه bachah.

PUPIL (*scholar*), شاگرد shágird, طلبه talabah.—(*of a holy man*) مرید muríd, تلمیذ talmíz.—(*of the eye*) بوبو búbú, مردمك چشم mardumak-i-chashm, چشملان chashmilán, ببه bibih (*vulg.*).

PUPILAGE, شاگردی shágirdí.

PUPPET, عروسك 'arúsak, عروسچه 'arúschah, علوچك 'alúchik (*vulg.*).

PURBLIND, شبکور shab-kúr.

PURCHASABLE, قابل خرید kábil-i-kharíd.

PURCHASE, خرید kharíd, اشترا ishtirá.

To PURCHASE, خریدن kharídan, اشترا نمودن ishtirá nimúdan, ابتیاع کردن ibtiyá' kardan, بر داشتن bar-dáshtan.

PURCHASER, مشتری mushtarí.

PURE, پاك pák, پاکیزه pákízah, صاف sáf, مصفی musaffá, طاهر táhir, مطهر mutahhar, نقی nakí, زلال zulál, منزه munazzah, معرا mu'arrá, صریح saríh, ناب náb, سارا sárá, مزکی muzakkí, سالم sálim.

PURELY, مخلصا mukhlisan, محضا mahzan.

PURGATIVE, مسهل mus-hil.

PURGATORY, مطهر mathar, اعراف a,ráf. [The latter is supposed to be a division between heaven and hell, regarding the precise nature of which there is some difference of opinion.]

PURGE, جلاب julláb, دوای مسهل davá,í-i-mus-hil.

To PURGE, تنقیه نمودن tankiyah nimúdan, اسهال نمودن is-hál nimúdan.—(*to be purged*) فعل کردن fi'l kardan, اسهال گرفتن is-hál giriftan.

PURGING, اسهال is-hál.

PURIFICATION, تنقیه tankiyah, تصفیه tasfiyah. — (*previous to prayer*) وضو vuzú, دستنماز dast-namáz, آبدست áb-dast.—(*ablution of the whole body*) غسل ghusl.—(*after calls of nature*) استنجا istinjá, طهارت tahárat, تطهیر tathír.—(*after touching a corpse or other unclean thing*) طهارت tahárat, شستگی shustagí.—(*of forty days after childbirth*) نفاس nifás.

PURIFIED, پاك pák, پاکیزه pákízah, صاف sáf, مصفی musaffá, طاهر táhir, مطهر mutahhar, نقی nakí, زلال zulál, منزه munazzah, معرا mu'arrá, صریح saríh, ناب náb, سارا sárá, مزکی muzakkí, سالم sálim.

To PURIFY, تنقیه کردن tankiyah kardan, تصفیه نمودن tasfiyah nimúdan, صاف کردن sáf kardan, پاك کردن pák kardan.

PURITY, پاکی pákí, پاکیزگی pákízagí, صفا safá, صفای safá,í, نظافت nazáfat, صراحت saráhat, نزاهت nazáhat, نقاوت nakávat, طهارت tahárat.

PURLIEU, اطراف atráf, حوالی haválí.

To PURLOIN, دزدیدن duzdídan, دزدی کردن duzdí kardan.

PURLOINER, دزد duzd.

PURPLE, قرمز تیره kirmiz-i-tírah, بنفش سیر binafsh-i-sír, ارغوانی arghaváni.

PURPORT, مطلب matlab, معنی ma'ní.

To PURPORT, قصد داشتن kasd dáshtan.

PURPOSE, ارادة irádah, مراد murád, عزم 'azm, عزیمت 'azímat, قصد kasd, مقصود maksúd, کام kám, نیت níyat, غرض gharaz, خواست khwást, طویت taviyat, مرکوز markúz, آهنگ áhang, سر sar, آرزو árzú, مرام marám, همت himmat, طلب talab, مطلب matlab, بنا biná, داعیة dá'iyah.—(*on purpose*) قصداً kasdan, عمداً amdan, دیدة و دانستة dídah va dánistah.

To PURPOSE, قصد کردن kasd kardan, خواستن khwástan, ارادة داشتن irádah dáshtan, بنا داشتن biná dáshtan.

To PURR (*as a cat*), خرخر کردن khur-khur kardan.

PURSE, کیسة kísah, صرة surrah.—(*leathern*) همیان himyán, جراب jiráb.—(*cut-purse*) طرار tarrár, کیسة بر kísah-burr.

PURSLAIN, خرفة kharfah, خلفة khalfah, بقلة الحمقاء baklatu-'l-hamká,.

PURSUABLE, قابل تعقب kábil-i-ta'akkub.

In PURSUANCE of, بموجب bi-mújib, حسب hasb.

To PURSUE, پس رفتن pas raftan, در پی رفتن dar pay raftan, پیروی نمودن pairaví nimúdan, عقب رفتن 'akab raftan, دنبال رفتن dumbál raftan, تعاقب کردن ta'ákub kardan.

PURSUIT, تعقب ta'akkub, تعاقب ta'ákub.—(*in war*) جنگ عقب jang-i-'akab.—(*in pursuit of*) به تعقیب bi-ta'kíb.

To PURVEY, حاضر کردن házir kardan.

PURVEYANCE, تهیة tahíyah, تدارک tadáruk.—(*for travellers*) سورسات súrsát, سیورسات suyúrsát, رسد rasad.

PURVEYOR, ذخیرة چی zakhírah-chí, سرکار sarkár.

PUS, ریم rím.

PUSH, هول húl, هل hul, سك suk, تکان takán, دفع daf', دسر dasr.

To PUSH, راندن rándan, هل دادن hul dádan, تکان دادن takán dádan, سك دادن suk dádan, له دادن lah dádan.—(*away*) وا راندن vá-rándan, دفع کردن daf' kardan.—(*in*) طپاندن tapándan.

PUSHING (*eager*), مبرم mubrim, سبقت جو sibkat-jú, تقدم گزین takaddum-guzín.

PUSILLANIMITY, بیدلی bí-dilí, کم جرائتی kam-jura,tí.

PUSILLANIMOUS, بی دل bí-dil, کم جرائت kam-jura,t.

PUSS, گربة gurbah.

PUSTULE, کورك kúrk, بثر basar, دانة dánah, جوش júsh.

To PUT, گذاشتن guzáshtan, گذاردن guzárdan, نهادن nihádan, وضع کردن vaz' kardan, کردن kardan, هشتن hishtan, هلیدن hilídan.—(*out, extinguish*) نشاندن nishándan, کشتن kushtan, اطفا نمودن itfá nimúdan, منطفی ساختن muntafí sákhtan, خاموش کردن khámúsh kardan, ساکت کردن sákit kardan.—(*eject*) بیرون کردن bírún kardan, راندن rándan, دفع نمودن daf' nimúdan, منع کردن mana' kardan.—(*on, dress*) پوشانیدن púshánídan, تلبیس نمودن talbís nimúdan.—(*off*) *vide* To UNDRESS.—(*to put in practice*) بکار بردن bi-kár burdan, بجا آوردن bi-já ávardan, ورزیدن varzídan, بعمل آوردن bi-'amal ávardan.—(*off, to procrastinate*) دست بدست کردن dast bi-dast kardan, در تعویق انداختن dar ta'vík andákhtan, تاخیر نمودن ta,khír nimúdan, لیت و لعل کردن lait va la'all kardan.—(*to put forth, extend*) دراز کردن diráz kardan, کشیدن kashídan.—(*to put forth, blossom*) شکوفتن shikúftan, شکفتن shikuftan, غنچه زدن ghunchah zadan.—(*to put forward, propose*) اقامت کردن ikámat kardan.—(*to become put out*) دلگیر شدن dil-gír shudan.—(*to put up with*) تاب آوردن táb ávardan, تاب داشتن táb dáshtan.—(*to put to, a horse*) بعرادة بستن bi-'arrádah bastan.

PUTREFACTION, پوسیدگی púsídagí.

PUTREFIED, پوسیده púsídah, گندیده gandídah, گنده gandah.

To PUTREFY, پوسیدن púsídan, گندیدن gandídan.

PUZZLE, رمز ramz, معما mu'ammá, لغز lughz, مشکله mushkilah.

To PUZZLE, دو چار کردن dú-chár kardan.—(*to be puzzled*) دو چار شدن dú-chár shudan, متحیر بودن mutahayyir búdan.

PUZZLING, مشکل mushkil.

PYRAMID, هرم haram (*pl.* اهرام ahrám, *or* هرام harám).

PYRE, وقود vakúd *or* vukúd.

Q

QUACK, عیار 'ayyár.

To QUACK (*as a duck*), وك وك نمودن vak-vak nimúdan.

QUACKERY, عیاری 'ayyárí.

QUADRANGLE, چهار گوشه chahár-gúshah.

QUADRANGULAR, مربع murabba', چهار گوشه chahár-gúshah.

QUADRANT, ربع دائرة rub'-i-dá,irah.

QUADRATE, مربع murabba'.

QUADRATURE, تربیع tarbí'.

QUADRILITERAL, رباعی rubá'í.

QUADRUPED, چهار پا chahár-pá, چار پایه chár-páyah.

QUADRUPLE, چار گانه chár-gánah, چار لا chár-lá, چهار تا chahár-tá.

QUAFF, نوش núsh.

To QUAFF, نوشیدن núshídan, آشامیدن áshámídan, خوردن khwurdan.

QUAGMIRE, *vide* SWAMP.

QUAIL, بودنه búdinah, سمانه samánah, بلدرچین bildarchín, وشم vashm.

To QUAIL (*to show the white feather, to flinch*), از میدان گریختن az maidán guríkhtan, کنار جستن kanár justan, تله گذاشتن tilah guzáshtan.

QUAINT, لطیف latíf, غریب gháríb, عجیب 'ajíb.

To QUAKE, ترسیدن tarsídan, هراسان شدن hirásán shudan, ترس داشتن tars dáshtan.

QUAKER, ترسان tarsán, ترسناك tarsnák, خائف khá,if, هراسان hirásán.

QUALIFICATION, توصیف tausíf, وصف vasf, قابلیت kábilíyat.

To QUALIFY, توصیف نمودن tausíf nimúdan, وصف نمودن vasf nimúdan.—(*to qualify oneself*) خودرا قابل ساختن khwudrá kábil sákhtan.

QUALITY, خاصیت khássíyat, سیرت sírat, خصلت khaslat, طبع tab', ذات zát, وصف vasf, صفت sifat, نهاد nihád, کیفیت kaifíyat, ماهیت máhíyat, عرض 'araz, حیثیت haisíyat.—(*of cloth*) قماش kumásh.

QUALM, غثیان ghasyán.—(*qualm of conscience*) شك shakk.

QUALMISH, بیمار bímár, نا خوش ná-khwush.

QUANDARY, مضیق mazík.

QUANTITY, قدر kadr, مقدار mikdár, مایه máyah, اندازه andázah, حسب hasb, کمیت kammíyat, کنه kunh, مقیاس mikyás.—(*great quantity*) افراط ifrát, فراوانی farávání, کثرت kasrat, افزونی afzúní, بسیاری bisyárí, وفرت vafrat, غنیمت ghanímat, زیادتی ziyádatí.

QUARANTINE, کرانتین karántín (*eur.*).

QUARREL, دعوی da'vá, نزاع nizá', منازعت munáza'at, مشاجرة mushájarah, جدل jadal, لجاج lajáj, قضیه

kazíyah, خرخشه kharkhishah, مناقشه munákashah, ستیزه sitízah, تکرار takrár, هیجان hayaján, اغتشاش ightishásh, جنگ jang.

To QUARREL, جنگ کردن jang kardan, منازعت کردن munáza'at kardan, تکرار کردن takrár kardan, دعوی کردن da'vá kardan, جنگیدن jangídan.

QUARRELSOME, لجوج lajúj, نزاع دوست nizá'-dúst, ستیزه جو sitízah-jú, جنگجو jang-jú.

QUARRY, کان سنگ kán-i-sang, معدن سنگ ma'dan-i-sang.

QUARTER (*one-fourth*), ربع rub', چهار یك chahár-yak, چارك chárik, حصه چهارم hissah-i-chahárum.—(*a quarter to* ...) ربع به ... مانده rub' bi ... mándah, یکربع کم ... ... yak-rub' kam.—(*a quarter past* ...) ربع از ... گذشته rub' az ... guzashtah.—(*region*) ملك mulk, ولایت valáyat, کشور kishvar, خطه khuttah, بلد balad, بلاد bilád, دیار diyár, اقلیم iklím, الکه ulkah, یورت yúrt.—(*of a town or city*) محل mahall, محله mahallah.—(*of the moon*) تربیع tarbí'.—(*mercy*) امان amán, دخیل dakhíl, پناه panáh, بخت bakht, زنهار zinhár.—(*to give quarter*) زنهار دادن zinhár dádan.—(*to seek quarter*) زنهار طلبیدن zinhár talbídan.

To QUARTER, مسکن دادن maskan dádan, جا دادن já dádan.—(*to be quartered*) مسکن گرفتن maskan giriftan, جا گرفتن já giriftan.—(*divide in parts*) چهار پاره ساختن chahár párah sákhtan.

QUARTERLY, در چار قسم dar chár kism.

To QUASH (*annul*), وا زدن vá-zadan, مبطل گردانیدن mubtal gardánídan, باطل کردن bátil kardan, ابطال نمودن ibtál nimúdan, نسخ ساختن naskh sákhtan, منسوخ کردن mansúkh kardan, موقوف کردن maukúf kardan.

QUATRAIN, مربع murabba', رباعی rubá'í.

QUAVER (*trill of the voice in singing*), تحریر آواز tahrír-i-áváz, غلط آواز ghalat-i-áváz.

QUAY, بندر گاه bandar-gáh, فرود گاه furúd-gáh, اسکله askalah (*eur.*)

QUEEN, ملکه málikah, سلطانه sultánah, زن شاه zan-i-sháh, حرم شاه haram-i-sháh, بیگم begum, بانو bánú.

QUEEN-DOWAGER, مالکهٔ زمانه málikah-i-zamánah.

QUEER, عجب 'ajab, عجیب 'ajíb, غریب gharíb.

QUEERLY, عجیباً 'ajíban.

To QUELL, آرام کردن árám kardan, آرامیدن árámídan, تسلی دادن tasallí dádan, تخفیف کردن takhfíf kardan, ساکن کردن sákin kardan, نشاندن nishándan.

To QUENCH (*thirst*), تسکین دادن taskín dádan, نشاندن nishándan.—(*fire*) نشاندن nishándan, کشتن kushtan, اطفا نمودن itfá nimúdan, منطفی ساختن muntafí sákhtan, خاموش کردن khámúsh kardan, ساکت کردن sákit kardan.

QUENCHABLE, قابل تسکین kábil-i-taskín, اطفا پذیر itfá-pazír.

QUERIST, سائل sá,il, مستفهم mustafhim.

QUERY, مسئله mas,alah.—(*question*) سؤال su,ál, پرسش pursish, استفهام istifhám, استفسار istifsár.

QUEST, *vide* SEARCH.

QUESTION, سؤال su,ál, پرسش pursish, استفهام istifhám, استفسار istifsár.—(*affair*) کار kár, امر amr, عمل 'amal, معامله mu'ámalah, سر و کار sar va kár, خصوص khusús, باب báb, بابت bábat, حال hál, ماده máddah.

To QUESTION, استفسار نمودن istifsár nimúdan, پرسیدن pursídan.

QUESTIONABLE, قابل اعتراض kábil-i-i'tiráz.—(*suspicious*) مشتبه mushtabih.

QUIBBLE, نکته nuktah, ابهام íhám.

To QUIBBLE, نکته گیری کردن nuktah-gírí kardan.

QUIBBLER, نکته گیر nuktah-gír.

QUICK, زود zúd, چابك chábuk, چالاك chálák, چست chust, مسرع musri',

جلد jald, تند tund, تیز tíz, شتاب shitáb, شتابان shitábán, زرنگ zaring, دو اسبه dú-asbah.—(*interj.*) بسرعت bih-sur'at, زود zúd. (*the quick*) احیا ahyá, زنده zindah, زندگان zindagán.

To QUICKEN (*trans.*), شتابانیدن shitábánídan.—(*intrans.*) شتافتن shitáftan, شتاب نمودن shitáb nimúdan, تعجیل نمودن taj,íl nimúdan. —(*make alive*) زنده ساختن zindah sákhtan.

QUICKLIME, آهک خام áhak-i-khám.

QUICKLY, زود zúd, بزودی bi-zúdí, سرعتاً sur'atan, بسرعت bi-su'rat. (*Vide* SOON).

QUICKNESS (*intelligence, facility of comprehending and learning*), سهولت تعلم suhúlat-i-ta'allum, سرعت فهم sur'at-i-fahm, صفای ذهن safá,í-i-zihn, چابکی chábukí, زرنگی zaringí, ذکاوت zakávat.—(*rapidity*) زودی zúdí, جلدی jaldí, شتاب shitáb.

QUICKSAND, ریگ روان ríg-i-rawán, شنار shinár.

QUICKSET (*thorny shrub*), دره dirrah.

QUICK-SIGHTED, تیز فهم tíz-fahm, زرنگ zaring, زیرک zírak, چابک chábuk, چست chust, ذکی zakí, چیره دست chírah-dast.

QUICKSILVER, سیماب sím-áb, زیبق zíbak, جیوه jívah.

QUIET (*at rest*), ساکن sákin, آرامیده árámídah, آسوده ásúdah, مطمئن mutma,inn, مرفه muraffah. —(*silent*) خاموش khámúsh, ساکت sákit, خب khab. —(*repose*) آرام árám, آسایش ásáyish, آسودگی ásúdagí, راحت ráhat, استراحت istiráhat, سکونت sukúnat, اطمینان itmínán, رفاهت rafáhat, رفاهیت rafáhiyat.—(*house*) رام rám, مطیع matí'.—(*man*) آرام árám.—(*to be quiet*) آرامیدن árámídan.

To QUIET, رام کردن rám kardan, آرام دادن árám dádan, تسلی دادن tasallí dádan, تسکین کردن taskín kardan.

QUIETLY, آهسته áhistah, یواش yavásh, سنگنك sanganak.

QUILL, شاه پر sháh-par, پر par.

QUILT, لحاف lahúf, رضائی razá,í.

To QUILT, آزدن ázadan.

QUILTED (*with cotton*), از پنبه پر کرده شده az pambah pur-kardah-shúdah, از پنبه آکنده az pambah-ákandah.

QUILTING, بخیه bakhyah.

QUINCE, به bih, بهی bihí, سفرجل safarjal.

QUININE, کنه کنه kinah-kinah (*eur.*).

QUINSY, خناق khunák.

QUINTESSENCE, سلاله sulálah, خلاصه khulásah, جوهر jauhar, عین 'ain, ذات zát.

QUINTUPLE, مخمس mukhammas.

QUIP, لطیفه latífah, بذله bazlah, مطائبه muta'ibah, شوخی shúkhí, باردی bárdí, فسوس fisús, کنایه kináyah, هزل hazl, مسخره maskharah.

To QUIP, دشنام دادن dushnám dádan, دشنامیدن dushnámídan, طعنه زدن ta'nah zadan, سب نمودن sabb nimúdan, زباندرازی کردن zabán-dirází kardan.

QUIRE (*of paper*) دستهٔ کاغذ dastah-i-kághaz.

To QUIT, گذاشتن guzáshtan, ترك کردن tark kardan.

QUITE, سراسر sar-á-sar, تماماً tamáman, بالکل bi-'l-kull, بالکلیت bi-'l-kullíyat, بالمره bi-'l-marrah, کلاً و قاطبةً kullan va kátibatan, کلیتاً kullíyatan, بعینه bi-'ainihi.

QUITTANCE (*discharge*), خط برائت ذمه khatt-i-bará,at-i-zimmah, مفاصای حساب mufasá,í-i-hisáb, فرخطی farkhatí.

QUIVER, ترکش tarkash, کیش kísh, جعبه ja'bah.

To QUIVER, طپیدن tapídan, لرزیدن larzídan, جنبیدن jumbídan.

QUOTATION (*from an author*), عبارت 'ibárat.

To Quote, ایراد نمودن írád nimúdan.
Quotidian, روزینه rúzínah, روزانه rúzánah, یومیه yaumíyah, هر روزه har-rúzah, یوما فیوما yauman fí-yaumin.
Quotient (*in arithmetic*), حاصل hásil, مقسوم maksúm.

R.

Rabbit, خرگوش khar-gúsh.
Rabble (*low people*), الواط alvát, لوطکی lútakí, عوام الناس 'avámmu-'n-nás.
Race (*family*), خاندان khándán, خانواده khánvádah, اصل asl, نسل nasl, نسب nasb, قوم kaum, آل ál, ال ill, نژاد nizhád, دودمان dúdmán, تبار tabár, قبیله kabílah.—(*running match*) شرط shart, مسابقت musábakat.
To Race, دوانیدن davánídan.
Race-course, میدان maidán.
Race-horse, اسب شرط asb-i-shart.
Racing, اسب دوانی asb-daváni.
Rack (*torture*), شکنجه shikanjah.
To Rack, شکنجه کردن shikanjah kardan, در شکنجه نهادن dar shikanjah nihádan.
Racked (*clarified*), مصفی musaffá, مروق muravvak.
Racy, مضحک muzhik, با مزه bá-mazah.
Radiance, نور núr, پرتو partav, تابش tábish.
Radiant, منور munavvar, پر نور pur núr, روشن raushan, منیر munír.
To Radiate, پرتو زدن partav zadan, تشعشع نمودن tasha'shu' nimúdan, تلالع نمودن tala'lu' nimúdan.
Radiation, تشعشع tasha'shu', تلالع tala'lu'.
Radical, اصلی aslí, ذاتی zátí.
Radically, اصلاً aslan.
Radish, تربزه turbizah, فجل fujl.—(*turnip radish*) ترب turb.
Radius (*of a circle*), نصف القطر nisfu-'l-kutr.
To Raffle, باختن bákhtan.
Raft, کلك kalak.
Rafter, چندل chandal, تیر tír, ورگه vargah.
Rag, پینه pínah, لته lattah, پاره párah, رقعه ruk'ah.—(*in rags and tatters*) ژنده پوش zhindah-púsh.—(*rag and bone man*) کهنه خر kuhnah-khar.
Rage, غضب ghazab, غیظ ghaiz, قهر kahr, خشم khishm, تهور tahavvur, حدت hiddat.
To Rage, رنجیدن ranjídan, آشوبیدن áshúbídan, نا راضی شدن ná-rází shudan, غضبناك شدن ghazab-nák shudan, تغضب نمودن taghazzub nimúdan, آشفتن áshuftan.—(*be prevalent*) مستولی شدن mustaulí shudan.
Ragged, دریده darídah, مرقع murakka', خلقان khulkán, پاره پاره párah-párah.
Raging (*animal*), ژیان zhiyán.
To Rail at, دشنام دادن dushnám dádan, دشنامیدن dushnámídan, طعنه زدن ta'nah zadan, سب نمودن sabb nimúdan, زباندرازی کردن zabán-dirází kardan.
Railer, سخره sukharah.
Railing (*balustrade, or fence of rails*), پنجره panjarah, معجر ma'jar.—(*round a tomb*) مقصوره maksúrah, ضریح zaríh.—(*hand railing*) دست انداز dast-andáz.—(*iron railings*) دیوار در آهنی dívár dar áhaní.
Raillery, هجو hajv, هجا hijá, مزاح mazáh, استهزا istihzá, طنز tanz, جفنگ jafang.
Railroad, راه آهن ráh-i-áhan.
Railway carriage, کالسکه بخار káliskah-i-bukhár, واگون vágún (*eur.*).
Raiment, جامه jámah, رخت rakht, پوشاك púshák, پوشش púshish, لباس libás, پوشن púshan, زی zí.

RAIN, باران bárán, بارش bárish, مطر matr. — (*untimely rain*) باران خمینه bárán-i-khamínah. — (*slight rain*) ترشح tarashshuh.— —(*want of rain*) انقطاع مطر inkitá'-i-matr. — (*threatening to rain*) مستعد باران musta'idd-i-bárán.— (*rains*) میاه miyáh.—(*heavy rain*) باران شدید bárán-i-shadíd.

To RAIN, باریدن barídan.

RAINBOW, قوس قزح kaus-i-kuzah, قوس القزح kausu-'l-kuzah, شمشیر علی shimshír-i-'alí.

RAINY, بارانی báráni.

To RAISE (*lift*), بر داشتن bar-dáshtan, افراختن afrákhtan, افراشتن afráshtan, بالا کردن bálá kardan. —(*excite*) انگیختن angíkhtan, تحریک نمودن tahrík nimúdan, خیزانیدن khízánídan.—(*an army, &c.*) جمع آوری کردن jam'-ávarí kardan. — (*plants*) عمل آوردن 'amal ávardan.—(*curtains, blinds, &c.*) بلند کردن buland kardan.— (*to raise oneself*) خودرا بلند کردن khwudrá buland kardan.

RAISINS, مویز maviz. — (*Sultana raisins*) کشمش kishmish.

RAKE, خاک کش khák-kash, اوسی ausí, اوچوم auchúm. — (*profligate*) رند rind, قلاش kallásh, اوباش aubásh, خراباتی kharábátí, زانی zání, شید باز shaid-báz, خوش گذران khwush-guzrán.

To RAKE, تراشیدن tiráshídan, تراش کردن tirásh kardan, رندیدن randídan, خاریدن khárídan.

RAKISH, بد کار bad-kár, شید باز shaid-báz.

To RALLY (*trans.*), جمع کردن jam' kardan. — (*intrans.*) جمع یافتن jam' yáftan.

RAM, غوچ ghúch, قوچ kúch.—(*of goats*), بزتکه buz-i-takkah.

To RAM, کوبیدن kúbídan, آکندن ákandan.

RAMBLE, تفرج tafarruj, گردش gardish.

To RAMBLE, گردیدن gardídan, سیر کردن sair kardan, گشت کردن gasht kardan.

RAMBLER, گردش کننده gardish-kunandah.

RAMBLING, گردش gardish.—(*incoherent*) درهم برهم darham-barham.

RAMIFICATION, شعبه shu'bah, تشعب tasha''ub.

To RAMIFY, منشعب شدن munsha'ib shudan.

RAMPARTS, بارو bárú, باره bárah, حصار hisár.

RAMROD (*of a gun*), سنبه sumbah, میل míl.

RANCID, ترش tursh.

RANCIDNESS, ترشی turshí.

RANCOUR, عداوت 'adávat, کین kín, کینه kínah, حقد hikd.

RANDOM (*chance*), عارضه 'árizah, قضا kazá.—(*at random*) بی مقصود bímaksúd, غافلانه ghafilánah, ولکی vilikí (*vulg.*).—(*to talk at random*) نا مربوط گفتن ná-marbút guftan.

RANGE (*row*), ردیف radíf, قطار kitár, رده radah.—(*of shot*) پرتاب partáb.

To RANGE, منظم کردن munazzam kardan, مرتب داشتن murattab dáshtan.—(*to range in battle*) مصافت نمودن musáffat nimúdan.

RANGED, مرتب murattab, منسوق mansúk.—(*to form ranks*) صف آرای نمودن saff-áráí nimúdan.

RANK (*line*), صف saff, قطار kitár, سلك silk, سلسله silsilah, ردیف radíf, رده radah. — (*degree*) قدر kadr, مقدار mikdár, مرتبه martabah, مثابه masábah, اندازه andázah, حد hadd, مقابله mukábalah, درجه darajah.—(*army*) عهده 'uhdah, منصب mansab.

To RANKLE, خلیدن khalídan.

To RANSACK, تاراج کردن táráj kardan, نهب نمودن nahb nimúdan.

RANSOM, فدا fidá, فدیه fidyah, تصدق tasadduk, نعلبندی na'l-bandí.

To RANSOM, فدا نمودن fidá nimúdan, فدیه نمودن fidyah nimúdan. —(*money paid to redeem from prison, servitude, &c.*) وجه آزادی vajh-i-ázádí, فدیه fidyah.

To RANT, غوغا کردن ghaughá kardan, داد زدن dád zadan.
RANUNCULUS, گل رعنازیبا gul-i-ra'ná-zíbá.
RAP, دستک dastak, سیلی sílí.
To RAP (*at a door*), در زدن dar zadan, دق الباب کردن daku-'l-báb kardan.
RAPACIOUS (*animal*), درنده darandah, ژیان zhiyán. — (*ravenous*) مفترس muftaris, اکول akúl. — (*greedy*) حریص harís, طمعکار tama'-kár, آرزومند árzú-mand, شائق shá,ik.
RAPACITY, درندگی darandagí.—(*greed*) حرص hirs, طمع tama', طمعکاری tama'-kárí, آز áz, بخل bukhl, خسیست khasísat, خست khissat, امساک imsák.
RAPE, زنا ziná, پرده دری pardah-darí, هتک عرض hatk-i-'irz.
To RAPE, بی عصمت کردن bí-'asmat kardan, مفتضح کردن muftazah kardan, بکارت بردن bikárat burdan, بزور زنا کردن bi-zúr ziná kardan, بی سیرت کردن bí-sírat kardan, ربودن rubúdan, هتک عرض کردن hatk-i-'irz kardan.
RAPE-SEED, راپه rápah (*eur.*).
RAPID, تند tund, تند رو tund-rau, زود zúd, سریع sarí'.—(*waterfall*) آب شار áb-shár.
RAPIDITY, زودی zúdí, تندی tundí, سرعت sur'at, تعجیل ta'jíl.
RAPIDLY, به تعجیل bi-ta'jíl, بسرعت bi-sur'at.
RAPIER, گزلک gazlak.
RAPINE (*plunder*) چپاو chapáw, غارت ghárat, تاراج táráj, نهب nahb, راهزنی ráh-zaní, ترک تازی turk-i-tází. — (*robbery*) دزدی duzdí.
RAPTURE, وجد vajd, شعف sha'af, خوشی khwushí.
RAPTUROUS, خوشحال khwush-hál.
RARE, نادر nádir, کم یاب kam-yáb, طرفه turfah (*precious*) عزیز 'azíz, نفیس nafís, ارجمند arjmand, قیمتی kaimatí, ثمین samín, فاخر fákhir, گران girán, گرانبها girán-bahá, گرانمایه girán-máyah.

RARELY, ندرةً nudratan, کمتر kamtar, کم kam, نادراً nádiran.
RARIFACTION, ترقیق tarkík.
To RARIFY, ترقیق نمودن tarkík nimúdan.
RARITY, نادری nádirí, ندرت nudrat. —(*rarities*) بدایع badáí', نفایس nafáís, نوادر navádir
RASCAL, فریبنده firíbandah, سر همبند sar-ham-band, دستکج dast-kaj, اوباش aubásh, حیله باز hílah-báz, نا بکار ná-bi-kár, غدار ghaddár, مکار makkár, نا درست ná-durust, قلابی kullábí, حیله ور hílah-var, دولابی dúlábí, دولابباز dúláb-báz.
RASCALITY, حیله بازی hílah-bází, نا درستی ná-durustí, دولاببازی dúláb-bází.
RASCALLY, بد bad, زشت zisht, اوباشانه aubáshánah.
RASH, دستپاچه dast-páchah, بی تدبیر bí-tadbír, متهور mutahavvir, گستاخ gustákh, جسور jasúr.—(*eruption*) دانه dánah, آبله ábilah, اوله aulah (*vulg.*).
RASHLY, گستاخانه gustákhánah, از سر انگشت az sar-i-angusht, غافلانه gháfilánah, عجلتاً 'ajalatan.
RASHNESS, گستاخی gustákhí, تهور tahavvur.
RASP, سوهان súhán.
To RASP, سوهان کردن súhán kardan.
RASPBERRY, گیهه gíhah. — (*bush*) درخت گیهه dirakht-i-gíhah.
RAT, موش músh.
RATE (*proportion*), اندازه andázah, حسب hasb, ازا izá,, قدر kadr, وفق vafk, قرار karár.—(*at the rate of*) بر وفق bar vafk, از قرار az karár, بازاء bi-izá,, بقدر bi-kadr.—(*at any rate*) در بهرحال dar bi-har hál.
To RATE, قیمت کردن kaimat kardan, اندازه نمودن andázah nimúdan, سنجیدن sanjídan.—(*chide*) سنجیدن sanjídan, نشان دادن nishán dádan.
RATHER, بیشتر bíshtar, اولاً avvalan.
RATIFICATION, تصدیق tasdík, قرار دار karár-dár, درستی durustí.

RATIFIED, قرار دار karár-dár.
To RATIFY, تصدیق نمودن tasdík nimúdan, درست کردن durust kardan.
RATIO, مقدار mikdár.
RATIONAL (*endowed with reason*), ناطق nátik. — (*judicious*) *vide* SENSIBLE).
RATIONALITY, سنجیدگی sanjídagí.
RATIONS (*daily allowance of provisions*), آذوقهٔ روزینه ázúkah-i-rúzínah, جیره jírah.
RATTAN, خیزران khaizurán.
RATTLE, چخچخی chakhchakhí, جنگجنگک jingjingak.
To RATTLE, صدای چخچخی کردن sadá,í - i - chakhchakhí kardan, صدا کردن sadá kardan.
RAVAGE, چپاو chapáw, غارت ghárat, تاراج táráj, نهب nahb, راهزنی ráhzaní, ترك تازی turk-i-tází.
To RAVAGE, چپاو کردن chapáw kardan, غارت کردن ghárat kardan, یغما کردن yaghmá kardan, سلب گرفتن salab giriftan, تاراج نمودن táráj nimúdan, نهب کردن nahb kardan, چپاولی کردن chapávalí kardan (*vulg.*).
RAVAGER, غارت کننده ghárat-kunandah, یغما چی yaghmá-chí.
To RAVE, شوریدگی کردن shúrídagí kardan, هذیان گفتن hazayán guftan, بیهوده حرف زدن bíhúdah harf zadan.
RAVELLED, پیچاپیچ pích-á-pích, بر هم زده bar-ham zadah, در هم dar-ham, ژولیده zhúlídah, پیچیده píchídah.
RAVEN, غراب ghuráb.
RAVENOUS, مفترس muftaris, اکول akúl. — (*animal*) جارحه járihah, درنده darandah.
RAVINE (*deep pass or hollow*), تنگ tang, کتل kutal, شعب sha'b, جای سراشیب já,í-i-saráshíb, جای پرت já,í-i-part, جای نشیب já,í-i-nishíb.
RAVING (*subs.*), شوریدگی shúrídagí, هذیان hazayán. — (*adj.*) شوریده shúrídah, پریشان paríshán.
To RAVISH, بی عصمت کردن bí-'asmat kardan, مفتضح کردن muftazah kardan, بکارت بردن bikárat burdan, بزور زنا کردن bi-zúr ziná kardan, بی سیرت کردن bí-sírat kardan, ربودن rubúdan, هتك عرض کردن hatk-i-'irz kardan.
RAVISHER, رباینده rubáyandah.—(*of women*) هتاك hatták, فاسخ fásikh.
RAVISHING, دلربا dil-rubá, دلاویز dil-áviz دلبر dil-bar, دلستان dil-sitán.
RAW, خام khám.
RAWNESS, خامی khámí.
RAY (*of light*), پرتو partav *or* partau, شعاع shu'á', لمعه lam'ah.
To RAZE, منهدم کردن munhadim kardan, خراب کردن kharáb kardan.
RAZOR, تیغ دلاکی tígh-i-dallákí, موس mús, موسی músá, استره usturah (*obs.*).
REACH, دست رس dast-ras.—(*out of reach*) دور دست dúr-dast.
To REACH, رسیدن rasídan, پیوسته شدن paivastah shudan, وصل کردن vasl kardan, واصل شدن vásil shudan, ملحق شدن mulhik shudan. —(*with the hand*) دست رسانیدن dast rasánídan, دست بردن dast burdan.
REACTION, انعکاس عمل in'ikás-i-'amal.
To READ, خواندن khwándan, مطالعه کردن mutála'ah kardan.
READER, خواننده khwánandah.—(*for the press*) مصحح musahhih.
READILY, قلباً kalban, از صمیم قلب az samím-i-kalb.
READINESS, آمادگی ámádagí.
READING, درس dars, مطالعه mutála'ah. — (*reading for the press*) تصحیح tashíh.
RE-ADMISSION, رجوع rujú', باز قبولی báz-kabúlí.
To RE-ADMIT, رجوع دادن rujú' dádan, باز قبول نمودن báz-kabúl nimúdan.
READY, حاضر házir, آماده ámádah, مهیا muhayyá, درست durust, تیار tayyár, موجود maujúd, مستعد

musta'idd, رو براه rú-bi-ráh.—(*ready money*) نقد nakd, پول púl.—(*ready made*) آماده ámádah.—(*to make ready*) ترتیب داشتن tarat-tub dáshtan, مهیا کردن muhayyá kardan.—(*to be ready*) مستعد شدن musta'idd shudan.

REAL, حقیقی hakíkí, راست rást, عینی 'ainí, صحیح sahíh, ذاتی zátí, واقعی váki'í.

To REALISE, محقق ساختن muhak-kak sákhtan. — (*money, &c.*) نقد ساختن nakd sákhtan, مضبوط ساختن mazbút sákhtan.—(*to be realised*) بظهور آمدن bi-zuhúr ámadan, صورت پذیر شدن súrat-pazír shudan.

REALITY, معنی ma'ní.—(*in reality*) تحقیق tahkík, یقیناً yakínan, فی الواقع fi-'l-váki', آری árí, فی الحقیقت fi-'l-hakíkat, واقعاً váki'an, انصافاً insáfan.

REALLY, تحقیق tahkík, یقیناً yakí-nan, فی الواقع fi-'l-váki', آری árí, فی الحقیقت fi-'l-hakíkat, واقعاً váki'an, انصافاً insáfan.

REALM, مملکت mamlakat, سلطنت sultanat, دولت daulat.

REAM, بسته bastah.

To RE-ANIMATE, باز زنده ساختن báz zindah sákhtan.

To RE-ANNEX, باز الحاق کردن báz ilhák kardan.

To REAP, درویدن diravídan, درو کردن dirau kardan, حصاد کردن hasád kardan.

REAPER, درو گر dirau-gar, درونده diravandah, حصاد hassád.

REAPING-HOOK, داس dás, داز dáz.

REAPING-MACHINE, اسباب درو کری asbáb-i-dirau-karí.

To RE-APPOINT, باز نصب کردن báz nasb kardan.

REAR, پس pas, عقب 'akab, دنبال dumbál.—(*of an army*) عقب سپاه 'akab-i-sipáh, چنداول chandával, پسرو pas-rau.—(*in the rear of*) از عقب az 'akab.

To REAR, پروردن parvardan, تربیت نمودن tarbiyat nimúdan, حضانت نمودن hizánat nimúdan.—(*as a horse*) سیخپا شدن síkh-pá shudan, چراغپا شدن chirágh-pá shudan, سر دو پا ایستادن sar-i-dú-pá ístádan.

To RE-ARRANGE, پس و پیش کردن pas va písh kardan.

To RE-ASCEND, باز بالا رفتن báz bálá raftan.

REASON (*faculty*), نطق nutk, عقل 'akl, ادراک ídrák, خرد khirad, قوت ناطقه kúvat - i - nátikah.—(*cause*) سبب sabab, موجب mújib, واسطه vásitah, وصیله vasílah, وسیله vasílah, جهت jihat, باعث bá'is.—(*by reason that*) برای اینکه baráy-i-án-kih, بهر bahr, از روی az rúy.—(*without reason*), بیمعنی bí-ma'ní.—(*for which reason*) من حیث min hays, از این سبب az ín sabab.

To REASON, بحث کردن bahs kardan, منازره کردن munázarah kardan.

REASONABLE, عقلمند 'akl - mand, درست durust, معقول ma'kúl.

REASONABLENESS, معقولیه ma'kúlí-yah.

REASONABLY, عقلانه 'aklánah.

To RE-ASSEMBLE (*trans.*), باز فراهم آوردن báz faráham ávardan, باز جمع کردن báz jam' kardan.—(*intrans.*) باز فراهم آمدن báz fará-ham ámadan, باز جمع شدن báz jam' shudan. — (*Court*) باز اجلاس کردن báz ijlás kardan.

To RE-ASSUME, باز گرفتن báz giriftan.

To REBATE, کم کردن kam kardan, کوچك کردن kúchik kardan, تخفیف نمودن takhfíf nimúdan.

REBEL, یاغی yághí, باغی bághí, عاصی 'ásí, طاغی tághí, گردن کش gardan-kash, مفسد mufsid, منحرف mun-harif, سر کش sar-kash, متمرد mu-tamarrid.

To REBEL, عصیان نمودن 'isyán ni-múdan, عاصی شدن 'ásí shudan, طغی کردن taghí kardan, یاغی شدن yághí shudan.

REBELLION, یاغیگری yághí - garí, بغی baghí, بغاوت baghávat, طغیان tughyán, سر کشی sar - kashí, گردنکشی gardan-kashí, فتنه fit-nah, انحراف inhiráf, فساد fasád, عناد 'inád, اغتشاش ightishásh, بلوا balvá.

Rebellious, سر کش sar-kash, گردنکش gardan-kash, طاغی tághí, عاصی 'ásí.

Rebound, نبوت nabvat, جستگی jastagí.

To Rebound, باز جستن báz jastan.

Rebuff, دفع daf'.

To Rebuff, مندفع نمودن mundafí' nimúdan.

To Rebuild, تعمیر نمودن ta'mír nimúdan, اصلاح ساختن isláh sákhtan.

Rebuke, سر زنش sar-zanish, زجر zajr, ملامت malámat, توبیخ taubíkh, نهیب nihíb, شتم shatm, ذم zamm, طعنه ta'nah, پیغاره paighárah, موٴاخذه mu,ákhazah.

To Rebuke, سر زنش نمودن sarzanish nimúdan, زجر نمودن zajr nimúdan.

To Recall (*dismiss*), معزول کردن ma'zúl kardan.

To Recede, *vide* To Retire.—(*cede back*) گذاشت نمودن guzásht nimúdan, وا گذاشتن vá-guzáshtan, تسلیم نمودن taslím nimúdan, حواله نمودن haválah nimúdan.

Receipt, رسید rasíd, داخله dákhilah. —(*prescription*) نسخه nuskhah. —(*written acknowledgment*) قبض kabz, قبض رسید kabz-i-rasíd, باز یافت báz-yáft.—(*receipts and disbursements*) جمع و خرج jam' va kharj, اخذ و مصرف akhz va masraf, مداخل و مخارج madákhil va makhárij.

Receivable, یافتنی yáftaní.

To Receive, گرفتن giriftan, اخذ کردن akhz kardan, حاصل کردن hásil kardan, پذیرفتن pazíruftan.—(*accept*) قبول کردن kabúl kardan, اجابت نمودن ijábat nimúdan.

Receiver (*collector*), تحصیلدار tahsíl-dár.—(*receiver of stolen goods*) شریك دزد sharík-i-duzd.

Recent, نو nau, تازه tázah.

Recently, جدیدا jadídan.

Receptacle, کفات kifát, جا já.

Reception, پذیرائی pazírá,í, قبول kabúl.—(*of doctrine, &c.*) تلقی talakkí.—(*evening reception*) شب نشینی shab-nishíní.—(*reception-room*) اطاق پذیرائی uták-i-pazírá,í, اطاق مجلس uták-i-majlis, دیوانخانه díván-khánah.

Recess (*nook*), گوشه gúshah, منفذ manfaz, خلل khalal.

Recipe, نسخه nuskhah.

Recipient, گیرنده gírandah.

Reciprocal, از طرفین az tarafain, از جانبین az jánibain, همدیگر hamdígar, یکدگر yak-digar.

Reciprocally, بالمفاوضه bi-'l-mufávazah.

To Reciprocate, از جانبین دادن az jánibain dádan.

Reciprocity, مفاوضه mufávazah.

Recitation, خواندگی khwándagí, قرائت kara,at, نشید nashíd, ذکر zikr, مذاکره muzákarah.

To Recite, خواندن khwándan.

Reckless, بیخبر bí-khabar, غافل ghâfil, بیپروا bí-parvá, بی احتیاط bí-ihtiyát, بی اندیشه bí-andíshah, کاهل káhil, بیهوش bí-húsh, زاهل záhil, بی مبالات bí-mubálát, لاقید lá-kaid.

To Reckon, شمردن shimurdan, حساب کردن hisáb kardan, تعداد نمودن ti'dád nimúdan, بر آورد کردن bar-ávard kardan. (*Vide* To Think, To Count.)

Reckoning, حساب hisáb, شمار shimár.

To Reclaim, اصلاح نمودن isláh nimúdan, تصحیح نمودن tashíh nimúdan.

Reclamation, استرداد istirdád.

To Recline, تکیه زدن takyah zadan, اتکا نمودن ittiká nimúdan, خوابیدن khwábídan, استراحت کردن istiráhat kardan.

Recluse, گوشه نشین gúshah-nishín, تنها نشین tanhá-nishín, ابدال abdál.

Recognition, شناخت shinákht.

Recognizance, اعتراف نامه i'tiráf-námah.

To Recognize, تشخیص دادن tashkhís dádan, باز شناختن báz-shinákhtan, دانستن dánistan.

To Recoil, *vide* To Shrink.

To Recollect, *vide* To Remember.

Recollection, یاد yád, حفظ hifz, ذکر zikr, خاطر khátir.

To Recommence, باز شروع کردن báz shurú' kardan.

To Recommend, سپارش کردن sipárish kardan, سفارش نمودن sifárish nimúdan.

Recommendation, سفارش sifárish, وسیله vasílah.—(*letter of recommendation*) سفارشنامه sifárish-námah, اعتبار نامچه i'tibár-námchah.

Recompense, عوض 'avaz, جزا jazá, پاداش pádásh, مکافات mukáfát, مثوبه masúbah, مزد muzd, اجر ajr, سزا sizá, تلافی taláfí.

To Recompense, مکافات کردن mukáfát kardan, اجر بخشیدن ajr bakhshídan.

Reconcilable, صلاح پذیر saláh-pazír.

To Reconcile, مصالحه نمودن musálahah nimúdan, آشتی کردن áshtí kardan.

Reconciler, مصلح muslih.

Reconciliation, صلح sulh, صلاح saláh, آشتی áshtí, التیام iltiyám, مصالحه musálahah.

Reconnaissance, کشفیات kashfíyát, جاسوسی jásúsí.

To Reconnoitre, کشفیات نمودن kashfíyát nimúdan.

To Record, ثبت کردن sabt kardan, نوشتن nivishtan.

Recorder, دفتر نویس daftar-nivís.

Records, دفتر daftar, دستک dastak.

To Recount, تقریر نمودن takrír nimúdan, گفتن guftan.

Recourse, مراجعت murája'at, توسل tavassul, رجوع rujú', التجا iltijá.—(*to have recourse to*) توسل نمودن tavassul nimúdan, رجوع کردن rujú' kardan, التجا نمودن iltijá nimúdan.

To Recover (*find*), باز یافتن báz yáftan. — (*in health*) شفا یافتن shifá yáftan, صحت یافتن sihhat yáftan, افاقه یافتن ifákah yáftan, به شدن bih shudan.

Recoverable, قابل تحصیل kábil-i-tahsíl.

Recovery, استرداد istirdád.—(*health*) شفا shifá, افاقه ifákah.

Recreant, نا مرد ná-mard, بز دل buz-dil, جبان jabbán, بیدل bí-dil, کمدل kam-dil, ترسو tarsú (*vulg.*).

Recreation, تفرج tafarruj, فرح farah, نزهت nuzhat, گشت gasht, صفا safá.—(*place of recreation*) جائی تعیش já,í-i-ta'ayyush.

To Recriminate, سر زنش کردن sarzanish kardan, ملامت نمودن malámat nimúdan, توبیخ نمودن taubíkh nimúdan.

Recrimination, سر زنش sar-zanish, ملامت malámat, توبیخ taubíkh.

Recruit (*new soldier*), جدید jadíd.

To Recruit (*levy soldiers*), جمع آوری کردن jam'-ávarí kardan.—(*health*) شفا یافتن shifá yáftan, صحت یافتن sihhat yáftan, افاقه یافتن ifákah yáftan, به شدن bih shudan.

Rectangular, قائم الزوایا ká,imu-'z-zaváyá.

Rectifiable, تصحیح پذیر tashíh-pazír.

Rectification, تصحیح tashíh, تعدیل ta'díl.

Rectifier, درست کننده durust-kunandah.—(*of spirits*) تصفیه کننده tasfiyah-kunandah.

To Rectify, راست ساختن rást sákhtan. — (*spirits*) تصفیه کردن tasfiyah kardan.

Rectitude, سداد sadád, صلاح saláh, صلاحیت saláhíyat, صواب saváb, صدق sidk, صداقت sadákat, راستی rástí, رشد rushd, دیانت diyánat.

To Recur, یاد آمدن yád ámadan. —(*occur*) واقع شدن váki' shudan, اتفاق افتادن ittifák uftádan, بظهور رسیدن bi-zuhúr rasídan, وارد شدن várid shudan.

Recurrence, مراجعت murája'at.

Recurrent, رجوع rujú'.

Red, سرخ surkh, احمر ahmar, قرمزی kirmizí.—(*red ink*) سرنج suranj, شنجرف shanjarf.—(*Society of the Red Crescent*) جمعیت هلال احمر

jam'íyat-i-hilál-i-ahmar.—(*Society of the Red Cross*) جمعیت صلیب احمر jam'íyat-i-salíb-i-ahmar.

To REDDEN, سرخ کردن surkh kardan.

REDDISH, مائل بسرخی má,il bi-surkhí.

To REDEEM, وا خریدن vá-kharídan, باز خریدن báz-kharídan, فدا کردن fidá kardan.—(*to redeem one's word*) وفا کردن vafá kardan.

REDEEMER, رهانندہ rihánandah, نجات دهندہ naját-dihandah.

To RE-DELIVER, باز تسلیم نمودن báz taslím nimúdan, باز حواله نمودن báz haválah nimúdan, باز سپردن báz sipurdan.—(*set free*) باز آزاد کردن báz ázád kardan, باز رهانیدن báz rihánídan, باز خلاص کردن báz khalás kardan.

REDEMPTION, فدیه fidyah, فدا fidá, رها rihá, رهائی rihá,í.

RED-HOT, تابیدہ شدہ tábídah-shudah, سرخ surkh.

RED-LEAD, شنگرف shangarf, سرنج suranj, زنجفره zinjifrah.

REDNESS, سرخی surkhí, احمرار ihmirár.

REDOLENCE, عطر 'itr, خوشبوی khwush-búí.

REDOLENT, معطر mu'attar, مشموم mashmúm.

To REDOUBLE, دو چندان کردن dú-chandán kardan, دو چندان شدن dú chandán shudan.

REDOUBT, قلعه kal'ah, ارك ark, حصار hisár, حصن hisn.

REDOUBTABLE, هول haul, هولناك haul-nák, مهیب mahíb.

REDRESS, تظلم tazallum, چارہ chárah.

To REDRESS, راست ساختن rást sákhtan.

To REDUCE (*conquer*), فتح کردن fath kardan, غلبه کردن ghalabah kardan, شکست دادن shikast dádan, ظفر یافتن zafar yáftan, گشادن gushádan, نصرت یافتن nusrat yáftan, فیروز شدن fírúz shudan, غالب آمدن ghálib ámadan.—(*lessen*) کم کردن kam kardan, کوچك کردن kúchik kardan, تخفیف نمودن takhfíf nimúdan.

REDUCIBLE, قابل تخفیف kábil-i-takhfíf.

REDUCTION, رعایت ri'áyat, کمی kamí.—(*arithmetical*) تحویل tahtahvíl.

REDUNDANCE, افراط ifrát, افزونی afzúní, کثرت kasrat, نهایت niháyat, زیادتی ziyádatí.

REDUNDANT, مزید mazíd, زیاد ziyád.

REED, نی nay, نای náy, قصب kasab.—(*for pens*) قلم kalam, کلك kilk, خامه khámah.—(*flag, rush*) پیزر pízur, چگن chagan, هردی hurdí, لخ lukh.—(*reed-bed or reedy place*) نیزار nay-zár, نیستان nay-istán.

To REEK, دود نمودن dúd nimúdan.

REEL (*for thread*), پیلی pílí, پیله pílah, پره pirrah.

To REEL (*totter*), یله رفتن yalah raftan, یله شدن yalah shudan, افتان و خیزان بودن uftán va khízán búdan.

To RE-ENTER, باز آمدن báz ámadan.

To RE-ESTABLISH, باز اثبات نمودن báz isbát nimúdan, باز وضع کردن báz vaz' kardan.—(*health*) تصحیح نمودن tashíh nimúdan.

RE-ESTABLISHMENT (*of health*), تصحیح tashíh, افاقه ifákah.

To REFER to, رجوع کردن rujú' kardan, حوالت کردن haválat kardan.—(*allude*) کنایه کردن kináyah kardan, اشارہ نمودن ishárah nimúdan.

REFERENCE, مراجعت murája'at. (*Vide* RELATION.)—(*official term*) مرجوعه marjú'ah (*pl.* مرجوعات marjú'át).—(*with reference to*) بالنسبه به bi-'n-nisbah bi, نظر به nazar bi, در باب dar báb, در خصوص dar khusús.

To REFINE (*clarify*), صاف کردن sáf kardan, تصفیه نمودن tasfiyah nimúdan.—(*metals, to smelt*) قال کردن kál kardan, قال گذاشتن kál guzáshtan.

REFINED (*clarified*), مصفی musaffá, صاف sáf, پاك pák, مزکی muzakká

—(*polite*) ادیب adíb, مؤدب mu,-addab, خلیق khalík, خوش اطوار khwush - atvár, خوش اخلاق khwush-akhlák.
REFINEMENT, صفائی safá,í.—(*politeness*) ادب adab, مردمی mardumí, تربیت tarbiyat.
REFINER (*of metals, smelter*), قالگر kál-gar, قالکن kál-kun, مصفی کننده musaffá-kunandah.
To REFLECT, عکس نمودن 'aks nimúdan, انعکاس کردن in'ikás kardan. (*Vide* To THINK.)
REFLECTED, منعکس muna'kis.
REFLECTION, عکس 'aks, انعکاس in'ikás. (*Vide* THOUGHT.)
REFLECTIVE, عکس انداز 'aks-andáz. —(*man*) متخیل mutakhayyil.
REFLECTOR, عکس انداز 'aks-andáz.
REFLEX (*subs.*), انقلاب inkiláb.—(*adj.*) منقلب munkalib.
REFLUX, جزر jazr.
REFORM, اصلاح isláh, تصحیح tashíh.
To REFORM, اصلاح نمودن isláh nimúdan, تصحیح نمودن tashíh nimúdan.
REFORMATION, اصلاح isláh, تصحیح tashíh.
REFORMER, مصلح muslih.
To REFRACT, انحراف نمودن inhiráf nimúdan.
REFRACTION, انحراف inhiráf.—(*of a ray of light*) انحراف شعاع inhiráf-i-shu'á'. — (*refracted ray*) شعاع منحرف shu'á'-i-munharif.
REFRACTIVE, قابل انحراف kábil-i-inhiráf.
REFRACTORINESS, عناد 'inád, بغاوت bagháwat, تمرد tamarrud.
REFRACTORY, معاند mu'ánid, عصی 'así, گردن کش gardan-kash, یاغی yághí.
REFRAIN (*of a song*) زمین zamín, زمینه zamínah.
To REFRAIN, باز ایستادن báz-ístádan, خودرا باز داشتن khwudrá báz-dáshtan, پرهیز کردن parhíz kardan, احتراز نمودن ihtiráz nimúdan, اجتناب ورزیدن ijtináb varzídan, وا ایستادن vá-ístádan.
To REFRESH, تازه ساختن tázah sákhtan.
REFRESHMENT, آسایش ásáyish, راحت ráhat, تازگی tázagí.—(*food*) اکل akl, غذا ghizá, طعام ta'ám, خوراک khwurák.—(*to take refreshment*) میل فرمودن mail firmúdan.
To REFRIGERATE, سرد کردن sard kardan.
REFRIGERATION, سرما sarmá, برد bard.
REFRIGERATOR, یخ چال yakh-chál.
REFUGE (*asylum*), پناه panáh, امن aman, مأمن ma,man, ملاذ maláz, ملجا maljá, عیاذ 'iyáz, مفر mafarr, بست bast.—(*to seek refuge*) ملتجی شدن multají shudan, بست گرفتن bast giriftan, التجا نمودن iltijá nimúdan.
REFUGEE, مهاجر muhájir.
REFULGENCE, روشنی raushaní, نور núr, تابش tábish, روشنائی raushaná,í, نورانی núrání, نیر nayyir, تجلی tajallí, جلوه jilvah, ضیا ziyá, فروغ furúgh.
REFULGENT, روشن raushan, منور munavvar, منیر munír, جوهر دار jauhar-dár, لامع lámi', جلی jalí, درخشان dirakhshán, تابان tábán, تابدار táb-dár, رخشان rukhshán.
To REFUND, استرداد نمودن istirdád nimúdan, وا دادن vá-dádan, باز دادن báz dádan.
REFUSAL, انکار inkár, دریغ dirígh, نفی nafy.
REFUSE (*leavings, dregs*), فضله fazlah, سفل sifl, درد durd, پس مانده pas-mándah.
To REFUSE, رد کردن radd kardan, ابا نمودن ibá nimúdan, نا پسند کردن ná-pasand kardan, حاشا کردن háshá kardan, نفی کردن nafy kardan, امتناع نمودن imtiná' nimúdan, دریغ کردن dirígh kardan.
REFUSER, منکر munkir.
REFUTATION, رد کلام radd-i-kalám, جرح jarh.
To REFUTE, رد کلام نمودن radd-i-kalám nimúdan, ردیه کردن radíyah kardan, جرح کردن jarh kardan.
REFUTED, رد radd, مردود mardúd.
To REGAIN, باز یافتن báz yáftan, باز

باز حاصل کردن báz hásil kardan, باز پیدا کردن báz paidá kardan.

REGAL, شاهوار sháh-vár.

To REGALE, مهمانی نمودن mihmání nimúdan.

REGALIA, دیهیم سلطنت dayhím-i-sultanat.

REGALITY, سلطنت sultanat, پادشاهت pádisháhat.

REGARD, حب hubb, مهر mihr, الفت ulfat, اخلاص ikhlás, التفات iltifát, اعزاز i'záz, احترام ihtirám.—(*reference to*) نسبت nisbat, دخل dakhl, علاقه 'alákah.—(*regarding, respecting*) نسبت به nisbat bi, در خصوص dar khusús, در باره dar bárah, در باب dar báb, در حق dar hakk.

To REGARD, نظر نمودن nazar nimúdan, دیدن dídan, نگرستن nigaristan, نگریستن nigarístan.—(*esteem*) محترم داشتن muhtaram dáshtan, مکرم داشتن mukarram dáshtan, معزز داشتن mu'azzaz dáshtan, احترام کردن ihtirám kardan.

REGARDFUL, خبردار khabar-dár, آگاه ágáh.

REGARDLESS, غافل ghákil, بیپروا bí-parvá, بی توجه bí-tavajjuh.

REGENCY (*government*), حکومت hukúmat, ایالت iyálat.—(*district*) حکومت hukúmat.—(*body of men*) مجلس نائب السلطنت majlis-i-ná,ibu-'s-sultanat.

To REGENERATE, از نو تولید نمودن az nau taulíd nimúdan.

REGENERATION, تولد نو tavallud-i-nau, تولد ثانی tavallud-i-sání, میلاد تازه mílád-i-tázah.

REGENT, نائب السلطنت ná,ibu-'s-sultanat.

REGICIDE, سلطان کشی sultán-kushí.

REGIME, اداره idárah.

REGIMEN, تدبیر غذا tadbír-i-ghizá.

REGIMENT, فوج fauj. [A Persian regiment of foot consists of one thousand men, namely: eight hundred سرباز sarbáz (private soldiers); one hundred and fifty-nine صاحب منصب sáhib-mansab (officers); and forty-one نقارچی nakkár-chí *or* طبلچی tabal-chí (drummers), شیپور چی shaifúr-chí (buglers), نیچی nay-chí (fifers), &c., belonging to the band; سرتیپ sartíp (colonel, commands two regiments); سرهنگ sarhang (lieutenant-colonel, commands one regiment); یاور yávar (major, of whom there are two to every regiment). The regiment is divided into ten دسته dastah (companies); and to each دسته dastah there are one سلطان sultán (captain), two نائب ná,ib (lieutenants), two بیگزاده beg-zádah (officers who look after the men), four وکیل vakíl (sergeants), four سر جوقه sar-jaukah (corporals). Each regiment has besides: a مشرف mushrif (head accountant), تحویلدار tahvíl-dár (cash-keeper), and five other accountants, علمدار 'alam-dár *or* بیرقدار bairak-dár (standard-bearers), وکیل باشی vakíl-báshí (sergeants major), اجودان ajúdán (adjutant). The غلام سواره ghulám-i-suvárah (cavalry) are divided into هزاره hazárah (regiments), commanded by سرتیپ sartíp (colonel) and سر کرده sar-kardah (lieutenant-colonel), assisted by سلطان sultán, نائب ná,ib, وکیل vakíl, یاور yávar, &c., as above; and some have a یوز باشی yúz-báshí (centurion) to every hundred men, a پنجاه باشی panjáh-báshí to every fifty, and a ده باشی dah-báshí *or* اون باشی aun-báshí to every ten. The Life Guards, or body of cavalry attendant on the Shah, are called غلام رکابی ghulám-i-rikábí.]

REGIMENTAL, فوجی faují, لشکری lashkarí.

REGION, قطر kutr, طرف taraf.

REGISTER, دفتر daftar, کتابچه kitáb-chah, فهرست fihrist.—(*ship's register*) قول kaul.

To REGISTER, ثبت کردن sabt kardan.

REGISTERED, ثبت sabt.
REGNANT, تخت نشین takht-nishín.
To REGRESS, باز رفتن báz raftan, مراجعت نمودن murája'at nimúdan.
REGRESSION, مراجعت murája'at.
REGRET, غم gham, الم alam, اندوه andúh, ملال malál, ملالت malálat, تأسف tá,assuf, کدورت kudúrat, رنج ranj, رنجه ranjah, درد dard, آزار ázár, حزن huzn, احزان ihzán, حسرت hasrat, عزا 'azá, دلتنگی dil-tangí, سوگ súg.—(*repentance*) پشیمانی pashímání, توبه taubah, ندامت nadámat, انابت inábat.
To REGRET, افسوس خوردن afsús khwurdan, ندامت کشیدن nadámat kashídan, پشیمان شدن pashímán shudan.
REGRETFUL, آرمانی ármání.
REGULAR, موافق قاعده muváfik-i-ká'idah, مستمری mustamirrí, علی القیاس 'ala-'l-kiyás.—(*ordinary*) مستمری mustamirrí, متداول mutadávil.—(*grammatical term*) سالم sálim.—(*regular troops*) عساکر نظمیه 'asákir-i-nazmíyah.
REGULARITY, انتظام intizám, ترتیب tartíb, نظام nizám, تدارك tadárúk, تدبیر tadbír, تمشیت tamshíyat.
REGULARLY, بترتیب bi-tartíb, با قاعده bá-ká'idah.
To REGULATE, انتظام نمودن intizám nimúdan, تدارك نمودن tadáruk nimúdan.
REGULATION, قاعده ká'idah, قانون kánún, آیین áyín, داب dáb.—(*army regulations*) تنسیقات tansíkát.
REGULATOR (*men*), مدیر mudír.—(*things*) مقیاس mikyás.
REHABILITATION, شفا shifá.
REHEARSAL, تکرار takrár, تکریر takrír.
To REHEARSE, تکرار نمودن takrár nimúdan, تکریر نمودن takrír nimúdan.
REIGN (*sway*), سلطنت sultanat, پادشاهی pádisháhí, داوری dávarí, حکمرانی hukm-rání, تسلط tasallut.—(*time of sovereignty*) عهد 'ahad, جلوس julús, عمل 'amal.
To REIGN, سلطنت نمودن sultanat nimúdan, تسلط نمودن tasallut nimúdan, حکمرانی کردن hukm-rání kardan, داوری کردن dávarí kardan.
To RE-IMBURSE, مسترد ساختن mustaradd sákhtan, ادا نمودن adá nimúdan.
REIN (*of a bridle*), عنان 'inán, زمام zamám, لجام lijám, لگام ligám, جلو jilau.—(*to rein, pull up*) جلو کشیدن jilau kashídan, جلو نگاه داشتن jilau nigah dáshtan.—(*to give or relax the rein*) ارخای عنان کردن irkhá,í-i-i'nán kardan, جلو ول کردن jilau vil-kardan.
To REINFORCE, امداد فرستادن imdád firistádan, مدد نمودن madad nimúdan.
REINFORCEMENTS, قوه امداد kúvah-i-imdád.
REINS, گرده gurdah, کلوه kulvah, کلیه kulyah.
To RE-INSTALL, باز نصب نمودن báz nasb nimúdan.
To REITERATE, اعاده کردن i'ádah kardan, تأکید نمودن ta,kíd nimúdan, باز گفتن báz guftan.
REITERATION, تأکید ta,kíd.
To REJECT, رد کردن radd kardan, پا زدن pá zadan, نفی کردن nafy kardan, وا زدن vá-zadan.
REJECTED, مردود mardúd, متروك matrúk, نا مقبول ná-makbúl, منفی manfy, ردی raddí.
REJECTION, دفع daf', نفع nafy, رد radd.
To REJOICE, خوشوقتی نمودن khwush-vaktí nimúdan, تهلیل نمودن tahlíl nimúdan, فخریه کردن fakhríyah kardan, شاد شدن shád shudan, ملتذ شدن multazz shudan, متعیش بودن muta'ayyish búdan.—(*make glad*) تفریح نمودن tafríh nimúdan.
REJOICING, شادی shádí, خوشوقتی khwush-vaktí, تهلیل tahlíl, فخریه fakhríyah, عیش و عشرت 'aish va 'ashrat.
To REJOIN, باز پیوستن báz paivastan,

باز پیوند کردن báz paivand kardan, باز وصل کردن báz vasl kardan.

REJOINDER, جواب javáb.

To RE-KINDLE, باز افروختن báz afrúkhtan.

RELAPSE (*medical term*), نکس nuks.

To RELAPSE (*medical term*), نکس نمودن nuks nimúdan.

To RELATE, آوردن ávardan.—(*to relate to*) راجع نمودن ráji' nimúdan.

RELATED, منتسب muntasib.

RELATION (*story*), قصه kissah, روایت riváyat, حکایت hikáyat, داستان dástán.—(*reference*) دخل dakhl, علاقه 'alákah, نسبت nisbat, انتساب intisáb, انتما intimá, سهم suhm, تعلق ta'alluk, رجوع rujú'.—(*kindred, relationship*) قرابت karábat, خویشی khwíshí, خویشاوندی khwísh-ávandí, نسبت nisbat, تعلقه ta'allukah.—(*relative, kinsman*) خویش khwísh, خویشاوند khwísh-ávand, قرابتدار karábat-dár, قریب karíb, قرین karín, متعلق muta'allik.—(*intercourse*) مناسبات munásabát.—(*diplomatic relations*), مناسبات دیپلوماتیك munásabát-i-díplúmátík. — (*suspension of relations*) قطع مراوده kat'-i-murávadah.—(*to have relations with*) مراوده داشتن murávadah dáshtan.

RELATIVE (*grammatical term*), خبر khabar.—(*concerning*) راجع ráji', نسبتی nisbatí. — (*relative to*) بالنسبه به bi-'n-nisbah bi, نظر به nazar bi, در باب dar báb, در خصوص dar khusús.

To RELAX, سست کردن sust kardan, اطلاق نمودن itlák nimúdan, ارخا نمودن irkhá nimúdan, ول کردن vil-kardan (*vulg.*).

RELAXATION, رخاوت rakhávat. (*Vide* REST (*repose*).)

RELEASE, خلاصی khalásí, رهائی rihá,í.

To RELEASE, خلاص دادن khalás dádan, رها کردن rihá kardan.

To RELENT, رحم کردن rahm kardan, شفقت نمودن shafakat nimúdan.—(*repent*) پشیمان شدن pashímán shudan, توبه کردن taubah kardan, ندامت کشیدن nadámat kashídan.

RELIABLE, معتمد mu'tamad, بطور موثوق bi-taur-i-mausúk.

RELIANCE, اعتماد i'timád, اعتبار i'tibár, اعتقاد i'tikád, تکیه takíyah, باور bávar.—(*on Providence*) توکل tavakkul.

RELICT, بیوه bívah, ارمله armalah (*pl.* ارامل arámil).

RELIEF, مدد madad, امداد imdád, پشتی pushtí, کمك kumak, عون 'aun, اعانت i'ánat, معاونت mu'ávanat, یاری yárí, تائید ta,ayyud, نصرت nusrat, دستگیری dast-gírí. —(*from pain*) تخفیف takhfíf, تسلی tasallí. — (*in high relief*) برجسته از دیوار bar-jastah az dívár. —(*in low relief*) چسبیده بدیوار chasbídah bi-dívár.

To RELIEVE, فارغ کردن fárigh kardan.—(*pain*) تخفیف نمودن takhfíf nimúdan.

RELIGION, دین dín, مذهب mazhab, ایمان ímán, ملت millat, مشرب mashrab, کیش kísh, امت ummat, اعتقاد i'tikád.—(*Christian*) ملت مسیحیه millat-i-masíhíyah, دین عیسوی dín-i-'ísaví.—(*Muhammadan*) اسلام islám, ملت محمدی millat-i-muhammadí.—(*true religion*) دین مبین dín-i-mubín.

RELIGIOUS, متدین mutadayyin, دیندار dín-dár, ایماندار ímán-dár, متقی muttakí, زکی zakí, خدا ترس khudá-tars.

RELIGIOUSNESS, دینداری dín-dárí, دیانت divánat.

To RELINQUISH, گذاشتن guzáshtan, ترك کردن tark kardan.—(*leave off*) وا ایستادن vá-ístádan, باز ایستادن báz-ístádan, قطع شدن kat' shudan, منقطع شدن munkati' shudan, موقوف بودن maukúf búdan, فراغت کردن farághat kardan.

RELINQUISHED, متروك matrúk.

RELINQUISHMENT, ترك tark, هجر hajr, هجران hijrán.

RELISH (*flavour*), مزه mazah, طعم ta'm, ذائقه zá,ikah, ذوق zauk.—

(*anything eaten with bread, rice, &c., in order to give a relish*) خورش khwurish, نان خورش nán-khwurish, قتوغ katúgh.

To RELISH, مزه بردن (از) mazah burdan (az).

RELUCTANCE, تردد taraddud, پس و پیش pas va písh, وسواس vasvás, اعراض i'ráz, ابا ibá.

RELUCTANT, متردد mutaraddid, ابی abí, معرض mu'arriz.

To RELY, اعتماد کردن i'timád kardan.

To REMAIN, ماندن mándan, بودن búdan, وا ماندن vá-mándan, پس ماندن pas-mándan. — (*last or endure*) ماندن mándan, پایدار بودن páyadár búdan, پاینده بودن páyandah búdan, دائم بودن dá,im búdan, دوام داشتن davám dáshtan, قائم بودن ká,im búdan, بقا داشتن baká dáshtan, پائیدن pá,ídan, امتداد دادن imtidád dádan, طول کشیدن túl kashídan.—(*to remain behind*) پس افتادن pas uftádan, واپس ماندن vápas mándan.

REMAINDER, باقی bákí, بقیه bakíyah, تتمه tatammah, ما بقی má-baká, پس مانده pas-mándah, میزان mízán.

REMAINS (*of a man*), جسد jasad, جنازه janázah.

REMAND, موقف muvakkaf, تاخیر ta,khír.

To REMAND, موقف نمودن muvakkaf nimúdan, تاخیر دادن ta,khír dádan.

REMARK (*saying*), گفتار guftár, قول kaul, مقوله makúlah.

To REMARK, گفتن guftan.—(*notice*) امعان نظر نمودن im'án-i-nazar nimúdan, ملتفت شدن multafit shudan, نظر نمودن nazar nimúdan, دیدن dídan, نگرستن nigaristan, نگریستن nigarístan.

REMARKABLE, عجیب 'ajíb, غریب gharíb. — (*celebrated*) مشهور mash-húr, معروف ma'rúf, موصوف mausúf, نامدار nám-dár, نامور nám-var, نیکنام ník-nám, ممدوح mamdúh.

REMARKABLY, غریبانه gharíbánah.

REMEDIABLE, تدارك پذیر tadáruk-pazír, اصلاح پذیر isláh-pazír.

REMEDIAL, اصلاح کن isláh-kun, علاج بخش 'iláj-bakhsh.

REMEDILESS, بیچاره bí-chárah, لا علاج lá-'aláj.

REMEDY, چاره chárah, علاج 'aláj, دوا davá, مداوا mudává, معالجه mu'álajah, اصلاح isláh, تدارك tadáruk, تلافی taláfí, سزا sizá.

To REMEDY, تلافی کردن taláfí kardan, تدارك نمودن tadáruk nimúdan.

To REMEMBER, یاد کردن yád kardan, یاد داشتن yád dáshtan, خاطر بودن khátir búdan.

REMEMBERER, یاد دار yád-dár.

REMEMBRANCE, یاد yád, حفظ hifz, ذکر zikr, خاطر khátir.

To REMIND, یاد آوردن yád ávardan, یاد دادن yád dádan, بخاطر آوردن bi-khátir ávardan.

REMINDER, یاد داشت yád-dásht.

REMINISCENCE, یاد yád, ذکر zikr.

REMISS, بیخبر bí-khabar, غافل ghá-fil, بیپروا bí-parvá, بی احتیاط bí-ihtiyát.

REMISSION (*pardon*), عفو 'afv, معافی mu'áfí, آمرزش ámurzish, بخشایش bakhsháyish, مسامحت musámahat, صفح safh, غفران ghufrán, مغفرت maghfirat, در گذر dar-guzar. —(*sending*) ارسال irsál, ترسیل tarsíl, روانگی ravánagí.—(*letting off payment*) آمرزش ámurzish, عفو 'afv, بخشش bakhshish.—(*abatement of payment*) رعایت ri'áyat, تخفیف takhfíf, تنزیل tanzíl.—(*of a fever or other disease*) تخفیف takhfíf, وقف vakf. — (*remission of sins*) غفران ghufrán.

To REMIT (*restore*), پس دادن pas dádan, رد کردن radd kardan, وا گذار کردن vá-guzár kardan.—(*forgive*) عفو کردن 'afv kardan, معاف کردن mu'áf kardan, بخشیدن bakhshídan, معذور داشتن ma'zúr dáshtan, در گذر کردن dar-guzar kardan, آمرزیدن ámurzídan, مغفور گردانیدن maghfúr gardánídan.

REMITTANCE, تسليم taslím, ادا adá, توفيه taufíyah.

REMNANT, باقى bákí, تتمه tatammah.

To REMODEL, تغير دادن taghayyur dádan.

REMONSTRANCE, تعرض ta'arruz, اعتراض i'tiráz, معارضه mu'árazah.

To REMONSTRATE, تعرض نمودن ta'arruz nimúdan, اعتراض نمودن i'tiráz nimúdan, معارضه نمودن mu'árazah nimúdan.

REMORSE, ندامت nadámat, تاسف ta,assuf, پشيمانى pashímání.

REMORSELESS, سنگدل sang-dil, بيرحم bí-rahm, ظالم zálim, بى مروت bí-murúvat.

REMOTE, بعيد ba'íd, دور dúr, قصى kasí, قاصى kásí, دور دست dúr-dast.

REMOTENESS, دورى dúrí, بعد bu'd.

To REMOUNT (*horse*), باز سوار شدن báz suvár shudan.—(*ascend*) باز بالا رفتن báz bálá raftan, باز صعود نمودن báz sa'úd nimúdan.

REMOVABLE, انتقال پذير intikál-pazír, نقل پذير nakl-pazír.

REMOVAL, نقل nakl, انتقال intikál.

To REMOVE (*oneself*), كوچيدن kúchídan, انتقال كردن intikál kardan, روانه شدن ravánah shudan, نقل مكان كردن nakl-i-makán kárdan.—(*a thing*) نقل كردن nakl kardan, بر داشتن bar-dáshtan, جا بجا كردن já-bi-já kardan.—(*to remove from a house*) رفتن raftan.

To REMUNERATE, اجرت دادن ujrat dádan.

REMUNERATION, اجرت ujrat, اجر ajr, مزد muzd.

REMUNERATIVE, مفيد mufíd, نافع náfi', فائده fá,idah, سود مند súd-mand.

RENCOUNTER (*meeting*), دو چار dú-chár, ملاقات mulákát, مقابله mukábalah.—(*battle*) جنگ jang, نبرد nabard, رزم razm, حرب harb, محاربه muhárabah, پرخاش purkhásh, هيجا haijá, كار زار kár-zár.—(*collision*) مصادمه musádamah, تصادم tasádum.

To RENCOUNTER (*fight*), جنگ كردن jang kardan, رزم ساختن razm sákhtan.—(*come into collision*) بهم خوردن bi-ham khwurdan.

To REND, دريدن darídan.

To RENDER (*pay*), دادن dádan, ادا كردن adá kardan.—(*inflict*) رسانيدن rasánídan.—(*translate*) ترجمه كردن tarjumah kardan.

RENDEZVOUS, مرجع marja', مجمع majma', ميعاد mí'ád.

RENEGADE (*apostate*), مرتد murtadd, منكر دين munkir-i-dín.

To RENEW, تجديد كردن tajdíd kardan, از سر نو كردن az sar-i-nau kardan, تكرير نمودن takrír nimúdan.—(*to renew a bill*) كاغذرا نو كردن kághazrá nau kardan.

RENEWAL, تجديد tajdíd, تجدد tajaddud.

RENEWED, مجدد mujaddad.

RENNET (*for cheese*), پنير مايه panír-máyah.

To RENOUNCE, انكار كردن inkár kardan, دوركشى نمودن dúr-kashí nimúdan, قطع علاقه نمودن kat'-i-'alákah nimúdan.

To RENOVATE, مجدد ساختن mujaddad sákhtan.

RENOVATION, تجديد tajdíd, تجدد tajaddud.

RENOVATOR, مجدد mujaddid.

RENOWN, نام nám, نيك نامى ník-námí, شهرت shuhrat, ناموس námús, ننگ nang, ذكر جميل zikr-i-jamíl.

RENOWNED, معلوم ma'lúm, مشهور mash-húr, نامدار nám-dár.

RENT (*tear*), چاك chák, شق shakk.—(*hire*) اجاره ijárah, اجرت ujrat, جيره jírah, كرا kirá, كرايه kiráyah, غله ghallah.—(*tax*) خراج khiráj, محصول mahsúl, باج báj.—(*revenue*) ماليات málíyát, مداخل madákhil.—(*rent-free*) بى اجاره bí-ijárah.

To RENT (*trans.*), بكرايه دادن bi-kiráyah dádan, اجاره دادن ijárah dádan, مستغل دادن mu.tághall dádan, غله كردن ghallah kardan.

—(*intrans.*) بکرایه گرفتن bi-kiráyah giriftan, کرایه کردن kiráyah kardan, اجیر کردن ajír kardan, اجیر گرفتن ajír giriftan.

RENTAL, اجاره ijárah, کرایه kiráyah.

RENTER, موءجر mu,jir, اجاره کار ijárah-kár.

RENUNCIATION, قطع علاقه kat'-i-'alákah, عزلت 'uzlat.

To REPAIR (*as buildings, &c.*), مرمت کردن marammat kardan, تعمیر کردن ta'mír kardan.—(*stitch*) رفو کردن rafv kardan, پیوند کردن paivand kardan.—(*broken articles*) تصلیح کردن taslíh kardan, مرمت کردن marammat kardan, درست کردن durust kardan.

REPAIRS (*buildings, &c.*), تعمیر ta'mír, مرمت marammat. — (*garments*) اصلاح isláh, وصله vaslah.

REPARABLE, اصلاح پذیر isláh-pazír.

REPARATION, تضمین tazmín.

REPARTEE, ظرافت zaráfat, حاضر جوابی házir-javábí, لطیفه latífah.

To REPASS, باز گذشتن báz guzashtan, باز گذر کردن báz guzar kardan, باز گذار آوردن báz guzár ávardan.

REPAST, جشن jashn, تغذیه taghziyah.

To REPAY, باز دادن báz dádan.

REPEAL, منسوخ mansúkh, معدوم ma'dúm, نسخ naskh.

To REPEAL, منسوخ کردن mansúkh kardan, نسخ نمودن naskh nimúdan, معدوم ساختن ma'dúm sákhtan, نا بود کردن ná-búd kardan, موقوف کردن maukúf kardan, مبطل گردانیدن mubtal gardánídan, باطل ساختن bátil sákhtan.

To REPEAT (*do again*), مکرر کردن mukarrar kardan, تکرار کردن takrár kardan, باز کردن báz kardan, بار دگر کردن bár-i-digar kardan.—(*say again*), باز گفتن báz guftan, باز گو کردن báz gú kardan, مکرر گفتن mukarrar guftan, تکرار نمودن takrár nimúdan.

REPEATEDLY, مکرراً mukarraran, بسیار بار bisyár bár, بار بار bár-bár.

REPEATER, مکرر mukarrir, تکرار کننده takrár-kunandah.

To REPEL, دفع نمودن daf' nimúdan, مدافعه نمودن mudáfa'ah nimúdan.

REPELLENT, دافع dáfi'.

To REPENT, پشیمان شدن pashímán shudan, توبه کردن taubah kardan, ندامت کشیدن nadámat kashídan.

REPENTANCE, پشیمانی pashímání, توبه taubah, ندامت nadámat, انابت inábat.

REPENTANT, توبه گذار taubah-guzár, پشیمان pashímán, تائب tá,ib.

REPERTORY, انبار ambár, مخزن makhzan.

REPETITION, تکرار takrár, تکرر takarrur, باز گوئی báz-gú,í, باز گفتار báz-guftár.

To REPINE, دلتنگ بودن dil-tang búdan, غم خوردن gham khwurdan, مکدر بودن mukaddar búdan, رنجیدن ranjídan.

REPINER, شاکی shákí.

To REPLACE (*exchange*), عوض کردن 'ivaz kardan, معاوضه کردن mu'ávazah kardan, بدل کردن badal kardan, مبادله کردن mabádalah kardan, تبدیل کردن tabdíl kardan, باز گذاشتن báz guzáshtan, واپس نهادن vápas nihádan, رجوع نمودن rujú' nimúdan.

To RE-PLANT, باز غرس کردن báz ghars kardan, باز نشاندن báz nishándan, باز کاشتن báz káshtan.

To REPLENISH, پر کردن pur kardan, تازه کردن tázah kardan.

REPLETE, پر pur, مملو mamlúw, سیر sír.

REPLETION, امتلا imtilá, سیری sírí.

REPLY, جواب javáb, پاسخ pásukh.

To REPLY, جواب دادن javáb dádan.

REPORT, *vide* NEWS, TALK.—(*of fire-arms*) شلیك shalík, صدای تفنگ sadá,í-i-tufang, آواز تفنگ áváz-i-tufang. — (*school*) کتابچه kitábchah.

To REPORT, شهرت دادن shuhrat dádan, خبر دادن khabar dádan, معروض داشتن ma'rúz dáshtan.——(*to be reported*) شایع شدن sháí' shudan.

Repose, آرام árám, آرمیدگی áramídagí, آسایش ásáyish, آسودگی ásúdagí, راحت ráhat, استراحت istiráhat, سکون sukún, فراغت farághat, رفاهیت rafáhiyat.

To Repose, آسودن ásúdan, استراحت کردن istiráhat kardan, آرام گرفتن árám giriftan, راحت کردن ráhat kardan, خوابیدن khwábídan.

Repository, خزانه khizánah, خزینه khazínah, مخزن makhzan, گنج ganj, انبار ambár, کنز kanz.

To Repossess, باز داشتن báz dáshtan, باز تصرف کردن báz tasarruf kardan.

To Reprehend, ملامت کردن malámat kardan, عیب گفتن 'aib guftan, ذم کردن zamm kardan, موأخذه کردن mu,ákhazah kardan.

Reprehensible, مقصر mukassar, لائق ملام lá,ik-i-malám, سزاور ملامت sazávar-i-malámat.

Reprehension, تعزیر ta'zír, زجر zajr, ملامت malámat, سر زنش sar-zanish, موأخذه mu,ákhazah, پیغاره paighárah, عتاب 'itáb.

To Represent, اظهار کردن izhár kardan, نمودن nimúdan, عرض کردن 'araz kardan, نشان دادن nishán dádan.—(*by petition*) عرض کردن 'arz kardan, معروض داشتن ma'rúz dáshtan, التماس کردن iltimás kardan.—(*imitate*) تقلید کردن taklíd kardan.

Representation, عرض 'arz, در خواست dar-khwást, التماس iltimás, تمنا tamanná. — (*written*) عریضه 'arízah, عرضداشت 'arz-dásht. —(*dramatic*) تقلید taklíd, تماشا tamáshá.

Representative, قائم مقام ká,im-makám.

Represented, معروض ma'rúz.—(*to be represented, at a meeting*) اعضا بودن a'zá búdan.

To Repress, فرو نشاندن furú nishándan.

Repression, فرو نشاندگی furú nishandagí.

Repressive, شدید shadíd, سخت sakht, موثر mu'assir.

Reprieve, مهلت muhlat.

To Reprieve, مهلت دادن muhlat dádan.

Reprimand, سر زنش sar-zanish, زجر zajr, ملامت malámat.

To Reprimand, ملامت کردن malámat kardan, عیب گفتن 'aib guftan, ذم کردن zamm kardan, موأخذه کردن mu,ákhazah kardan.

Reprisals, انتقام intikám, قصاص kisás, مکافات mukáfát. — (*to make reprisals*) تقاص نمودن takáss nimúdan.

Reproach, تعزیر ta'zír, زجر zajr, ملامت malámat, سر زنش sar-zanish, موأخذه mu,ákhazah, پیغاره paighárah, عتاب 'itáb.

To Reproach, ملامت کردن malámat kardan, عیب گفتن 'aib guftan, ذم کردن zamm kardan, موأخذه کردن mu,ákhazah kardan.

Reproachable, قابل ملامت kábil-i-malámat.

Reproachful, معیوب ma'yúb, شوخ shúkh, بد زبان bad-zabán, زبان دراز zabán-diráz. — (*infamous*) رسوا rusvá, فضیح fazíh, رو سیاه rú-siyáh.

Reproachfully, طعناً ta'nan.

Reprobate, مردود الایمان mardúdu-'l-ímán, مردود mardúd.

To Reproduce, باز آوردن báz ávardan, باز آفریدن báz áfirídan, باز پیدا کردن báz paidá kardan.

Reproduction, تجدید tajdíd.

Reproof, تعزیر ta'zír, زجر zajr, ملامت malámat, سر زنش sar-zanish, موأخذه mu,ákhazah, پیغاره paighárah, عتاب 'itáb.

Reprovable, قابل ملامت kábil-i-malámat.

To Reprove, ملامت کردن malámat kardan, عیب گفتن 'aib guftan, ذم کردن zamm kardan, موأخذه کردن mu,ákhazah kardan.

Reptile, خزنده khazindah, جنبنده jumbandah, حشرت hasharat (*pl.* حشرات hasharát).

Republic, دولت جمهوریه daulat-i-jumhúríyah.—(*President of the Republic*) رئیس الجمهور ra,ísu-'l-jumhúr.

Republican, جمهوری jumhúrí.
To Repudiate, منطلق ساختن muntalik sákhtan.
Repudiation, تطليق tatlík.
Repugnance (*dislike*), ابا ibá, اعراض i'ráz, نفرت nifrat, تنفر tanaffur, کراهيت karáhiyat. — (*reluctance*) تردد taraddud, پس و پيش pas va písh, وسواس vasvás, اعراض i'ráz, ابا ibá.
Repugnant, مخالف mukhálif, مغاير mugháyir, مناقض munakiz, منافی munáfí.—(*averse*) مانع máni', کاره kárih, مخالف mukhálif, راغم rághim, ضد zidd, متنفر matanaffir, مکره mukrih.
Repulse, دفع daf', اندفاع indifá', رفع raf', رد radd, حرمان harmán. —(*of an enemy, &c.*) شکست shikast, دفع daf', هزيمت hazímat.
To Repulse (*repel*), وا راندن várándan, باز راندن báz rándan, رد نمودن radd nimúdan, دور کردن dúr kardan, دفع کردن daf' kardan, رفع کردن raf' kardan.
Repulsed, مندفع mundafi', رد radd.
Repulsion, دفع daf', تدافع tadáfu', اندفاع indifá'.
Repulsive, بد چهره bad-chihrah, زشت zisht, مغص mughass.
Re-purchase, باز خريد báz-kharíd.
To Re-purchase, باز خريدن báz kharídan, باز اشترا نمودن báz ishtirá nimúdan, باز ابتياع کردن báz-ibtiyá' kardan.
Reputable, معتبر mu'tabar, محترم muhtaram.
Reputation, نام nám, نيکنامی níknámí, آبرو áb-rú, عرض 'irz, حرمت hurmat, عزت 'izzat, وقار vakár, ننگ nang, ناموس námús.
Request, در خواست dar-khwást, خواهش khwáhish, تمنا tamanná, آرزو árzú, التماس iltimás, نياز niyáz, دعا du'á, استدعا istid'á, مطلب matlab, طلب talab, الجاء iljá,.—(*at the request of*) بنا بر استدعائی biná bar istid'á,í.
To Request (*beg*), خواستن khwástan, در خواست نمودن dar-khwást nimúdan, التماس کردن iltimás kardan, تمنا نمودن tamanná nimúdan, نياز کردن niyáz kardan, دعا کردن du'á kardan, استدعا نمودن istid'á nimúdan.
To Require (*beg*), خواستن khwástan, در خواست نمودن dar-khwást nimúdan, التماس کردن iltimás kardan, تمنا نمودن tamanná nimúdan, نياز کردن niyáz kardan, دعا کردن du'á kardan, استدعا نمودن istid'á nimúdan.—(*to need, to want*) لازم داشتن lázim dáshtan, ضرور داشتن zarúr dáshtan, خواستن khwástan, حاجت داشتن hájat dáshtan, اقتضا کردن iktizá kardan, محتاج بودن muhtáj búdan, در کار شدن dar kár shudan.
Requirement, مقتضا muktazá.
Requisite (*subs.*), لوازمه lavázimah. — (*adj.*) ضرور zarúr, لازم lázim, ملتزم multazim, مقتضی muktazí, معتکد mu'takid, واجب vájib, در کار dar-kár, متحتم mutahattim.
Requital, مجازات mujázát, مکافات mukáfát, جزا jizá.
To Requite, مجازات کردن mujázát kardan, مکافات کردن mukáfát kardan.
Re-sale, وا فروخت vá-furúkht.
To Rescind, رد کردن radd kardan, باطل کردن bátil kardan, نسخ ساختن naskh sákhtan, قطع کردن kat' kardan.
Rescission, رد کردن radd-kardan, قطع کردن kat'-kardan.
Rescript, امر amr, تنظيم tanzím.
Rescue, رهائی rihá,í, رها rihá, خلاص khalás.
To Rescue, خلاص دادن khalás dádan.
Research, جستجو justujú, تفحص tafahhus.
To Re-sell, وا فروختن vá-furúkhtan.
Resemblance, برابری barábarí, تمثيل tamsíl, مثال misál, تشبيه tashbíh, مشابهه mushábahah, شبه shibh, موافقت muváfakat, شباهت shabáhat, نمايش nimáyish, حکم hukm.
To Resemble, مانستن mánistan,

تشبیه داشتن tashbíh dáshtan, مشابهه داشتن mushábahah dáshtan, تمثیل داشتن tamsíl dáshtan, مانند بودن mánand búdan, مثل بودن misl búdan, شباهت داشتن shabáhat dáshtan.

RESEMBLING, چون chún, چو chú, همچون ham-chún, چنان chunán, بکردار bi-kirdár, بسان bi-sán, مانند mánand, مثل misl, مثال misál, حکم hukm.

To RESENT, خشم نمودن khíshm nimúdan, آزرده شدن ázurdah shudan.

RESENTFUL, شریر sharír, بد نهاد bad-nihád, بد اندیش bad-andísh, بد خواه bad-khwáh, بد ذات bad-zát.

RESENTMENT, کین kín, خشم khishm, کینه kínah.

RESERVATION, تحاشی taháshá, احتیاط ihtiyát, استثنا istisná, باز داری báz-dárí.

RESERVE, برودت burúdat, توقیر taukír.—(*without reserve*) بی پروایانه bí-parváyánah.

To RESERVE, نگاه داشتن nigáh dáshtan.

RESERVED, برود barúd, موقر mu,akkar.—(*set apart*) مخصوص makhsús, مخصص makhassus.

RESERVOIR (*of water*), حوض hauz.—(*large public reservoir*) آب انبار áb-ambár.

To RESIDE, بودن búdan, ساکن بودن sákin búdan, بسر بردن bi-sar burdan, سکونت داشتن sukúnat dáshtan, ماندن mándan, اقامت کردن ikámat kardan, مستنزل بودن mustanzil búdan.

RESIDENCE, مکان makán, منزل manzil, مسکن maskan, مقام makám, خانه khánah, مأبد ma,bid, مقر makarr, مستقر mustakarr, ماوا mává.—(*residing*) اقامت ikámat, سکونت sukúnat. — (*official residence*) دولتخانه daulat-khánah.

RESIDENCY, بالیوزی bályúzí.

RESIDENT, ساکن sákin (*pl.* سکنه sakanah *and* سکان sukkán), باشنده báshandah (*pl.* باشندگان báshandagán), مکین makín, متمکن mutamakkin, مقیم makím, متوطن mutavattin, قاطن kátin, اهل ahl.—(*political or consular agent*) بالیوز bályúz (*eur.*), وکیل vakíl.

RESIDUE, باقی bákí, بقیه bakíyah, تتمه tatammah, ما باقی má-bákí, پس مانده pas-mándah, میزان mízán.

To RESIGN (*give up, intrust*), سپردن sipurdan, تحویل کردن tahvíl kardan, تفویض نمودن tafvíz nimúdan, تسلیم نمودن taslím nimúdan, حواله کردن haválah kardan.—(*give up office*) رخصت گرفتن rukhsat giriftan, استعفا گرفتن isti'fá giriftan.

RESIGNATION (*to Providence*), توکل tavakkul, رضا razá, تسلیم taslím.—(*of office, &c.*), استعفا isti'fá, عزل 'azl.—(*letter of resignation*) استعفا نامه isti'fá-námah.

RESIGNED, شکیب shikíb, صابر sábir.—(*religious term*) متوکل mutavakkil.

To RESIST, مقاومت نمودن mukávamat nimúdan, مخالفت کردن mukhálafat kardan, مقابلت کردن mukábalat kardan, مزاحم شدن muzáhim shudan, معاوضه نمودن mu'ávazah nimúdan, معارضه کردن mu'árazah kardan.—(*successfully withstand*) تاب آوردن táb ávardan.

RESISTANCE, مخالفت mukhálafat, مقاومت mukávamat, مقابلت mukábalat, تاب táb.

RESISTIBLE, مخالفت پذیر mukhálafat-pazír.

RESISTLESS, غیر مخالفت ghair-i-mukhálafat.

RESOLUTE, راسخ rásikh, بر قرار bar-karár, مستمر mustamirr, مصر musirr.

RESOLUTELY, جزماً و عزماً jazman va 'azman.

RESOLUTION (*fixed purpose*), نیت níyat, خوض khauz, ثبات sabát, تصمیم tasmím, رسوخ rusúkh.

RESOLVE, عزم 'azm, عزیمت 'azímat, جزم jazm, خوض khauz, تصمیم tasmím.

To Resolve, تصمیم کردن tasmím kardan, عزمرا جزم کردن 'azmrá jazm kardan, مصمم گشتن musammim gashtan, قراری دادن karárí dádan.
Resonance, صدا sadá.
Resort, مآب ma,áb, باز گشت báz-gasht.
To Resort (*frequent*), آمد و رفت نمودن ámad u raft nimúdan, مراودت کردن murávadat kardan.
To Resound, صدا دادن sadá dádan.
Resource, چاره chárah, علاج 'aláj, اصلاح isláh.
Resources, درمان darmán, نوا navá, معاش ma'ásh.
Respect, *vide* Veneration, Observance, Regard.—(*of persons, from external appearance*) ظاهر بینی záhir-bíní.
To Respect, احترام کردن ihtirám kardan, عزیز داشتن 'azíz dáshtan, محترم داشتن muhtaram dáshtan.
Respectable, معتبر mu'tabar, متشخص mutashakhkhis, صاحب وقار sáhib-vakár, محترم muhtaram.
Respected, معزز mu'azzaz, مشرف musharraf, محترم muhtaram, معتبر mutabar, معظم mu,azzam.
Respectful, متواضع mutavázi'.
Respectfully, خضوعانه khuzú'ánah, بطور مؤدب bi-taur-i-mu,addab.
Respecting, در باب dar báb, در باره dar bárah, نسبت به nisbat-bi, از az, در حق dar hakk, در خصوص dar khusús.
Respective, مخصوص makhsús, خاص kháss, خاصه khássah.
Respectively, یك یك yak yak, نسبة nisbatan, فی نفر fí-nafar.
Respects, سلام salám.
Respiration (*breathing*), تنفس tanaffus, نفس nafas.
To Respire, نفس کشیدن nafas kashídan.
Respite, مهلت muhlat, وقف vakf, فراغت farághat, دفع الوقت daf'u-'l-vakt.
To Respite, مهلت دادن muhlat dádan.
Resplendence, نور núr, تابش tábish, روشنی raushaní, جلوه jilvah, نیر nayyir, تجلی tajallí.
Resplendent, تابناك táb-nák, نورانی núrání, فروغمند furúgh-mand, رخشان rakhshán.
Resplendently, با نور bá-núr.
To Respond, جواب دادن javáb dádan.
Respondent (*legal term*), حریف haríf, مدعی علیه mudda'á 'alaihi.
Response, جواب javáb, پاسخ pásukh.
Responsible, جوابدار javáb-dár.—(*to be responsible*) بر ذمه داشتن bar zimmah dáshtan, جوابدار بودن javáb-dár búdan, ملتزم شدن multazim shudan, التزام نمودن iltizám nimúdan.
Responsibility, جوابداری javáb-dárí, ضمانت zamánat, التزام iltizám, ذمه zimmah.
Responsive, جواب ده javáb-dih.
Rest (*remainder*), باقی bákí, بقیه bakíyah, تتمه tatammah, ما باقی má-bákí, پس مانده pas-mándah, میزان mízán.—(*repose*) آرام árám, آرمیدگی áramídagí, آسایش ásáyish, آسودگی ásúdagí, راحت ráhat, استراحت istiráhat, سکون sukún, فراغت farághat, رفاهیت rafáhiyat. (*fork for resting a long rifle or musket*) دوشاخه dúshákhah, دایاق dáyák, دیاق dayák.—(*to be at rest*) آرامیدن árámídan.—(*to be at rest, volcano*) خاموش بودن khámush búdan.
To Rest, راحت نمودن ráhat nimúdan, مستریح گشتن mustaríh gashtan, آسودن ásúdan, استراحت کردن istiráhat kardan, رحل اقامت انداختن rahl-i-ikámat andákhtan.—(*remain*) توقف شدن tavakkuf shudan, مکث کردن maks kardan.
Restaurant, میخانه mai-khánah.
Resting-place, مقر makarr, مستقر mustakarr, ماوی mává, آرامگاه árám-gáh, نشیمن nishíman, مستراح mustaráh, منزل manzil, مسکن maskan, مقام makám.
Restitution, استرداد istirdád.—

(*to make restitution*) استرداد کردن istirdád kardan.

Restive, سر کش sar-kash, متمرد mutamarrid.

Restiveness, سر کشی sar-kashí.

Restless, متزلزل mutazalzil, بی تاب bí-táb.—(*to be restless*) بی تاب شدن bí-táb shudan.—(*at night*) نا راحت خوابیدن ná-ráhat khwábídan.

Restoration, استرداد istirdád.—(*of buildings*) اصلاح isláh, تعمیر ta'mír, مرمت marammat.

Restorative, شفابخش shifá-bakhsh, مقوی mukavví.

To Restore, وا پس دادن vá-pas dádan, باز رسانیدن báz rasánídan, رد نمودن radd nimúdan, استرداد نمودن istirdád nimúdan.—(*buildings*) اصلاح نمودن isláh nimúdan, تعمیر کردن ta'mír kardan, مرمت نمودن marammat nimúdan.—(*pension*) اجرار کردن ijrár kardan.

To Restrain, وا داشتن vá-dáshtan, باز داشتن báz dáshtan, ضبط نمودن zabt nimúdan.

Restrainable, قابل ضبط kábil-i-zabt.

Restrained, مجبور majbúr.

Restraint, منع mana', ضبط zabt.—(*self-restraint*) امتناع imtiná'.

To Restrict, منحصر نمودن mukhassar nimúdan.

Restriction, منع mana'.

Restringent, قابض kábiz, کشنده kashandah.

Result, نتیجه natíjah, انجام anjám, انصرام insirám, حاصل hásil, مال ma,ál, آخر ákhir, سر sar.

To Result, اتفاق افتادن ittifák uftádan, عارض شدن 'áriz shudan, روی نمودن rúy nimúdan, سر زدن sar zadan.

Resumable, قابل اخذ kábil-i-akhz, قابل عمل kábil-i-'amal.

Resumé, اختصار ikhtisár, ایجاز íjáz, اجمال ijmál, قصارت kasárat.

To Resume, باز گرفتن báz giriftan, وا پس گرفتن vá-pas giriftan, از نو گرفتن az nau giriftan. — (*the phrase "to resume"*) دیگر dígar, علاوه 'alávah.

Resumption, اخذ akhz.

Resurrection, رستخیز rastakhíz, قیامت kiyámat, حشر hashr, بعث و نشر ba's va nashr.—(*Day of Resurrection*) روز قیامت rúz-i-kiyámat, روز رستخیز rúz-i-rastakhíz, روز حساب rúz-i-hisáb, روز شمار rúz-i-shimár, روز مرصاد rúz-i-mirsád, روز جزا rúz-i-jizá, یوم النشور yaumu - 'n - nushúr, محشر mahshar. — (*interval between death and resurrection*) برزخ barzakh.

To Resuscitate, انشار نمودن inshár nimúdan, احیا نمودن ihyá nimúdan.

Resuscitation, احیا ihyá, انشار inshár, انتشار intishár.

Retail, خرده khurdah.

To Retail (*sell in small quantities*), خرده فروختن khurdah furúkhtan, جز فروختن juz furúkhtan.

Retailer, خرده فروش khurdah-furúsh.

To Retain, داشتن dáshtan, نگاه داشتن nigáh dáshtan.

To Retake, پس گرفتن pas giriftan.

To Retaliate, قصاص نمودن kisás nimúdan, مکافات نمودن mukáfát nimúdan.

Retaliation, جزا jizá, مجازات mujázát, عوض 'avaz, معاوضه mu'ávazah, بدله badlah, پاداش pádásh, ثار sár, قصاص kisás, مکافات mukáfát, انتقام intikám, مؤاخذه mu,ákhazah.

To Retard, تبطئه نمودن tabti'ah nimúdan, تأخیر نمودن ta,khír nimúdan, دیری کردن dírí kardan.

Retention, حفظ hifz, امساك imsák.—(*memory*) یاد yád, حفظ hifz, حافظ háfiz, خاطر khátir.

Retentive, حافظ háfiz, ممسك mumsik, نگاه دارنده nigáh-dárandah.

Retinue (*attendants, &c.*), خدم و حشم khadam va hasham, حشمت hashmat, جلو jilau, موکب maukab, کوکبه kaukabah, قبقبه kabkabah,

اتباع atbá', متعلقین muta'allikín, تابینها tábínhá (*vulg.*).

To RETIRE, *vide* To RETREAT, To WITHDRAW, To RESIGN.—(*withdraw from society*) متواری شدن mutavárí shudan, گوشه نشستن gúshah nishastan, خلوت گزیدن khalvat guzídan.

RETIRED, معزول ma'zúl.—(*modest*) محجوب mahjúb.

RETIREMENT (*from business, &c.*), فراغت farághat, عزلت 'uzlat, استیفا istífá, استعفا isti'fá, خلع khal', خلا khalá.—(*solitude*) خلوت khalvat, گوشه نشینی gúshah-nishíní, وحدت vahdat.

RETORT, حاضر جوابی házir-javábí.—(*chemical term*) انبیق ambík.

To RETORT, حاضر جوابی دادن házir-javábí dádan.

To RETRACE one's steps, باز گشتن báz gashtan, بر عقب رفتن bar 'akab raftan.

To RETRACT (*one's own words*), رد سخن نمودن radd-i-sukhun nimúdan, حرف دزدیدن harf duzdídan.

RETRACTION (*unsaying*), رد سخن radd-i-sukhun.

RETREAT (*place of privacy*), خلوتگاه khalvat-gáh, حرم haram, گوشه gúshah, خلوت khalvat.—(*of an army*), رجع raj', قهقرا kahkará.

To RETREAT, پساپس رفتن pas-á-pas raftan, پس نشستن pas nishastan, قهقرا نمودن kahkará nimúdan.

To RETRENCH, جلو گیری نمودن jilau-gírí nimúdan.—(*expenses*) ادارت کردن idárat kardan, کم خرج نمودن kam kharj nimúdan.

RETRENCHMENT, جلو گیری jilau-gírí.—(*of expenses*) خانه داری khánah-dárí, باریك روی baríkraví.

RETRIBUTION, جزا jizá, مجازات mujázát, عوض 'avaz, معاوضه mu'ávazah, بدله badlah, پاداش pádásh, ثار sár, قصاص kisás, مکافات mukáfát, انتقام intikám, مؤاخذه mu,ákhazah.

RETRIEVABLE, درمان پذیر darmán-pazír.

To RETRIEVE, یافتن yáftan, حاصل کردن hásil kardan.

RETROCESSION, واگذار شدن vá-guzár-shudan.

RETROGRADE, مدبر mudbir, راجع ráji', وا پس vá-pas.

To RETROGRADE, وا پس خزیدن vá-pas khazídan, رجع نمودن raj' nimúdan.

RETROGRESSION, وا گذار شدن vá-guzár-shudan.

RETROSPECT, ملاحظه ما مضی mulá-hazah-i-má mazá.

RETURN, مراجعت murája'at, باز گشت báz-gasht.

To RETURN (*come back*), باز آمدن báz ámadan, وا پس آمدن vá-pas ámadan, بر گشتن bar-gashtan, عودت کردن 'audat kardan.—(*go back*) باز رفتن báz raftan, بر گشتن bar-gashtan, رجوع کردن rujú' kardan, مراجعت نمودن murája'at nimúdan, باز گردیدن báz gardídan.—(*give back*) باز دادن báz dádan, وا پس دادن vá-pas dádan, رد نمودن radd nimúdan.

REUNION, وصل vasl, وصلت vuslat, دو چار dú-chár.—(*assembly*) مجلس majlis, بزم bazm, انجمن anjuman, محفل mahfil.

To RE-UNITE, فراهم آوردن faráham ávardan, موصول ساختن mausúl sákhtan.

RE-UNITED, موصول mausúl, متوصل mutavassil.

To REVEAL, مفوض داشتن mufavvaz dáshtan, افشا ساختن ifshá sákhtan, فاش کردن fásh kardan, اظهار کردن izhár kardan, کشف نمودن kashf nimúdan, آشکارا کردن áshkárá kardan, وحی نمودن vahy nimúdan. — (*in religious sense*) الهام نمودن ilhám nimúdan, تجلی نمودن tajallí nimúdan.

REVEALED, مکشوف makshúf, منکشف munkashif.—(*to be revealed*) فاش شدن fásh shudan.

REVEALER, کاشف káshif.

REVEL, بزم bazm, ولیمه valímah, جشن jashn.

To REVEL, تعيش كردن ta'ayyush kardan.

REVELATION, كشف kashf, فاش fásh, اظهار izhár.—(*from heaven*) الهام ilhám, مكاشفه mukáshafah, وحي vahy, تنزيل tanzíl.

REVELRY, قلاشي kalláshí, عيش و عشرت 'aish va 'ishrat, خوش گذراني khwush-guzrání.

REVENGE, انتقام intikám, كينه kínah, جزا jizá, سزا sizá, ثار sár.

To REVENGE, قصاص گرفتن kisás giriftan. —(*oneself*) انتقام كردن intikám kardan.

REVENGEFUL, پر انتقام pur-intikám, پر كينه pur-kínah.

REVENUE, ماليات máliyát, ارتفاع irtifá', محاصل mahásil, باج و خراج báj u khiráj, تعمير ta'mír.—(*management of revenues*) عاملي 'ámilí. —(*collector of revenue*) عامل 'ámil (*pl.* عمال 'ammál), مستوفي mustaufí, محصل muhassil.

To REVERBERATE, رد صدا نمودن radd-i-sadá nimúdan.

REVERBERATION (*of sound*), رد صدا radd-i-sadá, نوف núf.

To REVERE, محترم داشتن muhtaram dáshtan, اكرام نمودن ikrám nimúdan, تعظيم و تكريم كردن ta'zím va takrím kardan.

REVERENCE, تعظيم ta'zím, تكريم takrím, اعزاز i'záz, اعتبار i'tibár, احترام ihtirám.

To REVERENCE, محترم داشتن muhtaram dáshtan, اكرام نمودن ikrám nimúdan, تعظيم و تكريم كردن ta'zím va takrím kardan.

REVEREND (*revered*), محترم muhtaram, معزز mu'azzaz, معظم mu'azzam, مكرم mukarram.

REVERENT (*revering, respectful*), مؤدب mu'addab. اعتبار نما i'tibár-nimá, احترام نما ihtirám-nimá.

REVERENTIALLY, بتواضع bi-tavázu'.

REVERIE, خواب khwáb, خيال khiyál *or* khayál.

REVERSE, عكس 'aks, ضد zidd, خلاف khiláf, نقيض nakíz, ور var (*vulg.*). —(*change*) انقلاب inkiláb, تغيير taghyír, صارفت sárifat.—(*disaster*) نكبت nakbat, نكمت nakmat, شكست shikast, هزيمت hazímat.

To REVERSE, مقلوب كردن maklúb kardan, وارون كردن várún kardan.

REVERSED, وارونه várúnah, نگون nigún, معكوس ma'kús.

REVERSION, برگشت bar-gasht, رجوع rujú'.

To REVERT, رجوع نمودن rujú' nimúdan.

REVIEW (*of an army*), سان sán.—(*of book*), ملاحظه muláhazah.

To REVIEW (*book*), ملاحظه كردن muláhazah kardan. — (*army*) سان ديدن sán dídan.

To REVILE, *vide* To RAIL at, To SCOLD.

REVILER, مفتري muftarí, دشنام دهنده dushnám-dihandah.

REVISAL *or* REVISION, تصحيح tashíh.

REVISE, تصحيح tashíh.

To REVISE, تصحيح كردن tashíh kardan, درست كردن durust kardan.

To REVISIT, باز ديد نمودن báz-díd nimúdan, ملاقات كردن mulákát kardan.

REVIVAL, عود 'aud.

To REVIVE, اعاده نمودن i'ádah nimúdan.—(*get better*), به شدن bih shudan.—(*resuscitate*) انشار نمودن inshár nimúdan, احيا نمودن ihyá nimúdan.

REVIVER, مفرح mufarrih, محيي muhyí.

REVOCABLE, درمان پذير darmán-pazír.

REVOCATION, رد radd, نسخ naskh.

To REVOKE, رد كردن radd kardan, باطل كردن bátil kardan, نسخ ساختن naskh sákhtan, قطع كردن kat' kardan.

REVOLT, ياغيگري yághí-garí, بغاوت baghávat, فتنه fitnah, طغيان tughyán, عصيان 'isyán, فساد fasád, گردنكشي gardan - kashí, دغدغه daghdaghah, سر كشي sar-kashí, قهقرا kahkará, هرزگي harzagí.

REVOLUTION, گردش gardish, دور daur, دوران daurán, انقلاب inkiláb.—(*of the heavens*) دور گردون daur-i-gardún, تقلبات افلاك takallubát-i-aflák, گردش آسمان gardish-i-ásmán.—(*against a prince, &c.*) یاغیگری yághí-garí, بغاوت baghávat, فتنه fitnah, طغیان tughyán, عصیان 'isyán, فساد fasád, گردنکشی gardan-kashí, دغدغه daghdaghah, سر کشی sar-kashí, قهقرا kahkará, هرزگی harzagí.

To Revolve, گردیدن gardídan, گردش کردن gardish kardan, دور کردن daur kardan, چرخیدن charkhídan.

Revolver (*pistol*), رولور ravalvar (*eur.*).

Reward, مزد muzd, جزا jizá, اجر ajr, اجرت ujrat, حسنه hasanah, انعام in'ám, تلافی taláfí.—(*in the next world*) ثواب saváb, سعادت ابدی sa'ádat-i-abadí.

To Reward, پاداش کردن padásh kardan, جزا کردن jizá kardan.

Rhetoric, علم کلام 'ilm-i-kalám, علم فصاحت 'ilm-i-fasáhat, نطق nutk.

Rhetorical, منطقی mantikí.

Rhetorician, منطقی mantikí, اهل منطق ahl-i-mantik.

Rheum, زکام zukám.

Rheumatic, بادی bádí.

Rheumatism, باد bád, ریح ríh, وجع مفاصل vaj'-i-mafásil.

Rhinoceros, کرگدن kargadan.

Rhododaphne (*oleander*), خرزهره khar-zahrah, دفله diflah.

Rhombus (*in geometry*), معین ma'ín.

Rhubarb, ریوند rívand.—(*bastard rhubarb*) ریواس rívás, لیواس lívás.

Rhyme, قافیه káfiyah, سجع saj', نظم nazam.

To Rhyme (*trans.*), قافیه گفتن káfiyah guftan, شعر گفتن shi'r guftan.—(*intrans.*) قافیه بودن káfiyah búdan, قافیه داشتن káfiyah dáshtan.

Rib, استخوان پهلو ustukhwán-i-pahlú, دنده dandah.

Ribbon, بافته báftah, فیط fít, فتیله fatílah, پهنک pahnak, تافیه táfiyah.

Rice (*growing or in the husk*), شلتوک shaltúk, چلتوک chaltúk, شالی shálí.—(*cleared from the husk*) برنج birinj.—(*boiled*) چلاو chiláw.—(*rice and milk*) شیر برنج shír-birinj.—(*rice-broth*) شله shullah. (*rice and meat, spices, &c.*) پلاو piláw.—(*rice-field*) شلتوکزار shaltúk-zár, مزرع چلتوک mazra'-i-chaltúk.

Rich, مالدار mál-dár, تونگر tavangar, دولتمند daulat-mand, غنی ghaní, مستغنی mustaghaní, متمول mutammavvil, زر دار zar-dár, مایه دار máyah-dár, منعم muna''am.—(*as cookery, &c.*), چرب charb.—(*as a country or city, &c.*) زر خیز zar-khíz, مداخل خیز madákhil-khíz.

Riches, مال mál, دولت daulat, مایه máyah.

Richly, دولتمندانه daulat-mandánah.—(*fully*) تماما tamáman, بسیار bisyár.

Richness (*wealth*), مال mál, دولت daulat, مایه máyah.—(*fertility*) برومندی barú-mandí, خصب khisb.—(*of food*) چربی charbí.

Rick (*pile of corn, &c.*), توده غله túdah-i-ghallah, خرمن kharman; پر pir (*vulg.*).

Rickety (*infirm*), نا استوار ná-ustuvár, سست sust, لك lak.

To Rid, رهانیدن rihánídan.

Riddance, رهائی rihá,í, خلاص khalás.

Riddle (*enigma*), معما mu'ammá, رمز ramz.—(*sieve*) غربال gharbál, غلبار ghalbár, غلبیر ghalbír.

To Riddle, سوراخ سوراخ کردن súrákh súrákh kardan.

To Ride, سواره رفتن suvárah (*or* savárah) raftan, سواری کردن suvárí (*or* savárí) kardan, سوار شدن suvár (*or* savár) shudan.—(*to ride double, behind another person*) ترك نشستن tark nishastan.

Rider, سوار suvár (*or* savár), راکب rákib, فارس fáris.

Ridge, پشته pushtah, بالا bálá.—(*of a furrow*) کردو kurdú, کرزه kurzah.—(*division of a field or garden*) مرز marz.

Ridgeways, بطور پشت ماهی bi-taur-i-pusht-i-máhí.

Ridicule, خنده khandah, مزاح mizáh, مسخره maskharah, سخریه

sukhríyat, هجو hajv, استهزا istihzá, لابه lábah, بارده báradí, مضحکه mazhakah.

To RIDICULE, استهزا نمودن istihzá nimúdan, مسخره ساختن maskharah sákhtan.

RIDICULOUS, مضحك muzhik, مسخره maskharah.

RIDING-CLOAK (*large, with wide sleeves*) بارانی báráni, جبه jubbah. —(*furred and richly laced*) کاتبی kátíbí.

RIDING-COAT (*long-skirted*), ايمه uyamah, تکمه tikmah. —(*short jacket*) کلیجه kulíjah, کردی kurdí.

RIDING-HOOD, باشلق báshlúk.

RIFE, مستولی mustaulí, مروج muravvaj, طاری tárí, متداول mutadával, عموم 'umúm.

RIFLE (*gun*), تفنگ ششخانه tufang-i-shish-khánah (so called from its having usually six grooves or channels in the barrel).—(*long rifle*) جزائر jazá,ir, جزائل jazá,il, شمخال shamkhál, شخمال shakhmál.—(*groove in a rifle barrel*) خانه khánah, ناب náb.—(*different parts of a rifle*) *vide* MUSKET.

To RIFLE, چپاو کردن chapáw kardan, غارت کردن ghárat kardan, يغما كردن yaghmá kardan, سلب گرفتن salab giriftan, نهب کردن nahb kardan, چپاولی کردن chapáwlí kardan (*vulg.*).

RIFLED (*gun*), خانه دار khánah-dár, ناب دار náb-dár.

RIFLEMAN, جزائرچی jazá,ir-chí, شمخالچی shamkhál-chí, ششخانه تفنگچی shish-khánah-tufang-chí.

RIGGING, بند جهاز band-i-jaház, ريسمان rísmán.

RIGHT (*proper*), بجا bi-já, روا ravá, مناسب munásib, شایسته sháyistah, واجب vájib, لائق lá,ik, سزا sizá, لازم lázim, درست durust.—(*to deem right*) صواب دانستن savábdánistan.—(*correct*) درست durust, راست rást, صحیح sahíh, کامل kámil, بی غلط bí-ghalat.—(*straight*) راست rást, صائب sá,ib, سهی suhí, مستقیم mustakím.—(*not left*) راست rást, یمین yamín.—(*right and left*) چپ و راست chap u rást, یمین و یسار yamín u yasár, میمنه و میسره maimanah va maisarah.—(*on the right*) دست راست dast-i-rást, در یمین dar yamín.—(*right or wrong*) حق یا نا حق hakk yá ná-hakk.—(*due*) حق hakk, لازمه lázimah (*pl.* لوازم lavázim).—(*prerogative*) اختیار ikhtiyár, اقتدار iktidár, قدرت kudrat, حق hakk.—(*civil rights*) حقوق مدینه hukúk-i-madínah.—(*political rights*) حقوق سیاسیه hukúk-i-siyásíyah.—(*established rights*) حقوقیکه الان هست hukúkí kih al'án hast.—(*property*) *vide* PROPERTY.

To RIGHT, انصاف کردن insáf kardan.

RIGHTEOUS, صالح sálih, صادق sádik, عادل 'ádil, دیانتدار diyánat-dár, متدین mutadayyin.

RIGHTEOUSLY, براستی bi-rástí, عادلانه 'ádilánah.

RIGHTEOUSNESS, صداقت sadákat, صلاحیت saláhíyat, سداد sadád, صواب saváb, راستی rástí, دیانت diyánat.

RIGHTFUL, راست rást, درست durust, صحیح sahíh.

RIGHTLY, بطور درست bi-taur-i-durust.

RIGID, متصلب mutasallib, سخت sakht, درشت durusht, صلب salab.

RIGIDITY, صلابت salábat, سختی sakhtí, درشتی durushtí.

RIGIDLY, متصلبانه mutasallibánah.

RIGOROUSLY, بشدت bi-shiddat, بسختی bi-sakhtí.

RIGORS (*shivering of a fever*), قشعریره kusha'rírah, ارتعاش irti-'ásh.

RIGOUR, شدت shiddat, سختی sakhtí.

RILL, جوی júí, جوب júb (*vulg.*).

RIM, لب lab, کنار kanár, کناره kanárah, کران karán.

RIME, پژه puzhah, گچلك gachak (*vulg.*).

RIND, پوست púst, قشر kishr.

RING, حلقه halkah.—(*for the finger*) انگشتر angushtar, انگشترین angushtarín. — (*signet ring*) خاتم khátim.—(*earring*) گوشواره gúshvárah, حلقهٔ گوش halkah-i-gúsh. —(*ankle ring*) خلخال khalkhál, پای برنجن páy-baranjan. —(*nose-ring*) حلقهٔ بینی halkah-i-bíní, برسن bursan (*obs.*).—(*thumb-ring, worn by archers, and used in drawing the bow*) شست shast, انگشتوانه angushtavánah, زه گیر zih-gír.—(*for fighting*) کشتیگاه kushtí-gáh, زور خانه zúr-khánah.

To RING (*a bell, &c.*), تکان دادن takán dádan, زدن zadan, نواختن navákhtan, صدا دادن sadá dádan. —(*like glass*) آواز دادن áváz dádan.

RINGDOVE, قمری kumrí, فاخته fákhtah.

RINGLEADER, پیش رو písh-rau, سر حلقه sar-halkah.

RINGLET, زلف zulf, جعد ja'd, حلقه halkah, تاب táb.

RINGWORM, حصف hasaf, بهق bahak.

To RINSE (*wash*), شستن shustan.—(*to rinse the mouth with water*) مضمضه کردن mazmazah kardan, غرغره کردن ghargharah kardan.—(*to rinse the nostrils with water*) استنشاق کردن istinshák kardan.

RIOT (*tumult*), هنگامه hangámah, اغتشاش ightishásh, عربده 'urbadah, شورش shúrish, شماته shamátah, بلوا balvá, آشوب áshúb, فتنه fitnah, فساد fasad, غوغا ghaughá, غلبگی ghalabagí, شلتاق shilták, شلوک shulúk.

RIOTER, گردن کش gardan-kash, سر کش sar-kash, اوباش aubásh.

RIOTOUS, پر غوغا pur-ghaughá.—(*men*) با غوغا bá-ghaughá, غوغای ghaugháí.

To RIP, دریدن darídan.

RIPE, رسیده rasídah, پخته pukhtah, مستوی mistaví.—(*half ripe*) نیمرس ním-ras.—(*quite ripe*) تمام رس tamám-ras.

To RIPEN, رسیدن rasídan.

RIPENESS, رسیدگی rasídagí, پختگی pukhtagí.

RIPPLE, آبشار áb-shár, زنجیر zanjír.

To RIPPLE, زنجیر زدن *or* کشیدن zanjír zadan *or* kashídan.

To RISE (*up*) بر خاستن bar-khástan, ایستادن ístádan, پا شدن pá shudan.—(*as the sun*) طلوع کردن tulú' kardan, بر آمدن bar-ámadan, اشراق ساختن ishrák sákhtan.—(*issue*) صادر شدن sádir shudan, صدور کردن sudúr kardan, پیدا شدن paidá shudan.—(*as a blister*) آبله کردن ábilah kardan.

RISIBILITY, خنده انگیزی khandah-angízí.

RISIBLE, با خنده bá-khandah, مضحک muzhik.

RISING (*tumult*), هنگامه hangámah, اغتشاش ightishásh, عربده 'urbadah, شورش shúrish, شماته shamátah, بلوا balvá, آشوب áshúb, فتنه fitnah, فساد fasád, غوغا ghaughá, غلبگی ghalabagí, شلتاق shilták, شلوک shulúk.

RISK, خطر khatar, خطره khatrah, مخاطره mukhátarah, بیم bím, خدشه khadashah, تشویش tashvísh, باک bák, تنگنائی tangná,í.—(*to run a risk*) خودرا در خطر انداختن khwudrá dar khatar andákhtan. —(*at the risk of one's life*) جان در هلاک انداخته ján dar halák andákhtah.

RITE, رسم rasm, تکلف takalluf, ادب adab, تعارف ta'áruf.

RITUAL (*subs.*) رسوم rusúm.—(*adj.*) رسومی rusúmí.

RIVAL, حریف haríf, غیر ghair, رقیب rakíb.—(*rival wife*) هوو havú, هئو ha,ú, همشوئی ham-shú,í, انباغ ambágh (*obs.*).

To RIVAL, رقابت کردن rakábat kardan, هم چشمی نمودن ham-chashmí nimúdan, هم سری نمودن ham-sarí nimúdan.

RIVALRY, رقابت rakábat, تسابق tasábuk.

RIVER, رود rúd, رود خانه rúd-khánah, نهر nahr.—(*large river*) دریا daryá, شاه رود sháh-rúd.—(*small river or brook*) جوی júí, جوب júb (*vulg.*).

RIVET, پرچین parchín.—(*for glass*) گنگو gangú.

To RIVET, پرچین کردن parchín kardan.—(*glass*) گنگو کردن gangú kardan.

ROAD, راه ráh, ره rah, طریق tarík, سبیل sabíl, مسلک maslak, درب darb, صراط sarát, وتیره vatírah, سمت samt, طریقه taríkah.—(*high road*), شارع shári', شاه راه sháh-ráh, جاده jáddah.—(*foot road*) مرد رو mard-rau.—(*narrow road or pass*) تنگ tang, تنگ راه tang-ráh, گدوک gadúk.—(*path in a garden, or place for walking*) خیابان khiyábán.—(*path or track through deep snow*) رش rush, or rash, چقر chikkir. — (*carriage road*) راه کالسکه رو ráh-i-káliskah-rau.

ROADSTEAD, بندر bandar, کشتیگاه kashtí-gáh, لنگرگاه langar-gáh.

To ROAM, آواره گشتن ávárah gashtan.

ROAN (*horse*), سرختیره surkh-tírah, قزل kizil.

ROAR, بانگ báng, غرش ghurrish.—(*sea*) زخار zakhkhár.

To ROAR, غریدن ghurrídan, غرش کردن ghurrish kardan, بانگ زدن báng zadan. — (*as the sea*) زخار کردن zakhkhár kardan.

To ROAST, کباب کردن kabáb kardan, بریان کردن biryán kardan, برشتن burushtan.

ROASTER, تابه کباب tábah-i-kabáb.

ROAST MEAT, کباب kabáb, بریان biryán.

To ROB, دزدیدن duzdídan, دزدی کردن duzdí kardan.

ROBBER, دزد duzd, راهزن ráh-zan, سارق sárik, قاطع الطریق káti'u-'t-tarík, قطاع الطریق kattá'u-'t-tarík, لص liss, قزاق kazzák, قشاق kazzák, حرامی harámí, یغمائی yaghmá,í.

ROBBERY, دزدی duzdí, راهزنی ráh-zaní, سرقه sarikah, لصاصت lasásat, غصب ghasb, غارت ghárat, چپاو chapáw, تاراج táráj, نهب nahb, نهیب nihíb, چپاولی chapáwlí (*vulg.*).

ROBE, پوشاک púshák, جامه jámah, لباس libás, کسوت kisvat, پوشن púshan.

To ROBE, پوشیدن púshídan, آراستن árástan.

ROBUST, تنو مند tanú-mand, زور آور zúr-ávar, قوی kaví.

ROCK, صخره sakhrah, سنگ sang.

To ROCK (*trans.*), تکان دادن takán dádan, جنبانیدن jumbánídan, تکانیدن takánídan. — (*intrans.*) جنبیدن jumbídan, تکان نمودن takán nimúdan, لاندن lándan (*obs.*).

ROCKET (*firework*), تیر هوا tír-i-havá.—(*of war*) گلوله قپز gulúlah-i-kuppuz, تیر تخش tír-takhsh, گلوله قنفذ gulúlah-i-kunfuz.

ROCKY, سنگ لاخ sang-lákh, پر سنگ pur-sang, سنگی sangí.

ROD, عصا 'asá, چوب دستی chúb-dastí, ترکه tarkah.—(*surveying*) گز gaz.

ROE (*deer*), آهو áhú. [This is strictly the antelope.]—(*of fish*), اشپل ishpul, تخم ماهی tukhm-i-máhí. — (*hard roe*) سخت تخم sakht-tukhm.—(*soft roe*) نرم تخم narm-tukhm.

ROEBUCK, بز کوهی buz - i - kúhí. [This is strictly the ibex.)

ROGATION, دعا du'á, استدعا istid'á, سوءال su,ál.

ROGUE, حیله باز hílah-báz, حیله ور hílah-var, فریبنده firíbandah, سر همبند sar-ham-band, قلابی kul-lábí, دستکج dast - kaj, اوباش aubásh, نا بکار ná-bi-kár, غدار ghaddár, مکار makkár, دولابی dú-lábí, دولاب باز dúláb-báz.

ROGUERY, عیاری 'ayyárí, حیله بازی hílah-bází, سر همبندی sar-ham-bandí.

ROLE, رسم rasm.

ROLL (*of paper, &c.*), لوله lúlah, طومار túmár.—(*handkerchief, &c., rolled up in a ball*) چنبره chambarah.—(*muster-roll*) فهرست fihrist.

To ROLL (*trans.*), غلطانیدن ghaltánídan. — (*intrans.*) غلطیدن ghaltídan.—(*as a ship*) حرکت کردن harakat kardan, تکان دادن takán dádan.—(*roll up*) پیچانیدن píchánídan, نوردیدن navardídan, ته کردن

tah kardan, طی کردن tai kardan, تا کردن tá kardan.—(*roll out, flatten, as dough, &c.*) پهن کردن pahn kardan, پخش کردن pakhsh kardan.

Roller (*for levelling ground, &c.*), غلطک ghaltak.—(*for smoothing a house-top*) بان غلطان bán-ghaltán.

Rolling (*ship*), متزلزل mutazalzil.

Rolling-pin, تیره tírah.

Roman Catholic, پاپاوی papáví (*eur.*).

Roman Catholicism, دین پاپا dín-i-pápá (*eur.*).

Romance, افسانه afsánah, داستان dástán.

To Romance, افسانه پرداختن afsánah pardákhtan.

Romancer, افسانه پرداز afsánah-pardáz.

Romantic, افسانه وش afsánah-vash.

Romp (*person*), بازی گوش bází-gúsh, هرزه گر harzah-gar, ول کار vil-kár, لعاب la"áb.—(*thing*) بازی bází, لعب la'b.

To Romp, بازی نمودن bází nimúdan, لعب نمودن la'b nimúdan.

Roof, بام bám, بان bán.—(*interior or ceiling*) سقف sakf, عرش 'arsh.—(*exterior or flat terrace*) پشت بام pusht-i-bám.—(*platform upon the roof*) سکوی بام sakkú,í-i-bám.—(*parapet round roof*) معجر ma'jar, محجر mahjar.—(*eaves or border of roof*) طره turrah.—(*coping or face of roof*) رخبام rukh-bám.—(*cupola*) گنبد gumbad, گنبذ gumbaz, قبه kubbah.—(*gable or arched roof*) شیروانی shírvání.—(*palate of the mouth*) سق sakk.

Rook, کلاغ kalágh.

Room, اوطاق úták, اوطاغ útágh, حجره hujrah, اتاق uták, اطاق uták.—(*principal room in a Persian house*) دیوانخانه díván-khánah.—(*upper room, higher story*) بالا خانه bálá-khánah.—(*open room, supported on pillars*) تالار talár.—(*hall or reception-room*) ایوان aiván.—(*lumber room*) پستو pastú, صندوقخانه sandúk-khánah, میان پای miyán-i-páy.—(*private room*) اوطاق خلوت úták-i-khalvat. (*Vide also* House.)—(*to turn a room inside out*) پس و پیش کردن pas va písh kardan.

[The different compartments of a Persian room are: (the floor) زمین zamín, کف kaf; (skirting or level part of the wall, extending from the floor to the height of three or four feet, sometimes of slabs of marble, sometimes of fine plaster, rarely of boards) هزاره hizárah; (niches or small recesses, extending round three sides of the room above the skirting) طاقچه tákchah; (spaces between the niches) جرز jirz; (cornice or moulding above the row of niches) مقرنس mukarnas; (ceiling) سقف sakf; (level ceiling) سقف تخته sakf-i-takhtah; (ceiling with cross-beams rounded and ornamented) سقف مرجوک sakf-i-marjavak; (vaulted ceiling) سقف مقبب sakf-i-mukabbab, سقف مقوس sakf-i-mukavvas; (large window of coloured glass set in carved woodwork, in sashes, occupying the front of the room) ارسی urusí; (fire-place, generally opposite the large window) بخاری bukhárí; (threshold) درگاه dargáh; (upper part of a room, seat of honour) صدر sadr.]

Roomy, واسع vási', وسیع vasí'.

Roost, چوب chúb.

To Roost, بر چوب نشستن bar chúb nishastan.

Root, بیخ bíkh, ریشه ríshah, بن bun, اصل asl, دمار damár.—(*grammatical term*) اصل asl.—(*in arithmetic*) جذر jazr (*pl.* جذور juzúr).

To Root (*take root*), ریشه زدن ríshah zadan.—(*to root up*) بر کندن bar-kandan, از بیخ بیرون آوردن az bíkh bírún ávardan.

Rope, رسن rasan, ریسمان rísmán.—

(*tent-rope*) طناب tanáb, طناف tanáf (*vulg.*).—(*cable*) عمار ʻumár (*eur.*).—(*stretched rope, on which anything is hung*) ملسا milsá.—(*network of ropes suspended from the roof, and which serves to contain various articles*) چنبره chambarah, آونگ ávang.

Rope-dancer, بازیگر bází-gar, ریسمان باز rísmán-báz, بند باز band-báz, بمباز bambáz (*vulg.*).

Rope-maker, حبال habbál, رسنتاب rasan-táb.

Rosary, تسبیح tasbíh, سبحه sabhah. — (*place*) گلستان gulistán, گلشن gulshan, گلزار gul-zár.

Rose, گل gul, ورد vard.—(*large white rose*) نسترن nastaran. — (*hundred-leaved rose*) گل صدبرگ gul-i-sad-barg. — (*eglantine or sweet-briar*) نسرین nasrín.—(*Gueldres rose, snowball tree*) بداق budák, بداغ budágh.—(*cluster rose*) گل خوشه بسته gul-i-khúshah-bastah. (*rose-bush*) گلبن gul-bun.—(*rose-bower*) گلستان gulistán, گلشن gulshan, گلزار gul-zár.—(*rose-water*) گلاب gul-áb. — (*hot mixture of rosewater and sugar*) گلاب نبات gul-áb-nabát.—(*otto of roses*) عطر گل ʻitr-i-gul.—(*conserve of roses*) گلقند gul-kand. — (*rose-coloured*) گلگون gul-gún.

Rosette, گل gul.

Rosin, ساقز sákiz, زد zidd, سقز sakkiz.

Rosy (*hue*), گلگون gul-gún, گلفام gul-fám, گلرنگ gul-rang.—(*rosy-cheeked*) سرخ surkh.

Rot, پوسیدگی púsídagí, گندگی gandagí.

To **Rot**, پوسیدن púsídan, گندیدن gandídan. — (*to cause to rot*) پوسانیدن púsánídan.

Rotation, دوران daurán, دور daur, گردش gardish, انقلاب inkiláb.

Rotatory, گردان gardán.

Rotten, پوسیده púsídah, گنده gandah, گندیده gandídah.

Rottenness, پوسیدگی púsídagí, گندگی gandagí.

Rotund, گرد gird, مدور mudavvar.

Roué, خود سر khwud-sar, خوش گذران khwush-guzrán, رند rind, شید باز shaid-báz, قلاش kallásh.

Rouge, غازه gházah.

Rough, درشت durusht, زبر zibr, نا هموار ná-hamvár.—(*as the sea*) مواج mavváj, متلاطم mutalátim.—(*unpolished*) نا پرداخته ná-pardákhtah, غیر مصقول ghair-i-maskúl. — (*in temper*) تند tund, درشت durusht, بد خو bad-khú, عتل ʻutull.

To **Roughen** (*trans.*), نا هموار ساختن ná-hamvár sákhtan.—(*intrans.*) نا هموار شدن ná-hamvár shudan.

Roughly, با درشتی bá-durushti, با شدت bá-shiddat.

Roughness, درشتی durushtí, نا همواری ná-hamvárí.—(*sea*) تلاطم talátum, تموج tamavvuj.—(*temper*) تندی tundí, درشتی durushtí, بد خوئی bad-khú,í.

Round, گرد gird, مدور mudavvar.—(*around*) گرداگرد gird-á-gird, دور daur, پیرامون pairámún, در دوره dar daurah, دوراً dauran, در حوالی dar haválí.—(*of a ladder*), پله pillah. — (*of a race-course*) دوره daurah.

Rounded, مدور mudavvar.

Roundly, گرداگرد gird-á-gird, مدوراً mudavvaran. — (*openly*) ظاهراً záhiran, علانیةً ʻalániyatan, آشکاره áshkárah, عیاناً ʻayánan.

Roundness, گرد gird.

To **Rouse**, انگیختن angíkhtan, خیزانیدن khízánídan, برآشفتن bar-áshuftan, تحریک کردن tahrík kardan, بیدار کردن bídár kardan.

Rout (*defeat*), شکست shikast, هزیمت hazímat, انهزام inhizám.

To **Rout**, هزیمت دادن hazímat dádan, شکست دادن shikast dádan.—(*to be routed*) شکست خوردن shikast khwurdan.

Route, راه ráh, ره rah, طریق tarík, سبیل sabíl, مسلک maslak, درب darb, صراط sarát, وتیره vatírah, سمت samt, طریقه tarikah. — (*en route*) براه bi-ráh, رو براه rú bi-ráh.

To Rove, آواره گشتن ávárah gashtan, گرديدن gardídan, سير كردن sair kardan, گشت كردن gasht kardan.

Rover, آواره ávárah, گردش كننده gardish-kunandah.

Row (*line*), صف saff, قطار kitár, رديف radíf, رده raddah.—(*in rows*) بردیف bi-radíf.—(*tumult*) هنگامه hangámah, اغتشاش ightishásh, عربده 'urbadah, شورش shúrish, شماته shamátah, بلوا balvá, آشوب áshúb, فتنه fitnah, فساد fasád, غوغا ghaughá, شلتاق shilták, شلوك shulúk.—(*to lay in rows*) رديف نهادن radíf nihádan, رده گذاردن radah guzárdan.

To Row (*a boat*), پارو كشيدن párú kashídan, خاده زدن khádah zadan.

Rower, خاده كش khádah-kash, پارو كش párú-kash.

Royal, شاهی sháhí, پادشاهی pádisháhí, شاهانه sháhánah, پادشاهانه pádisháhánah, خاقانی khákání, سلطانی sultání, خسروی khusraví, كيانی kayání, شهرياری shahr-yárí, شاه وار sháh-vár.

Royalist, خير خواه سلطان khair-khwáh-i-sultán.

Royally, شاهانه sháhánah, پادشاهانه pádisháhánah.

Royalty, سلطنت sultanat, شاهی sháhí.

Rub, مالش málish.

To Rub, ماليدن málídan, سودن súdan, سائيدن sá,ídan, سابيدن sábídan.—(*to rub down a horse*) مالش كردن málish kardan, ماليدن málídan.—(*to rub off, dust*) زدودن zadúdan.—(*to rub out*) محو كردن mahv kardan.

Rubber (*person*), مالش دهنده málish-dihandah.—(*for grooming a horse*), كفی kafí, كفمال kaf-mál.

Rubbing, مالش málish.

Rubbish, خاشاك kháshák, خاكروبه khák-rúbah, اشكال ashkál, ادبار idbár, رشت rasht.

Ruby, لعل la'l, ياقوت احمر yákút-i-ahmar.

Rudder, سكان sukkán, دومن dúman, خله khallah.

Ruddiness, سرخی surkhí.

Ruddy, سرخ و سفيد surkh u safíd, سرخ surkh, سرخ رنگ surkh rang.

Rude, بی ادب bí-adab, درشت durusht, بی سليقه bi-salíkah, گستاخ gustákh, وحشی vahshí.—(*to be rude*) زباندرازی كردن zabán-dirází kardan.

Rudely, بی ادبانه bí-adabánah, گستاخانه gustákhánah.

Rudeness, بی ادبی bí-adabí, درشتی durushtí, گستاخی gustákhí, بی ساختگی bí-sákhtagí, بی تعارفی bí-ta'árufí.

Rudiment, اصل asl (*pl.* اصول usúl), قواعد kavá'id (*used in plural*), مصدر masdar.

Rudimental, اصلی aslí.

Rue (*herb*), سداب sudáb.

To Rue, *vide* To Regret.

Rueful, دلتنگ dil-tang, پريشان paríshán, ملول malúl, غمگين gham-gín, غمناك gham-nák.

Ruefully, غمناكانه gham-nákánah.

Ruefulness, غم gham, پريشانی paríshání, غمگينی gham-giní.

Ruffian, اوباش aubásh, جلاد jallád.

To Ruffle, درهم برهم ساختن darham-barham sákhtan, برهم زدن barham zadan.

Rug, فرش farsh, قالی kálí.

Rugged, درشت durusht, نا هموار ná-hamvár.

Ruggedly, با درشتی bá-durushtí.

Ruggedness, درشتی durushtí, نا هموارى ná-hamvárí.

Ruin, تلف talaf, تباهی tabáhí, خرابی kharábí, خلل khalal, اخلال ikhlál, خسارت khasárat.—(*place*) ويرانی vairání, خرابه kharábah, ويرانه vairánah.

To Ruin, خراب نمودن kharáb nimúdan, زير و زبر كردن zír u zabar kardan, تتبير كردن tatbír kardan.—(*persons*) متضرر گردانيدن mutazarrir gardánídan, شكسته حال گردانيدن shikastah-hál gardánídan.

Ruined, خراب kharáb, منهدم munhadam, رنبيده rumbídah, پايمال páy-mál, پخش pakhsh, بائر bá,ir.—

(*destroyed*) تباه tabáh, معدوم ma'-dúm, منهدم munhadam, تلف talaf, پايمال páy-mál, منقطع mun-kata'.—(*broken in fortune*) مفلس muflis, مستأصل musta,sal.—(*to fall in ruins*) خراب شدن kharáb shudan, رنبيدن rumbídan, منهدم شدن munhadam shudan.—(*to be ruined*) متضرر گرديدن mutazarrir gardídan.

RUINOUS, مهلك muhlik, متلف mut-lif.—(*desolate*) ويران vairán, خراب kharáb.

RUINOUSLY, متلفانه mutlifánah.

RULE (*government*) حكومت hukú-mat, حكمرانی hukm-rání, داوری dávarí, فرمانروائی firmán-ravá,í, فرمان گذاری firmán-guzárí, رئياست ri,ásat, تمشيت tamshíyat, عمل 'amal, ايالت iyálat, سلطنت sulta-nat, تسلط tasallut.—(*regulation*) قانون kánún, قاعده ká'idah, رسم rasm.—(*according to rule*) *vide* REGULAR.—(*mason's rule*) گونيه gúnyá, سه گوش sih-gúsh.—(*rule of three*) قانون مثلثی kánún-i-musallasí.—(*double rule of three*) مثلثی مضاعف musallasí-i-mu-zá'af.

To RULE, حكومت كردن hukúmat kardan, داوری نمودن dávarí nimú-dan.—(*to rule lines*) مسطر نمودن mistar nimúdan.

RULER (*for marking lines on paper, consisting of threads stretched upon a piece of pasteboard, in parallel order*), مسطر mistar.—(*king*) پادشاه pádisháh, شاه sháh, شه shah, ملك malk, سلطان sultán, خاقان khákán, كی kai.

RUM, روم rúm (*eur.*).

To RUMBLE (*thunder*), غريدن ghur-rídan.

RUMINANT *and* RUMINATION, نوشخوار núshkhwár.

To RUMINATE, نوشخوار كردن núsh-khwár kardan.—(*reflect*) فكر نمودن fikr nimúdan.

RUMMAGE, تلاش talásh.

To RUMMAGE, تلاش كردن talásh kar-dan.

RUMOUR, شهرت shuhrat, خبر khabar, گفتگو guftugú, گپ gap (*hind*).

To RUMOUR, خبر دادن khabar dá-dan.

RUMP, سرين surín, كفل kafal.—(*rump-bone*) عصعص 'us'us.

To RUMPLE, پيچ و چين پيدا كردن pích va chín paidá kardan.

RUN, دو dau.

To RUN, دويدن davídan, تاختن tákhtan, شتاب كردن shitáb kar-dan.—(*to flow*) جاری شدن jári shudan, روان شدن raván shudan.—(*to flee*) گريختن guríkhtan, فرار كردن firár kardan.—(*to run through*) *vide* To TRANSFIX.—(*melt*) گداختن gudákhtan, آب شدن áb shudan.—(*to run up and down*) تكاپو كردن takápú kardan, پوئيدن pú,ídan.—(*as ink on bad paper*) نشف كردن nashf kardan.—(*to run out*) ريختن ríkhtan.—(*to run over*) زير پا كردن zír-i-pá kardan.

RUNAWAY, فراری firárí.

RUNNER, دونده davandah.—(*mes-senger*) قاصد kásid, شاطر shátir, پيك paik.

RUNNING, دوان daván.

RUPEE, روپيه rúpiyah.

RUPTURE (*breach*), شكست shikast, شكاف shikáf, رخنه rikhnah.—(*dispute*) دعوی da'vá, نزاع nizá', منازعت munáza'at, مشاجره mushá-jarah, جدل jadal, لجاج lajáj, ستيزه sitízah, جنگ jang, مناقشه muná-kashah.—(*hernia*) فتق fatk.—(*between friends*) منقطع دوستی munkati'-i-dústí.

RURAL, صحرائی sahrá,í, دهقانی dih-kání, روستائی rústá,í.

RUSE, *vide* TRICK.

RUSH (*flag or reed*), پيزر pízur, لخ lukh, جگن jagan. — (*bulrush*) خونك khúnak, خنك khunak, هردی hurdí. — (*sudden spring*) جست jast, هجوم hujúm, تاخت tákht, حمله hamlah, يورش yúrish.

To RUSH, جستن jastan, هجوم آوردن hujúm ávardan.

RUSK, سخری sukhrí, كماج خشك kumáj-i-khushk, بست كماج bast-i-kumáj, نان چاهی nán-i-cháhí.

Rust, زنگ zang.

Rustic (*countryman*), روستائی rústá,í, دهقان dihkán.—(*rural*) صحرائی sahrá,í, دهقانی dihkání, روستائی rustá,í.

Rusticity, بی ادبی bí-adabí.

To Rustle, صدا کردن sadá kardan.

Rusty, زنگ گرفته zang-giriftah, زنگ آلوده zang-álúdah, زنگ زده zang-zadah.

Rut, گود gaud. [This is properly a ditch.]

Ruthless, جفا کار jafá-kár, بیرحم bí-rahm, درشت durusht, سنگدل sang-dil, ظالم zálim, بیمروت bí-murúvat, جبار jabbár, ستمکار sitam-kár.

Rye, گندم سیاه gandum-i-siyáh, گندم بهاره gandum - i - bahárah, چاودار cháwdár.

S.

Sabæan (*worshipper of the sun, moon, and host of heaven*), صابی sábí, نبطی nabatí.

Sabbath (*day*), سبت sabt, یوم السبت yaumu-'s-sabt. — (*Holy Sabbath*) سبت مقدس sabt-i-mu-kaddas.

Sable (*fur*), پوست سمور púst-i-sammúr. — (*the animal*) سمور sammúr.—(*black*) سیاه siyáh.—(*sables, mourning*) لباس مشکی libás-i-mishkí, لباس عزا libás-i-'azá.

Sabre, شمشیر shimshír.

Saccharine, شیرین shírín.

Sacerdotal, مقدس mukaddas.

Sack, جوال juvál, چوال chuvál.—(*storming of a town, &c.*) تسخیر taskhír, تاخت و تاراج tákht u táráj, غارت و خسارت ghárat va khasá-rat.

To Sack, غارت کردن ghárat kardan. تاراج نمودن táráj nimúdan.

Sack-cloth, پلاس palás.

Sacrament (*holy institute*), منسك مقدس mansik - i - mukaddas.—(*Baptism*) تعمید ta'míd, معمودیه ma'múdíyah, اصطباغ istibágh.—(*the Lord's Supper*) عشا ربانی 'ashá-i-rabbání, قداس kudás.

Sacred, مقدس mukaddas, قدسی kudsí, قدوس kudús, مبارك mu-bárak, مطهر mutahhar, منزه mu-nazzah, پاك pák, متبرك mutabar-rak.—(*sacred places*) اماکن مبارکه amákin-i-mubárakah.

Sacredness, مبارکی mubárakí, پاکی pákí, قدس kuds, تقدس takad-dus.

Sacrifice, کشتار kushtár, ذبح zibh. —(*thing offered up*) قربان kurbán, فدا fidá, تصدق tasadduk, نثار nisár.

To Sacrifice, فدا کردن fidá kardan, قربان نمودن kurbán nimúdan, ذبح نمودن zibh nimúdan, نحر کردن nahr kardan.—(*to sacrifice one's life*) جان در خطر انداختن ján dar khatar andákhtan.

Sacrificed, مذبوح mazbúh.

Sacrificial, قربانی kurbání.

Sacrilege, دزدی حرام duzdí-i-harám.

Sacrilegious, زشت zisht, نا مقدس ná mukaddas, خبیث مانند khabís-mánand, پلیدانه pilídánah.

Sad, دلتنگ dil-tang, دلفکار dil-fikár, دلگیر dil-gír, غمگین gham-gín,

غمناك gham-nák, مغموم maghmúm, حزين hazín, محزون mahzún, متعبس muta'abbis, ملول malúl, اندوه ناك andúh-nák, متألم muta'allim, سهمگين sahm-gín.—(*to be sad*) تأسف خوردن tá,assuf khwurdan, رنج كشيدن ranj kashídan, مبتلا شدن mubtalá shudan, مكدر شدن mukaddar shudan.

To SADDEN, دلتنگ ساختن dil-tang sákhtan, متفكر كردن mutafakkir kardan.

SADDLE, زين zín, سرج sarj.—(*bow of a saddle*) كوهه زين kúhah-i-zín, سر زين sar-i-zín, قربوس karbús, قاش زين kásh-i-zín.—(*stuffing or pad of a saddle*) تكلتو takaltú, تكلتى takaltí, تگل tagal.—(*hinder part of a saddle*) ترك tark.—(*saddle-girth*) تنگ tang.—(*crupper*) قشقون kashkún.—(*straps for tying up game when killed, &c.*) فتراك fitrák.—(*saddle-bags*) جوال juvál, تاچه táchah, خور جين khwur-jín.—(*saddle-cover*) زين پوش zín-púsh, غاشيه gháshiyah, دگدگى digdigí.—(*saddle-cloth, placed under the saddle*) جل jul, عرقگير 'arak-gír.—(*saddle-tree*) قلتاق kalták.—(*pack-saddle*) پالان pálán.—(*camel's saddle*) پالان شتر pálán-i-shutur, جهاز شتر jaház-i-shutur.—(*elephant's saddle*) حوده haudah, هودج haudaj, هوده haudah.

To SADDLE, زين كردن zín kardan, رخت نمودن rakht nimúdan.

SADDLER (*maker of the leather-work, &c.*), سراج sarráj.—(*maker of the saddle-tree*) زين ساز zín-sáz.

SADLY, با غم bá-gham.

SADNESS, دلتنگى dil-tangí, دلفكارى dil-fikárí, دلگيرى dil-gírí, غمگينى gham-gíní, حزن huzn, ملال malál, غم gham, الم alam.

SAFE, امين amín, ايمن íman, مسلم musallam, مأمون ma,mún, بسلامت bi-salámat, رستگار rastagár, سالم sálim, موتمن mu,taman.—(*for keeping provisions, &c.*), گنجه ganjah.—(*for jewels, &c.*), گنجينه ganjínah, صندوق آهن sandúk-i-áhan.

SAFEGUARD, حفاظت hifázat, پناه panáh, حمايت himáyat.

SAFELY, با سلامت ba-salámat.

SAFETY, سلامت salámat, امن aman, امان amán, حفاظت hifázat, رستگارى rastagárí.

SAFFRON, زعفران za'frán.—(*bastard saffron*) معصفر mu'asfar.

SAGACIOUS, عاقل 'ákil, ماهر máhir, زيرك zírak, زرنگ zaring, دانا dáná, بخرد bikhrad.

SAGACITY, فراست firásat, زكاوت zakávat, فطانت fatánat, بصيرت basírat, جزالت jazálat, بخردى bikhradí, دانائى dáná,í, زيركى zírakí, زرنگى zaringí.

SAGE (*herb*), سالبيه sálbiyah.—(*wise man*) حكيم hakím, فيلسوف failasúf, عالم 'álim, خرد مند khirdmand, دانشمند dánish-mand, بزرگ buzurg, حكمت پيشه hikmat-píshah.—(*sagacious*), عاقل 'ákil, ماهر máhir, زيرك zírak, زرنگ zaring, دانا dáná, بخرد bikhrad.

SAGELY, فرزانه وار farzánah-vár.

SAGO, ساگو ságú (*eur.*).

SAIL, پرده pardah, شراع shirá', جل jall, يلكن yalkan, بادبان bád-bán (*obs.*).—(*to hoist sail*) شراع كشيدن shirá' kashídan, شراع زدن shirá' zadan.—(*to take in sail*) شراع پيچيدن shirá' píchídan.—(*to take the wind out of one's sails*) پيش دستى كردن písh-dastí kardan.

To SAIL, سفر دريا كردن safar-i-daryá kardan.

SAILING, سفر دريا safar-i-daryá.

SAIL-MAKER, شراع ساز shirá'-sáz.

SAILOR, جاشو jáshú, ملاح malláh.

SAINT, ولى valí, پير pír.—(*one sanctified by Divine Grace*) مقدس mukaddas.—(*the Saints*) اصفياء asfiyá,, اوليا awliyá.

SAINTLY, بزرگوار buzurg-vár.

SAINTSHIP, تقدس takaddus, قداست kadásat.

SAKE, واسطه vásitah, براى baráy, اجل ajl, جهت jihat, بهر bahr.—(*for *the sake of*) از برای az baráy, پاس خاطر pás-i-khátir, از بهر az bahr, لاجل li ajli, بنا بخاطر biná bi-khátir, بواسطه bi-vásitah, بنا بر biná bar.

SALACIOUS, مست mast, شهوت پرست shahvat-parast.

SALACIOUSNESS, مستی mastí, شهوت shahvat, هوا havá, هوس havas, فسق fisk, نفس nafs.

SALAD, صلاته salátah (*eur*), سالات sálát (*eur.*).

SALAMANDER, سمندر samandar.

SAL-AMMONIAC, نوشادر naushádur.

SALARY, مواجبه mavájabah, مشاهره musháharah, وظیفه vazífah, جیره jírah.

SALE, فروش furúsh, بیع bai', فروخت furúkht.—(*by auction*) هراج harráj, لیلام lailám (*eur.*).—(*confirmed sale*) بیع قطعی bai'-i-kat'í.—(*conditional sale*) بیع خیار bai'-i-khıyár, شرط خیار فسخ shart-i-khiyár-i-faskh. — (*to exhibit for sale*) برای فروش چیدن baráy-i-furúsh chídan.

SALEABLE, قابل فروخت kábil-i-furúkht.

SALESMAN, فروشنده furúshandah, بایع báí'.

SALINE, نمکزار namak-zár, نمکسار namak-sár.

SALIVA, تف tuf, لعاب lu'áb, خیو khuyú, بزاق buzák, آب دهن áb-i-dahan, سلف suluf.

To be SALIVATED, دهان جوشیدن dahán júshídan, جوشش دهان بهم رسانیدن júshish-i-dahán bi-ham rasánídan.

SALLOW, زرد zard, اصفر asfar.

SALLY, یورش yúrish, خروج khurúj, هجوم hujúm.—(*sally-port*) دریچه daríchah.

To SALLY, یورش کردن yúrish kardan, هجوم آوردن hujúm ávardan, حمله کردن hamlah kardan.

SALMON, قزل ماهی kizil-máhí, آزاد ماهی ázád-máhí.

SALOON, تالار tálár, ایوان aiván, دیوانخانه díván-khánah.

SALT, نمك namak. — (*rock-salt*) نمك تبر زد namak-i-tabar-zad.—(*table-salt*) نمك طعام namak-i-ta'ám. — (*adj.*) نمکین namakín, شور shúr.

To SALT, نمك ریختن namak ríkhtan, نمکین کردن namakín kardan, نمك پاشیدن namak páshídan, نمك سود نمودن namak-súd nimúdan.

SALT-CELLAR, نمکدان namak-dán.

SALTER, نمك زن namak-zan.

SALTPETRE, شوره shúrah.

SALT-PIT, نمکسار namak-sár.

SALUBRIOUS, گواره guvárah, سازگار sáz-gár, صحت بخش sihhat-bakhsh.

SALUBRITY, عافیت 'áfiyat, صحت sihhat.

SALUTARY, مفید mufíd, نافع náfi'. —(*salubrious*) گواره guvárah, سازگار sáz-gár, صحت بخش sihhat-bakhsh.

SALUTATION, سلام salám, درود durúd, تحیه tahíyah.

SALUTE, سلام نظامی salám-i-nizámí, احترام نظامی ihtirám-i-nizámí.—(*with cannon*) شلیك shalík, تیر توپ tír-i-túp.

To SALUTE, تیر توپ شلیك انداختن tír-i-túp shalík andákhtan, توپ انداختن túp andákhtan.—(*as a soldier*) احترامات نظامی بعمل آوردن ihtirámát-i-nizámí bi-'amal ávardan, سلام نظامی دادن salám-i-nizámí dádan.

SALVAGE, سلویج salvíj (*eur.*).

SALVATION, رستگاری rastagárí, نجات naját, رهائی rihá,í, سلامت salámat, سعادت sa'ádat.

SALVE, مرهم marham, ضماد zamád.

SALVER, مجموعه majmú'ah, سینی síní.

SAME, همین hamín, همان hamán. —(*alike*) برابر barábar, یکسان yaksán, مشابه mushábih, نظیر nazír, مساوی musáví.—(*prefix in composition*) یك yak, هم ham.—(*same repeated, ditto*) مکرر mukarrar.

SAMENESS, مطابقت mutábakat.

SAMPLE, نمونه nimúnah, مثال misál.

SANATIVE, صحت بخش sihhat-bakhsh.

SANCTIFICATION, تقديس takdís, تنزيه tanzíh, تطهير tathír.

SANCTIFIED, مقدس mukaddas, قدسى kudsí, قدوس kudús, مبارك mubárak, مطهر mutahhar, منزه munazzah, پاك pák, متبرك mutabarrak.

To SANCTIFY, مقدس كردن mukaddas kardan, منزه كردن munazzah kardan, تطهير نمودن tathír nimúdan, تقديس نمودن takdís nimúdan.

SANCTIMONIOUS, زاهدانه záhidánah, صالح sálih, عابد 'ábid.

SANCTION, اجازت ijázat, اذن izn, اباحت ibáhat, رضا razá, رخصت rukhsat, دستور dastúr, جواز javáz. —(*approval*) تصديق tasdík.

To SANCTION, تصديق كردن tasdík kardan.

SANCTITY, مباركى mubárakí, پاكى pákí, قدس kuds, تقدس takaddus.

SANCTUARY (*holy place*), مكان مقدس makán-i-mukaddas. — (*asylum*) پناه panáh, امان aman, مأمن ma,-man, ملاذ maláz, ملجا maljá, عياذ 'iyáz, مفر mafarr, بست bast.

SANCTUM, حريم harím, خلوت khalvat.

SAND, ريگ ríg, ماسه mássah.—(*fine sand*) ماسه mássah.

To SAND, ريگ پاشيدن ríg páshídan.

SANDAL, نعلين na'lín. — (*sandal wood*) صندل sandal.

SANDBANK, پشته ريگ pushtah-i-ríg.

SANDINESS, پر ريگى pur-rígí.

SANDWICH, پيچيده گوشت píchídah-gúsht, گوشت پيچ gúsht-pích.

SANDY, ريگى rígí.—(*desert*) ريگستان rígistán.

SANE, صحيح sahíh, سالم sálim.

SANGUINARY, خونخوار khún-khwár, خونريز khún-ríz, خون آشام khún-áshám.

SANGUINE, اميدوار umíd-vár, متوقع mutavakki'.

SANGUINENESS, اميد umíd, توقع tavakku'.

SANITARY, صحى sihhí.

SANITY, صحت sihhat, تندرستى tandurustí, عافيت 'áfiyat, اوغر úghur.

SAP, شيره shírah, آب áb, عرق 'arak.

To SAP, كندن kandan, نقب زدن nakb zadan.

SAPIENCE, عقل 'akl, فراست firásat, ادراك idrák, ذهن zihn, زكاوت zakávat.

SAPIENT, عاقل 'ákil, دانشمند dánishmand, زرنگ zaring, زيرك zírak, چابك chábuk, چست chust.

SAPLESS, بى شيره bí-shírah, بى آب bí-áb, بى عرق bi-'arak.

SAPLING (*young shrub*), نهال nihál.

SAPONACEOUS, صابونى sábúní.

SAPPHIRE, ياقوت كبود yákút-i-kabúd, ياقوت ازرق yákút-i-azrak.

SAPPINESS, پر شيرگى pur-shíragí.

SAPPY, پر شيره pur-shírah.

SARCASM, هجو hajv, هجا hijá, مزاح mazáh, استهزا istihzá, طنز tanz.

SARCASTIC, طعنه زن ta'nah-zan, مستهزئى mustahz,í, با مزه bá-mazah.

SARCOPHAGUS, تابوت tábút, صندوق مقبره sandúk-i-makbarah.

SARSAPARILLA, عشبه 'ushbah.

SASH, شال كمر shál-i-kamar.—(*of a window*) درك darak, بالا رو bálá-rau.

SATAN, شيطان shaitán, ابليس iblís.

SATANIC, شيطانى shaitání.

SATCHEL, توشه دان túshah-dán.

SATELLITE, تابع tábi', خادم khádim.

To SATIATE, سير كردن sír kardan.

SATIATED, سير sír.—(*to be satiated*) سير شدن sír shudan.

SATIETY, سيرى sírí, شبع shab', شباعت shabá'at.

SATIN, اطلس atlas.

SATIRE, هجو hajv, هجا hijá.

SATIRICAL, هجو آمير hajv-ámíz.

SATIRIST, هجو گو hajv-gú.

To SATIRIZE, هجو كردن hajv kardan.

SATISFACTION (*content of mind*), دلآساى dil-ásáí, خوشدلى khwush-dilí, رضا مندى razá-mandí, رضا razá, خاطر جمعى khátir-jam'í, اطمئنان itmi,nán.—(*reparation for an injury*) عوض 'avaz, بدله badlah, جزا jazá, كفارت kaffárat,

مکافات mukáfát, مؤاخذه mu,ákhazah.

SATISFACTORY, دلخواه dil-khwáh, خاطر پسند khátir-pasand.

SATISFIED, راضی rází, خوش khwush, خوشنود khwush-núd, خرسند khursand, قانع káni', مستغنی mustaghní, سیر sír, آسوده ásúdah.—(*self-satisfied*) خود پسند khwud-pasand.

To SATISFY, راضی کردن rází kardan, خوشنود گردانیدن khwush-núd gardánídan.—(*to be satisfied with*) راضی شدن (از) rází shudan (az), خشنودی داشتن (از) khush-núdí dáshtan (az).

To SATURATE, اشباع کردن ishbá' kardan, سیر کردن sír kardan.

SATURATION, شبع shab'.

SATURDAY, شنبه shambah, روز شنبه rúz-i-shambah.

SATURN (*planet*), زحل zuhal, کیوان kaiván.

SATURNALIA, کلاشی kalláshí, عیاشی 'ayyáshí..

SATURNALIAN, کلاش kallásh.

SATURNINE, با وقار bá-vakár, با تمکین bá-tamkín.

SATYR, غول ghúl, افریت ifrít.

SAUCE, چاشنی cháshní.

SAUCEPAN, دیگ díg, دیگچه dígchah.

SAUCER, نلبکی nalbakí, نعلبکی na'lbakí, تشتری tashtarí.

SAUCILY, گستاخانه gustákhánah, بشوخی bi-shúkhí.

SAUCINESS, گستاخی gustákhí, شوخی shúkhí.

SAUCY (*impudent*), گستاخ gustákh, شوخ shúkh, طناز tannáz.

To SAUNTER, آواره گشتن ávárah gashtan, گردیدن gardídan, سیر کردن sair kardan, گشت کردن gasht kardan.

SAVAGE (*wild*), وحشی vahshí, بیابانی biyábání, دشتی dashtí, جنگلی jangalí.—(*cruel*) جفا کار jafá-kár, بیرحم bí-rahm, درشت durusht, سنگدل sang-dil, ظالم zálim, بیمروت bí-murúvat, جبار jabbár, ستمکار sitam-kár.—(*animal*) درنده darandah.—(*a wild man*) مرد وحشی mard-i-vahshí, آدم جنگلی ádam-i-jangalí.

SAVAGELY, با سنگدلی bá-sang-dilí.

SAVAGENESS, وحشیگری vahshígarí.—(*cruelty*) ظلم zulm, ستم sitam, سنگدلی sang-dilí, خشونت khushúnat.—(*animal*) درندگی darandagí.

SAVANT, حکیم hakím, عالم 'álim. بزرگ buzurg.

SAVE, بغیر bi-ghair, بجز ba-juz, غیر از ghair az, مگر magar.

To SAVE (*deliver*), رهانیدن rihánídan, خلاص کردن khalás kardan, نجات دادن naját dádan, رهائی دادن rihá,í dádan, آزاد کردن ázád kardan, رها کردن rihá kardan.——(*preserve*) نگاه داشتن nigáh dáshtan, احتیاط کردن ihtiyát kardan.—(*to save oneself*) رستن rastan.—(*to save one's life*) جان بدر بردن ján bi-dar burdan, جان بسلامت بردن ján bi-salámat burdan.

SAVIOUR, رهاننده rihánandah, نجات دهنده naját-dihandah.

SAVOUR, مزه mazah, گوار guvár.

To SAVOUR, مزه داشتن mazah dáshtan.

SAVOURY, گوار guvár.

SAW, اره arrah, اره irrah.—(*hand-saw*) دست اره dast-arrah.

To SAW, با اره بریدن bá-arrah burídan, اره کشیدن irrah kashídan.

SAWDUST, براده burádah.

SAWYER, اره کش arrah-kash.

To SAY, گفتن guftan, تقریر کردن takrír kardan.—(*respectfully*) فرمودن firmúdan.—(*one would say*) گویا gúyá.—(*that is to say*) یعنی ya'ní.

SAYING, گفتار guftár, سخن sukhun, مقالات makálat.

SCAB (*of a wound*), پوست ریش púst-i-rísh.—(*itch*) جرب jarab, گر gar.

SCABBARD, غلاف ghiláf, نیام niyám, میان miyán, جفیر jafír.

SCABBY, گرگین gar-gín.

SCAFFOLD (*wooden platform*), چوب بست chúb-bast, دار بست dárbást, تلواره talvárah.

To SCALD, از آب گرم سوختن az áb-i-garm súkhtan.
SCALDING, سوزان súzán.
SCALDINGS (*in passing urine*), سوزنك súzanak.
SCALE (*cup of a balance*), پله pillah. — (*of a crocodile*) سپر sipar. — (*of a fish*) پولك ماهی púlak-i-máhí, فلس fils.—(*gradation*) درجه darajah, تدریج tadríj. —(*for maps, &c.*) مقیاس mikyás.
SCALES, ترازو tarázú, میزان mízán.
SCALEY, فلس دار fils-dár, پولك دار púlak-dár.
SCAMMONY, سقمونیا sukmúniyá.
To SCAMPER, دویدن davídan, گریختن guríkhtan.
To SCAN, نظر نمودن nazar nimúdan, نگران گشتن nigrán gashtan.—(*poetry*) تقطیع کردن taktí' kardan.
SCANDAL, بهتان buhtán, تهمت tuhmat, غیبت ghíbat, افترا iftirá.
To SCANDALIZE, رنجانیدن ranjánídan, مذمت کردن mazammat kardan, بد نام ساختن bad-nám sákhtan.
SCANDALOUS, فرومایه furú-máyah, بد bad, زبون zabún.
SCANSION (*of verse*), تقطیع taktí'.—(*foot of a verse in scanning*) رکن rukn, جزء juz.
SCANTINESS, کمی kamí, قلت killat, تنگی tangí.
SCANTY, قلیل, kalíl, کم kam, تنگ tang.
SCAPEGOAT, بز طلیقه buz-i-talíkah.
SCAR, داغ dágh, نشان nishán.
To SCAR, داغ نمودن dágh nimúdan.
SCARCE (*rare*), نادر nádir, کم kam, کمیاب kam-yáb.—(*few*) کم عدد kam-'adad, کم kam, قلیل kalíl شاذ sház.
SCARCELY, با دشواری bá-dushvárí, مشکلانه mushkilánah, با دقت ba-dikkat.
SCARCITY, کمی kamí, قحط kaht, قلت killát, کم رسی kam-rasí, تنگی tangí, غلاً ghalá,.
SCARECROW (*in a cornfield*), مترس matars.
SCARF, گردنبند gardan-band.

SCARLET, سقرلات sakarlát (*eur.*), قرمزی kirmizí.
To SCATTER, پراکندن parákandan, پاشیدن páshídan, ریختن ríkhtan, پریشان کردن paríshán kardan, افشاندن afshándan, تار و مار کردن tár u már kardan.
SCATTERED, پراکنده parákandah, پریشان paríshán, افشانده afshándah, منتشر muntashir, ریخته ríkhtah, پاشیده páshídah, تار مار tár-már, پخش pakhsh. — (*scattered locality*) واسع vási', پهناور pahnávar. — (*to be scattered*) متفرق شدن mutafarrak shudan.
SCAVENGER, کناس kannás.
SCENE, منظر manzar, تماشا tamáshá. —(*stage*) پرده pardah.
SCENERY, نظر انداز nazar-andáz.
SCENT, بوی búy, بخور bukhúr, عطر 'itr.
To SCENT, خوش بو کردن khwush-bú kardan.
SCENT-BOX, عنبر دان 'ambar-dán.
SCENTED, معطر mu'attar.
SCEPTIC, شکاك shakkák, صوفی súfí. [The latter title was formerly given to learned and pious sages, but now most of this class are free-thinkers.]
SCEPTICISM, شك shakk, شبهه shubbah, تصوف tasavvuf.
SCEPTRE, عصا 'asá.
SCHEDULE, بند تفصیل band-i-tafsíl.
SCHEME (*contrivance*), ایجاد íjád, تجویز tajvíz, اختراع ikhtirá', ابداع ibdá', منسوبه mansúbah, تمهید tamhíd. — (*plot*) سازش sázish, معاهده mu'áhadah, وفاق vifák, اتفاق ittifák, توطئه tauti,ah, هم‌عهدی ham-'ahdí.
SCHEMER, مدبر mudabbir.
SCHISM, جدائی jidá,í, بدعت bid'at, رفض rafaz.
SCHISMATICAL, رافضی ráfizí, خارجی khárijí, اهل بدعت ahl-i-bid'at.
SCHOLAR, طالب العلم tálibu-'l-'ilm, طلبه talabah (*pl.* طلاب tulláb), تلمیذ talmíz, شاگرد shágird.—(*man of letters*) عالم 'álim, فاضل fázil, صاحب کمال sahib-kamál.

SCHOLARSHIP, دانش dánish, علم 'ilm, تحصیل tahsíl, معرفت ma'rifat, حکمت hikmat.
SCHOOL, مکتب maktab, مدرسه madrasah, کتاو kuttáv (*vulg.*), کتو kuttau (*vulg.*).—(*common school*) مکتب عوام maktab-i-'avámm.—(*high schools*) مکتبهای عالیه maktabaháí-i-'álíyah.—(*middle-class schools*) مکتبهای وسط maktabaháí-i-vasat.—(*military school*) مکتب عسکریه maktab-i-'askaríyah.—(*normal schools*) مکاتب رشدیه makátib-i-rashadíyah.—(*public school*) مدرسه madrasah.
SCHOOLFELLOW, هم مکتبی ham-maktabí, هم کتوی ham-kuttaví (*vulg.*).
SCHOOLMASTER, آخوند ákhwund, آخون ákhwun, استاد ustád, معلم mu'allim, ملا مکتبی mullá-maktabí.
SCHOONER, جهاز دو دقلی jaház-i-dú dakalí.
SCIATICA, نسا nasá.
SCIENCE, علم 'ilm, معرفت ma'rifat, حکمت hikmat, فن fann.—(*the exact sciences*) علوم ریاضیه 'ulúm-i-riyázíyah.—(*moral science*) علم اخلاق 'ilm-i-akhlák.—(*natural science*) علم طبیعیه 'ilm-i-tabí'íyah.
SCIENTIFIC, علمی 'ilmí.
SCIMITAR, شمشیر shimshír, سیف sayf.
SCISSORS, مقراض mikráz, قینچی kainchí.
SCOFF, استهزا istihzá, تسخر tasakhkhur, نکوهش nikúhish.
To SCOFF, استهزا نمودن istihzá nimúdan.
SCOFFER, مزخرف muzakhrif, مستهزئی mustahz,í, نکوهشکار nikúhish-kár.
SCOFFINGLY, با استهزا bá-istihzá.
SCOLD, زن گنده دهان zan-i-gandah-dahán.
To SCOLD, ملامت کردن malámat kardan, زباندرازی نمودن zabán-dirází nimúdan, عتاب کردن 'itáb kardan, طعن زدن ta'n zadan, ستیزه کردن sitízah kardan, مؤاخذه نمودن mu,ákhazah nimúdan, زجر نمودن zajr nimúdan, بانگ زدن báng zádan.
To SCOOP out, خالی ساختن khálí sákhtan, کاویدن kávídan.
To SCORCH, سوختن súkhtan, نیم سوختن ním súkhtan.
SCORCHED, مشتعل mushta'al, سوخته súkhtah.
SCORCHING, سوزان súzán.
SCORE (*twenty*), بیست bíst.—(*reckoning*) کنه kinah, نشان nishán, علامت 'alámat.—(*account*) سبب sabab, جهت jihat.
SCORIA (*of metal, &c.*), فلز filizz, ریم rím, فضله fazlah, درد durd.
SCORN, نکوهش nikúhish, تحقیر tahkír, اهانت ihánat.
To SCORN, خوار دیدن khwár-dídan, اهانت نمودن ihánat nimúdan, نکوهش کردن nikúhish kardan, تحقیر نمودن tahkír nimúdan.
SCORNFUL, نکوهشکار nikúhish-kár, مهین muhín, مستهزئی mustahz,í.
SCORNFULLY, بطور تحقیر bi-taur-i-tahkír, باهانت bi-ihánat, با نکوهش bá-nikúhish.
SCORPION, کژدم kazhdum, عقرب 'akrab.
SCOUNDREL, بد نفس bad-nafs, اوباش aubásh, بد نهاد bad-nihád.
To SCOUR, صیقل کردن saikal kardan, زدودن zadúdan, پرداختن pardákhtan.
SCOURER, لکه گیر lakkah-gír.
SCOURGE, تازیانه táziyánah, سوط saut, قمچی kamchí.
To SCOURGE, تازیانه زدن táziyánah zadan.
SCOUT, جاسوس jásús, خبر گیر khabar-gír.
SCRAMBLE, گیر و دار gír-u-dár, هنگامه hangámah, معرکه ma'rakah.
To SCRAMBLE, هجوم آوردن hujúm ávardan, گیر و دار کردن gír-u-dár kardan.
SCRAP (*small bit*), ریزه rízah, تکه tikkah, خورده khwurdah, پارچه párchah, ذره zarrah.
SCRAP-BOOK, مرقع murakka', بیاض bayáz.

Scrape, سختی sakhtí, مشکلی mush-kilí, دشواری dushvárí.
To Scrape, تراشیدن tiráshídan, خراشیدن khiráshídan.
Scraper (*rasp*), رنده randah.—(*at door*) کفش پاك کن kafsh-pák-kun.
Scratch, خراش khirásh.
To Scratch, خاریدن khárídan, خراشیدن khiráshídan.—(*to scratch out*) محو کردن mahv kardan, پاك کردن pák kardan.
Scratcher, خراشنده khiráshan-dah.
To Scrawl, بد نوشتن bad nivishtan, کلنجار کردن kalanjár kardan.
Scream or Screech, فریاد faryád, غریو gharív.
To Scream *or* Screech, غریو زدن gharív zadan, غریدن ghurrídan, فریاد کردن faryád kardan.
Screen, پرده pardah, حجاب hijáb, تجیر tajír.
To Screen, حفظ کردن hifz kardan, ستر کردن satr kardan.
Screw, پیچ pích, کیستاره kístárah (*obs.*).
To Screw, پیچ کردن pích kardan.
Screw-driver (*turn-screw*), آچار áchár, پیچکش pích-kash (*obs.*).
To Scribble, نوشتن nivishtan, کلنجار کردن kalanjár kardan.
Scribbler, نویسنده nivísandah.
Scribe, کاتب kátib, نویسنده ni-vísandah, محرر muharrir.
Scrip (*wallet*), انبان ambán, جلبند jul-band, توشه دان túshah-dán.
Scriptural, کتابی kitábí, تنزیلی tanzílí.
Scriptures (*sacred*), کلام الله kalamu-'llah, کتب سماوی kutub-i-samávi, کتب مقدس kutub-i-mukaddas.
Scrivener, کاتب kátib, نویسنده ni-vísandah.
Scrofula, خنازیر khanázír.
Scroll, دفتر daftar, طومار túmár.
Scrotum, فوطه fútah.
Scrub (*person*), کناس kannás.
To Scrub, زدودن zadúdan, سائیدن sá,ídan.
Scruple, تردد taraddud, شبهه shubhah, گمان gumán, شك shakk, ریب raib, وسواس vasvás, اشتباه ishtibáh.
To Scruple, تردید داشتن tardíd dáshtan, متردد بودن mutaraddid búdan, شك داشتن shakk dáshtan.
Scrupulous, وسواسی vasvásí, متعصب muta'assib, متورع muvarri'. —(*exact*) با دقت bá-dikkat.
Scrutable, یافتنی yáftaní.
Scrutineer, مفتش mufattish.
To Scrutinize, تفتیش نمودن taf-tísh nimúdan, تفحص کردن tafah-hus kardan.
Scrutiny, تفتیش taftish, تفحص ta-fahhus.
Scud, ابر abr, سحاب saháb, میغ mígh, غمامه ghamámah.
To Scud, مانند ابر درگذشتن mánand abr dar-guzashtan.
Scuffle, کشمکش kash-ma-kash, غوغا ghaughá, شلوك shulúk (*vulg.*)
Scull, سر sar, رأس ra,s, کله kallah, فرق fark.—(*oar*) پارو párú, خاده khádah.
Sculptor, نقاش nakkásh.
Sculpture, نقاشی nakkáshí, نقش naksh.
Scum (*froth*), کف kaf, تفش tafish, رغاوت raghávat. — (*mouldiness*) پرمك purmik, پورمك púrmik, رطوبت rutúbat.
Scurf (*of the skin*), بشره basharah.
Scurrility, بد زبانی bad-zabání, زبان درازی zabán-dirází, دشنام dush-nám, فحش fuhsh.
Scurrilous, بد زبان bad-zabán, زبان دراز zabán-diráz, فاحش fáhish.
Scurvy, جرب jarab.
Scuttle, زغال دان zughál-dán.
To Scuttle, دویدن davídan, گریختن gurikhtan.—(*a ship*) غرقاب ساختن gharkáb sákhtan.
Scythe, داس dás, دهره dahrah.
Sea, دریا daryá, بحر bahr, یم yamm, دنگز dangiz, اروند arvand.—(*land and sea*) بر و بحر bar u bahr, خشکی و دریا khushkí va daryá.—(*frozen or polar sea*) دریائی منجمد daryá,í-i-munjamad. — (*by sea*) بحراً

bahran, از راه دریا az ráh-i-daryá.

SEAFARING, دریائی daryá,í.

SEA-FOWL, مرغ دریا murgh-i-daryá, یاعو yá'ú, شالو shálú.

SEAL, مهر muhr, نشان nishán. —(*marine animal*) سگ ماهی sag-máhí.

To SEAL, ممهور ساختن mamhúr sákhtan, مهر کردن muhr kardan, مختوم ساختن makhtúm sákhtan. —(*respectfully speaking*) مزین فرمودن muzayyan firmúdan, طغرا گذاردن tughrá guzárdan.

SEALED, ممهور mamhúr, مختوم makhtúm.

SEALING-WAX, لاک lák.—(*strip of adhesive paper with which letters are fastened and sealed*) سر چسبان sar-chasbán.

SEAL-RING, خاتم khátim.—(*stone of seal-ring*) نگین nigín.

SEAM, درز darz, دوخته dúkhtah.—(*wide seam, basting*) بخیه bakhyah.

To SEAM, دوختن dúkhtan.

SEAMAN, جاشو jáshú, ملاح malláh.

SEANCE, مجلس majlis, مجالست mujálasat, نشیمن nishíman.—(*to hold a seance*) مجلس کردن majlis kardan.

SEA-NYMPH, دختر دریا dukhtar-i-daryá.

SEAPORT, بندر bandar, مینا míná.

To SEAR, داغ کردن dágh kardan.

SEARCH, تفتیش taftísh, تلاش talásh, تجسس tajassus.

To SEARCH, جستن justan (*root* جوی júí), جستجو کردن justujú kardan, کاویدن kávídan, تلاش کردن talásh kardan, تجسس نمودن tajassus nimúdan, تفتیش کردن taftísh kardan, پیجور بودن payjúr búdan (*vulg.*), پا پی شدن pá-pay shudan.

SEARCHER, متفحص mutafahhis, جویان júyán.

SEASHELL, دریا گوش daryá-gúsh.—(*larger seashell of the oyster kind*) صدف sadaf. —(*small sea-shells*) مهره muhrah.

SEASON, فصل fasl, موسم mausim, زمان zamán.—(*the four seasons*) فصول اربعه fusúl-i-arba'ah, چهار فصول chahár-fusúl.

To SEASON, نمك زدن namak zadan.

SEASONABLE, موافق muváfik, مناسب munásib, لائق lá,ik.

SEASONABLENESS, موافقت muváfakat, مناسبت munásabat.

SEASONING (*spices, &c.*), ادویه adviyah.

SEAT, تخت takht, کرسی kursí, صندلی sandalí, نشیمن nishíman, آرامگاه árám-gáh, مقعد mak'ad.—(*garden seat*) سکو sakú.—(*residence*) مقر makarr, خانه khánah.

To SEAT, نشاندن nishándan.

SEAWEED, خس دریا khas-i-daryá.

SECANT, قاطع káti'.

To SECEDE, اعتزال نمودن i'tizál nimúdan.

SECESSION, اعتزال i'tizál.

To SECLUDE, جدا ساختن jidá sákhtan.—(*to seclude oneself*) اعتزال نمودن i'tizál nimúdan, عزلت گزیدن 'uzlat guzídan.

SECLUSION, اعتزال i'tizál, عزلت 'uzlat, انزوا inzivá.

SECOND, دویم dúyum, دوم duvum, دویمین dúyumín, ثانی sání.—(*of time*) ثانیه sániyah, دقیقه dakíkah. —(*at a duel*) حامی hámí.

To SECOND, حمایت نمودن himáyat nimúdan.

SECOND-HAND (*used*), مستعمل musta'mal.

SECONDLY, ثانیاً sániyan.

SECOND-RATE, پست past, ادنا adná.

SECRECY, پنهانی panhaní, پوشیدگی púshídagí.

SECRET, راز ráz, سر sirr.—(*private*) نهان nihán, پنهان panhán, مخفی makhfí, پوشیده púshídah, مستور mastúr, در خفا dar khafá.

SECRETAIRE, پیشتخته písh-takhtah.

SECRETARIAT, دیوان díván.

SECRETARY, حضور نویس huzúr-nivís, منشی munshí, میرزا mírzá, کاتب kátib, مستوفی mustaufí, کاتب الاسرار kátibu-'l-asrár.—(*Secretary of Embassy*), نائب ná,ib, کاتب سفارت kátib-i-sifárat, سر کاتب sirrkátib.—(*Under Secretary of State*) مستشار mustashár.

SECRETARYSHIP, مستوفی گری mus-taufí-garí.

To SECRETE, نهفتن nihuftan, پوشیدن púshídan, پنهان کردن panhán kar-dan, نهان کردن nihán kardan, اخفا نمودن ikhfá nimúdan, مخفی ساختن makhfí sákhtan, متواری داشتن mutavárí dáshtan.

SECRETION, کتمان kitmán.—(*human*) مادّه máddah, ذخیره za-khírah.

SECRETLY, خفیاً khafíyan, سرّاً sirran, نهفته nihuftah, نهان nihán, در خفا dar khafá.

SECRETNESS, پوشیدگی púshídagí, پنهانی panhání, نهفتگی nihuftagí.

SECT (*class*), ذات zát, قوم kaum, شعبت shu'bat, فرقه firkah, ملت millat, امت ummat, جماعت ja-má'at, طائفه tá,ifah..

[The two great sects or religious classes of Muhammadans are:—The Sunnís (اهل تسنن ahl-i-tasannun, سنی sunní, چهار یاری chahár-yárí), who revere equally the four successors of Muhammad, and respect their precepts; Turks, Arabs, and most Indian Muslims are of this sect. The Shi'ahs (شیعه shí'ah, *pl.* شیعیان shí'ayán), who venerate 'Alí, the son-in-law of the Prophet; Persians and some Indians belong to this sect.]

SECTARIAN, بدعی bid'í.

SECTION (*of a chapter, &c.*), قطعه kat'ah, فصل fasl, باب báb. (*Vide* PART, SHARE, DIVISION.)

SECULAR, دنیوی dunyaví, دنیاوی dunyávi.

SECULARLY, بطور دنیاوی bi-taur-i-dunyávi.

SECURE, امین amín, ایمن íman, مسلم musallam, مأمون ma,mún بسلامت bi-salámat, رستگار rasta-gár, سالم sálim, مؤتمن mu,taman. —(*to feel secure*) مطمئن شدن mut-ma,inn shudan. — (*to render secure*) مأمون ساختن ma,mún sákhtan.

To SECURE, بدست آوردن bi-dast ávardan.

SECURELY, ایمنانه ímanánah.

SECURITY, سلامت salámat, امن aman, امان amán, حفاظت hifázat, رستگاری rastagárí.—(*bail*) ضمانت zamánat, کفالت kafálat.—(*pawn*) رهن rahn, گرو girau.

SEDAN-CHAIR, تخت روان takht-i-raván.

SEDATE, با وقار bá-vakár, با تمکین bá-tamkín.

SEDATENESS, وقار vakár, تمکین tam-kín.

SEDATIVE, مسکن musakkin, تسکین ده taskín-dih.

SEDENTARY, جالس jális.

SEDIMENT, درد durd, فضله fazlah, خلط khilt, لای lái, سفل sifl.

SEDITION, فتنه fitnah, فساد fasád, بغاوت baghávat, یاغیگری yághí-gari, دغدغه daghdaghah, بلوا balvá, هرزگی harzagí.

SEDITIOUS, فتنه انگیز fitnah-angíz, مفسد mufsid.

To SEDUCE, اغوا کردن ighvá kardan, فریفتن firíftan, ورغلانیدن var-gha-lánídan, ترغیب کردن targhíb kar-dan, مفتون گردانیدن maftún gar-dánídan, اضلال کردن izlál kardan. (*woman*) زنا کردن ziná kardan, زنا کار نمودن ziná-kár nimúdan, هتک عرض نمودن hatk-i-irz nimu-dan.

SEDUCER, فریبنده firíbandah. —(*of women*) زنا کار ziná-kár, هتاک عرض hatták-i-'irz.

SEDUCTION, اضلال izlál.—(*of women*) زنا ziná, پرده دری pardah-darí, هتک عرض hatk-i-irz.

SEDUCTIVE, دلاور dil-ávar, دلفریب dil-firíb.

SEDULOUS, متوجه mutavajjih, ساعی sá'í, مقید mukayyad, سرگرم sar-garm.

SEE! (*interj.*), اینك ínak, ببین bi-bín.

To SEE, دیدن dídan, نگریستن ni-garístan, نظر کردن nazar kardan,

نگاه کردن nigáh kardan, بنظر آوردن bi-nazar ávardan. — (*observe*) نگریستن nigarístan, مراکب بودن murákib búdan, ملاحظه mulázahah kardan. — (*to see a person, grant an interview*) حضور داشتن huzúr dáshtan, بار دادن bár dádan.—(*I see through it*) بر من پوشیده نیست bar man púshídah níst.—(*far-seeing*) باصر básir.— (*seeing that*) چون که chún-kih.

SEED, تخم tukhm, دانه dánah, بزر bazr, زرع zar‘, حب habb, هسته hastah.—(*semen genitale*) آب منی áb-i-muní, نطفه nutfah, آب انزال áb-i-inzál.

To SEED (*trans.*), تخم پاشیدن tukhm páshídan. — (*intrans.*) تخم کردن tukhm kardan.

SEEDLING, بیجه bíjah, زرع zar‘.

SEEDSMAN, بقال bakkál.

SEED-TIME, موسم زرع mausim-i-zar‘.

To SEEK, *vide* To SEARCH, To BEG. —(*to seek a person*) پی کسی گشته شدن páy-i-kasí gashtah shudan.

SEEKER, طالب tálib, جوینده júyandah.

To SEEM, نمودن nimúdan, نمودار شدن nimúdár shudan, مانستن mánistan, معلوم شدن ma‘lúm shudan, صورت پذیر شدن súrat-pazír shudan, ظاهر شدن záhir shudan.

SEEMING, ظاهر záhir.

SEEMINGLY, ظاهراً záhiran, ظاهرانه záhiránah, صورتاً súratan.

SEEMLINESS, حسن husn, لطافت latáfat, نزاکت nazákat, ناز náz.

SEEMLY, لطیف latíf, جمیل jamíl, نازك názuk.

SEER, غیب دان ghaib-dán, پیغمبر paigham-bar.

SEE-SAW, آورك ávarak.

To SEE-SAW, آورك خوردن ávarak khwurdan.

SEGMENT, قسمت kismat, حصه hissah.—(*of a circle*), قطاع kitá‘.

SEIGNORIAL, مالکانه málikánah.

To SEIZE, گرفتن giriftan, ربودن rubúdan, تسخیر کردن taskhír kardan, غصب کردن ghasb kardan, گرفتار کردن giriftár kardan, اخذ کردن akhz kardan, قبض کردن kabz kardan, بتصرف آوردن bi-tasarruf ávardan, کپیدن kapídan (*vulg.*).—(*to seize the idea*) درك فکرات نمودن dark-i-fikrát nimúdan.—(*to seize the occasion*) غنیمت شمردن ghanímat shimurdan.

SEIZURE, ربودگی rubúdagí, تسخیر taskhír, ضبط zabt, گرفتاری giriftárí, قبض kabz.

SELDOM, کم kam, کمتر kamtar, ندرتاً nudratan.

SELECT, ممتاز mumtáz.

To SELECT, گزیدن guzídan, چیدن chídan, انتخاب کردن intikháb kardan, اختیار کردن ikhtiyár kardan, مستخص کردن mustakhkhis kardan.

SELECTION, منتخب muntakhab, انتخاب intikháb.

SELF, خود khwud, خویش khwísh, خویشتن khwíshtan, نفس nafs.— (*I myself*) من خودم man khwudam, *or* خود من khwud-i-man.— (*thou thyself*) تو خودت tú khwudat, *or* خود تو khwud-i-tú.—(*he himself, she herself*) او خودش ú khwudash, *or* خود او khwud-i-ú. —(*we ourselves*) ما خودمان má khwudimán, *or* خود ما khwud-i-má.—(*you yourselves*) شما خودتان shumá khwuditán, *or* خود شما khwud-i-shumá. — (*they themselves*) ایشان خودشان íshán khwudishán, *or* خود ایشان khwud-i-íshán. — (*self-interest*) خود غرضی khwud-gharazí, نفس دوستی nafs-dústí.—(*self-conceit*) خود بینی khwud-bíní, خود پسندی khwud-pasandí.—(*self-defence*) توقی tavakkí, حفظ نفس hifz-i-nafs. — (*self-praise*) تصلف tasalluf, خود فروشی khwud-furúshí, خود نمای khwud-nimáy. — (*self-will*) عناد ‘inád.—(*self-possession*) خود داری khwud-dárí. — (*self-important*) خود بین khwud-bín, خود پسند khwud-pasand. — (*self-respect*) آبرو áb-rú, همت himmat, حمیت hamíyat, تشخص tashakhkhus, غیرت ghairat.—(*self-willed*) خود

رای khwud-rá,í, خود سر khwud-sar, مصر musirr, متمرد mutamarrid.

SELFISH, خود غرض khwud-gharaz, نفس دوست nafs-dúst, تن پرور tan-parvar.

To SELL, فروختن furúkhtan, بیع دادن bai' dádan.

SELLER, بایع báí'.

SEMBLANCE, برابری barábarí, تمثیل tamsíl, مثال misál, تشبیه tashbíh, مشابهه mushábabah, شبه shibh, موافقت muváfakat, شباهت shabáhat, نمایش nimáyish, حکم hukm.

SEMEN, آب منی áb-i-muní, نطفه nutfah, آب انزال áb-i-inzál.

SEMI, نیم ním, نصف nisf.

SEMI-CIRCLE, نیم دائره ním-dá,irah.

SEMI-CIRCULAR, نیم مدور ním-mudavvar.

SEMINARY, مکتب maktab, مدرسه madrasah, کتاو kuttáu, کتو kuttau (*vulg.*).

SENATE, مجلس majlis.

SENATOR, مشیر mushír, اهل مشورت ahl-i-mashvarat.

To SEND, فرستادن firistádan, ارسال داشتن irsál dáshtan, ارسال نمودن irsál nimúdan, رسانیدن rasánídan, روانه کردن ravánah kardan, مرسل نمودن mursal nimúdan, انفاذ نمودن infáz nimúdan.—(*to send for, to summon*) خواندن khwándan, احضار نمودن ihzár nimúdan, استحضار کردن istihzár kardan, طلب داشتن talab dáshtan, خواستن khwástan.—(*to send back*) بر گرداندن bar-gardándan.

SENIOR (*elder*), مهتر mihtar, مهین mihín, کلان kalán, اکبر akbar.

SENIORITY, کلانی kalání.

SENNA, سنا saná, سنائی مکی saná,í-i-makkí.

SENSE (*sensation*), حس hiss, احساس ihsás.—(*the five senses*) پنج حواس panj havâss, پنج مشاعر panj mashá'ir, قوائی بدن kuvá,í-i-badan. — (*seeing*) قوت باصرت kúvat-i-básirat. — (*hearing*) قوت سامعت kúvat-i-sámi'at.—(*tasting*) قوت ذائقه kúvat-i-zá,ikah.—(*smelling*) قوت شامه kúvat-i-shámmah.—(*touching*) قوت لامست kúvat-i-lámisat.—(*intellect*) عقل 'akl, فطانت fatánat, ادراك idrák, فهم fahm, هوش húsh, خرد khirad.—(*meaning*) معنی ma'ní, معنا ma'ná, فحوا fahvá. — (*common-sense*) کفایت kifáyat. — (*good sense*) درایت diráyat, فهم fahm, کفایت kifáyat. —(*to go out of one's senses*) سوار فیل شدن suvár-i-fíl shudan. — (*to have one's senses about one*) مشاعری بر جای گذاشتن mashá'irí bar jáy guzáshtan.—(*to lose one's senses*) بیهوش شدن bí-húsh shudan.—(*to recover one's senses*) بهوش آمدن bi-húsh ámadan.

SENSELESS (*without sensation*), بیهوش bí-húsh, بیجان bí-ján, بی حواس bí-haváss, بی حس bí-hiss. —(*foolish*) بی وقوف bí-vukúf, بی عقل bi-'akl, نا دان ná-dán.

SENSIBILITY, عقل 'akl, هوشمندی húsh-mandí, خرد مندی khirad-mandí, دانائی dáná,í, عقلمندی 'akl-mandí.

SENSIBLE (*endowed with senses*), ذو الحواس zu-'l-haváss, محس muhiss.—(*judicious, proper, fitting*) موجه muvajjah, مناسب munásib, با هوش bá-húsh, معقول ma'kúl.—(*acute, prudent, clever*) عاقل 'ákil, هوشمند húsh-mand, هوشیار húsh-yár, خردمند khirad-mand, دانا dáná, دانشمند dánish-mand, زیرك zírak, عقلمند 'akl-mand.—(*perceptible by feeling*) محسوس mahsús, قابل احساس kábil - i - ihsás. — (*visible*) ظاهر záhir, مرئی mar,í, مبین mubín, آشکاره áshkárah. — (*aware of*) منتقل muntakil, مخبر mukhbar, مستحضر mustahzar, آگاه ágáh, (*convinced of*) مجاب mujáb, مستدل mustadall, ملزم mulzam, مقر mukirr, قائل ká,il.

SENSIBLY, عاقلانه 'ákilánah.—(*manifestly*) ظاهرا záhiran.

SENSITIVE, ذو الحواس zu-'l-haváss, محس muhiss.

SENSUAL, نفسانی nafsání, نفس پرست nafs-parast, شهوتی shahvatí, مست mast.

SENSUALIST, *vide* VOLUPTUARY.

SENSUALITY, شهوت shahvat, نفس nafs, هوس havas, هوائی نفسانی havá,í-i-nafsání, نفس پرستی nafs-parastí, مستی mastí.

SENTENCE (*of a judge*), حکم hukm, فیصل faisal, فتوی fatvá.—(*period*) جمله jumlah, فقره fakarah.

To SENTENCE, حکم دادن hukm dádan.—(*to sentence to a term of imprisonment*) محبوسی مدت معین کردن mahbúsí muddat-i-mu'ayyan kardan.

SENTENTIOUS, مضبوط mazbút.

SENTIMENT, خیال khiyál, تصور tasavvur, اعتقاد i'tikád, پندار pindár.

SENTINEL, پاسبان pás-bán, حارس háris, کشیکچی kashík-chí, قراول karávul.

SEPARABLE, قابل تفریق kábil-i-tafrík, مفارقت پذیر mufárakat-pazír.

SEPARATE, جدا jidá, علحده 'alá-hiddah, متفرق mutafarrik, مباین mubáyan, جداگانه jidáganah.

To SEPARATE, تفریق نمودن tafrík nimúdan, جدا ساختن jidá sákhtan.

SEPARATED, مفروق mafrúk.

SEPARATELY, جداگانه jidáganah, یک یک yak yak, فردافرد fard-á-fard.

SEPARATION, جدائی jidá,í, فراق farák, مفارقت mufárakat, تفرقه tafrikah, هجر hajar, هجران hijrán, دوری dúrí, مباعدت mubá'adat, مهجوری mahjúrí, تباین tabáyun, تفریق tafrík.—(*severance*) انقطاع inkitá'.

SEPTEMBER, ایلول ailúl.

SEPTENTRIONAL, شمالی shimálí, شمالیه shimálíyah.

SEPULCHRE, گور gúr, مزار mazár, قبر kabr, مرقد markad, سر sirr.

SEPULTURE, دفن dafn.

SEQUEL, نتیجه natíjah, حاصل کلام hasil-i-kalám.

To SEQUESTRATE, ضبط کردن zabt kardan, مصادره نمودن musádarah nimúdan.

SEQUESTRATION (*confiscation*), ضبط zabt, قرق kurk.

SERAGLIO, زنانه zanánah, حرم haram, اندرون andarún, سرای saráí.

SERAPHIM, سرافی saráfí.

SERENE, با قرار bá-karár, با وقار bá-vakár.

SERENITY, بشاشت basháshat, کشایش kisháyish.

SERGEANT (*military term*), وکیل vakíl. — (*sergeant - major*) وکیل باشی vakíl-báshí.

SERIES, رشته rishtah, سلسله silsilah, تواتر tavátur.

SERIOUS (*true*), راست rást, حق hakk, صحیح sahíh.—(*grave*) موقر muvakkar, متعبس muta'abbis, با وقار bá-vakár, با تمکین bá-tamkín.

SERIOUSLY, عمدا 'amdan, بطور جدی bi-taur-i-jaddí, قصدا kasdan.

SERMON, خطبه khutbah, مواعظه muvá'azah, وعظ va'z.

SERPENT, مار már, افعی af'á.

SERVANT, نوکر naukar, چاکر chákar, خدمتکار khidmat-kár, پیشخدمت písh-khidmat, خادم khádam, ملازم mulázim, تابع tábi', اجیر ajír, بچه bachah. [Servants in Persia are always called for and addressed as their master's "children."] تابین tábín (*vulg.*) — (*servant who takes care of and educates children*) لله lallah, لالا lálá, لاله lálah. — (*bond-servant*) *vide* SLAVE.—(*nurse*) دایه dáyah, دده dadah. — (*your humble servant*) بنده مسکین شما bandah-i-maskín-i-shumá, نوکر خاکسار شما naukar-i-khák-sár-i-shumá. — (*servant-girl*) کنیز kaniz, زن خدمتکار zan-i-khidmat-kár. — (*servants, attendants*) خدام khaddám, نوکران naukarán, نوکر باب naukar-báb, ملازمان mulázimán, حشم و خدم hasham va khadam, بچها bachahá, تابینها tábínhá (*vulg.*).

To SERVE, ملازم شدن mulázim shudan, خدمت کردن khidmat kardan.

SERVICE, خدمت khidmat, ملازمت mulázamat, نوکری naukarí. —(*compulsory*) سخره sukhrah, خدمت بی جیرة khidmat-i-bí-jírah.—(*worship*) پرستاری parastárí, پرستش parastish. — (*On Her Majesty's Service*) خدمت دولتی khidmat-i-daulatí.—(*it is at your service*) پیشکش است písh-kash ast.

SERVICEABLE, قابل کار kábil-i-kár, مفید mufíd, فائدة fá,idah.

SERVILE, دون dún, پست past, خوار khwár, ذلیل zalíl.

SERVILITY, پستی pastí, دونی dúní, رذالت razálat, خواری khwárí.

SERVITUDE, بندگی bandagí, پستی pastí.

SESAMUM, کنجد kunjad, کنجید kunjíd, سمسم simsim.

SESSION, مجالست mujálasat, اجلاس ijlás.

SET (*complete suit*), دست dast. (*Vide* NUMBER.) — (*as jewels*) مکلل mukallal.

To SET, گذاشتن guzáshtan, گذاردن guzárdan, نهادن nihádan, وضع کردن vaz' kardan, هشتن hishtan, هلیدن hilídan. — (*as the sun*) غروب کردن ghurúb kardan, فرو رفتن furú raftan.—(*to set poultry*) خوابانیدن khwábánídan.—(*jewels*) ترصیع نمودن tarsí' nimúdan.—(*to set about*) عزیمت نمودن 'azímat nimúdan, شرع شدن shar' shudan, اقدام کردن ikdám kardan, پرداختن pardákhtan.—(*to set up*) بلند کردن buland kardan.—(*to set off on a journey*) راهی شدن ráhí shudan, روانه شدن ravánah shudan, براه افتادن bi-ráh uftádan.

SETTEE, نیم تخت ním-takht.

SETTER (*dog*), سگ شکاری sag-i-shikárí.

SETTING, غروب ghurúb, زوال zavál.

To SETTLE (*alight*), نشستن nishastan, نزول کردن nuzúl kardan, مستنزل گشتن mustanzal gashtan. —(*fix*) مقرر کردن mukarrar kardan, ثابت کردن sábat kardan, قرار دادن karár dádan.—(*decide*) صورت انجام دادن súrat-i-anjám dádan, قطع نمودن kat' nimúdan, فصل نمودن fasl nimúdan.—(*determine upon*) قراری دادن karárí dádan, مصمم گشتن musammim gashtan, تصمیم کردن tasmím kardan. — (*reside*) قرار گرفتن karár giriftan, وطن کردن vatan kardan, توطن کردن tavattun kardan. — (*subside, as dregs, &c.*) نشستن nishastan, ته کشیدن tah kashídan.—(*accounts*) مفروغ کردن mafrúgh kardan, کارسازی نمودن kár-sází nimúdan, ادا کردن adá kardan.—(*a dispute, amicably*), مصالحه کردن musálahah kardan.—(*the affairs of a country*) نظم دادن nazm dádan, تمشیت دادن tamshíyat dádan, نسق کردن nasak kardan.

SETTLED, معین mu'ayyan.

SETTLEMENT (*arrangement of business*), تعیین ta'yín, تمشیت tamshíyat, انتظام intizám, تنسیق tansík.—(*of the taxes upon tradespeople*) بنیچه بندی bunichah-bandí.

To SEVER, بریدن burídan *or* burrídan, قطع کردن kat' kardan, تراشیدن tiráshídan.—(*to sever friendship*) بهم خوردن bi-ham khwurdan.

SEVERAL, چند chand, چند تا chand-tá, بعضی ba'zí, چندین chandín.

SEVERALLY, جداگانه jidágánah, یك یك yak yak, فردافرد fard-á-fard.

SEVERE, درشت durusht, شدید shadíd, تند tund, قسی kasí, پر زور pur-zúr, زشت نهاد zisht-nihád, سخت sakht.

SEVERED, مجزوم majzúm, قطیع katí'.

SEVERELY, نهایت niháyat, بسیار bisyár.

SEVERITY, درشتی durushtí, شدت shiddat, تندی tundí, سختی sakhtí.

To SEW, دوختن dúkhtan.

SEWAGE, فضلة fazlah.

SEWER (*drain*), آبریز áb-ríz, آبگذر áb-guzar, بدر رو bi-dar-rau.—(*sink of a house*) آبشی áb-shí. — آبریز áb-ríz.—(*one who sews*) رفو گر rafv-gar.

SEX, جنس jins.

SEXTON, گورکن gúr-kan, حفار haffár.
SEXUAL INTERCOURSE, عشرت 'ashrat, مقاربت mukárabat, مجامعه mujáma'ah.
SHABBILY, بد bad.
SHABBINESS, ژنده پوشی zhindah-púshí.—(*meanness*) پستی pastí, دونی dúní.
SHABBY, ژنده پوش zhindah-púsh.—(*mean*) پست past, دون dún.
SHACKLE, پا بند pá-band.
To SHACKLE, بستن bastan, بند کردن band kardan.
SHADDOCK (*fruit*), بتاوی batáví [so called from Batavia, whence this fruit was first imported into Persia].
SHADE (*of glass*), لاله lálah, مردنگی mirdangí (*hind.*).—(*awning*) سایه بان sáyah-bán, چتر chatr.
To SHADE, سایه کردن sáyah kardan.
SHADOW, سایه sáyah, ظل zill.
To SHADOW, سایه افکندن sáyah afkandan.
SHADY, سایه دار sáyah-dár, چتر دار chatr-dár. — (*to be shady*) سایه داشتن sáyah dáshtan.
SHAFT, تیر tír, سهم sahm, ناوك navak, خدنگ khadang.—(*carriage*) چوب کالسکه chúb-i-káliskah.
SHAGGY, درشت durusht, شعرانی sha'rání.
SHAGREEN, ساغری ságharí.
SHAIKH, شیخ shaikh.
SHAKE, لرزه larzah, تکان takán.
To SHAKE (*trans.*), جنبانیدن jumbánídan, تکانیدن takánídan, تکان دادن takán dádan. — (*intrans.*) جنبیدن jumbídan, لرزیدن larzídan, تکان کردن takán kardan, لکیدن lakídan.—(*to brush off*) تکانیدن takánídan, پاك کردن pák kardan, افشاندن afshándan.
SHAKING, متزلزل mutazalzil.
SHALLOT, پیاز کوهی piyáz-i-kúhí.
SHALLOW, پایاب pá-yáb, نا عمیق ná-'amík, کم آب kam-áb.
SHALLOWNESS, کم آبی kam-ábí.
SHAM, بهانه bahánah, کاذب kázib, دروغ durúgh, زور zúr, ساختگی sákhtagí, قلابی kullábí.
To SHAM, بهانه نمودن bahánah nimúdan, تقلید کردن taklíd kardan.
SHAME, شرم sharm, شرمساری sharmsárí, شرمندگی sharmandagí, حیا hayá, خجلت khijlat, حجاب hijáb. —(*disgrace*) رسوائی rusváí, بد نامی bad-námí, ننگ nang, فضیحت fazíhat, عار 'ár.—(*ill-deed*) عیب 'aib, بدی badí, گناه gunáh, حیف haif, بیداد bí-dád, بی انصافی bí-insáfí. — (*put to shame*) مفتضح muftazih. — (*for shame!*) حاشا háshá, اف uf, تفو tufú, عیب ست 'aib ast.
To SHAME, شرمسار ساختن sharm-sár sákhtan, متخفر گردانیدن mutakhaffir gardánídan.
SHAMEFUL, معیوب ma'yúb, رذیل razíl, خبیث khabít.—(*it is shameful*) عیب است 'aib ast.
SHAMELESS, بیشرم bí-sharm, چشم دریده chashm-darídah, بیحیا bí-hayá.
SHAMPOOING (*rubbing and kneading the limbs*), مشت و مال musht va mál, دستمال dast-mál, مالش málish.
SHANK (*handle*), دسته dastah, قبضه kabzah.
SHAPE, شکل shakl, ترکیب tarkíb, صورت súrat, هئت hai,at, قواره kavárah, پیکر paikar.—(*ill-shaped*) بد اندام bad-andám. — (*strange-shaped*) عجیب الخلقه 'ajíbu-'l-khilkah.
To SHAPE, صورت دادن súrat dádan, تشکیل نمودن tashkíl nimúdan.
SHAPELESS, بد ترکیب bad-tarkíb.
SHAPELESSNESS, بد ترکیبی bad-tarkíbí.
SHARE, حصه hissah, تقسیم taksím, قسمت kismat, بخش bakhsh, سهم sahm, بهره bahrah, بخرا bakhrá. — (*document*) بلیت شراکت bilít-i-shirákat.
To SHARE (*trans.*), تقسیم کردن taksím kardan, دو قسمت کردن dú kismat kardan.—(*intrans.*) شارك بودن shárik búdan, شراکت داشتن sharákat dáshtan, حصه دار بودن

hissah-dár búdan, بهره داشتن bahrah dáshtan.
SHARK, بمبك bambak, سگ ماهی sag-máhí.
SHARP, تیز tíz, بران burrán, حاد hádd.—(*clever*) چابك chábuk, زیرك zírak, چست chust, زرنگ zaring, ذکی zakí, لوذعی lauza'í, چیره دست chírah-dast.
To SHARPEN, تیز کردن tíz kardan.—(*whet*) سنگ سای کردن sang-sáí kardan.
SHARPER, عیار 'ayyár, مکار makkár, فریبنده firíbandah, قلابی kullábí, دولابی dúlábí, صیاد shayyád, مزور muzavvir.
SHARPLY, به تیزی bi-tízí.
SHARPNESS, تیزی tízí.—(*quickness*) سهولت تعلم suhúlat-i-ta'allum, سرعت فهم sur'at-i-fahm, صفائی ذهن safá,í-i-zihn, چابکی chábukí, زرنگی zaringí, زکاوت zakávat.
SHARP-SIGHTED, تیز نظر tíz-nazar.
To SHATTER, شکستن shikastan, پاره پاره کردن párah-párah kardan, پخش کردن pakhsh kardan.
To SHAVE, تراشیدن tiráshídan, ستردن suturdan.—(*oneself*) ریش خودرا تراشیدن rísh-i-khwudrá tiráshídan.
SHAVER, تراشنده tiráshandah.—(*barber*) دلاك dallák, حجام hajjám, مزین muzayyin, سلمانی salmání (*vulg.*).
SHAVING (*of wood, &c.*), تراشه tiráshah.
SHAWL, شال shál.—(*fine shawl-stuff of Kashmir, &c.*) ترمه tirmah.
SHAWL-MERCHANT (*seller of shawls*), سمسار simsár.
SHAWL-WEAVER, شالباف shál-báf.
SHAWM, مزمار mizmár.
SHE, او ú.
SHEAF, بسته bastah, دسته dastah, بافه báfah.
To SHEAR (*sheep, &c.*), پشم بریدن pashm burídan, پشم چیدن pashm chídan, مقراض کردن mikráz kardan.
SHEARER, مقراض کن mikráz-kun.
SHEARS, مقراض mikráz, قینچی kainchí.—(*for ships, &c.*) آلت جر ثقیل álat-i-jarr-i-sakíl.
SHEATH, غلاف ghiláf, نیام niyám.
To SHEATHE, غلاف کردن ghiláf kardan.
SHED, سپنج sipanj, مظله mizallah, کپر kappar, کمند kumand, دستگاه dast-gáh.
To SHED, ریختن ríkhtan, افشاندن ifshándan.
SHEEP, گوسفند gúsfand, گوسپند gúspand.—(*ewe*) میش mísh.—(*ram*) غوچ ghúch.—(*wild sheep*) ارگلی argalí, پازن pázan.—(*fat-tailed sheep*) دمبه dumbah.
SHEEP-FOLD, آغل گوسفند ághil-i-gúsfand, محل گوسفند mahall-i-gúsfand, آگل ágil, سول súl.
SHEEPISH, شرمسار sharm-sár, خجل khijil, متخفر mutakhaffir, حیی hayí.
SHEEPISHNESS, خجلت khijlat, شرمساری sharm-sárí.
SHEET, چادر chádar, ردا ridá, شمد shamad.—(*of paper*) ورق varak, تخته takhtah.—(*in sheets, as an unbound book*) اوراق aurák.
SHELF, رفه raffah, طاقچه tákchah.
SHELL (*of an animal*), صدف sadaf.—(*of a nut, &c.*) پوست púst.—(*small shells*) مهره muhrah.—(*explosive*) خمبره khambarah. *Vide also* SEA-SHELL.
To SHELL, پوست کندن púst kandan, مقشر ساختن mukashshar sákhtan.
SHELTER, پوشش púshish, سایه sáyah.—(*protection*) پناه panáh, زنهار zinhár, ملجا maljá.—(*to seek shelter*) پناه بردن panáh burdan, التجا نمودن iltijá nimúdan, ملتجی شدن multají shudan.—(*place of shelter*) پناه panáh, بست bast, ملجا maljá, مأمن ma,man, ملاذ maláz.
To SHELTER, پناه دادن panáh dádan, حمایت دادن himáyat dádan, حفاظت نمودن hifázat nimúdan, صیانت کردن siyánat kardan, محارست نمودن muhárasat nimúdan.
SHELTERED, محفوظ mahfúz.
SHEPHERD, شبان shabán, چوپان

chaupán, گله بان gallah-bán, راعی rá'í.

SHERBET (*lemonade*), افشره afshurah. — (*of rose-water, &c.*) شربت sharbat.

SHEWBREAD (*loaves of unleavened bread, used by the Jewish priesthood in their sanctuary*), نان تقدمه nán-i-takaddumah.

SHIELD, سپر sipar, جنه junnah. — (*shield-bearer*) سپر دار sipar-dár.

To SHIELD, پناه دادن panáh dádan, حمایت دادن himáyat dádan, حفاظت نمودن hifázat nimúdan, صیانت کردن siyánat kardan, محارست نمودن muhárasat nimúdan.

SHIFT (*shirt*), پیراهن píráhan, قمیص kamís.—(*contrivance*) تمهید tamhíd, دسیسه dasísah. — (*evasion*) بهانه bahánah, عذر 'uzr, حیله hílah, تجاهل tajáhul, چنان چنین chunán chunín.

To SHIFT (*change places*), نقل کردن nakl kardan, انتقال کردن intikál kardan, جا بجا کردن já-bi-já kardan.—(*clothes*) تبدیل رخت کردن tabdíl-i-rakht kardan, رخوترا عوض کردن rukhútrá 'avaz kardan.

SHIFTER, حیله باز hílah-báz.

SHIFTLESS, بیچاره bí-chárah, نا چار ná-chár, نا دان ná-dán, احمق ahmak.

SHIFTLESSNESS, بیچارگی bí-cháragí, نا دانی ná-dání.

To SHILLY-SHALLY, دفع الوقت کردن daf'u-'l-vakt kardan, دل دل کردن dil dil kardan, لیت و لعل کردن lait u la'all kardan.

SHIN, ساق sák.

To SHINE, درخشیدن dirakhshídan, تابیدن tábídan, تافتن táftan, لامع شدن lámi' shudan, روشن بودن raushan búdan, شعله زدن shu'lah zadan, رخشیدن rakhshídan.

SHINING, درخشان dirakhshán, تابان tábán, روشن raushan, لامع lámi'.

SHIP, جهاز jaház, کشتی kashtí, مرکب markab, گمی gamí.—(*of war*) جهاز جنگی jaház-i-jangí, کشتی جنگ kashtí-i-jang, جهاز حربی jaház-i-harbí. — (*coasting vessel*) غراب ghuráb, بغله baghalah, بگله bagalah.—(*merchantman*) جهاز تجارتی jaház-i-tijáratí. —(*steamship*) کشتی بخار kashtí-i-bukhár.—(*sailing ship*) کشتی بادی kashtí-i-bádí, کشتی شراعی kashtí-i-shirá'í. — (*shipbuilding yard*) کشتی ساز خانه kashtí-sáz-khánah. —(*to go on board a ship*) بکشتی نشستن bi-kashtí-nishastan.—(*to go over a ship*) توی کشتیرا تماشا کردن túí-i-kashtírá tamáshá kardan.

SHIPWRECK, غرق ghark.

To SHIRK, طفره زدن tafrah zadan, تغافل نمودن tagháful nimúdan.

SHIRT, پیراهن píráhan, قمیص kamís.

To SHIVER (*tremble*), لرزیدن larzídan, رعشه کردن ra'shah kardan, ارتعاش نمودن irti'ásh nimúdan.—(*break in bits*) پاره پاره کردن párah-párah kardan, پخش کردن pakhsh kardan.

SHIVERING, لرزه larzah, متزلزل mutazalzil.

SHOAL (*shallow*), پا یاب pá-yáb, نا عمیق ná-'amík, کم آب kam-áb. —(*bank*) پایاب pá-yáb.—کم آب kam-áb.—(*of fish*) دسته dastah.

SHOCK, صدمه sadmah, هجوم hujúm, جنبش jumbish, تکان takán. — (*of corn*) حاصل hásil, بسته bastah, دسته dastah.

To SHOCK (*frighten*), ترسانیدن tarsánídan, تهدید کردن tahdíd kardan.—(*by collision*) تکان دادن takán dádan, تکانیدن takánídan. —(*make ashamed*) شرمنده ساختن sharmandah sákhtan, متخفر ساختن mutakhaffir sákhtan.

SHOCKED (*horrified, offended*), متنفر mutanaffir, آزرده ázurdah, رنجیده ranjídah, حیران hairán, مضطرب muztarib, سر گردان sar-gardán, مشوش mushavvash.

SHOCKING, هولناک haul-nák.

SHOE, کفش kafsh, پا افزار pá-afzár. —(*European shoes*) کفش ارسی kafsh-i-urasí.—(*strong knitted shoes with cloth soles*) ملکی malakí.—(*strong knitted shoes with long pointed leather toes, worn by mountaineers*) گیوه gívah.—(*horse-shoe*) نعل na'l.—(*shoeing horn*) پاشنه کش páshnah-kash.—(*shoes of green shagreen with high heels*) کفش ساغری kafsh-i-ságharí.—(*shoes with peak and heel*) شاهپسند sháh-pasand.—(*leathern buskin tied round the foot*) چارك chároak.—(*to put on shoes*) کفش پوشیدن kafsh púshídan.

SHOEMAKER, کفشدوز kafsh-dúz.—(*shoemaker's knife*) شفره shifrah, نشکرده nishkardah.—(*shoemaker's iron pestle*) مشته mushtah.

SHOE-STRING, کفش بند kafsh-band.

SHOOT (*of a plant or seed*), بنه bunah, پته pittah, تنج tinj, نهال nihál, تره tarh.

To SHOOT (*dart*), انداختن andákhtan.—(*strike*) زدن zadan.—(*fire a gun*) خالی کردن khálí kardan, تفنگ زدن tufang zadan.—(*as a plant or seed*) نبت کردن nabt kardan, رستن rustan, تنج زدن tinj zadan.—(*to shoot up*) جستن jastan (*root* جه jih).

SHOOTER, تفنگ چی tufang-chí.

SHOOTING, تفنگ زدن tufang-zadan.

SHOP, دکان dukán, حانوت hánút, حانوط hánút.

SHOPKEEPER, دکاندار dukán-dár, اهل دکان ahl-i-dukán. — (*petty shopkeeper*) بازار چی bázár-chí.

SHORE, کنار kanár, لب lab, ناحیه náhiyah, ساحل sáhil, کران karán.—(*on shore*) خشکی khushkí.

SHORT, کوتاه kútáh, کوته kútah, قصیر kasír.—(*of stature*) کوتاه قد kútah-kadd, کتولی kutúlí, کهپل khippil (*vulg.*).—(*to fall short of*) قاصر شدن kásir shudan, ناقص بودن nákis búdan.—(*shortly, soon*) زود zúd, بزودی bi-zúdí.—(*in short*) القصه al kissah, الغرض al-gharaz, اجمالاً ijmálan, الحاصل al-hásil, حاصل کلام hásil-i-kalám.—(*money*) بخس bakhs.—(*to cut short*) قطع کردن kat' kardan.

SHORT-BREAD (*cake of flour baked with butter, &c.*), کلوچه kulúchah.

To SHORTEN, کوتاه کردن kútáh kardan, کوتاهتر کردن kútáhtar kardan.

SHORTENED, مختصر mukhtasar.

SHORTNESS, کوتاهی kútáhí, کوتهی kútahí.

SHORT-SIGHTED, نزدیك بین nazdík-bín.—(*imprudent*) کوتاه بین kútáh-bín, کوتاه اندیش kútáh-andísh.

SHOT (*sound of a gun's discharge*), آواز ávaz, صدائی تفنگ sadá,í-i-tufang.—(*range of a ball, &c.*) پرتاب partáb.—(*volley of shot*) شلیك shalík.—(*ball*) غلوله ghulúlah, گلوله gulúlah, گله gullah.—(*small-shot*) ساچمه sáchmah.—(*slugs*) چار پاره chár-párah.—(*to be shot*) تیر تفنگی خوردن tír-i-tufangí khwurdan, گلوله خوردن gulúlah khwurdan.

SHOULDER, دوش dúsh, شانه shánah, کتف katif, کتف kitf.—(*shoulder blade*) شانه shánah. — (*shoulder belt, for a sword, &c.*) حمایل hamáyil. — (*broad shoulders*) شانه عریض shánah-i-'aríz.

To SHOULDER, بر دوش نهادن bar dúsh nihádan.

SHOUT, غریو gharív, بانگ báng, گلبانگ gulbáng, خروش khurúsh, غوغا ghaughá, آواز áváz, شغب shaghab, ولوله valvalah, غو ghau.—(*of joy*) تهلیل tahlíl, هبابك habábak, کل kill.

To SHOUT, آواز کردن áváz kardan, صدا کردن sadá kardan, بانگ زدن báng zadan.

SHOVE, هول húl, هل hul, سك suk, تکان takán, دفع daf', دسر dasr.

To SHOVE, راندن rándan, هل دادن hul dádan, هول دادن húl dádan, سك دادن suk dádan, له دادن lah dádan.

SHOVEL, بیل bíl, پارو párú.

SHOW (*spectacle*), تماشا tamáshá, منظر manzar, مظهر mazhar, مطمح mutmah.

To SHOW, نمودن nimúdan, نشان دادن nishán dádan. — (*demonstrate*) بیان کردن bayán kardan,

اظهار نمودن izhár nimúdan.—*to show a thing*) تماشا دادن tamáshá dádan.

SHOWER (*of rain*), باران bárán, بارش bárish, ترشح tarashshuh.—(*of arrows*), تیر باران tír-bárán, باران تیر bárán-i-tír.

To SHOWER, باریدن báridan, افشاندن afshándan.

SHOWERY, بارانی báráni.

SHOWY, خوشنما khwush-nimá, لطیف latíf, قشنگ kashang.

SHRED, پاره párah.

SHREW, زنکه zanakah.

SHREWD, چابک chábuk, زیرک zírak, چست chust, زرنگ zaring, ذکی zakí, چیره دست chírah-dast.

SHREWDLY, با ذهن bá-zihn.

SHREWDNESS, زیرکی zírakí, زرنگی zaringí, فراست firásat, زکاوت zakávat, ذهن zihn.

SHRIEK, فریاد faryád, غریو gharív.

To SHRIEK, غریو زدن gharív zadan, غریدن ghurrídan, فریاد کردن faryád kardan.

SHRILL (*as sound, voice*), تیز tíz.

SHRILLNESS, تیزی tízí.

SHRIMP, روبیان rúbiyán, ماهی میگو máhí-maigú.

SHRINE, درگاه dargáh, مزار mazár, زیارتگاه ziyárat-gáh, قدمگاه kadamgáh.

To SHRINK (*contract*), تنگ شدن tang shudan, در هم کشیدن dar-ham kashídan, خرد شدن khurd shudan.—(*away from*) کناره جستن kanárah justan, کنار گرفتن kanár giriftan, دور کشی نمودن dúr-kashí nimúdan.

To SHRIVEL, تنگ شدن tang shudan, در هم کشیدن dar-ham kashídan, خرد شدن khurd shudan.

SHROUD, کفن kafan.—(*shrouds of a ship*) رسن rasan, نردبان ریسمانی nardubán-i-rísmání.

To SHROUD, تکفین کردن takfín kardan.—(*cover*) پوشیدن púshídan, پوشانیدن púshánídan.

SHRUB, بوته bútah, درخت dirakht, بنه bunah.

SHRUBBERY, مشجره mashjarah, درختزار dirakht-zár.

SHRUG, تکان takán.

To SHRUG, تکان دادن takán dádan.

SHUCK, پوست púst, قشر kishr.

To SHUDDER, هراسان شدن harásán shudan, ترسیدن tarsídan.

SHUFFLE, آمیز ámíz, آمیزش ámízish.—(*evasion*) بهانه bahánah, حیله hílah, زبانبازی zabán-bází.

To SHUFFLE, آمیختن ámíkhtan.—(*prevaricate*) لیت و لعل کردن lait u la'all kardan.

SHUFFLER, مخلط mukhallit.—(*prevaricator*) زبان باز zabán-báz.

To SHUN, پرهیز کردن parhíz kardan, اجتناب نمودن ijtináb nimúdan, احتراز نمودن ihtiráz nimúdan, حذر کردن hazar kardan, پهلو تهی کردن pahlú-tuhí kardan, دور کشی نمودن dúr-kashí nimúdan, کنار رفتن kanár raftan.

To SHUT, بستن bastan, بند کردن band kardan, مسدود کردن masdúd kardan, روبهم کردن rúy-ham kardan, بهم گذاشتن bi-ham guzáshtan.—(*window*) پائین کردن pá,ín kardan.—(*door*) چفت کردن chift kardan.—(*window of train*) شیشه بستن shíshah bastan.—(*to shut off, water, &c.*) بستن bastan.

SHUTTER, دریچه daríchah, پنجره panjarah.

SHUTTLE (*weaver's*), ماکو mákú, ماکوب mákúb, مکوک makúk.

SHY, خجل khijil, شرمسار sharm-sár.

To SHY, رمیدن ramídan.

SICK, بیمار bímár, نا خوش ná-khwush, خسته khastah, مریض maríz, علیل 'alíl, نا مزاج ná-mizáj.—(*to be sick*) بی دماغ شدن bí-dimágh shudan.—(*vomit*) استفراغ نمودن istifrágh nimúdan, قی کردن kay kardan.

To SICKEN, بیمار شدن bímár shudan, نا خوش گردیدن ná-khwush gardídan.—(*disgust*) بیزار نمودن bízár nimúdan, تنفیر نمودن tanfír nimúdan.

SICKENING (*disgusting*), مغص mughass, مکروه makrúh, نفرت انگیز nifrat-angíz.

SICKLE, داس dás, داز dáz.

SICKNESS (*illness*), مرض marz, بیماری bímárí, علت 'illat, رنج ranj, آزار ázár, درد dard, نا خوشی ná-khwushí, تکسر مزاج takassar-i-mizáj.—(*inclination to vomit*) تهوع tahavvu', آشوب دل áshúb-i-dil.

SIDE, پهلو pahlú, کنار kanár, جنب jamb, جانب jánib. — (*direction*) طرف taraf, جانب jánib, کناره kanárah, سمت samt, سو sú, حوز hauz. —(*party, faction*) طرف taraf, قبل kibal, جانب jánib. — (*of paper*) صفحه safhah.—(*of medal, &c.*) روی rúy.—(*of vessel*) بغل baghal, دیوار dívár.—(*the sides*) اضلاع azlá'.—(*by side of*) در پهلوی dar pahlúy; در نزد dar nazd, پهلوی pahlúy.—(*on the wrong side*) وارونه várúnah. —(*from side to side*) از طرفین az tarafain, از هر طرف az har taraf.—(*on all sides*) از همه طرف az hamah taraf, از اطراف az atráf.

SIDEBOARD, میز míz.

SIDEWAYS, یك بری yak-barí.

SIEGE, محاصره muhásarah. — (*to raise the siege*) محاصره‌را موقوف کردن muhásarahrá maukúf kardan.

SIEVE, غربال gharbál, غلبار ghalbár, غلبیر ghalbír, غلبال ghalbál (*vulg.*).—(*fine sieve*) الك alik.

To SIFT, پیختن píkhtan, غربال زدن gharbál zadan.

SIFTER, غربال زن gharbál-zan.

SIGH, آه áh.

To SIGH, آه کشیدن áh kashídan.

SIGHT, نظر nazar, نگاه nigáh, دیدار dídár, دیده dídah. — (*spectacle*) تماشا tamáshá.—(*power of seeing*) بینائی bíná,í, باصرت básirat, دیدار dídár.—(*on the muzzle of a gun*) دید díd, دید پیش díd-i-písh.—(*hind-sight of a rifle or gun*) دید پس díd-i-pas. — (*to be lost to sight*) از نظر غائب شدن az nazar ghá,ib shudan, از چشم گم شدن az chashm gum shudan.

SIGHTLESS, نا بینا ná-bíná, کور kúr, اعما a'má, ضریر zarír.

SIGHTLY, مقبول makbúl, مرغوب marghúb, خوش منظر khwush-manzar.

SIGN, اشاره ishárah, نشان nishán, علامت 'alámat, اثر asar, سراغ surágh, ایما ímá, شعار shi'ár, دلالت dalálat.

To SIGN (*one's name*), صحیح کردن sahíh kardan, صح گذاردن sahh guzárdan, امضا نوشتن imzá nivishtan, ثبت کردن sabt kardan.—(*make a sign*) اشاره نمودن ishárah nimúdan. — (*to be signed*) بامضا رسیدن bi-imzá rasídan.—(*signed and sealed*) مسجل musajjal.

SIGNAL, اشاره ishárah, نشان nishán, علامت 'alámat, اثر asar, سراغ surágh, ایما ímá, شعار shi'ár, دلالت dalálat.—(*memorable*) مشهور mash-húr, معروف ma'rúf, موصوف mausúf. — (*train*) سیگنل sígnal (*eur.*).—(*signal-box*) قراولخانه karávul-khánah.

To SIGNAL, اشاره نمودن ishárah nimúdan.

To SIGNALIZE, نمودن nimúdan, اظهار نمودن izhár nimúdan.

SIGNALLY, معروفانه ma'rúfánah.

SIGNATORY, امضا کننده imzá-kunandah.

SIGNATURE, امضا imzá, نشان nishán.

SIGNET, خاتم khátim, مهر muhr.

SIGNIFICANCE (*matter of care*), مضایقه muzáyakah, پروا parvá.—(*sense*) معنی ma'ní, فحوا fahvá, مطلب matlab.—(*importance*) قدر kadr.

SIGNIFICANT, مهم muhimm.

SIGNIFICATION, معنی ma'ní, فحوا fahvá, مطلب matlab.

To SIGNIFY (*make known*), خبر کردن khabar kardan. — (*mean*) معنی داشتن ma'ní dáshtan.

SILENCE, خاموشی khámúshí, سکوت sukút, صمت samt. — (*interj.*) خاموش khámúsh. — (*to keep silence*) سکوت نمودن sukút nimúdan, خاموش شدن khámúsh shudan, لال ماندن lál mándan.

To SILENCE, ساکت کردن sákit kardan, اسکات نمودن iskát nimúdan.

SILENT, خاموش khámúsh, ساکت sákit, خب khab, صامت sámit.

SILENTLY, آهسته áhistah.

SILK, ابریشم abríshum.—(*silk cloth*) پارچهٔ ابریشمی párchah-i-abríshumí, حریر harír.—(*raw silk*) قز kazz, خز khaz.—(*silkworm*) کرم پیله kirm-i-pílah, کرم ابریشم kirm-i-abríshum.—(*cocoon of silkworm*) پیله pílah.—(*place where silkworms are reared*) تلمبار tilambár, تیلمبار tílambár. — (*satin*) اطلس atlas.—(*brocaded silk*) زری zarí.—(*silk stuff for making coats, &c.*) دارای dárái.—(*silk stuff for shirts, &c.*) علیچه 'alíchah.—(*stuff of silk and cotton mixed*) مشروع mashrú', گرمسوف garmasúf.—(*silk stuff for trousers, generally red*) قصب kasab.—(*shot silk*) استبرق istabrak.—(*silk cut up and put into an inkstand*) پرز purz, لیغه líghah, تلی tulí, لیقه líkah.—(*strong silk stuff, of any colour*) خارا khárá.—(*fine ditto, ditto*) تافته táftah.—(*silk cord or lace*) قیطان kaitán. — (*damasked silk*) اطلس مشجر atlas-i-mushajjar.

SILKEN, حریری harírí.

SILLINESS (*persons*), نادانی nádání, ابلهی ablahí, بلاهت baláhat, حماقت himákat, سفاهت safáhat, خبط khabt, قلت عقل killat-i-'akl, بیوقوفی bi-vukúfí, خریت kharíyat (*vulg.*).—(*things*) بیهودگی bíhúdagí, هرزگی harzagí.

SILLY (*persons*), نادان ná-dán, ناواقف ná-vákif, بیخبر bí-khabar, ساده لوح sádah-lauh. — (*things*) بیهوده bíhúdah, هرزه harzah, پوچ púch, بیمعنی bí-ma'ní, جفنگ jafang.

SILVAN, دهقانی dihkání.

SILVER, نقره nukrah, سیم sím.—(*made of silver*) سیمین símín, از نقره az nukrah.

To SILVER (*plate*), آب نقره دادن áb-i-nukrah dádan, مفضض کردن mufazzaz kardan.

SILVERED, سیم اندود sím-andúd, مفضض mufazzaz.

SILVER-GILT, نقره مطلا nukrah-mutillá, مفضض mufazzaz.

SILVERSMITH, جوهری jauharí, جواهری javáharí (*vulg.*).

SILVER THREAD, گلابتان gulábatán.

SIMILAR, برابر barábar, یکسان yaksán, موافق muváfik, مطابق mutábik, همتا ham-tá, مشابه mushábih, همانا hamáná, مانند mánand, مثل misl, مماثل mumásil, معادل mu'ádil.

SIMILARITY, برابری barábarí, تمثیل tamsíl, مثال misál, تشبیه tashbíh, مشابهه mushábabah, شبه shibh, موافقت muváfakat, شباهت shabáhat, نمایش nimáyish, حکم hukm.

SIMILE, تشبیه tashbíh, مثل masal, مجاز majáz, عبارت 'ibárat.

To SIMMER (*boil gently*), نیم جوش کردن ním-júsh kardan.

SIMPER, تبسم tabassum.

To SIMPER, تبسم نمودن tabassum nimúdan, خنده دروغ کردن khandah-i-durúgh kardan.

SIMPLE (*not compound*), مفرد mufrad, بسیط basít.—(*artless, harmless*) ساده لوح sádah-lauh, ساده دل sádah-dil, بی ریا bí-riyá.—(*herb*) گیاه giyáh, سبزی sabzí, علف 'alaf, نبات nabát.—(*plain*) ساده sádah.

SIMPLETON, ساده لوح sádah-lauh, ابله ablah, کودن kaudan, احمق ahmak, نا دان ná-dán, نا فهم ná-fahm, سفیه safíh, خوپله khwaplah, بیوقوف bí - vukúf, پخت pakht (*vulg.*).

SIMPLICITY, ساده دلی sádah-dilí, سادگی sádagí.

SIMPLY, محضاً mahzan, صرف sarf.

SIMULATION, تجاهل tajáhul, بهانه bahánah.

SIN, گناه gunáh, خطا khatá, جرم jurm, تقصیر taksír, عصیان 'isyán, اثم ism, جنایت janáyat, بزه bizah, ذنب zamb, گنه gunah, قصور kusúr.

To SIN, گناه کردن gunáh kardan, خطا کردن khatá kardan, تقصیر نمودن taksír nimúdan.

SINCE (*because that*), چونکه chúnkih, از آنجاکه az ánjá-kih, از بسکه az bas-kih.—(*from that time*) از آن وقت az án-vakt, پس از آن pas az án, من بعد min ba'd, بعد

از آن ba'd az án, از وقتیکه az vaktí-kih, تا tá.

SINCERE, صادق sádik, خالص khális, بیغرض bí-gharaz, بی ریا bí-riyá.

SINCERELY, اخلاصاً ikhlásan, صادقانه sádikánah, مخلصاً mukhlisan.

SINCERITY, صدق sidk, صداقت sadákat, اخلاص ikhlás, راستی rástí, خلوص khulús.

SINE, جیب jíb.—(*co-sine*) تمام جیب tamám-jíb.

SINEW, پی pay, عصب 'asab (*pl.* اعصاب a'sáb), وتر vatar (*pl.* اوتار autár).

SINEWY, عصب ناك 'asab-nák.

SINFUL, گناهکار gunáh-kár.

SINFULNESS, گناهکاری gunáh-kárí.

To SING, خواندن khwándan, سرائیدن sará,ídan.

To SINGE, سوختن súkhtan, نیم سوختن ním súkhtan.

SINGER, قوال kavvál, خواننده khwánandah, سراینده saráyandah, مغنی mughanní, مطرب mutrib.—(*comic singer*), مقلد خواننده mukallid-khwánandah.

SINGLE, یك yak, یکتا yak-tá, فرد fard, مفرد mufrad, واحد váhid, یگانه yagánah.

SINGLENESS, یگانگی yagánagí, وحدت vahdat.

SINGLY (*one by one*), یك یك yak yak, یگان یگان yagán yagán, فردافرد fard-á-fard.

SINGULAR (*strange*), غریب gharíb, عجیب 'ajíb.—(*single*) یك yak, یکتا yak-tá, فرد fard, مفرد mufrad, واحد váhid, یگانه yagánah.—(*singular number*) واحد váhid, مفرد mufrad.

SINGULARITY, غرابت gharábat, عجب 'ajab.

SINGULARLY, خصوصاً khusúsan.

SINISTER, زشت zisht, مشوم mashúm, قبیح kabíh.

SINK (*drain*), آبریز áb-ríz, آبشی áb-shí.

To SINK, فرو رفتن furú raftan, زوال کردن zavál kardan, پائین رفتن pá,ín raftan, نزول کردن nuzúl kardan.—(*cause to sink*) غرق کردن gharak kardan.—(*penetrate*) در رفتن dar raftan, نفاذ یافتن nafáz yáftan, تو رفتن tú raftan.—(*soak into*) خیسانیدن khísáníдan, نشر کردن nashr kardan.

SINLESS, بیگناه bí-gunáh, بیخطا bí-khatá, معصوم ma'súm, بیجرم bí-jurm.

SINNER, گناه کار gunáh-kár, خطا کار khatá-kár, خاطی khátí, عاصی 'ásí, مذنب muznib, آثم ásim, اثیم asím, فاجر fájir, سیه کار siyah-kár, بزه مند bizah-mand.

SIN-OFFERING, کفاره kaffárah.

SINUOSITY, عوج 'avaj, اعوجاج i'vijáj.

SIP, نوش núsh.

To SIP, نوشیدن núshídan, لیسیدن lísídan.

SIPHON, لوله lúlah.

SIR, آغا ághá, آقا áká, صاحب sáhib, خداوند khudávand.

SIRIUS (*the dog-star*), شعری shi'rá, الکلب al kalb.

SIRUP, شیره shírah, رب rubb.

SISTER, خواهر khwáhar, همشیره ham-shírah, دده dadah (*vulg.*).—(*full*) خواهر عین khwáhar-i-'ain.—(*half*) خواهر صلبی khwáhar-i-sulbí, خواهر بطنی khwáhar-i-batni. [The first is a sister by the father's, the second by the mother's side.]—(*adopted*) خواهر خوانده khwáhar-i-khwándah.—(*sister-in-law*) خواهر زوجه khwáhar-i-zaujah, زوجه برادر zaujah-i-birádar, خواهر زن khwáhar-i-zan.—(*sister of mercy*) خواهر ترحم دینی khwáhar-i-tarahhum-i-díní.

SISTERLY, خواهرانه khwáharánah.

To SIT, نشستن nishastan, جلوس کردن julús kardan, قعود کردن ka'úd kardan.—(*respectfully*) فرمودن firmúdan, استراحت فرمودن istirá-hat firmúdan.—(*in the Persian fashion, kneeling down and sitting backwards upon the heels*, دو زانو نشستن dú-zánú nishastan.—(*in the Turkish fashion, with the legs crossed*) چهار زانو نشستن chahár-zánú nishastan, مربع نشستن murabba' nishastan.—(*to sit on one's heels with the knees upwards*) سر پا نشستن sar-i-pá nishastan.

SITE, وضع vaz', جا já, جایگاه jáy-gáh.

SITUATED, واقع váki', موضوع mauzú', ایستاده ístádah, نشانده nishándah.

SITUATION, حال hál, حالت hálat, وضع vaz'. — (*appointment*) منصب mansab, تعیین ta'yín, عهده 'uhdah.

SIZE, اندازه andázah, قدر kadar, مقدار mikdár.—(*painter's size*) سیرشم sírishum, سریشم siríshum, سریش siríshum.

SKATE (*fish*), لقمه ماهی lukmah máhí.

SKEIN (*of thread*), کلافه kiláfah.

SKELETON, استخوان بندی ustakhwán-bandí, تشریح tashríh, تن سکلی tan-i-saklí.

SKETCH, مسوده musavvadah, سواد savád.—(*drawing or plan*) نقشه nakshah.

To SKETCH, کشیدن kashídan, تصویر کردن tasvír kardan, انگاشتن angáshtan.

SKEWER, سیخچه síkhchah.

SKIFF, زورق zaurak, کشتی kashtí, قایق káík.

SKILFUL, هنرمند hunar-mand, واقف vákif, قابل kábil, کار شناس kár-shinás, کار آموز kár-ámúz, ماهر máhir, دانا dáná, حاذق házik, مسلط musallat, زرنگ zaring.

SKILFULLY, با هنرمندی bá-hunar-mandí.

SKILL, هنر hunar, هنر مندی hunar-mandí, وقوف vukúf, معرفت ma'rifat, حکمت hikmat, مهارت mahárat, فن fann, قابلیت kábilíyat, تسلط tasallut, سر رشته sar-rishtah.

To SKIM, کف گرفتن kaf giriftan. (*pass lightly over*) سبک گذشتن subuk guzashtan.

SKIMMER, کفگیر kaf-gír, آب گردان áb-gardán.

SKIN, پوست púst, جلد jild, چرم charm, پوستگی pústagí.—(*cuticle or outer skin*) بشره basharah.—(*for holding water, wine, &c.*) مشك mashk, خیگ khíg.

To SKIN (*flay*), پوست کندن púst kandan, سلخ کردن salkh kardan, مجلد ساختن mujallad sákhtan.

SKINNY, پوست مانند púst-mánand, پر ریشته pur-ríshtah.—(*thin*) لاغر lághir, نزار nizár, ضعیف za'íf.

SKIP, جست jast.

To SKIP, جستن jastan (*root* جه jih).

SKIRMISH, زد و خوردی zad va khwurdí.

SKIRT, دامن dáman, ذیل zail, کنار kanár, اتك atak.—(*of a hill*) بغله baghalah, دامنه dámanah.

To SKIRT, از بغل رفتن az baghal raftan, خیز کردن khíz kardan.

SKIRTING (*of a wall*), هزاره hizáráh.

SKITTISH, ترسناك tars-nák, شوخ shúkh.

SKITTISHLY, بشوخی bi-shúkhí.

SKITTISHNESS, ترسناکی tars-nákí, شوخی shúkhí.

SKULK, کمین گر kamín-gar.

To SKULK, پنهان شدن panhán shudan, کمین کردن kamín kardan, نهفته شدن nihuftah shudan, متواری بودن mutavárí búdan.

SKULL, کاسه سر kásah-i-sar, کله kallah, جمجمه jumjumah.

SKULL-CAP, عرقچین 'arak-chín.

SKY, آسمان ásmán, فلك falak, هوا havá, اثیر asír.

SKYLARK, چکاوه chakávah, چکاوك chakávuk, قنبره kumbarah, قازلاق kázlák.

SKYLIGHT, تابدان táb-dán, سقف شیشه بلند sakf-i-shíshah - i - buland.

SLAB, تخته takhtah.

SLACK, سست sust, لك lak, شل shul.—(*persons*) سست sust, غافل ghá fil.

To SLACKEN, سست ساختن sust sákhtan.

SLACKNESS (*things*), سستی sustí.—(*persons*) سستی sustí, غفلت ghiflat.

SLAIN, مقتول maktúl.

To SLAKE (*thirst*), تسکین دادن taskín dádan, نشاندن nishándan.—(*fire*) نشاندن nishándan, کشتن kushtan; اطفا نمودن itfá nimúdan, منطفی ساختن muntafí sákhtan, خاموش کردن khámúsh kardan,

ساکت کردن sákit kardan.—(*lime*) فرو نشاندن furú nishándan.

SLANDER, بهتان buhtán, افترا iftirá, غیبت ghíbat, تهمت tuhmat, سعایت si'áyat.

To SLANDER, متهم کردن muttahim kardan, تهمت زدن tuhmat zadan, بهتان بستن buhtán bastan, افترا بستن iftirá bastan.

SLANDERER, بهتان انداز buhtán-andáz, نمام nammám, ساعی sá'í.

SLANDEROUS, افترا گو iftirá - gú, مفتری muftarí, بد سگال bad-sigál.

SLANG, زبان بازاری zabán-i-bázárí, کلام سوقی kalám-i-súkí.

SLANT, عوج 'ivaj, اعوجاج i'vijáj, میل mail.

To SLANT, تکیه دادن takyah dádan.

SLANTING, مائل má,il.

SLAP, طپانچه tapánchah, تماچه tamáchah, سیلی sílí, سله sallah.

To SLAP, سله زدن sallah zadan.

SLASH, سوراخ súrákh.

To SLASH, بریدن burídan *or* burrídan, قطع کردن kat' kardan.

SLATE, سنگ sang.—(*to write on*) لوح lauh.

SLAUGHTER, قتل katl, قتال katál, کشتار kushtár, خونریزی khún-rízí, خونفشانی khún-fisháni.

To SLAUGHTER, کشتن kushtan, قتل نمودن katl nimúdan, هلاك ساختن halák sákhtan, بقتل رسانیدن bi-katl rasánídan.

SLAUGHTER-HOUSE, سلاخ خانه sallakh-khánah, مسلخ maslakh.

SLAUGHTERMAN, قصاب kassáb.

SLAV, اسلاو isláv (*eur.*).

SLAVE, بنده bandah, عبد 'abd, غلام ghulám, برده bardah, پرستار parastár, مملوك mamlúk, قلی kullí, رهی rahí, حلقه بگوش halkah-bi-gúsh, کاکا káká [a cant term, literally signifying a younger brother].—(*slave girl*) کنیز kaníz, جاریه járiyah, دده dadah (*vulg.*)—(*fugitive slave*) آبق ábik, بنده فراری bandah-i-firárí.—(*slave freed at his master's death*) مدبر mudabbar, معتوق ma'túk.—(*slave purchasing or working out his own ransom*) مکاتب mukátib.—(*slave merchant*), غلام فروش ghulám-furúsh, بنده فروش bandah-furúsh.—(*slave trade*) بیع و شرای زنگیان 'bai' va shiráí-i-zangiyán.

SLAVERY, بندگی bandagí, عبودیت 'ubúdíyat.

SLAVISH, کمینه kamínah, پست past, دون dún.

SLAVISHNESS, کمینگی kamínagí, پستی pastí, دونی dúní.

To SLAY, کشتن kushtan, قتل نمودن katl nimúdan, هلاك ساختن halák sákhtan, بقتل رسانیدن bi - katl rasánídan.

SLEDGE, تخته takhtah.

SLEEK, املس amlas.

SLEEKNESS, صافی sáfí.

SLEEP, خواب khwáb, منام manám, نوم naum, رقاد rukád, هجوع hujú'. (*first sleep*) سر خواب sar-i-khwáb.

To SLEEP, خفتن khuftan (*root* خسپ khusp *or* خفت khuft), خسبیدن khusbídan, خوابیدن khwábídan, غنودن ghunúdan.—(*become torpid, as a limb*) بی حس شدن bí-hiss shudan, سست شدن sust shudan.—(*to put to sleep*) خوابانیدن khwábánídan.

SLEEPLESS, بیخواب bí-khwáb, بیدار bídár.

SLEEPLESSNESS, بیخوابی bí-khwábí, بیداری bí-dárí.

SLEEPY, خواب آلود khwáb-álúd, وا مانده vá-mándah, پینکی زده pínakí-zadah.

SLEET, برف باران barf-bárán.

SLEEVE, آستین ástín, کم kumm.

SLEEVE-LINKS, دکمه سر دست dugmah-i-sar-i-dast.

SLEIGHT OF HAND, شعبده shu'badah, شعبده بازی shu'badah-bází, چشم بندی chasm-bandí.

SLENDER, نازك názuk, تنك tang, رکیك rakík, باریك baríк, نزار nizár.

SLENDERNESS, باریکی báríkí, نزاری nizárí, نازکی názukí.

SLICE, قطعه kat'ah, شرحه sharhah, تراشه tiráshah.

To SLICE, تراشیدن tiráshídan.

To SLIDE, لغزیدن laghzídan, لخشیدن lakhshídan, سریدن surídan.
SLIGHT (*affront*), هتک آبرو hatk-i-áb-rú, شتم shatm, خفت khiffat, سر شکستگی sar-shikastagí, بی ساختگی bí-sákhtagí. — (*slender*), نازک názuk, تنگ tang, رکیک rakík, باریک bárík, نزار nizár. — (*little*) اندک andak, قلیل kalíl, کم kam.—(*meal*) مختصر mukhtasar.
To SLIGHT (*affront*), هتک آبرو کردن hatk-i-áb-rú kardan, خفت نمودن khiffat nimúdan, بی ساختگی نمودن bí-sákhtagí nimúdan.
SLIGHTINGLY, با خفت bá-khiffat.
SLIGHTLY, اندک andak, کم kam.
SLIGHTNESS, باریکی báríkí, نزاری nizárí, نازکی názukí.
SLIM, نازک názuk, تنگ tang, رکیک rakík, باریک bárík, نزار nizár.
SLIME, گل gil, لجن lajan.
SLIMY, گلناک gil-nák.
SLING, فلاخن falákhun, کلوه سنگ kulvah-sang, قلا سنگ kalá-sang.
To SLING (*across the shoulders*), هیکلوار انداختن haikal-vár andákhtan, بدوش انداختن bi-dúsh andákhtan.
To SLINK, افتادن uftádan.
SLIP, لغزش laghzísh.—(*error*) غلط ghalat, سهو sahv, خطا khatá, زلت zallat, علت zallat, مضلت mazallat, خبط khabt, قصور kusúr, تقصیر taksír.—(*slip of the pen*) سهو قلم sahv-i-kalam.
To SLIP, لغزیدن laghzídan, لخشیدن lakhshídan, سریدن surídan.
SLIPPER, کفش kafsh, پا پوش pá-púsh, پیزار paizár. — (*place where the slippers are deposited previous to stepping upon the carpetted floor of a room*), صف نعال saff-i-ni'ál, کفش کن kafsh-kan.
SLIPPERINESS, لغزانی laghzání, لغزندگی laghzandagí.
SLIPPERY, لغزنده laghzandah.
SLIPS (*for hounds*), مروس mirvas, مراس marás, مرس maras.
SLIT, چاک chák, شق shakk, درز darz.
To SLIT, چاک کردن chák kardan.

SLOE, آلوچه álúchah.
SLOPE, شیب shíb, نشیب nishíb.
SLOPING, نشیبدار nishíb-dár, مائل má,il, سرازیر sar-á-zír, سراشیب sar-á-shíb.
SLOTH, سستی sustí, غفلت ghiflat, تهاون tahávun, کاهلی káhilí, اهمال ihmál, تنبلی tambalí.—(*animal*) تنبل tambal.
SLOTHFUL, سست sust, کاهل káhil, تنبل tambal.
SLOTHFULLY, بسستی bi-sustí.
SLOVEN *and* SLOVENLY, پلشت pilisht.
SLOW, کند kund, دیر dír, سست sust.—(*slow to anger*) دیر غضب dír-ghazab, کاظم الغیظ kázimu-'l-ghaiz, حنان hannán.—(*watch*) دیر dír, کند kund.
SLOWLY, آهسته áhistah, رفته رفته raftah raftah, یواش yavásh.
SLOWNESS, آهستگی áhistagí, سستی sustí, دیری dírí.
SLUG (*small bullet*), چار پاره chár-párah.—(*grub*) کرم kirm.
SLUGGARD, تنبل tambal, آرام کار árám-kár.
SLUGGISH, کاهل káhil, تنبل tambal.
SLUGGISHLY, بسستی bi-sustí.
SLUICE, آبگیره áb-gírah.
SLUMBER, پینکی pínakí, خواب khwáb, منام manám, نوم naum, رقاد rukád, هجوع hujú'.
To SLUMBER, غنودن ghunúdan, خوابیدن khwábídan, پینکی زدن pínakí zadan.
SLUR (*slight disgrace*), عیب 'aib, داغ dágh, لکه lakkah. — (*to cast a slur upon one*) منافاتی داشتن munáfátí dáshtan.
SLUSH, شل shul.
SLUT, پلشت pilisht.
SLUTTISH, غافل gháfil, عاطل 'átil, نا پاک ná-pák.
SLY, روبه باز rúbah-báz, حیله باز hílah-báz, محتال muhtál, زیرک zírak.
SLYLY, با حیله بازی bá-hílah-bází.
SLYNESS, روبه بازی rúbah-bází, حیله بازی hílah-bází.

SMACK (*flavour*), مزه mazah.—(*sound*) آواز áváz.

SMALL, خورد khwurd, خرد khurd, کوچك kúchik, قليل kalíl, صغير saghír, پاچه páchah. — (*small in quantity*) کم kam, اندك andak.—(*small, as writing, gravel, shot, berries, peas, &c.*) ريزه rízah.

SMALLNESS, کوچکی kúchikí, صغر sighar.

SMALL-POX, آبله ábilah, جدری jadarí, چيچك chíchak (*obs.*), اوله aulah (*vulg.*).—(*pitted with the small-pox*) مجدر mujaddar, آبله زده ábilah-zadah, اوله زده aulah-zadah.

SMART (*active, sharp*), زرنگ zaring, قبراغ kibrágh, چابك chábuk, شاطر shátir.—(*pain*) درد dard.

To SMART, درد يافتن dard yáftan.

SMARTLY, با زرنگی bá-zaringí.

SMARTNESS, زرنگی zaringí, چابکی chábukí.

To SMASH (*to pieces*), پخش کردن pakhsh kardan, خورد کردن khwurd kardan, شکستن shikastan, حل کردن hall kardan, له کردن lih kardan.

SMASHED, مکسور maksúr, منکسر munkasir.—(*to be smashed*) خورد شدن khwurd shudan.

SMATTER, دانش خام dánish-i-khám, علم نا تمام 'ilm-i-ná-tamám.

To SMEAR, اندودن andúdan, آلودن álúdan, ماليدن málídan, پالودن pálúdan.

SMELL (*power of smelling*), شامه shámmah, شم shamm, مشام mushámm.—(*odour*) بو bú, بوی búy, رائحه rá,ihah. — (*sweet smell*) خوشبو khwush-bú, نفحه nafhah.—(*bad smell*) بد بو bad-bú, گند gand, عفونت 'ufúnat.

To SMELL (*trans.*), شميدن shamídan, شنيدن shinídan, بوئيدن bú,ídan, بو گرفتن bú giriftan.—(*intrans.*) بو دادن bú-dádan, گنديدن gandídan.

SMELLING-BOTTLE, بويدان búy-dán.

To SMELT, گداختن gudákhtan, گدازانيدن gudázánídan, حل کردن hall kardan, قال کردن kál kardan, قال گذاشتن kál guzáshtan.

SMILE, تبسم tabassum, نيم خنده ním-khandah, ابتسام ibtisám.

To SMILE, تبسم کردن tabassum kardan, ابتسام نمودن ibtisám nimúdan.

SMILING, ابتسام ibtisám, متبسم mutabassim.

SMILINGLY, متبسماً mutabassiman.

To SMITE, زدن zadan, ضرب کردن zarb kardan.

SMITH (*blacksmith*), آهنگر áhan-gar, حداد haddád.

SMOKE, دود dúd, دخان dukhán, دو dú (*vulg.*), دی dí (*vulg.*).

To SMOKE (*a pipe*), کشيدن kashídan.—(*fire*) دود دادن dúd dádan.—(*cure with smoke*) تدخين کردن tadkhín kardan.

SMOKER, قليان کش kalyán-kash.

SMOKY, دود آلود dúd-álúd.

SMOOTH, هموار ham-vár, صاف sáf, ساده sádah, مسطح musattah.—(*polished*) صيقلی saikalí, مصقول maskúl, زدوده zadúdah, مهره دار muhrah-dár, پرداخته pardákhtah.

To SMOOTH, تمهيد نمودن tamhíd nimúdan.

SMOOTHLY, هموار ham-vár, صاف sáf.

SMOOTHNESS, همواری ham-várí, صافی sáfí, سادگی sádagí.

SMOTHER, خفه khaffah.

To SMOTHER, خفه کردن khaffah kardan, دم بستن dam bastan.

To SMOULDER, سوختن súkhtan.

To SMUGGLE, در ادائی محصول گمرك دزدی کردن dar adá,í-i-mahsúl-i-gumruk duzdí kardan, بی ادائی عشور در آوردن bí-adá,í-i-'ushúr dar ávardan.

SMUGGLER, گريزاننده gurízánandah.

SMUT (*soot*), دوده dúdah.—(*dirty spot*) داغ dágh.—(*obscenity*) فحش fuhsh, زشتی zishtí, هرزگی harzagí, خباثت khabásat.

SMUTTY (*obscene*), هرزه harzah, پوچ púch, فاحش fáhish, خبيث khabís.

SNACK, حصه hissah.—(*meal*) خوراکی khwurákí, طعام ta'ám.

SNAIL, حلزون halazún. [This creature is scarcely known in Persia.]
SNAKE, مار már.—(*large snake or boa*) شاه مار sháh-már, افعی af'í.—(*viper*) تیره مار tírah-már, مار جعفری már-i-ja'farí. — (*huge fabulous snake or dragon*) اژدها azhdahá, تنین taníu, ثعبان sa'bán.—(*flexible tube of a pipe*) نیپیچ nay-pích, مار پیچ már-pích.—(*snake-gourd*) خیارزه khiyárzah.—(*snake-stone, bezoar*), پازهر pá-zahr, پادزهر pád-zahr.
SNAP, گسل gusil.—(*of the fingers*) پلنگک pilingak, بشکن bishkan.—(*bite*) گزندگی gazandagí, گزیدگی gazídagí.
To SNAP (*break, as a rope or other tough substance*) گسستن gusastan, گسیختن gusíkhtan, گسلانیدن gusilánídan. — (*the fingers*) پلنگک زدن pilingak zadan, بشکن زدن bishkan zadan. — (*bite at*) گزه گرفتن gazah giriftan.
SNAPPISH, غضوب ghazúb.
SNAPPISHLY, با غضب bá-ghazab.
SNAPPISHNESS, کج خلق kaj-khalk.
SNARE, دام dám, تله talah, کمند kamand.
To SNARE, کمند نمودن kamand nimúdan, کمند انداختن kamand andákhtan, دام انداختن dám andákhtan, به کمند آوردن bi-kamand ávardan.
SNARL, غره gharrah, اف اف af af.
To SNARL, غریدن ghurrídan.
To SNATCH, ربودن rubúdan, بدست گرفتن bi-dast giriftan, کپیدن kapídan (*vulg.*), کاپیدن kápídan (*vulg.*).
SNATCHER, رباینده rubáyandah.
SNEAK, بد نفس bad-nafs, بد نهاد bad-nihád, نا مرد ná-mard.
To SNEAK, غژیدن ghazhídan.
SNEER, استهزا istihzá, سخریه sukhríyah.
To SNEER, استهزا نمودن istihzá nimúdan, سخریه نمودن sukhríyah nimúdan.
SNEEZE, عطسه 'atsah.
To SNEEZE, عطسه زدن 'atsah zadan.
To SNIFF, استشمام نمودن istishmám nimúdan.
To SNIP, بریدن burídan *or* burrídan, قطع کردن kat' kardan.
SNIPE, پا شله pá-shallah, مرغ شلك murgh-i-shallak.
To SNIVEL, گریستن girístan, گریه کردن giryah kardan.
SNOB, اوباش aubásh.
SNORE, خره khurrah, خرخر khurkhur, خرنش khurnish.
To SNORE, خرخر کردن khurkhur, kardan, خره کشیدن khurrah kashídan, خرنش کشیدن khurnish kashídan.
To SNORT (*as a horse*), خره‌کشیدن khurrah kashídan.
SNOT, مرگ murg, خلط بینی khilt-i-bíní.
SNOUT, خرطوم khurtúm, پوز púz.
SNOW, برف barf.—(*snow-clad*) مملو از برف mamlú az barf, پر برف pur-barf.
To SNOW, برف باریدن barf báridan, برف آمدن barf ámadan.
SNOWSTORM, برف و بوران barf va búrán.—(*avalanche of snow*) شپه shappah.
SNOWY, برفناك barf-nák, برفین barfín.
SNUB, سر زنش sar-zanish, زجر zajr, ملامت malámat, توبیخ taubíkh, نهیب nihíb, شتم shatm, ذم zamm, طعنه ta'nah.
To SNUB, سر زنش نمودن sar-zanish nimúdan, زجر نمودن zajr nimúdan.
SNUFF, نشوق nushúk, سعوط sa'út, انفیه anfíyah. — (*of a candle*) گل gul.—(*to take snuff*) نشوق کردن nushúk kardan. — (*to snuff a candle*) گل گرفتن gul giriftan.
SNUFF-BOX, قوطی نشوق kútí-i-nushúk, قوطی انفیه kútí-i-anfíyah, انفیه دان anfíyah-dán.
SNUFFERS, گلگیر gul-gír.
SNUG, مناسب munásib, شایسته shayistah, لائق lá,ik, موافق muváfik.
So (*thus*), چنین chunín, همچنین ham-chunín, همچو ham-chú, همچی ham-chí (*vulg.*). [چنین and چنان are very generally pronounced in Persia "chinín"

and "chinán," but as they are evidently but an elliptic form of چون این chún-ín and چون آن chún-án, it seems necessary to spell them "chunín" and "chunán."] — (*so that*) تا tá, حتی hattá, تا که tá-kih, علی ان 'alá an. — (*so many or much*) اینقدر ín-kadar, چندین chandín, چندان chandán, آنقدر án-kadar.—(*so long as*) تا tá, مادامکه mádám-kih.—(*so to speak*) گویا gúyá.—(*so forth*) علی هذا 'alá házá, همچنین ham-chunín.—(*so and so, such an one*) فلان fulán, فلان کس fulán-kas, بیسار bísár, بیسار کس bísár-kas.

To SOAK (*steep*), آغشتن ághushtan.—(*sink into*) خیسانیدن khísání-dan, نشر کردن nashr kardan.

SOAP, صابون sábún.—(*cake of soap*) قالب صابون kálib-i-sábún.—(*soap-suds*) کف صابون kaf-i-sábún.

SOAPY, صابونی sábúní.

To SOAR, پریدن parídan *or* parrí-dan, پرواز نمودن parváz nimúdan, طیران نمودن tayarán nimúdan.

SOB, آه ah, ناله nálah, گریه giryah, فغان fighán.

To SOB, گریستن giristan, گریه کردن giryah kardan.

SOBER, نا سر خوش ná-sar-khwush, نا مست ná-mast, با هوش bá-húsh.

SOBERLY, با پرهیز گاری bá-parhíz-gárí.

SOBRIETY, پرهیز گاری parhíz-gárí.

SOBRIQUET, لقب lakab.

SOCIABLE *or* SOCIAL, مدنی madaní, آنس ánis.—(*social life*) استیناس istínás, انس uns.

SOCIABLENESS, اهلیت ahlíyat, استیناس istínás, انس uns.

SOCIALIST, سوسیالیست súsíálíst (*eur.*).

SOCIALITY, اهلیت ahlíyat, استیناس istínás, انس uns.

SOCIETY, معاشرت mu'ásharat, صحبت suhbat.—(*companionship*) صحبت suhbat, مصاحبت musáhabat, رفاقت rafákat, شراکت shirákat, مشارکت musharakat, همراهی ham-ráhí.

—(*mercantile term*) شرکت shir-kat.

SOCK, *vide* STOCKINGS.

SOCKET (*of the eye*), چشمخانه chashm-khánah.

SOD, کلوخ kulúkh.

SODA, نطرون natrún.

SODOMITE, فاعل fá'il, لاطی látí, لوطی lútí, بچه باز bachah-báz.

SODOMY, لواطه livátah, اغلام ighlám, ابنه ubnah, بچه بازی bachah-bází.—(*addiction to sodomy*) ناخوشی ابنه ná-khwushí-i-ubnah.—(*to entice to commit the crime*) پیله کردن pílah kardan.—(*the paihic, a catamite*) ملوط malút, مفعول maf'úl, مابون ma,bún, پشت pusht, مخنث mu-khannas, زن طبیعت zan-tabí'at.

SOFA, سریر sarír, مهاد mihád, پلنگ palang (*hind.*).

SOFT, نرم narm, ملایم muláyam, نازک názuk.

To SOFTEN, ملایم کردن muláyam kardan, نرم کردن narm kardan.

SOFTLY (*gently*) آهسته áhistah, یاواش yávásh, یواش yavásh, سنگنک sanganak.

SOFTNESS, نرمی narmí, ملایمت mu-láyamat, نازکی názukí.

SOIL (*ground*), زمین zamín, خاک khák, ارض arz, بر bar, تراب turáb.—(*dirt*) چرک chirk, لجن lajan, ادباری idbárí, کسافت kasáfat, دسومت dusúmat.

To SOIL, آلودن álúdan, نا پاک کردن ná-pák kardan, ملوث ساختن mu-lavvas sákhtan, نجس کردن najs kardan.

SOJOURN, اقامت ikámat.

To SOJOURN, اقامت نمودن ikámat nimúdan, مقیم نمودن mukím ni-múdan.

SOJOURNER, متوطن mutavattin, ساکن sákin, باشنده báshandah, مقیم mukím.

SOLACE, تسلی tasallí, دلاسائی dil-ásá,í.

To SOLACE, فرح بخشیدن farah bakh-shídan, علاقه دادن 'alákah dádan.

SOLAR, شمسی shamsí.

SOLD, فروخته furúkhtah. — (*to be*

sold) بفروش رفتن bi-furúsh raftan.

Solder, لحیم lahím, قلع kal'.

To Solder, لحیم کردن lahím kardan.

Soldier, سپاهی sipáhí, عسکری 'askarí, لشکری lashkarí, سرباز sarbáz.—(*of infantry*) سرباز sarbáz —(*of cavalry*) سوار suvár.—(*of king's body-guard*) جانباز ján-báz, فوج خاصه fauj-i-khássah, غلام رکابی ghulám-i-rikábí, غلام شاهی ghulám-i-sháhí.–(*artilleryman*) توپچی túp-chí.—(*pioneer*) بیلدار bíl-dár.

Sole, مجرد mujarrad, واحد váhid, وحد vahd, منفرد munfarid.—(*fish*) کوشك kaushak. — (*of the foot*) کف پا kaf-i-pá.—(*of a shoe*) ته کفش tah-i-kafsh, کف ارسی kaf-i-urusí.

Solecism, غلط ghalat.

Solely, محضاً mahzan, بس bas.

Solemn, هیبتوار haibat-vár, پر هیبت pur-haibat, محترم muhtaram, موقر mu,akkar, متعبس muta'abbis.

Solemnity, هیبت haibat, وقار vakár, تمکین tamkín.

Solemnization (*of marriage*), عقد 'akd, نکاح nikáh, عروسی 'arúsí.

To Solemnize (*marriage*), عقد نکاح بستن 'akd-i-nikáh bastan.

Solemnly, با هیبت bá-haibat.

To Solicit, خواستن khwástan, در خواست نمودن dar-khwást nimúdan, التماس کردن iltimás kardan, تمنا نمودن tamanná nimúdan, نیاز کردن niyáz kardan, نیازیدن niyázídan, التجا نمودن iljá, nimúdan, مستدع بودن mustadi' búdan, دعا کردن du'á kardan, استدعا نمودن istid'á nimúdan.

Solicitation, در خواست darkhwást, نیاز niyáz, استدعا istid'á.

Solicitor, وکیل vakíl.

Solicitous, مشتاق mushták, متفکر mutafakkir, مشوش mushavvash, اندیشمند andíshamand.

Solicitude, اعتنا i'tiná, دقت نظر dikkat-i-nazar, پروا parvá, اندیشه andíshah, اهتمام ihtimám.—(*to exhibit solicitude*) اعتنا نمودن i'tiná nimúdan.

Solid, مصمت musmit, صلد suld, میان پر miyán-pur, محکم muhkam, اصیل asíl, یك پارچه yak párchah.

Solidity, متانت matánat, رزانت razánat.

Solidly, قویاً kavíyan.

Soliloquy, مکالمه با نفس mukálamah bá-nafs.

Solitaire (*ornament worn by women, a spray of jewellery*), چتر chatr.

Solitary, تنها tanhá, تن تنها tan-i-tanhá, مفرد mufarrad, منفرد munfarid, واحد váhid, مجرد mujarrad, منهرد munharid, منزوی munzaví.

Solitude, وحشه vahshah, خلوت khalvat, تنهائی tanhá,í, وحدت vahdat.

Soluble, حل شدنی hall-shudaní.

Solution (*of a difficulty, question, &c.*), حل hall, کشف kashf, تعبیر ta'bír.—(*thing dissolved in water, &c.*) گداخته gudákhtah, آب شده áb-shudah.

To Solve, حل کردن hall kardan.

Solved, محلول mahlúl. — (*to be solved*) حل شدن hall shudan.

Sombre, تیره tírah, سیاه siyáh.

Some, چند chand, قدری kadarí, بعضی ba'zí. — (*somebody*) کسی kasí, شخصی shakhsí.—(*somehow*) بوجهی bi-vajhí, بنوعی bi-na. بطوری bi-taurí.—(*something*) چیزی chízí.—(*somewhat*) قدری kadarí, جزوی juzví, اندکی andakí, برخی barkhí, شطری shatrí.—(*sometimes*) گاه گاه gáh gáh, گاهی gáhí, احیاناً ahyánan, گاه وقتی gáh-vaktí, آناً آناً ánan ánan. — (*somewhere*) بجای bi-jáy, یك جای yak jáy.—(*somewhere else*) جای دیگر jáy-i-dígar.

Somersault, پشتك pushtak.—(*to make a somersault*) پشتك برداشتن pushtak bar-dáshtan, پشتك زدن pushtak zadan, واروه زدن várúnah zadan.

SOMNIFEROUS, خواب آور khwáb-ávar.

SON, فرزند farzand, پسر pisar, ولد valad, ابن ibn, پور púr (*obs.*).—(*in composition*) زاده zádah, اغلو ughlú, اوغلی úghlí.—(*son-in-law*) داماد dámád.—(*adopted son*) پسر متبنی pisar-i-mutabanná, پسر خوانده písar-i-khwándah.—(*god-son*) پسر خوانده pisar-i-khwándah.

SONG, سرود surúd, تصنیف tasníf, تصنیفک tasnífak, آواز áváz.—(*to sing a song*) تصنیفی آوازه خواندن tasnífí ávázah khwándan.

SONGSTER or SONGSTRESS, آوازه خوان ávázah-khwán, خواننده khwánandah, قوال kavvál.

SONNET, غزل ghazal.

SONOROUS, طنان tannán.

SOON, زود zúd, بزودی bi-zúdí, سرعتاً sur'atan, عنقریب 'an-karíb, زو zú (*vulg.*), زی zí (*vulg.*).—(*as soon as*) همان hamán, همانکه hamán-kih, همین hamín, همینکه hamín-kih, هرگاهکه har-gáh-kih, بمجرد bi-mujarrad, بمحض bi-mahz, در حالتیکه dar hálatí-kih, جخ jakh (*vulg.*).—(*sooner or later*) زود یا دیر zúd yá dír, خواه دیر خواه زود khwáh dír khwáh zúd, یک وقتی از اوقات yak vaktí az aukát.

SOOT, دوده dúdah.

SOOTHSAYER, فالچی fál-chí, عیاف 'ayyáf, غیب گو ghaib-gú.

SOOTY, پر دود pur-dúd.

SOP, لقمه lukmah.

SOPHISM (*doctrine of the free-thinkers of Persia*), تصوف tasavvuf.

SOPHIST (*freethinker*), صوفی súfí, اهل تصوف ahl-i-tasavvuf.

SOPHISTRY (*fallacious argument*), فلسفت falsafat.

SOPRANO, زیر zír.

SORCERER, جادو گر jádú-gar, ساحر sáhir, سحار sahhár, جادومان jádú-mán.

SORCERY, جادو jádú, جادوگری jádú-garí, افسون afsún, نیرنگ nairang.

SORDID, حریص haris, طمعکار tama'-kár, طامع támi', بخیل bakhíl, لئیم la,ím, ممسک mumsik, خسیس khasís.

SORDIDLY, پست فطرتانه past-fitra-tánah, با خست bá-khissat, با دنایت bá-dináyat.

SORE, ریش rísh, زخم zakhm, قرح kurh, جراحت jaráhat.—(*a running sore*) ناسور násúr, ناصور násúr.—(*painful*) پر درد pur-dard, درد مند dard-mand, دردناک dard-nák.

SORELY, بغایت bi-gháyat, بنهایت bi-niháyat, از حد زیاده az hadd ziyádah.

SORENESS, درد dard, درد مندی dard-mandí.

SORREL, لیواس lívás, ریواس rívás.

SORROW, غم gham, الم alam, اندوه andúh, ملال malál, ملالت malálat, تأسف ta,assuf, کدورت kudúrat, رنج ranj, رنجه ranjah, درد dard, آزار ázár, حزن huzn, احزان ihzán, حسرت hasrat, عزا 'azá, دلتنگی dil-tangí, هم hamm, وجع vaja', سوگ súg, تیمار tímár, هنجار hanjár, تنگنائی tangná,í.

SORROWFUL, دلتنگ dil-tang, دلفکار dil-fikár, دلگیر dil-gír, غمگین gham-gín, غمناک gham-nák, مغموم maghmúm, حزین hazín, محزون mahzún, متعبس muta'ab-bis, ملول malúl, اندوه ناک andúh-nák, متألم muta,allim, سهمگین sahm-gín.

SORRY, دلتنگ dil-tang, دلفکار dil-fikár, دلگیر dil-gír, غمگین gham-gín, غمناک gham-nák, مغموم maghmúm, حزین hazín, محزون mahzún, متعبس muta'abbis, ملول malúl, اندوه ناک andúh-nák, متألم muta,allim, سهمگین sahm-gín.—(*to be sorry*) افسوس خوردن afsús khwurdan, متألم شدن muta,allim shudan.

SORT, نوع nau' (*pl.* انواع anvá'), جنس jins, قسم kism (*pl.* اقسام ak-sám), گونه gúnah, صنف sinf, قبیل kabíl, طور taur, وجه vajh, نمط namt, جور júr.—(*out of sorts*) نا خوش ná-khwush, با کسالت bá-kasálat, بی دماغ bí-dimágh.—(*to be out of sorts*) بی دماغ شدن bi-dimágh

shudan, تکسر مزاجی داشتن takassur-i-mizájí dáshtan.
To SORT, چیدن chídan, ترتیب دادن tartíb dádan, آماده نمودن ámádah nimúdan, آراستن árástan.
SOT, بیهوش bí-húsh, بیخرد bí-khirad. (*drunkard*) می پرست mai-parast, شراب خور sharáb-khwur.
SOUL, روح rúh, نفس nafs, جان ján.
SOUND (*unbroken*), سالم sálim, درست durust, کامل kámil.—(*noise*) آواز áváz, صدا sadá, صوت saut.—(*loud noise*) بانگ báng, شورش shúrish, شماتة shamátah, غوغا ghaughá.—(*views, &c.*) مقرون بصواب makrún bi-saváb.—(*sound of voices*) قال و مقال kál va makál.
To SOUND (*a horn, &c.*), نواختن naválkhtan, زدن zadan, کشیدن kashídan.—(*measure the depth*) اندازه کردن andázah kardan.
SOUNDLY, بغایت bi-gháyat, بنهایت bi-niháyat, از حد زیاده az hadd ziyádah.
SOUNDNESS, درستی durustí, کمال kamál.
SOUP, شوربا shúrbá, آش ásh, آبگوشت áb-gúsht. — (*soup tureen*) شوربا خوری shúrbá-khwurí.
SOUR, ترش turush, حامض hámiz.
SOURCE, اصل asl, مصدر masdar, سر sar, منشا manshá, مبدا mabdá, منبع mamba'.—(*source of pride*) سرمایه افتخار sar-máyah-i-iftikhár.—(*from a good source*) از جای معتبر az jáy-i-mu'tabar.
SOURLY, ترشانه turushánah.
To SOUSE, آغشتن ághushtan.
SOUTH, جنوب junúb.—(*on the south*) جنوباً junúban.—(*south-wind*) باد جنوبی bád-i-junúbí.—(*south-east*) ما بین جنوب و مشرق mábain-i-junúb va mashrak.—(*south-west*) ما بین جنوب و مغرب má-bain-i-junúb va maghrab.
SOUTHERLY *or* SOUTHERN, جنوبی junúbi.
SOUTHERNWOOD (*plant*), قیصوم kaisúm, بومادران búmádarán.
SOUTHWARDS, بسمت جنوب bi-samt-i-junúb.
SOUVENIR, یاد گار yád-gár, یاد داشت yád-dásht, تذکره tazkarah.
SOVEREIGN, پادشاه pádisháh, شاه sháh, شه shah, ملك malk, سلطان sultán, خاقان khákán, کی kai.—(*sovereign of an order*) رئیس اداره نشان rá,ís-i-idárah-i-nishán.—(*money*) لیرا lírá (*eur.*).
SOVEREIGNTY, داوری dávarí, شاهی sháhí, سلطنت sultanat, پادشاهی pádishähí.
SOW, ماده خوگ mádah-khúg.
To SOW (*seed*), کشتن kishtan, کاشتن káshtan, تخم پاشیدن tukhm páshídan, کاریدن kárídan.
SOWER, کارنده kárandah, بذرگر bazargar, زارع zári', مزارع muzári'.
SPACE, فاصله fásilah, وسعت vus'at, ساحت sáhat. — (*of time*) عرصه 'arsah, مدت muddat, فاصله fásilah, مرور murúr, مسافت masáfat, اثنا asná. — (*between two near objects*) فرجه furjah.—(*open space*) وسعتگاه vas'at-gáh.—(*in the space of*) در ظرف dar zarf, بفاصله bi-fásilah.
SPACIOUS, وسیع vasí', واسع vási', عریض 'aríz, فراخ farákh, گشاد gushád.
SPADE, بیلچه bíl-chah.—(*large long-handled spade*) بیل bíl.
SPAN (*measure, from tip of thumb to tip of little finger*), وجب vajab. —(*width*) عرض 'arz, پهنائی pahna,í, قطر kutr.—(*of a bridge*) چشمه chashmah.
To SPAN, بدست پیمودن bi-dast paimúdan.
SPANGLE (*of gold, &c.*), پولك púlak.
To SPANK, سله زدن sallah zadan.
SPAR, دگل dagal, دقل dakal, دول dúl (*hind.*).
To SPAR, جنگ کردن jang kardan, منازعت کردن munáza'at kardan, تکرار کردن takrár kardan, دعوی کردن da'vá kardan, جنگیدن jangídan.
SPARE, لاغر lághir, نزار nizár, ضعیف za'íf.

To SPARE (*show mercy, forgive*), بخشیدن bakhshídan, عفو کردن 'afv kardan, امان دادن amán dádan, آمرزیدن ámurzídan, دخیل دادن dakhíl dádán, در گذر کردن darguzar kardan, پناه دادن panáh dádan, غفران نمودن ghufrán nimúdan.

SPARED, معاف mu'áf.

SPARING, خانه دار khánah-dár, کم خرج kam-kharj.

SPARK (*of fire*), اخگر akhgar, شراره sharárah, آتشپاره átish - párah, پرکاله parkálah.

To SPARKLE, درخشیدن dirakhshídan, شعله نمودن shu'lah nimúdan.

SPARKLING, تابان tábán, درخشان dirakhshán, رخشنده rakhshandah, لامع lámi'.

SPARROW, گنجشك gunjashk.—(*sparrow - hawk*) موشگیر múshgír.

SPASM, تشنج tashannuj.

SPATULA, مرهم کش marham-kash.

SPAVIN (*in a horse*), قرقوش karakaush.

SPAWN (*of fish*), تخم ماهی tukhm-i-máhí, اشپل ishpul.

To SPEAK, گفتن guftan, حرف زدن harf zadan, کلام کردن kalám kardan, سخن راندن sukhun rándan. —(*to speak to, address*) تکلم نمودن takallum nimúdan, متکلم شدن mutakallim shudan, عرض کردن 'arz kardan, مخاطب شدن mukhátib shudan.—(*to speak out*) بلندتر حرف زدن buland-tar harf zadan.

SPEAKER, قائل ká,il, گوینده gúyandah.—(*Speaker of the House of Commons*) رئیس مجلس ra,ís-i-majlis.

SPEAR, نیزه naizah, سنان sinán, رمح rumh, مزراق mizrák.—(*shaft of a spear*) چوب نیزه chúb-i-naizah.—(*head of spear*) سنان sinán, سر نیزه sar-i-naizah.—(*butt end of spear*) ته نیزه tah-i-naizah.

SPEARMAN, نیزه دار naizah-dár.

SPECIAL (*particular*), خاص kháss, مخصوص makhsús, مختص mukhtass.

SPECIALLY, خاصه khássah, خصوصاً khasúsan, مخصوصاً makhsúsan.—علی الخصوص 'ala-'l-khusus, سیما síyamá, لا سیما lá-síyamá.

SPECIES, نوع nau' (*pl.* انواع anvá'), جنس jins, قسم kism (*pl.* اقسام aksám), گونه gúnah, صنف sinf, قبیل kabíl, طور taur, وجه vajh, نمط namat, جور júr.

SPECIFIC, مخصوص makhsús, معین mu'ayyan.—(*against disease, &c.*) تریاق خاص tiryák-i-khâss.

SPECIFICALLY, مخصوصاً makhsúsan.

SPECIFICATION, تشخیص tashkhís, تعیین ta'yín.

SPECIFIED, معین mu'ayyan.

To SPECIFY, تعیین نمودن ta'yín nimúdan, تشخیص نمودن tashkhís nimúdan.

SPECIMEN, نمونه nimúnah.

SPECIOUS, مستحسن mustahsan, مقبول makbúl, مرغوب marghúb.

SPECK (*particle*), ذره zarrah, هوشه shúshah, همزه hamzah, شمه shammah, ریزه rízah.—(*spot*) داغ dágh, خال khál, لکه lakkah.

SPECKLED, لکه دار lakkah-dár, منقط munakkat, خالدار khál-dár.

SPECTACLE, تماشا tamáshá.

SPECTACLES (*glasses*), عینك 'ainak.

SPECTATOR, ناظر názir, تماشا چی tamáshá-chí.

SPECTRE, خیال khiyál, *or* khayál, شکل shakl.

To SPECULATE, فکر کردن fikr kardan, تصور نمودن tasavvur nimúdan, اندیشه کردن andíshah kardan. —(*in business*) معامله نمودن mu'ámalah nimúdan.

SPECULATION (*contemplation*), مشاهده musháhadah.—(*in business*) معامله mu'ámalah.—(*bad speculation*) مغبون maghbún.

SPEECH, سخن sukhun, زبان zabán, کلام kalám, گفتار guftár, قول kaul, نطق nutk, تنطق tanattuk.—(*harangue*) کلام kalám, نفس nafas, وعظ va'z, خطاب khitáb.—(*parts of speech*) جز کلام juz-i-kalám.—(*to make a speech*) نطقی کردن nutkí kardan.

SPEECHLESS, لا جواب lá-javáb.
SPEED, شتاب shitáb, سرعت sur'at, عجلت 'ajalat, چابکی chábukí, چالاکی chálákí, فور faur, زودی zúdí, مبادرت mubádarat, چستی chustí, اعجال i'jál, تعجیل ta'jíl, تندی tundí.
SPEEDILY, زود zúd, بزودی bi-zúdí, سرعتاً sur'atan, بسرعت bi-sur'at.
SPEEDY, زود zúd, چابك chábuk, چالاك chálák, چست chust, مسرع musri', جلد jald, تند tund, تیز tíz, شتاب shitáb, شتابان shitábán.
SPELL, نیرنگ nairang, افسون afsún.
To SPELL (*name the letters in a word*), هجا کردن hijá kardan, تهجی کردن tahajjí kardan.—(*use proper letters in writing, &c.*) املا کردن imlá kardan.
SPELLING, املا imlá.—(*error in spelling*) تصحیف tashíf.
SPELTER, روی rúí, روح rúh.
To SPEND, خرج کردن kharj kardan, صرف کردن sarf kardan, مصرف نمودن masraf nimúdan.
SPENDTHRIFT, مصرف musrif.
SPENT, مصروف masrúf.
SPERMA, *vide* SEED.
SPERMACETI, موم سفید múm-i-safíd.
To SPEW, قی کردن kay kardan.
SPHERE, کره kurrah, جرم jirm, مرکز markaz, گوی gúy. — (*celestial*) گردون gardún, سپهر sipihr.—(*one's own sphere*) مدار خود madár-i-khwud.
SPHERICAL, مستدیر mustadír.
SPHERICALLY, بطور کره bi-taur-i-kurrah.
SPHEROID, مدور mudavvar.
SPHINX, ابو الهول abu-'l-haul.
SPICE, ادویه adviyah, ادویجات adviyaját (*vulg.*).—(*spice-box*) ادویه دان adviyah-dán.
SPIDER, عنکبوت 'ankabút, جولاهك júláhak, کارتن kártan (*obs.*).—(*spider's web*) پرده عنکبوت pardah-i-'ankabút, تار عنکبوت tár-i-'ankabút, کنتره kinatrah.
SPIKE, مسمار mismár, میخ míkh.
SPIKENARD, سنبل الطیب sumbulu-'t-tíb, سنبل خطائی sumbul-i-khatá,í.
To SPILL, ریختن ríkhtan.
To SPIN, ریشتن ríshtan, تافتن táftan, تنبیدن tambídan, تنیدن tanídan.
SPINACH, اسفناج isfanáj.
SPINAL, صلبی sulbí, فقاری fakárí.
SPINDLE, دوك dúk, پره pirrah, پیلی pílí.
SPINE (*backbone*), پشتمهره pusht-muhrah, عصعص 'us'us, مهره پشت muhrah-i-pusht.—(*the os sacrum, or lower bone of the spine*) عجب 'ajb, عجب الذنب 'ajbu-'z-zanab.
SPINNER, ریسنده rísandah. — (*in comp.*) ریس rís.
SPINNING-WHEEL, چرخه charkhah.
SPINSTER, عزب 'azab.
SPIRAL, پیچ pích, پیچیده píchídah, پیچدار pích-dár.
SPIRE (*steeple or column*), منار manár, مناره minárah, میل míl.
SPIRIT (*soul*), روح rúh, نفس nafs, جان ján.—(*courage*) مردانگی mardánagí, دلیری dilírí, دلاوری dilávarí, همت himmat, جرأت jur,at, شجاعت shujá'at, غیرت ghairat, جسارت jasárat, شهامت shahámat, حمیت hamíyat, عصبیت 'asabíyat. (*ghost*) روح rúh, عفریت 'ifrít.— (*liquor*) عرق 'arak, خمر khamr.— (*essence*) خلاصه khulásah, زبده zubdah, جوهر jauhar, روح rúh.— (*an evil spirit*) روح مضر rúh-i-muzirr.—(*high spiril, honour, pluck*) همت himmat, غیرت ghairat, عصبیت 'asabíyat, حمیت hamíyat. —(*Holy Spirit*) روح خدا rúh-i-khudá, روح القدس rúhu-'l-kudus. (*spirits of wine*) عرق سه آتشی 'arak-sih-átishí.
SPIRITED, غیرت مند ghairat-mand.
SPIRITLESS, کم همت kam-himmat, بی غیرت bí-ghairat.
SPIRITUAL, معنوی ma'naví, روحانی rúhání.
SPIRITUALITY, روحانیت rúháníyat.
SPIRITUOUS DRINKS, جوهر jauhar, عرق 'arak, خمر khamr.
SPIT, سیخ síkh.

To SPIT, تف زدن tuf zadan, سلف انداختن suluf andákhtan, خیو افکندن khuyú afkandan.

SPITE, کینه kínah, بغض bughz, بد خواهی bad-khwáhí.—(*in spite of*) برغم انف bi-raghm-i-anf, با وجود که bá-vujúd-kih, علی رغم 'alá raghm.

To SPITE, رنجانیدن ranjánídan, جر آوردن jar ávardan.

SPITEFUL, شریر sharír, بد نهاد bad-nihád, بد اندیش bad-andísh, بد خواه bad-khwáh, بد ذات bad-zát.

SPITTING, تف سازی tuf-sází.

SPITTLE, تف tuf, آب دهن áb-i-dahan, لعاب la'áb, سلف suluf, بزاق buzák, خیو khuyú.

SPITTOON, سلفدان suluf-dán, تفلدان tafl-dán, سفلدان sifl-dán (*vulg.*).

To SPLASH, داغ انداختن dágh andákhtan.

SPLEEN, سپرز supurz, طحال tihál.—(*ill-humour*) سودائی saudá,í, بد خوئی bad-khú,í.

SPLENDID, درخشان dirakhshán, روشن raushan, تابناک táb-nák, تابان tábán.—(*magnificent*) معظم mu-'azzam, عظیم 'azím, جلیل jalíl, شگرف shigarf.

SPLENDIDLY, بخوبی bi-khúbí.

SPLENDOUR, رونق raunak, فر farr, جلال jalál, جلوه jálvah, تابش tá-bish, زینت zínat, احتشام ihtishám.

SPLENETIC, تند مزاج tund-mizáj, کجخلق kaj-khulk, افسرده afsur-dah.

SPLICE, وصل vasl.

To SPLICE, وصل کردن vasl kardan, چسبانیدن chasbánídan, ملحق کردن mulhak kardan.

SPLINT (*thin piece of wood, &c., used in bandaging a broken limb*), کمانچه kamánchah, جبیره jabírah. —(*disease in horses' legs*) گیچ دمبه gích-i-dumbah, قرقوش karakaush.

SPLINTER, پاره párah, ریزه rízah, تراشه tiráshah.

SPLIT, شکاف shikáf, شق shakk, چاک chák.

To SPLIT (*cleave*), شکافتن shikáf-tan, شق کردن shakk kardan, چاک کردن chák kardan.—(*crack*) شق شدن shakk shudan, چاک شدن chák shudan, مو داشتن mú dásh-tan. — (*burst*) پاره شدن párah shudan.

SPOIL, چپاو chapáu, غارت ghárat, تاراج táráj, نهب nahb, راهزنی rah-zaní, ترک تازی tark-i-tází.

To SPOIL, ضایع کردن zá'í' kardan, معیوب کردن ma'yúb kardan, مفسود کردن mafsúd kardan.—(*pillage*) چپاو کردن chapáu kardan, غارت کردن ghárat kardan, یغما کردن yaghmá kardan, سلب گرفتن salab giriftan, تاراج نمودن táráj nimú-dan, نهب کردن nahb kardan, چپاولی کردن chapáwalí kardan (*vulg.*).—(*rot*) پوسیدن púsídan, گندیدن gan-dídan.

SPOILER, غارت کننده ghárat-kunan-dah, یغماچی yaghmá-chí.

SPOILT (*damaged, destroyed*), معیوب ma'yúb, بائر bá'ir, ضایع zá'í'.

SPOKES (*of a wheel*), شمش shimsh, دیرک dírak.

SPOKESMAN, ترجمان tarjumán.

SPOLIATION, استلاب istiláb, غارت ghárat, تاراج táráz.

SPONGE, ابر abr, اسفند isfand, اسفنج isfanj.

SPONSOR, متضمن mutazammin.

SPONTANEOUS, خود بخود khwud bi-khwud, از خود az khwud, تبرعانه tabarru'ánah.

SPOON, چمچه chamchah, قاشق ká-shik, قاشوق kashúk.

SPOONFUL, یك قاشوق yak káshúk.

SPORT, بازی bází, بازیچه bázíchah, لعبت la'bat, تفرج tafarruj, ملاعبه mulá'abah.—(*hunting*) شکار shi-kár.

To SPORT, لهو نمودن lahv nimúdan, بازی کردن bází kardan.

SPORTIVE, خوشدل khwush-dil, شاد shád, شادمان shad-mán, خوش khwush, مشعوف mash'úf.

SPORTSMAN, شکارچی shikár-chí, شکار دوست shikár-dúst, شکار گر shikár-gar.

SPOT, داغ dágh, خال khál, لکه lak-kah, کلف kalaf, بیسه bísah, پیسه písah. — (*place*) مکان makán,

مقام makám, محل mahall, معرض ma'raz, موضع mauza', موقف mau-kif, حيز hayyiz, مطرح matrah, جا já, جاى jáy, جايگاه jáy-gáh, بقاع buká', موقع mauki'. — (*on the spot*) على الفور 'ala-'l-faur.

Spotless, بيداغ bí-dágh, بى عيب bí-'aib.

Spotted, لكه دار lakkah-dár, منقط munakkat, خالدار khál-dár.

Spousals, عروسى 'arúsí, تأهل ta,ahhul, ازدواج izdiváj, زواج ziváj.

Spouse, *vide* Husband, Wife.

Spout (*of an urn, &c.*), دهن شير dahan-i-shír.—(*on roof of a house, &c.*) ناودان náv-dán.

To Spout, جستن jastan.

Spouting, فوران favarán.

Sprain, پيچش píchish.

To Sprain, در رفتن dar raftan.

To Sprawl, ول گشتن vil-gashtan, هرزه گرى كردن harzah-garí kardan.

Spray (*of jewellery, worn on the head by a prince*) جيكا jíká.—(*similar ornament worn by women*) تيطه títah, چتر chatr. — (*of sea*) ترشح tarasshuh, رشحه rash-hah.

To Spread, انداختن andákhtan, گستردن gusturdan, گسترانيدن gus-turánídan, فرش كردن farsh kar-dan, پهن كردن pahn kardan.—(*strew or scatter*) پراكندن pará-kandan, پاشيدن páshídan, ريختن ríkhtan, افشاندن afshándan. — (*to spread abroad, trans.*) شايع نمودن sháí' nimúdan, شيوع كردن shuyú' kardan, انتشار كردن inti-shár kardan. — (*spread abroad, intrans.*) انتشار يافتن intishár yáftan, شايع شدن sháí' shudan.

Sprig, *vide* Twig.

Sprightliness, نشاط nishát, عشرت 'ishrat, فرح farah, شادى shádí, بهجت bihjat.

Sprightly, نشاطمند nishát-mand, شاد مان shád-mán.

Spring (*season*), بهار bahár, ربيع rabí'.—(*of steel, &c.*), كمان ka-mán.—(*of a watch*) فنر fanar.—(*spiral spring*) فنر fanar.—(*snare*) دام dám, تله talah, كمند kamand.

(*leap*) جست jast, خيز khíz.—(*of water*) چشمه chashmah, عين 'ain, منبع mamba'. — (*hot mineral springs*) آب گرم معدنى áb-i-garm-i-ma'daní.

To Spring (*forth*), جستن jastan, جهيدن jihídan, بر آمدن bar-áma-dan, صادر شدن sádir shudan.—(*grow*) نشو و نما كردن nashv va nimá kardan, رستن rustan, روئيدن rú,ídan.—(*as water*) جوشيدن júshí-dan, جستن jastan.

To Sprinkle, پاشيدن páshídan, ريختن ríkhtan, افشاندن afshándan.

Sprite, پرى parí.

Sprout, شاخه shákhah, غصن ghusn.

To Sprout (*as seed, germinate*), روئيدن rú,ídan, تنج زدن tinj za-dan, نمو كردن nimú kardan, بر آمدن bar-ámadan.

Spruce, پاكيزه pákízah, منقه munak-kah, آراسته árástah, قشنگ ka-shang, نظيف nazíf, خوشگل khwush-gil (*this applies only to persons*).

Spruceness, سليقت salíkat, نظافت nazáfat, قشنگى kashangí, پاكيزگى pákízagí.

Spur, مهميز mihmíz, خار khár.—(*of mountain*) شامخ shámikh.

To Spur, مهميز زدن mihmíz zadan.—(*incite*) ابرام نمودن ibrám nimú-dan, اغوا كردن ighvá kardan, تحريك دادن tahrík dádan, ترغيب نمودن targhíb nimúdan.

Spurious, دروغ durúgh, دغل daghal. (*money*) قلابى kullábí, قلب kalb, مغشوش maghshúsh, اشكيلى ishkílí.

Spurt, فش fish.

To Spurt, فش كردن fish kardan.

To Sputter (*pen*), مركب پرانيدن murakkab paránídan.

Spy, جاسوس jásús, خبرگير khabar-gír.

To Spy, جاسوسى كردن jásúsí kardan.

Spy-glass, دور بين dúr-bín.

Squabble, نزاع nizá', ستيزه sitízah, قرقشه karkashah, شلوك shulúk (*vulg.*).

To Squabble, ستيزه كردن sitízah kardan, دعوى كردن da'vá kardan, قرقشه كردن karkashah kardan, شلوك كردن shulúk kardan (*vulg.*).

SQUADRON, دسته dastah.
SQUALID, ناپاك ná-pák, پليد pilíd, پلشت pilisht, رنگ مرده rang-i-murdah, زرد رنگ zard-rang.
SQUALL, باد bád, هوا havá.
To SQUALL, گريستن giristan, گريه كردن giryah kardan.
SQUALLY, بادى bádí, هوائى havá,í.
SQUALOR, نا پاكى ná-pákí, نجاست najásat, آلودگى álúdagí.
To SQUANDER, اسراف نمودن isráf nimúdan, تلف كردن talaf kardan, بر باد دادن bar bád dádan, پراكندن parákandan, خرج بيجا كردن kharj-i-bí-já kardan, اخراج نا موجه كردن ikhráj-i-ná-muvajjah kardan.
SQUANDERER, مسرف musrif.
SQUARE, مربع murabba', چهار گوشه chahár-gúshah, مكعب muka''ab. —(*of soldiers*) قلعه kal'ah.—(*in a city*) چهار سو chahár-sú, ميدان maidán, صحن sahn.—(*instrument*) مربع murabba'. — (*square, in arithmetic*) مال mál (*pl.* اموال amvál).—(*square root, in arithmetic*) جذر jazr (*pl.* جذور juzúr), جدر jadr.
To SQUARE, مربع ساختن murabba' sákhtan. — (*accounts*) گذراندن guzrándan.
To SQUAT, نشستن nishastan.
To SQUEAK, مخ مخ كردن mikh mikh kardan.
SQUEAMISH, نازك طبع názuk-tab'.
To SQUEEZE, فشردن fishurdan, افشردن afshurdan, فشاردن fishárdan, چلاندن chilándan.
SQUIB, ماهتاب máh-táb.
SQUILLS, اسقيل iskail.
To SQUINT, احول شدن ahval shudan, دو ديدن dú dídan, كج ديدن kaj dídan, لوچ بودن lúch búdan.
SQUINTING, احول ahval, لوچ lúch, كج چشم kaj-chashm.
SQUIRE, كد خدا kad-khudá. [This is literally the headman of a village.]
SQUIRREL, كلهرى kalahrí (*hind.*), سنجاب sanjáb, سوسار súsár.
SQUIRT, آب دزدك áb-duzdak, حقنه huknah.

To STAB, زدن zadan, سپوختن sapúkhtan.
STABILITY, استوارى ustuvárí, ثبات sabát.
STABLE, طويله tavílah, اصطبل istabal. —(*firm*) بر قرار bar-karár, ثابت sábit, پايدار páyadár. — (*to be stable*) پاى داشتن páy dáshtan.
STACK (*of corn, &c.*), توده túdah, انبار ambár, خرمن kharman, پر pir.
To STACK, انبار كردن ambár kardan, انباشتن ambáshtan.
STAFF, چوب دستى chúb-dastí, عصا 'asá, كتك kutak, چماق chumák, دگنك daganak.—(*military term*) اتباع atbá', اجزا ajzá.—(*for surveying*) نيزه naizah.
STAG, گوزن gavazn.
STAGE (*on a journey*), منزل manzil, مرحله marhalah.—(*platform*) تخته takhtah, تلواره talvárah.—(*in a theatre*) مظهر mazhar. — (*in a building*) مرتبه martabah, طبقه tabakah, طاقه tákah.
To STAGGER, يله شدن yalah shudan, افتان و خيزان بودن 'uftán va khízán búdan, لطمه خوردن latmah khwurdan.
STAGNANT, گنده gandah, گنديده gandídah.
To STAGNATE, گنده شدن gandah shudan, گنديده شدن gandídah shudan.
STAGNATION, گندگى gandagí, گنديدگى gandídagí. — (*in trade*) كساد kasád.
STAIN, لكه lakkah, داغ dágh, عيب 'aib. — (*stigma*) لوث laus, عيب 'aib.
To STAIN, تيره كردن tírah kardan, آلودن álúdan, لكه گذاشتن lakkah guzáshtan.
STAINED, لكه وار lakkah-vár.
STAIR, نردبان nardubán, پله pillah, درجه darajah, اورچين úrchín, ارچين urchín, پلكان pillakán (*vulg.*).—(*spiral staircase*) پله پيچ پيچ pillah-i-pích-pích.
STAIR-ROD, ميل پله míl-i-pillah.
STAKE, چوب chúb, ميخ míkh.—(*at play*) داو dáv, شرط shart, گرو girau.

—(*for impalement*) خازوق kházúk, دار dár.
To STAKE, مایه گذاشتن máyah guzáshtan.
STALE, کهنه kuhnah, پوسیده púsídah, مانده mándah.—(*as victuals*) کهنه kuhnah, شبینه shabínah, شبمانده shab-mándah, بیات bayát, قدید kadíd.
STALENESS, کهنگی kuhnagí, پوسیدگی púsídagí, ماندگی mándagí.—(*victuals*) کهنگی kuhnagí, شبینگی shabínagí, شبماندگی shab-mándagí.
STALK (*of a plant*), ساقه sákah.—(*of corn*) شاخه shákhah.—(*of grapes*) چنبه chumbah, خوشه khúshah, خوشه خالی khúshah-i-khálí.
To STALK, *vide* To WALK.
STALL (*for cattle*), آخور ákhwur, آخر ákhur, معلف ma'laf.—(*bench, &c.*) دکانچه dukánchah, تخته takhtah.—(*at theatre*) لژ آخر lazh-i-ákhir.
STALLION, نریان naryán.
To STAMMER (*in speech*), الکن کردن alkan kardan, لکنت کردن luknat kardan.
STAMMERER, الکن alkan, گرفته زبان giriftah-zabán.
STAMMERING, لکنت luknat.
STAMP (*seal*), مهر muhr, سکه sikkah.—(*on weights, &c.*) عیار 'iyár.—(*impression*) نقش naksh, علامت 'alámat, نشان nishán, چاپ cháp, باسمه básmah.—(*adhesive stamp*) تکت چسپناک tikat-i-chasp-nák.
To STAMP, نشان دادن nishán dádan.—(*to stamp the feet*) پا زمین زدن pá-zamín zadan.
STANCH, استوار ustuvár, بر قرار bar-karár, راسخ rásikh, ثابت sábit.
To STANCH, سد کردن sadd kardan, موقوف کردن maukúf kardan.
STANCHLY, با دلیری bá-dilírí.
STANCHNESS, استواری ustuvárí, بر قراری bar-karárí.
STAND (*at races*), اطاق چوب uták-i-chúb.—(*bottom of a vessel, &c.*) کعب ka'b, پا pá.—(*of a coffee-cup*) ظرف zarf, زیر فنجان zír-finján.
To STAND, ایستادن ístádan, قائم شدن ká,im shudan, بر پا شدن bar pá shudan.—(*halt*) بودن búdan, وا ایستادن vá-ístádan.—(*to stand on end, hair*) بر پا شدن bar pá shudan, راست ایستادن rást ístádan.
STANDARD, نشان nishán, علم 'alam, رائیت ra,yat, لوا livá, بیرق bairak, بیراق bairák. — (*of versification*) رکن rukn (*pl.* ارکان arkán).—(*of weights, measures, &c.*) عیار 'iyár.
STANDARD-BEARER, بیرقدار bairak-dár, علم بردار 'alam-bar-dár, نشان بردار nishán-bar-dár.
STANDING, بر پا bar pá, استاده istádah.
STANZA (*couplet*), بیت bait (*pl.* ابیات abyát).
STAPLE, رزه rizah, ریزه rízah.—(*principal*) اول avval, عمده 'umdah.
STAR, ستاره sitárah, کوکب kaukab, اختر akhtar, نجم najm, یلدز yalduz, الوا ulvá.—(*fixed star*) ثابته sábitah, نجم ثابت najm-i-sábit.—(*planet*) سیاره sayyárah, نجم سائر najm-i-sá,ir.—(*falling star*) شهاب shaháb (*pl.* شهبان shuhbán).—(*fortunate aspect of stars*) قران kirán, سعد sa'd.—(*the fortunate stars, Jupiter and Venus*) سعدان sa'dán, سعدین sa'dain.—(*the unfortunate stars, Mars and Saturn*) نحسان nahsán, نحسین nahsain.—(*ill-starred*) بد طالع bad-táli', بد بخت bad-bakht.
STARBOARD, طرف راست taraf-i-rást, یمین yamín.
STARCH, نشاسته nishástah, آهار áhár.
To STARCH, نشاسته زدن nishástah zadan.
To STARE at, چشم خیره کردن chashm-i-khírah kardan, مراقب بودن murákib búdan.
STARK, تماماً tamáman, بکلی bikullí.
STARLING, سار sár.
STARRY, نجومی nujúmí.
START, بر جست bar-jast.—(*departure*) روانگی ravánagí, رحلت rihlat, جلا jalá, کوچ kúch, سفر safar.
To START, رم کردن ram kardan, بر

جستن bar-jastan, رمیدن ramídan. —(*depart*) روانه گشتن ravánah gashtan, رفتن raftan, نقل مکان کردن nakl-i-makán kardan, روانه شدن ravánah shudan, راهی شدن ráhí shudan. — (*a question*) اقامت کردن ikámat kardan.

STARTING-POINT, تکیه گاه takyah-gáh.

To STARTLE, رمانیدن ramánídan, ترسانیدن tarsánídan.

To STARVE, (*trans.*) تجویع نمودن tajví' nimúdan.—(*intrans.*) گرسنگی کشیدن gurisnagí kashídan, جوع کشیدن jú' kashídan.—(*with cold*) از سرما خشك شدن az sarmá khushk shudan, سرما کشیدن sarmá kashídan.

STARVING, گرسنه gurisnah, جوعان jú'án.

STATE (*condition*), حال hál, حالت hálat, احوال ahvál, کیفیت kaifíyat.—(*government*) سر کار sar-kár, دولت daulat, ملك mulk, مملکت mamlakat.—(*pomp*) شان shán, شوکت shaukat, حشمت hashmat, دبدبه dabdabah, عظمت 'azamat. —(*state of things*) صورت súrat.— (*state of the case*) واقع حال váki'-i-hál.

To STATE (*represent*), عرض کردن 'arz kardan, معروض داشتن ma'rúz dáshtan, تقریر نمودن takrír nimúdan, اظهار کردن izhár kardan.

STATELINESS, بزرگی buzurgí, جلالت jalálat, حشمت hashmat.

STATELY, با شوکت bá-shaukat, با جلالت bá-jalálat, با حشمت bá-hashmat.

STATEMENT, تقریر takrír, اقرار ikrár, گفتار guftár, مدعا mudda'á, توجیه taujíh.—(*public statement*) توضیح tauzíh.

STATESMAN, اهل تدبیر ahl-i-tadbír, اهل سیاست ahl-i-siyásat, مدبر mudabbir.

STATION (*place*), مکان makán, مقام makám, محل mahall, معرض ma'raz, موضع mauza', موقف maukif, حیز hayyiz, مطرح matrah, جا já, جای jáy, جایگاه jáy-gáh.—(*rank*) درجه darajah, جاه jáh, شان shán, مرتبه martabah, قدر kadr, پایه páyah. — (*railway station*) موقف maukif, منزل manzil.

STATIONARY, ساکن sákin, بی حرکت bí-harakat.

STATIONED, مقیم makím.

STATIONER, خرده فروش khurdah-furúsh, خراز kharráz.

STATIONERY, اسباب خرازی asbáb-i-kharrází.

STATISTICS, استاستیك istástík (*eur.*).

STATUARY, نقاشی nakkáshí.—(*man*) نقاش nakkásh.

STATUE, صنم sanam, صورت súrat, بت but, مجسم mujassam, مجسمه mujassamah.—(*equestrian statue*) مجسمه سواره mujassamah-i-suvárah.

STATURE, قامت kámat, قد kadd, اندام andám.—(*stature of man, a measure of five feet and a half*) کله kallah.

STATUTE, قاعده ká'idah, قانون kánún, آیین áyín.

To STAVE, شکستن shikastan.

STAY, عمود 'amúd, پشتی pushtí, ازا izá, عمدت 'umdat.

To STAY, ماندن mándan, بودن búdan, توقف کردن tavakkuf kardan, قرار گرفتن karár giriftan, اقامت ساختن ikámat sákhtan, سکونت نمودن sukúnat nimúdan, ساکن بودن sákin búdan.

STAYS, سینه بند sínah-band.

STEAD, عوض 'avaz *or* 'ivaz, جای jáy.

STEADFAST, استوار ustuvár, بر قرار bar-karár, راسخ rásikh, ثابت sábit.

STEADFASTLY, بااستواری bá-ustuvárí.

STEADINESS, استواری ustuvárí, بر قراری bar-karárí.

STEADY (*unmoved*), استوار ustuvár, بر قرار bar-karár, راسخ rásikh, ثابت sábit.—(*well-behaved, respectable*) صاحب وقار sáhib-vakár, متشخص mutashakhkhas, معتبر mu'tabar.

To STEAL, دزدیدن duzdídan, دزدی کردن duzdí kardan, سرقه کردن sarikah kardan.

STEALER, دزد duzd.

STEALTH, پنهانی panhání, دزدانه dúzdánah.

STEAM, بخار bukhár.—(*boat*) جهاز آتشی jaház-i-átishí, کشتی بخار kashtí-i-bukhár, جهاز دودی jaház-i-dúdí, گمی آتشی gamí-i-átishí, واپور vápúr (*eur.*) — (*merchant steamer*) واپور تجارت vápúr-i-tijárat.—(*engine*) آلت دودی álat-i-dúdí, منجنیق آتشی manjaník-i-átishí.—(*to go by steam*) با بخار حرکت کردن bá-bukhár harakat kardan.—(*steam launch*) قایق کوچکی بخاری káík-i-kúchikí-i-bukhárí.

STEED, اسب asb, اسپ asp, ستور sitúr, مرکب markab (*pl.* مراکب marákib), بارکی bárakí, اس as (*vulg.*).

STEEL (*crystallized or watered*), پولاد púlád, فولاد fúlád.—(*tempered, but not crystallized*) فنر fanar.—(*to strike a light with*) چخماق chakhmák, چقماق chakmák.

STEELYARD (*balance for weighing*), قبان kabbán.

STEEP, نشیبدار nishíb-dár, سراشیب sar-á-shíb, سرازیر sar-á-zír, پرت part.

To STEEP, آغشتن águshtan, خیسانیدن khísánídan.

STEEPLE, منار manár, منارة manárah, میل míl.

To STEER (*a vessel*), کشتی راندن kashtí rándan, راه جهاز انداختن ráh-i-jaház andákhtan.

STEERAGE, کشتی رانی kashtí-rání.

STEERSMAN, دومنچی dúman-chí, سکانی sukkání.

STEM, ساقه sákah.—(*of a ship*) سر جهاز sar-i-jaház, راس rás, جلو jilau.—(*flexible stem of a pipe*) مارپیچ már-pích.—(*wooden stem*) چوب چبوق chúb-i-chibúk.

To STEM, منع کردن mana' kardan, سد ساختن sadd sákhtan.—(*the tide*), مقابله کردن mukábalah kardan.

STENCH, بد بو bad-bú, عفونت 'ufúnat, گند gand.

STEP, قدم kadam, گام gám.—(*of a stair, &c.*) درجه darajah, پله pillah.—(*flight of steps*) جلوخان jilau khán. — (*quick step*) قدم تند kadam-i-tund. — (*slow step*) قدم kadam-i-sust.

To STEP, قدم زدن kadam zadan.

STEP-DAUGHTER, ربیبه rabíbah.

STEP-FATHER, عموئی ناپدری 'amu,í-ná-pidarí, راب ráb.

STEP-MOTHER, زن پدر zan-i-pidar, رابه rábah.

STEPS, نردبان nardubán, پله pillah, سد sidd, سلم sullam, اورچین úrchín.—(*to have steps, as stairs*) پله خوردن pillah khwurdan.—(*to take steps*) اقدام نمودن ikdám nimúdan.

STEP-SON, ربیب rabíb.

STEREOSCOPE, جهان نما jahán-nimá.

STERILE (*barren*), عقیم 'akím, ویرانه víránah, شوره shúrah, بائر bá,ir, بی بر bí-bar.

STERLING (*pure*), پاك pák, پاکیزه pákízah, صاف sáf, ناب náb.—(*honest*), صادق sádik, صالح sálih, متدین mutadayyin, راست rást, راستباز rast-báz.

STERN (*severe, grave*), موقر mu,akkar, متعبس muta'abbis, پفیوز pufyúz, زشت نهاد zisht-nihád.—(*of a ship*) دبوسه dabbúsah, تفر tafar. (*of the body*) کون kún, ماتحت mátaht, موضع معتاد mauza'-i-mu'tád, محل قعود mahall-i-ku'úd.

STERNLY, بدرشتی bi-durushtí.

STERNNESS, درشتی durushtí, سختی sakhtí, رنجش ranjish.

STEW (*dish*), قلیه kalyah, یخنی yakhní.—(*of meat*) مسمی musammá.—(*of meat and vegetables*) قاورمه kávurmah, قورمه kavurmah.—(*made with split almonds, &c.*) متنجنه mutanjanah. — (*brothel*) خیل خانه khail-khánah, کاولی خانه kávalá-khánah, زنا خانه ziná-khánah.

STEWARD, ناظر názir, سرکار sarkár.

STEWARDSHIP, سرکاری sar-kárí, نظارت nazárat.

STICK, چوب دستی chúb-dastí, عصا 'asá, کتک kutak, چماق chumák, دگنك daganak.

To STICK (*adhere to*), چسبیدن chasbídan, پیوستن paivastan, ملحق بودن mulhak búdan.—(*fasten to*) چسبانیدن chasbánídan, پیوند کردن paivand kardan, وصل کردن vasl kardan.—(*be impeded*) محکم شدن muhkam shudan, ماندن mándan, لاهم شدن láhim shudan, گیر آمدن gír-ámadan.—(*plant*) نشاندن nishándan, نصب ساختن nasb sákhtan, بر پا کردن bar pá kardan.—(*stab*) زدن zadan, سپوختن sapúkhtan.—(*be embarrassed or forgetful*) عاجز ماندن 'ájiz mándan, آشفته شدن áshuftah shudan, حیران شدن hairán shudan, سراسیمه گشتن sar-ásímah gashtan, متحیر بودن mu-tahayyir búdan.

STICKINESS, لزوجت luzújat, چسبندگی chasbandagí.

STICKY, چسپناك chasp-nák, لزوج luzúj, لذج lazij.

STIFF, سخت sakht, خشك khushk.—(*persons*) درشت durusht, شدید shadíd.

To STIFFEN (*trans.*), سخت کردن sakht kardan, خشك کردن khushk kardan.—(*intrans.*) سخت آمدن sakht ámadan, خشك بودن khushk búdan.

STIFFLY, با سختی ba-sakhtí.

STIFF-NECKED, معاند mu'ánid, عصی 'así, گردن کش gardan-kash, یاغی yághí.

STIFFNESS, سختی sakhtí, خشکی khushkí.—(*persons*) درشتی du-rushtí, شدت shiddat.

To STIFLE, خفه کردن khaffah kardan, دم بستن dam bastan.—(*suppress*) اخفا نمودن ikhfá nimúdan, پوشیدن púshídan, باطل گردانیدن bátil gardánídan.

STIGMA, لوث laus, عیب 'aib.

To STIGMATIZE, معیوب کردن ma'yúb kardan.

STIGMATIZED, معیوب ma'yúb.

STILETTO, گزلك gazlak.

STILL (*silent*), ساکت sákit, خاموش khámúsh, صامت sámit.—(*quiet*) ساکن sákin, آسوده ásúdah, آرامیده árámídah. —(*till now*) تا حال tá hál, تا هنوز tá hanúz.—(*nevertheless*) با وجود bá-vujúd, حال آنکه hál án-kih, مع کل هذا ma' kull házá. — (*for distillation*); قرنبیق karmbík, انبیق ambík, قرع انبیق kar'-ambík.—(*to keep still*) سکوت کردن sukút kardan.

To STILL, خاموش کردن khámúsh kardan, تسکین کردن taskín kardan, آرام دادن árám dádan.

STILLNESS, خاموشی khámúshí.—(*quietude*) آسودگی ásúdagí, آرامیدگی árámídagí, آرام árám.

STILTS, پای چوبین páy-i-chúbín.

STIMULANT, محرك muharrik, مقوی mukavví.

To STIMULATE, بر انگیختن bar-angíkhtan, خیزانیدن khízánídan, تحریك کردن tahrík kardan, تغیر ساختن taghayyur sákhtan.

STIMULATION, تحریك tahrík, ترغیب targhíb.

STING, نیش nísh, ناوك návak.

To STING, نیش زدن nísh zadan.

STINGINESS, حرص hirs, آز áz, طمع tama', طمعکاری tama'-kárí, بخل bukhl, خسیست khasísat, خست khissat, امساك imsák, لوئم lu,m.

STINGY, طمعکار tama'-kár, بخیل bakhíl, پول دوست púl-dúst, جوکی júkí, ممسك mumsik, کنس kinis.

STINK, بد بو bad bú, عفونت 'ufúnat, گند gand.

To STINK, بو کردن bú kardan, گندیدن gandídan, متعفن شدن muta'affin shudan.

STINKING, گنده gandah, گندیده gandídah, متعفن muta'affin.

STINT, دریغ dirígh, خست khissat.—(*without stint*) بی دریغ bí-dirígh.

To STINT, بخل ورزیدن bukhl varzídan, دریغ نمودن dirígh nimúdan.

STIPEND, علوفه 'alúfah, وظیفه vazífah, مواجب mavájib.

To STIPULATE, معاهده نمودن mu'áhadah nimúdan, قرار دادن karár dádan.

STIPULATION, شرط shart, قرار karár, عهد 'ahd.

STIR, هنگامه hangámah, غوغا ghaughá.

To STIR (*mix or agitate*), زیر رو کردن zír-rú kardan, جنبانیدن jumbánídan, در هم کردن dar-ham kardan, بر هم زدن bar-ham zadan.—(*move*) جنبیدن jumbídan, حرکت کردن harakat kardan, لاندن lándan (*obs.*). — (*to stir up*) بر انگیختن bar-angíkhtan, خیزانیدن khízánídan, تحریك کردن tahrík kardan, تغیر ساختن taghayyur sákhtan.

STIRRUP, رکاب rikáb. — (*leather*) دوال duvál, تسمه tasmah, ساقت sákat.—(*to take up the stirrups a hole*) رکابرا یك خانه بالا کردن rikáb-rá yak khánah bálá kardan, رکابرا یك سوراخ کوتاه کردن rikábrá yak súrákh kútáh kardan.

STITCH, بخیه bakhyah, دوخت dúkht.

To STITCH, دوختن dúkhtan.

STOCK (*of a gun*), قنداقه kundákah, قنداغ kundágh, کنده kundah (*obs.*). — (*capital*) سر مایه sar-máyah, راس المال rásu-'l-mál, بضاعت bizá'at, دستمایه dast-máyah.—(*lineage*) اصل asl, نسل nasl, نسب nasab.— (*of a tree*) ساقه sákah.—(*of a railway*) آلات álát.—(*flower*) شببو shab-bú.

To STOCK, آکندن akandan.

STOCKADE (*temporary fortification*), سنگر sangar, سیبه síbah, مترس matras.

STOCKINGS, جوراب júráb, پاکش pá-kash. — (*stocking-weaver*) جوراب باف júráb-báf.—(*of cloth, worn on ceremony*) چاقچور chákchúr.

STOCKJOBBER, محتکر muhtakir.

STOCKS, کنده kundah, کند kund, پالهنگ pá-lahang.

STOIC, رواقی riváki.

STOMACH, معده mi'dah, شکم shikm. —(*stomach-ache*) شکم درد shikm-dard, درد شکم dard-i-shikm, دل دردی dil-dardí.

STONE, سنگ sang, حجر hajar.—(*calculus in the bladder*) سنگ مثانه sang-i-masánah. — (*whet-stone*) سنگ سای sang-i-sáy, فسان fisán. — (*hailstone*) دانهٔ تگرگ dánah - i - tagarg.—(*touchstone*) سنگ محك sang-i-mihakk, عیار 'iyár, معیار mi'yár.—(*flagstone*) بلاط balát.—(*millstone*) سنگ آس sang-i-ás. — (*of fruit*) خسته khastah, خصه khassah, هسته hastah.—(*small stones or seeds of fruit*) دانه dánah.—(*precious stone*) جوهر jauhar, گوهر gauhar. —(*of a ring*) نگین nagín, فص fass. —(*stone-built*) سنگ بست sang-bast.

To STONE, سنگسار کردن sang-sár kardan, رجم کردن rajm kardan, سنگ زدن sang zadan.

STONEMASON, سنگتراش sang-tirásh.

STONY, سنگلاخ sang - lákh, قلبی kalbí. — (*made of stone*) سنگی sangí.

STOOL, کرسی kursí.—(*evacuation*) فعل fi'l, اطلاق itlák, غائط ghá,it براز biráz.—(*to go to stool*) بقضای حاجت نشستن bi-kazá,í-i-hájat nishastan, ریدن rídan, سر آب رفتن sar-i-áb raftan, متوضی رفتن mu-tavazzá raftan, ان کردن ann kar-dan.

To STOOP, خمیدن khamídan, سر فرو کردن sar-furú kardan.

STOP! (*interj.*), بایست bi-íst, باش básh, وا ایست vá-íst.—(*calling to an animal*) هش hush.—(*stop of a flute, &c.*) بند band.

To STOP, ایستادن ístádan, باز ماندن báz - mándan, بودن búdan, وا ایستادن vá-ístádan, توقف نمودن tavakkuf nimúdan. — (*hinder*) باز داشتن báz-dáshtan,. منع کردن mana' kardan, مزاحم شدن muzá-him shudan, کسیل کردن kisíl kar-dan.—(*arrest one's progress*) سر راه گرفتن sar-i-ráh giriftan. — (*watch*) (*trans.*) خوابانیدن khwá-bánídan.—(*intrans.*) وا ایستادن vá-ístádan, خوابیدن khwábídan.— (*train*) ایستادن ístádan.—(*to stop*

wages, as a fine) جیره بریدن jírah burídan, مواجب قطع کردن mavájib kat' kardan.—(*to stop up*) گرفتن giriftan, بستن bastan, مسدود کردن masdúd kardan.
STOPPAGE, بند band, سد sadd, ضیق سد zík-i-sadd.
STOPPER (*of a bottle*), سر شیشه sar-i-shíshah.
STORAX (*gum*), میعت mai'at, بخور مریم bukhúr-i-maryam.
STORE (*hoard*), ذخیره zakhírah, گنج ganj, خزانه khizánah, انبار ambár, مایه máyah.
To STORE, ذخیره کردن zakhírah kardan. — (*to be stored*) جمع آوری شدن jam'-ávarí shudan.
STOREHOUSE, مخزن makhzan, خزانه khizánah, خزینه khizínah, انبار ambár, گنجینه ganjínah, حاصل hásil.
STORK, لقلق laklak, لکلک laklak.
STORM, *vide* TEMPEST, ASSAULT.
To STORM, حمله کردن hamlah kardan, هجوم آوردن hujúm ávardan. —(*rage*) رنجیدن ranjídan, آشوبیدن áshúbídan, نا راضی شدن ná-rází shudan, غضبناك شدن ghazab-nák shudan, تغضب نمودن taghazzub nimúdan, آشفتن áshuftan.
STORMY, طوفانی túfání, پر باد pur-bád.
STORY, حکایت hikáyat, قصه kissah, داستان dástán, نقل nakl, افسانه afsánah, فسان fisán.—(*of a house*) طبقه tabakah, مرتبه martabah. —(*upper story*) مرتبه فوقانی martabah-i-faukání. — (*as the story goes*), چنانکه سمت ذکر یافت chunán - kih samt - i - zikr yáft. — چنانچه آورده اند chunán-chih ávardah and, چنانچه روایت میکنند chunán-chih riváyat mí-kunand. — (*story-book*) کتاب افسانه kitáb-i-afsánah, کتاب نقلی kitáb - i - naklí.
STORY-TELLER, قصه گو kissah-gú, نقال nakkál. — (*liar*) دروغگو durúgh-gú, کاذب kázib, کذاب kazzáb.
STOUT, مضبوط mazbút, قوی kaví, کلفت kuluft.—(*fat*) فربه farbih, چاق chák, جسیم jasím.
STOUTLY, دلیرانه dilíránah, باشجاعت bá-shajá'at.
STOUTNESS, مضبوطی mazbútí, قوت kúvat.—(*fatness*) فربهی farbihí.
STOVE, گلخن gulkhan, کوره kúrah, بخاری bukhárí.
To STOW, نهادن nihádan, گذاردن guzárdan, گذاشتن guzáshtan.
To STRADDLE, پا پهن کردن pá-pahn kardan.
To STRAGGLE, پراکنده رفتن parákandah raftan, آواره شدن ávárah shudan, بیراه شدن bí-ráh shudan.
STRAIGHT, راست rást, مستقیم mustakím, صائب sá,ib.— (*a straight line*) خط مستقیم khatt - i - mustakím.
To STRAIGHTEN, راست کردن rást kardan.
STRAIGHTFORWARD (*honest*), درست رفتار durust - raftár, خوشمعامله khwush - mu'ámalah. — (*to go straight forward*) راست پیش رفتن rást písh raftan.
STRAIGHTFORWARDNESS, صحت sihhat, راستی rástí.
STRAIGHTWAYS, در حل dar hal, فی الفور fi'l-faur.
STRAIN, پیچش píchish.—(*song*) آواز áváz.
To STRAIN (*filter*), پالودن pálúdan, صاف کردن sáf kardan, چلاندن chilándan.—(*the arm, &c.*) در رفتن dar raftan.
STRAINED, مصفی musaffá, مروق muravvak.
STRAINER, صافی sáfí, کفگیر kaf-gír. —(*large strainer for boiling rice*) سماق پالان sumák-pálán, چلاو صافی chiláu-sáfí, ترشپالان turush-pálán.
STRAIT (*narrow pass*), تنگ راه tang-ráh, تنگ tang, گدوك gadúk, گردن gardan.—(*difficulty*) مضایقه muzáyakah, مضیق mazík.
STRAITLY, با دقت bá-dikkat, نقیر و قطمیر nakír va katmír.
STRAITNESS (*poverty*), تنگی tangí, افلاس iflás, تنگ دستی tang-dastí, مسکنت maskanat, نا داری ná-dárí.

Stramonium (*thorn-apple*), جوز ماثل jauz-i-másal, بنج دشتی banj-i-dashtí, گوز گیاه gúz-i-giyáh.

Strange (*wonderful, uncommon*), عجب 'ajab, عجیب 'ajíb, غریب gharíb, نادر nádir, بدیع badí', بدیهی badíhí.

Strangely, عجباً 'ajaban.

Stranger, بیگانه bígánah, غریب gharíb, اجنبی ajnabí, غیر ghair.—(*newcomer*) خوش نشین khwush-nishín, تازه وارد tázah-várid.

To Strangle, خفه کردن khaffah kardan, خنق ساختن khanik sákhtan, طناب انداختن tanáb andákhtan, خناق کردن khunák kardan.

Strangulation, خفگی khaffagí, خناق khunák, اختناق ikhtinák.

Strangury, حبس البول habsu-'l-baul.

Strap, دوال duvál, تسمه tasmah.

Stratagem, حیله hílah, ساخته sákhtah, کید kaid, گول gúl.

Strategy, فن محاربه fann-i-muhárabah.

Stratum, طبقه tabakah.

Straw, کاه káh, که kah, پوش púsh.—(*of maize*) چوب ذرت chúb-i-zurrat.—(*of rice*) پوشال púshál, سراچینه saráchinah. — (*a single straw*) پر کاه par-i-káh.—(*bed of straw, for a horse*) تخت پئین takht-i-pa,ín. — (*to catch at a straw*) تشبث نمودن tashabbus nimúdan.

Strawberry, توت فرنگی tút-i-farangí, چمبو chambú, چنبل chambul.

To Stray, گمراه شدن gum-ráh shudan, بیراه شدن bí-ráh shudan, آواره شدن ávárah shudan.

Streak, خط khatt.

Streaked, مخطط mukhattat.

Stream, جوی júí, سیل sail, آبشار áb-shár.

To Stream, جاری شدن járí shudan, جریان نمودن jiryán nimudan, روان شدن raván shudan, سیلان شدن sayalán shudan, سیل نمودن sail nimúdan, ریزان شدن rízán shudan.

Streamer, علم 'alam, لوا livá, بیرق bairak.

Street, کوچه kúchah, کوی kúy, کو kú.—(*large or broad street*) شارع shári', معبر عام ma'bar-i-'ámm.—(*back street*) پس کوچه pas-kúchah.

Strength, زور zúr, زورآوری zúr-ávarí, توانائی tavánáí, نیرو nairú, نیرومندی nairú-mandí, برگ barg, زهره zahrah, قوت kúvat, *or* kuvvat, طاقت tákat, شدت shiddat, استواری ustuvárí, مکنت miknat, مجال majál, طرق tirak, نیو niyú, موجب mújat, اوغر úghur.—(*strength of mind*) قوت قلب kúvat-i-kalb.

To Strengthen, تاکید کردن ta,kíd kardan, مستحکم کردن mustahkim kardan, استحکام دادن istihkám dádan.

Strengthener, مقوی mukavví.

Strenuous, سخت sakht, شدید shadíd.

Strenuously, با سختی bá-sakhtí, با شدت bá-shiddat.

Strenuousness, سختی sakhtí, شدت shiddat.

Stress, تاکید ta,kíd.—(*force*) زور zúr, جور jaur, جبر jabr, قهر kahr.

To Stretch, کشیدن kashídan, دراز کردن diráz kardan, تطویل کردن tatvíl kardan.—(*extend*) پهن کردن pahn kardan, گستردن gusturdan.—(*to stretch oneself*) دراز کشیدن diráz kashídan.

To Strew, ریختن ríkhtan, افشاندن afshándan, گستردن gusturdan, گسترانیدن gusturánídan, پراکندن parákandan, پاشیدن páshídan.

Stricken (*in years*), مسن musinn.

Strict, اکید akíd.—(*complete*) کامل kámil.

Strictly, با دقت bá-dikkat, نقیر و قطمیر nakír va katmír.

Stricture (*blame*), زجر zajr, ملامت malámat, سر زنش sar-zanish, مواخذه mu,ákhazah, پیغاره paighárah, عتاب 'itáb.— (*medical term*) حبس البول habsu-'l-baul.

Stride, قدم kadam.

To Stride, قدم زدن kadam zadan.

STRIFE, ستیزه sitízah, منازعت munáza'at, نزاع nizá', مناقشه munákashah, جدال jadál, مجادله mujádaláh, مشاجره musliájarah, جنگ jang, فتنه fitnah, شلوك shulúk (*vulg.*).

To STRIKE, زدن zadan, کوبیدن kúbídan, کوفتن kúftan, کوتك زدن kútak zadan.—(*a tent*) انداختن andákhtan, کندن kandan, باز کردن báz-kardan. —(*as a workman*) دست از کار کشیدن dast az kár kashídan. — (*as a disease*) خوردن khwurdan.—(*as a ship on a rock*) بسنگ خوردن bi-sang khwurdan. —(*as a ship on a sandbank*) بریگ نشستن bi-ríg-nishastan, لاهم شدن láhim shudan.—(*a clock, a bell, &c.*) زدن zadan, آواز دادن áváz dádan.—(*out*) محو کردن mahv kardan, پاك کردن pák kardan.

STRIKING (*as likeness, &c.*), شگرف shigarf, موٴثر mu,assir.

STRING, ریسمان rísmán, رشته rishtah.—(*of a musical instrument*) تار tár.—(*bowstring*) زه zih, چله chillah.—(*to string a bow*) چله کردن chillah kardan, زه کردن zih kardan.—(*series*) سلسله silsilah, سلك silk, تواتر tavátur.

To STRING, برشته در آوردن bi-rishtah dar-ávardan.

STRINGY, پر ریشه pur-ríshah.

STRIP, پاره párah.

To STRIP, برهنه کردن barahnah kardan.—(*one's clothes*) لخت شدن lukht shudan.

STRIPE (*lash*), ضرب zarb, تازیانه tázyánah.—(*streak*) خط khatt.

STRIPED, مخطط mukhattat.

STRIPLING, بچه bachah.

STRIPPED, مجرد mujarrad, لخت lukht, برهنه barahnah.

To STRIVE, کوشش کردن kúshish kardan, جد و جهد کردن jadd va jahd kardan. تلاش کردن talásh kardan, ورزیدن varzídan.—(*contend*) مجادله کردن mujádalah kardán, دعوی کردن da'vá kardan, منازعت نمودن munáza'at nimúdan, معارضه کردن mu'árazah kardan. — (*to strive eagerly*) مبادرت ورزیدن mubádarat varzídan.

STROKE, ضرب zarb, ضربه zarbah, صدمه sadmah.

To STROKE (*with the hand*), با دست نواختن bá-dast navákhtan, از دست نوازش کردن az dast navázish kardan, دست مالیدن dast málídan.

STROLL, گردش gardish, تفرج tafarruj.

To STROLL, گردش کردن gardish kardan, تماشای اطراف نمودن tamáshái-i-atráf nimúdan.

STROLLER, گردش کننده gardish-kunandah, تفرج کن tafarruj-kun, متفرج mutafarrij.

STRONG, قوی kaví, زور آور zúr-ávar, توانا taváná, نیرومند nairú-mand, مضبوط mazbút, سترگ suturg, شدید shadíd, استوار ustuvár, تنومند tanú-mand, پر زور pur-zúr. — (*in phraseology*) سخت sakht, شدید shadíd, مضبوط mazbút.—(*firm*) واثق vásik. — (*as liquor, drug, &c.*) تند tund, سنگین sangín.

STRONGLY, قویاً kavíyan.

STROPHE, بیت bait (*pl.* ابیات abyát).

STRUCTURE (*human*), بنیه bunyah, جثه jussah.—(*building*) بنا biná, عمارت 'imárat, بنیان bunyán.

STRUGGLE, کشمکش kash-ma-kash, کشتی kushtí, شلوك shulúk (*vulg.*).

To STRUGGLE, چالش نمودن chálish nimúdan.

STRUMPET, فاحشه fáhishah, زانیه zániyah, لولی lúlí, جافجاف jáfjáf, روسپی rúspí, قحبه kahbah, لوند lavand, کاولی kávalí (*vulg.*), جنده jindah (*vulg.*).

To STRUT, خرامیدن khirámídan, چمیدن chamídan.

STUBBLE, کاهبن káh-bun, علف النگ 'alaf-ulang.

STUBBORN, خود سر khwud-sar, مرید maríd, متمرد mutamarrid, حرون harún, منخرط munkharit, معاند mu'ánid, اخلال ikhlál, لجوج lajúj.

STUBBORNLY, با سر کشی bá-sarkashí.

STUCCO, گچ بری gach-barí, گچ gach.

STUD (*of horses*), خیل khail, طویله tavílah, ایلخی ílkhí.—(*boss, ornament*) گلمیخ gul-míkh.—(*for fastening the collar of a shirt*) گل یقه gul-i-yakah.

STUDDED, آمود ámúd, آراسته árástah.—(*with jewels*) مرصع murassa', جوهرآمود jauhar-ámúd, جواهر آگین javáhir-ágín.—(*studded about, as houses, &c.*), تك تك tak-tak.

STUDENT, طلبه talabah, طالب العلم tálibu-'l-'ilm. — (*students*) طلاب tulláb.

STUDIED (*deliberate*), با عمد bá-'amd, بالقصد bi-'l-kasd.

STUDIOUS, درس خوان dars-khwán.

STUDIOUSLY (*deliberately*), دانسته dánistah.

STUDY, تحصیل tahsíl, مطالعه mutála'ah, ممارست mumárasat.

To STUDY, درس خواندن dars khwándan, طلب نمودن talab nimúdan, کارکردن kár kardan, علم تحصیل کردن 'ilm tahsíl kardan. — (*peruse*) مطالعه کردن mutála'ah kardan.

STUFF (*material, cloth, &c.*), قماش kumásh (*pl.* اقمشه akmishah).

To STUFF, آکندن ákandan, انپاشتن ampáshtan, چپانیدن chapánídan, طپانیدن tapánídan.

STUFFING, حشو hashv, آکندگی ákandagí.—(*for meat, &c.*) دولمه dúlmah.

To STUMBLE, سکندری خوردن sikandarí khwurdan, لغزیدن laghzídan, لخشیدن lakhshídan, رو رفتن rú raftan.

STUMBLER, لغزنده laghzandah, سکندری خور sikandarí-khwur, رو رونده rú-ravandah.

STUMBLING-BLOCK, سنگ تصادم sang-i-tasádum.

STUMP, کنده kundah, تنه tanah.

STUMPY, پر کنده pur-kundah, پر تنه pur-tanah.

To STUN, بی هوش کردن bí-húsh kardan, گیج کردن gíj kardan.—(*to be stunned*), از هوش رفتن az húsh raftan, از خود رفتن az khwud raftan, بی هوش شدن bí-húsh shudan.

To STUNT, کوتاه نمودن kútáh nimúdan.

STUPEFACTION, دمبستگی dam-bastagí, بیهوشی bí-húshí, تحیر tahayyur.

STUPEFIED, سراسیمه sarásímah, دمبسته dam-bastah, متحیر mutahayyir, مدهوش madhúsh, متغیر mutaghayyir, مبهوت mabhút.

To STUPEFY, سراسیمه ساختن sarásímah sákhtan, مدهوش گردانیدن madhúsh gardánídan.

STUPENDOUS, عجیب 'ajíb, غریب gharíb, حیرت انگیز hairat-angíz.

STUPENDOUSLY, با عجب bá-'ajab.

STUPID, کند رائی kund-ra,í, کودن kaudan, احمق ahmak, سفیه safíh, ابله ablah, غابی ghábí, خیره khírah, کند ذهن kund-zihn, بلید balíd, پخت pakht, خرف khirif.

STUPIDITY, حماقت hamákat, بلاهت baláhat, عدم عقل 'adam-i-'akl, خریت kharríyat.

STUPOR, بی هوشی bi-húshí, غش ghash, ضعف za'f.

STURDILY, سطبرانه sitabránah.

STURDINESS, سطبری sitabrí, تنومندی tanúmandí.

STURDY, سطبر sitabr, تنومند tanúmand.

STURGEON (*fish*), سگ ماهی sag-máhí, مرسین marsín.

To STUTTER, الکن کردن alkan kardan, لکنت کردن luknat kardan.

STUTTERER, الکن گو alkan-gú, لکنت کن luknat-kun.

STY, گراز دان guráz-dán.—(*in eye*) سنده سلامی sindah-salámí.

STYLE (*in composing*), اصطلاح istiláh, عبارت 'ibárat.—(*manner*) طور taur, طرح tarah, وجه vajh, طریق tarík, منوال minvál, رسم rasm, وتیره vatírah, وضع vaz', روش ravish, طرز tarz, راه ráh, سبیل sabíl, سلوك sulúk, دستور dastúr, گونه gúnah.—(*in the ... style*) ... بسبك bi-sabk-i- ... .

To STYLE, نامیدن námídan, نام گذاردن nám guzárdan, نام دادن nám dádan, اسم نهادن ism nihádan.

STYLISH, به موجب قاعده bi-mújib-i-ká'idah.

SUAVITY, ملايمت muláyamat, حلم hilm, لطف lutf.

SUBALTERN, زير دست zír-dast.

SUBDIVISION, شق shakk, قسمت kismat.

To SUBDUE, فتح كردن fath kardan, غلبه كردن ghalabah kardan, شكست دادن shikast dádan, ظفر يافتن zafar yáftan, گشادن gushádan, نصرت يافتن nusrat yáftan, فيروز شدن fírúz shudan, غالب آمدن ghálib ámadan.

SUBJECT, رعيت ra,íyat, تبيع tabí', فرمانبردار firmán-bardár.—(*foreign subjects*) تبعه اجنبيه taba'ah-i-ajnabíyah.—(*topic*) معنى ma'ní, مبحث mabhas, باب báb, موضوع mauzú', حجت hujjat, مدعى به mudda'á bihi, ماده máddah.—(*liable to*) مستوجب mustaujib, متحمل mutahammil, سزاوار sazávár, معرض mu'arraz.—(*purport*) مطلب matlab, مضمون mazmún, معنى ma'ní.—(*of a predicate or proposition*) مقدم mukaddam, مبتدا mubtadá, موضوع mauzú', محكوم عليه mahkúm 'alaihi.—(*on the subject of*) در باب dar báb, در باره dar bárah, نسبت به nisbat bi, از az, در حق dar hakk, در خصوص dar khusús.—(*to be on the subject*) بر سر مطلب شدن bar sar-i-matlab shudan.

To SUBJECT, فتح كردن fath kardan, غلبه كردن ghalabah kardan, شكست دادن shikast dádan, ظفر يافتن zafar yáftan, گشادن gushádan, نصرت يافتن nusrat yáftan, فيروز شدن fírúz shudan, غالب آمدن ghálib ámadan.—(*to subject oneself*) مطيع شدن mutí' shudan, باطاعت آمدن bi-itá'at ámadan, فرمان بردار شدن firmán-bardár shudan.

SUBJECTION, اطاعت itá'at, فرمان بردارى firmán-bardárí, انقياد inkiyád, خضوع khuzú', خشوع khushú', ابتهال ibtihál, وضاعت vazá'at, تواضع tavázu', ضراعت zará'at, تسليم taslím.

To SUBJOIN, اضافه كردن izáfah kardan, الحاق كردن ilhák kardan.

To SUBJUGATE, فتح كردن fath kardan, غلبه كردن ghalabah kardan, شكست دادن shikast dádan, ظفر يافتن zafar yáftan, گشادن gushádan, نصرت يافتن nusrat yáftan, فيروز شدن fírúz shudan, غالب آمدن ghálib ámadan.

SUBJUGATION, ظفر zafar, فيروز fírúz, غلبه ghalabah, فتح fath, شكست shikast.

SUBJUNCTIVE (*mood*), فعل مشروط fi-'l-i-mashrút, فعل مقيد fi-'l-i-mukayyad.

SUBLIME, رفيع rafí', عالى 'álí, سامى sámí, صمد samad, معلى mu'allá, والا válá, جليل jalíl.—(*the Sublime Porte*) آستان عاليشان ástán-i-'álí-shán, عتبه عليا 'atabah-i-'ulyá, سده سنيه suddah-i-saníyah.

SUBLIMELY, با جلالت bá-jalálat.

SUBLIMITY, علو 'ulúv, جلالت jalálat, رفعت rif'at, بلندى bulandí.

SUBLUNARY, دنيوى dunyaví, پست past, زمانى zamání.

SUBMARINE, زير دريائى zír-i-daryá,í.

To SUBMERGE, غرق نمودن gharak nimúdan.

SUBMERGED, غريق gharík.

SUBMERSION, غرق gharak.

SUBMISSION, اطاعت itá'at, فرمان بردارى firmán-bardárí, انقياد inkiyád, خضوع khuzú', خشوع khushú', ابتهال ibtihál, وضاعت vazá'at, تواضع tavázu', ضراعت zará'at, تسليم taslím.

SUBMISSIVE, مطيع mutí', متواضع mutavázi', فرمان بردار firmán-bardár.

SUBMISSIVELY, باطاعت bi-itá'at.

To SUBMIT, مطيع شدن mutí' shudan, باطاعت آمدن bi-itá'at ámadan, فرمان بردار شدن firmán-bardár shudan.—(*represent*) عرض كردن 'arz kardan, معروض داشتن ma'rúz dáshtan.

SUBORDINACY, *or* SUBORDINATION, زير دستى zír-dastí.

SUBORDINATE, زير دست zír-dast, تحت حكم taht-i-hukm.

To SUBORN (*influence*), تحريص كردن

tahrís kardan, سازش کردن sázish kárdan, آموختن ámúkhtan.

To SUBSCRIBE, زیر نوشتن zír nivishtan.—(*money*) اعانه نمودن i'ánah nimúdan, توزیع نمودن tauzí' nimúdan.

SUBSCRIBER, اعانه دهنده i'ánah-dihandah.

SUBSCRIPTION (*quota, share*), تقسیم taksím, حصه hissah, بهره bahrah. —(*signature*) دست خط dast-khatt, امضا imzá, نشان nishán, طغرا tughrá.—(*money*) اعانه i'ánah.—(*by subscription*) به طور تقسیم bi-taur-i-taksím. — (*subscription-list*) دفتر اعانه daftar-i-i'ánah.

SUB-SECTION, فصل fasl.

SUBSEQUENT, واپسین vá-pasín.

SUBSEQUENTLY, بعد از آن ba'd az án, من بعد min ba'd, از آن پس az án pas, بعده ba'dahu.

SUBSERVIENCY, اطاعت itá'at, فرمان بردارى firmán-bardárí, انقیاد inkiyád, خضوع khuzú', خشوع khushú', ابتهال ibtihál, وضاعت vazá'at, تواضع tavázu', ضراعت zará'at, تسلیم taslím.

SUBSERVIENT, متابع mutábi', متعلق muta'allak, منوط بر manút bar, زیر حکم zír-i-hukm.

To SUBSIDE, فرو رفتن furú raftan.—(*as rebellion, &c.*) فرو نشستن furú nishastan.

SUBSIDENCE, نشست nishast, فرو رفتگى furú-raftagí.

SUBSIDIARY, معاونتى mu'ávanatí.

SUBSIDY, وجه معاونت vajh-i-mu'ávanat.

To SUBSIST, زیستن zístan, زنده بودن zindah búdan, زندگى نمودن zindagí nimúdan.

SUBSISTENCE (*maintenance*), وجه گذران vajh-i-guzrán, مدد معاش madad-i-ma'ásh, روزى rúzí, زندگانى zindagání, گذران guzrán, معیشت ma'íshat.—(*a bare subsistence*) رمق ramik.

SUBSTANCE (*essential part*), اصل asl, مایه máyah, خلاصه khulásah, کنه kunah, مضغه muzghah. —(*in contradistinction to quality*) جوهر jauhar.—(*of a letter, &c.*) مال ma,ál, مطلب matlab.

SUBSTANTIAL, جوهرى jauharí, جسیم jasím.

SUBSTANTIALITY, تجسم tajassum, جسمانیت jismáníyat.

SUBSTANTIALLY, در واقع dar váki', فى الحقیقت fi-'l-hakíkat, الحق al-hakk.

To SUBSTANTIATE, اثبات نمودن isbát nimúdan, بر قرار نمودن bar-karár nimúdan.

SUBSTANTIVE (*noun*), اسم ذات ism-i-zát, اسم جنس ism-i-jins, اسم ism.

SUBSTITUTE, عوضى 'avazí, *or* 'ivazí.

To SUBSTITUTE, عوض کردن 'avaz kardan, تبدیل کردن tabdíl kardan, مبدل ساختن mubaddal sákhtan.

SUBSTITUTION, تبدیل tabdíl, مبادله mubádalah, عوض 'ivaz, استبدال istibdál.

SUBTERFUGE, بهانه bahánah, فریب firíb.

SUBTERRANEOUS, زیرزمینى zír-zamíní, تحت الارض tahtu-'l-arz.—(*vault or apartment*) سردابه sardábah, زیر زمین zír-zamín, ته خانه tahkhánah. — (*fold for cattle*) کند kand. — (*aqueduct*) کاریز káríz, قنات kanát.

SUBTILE, زرنگ zaring, زیرک zírak, چابک chábuk, چست chust.

SUBTILTY, نکته nuktah, دقیقه dakíkah.

SUBTLE, مکار makkár, حیله ور hílah-var, حیله باز hílah-báz, نا پاک ná-pák.

SUBTLETY, حیله hílah, مکر makr, نیرنگ nairang.

To SUBTRACT, تفریق نمودن tafrík nimúdan, منها کردن minhá kardan, وضع کردن vaz' kardan.

SUBTRACTION (*in arithmetic*), تفریق tafrík, منها minhá, وضع vaz', باد باقى bád-bákí, نقص naks.

SUBURB, پیرامون pairámún, سواد savád, حول و حوش haul u haush, حوالى haválí, نواحى naváhí.

SUBVERSION, شکست shikast, هزیمت hazímat, خلل khalal, خسارت khasárat.

To SUBVERT, شکست دادن shikast dádan, گشادن gushádan, هزیمت دادن hazímat dádan.

To SUCCEED (*follow*), پس آمدن pas ámadan, پیروی کردن pairaví kardan, عقب آمدن 'akab ámadan.—(*prosper*) کامیاب شدن kám-yáb shudan, بر آمدن bar-ámadan, مطلب یافتن matlab yáftan, بمراد رسیدن bi-murád rasídan, فیروز گشتن fírúz gashtan, بجای رسیدن bi-jáy rasídan, منتفع شدن muntafi' shudan, بر خوردار شدن bar-khwur-dár shudan. — (*inherit*) وارث شدن váris shudan, ارث گرفتن irs giriftan, میراث یافتن mírás yáftan.

SUCCEEDING (*coming after*) لاحق láhik, پیرو pay-rau, متعاقب muta'ákib.

SUCCESS, فلاح faláh, ظفر zafar, میمنه maimanah.

SUCCESSFUL, کامیاب kám-yáb, بهره مند bahrah-mand, فیروز fírúz, منتفع muntafi', بر خوردار bar-khwur-dár.

SUCCESSFULLY, بهرهمندانه bahrah-mandánah.

SUCCESSION (*heritage*), وراثت virásat, میراث mírás. — (*in succession*) توالی taválí, تواتر tavátur.

SUCCESSIVE *and* SUCCESSIVELY, پی در پی pay-dar-pay, متواتر mutavátir, متوالی mutaválí, متعاقب muta'ákib, مسلسل musalsal, مترادف mutarádif, خلفی khalafí.

SUCCESSOR, خلف khalaf, عقب 'akab (*pl.* اعقاب a'káb), جایگیر jáy-gír, جا نشین já-nishín.

SUCCINCT, مختصر mukhtasar.

SUCCINCTLY, بطور اختصار bi-taur-i-ikhtisár.

SUCCOUR, مدد madad, امداد imdád, مدد گاری madad-gárí, یاری yárí, یاوری yávarí, پشتی pushtí, نصرت nusrat, کمک kumak, عون 'aun, اعانت i'ánat, استعانت isti'ánat.

To SUCCOUR, متعرض حال شدن muta'arriz-i-hál shudan, مساعدت نمودن musá'adat nimúdan, کمک دادن kumak dádan, امداد کردن imdád kardan, مدد کردن madad kardan, پشتی کردن pushtí kardan.

SUCCULENT, آبدار áb-dár, تازه tázah.

SUCH, همچو ham-chú, همچون ham-chún, همچنان ham-chunán, چنان chunán, آنچنان án-chunán, آنچنین án-chunín, همیدون hamídún, چنین chunín.—(*such an one, so and so*) فلان fulán, بیسار bísár. — (*such as* ...) که عبارت از ... است kih 'ibárat az ... ast.

SUCK (*one gulp, draw, or inhalation*), مکه makkah, قرت kurt.

To SUCK, مکیدن makídan, رضع نمودن raz' nimúdan, رشف کردن rashf kardan, مجیدن majídan. — (*to suck up water*) آب کشیدن áb kashídan.

SUCKER, آب کش áb-kash.—(*of a plant*) شاخه shákhah, غصن ghusn.

SUCKING (*child*), طفل شیر خواره tifl-i-shír-khwárah, طفل رضیع tifl-i-razí'.

To SUCKLE, شیر دادن shír dádan.

SUCTION, مکش makish, مك makk, مکیدن makídan.

SUDDEN, دفعی daf'í, نا گهان ná-gahán, مفاجات mufáját.

SUDDENLY, نا گاه ná-gáh, نا گهان ná-gahán, بغتةً baghtatan, دفعةً daf'atan, یکسره yak sarah, یکباره yak bárah.

SUDDENNESS, نا گهانی ná-gahání.

To SUE, مرافعه کردن muráfa'ah kardan.—(*beg*) التماس کردن iltimás kardan, خواستن khwástan.

SUET, پیه píh, پی pí.

To SUFFER, کشیدن kashídan, خوردن khwurdan, بر داشتن bar-dáshtan, تحمل کردن tahammul kardan, متحمل بودن mutahammil búdan.—(*permit*) گذاشتن guzáshtan, بادن [illegible] dádan, دستور دادن dastúr dádan, اجازت دادن ijázat dádan, قائل بودن ká,il búdan, اذن دادن izn dádan, وا گذاشتن vá-guzáshtan, فرصت دادن fursat dádan, هشتن hishtan.

SUFFERABLE, قابل تحمل kábil-i-tahammul.

SUFFERER, مصیبت کش musíbat-kash.

SUFFERING, درد dard, رنج ranj, رنجش ranjish, عذاب 'azáb, آزار ázár, الم alam, زحمت zahmat, وجع vaja'.

To SUFFICE, کفاف دادن kafáf dádan, کفایت کردن kifáyat kardan, کافی بودن káfí búdan, بس بودن bas búdan.

SUFFICIENCY, کفایت kifáyat, بس bas, فراوانی farávání.

SUFFICIENT, بس bas, کافی káfí, وافی váfí, وافر váfir, فراوان farávân.

SUFFICIENTLY, بقدر کفایت bi-kadr-i-kifáyat.

SUFFIX, ملحق mulhak.

To SUFFOCATE, خفه کردن khaffah kardan, دم بستن dam bastan.

SUFFOCATED, منخنق munkhanik.

SUFFOCATING, خفه khaffah.

SUFFOCATION, خفه khaffah, حبس النفس habsu-'n-nafas.

SUFFRAGE, رأی ra,í.

To SUFFUSE, پر کردن pur kardan, انتشار دادن intishár dádan.—(*to be suffused*) انتشار یافتن intishár yáftan, پر شدن pur shudan.

SUFFUSION, انتشار intishár.

SUGAR, شکر shakar.—(*brown sugar*) شکر shakar. — (*lump sugar*) قند kand.—(*raw sugar*) شکر صاف نکرده shakar-i-sáf-na-kardah.—(*refined sugar*) شکر مصفی shakar-i-musaffá. — (*sugar candy*) نبات nabát, مصری misrí. — (*of roses*) گلقند gul-kand.—(*cane*) نی شکر nay-i-shakar, شکر قمیش shakar-kamísh.—(*plantation*) نیزار شکر nai-zár-i-shakar.—(*press or mill*) کار خانه شکر فشاری kár-khánah-i-shakar-fishárí, معصره ma'-sarah. — (*loaf of sugar*) کله قند kullah-i-kand. — (*sugar basin*) شکردان shakar-dán, کاسه شکر kásah-i-shakar.

To SUGGEST, اشاره دادن isharah dádan.

SUGGESTION, اشاره isharah. — (*according to the suggestion*) حسب الاشعار hasbu-'l-ish'ár.

SUICIDE, خودکشی khwud-kushí, قتل نفس katl-i-nafs, کشتن خود kushtan-i-khwud.

SUIT (*of clothes*), دست dast.—(*claim, &c.*) دعوی da'vá, مرافعه muráfa'ah, نزاع nizá', لجاج laják.

To SUIT, بکار خوردن bi-kár khwurdan, فراخور آمدن farákhwur ámadan.

SUITABILITY, شایستگی sháyistagí, مناسبت munásabat, سازکاری sáz-kárí.

SUITABLE, مناسب munásib, ساز کار sáz-kár, فراخور farákhwur, بجا bi-já.

SUITABLY, بطور شایستگی bi-taur-i-sháyistagí.

SUITE (*followers, &c.*), خدم و حشم khadam va hasham, نوکر باب naukar-báb, لواحق lavâhik, متعلقین muta'allikín.

SUITOR, مدعی mudda'í, شاکی shákí, داد خواه dád-khwáh, متظلم mutazallim.

SULLEN, پفیوز pufyúz, عبوس 'abús, سرکه فروش sirkah-furúsh, متعبس muta'abbas.

SULLENLY, بپفیوزی bi-pufyúzí.

SULLENNESS, پفیوزی pufyúzí, عبس 'abs, سرکه فروشی sirkah-furúshí.

To SULLY, فضیحت کردن fazíhat kardan, آلودن áludan.

SULPHATE, *vide* VITRIOL.

SULPHUR, کبریت kibrít, گوگرد gú-gird.

SULPHUROUS, کبریتی kibrítí.

SULTAN, سلطان sultán.

SULTANA (*raisin*), کشمش kishmish.

SULTRINESS, گرمی garmí.

SULTRY, گرم garm.

SUM (*of money*), مبلغ mablagh, موازی muvází.—(*in figures*) حساب hisáb, شمار shimár.—(*total*) جمله jumlah, جمع jam'.—(*to sum up*) الحاصل al-hásil.

SUMACH, سماق sumák.

SUMMARILY (*briefly*), مختصراً mukhtasaran, اجمالا ijmálan. — (*at once*) دفعتاً daf'atan.

To SUMMARIZE, منحصری ساختن munhasirí sákhtan.

SUMMARY, اجمال ijmál, مجمل mujmal.

SUMMER, تابستان tábistán, صيف saif. — (*summer residence*) ييلاق yailák, يائلاق yá,ilák.

SUMMER-HOUSE, كوشك kúshk, تالار tálár, تابستانى tábistání.

SUMMERSET, پشتك pushtak.—(*to turn a summerset*) پشتك بر داشتن pushtak bar-dáshtan, پشتك زدن pushtak zadan, وارونه زدن várúnah zadan.

SUMMIT, قله kullah, تيغ tígh, سر sar.

To SUMMON, احضار نمودن ihzár nimúdan, خواندن khwándan, طلب كردن talab kardan, طلب داشتن talab dáshtan, استحضار نمودن istihzár nimúdan.

SUMMONS (*written*), احضار ihzár.

SUMPTUOUS, عياش 'ayyásh. — (*to live sumptuously*) تعيش نمودن ta'ayyush nimúdan, خوش گذرانى نمودن khwush-guzrání nimúdan.

SUMPTUOUSLY, عياشانه 'ayyáshánah.

SUMPTUOUSNESS, عياشى 'ayyáshí.

SUN, آفتاب áftáb, مهر mihr, خورشيد khwurshíd, خور khwur, هور húr, شمس shams, يوح yúh, بيضا baizá, نير اعظم nayyir-i-a'zam. — (*disc of the sun*) قرص kurs. — (*sunbeam*) پرتو partav *or* partau, لمعه lam'ah, شعاع shu'á'.—(*sunburnt*) آفتاب زده áftáb-zadah. — (*sundial*) دائره هندى dá,irah-i-hindí, دائرهٔ ساعتى dá,irah-i-sá'atí.—(*sunflower*) گل آفتاب gul-i-áftáb.—(*sunrise*) طلوع آفتاب tulú'-i-áftáb, مطلع شمس matla'-i-shams, اشراق ishrák, آفتاب بر آمدن áftáb barámadan.—(*about a quarter of an hour before sunrise, time of prayer*) فجر fajr, فجر صبح fajr-i-subh. — (*about a quarter of an hour after sunset, time of prayer*) مغرب maghrib. — (*sunset*) غروب آفتاب ghurúb-i-áftáb, زوال شمس zavál-i-shams, وقوب vukúb.—(*sunshade*) آفتاب گردان áftáb-gardán. —(*sunshine*) تابش آفتاب tábish-i-áftáb.— (*sunstroke*) ضرب آفتاب zarb-i-aftáb.

SUNDAY, يكشنبه yak-shambah.

To SUNDER, بريدن burídan *or* burrídan, قطع كردن kat' kardan, دو پاره كردن dú-párah kardan, قيچى كردن kaichí kardan, دو نيم كردن dú-ním kardan.

SUNDRY, گوناگون gún-á-gún, مختلف mukhtalif.

SUNK, غريق gharík, مستغرق mustaghrak.

SUNNY, آفتابى áftábí.

To SUP, شام خوردن shám khwurdan.

To SUPERABOUND, موفور شدن maufúr shudan, كثير شدن kasír shudan, وافر شدن váfir shudan.

SUPERABUNDANCE, افراط ifrát, افزونى afzúní, فضل fazl.

SUPERABUNDANT, فاضل fázil, افزون afzún, زايد záíd.

SUPERANNUATED, سالى sálí.

SUPERB, معظم mu'azzam, عظيم 'azím, جليل jalíl, شگرف shigarf.

SUPERCILIOUS, مغرور maghrúr, متكبر mutakabbir.

SUPERCILIOUSLY, مغرورانه maghrúránah, متكبرانه mutakabbiránah.

SUPERCILIOUSNESS, اغماض ighmáz, تكبر takabbur.

SUPEREROGATION, نافله náfilah.

SUPERFICIAL (*external*), ظاهر záhir. بيرونى bírúní.—(*trifling*) سبكمايه subuk-máyah, هرزه harzah, خفيف khafíf, كوچك kúchik, جزئى juz,í, جز juz.

SUPERFICIES, بساط basát, بسيط basít, رو rú, سطح sath, صفحه safhah.

SUPERFINE, معظم mu'azzam, عظيم 'azím, جليل jalíl, شگرف shigarf.

SUPERFLUITY, افراط ifrát, افزونى afzúní, فضل fazl.

SUPERFLUOUS, زايد záíd, فاضل fázil, افزون afzún.

To SUPERINTEND, نظارت كردن nazárat kardan, رئسانه اداره نمودن ra,isánah idárah nimúdan.

SUPERINTENDENCE, نظارت nazárat,

کار گذاری kár-guzárí, کار رواج دهی kár-raváj-dihí.

SUPERINTENDENT, ناظر názir, کارگذار kár-guzár, سرکار sar-kár, مهتمم muhtamim, مدبر mudabbir.—(*to nominate or appoint a superintendent*) سر کار نمودن sar-kár nimúdar, بعهده کردن bi-'uhdah kardan.

SUPERIOR, برتر bartar, بالاتر bálátar, اعظم 'azam, اکبر akbar, فائق fá,ik, اعلی a'lá.

SUPERIORITY, سبقت sibkat, تفوق tafavvuk, استیلا istílá, پیش دستی písh-dastí, برتری bartarí.

SUPERLATIVE (*excellent*), افضل afzal, حسان hassán, احسن ahsan, اعلی a'lá.—(*superlative degree*) تفضیل tafzíl, رتبه تفضیل rutbah-i-tafzíl.

SUPERNATURAL, معجز mu'jiz.

SUPERNUMERARY, زیادتی ziyádatí.

To SUPERSCRIBE, زیر نوشتن zír nivishtan.

SUPERSCRIPTION, عنوان 'unván.

To SUPERSEDE (*abolish*) منسوخ کردن mansúkh kardan, نسخ نمودن naskh nimúdan, معدوم ساختن ma'dúm sákhtan, نا بود کردن ná-búd kardan, موکوف کردن maukúf kardan, مبطل گردانیدن mubtal gardánídan.—(*a person*) فائق آمدن fá,ik ámadan, برتری یافتن bartarí yáftan.

SUPERSTITION, وسواس vasvás, ایمان باطل ímán-i-bátil.—(*extra devotion*) تعبد ta'abbud.

SUPERSTITIOUS, وسواسی vasvásí.

SUPERVISION, رویت raviyat.

SUPERVISOR, ناظر názir, کار گذار kár-guzár, سرکار sar-kár, مهتمم muhtamim, مدبر mudabbir.

SUPINE, بیخبر bí-khabar, غافل ghافil, بیپروا bí-parvá, بی احتیاط bí-ihtiyát, بی اندیشه bí-andíshah, کاهل káhil, زاهل záhil.

SUPINELY, با غفلت bá-ghiflat, به اهمال bi-ihmál.

SUPINENESS, غفلت ghiflat, تغافل tagháful, بی پروائی bí-parvá,í, تهاون tahávun, اهمال ihmál, کاهلی káhilí, تساهل tasáhul, مساهلت musáhalat, مسامحت musámahat, مهلت muhlat.

SUPPER, شام shám, عشا 'ashá.—(*the Lord's Supper*) عشا ربانی 'ashá-i-rabbání, قداس kudás.

To SUPPLANT, پا در کف کردن pá dar kaf kardan, زیر پا زدن zír-i-pá zadan.

SUPPLANTER, زیر پا زن zír-i-pá-zan.

SUPPLE, نرم narm.

SUPPLEMENT, ضمیمه zamímah, تتمه tatammah.—(*grammatical term*) لاحق láhik, خاتمه khátamah.

SUPPLEMENTARY, علاوه 'alávah.

SUPPLIANT (*subst.*), دادخواه dád-khwáh, عارض 'áriz.—(*adj.*) نیازمند niyáz-mand, متضرع mutazarri'.

To SUPPLICATE, خواستن khwástan, در خواست نمودن dar-khwást nimúdan, التماس کردن iltimás kardan, تمنا نمودن tamanná nimúdan, نیاز کردن niyáz kardan, دعا کردن du'á kardan, مستدع بودن mustadi' búdan.

SUPPLICATION, نیاز niyáz, تمنا tamanná, التماس iltimás, دعا du'á, آرزو árzú, ابرام ibrám, الجا iljá.—(*to God*) نماز namáz, صلوت salát, دعا du'á.

SUPPLIES (*afforded to troops marching, travellers, &c.*), سیورسات suyúrsát.

To SUPPLY, دادن dádan, آماده کردن ámádah kardan, سر براه کردن sar-bi-ráh kardan.—(*to supply the want of* ...) تلافی عدم ... نمودن taláfí-i-'adam-i- ... nimúdan.

SUPPORT (*prop*), تکیه takyah, پشتی pushtí, ازا izá, عمدت 'umdat.—(*maintenance*) وجه گذران vajh-i-guzrán, مدد معاش madad-i-ma'ásh, روزی rúzí, زندگانی zindagání, گذران guzrán, معیشت ma'íshat.

To SUPPORT, بر داشتن bar-dáshtan, تحمل نمودن tahammul nimúdan, تاب آوردن táb ávardan, کشیدن kashídan.

SUPPORTABLE, متحمل mutahammil.

SUPPORTER, مدد گار madad-gár, مظاهر muzáhir.

SUPPOSABLE, محتمل muhtamal.
SUPPOSE (*for example*), اگر چنانچه agar chunánchih, فرضاً farzan, مثلاً masálan, فرض کن farz kun.
To SUPPOSE, قیاس کردن kiyás kardan, تصور کردن tasavvur kardan, مظنه داشتن mazannah dáshtan, گمان بردن gumán burdan, خیال کردن khiyál kardan, پنداشتن pindáshtan.
SUPPOSITION, تقدیر takdír, گمان gumán, فرض farz, توهم tavahhum.—(*on the supposition*) بخیال bikhiyál, فرضاً farzan.
SUPPOSITIVE, مظنون maznún, قیاسی kiyásí.
To SUPPRESS, وا زدن vá-zadan, مبطل گردانیدن mubtal gardánídan, باطل کردن bátil kardan, ابطال نمودن ibtál nimúdan, نسخ ساختن naskh sákhtan, منسوخ کردن mansúkh kardan, موقوف کردن maukúf kardan.—(*conceal*) نهفتن nihuftan, پوشیدن púshídan, پنهان کردن panhán kardan, نهان کردن nihán kardan, اخفا نمودن ikhfá nimúdan, مخفی ساختن makhfí sákhtan, متواری داشتن mutavárí dáshtan.
SUPPRESSION, تسکین taskín, توقیف taukíf.
SUPPRESSOR, مسکن musakkin.
To SUPPURATE, چرك کردن chirk kardan, ریم جمع نمودن rím jam' nimúdan.
SUPPURATION, چرك chirk, ریم rím.
SUPREMACY, تفوق tafavvuk.
SUPREME, أعلی a'lá, متسلط mutasallit, اعظم a'zam.
SUPREMELY, بسیار bisyár, خیلی khailí.
SURCHARGE, سر بار sar-bár.
To SURCHARGE, سر بار نمودن sar-bár nimúdan.
SURD, اصم asamm.
SURE, یقین yakín, محقق muhakkak, مقرر mukarrar, معین mu'ayyan, مسلم musallam.—(*interj.*) آری árí, البته albattah, بیشك bí-shakk, فی الحقیقت fi-'l-hakíkat.
SURETY (*security*), ضمانت zamánat, کفالت kafálat, گراو giráv.—(*sponsor*) ضامن zámin, کفیل kafíl, متکفل mutakaffil.
SURFACE, رو rú, روی rúy, وجه vajh, صفحه safhah, سطح sath, بشره basharah, بساط basát, کف kaf. —(*plane or level surface*) سطح متسوی sath-i-mutasavví.—(*convex surface*) سطح محدب sath-i-muhaddab. —(*concave surface*) سطح مقعر sath-i-muka''ar, صفحه مجوف safhah-i-mujavvaf.
SURFEIT, امتلا imtilá, شبع shab', شباعت shabá'at, سیری sírí.
To SURFEIT, تخمه شدن tukhmah shudan, سیر شدن sír shudan.
SURGE, موج mauj.
SURGEON, جراح jarráh.
SURGERY, جراحی jarráhí.—(*room*) خسته خانه khastah-khánah.
SURGICAL, جراحی jarráhí.
SURLILY, بسختی bi-sakhtí, بدرشتی bi-durushtí.
SURLINESS, سختی sakhtí, درشتی durushtí.
SURLY, ترش مزاج turush-mizáj, سخت sakht, پفیوز pufyúz, عبوس 'abús.
SURMISE, قیاس kiyás.
To SURMISE, پنداشتن pindáshtan, قیاس کردن kiyás kardan.
To SURMOUNT, برآمدن bar-ámadan, دست یافتن dast yáftan.
SURMOUNTABLE, حل پذیر hall-pazír.
SURNAME (*of relationship*), کنیه kunyah. —(*relating to family, trade, or country*) اسم منسوب ism-i-mansúb.—(*title or nickname*) لقب lakab (*pl.* القاب alkáb).
To SURPASS, رجحان داشتن rajahán dáshtan, سبقت بردن (بر) sibkat burdan (bar), فضیلت داشتن fazílat dáshtan, بهتر بودن bihtar búdan, قصب السبق ربودن kasabu-'s-sibk rubúdan, پیشی یافتن píshí yáftan, پیش دستی نمودن písh-dastí nimúdan, غالب شدن ghálib shudan, فائق بودن fá,ik búdan.
SURPASSING, متجاوز mutajáviz.
SURPLUS, افزونی afzúní, زیادتی ziyádatí, فضله fazlah, بقیه bakíyah, ما باقی má-bákí, تتمه tatammah.

—(*money*) مبلغ افزونی mablagh-i-afzúní.
SURPRISE, آشفتگی áshuftagí, حیرت hairat, تحیر tahayyur, عجب 'ajab, تعجب ta'ajjub, هکر hakar, دهشت dihshat, شش در shish-dar, تلواست talvásat.—(*by surprise*) سراسیمه sarásímah, مضطربانه muztaribánah.
To SURPRISE, تعجب نمودن ta'ajjub nimúdan, حیرت کردن hairat kardan, متعجب نمودن muta'ajjib nimúdan.—(*military term*) بر سر ریختن bar sar ríkhtan.
SURPRISING, *vide* WONDERFUL.
SURRENDER, تسلیم taslím.
To SURRENDER (*yield oneself*), خودرا تسلیم کردن khwudrá taslím kardan, سپر انداختن sipar andákhtan. — (*deliver up*) تسلیم نمودن taslím nimúdan, تفویض کردن tafvíz kardan, حواله نمودن haválah nimúdan, سپردن sipurdan.
To SURROUND, گرد آوردن gird ávardan, محاصره کردن muhásarah kardan, احاطه کردن ihátah kardan, گردش کردن gardish kardan, حاوی بودن háví búdan.
SURROUNDED, منحصر munhasir, مشمول mashmúl. — (*to be surrounded*) محاط شدن muhát shudan.
SURROUNDING, احاطه ihátah.
SURTOUT (*coat*), کلیچه kulíchah, کلیجه kulíjah.
SURVEILLANCE, نگاه nigáh, نگاهداری nigáh-dárí, معاینه mu'áyanah.
SURVEY, مساحت masáhat.
To SURVEY, مساحت نمودن masáhat nimúdan.—(*scan*) نگریستن nigristan, نظر کردن nazar kardan, نگاه کردن nigáh kardan, مشاهده کردن musháhadah kardan.
SURVEYOR, مساحت کن masáhat-kun.
To SURVIVE, ماندن mándan, زنده ماندن zindah mándan.
SURVIVOR, زنده zindah.
SUSCEPTIBLE, قابل kábil.
To SUSPECT, شبهه نمودن shubhah nimúdun, وهم نمودن vahm nimúdan, ظن بردن zann burdan احتمال داشتن ihtimál dáshtan.—(*think*) پنداشتن pindáshtan, گمان بردن gumán burdan.
SUSPECTED, مظنون maznún, متهم muttaham, محتمل muhtamal.
To SUSPEND, آویختن ávíkhtan, بر آویختن bar-ávíkhtan, تعلیق کردن ta'lík kardan, معلق کردن mu'allak kardan.
SUSPENDED, آویزان ávízán, متعلق muta'allik, معلق mu'allak.—(*held in suspense*) معلق mu'allak.
SUSPENSE, دلتنگی dil-tangí, اضطراب iztiráb, غم gham, فکر fikr, تشویش tashvísh.
SUSPENSION, آویزش ávízish.—(*of hostilities*) متارکه mutárakah.
SUSPICION, گمان gumán, شبهه shubhah, شائبه shá,ibah, اشتباه ishtibáh, وهم vahm, توهم tavahhum, ظن zann, مظنه mazannah, شك shakk, ریب raib, اندیشه andíshah, احتمال ihtimál.
SUSPICIOUS, محتمل muhtamal, متشکك mutashakkik, متوهم mutavahhim.
To SUSTAIN, بر داشتن bar-dáshtan, تحمل نمودن tahammul nimúdan, تاب آوردن táb ávardan, کشیدن kashídan.
SUSTENANCE (*food*), قوت kút, خوراك khwurák, طعام ta'ám, غذا ghizá, خورد khwurd, آذوقه ázúkah, مأکول ma,kúl.—(*maintenance*) وجه گذران vajh-i-guzrán, مدد معاش madad-i-ma'ásh, روزی rúzí, زندگانی zindagání, گذران guzrán.
SUZERAIN, متبوع matbú', متبوعه matbú'ah.
SWADDLING CLOTHS (*of a child*), قنداقه kandákah, قماط kimát.
SWAGGER, لاف láf, لاف و گزاف láf u gizáf.
To SWAGGER, لاف زدن láf zadan, قل رفتن kul raftan, گزاف زدن gizáf zadan.
SWALLOW, پرستك parastak, پرستوك parastúk. — (*large black swallow*) ابابیل abábíl.—(*gulp*) قرت kurt.

To SWALLOW, بلعیدن bal'ídan, فرو بردن furú burdan.

SWALLOW-WORT (*plant*), خرگ kharg, اشخر ishkhir, عشر 'ushar.

SWAMP, خلاب khaláb, مشیله mashílah, لجن lajan.

To SWAMP, غرق کردن gharak kardan.

SWAMPED, غریق gharík, مستغرق mustaghrak.

SWAMPY, مشیله ور mashílah-var.

SWAN, قو kau, غو ghau.

SWARM (*of bees, flies, &c.*), خیل khail, جماعت jamá'at, انبوه ambúh.

To SWARM, جمع شدن jam' shudan. —(*abound*) موفور شدن maufúr shudan, کثیر شدن kasír shudan, وافر شدن váfir shudan.

SWARTHY, گندم گون gandum-gún.

SWAY, حکومت hukúmat, حکمرانی hukm-rání, داوری dávarí, فرمانروائی firmán-ravá,í, فرمان گذاری firmán-guzárí, رئاست ri,ásat, تمشیت tamshíyat, عمل 'amal.

To SWAY, حکومت کردن hukúmat kardan, حکمرانی کردن hukm-rání kardan, فرمانروائی کردن firmán-ravá,í kardan, اداره کردن idárah kardan.

To SWEAR, قسم خوردن kasam khwurdan, سوگند خوردن saugand khwurdan, حلف کردن halaf kardan, سوگند یاد نمودن saugand yád nimúdan.—(*to be sworn in*) سوگند یاد کردن saugand yád kardan.

SWEARER, سوگند خور saugand-khwur.

SWEAT, عرق 'arak, خوی khway.

To SWEAT, عرق کردن 'arak kardan.

SWEATY, عرقناک 'arak-nák.

To SWEEP, رفتن ruftan, روفتن rúftan, جاروب کردن já-rúb kardan, رفت و رو کردن ruft u rú kardan.

SWEEPER, روبنده rúbandah, جاروب کش já-rúb-kash.

SWEEPINGS, خاکروبه khák-rúbah, خس khas, خاشاک kháshák, اشکال ashkál.

SWEET, شیرین shírín, خوش khwush, نوشین núshín, لذیذ lazíz, حلو halv. —(*water*) گوار guvár, گوارا guvárá

SWEETBRIAR, نسرین nasrín.

To SWEETEN, شیرین کردن shírín kardan.

SWEETENED, مقند mukannad, شیرین shírín.

SWEETHEART (*mistress*), معشوقه ma'shúkah, محبوبه mahbúbah, نگار nigár, شاهد sháhid, جانی jání.

SWEETMEATS, مربا murabbá, شیرینی shíríní.

SWEETNESS, شیرینی shíríní, حلاوت halávat. —(*freshness*), صفائی safá'í, طراوت taravat.

SWELL (*fop*), کج کلاه kaj-kuláh, قشنگ kashang.

To SWELL, آماسیدن ámásídan, آماس کردن ámás kardan, ورم کردن varam kardan, باد کردن bád kardan, لك شدن luk shudan (*vulg.*).

SWELLING, آماس ámás, ورم varam, باد bád, لك luk (*vulg.*).

To SWERVE, آواره شدن ávárah shudan, ترك کردن tark kardan, گذاشتن guzáshtan, کنار رفتن kanár raftan.

SWIFT, چابك chábuk, چست chust, تند tund, تیز tíz, جلد jald, زود zúd, سریع sarí', باد پا bád-pá.

SWIFTNESS, چابکی chábukí, چستی chustí, تندی tundí, تیزی tízí, جلدی jaldí, زودی zúdí, سرعت sur'at, چالاکی chálákí.

To SWIM, شنا کردن shiná kardan, شناویدن shinávídan.

SWIMMER, شناور shinávar, سباح sabbáh.

SWIMMING, شناوری shinávarí, سباحت sibáhat. —(*dress*) اسباب شناوری asbáb-i-shinávarí. —(*swimming in the head*) دوران سر daurán-i-sar.

To SWINDLE, فریفتن firíftan, فریب دادن firíb-dádan, گول خورانیدن gúl khwuránídan, گول زدن gúl zadan, غدر نمودن ghadar nimúdan, حیله کردن hílah kardan.

SWINDLER, فریبنده firíbandah, دستکج dast-kaj, غدار ghaddár, سر همبند sar-ham-band, حیله باز hílah-báz, دولاب باز dúláb-báz, دولابی dúlábí.

SWINE, خوگ khúg, خنزیر khinzír.

SWING (*of ropes*), باد خور bád-khwur, چنبلول chambalúl, چنچولی chanjúlí, اورک avarak.

To SWING (*hang loose*), آویختن ávíkhtan, آویزان بودن ávízán búdan, معلق بودن mu'allak búdan, فرو هشتن furú hishtan.—(*put in motion*) جنبانیدن jumbánídan, تکانیدن takánídan, تکان دادن takán dádan.—(*game*) اورک خوردن avarak khwurdan.

SWITCH, قمچی kamchí.

SWIVEL (*ring turning on a staple*), حلقۀ گردان halkah-i-gardán.—(*gun*) زنبورک zambúrak.

SWOLLEN, باد دار bád-dár, منتفخ muntafikh, لك luk (*vulg.*).

SWOON, بی هوشی bí-húshí, غش ghash, ضعف za'f.

To SWOON, غش کردن ghash kardan, بیهوش شدن bi-húsh shudan, غش شدن ghash shudan.

SWOOP, قبض kabz.

To SWOOP, ربودن rubúdan, قبض کردن kabz kardan, کپیدن kapídan (*vulg.*).

SWORD, شمشیر shimshír, تیغ tígh, سیف saif, پلارک pulárak.—(*black watered sword of Khurásán*) قره خراسانی karah-khurásání.—(*straight sword or tuck*) قداره kaddárah, کتاره kattárah.—(*blade of a sword*) تیغه tíghah.—(*water or temper of a sword*) جوهر jauhar, آب áb.—(*edge*) دم dam.—(*point*) سر sar, نوك nauk, نیش nísh.—(*hilt*) قبضه kabzah.—(*cross-guard*) برچاخ burchákh, برچك burchak.—(*pommel or knob*) کلاه kuláh.—(*sheath*) غلاف ghiláf, میان miyán, نیام niyám.—(*ferrule with ring*) قرباغه kurbághah, ور بند var-band, بند band.—(*end ferrule or chape*) ته غلاف tah-i-ghiláf.—(*belt, going round the waist*) بند شمشیر band-i-shimshír.—(*belt, crossing the shoulder*) حمایل hamáíl.—(*short, straight, broad-bladed sword or cutlas*) قمه kammah.—(*light sword with narrow curved blade*) قمچی kamchí.—(*small sword*) شمشیر قداره shimshír-i-kaddárah.—(*to take with the edge of the sword*) بزور شمشیر گرفتن bi-zúr-i-shimshír giriftan.

SWORDSMAN, شمشیر باز shimshír-báz.—(*sword-cutler*) شمشیر گر shimshír-gar.

SYCAMORE, جمیز jummaiz, توت انجیر tút-anjír, چنار chanár.

SYCOPHANCY, چاپلوسی cháplúsí, نوازش navázish, ریشخندی ríshkhandí.

SYCOPHANT, طفیلی tufailí, مداح maddáh, مفت خور muft-khwur.

SYLLABLE, هجا hijá, جز کلمه juz-i-kalimah, هجی hijí.

SYLLABUS, مجمل mujmal, موجز mújaz, مجموعه majmú'ah, وجیز vajíz.

SYLLOGISM, قیاس kiyás.

SYLVAN, جنگلی jangalí, پر درخت pur-dirakht.

SYMBOL, علامت 'alámat, نشان nishán.

SYMBOLICAL, باشاره bi-ashárah, با رمز bá-ramz.

To SYMBOLIZE, اشاره نمودن ishárah nimúdan, دلالت کردن dalálat kardan, علامت بودن 'alámat búdan.

SYMMETRICAL, معتدل mu'tadil, باندازه ba-andázah, هم میزان ham-mízán.

SYMMETRY, اعتدال i'tidál.

SYMPATHETIC, مشفق mushfik, مهربان mihrbán.

To SYMPATHISE with, همدرد بودن ham-dard búdan, با رقت دیدن bá-rikkat dídan.

SYMPATHY, رقت rikkat, همدردی ham-dardí.

SYMPTOM, اثر asar, علامت 'alámat.

SYNAGOGUE (*Jewish*), مجمع یهود majma'-i-yahúd.

SYNCOPE (*in grammar*), حذف hazf.—(*faint*) بی هوشی bí-húshí, غش ghash, ضعف za'f.

SYNDIC, مفتش mufattish.

SYNDICATE, شرکت صرافی shirkat-i-sarráfí.

SYNOD, سنود sanúd (*eur.*).

SYNONYM, لفظ مترادف lafz-i-mutarádif.

SYNONYMOUS, يكمعنى yak-ma'ní, هم معنى ham-ma'ní, مترادف mutarádif, مرادف murádif, مشترك المعنى mushtaraku-'l-ma'ná.

SYNOPSIS, اجمال ijmál.

SYNTAX, نحو nahv.

SYPHILIS, كوفت kúft, قروحات شهديه kurúhát-i-shahdíyah, مرض خبيث marz-i-khabís.

SYPHON, انبوب ambúb, قصابه kasábah.

SYRINGE, آب دزدك áb-duzdak, حقنه huknah. — (*medical*) دستور dastúr, اماله imálah, حقنه huknah.

SYRUP, رب rubb, شيره shírah.

SYSTEM, *vide* CUSTOM, MANNER, INSTITUTIONS.— (*to reduce to a system*) رابط نمودن rábit nimúdan.

SYSTEMATIC *or* SYSTEMATICALLY, مترتب mutarattib.

T.

TABERNACLE, خيمه khaimah.

TABLE, ميز míz, خوان khwán.

TABLE-CLOTH, سفره sufrah, سماط sumát. [These answer the purposes of table-cloths at meals, but are spread upon the floor, tables being unknown in Persian houses.]

TABLE-CUT (*flat, polished, as a jewel*) مسطح musattah, تخته takhtah.

TABLE D'HOTE, مشربه mashrabah. [This signifies "a place where people meet to drink." There is no precise equivalent in Persian for Table d'hôte.]

TABLET, لوح lauh, تخته takhtah.

TACIT, خاموش khámúsh, با سكوت básukút.

TACITLY, خاموشانه khámúshánah.

TACITURN, ساكت sákit, خاموش khámúsh, صامت sámit.

TACITURNITY, سكوت sukút, خاموشى khámúshí, صمت samt.

To TACK (*as a ship*), آمد شد نمودن ámad-shud nimúdan, عبور كردن 'ubúr kardan.

TACKLE, اسباب asbáb.

TACTICS, تدابير حربيه tadábír-i-harbíyah.

TADPOLE, بچه غوك bachah-i-ghúk, بچه قورباقه bachah-i-kurbákah.

TAFFETAS, مخمل makhmal.

TAIL, دم dum, ذنب zanab, دنبال dumbál.—(*an ox or horse's tail used as a standard, an insignia of rank among the Turks*) توغ túgh, پرچم parcham, غزغاو ghazhaghav, كتاس kitás.

TAILOR, خياط khayyát.

TAINT, شائبه shá,ibah.

To TAINT, رنگ كردن rang kardan, رنگ دادن rang dádan, آلودن álúdan, ملوث ساختن mulavvas sákhtan.

TAINTED, پوسيده púsídah, گنديده gandídah, گنده gandah.

TAINTLESS, بى شائبه bí-shá,ibah.

To TAKE, گرفتن giriftan, ستادن sitádan, اخذ كردن akhz kardan, كپيدن kapídan (*vulg.*).—(*receive*) پذيرفتن pazíruftan, قبول كردن kabúl kardan.—(*away, deprive of*) سلب كردن salab kardan, بر داشتن bar-dáshtan, بردن burdan, محروم ساختن mahrúm sákhtan.—(*care of*) متوجه بودن mutavajjih búdan, پرستارى كردن parastárí kardan, نگاهبانى كردن nigáhbání kardan, نگه داشتن nigah dáshtan.—(*away, remove*) بر داشتن bar-dáshtan, رفع نمودن raf' nimúdan, بردن burdan.—(*off*) بر كندن bar-kandan, بر آوردن bar-ávardan, خلع نمودن khal' nimúdan.—(*a fort, city, &c.*) تسخير كردن taskhír kardan, مسخر گردانيدن musakhkhar gardánídan, فتح نمودن fath nimúdan.—(*convey or conduct*) بردن burdan, بر داشتن bar-dáshtan,

کشیدن kashídan, راه نمودن ráh nimúdan. — (*captive*) اسیر گرفتن asír giriftan, گرفتار کردن giriftár kardan, دیل کردن díl kardan (*vulg.*). — (*back*) پس گرفتن pas giriftan, باز گرفتن báz giriftan.—(*medicine*) خوردن khwurdan.—(*in hand*) بر عهده گرفتن bar 'uhdah giriftan.—(*upon oneself*) به ذمت خود گرفتن bi-zimmat-i-khwud giriftan.—(*up*) بر داشتن bar-dáshtan, بلند ساختن buland sákhtan. —(*to be taken for* ...) پنداشته ... شدن ... pindáshtah shudan.

TAKE CARE! هان hán, هین hín, با هوش باش bá-húsh básh, خبر دار باش khabar-dár básh, حذر کن hazar kun, ده dah.—(*clear the way!*) سر حساب sar hisáb, راه بده ráh bi-dih, برو کنار bi-rau kanár, طرقو tarrakú.

TALC (*mica*), ابرق abrak.

TALE, قصه kissah, نقل nakl, حکایت hikáyat, داستان dástán, افسانه afsánah.

TALE-BEARER, سخن چین sukhun-chín, نمام nammám.

TALENT, عقل 'akl, فراست firásat, ادراك idrák, ذهن zihn, زکاوت zakávat, زرنگی zaringí.

TALISMAN, طلسم tilism.

TALK (*report, news*), سخن sukhun, خبر khabar, گپ gap (*hind.*).—(*there is a talk of*) سخن از ... است sukhun az ... ast.—(*mere talk*) محض صحبت mahz-i-suhbat.—(*foolish talk*) چرند charand.—لیچار líchár, جفنگ jafang. —(*small-talk*) صحبت suhbat.

To TALK, گفتن guftan, سخن راندن sukhun rándan, حرف زدن harf zadan.—(*to talk to oneself*) خود بخود حرف زدن khwud bi-khwud haraf zadan. — (*to talk over*) بگفتگوی پرداختن bi-guftagúí pardákhtan.

TALKATIVE, پر گو pur-gú, حرف مفت زن harf-i-muft-zan.

TALKATIVENESS, پر گوی pur-gúí, فضولی fuzúlí.

TALKER, متکلم mutakallim, سخن گو sukhun-gú.

TALL, بلند buland, طویل tavíl, کشیده kashídah, دراز diráz.

TALLOW, پی pí, پیه píh.

TALLOWY, چرب charb.

To TALLY with, مطابق شدن mutábik shudan.

TALMUD, تلمود talmúd.

TALON, چنگ chang, چنگل changal, چنگال changál, مخلب mikhlab, پنجه panjah, ناخن nákhun.

TAMARIND, تمر هندی tamar-i-hindí.

TAMARISK, گز gaz.

TAMBOURINE, دائره dá,irah, دمامه damámah.

TAME, رام rám, انسی unsí, دست آموز dast-ámúz.

To TAME, رام نمودن rám nimúdan, دست آموز کردن dast-ámúz kardan.

TAMELY, رامانه rámánah.

TAMENESS, رامی rámí, انس uns.

To TAMPER with, سازش کردن sázish kardan, تعلیم دادن ta'lím dádan, آموختن ámúkhtan. — (*meddle officiously*) فضولی کردن fuzúlí kardan.—(*garble or alter documents*) تحریف کردن tahríf kardan.

To TAN, دباغی کردن dabbághí kardan.

TANGENT, خط ملاقی khatt-i-mulákí, مماس mumáss.

TANGIBLE, مجسم mujassam.

To TANGLE, پیچانیدن píchánídan.

TANGLED, پیچیده píchídah, بر هم زده bar-ham-zadah, در هم dar-ham, ژولیده zhúlídah.

TANK, حوض hauz.—(*reservoir*) آب انبار áb-ambár.—(*large tank or pond*) دریاچه daryáchah, تالاب táláb (*hind.*).

TANNED, مدبوغ madbúgh.

TANNER, دباغ dabbágh.

TANNERY, دباغ خانه dabbágh-khánah.

TAN-PIT, مدبغه madbaghah.

To TANTALIZE, محروم کردن mahrúm kardan, نومید ساختن naumíd sákhtan.

TANTAMOUNT, برابر barábar.

TAP, دهن شیر dahan-i-shír.
TAPE, فیط fít, بافته báftah, پهنک pahnak.—(*red-tape, officiousness*) رسم دولتی rasm-i-daulatí.
TAPER, شمع sham', بال bál.
TAPERING, قلمی kalamí, گاو دم gáv-dum.
TAPESTRY, پرده منقش pardah-i-munakkash, قلابدوزی kulláb-dúzí, نقده دوزی nakdah-dúzí, لندره دوزی landarah-dúzí, بوته bútah, فرش صورتی farsh-i-súratí.
TAPIS, بساط bisát.—(*to come on the tapis*) بمیان آمدن bi-miyán ámadan.
TAR, قطران kitrán, قیر kír.
TARANTULA (*spider*), رتیل rutail, شتر زن shutur-zan.
TARDILY, بدرنگ bi-dirang.
TARDINESS, درنگ dirang, دیری dírí, سستی sustí.
TARDY, کاهل káhil, سست sust.
TARES, گندم دیوانه gandum-i-díványah, کاکلک kákulak.
TARGET, هدف hadaf, نشانه nishánah.
TARIFF, نرخ narkh.
To TARNISH, تیره کردن tírah kardan, بی جلا کردن bí-jalá kardan.
TARRAGON, ترخان tarkhán.
To TARRY, ماندن mándan, وا ماندن vá-mándan, پس ماندن pas-mándan.
TART (*slightly sour*), دبش dibash, تیزک tízak, ترش turush.
TARTAR, تاتار tátár, تتار tatár.
TARTLY, بتیزی bi-tízí.
TARTNESS, ترشی turushí, تیزکی tízakí.
TASK, کار معین kár-i-mu'ayyan, کار مقرری kár-i-mukarrarí, شغل shughl. — (*of a scholar*) سبق sabak, درس dars.
TASSEL, منگله mangulah, منگوله mangúlah, شرابه sharrábah.
TASTE (*flavour*), مزه mazah, طعم ta'm, ذوق zauk. — (*power of tasting*) ذائقه zá,ikah, قوت ذائقه kúvat-i-zá,ikah. — (*fancy, tastefulness*) سلیقه salíkah.—(*in good taste*) با ذوق bá-zauk. — (*after-taste*), مزه mazah, چاشنی cháshní.
— (*to have good taste*) سلیقه داشتن salíkah dáshtan.
To TASTE, چشیدن chashídan, ذائقه کردن zá,ikah kardan, مزه گرفتن mazah giriftan, طعم دیدن ta'm dídan, مزیدن mazídan.—(*have a relish of*) مزه داشتن mazah dáshtan. — (*to taste nice*) مزه دادن mazah dádan.
TASTEFUL, با سلیقه bá-salíkah.
TASTELESS, بیمزه bí-mazah.
TASTER (*to a prince*), چاشنیگیر cháshní-gír. [This is one who tastes victuals as a security against poison.]
TATTER, پینه pínah, لته lattah, پاره párah, رقعه ruk'ah.
To TATTER, دریدن darídan, پاره کردن párah kardan, چاک کردن chák kardan.
TATTLE, قیل و قال kíl u kál, گپ gap (*hind.*), حرف مفت harf-i-muft.
TATTLER, تفتاف taftáf, حراف harráf.
TATTOO (*marking the skin*), خال khál, دق dakk.—(*military term*), نوبت طبل naubat-i-tabl.
To TATTOO, خال کوفتن khál kúftan.
TAUNT, طعنه ta'nah, طنز tanz, زجر zajr.
To TAUNT, طعنه زدن ta'nah zadan.
TAUNTINGLY, طاعنانه tá,inánah.
TAURUS, *vide* ZODIAC.
TAUTOLOGICAL, پر تکرار pur-takrár.
TAUTOLOGY, تکریر سخن takrír-i-sukhun, حشو قبیح hashv-i-kabíh, تکرار لفظ takrár-i-lafz.
TAVERN, میخانه mai-khánah, شرابخانه sharáb-khánah, میکده mai-kadah, شیره خانه shírah-khánah (*vulg.*).
TAVERN-KEEPER, میخانه چی mai-khánah-chí.
TAWDRILY, مزخرفانه muzakhrafánah.
TAWDRINESS, مزخرفیت muzakhrafíyat.
TAWDRY, مزخرف muzakhraf.
TAWNY, گندم گون gandum-gún.
TAX, باج báj, خراج khiráj, محصول mahsúl, عشور 'ushúr, مال دیوانی mál-i-díváni, تکلیف taklíf, تعمیر

ta'mír.—(*on land*) مالیات máliyát, خراج زمین khiráj-i-zamín.—(*tithe*) ده یك dih-yak, عشر 'ushr (*pl.* عشور 'ushúr). — (*poll-tax*) جزیه jizyah, سر شماری sar-shimárí.—(*house-tax*) خانه شماری khánah-shimárí.—(*on professions, trades*) محترفه muhtarifah.—(*on cattle*) شاخ شماری shákh-shimárí.—(*irregular or emergent*) صادرات sádirát, صادر عوارض sádir-'aváriz. — (*presents to the Crown on New Year's Day*) پیشکش písh-kash.—(*duty on goods, &c., imported*) گمرك gumruk, محصول mahsúl, باج báj, عشور 'ushúr.—(*tax gatherer*) باجگیر báj-gír, گمرکچی gumruk-chí, محصل muhassil, مستوفی mustaufí.—(*chief collector of Customs and taxes*) گمرکچی باشی gumruk-chí-báshí.—(*office or house where taxes are paid*) گمرك خانه gumruk-khánah, باجگاه báj-gáh.

To TAX, بخرج بردن bi-kharj burdan. —(*to collect taxes*) تحصیل مالیات کردن tahsíl-i-máliyát kardan, عوارضرا گرفتن 'avárizrá giriftan.—(*to impose a tax*) اجرای بر قرار کردن ijráí bar-karár kardan.

TAXABLE, قابل محصول kábil-i-mahsúl.

TAXATION, عشور 'ushúr, خراج khiráj.

TEA, چای cháy, چاهی cháhí.—(*tea-urn*) سماور samávar (*eur.*)—(*tea-caddy*) چایدان cháy-dán.—(*teapot*) چایپز cháy-paz, قوری kúrí, پچ puch (*vulg.*)—(*tea-cup*) فنجان finján.—(*large tea-cup*) کاسه kásah. —(*black tea*) قره چای karah-cháy. —(*green tea*) چای سبز cháy-i-sabz. —(*Pekoe tea*) چای آقپر cháy-i-ákpar.—(*to take tea*) صرف چای نمودن sarf-i-cháy nimúdan, چای خوردن cháy khwurdan. — (*tea-things*) اسباب چای خوری asbáb-i-cháy-khwurí.

To TEACH, آموختن ámúkhtan, تعلیم دادن ta'lím dádan, یاد دادن yád dádan, درس دادن dars dádan.

TEACHABLE, قابل تعلیم kábil-i-ta'lím.

TEACHER, معلم mu'allim, آخوند ákhwund, آخون ákhwun, ملا مکتبی mullá-i-maktabí.

TEAK (*tree*), ساج sáj, ساگوان ság-ván.

TEAR, اشك ashk, سرشك sirishk, آب سیاه áb-i-siyáh, آب چشم áb-i-chashm, دمعه dam'ah.—(*flood of tears*) سیل اشك sail-i-ashk.—(*to shed tears*) گریستن giristan, گریه کردن giryah kardan, گریان کردن giryán kardan. — (*rent*) چاك chák, شق shakk.

To TEAR, دریدن darídan, پاره کردن párah kardan, چاك کردن chák kardan.

TEARFUL, اشکبار ashk-bár.

TEARLESS, بی اشك bí-ashk.

To TEASE, سر بسر گذاشتن sar-bi-sar guzáshtan, رنجانیدن ranjánídan, آزار رسانیدن ázár rasánídan, تصدیع دادن tasdí' dádan.

TEAT, سر پستان sar-i-pistán, ضرع zir'.

TECHNICAL, مخصوص بحکمت makhsús bi-hikmat. — (*technical terms*) اصطلاحات مخصوصه istiláhát-i-makhsúsah.

TECHNICALITY, اصطلاح istiláh.

TEDIOUS, طویل tavíl, مفصل mufassal, بی مزه bí-mazah.

TEDIOUSLY, علی التفصیل 'ala-'t-tafsíl, تفصیلا tafsílan, علی الطویل 'ala-'t-tavíl.

TEDIOUSNESS, تفصیل tafsíl, اطناب itnáb, تطویل tatvíl, درازی dirází.

To TEEM, پر بودن pur búdan.

TEETH, دندانها dandánahá, اسنان asnán. — (*back teeth, grinders*) ضرس zars (*pl.* ضروس zurús *or* اضراس azrás).

TELEGRAM, تلگرافنامه talagráf-námah (*eur.*), تلغرافنامه talaghráf-námah (*eur.*). — (*to send a telegram*) تلغراف کردن talaghráf kardan.

TELEGRAPH, تلگراف talagráf (*eur.*), تلغراف talaghráf (*eur.*). — (*on posts*) تلگراف هوائی talagráf-i-havá,í. — (*clerk*) نفر تلگرافچی nafar-i-talagráf-chí. — (*instrument*) دست گاه dast-gáh.—(*line of telegraph*) خط تلغراف khatt-i-talaghráf.—(*wire*) سیم sím.

TELEGRAPHIST, تلگرافچی talagráf-chí.

TELEPHONE, تلفون talfún. (*eur.*), تلیفون talífún (*eur.*).

TELESCOPE, دور بین dúr-bín.

To TELL, گفتن guftan, خبر کردن khabar kardan, اطلاع دادن ittilá' dádan, منتقل گردانیدن muntakil gardánídan.

TELLER, گویندہ gúyandah.

TELL-TALE, نمام nammám, ساعی sá'í.

TEMERITY, جسارت jasárat, تهور ta-havvur, گستاخی gustákhí.

TEMPER, *or* TEMPERAMENT, خو khú, خوی khúy, مزاج mizáj, خصلت khas-lat, طبع tab', طبیعت tabí'at, نهاد nihád, سیرت sírat, سرشت sirisht, طینت tínat.—(*of steel*) آب áb, گهر guhar, جوهر jauhar.—(*in good temper*) خوش مزاج khwush-mizáj, سر دماغ sar-i-dimágh. — (*out of temper*) کج خلق kaj-khulk. — (*good tempered*) شیرین مزاج shírín-mizáj.—(*bad tempered*) بد مزاج bad-mizáj.

To TEMPER, اعتدال دادن i'tidál dádan, ممزوج ساختن mamzúj sákh-tan.

TEMPERANCE, اعتدال i'tidál, پرهیز parhíz, پرهیز گاری parhíz-gárí, ریاضت riyázat.

TEMPERATE, معتدل mu'tadil.—(*per-sons*) پرهیز گار parhíz-gár.

TEMPERATURE, درجه هوا darajah-i-havá.

TEMPEST, طوفان túfán, باد تند bád-i-tund, باد شدید bád-i-shadíd.

TEMPESTUOUS, طوفانی túfání, پر باد pur-bád.

TEMPLE, هیکل haikal, عبادتگاه 'ibádat-gáh, معبد ma'bad.—(*idol temple*) بتکده but-kadah, بتخانه but-khánah. — (*Muhammadan mosque*) مسجد masjid, نماز گاه na-máz-gáh, مشکو mashkú.—(*Chris-tian church*) کلیسیا kalísiyá, کنیسه kanísah. — (*fire temple*) آتشکده átish-kadah, کنشت kunisht.—(*of Makkah*) بیت الله baitu-'llah, مشعر mash'ar, بیت الحرام baitu-'l-harám, قبله kiblah. — (*square building in the temple of Makkah*) کعبه ka'bah.—(*of the forehead*) شقیقه shakíkah, صدغین sudghain.

TEMPORAL, دنیوی dunyaví, زمانی zamání.

TEMPORALLY, بطور دنیاوی bi-taur-i-dunyáví.

TEMPORARILY, موقتاً muvakkatan.

TEMPORARY, موقت muvakkat.

To TEMPORIZE, وقت گذراندن vakt guzrándan, وقت بوقت کردن vakt bi-vakt kardan.

To TEMPT, امتحان نمودن imtihán nimúdan, اغوا نمودن ighvá nimú-dan, ور غلانیدن var-ghalánídan, ترغیب کردن targhíb kardan, آزمایش نمودن ázmáyish nimúdan, مفتون ساختن maftún sákhtan.

TEMPTATION, آزمایش ázmáyish, امتحان imtihán, اغوا ighvá, ترغیب targhíb.—(*of the devil*) وسوسه vasvasah.

TEMPTER, مغوی mughví, وسواس vas-vás, امتحان کننده imtihán-kunan-dah, ممتحن mumtahin.

TENABLE, صاف sáf, قابل گرفت kábil-i-girift.

TENACIOUS (*grasping*), طمعکار ta-ma'-kár. — (*adhesive*) چسبنده chasbandah.

TENANT, مستاجر mustájir, اجاره دار ijárah-dár, ساکن sákin.

TENANTABLE, لائق آباد lá,ik-i-ábád.

To TEND (*incline towards*), مائل بودن má,il búdan, میل داشتن mail dáshtan.—(*the sick*) پرستاری کردن parastárí kardan, تیمار کردن tímár kardan.—(*flocks, &c.*) رعایت کردن ri'áyat kardan, چوپانی کردن chau-pání kardan, چرانیدن charánídan. —(*lead to*) کشیدن kashídan, مائل بودن má,il búdan, مودی بودن mu,addí búdan, مبلغ بودن mu-balligh búdan.

TENDENCY, میل mail, میلان mailán, توجه tavajjuh.

TENDER (*soft*), نازک názuk, ملایم muláyam, نرم narm. — (*gentle*)

مشفق mushfik, مهربان mihr-bán.—(*legal tender*) حق شرعی hakk-i-shar'í.

To TENDER, پیش آوردن písh ávardan, تقدیم کردن takdím kardan, تقریب نمودن takríb nimúdan.

TENDERLY, آهسته áhistah, با شفقت bá-shafakat.

TENDERNESS (*softness*), نازکی názukí, ملایمت muláyamat, نرمی narmí.—(*gentleness*) شفقت shafakat, مهربانی mihr-bání.—(*of years*) صغر sighar.

TENDON, پی pay, عصب 'asab (*pl.* اعصاب a'sáb), وتر vatar (*pl.* اوتار autár).

TENDRIL, ریشه ríshah.

TENET, عقیده 'akídah.

TENFOLD, ده چند dah-chand, ده چندان dah-chandán, ده تا dah-tá.

TENOR, قرار karár, مضمون mazmún.

TENSE (*in grammar*), حالت hálat, صیغه síghah.—(*future tense*) زمان مستقبل zamán-i-mustakbil.—(*imperfect*) ماضی استمراری mází-i-istimrárí. —(*past*) ماضی mází, ماضی مطلق mází-i-mutlak.—(*pluperfect*) ماضی بعید mází-i-ba'íd.—(*present*) زمان حال zamán-i-hál.

TENSION, امتداد imtidád.

TENT, خیمه khaimah, چادر chádar, خرگاه khargáh.—(*flat-roofed tent*) چادر مسطح chádar-i-musattah.—(*peak-roofed tent*) چادر چلندری chádar-i-chalandarí, خیمه قلندری khaimah-i-kalandarí.—(*wall of curtains surrounding a tent*) سراپرده sar-á-pardah.—(*tents packed up, &c. on a journey*) بارخانه bár-khánah, بنه bunah.—(*tent-pitcher*) فراش farrásh.—(*tent-rope*) رسن خیمه rasan-i-khaimah, طناب tanáb.—(*wall of tent*) اتك atak, تجیر tijír.—(*fly of tent*) طاق خیمه ták-i-khaimah, سقف خیمه sakf-i-khaimah, قلندری kalandarí. —(*door of tent*) رواق ravák, در خیمه dar-i-khaimah.—(*tent-pole*) دیرك dírak, چوب chúb, ستون sutún, عمود 'amúd.—(*tent-peg*) میخ míkh, وتد vatad.—(*sack for packing a tent in*) جوال juvál, شلیطه shalítah.—(*loops of the tent*) مادگی mádagí.—(*circular piece of wood at the upper end of the tent-pole, upon which the fly rests*) کماچ kumách, کماج kumáj.—(*tent of camel or goat's hair*) خبا khibá, چادر سیاه chádar-i-siyáh.—(*small tent*) آفتاب گردان áftáb-gardán, چادرك chádarak.

TENTH, ده یك dah-yak.—(*tenth part*) عشر 'ushr.

TENUITY, باریکی báríkí, نزاری nizárí, نازکی názukí.

TENUOUS, نازك názuk, تنگ tang, رکیك rakík, باریك bárík, نزار nizár.

TENURE, مستمسك mustamsak.

TEPID, شیر گرم shír-garm, نیم گرم ním-garm, ملول malúl.

TEPIDNESS, نیم گرمی ním-garmí.

TERM (*appellation*), نام nám, اسم ism (*pl.* اسامی asámí *or* اسما asmá).—(*condition, stipulation*) شرط shart, عهد 'ahd, وعده va'dah, قرار karár.—(*space of time*) مدت muddat, عرضه 'arzah, مهلت muhlat.—(*phrase*) اصطلاح istiláh, طرز کلام tarz-i-kalám, ضرب مثل zarb-i-masal.

To TERM, نامیدن námídan, نام گذاردن nám guzárdan, نام دادن nám-dádan, مسمی نمودن musammá nimúdan.

TERMAGANT, زنکه zanakah.

TERMINABLE, متناهی mutanáhí, آخر شدنی ákhir-shudaní.

To TERMINATE (*finish*), تمام کردن tamám kardan, باخر رسانیدن bi-ákhir rasánídan, پرداختن pardákhtan, انجام کردن anjám kardan. (*end in*) تمام شدن (به) tamám shudan (bi).

TERMINATED, متناهی mutanáhí, منقرض munkariz, منتهی muntahá.

TERMINATION, آخر ákhir, آخرت ákhirat, عاقبت 'ákibat, اتمام itmám, تمام tamám, تتمه tatammah, سر sar, انجام anjám, نهایت niháyat.

TERMINUS, گار gár (*eur.*), سر راه آهن sar-i-ráh-i-áhan.

Terrace (*before a house*), سکو sakkú, مرتبه martabah. — (*flat roof of a house*) بان bán, بام bám, پشت بام pusht-i-bám.

Terrestrial, زمینی zamíní, ارضی arzí.

Terrible, هولناك haul-nák, هائل há,il, مهیل mahíl, مخوف mukhavvif, سهمناك sahm-nák, ترسناك tars-nák, مرهوب marhúb, مهیب muhíb, خطر ناك khatar-nák, سهمکین sahm-kín.

Terribly, بسیار bisyár, نهایت niháyat, خیلی khailí.

Terrific, هولناك haul-nák, ترسناك tars-nák, مخوف mukhavvif, هائل há,il, مهیب muhíb.

To Terrify, ترسانیدن tarsánídan, تهدید کردن tahdíd kardan.

Territorial, ملکی mulkí, بلدی baladí.

Territory, ملك mulk, ولایت valáyat, کشور kishvar, خطه khuttah, بلد balad, بلاد bilád, دیار diyár, اقلیم iklím, الکه ulkah, یورت yúrt, مرز و بوم marz u búm.

Terror, ترس tars, بیم bím, باك bák, دهشت dihshat, هول haul, هراس hirás, خوف khauf, ستوه sutúh, وحشت vahshat, نهیب nihíb, خشیت khashyat, هیبت haibat, مهابت mahábat.—(*object of terror*) مخافه makháfah.

Terse, مختصر mukhtasar, مجمل mujmal, وجیز vajíz.

Tertian, مثلثی musallasí.

Test (*touchstone*), محك mihakk, عیار 'iyár, معیار mi'yár.—(*trial*) امتحان imtihán, آزمایش ázmáyish, تجربه tajribah.

To Test, آزمودن ázmúdan, محك زدن mihakk zadan.

Testament (*will*), وصیت vasíyat, وثیقه vasíkah.—(*Old Testament*) عهد عتیق 'ahd-i-'atík, پیمان قدیم paimán-i-kadím. — (*Pentateuch*) توریت taurát.—(*New Testament*) عهد جدید 'ahd-i-jadíd, پیمان تازه paimán-i-tázah.—(*Gospel*) انجیل injíl.

Testamentary, شهادتی shahádatí.

Testate, وصیت دار vasíyat-dár, موصی músí.

Testator (*to a will, &c.*), موصی músí *or* muvassí.

Testatrix, موصیه musíyah *or* muvassíyah.

Testicle, خایه kháyah, خصیه khusyah, تخم tukhm, بیضه baizah.

Testified, مشهود mash-húd.

Testifier, گواه guváh, شاهد sháhid.

To Testify, شهادت دادن shahádat dádan.

Testimonial, شهادتنامه shahádat-námah.

Testimony, شهادت shahádat, گواهی guváhí.

Testy, محرور المزاج mahrúru-'l-mizáj.

Tête-à-tête, سر بسر sar-bi-sar, رو برو rú-bi-rú.

Tether, پالهنگ pá-lahang *or* pál-hang, شکال shikál.

Tetragon, چار گوشه chár-gúshah, مربع murabba'.

Tetrarch, بیگلر بیگ beglar-beg, بگلر بگ baglar-bag, والی válí, حاکم hákim.

Text (*of a book*) متن matan.—(*single verse*) آیت áyat.—(*religious term*) نص nass.

Texture (*of cloth, &c.*), بافته báftah, نساجه nasájah.

Than, از az, ز zi, من min, تا tá.

To Thank, اظهار رضامندی کردن izhár-i-razá-mandí kardan, تشکر کردن tashakkur kardan.—(*thank you*) لطف شما زیاد lutf-i-shumá ziyád, التفات شما زیاد iltifát-i-shumá ziyád, از لطف شما az lutf-i-shumá, از شفقت شما az shafakat-i-shumá, مرهون منت ساختید marhún-i-minnat sákhtíd.

Thankful, شاکر shákir, شکور shakúr, شکر گذار shukr-guzár, حق شناس hakk-shinás.

Thankfulness, شکر گذاری shukr-guzárí, حق شناسی hakk-shinásí.

Thankless, نا سپاس ná-sipás, نا حق شناس ná-hakk-shinás, کافر نعمت káfir-i-ni'mat, نا شکور ná-shakúr.

Thanks, شکر shukr, شکران shukrán,

ستایش sitáyish, نیایش niyáyish.—(*to give thanks*) تشکر کردن tashakkur kardan, شکرگذاری کردن shukr-guzárí kardan.

THANKSGIVING, شکر shukr, شکران shúkrán, ستایش sitáyish, نیایش niyáyish.

THAT (*pronoun*), آن án.—(*adverb*) که kih.—(*so that*) تا tá, تا که tá-kih, حتی hattá.—(*that is to say, viz.*) یعنی ya'ní, اعنی a'ní, ای ai, گویا gúyá.

THATCH, کاه káh, پوش púsh, کپر kappar.

To **THATCH**, کپر زدن kappar zadan, با گیاه پوشیدن bá-giyáh púshídan.

THAW, یخ آب yakh-áb.

To **THAW**, یخ آب شدن yakh-áb shudan, برف آب شدن barf-áb shudan.

THE, ال al.

THEATRE, تماشا خانه tamáshá-khánah.—(*in which religious dramas are performed at the time of the Muharram festival*) تکیه takyah.

THEATRICAL, قابل تماشا kábil-i-tamáshá.

THEFT, دزدی duzdí, سرقه sarikah.

THEIR, مال ایشان mál-i-íshán.

THEME, مصدر masdar.

THEN, پس pas, آنوقت án-vakt, آنگاه án-gáh.—(*after that*) از آن پس az án pas, بعد از آن ba'd az án, بعده ba'dahu, من بعد min ba'd.—(*for that reason*) پس pas, از آن جهت az án jihat, لهذا liházá, از برای آن az baráy-i-án.

THENCE, از آنجا az án-já.—(*from that cause*) از آن سبب az án sabab, از برای آن az baráy-i-án.—(*from that time*) از آن باز az án báz, از آن زمان az án zamán, از آنوقت án-vakt, بعده ba'dahu.

THEOLOGIAN, حکیم الاهی hakím-i-iláhí.

THEOLOGY, حکمت الاهی hikmat-i-iláhí.

THEOREM, مسئله mas,alah, مشکله mushkilah.

HEORETICAL, قیاسی kiyásí.

THEORY, قیاس kiyás, حدس hads, خیال khiyál, منصوبه mansúbah.

THERE, آنجا án-já.—(*here and there*) جا بجا já-bi-já, اینجا آنجا ín-já án-já.

THEREABOUTS (*near a place*), در آن حوالی dar án haválí, در آن نزدیکی dar án nazdíkí.—(*near a quantity, number, &c.*) تخمیناً takhmínan, مظنه mazannah, تقریباً takríban, قریب karíb, گویا gúyá.

THEREAFTER, بعده ba'dahu, بعد از آن ba'd az án, در اثر dar isr.

THEREAT, در آن جا dar án já.—(*then*) پس pas, آنوقت án-vakt, آنگاه án-gáh.—(*for that reason*) پس pas, از آن جهت az án jihat, لهذا liházá, از برای آن az biráy-i-án.

THEREBY, از آن az án, بان bi-án.

THEREFORE, لهذا liházá, بنا بر banábar, باعث بر آن bá'is bar án, از آن سبب az án sabab, از آن جهت az án jihat, از برای آن az baráy-i-án, من ثم min summa.

THEREFROM, از آن جا az án já.

THEREIN, در آن dar án, درین dar ín.

THEREOF, از آن az án.

THEREWITH, با آن bá-án, معاً ma'an.

THERIAC, تریاق tiryák, طریاق tiryák, دافع زهر dáfi'-i-zahr.

THERMOMETER, درجه darajah, میزان حرارت mízán-i-harárat.

THESE, این ín, اینها ínhá.

THESIS, مصدر masdar.

THEY, ایشان íshán, آنها ánhá, اینها ínhá, اوشان úshán.—(*they who*) کسانیکه kasání-kih, آنهاکه ánhá-kih.

THICK, گنده gundah, درشت durusht, کلفت kuluft, ستبر sitabr, ضخیم zakhím, سطبر sitabr.—(*large*) جسیم jasím, توفال túfál.—(*muddy*) غلیظ ghalíz, سخت sakht, سفت sift, منجمد munjamad.—(*crowded together*) متصل muttasil, درهم dar-ham, جنجال janjál.

To **THICKEN**, غلیظ ساختن ghalíz sákhtan.

THICKET, درختزار dirakht-zár.

THICKNESS, کلفتی kuluftí, ضخامت zakhámat, سطبری sitabrí.—(*closeness*) هجوم hujúm.—(*muddi-

ness) سختی sakhtí, غلیظت ghalízat.

THIEF, دزد duzd, سارق sárik, لص liss, قزاق kazzak.

THIEF-CATCHER, دزد بگیر duzdí-bigír.

To THIEVE, دزدی نمودن duzdí nimúdan, دزدیدن duzdídan.

THIEVERY, دزدی duzdí, سرقه sarikah.

THIEVISH, دزدانه duzdánah.

THIGH, ران rán, فخذ fakhiz.—(*thigh-bones*) استخوان ران ustukhwán-i-rán.

THIMBLE, انگشتانه angushtánah.

THIN, تنگ tang, رقیق rakík, باریك báríк. — (*lean, emaciated*) لاغر lághir, نزار nizár.—(*as fluid*) رقیق rakík, شل shul, آبکی ábakí.—(*thin, as long objects, such as a stick, a cord, thread, &c.; also a slender man*) باریك báríк.—(*as flat objects, such as cloth, paper, cake of bread, &c.*) نازك názuk.

THINE, مال تو mál-i-tú.

THING, چیز chíz, شی shai (*pl.* اشیا ashyá.—(*it is the same thing*) یکی است yakí ast, یکسان است yak-sán ast.—(*it is another thing*) امریست علحده amríst 'aláhiddah.

To THINK, اندیشیدن andíshídan, مظنه داشتن mazannah dáshtan, قیاس کردن kiyás kardan, گمان بردن gumán burdan, خیال کردن khiyál kardan, پنداشتن pindáshtan, تصور کردن tasavvur kardan, فکر کردن fikr kardan, سگالیدن sigálídan, خاطر بستن khátir bastan.—(*without thinking*) غفلةً ghiflatan.

THINLY, لاغرانه lághiránah. —(*sparsely*) کم kam, اندك andak.

THINNESS, تنگی tangí, رقت rikkat, باریکی báríkí.—(*leanness*) لاغری lághirí, نزاری nizárí.—(*as fluid*) رقت rikkat.

A THIRD, سه یك sih-yak, ثلث suls.

THIRST, تشنگی tishnagí, عطش 'atash, جواد juvád.

THIRSTY, تشنه tishnah, عطشان 'atshán, غل ghall.—(*to be thirsty*) عطش داشتن 'atash dáshtan, تشنه شدن tishnah shudan.

THIS, این ín, هذا házá.

THISTLE, خسك khasak, کنگر kangar, شکر تغار shakr-taghár.

THITHER, آنجا án já, بآنجا bi-án já, آنسو án sú.

THONG (*of leather*), تسمه tasmah, دوال duvál.

THORN, خار khár, شوك shauk.—(*thorn-bush*) خار بن khár-bun.—(*thorn in the side*) خار بغل khár-i-baghal.

THORN-APPLE, جوز ماثل jauz-i-másal, بنج دشتی banj-i-dashtí, گوز گیاه gauz-i-giyáh.

THORNY, خار دار khár-dár, پر خار pur-khár.

THOROUGH, تمام tamám, تام tamm, کامل kámil, سالم sálim, صحیح sahíh.

THOROUGHBRED, خالص khális, اصیل asíl.

THOROUGHFARE, راه ráh, ره rah, طریق taríк, شارع shári'.—(*leading thoroughfare*) شاه راه sháh-ráh, برزن barzan.

THOROUGHLY, بالمره bi-'l-marrah.

THOU, تو tú.—(*thou thyself*) تو خودت tú khúdat.

THOUGH, اگرچه agarchih, گرچه garchih, هرچند که har-chand kih, علی ان 'alá án, با وجود که bá-vujúd kih.

THOUGHT, اندیشه andíshah, فکر fikr, قیاس kiyás, وهم vahm, رائی ra,í, تصور tasavvur, ظن zann, مظنه mazannah, گمان gumán, خیال khiyál, زعم za'm.

THOUGHTFUL, فکرمند fikr-mand, متفکر mutafakkar, متأمل muta,ammil.

THOUGHTFULNESS, تأمل tá,ammul, فکر fikr.

THOUGHTLESS, بی فکر bí-fikr, بی اندیشه bí-andíshah, غافل ghâfil.

THRALDOM, وا بستگی vá-bastagí, بند band, گرفتاری giriftárí, اسر usr, اسیری asírí.

To THRASH (*beat*), زدن zadan, کوفتن kúftan.—(*grain*) مالش کردن málish kardan, کوبیدن kúbídan.

THRASHER (*who sits on the machine and drives it*) چوم کش chúm-kash, بره کش burrah-kash.—(*person who follows the thrashing-machine, and arranges and winnows the corn with a long fork*) بوجار bújár.

THRASHING-FLOOR, خرمن گاه khirman-gáh, زمین خرمن zamín-i-khirman, زمین درك zamín-i-dirk.

THRASHING-MACHINE (*sledge drawn by bullocks or horses over the corn spread out, and having numerous sharp-edged small wheels*) تخته خرمن کوبی takhtah-i-khirman-kúbí, چوم chúm, بره burrah.

THREAD, ریسمان rísmán, رشته rishtah, سلك silk, خیاطه khiyátah, نخ nakh. — (*of gold or silver*) گلابتان gulábatán, قلابتون kulábatún.

To THREAD (*string*), بر سلك کشیدن bar silk kashídan.

THREADBARE, مندرس mundaris, کهنه kuhnah.

THREAT, تهدید tahdíd, تخویف takhvíf.

To THREATEN, ترسانیدن tarsánídan, تهدید نمودن tahdíd nimúdan.—(*to threaten to rain*) بنا باریدن داشتن baná-i-báridan dáshtan.

THREATENING, تهدید tahdíd.

THREEFOLD, سه چند sih-chand.

THRESHOLD, آستانه ásitánah, آستان ásitán, سده suddah, در گاه dargáh.

THRICE, سه بار sih bár, سه دفعه sih daf'ah, سه مرتبه sih martabah, سه گانه sih gánah.

THRIFT (*frugality*), لئامت li,ámat, باریك روی bárík-raví.

THRIFTILY, با باریك روی bá-bárík-raví.

THRIFTLESS, مسرف musrif, سرف saraf.

THRILL, قشعریره kusha'rírah.

To THRILL, قشعریره شدن kusha'rírah shudan.

To THRIVE (*prosper*), بختیار شدن bakht-yár shudan, کامیاب شدن kám-yáb shudan, منتفع شدن muntafi' shudan, سعادتمند بودن sa'ádat-mand búdan, دولت یافتن daulat yáftan, بهره مند بودن bahrah-mand búdan, نیکبخت بودن ník-bakht búdan, ترقی یافتن tarakkí yáftan, بر خوردار شدن bar-khwurdár shudan, بهم رسیدن biham rasídan.

THROAT, گلو gulú, حلق halk, حلقوم halkúm. —(*sore throat*) گلو درد gulú-dard, سرفه surfah.—(*to cut the throat*) سر بریدن sar burídan.

THROB, حرکت harakat.

To THROB, حرکت نمودن harakat nimúdan.

THRONE, تخت takht, مسند masnad, سریر sarír, اورنگ aurang, اریکه aríkah.—(*to ascend the throne*) جلوس کردن julús kardan.

THRONG, جماعت jamá'at, جمع jam', انبوه ambúh, هنگامه hangámah, گروه gurúh, غلبه ghalabah, ازدحام izdihám, هجوم hujúm.

To THRONG, جمع زدن jam' zadan, فراهم آمدن faráham ámadan.

To THROTTLE, خفه کردن khaffah kardan.

THROUGH, از az, عبور 'ubúr, سراسر sar-á-sar, از میان az miyán.—(*by means of*) از az, به bih, از وسیله az vasílah, از وساطت az visátat.

THROUGHOUT, درون و بیرون darún va bírún.

To THROW, افکندن afkandan, انداختن andákhtan. —(*to throw down, a person*) خوابانیدن khwábánídan. — (*a thing*) افکندن afkandan, پرت کردن part kardan (*vulg.*).

THRUSH (*bird*), سار sár, طرقه tarkah. —(*disease*) بثورات busúrát.

THRUST (*with a weapon*), هل hul, هول húl, سك suk.

To THRUST, راندن rándan, زدن zadan, هل دادن hul dádan, سك دادن suk dádan.—(*to thrust in*) طپاندن tapándan.

THUMB, شست shast, ابهام ibhám, انگشت بزرگ angusht-i-buzurg.

THUMP, مشت musht, طپانچه tapánchah, لس lus, زد zad, ضرب zarb.
To THUMP, زدن zadan, کوفتن kúftan.
THUNDER, رعد ra'd.
To THUNDER, رعد کردن ra'd kardan.
THUNDERBOLT, صاعقه sá'ikah, برقی barkí.
THUNDERCLAP, صدائی رعد sadá,í-i-ra'd.
THUNDERSTRUCK, حیران hairán, متحیر mutahayyir, متعجب muta-'ajjib, سراسیمه sarásímah, سرگردان sar-gardán, مات mát, آشفته áshuftah, مدهوش madhúsh, دنگ dang.
THURSDAY, پنجشنبه panj-shambah.
THUS, چنین chunín, همچنین hamchunín, اینطور ín-taur, باین وجه bi-ín vajh, همچو ham-chú, همچی ham-chí (*vulg.*).
To THWART, مخالفت نمودن mukhálafat nimúdan, مخالف بودن mukhálif búdan, مقاومت کردن mukávamat kardan, مزاحم شدن muzáhim shudan, اعتراز نمودن i'tiráz nimúdan, بر ضد شدن bar zidd shudan.
THY, مال تو mál-i-tú.
THYME, اپار ipár.
THYSELF, تو خود tú-khúd, تو خودت tú-khúdat, نفسك nafsak.
TIARA, تاج táj.
TIC-DOULOUREUX (*neuralgia*), صداع شمسی sudá'-i-shamsí.
TICK (*louse on cattle*), کنه kanah.—(*large kind of tick*) شبگز shabgaz.—(*of a clock*) چرنگ chiring.
To TICK, چرنگ نمودن chiring nimúdan.
TICKET, تکت tikat (*eur.*).
TICKET-OFFICE, حساب خانه hisábkhánah, دار الحساب dáru-'l-hisáb.
TICKING (*for bed*) دو پود dú-púd, دو گردی باف dú-gardí-báf.
To TICKLE, قلقلی کردن kilkilí kardan.
TICKLING, قلقل kilkil.
TICKLISH, قلقلی شدن kilkilí-shudan; thus: *I am ticklish*, قلقلیم شد kilkilí-am shud.
TIDE, مد و جزر madd va jazr.—(*ebb-tide*) جزر jazr. — (*flood-tide*) مد madd.—(*to go against the tide*) بر خلاف جریان آب رفتن bar khiláf-i-jiryán-i-áb raftan.—(*the river is tidal*) رود خانه جزر و مد دارد rúdkhánah jazr va madd dárad, آب رود خانه زیاد و کم است áb-i-rúdkhánah ziyád va kam ast.
TIDINGS, اخبار akhbár, افواه afváh, آوازه ávázah. — (*glad tidings*) مژده muzhdah, نوید navíd, بشارت bishárat, خوشخبر khwush-khabar.
TIDY, پاك pák, قشنگ kashang, پاکیزه pakízah, منقه munakkah, نظیف nazíf.
TIE, عقد 'akd, عقده 'ukdah.
To TIE, بستن bastan, ربط کردن rabt kardan, بند کردن band kardan.
TIED, بسته bastah, معقود ma'kúd, منعقد muna'kid.
TIER (*range*), ردیف radíf, طبقه tabakah, رده raddah.
TIGER, پلنگ palang, ببر babar.—[The first commonly signifies the leopard, and the second the royal tiger, an animal sometimes, but rarely, found in Persia.]
TIGHT, تنگ tang, چست chust, استوار ustuvár, محکم muhkam, سفت sift.
To TIGHTEN, تنگ کشیدن tang kashídan, محکم کشیدن muhkam kashídan. — (*become tight*) تنگ شدن tang shudan, سفت شدن sift shudan.
TIGHTLY, بتنگی bi-tangí.
TIGHTNESS, تنگی tangí, استواری ustuvárí.
TIGHTS (*clothes*), لباس تنگ libás-i-tang, رخت تنگی rakht-i-tangí.
TIGRESS, پلنگ ماده palang-i-mádah, ببر ماده babar-i-mádah.
TILE, طوب túb, کوارة ku,árah.—(*coloured and glazed tiles*) کاشی káshí, کاچی káchí.—(*mosaic work in coloured tiles*) کاشیکاری kashíkárí.
TILL, تا tá, الی ilá, حتی hattá.—

(*till when?*) تا کی tá kai, تا کجا tá kujá.—(*till then*) تا آنوقت tá án vakt, تا وقتیکه tá vaktí kih.—(*till now*) تا هنوز tá hanúz, تا حال tá hál, الی الآن 'ila-'l-án.

To TILL, زرع نمودن zar' nimúdan.

TILLABLE, قابل زرع kábil-i-zar'.

TILLAGE, زراعت zirá'at, کشتکاری kisht-kárí, فلاحت faláhat.

TILLER (*nautical term*), زبانهٔ سکان zabánah-i-sukkán.—(*cultivator*) زارع zári', فلاح falláh, بذرگر bazr-gar, کشتکار kisht-kár.

TILT (*cover or awning*), سایه بان sáyah-bán, چتر chatar.

To TILT, ریختن ríkhtan.

TILT-RIDE (*roundabout*), چرخک charkhak.

TIMBER, چوب chúb.

TIMBREL, طبل tabal.

TIME, وقت vakt, گاه gáh, زمان zamán, زمانه zamánah, هنگام hangám *or* hingám, اوان aván, مدت muddat.—(*epoch or period*) عهد 'ahd, زمان zamán, ایام ayyám, عصر 'asr.—(*a time or occasion*) بار bár, مره marrah, دفعه daf'ah, مرتبه martabah, کره kirrah.—(*a degree, fold or measure*) مقابل mukábil, چندان chandán, چند chand, برابر bar-á-bar, مساوی musáví, تا tá.—(*present time*) حال hál, وقت حال vakt-i-hál, الآن alán, اینوقت ín-vakt.—(*past time*) زمان ماضی zamán-i-mází, وقت گذشته vakt-i-guzashtah, عهد سالف 'ahd-i-sálif, زمان سابق zamán-i-sábik, وقت پیشین vakt-i-píshín. — (*at the time when*) حین hín, آنگاه án-gáh, وقتیکه vaktí-kih. — (*a short time*) قدری kadrí, یکچندی yak-chandí, اندکی andakí, زمان قلیل zamán-i-kalíl. — (*in time, opportunely*) بر وقت bar vakt, بموقع bi-mauki'. —(*out of time, inopportune*) بیگاه bí-gáh, بی موقع bí-mauki'.—(*in time, musical term*) آهنگ áhang.—(*for all time*) همیشه hamíshah, جهت همهٔ وقت jihat-i-hamah vakt.—(*a long time*) وقت اوسع vakt-i-ausa'. — (*at one time ... at another* ...) ... گاه ... گاه gáh ... gáh ... , ... یک بار ... یک بار yak bár ... yak bár ....—(*in a short time*) در اندک مدت dar andak muddat, در قلیل زمان dar kalíl zamán. — (*in multiplication*) بر bar, *as* سه بر دو شش است sih bar dú shish ast (three times two are six), پنج بر هشت چهل است panj bar hasht chihal ast (five times eight are forty). —(*by London time*) بکوک ساعت لندن bi-kúk-i-sá'at-i-landan. — (*from time to time*) گاه گاه gáh-gáh, دم بدم dam bi-dam.—(*in time to come*) سپس sipás.—(*in good time*) زود zúd.—(*at the same time*) مقارب این حال mukárib-i-ín hál.—(*at the very time*) عین وقت 'ain-i-vakt. — (*immediately upon, as soon as*) بمجرد bi-mujarrad, بمحض bi-mahz, همانکه hamán-kih, همینکه hamín-kih, جخ jakh (*vulg.*).—(*to take one's time*) تمهل نمودن tamahhul nimúdan.

TIMELY, با محل bá-mahall, با موقع bá-mauki', بجا bi-já.

TIME-PIECE, ساعت مجلسی sá'at-i-majlisí.

TIMID, ترسان tarsán, هراسان hirásán, خائف khá,if, خاشع kháshi', کم جرات kam-jur,at, محجوب mahjúb.

TIMIDITY, ترس tars, هراس hirás, خوف khauf.

TIN, ارزیز irzíz, قلع kal'.—(*sheet tin or tinned iron*) حلبی halabí.

To TIN (*whitewash with tin*) سفید کردن safíd kardan.

TINCTURE, رنگ rang, رز raz.

TINDER (*burnt rags*), سوخته súkhtah, پرز purz.—(*German tinder*) قو kau, قاو káw.

TINGE, رنگ rang.

To TINGE, رنگ زدن rang zadan, رنگ کردن rang kardan.

TINGED, مصبغ musabbagh, مصبوغ masbúgh.

To TINGLE (*fingers*), مور مور کردن múr múr kardan.—(*ear*) دنگ شدن dang shudan.

TINKER, مسگر mis-gar.
To TINKLE, صدا کردن sadá kardan.
TINMAN (*person who tins pots and dishes, &c.*) سفید گر safíd-gar.
TINSEL, آرایش áráyish, زیور zívar.
TINT, رنگ rang.
To TINT, رنگ زدن rang zadan, رنگ کردن rang kardan.
TINY, خورد khwurd, خرد khurd, کوچك kúchik, قلیل kalíl, صغیر saghír, پاچه páchah.
TIP, سر sar, نوك nauk, بن bun.—(*tip of the finger*) سر انگشت sar-i-angusht.—(*tip of the tongue*) نوك زبان nauk-i-zabán.
TIP-CAT, چلك مسته chalak-mastah.
To TIPPLE, بسیار آشامیدن bisyar áshámídan.
TIPPLER, شراب خور sharáb-khwur, می پرست mai-parast, باده آشام bádah-ásham..
TIPSY, مست mast, سر مست sar-mast, مخمور makhmúr, سر گران sar-girán.
TIPTOE, سر انگشت sar-angusht.
TIRE (*row*), طبقه tabakah, صف saff, قطار kitár, ردیف radíf, رده raddah.—(*tiara*) تاج táj.—(*of a wheel*) کمانه kamánah.
To TIRE, خسته کردن khastah kardan.
TIRED (*fatigued*), مانده mándah, خسته khastah, افگار afgár.—(*weary of, disgusted*) بیزار bí-zár متنفر mutanaffir.—(*to be tired*) مانده شدن mándah shudan, خسته شدن khastah shudan, کوفته شدن kúftah shudan.—(*to be tired of*) سیر شدن از sír shudan az.
TIRESOME, نفرت انگیز nifrat-angíz, مصدع musaddi', زحمت دار zahmat-dár.
TIRE-WOMAN, مشاطه mashshátah.
TISSUE (*gold or silver stuff*), زری zarí. (*Vide also* TEXTURE.)
TIT-BIT, لقمه lukmah.
TITHE, ده یك dih-yak, عشیر 'ashír, عشر 'ushr.—(*tithe-land*) ارض عشریه arz-i-'ushríyah.
TITILLATION, قلقل kilkil.
TITLE (*person*), لقب lakab (*pl.* القاب alkáb), خطاب khitáb.—(*book*) اسم ism, سر نامه sar-námah—(*title-page of a book*) عنوان 'inván.—(*claim*) دعوی da'vá, ادعا iddi'á, طلب talab, اقتضا iktizá.
TITLED, متلقب mutalakkib, معنون mu'anvan.
To TITTER, خندیدن khandídan, خنده کردن khandah kardan.
TITTLE, شوشه shúshah, همزه hamzah, نکته nuktáh, ذره zarrah, شمه shammah.
TITTLE-TATTLE, پر گوی pur-gúí, زیاده گوی ziyádah-gúí.
TITULAR, لقبی lakabí, اسمی ismí.
To, ب bi, به bih, الی ilá, دم dam.—(*to go to and fro*), آمد و رفت کردن ámad u raft kardan.
TOAD, قرباغه kurpághah, وزغ wazagh.
TOADSTOOL, قارچ kárch, چتر مار chatr-i-már, قارچ مار kárch-i-már.
TOAST, نان برشته nán-i-burushtah.
To TOAST, نیم سوختن ním súkhtan.
TOAST-RACK, برشته دان burushtah-dán.
TOBACCO, تنباکو tambákú, طنبقو tam-bakú (*vulg.*).—(*Turkish tobacco*) تتن tutun, توتون tútún.
TOBACCONIST, تنباکو فروش tambákú-furúsh, تتن فروش tutun-furúsh.
TOBACCO-POUCH, تنباکو دان tambákú-dán, کیسه تنباکو kísah-i-tambákú.
TO-DAY, امروز imrúz, الیوم al-yaum.
TOE, انگشت پای angusht-i-páy.—(*of a slipper or boot*) نوك nauk.
TOGETHER, با هم bá-ham, بهم bi-ham, همراه ham-ráh, بمصاحبت bi-sahábat. — (*together with*) بهمراه bi-hamráh, با هم bá-ham.—(*in addition to*) بانضمام bi-inzimám.
TOIL, محنت mihnat, رنج ranj, جد و جهد jadd va jahd, زحمت zahmat.
To TOIL, عمل نمودن 'amal nimú-dan, کار کردن kár kardan.
TOILET, لباس libás, زینت zínat.—(*to perform one's toilet*) زیور زدن zívar zadan, تحلی نمودن tahallí nimúdan.
TOILSOME, مشکل mushkil, سخت sakht.
TOILSOMENESS, محنت mihnat, رنج ranj, جد و جهد jadd va jahd, زحمت zahmat.

Token, اشاره isháraḥ, نشان nishán, علامت 'alámat, اثر asar, سراغ surágh, ایما ímá, شعار shi'ár, دلالت dalálat.
Tolerable, تحمل پذیر tahammul-pazír.
Tolerably, میانه miyánah, طوری taurí, همچنین ham-chunín, معتدل mu'tadil.
Tolerant, شکیبسار shikíb-sár, صابر sábir, صبور sabúr.
To Tolerate (*permit*), روا داشتن ravá dáshtan, روا دیدن ravá dídan, جائز داشتن já,iz dáshtan, اجازت دادن ijázat dádan.—(*put up with*) تحمل نمودن tahammul nimúdan.
Toleration, اجازت ijázat, تحمل tahammul, مقاسات mukását.
Toll (*tax*), باج báj, محصول mahsúl, خراج khiráj, عشور 'ushúr, گمرك gumruk.
To Toll, تکان دادن takán dádan, زدن zadan, نواختن navákhtan, صدا دادن sadá dádan.
Tollman, راهدار ráh-dár.
Tomata, بادنجان فرنگی bádinján-i-farangí.
Tomb, قبر kabr, مقبره makbarah, مزار mazár, تربت turbat, سر sirr, دخمه dakhmah.—(*tombstone*) لوح مزار lauh-i-mazár, سنگ قبر sang-i-kabr, سنگ لحد sang-i-lahd.—(*building over the grave, six or seven feet long*) سکوی قبر sakkú,í-i-kabr. — (*the grave or pit*) گور gúr, حفره hufrah.—(*railings round the grave*) ضریح zaríh, مقصوره maksúrah, پنجره panjarah.—(*tomb of a holy personage*) امامزاده imám-zádah, مزار mazár, روضه rauzah, درگاه dar-gáh.
Tome, جلد jild.
To-morrow, فردا fardá, صباح sabáh, روز بعد rúz-i-ba'd.—(*day after to-morrow*) پس فردا pas fardá.
Tone, نوا navá, صدا sadá, بانگ báng.
Tongs, انبر ambur, دستپناه dast-panáh, ماشه máshah.
Tongue, لسان lisán, زبان zabán.—(*native tongue*) زبان اصلی zabán-i-aslí.—(*of flame*) زبانه zabánah.—(*to hold one's tongue*) سکوت نمودن sukút nimúdan, خاموش شدن khámúsh shudan, لال ماندن lál mándan.—(*hold your tongue*) سکوت sukút.
Tongue-tied, مربوط اللسان marbútu-'l-lisán, منعقد اللسان mun'akidu-'l-lisán.
Tonic, دوائی مقوی davá,í-i-mukavví.
Tonnage, ظرفیت zarfíyat, گنجایش gunjáyish.—(*vessels of light tonnage*) کشتی کوچك kashtí-i-kúchik.
Tonsure, طاسی tásí.
Too (*much*), زائد zá,id, افراط ifrát, پر pur, زیاد ziyád, خیلی khailí, بسیار bisyár.—(*also*) نیز níz, هم ham.
Tool, آلت álat, ادات adát, دست افراز dast-afráz (*obs.*). — (*tools, implements*) اوضاع auzá', آلات álát, یراق yarák, ساز sáz.
Tooth, دندان dandán. — (*front tooth*) سن sinn (*pl.* اسنان asnán).—(*canine tooth*) ناب náb (*pl.* انیاب anyáb).—(*back tooth*) دندان آسیا dandán-i-ásyá, ضرس zars (*pl.* اضراس azrás, *or* ضروس zurús).—(*of a saw, a comb, &c.*) دندانه dandánah.—(*tooth-ache*) درد دندان dard-i-dandán, وجع الاسنان vaj'u-'l-asnán. — (*tooth-brush*) مسواك misvák.—(*toothless*) بی دندان bí-dandán.—(*tooth-pick*) خلال khilál.—(*wisdom tooth*) دندان عقل dandán-i-'akl. — (*tooth-powder*) دندانشو dandán-shú, گرتك gartak.—(*to clean one's teeth*) مسواك کردن misvák kardan.
Top, سر sar, رأس ra,s, تار tár, تارك tárak, بالا bálá, قله kullah, کله kallah, ذروت zurvat, اوج auj.—(*of a mountain*) سر کوه sar-i-kúh, قله کوه kullah-i-kúh, رأس الجبل ra,su-'l-jabal, تیغ کوه tígh-i-kúh.—(*lid or cover*) سر پوش sar-púsh, سر sar.—(*plaything*) پرپرك pir-pirak.—(*of the head*) فرق fark.—(*upon the top of*) بر سر bar sar, بالا bálá, از روی az rúy.
Topaz, زبرجد zabarjad, یاقوت زرد

yákút-i-zard, یاقوت اصفر yákút-i-asfar, طوباز túbáz, تلیا tilyá.

To TOPE, . شراب خوردن sharáb khwurdan.

TOPER, شراب خور sharáb-khwur, باده پیما bádah-paimá.

TOPIC, معنی ma'ní, مبحث mabhas, باب báb, ماده máddah.

TOPICAL, محلی mahallí, محلیه mahallíyah, موقعی mauki'í.

TOPMOST, اعلا a'lá.

TOPOGRAPHY, بیان محل bayán-i-mahall.

TOPSAIL, شراع بالای shirá'-i-báláí.

TOPSY-TURVY, سر نگون sar-nigún, واژ گون vázh-gún, وارونه várúnah, زیر زبر zír-zabar, بر گشته bar-gashtah.—(*to turn topsy-turvy*) زیر زبر کردن zír-zabar kardan.

TORCH, مشعل mash'al.

TORCH-BEARER, مشعلچی mash'al-chí.

TORMENT, عذاب 'azáb, عقاب 'ikáb, آزار ázár, رنج ranj, شکنجه shikanjah.

To TORMENT, عذاب نمودن 'azáb nimúdan, آزردن ázurdan, الم رسانیدن alam rasánídan, آزار کردن ázár kardan, اذیت کردن azíyat kardan.—(*to tease*) رنجانیدن ranjánídan, تصدیع دادن tasdí' dádan.

TORMENTED, مضطرب muztarib, معذب mu'azzab.

TORMENTOR, ظالم zálim, جفا کار jafá-kár.

TORN (*rent*), دریده darídah, چاک chák, پاره párah.—(*in pieces*) پاره پاره párah-párah, مضمحل muzmahill.—(*to be torn*) پاره شدن párah shudan.

TORNADO, طوفان túfán.

TORPEDO (*electric fish*), لرز ماهی larz-máhí, رعاد ri''ád.

TORPID, سست sust.

TORPOR, سستی sustí.

TORRENT, سیل sail, سیلان sayalán, سیلاب sailáb.

TORRID, گرم garm.—(*torrid zone*) اقلیم حار iklím-i-hárr, منطقه حاره muntakah-i-hárrah.

TORTOISE, لاک پشت lák-pusht, کاسه پشت kásah-pusht, کشف kashaf, سنگ پشت sang-pusht (*obs.*).—(*tortoise-shell*) پوست کاسه پشت púst-i-kásah-pusht.

TORTUOSITY, پیچ pích.

TORTUOUS, کج kaj, معوج mu'avvaj, با پیچ و خم bá-pích va kham.

TORTURE, شکنجه shikanjah, عقوبت 'ukúbat, عذاب 'azáb, تعذیب ta'zíb.

To TORTURE, شکنجه دادن shikanjah dádan, تعذیب نمودن ta'zíb nimúdan, اذیت کردن azíyat kardan.

TOSS, انداخت andákht, اندازی andází.—(*of the head*) تکان takán.—(*gambling*) بازی bází.'

To TOSS (*throw*) انداختن andákhtan, افکندن afkandan.—(*gamble*) قمار بازی کردن kimár-bází kardan, باختن bákhtan.—(*shake*) جنبیدن jumbídan, لرزیدن larzídan, تکان کردن takán kardan, لکیدن lakídan.—(*as a ship*) در تلاطم افتادن dar talátum uftádan.—(*as waves*) متلاطم شدن mutalátim shudan.

TOSSING (*of waves*), تلاطم talátum.

TOTAL, مجموع majmú', جمع jam', جمله jumlah. — (*complete*) کامل kámil, تام tamm, تمام tamám.

TOTALITY, کلیه kullíyah, مجموعت majmú'at.

TOTALLY, سراسر sar-á-sar, تماما tamáman, بالکل bi-'l-kull, بالکلیت bi-'l-kulliyat, بالمره bi-'l-marrah, کلا و قاطبة kullan va kátibatan.

To TOTTER, تزلزل کردن tazalzul kardan, طپیدن tapídan, یله شدن yalah shudan.

TOUCH, دست زدن dast-zadan, مس mass, لمس lams.—(*of an instrument*) پرده pardah.

To TOUCH, مس کردن mass kardan, لمس کردن lams kardan, دست بردن dast burdan, دست رسانیدن dast rasánídan.

TOUCH-HOLE (*of a gun*), برمه burmah, گداره gudárah.

TOUCHING, در باب dar báb, در باره dar bárah, نسبت به nisbat bi, از az, در حق dar hakk, در خصوص dar khusús.

TOUCHSTONE, محک mihakk, عیار 'iyár, معیار mi'yár.

Touchwood, پیفه pífah, پرز purz.
Touchy, محرور المزاج mahrúru-'l-mizáj.
Tough, سخت sakht, قدید kadíd.
To Toughen (*trans.*), سخت ساختن sakht sákhtan.—(*intrans.*) سخت گشتن sakht gashtan.
Tour, سفر safar, سیر sair, مسیر masír, کوچ kúch, مسافرت musáfarat.
Tow, کنب kanab, کنف kanaf, اسطبه ustubbah.
To Tow, کشیدن kashídan.
Towards, سوی suví, بجانب bi-jánib, طرف taraf, سمت samt.—(*towards evening*) طرف عصر taraf-i-'asr.—(*towards one another*) در حق همدیگر dar hakk-i-ham-dígar.
Towel, دستمال dast-mál, پیشگیر písh-gír, حولی húlí.
Tower, برج burj.
To Tower, برآمدن bar-ámadan.
Town, شهر shahr, مدینه madínah, بلده baladah (*pl.* بلدان buldán).
Toy, لعبت la'bat, بازیچه bázíchah, اسباب بازی asbáb-i-bází.
To Toy, نوازش کردن navázish kardan, عشقبازی نمودن 'ishk-bází nimúdan.
Trace, سراغ surágh, اثر asar, نشان nishán, علامت 'alámat.—(*harness*) یراق yarák, ساز sáz.
To Trace (*on paper, in copying, &c.*) گرته زدن gartah zadan, گرده زدن gardah zadan.—(*follow up*) پیروی نمودن pay-raví nimúdan, عقب رفتن 'akab raftan, دنبال رفتن dumbál raftan.
Tracery (*pattern-work*), نقش naksh.
Track (*foot-marks*), سراغ surágh, نشان nishán, اثر asar (*pl.* آثار ásár), قدم kadam.—(*path*) راه ráh, جاده jáddah, سبیل sabíl.—(*on water*) کف kaf.—(*path through deep snow*) چقر chikkir, رش rash or rush.
To Track, پی زدن pay zadan.
Tracker (*one who pursues another by his tracks or foot-marks*) پی زن pay-zan, پی رونده pay-ravandah, معاقب mu'ákib.
Tract (*of land*), ناحیه náhiyah, ساحت sáhat, قطعه kat'ah, بقعه buk'ah.—(*small book*) رساله risálah.
Tractable, رام rám, مطیع mutí', دست آموز dast-ámúz.
Trade (*traffic*), سوداگری saudágarí, تجارت tijárat, متجر matjar, معامله mu'ámalah, داد و ستد dád u sitad, اشترا ishtirá.—(*employment or profession*) پیشه píshah, کار kár, کسب kasb, حرفت hirfat, فن fann, صنعت san'at.—(*Secretary to the Board of Trade*) وزیر تجارت vazír-i-tijárat.—(*trade is bad*) بازار کاسد است bázár kásid ast.
To Trade, تجارت کردن tijárat kardan, مشغول تجارت شدن mashghúl-i-tijárat shudan.
Trader, بازارگان bázárgán, تاجر tájir (*pl.* تجار tujjár), سوداگر saudá-gar, خواجه khwájah.
Tradesman, پیشه ور píshah-var.
Tradition, روایت riváyat, اثر asar, خبر khabar, اخبار akhbár.—(*traditions of the prophet Muhammad*) حدیث hadís, احادیث ahádís.

[These sacred traditions are classed in four orders, as follow: (1) حدیث صحیح hadís-i-sahíh (*perfect or indubitable tradition*), ascribed to one of the fourteen معصوم ma'súm (*sinless or holy personages*), namely, Muhammad himself, Fátimah his daughter, and the twelve Imáms, who are 'Alí, the cousin of Muhammad and husband of Fátimah, their two sons, Hasan and Husain, and other descendants to the ninth generation. This tradition must have been handed down to posterity by one who is عادل 'ádil (*a true and just Musulmán*), whether Shí'ah or Sunní; (2) حدیث حسن hadís-i-hasan (*excellent tradition*), the same as above, but the narrator a Shí'ah; (3) حدیث موثق hadís-i-muvassik (*credible tradition*), the same as the foregoing, but the narrator any person worthy of belief, whether a Musulmán or otherwise; (4) حدیث ضعیف hadís-i-za'íf (*weak or dubious tradition*)—any sort of tradition resting on no very sure authority.]

TRADITIONAL, نقلی naklí.

To TRADUCE, بد گفتن bad guftan, افترا کردن iftirá kardan, بهتان بستن buhtán bastan.

TRADUCER, بهتان انداز buhtán-andáz, بد زبان bad-zabán, نمام nammám.

TRADUCEMENT, تهمت tuhmat, افترا iftirá, بهتان buhtán, غیبت ghíbat, سعایت si'áyat.

TRAFFIC, عبور و مرور 'ubúr va marúr, آمد شد ámad-shud. — (*trade*) سوداگری saudá-garí, تجارت tijárat, متجر matjar, معامله mu'ámalah, داد و ستد dád u sitad, اشترا ishtirá.

To TRAFFIC, تجارت کردن tijárat kardan, مشغول تجارت شدن mashghúl-i-tijárat shudan.

TRAGACANTH (*plant*), گون gavan, قتاد katád.—(*gum*) کتیرا katírá.

TRAGEDIAN, مرثیه ساز marsiyah-sáz.

TRAGEDY, مرثیه marsiyah.

TRAGIC, دلتنگ dil-tang, دلفکار dil-fikár, دلگیر dil-gír, غمگین gham-gín, مغموم maghmúm.

TRAIL, سراغ surágh, نشان nishán, اثر asar, قدم kadam.

To TRAIL, کشیدن kashídan.

TRAIN (*long skirt*), دامن dáman, ذیل zail.—(*of gunpowder, &c.*), سلسله silsilah.—(*railway*) کالسکه káliskah. — (*passenger train*) کالسکهٔ مسافرین káliskah-i-musáfirín.

To TRAIN (*to allure*), کشیدن kashídan, ترغیب کردن targhíb kardan. —(*to exercise, teach*) آموختن ámúkhtan, پروردن parvardan, تعلیم دادن ta'lím dádan. — (*in hard training, a horse*) سوغان saughán.

TRAIT, رسم rasm.

TRAITOR, خائن khá,in, خوان khav-ván, خیانتگر khiyánat-gar, غدار ghaddár.

To TRAJECT, افکندن afkandan.

To TRAMMEL, مرتبك ساختن murtabik sákhtan, در اشکال انداختن dar ishkál andákhtan.

TRAMP, پیسپار pay-sipár, آواره ávárah, در بدر dar-bi-dar.

To TRAMPLE on, پایمال کردن páy-mál kardan, لگد زدن lagad zadan.

TRAMWAY, تراموای tarámvái (*eur.*). —(*tramway-car*) عربهٔ تراموای 'arabah-i-tarámvái.

TRANCE, بی خودی bí-khwudí, غش ghash, بی هوشی bí-húshí.

TRANQUIL, آرام árám, راحت ráhat, آسوده ásúdah, آسوده حال ásúdah-hál.—(*to be tranquil*) آسودن ásúdan, آرام بودن árám-búdan.

TRANQUILLITY, آسایش ásáyish, راحت ráhat, آرام árám, اطمئنان itmi,nán, رفاهیت rafáhiyat, ترفیه tarfíh, سکونت sukúnat.

To TRANQUILLIZE, آسوده کردن ásúdah kardan, مطمئن نمودن mutma,inn nimúdan, آرام دادن árám dádan.

To TRANSACT (*perform, conduct*), اجرا کردن ijrá kardan, تمشیت نمودن tamshíyat nimúdan, بکار بردن bi-kár burdan, بجا آوردن bi-já ávardan, ادا کردن adá kardan.

TRANSACTION, کار kár, امر amr, عمل 'amal, معامله mu'ámalah, سر و کار sar va kár, خصوص khusús, باب báb, بابت bábat, حال hál, ماده máddah. — (*performance*) سر براهی sar-bi-ráhí, آدا ádá, اتمام itmám, اجرا ijrá, ایفا ífá, کار kár.

To TRANSCEND, سبقت بردن sibkat burdan, فضیلت داشتن fazílat dáshtan, غالب شدن ghálib shudan.

TRANSCENDENCE, سبقت sibkat, فضیلت fazílat.

TRANSCENDENT, به bih, بهتر bihtar, خوبتر khúbtar.

TRANSCENDENTLY, بنهایت bi-niháyat, بغایت bi-gháyat.

To TRANSCRIBE, نقل کردن nakl kardan, نقل بر داشتن nakl bar-dáshtan.

TRANSCRIPT, نقل nakl, نسخه nuskhah.

TRANSFER, نقل nakl, تحویل tahvíl.

To TRANSFER, نقل کردن nakl kardan.

TRANSFIGURATION, تبدیل صورت tabdíl-i-súrat.

To TRANSFIX (*pierce through*), گذرانیدن guzránídan, سوراخ کردن súrákh kardan, سفتن suftan, سنبیدن sumbídan, دوختن dúkhtan, گذر کردن guzar kardan.—(*to become transfixed*) خشک شدن khushk shudan.

To TRANSFORM, تبدیل کردن tabdíl kardan, تغییر دادن taghyír dádan.

TRANSFORMATION, تبدیل صورت tabdíl-i-súrat, تغییر شکل taghyír-i-shakl, مسخ maskh, نسخ naskh.

TRANSFORMED, متغیر mutaghayyir.

To TRANSGRESS, از حد گذشتن az hadd guzashtan, تجاوز نمودن tajávuz nimúdan, متجاوز بودن mutajáviz búdan. — (*offend against*) تجاوز نمودن tajávuz nimúdan, عدول کردن 'udúl kardan, گردن کشي نمودن gardan-kashí nimúdan, نقض کردن nakz kardan, نا فرمانی کردن ná-firmání kardan.

TRANSGRESSION (*passing beyond*), تعدی ta'addí, تجاوز tajávuz.—(*fault*) عیب 'aib, خطا khatá, قصور kusúr, غلط ghalat, گناه gunáh, سهو sahv, ذنب zamb, ضل zall, تقصیر taksír, زلت zallat, نقص nuks.

TRANSGRESSOR, متجاوز mutajáviz, تجاوز کننده tajávuz-kunandah, گناه کار gunáh-kár.

TRANSIENT, نا پایدار ná-páyadár, فانی fání, فنا پذیر faná-pazír.

TRANSIT and TRANSITION, عبور 'ubúr, مرور murúr.—(*transit-duty*) حق مرور hakk-i-murúr, باج عبور báj-i-'ubúr.

TRANSITIVE (*grammatical term*), متعدی muta'addí.

TRANSITORY, نا پایدار ná-páyadár, فانی fání, فنا پذیر faná-pazír.

To TRANSLATE, ترجمه نمودن tarjumah nimúdan.

TRANSLATION, ترجمه tarjumah.

TRANSLATOR, مترجم mutarjim, ترجمان turjumán, دلماج dilmáj.

TRANSLITERATION, نقل حروف nakl-i-hurúf.

TRANSMIGRATION (*in human form*), تناسخ tanásukh, نسخ naskh.—(*in bestial form*) مسخ maskh.

TRANSMISSION, ارسال irsál, انفاذ infáz.

To TRANSMIT, فرستادن firistádan, ارسال داشتن irsál dáshtan, ارسال نمودن irsál nimúdan, رسانیدن rasánídan, روانه کردن ravánah kardan, مرسل نمودن mursal nimúdan, انفاذ نمودن infáz nimúdan.

TRANSMUTABLE, قابل تبدیل kábil-i-tabdíl.

TRANSMUTATION, تبدیل tabdíl.—(*of metals*) کیمیا kímiyá, کیمیائی اکبر kímiyá,í-i-akbar.

To TRANSMUTE, تبدیل کردن tabdíl kardan, تغییر دادن taghyír dádan.

TRANSPARENCY, اشتشفاف ishtishfáf.

TRANSPARENT, شفاف shaffáf.

To TRANSPIRE, واقع شدن váki' shudan, اتفاق افتادن ittifák uftádan, بظهور رسیدن bi-zuhúr rasídan, عارض شدن 'áriz shudan, بهم شدن bi-ham shudan, وارد شدن várid shudan.

To TRANSPLANT, جا بجا نشاندن já-bi-já nishándan, تولکی کردن túlakí kardan, تولك نمودن túlak nimúdan.

TRANSPLANTATION, تولکی túlakí, تولك túlak.

TRANSPORT, نقل nakl.—(*means of transport*) واسطه نقلیه vásitah-i-naklíyah.—(*ship*) واپور حمل و نقل لشکر vápúr-i-haml va nakl-i-lashkar. — (*delight*) لذت lazzat, دلخوشی dil-khwushí, عیش 'aish, عشرت 'ishrat, حظ hazz, شادی shádí.

To TRANSPORT (*goods*), نقل کردن nakl kardan.—(*persons*) نفی کردن nafí kardan, اخراج ملك کردن ikhráj-i-mulk kardan, جلائی وطن کردن jilá,í-i-vatan kardan. — (*to delight*) لذت دادن lazzat dádan, ممنون کردن mamnún kardan.—(*to be transported*) نفی و تبعید کرده شدن nafí va tab'íd-kardah shudan.

جلائی وطن کرده شدن jilá,í-i-vatan-kardah shudan.

TRANSPORTATION, نفی nafí, تبعید tab'íd.

To TRANSPOSE, تبدیل نمودن tabdíl nimúdan, تحریف نمودن tahríf nimúdan.

TRANSPOSITION, تبدیل tabdíl, تحریف tahríf.

TRANSUBSTANTIATION, تبدیل tabdíl.

TRANSUDATION, عرق نشینی 'arak-nishíní.

To TRANSUDE, عرق نشستن 'arak nishastan.

TRAP, تله talah, دام dám, کمند kamand.

To TRAP, کمند نمودن kamand nimúdan, دام انداختن dám andákhtan, بکمند آوردن bi-kamand ávardan.

TRAP-DOOR, دربچه dar-bachah.

TRAPEZIUM (*in geometry*), منحرف munharaf.

TRAPPINGS, یراق yarák, اسباب asbáb.

TRASH, اسفناك isfinák.

TRAVAIL, عنا 'aná, تعب ta'ab, محنت mihnat. — (*child - birth*) درد زه dard-i-zih, طلق talk, مخاض makház.

To TRAVAIL, زحمت کشیدن zahmat kashídan, رنج بردن ranj burdán.

TRAVEL, سفر safar, مسافرت musáfarat, سیر sair, سیاحت siyáhat.

To TRAVEL, کوچیدن kúchídan, سیاحت کردن siyáhat kardan, راه رفتن ráh raftan, سفر کردن safar kardan.

TRAVELLER, مسافر musáfir, سیاح sayyáh, راهرو ráh-rau, سالك sálik. —(*fellow-traveller*) همسفر ham-safar.—(*fellow-traveller who clubs means with another*) همدبش ham-dabish.

To TRAVERSE, پیمودن paimúdan, طی کردن tai kardan, نوردیدن navardídan.

TRAVESTY, متنکر mutanakkir.

TRAY (*of metal*), مجموعه majmú'ah, مجمعه majmu'ah, سینی síní.—(*of wood*) خوان khwán, خوانچه khwán-chah.—(*small tray*) دوری daurí.—(*tray in which dough is kneaded, clothes washed, &c.*) حسین hasín, تغار taghár.

TREACHEROUS, بیوفا bí-vafá, بی ایمان bí-ímán, حیله ور hílah-var, خائن khá,in, غدار ghaddár.

TREACHERY, خیانت khiyánat, غدر ghadr, دغا daghá, بیوفائی bí-vafá,í.

TREACLE, طریاق tiryák, تریاق tiryák, شیره قند shírah-i-kand, تریاك tir-yák.

TREAD, گام gám.

To TREAD on, پای گذاردن páy guzárdan.—(*trample*) پایمال کردن páy-mál kardan, لگد زدن lagad zadan. —(*grapes*) فشردن fishurdan, فشاردن fishárdan.

TREADLE (*of a loom, &c.*), چوب پا چال chúb-i-pá-chál.

TREASON, خیانت khiyánat, غدر ghadr, دغا daghá, بیوفائی bí-vafá,í.

TREASURE, گنج ganj, ذخیره zakhírah, خزانه khizánah, خزینه khizínah.—(*hidden treasure*) کنز kanz, دفینه dafínah, رکاز rikáz.

To TREASURE, اندوختن andúkhtan, جمع کردن jam' kardan, فراهم آوردن faráham ávardan.

TREASURER, خزانچی khazán-chí, خزینه دار khizínah-dár.

TREASURY, مخزن makhzan, خزانه khizánah, خزینه khizínah, گنج ganj, گنجینه ganjínah.—(*public*) بیت المال baitu-'l-mál, خالصه khálisah.

TREAT, ضیافت ziyáfat.

To TREAT (*medically*), مداوات نمودن mudávát nimúdan — (*commercially*) معامله نمودن mu'ámalah nimúdan.—(*give a treat*) ضیافت کردن ziyáfat kardan.

TREATISE, رساله risálah, نسخه nuskhah.

TREATMENT, رفتار raftár, سلوك sulúk. —(*medical term*) شفا shifá, علاج 'iláj, معالجه mu'álajah, دارو dárú, چاره chárah, دوا davá.

TREATY, عهد 'ahd, مصلحت maslahat, قرار karár, پیمان paimán, وعده va'dah.—(*of navigation*) معاهده در خصوص تردد کشتیها mú'áhadah dar khusús-i-taraddud-i-kashtíhá.—(*defensive*) معاهده دفعی mu'áhadah-i-daf'í. — (*offensive*) معاهده تجاوزی mu'áhadah-i-tajávuzí.—(*of commerce*) معاهده تجارتی mu'áhadah-i-tijáratí.—(*to conclude a treaty*) معاهده نمودن mu'áhadah nimúdan.

TREBLE (*voice*), صدا باریك sadá-i-bárík.—(*triple*) سه تا sih-tá, سه چند sih-chand, مثلث musallas, سه گانه sih-gánah.

TREE, درخت dirakht, دار dár, شجر shajar.—(*forest tree*) درخت جنگلی dirakht-i-jangalí. — (*fruit tree*) درخت میوه dirakht-i-mívah.

TREFOIL, شبدل shabdul, شفدر shafdar, سه برگه sih-bargah.

TRELLIS (*for training creepers, vines, &c., on*), دار بست dárbast, چفته chiftah, تالانه tálánah.—(*trellis-work*) شبکه shabakah.

To TREMBLE, لرزیدن larzídan, ارتعاش نمودن irti'ásh nimúdan, زلزله نمودن zalzalah nimúdan. — (*to make tremble*) لرزه باندام انداختن larzah bi-andám andákhtan.

TREMBLING (*tremor*), لرزش larzish, لرزه larzah, رعشه ra'shah, تزلزل tazalzul.

TREMENDOUS, مهیب mahíb, هولناك haul-nák, ترسناك tars-nák, هائل há,il, سخت sakht.

TRENCH, خندق khandak, گودال gaudál, گود gaud.

To TRENCH, کندن kandan.

TRENCHANT, تیز tíz, قاطع káti'.

TRENCHER, خوان khwán, خوانچه khwán-chah.

TREPIDATION, ترس tars, بیم bím, باك bák, دهشت dihshat, هول haul, هراس hirás, خوف khauf, ستوه sutúh, وحشت vahshat, نهیب nihíb, هیبت haibat, مهابت mahábat.

TRESPASS (*passing beyond*), تعدی ta,addí, تجاوز tajávuz. — (*fault*) عیب 'aib, خطا khatá, قصور kusúr, غلط ghalat, گناه gunáh, سهو sahv, ذنب zamb, ضل zall, تقصیر taksír, زلت zallat, نقص nuks.

TRESSES (*hair on back of head*), گیسو gísú, گیس gís.

TRIAL (*experiment*), آزمایش ázmáyish, تجربه tajribah, امتحان imtihán.—(*attempt*) قصد kasd, کوشش kúshish, تلاش talásh, سعی sa'í.—(*temptation*) امتحان imtihán, اغوا ighvá, تجربه tajribah, آزمایش ázmáyish, وسوسه vasvasah.—(*examination*) تجویز tajvíz, تحقیق tahkík, تفحص tafahhus, امتحان imtihán.

TRIANGLE, سه گوشه sih-gúshah, مثلث musallas.—(*of sticks or guns piled, &c.*) سه پایه sih-páyah.—(*equilateral triangle*) مثلث متساوی الاضلاع musallas-i-mutasávíu-'l-azlá'.—(*isosceles triangle*) مثلث متساوی الساقین musallas-i-mutasávíu-'s-sákain. — (*scalene triangle*) مثلث مختلف الاضلاع musallas-i-mukhtalifu-'l-azlá'.—(*right-angled triangle*) مثلث قائم الزاویه musallas-i-ká,imu-'z-záviyah. — (*obtuse-angled triangle*) مثلث منفرج الزاویه musallas-i-munfariju-'z-záviyah. — (*acute-angled triangle*) مثلث حاد الزاویه musallas-i-háddu-'z-záviyah.

TRIANGULAR, مثلث musallas.

TRIBE, قوم kaum, طائفه tá,ifah, ذات zát, گروه gurúh, تبار tabár, ایل íl, شعبه shu'bah.—(*large tribe or clan*), قبیله kabílah, شعب sha'b, ایل íl (*pl.* ایلیات íliyát).—(*family or sept*) سبط sabt, فرقه firkah, جیل jíl, عشیره 'ashírah.

TRIBUNAL, خانه شرع khánah-i-shar',محکمه mahkamah.

TRIBUTARY, باجگذار báj-guzár, خراجگذار khiráj-guzár, ذمی zimmí.—(*subs.*) اهل ذمت ahl-i-zimmat.

TRIBUTE, باج báj, غرامت gharámat, پیشکش písh-kash, خراج khiráj, تکلیف taklíf, ساو sáv.

TRICE, لحظه lahzah, لمحه lamhah, آن án, دم dam.

TRICK, ساخته sákhtah, گول gúl, رنگ rang, نیرنگ nairang, کید kaid, بهانه bahánah, مکر makr, فریب firíb, حیله hílah, حیله بازی hílah-bází, دولاب بازی dúláb-bází.—(*to play a trick upon a person*) گول زدن gúl zadan.

To TRICKLE, چکیدن chakídan, قطره قطره افتادن katrah katrah uftadan, چکه کردن chakkah kardan.

TRICOLOR, سه رنگ sih-rang.

TRIDENT, نیزه naizah.

TRIENNIAL, سه ساله sih-sálah, سه سال sih-sál.

TRIFLE, نا چیز ná-chíz, لا شی lá-shai, هرزه harzah, خرده khurdah, پوچ púch, جزوی juzví, جز juz, امر جزئی amr-i-juz,í, امر سبك amr-i-subuk.—(*trifles*) ترهات turrahát, مزخرفات muzakhrafát, هرزوات harzavát.

To TRIFLE, نا چیز دانستن ná-chíz dánistan, لا ابالی گری کردن lá-ubálí-garí kardan.

TRIFLER, هرزه گرد harzah-gard, بی پروا bí-parvá, لا ابالی lá-ubálí.

TRIFLING, رقیق rakík, اندك andak, کم kam.

TRIGGER (*of a gun*), پایه páyah, پاشنه páshnah, ماشه máshah.

TRIGONOMETRY, زوایائی مثلث zavá-yá,í-i-musallas.

TRILATERAL, مثلث musallas, سه پهلو sih-pahlú.

TRILITERAL, ثلاثی sulásí.

TRILL (*quaver in singing*), تحریر آواز tahrír-i-áváz, غلط آواز ghalat-i-áváz.

TRIM, پاکیزه pákízah, منقه munakkah, آراسته árástah, قشنگ kashang, نظیف nazíf.

To TRIM, آراستن árástan, تراشیدن tiráshídan.

TRIMMING (*of a garment, &c.*), سجاف sijáf, ریشه ríshah, حاشیه háshiyah, لبك labak.

TRINITARIAN, معتقد بثالوث اقدس mu'takid bi-sálús-i-akdas.

TRINITY, ثالوث sálús.—(*Person of the Trinity*) اقنوم aknúm (*pl.* اقانیم akáním). — (*the Holy Trinity*) ثالوث اقدس sálús - i - akdas.

TRINKET, جوهر jauhar, گوهر gauhar.

TRIP, گردش gardish.—(*error*) غلط ghalat, سهو sahv, خطا khatá, زلت zallat, تقصیر taksír. — (*stumble*) پرت part.

To TRIP (*stumble*), سکندری خوردن sikandarí khwurdan, پا لخشیدن pá lakhshídan, پا لغزیدن pá laghzídan.—(*to trip up another person*) پاهارا لخشك زدن páhárá lakhshak zadan, پاهارا لغزانیدن páhárá laghzánídan. — (*to catch the ground with the hoof, a horse*) ناخن بند کردن nákhun-band kardan.—(*to knock the fore-feet together, a horse*) تپق زدن tupuk zadan.

TRIPARTITE, مثلث musallas.

TRIPE, شکنبه shikambah.

TRIPLE, سه تا sih-tá, سه چند sih-chand, مثلث musallas, سه گانه sih-gánah.

TRIPLICATE, مثلث musallas, سه گونه sih-gúnah.

TRIPOD, سه پایه sih-páyah.

TRIPTOTE, المعرب al-mu'rab.

TRISECTION, تثلیث taslís.

TRITE, کهنه kuhnah.

To TRITURATE, مالیدن málídan, سودن súdan, سائیدن sá,ídan, سابیدن sábídan.

TRITURATION, مالش málish.

TRIUMPH, ظفر zafar, فیروز fírúz, شکست shikast, غلبه ghalabah.

To TRIUMPH, فتح کردن fath kardan, غلبه کردن ghalabah kardan, شکست دادن shikast dádan, ظفر یافتن zafar yáftan, گشادن gushádan, غالب آمدن ghálib ámadan.

TRIUMPHAL, فتحی fathí, ظفر یاب zafar-yáb.

TRIUMPHANT, فیروز مند fírúz-mand, غالب ghálib, ظفر مند zafar-mand, مظفر muzaffar, منصور mansúr.

TRIUMPHANTLY, غالباً ghálíban, غالبانه ghálibánah.

TRIUMPHER, فیروز fírúz, مظفر muzaffar, منصور mansúr.

TRIVET, سه پایه sih-páyah.

TRIVIAL, رقیق rakík, اندك andak, کم kam.

TROOP, دسته dastah, فوج fauj.—(*crowd*) گروه gurúh, انبوه ambúh, ازدحام izdihám.—(*of horse*) دسته dastah, خیل khail, رساله risálah.

TROOPER, سوار suvár.

TROPHY, علامت ظفر 'alámat-i-zafar.

TROPIC, خط khatt, دائره dá,irah.—(*of Cancer*) خط سرطان khatt-i-saratán, دائره راس السرطان dá,irah-i-ra,su-'s-saratán. — (*of Capricorn*) خط جدی khatt-i-jadí, دائره راس الجدی dá,irah-i-ra,su-'l-jadí.

TROPICAL, گرمسیر garm-sír.

To TROT, لکه رفتن lukkah raftan, لك لك رفتن luk luk raftan.

TROUBADOUR, قوال kavvál.

TROUBLE, تصدیع tasdí', زحمت zahmat, ایذا ízá, اذیت azíyat, محنت mihnat, آزار ázár, رنج ranj, کربت kurbat, کلفت kulfat, تکلیف taklíf.—(*to have one's trouble for one's pains*) مایوس و خسته شدن máyús va khastah shudan.—(*to take the trouble*) زحمت کشیدن zahmat kashídan.

To TROUBLE, آزار کردن ázár kardan, آزردن ázurdan.—(*to trouble one's head about a person*) متعرض حال کسی شدن muta'arriz-i-hál-i-kasí shudan.

TROUBLED, مضطرب muztarib, رنجیده ranjídah, آشفته áshuftah.—(*as water*) تیره tírah, مکدر mukaddar, غلیظ ghalíz.—(*to be troubled*) زحمت کشیدن zahmat kashídan.—(*as water*) تیره شدن tírah shudan.

TROUBLESOME, مصدع musaddi', شاق shákk, رنجاور ranj-ávar. — (*difficult*) مشکل mushkil, دشوار dushvár, سخت sakht, صعب sa'b.

TROUGH, ناوه návah, ناو náv, نو nau.—(*kneading trough*) حسین hasín, تغار taghár. — (*watering trough, generally attached to a well*) سنگاب sang-áb.

TROUSERS, زیر جامه zír-jámah.—(*riding trousers*) شلوار shalvár.

TROUSSEAU, لباس عروسی libás-i-'arúsí, جهاز jaház.

TROUT (*fish*), قزل آلا kizil-álá.

TROWEL, ماله بنائی málah-i-banná,í, ماله málah.

TRUANT, مکتب گریز maktab-guríz, کتو گروز kutau-gurúz (*vulg.*).—(*to play the truant*), طفره زدن tafrah zadan.

TRUCE, مهلت muhlat, مهلت جنگ muhlat-i-jang, متارکه mutárakah.

To TRUCKLE, اطاعت کردن itá'at kardan, مطیع شدن mutí' shudan, فرمان بردار شدن firmán-bardár shudan.

TRUCULENCE, ظلم zulm, ستم sitam, سنگدلی sang-dilí, خشونت khushúnat.

TRUCULENT, جفا کار jafá-kár, بیرحم bí-rahm, درشت durusht, سنگدل sang-dil, ظالم zálim, بیمروت bí-murúvat, جبار jabbár, ستمکار sitam-kár.

TRUE, راست rást, درست durust, حق hakk, حقیقی hakíkí, صحیح sahíh, هوده húdah, عینی 'ainí, صادق sádik, صریح saríh.

TRUISM, بدیهی badíhí, بداهت badáhat.

TRULY, بدرستی bi-durustí, حقاً hakkan, حقا hakká, تحقیقاً tahkíkan, فی الحقیقت fi-'l-hakíkat, بالحق bi-'l-hakk, یقیناً yakínan, عیناً 'ainan, بالفرض bi-'l-farz, ان inna, آری árí, صحیحاً sahíhan, خاطر جمع khátir-jam' (*vulg.*).

TRUMPERY (*old worthless articles*), خورده مرده khwurdah-murdah, کهنه kuhnah.—(*a seller of trumpery, old goods, &c.*) بساط انداز bisát-andáz.

TRUMPET, کرنا karná, بوق búk, صور súr. — (*speaking-trumpet*) دور شنو dúr-shinú.—(*to blow a trumpet*) کرنا زدن karná zadan, بوق زدن búk zadan, صور زدن súr zadan.

TRUMPETER, کرناچی karná-chí.

TRUNCHEON, چوب chúb, عصا 'asá.

To TRUNDLE, چرخاندن charkhándan, غلطاندن ghaltándan.

TRUNK (*of a tree*), تنه درخت tanahi-dirakht, کنده kundah, ساق sák. —(*box*) صندوق sandúk, یخدان yakh-dán, بنه bunah. — (*of an elephant*) خرطوم khartúm.

TRUSS, دسته dastah. — (*medical*) آلت جراحی álat-i-jarráhí.

TRUST (*confidence*), اعتماد i'timád, اعتقاد i'tikád, اعتبار i'tibár, اتکال ittikál, توکل tavakkul, امید umíd, وثوق vusúk, باور bávar.—(*charge*) سپرد sipurd, حواله haválah, ذمه zimmah.—(*deposit*) ودیعت vadí'at, امانت amánat, گرو girau.—(*credit*) وعده va'dah, نسیه nasyah. —(*in God*) توکل tavakkul.

To TRUST, اعتبار کردن i'tibár kardan, اعتماد کردن i'timád kardan, اعتقاد بردن i'tikád burdan, واثق شدن vásik shudan.—(*in God*) توکل نمودن tavakkul nimúdan.

TRUSTEE, أمین amín, وکیل vakíl, وصی vasí.

TRUSTWORTHY, معتمد mu'tamad.

TRUTH, راستی rástí, درستی durustí, حق hakk, صدق sidk, حقیقت hakíkat, سداد sadád, هوده húdah, صحت sihhat, تحقیق tahkík.—(*in truth*) حقیقت hakíkat, انصافاً insáfan, راستی rástí, واقعاً váki'an.

TRUTHFULNESS, صادقی sádikí, صداقت sadákat, راستی rástí, درستی durustí, حق hakk, صدق sidk, حقیقت hakíkat, تحقیق tahkík.

To TRY, سعی کردن sa'í kardan, کوشش کردن kúshish kardan, تلاش کردن talásh kardan, تجربه کردن tajribah kardan.—(*investigate*) تحقیق کردن tahkík kardan, تنقیح کردن tankíh kardan, تجویز کردن tajvíz kardan, تفتیش نمودن taftísh nimúdan.—(*prove or put to test*) آزمایش کردن ázmáyish kardan, آزمودن ázmúdan, امتحان کردن imtihán kardan, تجربه کردن tajribah kardan.—(*to essay metals*) قال گذاشتن kál-guzáshtan, خلاص گذاردن khilás guzárdan.

TUB (*wooden bucket*), بالدی báldí (*hind.*).—(*of metal*) ستل satl, سطل satl.

TUBA (*tree in Paradise*), طوبی túbá.

TUBE, لوله lúlah, نی nay, نال nál.—(*india-rubber tubing*) لوله گسم الاستیک lúlah-i-gum-alástík (*eur.*).

TUBERCLE, دنبل dumbal, دمل dummal, آماس ámás, کورک kúrk (*vulg.*), لك luk (*vulg.*).

TUBEROSE, گل مریم gul-i-maryam.

TUBULAR, لوله دار lúlah-dár.

TUCK, قور بخیه kúr-bakhyah, مغزی maghzí.

TUESDAY, سه شنبه sih-shambah.

TUFT, طره turrah.

TUFTY, طره دار turrah-dár.

To TUG, کشیدن kashídan.

TUITION, تربیت tarbiyat, تعلیم ta'lím, تأدیب ta,díb, افاد ifád, افاده ifádah.

TULIP, لاله lálah.

To TUMBLE, اوفتادن úftádan, افتادن uftádan, سقوط کردن sukút kardan, پرت شدن part shudan, زمین خوردن zamín khwurdan.—(*to tumble on one's legs*) کامیاب شدن kám-yáb shudan.—(*to tumble out*) بدر افتادن bi-dar uftádan.

TUMBLER (*glass*), استیکان istíkán. —(*of a gunlock*) چرخ charkh.—(*dancer, buffoon*), بند باز bandbáz, لوطی lútí, رقاص rakkás, بازیگر bází-gar. — (*pigeon*) کفتر معلقی kaftar-i-mu'allakí.

TUMOUR, دنبل dumbal, دمل dummal, آماس ámás, کورک kúrk (*vulg.*), لك luk (*vulg.*).

TUMULT, هنگامه hangámah, اغتشاش ightishásh, عربده 'urbadah, شورش shúrish, شماته shamátah, بلوا balvá, آشوب áshúb, فتنه fitnah, فساد fasád, غوغا ghaughá, غلبگی ghalabagí, شلتاق shilták, شلوك shulúk.

TUMULTUOUS, جنگ جو jang-jú, لجوج lujúj, متمرد mutamarrid, گردن کش gardan-kash.

TUNE, آهنگ áhang, آواز áváz, هوائی ساز havá,í-sáz.—(*to tune an instrument*) کوك کردن kúk kardan.

TUNER, کوك کننده kúk-kunandah, نغمه ده naghmah-dih.

TUNIC, قبا kabá.
TUNNEL, سوراخ کوه súrákh-i-kúh.—(*to pierce a tunnel*) سوراخ باز کردن súrákh báz kardan.—(*to pass through a tunnel*) از سوراخ عبور نمودن az súrákh 'ubúr nimúdan.
TURBAN, دستار dastár, عمامه 'imámah, دولبند dúl-band, مندیل mandíl.
TURBID, تیره tírah, غلیظ ghalíz, مکدر mukaddar.
TURBOT, جریث jirrís.
TURBULENCE, گردنکشی gardan-kashí, فتنه fitnah, سر کشی sar-kashí, فساد fasád.
TURBULENT, جنگ جو jaug-jú, لجوج lujúj, متمرد mutamarrid, گردن کش gardan-kash.
TURF, کسك kasak, عزق 'azk.
TURGID, ورم شده varam-shudah, آماس کرده ámás-kardah, بر آماسیده bar-ámásídah, لك شده luk-shudah.
TURK, ترك turk. — (*Constantinopolitan*) عثمانلی 'usmánlí.
TURKEY, ملك روم mulk-i-rúm, مملکت عثمانلو mamlakat-i-'usmánlú, ممالك عثمانیه mamálik-i-'usmáníyah.—(*the fowl*) فیل مرغ fíl-murgh, بو قلمون bú-kalamún. [This bird is scarcely known in Persia.]
TURKISH, ترکی turkí, رومی rúmí, عثمانی 'usmání.
TURKISTAN (*Western Tartary or Bucharia*), ترکستان turkistán, بخارا bukhárá.
TURMERIC, زرد چوبه zard-chúbah.
TURMOIL, هنگامه hangámah, اغتشاش ightishásh, عربده 'urbadah, شورش shúrish, شماته shamátah, بلوا balvá, آشوب áshúb, فتنه fitnah, فساد fasád, غوغا ghaughá, غلبگی ghalabagí, شلتاق shilták, شلوك shulúk.
TURN (*change*), انقلاب inkiláb, قلب kalb, تبدیل tabdíl.—(*taste*) میل mail, شوق shauk. — (*by turns*) بنوبت bi-naubat, نوبت بنوبت naubat bi-naubat.
To TURN (*intrans.*), گردیدن gardídan, گردش کردن gardish kardan, دور کردن daur kardan.—(*trans.*) گردانیدن gardánídan. — (*become*) شدن shudan, گشتن gashtan.—(*back*) بر گشتن bar-gashtan, باز گردیدن báz gardídan, رجوع کردن rujú' kardan, مراجعت نمودن murája'at nimúdan. — (*with a lathe*) خراطی کردن kharrátí kardan.—(*a handle*) چرخانیدن charkhánídan.—(*the back*) پشت دادن pusht dádan. — (*on water, &c.*) باز کردن báz kardan.—(*away*) اخراج کردن ikhráj kardan, بیرون کردن bírún kardan, معزول کردن ma'zúl kardan, بر طرف کردن bar taraf kardan. — (*aside*) کناره جستن kanárah justan, خودرا بکناره کشیدن khwudrá bi-kanárah kashídan.—(*aside, err*) خطا کردن khatá kardan.—(*to cause to turn aside*) حبط کردن habt kardan, احباط نمودن ihbát nimúdan.
TURNER, خراط kharrát, خرادی kharádí.
TURNING-LATHE, چرخ خراطی charkh-i-kharrátí.
TURNIP, شلغم shalgham, شلجم shaljam.
TURPENTINE, طرمنتین tarmantín (*eur.*).
TURNPIKE, راه دار خانه ráh-dár-khánah.
TURNSCREW, آچار áchár.
TURPITUDE, خساسة khasásat, خست khissat, دونی dúní, ذلت zillat, شنعت shan'at, خواری khwárí, خباثت khabásat, ذل zull, سگیت sagíyat (*vulg.*).
TURQUOISE, فیروزه fírúzah.
TURRET, کنگره kungirah, برج burj.
TURTLE, کاسه پشت kásah-pusht, سنگ پشت sang-pusht (*obs.*).—(*dove*) فاخته fákhtah, موسیچه músíchah, قمری kumrí.
TUSH, خاموش khámúsh, سکوت sukút.
TUSK, دندان dandán, ناب náb (*pl.* انیاب anyáb).
TUTELAGE, شاگردی shágirdí.
TUTELAR, محافظ muháfiz.

Tutenague (*kind of bell-metal*), چدن chudan, مفرق mafrak.
Tutor, استاد ustád, اوستاد ústád, اتالیق atálík, لالا lálá, وصی vasí, لله lallah (*vulg.*), ددہ dadah (*vulg.*).
To Tutor, تعلیم کردن ta'lím kardan, تادیب نمودن ta,díb nimúdan, یاد دادن yád dádan, تربیت نمودن tarbiyat nimúdan.
Tutorage, تربیت tarbiyat.
Twain, دو dú.
Twang, آواز áváz.
To Twang, بصدا آوردن bi-sadá ávardan, رنگیدن ringídan (*vulg.*).
Tweezers, منقاش minkásh.
Twice, دو بار dú-bár, دو مرتبه dú-martabah, دو دفعه dú-daf'ah, دو گانه dú gánah.—(*twice as many*) دو چند dú-chand.
Twig, نهال nihál, شاخه shákhah, ترّہ tarrah, بنه bunah.
Twilight, شفق shafak, غسق ghasak, هوائی گرگ و میش havá,í-i-gurg u mísh.
Twin, توأم tava,m (*pl.* توأمان tava,mán), همزاد ham-zád.
Twine, ریسمان rísmán, رشته rishtah.
To Twine (*trans.*), تافتن táftan, پیچانیدن píchánídan.—(*intrans.*) پیچیدن píchídan.
Twinge, درد dard, رنج ranj, محنت mihnat.
To Twinge, شکنجه کردن shikanjah kardan.
To Twinkle, درخشیدن dirakhshídan.
Twinkling, درخشان dirakhshán.—(*instant*) لحظه lahzah, لمحه lamhah, آن án, دم dam, طرفة العین tarfatu-'l-'ain.
Twirl, گردش gardish, دوران daurán, دور daur.
To Twirl, گردیدن gardídan, گردش کردن gardish kardan, دور کردن daur kardan, چرخیدن charkhídan. (*twist*) پیچانیدن píchánídan.

Twist (*coil*), پیچ píchh, حلقه halkah.—(*twists and turns*) پیچ و خم píchh va kham.
To Twist (*trans.*), تافتن táftan, پیچانیدن píchánídan.—(*intrans.*) پیچیدن píchídan.
Twisted, تابدار táb-dár, مفتول maftúl.
To Twit, ملامت کردن malámat kardan, عیب گفتن 'aib guftan, ذم کردن zamm kardan, سر بسر گذاشتن sar bi-sar guzáshtan.
Twitch, انقباض inkibáz, قلع kal'.
To Twitch, قلع نمودن kal' nimúdan, منقبض ساختن munkabiz sákhtan.
To Twitter, ویك ویك کردن vík vík kardan.
Two-fold, دولا dú-lá, دو تا dú-tá.
Tymbal, نقاره nakkárah.
Type, نشان nishán, علامت 'alámat.—(*for printing*) حرف چاپ harf-i-cháp, حرف طبع harf-i-tab'.
Typical, نشانه nishánah.
Typographer, باسمه چی básmah-chí, چاپچی cháp-chí.
Typography, چاپ cháp, طبع tab'.
Tyrannical, ظالم zálim, جفا پیشه jafá-píshah, ستم گر sitam-gar, جور پیشه jaur-píshah, دراز دست diráz-dast.
Tyrannically, ظالمانه zálimánah.
To Tyrannize, ظلم کردن zulm kardan.
Tyranny, ستم sitam, ظلم zulm, جور jaur, جفا jafá, جبر jabar, تعدی ta'addí, دراز دستی diráz-dastí, تطاول tatávul, استبداد istibdád, آوار ávár.
Tyrant, ظالم zálim, ستمگر sitamgar, ستمکار sitam-kár, جفا کار jafákár, جبار jabbár.— (*blood-spiller*) خون خوار khún-khwár, خونریز khúnríz, خون آشام khún-ásham, خونفشان khún-fishán.
Tyro, نوآموز nau-ámuz, مبتدی mubtadí.

U.

UBIQUITOUS, همه جا حاضر hamah-já-házir, هر جائی har-já,í.
UBIQUITY, همه جا حاضری hamah-já-házirí.
UDDER, پستان pistán.
UGLINESS, زشتی zishtí, بد نمائی bad-nimá,í.
UGLY, زشت zisht, بد صورت bad-súrat, بد منظر bad-manzar, کریه المنظر karíhu-'l-manzar, بد گل bad-gil.
ULCER, قرح kurh, ریش rísh.
ULCERATED, قریح karíh.
ULTIMATE, آخر ákhir.
ULTIMATELY, عاقبت 'ákibat, بالاخره bi-'l-ákhirah, نهایت الامر niháyatu-'l-amr.
UMBILICUS (*the navel*), ناف náf.—(*umbilical cord*), خصم khasm.
UMBRAGE, شتم shatm, خفت khiffat. —(*to take umbrage*) خشم گرفتن khishm giriftan.
UMBRELLA, چتر chatr, افتابگیر áftáb-gír —(*to put up an umbrella*) چتر بر گرفتن chatr bar-giriftan.
UMPIRE, منصف munsif, حکم hakam, میاندار miyán-dár, میانچی miyán-chí.
UNABASHED, بی شرم bí-sharm.
UNABLE, نا توان ná-taván.
UNACCEPTABLE, نا مرضی ná-marzí, نا پسند ná-pasand, نا قبول ná-kabúl.
UNACCOUNTABLE, بیان نا پذیر bayán-ná-pazír, بی حساب bí-hisáb.
UNACCUSTOMED, غیر معتاد ghair-i-mu'tád, غیر عادی ghair-i-'ádí.
UNACQUAINTED, غیر آشنا ghair-i-áshná.
UNADORNED, ساده sádah.
UNADULTERATED, ناب náb.
UNAFFECTED, ساده sádah.
UNALLOYED, ناب náb.
UNALTERABLE, لایتغیر lá-yataghay-yur, بی تغییر bí-taghyír.
UNAMBIGUOUS, واضح vázih, نا مبهم ná-mubham, صریح saríh.
UNAMIABLE, نا مرغوب ná-marghúb.
UNANIMITY, وفاق vafák, یکجهتی yak-jihatí, ایتلاف افکاری ítiláf-i-ifkárí.
UNANIMOUS, یکدل yak-dil, متفق muttafik, همساز ham-sáz.
UNANIMOUSLY, متفقاً muttafikan.
UNANSWERABLE, لا جواب lá-javáb.
UNANSWERED, بی جواب bí-javáb.
UNAPPROACHABLE, دست نا رس dast-ná-ras, وصول نا پذیر vusúl-ná-pazír.
UNARMED, بی سلاح bí-siláh.
UNASPIRATED, ساکنه sákinah, خفیفه khafífah.
UNASSISTED, بی امداد bí-imdád, بی یاری bí-yárí.
UNAUTHORIZED, بی حکم bí-hukm.
UNAVAILING, بی فائده bí-fá,idah.
UNAVOIDABLE, ضرور zarúr, نا گزیر ná-guzír.
UNAWARES, نا گاه ná-gáh, نا گهان ná-gahán, خطاء khatá,an, نا دانسته ná-dánistah, علی الفور 'ala-'l-faur.
UNBECOMING, نا سزا ná-sazá, نا مناسب ná-munásib, نا شایسته ná-sháyistah.
UNBELIEF, عدم اعتقاد 'adam-i-i'ti-kád, سستی ایمان sustí-i-ímán, بی اعتقادی bí-i'tikádí.
UNBELIEVER (*anyone not a Muslim*), کافر káfir, بی دین bí-dín.—(*idolater*) بت پرست but-parast.—(*magian*) گبر gabr, گور gaur, مجوسی majúsí. — (*polytheist*) مشرک mushrik.—(*Sabœan*) صابی sábí, نبطی nabatí. — (*Christian*) ترسا tarsá, نصرانی nasrání, عیسوی 'ísaví.—(*one who denies a future state of existence*), ملحد mulhid. —(*fatalist*) دهری dahrí.—(*Jew*) یهودی yahúdí, اسرائلی isrá,ilí, نغوك nighúk.—(*atheist*) منکر وجود خدای munkir-i-vujúd-i-khudaí

[The Persians have no single word for an atheist, a phase of unbelief considered scarcely possible.]

UNBIDDEN, غیر ماٴمور ghair-i-ma,-múr.

UNBLAMEABLE, بی عیب bí-'aib, بیگناه bí-gunáh.

UNBLEMISHED, پاك pák, بی داغ bí-dágh.

To UNBOSOM, ظاهر کردن záhir kardan.

UNBOUNDED, بی حد bí-hadd, بی پایان bí-páyán, بی نهایت bí-nihá-yat, غیر محیط ghair-i-muhít, نا محدود ná-mahdúd, بلا انتها bilá intihá.

UNBROKEN (*horse*), نا رام ná-rám.

To UNBURTHEN, بار بر داشتن bár bar-dáshtan.

To UNBUTTON, تکمه گشادن tukmah gushádan.

UNCEASING, مدام mudám, بلا فاصله bilá fásilah.

UNCERTAIN, غیر معین ghair-i-mu'ay-yan, غیر محقق ghair-i-muhakkak, مشکوك mashkúk, مشتبه mushta-bih.

UNCERTAINTY, اشتباه ishtibáh, گمان gumán, شك shakk, شبهه shubhah.

UNCHANGEABLE, بلا تغییر bilá tagh-yír, بی تبدیل bí-tabdíl.

UNCHARITABLE, بی محبت bí-ma-habbat, خلاف مروت khiláf-i-murúvat.

UNCHASTE, تر دامن tar-dáman, دامن آلوده dáman-álúdah.

UNCIRCUMCISED, نا مختون ná-makhtún.

UNCIRCUMCISION, نا مختونی ná-makhtúní.

UNCIVIL, بی ادب bí-adab, گستاخ gustákh.

UNCIVILIZED, وحشی vahshí, غیر متمدن ghair-i-mutamaddin.

UNCIVILLY, بی ادبانه bí-adabánah.

UNCLE (*paternal*), عم 'amm, عمو 'amú, اودر audar. — (*maternal*) خال khál, خالو khálú, دائی dá,í (*vulg.*).

UNCLEAN, نا پاك ná-pák, ملوث ma-lavvas, چرکین chirkín, کسیف kasíf.—(*defiled*) نجس najis, جنب junub.

UNCLEANNESS, نا پاکی ná-pákí, کسافت kasáfat, نجاست najásat.

UNCOMFORTABLE, بی آرام bí-árám, نا گواره ná-guvárah, نا مرغوب ná-marghúb.

UNCOMMON, نادر nádir, کمیاب kam-yáb, شاذ sházz.

UNCONCERNED, غافل gháfil, کاهل káhil.

UNCONDITIONAL, بدون شرط bidún-i-shart.

UNCONNECTED, نا مربوط ná-marbút.

UNCONQUERABLE (*persons*), مغلوب نا شدنی maghlúb-ná-shudaní.—(*things*) فتح نا پذیر fath-ná-pazír.

UNCONSCIOUS, بیخود bí-khwud.

UNCONSTITUTIONAL, غیر مشروط ghair-i-mashrút.

To UNCORK, سر شیشهرا بیرون آوردن sar-i-shíshahrá bírún ávardan.

UNCOUTH, بد ترکیب bad-tarkíb, بد هیئت bad-hí,at, بد قواره bad-kavárah, نا تراشیده ná-tiráshídah. —(*uncouth, as language*) نا مربوط ná-marbút, مزخرف muzakhraf.

To UNCOVER, گشادن gushádan, پرده بر داشتن pardah bar-dáshtan, برهنه کردن barahnah kardan.

UNCOVERED, منکشف munkashif.

UNCTION, تدهین tadhín, تمریخ tam-ríkh.

UNCTUOUS, چرب charb, روغنی rau-ghaní.

UNCULTIVATED, نا مزروع ná-mazrú', مخروبه makhrúbah, ویران vairán, بائر bá,ir.

UNDAUNTED, بی باك bí-bák.

To UNDECEIVE, رفع خطا کردن raf'-i-khatá kardan, مطلع گردانیدن mut-tali' gardánídan, مخبر ساختن mukhbar sákhtan.

UNDECIDED, مردد muraddad, متوقف mutavakkif, معلق mu'allak.

UNDECORATED, ساده sádah, سفید کار safíd-kár.

UNDEFINABLE, حد نا پذیر hadd-ná-pazír, غیر منحل ghair-i-munhall.

UNDEFINED, غیر معروف ghair-i-ma'rúf, غیر محدود ghair-i-mahdúd.

UNDENIABLE, نا قابل انکار ná-kábil-i-inkár, بلا اعتراض bilá i'tiráz, ممتنع الاعتراض mumtani'u-'l-i'tiráz.

UNDER, پائین pá,ín, زیر zír, تحت taht, دامن dáman (*vulg.*), دومن dúman (*vulg.*).

To UNDERGO, کشیدن kashídan.

UNDERHAND, نهان nihán, پنهان panhán, مخفی makhfí, پوشیده púshídah.

To UNDERLINE, کشیدن kashídan.

To UNDERMINE, نقب کندیدن nakb kandídan.

UNDERMOST, زیرترین zírtarín.

UNDERNEATH, در زیر dar zír, پائین pá,ín.

To UNDER-RATE, بنظر کم دیدن bi-nazar kam dídan.

To UNDER-SELL, ارزان فروختن arzán furúkhtan, بقیمت کم فروختن bi-kaimat-i-kam furúkhtan.

The UNDERSIGNED, گذارندهٔ امضا guzárandah-i-imzá.

To UNDERSTAND, فهمیدن fahmídan, در یافتن dar-yáftan, در یافت کردن dar-yáft kardan, معلوم کردن ma'lúm kardan, درك کردن darak kardan, ملتفت شدن multafit shudan.—(*have a knowledge of*) شناختن shinákhtan.—(*do you understand me?*) می‌یابی mí-yábí, می رسی mí-rasí, می فهمی mí-fahmí.—(*to give to understand*) تفهیم نمودن tafhím nimúdan, مطلع گردانیدن muttali' gardánídan.

UNDERSTANDING, عقل 'akl, فطانت fatánat, ادراك idrák, فهم fahm, هوش húsh, خرد khirad.—(*arrangement*) اتفاق ittifák, موافقت muváfakat.—(*to come to an understanding*) اتفاق کردن ittifák kardan, موافقت نمودن muváfakat nimúdan.

UNDERSTOOD (*not expressed*) مقدر mukaddar.

To UNDERTAKE, ارتکاب نمودن irtikáb nimúdan, مباشرت کردن mubásharat kardan, عزم کردن 'azm kardan.

UNDERTAKER, مرده شو murdah-shú, دفان daffán.

UNDERTAKING (*work*), کار kár, امر amr, عزم 'azm, عمل 'amal, سعی sa'í.

UNDESERVED, نا مستحق ná-mustahakk, غیر واجب ghair-i-vájib.

UNDESERVING, نا مستحق ná-mustahakk.

UNDESIRABLE, نا مرغوب ná-marghúb.

UNDISCIPLINED, نا آموخته ná-ámúkhtah, بی انتظام bí-intizám.

To UNDO, وا کردن vá-kardan, حل کردن hall kardan.

UNDOUBTEDLY, بی شبهه bí-shubhah, بلا شك bilá shakk, بی همه چیز bí-hamah chíz.

To UNDRESS, جامه از بر کندن jámah az bar kandan, جامه بیرون آوردن jámah bírún ávardan, لباسرا خلع نمودن libásrá khal' nimúdan.

To UNDULATE, لرزیدن larzídan, اهتزاز نمودن ihtizáz nimúdan.

UNDULATION, اهتزاز ihtizáz.

UNDUTIFUL (*as a son, relative, &c.*), عاق 'ákk, متمرد mutamarrid.—(*as a wife*) ناشزه náshizah.

UNEASINESS, اضطراب iztiráb.

UNEASY, بی آرام bí-árám, مضطرب muztarib, دلفکار dil-fikár, مشوش mushavvash.

UNEMPLOYED, بیکار bí-kár.

UNEQUAL, نا مساوی ná-musáví, نا هموار ná-hamvár, نا برابر ná-barábar.

UNEQUALLED, بیمثال bí-misál, بی نظیر bí-nazír.

UNEQUIVOCAL, ظاهر záhir.

UNEQUIVOCALLY, ظاهرانه záhiránah.

UNERRING, بیگناه bí-gunáh.—(*certain*) درست durust, راست rást.

UNEVENNESS, نا همواری ná-hamvárí.

UNEXAMPLED, بی مثل bí-misl.

UNEXCEPTIONABLE, بی استثنا bí-istisná.

UNEXPECTED, نا گهان ná-gahán, غیر مترصد ghair-i-mutarassid, نا متوقع ná-mutavakki'.

UNFAIR, نا پسند ná-pasand, نا مناسب munásib, نا شایسته ná-sháyistah.
UNFAIRNESS, تغلب taghallub.
UNFAITHFUL, بی وفا bí-vafá.
UNFASHIONABLE, نا مرغوب ná-marghúb.
UNFATHOMABLE, عمیق 'amík, بی ته bí-tah.
UNFAVOURABLE, نا موافق ná-muváfik, نا مسعود ná-mas'úd.
UNFEELING, سنگدل sang-dil.
UNFEIGNED, مخلص mukhlis, مخلصانه mukhlisánah.
UNFINISHED, نا تمام ná-tamám, نا کامل ná - kámil, بی انجام bí-anjám.
UNFIT, نا لائق ná-lá,ik, نا مناسب ná-munásib, نا سزا ná-sazá.
UNFLINCHING, متجاسر mutajásir.
To UNFOLD, گشادن gushádan, باز کردن báz kardan.
UNFORESEEN, نا گهان ná-gahán, غیر مترصد ghair-i-mutarassid, نا متوقع ná-mutavvaki'.
UNFORTUNATE, بد بخت bad-bakht, کم بخت kam-bakht, بی نصیب bí-nasíb, سیه روز siyah-rúz, منحوس manhús, محروم mahrúm, مدبر mudbir, میشوم maishúm, نحس nahs.
UNFORTUNATELY, بد بختانه bad-bakhtánah.
UNFOUNDED, بی سبب bí-sabab, باطل bátil, بی اصل bí-asl.
UNFREQUENTED, بی آمد و شد bí-ámad-u-shud.
UNFRIENDLY, نا مهربان ná-mihrbán.
UNFRUITFUL, غیر مثمر ghair-i-musmir.
UNFULFILLED, نا تمام ná-tamám.
UNFURNISHED, غیر مفروش ghair-i-mafrúsh.
UNGENEROUS, بی کرم bí-karm, نا نجیب ná-najíb.
UNGODLINESS, عدم اعتقاد 'adam-i-i'tikád, سستی ایمان sustí-i-ímán, بی اعتقادی bí-i'tikádí.
UNGODLY, بی دین bí-dín, کافر káfir.
UNGOVERNABLE, غیر محکوم ghair-i-mahkúm.
UNGRACEFUL, بد نما bad-nimá.
UNGRATEFUL, نا سپاس ná-sipás, نا حق شناس ná-hakk-shinás, نا شکر گذار ná-shukr-guzár, بی وفا bí-vafá, نمک حرام namak-harám, کافر نعمت káfir-i-ni'mat, بد عهد bad-'ahd.
UNGUENT, مرهم marham, ضماد zamád.
UNHAPPINESS, دردمندی dard-mandí, دلتنگی dil-tangí, مستمندی mustamandí, ملولی malúlí.
UNHAPPY, دلتنگ dil-tang, مستمند mustamand, غمگین gham-gín, اندوهناک andúh-nák, ملول malúl.
To UNHARNESS, ساز وا کردن sáz vá-kardan.
UNHEALTHINESS, نا خوشی ná-khwushí.
UNHEALTHY, نا موافق ná-muváfik, نا گواره ná-guvárah.—(*diseased*) نا خوش ná-khwush, غیر سالم ghair-i-sálim.
UNHEARD of, نا شنیده ná-shiní-dah.
UNHEEDFUL, غافل gháfil.
UNHESITATINGLY, بی دریغ bí-dirígh.
UNHOLINESS, نا مقدسی ná-mukad-dasí, نا پاکی ná-pákí, بیدینی bí-díní.
UNHOLY, نا مقدس ná-mukaddas, نا پاک ná-pák, پلید pilíd, بیدین bí-dín.
UNICORN, کرگدن kargadan. [This is, strictly speaking, the "rhinoceros."]
UNIFORM (*of a soldier*), رخت نظام rakht-i-nizám. — (*alike*) متفق muttafik, یك رنگ yak-rang.
UNIFORMITY, مطابقت mutábakat, یکرنگی yak-rangí.
UNIFORMLY, یك رنگانه yak-rangá-nah, هم شکلانه ham-shaklánah.
UNINHABITABLE, نا قابل ماندن ná-kábil-i-mándan, نا لائق سکونت ná-lá,ik-i-sukúnat.
UNINHABITED, غیر مسکون ghair-i-maskún, نا آباد ná-ábád, نا معمور ná-ma'múr.
UNINTELLIGIBLE, لا یفهم lá-yafham, نا قابل فهم ná-kábil-i-fahm, نا

سمکن ادراک ná-mumkin-i-idrák, بی معنی bí-ma'ní, گنگ gung.

UNINTENTIONALLY, *vide* UNWITTINGLY.

UNINTERESTING, بی مزه bí-mazah.

UNINTERRUPTED, نا مقطوع ná-maktú', لا تقطع lá-takattu', متواتر mutavátir, دائم dá,im.

UNION, اتحاد ittihád, اتفاق ittifák, اتصال ittisál, وصل vasl, اقتران iktirán.—(*marriage*) عروسی 'arúsí, تأهل tá,ahhul, ازدواج izdiváj, زواج ziváj.—(*trades union*) اصناف asnáf, طائفه tá,ifah.

UNIQUE, بی عدیل bí-'adíl, واحد váhid, یکتا yak-tá, لنگه lingah (*vulg.*).

UNISON, هم آهنگی ham-áhangí.

UNITARIAN, اهل وحدت ahl-i-vahdat. [This is rather a Pantheist, or one who holds that the Divine Spirit pervades everywhere. All Muhammadans are in fact Unitarians.]

To UNITE, پیوستن paivastan, وصل کردن vasl kardan, اتحاد نمودن ittihád nimúdan, متفق شدن muttafik shudan.—(*in marriage*) عقد نکاح بستن 'akd-i-nikáh bastan.

UNITED, متحد muttahid, متفق muttafik, موصول mausúl, پیوسته paivastah.

UNITY, اتحاد ittihád.—(*of the Deity*) توحید tauhíd.

UNIVERSAL, عمومی 'umúmí, کلی kullí, جامع jámi', شامل shámil.

UNIVERSALITY, کلیت kullíyat, جملگی jumlagí, عمومیت 'umúmíyat.

UNIVERSALLY, بالجمله bi-'l-jumlah, بالکلیت bi-'l-kullíyat, عموماً 'umúman, علی الاطلاق 'ala-'l-itlák.

UNIVERSE, عالم 'álim, کون و مکان kaun va makán, جمله کائنات jumlah-i-ká,inát, جهان jahán.

UNIVERSITY (*college*), مدرسه madrasah.

UNJUST, بی داد bí-dád, نا حق ná-hakk, جفا کار jafá-kár, حیف haif, بی انصاف bí-insáf, ظالم zálim.

UNJUSTIFIABLE, تصدیق نا پذیر tasdík-ná-pazír.

UNJUSTLY, ظالمانه zálimánah, نا حق ná-hakk.

UNKIND, نا مهربان ná-mihr-bán, بی شفقت bí-shafakat.

UNKINDLY, نا مشفقانه ná-mushfikánah.

UNKINDNESS, نا مهربانی ná-mihr-báni.

UNKNOWN, نا معلوم ná-ma'lúm, مجهول majhúl, نا معروف ná-ma'rúf.

UNLAMENTED, ماتم نا گرفته mátam-ná-giriftah, بی ماتم bí-mátam.

UNLAWFUL, خلاف شرع khiláf-i-shar', نا مشروع ná-mashrú', حرام harám, نا حق ná-hakk.

UNLAWFULLY, غیر مشروعانه ghair-i-mashrú'ánah.

UNLEARNED (*uneducated*), امی ummí, بی سواد bí-savád, نا خوانده ná-khwándah.

UNLEAVENED, فطیری fatírí.—(*unleavened bread*) نان فطیری nán-i-fatírí. — (*feast of unleavened bread*) عید فطیر 'íd-i-fatír.

UNLESS, الا illá, اگرنه agarnah, وگرنه vagarnah, مگر magar, بغیر bi-ghair, سوای آن siváí-i-án.

UNLETTERED, نا دان ná-dán.

UNLIKE, غیر مشابه ghair-i-mushábih, بی تمثیل bí-tamsíl, بی مشابهت bí-mushábahat.

UNLIMITED, بیحد bí-hadd, بی نهایت bí-niháyat.

To UNLOAD, از متاع خالی کردن az matá' khálí kardan, در کردن dar-kardan.

To UNLOOSE, حل کردن hall kardan, وا کردن vá-kardan.

UNLOVELINESS, غیر محبوبیت ghair-i-mahbúbíyat.

UNLOVELY, غیر محبوب ghair-i-mahbúb.

UNLUCKILY, بد بختانه bad-bakhtánah.

UNLUCKY (*unfortunate*), بد بخت bad-bakht, کم بخت kam-bakht, بی نصیب bí-nasíb, سیه روز siyah-rúz, منحوس manhús, محروم

mahrúm, مدبر mudbir, میشوم maishúm, نحس nahs.—(*unpropitious*) نا موافق ná-muváfik, نا مسعود ná-mas'úd, مخالف mukháIif, نحس nahs.

To UNMAN, نا مرد ساختن ná-mard sákhtan, بی جرأت ساختن bí-jur,at sákhtan.

UNMANLY, نا مرد ná-mard, نا مردانه ná-mardánah.

UNMANNERLY (*adj.*), بی ادب bí-adab, درشت durusht, بی سلیقه bí-salíkah, گستاخ gustákh.—(*adv.*) بی ادبانه bí-adabánah, گستاخانه gustákhánah.

UNMARRIED (*man*), مجرد mujarrad, عزب 'azab, نا مزوج ná-muzavvaj, غیر متأهل ghair-i-muta,ahhil.—(*woman*) نا کد خدا ná-kad-khudá, نا مزوجه ná-muzavvajah, غیر منکوحه ghair-i-mankúhah.

To UNMASK, از پرده بیرون آوردن az pardah bírún ávardan, بمیدان آوردن bi-maidán ávardan, ظاهر ساختن záhir sákhtan, کشف کردن kashf kardan.

UNMEANING, بی معنی bí-ma'ní, جفنگ jafang, هرزه harzah, پوچ púch, بیهوده bíhúdah.

UNMERCIFUL, بی رحم bí-rahm, بی مروت bí-muravvat, سنگدل sang-dil.

UNMERCIFULLY, نا مهربانه ná-mihrbánah.

UNMIXED, نا آمیخته ná-ámíkhtah.—(*pure*) صاف sáf, ناب náb, ساده sádah.—(*mere*) محض mahz.

UNNATURAL, خلاف طبیعت khiláf-i-tabí,at, خلاف طبع khiláf-i-tab'.

UNNATURALLY, خلاف طبیعت khiláf-i-tabí'at.

UNNECESSARY, غیر لازم ghair-i-lázim.

UNNEIGHBOURLY, خلاف همسایگی khiláf-i-ham-sáyagí.

To UNNERVE, بیطاقت کردن bí-tákat kardan.

UNNUMBERED, بی حساب bí-hisáb, نا معدود ná-ma'dúd, بیشمار bi-shimár, لا یعد و لا یحصی lá-yu'add va lá-yuhsá.

UNOBSERVED, نا دیده ná-dídah.

UNOBTAINABLE, حصول نا پذیر husúl-ná-pazír.

UNOCCUPIED (*person*), نا مشغول ná-mashghúl.—(*place, &c.*) غیر سکون ghair-i-sukún.

UNOFFENDING, نا مضر ná-muzirr, نا موذی ná-mu,zá.

UNOFFICIAL, غیر رسامی ghair-i-rassámí.

UNPAID, مفت muft, بلا عوض bilá 'ivaz.

UNPALATABLE, نا گوار ná-guvár, بد مزه bad-mazah.

UNPARALLELED, بی نظیر bí-nazír, بی مثال bí-misál, بی بدل bí-badal, بی همال bí-hamál.

UNPARDONABLE, مغفرت نا پذیر maghfirat-ná-pazír.

UNPLEASANT, نا پسند ná-pasand, غیر لطیف ghair-i-latíf, نا دلپذیر ná-dil-pazír, نا مرغوب ná-marghúb, نا گواره ná-guvárah.

UNPLEASANTLY, نا خوش آیندانه ná-khwush-áyandánah.

UNPLEASING, غیر مرضی ghair-i-marzí, نا خوش آیند ná-khwush-áyand.

UNPOLITE, بی ادب bí-adab, درشت durusht, بی سلیقه bí-salíkah, گستاخ gustákh.

UNPOLLUTED, بی عیب bí-'aib, صاف sáf, پاك pák.

UNPOPULAR, نا پسند ná-pasand.

UNPRACTISED, خام khám, نا آزموده ná-ázmúdah.

UNPRECEDENTED, غیر مسبوق ghair-i-masbúk.

UNPREPARED, نا مهیا ná-muhayyá, غیر آماده ghair-i-ámádah.

UNPRINCIPLED, بی محابا bí-muhábá, بی حیا bí-hayá, بد نفس bad-nafs, مفسد mufsid.

UNPROFITABLE, بیفائده bí-fá,idah, بینفع bí-naf', غیر مفید ghair-i-mufíd, نا سودمند ná-súd-mand.

UNPROFITABLY, غیر مفیدانه ghair-i-mufídánah, بدون فائده bidún-i-fá,idah.

UNPROPITIOUS, نا موافق ná-muváfik, نا مسعود ná-mas'úd, مخالف mukhálif, نحس nahs.

Unprotected, بی حمایت bí-himáyat, نا محفوظ ná-mahfúz, غیر محروس ghair-i-mahrús, بی صاحب bí-sáhib.

Unpunctuality, بی وقت bí-vakt.

Unqualified, نا قابل ná-kábil.

Unquenchable, اطفا نپذیر itfá-napazír.

Unquestionably, بلا شک bilá shakk.

Unquiet, بی تاب bí-táb, متزلزل mutazalzil.

To **Unravel**, حل کردن hall kardan, باز کردن báz kardan.

Unreasonable (*excessive*), بی اعتدال bí-i'tidál, بی حد bí-hadd, متجاوز mutajáviz, نهایت niháyat, فزون fuzún. — (*against reason*) نا معقول ná-ma'kúl, خلاف عقل khiláf-i-'akl.

Unreasonably, نا معقولانه ná-ma'kúlánah.

Unrelenting, سخت دل sakht-dil.

Unreliable, متبدل mutabaddil, بی بقا bí-baká, بیقرار bí-karár.

Unrepentant, نا توبه کار ná-taubah-kár, بی ندامت bí-nadámat, غیر تائب ghair-i-tá,ib.

Unresisting, بدون ابا bidún-i-ibá.

Unrestrained, مطلق mutlak.

Unrewarded, بی مزد bí-muzd, بی جزا bí-jazá.

Unripe, خام khám, نا رسیده ná-rasídah, نا رس ná-ras, نا پخته ná-pukhtah.—(*unripe fruit, not attained the proper size*) چغله chughulah, چاغاله chághálah.—(*unripe dates*) بسر busr, مذنب muzannib.—(*unripe grapes*) غوره ghúrah, باغچ bághich.—(*unripe melon*) کرکو karkú, کنبزه kumbizah.

Unrivalled, بی مثال bí-misál, بی نظیر bí-nazír.

To **Unroll**, گشادن gushádan.

Unruly, سرکش sar-kash.

Unsafe, بی سلامت bí-salámat, خطرناک khatar-nák, نا امن ná-aman.

Unsatisfactory, نا پسند ná-pasand, نه بطور دلخواه nah-bi-taur-i-dil-khwáh.

Unsavoury, بی مزه bí-mazah.

To **Unscrew**, پیچ وا کردن pích vá kardan.

To **Unseal**, مهر شکستن muhr shikastan.

Unsearchable, تفحص نا پذیر tafahhus ná-pazír.

Unseasonable, بی وقت bí-vakt, بیگاه bí-gáh, بی زمان bí-zamán, بی موقع bí-mauki'.

Unseemly, نا شایسته ná-sháyistah.

Unserviceable, نه قابل کار nah kábil-i-kár, نا کاره ná-kárah.

Unsettled, بی قرار bí-karár, بی ثبات bí-sabát.—(*the weather was unsettled*) هوا انقلابرا داشت havá inkilábrá dásht.

To **Unsew**, شکافتن shikáftan.

Unshaken, غیر متحرک ghair-i-mutaharrik, ثابت sábit.

To **Unsheathe**, بیرون کشیدن bírún kashídan.

Unsightly, زشت zisht, بد نما bad-nimá.

Unskilful, غیر ماهر ghair-i-máhir.

Unskilfulness, بی مهارتی bí-mahá-ratí.

Unsociable, نا مأنوس ná-ma,nús, انس نا پذیر uns-ná-pazír.

Unsound, نا صحیح ná-sahíh, غیر سالم ghair-i-sálim.

Unsparingly, بی دریغ bí-dirígh.

Unspeakable, نا گفتنی ná-guftaní.

Unspeakably, بطور نا گفتنی bi-taur-i-ná-guftaní.

Unstable, بی بقا bí-baká, بیقرار bí-karár.

Unsteadily, متزلزلانه mutazalzilánah.

Unsteady, نا قائم ná-ká,im, نا مضبوط ná-mazbút, نا استوار ná-ustuvár, لک lak (*vulg.*)

Unsubdued, نا مغلوب ná-maghlúb.

Unsuccessful, نا کام ná-kám, نا کامیاب ná-kám-yáb, بینصیب bí-nasíb, بیمقصد bí-maksad, نا بختیار ná-bakht-yár, نا مراد ná-murád, محروم mahrúm, منحوس manhús.

Unsuitable, نا مناسب ná-munásib, بیجا bí-já, نا لائق ná-lá,ik, نا موافق ná-muváfik, نا سزا ná-sazá.

UNSUITABLENESS, نا شایستگی ná-sháyistagí.

UNSUSPECTED, بی بد گمان bí-bad gumán, نا مظنون ná-maznún, بی شائبه bí-shá,ibah, غیر متهم ghair-i-muttahim.

UNTAMED, نا رام ná-rám.

To UNTIE, حل کردن hall kardan, وا کردن vá-kardan.

UNTIL, تا tá, تا که tá-kih, حتی hattá, الی ilá.

UNTIMELY, بیگاه bí-gáh, بی محل bí-mahal, بی وقت bí-vakt, بی موقع bí-mauki'.

UNTOWARD, بد بخت bad-bakht, کم بخت kam-bakht, بی نصیب bí-nasíb, سیه روز siyah-rúz, منحوس manhús, محروم mahrúm, مدبر mudbir, میشوم maishúm, نحس nahs.

UNTRUE, دروغ durúgh, کاذب kázib, نا راست ná-rást.

UNTRULY, نا راستانه ná-rástánah.

UNTRUTH, دروغ durúgh, کذب kizb, تزویر tazvír, غدر ghadr, ارجاف irjáf.

To UNTWIST, وا تابیدن vá-tábídan.

UNUSED, بی عادت bí-'ádat, عادت نکرده 'ádat-na-kardah.

UNUSUAL, غیر معمول ghair-i-ma'múl, غیر معهود ghair-i-ma'hud, خلاف عادت khiláf-i-'ádat.

UNUTTERABLE, نا گفتنی ná-guftaní.

To UNVEIL, از پرده بیرون آوردن az pardah bírún ávardan, بمیدان آوردن bi-maidán ávardan, ظاهر ساختن záhir sákhtan, کشف کردن kashf kardan.

UNWARILY, غافلانه gháfilánah, بغفلت bi-ghiflat.

UNWARLIKE, نا شایسته جنگ ná-sháyistah-i-jang.

UNWARRANTABLE, تصدیق نا پذیر tasdík-ná-pazír.

UNWARY, غافل gháfil, بی احتیاط bí-ihtiyát, نا هوشیار ná-húsh-yár.

UNWEARIED, بی ملال bí-malál.

UNWELCOME, نا خواسته ná-khwástah, نا مطلوب ná-matlúb.

UNWELL, بی دماغ bí-dimágh, نا خوش ná-khwush, با کسالت bá-kasálat.

UNWHOLESOME, نا گوارة ná-guvárah, نا موافق ná-muváfik, مضر muzirr, موذی mu,zí.

UNWIELDY, جسیم jasím, بزرگ buzurg.

UNWILLING, نا راضی ná-rází, نا خوشنود ná-khwush-núd, نا خواه ná-khwáh, نخواسته na-khwástah, شاکی shákí.

UNWILLINGLY, بی اختیار bí-ikhtiyár.

UNWISE, نا دان ná-dán, بیوقوف bí-vukúf.

UNWISELY, غافلاً gháfilan, احمقانه ahmakánah, بی بصیرت bí-basírat.

UNWITTINGLY, لا عن شعور lá-'an shu'úr, سهواً sahvan, نا دانسته ná-dánistah, عارضاً 'árizan.

UNWORTHILY, نا شایستانه ná-sháyistánah, نا لائقانه ná-lá,ikánah.

UNWORTHY, نا مستحق ná-mustahakk, نا سزاوار ná-sazávár, نا لائق ná-lá,ik, نا شایسته ná-sháyistah.

To UNYOKE, جوغ کشادن júgh gushádan, یوغ باز کردن yúgh báz kardan.

UP (*adv.*), بالا bálá. — (*prep.*) قائم ká,im.—(*up and down*) سر بالا سرازیر sar-bálá sar-á-zír.

To UPBRAID, ملامت کردن malámat kardan, عیب گفتن 'aib guftan, ذم کردن zamm kardan, مواخذه کردن mu,ákhazah kardan.

To UPHOLD, حمایت کردن himáyat kardan.

UPON, بر bar, بالا bálá, فراز faráz, فوق fauk, علی 'alá, کف kaf, روی rúy.

UPPER, بالاتر bálátar, برتر bartar, اعلی a'lá. — (*upper room, upstairs apartment*) کوشک kúshk, بالا خانه bálá-khánah.—(*upper seat, at the further end of a room*) صدر sadr. —(*the upper part*) فراز faráz, فوق fauk.

UPRIGHT (*perpendicular*), قائم ká,im, مستقیم mustakím, صحی sahí or suhí, راست rást, بر پا bar pá.—(*honest*) صادق sádik, صالح sálih, راست rást, راستباز rást-báz.

UPRIGHTNESS, راستی rástí.—(*honesty*) راستی rástí, انصاف insáf, صداقت sadákat.

UPROAR, هنگامه hangámah, غوغا ghaughá, قیل و قال kíl u kál, دمدمه damdamah, همهمه hamhamah.

UPSET, وارونه várúnah, منقلب munkalib.

To UPSET, سر نگون کردن sar-nigún kardan, سر زیر کردن sar-zír kardan, وارونه کردن várúnah kardan, واژگون ساختن vázhgún sákhtan, بر گشته ساختن bar-gashtah sákhtan, بر گردانیدن bar-gardánídan.

UPSHOT, نتیجه natíjah, انجام anjám, انصرام inzirám, حاصل hásil, مال ma,al, آخر ákhir, سر sar.

UPSIDE-DOWN, زیر زبر zír-zabar, سر نگون sar-nigún, وارونه várúnah, واژگون vázhgún, سر زیر sar-zír, نگون nigún, نگونسار nigún-sár, مقلوب maklúb, بر گشته bar-gashtah.

UPSTART, نو کیسه nau-kísah, نو خیز nau-khíz.

UPWARDS, بالا bálá.—(*upwards and downwards*) شیب و فراز shíb va faráz.

URBAN, شهری shahrí, مدنی madaní, بلدی baladí.

URBANITY, ادب adab.

URCHIN, کودك kúdak.

URETHRA, مبال mabál.

To URGE, تقاضا کردن takázá kardan, اغوا کردن ighvá kardan, ابرام نمودن ibrám nimúdan, تحریك نمودن tahrík nimúdan, الحاح نمودن ilháh nimúdan, بر آن داشتن bar án dáshtan, القا نمودن ilká nimúdan.

URGENCY, ضرورت zarúrat, لزوم luzúm.

URGENT, ضرور zarúr, لازم lázim.

URINAL, قاروره kárúrah.

URINE, پیشاب písh-áb, بول baul, شاش shásh, ادرار idrár, زهراب zahr-áb.

To URINE, شاشیدن sháshídan, پیشاب کردن písh-áb kardan, بول کردن baul kardan, ادرار کردن idrár kardan, تشرشر کردن tasharshur kardan.

URN (*for tea-making*), سماور samávar (*eur.*), سماوار samávár (*eur.*).—(*vase*) ظرف zarf.

US, مارا márá.

USAGE (*treatment*), سلوك sulúk, وضع vaz‘, استعمالی ísti‘málí, رفتار raftár, معمول ma‘múl.

USE, کار kár, فائده fá‘idah, عمل ‘amal, مصرف masraf.—(*in use*) روان raván, مستعمل musta‘mal.—(*what is the use*) چه حاصل chih hásil.—(*to be of use*) بکار آمدن bi-kár ámadan, بکار خوردن bi-kár khwurdan, کار گر آمدن kár-gar ámadan, مفید بودن mufíd búdan, بعمل آمدن bi-‘amal ámadan, مصرف داشتن masraf dáshtan, نافع بودن náfi‘ búdan, فائده داشتن fá,idah dáshtan.

To USE (*make use of*) بکر بردن bi-kár burdan, تصرف نمودن tasarruf nimúdan, بعمل آوردن bi-‘amal ávardan.—(*be in the habit of*) استعمال کردن isti‘mál kardan, عادت داشتن ‘ádat dáshtan, معتاد بودن mu‘tád búdan, قاعده داشتن ká‘idah dáshtan, خو گرفتن khú giriftan, پیش نهاد نمودن písh-nihád nimúdan.

USEFUL, بکار bi-kár, مفید mufíd, کار آمدنی kár-ámadaní.

USELESS, بیکاره bí-kárah, نا بکار ná-bi-kár, بیفائده bí-fá,idah, بیمصرف bí-masraf, از روی هوا az rúy-i-havá.—(*to render useless*) ابطال نمودن ibtál nimúdan.

USELESSLY, باطلاً bátilan.

USHER (*at a court*), عرضبیگی ‘arz-begí.—(*at a school*) نائب ná,ib.

USUAL, معمول ma‘múl, متعارف muta‘árif, متداول mutadával, معهود ma‘húd, مروج muravvaj, معتاد mu‘tád, حسب استعمال hasb-i-isti‘mál, مستمری mustamarrí.

USUALLY, عموماً ‘umúman.

USUFRUCT (*temporary profit*), سود súd, نفع naf‘, حاصل hásil.—(*partition of usufruct*) مهایات muháyát.

USURER, ربا خور ribá-khwur, سود خوار súd-khwár, رابح rábih.
USURIOUS, رباى ribáí.
To USURP, بغير حق متصرف شدن bi-ghair-i-hakk mutasarrif shudan, بظلم گرفتن bi-zulm giriftan, غصب نمودن ghasb nimúdan.
USURPATION, غصب ghasb, ظلم zulm, تعدى ta'addí.
USURPER, ظالم zálim, جبار jabbár.
USURY, ربا ribá, ربح ribh, مرابحه murábahah.
UTENSIL, ظرف zarf. — (tools), اوضاع auzá', آلات álát, يراق yarák, ساز sáz, ادات adát.
UTERINE, شکمى shikmí.
UTILITY, افاده ifádah, فائده fá,idah, نفع naf', منفعت marfa'at.
To UTILIZE, صرف کردن sarf kardan.
UTMOST, غايت gháyat, نهايت niháyat, اقصى aksá, آخر akhir.—(at the utmost) انتهائى مراتب intihá,í-i-marátib, بنهايت bi-niháyat, بآخر bi-ákhir, بهمه جهت bi-hamah-jihat. — (to the utmost of one's ability) حتى المقدور hattu-'l-makdúr, بقدر مقدور bi-kadar-i-makdúr.
UTTER, کامل kámil, کل kull.
To UTTER, گفتن guftan.
UTTERABLE, گفتنى guftaní.
UTTERANCE (pronunciation), تلفظ talaffuz, مخرج makhraj, تجويد tajvíd.
UTTERER, قائل ká,il, گوينده gúyandah.
UTTERLY, سراسر sar-á-sar, تماماً tamáman, بالکل bi-'l-kull, بالکليت bi-'l-kullíyat, بالمره bi-'l-marrah, کلاً و کاطبةً kullan va kátibatan, کليتاً kullíyatan, بعينه bi-'ainihi.
UVULA, کنج kanj, زبان کوچك zabán-i-kúchik.

V.

VACANCY, خلو khulú. — (appointment) جا já, ضرورت zarúrat.
VACANT, خالى khálí.—(to be vacant) بطال شدن battál shudan, منحل شدن munhall shudan.
To VACATE, خالى نمودن khálí nimúdan, تخليه كردن takhliyah kardan.
VACATION (time of intermission from business, &c.), تعطيل ta'tíl, فراغت farághat, ايام استراحت ayyám-i-istiráhat.
To VACCINATE, آبله کوبيدن ábilah kúbídan.
VACCINATION, آبله کوبى ábilah-kúbí, اوله کوبى aulah-kúbí (vulg.).
VACCINE LYMPH, ماده آبله máddah-i-ábilah.
To VACILLATE, دل دل نمودن dil dil nimúdan, دو دل بودن dú dil búdan, ليت و لعل کردن lait u la'all kardan.
VACILLATION, تردد taraddud.
VACUUM, خلو khulú, خلا khalá.
VAGABOND, اوباش aubásh, آواره ávárah, بيکار bí-kár, مطرود matrúd.
VAGARY, وسواس vasvás.
VAGRANCY, آوارگى áváragí.
VAGRANT, آواره ávárah.
VAGUE, بى قرار bí-karár, غير معين ghair-i-mu'ayyan, مشتبه mushtabih, نا معهود ná-ma'húd, بى ثبات bí-sabát.
VAIN (fruitless), بى فائده bí-fá,idah, عبث 'abas, باطل bátil, بطال battál, بى مصرف bí-masraf, از روى هوا az rúy-i-havá.—(conceited) خود پسند khwud-pasand, خود بين khwud-bín, مغرور maghrúr, هوا دار havá-dár, باد دار bád-dár, يالبند yál-band.—(in vain) عبثاً 'abasan, باطلاً bátilan, به بطلان bi-batlán.
VAINGLORIOUS, مغرور maghrúr, لاف زن láf-zan, يالبند yál-band.
VAINGLORY, مباهات mubáhát, تصلف tasalluf.

VALET (*personal servant*), پیشخدمت písh-khidmat.

VALETUDINARIAN, وسواسی vasvásí, احتیاط کار ihtiyát-kár.

VALIANT, دلیر dilír, دلاور dilávar, بیباك bí-bák, جانباز ján-báz, شجاع shujá‘, شجیع shají‘, جری jarí, بهادر bahádur, شیر مرد shír-mard, رشید rashíd.

VALIANTLY, با دلیری bá-dilírí, با جسارت bá-jasárat, دلیرانه dilíránah.

VALID, کامل kámil, درست durust, مقرون بصواب makrún bi-saváb.

VALIDITY, درستی durustí, کمال kamál.

VALLEY, دره darrah, وادی vádí, جلگه julgah, گود gaud, ویل vail.

VALOROUS, دلیر dilír, دلاور dilávar, بیباك bí-bák, جانباز ján-báz, شجاع shujá‘, شجیع shají‘, جری jarí, بهادر bahádur, شیر مرد shír-mard, رشید rashíd.

VALOUR, دلیری dilírí, دلاوری dilávarí, جرأت jur,at, جسارت jasárat, شجاعت shajá‘at, غیرت ghairat, بیباکی bí-bákí, شراعت shará‘at.

VALUABLE, گرانمایه girán-máyah, گران بها girán-bahá, بیش قیمت bísh-kaimat, عزیز ‘azíz, اعلی a‘lá.

VALUATION (*estimate*), بر آورد bar-ávard, تخمین takhmín.

VALUE, قیمت kaimat, ارزش arzish, بها bahá, قدر kadar, ثمن saman.—(*utility*) مصرف masraf, فائده fá‘idah.

TO VALUE, قیمت کردن kaimat kardan, نرخ گذاشتن narkh guzáshtan, ارزش نهادن arzish nihádan.—(*appreciate*) غنیمت دانستن gha, nímat dánistan.

VALUELESS, بی بها bí-bahá, بی قیمت bí-kaimat.

VALVE, پرده pardah, غطا ghitá.

VAN (*of an army*), طلایه taláyah, پیشرو písh-rau, قراول karávul.

VANE, باد نما bád-nimá.

VANGUARD, مقدمت الجیش mukaddamatu-'l-jaish.

TO VANISH, غائب شدن ghá,ib shudan, نا پیدا گشتن ná-paidá gashtan, مضمحل شدن muzmahill shudan.

VANITY (*inutility*), بطلان batlán, عدم فائده ‘adam-i-fá‘idah, بطالت batálat. — (*conceit*) غرور ghurúr, مغروری maghrúrí, کبریا kibriyá,, تکبر takabbur, نفس nafs, خود پسندی khwud-pasandí, نخوت nakhvat, عجب ‘ujb, خود نمائی khwud-nima,í. —(*nothingness*) هبا habá, نیستی nístí, تباهی tabáhí, بطالت batálat.

TO VANQUISH, فتح کردن fath kardan, غلبه کردن ghalabah kardan, شکست دادن shikast dádan, ظفر یافتن zafar yáftan, گشادن gúshádan, نصرت یافتن nusrat yáftan, فیروز شدن fírúz shudan, غالب آمدن ghálib ámadan.

VANQUISHER, فیروز fírúz, مظفر muzaffar, منصور mansúr.

VANTAGE, نفع naf‘, فائده fá,idah, منفعت manfa‘at, سود súd, صرفه sarfah.

VAPID, بیروح bí-rúh, بیجان bí-ján.

VAPIDNESS, کسالت kasálat.

VAPOROUS, پر بخار pur-bukhár.

VAPOUR, بخار bukhár, غبار ghubár, تف taf.

VARIABLE, بی قرار bí-karár, نا پایدار ná-páyadár, متغیر mutaghayyir, بی ثبات bí-sabát, متلون mutalavvin, دو رو dú-rú, سبك پا subuk-pá.

VARIANCE, اختلاف ikhtiláf, فتنه fitnah, ستیزه sitízah.

VARIATION, تفاوت tafávut.

TO VARIEGATE, ملون ساختن mulavvan sákhtan.

VARIEGATED, رنگارنگ rang-á-rang, گوناگون gún-á-gún, ملون mulavvan.

VARIEGATION, گوناگونی gún-á-gúní.

VARIETY, اختلاف ikhtiláf.

VARIOUS, متفرق mutafarrik, مختلف mukhtalaf, گوناگون gún-á-gún.

VARNISH, روغن کمان raughan-i-kamán.

TO VARNISH, مستحکم تر کردن mustahkim-i-tar kardan, روغن زدن raughan zadan.

TO VARY, (به) تفاوت داشتن tafávut dáshtan (bi).—(*change*) بدل کردن

badal kardan, تبدیل نمودن tabdíl nimúdan, عوض کردن 'ivaz kardan, تغییر نمودن taghyír nimúdan.—(*to vary the operation with* ...) در بین کار ... مخلوط کردن dar bain-i-kár ... makhlút kardan.

Vase, ظرف zarf, سبو sabú, کوارہ kuvárah *or* کوارہ ku,árah, کلوك kulúk, بلونی bulúní, بستو bastú.

Vassal, رعیت ra'íyat, تبیع tabí', فرمانبردار firmán-bardár.

Vassalage, بندگی bandagí, رعیتی ra'iyatí.

Vast, وسیع vasí', بی اندازہ bí-andázah, بی حد bí-hadd, اعظم a'zam.

Vastly, بسیار bisyár, خیلی khailí.

Vat, حوض hauz.

Vatican, عمارت واتیگان 'imárat-i-vátígán (*eur.*).

Vault (*dome*), گنبذ gumbaz, گنبد gumbad, قبه kabbah.—(*underground*) ته خانه tah-khánah, سردابه sardábah, زیر زمین zír-i-zamín.

To **Vault**, مسقف ساختن musakkaf sákhtan.—(*jump*) جستن jastan, خیز کردن khíz kardan.

Vaulted, مسقف musakkaf.

To **Vaunt**, قل رفتن kul raftan, مفاخرت نمودن mufákharat nimúdan, گزاف زدن gizáf zadan, لاف زدن láf zadan.

Vaunting, لافزنی láf-zaní, فخر fakhr, مفاخرت mufákharat.

Vauntingly, با لافزنی bá-láf-zaní.

Veal, گوشت گوساله gúsht-i-gúsálah.

To **Veer**, تبدیل یافتن tabdíl yáftan, متغیر شدن mutaghayyir shudan.

Vegetable, سبزی sabzí, نبات nabát, رستنی rustaní.

Vegetation, نما namá, علف 'alaf, ورق varak.

Vehemence, تندی tundí, سختی sakhtí, درشتی durushtí.

Vehement, تند tund, سخت sakht, درشت durusht.

Vehicle, مرکب markab.

Veil (*covering the face*), رو بند rú-band, رو بنده rú-bandah, برقع burka', مقنع mikna', نقاب nikáb.—(*covering the person*) چادر chádar, ستاره satárah, ایزار ízár.—(*curtain*) پرده pardah, حجاب hijáb, تجیر tajír.

To **Veil**, نهفتن nihuftan, پوشیدن púshídan, پنهان کردن panhán kardan, نهان کردن nihán kardan, مخفی ساختن makhfí sákhtan.—(*to veil oneself*) برقع زدن burka' zadan, نقاب انداختن nikáb andákhtan.

Vein, رگ rag, عرق 'irk (*pl.* عروق 'urúk).

Vellum, رق rikk, پوست آهو púst-i-áhú.

Velocity, سرعت sur'at, زودی zúdí, تندی tundí.

Velvet, مخمل makhmal, قطیفه katífah.

Venal, فروختنی furúkhtaní, قابل فروش kábil-i-furúsh, قابل بخشش kábil-i-bakhshish.

Venality, آمادگی ámádagí.

To **Vend**, فروختن furúkhtan, بیع دادن bai' dádan.

Vender, بایع báí'.

Vendible, قابل فروخت kábil-i-furúkht.

Venerable, محترم muhtaram, گرامی garámí, معزز mu'azzaz, مکرم mukarram.

To **Venerate**, محترم داشتن muhtaram dáshtan, مکرم داشتن mukarram dáshtan, معزز داشتن mu'azzaz dáshtan, اکرام کردن ikrám kardan, عزیز داشتن 'azíz dáshtan.

Venerated, محترم muhtaram, مکرم mukarram.

Veneration, احترام ihtirám, اکرام ikrám, اعزاز i'záz, تعظیم ta'zím, تکریم takrím, آزرم ázarm, توقیر taukír.

Venereal disease (*gonorrhœa*), سوزنك súzanak, آتشك átishak, کم سوزه gum-súzah (*vulg.*), سوزاك súzák (*obs.*).—(*syphilis*) کوفت kúft, قروحات شهدیه kurúhát-i-shahdíyah, مرض خبیث marz-i-khabís.

Venery, مضاجعت muzája'at.

Vengeance, انتقام intikám, کینه kínah, قهر kahr, ثار sár.

VENGEFUL, پر انتقام pur-intikám, پر کینه pur-kínah.
VENIAL, عفو پذیر 'afv-pazír, سزاوار مغفرت sazávar-i-maghfirat.
VENIALNESS, معذوریت ma'zúriyat, عذر پذیری 'uzr-pazírí.
VENISON, گوشت آهو gúsht-i-áhú, گوشت نخچیر gúsht-i-nakhchír.
VENOM, زهر zahr, سم samm.
VENOMOUS, زهر دار zahr-dár, زهر ناك zahr-nák, موذی mu,zí, سام sámm.
VENT, باد گیر bád-gír, منفذ manfaz, منفس manfas.
To VENT, ول کردن vil kardan, بیرون دادن bírún dádan, بیرون ریختن birún ríkhtan.
To VENTILATE, هوا دادن havá dádan.
VENTILATION, هوا havá.
VENTILATOR (*fan*), باد بزن bád-bizan, مروحه mirvahah.—(*wind-sail*) باد گیر bád-gír.
VENTRICLE, شکنبه shikambah.
VENTRILOQUISM, فوتك گوی fútak-gúí.
To VENTURE, جرأت کردن jur,at kardan, جسارت ورزیدن jasárat var-zídan.
VENTURESOME, جسور jasúr; متهور mutahavvir.
VENUS (*the planet*), زهره zuhrah, ناهید náhíd.
VERACIOUS, صادق القول sádiku-'l-kaul.
VERACITY (*honesty*) صدق sidk, صداقت sadákat, راستی rástí, دیانت diyá-nat, صلاح salāh.—(*truth*) راستی rástí, درستی durustí, حق hakk, صدق sidk.
VERANDAH (*porch*), طاق tak, رواق rivák.—(*projecting from a house*) بر آمده bar-ámadah.
VERB, فعل fi'l.—(*active transitive verb*) فعل متعدی fi'l-i-muta'addí.—(*causal verb*) فعل مجبور fi'l-i-majbúr.—(*intransitive or neuter verb*) فعل لازم fi'l-i-lázim.—(*active voice*) فعل معروف fi'l-i-ma'rúf.—(*passive voice*) فعل مجهول fi'l-i-majhúl.—(*auxiliary verb*) فعل رابطه fi'l-i-rábitah.—(*perfect verb*) فعل تام fi'l-i-támm.—(*imperfect or defective verb*) فعل ناقص fi'l-nákis.—(*reflective verb*) فعل متعدی بنفس fi'l-i-muta'addí bi-nafs.—(*affirmative verb*) فعل مثبت fi'l-i-musbit.—(*negative verb*) فعل منفی fi'l-i-munfí.
VERBAL, شفاهی shifáhí.—(*verbal noun*) مصدر masdar.
VERBALLY (*viva voce*), زبانی zabání—(*literally*) لفظاً بلفظ lafzan bi-lafz.
VERBATIM, لفظ بلفظ lafz bi-lafz.
VERBERATION, مصادمه musádamah.
VERBOSE, طویل tavíl, مفصل mufas-sal, دراز diráz.
VERBOSITY, تفصیل tafsíl, اطناب itnáb, تطویل tatvíl.
VERDANT, سبز sabz, تر tar.
VERDICT, فتوی fatvá, حکم hukm.
VERDIGRIS, زنگار zaugár.
VERDURE, سبزی sabzí, سبزه sabzah.
VERGE, دم dam, لب lab, کنار kanár.—(*to be on the verge of*) مشرف بودن (به) mushrif búdan (bi).
VERIFICATION, تحقیق tahkík, تصدیق tasdík, تصحیح tashíh.
To VERIFY, تصدیق کردن tasdík kar-dan, محقق نمودن muhakkak ni-múdan, تحقیق کردن tahkík kar-dan.
VERILY, *vide* TRULY.
VERITY, *vide* TRUTH.
VERMICELLI, رشته rishtah.
VERMILION, شنجرف shanjarf, زنجفره zinjifrah, سرنج suranj.
VERMIN, حشرات hasharát, جانورك jánvarak.
VERNACULAR (*speech*), خاص زبان kháss-zabán.
VERNAL, بهاری bahárí, ربیعی rabí'í, ربعی rib'íy.
VERSATILE, بی قرار bí-karár, نا پایدار ná-páyadár, متغیر mutaghayyir, بی ثبات bí-sabát, متلون mutalav-vin, دو رو dú-rú, سبك پا subuk-pá.
VERSATILITY, چالاکی chálákí, زرنگی zaringí.
VERSE (*poetry*), نظم nazm, شعر shi'r.—(*couplet*) بیت bait (*pl.*

ابیات abyát).—(*hemistich*) مصراع misrá'.—(*quatrain*) رباعی rubá'í. (*strophe*) قطعة kat'ah.—(*of the Kur,án, &c.*) آیت áyat (*pl.* آیات áyát).—(*of a song*) بند band.—(*blank verse, or prose in poetic measure*) مرجز murajjaz.—(*rhyme without measure*) مسجع musajja'. —(*Persian and Arabic verses mixed*) ملمع mulamma'.—(*a foot in verse*) رکن rukn (*pl.* ارکان arkán), جز juz (*pl.* اجزا ajzá).

Versed, واقف vákif, کار شناس kár-shinás.

Versification, تنظیم tanzím.

Versifier, شاعر shá'ir.

To Versify, بنظم در آوردن bi-nazm dar ávardan.

Version (*translation*), ترجمة tarjumah.—(*statement*) کول kaul, گفتة guftah.

Verst, ورست varst (*eur.*).

Vertebral, فقاری fakárí.

Vertebræ (*of the spine*), مهرة muhrah, فقار fakár.

Vertex, فرق fark, ناصیة násiyah.

Vertical, قائم ká,im.

Vertigo, خیرگی khíragí, سر گردانی sar-gardání, دوران سر daurán-i-sar, دوار davár.

Very, بسیار bisyár, نهایت niháyat, بغایت bi-gháyat, خیلی khailí, بس bas, بسا basá.—(*very, identical*) همین hamín, همان hamán, خود khwud, عینی 'ainí. — (*the very act*) عین فعل 'ain-i-fi'l.—(*on that very day*) در خود آن روز dar khwud-i-án rúz, همان روز hamán-rúz.

Vesicle, تول tuvul, آبلة ábilah, اولة aulah (*vulg.*).

Vesicular, آبلة دار ábilah-dár.

Vesper, شام shám.

Vespers, نماز شام namáz-i-shám.

Vessel (*ship*), جهاز jaház, کشتی kashtí, مرکب markab, گمی gamí. —(*vase*) ظرف zarf, سبو sabú, کوارة kuvárah, کلوك kulúk, بلونی bulúní, بستو bastú.

Vest (*inner coat*), ارخالق arkhálik, الخلق alkhuluk, قفتان kaftán.

To Vest (*adorn*), آراستن árástan, پوشانیدن púshánídan.—(*to vest in*) قرار گرفتن karár giriftan, استقرار یافتن istikrár yáftan.

Vestal, پاك دامن pák-dáman, عفیف 'afíf, پرهیزگار parhíz-gár.

Vestibule, پیشگاه písh-gáh, دالان dálán.

Vestige, اثر asar, نشان nishán.

Vestment, پوشاك púshák, جامة jámah, لباس libás, کسوت kisva پوشن púshan.

Vesture, پوشاك púshák, جامة jámah, لباس libás, کسوت kisvat پوشن púshan.

Vestry, مشورتخانة mashvarat-khánah.

Vetches (*cicer arietinum*), نخود nukhúd. — (*vicia faba*) کشنة kashanah, کسنة kasannah, کرسنة karsannah.

Veteran, کهن kuhan, کار آزمودة kár-ázmúdah.—(*military term*), سرباز پیر قدیم sarbáz-i-pír-i-kadím.

Veterinary surgeon, بیطار baitár.

To Vex, رنجانیدن ranjánídan, آزردن ázurdan, ایذا رسانیدن ízá rasánídan, مکدر گردانیدن mukaddar gardánídan, رنج دادن ranj dádan, متنفر گردانیدن mutanaffir gardánídan, آزار دادن ázár dádan, تلخ جان گردانیدن talkh-ján gardánídan, گزیدن gazídan.—(*to be vexed*) آزردة شدن ázurdah shudan, کجخلق شدن kaj-khulk shudan, ملول شدن malúl shudan, متنفر شدن mutanaffir shudan, رنجیدن ranjídan, رنجیدة شدن ranjídah shudan, اوقات تلخ شدن aukát talkh shudan, حواس مغشوش گردیدن haváss maghshúsh gardídan, مضطرب گشتن muztarib gashtan, طبیعت بر هم زدة شدن tabí'at bar-hamzadah shudan, متالم شدن muta,allim shudan.

Vexation, آزار ázár, رنج ranj, افسوس afsús, آشوب áshúb, کدورت kadúrát.

Vexatious, دل آزار dil-ázár.

Vexed, مضطرب muztarib, کج خلق kaj-khulk, رنجیدة ranjídah, غمگین gham-gín, متغیر mutaghayyir.—

(*to be vexed with*) (از) رنجیدن ranjídan (az).
VIAL, شیشه shíshah.
VIANDS, آذوقه ázúkah, خوراك khwurák, خوردنی khwurdaní, اکل akal, ماکولات ma,kúlát, غذا ghizá, توشه túshah, زاد zád, روزی rúzí, قوت kút.
TO VIBRATE, جنبیدن jumbídan, طپیدن tapídan, لرزیدن larzídan, تکان نمودن takán nimúdan.
VIBRATION, لرزه larzah, تکان takán.
VICE (*wickedness*), بدی badí, بد کاری bad-kárí, شر sharr, شرارت sharárat, زبونی zabúní, قباحت kabáhat, فساد fasád, گناه gunáh, رذیله razílah.—(*large, carpenter's or blacksmith's vice*) گیره gírah.—(*small hand-vice*) گیره دست gírah-i-dast.
VICEROY, نائب ná,ib, نائب مناب ná,ib-i-manáb, وکیل vakíl, نواب navváb, نظام nazzám.—(*Governor-General*) فرمانفرمای firmán-firmáí.
VICEROYALTY, فرمان فرمائی firmán-firmá,í.
VICE-VERSÂ, به عکس bi-'aks.
VICINITY (*neighbourhood*), همسایگی ham-sáyagí, جوار javár, مجاورت mujávarat, قرب kurb, نواحی naváhí. — (*proximity*) نزدیکی nazdíkí, قربت kurbat, قرابت karábat, تقریب takríb.
VICIOUS, فاسد fásid, شریر sharír, معیوب ma'yúb, بد خو bad-khú, بد نفس bad-nafs.
VICISSITUDES (*of fortune*), انقلابات inkilábát, دوران فلك daurán-i-falak, دور گردون daur-i-gardún, گردش چرخ gardish-i-charkh, حوادث زمان havádis-i-zamán, تقالیب روزگار takálíb-i-rúzigár, اختلافات روزگار ikhtiláfát-i-rúzigár.
VICTIM, فدا fidá, فدیه fidyah, قربان kurbán, تصدق tasadduk.
VICTOR, غالب ghálib, مظفر muzaffar, منصور mansúr, فیروز fírúz.
VICTORIOUS, فیروز fírúz, مظفر muzaffar, منصور mansúr, غالب ghálib.
VICTORIOUSLY, غالبانه ghálibánah, غالبا ghálibạn.
VICTORY, فتح fath, ظفر zafar, غلبه ghalabah, فیروزی fírúzí, دستبرد dast-burd, نصرت nusrat, فوز fauz, استیلا istílá, نصر nasr. — (*to gain a victory*) فتح یافتن fath yáftan, غالب آمدن ghálib ámadan, ظفر یافتن zafar yáftan. — (*to claim a victory*) ادعائی فتح نمودن iddi'á,í-i-fath nimúdan, ادعائی ظفر کردن iddi'á,í-i-zafar kardan.
TO VICTUAL, خورانیدن khwúránídan, پروردن parvardan, تغذیه نمودن taghziyah nimúdan.
VICTUALS, آذوقه ázúkah, خوراك khwurák, خوردنی khwurdaní, اکل akal, ماکولات ma,kúlát, غذا ghizá, توشه túshah, زاد zád, روزی rúzí, قوت kút.—(*not requiring to be cooked, but always ready, such as bread, cheese, fruit, preserves, &c.*), حاضری házirí.—(*requiring cookery, such as meat, &c.*) پختنی pukhtaní, خورش khwurish.
VIDELICET, یعنی ya'ní, اعنی a'ní, ای ai.
TO VIE, رقابت نمودن rakábat nimúdan.
VIEW, نظر nazar, نگاه nigáh, منظر manzar.—(*opinion*) رأی ra,í, رای ráy, گمان gumán, اندیشه andíshah, قیاس kiyás, خیال khiyál, حدس hads, تصور tasavvur, فکر fikr. —(*in view*) نصب العین nasbu-'l-'ain, بنظر آمده bi-nazar ámadah.—(*in this view*) نظر بر این nazar bar ín. —(*to forward the views*) ممد خیالات بودن mumidd-i-khiyálát búdan. —(*to keep in view*) به مد نظر آوردن bi-madd-i-nazar ávardan.
TO VIEW, نظر نمودن nazar nimúdan. —(*consider*) دانستن dánistan, انگاشتن angáshtan.
VIGIL (*keeping watch*), پاسبانی pásbání, نگهبانی nigah-bání, کشیك kashík. — (*study or devotion at night*) سهران sahrán, سهر sahar.
VIGILANCE, آگهی ágahí, آگاهی ágáhí, احتیاط ihtiyát, بصیرت basírat, بیداری bídárí, خبرداری khabar-dárí, هوشیاری húsh-yárí, انتباه intibáh.

VIGILANT, آگاه ágáh, بیدار bídár, هوشیار húsh-yár, متنبه mutanabbih.

VIGILANTLY, بهوشیاری bi-húsh-yárí.

VIGNETTE, نیم تنه ním-tanah.

VIGOROUS, قوی kaví, زور آور zúr-ávar, توانا tavána, نیرو مند nairú-mand, پر زور pur-zúr.

VIGOROUSLY, بطور جدی bi-taur-i-jiddí.

VIGOUR, زور zúr, زور آوری zúr-ávarí, توانائی taváná,í, نیرو nairú, نیرو مندی nairú-mandí, قوت kúvat or kuvvat, موجت mújat.

VILE, خوار khwár, پست past, نا کاره ná-kárah, زلیل zalíl, کمینه kamínah, فرو مایه furú - máyah, حقیر hakír, نا کس ná-kas, مخذول makhzúl, دون dún, خسیس khasís, سفله siflah, رذیل razíl, ول vil.

VILELY, حقیرانه hakíránah.

VILENESS, خواری khwárí, پستی pastí, ذلت zillat, دونی dúní, سفلگی siflagí.

To VILIFY, بد نام کردن bad-nám kardan, دشنام دادن dushnám dádan, دشنامیدن dushnámídan.

VILLA, سرا sará, قصر kasr.

VILLAGE, قریه karyah, ده dih, موضع mauza', روستا rústá, الکه ulkah.—(*small village, hamlet*) حشم hasham, احشام ihshám.—(*number of contiguous villages, forming a district*) بلوك bulúk.

VILLAGER, روستائی rústá,í, دهقان dihkán.—(*head villager, or chief man of a village*) کد خدا kad-khudá, ده خدا dih-khudá, پیر ده pír-i-dih, رئیس ra,ís, مقدم mukaddam, ریش سفید rísh-safíd.

VILLAIN, شریر sharír, اوباش aubásh, شقی skakí, فاسد fásid, بد ذات bad-zát.

VILLAINOUS, بد bad, بد کار bad-kár, شریر sharír, بد ذات bad-zát.

VILLAINOUSLY, شریرانه sharíránah.

VINCIBLE, مغلوب شدنی maghlúb-shudaní.

To VINDICATE, حمایت کردن himáyat kardan, هواداری نمودن havá-dárí nimúdan.

VINDICATION, تزکیه tazkiyah, اعتزار i'tizár, معذرت ma'zarat.

VINDICTIVE, کینه ور kínah-var, منتقم muntakim, کینه خواه kínah-khwáh.

VINE, درخت انگور dirakht-i-angúr, تاك ták, بنه رز bunah-i-raz, درخت مو dirakht-i-mau.

VINE-DRESSER, تاکبان ták-bán.

VINEGAR, سرکه sirkah, خل khall.

VINE-LEAF, برگ رز barg-i-raz, برگ مو barg-i-mau.

VINEYARD, تاکستان tákistán, انگورستان angúrıstán, باغ مو bágh-i-mau.

VINOUS, شرابی sharábí.

VINTAGE (*time of gathering grapes*), قطاف katáf, چیدن انگور chídan-i-angúr.

VINTNER, می فروش mai-furúsh.

VIOL, کمانچه kamánchah.

VIOLABLE, نقض پذیر naks-pazír.

To VIOLATE (*ravish*), بکارت بردن bi-kárat burdan, بی عصمتی کردن bí-'asmatí kardan, بی سیرت کردن bí-sírat kardan, بزور زنا کردن bi-zúr ziná kardan.—(*a promise*) عهد شکستن 'ahd shikastan, جر زدن jir zadan, فسخ عهد کردن faskh-i-'ahd kardan, خلف وعده کردن khulf-i-va'dah kardan.

VIOLATION (*ravishment*), زنا ziná, پرده دری pardah-darí, هتك عرض hatk-i-'irz.—(*of a promise*) عهد شکستگی 'ahd - shikastagí, فسخ faskh, نقض nakz.

VIOLATOR, جنایتکار jináyat-kár.—(*of women*) زنا کار ziná-kár, هتاك عرض hatták-i-'irz.

VIOLENCE, زور zúr, جور jaur, جفا jafá, ستم sitam, جبر jabr, ظلم zulm, تهور tahavvur, تعدی ta'addí, دست درازی dast-dirází, غصب ghasb, شدت shiddat.—(*of cold, fever, &c.*) سورت súrat.—(*of wind*) صدمات sadamát.

VIOLENT, شدید shadíd, سخت sakht, متهور mutahavvir, جفا کار jafá-kár.

VIOLENTLY, متهورانه mutahavviránah, بزور bi-zúr, زجرا zajran, بشدت bi-shiddat.

VIOLET, بنفشه binafshah.—(*colour*) رنگ بنفش rang-i-binafsh, بنفشه binafshah.

VIOLIN, کمانچه kamánchah.—(*player*) کمانچه زن kamánchah-zan.—(*to play the violin*) کمانچه زدن *or* کشیدن kamánchah zadan *or* kashídan.

VIPER, افعی af'í, مار már, تیره مار tírah-már, مار جعفری már-i-ja'farí.

VIRAGO, زنکه zanakah.

VIRGIN, باکره bákirah, بالست bálist, دوشیزه dúshízah, عذرا 'azrá, دختر dukhtar.

VIRGINITY, بکریت bikríyat, بکارت bikárat, دوشیزگی dúshízagí.—(*to deprive of virginity*) بکارت بردن bikárat burdan, بی عصمتی کردن bí-'asmatí kardan, بی سیرت کردن bí-sírat kárdan, بزور زنا کردن bi-zúr ziná kardan.—(*woman who has lost her virginity*) ثیبه sayyibah.

VIRILE, مردانه mardánah.

VIRILITY, مردانگی mardánagí, مردی mardí, مروت murúvat.

VIRTUAL, معنوی ma'naví, معناوی ma'náví.

VIRTUALLY, در حقیقت dar kakíkat.

VIRTUE (*chastity*), عصمت 'asmat, عفت 'iffat, پاکدامنی pák-dámaní, پارسائی pársá,í, زهد zuhd, تقاوت takávut, رهبانیت ruhbáníyat, پرهیز گاری parhíz-gárí.—(*quality*) خاصیت khássíyat, ذات zát, کیفیت kaifíyat, حیثیت haisíyat.

VIRTUOSO, اهل هنر ahil-i-hunar.

VIRTUOUS, پاك pák, پاکیزه pákízah, پاکدامن pák-dáman, پارسا pársá, عفیف 'afíf, عاصم 'ásim, طاهر táhir, پرهیز گار parhíz-gár, حصور hasúr, محتاط muhtát, معصوم ma'súm.

VIRULENCE, شدت shiddat, مرارت marárat, تلخی talkhí, سختی sakhtí.

VIRULENT, شدید shadíd, تلخ talkh, سخت sakht.

VIRULENTLY, با شدت bá-shiddat, با سختی bá-sakhtí.

VIRUS, ریم rím.

VIS-À-VIS, مقابل mukábil, رو برو rú-bi-ru, پیشاپیش písh-á-písh, در برابر dar barábar.

VISAGE, رو rú, روی rúy, وجه vajh, چهره chihrah, جبین jabín, منظر manzar, رخ rukh, لقا liká, پیکر paikar, سیما símá, صورت súrat.

VISCERA, رودها rúdahá, امعا am'á, احشا ahshá.

VISCOUS (*tenacious*), چسبان chasbán, چسبنده chasbandah.—(*clammy*) لزج lazij.

VISCOUSNESS (*tenacity*), چسبانی chasbání, چسبندگی chasbandagí.—(*clamminess*) لزوجت luzújat.

VISIBILITY, شهادت shahádat, رؤیت ru,yat.

VISIBLE, ظاهر záhir, هویدا huvaidá, نمودار nimúdár, آشکار áshkár, آشکاره áshkárah, منظور manzúr, مرئی mar,í, نمایان nimáyán, پدید padíd, عیان 'ayán, فاش fásh, مبین mubín. — (*to be visible*) ملحوظ افتادن malhúz uftádan.

VISIBLY, ظاهراً záhiran, ظاهرانه záhiránah, آشکاره áshkárah.

VISION (*sight*), بینائی bíná,í, بصارت basárat, نظر nazar, قوت باصرت kúvat-i-básirat.—(*apparition*) روح rúh, خیال khiyál.—(*dream*) خواب khwáb, حلم hilm, رؤیا ru,yá.

VISIONARY, خیالی khiyálí, وهمی vahmí.

VISIT, ملاقات mulákát, دید díd, دیدن dídan.—(*to sick persons*) عیادت 'iyádat. — (*to tombs of saints, sacred spots, &c.*) زیارت ziyárat.—(*interchange of visits*) دید و باز دید díd u báz-díd.—(*to return a visit*) بباز دید رفتن bi-báz-díd raftan.

To VISIT, عیادت کردن 'iyádat kardan, زیارت نمودن ziyárat nimúdan, ملاقات کردن mulákát kardan.

VISITATION, ملاقات mulákát, تفقد tafakkud.—(*of God*) تلاقی talákí, لقا liká.

VISITOR, زائر zá,ir.—(*of the sick*) عائد 'á,id.

VISOR, برقع burka'.

VISTA, چشم انداز chashm-andáz, نظر گاه nazar-gáh.
VISUAL, باصره básirah.
VITAL, حیاتی hayátí, اصلی aslí, ضروری zarúrí.
VITALITY, زندگی zindagí, اثر حیات asar-i-hayát.
VITALS, ادوات حیات adavát-i-hayát, آلات زندگی álát-i-zindagí.
To VITIATE, فاسد کردن fásid kardan, تباه ساختن tabáh sákhtan, معیوب ساختن ma'yúb sákhtan.
VITIATED, تباه tabáh, فاسد fásid, معیوب ma'yúb.
VITIATION, فساد fasád, تباهی tabáhí, افساد ifsád.
VITRIFACTION, گداز gudáz.
To VITRIFY, گداختن gudákhtan.
VITRIOL, زاج záj, زاق zák, توتیا tútiyá.—(*blue vitriol, sulphate of copper*) زنگبار zangbár, زاج کبود záj-i-kabúd, توتیای هندی tútiyá,í-i-hindí.—(*white vitriol, sulphate of zinc*) توتیای روح tútiyá,í-i-rúh, توتیای بصره tútiyá,í-i-basrah.—(*green vitriol, sulphate of iron*) توتیای آهن tútiyá,í-i-áhan, توتیای سبز tútiyá,í-i-sabz. — (*spirit of vitriol, sulphuric acid*) روح توتیا rúh-i-tútiyá, جوهر توتیا jauhar-i-tútiyá.
To VITUPERATE, ملامت کردن malámat kardan, عیب گفتن 'aib guftan, ذم کردن zamm kardan.
VITUPERATION, زجر zajr, ملامت malámat, سرزنش sar-zanish, مؤاخذه mu,ákhazah, پیغاره paighárah, عتاب 'itáb.
VIVACIOUS, زرنگ zaring, شوخ shúkh.
VIVACITY (*liveliness*), زرنگی zaringí, شوخی shúkhí, جلفی jilfí.
VIVID, روشن raushan, منور munavvar, منیر munír, لامع lámi', تابان tábán, رخشان rukhshán.
VIVIDNESS, روشنی raushaní, تابانی tábání, تاب táb, تابش tábish, رخشندگی rakhshandagí.
VIVIFIC, جانبخش ján-bakhsh.
VIVIFICATION, جانداری ján-dárí, رستخیز rustakhíz.

To VIVIFY, احیاء کردن ahyá, kardan, زنده کردن zindah kardan.
VIXEN, زنکه zanakah.
VIZARD, برقع burka'.
VIZIER, وزیر vazír, مدبر mudabbir, مشیر mashír, دبیر dabír.
VOCABULARY, فرهنگ farhang, لغت lughat.
VOCAL, صوتی sautí, نوائی navá,í.
VOCALLY, با آواز bá-áváz.
VOCATION, شغل shughl, کار kár, پیشه píshah, کسب kasb, حرفت hirfat.
VOCATIVE, منادا munádá,.—(*vocative particle*) حرف ندا harf-i-nidá,.
To VOCIFERATE, نعره زدن na'rah zadan.
VOCIFERATION, نعره na'rah, بانگ báng.
VOCIFEROUS, غوغائی ghaughá,í.
VOGUE, رسم rasm, روش ravish, عادت 'ádat, شیوه shívah, طریق tarík, سلوک sulúk.—(*to be in vogue*) رواج یافتن raváj yáftan, معمول شدن ma'múl shudan.
VOICE, آواز áváz, صوت saut, صدا sadá, صیت sít, نوا navá, بانگ báng.—(*weak voice*) صدا کم sadá-i-kam.—(*the public voice*) افکار عمومیه afkár-i-'umúmíyah.—(*active voice*) فعل معروف fi'l-i-ma'rúf. — (*passive voice*) فعل مجهول fi-'l-i-majhúl.
VOID, تهی tuhí, خالی khálí, فارغ fárigh, پوک púk (*vulg.*). — (*null*) باطل bátil, معطل mu,attal, فاسد fásid, منسوخ mansúkh, مبطل mubtal.
To VOID, خالی ساختن khálí sákhtan, تهی نمودن tuhí nimúdan.
VOLANT, طیران tayarán, پرواز parváz.
VOLATILE, لطیف latíf, رقیق rakík, پریدنی parídaní.
VOLATILENESS, لطافت latáfat, رقت rikkat, پریدگی parídagí.
VOLCANO, کوه آتشین kúh-i-átishín, کوه سوزنده kúh-i-súzandah, کوه آتش فشان kúh-i-átish-fishán.
VOLENS NOLENS, خواسته نخواسته khwástah na-khwástah, خواه مخواه khwáh ma-khwáh, طوعاً

کرهن tau'an karahan, چار نا چار chár ná-chár, خواهی نخواهی khwáhí na-khwáhí.

VOLLEY (*of shot*), شلیك shalík.—(*volley firing*) مشك شلیك mashk-i-shalík.—(*to fire a volley*) شلیك کردن shalík kardan.

VOLUBILITY, فصاحت fasáhat, زبان آوری zabán-ávarí.

VOLUBLE, فصیح fasíh, زبان آور zabán-ávar.

VOLUME, جلد jild, دفتر daftar, صحیفه sahífah.

VOLUMINOUS (*writer*), زیاد نویس ziyád-nivís.—(*book*) بزرگ buzurg, حجیم hajím.

VOLUMINOUSNESS (*writer*), زیاد نویسی ziyád-nivísí.—(*book*) بزرگی buzurgí.

VOLUNTARILY, باختیار bi-ikhtiyár, بمیل خود bi-mail-i-khwud, اختیاراً ikhtiyáran.

VOLUNTARY, مفت muft, اختیاری ikhtiyárí.

VOLUPTUARY, عیاش 'ayyásh, قلاش kallásh, خوش گذران khwush-guzrán.

VOLUPTUOUS, نفسانی nafsání, نفس پرست nafs-parast, شهوتی shahvatí, مست mast.

VOLUPTUOUSNESS, شهوت shahvat, نفس nafs, هوس havas, هوائی نفسانی havá,í-i-nafsání, نفس پرستی nafs-parastí, مستی mastí.

VOMIT (*emetic*), دوائی قی davá,í-i-kai, دوائی مقیی davá,í-i-mukayyí, مستفرغ mustafrigh.

To VOMIT, قی کردن kai kardan, استفراغ کردن istifrágh kardan.

VOMITING, استفراغ istifrágh, قی kai.

VORACIOUS, اکول akúl, شکمو shikamú (*vulg.*).

VORACIOUSLY, حریصانه harísánah.

VORACIOUSNESS, حرص hirs, حریصی harísí.

VORTEX, گرد آب gird-áb.

VOTARESS, عابده 'ábidah.

VOTARY, عابد 'ábid, عاکف 'ákif.—(*religious term*) اهل ahl.

VOTE, قول kaul, سخن sukhun, رائی ra,í.

To VOTE, رائی زدن ra,í zadan.

VOTER, رائی دهنده ra,í-dihandah.

To VOUCH (*declare*), عرض کردن 'arz kardan, معلوم نمودن ma'lúm nimúdan.—(*bear witness*) گواه دادن guváh dádan.

VOUCHER, ضامن zámin.

To VOUCHSAFE (*trans.*), موهبت کردن mauhabat kardan. — (*intrans.*) عنایت فرمودن 'ináyat firmúdan.

VOW, نذر nazr, عهد 'ahd, شرط shart.—(*abandonment of a sin*) توبه taubah.—(*conditional vow*) یمین yamín.—(*not to cohabit with one's wife for a certain period, as a religious penance*) ایلا i,lá.

To VOW, نذر کردن nazr kardan, شرط نمودن shart nimúdan.

VOWEL (*long*), حرف علت harf-i-'illat.—(*short*) حرکت harakat.—(*vowel points*) حرکات harakát, اعراب i'ráb.

VOYAGE, سفر safar, سفر دریا safar-i-daryá.

VOYAGER, سافر sáfir, راه آور ráh-ávar.

VULGAR, عام 'ámm, عموم 'umúm, مبتذل mubtazall, رزیل razíl, رکیك rakík, پوچ púch, ول vil, خوار khwár, پست past, مستهجن mustahjan.—(*vulgar phraseology*) گفتار عوام guftár-i-'avámm, محاورت عوام muhávarat-i-'avámm. — (*vulgar tongue*) لسان متداوله lisán-i-mutadávalah.

VULGARITY, غلظت ghilzat, پستی pastí (*vulg.*).

VULGARLY, عوامانه 'avámmánah.

VULNERABILITY, زخم برداری zakhm-bardárí, تأذی ta,azzí.

VULNERABLE, زخم بردار zakhm-bardár, جرح پذیر jurh-pazír.

VULPINE, حیله باز hílah-báz.

VULTURE, کرکس karkas, لاشه خور láshah-khwur. — (*black vulture*) قرقوش karakúsh, دال dál.

W.

WADDING (*for a gun*), کهنه kuh-nah.

To WADDLE, متمایل شدن mutamáyil shudan.

WADDLER, شخص متمایل shakhs-i-mutamáyil.

To WADE, غور کردن ghaur kardan.

WAFER, کلوچه kulúchah, رقیق rakík.

To WAFT, رسانیدن rasánídan.

WAG, مسخره maskharah.

To WAG (*trans.*), جنبانیدن jumbánídan, تکانیدن takánídan, تکان دادن takán dádan.—(*intrans.*) جنبیدن jumbídan, لرزیدن larzídan, تکان کردن takán kardan, لکیدن lakídan.

To WAGE, بحس نمودن bahs nimúdan, شرط بستن shart bastan, نذر بستن nazr bastan.—(*to wage war*) جنگ کردن jang kardan, هجوم آوردن hujúm ávardan.

WAGER, بحث bahs, شرط shart, گرو girau, سبق sabak, اوچ úch.

To WAGER, بحث نمودن bahs nimúdan, شرط بستن shart bastan, نذر بستن nazr bastan.

WAGES, مواجب mavájib, اجرت ujrat, اجر ajr, وظیفه vazífah, علوفه 'alúfah, مزد muzd.

WAGGERY, شوخی shúkhí.

WAGGISH, ظریف zaríf, خوشدل khwush-dil, شاد shád, شادمان shád-mán, خوش khwush, مشعوف mash'úf.

WAGGISHLY, از روی شوخی az rúy-i-shúkhí.

WAGGON, عراده 'arrádah, عرابه 'arábah.

WAGGONER, عراده چی 'arrádah-chí.

WAGTAIL (*small bird*), صعوه sa'vah, گاذرشك gázurishk, گنجشك سقوی gunjashk-i-sakaví, سقاچی sakkáchí.

WAIF (*thing found without owner*), لقطه luktah.

WAIL (*lament*), ناله náláh, زاری zárí, نوحه nauhah, نیاح niyáh.—(*for the dead*) نوحه nauhah, شیون shívan.—(*persons who bewail the dead*) نوحه گران nauhah-garán, نوحه کنندگان nauhah-kunandagán.

To WAIL, نوحه گری نمودن nauhah-garí nimúdan, عزاداری نمودن 'azádárí nimúdan, نالیدن nálídan, شیون کردن shívan kardan.

WAINSCOT, هزاره hizárah.

WAIST, کمر kamar, میان miyán, نطاق niták.

WAISTCOAT, جلیدکه jalídkah, ژیلتکه zhílitkah.

To WAIT, ماندن mándan, بودن búdan, انتظار کشیدن intizár kashídan, منتظر بودن muntazir búdan, صبر کردن sabr kardan, مکث نمودن makas nimúdan. — (*to wait upon*) ملازم بودن mulázim búdan, اداثی خدمت نمودن adá,í-i-khidmat nimúdan, خدمت رسیدن khidmat rasídan.—(*to lie in wait*) کمین کردن kamín kardan, در کمینگاه نشستن dar kamín-gáh nishastan.—(*wait a bit*) قدری صبر بکنید kadrí sabr bi-kuníd, اندکی صبر کنید andakí sabr-kuníd. — (*after waiting some time*) بعد از چند دقیقه مکث ba'd az chand dakíkah-i-makas.

WAITER, غلام ghulám, ملازم mulázim.—(*tray*) مجموعه majmú'ah, مجمعه majmu'ah, سینی síní, خوان khwán.

WAITING-ROOM, اطاق گار uták-i-gár (*eur.*).

To WAIVE (*relinquish*), گذاشتن guzáshtan, ترك كردن tark kardan.

WAKE (*in the wake of*), عقب سر 'akb-i-sar.

To WAKE, بیدار شدن bídár shudan.—(*awaken another*) بیدار کردن bídár kardan.

WAKEFUL, بیخواب bí - khwáb.—(*watchful*) بیدار bídár, متنبه mutanabbih, خبردار khabar-dár.

WAKEFULNESS, بیخوابی bí-khwábí.

(*watchfulness*) بیداری bídárí, خبرداری khabar-dárí.

WALK, گردش gardish.—(*in a garden, &c., paved or gravelled*) خیابان khiyábán. — (*to go for a walk*) بگردش رفتن bi-gardish raftan, تفرج گردش کردن tafarruj gardish kardan.

To WALK (*persons*), از پا رفتن az pá raftan, پیاده رفتن piyádah raftan, خرامیدن khirámídan, قدم زدن kadam zadan, راه رفتن ráh raftan. —(*animals*) قدم رفتن kadam raftan.—(*up and down*) گشت کردن gasht kardan.

WALKER, متفرج mutafarrij.

WALKING-STICK, چوب دستی chúb-dastí, عصا ʻasá, چماق chumák.

WALL, دیوار dívár, حائط há,it, جدار jidár.—(*walls of a town*) بارو bárú, دیوار dívár. — (*fortified walls*) حصار hisár, دیوار قلعه dívár-i-kalʻah.—(*canvas walls*) سراپرده sar-á-pardah.—(*coping of a wall*) رخبام rukh-bám, تاج دیوار táj-i-dívár. — (*parapet wall*) معجر maʻjar, محجر mahjar. — (*wall constructed of layers of mud*) چینه chínah.—(*party-wall*) دیوار مشترك dívár-i-mushtarak.

To WALL, دیوار ساختن dívár sákhtan.

WALLET, انبان ambán, جلبندی julbandí, خورجین khúrjín.—(*small wallet fastened behind the saddle*) ترك tark.

WALLFLOWER, گول شب بو gúl-i-shab-bú.

To WALLOW, غلطیدن ghaltídan.

WALNUT, گردو girdú, گردکان girdgán.

WALTZ, والتز váltz (*eur.*).

To WALTZ, والتز نمودن váltz nimúdan (*eur.*).

WAN, سست sust, فاتر fátn, مانده mándah.

WAND, عصا ʻasá, چوب chúb.

To WANDER, گردیدن gardídan, گشت کردن gasht kardan, آواره گردیدن ávárah gardídan, سیر کردن sair kardan, بیراه شدن bí-ráh shudan, گمراه شدن gum-ráh shudan.—(*to wander from one's subject*) از مطلب دور افتادن az matlab dúr uftádan.

WANDERER, آواره ávárah, سیار sayyár, دربدر dar-bi-dar, سرگشته sargashtah.—(*wandering or nomadic tribe*) ایل íl (*pl.* ایلیات íliyát).—(*man of a nomadic tribe*) ایلیاتی íliyátí.—(*chief of the wandering tribes*) ایلخانی íl-khání, ایلبیگی íl-begí.

To WANE, کاستن kástan, کم شدن kam shudan.

WANT (*wish*), خواهش khwáhish, مطلب matlab, آرزو árzú, مراد murád. — (*need*) حاجت hájat, احتیاج ihtiyáj, ضرورت zarúrat, کار kár.—(*deficiency*) کمی kamí, کم رسی kam-rasí, نقص naks, قصور kusúr, عدم ʻadam. — (*poverty*) تنگی tangí, قحط kaht, گدائی gadá,í, نیاز مندی niyáz-mandí, بینوائی bí-navá,í.—(*for want of, lacking*) از عدم az ʻadam, از سبب نقص az sabab-i-naks, از سبب قصور az sabab-i-kusúr, بنابر نا بودن banábar-i-ná-búdan.

To WANT (*wish*), خواهش نمودن khwáhish nimúdan, خواستن khwástan. — (*need*) لازم داشتن lázim dáshtan, ضرور داشتن zarúr dáshtan, خواستن khwástan, حاجت داشتن hájat dáshtan, محتاج بودن muhtáj búdan.—(*it wanted two hours to sunset*) دو ساعت بغروب مانده بود dú sáʻat bi-ghurúb mándah búd.

WANTON, شوخ shúkh, مست mast, شهوتی shahvatí.

WANTONLY, با شوخی bá-shúkhí, با شهوت bá-shahvát.

WANTONNESS, شوخی shúkhí, مستی mastí.

WAR, جنگ jang, کار زار kár-zár, جدال jadál, نبرد nabard, رزم razm, حرب harb, مبارزت mubárazat, پرخاش parkhásh, پیکار paikár, هیجا haijá, وغا vaghá. — (*war against infidels*) جهاد jahád, غزا ghazá.—(*Secretary for War*) سر

عسکر sar-'askar.—(*declaration of war*) اعلان حرب i'lán-i-harb. —(*materials of war*) آلات جنگ álát-i-jang.

To WAR, جنگیدن jangídan, جنگ کردن jang kardan.

To WARBLE, سرائیدن sará,ídan, ترنم کردن tarannum kardan, نغمه پرداختن naghmah pardákhtan.

WARBLER, قوال kavvál, خوانندہ khwánandah, سرایندہ saráyandah, مغنی mughanní.

WARD (*one under a guardian*), موصی له músá lahu.

To WARD off, رد کردن radd kardan, دفع کردن daf' kardan, وا زدن vá-zadan, وا داشتن vá-dáshtan.

WARDEN, محافظ muháfiz.

WARDROBE, توشه خانه túshah-khánah, قور خانه kúr-khánah.

WARDSHIP, محافظت muháfazat.

WARE, متاع mutá' (*pl.* امتعه amti'ah), اسباب asbáb (*only used in the plural*).

WAREHOUSE, مخزن makhzan, خزینه khizínah, کار خانه kár-khánah, بار خانه bár-khánah, انبار ambár.

To WAREHOUSE, امانت گذاشتن amánat guzáshtan, ودیعت نهادن vadí'at nihádan.

WARFARE, جنگ jang, کار زار kár-zár, جدال jadál, نبرد nabard, رزم razm, حرب harb, مبارزت mubárazat, پرخاش parkhásh, پیکار paikár, هیجا haijá, وغا vaghá.

WARILY, بخبرداری bi-khabar-dárí.

WARINESS, خبر khabar, خبرداری khabar-dárí, احتیاط íhtiyát, حذر hazar, هوشیاری húsh-yárí, دیده بانی dídah-bání.

WARLIKE, جنگ آزموده jang-ázmúdah, رزم پیشه razm-píshah, جنگی jangí.

WARM, گرم garm, حار hárr.

To WARM (*trans.*), گرم ساختن garm sákhtan. — (*intrans.*) گرم شدن garm shudan, تفسیدن tafsídan.

WARMLY, با گرمی bá-garmí.

WARMTH, گرمی garmí, حرارت hará-rat.

To WARN, متنبه ساختن mutannabbih sákhtan, تنبیه نمودن tambíh nimúdan, اطلاع دادن ittilá' dádan, ملهم گردانیدن mulham gardánídan, آگهی دادن ágahí dádan, آگاهانیدن ágáhánídan, خبر دادن khabar dádan.

WARNING, آگهی ágahí, اطلاع ittilá', تنبیه tambíh. — (*example*) عبرت 'ibrat. — (*to take warning by*) عبرت گرفتن 'ibrat giriftan.

WARP (*of cloth*), تار tár.

To WARP (*trans.*), مائل گردانیدن má,il gardánídan. — (*intrans.*) مائل شدن má,il shudan.

WARRANT (*order*), فرمان firmán, سند sanad, دستک dastak, حکم hukm.

To WARRANT (*guarantee*), ضمانت کردن zamánat kardan.—(*authorize*) اجازه دادن ijázah dádan, امر کردن amr kardan.

WARRANTABLE, قابل تصدیق kábil-i-tasdík.

WARREN, خرگوش گاه khár-gúsh-gáh.

WARRIOR, دلاور dilávar, پهلوان pahlaván, غازی ghází, بهادر bahádur, محارب muhárib, مجاهد mujáhid, یل yal, ناضل názil, صفدر saf-dar, گرد gurd, تهمتن taham-tan.

WART, توتولی tútúlí, خال میخکی khál-i-míkhakí, گوک gúk (*vulg.*), ژخ zhakh (*obs.*).

WARY, متنبه mutanabbih, محترز muhtariz.

To WASH, شستن shustan, شستشو کردن shustushú kardan, شوریدن shúrídan.—(*the body*) غسل کردن ghusl kardan. — (*to be washed away*) برد شدن burd shudan.—(*to wash one's hand of an affair*) بیزار شدن bízár shudan.

WASHER (*of cloth in the web*), گازر gázar, قصار kassár.—(*of clothes, &c.*) رختشو rakht-shú, قصار kassár. —(*of the dead*) مرده شو murdah-shú, غسال ghassál.

WASH-HOUSE, گازر خانه gázar-khánah.

WASP, زنبور zambúr, زنبور خر zambúr-i-khar.—(*wasp's nest*) چال زنبور chál-i-zambúr.

WASPISH, غضوب ghazúb.
WASPISHLY, با غضب bá-ghazab.
WASPISHNESS, کج خلق kaj-khalk.
WASTE (*land*), ویرانه vairánah, مخروب makhrúb, شوره زار shúrah-zár.—(*of things, &c.*) اسراف isráf, تلف talaf, اتلاف itláf.
To WASTE (*become less*), کاستن kástan, زائل شدن zá,il shudan, کم شدن kam shudan, کاهیدن káhídan. — (*expend profusely*) اسراف کردن isráf kardan, تلف کردن talaf kardan, بر باد دادن bar bád dádan, ضایع ساختن záí' sákhtan, خرج کردن kharj kardan.—(*to waste time*) فرصترا از دست دادن fursatrá az dast dádan, اوقاترا ضایع کردن aukátrá záí' kardan.
WASTEFUL, مسرف musrif.
WATCH (*timepiece*), ساعت sá'at.—(*hunting watch*) ساعت شکاری sá'at-i-shikárí. — (*gold watch*) ساعت طلا sá'at-i-tilá. — (*silver watch*) ساعت نقره sá'at-i-nukrah. —(*pocket watch*) ساعت بغلی sá'at-i-baghalí. — (*chain*) زنجیر ساعت zanjír-i-sá'at.—(*case of a watch*) قاب káb.—(*spring*) فنر fanar.—(*balance*) رقاص rakkás. — (*regulator*) چرخ کند و تند charkh-i-kund va tund.—(*face*) صفحه safhah.—(*hands*) عقرب 'akrab, عقربك 'akrabak. — (*barrel*) قوطی فنر kútí-i-fanar. — (*watch-key*) کلید ساعت kilíd - i - sá'at.—(*watch - maker*) ساعت ساز sá'at-sáz. — (*period of three hours*) پاس pás (*obs.*).—(*keeping guard*) نوبت naubat, پاس pás, کشیك kashík, پاسبانی pás-bání.—(*guard*) کشیك kashík, پاس pás, قراول karávul.—(*night-guard*) گزمه gazmah.
To WATCH (*be vigilant and awake*), بیدار بودن bídár búdan, متنبه بودن mutanabbih búdan. — (*guard*) کشیك کشیدن kashík kashídan, پاسبانی کردن pás-bání kardan.
WATCHFUL, بیدار bídár, متنبه mutanabbih, خبر دار khabar-dár, هوشیار húsh-yár.
WATCHFULNESS, بیداری bídárí, خبرداری khabar - dárí, هوشیاری húsh-yárí.
WATCHMAN, کشیکچی kashík-chí, پاسبان pás-bán, نگاهبان nigáh-bán, حارس háris, دیده بان dídah-bán.
WATCH-TOWER, قراول خانه karávul-khánah, راه دار خانه ráh-dár-khánah, محرس mahras.
WATCHWORD, اسم شب ism-i-shab.
WATER, آب áb, او au (*vulg.*), ماء má,.—(*fresh water*) آب شیرین áb-i-shírín. — (*salt water*) آب شور áb-i-shúr, شور آب shúr-áb.—(*drinking-water*) آب برای نوشیدن áb-baráy-i-núshídan. — (*running water*) آب روان áb-i-raván.—(*rose-water*) گلاب gul-áb, ماء الورد má,ul-vard.—(*lustre of a gem*) آب áb.—(*of a sword, damask*) جوهر jauhar, آب áb. — (*water-carrier*) سقا sakká.—(*water - closet*) جای ضرور jáy-i-zarúr, مبرز mabraz, مزبله mazbalah, بیت الخلا baitu-'l-khalá, مستراح mustaráh, منجلاب خانه manjaláb-khánah. — (*water-course, above ground*) جوی júy, جوب júb (*vulg.*).—(*watercourse, underground*) کاریز káríz, قنات kanát.—(*water-pipe*) لوله lúlah, تنبوشه tambúshah, دس das.—(*large water-skin for camels*) راویه ráviyah. — (*smaller water - skin, carried by asses or men*) مشك mashk, قربه kirbah. — (*small channel, irrigating a garden-bed, field, &c.*) جدول jadval.—(*water-course leading over a hollow*) پلخنگ pul-khung, سواره suvárah. —(*inclined plane of stonework, through which water flows*) شرشرك shurshurak, آبشار áb - shár.—(*reservoir in which rain-water is collected*) آب انبار áb-ambár.—(*water-cresses*) تره تیزك tarah-i-tízak. — (*water-fall*) آبشیب áb-shíb, آبشار áb-shár.—(*fountain, jet d'eau*) فواره favvárah.—(*water-flash, of metal*) آفتابه áftábah.—(*ditto, of leather*) مطاره matárah, مطهره matharah.—(*water-fowl*) مرغ آبی murgh-ábí.—(*house or place*

where water is provided, by way of charity, to passengers and travellers) سقا خانه sakká-khánah.—(*spring of water*) چشمه chashmah, عین 'ain, منبع mamba'.—(*water-lily*) ابو abú, نیلوفر nílúfar.—(*water - mark*) نشان nishán.—(*water - melon*) هندوانه hinduvánah, قارپوز kár-púz, تربوز tar-búz, تربزه tar - buzah. — (*water-mill*) آسیائی آب ásyá,í-i-áb. — (*water-parting*) خط فاصل khatt-i-fásil, تقسیم آبهای taksím-i-ábaháí. — (*water-proof, subs.*) بارانی báráni. —(*adj.*) آب آزما áb-ázmá, دفع المطر daf'u-'l-matar, آب در مشو áb-dar-ma-shav. — (*water - way*) مجرا majrá. — (*water - wheel*) *vide* WHEEL. — (*officer who superintends watercourses and irrigation of lands*) میر آب mír-áb. — (*by water*) از روی آب az rúy-i-áb.—(*to draw water*) استسقا کردن istiská kardan, آب کشیدن áb kashídan.—(*to make the mouth water*) آب در دهن آوردن áb dar dahan ávardan. —(*to lay water on a house*) آبی بخانه راه دادن ábí bi-khánah ráh dádan.

To WATER, آب بخشیدن áb bakhshídan, آبیاری کردن áb-yárí kardan, آب دادن áb dádan.—(*to make water*) شاشه کردن sháshah kardan, بول کردن baul kardan, شاشیدن sháshídan.—(*to water a horse*) اسبرا آب دادن asbrá áb dádan.

WATERY, آبناك áb-nák, آبکی ábakí.

WAVE, موج mauj.

To WAVE (*trans.*) تکان دادن takán dádan.—(*intrans.*) موج زدن mauj zadan.

To WAVER, تردید داشتن tardíd dáshtan, تردد نمودن taraddud nimúdan, متردد بودن mutaraddid búdan, دو دل بودن dú-dil búdan.

WAVERING, مذبذب muzabzib, متردد mutaraddid.

WAVING, متمایل mutamáyil, مواج mavváj.

WAX, موم múm, شمع sham'.—(*of the ears*) چرك گوش chirk-i-gúsh. —(*sealing-wax*) لاك lák.—(*wax-cloth*) پارچه مشمع párchah-i-mushamma'.—(*adj.*) مومی múmí.

To WAX, مشمع کردن mushamma' kardan.—(*become*) شدن shudan, گشتن gashtan, گردیدن gardídan.

WAXED, مشمع mushamma'.

WAY, راه ráh, ره rah, طریق tarík, سبیل sabíl, مسلك maslak, درب darb, صراط sarát, وتیره vatírah, سمت samt, طریقه taríkah.—(*method*) طور taur, طریق tarík, وجه vajh, دستور dastúr, منوال minvál, رسم rasm, طرز tarz, روش ravish, اسلوب uslúb, طرح tarah, قاعده ká'idah, نمط namat.—(*in any way*) بهمه جهت bi-hamah jihat. — (*in no way*) بهیچ وجه bi-hích vajh. — (*in a general way*) عادتا 'ádatan.—(*to make the best of one's way*) افتان خیزان خودرا رسانیدن uftán khízán khwudrá rasánídan.—(*to proceed on one's way*) راه رفتن ráh raftan.—(*to see one's way clear*) پیشرو کار خود دیدن písh-rau-i-kár-i-khwud dídan. — *to put oneself out of the way*) کلفت نمودن kulfat nimúdan.—(*right of way*) حق مرور hakk-i-murúr.—(*to have a right of way*) راه داشتن ráh dáshtan.—(*to go one's own way*) راه خود گرفتن ráh-i-khwud giriftan.—(*to give way, as the mind*) زائل گردیدن zá,il gardídan.

WAYFARER, مسافر musáfir, سیاح sayyáh, راهرو ráh-rau, سالك sálik.

To WAYLAY, راه زدن ráh zadan.

WAYWARD, خود پسند khwud-pasand.

WE, ما má, مایان máyán, ماها máhá.

WEAK, ضعیف za'íf, نا توان ná-taván, نحیف nahíf, سست sust, رکیك rakík, عاجز 'ájiz, کم زور kam-zúr, علیل 'alíl.—(*bending, as a fragile plant, &c.*) لس las, لاسیده lásídah. —(*tea, &c.*) سبك subuk.

To WEAKEN, ضعیف کردن za'íf kardan, بی حال کردن bí-hál kardan, علیل کردن 'alíl kardan, از قوت انداختن az kúvat andákhtan, کم

زور کردن kam-zúr kardan, نا توان گردانیدن ná-taván gardánídan.

WEAKNESS, ضعف za'f, ضعیفی za'ífí, نا توانی ná-taváni, عجز 'ajz, رکاکت rakákat, کلال kalál, سستی sustí, وهن vahn. — (*weakness in the loins, a disease in horses*) سگ باد sag-bád.

WEALTH, مال mál, مالداری mál-dárí, دولت daulat, غنا ghaná, توانگری tavangarí, رزق rizk, نعمت ni'mat, غنیمت ghanímat, املاک amlák.

WEALTHY, دولتمند daulat-mand, توانگر tavangar, غنی ghaní, مالدار mál-dár, زر دار zar-dár, مایه دار máyah-dár, متمول mutamavvil, متنعم mutana''im, با دولت bá-daulat.

To WEAN (*a child*), باز داشتن از شیر báz-dáshtan az shír, از شیر بریدن az shír burídan.

WEANED, فطیم fatím.

WEAPON, آلت جنگ álat-i-jang, سلاح saláh, حربه harbah, ساز sáz.

WEAR, دوام davám, قماش kumásh.

To WEAR (*put on*), پوشیدن púshídan, ملبس بودن mulabbas búdan. —(*wear out*) سائیدن sá,ídan, سابیدن sábídan, فرسودن farsúdan, مندرس شدن mundaris shudan.

WEARER, پوشنده púshandah.

WEARINESS, ماندگی mándagí, خستگی khastagí, ملال malál, ملالت malálat, کسل kasal.

WEARISOME, مشکل mushkil, سخت sakht.

WEARY, افکار ifkár, مانده mándah, خسته khastah, کوفته kúftah, کسل kasil, ملول malúl. — (*impatient of*) بیزار bízár, متنفر mutanaffir.

To WEARY, ملول کردن malúl kardan, خسته کردن khastah kardan.

WEASEL, راسو rású.—(*large species of weasel*) خز khaz.

WEATHER, هوا havá, ایام ayyám, آب و هوا áb u havá. — (*hot weather*) گرمی garmí.—(*cold weather*) سرما sarmá. — (*fair weather*) هوا خوب havá-i-khúb.

WEATHERCOCK, باد نما bád-nimá.

To WEAVE, بافتن báftan, نسج کردن nasj kardan.

WEAVER, بافنده báfandah, نساج nassáj, جلاه julláh, چولاه chúláh.

WEB, پارچه párchah, طاقه tákah, ثوب saub, توپ túp (*vulg.*).—(*of a spider*) پرده عنکبوت pardah-i-'ankabút, تار عنکبوت tár-i-'ankabút, کنتره kinatrah.

WEB-FOOTED (*as water-fowl, &c.*) وصل پا vasl-pá.

To WED, *vide* To MARRY.

WEDDING, عروسی 'arúsí, سور súr, عقد 'akd, نکاح nikáh.

WEDGE, میخ míkh, گاوه gávah, گوه gavvah, اخی akhí, گاز gáz.

WEDNESDAY, چهارشنبه chahár-shambah.

WEED, خس khas, کاه káh, سبزه sabzah, علف 'alaf.

To WEED, پاک کردن pak kardan.

WEEK, هفته haftah, اسبوع usbú'.—(*every week*) هر هفته har-haftah.

WEEKLY, هفتگی haftagí.

To WEEP, گریستن girístan, گریه کردن giryah kardan, ناله کردن nálah kardan, دموع نمودن dumú' nimúdan.

WEEPER, اشکبار ashk-bár, اشکریز ashk-ríz.

WEEPING, گریه giryah.

WEEVIL, کرم kirm, کو kau, لنبه lambah.

To WEIGH (*trans.*), سنجیدن sanjídan, وزن کردن vazn kardan, کشیدن kashídan, سختن sukhtan (*obs.*). —(*intrans.*) وزن بودن vazn búdan, وزن داشتن vazn dáshtan.

WEIGHT, وزن vazn, گرانی giráni, بار bár, ثقل sikl.—(*mass by which things are weighed*) سنگ sang, وزنه vaznah. — (*good weight*) وزن تمام vazn-i-támám, وزن درست vazn-i-durust, سنگین sangín.—(*light weight*) سبک subuk, وزن سبک vazn-i-subuk.—(*the same weight*) همسنگ ham-sang.

WEIGHTILY, با گرانی bá giráni.

WEIGHTINESS, گرانی giráni, سنگینی sangíní, ثقلت saklat.

Weighty, گران girán, سنگین sangín, وزنی vazní, ثقیل sakíl.

Welcome, ترحیب tarhíb, مرحبا marhabá.—(*to be welcome*) خوش آمدن khwush ámadan.

Welcomer, ترحیب گوینده tarhíb-gúyandah, مرحبا گو marhabá-gú.

To Weld, کوفتن kúftan, ترکیب آوردن tarkíb ávardan, جمع کردن jam' kardan.

Welfare, اقبال ikbál, سعادت sa'ádat, سعادتمندی sa'ádat-mandí, نیکبختی ník-bakhtí, بختیاری bakht-yárí, فرخندگی farkhundagí, دولت daulat, بهره مندی bahrah-mandí, بهبودی bih-búdí, فیروزمندی fírúz-mandí, ترقی tarakkí, میمنت maimanat, فلاح faláh, برکت barakat, بر خور داری bar-khwur-dárí, خیریت khairíyat.

Well, چاه cháh, چه chah.—(*parapet or mouth of a well*) لبه چاه labah-i-cháh, دهنه چاه dahanah-i-cháh.—(*trough of a well*) سنگاب sang-áb. — (*well or shaft going down into an aqueduct*) شتر گلو shutur-gulú. — (*brick-well*) چاه پخته cháh-i-pukhtah.—(*well in health*), خوش khwush, بخیر bi-khair, چاق chák, تندرست tan-durust.—(*good!*) خوب khúb, خیر khair, فبها fabihá.

Well-a-day, دریغ dirígh, دریغا dirígha, هیهات haihát.

Well-being, خیر khair, خیریت khairíyat, خوشگذرانی khwush-guzrání.

Well-bred, خوش اطوار khwush-atvár, خوش اخلاق khwush-akhlák, مؤدب mu,addab.

Well-done! واه واه váh váh, به به bah bah, آفرین áfirín, احسن ahsan, حبذا habbazá, مرحبا marhabá, بارک الله bárak allah, زه zih, زهی zihí.

Well-founded, سخت بنیاد sakht-bunyád.

Well-liking, خوش گذشت khwush-guzasht.

Well-wisher, خیر خواه khair-khwáh, دولت خواه daulat-khwáh.

Welt, حاشیه háshiyah, زه ور zah-var.

To Welter, غلطیدن ghaltídan.

Wen, غده ghuddah, دشول dushvil.

Wench, کنیز kaníz.

West, مغرب maghrib, غرب gharb.—(*west wind*) دبور dabúr, باد غربی bád-i-gharbí.—(*on the west*), غرباً gharban.

Western, مغربی maghribí, غربی gharbí.

Wet, تر tar, نم nam, باران bárán, بارش bárish, مطر matar.—(*to get wet*) تر شدن tar shudan, نم شدن nam shudan.

To Wet, تر ساختن tar sákhtan.—(*to wet through*) از سر تا پا تر کردن az sar tá pá tar kardan.

Wether (*sheep*), گوسفند خصی gúsfand-i-khusí, گوسفند آخته gúsfand-i-ákhtah.

Wetness, رطوبت rutúbat, تری tarí, نمی namí.

Whale, حوت hút.

Whaler (*ship*), کشتی حوتی kashtí-i-hútí.

Wharf, بندر گاه bandar-gáh, اسکله askalah.

What (*relat.*), آنچه án-chih, آنکه án-kih, چه chih, که kih.—(*interrog.*) چه chih, کدام kudám. — (*what then?*) چه چه chih chih, یعنی چه ya'ní chih.

Whatever, هر چه har-chih, هر آنچه har-án-chih.

Wheat, گندم gandum.

Wheaten, گندمی gandumí, از گندم az gandum.

To Wheedle, دمدمه ساختن dam-damah sákhtan, ور غلانیدن var-ghulánídan, ریشخندی کردن rísh-khandí kardan, تملق نمودن tamalluk nimúdan, چاپلوسی کردن cháplúsí kardan, دم بازی نمودن dam-bází nimúdan.

Wheel, چرخ charkh, دولاب dúláb.—(*spinning wheel*) چرخه charkhah.—(*for raising water by a large leathern bucket*) چرخ چاه charkh-i-cháh, چرخاب charkh-áb.—(*potter's wheel*) چرخ فخاری

charkh-i-fakhkhárí, چرخ کوزه گر charkh - i - kúzah - gar.—(*fire-wheel*) چرخ آتشین charkh-i-átishín. —(*nave of a wheel*) چنبره chambarah.—(*spoke of a wheel*) پره parrah, شمش shimsh, دیرک dírak. —(*felloe of a wheel*) دائره dá,irah. —(*cogs of a wheel*) دستک dastak, پرک parrak, دندانه dandánah.—(*axle of a wheel*) تیر tír, مشون mashún.

To WHEEL (*trans.*), چرخانیدن charkhánídan. — (*intrans.*) چرخیدن charkhídan.

WHEELBARROW, گاری کوچك garí-i-kúchik.

To WHEEZE, خس خس کردن khis khis kardan.

WHEEZING, خس خس khis khis.

WHELP, بچه bachah.

WHEN (*interrog.*) کی kai, چوقت chi-vakt. — (*relat.*) چو chú, چون chún, آنگاه án-gáh, وقتیکه vaktí-kih.—(*after which*) بعد از این که ba'd az ín kih.

WHENCE (*from where?*) از کجا az kujá, از چه طرف az chih taraf, از کو az kú.—(*for which reason*) من حیث min hais.

WHENSOEVER, هر گاه که har-gáh kih, هر وقتیکه har vaktí kih.

WHERE (*interrog.*), کو kú, کجا kujá.—(*relat.*) آنجا án-já, جایکه jáy-kih. — (*where to*) تا کجا tá kujá.—(*nowhere*) هیچ جا hích-já.

WHEREABOUTS, از کدام طرف az kudám taraf.

WHEREAS, از بسکه az bas kih, از آنجا که az án-já kih.

WHEREAT, از آن جهت az án jihat, در آن باب dar án báb.

WHEREBY, که kih.

WHEREFORE (*interrog.*), چرا chirá, از چه سبب az chih sabab, برای چه baráy-i-chih, واسه چه vásah-i-chih (*vulg.*).—(*for this reason*) از برای آن az baráy-i-án, از این جهت az ín jihat, از این سبب az ín sabab, لهذا liházá.

WHEREOF, که از آن kih áz án, کش kish (a contraction of که از اش).

WHERESOEVER, هر کجا har kujá, هر جای که har jáy kih.

WHEREUPON, که بر آن kih bar án.

WHEREWITH, با که bá-kih, با چه bá-chih, از چه az chih.

WHERRY, قایق káík.

To WHET, سنگ سای کردن sang-i-sáy kardan.

WHETHER, خواه khwáh, یا yá, آیا áyá.—(*whether* ... *or* ...) ... چه ... چه chih ... chih ..., ... خواه .. خواه khwáh ... khwáh ..., اعم از اینکه ... یا ... a'amm az ín kih ... yá ....

WHETSTONE, سنگ سای sang-i-sáy, سنگ فسان sang-i-fisán, سنگ رومی sang-i-rúmí.

WHEY, آب پنیر áb-i-panír, پنیر آب panír-áb.

WHICH (*interrog.*), چه chih, که kih, کی kí, کدام kudám, کدامین kudámín.—(*relat.*) آنچه án-chih, آنکه án-kih, چه chih, که kih.

WHICHEVER, هر آنچه har-án chih, هر چه har chih, هرکدام har kudám.

WHIFF, نفحه nafhah.—(*gulp*) جرعه jur'ah, قرت kurt.

WHILE (*a time*), مدتی muddatí, چند وقت chand vakt, یکچندی yak-chandí, زمانی zamání.—(*a little while ago*) اندکی پیش از این an-dakí písh az ín, یکچندی قبل از این yak-chandí kabl az ín.—(*a long while ago*) مدتی مدید شد muddatí-i-madíd shud, مدتی طویل قبل از این muddatí-i-tavíl kabl az ín, دیر باز dír-báz.—(*in a little while, soon*) بزودی bi-zúdí, بعد از زمان قلیل ba'd az zamán-i-kalíl.—(*after a while*) بعد زمان ba'd zamán, بمرور bi-murúr.—(*to while away*) وقت گذراندن vakt guzrándan.

WHILST, مادام mádám, مادامکه mádám-kih, در بین dar bain, در اثنا dar asná, تا که tá kih, تا tá.

WHIM, وهم vahm, خیال باطل khiyál-i-bátil, خود سری khwud-sarí.

To WHIMPER, گریستن giristan, گریه کردن giryah kardan.

WHIMSICAL, وسواسی vasvásí, خود سر khwud-sar.

To WHINE, دوله زدن dúlah zadan.
To WHINNY, شیهه کردن shaihah kardan, صهیل کردن sahíl kardan.
WHIP, قمچی kamchí, تازیانه tázi-yánah (*obs.*).—(*rod*) چوب chúb.
To WHIP, قمچی زدن kamchí zadan.
WHIPPER, قمچی زن kamchí-zan.
WHIRL, دوار davár, دور daur, گردش gardish.
To WHIRL (*trans.*), گردانیدن gar-dánídan, گردش کردن gardish kar-dan.—(*intrans.*) گردیدن gardídan.
WHIRLIGIG (*tilt - ride*), چرخك charkhak.
WHIRLPOOL, گرداب gird-áb, ورطه vartah.
WHIRLWIND, گردباد gird-bád, لوله باد lúlah-bád.
WHISK, منقات minkát.
To WHISK, تکان دادن takán dádan.
WHISKERS, بروت burút, سبیل sibíl.
WHISKY, سفید آب safíd-áb.
WHISPER, فچفچ fichfich.
To WHISPER, آهسته گفتن áhistah guftan, تو گوشی گفتن tú-i-gúshí guftan, سر بگوش گفتن sar-bi-gúsh guftan, سر گوشی گفتن sar-gúshí guftan, زیر لب گفتن zír-i-lab guf-tan, یواش گفتن yavásh guftan.
WHISPERER, فچفچ کننده fichfich-kunandah.
WHIST! خاموش khámúsh, سکوت sukút.
WHISTLE, شافوت sháfút, شفوتك shufútak, صفیر safír, فوتك fútak (*vulg.*).
To WHISTLE, شافوت زدن sháfút zadan, صفیر زدن safír zadan.
WHISTLER, صفیر زن safír-zan.
WHITE, سفید safíd, سفید رنگ safíd rang, سپید sapíd, ابیض abyaz, آق ák.—(*white of egg*) سفیده safídah. —(*white of the eye*) سفیده چشم safídah-i-chashm.
To WHITEN, سفید کردن safíd kar-dan, تبییض نمودن tabyíz nimú-dan.
WHITENING (*of a wall*), سفید کاری safíd-kárí, گچکاری gach-kárí.
WHITENESS, بیاض bayáz, سفیدی safídí.
To WHITEWASH, سفیدی کردن safídí kardan, گچکاری نمودن gach-kárí nimúdan.
WHITHER (*interrog.*), کو kú, کجا kujá. — (*relat.*) آنجا án-já, جایکه jáy-kih.
WHITLOW, گزدمك gazhdumak, دانه dánah.
WHIZ, وز viz.
To WHIZ, وز وز کردن viz viz kardan.
WHO (*interrog.*), که kih, کی kí.—(*relat.*) که kih, آنکه án kih.—(*who am I?*) سگ که هستم sag-i-kih hastam (*vulg.*).
WHOEVER, هر که har kih, هر آنکه har án kih.
WHOLE (*entire*), کامل kámil, درست durust, سالم sálim, مسلم musal-lam.—(*the whole*) جمله jumlah, همگی hamagí, تمام tamám, جمیع jamí‘, تمامی tamámí, جمهور jam-húr, همه hamah, سراپسر sar-á-sar, همه روی هم رفته hamah rúy ham raftah.—(*upon the whole*) بعد همه ba‘d hamah, فی الجمله fi-'l-jumlah, الحاصل al-hásil, القصه al-kissah.
WHOLESALE, یك جا yak-já.
WHOLESOME, سازگار sáz-gár, خوشگوار khwush-guvár, موافق muváfik, گوار guvár.
WHOLESOMENESS, سازگاری sáz-gárí, خوشگواری khwush-guvárí, موافقت muváfakat, گواری guvárí.
WHOLLY, مطلقاً mutlakan, بالکل bi-'l-kull.
WHOOP, بانگ báng, غریو gharív, آواز áváz.
WHORE, فاحشه fáhishah, زانیه záni-yah, لولی lúlí, جافجاف jáfjáf, روسپی ruspí, قحبه kahbah, لوند lavand, کاولی kávalí (*vulg.*), جنده jindah (*vulg.*).
WHOREDOM, زنا ziná, شید shaid, فاحشگی fáhishagí, جنده گری jin-dah-garí.
WHOREMONGER, زنا کار ziná-kár, زانی zání, شید باز shaid-báz.
WHOSE (*interrog.*) از آن که az án-i-kih, مال که mál-i-kih.
WHOSESOEVER, مال هر که mál-i-har kih.

WHY, چرا chirá, بچه bi-chih, چه سبب chih sabab, از برای چه az baráy-i-chih, واسه چه vásah-i-chih (*vulg.*).—(*why and wherefore*) چون و چرا chún u chirá.

WICK, فتیله fatílah.

WICKED, بد bad, بد کار bad-kár, شریر sharír, فاسد fásid, مفسد mufsid, بد نفس bad-nafs, بد آیین bad-áyín, شقی shakí, بد ذات bad-zát, بد خو bad-khú, طالح tálih.

WICKEDNESS, بدی badí, شرارت sharárat, شر sharr, فساد fasád, شنعت shun'at, بد خوی bad-khúí, بد کرداری bad-kirdárí, قباحت kabáhat, شقاوت shakávat.

WICKER-WORK, سبد بافی sabad-báfí.

WICKET (*small gate*), دریچه daríchah.

WIDE, پهنا pahná, پهناور pahn-ávar, واسع vási', وسیع vasí', فراخ farákh, بسیط basít, عریض 'aríz, گشاده gushádah, گشاد gushád.

WIDELY, بنهایت bi-nihàyat, در هر جا dar har já, علی الاتساع 'ala-'l-ittisá'.

To WIDEN, پهن ساختن pahn sákhtan, وسعت دادن vus'at dádan.

WIDOW, بیوه bívah, ارمله armalah (*pl.* ارامل arámil).

WIDOWER, ارمل armal.

WIDOWHOOD, بیوگی bívagí.

WIDTH, پهن pahn, عرض 'arz, وسعت vus'at, پهنای pahnáí.—(*in width*) عرضاً 'arzan.

To WIELD, گرفتن giriftan, قبض نمودن kabz nimúdan.

WIELDY, باب دست báb-i-dast, قابل اخذ kábil-i-akhz.

WIERY, سیمی símí.

WIFE, زن zan, زوجه zaujah, منکوحه mankúhah, قعاده ku'ádah, حلاله halálah, کوچ kúch (*vulg.*).—(*regular wife, of whom four are permitted*) زن عقدی zan-i-'akdí, کوچ عقدی kúch-i-'akdí.—(*temporary wife or concubine*) زن متعه zan-i-mut'ah, خاصه گی khássah-gí, زن صیغه zan-i-síghah.—(*rival or fellow wife*) هوو havú, هئو ha,ú, همشوی ham-shaví, شریکه sharíkah, انباغ ambágh (*obs.*).—(*wife separated from her husband*) طالق tálik, مطلقه matlakah.—(*man and wife*) زوجین zaujain.

WIG موی عملی múí-i-'amalí.

WILD, وحشی vahshí, دشتی dashtí, جنگلی jangalí.—(*untamed*) نا رام ná-rám, نا دست آموز ná-dast-ámúz, وحشی vahshí.—(*wild-fowl*) مرغ دشتی murgh-i-dashtí.—(*flowers, &c.*) خود رو khwud-rú.—(*wild beast*) درنده darandah.

WILDERNESS, بیابان biyábán, ویرانه vairánah, دشت dasht, بادیه bádiyah, بیدا baidá, چول chaul, قاع ká', تیه tíh, بریه barriyah, مفازت mafázat, سهب sahb.

WILDNESS, وحشیه vahshíyah.

WILE, گول gúl, رنگ rang, حیله hílah, حیله بازی hílah-bází.

WILFUL, خود سر khwud-sar, گردن کش gardan-kash.

WILFULLY, قصداً kasdan, عمداً 'amdan, دیده و دانسته dídah va dánistah.

WILL, خواهش khwáhish, آرزو árzú, کام kám, مراد murád, ارادت irádat.—(*of God*) رضائی حق razá,í-i-hakk, مشیت mashíyat, قدر kadr.—(*testament*) وصیت vasíyat, وثیقه vasíkah.—(*to make a will*) توصیه نمودن tausiyah nimúdan, وصیت نمودن vasíyat nimúdan.—(*against one's will*) کرهاً karahan.

WILLING, خواهان khwáhán.—(*willing or unwilling*) خواهی نخواهی khwáhí na-khwáhí, طوعاً و کرهاً tau'an va karahan, کام نا کام kám ná-kám.

WILLINGLY, بچشم bi-chashm, بسر و چشم bi-sar u chashm, علی الراس و العین 'ala-'r-rás va-'l-'ain, خواسته khwástah, از دل و جان az dil u ján.—(*designedly*) خواسته khwástah, عمداً 'amdan, اختیارانه ikhtiyáránah, قصداً kasdan, دانسته dánistah.—(*most willingly*) با نهایت رغبت bá-nihàyat-i-raghbat.

WILLINGNESS, خواهش khwáhish.

WILLOW, بید bíd.—(*weeping willow*) بید معلق bíd-i-mu'allak.—(*sweet *or Oriental willow*) بید مشك bíd-mishk, خلاف khiláf, بان bán.

WILY, حیله ور hílah-var, بیوفا bí-vafá, غدار ghaddár.

WIMBLE (*borer*), مته mattah, برمه barmah.

To WIN, بردن burdan, غالب شدن ghálib shudan, فیروز شدن fírúz shudan.—(*a race*) پیش آمدن písh ámadan.—(*at cards*) بازی بردن bází burdan.

To WINCE, رمیدن ramídan, تکان خوردن takán khwurdan.

WIND, باد bád, هوا havá, ریح ríh.—(*violent wind*) تند باد tund-bád, باد شدید bád-i-shadíd.—(*gentle wind*) صبا sabá, نسیم nasím, هوائی ملایم havá,í-i-muláyam.—(*hot wind*) سموم samúm, باد سام bád-i-sámm, هوائی گرم havá,í-i-garm.—(*cold wind*) صرصر sarsar, باد سرد bád-i-sard.—(*favourable wind*) باد مراد bád-i-murád.—(*to break wind*) گوزیدن gúzídan, تیزیدن tízídan, تیز دادن tíz dádan, گوز دادن gúz dádan.

To WIND, رشتن rishtan.—(*roll up*) پیچانیدن píchánídan, نوردیدن navardídan, تافتن táftan.—(*a horn*) کشیدن kashídan, نواختن navákhtan, زدن zadan.—(*up a watch*) کوك کردن kúk kardan, کلید دادن kilíd dádan.—(*meander*) گردیدن gardídan, پیچیدن píchídan, پیچ خوردن píchkhwurdan.

WINDER, دولاب dúláb.

WINDFALL, باد آور bád-ávar.—(*fruit, &c.*) باد ریخته bád-ríkhtah.

WINDING, پیچاپیچ pích-á-pích.

WINDING-SHEET, کفن kafan.

WINDLASS, منجنیق manjaník.

WINDMILL, آسیائی باد ásyá,í-i-bád.

WINDOW, پنجره panjarah, روزن rauzan, دریچه daríchah, تابدان tábdán, شمسه shamsah.—(*large window of coloured glass in sashes*) ارسی urusí.—(*sash of window, composed of small coloured panes*) درك darrak, بالارو bálá-rau.—(*of a coach*) دریچه daríchah.—(*of a train*) شیشه shíshah.—(*lattice or grated window*) پنجره panjarah.—(*of venetian blinds*) کرکری kirkirí (*hind.*).—(*frame of a window*) چهار چوبه chahár-chúbah, چار چوبه chár-chúbah.—(*window-sill*) آستانه پنجره ásitánah-i-panjarah.

WINDPIPE (*trachæa*), نای گلو náy-i-gulú, حنجره hanjarah, حلقوم hulkúm.

WINDWARD, طرف باد taraf-i-bád.

WINDY, بادی bádí.

WINE, شراب sharáb, می mai, باده bádah, مل mul, مدام mudám, خمر khamr, نبیذ nabíz, رهیق rahík, رحیق rahík, ام الخبائث ummu-'l-khabá,is (*lit.* "*mother of all evil*"), گوشت بلبل gúsht-i-bulbul (*lit.* "*nightingale's flesh,*" *slang term*).—(*new wine*) شیره shírah.—(*wine-press*) شیره خانه shírah-khánah, آخوره انگور ákhwurah-i-angúr, حوض hauz.—(*wine-seller*) می فروش mai-furúsh, باده فروش bádah-furúsh.—(*wine of Paradise, which will not intoxicate, to be drunk by the faithful hereafter*) شراب طهور sharáb-i-tahúr.—(*wine-biber*) باده پیما bádah-paimá, باده نوش bádah-núsh, میخور mai-khwur.—(*wine-shop*) شرابخانه sharáb-khánah, میخانه mai-khánah.—(*to make wine*) شراب انداختن sharáb andákhtan.

WING, بال bál, پر par, جناح janáh.—(*of an army*) جناح janáh, جانب jánib.

WINGED, بالدار bál-dár.

WINK, غمزه ghamzah, چشمك chashmak.

To WINK, پلك زدن palk zadan, چشمك زدن chashmak zadan.—(*to wink or connive at a thing*) قطع نظر نمودن kat'-i-nazar nimúdan.

WINNER, بازی بر bází-bar, بازی برنده bází-barandah.

WINNINGS, گرو برده girau-burdah.

WINNOW (*fan for winnowing corn*), طبق tabak.—(*fork*) اوچوم auchúm, اوسی ausí.

To WINNOW, هوا افکندن havá afkandan, افشاندن afshándan.—(*a winnower of corn*) بوجار bújár.

WINTER, سرما sarmá, زمستان zamistán, شتا shitá.—(*winter-quarters*) قشلاق kishlák, غیشلاق ghíshlák.

To WINTER, زمستان کردن zamistán kardan.

WINTRY, زمستانی zamistání.

To WIPE, پاك کردن pák kardan, صاف کردن sáf kardan, تمییز کردن tamyíz kardan.—(*to wipe out, efface*) پاك کردن pák kardan, محو کردن mahv kardan.

WIPER, پاك کننده pák-kunandah.

WIRE, تار tár.—(*thick wire or rod of metal*) مفتول maftúl.—(*fine wire of silver, brass, &c.*) سیم sím.—(*telegraph*) سیم sím.—(*thin telegraphic wire*) مفتول maftúl.—(*wire strainer, telegraphic instrument*) گاو سر gáv-sar.

To WIREDRAW, سیم ساختن sím sákhtan.

WISDOM, دانائی dáná,í, دانش dánish, حکمت hikmat, علم 'ilm, خرد khirad, بخردی bikhradí, عقل 'akl, شعور shu'úr, فرزان farzán, فطانت fatánat.

WISE, دانشمند dánish-mand, دانا dáná, خردمند khirad-mand, عقلمند 'akl-mand, هوشمند húsh-mand, عالم 'álim, عاقل 'ákil, عارف 'árif, حکیم hakím, فرزانه farzánah.—(*manner*) طور taur, طرح tarah, وجه vajh, طریق tarík, رسم rasm, گونه gúnah, قسم kism.

WISEACRE, فضول fuzúl, ابله ablah, احمق ahmak.

WISELY, عاقلانه 'ákilánah, بطور معقول bi-taur-i-ma'kúl, از روی بصیرت az rúy-i-basírát.

WISH, خواهش khwáhish, مراد murád, مطلوب matlúb, آرزو árzú, شوق shauk, میل mail, مرضی marzí, تمنا tamanná, اراده irádah.

To WISH, خواستن khwástan, خواهش کردن khwáhish kardan.—(*if you wish*) اگر چنانچه دلت بخواهد agar chúnán-chih dilat bikhwáhad.—(*as you wish*) اختیار با شما است ikhtiyár ba-shumá ast.—(*against the wishes*) بر خلاف رای bar khiláf-i-ráy.

WISHER, خواهنده khwáhandah.

WISHFUL, آرزومند árzú-mand.

WISHFULLY, بآرزومندی bi-árzú-mandí.

WISP, دسته dastah.

WISTFUL, متوجه mutavajjih, آگاه ágah, ملتفت multafit.

WISTFULLY, بدقت bi-dikkat, رو بکار rú-bi-kár.

WIT, ذهن zihn, فراست firásat, زیرکی zírakí, عقل 'akl.—(*pleasantry*) ظرافت zaráfat, مزاح mizáh, شوخی shúkhí, لطافت latáfat.—(*to sharpen one's wits*) فهم خودرا تیز گردانیدن fahm-i-khwudrá tíz gardánídan.—(*to lose one's wits*) عقلرا گم کردن 'aklrá gum kardan.

WITCH, زن جادوگر zan-i-jádú-gar, ساحره sáhirah, صاحبه اجنه sáhibah-i-ajinnah.

WITCHCRAFT, نیرنج nairanj, جادو jádú, سحر sihr.

WITH, با bá, ب bi, به bih, از az, مع ma'.

WITHAL, علاوه 'alávah, بجز آن bi-juz-i-án.

To WITHDRAW (*retire*), کنار گرفتن kanár giriftan, باز گشتن báz gashtan, متواری شدن mutavárí shudan, پس رفتن pas raftan.—(*to take away*) سلب کردن salab kardan, بر داشتن bar-dáshtan, بردن burdan, محروم ساختن mahrúm sákhtan.

WITHDRAWAL, پس کشیدن pas-kashídan.

To WITHER, پژمرده شدن pazhmurdah shudan, خشکیدن khushkídan, پوسیدن púsídan, افسردن afsurdan, کاهیدن káhídan, خوشیدن khúshídan.

WITHERED, پوسیده púsídah, پژمردن pazhmurdah, افسرده afsurdah.

WITHERS (*part between neck and shoulders of a horse*), سر کتف sar-i-katf, حارك hárik.

To WITHHOLD, وا داشتن vá-dáshtan, باز داشتن báz dáshtan, دریغ داشتن dirígh dáshtan, تعویق

انداختن ta'vík andákhtan.—(*refuse*) رد کردن radd kardan, نفی کردن nafy kardan, ابا نمودن ibá nimúdan.

WITHIN, اندر andar, درون darún, اندرون andarún, داخل dákhil, تو tú, توی túí.

WITHOUT (*outside*), بیرون bírún, بدر bi-dar, خارج khárij.—(*wanting*) بی bí, بدون bidún, غیر ghair, بغیر bi-ghair, بلا bilá.—(*without fail*) بلا قصور bilá kusúr, بلا اهمال bilá ihmál, بی کوتاهی bí-kútáhí.

To WITHSTAND, مقاومت نمودن mu-kávamat nimúdan, ایستادگی کردن ístádagí kardan, مخالفت کردن mukhálafat kardan.

WITNESS, شاهد sháhid, گواه guváh, شهید shahíd.—(*evidence*) شهادت shahádat, گواهی guváhí.—(*to bear witness*) گواهی دادن guváhí dádan, شهادت بردن shahádat burdan.—(*false witness*) شهادت دروغ shahádat-i-durúgh, شهادت زور shahádat-i-zúr, گواهی دروغ gu-váhí,-i-durúgh.—(*a truth-telling witness*) شاهد عادل sháhid-i-'ádil, گواه عادل guváh-i-'ádil.—(*witness-box*) محضر تدافع mahzar-i-tadáfu'.

WITNESSED, مشهود mash-húd.—(*to be witnessed*) مشهود افتادن mash-húd uftádan.

WITTICISM, لطیفه latífah, بذله baz-lah, شوخی shúkhí, مسخره mas-kharah.

WITTILY, با شوخی bá-shúkhí.

WITTINGLY, قصداً kasdan, عمداً 'amdan, دیده و دانسته dídah va dánistah.

WITTY, ظریف zaríf, لطیفه گو latífah-gú.

WIZARD, افسونگر afsún-gar, جادو گر jádú-gar.

WOE, غم gham, الم alam, اندوه an-dúh, ملال malál, ملالت malálat, تأسف ta,assuf, کدورت kudúrat, رنج ranj, رنجه ranjah, درد dard, آزار ázár, حزن huzn, احزان ihzán, حسرت hasrat, عزا 'azá, دلتنگی dil-tangí, هم hamm, وجع vaja', سوگ súg, تیمار tímár, هنجار han-jár, تنگنائی tangná,í.—(*interjection*) وای váy, تبا tabban.—(*woe is me!*) وای بر من váy bar man.—(*woe on it!*) وای بر آن váy bar án.

WOEFUL, دلتنگ dil-tang, دلفکار dil-fikár, دلگیر dil-gír, غمگین gham-gín, غمناک gham-nák, مغموم maghmúm, حزین hazín, محزون mahzún, متعبس muta'abbis, ملول malúl, اندوه ناک andúh-nák, متألم muta,allim, سهمگین sahm-gín.

WOEFULLY, با غم bá-gham.

WOEFULNESS, دلتنگی dil-tangí, دلفکاری dil-fikárí, دلگیری dil-gírí, غمگینی gham-giní, حزن huzn, ملال malál, غم gham, الم alam.

WOLF, گرگ gurg.

WOMAN, زن zan, ضعیفه za'ífah, امرأة imra,at (*pl.* نسا nisá, نسوات nisvát, نسوان nisván).

WOMANHOOD, انثت unusat.

WOMANLY, زنانه zanánah, زن آسا zan-ásá, زن صفت zan-sifat.

WOMB, رحم rahm, مشیمه mashí-mah.

WONDER, آشفتگی áshuftagí, حیرت hairat, تحیر tahayyur, عجب 'ajab, تعجب ta'ajjub, هکر hakar, دهشت dihshat, ششدر shish-dar, تلواسه talvásah.—(*miracle*) کرامت kará-mat, اعجوبه u'júbah, آیت áyat.

To WONDER, تعجب کردن ta'ajjub kardan, متعجب بودن muta'ajjib búdan, عجب ماندن 'ajab mán-dan, شگفتن shikiftan, متحیر شدن mutahayyir shudan, حیران بودن hairán búdan.

WONDERFUL, عجب 'ajab, عجیب 'ajíb, غریب gharíb, بدیع badí', نادر nádir.—(*exclamation*) مرحباً marhaban.

WONDERFULLY, عجیبانه 'ajíbánah.

WONTED, معتاد mu'tád, مستعمل musta'mal, معهود ma'húd.

To WOO, عشق بازی کردن 'ishk-bází kardan, دم دادن dam dádan (*vulg.*).

WOOD (*timber*), چوب chúb.—(*fire-wood*) هیزم hízum, هیمه hímah, حطب hatab.—(*forest*) جنگل jangal, بیشه bíshah, درختستان dirakhtistán, درختزار dirakht-zár.

Woodcock, یلوه قوشی yalvah-kaushí, هیوه hívah, مرغ زیرک murgh-i-zírak.

Wood-cutter, تبر زن tabar-zan.

Wooded, مشجر mushjir.

Wooden, چوبین chúbín, از چوب az chúb.

Woodlouse, خرخاکی khar-khákí.

Woodman, هیمه فروش hímah-furúsh.

Woodpecker, درختکن dirakht-kan.

Wood-work, چوبها chúbhá.

Wooer, عشق باز 'ishk-báz, عاشق 'áshik.

Woof (*of cloth*), پود púd.

Wool, پشم pashm, صوف súf.—(*nap of wool*) کلك kulk, خواب khwáb. —(*woollen cloth*) ماهوت máhút, پشمی pashmí. —(*coarse woollen cloth*) پتو pattú.—(*thick woollen stuff*) نمد namad, لبد libd.

Woollen, پشمین pashmín.—(*woollen goods*) قماش kumásh, ماهوت máhút.

Word, سخن sukhun, کلمه kalimah, کلام kalám, لفظ lafz.—(*soft words*) سخنها باریك sukhunhá-i-bárík.—(*in a word*) الحاصل al-hásil, الغرض al-gharaz, القصه al-kissah, غایتش gháyatash. — (*in other words*) عبارةً اخری 'ibáratan ukhrá.—(*word by word*) لفظ بلفظ lafz bi-lafz.

To Word, بعبارت در آوردن bi-'ibárat dar ávardan, عبارت پردازی کردن 'ibárat-pardází kardan.

Work, کار kár, کار و بار kár u bár, عمل 'amal, فعل fi'l, شغل shughl. —(*embroidery*) نقش naksh, قیطان دوزی kaitán-dúzí, قلاب دوزی kul-láb-dúzí.—(*works of an author*) کلیات kullíyát, مؤلفات mu,allafát. —(*composition*) مصنف musannaf, تصنیف tasníf, تألیف ta,líf.—(*good works*) محاسن mahásin.

To Work, کار کردن kár kardan, ورزیدن varzídan, عمل کردن 'amal kardan.—(*to work a ship*) خدمت کشتی کردن khidmat-i-kashtí kardan.—(*a farm, &c.*) باجاره دادن bi-ijárah dádan, ایجار نمودن íjár nimúdan.

Workman, کاریگر kárí-gar, صنعتگر san'at-gar, صانع sáni', فاعل fá'il (*pl.* فعله fa'alah), پیشه ور píshah-var, عامل 'ámil (*pl.* عمله 'amalah *or* عمال 'ummál).—(*hired*) مزدور mazdúr, اجیر ajír.

Workmanship, عمل 'amal, صنعت san'at.

Workshop, کارخانه kár-khánah.

World, جهان jahán, عالم 'álam, دنیا dunyá, گیتی gítí, دهر dahr, گیهان gaihán, گردون gardún, روزگار rúzi-gár, زمانه zamánah.—(*division of the world*) کشور kishvar, اقلیم iklím.—(*both worlds, this and the next*) دارین dárain, کونین kaunain, دنیا و آخرت dunyá va ákhirat, دو جهان dú jahán, نشاتین nishátain. —(*the world to come*) عالم بقا 'álam-i-baká, دار بقا dár-i-baká.—(*the world below*) عالم شهادت 'álam-i-shahádat, عالم فانی 'álam-i-fání.

Worldliness, دنیویت dunyavíyat.

Worldling, مرد دنیوی mard-i-dun-yaví.

Worldly, دنیوی dunyaví, دنیاوی dunyáví, زمانه zamánah.

Worm, کرم kirm. — (*earth-worm*) خراطین kharatín. — (*glow-worm*) کرم شبتاب kirm-i-shab-táb.—(*silk-worm*) کرم پیله kirm-i-pílah, کرم ابریشم kirm-i-abríshum.—(*palmer-worm*) هزار پا hazár-pá. —(*worm of a screw*) پیچ pích.—(*worm of a still*) انبوبه ambúbah, لوله انبیق lúlah-i-ambík.—(*to have the worms*) کرم داشتن kirm dáshtan, کرم گرفتن kirm giriftan.

Worm-eaten, کرم خورده kirm-khwurdah, کرم زده kirm-zadah.

Wormwood, افسنتین afsantín, درمنه dirmanah.

Worn (*fatigued*), کسل kasil, خسته khastah, کوفته kúftah. — (*worn out*) مندرس mundaris, سابیده sábídah, کهنه kuhnah, فرسوده farsúdah.

To Worry, اذیت کردن azíyat kardan, آزردن ázurdan.

Worse, بدتر badtar, بتر batar, اشر asharr. — (*worse and worse*) بد اندر بد bad andar bad, بدتر از بدتر badtar az badtar.

Worship, پرستش parastish, عبادت 'ibádat. — (*place of worship*) مسجد masjid, عبادتخانه 'ibádat-khánah, سجده گاه sijdah-gáh.

To Worship, پرستیدن parastídan, سجده نمودن sijdah nimúdan.

Worshipful, مطاع mutá', واجب الاطاعت vájibu-'l-itá'at.

Worshipfully, مطیعانه mutí'ánah.

Worshipper, پرستنده parastandah, متعبد muta'abbid, عابد 'ábid.— (*in composition*) پرست parast.

Worst, بدترین badtarín, بترین batarín.

Worsted (*spun wool*), پشم ریشته pashm-i-ríshtah, قاطمه kátmah.

Worth, قیمت kaimat, ارزش arzish, بها bahá, قدر kadr, ثمن saman.— (*to be worth*) ارزیدن arzídan, قیمت داشتن kaimat dáshtan, قدر داشتن kadar dáshtan, گنجایش داشتن gunjáyish dáshtan, مصرف داشتن masraf dáshtan.—(*be equivalent*) معادل شدن mu'ádil shudan, نظیر شدن nazír shudan.—(*it is not worth the trouble*) برحمت نمی ارزد bi zahmat na-mí arzad, قابل آن نیست که kábil-i-án-níst kih.

Worthily, بالواجب bi-'l-vájib

Worthiness, لیاقت liyákat, قدر kadr, فضیلت fazílat, سزاوری sazávarí.

Worthless, بی مصرف bí-masraf, بیقدر bí-kadar, بی لیاقت bí-liyákat, بیکاره bí-kárah. — (*spoilt, good for nothing*) معیوب ma'yúb, ادبار idbár, بی مصرف bí-masraf, ضایع zái'. — (*cowardly, indolent, person*) لجاره lajjárah, رجاله rajjálah.

Worthy, سزاوار sazávár, لائق lá,ik, واجب vájib, مستوجب mustaujib, مستحق mustahakk, شایسته sháyistah, سزا sazá, مستعد musta'idd.

Wound, زخم zakhm, ریش rísh, جراحت jaráhat, خستگی khastagí. — (*mortal wound*) زخم کاری zakhm-i-kárí, زخم مهلک zakhm-i-muhlak.

To Wound, زخم زدن zakhm zadan, مجروح ساختن majrúh sákhtan, زخمدار کردن zakhm-dár kardan.

Wounded, مجروح majrúh, زخم خورده zakhm-khwurdah, زخمدار zakhm-dár.

Wrangle, قال و مقال kál va makál, منازعت munáza'at, ستیزه sitízah.

To Wrangle, دعوی کردن da'vá kardan, منازعت کردن munáza'at kardan, ستیزه نمودن sitízah nimúdan.

Wrangler, مباحث mubáhis.

To Wrap (*envelop*), لفافه کردن lifáfah kardan, ملفوف کردن malfúf kardan, لف کردن laff kardan.— (*roll up*) پیچیدن píchídan, ملتف ساختن multaff sákhtan. — (*to wrap oneself up*) لباس بر خود پیچیدن libás bar khwud píchídan.

Wrapper (*cover or envelope*), لفافه lifáfah, غلاف ghiláf.—(*cover of a book*) قولق kauluk, قولیق kaulíuk. —(*of linen, used while bathing*) لنگ lung, لنگ رشتی lung-i-rashtí.—(*used after bathing*) قطیفه katífah.

Wrath, غیظ ghaiz, غضب ghazab, قهر kahr, سورت saurat, بطش batsh, حدت hiddat, خشم khishm.— (*divine*) سخط sukht, مواخذه mu,-ákházah.

Wrathful, غضبناک ghazab-nák, خشمناک khishm-nák, بر آشفته bar-áshuftah, کجخلق kaj-khulk, متنفر mutanaffir, گرم garm, آزرده ázurdah, مکدر mukaddar, رنجیده ranjídah, در هم dar-ham, خفا khafá (*obs.*).

Wrathfully, با غضب bá-ghazb.

To Wreak, بیرون دادن bírún dádan.

Wreath (*of flowers*), تاج گل táj-i-gul, سهره sihrah.

Wreck, شکست shikast, تباهی tabáhí.—(*to be wrecked*) شکسته شدن

shikastah shudan, تباه شدن tabáh shudan.

WRENCH (*twist*), پیچ pích, پیچش píchish, تاب táb.

To WRENCH, ربودن rubúdan, بیرون کشیدن bírún kashídan.

To WRESTLE, کشتی گرفتن kushtí giriftan, مصارعت کردن musára'at kardan.

WRESTLER, کشتیگیر kushtí-gír, مصارع musári', پهلوان pahlaván.

WRESTLING, کشتی kushtí.

WRETCH, بد بخت bad-bakht, شقی shakí.

WRETCHED, دلتنگ dil-tang, مستمند mustamand, غمگین gham - gín, اندوهناک andúh-nák, ملول malúl.

WRETCHEDLY, با دلتنگی bá-dil-tangí.

WRETCHEDNESS, درد مندی dard-mandí, دلتنگی dil-tangí, مستمندی mustamandí, ملولی malúlí.

To WRIGGLE, غربیله کردن gharbílah kardan.

To WRING, پیچیدن píchídan, فشردن fishurdan, فشاردن fishárdan, چلاندن chilándan, پیچانیدن píchánídan, آب گرفتن áb giriftan.

WRINKLE, چین chín, چروت churút (*vulg.*), چورت chúrut (*vulg.*).

To WRINKLE, پر چین شدن pur-chín shudan.

WRINKLED, پر چین pur-chín, چورت زده chúrut-zadah.

WRIST, بند دست band-i-dast, ساعد sá'id, مچ دست much - i - dast (*vulg.*).

To WRITE, نوشتن nivishtan, نبشتن nibishtan, قلمی کردن kalamí kardan, نگاشتن nigáshtan, تحریر نمودن tahrír nimúdan, مسطور ساختن mastúr sákhtan, ترقیم نمودن tarkím nimúdan, ثبت کردن sabt kardan. — (*compose*) تصنیف کردن tasníf kardan.—(*to write clearly*) پاک نویسی کردن pák-nivísí kardan. —(*to write one's name*) اسم خودرا ثبت کردن ism-i-khwudrá sabt kardan.

WRITER, نویسنده nivísandah, راقم rákim, محرر muharrir, کاتب kátib. —(*secretary*) منشی munshí, میرزا mírzá.—(*fine writer*) خوش نویس khwush-nivís. — (*author*) مصنف musannif, مؤلف mu,allif.

To WRITHE, پیچیدن píchídan, غلطیدن ghaltídan.

WRITING, خط khatt, تحریر tahrír, رقم rakm, نوشت nivisht.—(*large text*) خط جلی khatt-i-jalí.—(*middle sized*) خط وسط khatt-i-vasat.—(*small sized*) خط خفی khatt-i-khafí, خط ریزه khatt-i-rízah.—(*in writing*) تحریرا tahríran.—(*to put down in writing*) اکتتاب نمودن iktitáb nimúdan.

The most common kinds of writing are the following: نسخ *naskh*, a plain bold legible hand, much used in transcribing books, and all manner of writings; تعلیق *ta'lík*, an elegant sloping hand, much employed in transcribing poetry, &c.; نستعلیق *nasta'lík*, a mixture of the above two; ثلث suls, a common Arabic hand, more stiff and formal than the نسخ *naskh*; کوفی *kúfí*, the old Arabic character, now disused; شکسته *shikastah*, a rapid cursory hand, much employed in letter writing, &c., and often not very legible; شکستامیز *shikast-ámiz*, any other hand mixed with شکسته *shikastah*; ترسل *tarassul*, a very rapid and illegible kind of شکسته *shikastah*; رقاع *ruká'*, علفی *saulfí*, دیوانی *díváni*, یاقوتی *yákúti*, طأوسی *táu,si*, طغرائی *tughrá,í*, various styles of writing not in general use.

WRITING-MASTER, استاد نویسنده ustád - i - nivísandah, صاحب خط sáhib-i-khatt.

WRITTEN, نوشته nivishtah, قلمی kalamí, مرقوم markúm, مکتوب maktúb, مسطور mastúr, رقمزده rakm-zadah. — (*MS.*) خط khat, خطی khatí.

WRONG, غلطی ghalatí, بیجا bí-já, نا مناسب ná-munásib, نا راست ná-

. rást, نا درست ná-durust, غیر صحیح ghair-i-sahíh, نا صواب ná-suváb, خطا khatá, نا حق ná-hakk.—(*hurt*) ضرر zarar, زیان ziyán, آزار ázár, آسیب ásíb, تطاول tatávul.—(*to be wrong*) گه خوردن guh khwurdan (*vulg.*).—(*to do wrong*) خبط کردن khabt kardan, غلط کردن ghalat kardan, گه خوردن guh khwurdan (*vulg.*).

To WRONG, زحمت نمودن zahmat nimúdan, تصدیع دادن tasdí' dádan.

WRONGED, متضرر mutazarrir.

WRY (*crooked*), کج kaj, معوج mu'-vajj *or* mu'avvaj, چوله chaulah (*vulg.*).

Y.

YACHT, قایق káík, زورق zaurak, سنبوق sumbúk.

YAM, سیب زیر زمینی síb-i-zír-zamíní.

YARD (*court of a house*), حیاط ha-yát, صحن sahn. — (*measure of forty inches*) ذرع zar', گز gaz.—(*of a sail*) صرن saran, فرمن farman, فروند farvand.—(*place where beasts of burden are tethered*) بار بند bár-band.

YARN, رشتهٔ خام rishtáh-i-khám.

YAWL, زورق zaurak, قایق káík, سنبوق sumbúk.

YAWN, خمیازه khamyázah.

To YAWN, خمیازه کردن khamyázah kardan.

YEA, بلی balí, بله balah, آری árí, نعم na'am.

YEAR, سال sál, سنه sanah, سن sinn, ایل íl, عام 'ám.—(*solar year*) سال شمسی sál-i-shamsí, سنه شمسیه sanah - i - shamsíyah. — (*lunar year*) سال قمری sál-i-kamarí, سنه قمریه sanah-i-kamaríyah. — (*this year*) امسال imsál, سنه حال sanah-i-hál.—(*last year*) سال گذشته sál-i-guzashtah, پار سال pár-sál, سنه سابقه sanah-i-sábikah, سال قبل sál-i-kabl. — (*year before last*) پیرار سال pírár-sál, پیلار سال pílár-sál (*vulg.*).—(*next year*) سال آینده sál-i-áyandah, سال دیگر sál - i - dígar.—(*years*) سالها sálhá, سنوات sanavát, سنین sanín, اعوام a'vám.—(*leap-year*) سال کبیسه sál-i-kabísah.—(*many years ago*) سالهای سال sálhái-i-sál. — (*Christian year*) سال میلادی sál-i-míládí, سنه عیسویه sanah-i-'ísavíyah, سال مسیحی sál-i-masíhí.—(*new year*) سال جدید sál-i-jadíd.—(*New Year's Day*) نو روز nau rúz.—(*a man of years*) مرد معمر mard-i-mu'ammar.

The Persians have a cycle of twelve years, denominated سنوات ترکی sanavát-i-turkí (*Turkí or Turkish years*), which are solar like the ancient Persian year; and each year has a separate name. In deeds, bonds, accounts of transactions, historical or other records, the name of the Turkí solar year and the date of the Muhammadan lunar year are mentioned together. Thus: A.D. 1851 is A.H. 1267–8, and the تنگوز ایل tangúz-íl (*hog year*); the latter commencing at the Vernal equinox, or 21st of March. The cycle when completed, commences again. The following are the names of these years, which are old Turkish terms:—

سیچقان ایل síchkán-íl (*the mouse year*).

اود ایل úd-íl (*the cow year*).

پارس ایل párs-íl (*the leopard year*).

توشقان ایل tavishkán-íl (*the hare year*).

لوی ایل lúí-íl (*the crocodile year*).

ايل يلان yalán-íl (*the snake year*).
ايل يونت yúnt-íl (*the horse year*).
ايل قوى kúí-íl (*the sheep year*).
ايل پيچى píchí-íl (*the monkey year*).
ايل تخاقو takhákú-íl (*the fowl year*).
ايل ايت ít-íl (*the dog year*).
ايل تنگوز tangúz-íl (*the hog year*).

YEARLING, يك ساله yak-sálah.

YEARLY, ساليانه sáliyánah, سنوى sanaví.—(*every year*) هر سال har sál, هر سنه har sanah, هر ساله har sálah.

To YEARN after, خون بجوش آمدن khún bi-júsh ámadan, رقت داشتن rikkat dáshtan, آرزو كردن árzú kardan.

YEAST, مايه máyah.

YELL (*cry*), نعره na'rah, غريو gharív, فرياد faryád, صراخ sarákh, صيحه saihah.

To YELL, بانگ زدن báng zadan, آواز دادن áváz dádan, غوغا كردن ghaughá kardan, نعره بر آوردن na'rah bar-ávardan, فرياد بر آوردن faryád bar-ávardan, صيحه زدن saihah zadan.

YELLOW, زرد zard, اصفر asfar.—(*yellow of an egg*) زرده zardah.

YELLOWISH, زرد فام zard-fám.

YELLOW-OCHRE, گل زرد gil-i-zard.

To YELP, وع وع كردن va' va' kardan, عو عو كردن 'av 'av kardan, عف عف كردن 'af 'af kardan.

YEW (*tree*), كاج káj.

YES, بلى balí, بله balah, آرى árí, نعم na'am. —(*when used towards a superior, indicating that the command will be obeyed*) بچشم bi-chashm.

YESTERDAY, ديروز dí-rúz, دى dí, روز قبل rúz-i-kabl, ديگنه dígunah (*vulg.*).—(*day before yesterday*) پريروز parí-rúz.

YESTERNIGHT, ديشب dí-shab, دوش dúsh, بارحه bárihah.

YET, اما ammá, بلكه bal-kih, لكن lákin, ولى valí, مگر magar.—(*till now*) هنوز hanúz, تاحال ta-hál, الى الان ila-'l-án.—(*not yet*) نه هنوز nah hanúz, هنوز نه hanúz nah, خير هنوز khair hanúz.

To YIELD (*produce*), بار دادن bár dádan, پيدا كردن paidá kardan, بعمل آوردن bi-'amal ávardan.—(*submit*) خودرا تسليم كردن khwudrá taslím kardan.

YOKE, يوغ yúgh, جوغ júgh, غل ghul, پالهنگ pálhang. — (*pair*) جفت juft, جور júr, زوج zauj, بند band.

To YOKE, جفت كردن juft kardan.

YOKEL, ترك turk.

YOLK (*of an egg*), زرده zardah.

YONDER, آنجا án-já.

YORE, قديم kadím, كهنه kuhnah.

YOU, شما shumá, شماها shumáhá, شمايان shumáyán.

YOUNG, جوان javán, خورد سال khwurd-sál, تازه tázah, جاهل jáhil (*vulg.*). — (*of animals*) بچه bachah, بچها bachahá, نتاج nitáj. —(*while young*) در كوچكى dar kúchikí.—(*young and old*) پير و برنا pír va barná.

YOUR, مال شما mál-i-shumá.

YOURSELF, خود شما khwud-i-shumá.

YOUTH, جوانى javání, شباب shabáb. —(*young man*) جوان javán, برنا barná, شاب shább.—(*beardless youth*) غير ملتحى ghair-i-multahí, مزلف muzallif.

YOUTHFUL, جوان javán, خورد سال khwurd-sál, تازه tázah, جاهل jáhil (*vulg.*).

Z.

ZANY, مسخره maskharah, لوطی lútí.

ZEAL, غیرت ghairat, حمیت hamíyat, شوق shauk, اشتیاق ishtiyák, اجتهاد ijtihád.

ZEALOT (*religious bigot or fanatic*), زاهد záhid, اهل غیرت ahl-i-ghairat, وسواسی vasvásí.

ZEALOUS, شوقمند shauk-mand, غیور ghuyúr, جهود jahúd.

ZEALOUSLY, غیورانه ghuyúránah.

ZEBRA, گور اسب gúr-asb.

ZENITH, سمت الرأس samtu-'r-ra,s.

ZEPHYR, باد صبا bád-i-sabá, نسیم nasím.

ZERO, صفر sifr (*pl.* اصفار asfár).

ZEST (*relish*), مزه mazah, ذائقه zá,ikah, ذوق zauk, میل mail.

ZIG-ZAG, پیچ و خم píchva kham, پیچ در پیچ pích dar pích, کج و معوج kaj va mu'avvaj.

ZINC, روی rúí, روح rúh (*vulg.*).

ZODIAC, منطق البروج mintaku-'l-burúj.—(*a sign*) برج burj (*pl.* بروج burúj).—(*Aries*) حمل hamal, بره barrah. — (*Taurus*) ثور saur.—(*Gemini*) جوزا jauzá, دو پیکر dú-paikar.—(*Cancer*) سرطان saratán. —(*Leo*) اسد asad, شیر shír.—(*Virgo*) سنبله sumbulah, خوشه khúshah.—(*Libra*) میزان mízán. —(*Scorpio*) عقرب 'akrab.—(*Sagittarius*) قوس kaus, کمان kamán. — (*Capricornus*) جدی jadí. — (*Aquarius*) دلو dalv, آبی ábí.— (*Pisces*) حوت hút.

ZONE (*girdle*), کمر kamar, کمر بند kamar-band, منطق mintak, حزام hizám.—(*circle dividing the earth*) منطق mintak, منطقه mintakah.— (*frigid zone*) منطقه مبروده mintakah-i-mabrúdah. — (*temperate zone*) منطقه معتدله mintakah-i-mu'tadilah.—(*torrid zone*) منطقه محروقه mintakah-i-mahrúkah.

ZOOLOGICAL GARDENS, باغ حیوانات bágh-i-haivánát, باغ وحوش bágh-i-vuhúsh.

ZOOLOGIST, معلم علم حیوانات mu'allim-i-'ilm-i-haivánát.

ZOOLOGY, علم حیوانات 'ilm-i-haivánát.

ZOOPHYTE, گل دریا gul-i-daryá.

ZOROASTER (*founder of the Magian faith*), زردهشت zardusht, زرتشت zartusht.

ZOROASTRIAN, *vide* MAGIAN.

ZOUAVE, زواو zúáv (*eur.*).

APPENDIX.

NUMBERS.—THE ABJAD.—SIYAK.

PERSIAN MONEY, WEIGHTS AND MEASURES,

NAMES OF PERSONS AND PLACES,

AND

COMPARATIVE TABLE

OF THE

MUHAMMADAN AND CHRISTIAN ERAS.

APPENDIX.

NUMBERS.

The Persians, like ourselves, have borrowed their numeral figures from the Arabs, who probably, as traders, obtained them, at an early period, from India, with which country they held extensive dealings; to this day, indeed, they term them رقم الهندی rakmu-'l-hindí (Indian numerals). The following are the figures :—

1	2	3	4	5	6	7	8	9	0
١	٢	٣	۴	٥	٦	٧	٨	٩	٠

The variations in the lower line are occasionally to be met with in manuscripts, &c. The numbers in the line above are the more correct forms generally used in printed books and in careful and accurate writings. These numerals are written from left to right. The following are examples of numeration :—

21	300	6052	1845	&c.
٢١	٣٠٠	٦٠٥٢	١٨۴٥	

Fractional numbers are usually written, as with us, by placing the numerator above the denominator, as—

$\frac{1}{3}$ ١/٣ $\frac{3}{7}$ ٣/٧ $\frac{4}{5}$ ۴/٥ &c.

In money accounts, a dot (.) stands for half a dínár. *Vide* the following sections on Siyák and Persian money.

Cardinal Numbers.

اعداد a'dád.

1 یك yak.
2 دو dú.
3 سه sih.
4 چهار chahár (contracted چار chár).
5 پنج panj.
6 شش shish.
7 هفت haft.
8 هشت hasht.
9 نه nuh *or* نوه núh.
10 ده dah.
11 یازده yázdah *or* یانزده yánzdah.
12 دوازده davázdah.
13 سیزده sízdah.
14 چهارده chahárdah.
15 پانزده pánzdah.

16 شانزده shánzdah.
17 هفده hafdah.
18 هجده hajdah *or* هشده hashdah.
19 نوزده núzdah *or* نوازده navázdah.
20 بیست bíst (contracted بست bist).
21 بیست و یك bíst u yak.
22 بیست و دو bíst u dú.
&c. &c.
30 سی sí.
31 سی و یك sí u yak.
&c. &c.
40 چهل chihil (contracted چل chil).
50 پنجاه panjáh.
60 شست shast *or* شصت shast.
70 هفتاد haftád.
80 هشتاد hashtád.
90 نود navad.
100 صد sad.
101 یکصد و یك yak sad u yak.
121 یکصد و بیست و یك yak sad u bíst u yak.
132 یکصد و سی و دو yak sad u sí u dú.
&c. &c.
200 دویست davíst *or* دو صد dú sad.
300 سیصد sí sad.
400 چهارصد chahár sad.
500 پانصد pán sad.
600 ششصد shish sad.
700 هفصد haf sad.
800 هشصد hash sad.
900 نهصد nuh sad.
1000 هزار hazár.
2000 دو هزار dú hazár.
&c. &c.
100,000 make one لك lak (lakh), and five laks one کرور karúr (krore). These two terms of number have been borrowed from the Indian system of calculation; but in India the "krore" signifies one hundred laks or ten millions.

Ordinal Numbers.

The Ordinal numbers are thus formed:—

1st اول avval, نخستین nakhustín, *or* یکم yakum.
2nd دوم duvum *or* دویم dúyum.
3rd سیوم síyúm *or* سیم siyyum.
4th چهارم chahárum.
5th پنجم panjum.
6th ششم shishum.
7th هفتم haftum.
8th هشتم hashtum.
9th نهم nuhum.
10th دهم dahum.
11th یازدهم yázdahum, &c.
19th نوزدهم núzdahum.
20th بیستم bístum.
21st بیست و یکم bíst u yakum, &c.
30th سی ام sí-um.
40th چهلم chihilum.
50th پنجاهم panjáhum.
60th شستم shastum *or* شصتم shastum.
70th هفتادم haftádum.
80th هشتادم hashtádum.
90th نودم navadum.
100th صدم sadum, &c.

Fractions are usually formed by placing the denominator before the numerator, as چهار یك chahár-yak (one-fourth), هفت دو haft-dú (two-sevenths). The Arabic fractional terms are also sometimes used. The following will serve as examples:—

One-fourth, چهار یك chahár-yak, ربع rub', چارك chárak (*vulg.*).
A half, نیم ním, نصف nisf.
Three-fourths, چهار سه chahár-sih, سه ربع sih-rub', سه چارك sih-chárak.
One-third, سه یك sih-yak, ثلث suls.
Two-thirds, سه دو sih-dú, ثلثین sulsain.
One-fifth, پنج یك panj-yak, خمس khums.
One-sixth, شش یك shish-yak, سدس suds.

Five-sixths, پنج شش shish-panj.
A tenth, ده یك dah-yak, عشر ʻushr.
Nine-tenths, ده نه dah-nuh.
One-hundredth, صد یك sad-yak.
Ninety-nine-hundredths, فی صد نود و نه fí sad navad u nuh.
A thousandth part, هزار یك hazár-yak, &c.

Reduplicative numbers are as follow:—

Single, مفرد mufrad, یکتا yak-tá, یگانه yagánah.
Double, مضاعف muzáʻaf, دو تا dú-tá, دو چند dú-chand, دو گانه dú-gánah, دولا dú-lá.
Treble, مثلث musallas, سه تا sih-tá, سه چند sih-chand, سه گانه sih-gánah.
Fourfold, چهار تا chahár-tá, چهار چند chahár-chand, مربع murabbaʻ, اربعه اضعاف arbaʻah-i-azʻáf.
Twentyfold, بیست چندان bíst-chandán, بیست مقابله bíst-mukábalah, بیست تا bíst-tá.
A hundredfold, صد چندان sad-chandán, صد مقابله sad-mukábalah, صد تا sad-tá, &c.

Distributives are thus expressed:—

One by one, یکی یکی yakí yakí, هو هو huva huva.
By twos, دو تا دو تا dú-tá dú-tá, دو دو dú dú.
By tens, ده ده dah dah.
Alternately, یکی در میان yakí dar miyán.
On alternate days, غبا ghibban, یك روز در میان yak rúz dar miyán.
Once every ten days, هر ده روز یك مرتبه har dah rúz yak martabah, &c.

Nouns joined with Cardinal numbers should always be put in the singular, as ده اسب dah asb (ten horses), هزار مرد hazár mard (a thousand men), &c. Arabic plurals are, however, sometimes employed, as ده فعله dah faʻalah (ten workmen).

Numbers from 20 upwards are usually arranged by having the greatest number expressed first, and the lesser added with the conjunction "and," as 254,783 دویست و پنجاه و چهار هزار و هفصد و هشتاد و سه davíst u panjáh u chahar hazár u hafsad u hashtád u sih. From 20 up to 50 the smaller number may be expressed first, as دو بیست dú bíst (twenty-two), چهار سی chahár sí (thirty-four), &c.; but it is considered more correct and idiomatic to place the larger number first, with the conjunction, as بیست و دو bíst u dú (twenty-two), &c.

ابجد ABJAD.

The twenty-eight letters of the Arabic alphabet possess each a numerical value, as expressed in the following unmeaning words :—

zazigh	sakhiz	karashat	sa'fas	kalaman	huttí	havvaz	abjad
ضظغ	تخذ	قرشت	سعفص	كلمن	حطى	هوز	ابجد
800 900 1000	500 600 700	100 200 300 400	60 70 80 90	20 30 40 50	8 9 10	5 6 7	1 2 3 4

This numerical mode, which is generally called ابجد abjad, from the first word, is much employed in forming chronograms denoting dates of events. These are indicated by a short sentence, the numerical values of the letters composing which, being added up, give the date required. The following chronograms will serve as examples :—

The date of the death of the celebrated piratical Basha of Algiers and Tunis, Khairu-'d-Dín, surnamed Barbarossa, is expressed by the Arabic sentence مات رئيس البحر máta ra,isu-'l-bahr (the chieftain of the sea is dead), and the numbers denoted by the letters composing this sentence being added up, give a quotient of 952, in which year of the Hijrah, corresponding with A.D. 1545–46, Barbarossa died.

The demise of the famous Tamerlane is contained in the following: وداع شهرياری vidá'-i-shahr-yárí (adieu to royalty), equivalent to A.H. 807, or A.D. 1404–5.

Nádir Sháh, when proclaimed sovereign of Persia, had coinage struck in his name, with the inscription in Arabic: الخير فی ما وقع al-khairu fí má vaka'a (what has happened is best), the numbers of which motto amount to A.H. 1148, the year corresponding with our 1735–36, in which he obtained the crown.

The celebrated Sultan Baber, the Napoleon of the East, was born on the sixth of the Muharram month. It is singular that the Persian date of the month, شش محرم shish-i-muharram, gives the year in which this prince was born, namely A.H. 888, corresponding with A.D. 1483–84.

The practise of commemorating events by these chronograms is common in all Muhammadan countries.

Numbers are often formed by letters as well as figures, according to this method, for example :—

11	12	13	14	15	16	17	18	19	21	22	23	24	25	26
يا	يب	يج	يد	يه	يو	يز	يح	يط	كا	كب	كج	كد	كه	كو

27	28	29	31	32	33	34	&c.
كز	كح	كط	لا	لب	لج	لد	

The units, tens, and hundreds, &c., have already been given.

SIYÁK.

The سياق siyák is a species of figures commonly used in all money transactions, accounts of shopkeepers and merchants, &c. Accounts are reckoned in *dínárs*, an imaginary coin, of the lowest value, being the ten-thousandth part of the *túmán*, the current gold coin in Persia, now worth about eight shillings. The figure in *Siyák* always indicates the number of *dínárs.* The *Siyák* used in India (in which country it is called رقم rakm), differs somewhat from the Persian system. (*Vide* the Introduction to "Stewart's Persian Letters.") The units in combination with the tens are nearly the same in both, but the simple units are entirely different, as well as many of the higher numbers. A knowledge of this figure will be found absolutely necessary for those connected with business and trade, as accounts are seldom written in any other.

The following are the simple units :

1 2 3 4 5 6 7 8 9

The following are the tens :

10 20 30 40 50 60 70 80 90

The units and tens in combination :

11 12 13 14 15 16 17 18

19 21 22 23 35 62 99

The higher numbers :

100 200 300 400 500 600 700

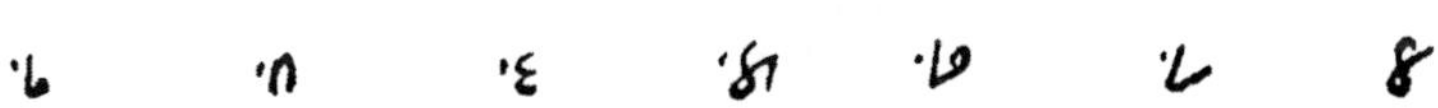

800 900 1,000 1,100 1,200 1,300

2,000 3,000 4,000 5,000 6,000 7,000

8,000 9,000 10,000 20,000 30,000 40,000

50,000	60,000	70,000	80,000	90,000	100,000

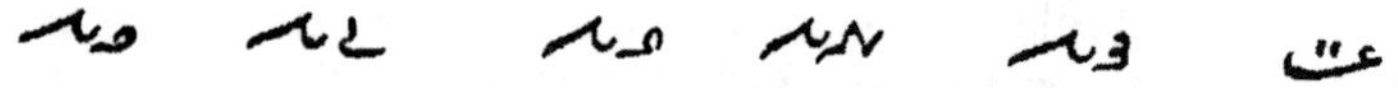

110,000	120,000	130,000	150,000	200,000	1,000,000

MONEY.

The following are the moneys now current in Persia:—

دینار **dínár**, an imaginary infinitesimal coin, in which accounts are reckoned. Its value will amount to something less than one-twentieth of a farthing sterling.

5 دینار dínár=1 غاز ghāz; also a nominal money.

10 غاز ghāz=50 دینار dínár=1 شاهی shāhí, about $\frac{1}{2}$d. sterling.

2 شاهی shāhí=100 دینار dínár=1 محمدی muhammadí, about 1d.

4 شاهی shāhí=200 دینار dínár=1 عباسی ʻabbásí, about 2d.

5 عباسی ʻabbásí=20 شاهی shāhí=1,000 دینار dínár=1 قرانی kirání *or* صاحب قرانی sáhib-kirání.

10 قرانی kirání=10,000 دینار dínár=1 تومان túmán, a gold coin, generally reckoned at 9s. in value, but in reality not worth more than 8s. or thereabouts.

The تومان túmán was formerly worth much more. In the reign of Sháh ʻAbbás I. its value was nearly £3 sterling; and when Sir John Malcolm visited Persia, at the commencement of the present century, it was then worth from 18s. to £1. It is now equivalent to a trifle over 7s. 11d.

The پول سیاه púl-i-siyáh (black money) is a copper coin, of various sizes and values; but it is commonly worth from one-half to one-third of a farthing. The name applies to copper coins in general. The پول سیاه púl-i-siyáh is not used in accounts.

The ریال riyál, which is worth about $1\frac{1}{4}$ kirání, is properly the Spanish dollar; but that coin is now rarely seen in Persia.

The Turkish piastre, called قروش kurúsh *or* غروش ghurúsh, is current in the northern provinces of Persia. Its value in former times was about 2s. 6d.; it is now worth no more than $2\frac{1}{2}$d.

The پناهبادی panáhbádí *or* پهنابادی pahnábádí is a silver coin, worth somewhat less than half a قرانی kirání; *e.g.* 23 پهنابادی pahnábádí= 10 قرانی kirání=1 تومان túmán.

European ducats, called مجر majar and باجغلی bájughlí, are current in many places. Their value fluctuates, but it is usually nearly equal to that of the تومان túmán, sometimes a little more or less.

The muhammadí, ʻabbásí, and riyál are not represented by any coin. The terms are used much in the same way as the English "guinea." It may be added also that the first-mentioned of these is never used for any lesser number than three muhammadís, sums amounting to no more than one or two muhammadís being expressed in dínárs.

Accounts are kept in the system called سياق siyák, already detailed, in the following manner:—

• Half a دينار dínár.

 1 دينار dínár.

 2 دينار dínár.

 3 دينار dínár.

 4 دينار dínár.

 5 دينار dínár=1 غاز gház.

 50 دينار dínár=1 شاهى sháhí.

 200 دينار dínár=1 عباسى ‘abbásí.

 or  1,000 دينار dínár= 1 قرانى kiráuí.

 or  2,000 دينار dínár= 2 قرانى kiráni.

 10,000 دينار dínár=1 تومان túmán.

 20,000 دينار dínár=2 تومان túmán.

 10 تومان túmán.

 11 تومان túmán.

 20 تومان túmán.

 30 تومان túmán.

 100 تومان túmán.

WEIGHTS.

Persian weights are the following. In Persia, as in most Muhammadan countries, grain, liquids, &c., are sold by weight, not by measure.

نخود nukhúd, a small chick-pea (*cicer arietinum*), called in India "Bengal gram," weighing about $\frac{1}{144}$ of an ounce.

24 نخود nukhúd=1 مثقال miskál, nearly $\frac{1}{6}$ of an oz. avoirdupois.

90 مثقال miskál=1 وقه vakkah, about 14 oz. avoirdupois.

8 وقه vakkah=720 مثقال miskál=1 من تبریزی mann-i-tabrízí (Tabriz mann), weighing from $7\frac{1}{4}$ to $7\frac{1}{2}$ lbs. avoirdupois.

2 من تبریزی mann-i-tabrízí=1 من شاهی mann-i-sháhí (Royal mann), from $14\frac{1}{2}$ to 15 lbs.

4 من تبریزی mann-i-tabrízí=1 من ری mann-i-rai (mann of Rai), nearly 30 lbs.

16 من تبریزی mann-i-tabrízí=1 من هاشمی mann-i-háshimí (Hashimi mann), used only in the southern provinces, 116 lbs.

100 من تبریزی mann-i-tabrízí=1 خروار kharvár (donkey-load), 725 lbs.

The quarter of a Tabriz mann, or about 1 lb. 12 oz. avoirdupois, is usually called a چارک chárik; and this term is also sometimes used to signify the quarter of a Royal mann, or about 3 lbs. 10 oz.

The باتمان bátmán *or* بطمن batman is a Turkish weight, used in Western Persia. It is the same as the Royal mann, or nearly 15 lbs.

The قیراط kírát *or* قراط karrát (carat) is an Arabian weight, varying from three to four English grains in different places. It is occasionally employed in weighing jewels and drugs.

MEASURES OF LENGTH.

موی شتر múí-i-shutur, the breadth of a camel's hair.

جو jau, a barleycorn.

انگشت angusht, a finger-breadth.

بهر bahar, length of one joint of the thumb, or about $1\frac{1}{4}$ inch.

2 بهر bahar=1 گره girah, or about $2\frac{1}{2}$ inches.

16 گره girah=1 ذرع zar' *or* گز gaz, the Persian ell of about 40 inches.

ارشین arshín, the Turkish ell; much the same as the above.

وجب vajjab, a span, from tip of thumb to tip of little finger extended.

ارج araj, دست dast, *or* ذراع zirá', a cubit, from the elbow to the tip of the middle finger.

قدم kadam, a short pace of 20 inches.

بغل baghal, a fathom, or space between the tips of the fingers of the two hands, when the arms are extended.

کله kallah, the ordinary stature of a man, about $5\frac{1}{2}$ feet.

12,000 قدم kadam=6,000 گز gaz=1 فرسخ farsákh *or* فرسنگ farsang, a parasang of about $3\frac{3}{4}$ English miles.

NAMES OF PERSONS AND PLACES.

A.

Aaron, هرون harún, هارون hárún.
Abadan, عبادان 'abbádán, آبادان ábádán.
Abbasides, عباسیان 'abbásiyán.
Abel, حابل hábil, هابیل hábíl, حبیل habíl.
Abiverd, ابیورد abívard.
Abraham, ابراهیم ibráhím.
Abu-bakr, ابو بکر abú-bakr.
Abu-'l-fazl, ابولفضل abu-'l-fazl.
Abyssinia, حبش habash, حبشستان habashistán.
Abyssinian, حبشی habashí.
Achin, آچین áchín.
Acre, عکا 'akká.
Adam, آدم ádam.
Adelaide, ادلاید adaláyid.
Aden, عدن 'adan.
Adrianople, ادرنه adranah, ادریانوپل adriyánúpal.
Adriatic Sea, دریائی ادریاتیك daryá,í-i-adriyátík.
Ægean Sea, بحر یونان bahr-i-yúnán.
Afghan, افغان afghán.
Afghanistan, افغانستان afghánistán.
Afrasyab, افراسیاب afrásyáb.
Africa, افریقا afríká, افریق afrík, افریقه afríkah.
African, مغربی maghribí.
Afridí, افریدی afrídí.
Agra, آگره ágrah.
Ahmedabad, احمداباد ahmadábád.
Ahmednagar, احمدنگر ahmadnagar.
Aix-la-chapelle, اکسلاشاپل aksláshápal.
Ajmir, اجمیر ajmír.
Albanian, ارنودی arnaudí.
Albert, البر albar.
Aleppo, حلب halab.
Alexander, اسکندر iskandar, سکندر sikandar.
Alexander the Great, ذو القرنین zu-'l-karnain, اسکندر رومی iskandar-rúmí.
Alexandra, الکسندرا alaksandrá.
Alexandretta, اسکندرون iskandarún.
Alexandria, اسکندریه iskandariyah, سکندریه sikandariyah.
Alfred, الفرد alfrad.
Algeria, الجزایر aljazáír.
Algiers, الجزائر al jazá,ir.
Ali, علی 'alí.—(*descendants of Ali*) علویان 'alavíyán.
Alice, الیس alís.
Allahabad, الله آباد allah-ábád.
Alma, الما almá.
Alps, الپ alp.
Alsace, آلزاس alzás.
Amadeus, امده amadah.
Amalek, عملیق 'imlík.
America, ینگی دنیا yangí-dunyá.—(*North America*) ینگی دنیا شمالی yangí-dunyá-i-shimálí. — (*South America*) ینگی دنیا جنوبی yangí-dunyá-i-junúbí.
American, ینگی دنیائی yangí-dunyá,í.
Amerkote, امرکوت amrkút.
Amsterdam, امستردام amstardám.
Anatolia, اناطولی anátúlí.
Andalusia, اندلس andalas.
Angora, انقره ankarah.
Antioch, انطاکیه antákiyah.
Arab, عرب 'arab.
Arabia, عرب 'arab, عربستان 'arabistán.
Arabia Felix, یمن yaman.
Arabia Petræa, حجاز hijáz.
Arabian, عربی 'arabí, تازی tází.
Arabic, عربی 'arabí, زبان عربی zabán-i-'arabí.
Ararat, آغر طاغ ághir-tágh, آغر داغی ághir-dághí.

Araxes, ارس aras.
Archimedes, ارشمیدس arshimíds.
Ardahan, اردهان ardahán.
Ardistan, آردستان árdistán.
Aristotle, ارسطو aristú, ارسط arast.
Armenia, ارمنیه armaniyah.
Armenian, ارمنی armaní (*pl.* ارامنه aráminah).
Arnot, ارناوت arnáút.
Arracan, ارخنگ arakhang.
Artaxerxes, اردشیر ardshír, ارتاهاشت artáhásht.
Artemisia, شویلا shuvílá.
Arthur, ارتور artúr.
Ashurada, عاشورادة 'áshúrádah.
Asia, اسیائی asiyá,í.—(*Asia Minor*) اسیائی کوچك asiyá,í - i - kúchik, اناطولی anátúlí.—(*Central Asia*) اسیائی وسطی asiyá,í-i-vasatí.
Askelon, اسقلان askalán.
Astarabad, استراباد astarábád.
Athens, اثنة atanah, اثنة atanah, اثن atan, اثانیه atániyah.
Atlantic Ocean, بحر اتلانتیك bahr-i-atlántík.
Atlas, اطلس atlas.
Attock, اتك atak.
Aurangzib, اورنگزیب aurangzíb.
Australia, اوسترالی ústarálí, استرالی ustarálí.
Austria, اطریش atrísh, اوستریا ústriyá.
Ayishah, عایشة 'áyishah.
Azarbijan, آذربایجان ázarbáíján, آذربیجان ázarbaiján.

B.

Baal, بعل ba'l.
Baalbak, بعلبك ba'albakk.
Babelmandeb, باب المندب bábu-'l-mandib.
Babylon, بابل bábul.
Babylonia, عراق 'irák.
Bacchus, باخوس bákhús.
Badakhshan, بدخشان badakhshán, بداخشان badákhshán.
Baghdad, بغداد baghdád.
Bahavul, بهاول bahával.
Bahrain, بحرین bahrain.
Baku, بادکوبه bádkúbah.
Balasore, بالیسر bálísar.
Balkh, بلخ balkh.
Balkhans, بلخان balkhán, بلقانها balkánahá, بالقان bálkán.
Baltic, بالتك báltik.
Bamian, بامیان bámiyán.
Bangalore, بنگلور bangalúr.
Bangkok, بانگکك bángkak.
Banswara, بانسوارة bánsvárah.
Barca, برقه barkah.
Barcelona, برشلونه barshalúnah.
Bareilly, بریلی barílí.
Baroach, بارروج bárrúj.
Bavaria, باویر bávír.
Bayazid, بایزید báyizíd.
Beatrice, بیاتریس biyátrís.
Behar, بهار bihár.
Belgium, بلجیك baljík, بلژیك balzhík.
Benares, بنارس banáras, بانارس bánáras.
Bengal, بنگاله bangálah.
Benjamin, ابن یامین ibnyámín.
Beor, باعورا bá'úrá.
Berar, برار barár.
Berlin, برلن barlin, برلین barlín.
Bermuda, برمود barmúd.
Bern, برن barn.
Bessarabia, بسارابیا basárábiyá.
Bethlehem, بیتالحم baitálahm, بیت لحم baitlahm.
Beyrout, بیروت bírút, باروط bárút, برود barúd.
Bhopal, بپل bapal.
Bidur, بیدر bídar.
Bijapur, بیجاپور bíjápúr.
Bijnur, بجنور bijnúr.
Bilaspur, بلاسپور biláspúr.
Biluchistan, بلوچستان bilúchistán.
Birbhum, بیربهوم birbhúm.
Black Sea *or* Euxine, بحر سیاه bahr-i-siyáh, قره دنگز karah-dingiz.
Bohemian, زنگی فرنگی zangí-i-firangí, قبطی kibtí.
Bolivia, بولیوی búlíví, بولیوار búlívár.
Bombay, بمبی bambí
Bordeaux, بردال burdál.
Borneo, برنیو barniú.
Bosnia, باسنه básnah, بوسنه búsnah.

Bosphorus, بوغاز بزرگ búgház-i-buzurg.
Boston, بستن bustan.
Bourbon (Isle of), جزيرهٔ بوربان jazírah-i-búrbán.
Brindisi, برانديزى birindízí.
Broach, بروج barvaj.
Brussels, بروكسل barúksal.
Bucharest, بكرش bakarash.
Bujnurd, بجنورد bujnúrd.
Bukhara, بخارا bukhárá.
Bulgaria, بلغار bulghár.
Bundi, بوندى búndí.
Burdwan, بردوان bardván.
Burhanpur, برهانپور barhánpúr.
Bushire, بوشهر bú-shahr, بندر البوشهر bandaru-'l-bú-shahr.
Bussorah, بصره basarah.
Bustam, بسطام bustám.
Buxar, بكسر baksir.
Byzantium, بزنطيه bizantíh.

C.

Cadiz, قادس kádis.
Cæsar, قيصر kaisar.
Cæsarea, قيصريه kaisariyah.
Cain, قابل kábil, قابيل kábíl.
Cairo, قاهره káhirah.
Calais, كاله kálah.
Calcutta, كلكته kalkattah.
California, كاليفورنى kálífúrní.
Calmuck, قلماق kalmák.
Canaan, كنعان kin'án.
Canada, كانادا kánádá.
Candia, قانديه kándiyah, قنديد kandíd, قنديه kandiyah.
Canton, خانقو khánkú.
Cape of Good Hope, دماغهٔ افريقيه dimághah-i-afríkíyah, دماغهٔ اميد dimághah-i-umíd.
Cape Noir, سادهٔ قهوه sádah-kahvah.
Carlist, كارليست kárlíst.
Carmel, كرمل kirmil.
Carnatic, كرناتك karnátak.
Caroline, كارولين kárúlín.
Carpathians, الامان طاغى alámán-tághí.
Carthage, قرطاجنه kurtájannah.
Caspian Sea, بحر خزر bahr-i-khazar, درياى قلزوم daryá,í-i-kulzúm, درياى حاجيطرخان daryá,í-i-hájí-tar-khán, بحر گيلان bahr-i-gílán.
Castile, قسطله kastalah, قسطيليه kastílíyah.
Catalan, قاتلان kátlán.
Catherine, كاترين kátrín.
Caucasus, قفقاز kafkáz.
Cawnpur, خانپور khánpúr.
Ceuta, سيته sítah, سبته sabtah.
Ceylon, سرانديپ sarándíp, سيلان sailán.
Chaldea, عراق 'irák.
Champarun, چنپارن chumpárun.
Charles, شارل shárl.
Chili, شيلى shílí.
China, چين chín, صين sín.—(*Emperor of China*) فغفور faghfúr, خاقان چين khákán-i-chín.
Chinese (*people*), اهل چين ahl-i-chín.—(*adj.*) چينى chíní.
Christiania, كريستيانيا kiristiyániyá.
Circassian, چركس charkas.
Cobourg, كبورغ kabúrgh.
Columbia, كولمبى kúlambí.
Constantine, قسطنطين kustantín.
Constantinople, اسلامبول islámbúl, استانبول istámbúl.
Copenhagen, كوپانهاك kúpánák, كوپنهاك kúpanhák.
Copt, قبط kibt.
Coptic, قبطى kibtí.
Corfu, كرفو karfú.
Corsica, كورسيكا kúrsíká, كرس kars, قورسيقه kúrsíkah.
Corunna, قلنه kalannah.
Cossack, قزاق kazák.
Cosseir, قصير kusair.
Crete, گرد girid, كريد kiríd, اقريطش akrítish, قانديه kándiyah, قنديه kandiyah.
Crimea, قريم karím.
Cronstadt, كرنستاد karanstád, كرونستاد karúnstád.
Cyclops, سيكلپ síklap.
Cyprus, قبريس kabrís, قبرس kabris.
Cyrene, قيروان kairaván.
Cyrus, كسرى kasrá, كورش kúrash.

D.

Dadur, دادر dádar.
Dalmatia, دالماچیا dálmáchiyá.
Damaghan, دامغان dámaghán.
Damascus, شام shám, دمشق dimashk.
Damietta, دمیاط dimyát.
Daniel, دانال dánál, دانیال dániyál.
Danube, طونه túnah, تونه túnah, دانوب dánúb.
Dardanelles, بوغاز دریای سیاه búgház-i-daryá,í-i-siyáh, بوغاز قلعه سلطانیه búgház-i-kal'ah-i-sultaníyah, بوغاز داردانال búgház-i-dárdánál, بوغاز چناق قلعه búgház-i-chanák-kal'ah.
Darius, دارا dárá.
David, داؤد da,úd.
Dead Sea, بحر لوط bahr-i-lút.
Deccan, دکن dakan, دکهن dakhan.
Dehra Ghazí Khan, دیره غازیخان dírah ghází-khán.
Delhi, دهلی dihlí.
Denmark, دانمارك dánmárk.
Dholepur, دهولپور dhúlpúr.
Dhurumpur, دهرمپور dharampúr.
Diana, ارطمیس artamís.
Diarbekr, دیاربکر diyárbakr.
Dinah, دینا díná.
Dizful, دزفول dizfúl.
Dniester, طورلا túrlá.
Doab, دوآب dú-áb.
Don, دن dan.
Dorcas, ظبیه zabyah.
Dowlutabad, دولتاباد daulutábád.
Dresden, درسد darasd.

E.

Ecuada, اکواتر akvátar.
Eden, عدن 'adan.
Edur, ایدر ídar.
Egypt, مصر misr.—(*Lower Egypt*) مصر سفلا misr-i-suflá, بحیرة bahairah.—(*Upper Egypt*) مصر علیا misr-i-'ulyá, سعید sa'íd.
Egyptian, مصری misrí.
Elias, الیاس ilyás.
Elizabeth, الزابت alizábat.
Emmaus, عمواس 'amvás.
England, انگلستان inglistán, انگلاند inglánd.
English, انگلیس inglís, انگریز ingríz.
English Channel, دریای مانش daryá,í-i-mánsh.
Enoch, ادریس idrís, اخنوخ akhnúkh.
Enzeli, انزلی anzalí.
Ephesus, فسوس fasús.
Erivan, ایروان iraván.
Erzeroum, ارضروم arzirúm, ارض روم arz-i-rúm, ارزن الروم arzanu-'r-rúm.
Esaias, اشعیا ish'iyá.
Esau, عیص 'ais, عیصو 'ísú.
Etawah, اتاوه itávah.
Ethiopia, زنگ zang, حبشه habashah.
Ethiopian, زنگی zangí, زنج zanj, حبش habash, حبشی habashí.
Etna, اتنا atná, اطنا atná.
Eugenie, اوژنی úzhaní.
Europe, فرنگستان firingistán, اوروپ úrúp, اروپ urúp, اوروپا úrúpá.
European, فرنگ firing, فرنج firinj, افرنج afranj.—(*adj.*) فرنگی firingí.
Euxine, *vide* Black Sea.
Eve, حوا havá.
Ezekiel, حزقیل hizkíl.

F.

Falkland Isles, جزائر فالکلاند jazá,ir-i-fálklánd.
Faridun, فریدون farídún.
Fars, فارس fárs.
Fatimah, فاطمه fátimah.
Ferdinand, فردیناند fardínánd, فردینان fardínán.
Ferghana, فرغانه farghánah.
Firuzpur, فیروزپور fírúzpúr.
Flanders, فلمنگ falmang.
Fleming, فلمنگ falmang.
Flemish, فلمنگی falmangí.
Florence, فلورانس falúráns.
Fontainbleau, فونتنبلو fúntambalú.

France, فرانسه faránsah.
Frank, فرنك firink, فرنج firing, افرنج afranj.
Frederick, فردريك fardarík.
French, فرانسه faránsah.
Furrah, فره farah.
Futtehpur, فتحپور fathpúr.

G.

Gabriel, جبريل jibríl, جبرئيل jabra,íl.
Galatz, قلاص kalás.
Gallipoli, گاليپولى gálípúlí, گليپولى galípúlí.
Ganges, گانگ gáng, گنگ gang, غانج ghánj, غانغا ghánghá.
Geneva, ژنو zhanv. — (*Lake of Geneva*) درياچهٔ ژنو daryáchah-i-zhanv.
Genoa, جنو janv, شنوه shanvah.
Genoese, جنويز janavíz.
George, ژوژ zhúzh.
Georgia, گرجستان gurjistán.
Georgian, گرجى gurjí.
German, المان almán, نمسى nimsí.
Germany, نيمچه nímchah, نمسستان nimsistán, المانيا almániyá.
Ghazipur, غازيپور gházípúr.
Ghuzni, غزنى ghazní.
Gibraltar, جبل الطارق jabalu-'t-tárik, مضيق masík.
Gilan, گيلان gílán, جيلان jílán.
Godavery, گوداورى gúdávarí.
Gog, ياجوج yájúj.
Golconda, گلكنده gulkundah.
Gold Coast, بلاد التبر biládu-'t-tibr.
Gomorrah, غموره ghumúrah, غمره ghumurah.
Gondal, گوندل gúndal.
Goruckpur, گورکهپور gúrakhpúr.
Great Britain, غرات بريتانيا ghirát brítániyá.
Grecian, يونانى yúnání, رومى rúmí.
Grecian Archipelago, بحر ابيض bahr-i-abyaz.
Greece, يونان yúnán, روم rúm, يونانستان yúnánistán.
Greek, يونانى yúnání, رومى rúmí.
Greeks (The), اروام arvam.
Greenland, دشت سبز dasht-i-sabz, گرينلاند grínlánd.
Grenada, غرناطه gharnátah.
Guadalquiver, وادى الكبير vádíu-'l-kabír.
Guatemala, گواتمالا guvátamálá.
Gujerat, گجرات gujrát.
Gurgan River, گرگانرود gurgán-rúd.
Gushtasp, گشتاسپ gushtásp.
Gwalior, گواليار guváliyár.

H.

Hadramaut, حضرموت hazramaut.
Hagar, آجر ájar.
Haiderabad, حيدراباد haidarábád.
Ham, حام hám, يام yám.
Hamazan, همزان hamazán.
Hamburg, هامبورگ hámbúrg.
Hanover, هانوور hánúvar.
Harun - al - Rashid, هارون الرشيد hárúnu-'r-rashíd.
Hayti, هايتى háítí.
Hazarah, هزاره hazárah.
Hebrew, عبرانى 'ibrání, عبرى 'ibrí.
Hecla, هكلا haklá.
Helen, هلن halan.
Helena, النه alnah.
Heliopolis, بعلبك ba'albakk.
Helvetia, هلوچيا halvachiyá.
Herat, هرات hirát.
Herod, هيروديس hírúdís.
Herzegovina, هرسك harasak.
Hesse Cassel, هس كاسل has kásal.
Hijaz, حجاز hijáz.
Himalayas, جبل هيمالها jabal-i-hímálahá.
Hindustan, هند hind, هندوستان hindústán.
Hippocrates, بقراط bukrát.
Holland, پى با páy-bá, هلاند huland, هولاند húlánd.
Honduras, هندوراس handúrás, هندورا handúrá.
Hong Kong, هونگ كونگ húng-kúng.
Honolulu, هنولولو hanúlúlú.
Hormuz, هرمز hurmuz.

Humbert, همبر hambar.
Hungarian, مجار majár.
Hungary, مجارستان majáristán.

I.

Ighriras, اغريرث ighríras.
Imran, عمران 'imrán.
India, هند hind, هندوستان hindústán.
Indian Ocean, بحر الهند bahru-'l-hind.
Indus, رود خانه سنده rúd-khánah-i-sindh, نيلاب níláb.
Innspruch, انسپروك insparúk.
Iram, ارم iram.
Ireland, ايرلند írland, ايرلاند írlánd.
Isaac اسحاق ishák, اسحق ishák.
Isaiah, اشعيا isha'yá.
Isfahan, اصفهان isfahán, صفاهان sifáhán.
Isfandyar, اسفنديار isfandyár.
Ishmail, اسمعيل isma'íl, اسماعيل ismá'íl.
Israel, اسرائيل isrá,íl.—(*Children of Israel*) بنى اسرائيل baní-i-isrá,íl.—(*Twelve tribes of Israel*) دوازده اسباط اسرائيل davázdah asbát-i-isrá,íl.
Italian, اتاليان itáliyán, اطاليان itáliyán.
Italy, ايتالى ítálí, اطاليا itáliyá.

J.

Jack, ژاك zhák.
Jacob, يعقوب ya'kúb.
Jaffa, يافا yáfá.
Jaipur, جيپور jaipúr.
Jaitpur, جيتپور jaitpúr.
James, يعقوب ya'kúb.
Jalalabad, جلالاباد jalálábád.
Jamshíd, جمشيد jamshíd.
Japan, ژاپون zhápún, ژاپن zhápun.
Japhet, يافث yáfis.
Jaunpur, جونپور jaunpúr.
Java, جاوه jávah.
Jaxartes, سيحون saihún.
Jeddah, جده juddah.
Jellasore, جاليسر jalísar.
Jeremiah, ارميا armiyá.
Jericho, اريحا ariyá.
Jeroboam, ياروبعام yárúb'ám.
Jerusalem, اورشليم úrishalím, القدس al-kuds, بيت المقدس baitu-'l-mukaddas.
Jesse, آشى áshá.
Jesus, عيسى 'ísá.
Jethro, شعيب shu'aib.
Jeysulmir, جيسلمير jaisulmír.
Jhallavar, جهلاور jhalávar.
Jind, جيند jínd.
Jingiz Khan, جنگيز jingíz, چنگيز chingíz.
Job, عيوب 'ayúb, ايوب ayyúb.
John, يحنا yuhanná.
John the Baptist, يحيى yahyá.
Jonas, يونس yúnas, يوناس yúnás.
Joppa, يافا yáfá.
Jordan, اردن urdunn *or* ardan, هردوم hardúm, يوردان yúrdán.
Joseph, يوسف yúsif.
Judah, يهودا yahúdá.
Judas Iscariot, يهوداى اسخريوتى yahúdá,í-i-iskhariyútí.
Jullundhur, جالندهر jálandhur.
Jummu, جمو jammú.
Jumna, جمنا jumná.
Jyntia, جينتيا jaintiyá.

K.

Kabul, كابل kábul.
Kaf, قاف káf.
Kai Kaus, كيكاوس kai-káús.
Kai Khusrau, كيخسرو kai-khusrau.
Kai Kubad, كيقباد kai-kubád.
Kalat, كلات kalát.
Kalmuck, قالمق kálmak.
Kalpi, كالپى kálpí.
Kampta, كامتا kámtá.
Kandahar, قندهار kandahár.
Kangra, خنگره khangarah, كانگر kángar.
Karasu, قراسو karású (="black water").

Kars, قارص kárs.
Kashan, کاشان káshán.
Kashghar, کاشغر káshghar.
Kashmir, قاشمیر káshmír, کشمیر kashmír.
Kaswin, قزوین kazvín.
Kathay, خطای khatáí.
Kerbela, کربلا karbalá.
Khaibar, خیبر khaibar.
Khiva, خیوه khívah, خوارزم khavárizm.
Khojand, خجند khajand.
Khokand, کوکن kúkan, خوقند khúkand.
Khotan, ختن khutan, خلم khulum
Khurasan, خراسان khurásán.
Khurum, خـــرم khurum, خـــورم khúrum.
Kirman, کرمان kirmán.
Kirmanshah, کرمانشاه kirmánsháh.
Konigsburg, کنیکسبرگ kaníksburg.
Kotah, کوتا kútá.
Kremlin, کرملین karmlín.
Kronstadt, کورنستاد kúrnstád.
Kufa, کوفان kaufán *or* kúfán.
Kuldja, قولچه kúlchah.
Kum, قم kum.
Kurd, کرد kurd (*pl.* اکراد akrád).
Kurdistan, کردستان kurdistán.
Kurnal, کرنال kurnál.
Kurrachi, کراچی karáchí.
Kuttach, کتك katak.

L.

Lahore, لاهور láhúr.
Laodicæa, لادق ládik.
Laristan, لرستان luristán, لورستان lúristán, لارستان láristán.
Lahsá, لحسا lahsá.
Lar, لار lár.
Lazarus, لعازر la'ázar, لاز láz, لازوری lázúrí.
Leander, اندروس andarús.
Lebanon, لبنان labnán.
Leghorn, لیگورن lígúrn.
Leopold, لیوپلد líúpuld.
Levantine, اهل شرق ahl-i-shark.
Limri, لیمری límrí.
Lingah, لنگا lingá.
Lisbon, لیزبن lízbun, اشبونه ashbúnah.
Livadia, لیوادیا lívádiyá, لوادیا livádiyá.
Llama, لاما lámá.
Lombardy, لـــنـبـــردیـه lumbardíh, لومباردی lúmbárdí.
London, لندن landan.
Lorraine, لورن lúran, لورینه lúrínah.
Lot, لوط lút.
Louis, لوی lúí.
Louise, لویز lúíz.
Lucknow, لکهنو lakhnau.
Ludhiana, لودهینه lúdhínah.
Luke, الوك alúk, لوك lúk, لوقا lúká.
Luxemburg, لوکسانبـــورگ luksámbúrg.
Lybia, لوبه lúbah.
Lyons, لیون líún.

M.

Macedonia, ماقدونیه mákdúniyah, ماکدونیا mákdúniyá, ماکدون mákdún, ماقدونیا mákdúniyá, مقدونیه makdúniyah.
Macon, ماکن mákan.
Madagascar, ماداگاسکار mádágáskár.
Madina, مدینه madínah.
Madras, مدراس madrás.
Madrid, مادرید mádríd.
Magog, ماجوج májúj.
Magyar, مجار majár.
Malabar, ملیبار malíbár, مالابار málábár, مالبار málabár.
Malacca, ملاخ malákh.
Malaga, مالقه málakah.
Mallia, مالیا máliyá.
Malta, مالت mált, مالطه máltah, مالته máltah.
Malwah, مالوه málvah.
Mamalouk, مملوك mamlúk (pl. ممالیك mamálík).
Manchu, مانچو mánchú, منچو manchú.
Manchuria, منچهر manchhar.
Mandavi, ماندوی mándaví, مندوی mandaví.
Mani, مانی mání.

Marguerite, مارگوریت márgúrít, مروارید marváríd (=" pearl ").
Mark, مارک márk.
Marseilles, مرسلیا marsaliyá.
Marwar, ماروار márvár.
Mary, ماری márí, مریم maryam.
Massowah, مصوق masúk.
Matthew, متهی mathá, متتی mattá.
Mauritius, موریس múrís.
Maximilian, ماکسیملین máksímilín, ماکزیمیلین mákzímílín.
Mazindaran, مازندران mázhindarán, مازندران mázindarán.
Mecca, مکه makkah, مکه معظمه makkah-i-mu'azzamah. — (*Temple of Mecca*) بیت الحرام baitu-'l-harám.
Mede, شروانی shirvání.
Media, شروان shirván.
Mediterranean, بحر الابیض bahru-'l-abyaz, بحر روم bahr-i-rúm, آق دنگز ák-dangiz, دریای سفید daryá,í-i-safíd.
Mekran, مکران makrán.
Merv, مرو marv.
Meshed, مشهد mashhad.
Mesopotamia, بلاد بین النهرین bilád bainu-'n-nahrín, الجزیرة al-jazírah, دیار بکر diyár-bakr.
Messinah, مسینه masínah.
Metz, متز matz.
Mexican, مکسیک maksík, مکزیک makzík.
Mexico, مکسیکو maksíkú.
Meywar, میوار mívár.
Miani, میانی míání.
Michael, میکائیل míká,íl.
Michní, میچنی michní.
Midian, مدین madyan.
Milan, ملان milán, میلان mílán.
Milo, میلو mílú.
Mirpur, میرپور mírpúr.
Mirut, مراٹ mirát.
Mitylene, مدل madal.
Mocha, مخا mukhá.
Moldavia, افلاک aflák, قره افلاک karah-aflák, بغدان baghdán.
Mongolia, مغلستان mughulistán.
Mont Blanc, مون بلان mún-bilán.
Mont Cenis, مون سنی mún-siní.
Montenegro, قره طاغ karah-tágh.
Montevideo, منتویداو mantivídáv.
Morea, موره múrah.
Morocco, ماروک márúk, مغرب maghrib.
Moscow, مسقوا muskuvá, مسکو muskú.
Moses, موسی músá.
Mosul, موصول músúl.
Mount St. Gothard, کوه سن کوتار kúh-i-san kútár.
Muhammerah, محمره muhammarah.
Multan, ملتان multán, مولتان múltán.
Munich, مونیک múník.
Muscovite, مسقو muskú.
Muskat, مسقط maskat.
Muttra, متهرا matthrá.

N.

Nadir Shah, نادر شاه nádir sháh.
Nagarkot, نگرکوٹ nagarkút.
Nahawand, نهاوند nahávand.
Najd, نجد najd.
Naples, ناپل nápul, ناپولی nápúlí.
Napoleon, ناپلیون nápaliyún.
Nardin, نردین nardín.
Natal, ناتال nátál.
Naushirawan, نوشروان naushiraván, نوشیروان naushíraván.
Navarino, ناوارن náváran.
Nazareth, ناصره násirah.
Nebuchadnezzar, بخت النصر bakhtu-'n-nassar.
Nestorian, نسطوری nastúrí.
Nestorius, نسطور nastúr.
Netherlands, پای با páy-bá, هلاند haland, ندرلانده nadarlándah.
New York, نیورک niyúrk, نویرک núyurk.
New Zealand, نوزلاند núzaland.
Nicaragua, نیکاراگا níkárágá.
Nice, نیس nís.
Nicholas, نیکلا níklá.
Nile, نیل níl.
Nimranah, نیمرانه nímránah.
Nineveh, نینوا nínavá, نینوی nínuví.
Nishapur, نیشاپور níshápúr, نشاپور nishápúr.

Noah, نوح núh.—(*Noah's ark*) کشتی نوح kashtí-i-núh, سفینه نوح safínah-i-núh.
North Sea, دریای شمال daryá,í-i-shimál.
Norway, نروج nurúj, نوروج núrúj.
Nowanagar, نوانگر navánagar.
Nubia, نوبیار núbiyár, نوبه núbah.
Nuddea, ندیا nadyá.
Nusirabad, نصراباد nasirábád, نصیراباد nasírábád.

O.

Oceania, اوقیانوس úkiyánús, اقیانوس ukiyánús.
Odessa, اودیسه údísah.
Olympus, جبل اناطولی jabal-i-anátúlí, جبل کریم jabal-i-karím.
Oman, عمان 'umán *or* 'ummán.
Orissa, اریسه urísa.
Osborne, اوزبون úzbún.
Oscar, اسکار uskár.
Otaheite, جزیره تایتی jazírah-i-táyití.
Oxus, جیحون jaihún.

P.

Pacific Ocean, بحر پاسیفیك bahr-i-pásífík, بحر پاسفیك bahr-i-pásifík.
Palanpur, پالهنپور pálhanpúr.
Palestine, فلستین filastín, فلسطون filastún.
Panama, پاناما pánámá.
Paniput, پانیپت pániput.
Paraguay, پاراگی parágí.
Paris, پاریس párís.
Parthia, کوهستان kúhistán.
Pashang, پشنگ pashang.
Patiala, پتیاله patiyálah.
Patna, پتنه patnah.
Paul, پاؤل pa,úl, بولس búlus, پاولوس páwlús.
Pegu, پیگو pígú.
Pekin, پکین pakín, پکن pakin.
Penelope, پنلوب panalúb.
Persepolis, استخر istakhr, تخت جمشید takht-i-jamshíd.
Persia, ایران írán, عجم 'ajam.
Persian, فارسی fársí, ایرانی íráni, عجمی 'ajamí.
Persian Gulf, خلیج فارس khalíj-i-fárs, دریای عمان daryá,í-i-'ummán, بحر العجم bahru-'l-'ajam, خلیج بصره khalíj-i-basarah.
Peshawur, پیشاور píshávur.
Pesth, پسته pastah, پست past.
Peter, پطر patar, پتر patar.
Peter the Great, پطر کبیر patar-i-kabír.
Pharaoh, فرعون fir'aun.
Phillipopolis, فلبه falabah, فلپلس falapalas.
Philistine, فلسطی filastí.
Phœnicia, ساحل sáhil.
Piedmont, پیدمون pídmún.
Pishin, پیشین píshín.
Plato, افلاطون aflátún.
Pliny, بولینس bulínas.
Po, پو pú.
Poland, له lah, لهستان lahistán.
Pole, له lah.
Polydore, پولیدور púlídúr.
Porebundar, پوربندر púrbundur.
Port Said, سعید sa'íd.
Porte, دولت علیه daulat-i-'alíyah, باب عالی báb-i-'álí.
Portugal, پرتگال purtagál, پرتقال purtakál, پرتغال purtaghál, پورتوغال púrtúghál, پورتگال púrtagál.
Potí, پوتی pútí.
Priam, پریام puriyám.
Prussia, پروس prús.
Pruth, پروت prút.
Psyche, نفس nafs.
Puna, پونه púnah.
Punjab, پنجاب panjáb.
Punnah, پنه panah.
Pyrenees, جبل الابواب jabalu-'l-abváb.
Pythagoras, فیثاغورث fisághúras.

R.

Radhunpur, رادهنپور rádhanpúr.
Rai Bareilly, رای بریلی raí barailí.
Rajpur, راجپور rájpúr.

Rajputana, راجپوتانه rájpútánah.
Ramah, رامه rámah.
Ramghur, رامگر rámgar.
Rampur, رامپور rámpúr.
Rangpur, رنگپور rangpúr.
Ray, ری rai.
Red Sea, دریای احمر daryá,í-i-ahmar, بحر الاحمر bahru-'l-ahmar, بحر اليمن bahru-'l-yaman, بحر الحجاز bahru-'l-hijáz.
Resht, رشت rasht.
Reunion, جزيرهٔ بوربان jazírah-i-búrbán.
Rhodus, رودس rúdis.
Rio Janeiro, ريو زانرو ríú-zánrú.
Rohtak, رهتك rahtak.
Roman, رومی rúmí.
Romans (The), روميان rúmiyán.
Rome, روم rúm, روما rúmá, رومه rúmah.
Romulus, روملش rúmlush.
Rosetta, رشيد rashíd.
Roumania, روميه rúmíyah.
Roumelia, روم‌ايلی rúmáílí.
Rudolph, ردلف rudulf.
Russia, روس rús, روسيه rúsiyah.
Russian, روس rús.
Rustam, رستم rustam, روستم rústam.
Rutlam, رتلام rutlám.

S.

Sabuktigin, سبکتگين subuktigín.
Sabzwar, سبزوار sabzvár.
Sadi, سعدی saʿdí.
Saharunpur, سهارنپور sahárunpúr.
Saint Helena, سنت هلن sant-halan,
St. John the Baptist, يحيی تعميد دهنده yahyá-i-taʿmíd-dihandah, يحيی الاصطباغی yahya-'l-istibághí.
St. John the Evangelist, يوحنای انجيلی yúhnáí-i-injílí.
St. Petersburg, سن پتربورغ san-patarbúrgh.
St. Salvador, سن سالوادر san-sálvádar.
St. Sophia, ايا صوفيه ayá-súfiyah.
St. Stephano, ايا ستفانوس ayá-stafánús.

Salonica, سلانيك salánik.
Samaria, سامريا sámariyá, سامريه sámariyah.
Samarkand, سمرقند samarkand.
Samos, ساموز sámúz, سوسام súsám, شامس shámis.
San Domingo, سن دومنغ san-dúmingh.
San Francisco, سانفرانسيسکو sán-fránsískú.
Sandwich Isles, جزيرهٔ ساندويچ jazírah-i-sándvích.
Santiago, سانتياگو sántíágú.
Saragossa, سرقسطه sarakustah.
Sarah, ساره sárah.
Sarakhs, سرخس sarakhs.
Sardinia, سردانيه sardániyah, ساردن sárdan, شارده shárdah.
Sassanian, ساسانی sásání.
Saul, سولس saulus.
Save, ساوه sávah.
Savoy, ساووا sáúvá.
Saxony, ساکس sáks, ساکسونيا sáksúniyá.
Scio, جزيرة المصطکی jazírahu-'l-mastakí.
Sclav, سقالبه skálabah.
Sclavonia, سقلاب sakláb.
Scotch, اکوسی akúsí.
Scotland, اسکاتلند askátland.
Scutari, اسکداری askudárí, اشقودره ashkúdarah.
Sea of Azof, بحر القرم bahru-'l-kirim.
Sea of Marmora, دريای مرمره daryá,í-i-marmarah, بحر سفيد bahr-i-safíd.
Sea of Tiberias, بحيرهٔ طبريه buhayrah-i-tabariyah.
Sebastopol, سواستاپول savástápúl, سيواستاپول sívástápúl.
Senegal, سنکال sanakál.
Servia, صربستان sarbistán.
Seth, شيث shís.
Seville, اسبيل isbíl.
Shahpur, شاهپور sháhpúr.
Shahrisabs, شهر سبز shahr-i-sabz.
Shahrud, شاهرود sháhrúd, شهرود shahrúd.
Sheba, Queen of, بلقيس bilkís.
Shem, سام sám.

Shikarpur, شکارپور shikárpúr, شیخپور shaikhpúr, شیخوپور shaikhúpúr.
Shiraz, شیراز shíráz.
Shirpur, شیرپور shírpúr.
Shirvan, شیروان shírván.
Shorepur, شورپور shúrpúr.
Shuster, شوشتر shúshtar, ششتر shustar.
Sialkote, سیالکوت siyálkút.
Siam, سیام siyám.
Siberia, سبیر sabír.
Sicily, سیسیل sísíl.
Sidon, اربل irbil, صیدا saidá.
Sierra Leone, سیرالون sírálún, سرالون sirálún.
Simeon, سمعان sim'án.
Simla, شمله shimlah.
Simon, سمعان sim'án.
Sinai, طور túr, سینا sainá, جبل سینا jabal-i-sainá, جبل موسی jabal-i-músá.
Sind, سند sind, سنده sindh.
Sinope, سنوب sinúb, سینوب sínúb.
Sirhind, سرهند sarhind.
Sirsa, سرسا sirsá.
Sistan, سیستان sístán.
Socotra, سقطره sukutrah, سقوطره sukútarah, سقرطا sukrutá.
Socrates, سقراط sukrát, سقراث sukrát.
Sodom, سدوم sudúm.
Sogdiana, سغد sughd.
Solomon, سلیمان sulaimán.
Somnath, سومنات súmnát.
Soudan, سودان súdán.
Sophia, صفیه safiyah.
Spain, اسپانیا ispániyá, اندلس andalus, اسپانیول ispániyúl.
Stockholm, استکهم ustakham, استکهلم ustakhalm.
Straits of Messina, بوغاز مسینا bugház-i-masíná.
Stutgardt, استوتگار ustútgár.
Suez, سویش savísh.
Sumatra, سوماطرا súmátrá.
Surat, سورت súrat.
Susa, ششتر shustar, شوشتر shúshtar.
Susanna, سوسنا súsanná.
Sutlej, ستلج satlaj.
Sweden, اسوج asvaj, سود súd, زوژ zúzh.
Swedish, اسوج asvaj.
Swiss, سویس savís.
Swiss Republic, جمهوری سویس jamhúrí-i-savís.
Switzerland, هلوچیا halvachiyá.
Syria, شام shám.

T.

Tabriz, تبریز tabríz.
Tahmasp, طهماسب tahmásb.
Tamerlane, تیمور اعرج taimúr-a'raj, تیمور لنک taimúr-lang.
Tangiers, تنجا tanjá, تنجیا tanjiyá, طنجه tanjah.
Tanna, تانه tánah.
Tapti, تپتی taptí.
Tarragona, تاکرونا tákurruná.
Tarsus, طرسوس tarsús.
Tartar, تاتار tátár, تتار tatár, تاتار tátár.
Tartary, توران túrán. — (*Chinese Tartary*) ختن khutan.
Tashkend, تاشکند táshkand.
Teheran, طهران tahrán.
Telemachus, تلماك talamák, تلمارك talamárk.
Therapia, طرابیه tarábiyah.
Thomas, توما túmá.
Thrace, تیراس tírás.
Tiberias, طبریه tabariyah.
Tibet, تبت tibbat.
Tiflis, تفلیس tiflís.
Tigris, دجله dijlah.
Timothy, تمتهی tamtahí.
Tipperah, تپره taprah.
Tirhoot, ترهت tarhat.
Tirnova, طرنوی tarnúí.
Tortosa, طرطوشه turtúshah.
Transoxiana, ماور النهر mávaru-'n-nahr.
Transylvania, اردل ardal.
Trebizonde, طربزان tirabazán, طرابزون tirábazún, طربزون tirabazún, طرابزان tirábazán.
Tripolis, طرابلس tarábulus.
Troy, تروا tarvá, تروا tarúvá.
Tunis, تنیس tunís, تونس túnis, تونیز túníz.

Tur, تور túr.
Turin, تورن túran.
Turk, عثمانی 'usmání.
Turkey, ملك روم mulk-i-rúm, مملکت عثمانلو mamlikat-i-'usmánlú, ممالك عثمانیه mamálik-i-'usmániyah.
Turkish, عثمانی 'usmání. — (*language*) ترکی turkí.
Turkistan, ترکستان turkistán.
Turkoman, ترکمان turkmán (*pl.* تراکمه tarákimah.—(*Tekke Turkomans*) ترکمانان تکه turkmánán-i-takah.
Turkomanchai, Treaty of, مصالحه ترکمان چای musálahah-i-turkmán-cháí.
Tus, طوس tús.
Tyre, صور súr.
Tyrol, تیرول tírúl.

U.

Udaipur, اودیپور údaipúr.
Ujain, اجین ujain.
Ulysses, اولیس úlís.
Umballah, انباله ambálah.
Umreilly, امریلی umrailí.
United States, دول متحده duval-i-muttahidah.
Uriah, اوریا úriyá.
Urmuz, ارمز urmuz.
Uzbek, اوزبك úzbak.

V.

Valentia, بلنسیه balansiyah.
Varna, وان ván.
Venezuela, ونزولا vanizúlá.
Venice, ونیس vanís.
Venus, زهره zuharah.
Versailles, ورسایل varsáil.
Victoria, ویکتوریا víktúriyá.
Vienna, وین vín, ویانا víáná.
Virgil, ویرژیل vírzhíl.
Vistula, ویستول vístúl
Vladimir, والدمار váldamár.

W.

Wahabees, وهابی vahábí.
Wallachia, افلاق aflák, بوغدان búghdán.
Warsaw, وارشاو várshâv.
Washington, وازنگتون vázingtún, واشنگتن váshingtun.
Waterloo, واطرلو vátarlú.
West Indies, هند الغربی hindu-'l-gharbí.
White Sea, بحر ابیض bahr-i-abyaz.
William, گیلیوم gíliyúm.
Windsor, وینسور vínsúr.
Wurtemburg, ورتمبرغ vartamburgh.

Y.

Yaman, یمین yamín, یمن yaman.
Yazd, یزد yazd.
Yazdagird, یزدگرد yazdagird, یزدجرد yazdajird.
Yeddo, یدو yadú.
Yokohama, یوکوهوما yúkúhúmá.

Z.

Zacharias, ذکریا zakariyá, زکریا zakariyá, زکری zakarí.
Zal, زال zál.
Zamindawar, زمین داور zamíndávar.
Zanzibar, زنگبار zangbár.
Zenocrates, ذیمقراطیس zímkarátís.
Zipporah, صفورا safúrá, صفوره safúrah.
Zoroaster, زاردهشت zárdusht, زارهشت zárhusht, زارتشت zártusht, زرادهشت zarádusht, زرادهشت zaráduhsht.
Zulu, زولو zúlú.

COMPARATIVE TABLE

OF THE

MUHAMMADAN AND CHRISTIAN ERAS.

Hijrah Year.	Christian Year.	Hijrah Year.	Christian Year.	Hijrah Year.	Christian Year.
1	622 16 July	36	656 30 June	71	690 15 June
2	623 5 July	37	657 19 June	72	691 4 June
3	624 24 June	38	658 9 June	73	692 23 May
4	625 13 June	39	659 29 May	74	693 13 May
5	626 2 June	40	660 17 May	75	694 2 May
6	627 23 May	41	661 7 May	76	695 21 April
7	628 11 May	42	662 26 April	77	696 10 April
8	629 1 May	43	663 15 April	78	697 30 March
9	630 20 April	44	664 4 April	79	698 20 March
10	631 9 April	45	665 24 March	80	699 9 March
11	632 29 March	46	666 13 March	81	700 26 Feb.
12	633 18 March	47	667 3 March	82	701 15 Feb.
13	634 7 March	48	668 20 Feb.	83	702 4 Feb.
14	635 25 Feb.	49	669 9 Feb.	84	703 24 Jan.
15	636 14 Feb.	50	670 29 Jan.	85	704 14 Jan.
16	637 2 Feb.	51	671 18 Jan.	86	705 2 Jan.
17	638 23 Jan.	52	672 8 Jan.	87	705 23 Dec.
18	639 12 Jan.	53	672 27 Dec.	88	706 12 Dec.
19	640 2 Jan.	54	673 16 Dec.	89	707 1 Dec.
20	640 21 Dec.	55	674 6 Dec.	90	708 20 Nov.
21	641 10 Dec.	56	675 25 Nov.	91	709 9 Nov.
22	642 30 Nov.	57	676 14 Nov.	92	710 29 Oct.
23	643 19 Nov.	58	677 3 Nov.	93	711 19 Oct.
24	644 7 Nov.	59	678 23 Oct.	94	712 7 Oct.
25	645 28 Oct.	60	679 13 Oct.	95	713 26 Sept.
26	646 17 Oct.	61	680 1 Oct.	96	714 16 Sept.
27	647 7 Oct.	62	681 20 Sept.	97	715 5 Sept.
28	648 25 Sept.	63	682 10 Sept.	98	716 25 Aug.
29	649 14 Sept.	64	683 30 Aug.	99	717 14 Aug.
30	650 4 Sept.	65	684 18 Aug.	100	718 3 Aug.
31	651 24 Aug.	66	685 8 Aug.	101	719 24 July
32	652 12 Aug.	67	686 28 July	102	720 12 July
33	653 2 Aug.	68	687 18 July	103	721 1 July
34	654 22 July	69	688 6 July	104	722 21 June
35	655 11 July	70	689 25 June	105	723 10 June

Hijrah Year.	Christian Year.	Hijrah Year.	Christian Year.	Hijrah Year.	Christian Year.
106	724 29 May	155	771 13 Dec.	204	819 28 June
107	725 19 May	156	772 2 Dec.	205	820 17 June
108	726 8 May	157	773 21 Nov.	206	821 6 June
109	727 28 April	158	774 11 Nov.	207	822 27 May
110	728 16 April	159	775 31 Oct.	208	823 16 May
111	729 5 April	160	776 19 Oct.	209	824 4 May
112	730 26 March	161	777 9 Oct.	210	825 24 April
113	731 15 March	162	778 28 Sept.	211	826 13 April
114	732 3 March	163	779 17 Sept.	212	827 2 April
115	733 21 Feb.	164	780 6 Sept.	213	828 22 March
116	734 10 Feb.	165	781 26 Aug.	214	829 11 March
117	735 31 Jan.	166	782 15 Aug.	215	830 28 Feb.
118	736 20 Jan.	167	783 5 Aug.	216	831 18 Feb.
119	737 8 Jan.	168	784 24 July	217	832 7 Feb.
120	737 29 Dec.	169	785 14 July	218	833 27 Jan.
121	738 18 Dec.	170	786 3 July	219	834 16 Jan.
122	739 7 Dec.	171	787 22 June	220	835 5 Jan.
123	740 26 Nov.	172	788 11 June	221	835 26 Dec.
124	741 15 Nov.	173	789 31 May	222	836 14 Dec.
125	742 4 Nov.	174	790 20 May	223	837 3 Dec.
126	743 25 Oct.	175	791 10 May	224	838 23 Nov.
127	744 13 Oct.	176	792 28 April	225	839 12 Nov.
128	745 3 Oct.	177	793 18 April	226	840 31 Oct.
129	746 22 Sept.	178	794 7 April	227	841 21 Oct.
130	747 11 Sept.	179	795 27 March	228	842 10 Oct.
131	748 31 Aug.	180	796 16 March	229	843 30 Sept.
132	749 20 Aug.	181	797 5 March	230	844 18 Sept.
133	750 9 Aug.	182	798 22 Feb.	231	845 7 Sept.
134	751 30 July	183	799 12 Feb.	232	846 28 Aug.
135	752 18 July	184	800 1 Feb.	233	847 17 Aug.
136	753 7 July	185	801 20 Jan.	234	848 5 Aug.
137	754 27 June	186	802 10 Jan.	235	849 26 July
138	755 16 June	187	802 30 Dec.	236	850 15 July
139	756 5 June	188	803 20 Dec.	237	851 5 July
140	757 25 May	189	804 8 Dec.	238	852 23 June
141	758 14 May	190	805 27 Nov.	239	853 12 June
142	759 4 May	191	806 17 Nov.	240	854 2 June
143	760 22 April	192	807 6 Nov.	241	855 22 May
144	761 11 April	193	808 25 Oct.	242	856 10 May
145	762 1 April	194	809 15 Oct.	243	857 30 April
146	763 21 March	195	810 4 Oct.	244	858 19 April
147	764 10 March	196	811 23 Sept.	245	859 8 April
148	765 27 Feb.	197	812 12 Sept.	246	860 28 March
149	766 16 Feb.	198	813 1 Sept.	247	861 17 March
150	767 6 Feb.	199	814 22 Aug.	248	862 7 March
151	768 26 Jan.	200	815 11 Aug.	249	863 24 Feb.
152	769 14 Jan.	201	816 30 July	250	864 13 Feb.
153	770 4 Jan.	202	817 20 July	251	865 2 Feb.
154	770 24 Dec.	203	818 9 July	252	866 22 Jan.

Hijrah Year.	Christian Year.	Hijrah Year.	Christian Year.	Hijrah Year.	Christian Year.
253	867 11 Jan.	302	914 27 July	351	962 9 Feb.
254	868 1 Jan.	303	915 17 July	352	963 30 Jan.
255	868 20 Dec.	304	916 5 July	353	964 19 Jan.
256	869 9 Dec.	305	917 24 June	354	965 7 Jan.
257	870 29 Nov.	306	918 14 June	355	965 28 Dec.
258	871 18 Nov.	307	919 3 June	356	966 17 Dec.
259	872 7 Nov.	308	920 23 May	357	967 7 Dec.
260	873 27 Oct.	309	921 12 May	358	968 25 Nov.
261	874 16 Oct.	310	922 1 May	359	969 14 Nov.
262	875 6 Oct.	311	923 21 April	360	970 4 Nov.
263	876 24 Sept.	312	924 9 April	361	971 24 Oct.
264	877 13 Sept.	313	925 29 March	362	972 12 Oct.
265	878 3 Sept.	314	926 19 March	363	973 2 Oct.
266	879 23 Aug.	315	927 8 March	364	974 21 Sept.
267	880 12 Aug.	316	928 25 Feb.	365	975 10 Sept.
268	881 1 Aug.	317	929 14 Feb.	366	976 30 Aug.
269	882 21 July	318	930 3 Feb.	367	977 19 Aug.
270	883 11 July	319	931 24 Jan.	368	978 9 Aug.
271	884 29 June	320	932 13 Jan.	369	979 29 July
272	885 18 June	321	933 1 Jan.	370	980 17 July
273	886 8 June	322	933 22 Dec.	371	981 7 July
274	887 28 May	323	934 11 Dec.	372	982 26 June
275	888 16 May	324	935 30 Nov.	373	983 15 June
276	889 6 May	325	936 19 Nov.	374	984 4 June
277	890 25 April	326	937 8 Nov.	375	985 24 May
278	891 15 April	327	938 29 Oct.	376	986 13 May
279	892 3 April	328	939 18 Oct.	377	987 3 May
280	893 23 March	329	940 6 Oct.	378	988 21 April
281	894 13 March	330	941 26 Sept.	379	989 11 April
282	895 2 March	331	942 15 Sept.	380	990 31 March
283	896 19 Feb.	332	943 4 Sept.	381	991 20 March
284	897 8 Feb.	333	944 24 August	382	992 9 March
285	898 28 Jan.	334	945 13 August	383	993 26 Feb.
286	899 17 Jan.	335	946 2 August	384	994 15 Feb.
287	900 7 Jan.	336	947 23 July	385	995 5 Feb.
288	900 26 Dec.	337	948 11 July	386	996 25 Jan.
289	901 16 Dec.	338	949 1 July	387	997 14 Jan.
290	902 5 Dec.	339	950 20 June	388	998 3 Jan.
291	903 24 Nov.	340	951 9 June	389	998 23 Dec.
292	904 13 Nov.	341	952 29 May	390	999 13 Dec.
293	905 2 Nov.	342	953 18 May	391	1000 1 Dec.
294	906 22 Oct.	343	954 7 May	392	1001 20 Nov.
295	907 12 Oct.	344	955 27 April	393	1002 10 Nov.
296	908 30 Sept.	345	956 15 April	394	1003 30 Oct.
297	909 20 Sept.	346	957 4 April	395	1004 18 Oct.
298	910 9 Sept.	347	958 25 March	396	1005 8 Oct.
299	911 29 Aug.	348	959 14 March	397	1006 27 Sept.
300	912 18 Aug.	349	960 3 March	398	1007 17 Sept.
301	913 7 Aug.	350	961 20 Feb.	399	1008 5 Sept.

Hijrah Year.	Christian Year.	Hijrah Year.	Christian Year.	Hijrah Year.	Christian Year.
400	1009 25 Aug.	449	1057 10 March	498	1104 23 Sept.
401	1010 15 Aug.	450	1058 28 Feb.	499	1105 13 Sept.
402	1011 4 Aug.	451	1059 17 Feb.	500	1106 2 Sept.
403	1012 23 July	452	1060 6 Feb.	501	1107 22 Aug.
404	1013 13 July	453	1061 26 Jan.	502	1108 11 Aug.
405	1014 2 July	454	1062 15 Jan.	503	1109 31 July
406	1015 21 June	455	1063 4 Jan.	504	1110 20 July
407	1016 10 June	456	1063 25 Dec.	505	1111 10 July
408	1017 30 May	457	1064 13 Dec.	506	1112 28 June
409	1018 20 May	458	1065 3 Dec.	507	1113 18 June
410	1019 9 May	459	1066 22 Nov.	508	1114 7 June
411	1020 27 April	460	1067 11 Nov.	509	1115 27 May
412	1021 17 April	461	1068 31 Oct.	510	1116 16 May
413	1022 6 April	462	1069 20 Oct.	511	1117 5 May
414	1023 26 March	463	1070 9 Oct.	512	1118 24 April
415	1024 15 March	464	1071 29 Sept.	513	1119 14 April
416	1025 4 March	465	1072 17 Sept.	514	1120 2 April
417	1026 22 Feb.	466	1073 6 Sept.	515	1121 22 March
418	1027 11 Feb.	467	1074 27 Aug.	516	1122 12 March
419	1028 31 Jan.	468	1075 16 Aug.	517	1123 1 March
420	1029 20 Jan.	469	1076 5 Aug.	518	1124 19 Feb.
421	1030 9 Jan.	470	1077 25 July	519	1125 7 Feb.
422	1031 29 Dec.	471	1078 14 July	520	1126 27 Jan.
423	1031 19 Dec.	472	1079 4 July	521	1127 17 Jan.
424	1032 7 Dec.	473	1080 22 June	522	1128 6 Jan.
425	1033 26 Nov.	474	1081 11 June	523	1128 25 Dec.
426	1034 16 Nov.	475	1082 1 June	524	1129 15 Dec.
427	1035 5 Nov.	476	1083 21 May	525	1130 4 Dec.
428	1036 25 Oct.	477	1084 10 May	526	1131 23 Nov.
429	1037 14 Oct.	478	1085 29 April	527	1132 12 Nov.
430	1038 3 Oct.	479	1086 18 April	528	1133 1 Nov.
431	1039 23 Sept.	480	1087 8 April	529	1134 22 Oct.
432	1040 11 Sept.	481	1088 27 March	530	1135 11 Oct.
433	1041 31 Aug.	482	1089 16 March	531	1136 29 Sept.
434	1042 21 Aug.	483	1090 6 March	532	1137 19 Sept.
435	1043 10 Aug.	484	1091 23 Feb.	533	1138 8 Sept.
436	1044 29 July	485	1092 12 Feb.	534	1139 28 Aug.
437	1045 19 July	486	1093 1 Feb.	535	1140 17 Aug.
438	1046 8 July	487	1094 21 Jan.	536	1141 6 Aug.
439	1047 28 June	488	1095 11 Jan.	537	1142 27 July
440	1048 16 June	489	1095 31 Dec.	538	1143 16 July
441	1049 5 June	490	1096 19 Dec.	539	1144 4 July
442	1050 26 May	491	1097 9 Dec.	540	1145 24 June
443	1051 15 May	492	1098 28 Nov.	541	1146 13 June
444	1052 3 May	493	1099 17 Nov.	542	1147 2 June
445	1053 23 April	494	1100 6 Nov.	543	1148 22 May
446	1054 12 April	495	1101 26 Oct.	544	1149 11 May
447	1055 2 April	496	1102 15 Oct.	545	1150 30 April
448	1056 21 March	497	1103 5 Oct.	546	1151 20 April

Hijrah Year.	Christian Year.	Hijrah Year.	Christian Year.	Hijrah Year.	Christian Year.
547	1152 8 April	596	1199 23 Oct.	645	1247 8 May
548	1153 29 March	597	1200 12 Oct.	646	1248 26 April
549	1154 18 March	598	1201 1 Oct.	647	1249 16 April
550	1155 7 March	599	1202 20 Sept.	648	1250 5 April
551	1156 25 Feb.	600	1203 10 Sept.	649	1251 26 March
552	1157 13 Feb.	601	1204 29 Aug.	650	1252 14 March
553	1158 2 Feb.	602	1205 18 Aug.	651	1253 3 March
554	1159 23 Jan.	603	1206 8 Aug.	652	1254 21 Feb.
555	1160 12 Jan.	604	1207 28 July	653	1255 10 Feb.
556	1160 31 Dec.	605	1208 16 July	654	1256 30 Jan.
557	1161 21 Dec.	606	1209 6 July	655	1257 19 Jan.
558	1162 10 Dec.	607	1210 25 June	656	1258 8 Jan.
559	1163 30 Nov.	608	1211 15 June	657	1258 29 Dec.
560	1164 18 Nov.	609	1212 3 June	658	1259 18 Dec.
561	1165 7 Nov.	610	1213 23 May	659	1260 6 Dec.
562	1166 28 Oct.	611	1214 13 May	660	1261 26 Nov.
563	1167 17 Oct.	612	1215 2 May	661	1262 15 Nov.
564	1168 5 Oct.	613	1216 20 April	662	1263 4 Nov.
565	1169 25 Sept.	614	1217 10 April	663	1264 24 Oct.
566	1170 14 Sept.	615	1218 30 March	664	1265 13 Oct.
567	1171 4 Sept.	616	1219 19 March	665	1266 2 Oct.
568	1172 23 Aug.	617	1220 8 March	666	1267 22 Sept.
569	1173 12 Aug.	618	1221 25 Feb.	667	1268 10 Sept.
570	1174 2 Aug.	619	1222 15 Feb.	668	1269 31 Aug.
571	1175 22 July	620	1223 4 Feb.	669	1270 20 Aug.
572	1176 10 July	621	1224 24 Jan.	670	1271 9 Aug.
573	1177 30 June	622	1225 13 Jan.	671	1272 29 July
574	1178 19 June	623	1226 2 Jan.	672	1273 18 July
575	1179 8 June	624	1226 22 Dec.	673	1274 7 July
576	1180 28 May	625	1227 12 Dec.	674	1275 27 June
577	1181 17 May	626	1228 30 Nov.	675	1276 15 June
578	1182 7 May	627	1229 20 Nov.	676	1277 4 June
579	1183 26 April	628	1230 9 Nov.	677	1278 25 May
580	1184 14 April	629	1231 29 Oct.	678	1279 14 May
581	1185 4 April	630	1232 18 Oct.	679	1280 3 May
582	1186 24 March	631	1233 7 Oct.	680	1281 22 April
583	1187 13 March	632	1234 26 Sept.	681	1282 11 April
584	1188 2 March	633	1235 16 Sept.	682	1283 1 April
585	1189 19 Feb.	634	1236 4 Sept.	683	1284 20 March
586	1190 8 Feb.	635	1237 24 Aug.	684	1285 9 March
587	1191 29 Jan.	636	1238 14 Aug.	685	1286 27 Feb.
588	1192 18 Jan.	637	1239 3 Aug.	686	1287 16 Feb.
589	1193 7 Jan.	638	1240 23 July	687	1288 6 Feb.
590	1193 27 Dec.	639	1241 12 July	688	1289 25 Jan.
591	1194 16 Dec.	640	1242 1 July	689	1290 14 Jan.
592	1195 6 Dec.	641	1243 21 June	690	1291 4 Jan.
593	1196 24 Nov.	642	1244 9 June	691	1291 24 Dec.
594	1197 13 Nov.	643	1245 29 May	692	1292 12 Dec.
595	1198 3 Nov.	644	1246 19 May	693	1293 2 Dec.

Hijrah Year.	Christian Year.	Hijrah Year.	Christian Year.	Hijrah Year.	Christian Year.
694	1294 21 Nov.	743	1342 6 June	792	1389 20 Dec.
695	1295 10 Nov.	744	1343 26 May	793	1390 9 Dec.
696	1296 30 Oct.	745	1344 15 May	794	1391 29 Nov.
697	1297 19 Oct.	746	1345 4 May	795	1392 17 Nov.
698	1298 9 Oct.	747	1346 24 April	796	1393 6 Nov.
699	1299 28 Sept.	748	1347 13 April	797	1394 27 Oct.
700	1300 16 Sept.	749	1348 1 April	798	1395 16 Oct.
701	1301 6 Sept.	750	1349 22 March	799	1396 5 Oct.
702	1302 26 Aug.	751	1350 11 March	800	1397 24 Sept.
703	1303 15 Aug.	752	1351 28 Feb.	801	1398 13 Sept.
704	1304 4 Aug.	753	1352 18 Feb.	802	1399 3 Sept.
705	1305 24 July	754	1353 6 Feb.	803	1400 22 Aug.
706	1306 13 July	755	1354 26 Jan.	804	1401 11 Aug.
707	1307 3 July	756	1355 16 Jan.	805	1402 1 Aug.
708	1308 21 June	757	1356 5 Jan.	806	1403 21 July
709	1309 11 June	758	1356 25 Dec.	807	1404 10 July
710	1310 31 May	759	1357 14 Dec.	808	1405 29 June
711	1311 20 May	760	1358 3 Dec.	809	1406 18 June
712	1312 9 May	761	1359 23 Nov.	810	1407 8 June
713	1313 28 April	762	1360 11 Nov.	811	1408 27 May
714	1314 17 April	763	1361 31 Oct.	812	1409 16 May
715	1315 7 April	764	1362 21 Oct.	813	1410 6 May
716	1316 26 March	765	1363 10 Oct.	814	1411 25 April
717	1317 16 March	766	1364 28 Sept.	815	1412 13 April
718	1318 5 March	767	1365 18 Sept.	816	1413 3 April
719	1319 22 Feb.	768	1366 7 Sept.	817	1414 23 March
720	1320 12 Feb.	769	1367 28 Aug.	818	1415 13 March
721	1321 31 Jan.	770	1368 16 Aug.	819	1416 1 March
722	1322 20 Jan.	771	1369 5 Aug.	820	1417 18 Feb.
723	1323 10 Jan.	772	1370 26 July	821	1418 8 Feb.
724	1323 30 Dec.	773	1371 15 July	822	1419 28 Jan.
725	1324 18 Dec.	774	1372 3 July	823	1420 17 Jan.
726	1325 8 Dec.	775	1373 23 June	824	1421 6 Jan.
727	1326 27 Nov.	776	1374 12 June	825	1421 26 Dec.
728	1327 17 Nov.	777	1375 2 June	826	1422 15 Dec.
729	1328 5 Nov.	778	1376 21 May	827	1423 5 Dec.
730	1329 25 Oct.	779	1377 10 May	828	1424 23 Nov.
731	1330 15 Oct.	780	1378 30 April	829	1425 13 Nov.
732	1331 4 Oct.	781	1379 19 April	830	1426 2 Nov.
733	1332 22 Sept.	782	1380 7 April	831	1427 22 Oct.
734	1333 12 Sept.	783	1381 28 March	832	1428 11 Oct.
735	1334 1 Sept.	784	1382 17 March	833	1429 30 Sept.
736	1335 21 Aug.	785	1383 6 March	834	1430 19 Sept.
737	1336 10 Aug.	786	1384 24 Feb.	835	1431 9 Sept.
738	1337 30 July	787	1385 12 Feb.	836	1432 28 Aug.
739	1338 20 July	788	1386 2 Feb.	837	1433 18 Aug.
740	1339 9 July	789	1387 22 Jan.	838	1434 7 Aug.
741	1340 27 June	790	1388 11 Jan.	839	1435 27 July
742	1341 17 June	791	1388 31 Dec.	840	1436 16 July

Hijrah Year.	Christian Year.	Hijrah Year.	Christian Year.	Hijrah Year.	Christian Year.
841	1437 5 July	890	1485 18 Jan.	939	1532 3 Aug.
842	1438 24 June	891	1486 7 Jan.	940	1533 23 July
843	1439 14 June	892	1486 28 Dec.	941	1534 13 July
844	1440 2 June	893	1487 17 Dec.	942	1535 2 July
845	1441 22 May	894	1488 5 Dec.	943	1536 20 June
846	1442 12 May	895	1489 25 Nov.	944	1537 10 June
847	1443 1 May	896	1490 14 Nov.	945	1538 30 May
848	1444 20 April	897	1491 4 Nov.	946	1539 19 May
849	1445 9 April	898	1492 23 Oct.	947	1540 8 May
850	1446 29 March	899	1493 12 Oct.	948	1541 27 April
851	1447 19 March	900	1494 2 Oct.	949	1542 17 April
852	1448 7 March	901	1495 21 Sept.	950	1543 6 April
853	1449 24 Feb.	902	1496 9 Sept.	951	1544 25 March
854	1450 14 Feb.	903	1497 30 Aug.	952	1545 15 March
855	1451 3 Feb.	904	1498 19 Aug.	953	1546 4 March
856	1452 23 Jan.	905	1499 8 Aug.	954	1547 21 Feb.
857	1453 12 Jan.	906	1500 28 July	955	1548 11 Feb.
858	1454 1 Jan.	907	1501 17 July	956	1549 30 Jan.
859	1454 22 Dec.	908	1502 7 July	957	1550 20 Jan.
860	1455 11 Dec.	909	1503 26 June	958	1551 9 Jan.
861	1456 29 Nov.	910	1504 14 June	959	1551 29 Dec.
862	1457 19 Nov.	911	1505 4 June	960	1552 18 Dec.
863	1458 8 Nov.	912	1506 24 May	961	1553 7 Dec.
864	1459 28 Oct.	913	1507 13 May	962	1554 26 Nov.
865	1460 17 Oct.	914	1508 2 May	963	1555 16 Nov.
866	1461 6 Oct.	915	1509 21 April	964	1556 4 Nov.
867	1462 26 Sept.	916	1510 10 April	965	1557 24 Oct.
868	1463 15 Sept.	917	1511 31 March	966	1558 14 Oct.
869	1464 3 Sept.	918	1512 19 March	967	1559 3 Oct.
870	1465 24 Aug.	919	1513 9 March	968	1560 22 Sept.
871	1466 13 Aug.	920	1514 26 Feb.	969	1561 11 Sept.
872	1467 2 Aug.	921	1515 15 Feb.	970	1562 31 Aug.
873	1468 22 July	922	1516 5 Feb.	971	1563 21 Aug.
874	1469 11 July	923	1517 24 Jan.	972	1564 9 Aug.
875	1470 30 June	924	1518 13 Jan.	973	1565 29 July
876	1471 20 June	925	1519 3 Jan.	974	1566 19 July
877	1472 8 June	926	1519 23 Dec.	975	1567 8 July
878	1473 29 May	927	1520 12 Dec.	976	1568 26 June
879	1474 18 May	928	1521 1 Dec.	977	1569 16 June
880	1475 7 May	929	1522 20 Nov.	978	1570 5 June
881	1476 26 April	930	1523 10 Nov.	979	1571 26 May
882	1477 15 April	931	1524 29 Oct.	980	1572 14 May
883	1478 4 April	932	1525 18 Oct.	981	1573 3 May
884	1479 25 March	933	1526 8 Oct.	982	1574 23 April
885	1480 13 March	934	1527 27 Sept.	983	1575 12 April
886	1481 2 March	935	1528 15 Sept.	984	1576 31 March
887	1482 20 Feb.	936	1529 5 Sept.	985	1577 21 March
888	1483 9 Feb.	937	1530 25 Aug.	986	1578 10 March
889	1484 30 Jan.	938	1531 15 Aug.	987	1579 28 Feb.

Hijrah Year.	Christian Year.	Hijrah Year.	Christian Year.	Hijrah Year.	Christian Year.
988	1580 17 Feb.	1037	1627 12 Sept.	1086	1675 28 March
989	1581 5 Feb.	1038	1628 31 Aug.	1087	1676 16 March
990	1582 26 Jan.	1039	1629 21 Aug.	1088	1677 6 March
991	1583 25 Jan.	1040	1630 10 Aug.	1089	1678 23 Feb.
992	1584 14 Jan.	1041	1631 30 July	1090	1679 12 Feb.
993	1585 3 Jan.	1042	1632 19 July	1091	1680 2 Feb.
994	1585 23 Dec.	1043	1633 8 July	1092	1681 21 Jan.
995	1586 12 Dec.	1044	1634 27 June	1093	1682 10 Jan.
996	1587 2 Dec.	1045	1635 17 June	1094	1682 31 Dec.
997	1588 20 Nov.	1046	1636 5 June	1095	1683 20 Dec.
998	1589 10 Nov.	1047	1637 26 May	1096	1684 8 Dec.
999	1590 30 Oct.	1048	1638 15 May	1097	1685 28 Nov.
1000	1591 19 Oct.	1049	1639 4 May	1098	1686 17 Nov.
1001	1592 8 Oct.	1050	1640 23 April	1099	1687 7 Nov.
1002	1593 27 Sept.	1051	1641 12 April	1100	1688 26 Oct.
1003	1594 16 Sept.	1052	1642 1 April	1101	1689 15 Oct.
1004	1595 6 Sept.	1053	1643 22 March	1102	1690 5 Oct.
1005	1596 25 Aug.	1054	1644 10 March	1103	1691 24 Sept.
1006	1597 14 Aug.	1055	1645 27 Feb.	1104	1692 12 Sept.
1007	1598 4 Aug.	1056	1646 17 Feb.	1105	1693 2 Sept.
1008	1599 24 July	1057	1647 6 Feb.	1106	1694 22 Aug.
1009	1600 13 July	1058	1648 27 Jan.	1107	1695 12 Aug.
1010	1601 2 July	1059	1649 15 Jan.	1108	1696 31 July
1011	1602 21 June	1060	1650 4 Jan.	1109	1697 20 July
1012	1603 11 June	1061	1650 25 Dec.	1110	1698 10 July
1013	1604 30 May	1062	1651 14 Dec.	1111	1699 29 June
1014	1605 19 May	1063	1652 2 Dec.	1112	1700 18 June
1015	1606 9 May	1064	1653 22 Nov.	1113	1701 8 June
1016	1607 28 April	1065	1654 11 Nov.	1114	1702 28 May
1017	1608 17 April	1066	1655 31 Oct.	1115	1703 17 May
1018	1609 6 April	1067	1656 20 Oct.	1116	1704 6 May
1019	1610 26 March	1068	1657 9 Oct.	1117	1705 25 April
1020	1611 16 March	1069	1658 29 Sept.	1118	1706 15 April
1021	1612 4 March	1070	1659 18 Sept.	1119	1707 4 April
1022	1613 21 Feb.	1071	1660 6 Sept.	1120	1708 23 March
1023	1614 11 Feb.	1072	1661 27 Aug.	1121	1709 13 March
1024	1615 31 Jan.	1073	1662 16 Aug.	1122	1710 2 March
1025	1616 20 Jan.	1074	1663 5 Aug.	1123	1711 19 Feb.
1026	1617 9 Jan.	1075	1664 25 July	1124	1712 9 Feb.
1027	1617 29 Dec.	1076	1665 14 July	1125	1713 28 Jan.
1028	1618 19 Dec.	1077	1666 4 July	1126	1714 17 Jan.
1029	1619 8 Dec.	1078	1667 23 June	1127	1715 7 Jan.
1030	1620 26 Nov.	1079	1668 11 June	1128	1715 27 Dec.
1031	1621 16 Nov.	1080	1669 1 June	1129	1716 16 Dec.
1032	1622 5 Nov.	1081	1670 21 May	1130	1717 5 Dec.
1033	1623 25 Oct.	1082	1671 10 May	1131	1718 24 Nov.
1034	1624 14 Oct.	1083	1672 29 April	1132	1719 14 Nov.
1035	1625 3 Oct.	1084	1673 18 April	1133	1720 2 Nov.
1036	1626 22 Sept.	1085	1674 7 April	1134	1721 22 Oct.

Hijrah Year.	Christian Year.	Hijrah Year.	Christian Year.	Hijrah Year.	Christian Year.
1135	1722 12 Oct.	1184	1770 27 April	1233	1817 11 Nov.
1136	1723 1 Oct.	1185	1771 16 April	1234	1818 31 Oct.
1137	1724 20 Sept.	1186	1772 4 April	1235	1819 20 Oct.
1138	1725 9 Sept.	1187	1773 25 March	1236	1820 9 Oct.
1139	1726 29 Aug.	1188	1774 14 March	1237	1821 28 Sept.
1140	1727 19 Aug.	1189	1775 4 March	1238	1822 18 Sept.
1141	1728 7 Aug.	1190	1776 21 Feb.	1239	1823 7 Sept.
1142	1729 27 July	1191	1777 9 Feb.	1240	1824 26 Aug.
1143	1730 17 July	1192	1778 30 Jan.	1241	1825 16 Aug.
1144	1731 6 July	1193	1779 19 Jan.	1242	1826 5 Aug.
1145	1732 24 June	1194	1780 8 Jan.	1243	1827 25 July
1146	1733 14 June	1195	1780 28 Dec.	1244	1828 14 July
1147	1734 3 June	1196	1781 17 Dec.	1245	1829 3 July
1148	1735 24 May	1197	1782 7 Dec.	1246	1830 22 June
1149	1736 12 May	1198	1783 26 Nov.	1247	1831 12 June
1150	1737 1 May	1199	1784 14 Nov.	1248	1832 31 May
1151	1738 21 April	1200	1785 4 Nov.	1249	1833 21 May
1152	1739 10 April	1201	1786 24 Oct.	1250	1834 10 May
1153	1740 29 March	1202	1787 13 Oct.	1251	1835 29 April
1154	1741 19 March	1203	1788 2 Oct.	1252	1836 18 April
1155	1742 8 March	1204	1789 21 Sept.	1253	1837 7 April
1156	1743 25 Feb.	1205	1790 10 Sept.	1254	1838 27 March
1157	1744 15 Feb.	1206	1791 31 Aug.	1255	1839 17 March
1158	1745 3 Feb.	1207	1792 19 Aug.	1256	1840 5 March
1159	1746 24 Jan.	1208	1793 9 Aug.	1257	1841 23 Feb.
1160	1747 13 Jan.	1209	1794 29 July	1258	1842 12 Feb.
1161	1748 2 Jan.	1210	1795 18 July	1259	1843 1 Feb.
1162	1748 22 Dec.	1211	1796 7 July	1260	1844 22 Jan.
1163	1749 11 Dec.	1212	1797 26 June	1261	1845 10 Jan.
1164	1750 30 Nov.	1213	1798 15 June	1262	1845 30 Dec.
1165	1751 20 Nov.	1214	1799 5 June	1263	1846 20 Dec.
1166	1752 8 Nov.	1215	1800 25 May	1264	1847 9 Dec.
1167	1753 29 Oct.	1216	1801 14 May	1265	1848 27 Nov.
1168	1754 18 Oct.	1217	1802 4 May	1266	1849 17 Nov.
1169	1755 7 Oct.	1218	1803 23 April	1267	1850 6 Nov.
1170	1756 26 Sept.	1219	1804 12 April	1268	1851 27 Oct.
1171	1757 15 Sept.	1220	1805 1 April	1269	1852 15 Oct.
1172	1758 4 Sept.	1221	1806 21 March	1270	1853 4 Oct.
1173	1759 25 Aug.	1222	1807 11 March	1271	1854 24 Sept.
1174	1760 13 Aug.	1223	1808 28 Feb.	1272	1855 13 Sept.
1175	1761 2 Aug.	1224	1809 16 Feb.	1273	1856 1 Sept.
1176	1762 23 July	1225	1810 6 Feb.	1274	1857 22 Aug.
1177	1763 12 July	1226	1811 26 Jan.	1275	1858 11 Aug.
1178	1764 1 July	1227	1812 16 Jan.	1276	1859 31 July
1179	1765 20 June	1228	1813 4 Jan.	1277	1860 20 July
1180	1766 9 June	1229	1813 24 Dec.	1278	1861 9 July
1181	1767 30 May	1230	1814 14 Dec.	1279	1862 29 June
1182	1768 18 May	1231	1815 3 Dec.	1280	1863 18 June
1183	1769 7 May	1232	1816 21 Nov.	1281	1864 6 June

Hijrah Year.	Christian Year.	Hijrah Year.	Christian Year.	Hijrah Year.	Christian Year.
1282	1865 27 May	1329	1911 2 Jan.	1376	1956 8 Aug.
1283	1866 16 May	1330	1911 22 Dec.	1377	1957 29 July
1284	1867 5 May	1331	1912 11 Dec.	1378	1958 18 July
1285	1868 24 April	1332	1913 30 Nov.	1379	1959 7 July
1286	1869 13 April	1333	1914 19 Nov.	1380	1960 26 June
1287	1870 3 April	1334	1915 9 Nov.	1381	1961 15 June
1288	1871 23 March	1335	1916 28 Oct.	1382	1962 4 June
1289	1872 11 March	1336	1917 17 Oct.	1383	1963 25 May
1290	1873 1 March	1337	1918 7 Oct.	1384	1964 13 May
1291	1874 18 Feb.	1338	1919 26 Sept.	1385	1965 2 May
1292	1875 7 Feb.	1339	1920 15 Sept.	1386	1966 22 April
1293	1876 28 Jan.	1340	1921 4 Sept.	1387	1967 11 April
1294	1877 16 Jan.	1341	1922 24 Aug.	1388	1968 31 March
1295	1878 5 Jan.	1342	1923 14 Aug.	1389	1969 20 March
1296	1878 26 Dec.	1343	1924 2 Aug.	1390	1970 9 March
1297	1879 15 Dec.	1344	1925 22 July	1391	1971 27 Feb.
1298	1880 4 Dec.	1345	1926 12 July	1392	1972 16 Feb.
1299	1881 23 Nov.	1346	1927 1 July	1393	1973 4 Feb.
1300	1882 12 Nov.	1347	1928 20 June	1394	1974 25 Jan.
1301	1883 2 Nov.	1348	1929 9 June	1395	1975 14 Jan.
1302	1884 21 Oct.	1349	1930 29 May	1396	1976 3 Jan.
1303	1885 10 Oct.	1350	1931 19 May	1397	1976 23 Dec.
1304	1886 30 Sept.	1351	1932 7 May	1398	1977 12 Dec.
1305	1887 19 Sept.	1352	1933 26 April	1399	1978 2 Dec.
1306	1888 7 Sept.	1353	1934 16 April	1400	1979 21 Nov.
1307	1889 28 Aug.	1354	1935 5 April	1401	1980 9 Nov.
1308	1890 17 Aug.	1355	1936 24 March	1402	1981 30 Oct.
1309	1891 7 Aug.	1356	1937 14 March	1403	1982 19 Oct.
1310	1892 26 July	1357	1938 3 March	1404	1983 8 Oct.
1311	1893 15 July	1358	1939 21 Feb.	1405	1984 27 Sept.
1312	1894 5 July	1359	1940 10 Feb.	1406	1985 16 Sept.
1313	1895 24 June	1360	1941 29 Jan.	1407	1986 6 Sept.
1314	1896 12 June	1361	1942 19 Jan.	1408	1987 26 Aug.
1315	1897 2 June	1362	1943 8 Jan.	1409	1988 14 Aug.
1316	1898 23 May	1363	1943 28 Dec.	1410	1989 4 Aug.
1317	1899 12 May	1364	1944 17 Dec.	1411	1990 24 July
1318	1900 1 May	1365	1945 6 Dec.	1412	1991 13 July
1319	1901 20 April	1366	1946 25 Nov.	1413	1992 2 July
1320	1902 10 April	1367	1947 15 Nov.	1414	1993 21 June
1321	1903 30 March	1368	1948 3 Nov.	1415	1994 10 June
1322	1904 18 March	1369	1949 24 Oct.	1416	1995 31 May
1323	1905 8 March	1370	1950 13 Oct.	1417	1996 19 May
1324	1906 25 Feb.	1371	1951 2 Oct.	1418	1997 9 May
1325	1907 14 Feb.	1372	1952 21 Sept.	1419	1998 28 April
1326	1908 4 Feb.	1373	1953 10 Sept.	1420	1999 17 April
1327	1909 23 Jan.	1374	1954 30 Aug.	1421	2000 6 April
1328	1910 13 Jan.	1375	1955 20 Aug.		

January. Year. Com.	January. Year. Leap	January. Day of the Year.	February. Year. Com.	February. Year. Leap	February. Day of the Year.	March. Year. Com.	March. Year. Leap	March. Day of the Year.	April. Year. Com.	April. Year. Leap	April. Day of the Year.	May. Year. Com.	May. Year. Leap	May. Day of the Year.	June. Year. Com.	June. Year. Leap	June. Day of the Year.
1	1	1	1	1	32	1		60	1		91	1		121	1		152
2	2	2	2	2	33	2	1	61	2	1	92	2	1	122	2	1	153
3	3	3	3	3	34	3	2	62	3	2	93	3	2	123	3	2	154
4	4	4	4	4	35	4	3	63	4	3	94	4	3	124	4	3	155
5	5	5	5	5	36	5	4	64	5	4	95	5	4	125	5	4	156
6	6	6	6	6	37	6	5	65	6	5	96	6	5	126	6	5	157
7	7	7	7	7	38	7	6	66	7	6	97	7	6	127	7	6	158
8	8	8	8	8	39	8	7	67	8	7	98	8	7	128	8	7	159
9	9	9	9	9	40	9	8	68	9	8	99	9	8	129	9	8	160
10	10	10	10	10	41	10	9	69	10	9	100	10	9	130	10	9	161
11	11	11	11	11	42	11	10	70	11	10	101	11	10	131	11	10	162
12	12	12	12	12	43	12	11	71	12	11	102	12	11	132	12	11	163
13	13	13	13	13	44	13	12	72	13	12	103	13	12	133	13	12	164
14	14	14	14	14	45	14	13	73	14	13	104	14	13	134	14	13	165
15	15	15	15	15	46	15	14	74	15	14	105	15	14	135	15	14	166
16	16	16	16	16	47	16	15	75	16	15	106	16	15	136	16	15	167
17	17	17	17	17	48	17	16	76	17	16	107	17	16	137	17	16	168
18	18	18	18	18	49	18	17	77	18	17	108	18	17	138	18	17	169
19	19	19	19	19	50	19	18	78	19	18	109	19	18	139	19	18	170
20	20	20	20	20	51	20	19	79	20	19	110	20	19	140	20	19	171
21	21	21	21	21	52	21	20	80	21	20	111	21	20	141	21	20	172
22	22	22	22	22	53	22	21	81	22	21	112	22	21	142	22	21	173
23	23	23	23	23	54	23	22	82	23	22	113	23	22	143	23	22	174
24	24	24	24	24	55	24	23	83	24	23	114	24	23	144	24	23	175
25	25	25	25	25	56	25	24	84	25	24	115	25	24	145	25	24	176
26	26	26	26	26	57	26	25	85	26	25	116	26	25	146	26	25	177
27	27	27	27	27	58	27	26	86	27	26	117	27	26	147	27	26	178
28	28	28	28	28	59	28	27	87	28	27	118	28	27	148	28	27	179
29	29	29		29	60	29	28	88	29	28	119	29	28	149	29	28	180
30	30	30				30	29	89	30	29	120	30	29	150	30	29	181
31	31	31				31	30	90		30	121	31	30	151		30	182
							31	91					31	152			

July. Year. Com.	July. Year. Leap	July. Day of the Year.	August. Year. Com.	August. Year. Leap	August. Day of the Year.	September. Year. Com.	September. Year. Leap	September. Day of the Year.	October. Year. Com.	October. Year. Leap	October. Day of the Year.	November. Year. Com.	November. Year. Leap	November. Day of the Year.	December. Year. Com.	December. Year. Leap	December. Day of the Year.
1		182	1		213	1		244	1		274	1		305	1		335
2	1	183	2	1	214	2	1	245	2	1	275	2	1	306	2	1	336
3	2	184	3	2	215	3	2	246	3	2	276	3	2	307	3	2	337
4	3	185	4	3	216	4	3	247	4	3	277	4	3	308	4	3	338
5	4	186	5	4	217	5	4	248	5	4	278	5	4	309	5	4	339
6	5	107	6	5	218	6	5	249	6	5	279	6	5	310	6	5	340
7	6	188	7	6	219	7	6	250	7	6	280	7	6	311	7	6	341
8	7	189	8	7	220	8	7	251	8	7	281	8	7	312	8	7	342
9	8	190	9	8	221	9	8	252	9	8	282	9	8	313	9	8	343
10	9	191	10	9	222	10	9	253	10	9	283	10	9	314	10	9	344
11	10	192	11	10	223	11	10	254	11	10	284	11	10	315	11	10	345
12	11	193	12	11	224	12	11	255	12	11	285	12	11	316	12	11	346
13	12	194	13	12	225	13	12	256	13	12	286	13	12	317	13	12	347
14	13	195	14	13	226	14	13	257	14	13	287	14	13	318	14	13	348
15	14	196	15	14	227	15	14	258	15	14	288	15	14	319	15	14	349
16	15	197	16	15	228	16	15	259	16	15	289	16	15	320	16	15	350
17	16	198	17	16	229	17	16	260	17	16	290	17	16	321	17	16	351
18	17	199	18	17	230	18	17	261	18	17	291	18	17	322	18	17	352
19	18	200	19	18	231	19	18	262	19	18	292	19	18	323	19	18	353
20	19	201	20	19	232	20	19	263	20	19	293	20	19	324	20	19	354
21	20	202	21	20	233	21	20	264	21	20	294	21	20	325	21	20	355
22	21	203	22	21	234	22	21	265	22	21	295	22	21	326	22	21	356
23	22	204	23	22	235	23	22	266	23	22	296	23	22	327	23	22	357
24	23	205	24	23	236	24	23	267	24	23	297	24	23	328	24	23	358
25	24	206	25	24	237	25	24	268	25	24	298	25	24	329	25	24	359
26	25	207	26	25	238	26	25	269	26	25	299	26	25	330	26	25	360
27	26	208	27	26	239	27	26	270	27	26	300	27	26	331	27	26	361
28	27	209	28	27	240	28	27	271	28	27	301	28	27	332	28	27	362
29	28	210	29	28	241	29	28	272	29	28	302	29	28	333	29	28	363
30	29	211	30	29	242	30	29	273	30	29	303	30	29	334	30	29	364
31	30	212	31	30	243		30	274	31	30	304		30	335	31	30	365
	31	213		31	244					31	305					31	366

Muharram.		Safar.		Rabí I.		Rabí II.		Jumádi I.		Jumádá II.	
Day of the		Day of the		Day of the		Day of the		Day of the		Day of the	
Month	Year.	Month	Year.	Month	Year.	Month	Year.	Month	Year.	Month	Year.
1	1	1	31	1	60	1	90	1	119	1	149
2	2	2	32	2	61	2	91	2	120	2	150
3	3	3	33	3	62	3	92	3	121	3	151
4	4	4	34	4	63	4	93	4	122	4	152
5	5	5	35	5	64	5	94	5	123	5	153
6	6	6	36	6	65	6	95	6	124	6	154
7	7	7	37	7	66	7	96	7	125	7	155
8	8	8	38	8	67	8	97	8	126	8	156
9	9	9	39	9	68	9	98	9	127	9	157
10	10	10	40	10	69	10	99	10	128	10	158
11	11	11	41	11	70	11	100	11	129	11	159
12	12	12	42	12	71	12	101	12	130	12	160
13	13	13	43	13	72	13	102	13	131	13	161
14	14	14	44	14	73	14	103	14	132	14	162
15	15	15	45	15	74	15	104	15	133	15	163
16	16	16	46	16	75	16	105	16	134	16	164
17	17	17	47	17	76	17	106	17	135	17	165
18	18	18	48	18	77	18	107	18	136	18	166
19	19	19	49	19	78	19	108	19	137	19	167
20	20	20	50	20	79	20	109	20	138	20	168
21	21	21	51	21	80	21	110	21	139	21	169
22	22	22	52	22	81	22	111	22	140	22	170
23	23	23	53	23	82	23	112	23	141	23	171
24	24	24	54	24	83	24	113	24	142	24	172
25	25	25	55	25	84	25	114	25	143	25	173
26	26	26	56	26	85	26	115	26	144	26	174
27	27	27	57	27	86	27	116	27	145	27	175
28	28	28	58	28	87	28	117	28	146	28	176
29	29	29	59	29	88	29	118	29	147	29	177
30	30			30	89			30	148		

Rajab.		Sha'bán.		Ramazán.		Shavvál.		Zu-'l-kadah.		Zu-'l-hijjah.	
Day of the		Day of the		Day of the		Day of the		Day of the		Day of the	
Month	Year.	Month	Year.	Month	Year.	Month	Year.	Month	Year.	Month	Year.
1	178	1	208	1	237	1	267	1	296	1	326
2	179	2	209	2	238	2	268	2	297	2	327
3	180	3	210	3	239	3	269	3	298	3	328
4	181	4	211	4	240	4	270	4	299	4	329
5	182	5	212	5	241	5	271	5	300	5	330
6	183	6	213	6	242	6	272	6	301	6	331
7	184	7	214	7	243	7	273	7	302	7	332
8	185	8	215	8	244	8	274	8	303	8	333
9	186	9	216	9	245	9	275	9	304	9	334
10	187	10	217	10	246	10	276	10	305	10	335
11	188	11	218	11	247	11	277	11	306	11	336
12	189	12	219	12	248	12	278	12	307	12	337
13	190	13	220	13	249	13	279	13	308	13	338
14	191	14	221	14	250	14	280	14	309	14	339
15	192	15	222	15	251	15	281	15	310	15	340
16	193	16	223	16	252	16	282	16	311	16	341
17	194	17	224	17	253	17	283	17	312	17	342
18	195	18	225	18	254	18	284	18	313	18	343
19	196	19	226	19	255	19	285	19	314	19	344
20	197	20	227	20	256	20	286	20	315	20	345
21	198	21	228	21	257	21	287	21	316	21	346
22	199	22	229	22	258	22	288	22	317	22	347
23	200	23	230	23	259	23	289	23	318	23	348
24	201	24	231	24	260	24	290	24	319	24	349
25	202	25	232	25	261	25	291	25	320	25	350
26	203	26	233	26	262	26	292	26	321	26	351
27	204	27	234	27	263	27	293	27	322	27	352
28	205	28	235	28	264	28	294	28	323	28	353
29	206	29	236	29	265	29	295	29	324	29	354
30	207			30	266			30	325	30	355